# THE
# HILLIER MANUAL
## OF
# TREES
# & SHRUBS

EST
1864

BY APPOINTMENT TO
H.M. THE QUEEN
NURSERYMEN AND SEEDSMEN

BY APPOINTMENT TO
H.M. QUEEN ELIZABETH
THE QUEEN MOTHER
NURSERYMEN AND SEEDSMEN

# THE HILLIER MANUAL OF TREES & SHRUBS

## SIXTH EDITION

DAVID & CHARLES

First published 1972
Reprinted 1973
Reprinted 1974
Reprinted 1975
New Edition 1977
Fifth Edition 1981
Reprinted 1984
Reprinted 1988
Reprinted 1989
Reprinted 1990
Reprinted 1991
New Edition 1991

British Library Cataloguing in Publication Data
The Hillier manual of trees and shrubs. — 6th ed.
  I. Hillier Nurseries (Winchester) Ltd
  635.03

  ISBN 0-7153-9942-X

Typeset by APS, Salisbury, Wiltshire

and printed in Great Britain by Redwood Press Ltd., Melksham, Wiltshire
for David & Charles plc
Brunel House Newton Abbot Devon

# Contents

# Preface

A new, updated version of this work is most welcome. The *Hillier Manual* has already gone through five editions and many reprints and has become an indispensable guide for anyone who has an interest in or requires information about cultivated trees and shrubs. The key to its success is accurate botanical and horticultural information, in sufficient detail, well presented, and produced at a price that permits individual rather than exclusively library ownership.

I am delighted by the accuracy of the botanical information, which also now includes details of the number of species and range of each genus. The 1,000 plus new entries and the many amendments to nomenclature ensure up-to-date naming, with cross-references to earlier synonyms. So much information on our garden plants is lost to us through lack of recording but, in this Manual, we have the authoritative documentation that enriches our understanding of trees and shrubs.

The usefulness of the notes on each plant comes also from the experience and knowledge gained from the performance throughout the country of the millions of plants that Hillier's have produced over many years. Thus the Manual also assesses the horticultural value of plants and guides suitably as to their siting. This is particularly useful with new introductions.

The sections on *Choisya*, *Cotinus*, *Daphne* and *Phygelius*, for example, also illustrate that Hillier's, through the dedicated skills of their propagators and hybridists, are still involved in the introduction of worthy new garden plants.

In many ways, this work stands as a tribute to the late Sir Harold Hillier. His contributions to horticulture were outstanding and it was his foresight that created the base for the modern commercial success of the company and its worldwide recognition as a source of new introductions. His greatness can perhaps best be seen in the Hillier Gardens and Arboretum, his remarkable visionary gift to future generations. Now managed successfully by Hampshire County Council, the Arboretum continues to grow in national and international status.

The Manual appropriately describes both family and arboretum, but it is the encyclopedic information that underlines the truth of the remark in an earlier preface by the late Sir Harold Fletcher that this is an unrivalled and essential work. It is encouraging to see a family tradition upheld by the present representatives of the Hillier family, John and Robert, who continue to maintain an extensive interchange of plants and information that has given both Hillier's and the Manual the good reputation that they so justly deserve.

Ghillean T. Prance
Director
Royal Botanic Gardens, Kew
1991

# Introduction
## to the Sixth Edition

Like most plantsmen, the Hillier family have always made copious notes - sometimes in pocket notebooks but often on any scrap of paper which happened to be handy.

These served many purposes - as botanical, cultural, commercial management and cost records, as the basis for future plans, for the production of generations of catalogues and as a source of material for authoritative articles on a wide variety of horticultural and environmental topics.

By the 1960s the range of Hillier woody plants extended to over 8,000, representing 638 genera, and for the late Sir Harold Hillier to compile and publish a comprehensive and informative catalogue was a mammoth task. But thus was born, through years of diligent research with acknowledged help from people such as Desmond Clarke, Roy Lancaster and Mr P.H.B. Gardner, the *Hillier Manual of Trees and Shrubs*.

First published in 1971, effectively as a catalogue of plants then grown on the nursery, the Manual quickly became established as a standard work, recognised and respected by professional horticulturists and enthusiastic amateurs alike.

Regretfully, it has long been commercially impractical for any one nursery to produce all of the plants described - although Hillier's still grow what is believed to be the world's widest range of trees and shrubs for temperate climates. Fortunately, however, representative specimens of every tree, shrub, climber and conifer may be found in the Hillier Gardens and Arboretum or in other arboreta, public parks and private gardens in Britain. More and more valuable work is being done by a variety of organisations, groups and individuals (in particular by the guardians of National Collections) to ensure the conservation and continuing propagation of this living heritage.

There is still, too, the excitement of introducing newly discovered or developed plants to general cultivation. This sixth edition of the *Hillier Manual of Trees and Shrubs* has been substantially updated and expanded both as a hopefully valid contribution to the perpetuation of past and present plantsmanship values and as a spur to innovation.

As with earlier editions of the Manual, much help has been forthcoming from a number of botanical friends, but particular thanks and appreciation are due for the tremendous amount of research and detailed work carried out by Allen J. Coombes. Additional measurements for this edition were made by Mr P.H.B. Gardner.

Ampfield House
1991

# The Story of Hillier Plantsmanship

In a preface to the first edition of the *Hillier Manual of Trees and Shrubs*, the late Sir Harold Fletcher, a former Regius Keeper of the Royal Botanic Garden, Edinburgh, gave a very brief outline of the history of Hillier Nurseries. Since that time, there have been many requests for more information about the milestones and philosophies of a family business which spans five generations, and is still growing in every sense of the word.

The publication of this new edition of the Manual is an opportune time to tell at least some of the story behind more than a century and a quarter of plantsmanship, which blends traditional skills with the dynamic needs of markets and technology, and is at the same time attuned to an inherent yet increasing need for environmental conservation and improvement.

## In the Beginning...

In 1864, Edwin Hillier and his wife Betsy had an important decision to make. Although only twenty-four years old, Edwin had gained wide experience in some of the leading gardens and nurseries of the day, not least the world-famous Veitch's nursery at Chelsea. Like Veitch, Edwin combined plantsmanship with entrepreneurial ambition - but, unfortunately, without the same level of financial resources. Despite this, the couple felt that the time was right to launch out on their own.

The choice lay between purchasing a small florist and nursery business in Winchester, or acquiring a similar business in Richmond. In the end, the issue was decided on the spin of a 'trencher' - and we're not quite sure whether this was a wooden plate or a coin. But thus was founded, in the former capital of the Kingdom of Wessex, the family business which was to become internationally renowned as growers of the world's widest range of temperate zone trees and shrubs.

Initially just two acres of land were acquired, primarily to produce flowers and plants for sale in the little shop. In the following year, both the business and the family expanded. Another three acres of land were acquired, and, more importantly, Edwin and Betsy celebrated the birth of their first son, Edwin Lawrence Hillier. They were able to move from their rented accommodation to 14, Jewry Street, which served as home, office and shop.

In 1874, Edwin entered into an agreement with a Dr Hitchcock to buy a parcel of land adjoining the County Gaol, and this, the 'Home Nursery', or 'No 1' as it became known, eventually encompassed some 14 acres. Today, part of it is still used as a Hillier Garden Centre - officially designated as such in 1962, and the first of a growing chain of such centres of which there are now eight, mostly on the sites of formerly famous nurseries.

Meanwhile, as the business grew, thanks to a combination of green-fingered acumen and extraordinarily long hours of work, so did the scope of goods and services offered. Floristry

*Edwin Hillier*     *Edwin Lawrence Hillier*     *Arthur Richard Hillier*

was still important both for shop sales and for staging displays in private homes and civic buildings for special events. A wide range of seeds and bulbs was offered. Stove plants and even hot-house-grown grapes and peaches were supplied by horse and cart delivery to the great houses in the locality, along with an ever-widening list of trees, shrubs, roses, fruits, herbaceous and bedding plants. Landscaping and garden maintenance services (at what nowadays seems unbelievably low cost) no doubt provided greater opportunities for the supply of seasonal and permanent plantings. The Hillier reputation for quality began to spread - and greater use of the nearby railway was made to despatch plants and expertise further afield.

In 1877 a second son, Arthur Richard, was born. As the two boys grew up, they developed a balance of talents and skills. From his earliest days, Edwin Lawrence shone as a plantsman with a dedication to procuring and raising new plants whilst Arthur, albeit horticulturally knowledgeable, soon demonstrated the keen business mind which subsequently led to him becoming the firm's administrative head.

# The Golden Age

This was the age of the 'great collectors', when wealthy patrons, such as the Rothschilds of Exbury and the Williams of Caerhays, Cornwall, vied with each other to finance expeditions to source new and rare plants to adorn their gardens and greenhouses. In general, nurserymen were kept well away from these estates lest they should acquire propagating material. A few, however, such as London and Wise, C. Louden and the house of Veitch, did have the resources to finance some of the great collectors such as Ernest Wilson and George Forrest. Despite the difficulties, Hillier's were already introducing new plants - the first recorded example being *Primula sinensis* 'Annie Hillier' introduced in 1875 and awarded the Royal Horticultural Society's First Class Certificate in 1880.

In 1873, the firm took two major steps forward. Premises purchased at 95 High Street, Winchester, provided a new shop, with rear storage, office space and upstairs living accommodation for staff. Probably much more important to Edwin Lawrence, however, was the fact that his father borrowed £2,000 to buy Shroner Wood, a 130 acre site on the London Road, about six miles north of the city. The loan was repaid within two years.

Young Edwin Lawrence's first love was palms, and he was a frequent visitor to the Palm House at Kew. However, having a practical frame of mind, he devoted his attention to hardy plants, especially conifers, of which he was reputed to have a greater knowledge than probably any of his contemporaries. At Shroner Wood he established a pinetum, said to have been the most complete collection of its day. *Thuja plicata* 'Hillieri', selected there in the 1880s, is still

**9**

*Harold Hillier as a boy*

popular today as a slow-growing form of the Western Red cedar, with a dense, rounded habit.

Sadly, Edwin sold Shroner Wood in 1913, probably to make financial provision for his daughters, thus balancing the 'ownership' and management benefits (and responsibilities) which he was progressively handing over to his sons, although he still took a keen interest in the business until his death in 1926. Other land purchases had been made in the preceding few years, notably at St Cross, where herbaceous plants, aquatics and alpines were grown, and Pitt Corner, for tree and shrub production.

The demise of Shroner Wood coincided with the break-up of the Veitch nurseries, and as a result of the latter, Edwin Lawrence no doubt found some consolation in being able to acquire a wealth of choice plant material of the type sent home by Wilson, Forrest and, later, Kingdon-Ward.

World War I brought devastation among the leading nurseries of Europe. Many skilled Hillier employees departed on active service - some of them, sadly, never to return. However, despite all the problems associated with labour shortages and enforced changes in cropping, Hillier's survived to identify and fill the post-war need for a nursery which was prepared to grow and offer the vast range of hitherto unknown plants which were pouring into cultivation.

This was the atmosphere in which Edwin Lawrence's son, Harold Hillier, spent his formative years, developing a love of plants and a determination to share that love with others. By the time he became an 'official' member of staff in 1921, he had already spent a great deal of time on the nurseries, looking and learning, and had visited many of the great gardens and estates with his father (including Glamis, where he reputedly had his first introduction to the young Elizabeth Bowes-Lyon).

Initially he was placed under the watchful eye of Harry Bryce, a propagator who had recently joined the firm after learning his skills at Edinburgh Botanic Garden, and who in 1989, at the age of ninety-two, became an Associate of Honour of the Royal Horticultural Society. Harry's firm instructions were to teach Harold everything possible about the propagation and gentle raising of plants - but without allowing him to acquire any bad habits. Like his father, Harold became an avid plant collector - not until much later by collecting in the wild, but through initiating and maintaining correspondence with leading plantsmen, botanic gardens and centres of horticultural excellence around the world. He developed many long-lasting friendships, based upon mutual respect and the sharing of both knowledge and precious plant material.

More plants, of course, demanded more space. In the years between the two World Wars, eight acres of acid land were purchased at Hiltingbury, near Chandler's Ford - motivated in part by a gift from Lionel de Rothschild of some new large-leaved Himalayan Rhododendron species which could not have thrived in the lime-laden soil around Winchester. In Sarum Road, thirteen and later a further eighteen acres were devoted increasingly to the production of larger trees, above normal nursery size, which were much appreciated by local authorities who, even in those days, were having to contend with the ravages of vandalism. In 'amenity planting' terms Hillier's were also pioneering planned roadside plantings of trees and shrubs, especially along the new-fangled dual carriageways.

# Another War - More Challenges

By 1939, the area under cultivation totalled some 80 acres, but the onset of World War II posed yet more challenges. Again, many staff saw active service and vegetable crops replaced trees, shrubs and herbaceous plants over a considerable area, some of them tended by members of the Women's Land Army.

However, the war also led to the development of yet more areas of expertise. At the request of the Air Ministry, Hillier's developed techniques for lifting and transplanting large trees - thirty to fifty feet high - to camouflage aircraft hangars. Subsequent research enabled them to demonstrate, at a 'hush-hush' display at the RHS Hall, that smaller trees could also be used to good effect and that 'portable' hedgerows could be constructed and wheeled into place to disguise airfield runways between sorties.

'Big tree' lifting, transporting and transplanting was to become one of Harold Hillier's specialities, and in post-war years the technique was successfully applied - to the delight of the news-hungry journalists and cameramen - to such projects as the 'instant' maturity of the 1951 Festival of Britain site on London's South Bank.

*The* Daily Mirror *October 1950*

# The Dream - and the Reality

Edwin Lawrence Hillier died in 1944 - two years after being awarded the Royal Horticultural Society's prestigious Victoria Medal of Honour - and Arthur retired two years later, having combined plantsmanship with commercial management. In pursuit of his forebears' and his own dreams, and in anticipation of his descendants providing caring and yet commercially viable succession, Harold embarked on a period of considerable expansion. He wanted to increase the Hillier range of plants and to provide hospitable soil conditions in which to raise them. At the same time, he was anticipating and accepting (whether he approved or not) that the marketplace would change and that techniques would need to be developed, for instance to enable container-grown stock to be marketed through garden centres and other outlets throughout the year.

Perhaps partly because of this awareness, and the potential restraints that it implied, he was determined to fulfil his ambition to create an arboretum and garden which would become a definitive and comprehensive legacy of temperate-zone woody plants, to provide a priceless conservation and educational 'bank'. He drew a triangle linking Winchester, Southampton and Romsey, and decided he must acquire such land as he could to answer his needs.

Thus between 1950 and the late 1970s Hillier plants were grown on sites totalling some 700 acres in Eastleigh, Ampfield, Braishfield and the edge of Romsey. Some of these locations subsequently proved to be less than ideal, while others remain as outstanding. Jermyns and adjoining land became not only Harold and Barbara Hillier's home, but the site of the Hillier Gardens and Arboretum, now in the care of Hampshire County Council and extending to over 160 acres as a resource centre and a source of pleasure and erudition of international renown (see p.704).

Brentry House became a hostel for students from around the world who came to acquire the Hillier 'magic' and expertise, and to take it back to their homelands. The adjoining land has become one of Britain's largest container-plant production areas, supplying literally millions of quality plants to individual gardeners, to amenity planting customers, and to reputable garden centres and other 'top-name' retail outlets.

Ampfield House, with surrounding land, was acquired in 1977 and became the firm's headquarters. At that time, Hillier and Sons became Hillier Nurseries, (Winchester) Limited, with Harold Hillier as President (an office now held by Lady Hillier) and his two sons, John and Robert, as Managing Directors. Both had received extensive horticultural training in the UK and overseas as well as on the family nurseries, in preparation for the responsibilities which they now shouldered. The move to Ampfield House, a handsome listed building, provided space for pioneering of a different kind. In 1969, there was a major (and still continuing) investment in developing and applying computer technology to the day-to-day running of the business.

Freed from management duties, Harold Hillier was at last able to travel extensively and to collect hundreds of species 'in the wild' in such locations as southern Russia, eastern Asia, Australasia, southern Africa and the Americas. Although modest to the point of self-deprecation, he received many honours and awards over the years, including the CBE, the Victoria Medal of Honour, and the Veitch Memorial Medal. He was a fellow of the Linnaean Society and both an Honorary Fellow and a Vice-President of the Royal Horticultural Society. In 1983, he received the accolade of Knighthood from Her Majesty Queen Elizabeth the Queen Mother, and thus became Sir Harold Hillier, CBE, FLS, VMH.

In a memorial tribute to Sir Harold, following his death in 1985, the Lord Aberconway, President Emeritus of the Royal Horticultural Society, said, "The words on Christopher Wren's tomb in St Paul's Cathedral could equally come to mind for Harold as one walks around Britain's gardens - *If you seek his memorial, look around you.*"

# The Continuing Quest

Progress in the introduction, propagation and production of a wide range of worthy high-quality plants continues, blending traditional skills and values with investment in the development and adoption of 'space-age' horticultural techniques.

At Liss in eastern Hampshire, clonal selection is playing an important role in the open-ground production of 'new generation' trees on 270 acres of deep sandy loam purchased in 1984. At the propagation unit adjoining the Hillier Gardens and Arboretum, skills which Edwin Hillier and his successors practised are supported and enhanced in computer-controlled conditions. Nearby at Brentry, new, scientifically developed composts are helping in the production of millions of healthy, well-presented container-grown plants of uniformly high quality.

In 1989 Hillier's acquired the business of Broadmead Trees, widely regarded as Britain's premier producer of large, container-grown trees for amenity planting. Special techniques have

*John Hillier*

*Robert Hillier*

*Sir Harold and Lady Hillier 1983*

been developed to enable specimen trees 6m or more in height and with girths up to 50cm to be successfully transplanted on a 'year-round' basis - even when in full leaf.

Whether on the nurseries, at the garden centres, in the landscaping and wholesaling divisions, or in the administrative offices, over three hundred Hillier people are 'growing together', to meet the gardening and environmental needs and challenges of today - and tomorrow - in Britain and in export markets. Edwin and Betsy would no doubt be happy to know that five of their great-great-grandchildren are currently either working at Hillier's or undergoing horticultural training.

# The 'Good Old Days'

I remember the days when my father, my uncle and the staff worked from 6.00am to 6.00pm, finishing at 4.00pm on Saturdays, using hurricane lamps in the winter, early mornings and evenings. In the days of Shroner, this meant a walk of six miles before 6.00am. Only if one was lucky was there a lift in a wagon. After a high tea, my father would work in the office at the back of 95 High Street, returning home in time for bed at 11.30pm.

**Sir Harold Hillier**

When Edwin Hillier started in business, long hours and low pay were the norm - a situation which prevailed for many years. A wages book spanning the period of 1893-1909 shows that workers' pay ranged from ten shillings to little more than one pound per week - and increases were both small and rare!

Then, as now, weather and seasonal vagaries often made life harder, both for the people and for the plants they tended. Despite (or perhaps because of) discomforts and difficulties, 'Hillier people' tended to stick together, establishing and maintaining tradition and continuity. There are many examples of several generations of the same family being employed simultaneously or successively, and individual long service records of up to sixty years. Hillier's even earned the reputation of being something of a 'marriage market'!

Time and energy were somehow found for a variety of social activities, shared by employers and employees. Prominent among these (and a tradition which still

*The annual cricket match. This family group at the
1923 match (above) includes Edwin, Edwin Lawrence,
Arthur and Harold Hillier*

continues) was cricket. Fixtures were very much family occasions and an annual highlight was the 'Home Nursery' v 'The Rest' match.

Life is still by no means 'soft' in the nursery business, but at Hillier's conditions have radically improved, with more and better staff facilities, comprehensive training programmes and career advancement opportunities. Today's remuneration structure is geared to the recognition of performance, experience and commitment, and there is still a healthy flow of social and community service activities, many of which help to raise funds for worthy causes.

# Royal Pride

Among the contacts which Hillier's have been privileged to enjoy with many distinguished people, none has generated more pride than the continuing interest shown by the members of the Royal Family - whether at Chelsea Shows, in the contexts of their own gardens, at tree-planting ceremonies or on visits to our nurseries.

Their Royal Highnesses, the Duke and Duchess of York visited Hillier's West Hill nursery - at literally an hour's notice - in 1936. Two years later, in January 1938, a Royal Warrant of Appointment was granted to Hillier and Sons as Nurserymen to HRH the Prince of Wales. Later in the same year, this was replaced when the present Queen Mother granted hers as Nurserymen and Seedsmen. Her Majesty Queen Elizabeth granted a similar Warrant in 1983 adding to that which already existed and is still proudly held in respect of HM Queen Elizabeth the Queen Mother.

*Their Royal Highnesses the Duke and Duchess of York visited Hillier's West Hill Nursery in 1936*

(Left, below) *Her Majesty Queen Elizabeth the Queen Mother accepted the gift of the Hillier Arboretum on behalf of Hampshire County Council in May 1978*

(Below) *Her Majesty Queen Elizabeth granted a Royal Warrant of Appointment to Hillier's in 1983*

# Show Business

Soon after the business was founded, Hillier's earned a reputation for staging breathtaking exhibits at horticultural shows. When the Royal Horticultural Society's Great Spring Show arrived at its new venue in the grounds of the Royal Hospital, Chelsea, in 1913, Hillier's were there - as they were at earlier Great Spring Shows at Temple Gardens, and have been at every Chelsea Show to the present day. In 1990 they were proud to be awarded their 45th consecutive Chelsea Gold Medal.

Hillier exhibits have been a regular feature at the RHS Halls too, where in 1964 (their centenary year) a collection of over 800 conifers was awarded the Lawrence Medal.

In addition to their RHS show successes, Hillier's have staged countless award-winning exhibits at major horticultural shows and garden festivals throughout Britain and overseas.

# How to use the Manual

The descriptions in this Manual have, wherever possible, been based on typical plants growing in our nurseries or in the Hillier Gardens and Arboretum. However, as species and varieties are often variable, such characteristics as leaf shape, colour and texture, colour of flower, occurrence of flower and fruit, habit of plant and autumn colour may vary (within the limitations of the species) from those described. Autumn colours are particularly influenced by local and seasonal conditions, but some clones of a species are more reliable than others.

## HEIGHTS

The ultimate height of a tree or shrub is largely dependent on such factors as soil, aspect and local weather conditions. With British gardens in mind we have devised the following scale to give the probable range of each plant growing under average conditions. Allowances must be made for specimens growing in shade, against walls and under exceptional circumstances.

**Trees**
**Large**—Over 18m (over 60ft)
**Medium**—10 to 18m (35 to 50ft)
**Small**—4.5 to 9m (15 to 30ft)

**Shrubs**
**Large**—Over 3m (over 10ft)
**Medium**—1.5 to 3m (6 to 10ft)
**Small**—1 to 1.5m (3 to 5ft)
**Dwarf**—0.3 to 0.6m (1 to 2ft)
**Prostrate**—Creeping

## FLOWERING PERIODS

Flowering periods in this Manual should be taken as being approximate, as they will vary according to locality and from year to year depending on the vagaries of the season.

## SOIL pH AND THE PLANT

The term pH is used to designate the acid or alkaline reaction of the soil. A pH reading of seven is neutral while below this the soil becomes increasingly acid and above it progressively alkaline. In this work, the symbol ‡ is used to denote plants unsuitable for chalky soils. It should, however, be realised that there are many trees and shrubs which, weak and miserable in a *shallow* soil over chalk, will grow well in a *deep* soil over chalk.

## HARDINESS

The hardiness of plants is something about which the gardener is forever wondering. It is a subject full of pitfalls, surprises, disappointments and exceptions to the rule. The term hardy is used to indicate that a plant is able to withstand an average winter in any given area. Some plants, particularly those from northerly latitudes, may be perfectly hardy but may be induced into growth during mild periods in spring and then cut back by late frosts, while others may only be hardy if they have had sufficient summer sun to ripen their growth. While the former should not be planted in sheltered positions or frost pockets the latter should receive as much sun as possible during the year.

Plants that are not generally hardy can often be accommodated by planting in positions that offer a favourable microclimate, such as against a wall or amongst or under other trees and shrubs. A surprising number of supposedly tender plants can often be grown in this way. It should be remembered that the small garden, particularly in a built-up area, can usually provide much more shelter and warmth than the large garden or park. Tender plants that need protection except in the milder areas are indicated by the symbol †.

## NOMENCLATURE AND CLASSIFICATION

Plant nomenclature is controlled by two internationally accepted codes.

The botanical names of plants (necessary for both wild and cultivated plants) are covered by the 'International Code of Botanical Nomenclature', while the use of cultivar and group epithets as well as the names of graft hybrids (which are only required for cultivated plants) are covered by the 'International Code of Nomenclature for Cultivated Plants'.

Advances in our knowledge both of plant variation and plant relationships has inevitably resulted in the re-classification of many plants. This, plus the application of the 'Rule of Priority' (ie the use of the earliest legitimate name) has necessitated a number of name changes. For various reasons not all changes are accepted in this Manual, but where a plant has been re-named it has been cross-referenced under its old name, which is also included as a synonym after the accepted name.

The following notes are provided to assist readers with the use and arrangement of plant names in this work.

**GENERA** These are shown in bold type and capital letters
> eg **ACER, PRUNUS, PINUS**

**FAMILIES** These are shown in bold type with a capital initial and follow the generic names
> eg **MALUS—Rosaceae**
> (genus)    (family)

**SPECIES** These are shown in bold type with a small initial and are listed under the genus to which they belong
> eg **RHODODENDRON**
> **ponticum**
> **racemosum**

**SUBSPECIES & VARIETIES** Botanically recognised subdivisions of a species (distinct forms which occur in the wild) are shown in bold type with a small initial and follow the species to which they belong. These can be subspecies (subsp.), varietas (var.) or forma (f.)
> eg **SARCOCOCCA hookeriana var. digyna**
> (genus)        (species)        (variety)

It should be appreciated that when subdivisions of a species are recognised, the name of the species includes these. Thus, in the above example, *Sarcococca hookeriana* refers to var. *digyna* as well as to the typical plant usually known as *S. hookeriana* and often called the typical variety or 'type', which, to be technically accurate, should be referred to as *S. hookeriana* var. *hookeriana*.

**CULTIVARS** These are distinct forms which are not considered to warrant botanical recognition, selected either from garden or wild plants and maintained in cultivation by propagation. They normally follow the species to which they belong and are shown in bold type with a capital initial and are enclosed in single quotation marks
> eg **CAMELLIA japonica 'Jupiter'**
> **FAGUS sylvatica 'Cristata'**
> (genus) (species) (cultivar)

**19**

**GROUPS** In status these lie between the cultivar and botanical subdivisons of species. Whereas a cultivar should, ideally, show little or no variation, the members of a group can vary considerably but are still not considered to warrant botanical status. A group can include cultivars with similar features, all the products of a cross between two plants, or it can be a previously recognised botanical category which is no longer afforded botanical status. In this work the term **grex**, often used for certain types of plant, particularly rhododendrons, to indicate the products of one cross, is not recognised as distinct from **group**

> eg **ACER palmatum Dissectum group** includes the forms of *Acer palmatum* with foliage similar to 'Dissectum'.
> **RHODODENDRON Loderi group** includes all crosses between *R. fortunei* and *R. griffithianum.*
> **CEDRUS atlantica Glauca group** includes the blue-foliaged forms of *C. atlantica* previously referred to as *C. atlantica* f. *glauca.*

**GREX** See under **GROUPS**.

**CLONE** A group of individuals derived originally from a single individual and maintained in cultivation by vegetative propagation. All such individuals of a clone are exactly alike and are identical with the original. The majority of the cultivars in this Manual are clonal in origin and are normally propagated vegetatively.

**FORMS** Although *forma* is a recognised botanical category below variety, the term form is often used in a more general manner and may refer to a variety, subspecies or cultivar.

**HYBRIDS** Hybrids between two species are normally given a collective name in Latin form. These are shown as for a species but are preceded by a multiplication sign

> eg **QUERCUS × hispanica**

For hybrids given a collective name in English see under **GROUPS**.

Where no collective name is available for a hybrid, its cultivar name is given and treated in the same way as a cultivar

> eg **CISTUS 'Silver Pink'**
> **SORBUS 'Winter Cheer'**

Where neither collective name nor cultivar name exists for a hybrid, the names of the parents are given, connected by a multiplication sign

> eg **QUERCUS canariensis × robur**

Parents of hybrids, where known, are shown in italics and enclosed in parentheses after the name of the hybrid, or in a few instances are mentioned in the description. Unless otherwise indicated, the sequence of the parents is purely alphabetical

> eg **VIBURNUM × hillieri** (*V. erubescens × V. henryi*)
>    (hybrid)              (parents)

**INTERGENERIC HYBRIDS** Natural (sexual) hybrids between species of two different genera are shown in bold type and are preceded by a multiplication sign

> eg **× MAHOBERBERIS** (*Mahonia × Berberis*)
>   (intergeneric hybrid)     (parents)

Graft hybrids (chimaeras) between species of two different genera are shown in bold type and are preceded by a plus sign

> eg **+ LABURNOCYTISUS** (*Laburnum + Cytisus*)
>   (graft hybrid)        (parents)

**SUBGENERA, SECTIONS etc.** The larger genera are normally subdivided into Subgenera, Sections, Subsections or Series. Where it is felt these may be of use as a reference they have been added in parentheses after the individual species

> eg **FRAXINUS mariesii** (Sect. Ornus)
> **RHODODENDRON forrestii** (Subgenus Hymenanthes, Subsect. Neriiflora)

**SYNONYMS** Old or invalid names (those by which a plant was previously known), also those names not accepted in this Manual, are shown in italics and placed in parentheses after the accepted name.

> eg **PONCIRUS trifoliata** (*Aegle sepiaria*)
>
> **THUJA plicata** (*T. lobbii*)
>
> (accepted name) (synonym)

Where a synonym is accompanied by the abbreviation HORT., it indicates that the plant in question is often known incorrectly by this name in Horticulture (Gardens)

> eg **HEBE brachysiphon** (*H. traversii* HORT.)

**FOREIGN NAMES OF CULTIVARS** Names of cultivars enclosed in brackets as against parentheses indicate prior names (correct names) of foreign origin which have been given an English equivalent.

> eg **HAMAMELIS** × **intermedia 'Magic Fire'** ['Feuerzauber']
>
> (translation) (prior name)

**COMMON NAMES** Common or colloquial names of common usage are included in double quotation marks before the description. In recent years it has been common practice to invent common names often by translating the botanical name; these are not accepted here

> eg **QUERCUS coccinea** "Scarlet Oak"
>
> (botanical name)    (common name)

In addition, the more familiar common names are included in the text and are cross-referenced to the appropriate botanical name.

**AUTHORITIES** Following names of genera, species, subspecies and varieties, etc, are the names in capitals, usually abbreviated, of the authority responsible for publishing that particular combination

> eg **OSMANTHUS delavayi** FRANCH. name given by the botanist Franchet
>
> **ILEX aquifolium** L. name given by Linnaeus
>
> **COTONEASTER floccosus** (REHD. & WILS.) FLINCK & HYLMÖ name given by Rehder and Wilson to a variety of *C. salicifolius* and later recognised as a species by Flinck & Hylmö

## ORIGINS

The countries of origin of wild species and varieties, where known, have been included, normally at the end of the description. Distribution of individual plants may vary depending on one's concept of a species. The recommended and now accepted Pinyin system has been adopted for Chinese placenames except for Tibet which should now correctly be referred to as Xizang.

## DATES OF INTRODUCTION

The dates of introduction into western gardens of species and varieties, where known, have been included at the end of each description, eg I 1869.

Where no date of introduction is known, the earliest known date of cultivation is included, eg C 1658.

## AWARDS

Many plants have been given awards by the Royal Horticultural Society, but the criteria and procedures vary considerably according to the type of award.

**First Class Certificate (FCC)** - instituted 1859

**Award of Merit (AM)** - instituted 1888

Recommendations for these awards are made by the appropriate committee to the RHS council, usually after viewing as a cut specimen in a vase, occasionally as a specimen plant. Judgement is therefore 'as seen' on the day, in an 'exhibition' context.

**FCCT and AMT**

Recommendations are again made to the RHS council, by the appropriate committee, but only after trials at the RHS Gardens, Wisley.

**Award of Garden Merit (AGM)** - instituted 1921

Subjects for this award are recommended to the council by the Award of Garden Merit Committee on the basis of their assessment as valuable garden plants.

Between 1982 and 1984, the committee re-assessed all plants to which the award had already been granted, and made further recommendations. It has not met since that time. In this edition of the Manual, any AGM awards preceding the 1984 list have been disregarded.

**Cory Cup** The Reginald Cory Memorial Cup, awarded to the raiser of the best deliberately raised hybrid of that year.

At the time of going to press, the whole system of RHS awards is under review (1991).

## WORKS OF REFERENCE

The following is a selection from the many books referred to during the preparation of this work.

Ahrendt, L. W. A. (1961) *Berberis and Mahonia*. J. Linn. Soc. (Botany) vol 57.

Allan, H. H. (1961) *Flora of New Zealand*. Vol 1. Wellington.

Bailey, Liberty Hyde, Hortorium (1976) *Hortus Third*. New York.

Bean, W. J. (1972-80) *Trees and Shrubs Hardy in the British Isles*. Vols 1-4. Supplement (1988) by D. L. Clarke.

Brickell, C. D. and Mathew, B. (1976) *Daphne. The Genus in the Wild and in Cultivation*. Alpine Garden Society.

Brickell, C. D. et al (eds) (1980) *International Code of Nomenclature for Cultivated Plants*.

Chalk, D. (1988) *Hebes and Parahebes*. London.

Chao, C. S. (1989) *A Guide to Bamboos Grown in Britain*. Royal Botanic Gardens, Kew.

Cox, Peter A. and Cox, Kenneth N. E. (1988) *Encyclopedia of Rhododendron Hybrids*. London.

Cox, Peter A. (1985) *The Smaller Rhododendrons*. London.

Curtis, W. M. (1956-67) *A Student's Flora of Tasmania*. Parts 1-3. Hobart.

Dallimore, W. and Jackson, A. B. (1966) *A Handbook of Coniferae and Ginkgoaceae*. 4th ed. London.

Dirr, M. A. (1983) *Manual of Woody Landscape Plants*. 3rd ed. Champaign, Illinois.

Fernald, M. L. (1950, corrected printing 1970) *Gray's Manual of Botany*. New York.

Flower Association of Japan (1983) *Manual of Japanese Flowering Cherries*. Tokyo.

Galbraith, J. (1977) *Collins Field Guide to the Wild Flowers of South-East Australia*. Sydney.

Galle, Fred C. (1987) *Azaleas*. Portland, Oregon.

Gardiner, J. M. (1989) *Magnolias, Their Care and Cultivation*. London.

Gelderen, D. M. van and Hoey-Smith, J. R. P. (1986) *Conifers*. London.

Grierson, A. J. C. and Long, D. G. (1983) *Flora of Bhutan*. Royal Botanic Garden, Edinburgh.

Hara, H., Stearn, W. T. and Williams, L. H. J. (1978-82) *An Enumeration of the Flowering Plants of Nepal*. London.

Haworth-Booth, M. (1984) *The Hydrangeas*. 5th ed. London.

Krüssmann, G. (1986) *Manual of Cultivated Broad-Leaved Trees and Shrubs*. London.

Krüssmann, G. (1985) *Manual of Cultivated Conifers*. London.

Mabberley, D. J. (1987) *The Plant-Book*. Cambridge.

Meikle, R. D. (1977 and 1985) *Flora of Cyprus*. The Bentham-Moxon Trust, Royal Botanic Gardens, Kew.

Meikle, R. D. (1984) *Willows and Poplars of Great Britain and Ireland*. BSBI.

Metcalf, L. J. (1987) *The Cultivation of New Zealand Trees and Shrubs*. Wellington.

Munz, P. A. (1968) *A California Flora and Supplement*. University of California Press.

Munz, P. A. (1974) *A Flora of Southern California*. University of California Press.

Ohwi, J. (1965) *Flora of Japan*. Washington, DC.

Ouden, P. den and Boom, B. K. (1982) *Manual of Cultivated Conifers*. The Hague.

Radford, A. E., Ahles, H. E. and Bell, C. R. (1964) *Manual of the Vascular Flora of the Carolinas*. The University of North Carolina Press.

Rehder, A. (1940) *Manual of Cultivated Trees and Shrubs*. 2nd ed. New York.

Richens, R. H. (1983) *Elm*. Cambridge.

Rose, P. Q. (1980) *Ivies*. Poole.

Royal Horticultural Society (1980) *The Rhododendron Handbook*.

Rushforth, K. D. (1987) *Conifers*. London.

Salley, Homer E. and Greer, Harold E. (1986) *Rhododendron Hybrids: A Guide to their Origins*. London.

Stearn, W. T. (1983) *Botanical Latin*. 3rd ed. Newton Abbot.

Thomas, G. S. (1980) *Shrub Roses of Today*.

Thomas, G. S. (1978) *Climbing Roses Old and New*.

Treseder, N. G. (1978) *Magnolias*. London.

Tutin, T. G., Heywood, V. H., et al (eds) (1964-80) *Flora Europaea*. Cambridge.

Walters, S. M. et al (eds) (1984) *The European Garden Flora*. Cambridge.

Welch, H. J. (1979) *Manual of Dwarf Conifers*. New York.

Willis, J. C. (1973) *A Dictionary of the Higher Plants and Ferns*. 8th ed, revised by H. K. Airy Shaw. Cambridge.

# GLOSSARY

Technical and botanical terms have been used only when necessary for precision and brevity.

**Acicular**—Needle-shaped

**Acuminate**—Tapering at the end, long pointed

**Acute**—Sharp pointed

**Adpressed**—Lying close and flat against

**Anther**—The pollen-bearing part of the stamen

**Aristate**—Awned, bristle-tipped

**Articulate**—Jointed

**Ascending**—Rising somewhat obliquely and curving upwards

**Auricle**—An ear-shaped projection or appendage

**Awl-shaped**—Tapering from the base to a slender and stiff point

**Axil**—The angle formed by a leaf or lateral branch with the stem, or of a vein with the midrib

**Axillary**—Produced in the axil

**Bearded**—Furnished with long or stiff hairs

**Berry**—Strictly a pulpy, normally several-seeded, indehiscent fruit

**Bifid**—Two-cleft

**Bipinnate**—Twice pinnate

**Bisexual**—Both male and female organs in the same flower

**Blade**—The expanded part of a leaf or petal

**Bloomy**—With a fine powder-like waxy deposit

**Bole**—Trunk, of a tree

**Bract**—A modified, usually reduced leaf at the base of a flower-stalk, flower-cluster, or shoot

**Bullate**—Blistered or puckered

**Calcareous**—Containing carbonate of lime or limestone, chalky or limy

**Calcifuge**—Avoiding calcareous soils

**Calyx**—The outer part of the flower, the sepals

**Campanulate**—Bell-shaped

**Capitate**—Head-like, collected into a dense cluster

**Capsule**—A dry, several-celled pod

**Catkin**—A normally dense spike or spike-like raceme of tiny, scaly-bracted flowers or fruits

**Ciliate**—Fringed with hairs

**Cladode**—Flattened leaf-like stems

**Clone**—See under Nomenclature and Classification (p. 19)

**Columnar**—Tall, cylindrical or tapering, column-like

**Compound**—Composed of two or more similar parts

**Compressed**—Flattened

**Conical**—Cone-shaped

**Cordate**—Shaped like a heart, as base of leaf

**Coriaceous**—Leathery

**Corolla**—The inner normally conspicuous part of a flower, the petals

**Corymb**—A flat-topped or dome-shaped flowerhead with the outer flowers opening first

**Corymbose**—Having flowers in corymbs

**Crenate**—Toothed with shallow, rounded teeth, scalloped

**Cultivar**—See under Nomenclature and Classification (p. 19)

**Cuneate**—Wedge-shaped

**Cuspidate**—Abruptly sharp pointed

**Cyme**—A flat-topped or dome-shaped flowerhead with the inner flowers opening first

**Cymose**—Having flowers in cymes

**Deciduous**—Soon or seasonally falling, not persistent

**Decumbent**—Reclining, the tips ascending

**Decurrent**—Extending down the stem

**Deltoid**—Triangular

24

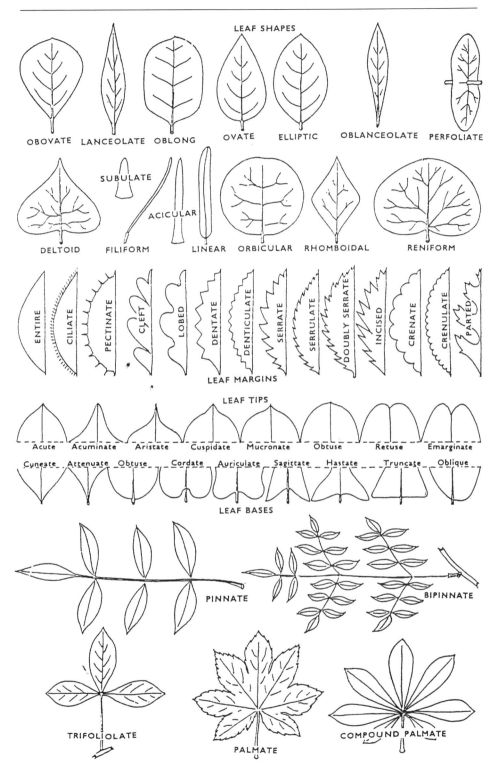

LEAF SHAPES

OBOVATE    LANCEOLATE    OBLONG    OVATE    ELLIPTIC    OBLANCEOLATE    PERFOLIATE

SUBULATE    ACICULAR

DELTOID    FILIFORM    LINEAR    ORBICULAR    RHOMBOIDAL    RENIFORM

ENTIRE    CILIATE    PECTINATE    CLEFT    LOBED    DENTATE    DENTICULATE    SERRATE    SERRULATE    DOUBLY SERRATE    INCISED    CRENATE    CRENULATE    PARTED

LEAF MARGINS

LEAF TIPS

Acute    Acuminate    Aristate    Cuspidate    Mucronate    Obtuse    Retuse    Emarginate

Cuneate    Attenuate    Obtuse    Cordate    Auriculate    Sagittate    Hastate    Truncate    Oblique

LEAF BASES

PINNATE    BIPINNATE

TRIFOLIOLATE    PALMATE    COMPOUND PALMATE

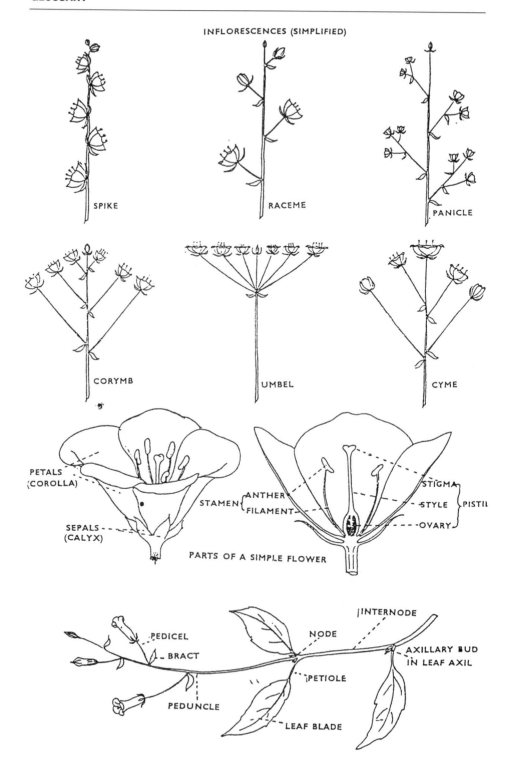

INFLORESCENCES (SIMPLIFIED)

SPIKE

RACEME

PANICLE

CORYMB

UMBEL

CYME

PETALS
(COROLLA)

STAMEN { ANTHER
FILAMENT

STIGMA

STYLE } PISTIL

OVARY

SEPALS
(CALYX)

PARTS OF A SIMPLE FLOWER

PEDICEL

BRACT

PEDUNCLE

INTERNODE

NODE

AXILLARY BUD
IN LEAF AXIL

PETIOLE

LEAF BLADE

**Dentate**—Toothed with teeth directed outward
**Denticulate**—Minutely dentate
**Depressed**—Flattened from above
**Diffuse**—Loosely or widely spreading
**Digitate**—With the members arising from one point (as in a digitate leaf)
**Dioecious**—Male and female flowers on different plants
**Dissected**—Divided into many narrow segments
**Distichous**—Arranged in two vertical ranks: two-ranked
**Divaricate**—Spreading far apart
**Divergent**—Spreading
**Divided**—Separated to the base
**Double**—(flowers) with more than the usual number of petals, often with the style and stamens changed to petals
**Doubly serrate**—Large teeth and small teeth alternating
**Downy**—Softly hairy
**Elliptic**—Widest at or about the middle, narrowing equally at both ends
**Elongate**—Lengthened
**Emarginate**—With a shallow notch at the apex
**Entire**—Undivided and without teeth
**Evergreen**—Remaining green during winter
**Exfoliating**—Peeling off in thin strips
**Exserted**—Projecting beyond (eg stamens from corolla)
**Falcate**—Sickle-shaped
**Fascicle**—A dense cluster
**Fastigiate**—With branches erect and close together
**Fertile**—Stamens producing good pollen or fruit containing good seeds, or of stems with flowering organs
**Ferruginous**—Rust-coloured
**Filament**—The stalk of a stamen
**Filiform**—Thread-like
**Fimbriate**—Fringed
**Flexuous**—Wavy or zig-zag
**Floccose**—Clothed with flocks of soft hair or wool
**Florets**—Small, individual flowers of a dense inflorescence
**Floriferous**—Flower-bearing, usually used to indicate profuse flowering
**Gibbous**—Swollen, usually at the base (as in corolla)
**Glabrous**—Hairless
**Glandular**—With secreting organs
**Glaucous**—Covered with a bloom, bluish-white or bluish-grey
**Glutinous**—Sticky
**Hermaphrodite**—Bisexual, both male and female organs in the same flower
**Hirsute**—With rather coarse or stiff hairs
**Hispid**—Beset with rigid hairs or bristles
**Hoary**—Covered with a close whitish or greyish-white pubescence
**Hybrid**—A plant resulting from a cross between different species
**Imbricate**—Overlapping, as tiles on a roof
**Impressed**—Sunken (as in veins)
**Incised**—Sharply and usually deeply and irregularly cut
**Indehiscent**—Fruits which do not (burst) open
**Indumentum**—Dense hairy covering
**Inflorescence**—The flowering part of the plant
**Internode**—The portion of stem between two nodes or joints
**Involucre**—A whorl of bracts surrounding a flower or flower cluster
**Keel**—A central ridge

**Lacerate**—Torn, irregularly cut or cleft

**Laciniate**—Cut into narrow pointed lobes

**Lanceolate**—Lance-shaped, widening above the base and long tapering to the apex

**Lanuginose**—Woolly or cottony

**Lateral**—On or at the side

**Lax**—Loose

**Leaflet**—Part of a compound leaf

**Linear**—Long and narrow with nearly parallel margins

**Lip**—One of the parts of an unequally divided flower

**Lobe**—Any protruding part of an organ (as in leaf, corolla or calyx)

**Lustrous**—Shining

**Membranous**—Thin and rather soft

**Midrib**—The central vein or rib of a leaf

**Monoecious**—Male and female flowers separate, but on the same plant

**Monotypic**—Of a single species (genus)

**Mucronate**—Terminated abruptly by a spiny tip

**Nectary**—A nectar-secreting gland, usually a small pit or protuberance

**Node**—The place upon the stem where the leaves are attached, the 'joint'

**Nut**—A non-splitting, one-seeded, hard and bony fruit

**Oblanceolate**—Inversely lanceolate

**Oblique**—Unequal-sided

**Oblong**—Longer than broad, with nearly parallel sides

**Obovate**—Inversely ovate

**Obtuse**—Blunt (as in apex of leaf or petal)

**Orbicular**—Almost circular in outline

**Oval**—Broadest at the middle

**Ovary**—The basal 'box' part of the pistil, containing the ovules

**Ovate**—Broadest below the middle (like a hen's egg)

**Ovule**—The body which, after fertilisation, becomes the seed

**Palmate**—Lobed or divided in hand-like fashion, usually five or seven-lobed

**Panicle**—A branching raceme

**Paniculate**—Having flowers in panicles

**Parted**—Cut or cleft almost to the base

**Pea-flower**—Shaped like a sweet-pea blossom

**Pectinate**—Comb-like (as in leaf margin)

**Pedicel**—The stalk of an individual flower in an inflorescence

**Peduncle**—The stalk of a flower cluster or of a solitary flower

**Pellucid**—Clear, transparent (as in gland)

**Pendulous**—Hanging, weeping

**Perfoliate**—A pair of opposite leaves fused at the base, the stem appearing to pass through them

**Perianth**—The calyx and corolla together; also commonly used for a flower in which there is no distinction between corolla and calyx

**Persistent**—Remaining attached

**Petal**—One of the separate segments of a corolla

**Petaloid**—Petal-like (as in stamen)

**Petiole**—The leaf-stalk

**Pilose**—With long, soft straight hairs

**Pinnate**—With leaflets arranged on either side of a central stalk

**Pinnatifid**—Cleft or parted in a pinnate way

**Pistil**—The female organ of a flower comprising ovary, style and stigma

**Plumose**—Feathery, as the down of a thistle

**Pollen**—Spores or grains contained in the anther, containing the male element

**Polygamous**—Bearing bisexual and unisexual flowers on the same plant

28

**Procumbent**—Lying or creeping

**Prostrate**—Lying flat on the ground

**Pruinose**—Bloomy

**Puberulent**—Minutely pubescent

**Pubescent**—Covered with short, soft hairs, downy

**Punctate**—With translucent or coloured dots or depressions

**Pungent**—Ending in a stiff, sharp point, also acid (to the taste) or strong-smelling

**Pyramidal**—Pyramid-shaped (broad at base tapering to a point)

**Raceme**—A simple elongated inflorescence with stalked flowers

**Racemose**—Having flowers in racemes

**Rachis**—An axis bearing flowers or leaflets

**Recurved**—Curved downward or backward

**Reflexed**—Abruptly turned downward

**Reniform**—Kidney-shaped

**Reticulate**—Like a network (as in veins)

**Revolute**—Rolled backwards, margin rolled under (as in leaf)

**Rib**—A prominent vein in a leaf

**Rotund**—Nearly circular

**Rufous**—Reddish-brown

**Rugose**—Wrinkled or rough

**Runner**—A trailing shoot taking root at the nodes

**Sagittate**—Shaped like an arrow-head

**Scabrous**—Rough to the touch

**Scale**—A minute leaf or bract, or a flat gland-like appendage on the surface of a leaf, flower or shoot

**Scandent**—With climbing stems

**Scarious**—Thin and dry, not green

**Semi-evergreen**—Normally evergreen but losing some or all of its leaves in a cold winter or cold area

**Sepal**—One of the segments of a calyx

**Serrate**—Saw-toothed (teeth pointing forward)

**Serrulate**—Minutely serrate

**Sessile**—Not stalked

**Setose**—Clothed with bristles

**Sheath**—A tubular envelope

**Shrub**—A woody plant which branches from the base with no obvious trunk

**Simple**—Said of a leaf that is not compound or an unbranched inflorescence

**Sinuate**—Strongly waved (as in leaf margin)

**Sinus**—The recess or space between two lobes or divisions of a leaf, calyx or corolla

**Spathulate**—Spoon-shaped

**Spicate**—Flowers in spikes

**Spike**—A simple, elongated inflorescence with sessile flowers

**Spine**—A sharp pointed end of a branch or leaf

**Spur**—A tubular projection from a flower; or a short stiff branchlet

**Stamen**—The male organ of a flower comprising filament and anther

**Staminode**—A sterile stamen, or a structure resembling a stamen, sometimes petal-like

**Standard**—The upper, normally broad and erect petal in a pea-flower; also used in nurseries to describe a tall single-stemmed young tree

**Stellate**—Star-shaped

**Stigma**—The summit of the pistil which receives the pollen, often sticky or feathery

**Stipule**—Appendage (normally two) at base of some petioles

**Stolon**—A shoot at or below the surface of the ground which produces a new plant at its tip

**Striate**—With fine, longitudinal lines

**Strigose**—Clothed with flattened fine, bristle-like, hairs

**Style**—The middle part of the pistil, often elongated between the ovary and stigma

**Subulate**—Awl-shaped

**Succulent**—Juicy, fleshy, soft and thickened in texture

**Suckering**—Producing underground stems; also the shoots from the stock of a grafted plant

**Tendril**—A twining thread-like appendage

**Ternate**—In threes

**Tessellated**—Mosaic-like (as in veins)

**Tomentose**—With dense, woolly pubescence

**Tomentum**—Dense covering of matted hairs

**Tree**—A woody plant that produces normally a single trunk and an elevated head of branches

**Trifoliate**—Three-leaved

**Trifoliolate**—A leaf with three separate leaflets

**Turbinate**—Top-shaped

**Type**—Strictly the original (type) specimen, but often used in a general sense to indicate the typical form in cultivation

**Umbel**—A normally flat-topped inflorescence in which the pedicels or peduncles all arise from a common point

**Umbellate**—Flowers in umbels

**Undulate**—With wavy margins

**Unisexual**—Of one sex

**Urceolate**—Urn-shaped

**Velutinous**—Clothed with a velvety indumentum

**Venation**—The arrangement of the veins

**Verrucose**—Having a wart-like or nodular surface

**Verticillate**—Arranged in a whorl or ring

**Villous**—Bearing long and soft hairs

**Viscid**—Sticky

**Whorl**—Three or more flowers or leaves arranged in a ring

# A Brief History of Plant Hunting

(as it concerns woody plants)

## ROY LANCASTER

In 1873, Jules Verne's famous character Phileas Fogg created a sensation by travelling around the world in 80 days. Today it is possible to achieve the same feat in less than 80 minutes. All one needs is a garden and a good book plus a little imagination to make the journey more lively and enjoyable. This is made possible by the fact that gardens are filled with plants from foreign lands introduced over a period of many centuries. Even the smallest gardens contain representatives of several countries, among which one is sure to find China, the United States and probably Italy and Spain. Larger gardens might also have Japan, India and Russia represented whilst the gardens, large or small, of really keen gardeners and specialists are likely to include New Zealand, Australia, South Africa, Chile, Mexico, Nepal and Kashmir with others such as Greece and Turkey thrown in for good measure.

Botanic gardens and other major collections such as the Hillier Gardens and Arboretum and the Royal Horticultural Society's Garden at Wisley offer a wealth of plants from most if not all points of the globe and, what's more, they are normally labelled. A garden therefore contains the potential for an adventure in which people of all ages and persuasions can participate. The keys to the adventure are the names of the plants and a good reference book. In the case of woody plants - trees, shrubs, conifers, climbers and bamboos - Bean's *Trees and Shrubs Hardy in the British Isles* is the classic reference work in English, but it is bulky, perfect for consulting in one's home but not for carrying around gardens. For this purpose the *Hillier Manual* is ideal.

Thus prepared, one can set out into the garden or arboretum in search of adventure. One of the first things one learns on these occasions is the importance of plant collectors in providing our gardens with the curious and the lovely. Without them there would be no gardens except those formal associations where grass, gravel, water and hedge obey the whims of man, or else the contrived wilderness where native herbs run amok. Important though these gardens are in the general scheme of things they have their limitations and cannot replace the excitement and satisfaction of growing plants from foreign locations, nor can they compete with the range of effects, especially in flower, foliage, fruit and bark.

As far as Britain is concerned, the earliest trees and shrubs from foreign shores were introduced in ancient times eg the Sweet Chestnut (*Castanea sativa*) and the Bay (*Laurus nobilis*) from southern Europe and the Walnut (*Juglans regia*) from the Caucasus and SW Asia. Most of these early introductions were made for their food value or medicinal properties, including such familiar shrubs as Lavender (*Lavandula angustifolia*), Wall Germander (*Teucrium chamae-drys*), Rue (*Ruta graveolens*) and Rosemary (*Rosmarinus officinalis*), all from Europe, while the Summer Jessamine (*Jasminum officinale*) has been cultivated in Britain, according to Bean, since time immemorial, presumably for its sweetly scented flowers. We have no record of the exact date these plants arrived here, nor by whom they were introduced, and this state of affairs continued until well into the 16th century, when a goodly number of what we now regard as ornamental plants were finding their way here from Europe. Thus *Staphylea pinnata* was recorded by the herbalist John Gerard as growing in London "by the Lord Treasurer's House". *Vitex agnus-castus*, *Clematis viticella*, *Cupressus sempervirens*, *Platanus orientalis* and *Pinus pinaster* are just a few of the many ornamental woody plants recorded as growing in Britain at this time.

The first organised plant collecting for British gardens took place in the early 17th century when John Tradescant, then gardener to Sir Robert Cecil the first Lord Salisbury, was sent by his employer on a visit to France and Holland to buy plants from nursery gardens. In 1618, after the death of Lord Salisbury, Tradescant left on a far more ambitious expedition to Russia where he is said to have collected several trees and shrubs new to Britain, though what these were is open to dispute. This was followed by an expedition to the Mediterranean whence many new plants including *Cistus* and *Cytisus* species were introduced. Tradescant had a son, also John, who followed in his father's footsteps as a plant collector, choosing an entirely different territory however, when in 1637 he sailed for Virginia and the "New World".

A host of new plants were sent back from this expedition and from further visits there in 1642 and 1654. Among his introductions were the Black Locust - *Robinia pseudoacacia* - and the Tulip Tree - *Liriodendron tulipifera*. Later that century and from the same area, Virginia, a missionary, John Bannister, began sending native plants, especially trees and shrubs, to Henry Compton, Bishop of London. These included maples, red oaks and walnuts.

The following century saw a great increase in plant introductions with John Bartram and his son in Philadelphia increasing the flow of novelties chiefly from the SE United States. In 1772, Francis Masson, often described as the first of the professional plant collectors and the first of a long line to be employed by the Royal Botanic Gardens, Kew, was sent to South Africa at the instigation of Sir Joseph Banks, himself a collector in Australia and the South Pacific. Masson was a hard-working and diligent collector but his collections were mostly restricted to non-woody plants, though he did introduce some of the Cape Heaths (*Erica* spp.) and similarly exotic but tender shrubs. In the last two decades of the 18th century a great number of plants, especially woody plants, were introduced to Britain from the eastern United States, particularly from the south-east, by Scotsman John Fraser. These included *Magnolia fraseri* and *Pieris floribunda*.

As far as woody plants are concerned, the introductions of the 19th century far exceeded all those made before. For Britain it was the age of an expanding empire and her merchant ships pursued an increasing trade with countries all over the globe. This had a great influence on plant introduction and many collectors were sent by Kew and the Royal Horticultural Society, as well as by private patrons, to scour the world's wild places for new plants to feed the ever-increasing interest in gardening.

In 1824 one of the greatest plant collectors of all time, David Douglas, set out on the first of two expeditions to western North America and over the next three years (to 1827) he travelled widely, collecting a huge number of seeds including many fine shrubs and trees, especially conifers. These included *Pinus ponderosa* and *P. lambertiana* as well as *Mahonia aquifolium* and the Flowering Currant - *Ribes sanguineum*. He also introduced seed of the tree that bears his name, the Douglas Fir - *Pseudotsuga menziesii*, discovered some thirty years earlier by Archibald Menzies. Douglas's second expedition lasted from 1829 until 1834 during which time he travelled from British Columbia south to California collecting, among other plants, *Garrya elliptica*. He died tragically in Hawaii in July 1834 having fallen into a pit containing a wild bull.

Douglas was a Scotsman and in 1843 another great plant-collecting Scot, Robert Fortune, was sent by the Royal Horticultural Society to the east coast of China. Over the next three years he made a large collection of plants, most of which he purchased in nursery gardens. He returned to China on two separate occasions and made a final expedition to Japan and China before returning to Scotland. During these visits he is said to have introduced to Britain for the first time nearly 190 species and varieties of plants including many trees, shrubs and climbers. These included such well known garden standards as *Jasminum nudiflorum*, *Lonicera fragrantissima*, *Viburnum plicatum* and *Weigela florida*.

Meanwhile, many Japanese plants had found their way into Britain via the Dutch nursery of Dr Philip von Siebold, a German eye surgeon who lived and collected in Japan for many years. The middle years of the last century must have been an exciting time for gardeners with the fruits of Fortune's Chinese expeditions being distributed, plus the results of Sir Joseph Hooker's expedition to the Sikkim Himalaya where so many fine Rhododendrons were discovered, and the expeditions to Chile and then California and Oregon by the Cornishman, William Lobb. From his two Chilean visits Lobb introduced *Berberis darwinii*, *Lapageria rosea*, *Desfontainia spinosa* and *Embothrium coccineum* as well as numerous other woody plants.

During the latter half of the 19th century a great deal of plant activity was taking place in China as a result of French missionaries in remote areas pursuing a second "career" as plant collectors. Armand David, Jean Delavay and Paul Farges were the most productive in this field, most of their collections going to the Natural History Museum in Paris and any living plants or seed being grown in the gardens there or put into commerce via French nurseries such as Vilmorin. All three missionaries are commemorated in the names of many of the plants they discovered eg *Davidia involucrata* - the Dove Tree, *Abies delavayi* and *Catalpa fargesii*.

Between 1877 and 1879 an Englishman, Charles Maries, was also in China, Taiwan and Japan collecting on behalf of the Veitch nursery of Chelsea. He was the first to introduce, among other things, the Chinese Witch Hazel - *Hamamelis mollis*. Almost twenty years earlier John Gould Veitch had introduced from Japan a rich selection of new conifers including *Larix kaempferi*, the Japanese Larch.

What is generally referred to as the Golden Age of Chinese plant introductions was ushered in by an Irishman, Augustine Henry, who, during seven years as an official for the Imperial Maritime Customs Service based at Ichang in Hubei province, helped make known to Britain and the West the botanical riches of central and western China. Of the plants first discovered by Henry, *Tilia henryana* and *Parthenocissus henryana* are two that bear his name.

It was as a result of Henry's discoveries that another great plant collector appeared on the scene in the shape of Ernest Henry Wilson, who between 1899 and 1911 made four expeditions to central and western China. The first two were for the Veitch nursery, the last two on behalf of the Arnold Arboretum, Massachusetts. He is said to have introduced over a thousand plants new to western cultivation, most of them woody and many still considered as garden standards today. They included the Chinese Paperbark Maple - *Acer griseum*, *Ceratostigma willmottianum*, *Rhododendron lutescens* and *Berberis wilsoniae*. Wilson later went on to collect in Taiwan, Japan and Korea.

China, in the first three decades of the present century, was a hive of activity as first one, then another plant collector arrived, charged with finding and introducing new hardy ornamentals. One of the most famous of these was the Scot, George Forrest, who spent most of thirty years and a total of seven expeditions in the border areas of China, Burma and Tibet. Whereas Wilson concentrated on Sichuan and Hubei, Forrest made the province of Yunnan his main collecting ground and during an active and gruelling but productive career, introduced large numbers of seeds and plants to British cultivation. He is remembered by gardeners for, among other plants, *Pieris formosa* var. *forrestii*, *Magnolia campbellii* var. *mollicomata* and innumerable Rhododendrons. Other major plant collectors in China at this time included Reginald Farrer who concentrated mainly on alpines and perennials, Frank Kingdon-Ward and Joseph Rock. Kingdon-Ward, like Forrest, was initially employed by A.K. Bulley, a businessman who founded Bees nursery of Chester as well as Ness Gardens in the Wirral. Between 1911 and his death in 1958, Kingdon-Ward, who was probably the longest-serving professional plant collector, made 25 expeditions mainly to Yunnan, Tibet, Assam and Burma during which time he introduced an enormous range of plants and seeds including, for the first time, *Rhododendron wardii*, *R. macabeanum* and *Sorbus wardii*.

Joseph Rock, an American of Austrian birth, also spent a good deal of his life in Yunnan. Indeed, he first visited the province in 1922 and was the last major western plant collector to leave when the People's Republic was declared in 1949. He is mainly remembered by gardeners for the *Sorbus* which bears his name and by Rhododendron enthusiasts for the many good forms of species he introduced. Meanwhile, in the eastern Himalaya, two plant collectors, Frank Ludlow and Major George Sherriff pursued a highly successful partnership in the mountains of Bhutan and SE Tibet, whence, in a series of expeditions lasting from 1933 to 1949, they introduced a wealth of new plants among which woody plants were in the minority. They did collect, however, many fine Rhododendrons and other trees and shrubs including *Berberis sherriffii* and *Paeonia lutea* var. *ludlowii*.

With the death of Kingdon-Ward, the last of the major plant collectors, in 1958, the so-called "Golden Years" of plant hunting came to an end. But plant collecting itself did not die. With the opening up of Nepal in the 1960s and the reopening of China in the 1970s, new opportunities for plant introduction presented themselves and from these two countries alone has flowed, in the past two decades, a steady stream of new plants including trees and shrubs. In addition, in the search for species new to cultivation as well as improved forms of those previously introduced, many of the old collecting areas have been revisited and looked at with new eyes. Of course, given the requirements of conservation world-wide, the priorities of the plant hunter have changed. In the old days two years was the average period for an expedition, with enough time to do a thorough reconnaissance in the flowering season and return the following autumn for the seed harvest, and harvest is the word. Baskets of plants and mule-loads of seed were regularly collected to satisfy the demands of patrons and, as is often the case when there is an abundance of riches, wastage and losses occurred through carelessness and neglect.

Today's plant hunter, by comparison, is well aware of the conservation priorities in his or her collecting area and collecting proceeds with these priorities in mind. Expeditions are relatively short-term affairs while the individual collections may comprise a seedling, a cutting, a rooted piece or a pinch of seed; but then that is often all that is required. Modern air travel can have collected material at its destination within one to three days and the collector, having ensured beforehand that the material goes to the sources most likely to establish it, can be reasonably confident of its success.

Gardeners have benefitted and will continue to benefit from the recent co-operation between botanical institutions in China on the one hand and those in Britain and North America. The British collectors most involved in recent introductions of woody plant species to Britain include Chris Brickell, Peter Cox, Brian Halliwell, Harold Hillier, Roy Lancaster, Keith Rushforth, Jim Russell, Tony Schilling and John Whitehead.

Thus ends a short account of plant collecting as it concerns hardy woody plants. Throughout the last four hundred years, trees and shrubs, with other plants, have found their way into British and Western cultivation by a bewildering variety of means. All the writer has done so far is to draw attention to some of the more successful and dedicated individuals, all of whom risked and, in a few instances, lost their lives in pursuing their chosen career. Space does not permit a mention of those countless people, mostly forgotten, who have caused the occasional foreign plant to be introduced to our gardens. They include travellers of all kinds, legation officials and their spouses, sea captains, medical practitioners, botanists and of course gardeners.

Following is a selection of the major collectors involved in introducing hardy woody plants to Britain together with brief lists of some of their most notable introductions. It must be emphasised that plants in these lists are, as far as we can ascertain, *first* introductions. Many plants in cultivation today are descended from subsequent introductions by other collectors. It should be pointed out that many of the early plant introductions from Australia and New Zealand appear to have gone unrecorded, at least there is a paucity of dates in Bean's work, nor has it been possible to include the plant introductions of the French missionaries David and Delavay as it has proved impossible to differentiate seed and plant collections from the much greater collections for the herbarium. In this connection one should also acknowledge the plant collecting activities of others, especially the Russians who, mainly in the 19th century, caused many plants to be introduced from central and eastern Asia.


**John Tradescant the Elder** (d. 1638) Mediterranean region (reputedly introduced)
*Cistus monspeliensis, C. albidus, C. ladanifer, C. populifolius, C. crispus, Cytisus canariensis, Danae racemosa, Halimium halimifolium, Jasminum grandiflorum, Prunus laurocerasus, Salix elaeagnos, Syringa × persica.*


**John Tradescant the Younger** (1608-62) SE United States
*Acer rubrum, Celtis occidentalis, Juglans cinerea, Liriodendron tulipifera, Lonicera sempervirens, Parthenocissus quinquefolia, Platanus occidentalis,* ? *Robinia pseudoacacia, Taxodium distichum, Vitis labrusca,* ? *Yucca filamentosa.*


**John Fraser** (1752-1811) SE United States
*Abies fraseri, Aesculus parviflora, Magnolia fraseri, Pieris floribunda, Rhododendron maximum.*

**David Douglas** (1798-1834) Western North America
*Arbutus menziesii, Abies grandis, A. procera, Acer macrophyllum, A. circinatum, Castanopsis chrysophylla, Garrya elliptica, Gaultheria shallon, Holodiscus discolor, Mahonia aquifolium, Mahonia nervosa, Picea sitchensis, Pinus contorta, P. coulteri, P. monticola, P. ponderosa, P. radiata, Pseudotsuga menziesii, Quercus garryana, Ribes sanguineum, Rubus parviflorus, R. spectabilis, Spiraea douglasii, Umbellularia californica.*

**Philip F. von Siebold** (1796-1866) Japan
*Fraxinus sieboldiana, Forsythia suspensa* var. *sieboldii, Hamamelis japonica* 'Arborea', *Ilex latifolia, Ligustrum japonicum, Lespedeza thunbergii, Malus sieboldii, Pinus densiflora, Spiraea nipponica, S. prunifolia* 'Plena', *Trachycarpus fortunei, Wisteria floribunda.*

**William Lobb** (1809-1863) Chile and California
*Abies bracteata, Berberis darwinii, Desfontainia spinosa, Embothrium coccineum, Nothofagus obliqua, Fitzroya cupressoides, Sequoiadendron giganteum, Thuja plicata.*

**Robert Fortune** (1812-1880) China and Japan
*Abelia uniflora, Akebia quinata, Callicarpa dichotoma, Cephalotaxus fortunei, Clematis lanuginosa, Cupressus funebris, Cryptomeria japonica, Exochorda racemosa, Forsythia viridissima, F. suspensa* var. *fortunei, Ilex cornuta, Jasminum nudiflorum, Lonicera fragrantissima, L. standishii, Mahonia japonica* 'Bealei', *Pinus bungeana, Prunus triloba* 'Multiplex', *Pseudolarix amabilis, Rhododendron fortunei, R. degronianum* subsp. *heptamerum, R. Obtusum, Skimmia japonica* subsp. *reevesiana, Spiraea japonica* var. *fortunei, Viburnum macrocephalum* 'Sterile', *V. plicatum* 'Sterile', *Weigela florida.*

**J.G. Veitch** (1839-1870) Japan
*Abies firma, Larix kaempferi, Picea bicolor, P. jezoensis* var. *hondoensis, P. polita, Pinus koraiensis, P. parviflora, P. thunbergii.*

**Sir Joseph Hooker** (1817-1911) Sikkim Himalaya
*Juniperus wallichiana, Magnolia campbellii, Rhododendron arboreum, R. barbatum, R. campanulatum, R. campylocarpum, R. cinnabarinum, R. dalhousiae, R . falconeri, R. grande, R. griffithianum, R. thomsonii* and many more.

**Charles Maries** (1851-1902) Japan and China
*Abies veitchii, A. mariesii, Acer carpinifolium, A. davidii, A. palmatum* (many cultivars of), *A. rufinerve, Carpinus cordata, Enkianthus campanulatus, Hamamelis mollis, Rhododendron oldhamii, Styrax obassia, Viburnum plicatum* 'Mariesii'.

**E.H. Wilson** (1876-1930) W China
*Acer griseum, Actinidia chinensis, Berberis julianae, B. sargentiana, B. wilsoniae, Catalpa fargesii, Ceratostigma willmottianum, Clematis armandii, Clematis montana* var. *rubens, Corylopsis veitchiana, Cornus kousa* var. *chinensis, Cotoneaster dammeri, Cotoneaster salicifolius, Daphne genkwa, D. retusa, Deutzia longifolia, Dipelta floribunda, Ilex pernyi, Jasminum mesnyi, Kolkwitzia amabilis, Lonicera nitida, Magnolia delavayi, M. dawsoniana, M. sargentiana, M. wilsonii, Malus hupehensis, Photinia davidiana, Prunus serrula, Rhododendron rex* subsp. *fictolacteum, R. lutescens, R. williamsianum, Rosa moyesii, R. willmottiae, Salix magnifica, Sorbus sargentiana, S. megalocarpa, Viburnum davidii.*

**George Forrest** (1873-1932) SW China
*Abies forrestii, Acer forrestii, Berberis jamesiana, Buddleja fallowiana, B. forrestii, Camellia reticulata* (wild form), *C. saluenensis, Cotoneaster lacteus, Deutzia monbeigii, Gaultheria forrestii,*

*Hypericum forrestii, Jasminum polyanthum, Osmanthus suavis, Pieris formosa* var. *forrestii, Pyracantha rogersiana, Rhododendron griersonianum, R. neriiflorum, R. protistum* var. *giganteum, R. sinogrande, R. souliei, Sorbus harrowiana, Syringa yunnanensis.*

**Frank Kingdon-Ward** (1885-1958) SW China, Upper Burma, SE Tibet
*Acer wardii, Berberis calliantha, B. hypokerina, B. wardii, Cassiope wardii, Cornus chinensis, Cotoneaster conspicuus, C. wardii, Gaultheria wardii, Leycesteria crocothyrsos, Rhododendron calostrotum, R. charitopes* subsp. *tsangpoense, R. leucaspis, R. macabeanum, R. uniflorum* var. *imperator, R. wardii, Sorbus poteriifolia, S. wardii.*

**Recent collections** (Various collectors in many countries)
*Acer pycnanthum, Alnus jorullensis, Aucuba omeiensis, Betula calcicola, B. tianschanica, Camellia chrysantha, Carpinus pubescens, C. schuschaensis, Clematis marmoraria, Colutea buhsei, Craibiodendron yunnanense, Eucalyptus debeuzevillei, Euonymus vagans, Hedera nepalensis* var. *sinensis, H. pastuchowii, Heptacodium jasminoides, Hypericum lancasteri, H. maclarenii, Larix himalaica, Lonicera infundibulum* var. *rockii, L. prostrata, Magnolia dealbata, Mahonia confusa, M. gracilipes, M. russellii, Nothopanax delavayi, Pinus bhutanica, P. culminicola, Pernettya poeppigii, Populus jacquemontii* var. *glauca, Quercus durata, Q. monimotricha, Q. rysophylla, Rhododendron kesangiae, Salix elbursensis, Sinocalycanthus chinensis, Sorbus aronioides, S. gonggashanica, Telopea truncata* f. *lutea, Tilia begoniifolia, T. nobilis, Viburnum chingii.*

# TREES AND SHRUBS

This section does not include CLIMBERS, CONIFERS or BAMBOOS, which are listed under separate headings at the end of this manual.

---

\* Indicates that the plant is evergreen.

† Indicates that the plant is too tender for exposed positions in all but the mildest localities, though most of them are hardy on walls, or when given evergreen, woodland, or similar protection.

‡ Indicates that the plant requires lime-free or neutral soil, and will not tolerate alkaline or chalky conditions.

× Indicates that the plant is of hybrid origin.

+ Indicates that the plant is a graft chimaera (graft hybrid).

I Indicates the date of original introduction into western gardens.

C Indicates the first recorded date of cultivation where the exact date of introduction is not known.

---

Awards – See p. 21
Heights – See p. 18

---

**ABELIA** R. BR.—**Caprifoliaceae**—A genus of about 30 species of deciduous and evergreen shrubs natives of E Asia and Mexico with opposite leaves and profusely borne funnel-shaped or tubular flowers. In many species the persistent calyx is attractive after the corolla has fallen. Best in full sun.

**chinensis** R. BR. A small shrub with fragrant white, rose-tinted flowers, freely produced. July to October. C and E China. C 1844. AM 1976.

**'Edward Goucher'** (*A.* × *grandiflora* × *A. schumannii*). Small, semi-evergreen shrub with bright, glossy green leaves bronze when young. Lilac-pink flowers are profusely borne during summer and autumn. Sepals 2. Raised in the United States in 1911. A first class shrub for the small garden.

†**floribunda** DECNE. A medium-sized, evergreen or semi-evergreen shrub producing abundant tubular flowers up to 5cm long, of a brilliant cherry-red in June. Best against a warm wall. Mexico. I 1841.

**graebneriana** REHD. A rare species, a vigorous medium-sized shrub with reddish shoots and glossy green, taper-pointed leaves; flowers apricot with yellow throat. C China. I 1910 by Ernest Wilson.

**'Vedrariensis'** A form with larger leaves and broader blotches in the throat of the flower.

×**grandiflora** REHD. (*A. chinensis* × *A. uniflora*). A vigorous, arching, medium-sized semi-evergreen shrub with dark glossy green leaves which are sometimes borne in threes or even fours on vigorous shoots. Flowers slightly fragrant, white tinged pale pink, borne over a long period from July to October or later followed by attractive pink-tinged sepals. Raised in Italy before 1866 and possibly elsewhere. AGM 1984.

**'Francis Mason'** Leaves dark green with a golden yellow margin. Originated at Mason's Nurseries in New Zealand in the early 1950s as a sport. The variegation is best developed in full sun in a dry soil. Often sports to produce a form with all-gold leaves which has been called 'Goldsport', 'Goldspot' or 'Gold Strike'. AGM 1984.

**schumannii** (GRAEBN.) REHD. A small shrub giving a continuous display of abundant, lilac-pink, slightly fragrant flowers blotched with orange over a long period during late summer and autumn. Very hardy and subject to injury only in very cold winters. W China. I 1910 by Ernest Wilson. AM 1926. AGM 1984.

**serrata** SIEB. & ZUCC. A dwarf to small shrub of slow growth; flowers white or blush, tinged orange, May to June. Not recommended for shallow chalk soils. Japan. I 1879 by Charles Maries.

**ABELIA**—*continued*

**spathulata** SIEB. & ZUCC. A small, very hardy shrub with taper-pointed leaves, bronze-margined when young. The showy white flowers marked with orange are borne in June. Japan. I 1880 by Charles Maries.

**triflora** R. BR. ex WALL. A large, erect shrub of graceful habit. Flowers produced in June in threes in dense clusters, white tinged pink, and exquisitely scented. NW Himalaya. I 1847. AM 1959.

**umbellata** REHD. A vigorous medium-sized to large shrub of spreading habit. The pure white flowers are produced in early June. C and W China. I 1907 by Ernest Wilson.

**ABELIOPHYLLUM** NAKAI—**Oleaceae**—A monotypic genus related to *Forsythia* but with white flowers. Very hardy but needs hot sun to thrive.

**distichum** NAKAI A small shrub of slow growth. The fragrant white, pink-tinged flowers are produced on the purplish, leafless stems during February. The leaves sometimes turn purple in autumn. Korea. I 1924. AM 1937. FCC 1944.

†**ABUTILON** MILL.—**Malvaceae**—A large genus of more than 100 species of trees, shrubs and herbs found in tropical and subtropical regions of both hemispheres. The plants described here are small to large shrubs suitable for a south wall or cool greenhouse. Flowers often large, bell-shaped or open and saucer-shaped, produced over a long period.

**'Ashford Red'** A medium-sized shrub with large apple-green leaves and flowers of good texture, size and substance, best described as a deep shade of crushed strawberry. An outstanding plant.

**'Kentish Belle'** (*A.* × *milleri* × *A.* 'Golden Fleece'). A small to medium-sized shrub with purplish stems and dark green, long-pointed triangular leaves. Flowers bell-like, pendulous on long stalks over a long period during summer and autumn; 4cm long with a red calyx and soft apricot petals, the veins faintly stained with red. Raised by A.V. Pike, once Head Gardener at Hever Castle, Kent. AM 1968.

**'Margherita Manns'** See *A. ochsenii.*

**megapotamicum** ST.HIL. & NAUD. (*A. vexillarium* MORR.) A small to medium-sized shrub for a warm wall. The conspicuous pendulous flowers have a red calyx, yellow petals and purple anthers. Summer and autumn. Brazil. I 1804. AM 1949.

**'Variegatum'** Leaves with mottled yellow variegation. AM 1988.

× **milleri** HORT. (*A. megapotamicum* × *A. pictum*). A medium-sized shrub. Flowers bell-shaped, orange, with crimson stamens; leaves dark green. Continuous flowering.

**'Variegatum'** Leaves mottled yellow.

**ochsenii** (PHIL.) PHIL. (*A.* 'Margherita Manns') A medium to large, slender shrub for a sunny wall, with cup-shaped flowers of a lovely lavender-blue, darker at centre. Chile. I about 1957. AM 1962.

× **suntense** BRICKELL (*A. ochsenii* × *A. vitifolium*). Intentionally raised by our propagator Peter Dummer in 1967 and accidentally from Highdown seed by Richard Gorer of Sunte House after which it is named. A large, fast-growing shrub flowering freely between May and July. AGM 1984 (to selected forms).

**'Gorer's White'** Flowers white. A selection of the Sunte House seedlings. AM 1977.

**'Jermyns'** A form selected from the original cross made in our Winchester nursery in 1967, using the form of *A. vitifolium* known as 'Veronica Tennant'. Flowers clear, dark mauve.

**'Violetta'** Flowers deep violet-blue.

**'White Charm'** Flowers white, slight , , shaped, up to 5cm across. Originated as a chance seedling in the Hillier Gardens and Arboretum in 1975.

**vexillarium** See *A. megapotamicum.*

**vitifolium** (CAV.) PRESL. A large, handsome shrub needing a sunny sheltered site. Flowers saucer-shaped, pale to deep mauve. May to July. The vine-shaped leaves are downy and grey. Chile. I 1836. FCC 1888. AGM 1984 (to selected forms).

**'Album'** Flowers white. AM 1961.

**'Tennant's White'** A form with large, pure white flowers freely borne.

**'Veronica Tennant'** A free-flowering selection with large, mauve flowers.

†*ACACIA MILL.—**Leguminosae**—The "Wattles" are a very large genus of more than 1000 species of trees and shrubs (very rarely herbs) found throughout tropical and subtropical regions particularly Africa and Australia. The leaves are often bipinnate but in many species are reduced to phyllodes (a development of the leaf stalk). The acacias are mostly winter or spring-flowering cool-greenhouse shrubs but several species attain tree size out-of-doors in favoured localities. Flowers usually yellow, in small rounded heads or bottlebrushes, the conspicuous feature of which is the stamens. Most become chlorotic on chalk soils.

**armata** R. BR. "Kangaroo Thorn". A small-leaved prickly species of dense bushy habit. Phyllodes small and narrow, dark green. Masses of yellow flowers all along the branches in spring. I 1803.

**baileyana** F. MUELL. "Cootamundra Wattle". Small tree or large shrub with attractive glaucous, bipinnate leaves and racemes of bright yellow flowers freely produced. Winter and spring. New South Wales. I 1888. AM 1927. FCC 1936.

  **'Purpurea'** A spectacular form with the young foliage deep purple contrasting with the blue-green older leaves.

**dealbata** LINK (*A. decurrens* var. *dealbata* (LINK) F. MUELL.) "Silver Wattle". A large shrub or small tree for a sheltered wall. The fern-like leaves are silvery green. Flowers produced in late winter to early spring, fragrant. The popular golden "Mimosa" of florists. SE Australia, Tasmania. I 1820. AM 1935. FCC 1971.

**decurrens var. dealbata** See *A. dealbata*.

**diffusa** KER. A large, lax, genista-like shrub with narrow, sharp-pointed phyllodes; sulphur-yellow flowers are borne in small heads. I 1818. AM 1934.

**'Exeter Hybrid'** (*A. longifolia* × *A. riceana*). (*A.* 'Veitchiana') A beautiful medium to large-sized shrub raised by Veitch in Exeter. The arching branches bear narrow leaves and spikes of rich yellow, fragrant flowers. AM 1961.

**longifolia** (ANDR.) WILLD. "Sydney Golden Wattle". Large shrub with long, lance-shaped, dark green phyllodes and bright yellow flowers in 4-8cm spikes. One of the hardiest species, and fairly lime tolerant. Australia, Tasmania. I 1792.

  **var. sophorae** (LABILL.) F. MUELL. Phyllodes somewhat shorter and broader. Moderately hardy in favoured areas.

**melanoxylon** R. BR. "Blackwood Acacia". A tree-like species allied to *A. longifolia*, but with pinnate juvenile foliage. S Australia, Tasmania. I 1808.

**mucronata** WILLD. A large shrub related to and resembling *A. longifolia*, but with much narrower phyllodes. SE Australia, Tasmania. AM 1933.

**pendula** A. CUNN. "Weeping Myall". Small tree with pendulous stems, narrow, rigid, silvery-grey phyllodes and cylindrical panicles of yellow flowers. E Australia.

**pravissima** F. MUELL. "Oven's Wattle". A large shrub or small tree with slender arching shoots. Phyllodes triangular, two-veined, glaucous on both sides with a single spine on the lower side of the broad apex. Flowers yellow in small clusters early spring. SE Australia.

**rhetinodes** SCHLECHT. A small tree with narrow, grey-green, willow-like phyllodes. Flowers freely carried in large, loose panicles during the summer. One of the most lime-tolerant species. SE Australia, Tasmania. I 1871. AM 1925.

**riceana** HENSLOW "Rice's Wattle". A large shrub or small tree of graceful habit with slender weeping shoots and dark green, sharp-pointed phyllodes. Flowers pale yellow, in drooping clusters in spring. Tasmania. AM 1926.

**verticillata** (L'HERIT.) WILLD. "Prickly Moses". A large shrub or small tree with dark green, whorled needle-like phyllodes and cylindrical spikes of bright yellow flowers. SE Australia, Tasmania. I 1780 by Sir Joseph Hooker. AM 1926.


**"ACACIA, FALSE"** See *Robinia pseudoacacia*.


**ACANTHOPANAX** See *Eleutherococcus*.

  **pentaphyllus** See *E. sieboldianus*.

  **ricinifolius** See *Kalopanax pictus*.

  **spinosus** See *E. sieboldianus*.

**ACER** L.—**Aceraceae**—The "Maples" comprise more than 100 species of mainly deciduous trees and shrubs found throughout N temperate regions with a large number in E Asia. Leaves opposite, palmately lobed in most species, entire or compound. They are mostly very hardy and of easy culture. Those referred to as "Japanese Maples" will be found under *A. japonicum* and *A. palmatum*. Flowers small but often attractive, usually opening with the young leaves.

**acuminatum** WALL. ex D. DON A small tree closely related to *A. caudatum*. Leaves on scarlet petioles, usually three-lobed and sharply toothed, the lobes with slender tail-like points. W Himalaya.

**amplum** REHD. A small tree with polished, green stems. Leaves like those of the "Norway Maple", five-lobed, bronze when young. C China. I 1901 by Ernest Wilson.

‡**argutum** MAXIM. A small, upright tree with elegant, five-lobed, pale green leaves, made conspicuous by the reticulate venation. Long-stalked, greenish flowers open with the leaves. Japan. I 1881.

**buergerianum** MIQ. (*A. trifidum* HOOK. & ARN. not THUNB.) Small, bushy tree with three-lobed, long-persistent leaves often red or orange in autumn. E China and Korea. C 1890.

†**campbellii** HOOK. f. & THOMS. Medium-sized tree with palmately lobed leaves, red when young and often colouring well in autumn. Hardy here in sheltered woodland. E Himalaya, Burma. I about 1851 by Sir Joseph Hooker.

　**var. yunnanense** See *A. flabellatum* var. *yunnanense*.

**campestre** L. "Field Maple" "Hedge Maple". A picturesque medium-sized tree frequently used in rustic hedges; foliage turns clear yellow, sometimes flushed red, in autumn. Europe (incl British Isles), W Asia. AGM 1984.

　**'Compactum'** A shrubby form of dense, bushy habit. C 1893.

　**'Elsrijk'** A Dutch selection of dense, conical habit. A good street tree. C 1953.

　**'Postelense'** Young leaves golden yellow, later yellow-green, red-stalked. Shrubby or a mop-headed small tree. C 1896.

　**'Pulverulentum'** Leaves thickly speckled and blotched with white. C 1859.

　**'Schwerinii'** A form with purple leaves. C 1897.

**capillipes** MAXIM. A small tree with striated bark and bright green, three-lobed leaves, the young growths coral-red. Attractive autumn tints of orange and red. Japan. I 1892 by Charles Sargent. AM 1975. AGM 1984.

**cappadocicum** GLEDITSCH (*A. laetum* C.A. MEY.) A medium-sized to large tree with broad, five to seven-lobed, glossy leaves turning to rich butter-yellow in autumn. Caucasus and W Asia to the Himalaya. I 1838.

　**'Aureum'** A striking form with red young leaves, turning golden yellow and remaining so for many weeks. C 1914. AGM 1984.

　**'Rubrum'** Young growths blood-red. A most attractive form. I 1838. AGM 1984.

　**var. sinicum** REHD. A very attractive variety with smaller, usually five-lobed leaves; young growths coppery-red. Fruits red in autumn. China. I 1901 by Ernest Wilson. AM 1958.

**carpinifolium** SIEB. & ZUCC. "Hornbeam Maple". Small to medium-sized tree with leaves remarkably like those of the "Common Hornbeam" but opposite, turning gold and brown in autumn. Japan. I 1879 by Charles Maries.

**caudatum** WALL. (*A. papilio* KING) A medium-sized tree with glabrous shoots and five-lobed, coarsely-toothed leaves, downy beneath. E Himalaya.

**circinatum** PURSH "Vine Maple". A large shrub, or occasionally a small tree, with almost circular leaves prettily tinted in summer, and turning orange and crimson in autumn. The wine-red and white flowers in April are quite decorative. Grows well even in dry, shady positions. W North America. I 1826 by David Douglas.

　**'Monroe'** A small shrub, the leaves divided to the base into usually 5 deeply cut lobes. Found in the Willamette National Forest, Oregon in 1960 by Mr Warner Monroe.

**cissifolium** (SIEB. & ZUCC.) K. KOCH A small tree with trifoliolate, bronze-tinted leaves which turn to red and yellow in autumn. Similar to *A. henryi*. Not very tolerant of chalk soils. Japan. I before 1870.

×**coriaceum** TAUSCH (*A. monspessulanum* × *A. pseudoplatanus*). Small tree of neat, rounded habit with rather leathery, shallowly three-lobed leaves which are often retained well into winter turning rich yellow before they fall. C 1790.

**ACER**—*continued*

**crataegifolium** SIEB. & ZUCC. A small tree or large shrub with prettily marked bark and small leaves of variable shape; flowers mustard-yellow in slender racemes. Japan. I 1879 by Charles Maries.

**'Veitchii'** Leaves heavily mottled with white and pink, brilliant pink and purple in autumn. C 1881.

**creticum** See *A. sempervirens*.

**dasycarpum** See *A. saccharinum*.

**davidii** FRANCH. A small tree with attractively striated green and white bark. The shining, dark green, ovate leaves colour richly in the autumn. The green fruits are often attractively suffused red and hang all along the branches in autumn. C China. I 1879 by Charles Maries. AGM 1984.

**'Ernest Wilson'** Rare in cultivation. A more compact tree with branches ascending then arching. Leaves pale green, orange-yellow in autumn, rather cup-shaped at base, petioles pink at first. The original form from W Hubei and W Yunnan, introduced by Maries and later by E.H. Wilson and Kingdon-Ward.

**'George Forrest'** ('Horizontale') This is the form most commonly met with in cultivation. An open tree of loose habit with vigorous spreading branches and large, dark green leaves with rhubarb-red stalks. Introduced by George Forrest from Yunnan in 1921-22. AM 1975 (for fruit). AGM 1984.

**'Madeline Spitta'** A columnar form with erect branches. Raised at Winkworth. Leaves dark glossy green, retained until late autumn, turning orange before they fall.

**diabolicum** K. KOCH "Horned Maple". A medium-sized dioecious tree with large, five-lobed leaves, pendulous corymbs of yellow flowers in April and distinctive, bristly, reddish fruits. Japan. I 1880 by Charles Maries.

**f. purpurascens** (FRANCH. & SAV.) REHD. A most ornamental tree with purple-tinged young leaves red in autumn, its branches in spring draped with innumerable drooping clusters of salmon-coloured flowers. Japan. C 1878.

×**dieckii** PAX (*A. lobelii* × *A. platanoides*). A medium-sized to large tree of rapid growth. Leaves large, five-lobed, turning to dark red-brown or old gold in the autumn. Garden origin.

**distylum** SIEB. & ZUCC. A medium-sized tree with lime-like, undivided, glossy green leaves, which when unfolding are attractively tinted cream and pink. Rich yellow autumn colour. Japan. I 1879 by Charles Maries.

**divergens** PAX (*A. quinquelobum* K. KOCH not GILIB.) Large shrub or small tree with small, polished five or occasionally three-lobed leaves bronze-edged when young. Related to *A. campestre*. Transcaucasus. I 1923.

**erianthum** SCHWER. A small tree with five to seven-lobed leaves marked beneath by white tufts of hair in the vein axils. Often abundant crops of attractive, pink-winged fruits. Not very tolerant of chalk soils. W China. I 1907 by Ernest Wilson.

†**fabri** HANCE A small, semi-evergreen tree with bloomy young stems and oblong-lanceolate, slender-pointed leaves similar to those of *A. laevigatum* but more prominently veined and with axillary tufts of hair beneath. Originally listed as *A. wardii*. China, E Himalaya.

**flabellatum** REHD. A small, shrubby tree, resembling *A. campbellii*. Leaves broadly palmate, seven to nine-lobed, the lobes sharply serrate. Not hardy enough for coldest areas. C China. I 1907 by Ernest Wilson.

**var. yunnanense** (REHD.) FANG (*A. campbellii* var. *yunnanense* REHD.) A slender tree with deeply five-lobed leaves and red petioles. Yunnan, China.

**forrestii** DIELS A most beautiful small tree with striated bark; young stems and petioles an attractive coral-red. Not very tolerant of chalk soils. China. I 1906 by George Forrest.

**franchetii** PAX A small, slow-growing tree with large three-lobed leaves, suggesting kinship with *A. sterculiaceum*. Relatively large, green, thick-petalled flowers are borne in drooping clusters with the leaves. C China. I 1901 by Ernest Wilson.

**ginnala** MAXIM. "Amur Maple". A large shrub or small tree of vigorous, spreading habit. The bright green, three-lobed leaves turn to orange and vivid crimson in autumn. Manchuria, China and Japan. I 1860.

**var. semenowii** (REG. & HERD.) PAX Shrubby variety with smaller occasionally five-lobed leaves. Turkestan. C 1880.

**ACER**—*continued*

**giraldii** PAX A medium-sized to large tree, similar to *A. sterculiaceum* but differing in its bloomy young stems and leaves which have broader, less acuminate lobes, coarser serrations and are glaucous and reticulate beneath. Yunnan, China. I by George Forrest.

**glabrum** TORR. "Rock Maple". A large shrub or small tree of upright habit with variable leaves which may be three to five-lobed or trifoliolate. W North America. I about 1884.

> **var. douglasii** (HOOK.) DIPP. A variety with three-lobed leaves. I 1902.

**grandidentatum** See *A. saccharum* subsp. *grandidentatum*

**griseum** (FRANCH.) PAX "Paperbark Maple". One of the most beautiful of all small trees. Leaves trifoliolate, often gorgeously coloured red and scarlet in autumn. Old bark on trunk and primary branches flakes and curls back to reveal the cinnamon-coloured underbark. C China. I by Ernest Wilson in 1901. AM 1922. AGM 1984.

**grosseri** PAX One of the most beautiful of the "Snakebark" maples. A small tree, the leaves of which colour magnificently in autumn. C China. I about 1923.

> **var. hersii** (REHD.) REHD. (*A. hersii* REHD.) A small tree with wonderfully marbled bark. Leaves with or without lobes. Fruits in conspicuous long racemes. Rich autumn colour. C China. I 1921. AGM 1984.

**heldreichii** BOISS. A very handsome, medium-sized tree. Distinctive on account of its deeply cleft three-lobed leaves which almost resemble those of the "Boston Ivy". SE Europe. I 1879.

> **subsp. visianii** K. MALY Some plants grown as the typical form belong here. It differs in its larger leaves and fruits. Yugoslavia, Bulgaria.

**henryi** PAX A small to medium-sized spreading tree, having stems marked with bluish striations; young leaves beautifully tinted and brilliant red in autumn, resembling those of *A. cissifolium*, but leaflets nearly entire. Flowers yellow, in slender drooping catkins appearing with the unfolding leaves. C China. I 1903 by Ernest Wilson.

**hersii** See *A. grosseri* var. *hersii*.

×**hillieri** LANCASTER (*A. cappadocicum* × *A. miyabei*). This hybrid, described in 1979, can occur whenever the two parents grow together. It was first recognised in our West Hill nursery.

> **'Summergold'** Leaves golden yellow, young growths red in summer. Best if slightly shaded. One parent of this form was *A. cappadocicum* 'Aureum'.

> **'West Hill'** The original form raised in our West Hill nursery before 1935 from seed of *A. miyabei* received from Kew. A small to medium-sized, round-headed tree with slightly glossy, five or seven-lobed leaves turning butter-yellow in autumn. Previously listed as *A.* × *hillieri*.

†**hookeri** MIQ. Medium-sized, semi-evergreen tree with red young shoots and large, usually entire leaves. Only suitable for the mildest areas. E Himalaya. I 1892.

×**hybridum** SPACH (*A. monspessulanum* × *A. opalus*). A medium-sized to large tree with three-lobed leaves and drooping panicles of yellow-green flowers in May. Plants of this parentage occur in the wild with the parents.

**hyrcanum** FISCH. & MEY. Small tree of compact habit and slow growth with three or five-lobed leaves, allied to *A. opalus*. SE Europe, Crimea, Caucasus and Asia Minor. C 1865.

**japonicum** THUNB. A small tree or large bush with foliage of a soft green, beautifully coloured in autumn, petioles softly hairy. Flowers red with yellow anthers, appearing in delicate drooping clusters with the young leaves. There are a number of forms, and all do best in a moist well drained position sheltered from cold winds. Japan. I 1864.

> **'Aconitifolium'** ('Laciniatum') ('Filicifolium') Leaves deeply lobed and cut, colouring rich ruby-crimson in autumn. C 1888. AGM 1984.

> **'Aureum'** See *A. shirasawanum* 'Aureum'.

> **'Filicifolium'** See 'Aconitifolium'.

> **'Laciniatum'** See 'Aconitifolium'.

> **'Vitifolium'** Broad, fan-shaped leaves with ten to twelve lobes. An extremely beautiful form colouring brilliantly in the autumn. C 1882. FCC 1974 (for autumn foliage). AGM 1984.

†**laevigatum** WALL. A small, semi-evergreen tree with smooth green shoots, bloomy when young. Leaves oblong-lanceolate, acuminate, 15cm or more long, bright green and

**ACER laevigatum**—*continued*

lustrous, reticulate beneath; adpressed serrate, at least when young. This species has been received from various sources as *A. fargesii*. Himalaya, China. I 1907.

**laxiflorum** PAX A rare, small, spreading tree, the bark streaked with green and white. Leaves dark green above, with dark brown hairs on the veins beneath, taper-pointed and shallowly lobed below the middle. Inclined to be calcifuge. W China. I 1908.

**leucoderme** See *A. saccharum* subsp. *leucoderme*.

**lobelii** TEN. A fast-growing, medium to large tree related to *A. cappadocicum* with bloomy young shoots and wavy-edged dark green leaves with taper-pointed lobes. Its ascending branches form a compact, conical head, broadening with age. Good for restricted spaces. S Italy. I 1683.

**macrophyllum** PURSH "Oregon Maple". A large tree with very large, handsome, dark, shining green leaves which turn a bright orange in the autumn. The large, drooping clusters of fragrant yellow flowers and later bristly fruits are very ornamental. W North America. I 1826 by David Douglas.

**'Seattle Sentinel'** A dense, columnar form with upright branches. Originated in Seattle, Washington about 1920.

**mandshuricum** MAXIM. A large shrub or small tree with trifoliolate leaves and red petioles. Allied to *A. maximowiczianum* but leaves glabrous. Rich autumn colour. Manchuria, Korea. C 1904.

**maximowiczianum** MIQ. (*A. nikoense* (MAXIM.) MIQ.) "Nikko Maple". A very hardy and beautiful tree of small to medium size. The hairy, trifoliolate leaves, glaucous beneath, turn a glorious orange and flame in autumn. Now a rare tree in its native lands. Japan, C China. I 1881. FCC 1971.

**maximowiczii** PAX An attractive small tree with striated stems and three or five-lobed leaves, which are attractively red-tinted throughout the growing season, becoming more colourful as autumn approaches. C China. I 1910 by Ernest Wilson.

**micranthum** SIEB. & ZUCC. A large shrub or small tree. The small, five-lobed leaves are beautifully tinted throughout the growing season. Autumn foliage usually red. Japan. I 1879.

**miyabei** MAXIM. A small to medium-sized tree of rounded habit. The large, three to five-lobed leaves recall those of the "Norway Maple". Japan. I 1892 by Charles Sargent.

**mono** MAXIM. (*A. pictum* THUNB.) A medium-sized tree with palmately five to seven-lobed leaves, which usually turn bright yellow in autumn. Japan, China, Manchuria, Korea. I 1881 by Charles Maries.

**f. ambiguum** (DIPP.) REHD. A rare variety with leaves minutely downy beneath. Autumn colour usually yellow. Origin unknown. C 1892.

**var. tricuspis** REHD. A variety with smaller, three-lobed, rather persistent, leaves. C China. I 1901 by Ernest Wilson.

**monspessulanum** L. "Montpelier Maple". Usually a small tree of neat habit; occasionally shrubby. In general appearance it resembles our native field maple but the three-lobed leaves are perfectly glabrous and glaucous beneath, and the stalks do not possess the milky juice of the common species. S Europe, W Asia. I 1739.

**multiserratum** MAXIM. (*A. caudatum* var. *multiserratum* (MAXIM.) REHD.) A small tree with downy shoots and five to seven-lobed leaves, nearly glabrous beneath. China. I 1907 by Ernest Wilson.

**neglectum** See *A. × zoeschense*.

**negundo** L. "Box Elder". A fast-growing, bushy-headed tree of medium to large size. The young shoots are bright green and the leaves are pinnate with 3-5, sometimes 7-9, leaflets of a bright green above, paler beneath. A very popular maple. Reverting shoots on variegated forms should be removed. North America. C 1688.

**'Auratum'** Leaves bright golden yellow. AM 1901.

**var. californicum** (TORR. & GRAY) SARG. A form with softly hairy shoots and leaves. The male tree has flowers in showy pink tassels. California.

**'Elegans'** ('Elegantissimum') Leaves with bright yellow marginal variegation. Young shoots with white bloom. C 1885. FCC 1898.

**'Flamingo'** Young leaves with a broad soft pink margin changing to white, often green at first, shoots glaucous bloomed. This form is often grown as a shrub but will reach tree size.

**ACER negundo**—*continued*

'**Variegatum**' ('Argenteovariegatum') Leaves with broad, irregular white margin. A most effective tree but tends to revert if not carefully pruned.

**var. violaceum** (KIRCHN.) JAEG. Young shoots purple or violet covered by a white bloom. Leaflets usually 5-7. An attractive tree in spring when draped with its long, pendulous, reddish-pink flower tassels. AM 1975.

**nigrum** See *A. saccharum* subsp. *nigrum*.

**nikoense** See *A. maximowiczianum*.

†**oblongum** DC. A small tree or large shrub suitable only for mild areas. The oblong, semi-persistent leaves are entire though sometimes three-lobed on young trees, glabrous above, glaucous beneath. Himalaya, C and W China. I 1824.

**var. concolor** PAX Leaves green on both sides. Our stock is a fairly hardy form introduced by Ernest Wilson from China.

*\***obtusifolium** SIBTH. & SM. (*A. syriacum* BOISS. & GAILL.) A large shrub or small bushy tree with ovate, entire or three-lobed, dark green rigid leaves. Very hardy. Syria, Cyprus. C 1903.

**oliverianum** PAX A handsome species forming a large shrub or small tree. Leaves deeply five-lobed, somewhat resembling *A. palmatum* but cleaner cut, turning subtle shades of orange, red and purple over a long period in autumn. C China. I 1901 by Ernest Wilson.

**opalus** MILL. "Italian Maple". A medium-sized tree of rounded habit with shallowly five-lobed leaves which are glabrous above, downy, occasionally glabrous beneath. The yellow flowers are conspicuous and appear in crowded corymbs on the leafless stems in March. S Europe. I 1752. AM 1967.

**var. obtusatum** (WILLD.) HENRY A variety with usually larger leaves softly downy beneath, the lobes short and rounded. SE Europe and Italy. I 1805.

**orientale** See *A. sempervirens*.

†**osmastonii** GAMBLE Small tree, the young shoots covered by a conspicuous almost chalky white bloom changing to white striations on the pale green older bark. Leaves large, deeply five-lobed, green on both surfaces, purplish when unfolding, petioles red. Intermediate between *A. campbellii* and *A. laevigatum* but probably not a hybrid. Sikkim Himalaya.

**palmatum** THUNB. "Japanese Maple". Generally a large shrub or small tree with a low, rounded head. Leaves five or seven-lobed of a bright green. Japan, C China, Korea. I 1820. Many cultivars have been raised from this species, which exhibit a wide range of forms both in leaf and habit. The majority attain the size of a large bush or occasionally a small tree, and give gorgeous red, orange or yellow autumnal colours. Though the typical and certain stronger forms will tolerate chalk soils, the "Japanese Maples" are at their best in a moist but well drained loam, sheltered from cold winds especially from the east.

'**Albomarginatum**' ('Argenteomarginatum') Leaves smaller than normal, green with a white marginal variegation. Liable to revert.

'**Asahi Zuru**' A fast-growing, large, spreading shrub. Leaves variously blotched with white, sometimes nearly all white or pink when young. One of the best variegated forms.

**Atropurpureum group** The most popular "Japanese Maple". A striking colour form; leaves bronzy-crimson throughout the summer, brilliant red in autumn. C 1857. AGM 1984 (to selected forms only).

'**Aureum**' Leaves suffused soft yellow becoming golden yellow in summer. C 1881.

'**Beni Maiko**' A small, bushy shrub with brilliant red young foliage later pinkish then greenish-red.

'**Beni Schichihenge**' A striking and rare form. Leaves blue-green, deeply five to seven-lobed, the lobes margined with pinkish white or almost entirely bright orange-pink.

'**Bloodgood**' Leaves very deep reddish-purple, holding their colour well, red in autumn. The red fruits are also attractive.

'**Burgundy Lace**' A small, spreading tree. Leaves rich wine-red, divided to the base into narrow, sharply-toothed lobes.

'**Butterfly**' A medium-sized shrub of upright habit. Leaves rather small, deeply cut, grey-green margined cream, pink-tinged when young. The margin turns red in autumn.

**ACER palmatum**—*continued*

'**Chitoseyama**' A superb clone with deeply cut greenish-bronze leaves which colour richly in autumn. Old plants possess a dense mound-like habit with gracefully drooping branches.

'**Corallinum**' A rarely seen, most distinct cultivar of slow growth, forming a compact small shrub. Young stems soft coral-pink; leaves usually less than 5cm long, five-lobed, bright shrimp-pink when unfolding, changing to pale mottled green by midsummer.

**var. coreanum** See 'Koreanum'.

'**Crimson Queen**' (Dissectum group) Leaves very deep reddish-purple, the colour long-lasting, deeply divided into slender, finely cut lobes.

'**Crippsii**' A slow-growing elegant form with bronze-red leaves finely cut into grasslike segments. A plant of weak constitution. AM 1903.

'**Deshojo**' An upright shrub of medium size, leaves with slender-pointed lobes, brilliant red when young turning bright green.

**Dissectum group** A group of clones in which the leaves are divided to the base into 5, 7 or 9 pinnatifid lobes. They are generally shrubby in habit, mushroom-shaped when young, ultimately a dense, rounded bush, the branches falling from a high crown. Train carefully when young to produce a standard.

'**Dissectum**' Leaves green. AGM 1984.

'**Dissectum Atropurpureum**' Leaves deep purple. AGM 1984.

'**Dissectum Flavescens**' Leaves soft yellow-green in spring.

'**Dissectum Nigrum**' ('Ever Red') Dense habit, the deep bronze-red leaves turning red in autumn. C 1938.

'**Dissectum Ornatum**' Leaves bronze-tinted.

'**Dissectum Palmatifidum**' More finely cut foliage than 'Dissectum', but not very constant. FCC 1869.

'**Dissectum Variegatum**' Leaves bronze-red, some tipped pink and cream.

**Elegans group** (Heptalobum group) (Septemlobum group) A group of clones having leaves larger and usually seven-lobed, the lobes finely doubly serrate, broadest about the middle.

'**Elegans**' Leaves up to 13cm long, green, deeply and attractively toothed.

'**Elegans Purpureum**' See 'Hessei'.

'**Filigree**' (Dissectum group) A very beautiful and unusual form. Leaves with 7 deeply and finely divided lobes, pale yellow-green with darker veins, turning gold in autumn.

'**Garnet**' (Dissectum group) A strong-growing form, the large deep garnet-red leaves with finely cut lobes. Raised in Holland. C 1960.

'**Hagoromo**' See under 'Koshimino'.

**Heptalobum group** See Elegans group.

'**Hessei**' ('Elegans Pupureum') (Elegans group) Leaves dark bronze-crimson.

'**Inaba Shidare**' (Dissectum group) Large, red-stalked leaves deeply divided into finely pointed deep purplish lobes, crimson in autumn. Strong-growing, retaining its colour well.

'**Kagiri Nishiki**' ('Roseomarginatum') Leaves pale green, irregularly edged with coral-pink. Charming but not constant and liable to revert. FCC 1865.

'**Karasugawa**' Leaves deeply five to seven-lobed, pink when young becoming streaked and speckled with white and pink.

'**Koreanum**' (var. *coreanum* HORT. not NAKAI) Leaves becoming rich crimson in autumn, lasting longer than most. The name is not clonal as this plant has been raised from seed for many years.

'**Koshimino**' ('Sessilifolium') ('Decompositum') A small tree of erect habit with short-stalked, deeply cut leaves colouring well in autumn. The dwarf plant grown as 'Sessilifolium' or 'Decompositum' is 'Hagoromo'.

'**Linearilobum**' Leaves divided to the base into long, narrow, remotely serrate lobes. AM 1896. AGM 1984.

'**Linearilobum Atropurpureum**' ('Atrolineare') Similar to 'Linearilobum' but leaves bronze-red. AGM 1984.

'**Lutescens**' Leaves glossy green turning clear butter-yellow in autumn.

'**Nigrum**' A form with leaves of deep purple.

**ACER palmatum**—*continued*

**'Osakazuki'** (Elegans group) Leaves green, turning in autumn to fiery scarlet, probably the most brilliant of all Japanese Maples. AGM 1984.

**'Oshio Beni'** Leaves deep orange-red later bronze-green, brilliant scarlet in autumn. C 1898.

**'Red Pygmy'** A slow-growing, shrubby form resembling 'Linearilobum Atropurpureum' but less than 2m tall and across and retaining its colour longer. Leaves reddish-purple, often divided to the base into long, very slender lobes with some leaves bearing broader lobes. Selected in Holland before 1969.

**'Reticulatum'** Leaves soft yellow-green with green margins and dark veins.

**'Ribesifolium'** ('Shishigashira') A slow-growing form of distinctive upright growth almost fastigiate but with a broad crown. Leaves dark green, deeply cut, changing to old gold in autumn.

**'Roseomarginatum'** See 'Kagiri Nishiki'.

**'Rubrum'** Large leaves blood-red in spring, paling towards late summer.

**'Rufescens'** A distinct, wide-spreading shrub with broad, deeply cleft leaves, green in summer and attractively tinted in autumn.

**'Seiryu'** (Dissectum group) An unusual form of upright habit. Leaves bright green, red-tinged when young, the lobes finely cut, orange-yellow splashed crimson in autumn. Makes a large shrub.

**'Senkaki'** ('Sango Kaku') "Coral Bark Maple". An invaluable shrub or small tree for winter effect, all the younger branches being of a conspicuous and attractive coral-red. Leaves turning soft canary-yellow in autumn. AM 1950. AGM 1984.

**Septemlobum group** See Elegans group.

**'Sessilifolium'** See 'Koshimino'.

**'Shishigashira'** See 'Ribesifolium'.

**'Shishio Improved'** A dense, bushy, medium-sized to large shrub. Leaves small, brilliant red when young, later green.

**'Trompenburg'** A large shrub, leaves deep purplish-red later green, red in autumn, divided nearly to the base, the lobes narrow with the margins rolled under. An outstanding plant raised in Holland.

**'Ukigumo'** A striking variegated form, the deeply five-lobed leaves heavily mottled and edged white and pink. A small to medium-sized shrub. The name means "passing cloud".

**'Versicolor'** Leaves green with white, pink-tinged blotches and spots. Liable to revert.

**'Villa Taranto'** Similar to 'Linearilobum' but making a dome-shaped bush, the leaves with 5 slender leaflets. Reddish young leaves contrast well with the green older foliage, yellow in autumn.

**papilio** See *A. caudatum*.

†**paxii** FRANCH. A small, striking, semi-evergreen tree with three-lobed leathery leaves, glaucous beneath. China.

**pensylvanicum** L. (*A. striatum* DUROI) A small tree, young stems green, beautifully striped with white and pale jade-green. Leaves up to 18cm across, three-lobed, turning bright yellow in the autumn. Not very tolerant of chalk soils. E North America. I 1755. AGM 1984.

**'Erythrocladum'** A lovely form in which the young shoots in winter are a brilliant candy-pink with white striations. A plant of weak constitution but attractive when young. AM 1976. FCC 1977.

†**pentaphyllum** DIELS A rare, handsome but tender species making a small tree. Leaves on long, slender scarlet petioles, divided to the base into 5 linear-lanceolate segments which are green above, glaucous and reticulate below. Sichuan, China. I 1929 by Joseph Rock.

**pictum** See *A. mono*.

**platanoides** L. "Norway Maple". A handsome, fast-growing tree of large size. The conspicuous clusters of yellow flowers are produced on the bare stems in April, usually following those of *A. opalus*. In autumn the foliage turns a clear bright yellow, occasionally red. Europe, Caucasus. Long cultivated. AM 1967. AGM 1984.

**'Cleveland'** A selection of strong, upright habit making an oval head of branches with large, deep green leaves. Popular as a street tree in North America.

**'Columnare'** A large, erect form of columnar habit. Raised in France in 1855.

**ACER platanoides**—*continued*

**'Crimson King'** A large, handsome tree; leaves of a deep crimson-purple. Flowers deep yellow tinged red. A seedling of 'Schwedleri'. C 1946. AGM 1984.

**'Crimson Sentry'** A narrowly columnar form with reddish-purple leaves, not as dark as 'Crimson King'.

**'Cucullatum'** A large, erect tree. Leaves long-stalked, fan-shaped at the base, prominently seven to nine-veined and shallowly seven to nine-lobed, each lobe divided into three or more, slender-pointed teeth. Similar in effect to 'Laciniatum' but lobes not as pointed. C 1881.

**'Deborah'** Young leaves brilliant red with wavy margins, turning to dark green. A seedling of 'Schwedleri' raised in the United States.

**'Dissectum'** ('Palmatifidum') Almost identical to 'Lorbergii', but leaves darker and glossier green, the lobes with crinkled margins and straight or down-pointing lobes. C 1869.

**'Drummondii'** A very striking cultivar, the leaves with a broad marginal creamy-white band. Any reverting shoots should be removed. C 1903. AM 1956. AGM 1984.

**'Emerald Queen'** A vigorous form with dark, glossy green leaves. Upright when young, broadening with age. Raised in 1959.

**'Erectum'** An erect, usually slow-growing cultivar of medium size with short ascending branches.

**'Globosum'** A striking small tree, the short branches forming a dense mop-shaped head. C 1873.

**'Laciniatum'** "Eagle's Claw Maple". An erect-growing, large tree, the leaves fan-shaped at the base, five-veined and deeply five-lobed, the lobes ending in long, slender, claw-like points. C 1683.

**'Lorbergii'** Medium-sized tree; leaves deeply five-lobed, pale green; the lobes with entire margins and long-pointed tips ascending from the leaf plane. C 1866.

**'Meyering'** A Dutch selection of upright habit. Young leaves bronze-tinged, soon green, brilliant orange-red in autumn. C 1958.

**'Palmatifidum'** See 'Dissectum'.

**'Reitenbachii'** A medium-sized tree. Leaves red on emerging, gradually turning to green and finally assuming red autumn tints. C 1874.

**'Schwedleri'** Leaves and young growths rich crimson-purple. Most effective when pruned hard every other autumn. C 1864.

**'Walderseei'** An unusual form in which the leaves are densely speckled with white flecks, greyish from a distance. A tree of rather weak constitution and difficult to propagate. C 1904.

**pseudoplatanus** L. "Sycamore". A picturesque, large tree, and one of the best for exposed situations in any soil. Long planted and naturalised in many parts of the British Isles. Native of Europe and W Asia.

**'Atropurpureum'** ('Purpureum Spaethii') A selected form with leaves purple beneath. C 1883.

**'Brilliantissimum'** A distinct small tree of slow growth. The young leaves in spring are a glorious shrimp-pink later changing to pale yellow-green and finally green. C 1905. AM 1925. FCC 1977. AGM 1984.

**'Corstorphinense'** "Corstorphine Plane". Leaves golden yellow when young. It was under this tree at Corstorphine near Edinburgh in 1679 that Lord Forrester was murdered with his own sword by his first wife's sister who was later executed for the deed. The original tree was said to be haunted by their ghosts.

**'Erectum'** ('Fastigiatum') A large tree with erect branches. C 1935.

**f. erythrocarpum** (CARR.) PAX A form with conspicuous and attractive red seed wings. C 1864.

**'Fastigiatum'** See 'Erectum'.

**'Leopoldii'** Leaves yellowish-pink at first, later green, speckled and splashed yellow and pink. FCC 1865.

**'Negenia'** Vigorous and conical with large, dark green, red-stalked leaves. Selected in 1948 in Holland where it is planted as a street tree.

**ACER pseudoplatanus**—*continued*

**'Nizetii'** Leaves heavily blotched and streaked pale green and white, purple-tinged beneath. C 1887.

**'Prinz Handjery'** A small slow-growing tree similar to 'Brilliantissimum' but slightly larger, and with leaves purple-tinged beneath. FCC 1890.

**Purpureum group** (f. *purpureum* LOUD.) A large, pictorial tree, the under-surfaces of the leaves being conspicuously coloured purple; effective in a breeze.

**'Purpureum Spaethii'** See 'Atropurpureum'.

**'Simon-Louis Frères'** Leaves pink when young becoming blotched and streaked green and white, green beneath. C 1881.

**'Worleei'** "Golden Sycamore". Medium-sized tree. Leaves soft yellow-green at first then golden, finally green. Raised in Germany before 1893.

**quinquelobum** See *A. divergens.*

‡**rubrum** L. "Red Maple" "Canadian Maple". A free-growing, ultimately large tree. The palmate leaves are dark green above, glaucous beneath and turn rich red and scarlet in autumn. Although fairly lime-tolerant, it rarely colours as well on chalky soils. E North America. C 1656. AM 1969.

**'Columnare'** Eventually a tall tree of narrowly columnar habit, a fiery pillar in autumn. C 1889.

**'October Glory'** An American selection with long-lasting, brilliant red autumn colour. C 1964. AM 1988.

**'Red Sunset'** A form of upright habit with particularly good red autumn colour. C 1968.

**'Scanlon'** A medium-sized tree of American origin eventually forming a broadly columnar head of branches. Rich autumn colour. C 1948.

**'Schlesingeri'** A clone notable for its outstanding, very early autumn colour which is a rich deep scarlet. C 1888. AM 1976.

**rufinerve** SIEB. & ZUCC. A medium-sized tree; young stems glaucous, older stems and trunk green with conspicuous white striations. Leaves three-lobed, recalling those of *A. pensylvanicum.* Bright red and yellow autumn colours. Japan. I 1879. AM 1986 (for autumn colour).

**f. albolimbatum** (HOOK. f.) SCHWER. Leaves mottled and margined white. Autumn colour brilliant red and purple. C 1869.

**saccharinum** L. (*A. dasycarpum* EHRH.) (*A. eriocarpum* MICHX.) "Silver Maple". A large, fast-growing tree. Leaves deeply five-lobed, silvery-white beneath, creating a delightful effect when ruffled by the wind. Attractive autumn tints. E North America. I 1725. AGM 1984.

**'Fastigiatum'** See 'Pyramidale'.

**Laciniatum group** (f. *laciniatum* (CARR.) REHD.) This name covers forms with deeply cut leaves. See also 'Wieri'.

**'Lutescens'** Leaves soft yellow-green during summer, orange-yellow when young. C 1881.

**'Pendulum'** A form with somewhat pendulous branches. C 1875.

**'Pyramidale'** ('Fastigiatum') An upright-growing form. C 1885.

**'Wieri'** (Laciniatum group) A selection with pendulous lower branches and the leaves deeply divided into sharply cut lobes. Found in 1873.

**saccharum** MARSH. "Sugar Maple". An ornamental, ultimately large tree resembling the "Norway Maple". One of America's finest autumn-colouring trees but usually not as good in this country. The colour varies, orange, gold, scarlet and crimson being exhibited by different individuals. C and E North America, where the sap is used to make maple syrup. I 1735.

**subsp. grandidentatum** (NUTT. ex TORR. & GRAY) DESMARAIS (*A. grandidentatum* NUTT.) Usually a small, rather slow-growing tree with three-lobed leaves. Attractive autumn tints of red and orange. W North America, New Mexico. I 1882.

**subsp. leucoderme** (SMALL) DESMARAIS (*A. leucoderme* SMALL) A small tree with three to five-lobed leaves. Lovely autumn tints. SE United States. C 1900.

**'Newton Sentry'** ('Columnare') A striking but slow-growing form of columnar habit, with upright branches and no central leader; in early autumn turning into a pillar of orange. See also 'Temple's Upright'. C 1871.

**ACER saccharum**—*continued*

**subsp. nigrum** (MICHX. f.) DESMARAIS (*A. nigrum* MICHX. f.) "Black Maple". A medium to large tree with deeply furrowed bark and large three sometimes five-lobed leaves of a dull, dark green, turning yellow in autumn. The petioles have stipules near the base. E North America. I 1812.

**'Temple's Upright'** ('Monumentale') A conical tree with a strong central leader and ascending branches. Has been confused with 'Newton Sentry'. C 1887.

**sempervirens** L. (*A. creticum* AUCT. not L.) (*A. orientale* AUCT. not L.) "Cretan Maple". A slow-growing large shrub or small tree. The leaves are of various shapes, ovate and entire to three-lobed, up to 4cm long, glabrous and bright green and often retained until Christmas. Related to *A. monspessulanum*. E Mediterranean region. I 1752.

**shirasawanum** KOIDZ. A small, bushy tree or large shrub of elegant habit related to *A. japonicum* with bloomy shoots. The rounded, bright green leaves, with the petioles glabrous or nearly so, have usually 11 sharply-toothed lobes and turn orange and red in autumn. Flowers with a pink calyx and cream petals, in spreading or almost upright clusters. Japan. C 1888.

**'Aureum'** (*A. japonicum* 'Aureum') A beautiful, slow-growing form with soft yellow leaves. Can scorch in full sun. FCC 1884. AGM 1984.

**sieboldianum** MIQ. A small tree or large shrub similar to *A. japonicum* but flowers yellow not red and leaves finely-toothed. Japan. C 1880. AM 1966.

**'Silver Vein'** (*A. laxiflorum* × *A. pensylvanicum* 'Erythrocladum'). A strong-growing, snake bark maple, the arching branches conspicuously streaked green and white. Leaves large, three-lobed above the middle with a tapering point, rich green above, on long red stalks, turning butter-yellow in autumn. Raised in our Chandlers Ford nursery by Peter Douwsma from a cross made in 1961.

**spicatum** LAM. "Mountain Maple". A small tree or large shrub. Leaves three, sometimes five-lobed, colouring red and yellow in autumn. Flowers in slender, erect panicles, later replaced by attractive red fruits. Not very tolerant of chalk soils. C and E North America. I 1750.

**stachyophyllum** HIERN A rare, small tree closely related to *A. tetramerum* the young shoots and petioles flushed scarlet. Leaves ovate, sharply three-lobed and dentate, ending in a long point. E Himalaya, W China.

**sterculiaceum** WALL. (*A. villosum* WALL.) A remarkable tree with very large palmately lobed leaves, and drooping clusters of large fruits. Often gives good autumn colour. Himalaya. I before 1850.

**striatum** See *A. pensylvanicum*.

**syriacum** See *A. obtusifolium*.

**tataricum** L. "Tatarian Maple". A large shrub or small tree of spreading habit. The leaves are dull, pale green and doubly-toothed, tapering to a slender point. On young plants and vigorous shoots they may be lobed and resemble those of *A. ginnala* to which it is closely related. Flowers greenish-white, produced in erect panicles in May and June. SE Europe, SW Asia. I 1759.

**tetramerum** PAX Medium-sized tree of graceful habit with ovate, incisely serrate leaves. E Himalaya to C China. I 1901.

**trautvetteri** MEDWED. A medium-sized tree with large, deeply five-lobed leaves deep golden yellow in autumn; flowers in upright panicles. Fruits with showy, broad red wings in summer. A handsome foliage tree, conspicuous when the bright red buds open in spring. Caucasus, SW Asia. I 1866. AM 1975.

**trifidum** See *A. buergerianum*.

**triflorum** KOMAR. A very rare, slow-growing, small tree related and similar to *A. maximowiczianum*, but with characteristic pale grey-brown, flaking bark. Leaves trifoliolate, glaucous beneath. One of the most consistent small trees for the brilliance of its autumn colour. Manchuria, Korea. I 1923.

**truncatum** BUNGE A small, round-headed tree bearing five to seven-lobed, bright green leaves which are truncate or occasionally heart-shaped at the base. Corymbs of showy, yellow-green flowers emerge with the leaves. China. I 1881.

**tschonoskii** MAXIM. A very rare, small tree or large shrub with five-lobed leaves which turn a lovely colour in autumn. Not very tolerant of chalk soils. Japan. I 1902.

**ACER**—*continued*

**turkestanicum** PAX A large shrub or small bushy tree with three to five-lobed leaves. W Asia.

**ukurunduense** TRAUTV. & MEY. (*A. caudatum* var. *ukurunduense* (TRAUTV. & MEY.) REHD.) A small tree with five-lobed leaves, deeply veined above and densely pubescent beneath. Flowers tiny, in slender, upright panicles. Colourful autumn tints. Not very tolerant of chalk soils. E Asia.

**velutinum** BOISS. (*A. insigne* BOISS.) A large tree with broad, three to five-lobed sycamore-like leaves softly downy beneath. Flowers bright yellow in dense, upright panicles after the leaves emerge. Caucasus, N Iran.

**f. glabrescens** (BOISS. & BUHSE) REHD. Leaves smooth and glaucous beneath.

**var. vanvolxemii** (MAST.) REHD. Leaves very large, blue-green beneath and hairy only on the veins. I 1873.

**villosum** See *A. sterculiaceum*.

†**wardii** W.W. SM. A small, semi-evergreen tree with bloomy young stems, and oblong-lanceolate, slender-pointed leaves which are similar to those of *A. laevigatum* but are more prominently veined, and with axillary tufts of hair beneath. Upper Burma, Yunnan, Tibet. I by George Forrest.

**wilsonii** REHD. A large shrub, or sometimes a small tree. Leaves generally three-lobed, occasionally with 2 small basal lobes, glabrous. Young foliage bright shrimp to coral-pink, passing with age to soft pale green. SW China. I 1907 by Ernest Wilson.

×**zoeschense** PAX (*A. neglectum* LANGE not HOFFMANNS.) A medium-sized tree with five-lobed dark green, somewhat purple-tinged leaves. Clearly a hybrid of *A. campestre* possibly with *A. cappadocicum* but leaves larger and more angular. Garden origin.

*†**ACRADENIA** KIPPIST—**Rutaceae**—A genus of 2 species. Apart from the following, *A. euodiiformis* occurs in E Australia.

**frankliniae** KIPPIST A small to medium-sized evergreen shrub of upright habit succeeding well in mild areas. Dark green trifoliolate, aromatic leaves and flat clusters of white flowers in May. W Tasmania. I 1845.

**"ADAM'S NEEDLE"** See *Yucca gloriosa*.

*†**ADENOCARPUS** DC.—**Leguminosae**—Very leafy, evergreen shrubs related to *Laburnum* with trifoliolate leaves and broom-like, golden yellow flowers. About 15 species, natives of the Mediterranean region, Canary Islands and mountains of tropical Africa.

†**anagyrifolius** COS. & BAL. Small to medium-sized shrub with glandular stems and slightly glaucous trifoliolate leaves. Golden yellow pea flowers in summer. Pods warty. Morocco.

**var. leiocarpus** MAIRE A form with smooth pods.

**decorticans** BOISS. Essentially a shrub for a sunny wall. Vigorous, densely clothed with silvery hairy trifoliolate leaves. Flowering in May and June. Spain. AM 1947.

†**foliolosus** (AIT.) DC. A small shrub with small hairy leaves densely crowded along the stems and numerous short, dense terminal racemes of yellow pea flowers in spring.

**AESCULUS** L.—**Hippocastanaceae**—The "Horse Chestnuts" and "Buckeyes" are among the most ornamental of late spring and early summer-flowering trees. All have compound, palmate leaves and flowers in panicles, and all are easily cultivated, thriving in any soil. About 13 species in North America, SE Europe and E Asia.

**arguta** BUCKL. "Texas Buckeye". Small shrubby tree related to *A. glabra* but leaves with 7-9 leaflets which are deeply double-toothed. Flowers soft cream in May. Oklahoma, Texas (United States). I 1909.

×**bushii** SCHNEID. (*A. discolor* × *A. glabra*). A small to medium-sized tree with individual flowers of red, pink and yellow in May or June. Mississippi, Arkansas (United States).

**californica** (SPACH) NUTT. A low, wide-spreading tree or shrub. Leaves relatively small, with 5-7 rather blue-green leaflets. The fragrant white or pink-tinted flowers are borne in dense, erect panicles up to 20cm long during summer. California. I about 1850 by William Lobb.

**AESCULUS**—*continued*

× **carnea** HAYNE (*A. hippocastanum* × *A. pavia*). (*A. rubicunda* LOISEL.) "Red Horse Chestnut".
A large tree, much used for avenues and parks. Flowers rose-pink in panicles up to
20cm long. Similar to *A. hippocastanum* but generally smaller and more compact with
smaller, darker green leaflets. C 1820.

'**Briotii**' A compact form with deeper coloured flowers. Raised in 1858. AM 1965. AGM
1984.

'**Plantierensis**' (*A.* × *carnea* × *A. hippocastanum*) Perhaps the best form, a large tree
resembling *A. hippocastanum* but with pale pink flowers. A back-cross that does not set
seed. Raised in France in about 1894.

**chinensis** BUNGE The "Chinese Horse Chestnut" is a very distinct small, slow-growing and
rare tree with small white flowers carried in long, slender, cylindrical racemes. The leaves
have 5 or 7 narrow, bright green leaflets. Some plants received under this name are *A.
indica*. N China. I 1912 by William Purdom.

**flava** SOLAND. (*A. octandra* MARSH.) "Sweet Buckeye". A medium-sized or large tree; flowers
nearest to yellow in a "Horse Chestnut", borne in May and June; leaves with 5-7 leaflets,
usually giving good autumn tints. SE United States. I 1764.

**georgiana** SARG. (*A. neglecta* var. *georgiana* (SARG.) SARG.) A large shrub or small tree with
dense panicles of orange-red flowers. SE United States. I 1905.

**glabra** WILLD. "Ohio Buckeye". A small to medium-sized tree with rough bark, leaves with
usually 5 leaflets, orange-yellow in autumn. Flowers yellow-green, with exserted stamens,
May, followed by prickly fruits. SE and C United States. C 1809.

**f. pallida** (WILLD.) SCHELLE Habit of branching more erect. I 1812.

**glaucescens** SARG. A shrub or a small, slow-growing tree with yellow-green flowers and
leaves with 5 leaflets, bright green above, glaucescent beneath. SE United States.

**hippocastanum** L. "Common Horse Chestnut". Possibly the most beautiful of large flowering
trees hardy in the British Isles. Exceptionally attractive when covered with its stout
candles of flowers in May, white with a yellow then red blotch. Providing the familiar
conkers of children's games in autumn. Native of the wild border region between Greece
and Albania. I into W Europe in 1576 and to the British Isles early in the 17th century.
AGM 1984.

'**Baumannii**' ('Florc Pleno') Flowers double, white; does not set seed. Arose as a sport in
about 1820. AGM 1984.

'**Digitata**' ('Pumila') A curious dwarf form with smaller, deeply incised leaves.

'**Flore Pleno**' See 'Baumannii'.

'**Hampton Court Gold**' Leaves soft yellow when young becoming greenish-yellow. Slow-
growing and can burn in full sun. Derives from a tree in the 'Wilderness' garden at
Hampton Court which is about 12m tall.

**Laciniata group** (*f. laciniata* (JACQUES) SCHELLE) A slow-growing form with leaves
narrowly, deeply and irregularly incised. Old plants have slender, drooping branches.

'**Pumila**' See 'Digitata'.

'**Pyramidalis**' An unusual form of broadly pyramidal habit. C 1895.

× **hybrida** DC. (*A. flava* × *A. pavia*). (*A. lyonii* HORT.) (*A. versicolor* WENDER.) Small to medium-
sized tree with dark glossy green leaves producing red and yellow flowers in panicles 10-
18cm long in June. Occurs wild in the Alleghany mountains and has arisen in cultivation.

**indica** (COLEBR. EX CAMBESS.) HOOK. "Indian Horse Chestnut". A magnificent large tree
with panicles of pink-flushed flowers, occasionally as much as 40cm long and 13cm wide,
in June and July. Leaves with 7 leaflets, bronze when young becoming dark glossy green,
turning orange or yellow in autumn. A splendid specimen grows on chalk soil on the
site of our West Hill nursery in Winchester where it was 15m tall in 1990. NW Himalaya.
I 1851. AM 1922. FCC 1933. AGM 1984.

'**Sydney Pearce**' A free-flowering form of upright habit, with dark olive-green leaves.
Flowers in large panicles with individual blossoms up to 2.5cm across, petals white,
marked yellow and prettily suffused pink. Raised at Kew in 1928. AM 1967.

× **mississippiensis** SARG. (*A. glabra* × *A. pavia*). Small tree with flowers dark red and yellow,
the stamens protruding beyond the petals. Occurs in the wild with the parents.

× **mutabilis** (SPACH) SCHELLE (*A. pavia* × *A. georgiana*). A large shrub or small tree with red
and yellow flowers in May and June. C 1834.

**AESCULUS × mutabilis**—*continued*

**'Harbisonii'** A form raised at the Arnold Arboretum with bright red flowers. C 1905.

**'Induta'** ('Rosea Nana') Flowers apricot with yellow markings during summer. C 1905. AM 1959.

×**neglecta** LINDL. (*A. flava* × *A. sylvatica*). A medium-sized tree bearing panicles of pale yellow flowers in May and June. Rich autumn colour. SE United States. C 1826.

**'Erythroblastos'** A spectacular, rather slow-growing form in which the young leaves are a brilliant shrimp-pink changing to a pale yellow-green later in the season. C 1935. AM 1962.

**var. georgiana** See *A. georgiana*.

**octandra** See *A. flava*.

**parviflora** WALT. A spreading shrub 2.5m or more high, flowering freely in July and August. Flowers white, with long-exserted red anthers, in slender panicles 20-30cm long. Leaves bronze when young and attractively coloured yellow in autumn. SE United States. I 1785. AM 1955. AGM 1984.

**pavia** L. "Red Buckeye". A beautiful medium-sized to large shrub or small tree, leaves with 5 glossy green leaflets; flowers crimson, in panicles 15cm long, opening in June to July. S United States. I 1711.

**'Atrosanguinea'** Flowers a little deeper red.

**'Humilis'** Of low, spreading growth; flowers red. C 1826.

**splendens** SARG. A shrubby species, with long panicles of scarlet flowers in May. Perhaps the handsomest of the "Buckeyes". This species is now included in *A. pavia*.

**turbinata** BLUME "Japanese Horse Chestnut". A large tree with outsize foliage attractively veined and tinted in autumn. Flowers in long panicles, yellowish-white with a red spot, appearing in May or June, a little later than those of *A. hippocastanum*. Japan. Fruits large, pear-shaped, not spiny. I before 1880.

**wilsonii** REHD. A very rare tree with larger leaves than those of *A. chinensis*. Small white flowers in June with a yellow, later red centre. Introduced by Ernest Wilson from China in 1908.

‡†*****AGAPETES** D. DON ex G. DON (*Pentapterygium* KLOTZSCH)—**Ericaceae**—A genus of about 95 species of usually bristly, often epiphytic shrubs, native from the Himalaya and E Asia to NE Australia. Suitable for cool conservatory cultivation or for a sheltered shaded wall in the mildest areas.

**'Ludgvan Cross'** (*A. rugosus* × *A. serpens*). (*Pentapterygium* 'Ludgvan Cross') A striking hybrid, intermediate in size and character between its parents. Flowers large, pale pink, conspicuously veined with deeper pink, and with a crimson calyx. Garden origin.

**rugosus** (HOOK. f.) K. HARIDASAN (*Pentapterygium rugosum* HOOK. f.) A handsome, small shrub from the Khasia Hills, Assam and Bhutan. Stems rather stiff and upright; leaves larger and broader than those of *A. serpens*, 7.5-10cm long, rugose and toothed. Flowers 2.5cm long, white marbled purple or red, nodding; fruits purple. C 1860. AM 1934.

**serpens** (WIGHT) SLEUM. (*Pentapterygium serpens* (WIGHT) KLOTZSCH) A beautiful, long-flowering, Himalayan shrub up to 2m with long sinuous, arching branches. Leaves lanceolate, 12mm long. Flowers bright red with darker markings, pendulous, borne all along the slender, arching branches like curious Japanese lanterns. E Himalaya. C 1884. AM 1900.

‡*****AGARISTA** D. DON ex G. DON—**Ericaceae**—About 30 species of evergreen shrubs and trees related to *Lyonia* and *Pieris*, natives of S and C America, the SE United States and Africa.

**populifolia** (LAM.) JUDD (*Leucothoe populifolia* (LAM.) DIPP.) A vigorous, medium-sized shrub of considerable quality. Leaves lanceolate to ovate-lanceolate, up to 10cm long. Flowers white, in short racemes. Subject to injury in the coldest areas. SE United States. I 1765.

†*****AGATHOSMA** WILLD.—**Rutaceae**—A genus of about 135 species of heath-like evergreens, natives of S Africa.

**pulchella** (L.) LINK (*Barosma pulchella* (L.) BARTL. & WENDL.) (*Diosma pulchella* L.) An attractive, aromatic, heath-like shrub with terminal clusters of lilac-pink flowers. A pleasing plant but only suitable for the mildest areas or cool greenhouses. I 1787.

**AILANTHUS** DESF.—**Simaroubaceae**—Handsome, fast-growing trees with large, pinnate leaves. Extremely tolerant of atmospheric pollution. About 5 species from E Asia to Australia.

**altissima** (MILL.) SWINGLE (*A. giraldii* DODE) (*A. glandulosa* DESF.) "Tree of Heaven". A large imposing tree with distinct ash-like leaves which on young specimens are up to 1m long. Female trees produce large conspicuous bunches of reddish "key"-like fruits. N China. I 1751 by Peter Collinson. AM 1953.

**'Pendulifolia'** A graceful tree with very large drooping leaves. C 1899.

**giraldii** See *A. altissima*.

**glandulosa** See *A. altissima*.

**vilmoriniana** DODE Very close to *A. altissima* from which it differs in the occasional bristly shoots, and sometimes rich red rachis. W China. I 1897 by Père Farges.

**ALANGIUM** LINDL.—**Alangiaceae**—A genus of about 20 species of trees, shrubs and climbers found mainly in warm regions of the Old World. *A. platanifolium* makes an attractive foliage plant with unusual flowers shaped like a miniature lily.

**chinense** (LOUR.) HARMS A handsome shrub with large maple-like leaves. The fragrant flowers have 6 recurved petals and open in June and July. Widely distributed in E Asia and Africa.

**platanifolium** HARMS Large shrub with three to five, occasionally seven-lobed leaves and cymes of white, yellow-anthered flowers in June and July. Japan, China, Korea, Manchuria, Taiwan. I 1879 by Charles Maries.

**ALBIZIA** DURAZZ.—**Leguminosae**—Deciduous mimosa-like shrubs or small trees valuable for their handsome foliage and attractive fluffy heads of flowers. Full sun. About 150 species mainly in the Old World tropics and S America.

**†distachya** (VENTEN.) MACBR. (*A. lophantha* (WILLD.) BENTH.) A large shrub or small tree with beautiful pinnate or doubly pinnate leaves and sulphur-yellow bottlebrush-like racemes of flowers, produced in spring or earlier under glass. Only suitable for the mildest localities. W Australia. I 1803.

**julibrissin** (WILLD.) DURAZZ. The hardiest species; a small, spreading, graceful tree, flower heads pink, produced in late summer to early autumn. Iran to China, Taiwan. I 1745.

**'Rosea'** A very hardy form with dense heads of bright pink flowers. I 1918 by Ernest Wilson from Korea.

**lophantha** See *A. distachya*.

**"ALDER"** See *Alnus*.

**"ALLSPICE"** See *Calycanthus*.

**"ALMOND"** See *Prunus dulcis*.

**ALNUS** EHRH.—**Betulaceae**—The "Alders" will grow in almost any soil, except very shallow chalk soils, and are particularly useful for damp situations. The most lime-tolerant species are *A. cordata*, *A. glutinosa* and *A. viridis*. Deciduous trees and shrubs with about 35 species mainly in N temperate regions but extending to the Andes. Male and female flowers are borne on the same plant, the male catkins long and drooping, the females short, becoming a woody cone.

**cordata** DESF. "Italian Alder". A splendid medium to large-sized conical-shaped tree for all types of soil, growing rapidly even on chalk soils; notable for its bright green, glistening foliage. Corsica and S Italy. I 1820. AM 1976. AGM 1984. FCC 1987.

**crispa** See *A. viridis* subsp. *crispa*.

**fauriei** LEV. A dense large shrub or small tree with glabrous young shoots. Leaves broadly wedge-shaped, to 10cm long and 13cm across, rounded to cuneate and entire at the base with a broad, truncate and emarginate apex, glabrous above with conspicuous tufts of brown hairs in the vein axils and along the midrib at the base beneath. N and C Japan.

**ALNUS**—*continued*

**firma** SIEB. & ZUCC. A densely branched small tree or large shrub with occasionally downy branches and ovate, acuminate, sharply-toothed leaves often remaining green until late autumn. Kyushu, Japan. The following variety is the plant most often cultivated.

**var. hirtella** FRANCH. & SAV. A graceful variety making a large shrub or small tree with handsome hornbeam-like foliage. Japan. I 1894.

**glutinosa** (L.) GAERTN. "Common Alder". A small to medium-sized bushy tree with sticky young growths and yellow catkins in March. Once used extensively in the manufacture of clogs in the north of England. Europe (incl British Isles), W Asia, N Africa.

**'Aurea'** Leaves pale yellow, particularly noticeable in spring and early summer. Raised about 1860. FCC 1867.

**'Fastigiata'** See 'Pyramidalis'.

**'Imperialis'** An attractive and very graceful form with deeply and finely cut leaves. C 1859. AM 1973. AGM 1984.

**Incisa group** (f. *incisa* (WILLD.) KOEHNE) Leaves small, deeply cut or pinnate with broad, rounded, dentate lobes. There are shrubby and arboreal forms of this group.

**'Laciniata'** Like 'Imperialis' but stronger-growing with a stiffer habit and the leaves not so finely divided. Arose in France before 1819.

**'Pyramidalis'** ('Fastigiata') A form with branches at an acute angle making a narrowly conical tree.

**hirsuta** (SPACH) RUPR. (*A. tinctoria* SARG.) A medium-sized tree similar in many respects to *A. incana* but the leaves are generally larger and more deeply lobed. NE Asia and Japan. I 1879 by Charles Maries.

**incana** (L.) MOENCH "Grey Alder". An exceptionally hardy tree or large shrub with leaves grey beneath. Ideal for cold or wet situations. The North American plant once referred to this species is now known as *A. rugosa* (DUROI) SPRENG. Europe, Caucasus. I 1780.

**'Aurea'** Young shoots and foliage yellow and catkins conspicuously red-tinted.

**'Laciniata'** ('Acuminata') Leaves dissected. C 1861. FCC 1873.

**'Pendula'** A handsome, small, weeping tree forming a large mound of pendulous branches and grey-green leaves. Originated in Holland before 1900.

**'Ramulis Coccineis'** This attractive tree does not appear to differ from 'Aurea', which see.

**japonica** (THUNB.) STEUD. A striking species in time making a medium-sized to large tree. Leaves elliptic, relatively narrow and pointed. Korea, Manchuria, Japan, Taiwan. I before 1880.

**maritima** (MARSH.) NUTT. A large shrub or small tree with downy young shoots. Leaves to 8cm long, broadly elliptic to obovate, broadly cuneate at the base, double-toothed at the margin, glossy green above, downy beneath. The catkins form in summer and expand in autumn. Delaware and Maryland (United States). I 1878.

**maximowiczii** CALLIER A large shrub with rather thick twigs, broad leaves and clusters of short, fat, yellow catkins in late spring. Japan, Kamchatka, Korea. I 1914.

**nitida** (SPACH) ENDL. "Himalayan Alder". Medium-sized tree with ovate, normally entire leaves. Distinct on account of its long male catkins being produced in autumn. NW Himalaya. I 1882 by R.E. Ellis.

**oregona** See *A. rubra*.

**orientalis** DECNE. "Oriental Alder". Medium-sized tree with sticky buds, glossy green, ovate, coarsely-toothed leaves and clusters of yellow catkins in March. Syria, Cilicia, Cyprus. I 1924.

**rhombifolia** NUTT. "White Alder". Medium-sized to large tree of spreading habit with often diamond-shaped leaves. W North America. I 1895.

**rubra** BONG. (*A. oregona* NUTT.) Medium-sized, fast-growing tree of graceful habit festooned in spring with the 10-15cm long male catkins. Leaves large. W North America. I before 1880.

**rugosa** (DUROI) SPRENG. "Speckled Alder". A small tree or shrub related to *A. incana* and sometimes regarded as a subspecies of it. Leaves ovate-elliptic, branches with pale lenticels. E North America.

**serrulata** (AIT.) WILLD. "Smooth Alder". A large shrub or small tree with long catkins in spring before the leaves appear, related to *A. incana* but differing in its obovate leaves, green beneath. E United States. I 1769.

**ALNUS**—*continued*

**sinuata** (REG.) RYDB. (*A. sitchensis* SARG.) "Sitka Alder". A small tree or large shrub related to *A. viridis* with broad leaves. The male catkins are conspicuous, up to 13cm long, hanging in great profusion. W North America, NE Asia. I 1903.

**sitchensis** See *A. sinuata*.

× **spaethii** CALLIER (*A. japonica* × *A. subcordata*). A fast-growing tree of medium size, with large leaves purplish when young. Outstanding when in catkin. Garden origin. C 1908.

**subcordata** C. A. MEY. "Caucasian Alder". A fast-growing medium-sized to large tree with broad sometimes slightly heart-shaped leaves up to 15cm long. Long male catkins are borne very early. Caucasus, N Iran. I 1838.

**tenuifolia** NUTT. Small tree or large shrub with oval leaves, cordate or rounded at the base. W North America. I 1891.

**viridis** (CHAIX) DC. "Green Alder". A medium-sized to large shrub forming a clump of long, erect, hazel-like stems. The common alder of the C European Alps. Europe. I 1820.

> **subsp. crispa** (AIT.) TURRILL (*A. crispa* (AIT.) PURSH) "American Green Alder". This differs from the European form in its larger size and its larger, more finely-toothed leaves. E North America. **var. mollis** (FERN.) FERN. (*A. crispa* var. *mollis* FERN.) is a form of this with the shoots and undersides of the leaves softly downy.

†**ALOYSIA** JUSS.—**Verbenaceae**—About 35 species of aromatic shrubs, natives of the SW United States, C and S America. Only *A. triphylla* is commonly grown.

*****chamaedryfolia** CHAM. A medium-sized to large, aromatic shrub of open, spreading habit. Leaves opposite, broadly ovate, sharply-toothed and scabrid. Tiny scented flowers, lavender becoming white are borne in slender spikes in late summer and autumn. Brazil, Argentina.

**triphylla** (L'HERIT.) BRITT. (*Lippia citriodora* (ORT.) H.B.K.) "Lemon Verbena". A medium-sized to large shrub with lanceolate, lemon-scented leaves normally in whorls of 3. The tiny, pale purple flowers are profusely borne in terminal panicles in August. Best against a warm wall. Chile. I 1784.

**AMELANCHIER** MEDIKUS—**Rosaceae**—Commonly known as "June Berry", "Serviceberry" or "Snowy Mespilus" this is a genus of about 10 species of beautiful and very hardy small trees or shrubs, mainly natives of North America, but also found in Europe and Asia. They thrive in moist, well drained, lime-free soils, the most lime-tolerant species being *A. alnifolia*, *A. asiatica*, and *A. rotundifolia* (*A. ovalis*). The abundant racemes of white flowers are produced in spring before the leaves are fully developed. The foliage is often richly coloured in the autumn. Several of the European species are presumed to have originated from plants introduced from North America.

**alnifolia** (NUTT.) NUTT. A medium-sized shrub with rounded leaves. Short, dense, terminal racemes of flowers in spring open after the leaves, followed by black fruits. W North America. I 1918.

> **var. cusickii** (FERN.) C.L.HITCHC. (*A. cusickii* FERN.) Flowers relatively large, in few flowered racemes after the smooth leaves emerge. Fruits at first scarlet gradually turning black. NW United States. C 1934.

> **var. semiintegrifolia** (HOOK.) C.L.HITCHC. (*A. florida* LINDL.) An erect-branched large shrub or small tree with rounded or oval leaves and purplish fruits. Flowers borne in upright racemes in May. Autumn tints include a rich clear yellow. W North America. I 1826 by David Douglas.

**asiatica** (SIEB. & ZUCC.) WALP. An elegant large shrub with slender arching shoots flowering in May after the leaves emerge and intermittently over a long period. Leaves pale green and smooth above when young, silky white hairy beneath, becoming dark green, orange-red in autumn. Fruits like blackcurrants. E Asia. I 1865.

**'Ballerina'** A vigorous large shrub or small tree with finely-toothed leaves bronze when young. Large white flowers are very profusely borne. Selected in Holland from plants sent from our nursery in 1970. Probably a hybrid of *A. laevis*.

**AMELANCHIER**—*continued*

**canadensis** (L.) MEDIKUS (*A. oblongifolia* ROEM.) Medium to large-sized suckering shrub with tall erect stems, oblong leaves and erect racemes. Grows well in moist situations. See also *A. lamarckii* and *A. laevis* with which this species has been confused. North America. AM 1938.

**cusickii** See *A. alnifolia* var. *cusickii*.

**florida** LINDL. See *A. alnifolia* var. *semiintegrifolia*.

× **grandiflora** REHD. (*A. arborea* × *A. laevis*). A large spreading shrub with bronze young leaves and profuse clusters of large white flowers. This hybrid has originated in the wild as well as in cultivation. Best known here in the following forms. See also *A. lamarckii*.

**'Robin Hill'** A large shrub or small tree of dense, upright habit. Flowers pink in bud opening pale pink, becoming white.

**'Rubescens'** An attractive form with pale pink flowers deep pink in bud. Raised in New York before 1920.

**humilis** WIEG. Erect-growing, suckering shrub of medium size. Shoots deep red, leaves elliptic oblong. Flowers in dense, upright racemes in May as the leaves emerge, which are densely white tomentose beneath. Fruits almost black, bloomy. E United States. I 1904.

**laevis** WIEG. A small tree or occasionally large shrub usually grown, wrongly, as *A. canadensis*. A picture of striking beauty in early May, when the profusion of white fragrant flowers is interspersed with delicate pink young foliage. The leaves assume rich autumnal tints. North America. C 1870.

**lamarckii** SCHRÖDER A large shrub or small tree of bushy, spreading habit. Leaves oval to oblong, coppery-red and silky when young, colouring richly in autumn. Flowers in lax, ample racemes scattered along the branches as the young leaves unfold. Fruits black. The best species for general planting, a tree in full flower being a beautiful spectacle. Naturalised in Belgium, Holland, NW Germany and several parts of England where it has been variously, but wrongly, referred to the following species:—*A. canadensis, A. laevis* and *A. confusa*. AM 1976. AGM 1984.

**'Rubescens'** See *A.* × *grandiflora* 'Rubescens'.

**oblongifolia** See *A. canadensis*.

**ovalis** See *A. rotundifolia*.

**rotundifolia** (LAM.) DUM.-COURS. (*A. ovalis* MEDIKUS), (*A. vulgaris* MOENCH) A medium-sized to large shrub of upright habit. Flowers large in short erect racemes. Leaves ovate, dark green above, white woolly beneath when young. Fruit red becoming black. C and S Europe, N Africa, W Asia. I 1596.

**sanguinea** (PURSH) DC. Medium-sized shrub with oval-oblong or rounded leaves and loose, lax racemes in May after the leaves have emerged. Fruits black, bloomy. SE Canada, NE United States. I 1824.

**spicata** (LAM.) K. KOCH A medium-sized to large, erect-branched suckering shrub of bushy habit with the leaves white hairy beneath when young. Flowers in dense, erect racemes in April and May before or with the leaves. Fruits blue-black. North America.

**stolonifera** WIEG. A small to medium-sized suckering shrub forming a dense thicket of erect stems. Flowers in short erect racemes in May as the white hairy young leaves emerge. North America. I 1883.

**vulgaris** See *A. rotundifolia*.

× **AMELASORBUS** REHD.—**Rosaceae**—An interesting natural intergeneric hybrid between *Amelanchier* and *Sorbus*. Occurs with the parents in Idaho and Oregon, United States.

**jackii** REHD. (*Amelanchier alnifolia* × *Sorbus scopulina*). This unusual shrub has oval to elliptic leaves sometimes with distinct leaflets at the base. In spring 5cm long clusters of white flowers are produced followed by dark red fruits which are covered with a blue bloom.

†**AMICIA** KUNTH—**Leguminosae**—A small genus of about 8 species of C and S American sub-shrubs. The following is the only one in general cultivation and requires a well drained soil and a warm, sunny, sheltered site.

**AMICIA**—*continued*

**zygomeris** DC. A medium-sized shrub of extremely vigorous habit, with erect, greenish, downy stems which are hollow and generally herbaceous in nature. Leaves pinnate, with 4 obovate notched leaflets, arising from a pair of inflated, purple-tinged leafy stipules. The yellow, purple-splashed, pea flowers are produced in short axillary racemes during autumn, often too late to avoid early frosts. Mexico. I 1826.

**AMORPHA** L.—**Leguminosae**—A genus of about 15 species of deciduous sun-loving shrubs or sub-shrubs with pinnate leaves and dense, spike-like racemes of small, usually violet or blue pea flowers in summer. The flowers are unusual in having only one petal. Natives of North America and Mexico.

**canescens** NUTT. "Lead Plant". A small sub-shrub with grey-hairy pinnate leaves; flowers violet, with orange anthers, produced in dense cylindrical racemes 10-15cm long in the late summer and early autumn. E North America. I 1812.

**fruticosa** L. "False Indigo". A variable shrub of medium to large size with pinnate leaves and slender racemes of purplish-blue flowers in July. S United States. I 1724.

**'Pendula'** A form with pendulous branches.

**AMPHIRAPHIS albescens** See *Aster albescens*.

†**ANAGYRIS** L.—**Leguminosae**—A genus of 2 tender sun-loving shrubs or small trees related to *Piptanthus*. *A. latifolia* BROUSS. is a rare native of the Canary Islands.

**foetida** L. A large shrub or small tree with sage-green trifoliolate leaves, which are foetid when crushed, and short racemes of yellow pea flowers in late spring. Mediterranean region. C 1750.

**ANDRACHNE** L.—**Euphorbiaceae**—A small genus of about 20 species of herbs and small shrubs native mainly of N temperate regions. They need a well drained soil in full sun and are largely of botanical interest.

**colchica** BOISS. A dense, dwarf shrub bearing clusters of small, yellowish-green flowers in summer and autumn. Caucasus. C 1900.

‡*****ANDROMEDA** L.—**Ericaceae**—A genus of 2 species of low-growing slender-stemmed shrubs for the peat garden or damp acid soils.

**glaucophylla** LINK. A dwarf shrub with slender erect stems, narrow leaves and terminal clusters of pale pink pitcher-shaped flowers in late spring and early summer. Differs from *A. polifolia* in the leaves being minutely white tomentulose beneath. NE North America. C 1879.

**f. latifolia** (AIT.) REHD. A form of looser, more straggly growth with broader leaves.

**polifolia** L. "Bog Rosemary". A charming dwarf shrub, a rare native of the British Isles. The slender stems bear narrow glaucous-green leaves glabrous and white beneath, and terminal clusters of soft pink flowers in May or early June. Europe, N Asia, North America. C 1768.

**'Alba'** A rather straggly form with light blue foliage and white flowers.

**'Compacta'** A gem for a cool peat bed; bears clusters of bright pink flowers from May onwards. Compact habit. AM 1964.

**'Macrophylla'** A form with relatively broad leaves and deep pink flowers. FCC 1981.

**'Major'** A taller form with broader leaves.

**'Minima'** A decumbent or nearly prostrate form with dark green linear leaves and pink flowers. AM 1985.

**'Nikko'** A neat-growing form of compact habit. An improvement on 'Compacta'.

†*****ANOPTERUS** LABILL.—**Escalloniaceae**—A genus of 2 species related to *Escallonia*.

**glandulosa** LABILL. A rare, Tasmanian evergreen shrub or small tree, with coarsely-toothed obovate, leathery leaves. A beautiful plant, producing terminal racemes of lily-of-the-valley-like flowers in April and May. Hardy only in favoured localities. I about 1840. AM 1926.

**ANTHYLLIS** L.—**Leguminosae**—A genus of some 20 species of annual and perennial herbs and shrubs with usually pinnate leaves and clustered pea-like flowers. Natives of Europe, W Asia and N Africa. The following require full sun and a well drained soil.

†\***barba-jovis** L. "Jupiter's Beard". A medium-sized shrub with pinnate, silvery leaves and cream coloured flowers borne in terminal clusters in early summer. SW Europe, Mediterranean region. C 1640.

**hermanniae** L. An attractive dwarf shrub suitable for the rock garden with small, narrow, simple, sometimes trifoliolate leaves; masses of small, pea-shaped, yellow flowers with orange markings on the standards, in June and July. Mediterranean region. I early 18th century.

**montana** L. A prostrate sub-shrub with silky hairy pinnate leaves bearing 17-31 leaflets. Pink flowers are borne in dense, clover-like heads in June. S Europe.
**'Rubra'** A selection with crimson flowers. AM 1956.

**APHANANTHE** PLANCH.—**Ulmaceae**—About 5 species of deciduous and evergreen trees, natives of E Asia, Australia and Madagascar.

**aspera** (THUNB.) PLANCH. A small tree in this country but reaching a large size in the wild. Shoots and leaves with adpressed hairs making them rough to the touch. Leaves ovate, long acuminate, prominently serrate, usually truncate and somewhat oblique at the base, to 10cm long. Japan, Korea, China. I 1895.

**ARALIA** L.—**Araliaceae**—More than 35 species of perennial herbs and deciduous shrubs, rarely climbers, native mainly of North America and E Asia but also found in C and S America and SE Asia. The following are mainly grown for the beauty of their large compound leaves.

**chinensis** L. "Chinese Angelica Tree". A tall, suckering shrub or small tree, with stout, spiny stems. Leaves doubly pinnate, 1-1.25m long and 0.6m or more wide; flowers small, white, in huge panicles, the panicles with a central axis, appearing in August and September. NE Asia. I about 1830.

**elata** (MIQ.) SEEM. "Japanese Angelica Tree". Usually seen as a large suckering shrub but occasionally making a small sparsely branched tree. The huge, doubly pinnate leaves are gathered mainly in a ruff-like arrangement towards the tips of the stems and often colour well in autumn. Flowers white, in large panicles, the panicles branched from base, in early autumn. Japan. I about 1830. AM 1959.
**'Aureovariegata'** Leaflets irregularly margined and splashed with yellow. The 2 variegated forms are distinct in the spring but later in the summer the leaves of both become variegated silver-white.
**'Variegata'** A handsome form with leaflets irregularly margined and blotched creamy-white. I 1865. AM 1902. AGM 1984. See note under 'Aureovariegata'.
**sieboldii** See *Fatsia japonica*.
**spinosa** L. "Hercules' Club" "Devil's Walking-Stick". A North American species with viciously spiny stems. Panicles with a central axis, flowers greenish-white, much earlier than *A. elata* and *A. chinensis*, but less showy. July. In fruit when the other two are in flower. SE United States. I 1688. AM 1974 (for fruit).

\***ARBUTUS** L.—**Ericaceae**—The "Strawberry Trees" are amongst the most ornamental and highly prized of small evergreen trees, belonging to the Old and New Worlds and attaining, with few exceptions, 3-6m. The dark, glossy green leaves, panicles of white, pitcher-shaped flowers and strawberry-like fruits are very attractive. There are about 15 species which apart from the following occur in the Canary Islands, SW United States, Mexico and C America.

†**andrachne** L. The beautiful Grecian "Strawberry Tree". White pitcher-shaped flowers produced in the spring. Stems cinnamon-brown with flaking bark. Tender when young; hardy when mature, if rightly sited. SE Europe. I 1724.

×**andrachnoides** LINK (*A. andrachne* × *A. unedo*). (*A.* × *hybrida* KER-GAWLER) Intermediate between the "Killarney Strawberry Tree" and the Grecian species. Remarkably beautiful

**ARBUTUS** × **andrachnoides**—*continued*

cinnamon-red branches, lime-tolerant and quite hardy. Flowers during late autumn and winter. Found in the wild in Greece. C 1800. AM 1953. AGM 1984.

‡**menziesii** PURSH The noble "Madroña" of California, occasionally seen as a tree up to 18m with beautiful, smooth, reddish-brown bark, peeling in late summer to reveal the young green bark. Flowers in conspicuous panicles in late spring, followed by small, orange-yellow fruits. Hardy in the home counties when rightly sited. One of the many fine introductions of David Douglas. W North America. I 1827 by David Douglas. AM 1926. AGM 1984.

**unedo** L. "Killarney Strawberry Tree". A small tree often of gnarled appearance when old, bark deep brown and shredding. Flowers and fruits produced simultaneously in late autumn. Withstands gales in coastal districts. Unusual among ericaceous plants for its lime tolerance. Mediterranean region, SW Ireland. FCC 1933. AGM 1984.

‘**Elfin King**’ A bushy form making a medium-sized shrub, free-flowering and fruiting when small.

‘**Integerrima**’ A slow-growing shrubby form with entire leaves. White flowers occasionally produced.

‘**Quercifolia**’ A distinct form with coarsely-toothed leaves tapering to an entire base.

‘**Rubra**’ A choice form with pink-flushed flowers and abundant fruits. C 1835. AM 1925. AGM 1984.

**ARCTERICA nana** See *Pieris nana*.

‡*ARCTOSTAPHYLOS** ADANS.—**Ericaceae**—Distinctive evergreens, varying from prostrate shrubs to small trees, the larger species usually with attractive bark. Flowers white to pink, small and nodding, borne in clusters followed by berry-like fruits. About 50 species mainly in W North America and Mexico. Allied to *Rhododendron* they succeed under like soil conditions but love the sun.

**alpina** See *Arctous alpinus*.

†*diversifolia** PARRY (*Comarostaphylis diversifolia* (PARRY) GREENE) "Summer Holly". A medium to large shrub or small tree recalling *Arbutus unedo*. Leaves elliptic-obovate, to 4.5cm long, coarsely-toothed at the margin, blunt to shallowly emarginate at the apex, glossy green above, thinly downy beneath. Flowers white in more or less erect or spreading terminal racemes in spring followed by small, deep red fruits. S California. C 1896.

**manzanita** PARRY "Common Manzanita". A beautiful tall-growing evergreen shrub, with attractive dark red-brown peeling bark, sea-green leaves and spikes of pink or white pitcher-shaped flowers. California. I 1897. FCC 1923.

**myrtifolia** PARRY "Ione Manzanita". A rare, tiny Californian shrublet with white, bell-shaped flowers, tipped pink.

**nevadensis** A. GRAY "Pinemat Manzanita". A prostrate, Californian species bearing its white urn-shaped flowers in racemes or panicles. Fruits red.

**pumila** NUTT. "Dune Manzanita". A very attractive prostrate species with small, downy, grey-green leaves. Flowers white or pinkish, followed by brown fruits. California. C 1933.

†**tomentosa** (PURSH) LINDL. "Shaggy-barked Manzanita". A small shrub with attractive shreddy bark and densely grey tomentose branches. Leaves sage-green, densely hairy beneath; flowers white in spring. W North America. C 1835.

**uva-ursi** (L.) SPRENG. "Red Bearberry". An interesting, native, creeping alpine shrub; flowers small, white tinged pink; fruits red. A good plant for sandy banks. Cool temperate regions of N hemisphere.

‘**Clyde Robin**’ A low-growing, wide-spreading form with bright green leaves.

‘**Point Reyes**’ Prostrate with arching branches, peeling bark and grey leaves. Flowers blush-pink.

‡**ARCTOUS** (A. GRAY) NIEDENZU—**Ericaceae**—A small genus, sometimes regarded as monotypic, related to *Arctostaphylos* but differing in the deciduous, always toothed leaves. Low-growing shrubs for cool, peaty soils.

**ARCTOUS**—*continued*

**alpinus** (L.) NIEDENZU (*Arctostaphylos alpina* (L.) SPRENG.) "Black Bearberry". A rare native shrublet forming a dense mat of prostrate reddish stems. Flowers in terminal clusters, urn-shaped, white flushed pink, in late spring. Fruits black. Northern latitudes of Europe (incl Scotland), Asia, North America. C 1789.

‡†**\*ARDISIA** SWARTZ—**Myrsinaceae**—A large genus of some 250 species of mainly tropical evergreen trees and shrubs found largely in E Asia and C and S America.

**japonica** (THUNB.) BLUME An attractive dwarf evergreen for pot culture or a lime-free soil in very mild areas. Reaching 30cm in height, it produces whorls of glossy leaves and bright red berries. China, Japan. C 1834.

**ARISTOTELIA** L'HERIT.—**Elaeocarpaceae**—A small genus of about 5 species of mainly evergreen Australasian and S American shrubs needing some protection in cold districts. Male and female flowers often occur on separate plants.

†**\*chilensis** (MOL.) STUNTZ (*A. macqui* L'HERIT.) An interesting evergreen attaining 5m in mild districts. Leaves 13cm long, lustrous green; berries small, black, on female plants. Suitable for maritime exposure. Chile. I 1773.

'**Variegata**' Leaves conspicuously variegated yellow.

**\*fruticosa** HOOK. f. "Mountain Wineberry". An intricately branched and remarkably hardy, medium-sized shrub recalling *Corokia cotoneaster;* leaves leathery, varying from linear to oblong-obovate. The tiny flowers are followed by small berries variable in colour. New Zealand.

†**serrata** (FORST. & FORST. f.) W.R. OLIV. (*A. racemosa* (A.CUNN.) HOOK. f.) "Wineberry". A graceful small tree from New Zealand, with heart-shaped, long-pointed leaves 5-10cm long, which are jaggedly-toothed and downy when young, small rose-pink flowers and dark red berries. Well-developed specimens may be seen in mild areas. I 1873.

**ARONIA** MED.—**Rosaceae**—The "Chokeberries" are attractive shrubs related to *Pyrus* and *Sorbus*, with white flowers in spring followed by conspicuous clusters of red or black fruits, and brilliant autumn colours. Not recommended for shallow chalk soils. 3 species in North America.

**arbutifolia** (L.) PERS. "Red Chokeberry". A medium-sized shrub with narrow, dark green leaves grey felted beneath. Notable for its bright red fruits and exceptionally brilliant autumn colours. E North America. C 1700.

'**Brilliant**' ('Brilliantissima') A form selected in North America for its fruit. Previously listed as *A. melanocarpa* 'Brilliant'. It has apparently been raised from seed and several forms may be grown under this name.

'**Erecta**' A compact, erect-branched shrub, arching with age, with rich autumn colour. AM 1974.

**floribunda** See *A. prunifolia*.

**melanocarpa** (MICHX.) ELLIOTT "Black Chokeberry". Small shrub with obovate, dark glossy green leaves colouring brilliantly in autumn and white, hawthorn-like flowers in spring followed by lustrous black fruits. E North America. I about 1700. AM 1972. FCC 1980.

'**Brilliant**' See *A. arbutifolia* 'Brilliant'.

**prunifolia** (MARSH.) REHD. (*A. floribunda* SPACH) Intermediate in character between the 2 preceding species. Fruits purple-black. SE United States. I 1800.

**ARTEMISIA** L.—**Compositae**—A large genus of some 300 species of often aromatic, perennial herbs, shrubs and sub-shrubs with attractive green or grey foliage. Natives mainly of the temperate N hemisphere but also found in S Africa and S America. They prefer a dry, well drained soil in full sun.

**abrotanum** L. The "Southernwood" or "Lad's Love" of cottage gardens. A small erect grey-downy shrub with sweetly aromatic, finely divided leaves. S Europe. C in England since 16th century.

†**arborescens** L. A small shrub of rounded habit. The billowy filigree of its silvery leaves makes it a charming subject for the grey or blue border. S Europe. I 1640. AM 1966.

**ARTEMISIA arborescens**—*continued*

**'Faith Raven'** A particularly hardy form collected at high altitude in Crete by John Raven.

**'Powis Castle'** (*A. absinthium* × *A. arborescens*). A beautiful small shrub with deeply cut silvery-grey leaves which originated at the National Trust garden at Powis Castle. It is hardier than *A. arborescens* and as it does not flower retains its compact habit. The best of its type for general garden use and excellent ground-cover in full sun. AM 1983. AGM 1984.

**tridentata** NUTT. "Sage Brush". A medium-sized shrub of spreading habit. The grey, aromatic leaves are wedge-shaped, three-toothed at the apex and occur in clusters along the stems. Large clusters of small, yellow flower heads are borne in late summer and autumn. W United States. I 1895.

**"ASH"** See *Fraxinus*.

**ASIMINA** ADANS.—**Annonaceae**—A small genus of about 8 species of evergreen and deciduous shrubs and small trees. The following is the only hardy member of the family which includes the "Custard Apple" (*Annona cherimola* MILL.). Not to be confused with the true "Pawpaw" (*Carica papaya* L.) a tender tree from tropical S America widely grown in the tropics for its fruit.

**triloba** (L.) DUNAL In this country the "Pawpaw" forms a large deciduous shrub with obovate leaves up to 20cm long. The unusual purplish flowers are borne in May to June as the leaves emerge. The curious fruits, which frequently form on a plant in the Hillier Gardens and Arboretum, are edible when ripe. SE United States. One of the first American plants to be introduced by Peter Collinson in 1736.

**"ASPEN"** See *Populus tremula*.

**†\*ASTELIA** BANKS & SOLANDER—**Asteliaceae**—A small genus of 25 species of evergreen, dioecious, clump-forming perennials native to the Pacific Islands, Australia and New Zealand.

**nervosa** BANKS & SOLANDER Dense tufts of sedge-like, green, conspicuously veined leaves; flowers small, fragrant, in dense panicles; female plants bear orange berries. New Zealand.

**ASTER** L.—**Compositae**—A large genus of some 250 species of mainly perennial herbs widely distributed. The following is suitable for any well drained soil in a sunny position.

**albescens** (DC.) HAND.-MAZZ. (*Microglossa albescens* (DC.) C.B. CLARKE) (*Amphiraphis albescens* DC.) A small shrub up to 1m tall, producing its pale lilac-blue, daisy-like flowers in terminal corymbs in July. Himalaya, China. I about 1840.

**ASTERANTHERA ovata** See under CLIMBERS.

**ASTRAGALUS** L.—**Leguminosae**—The "Goat's Thorns" are a large genus of about 2000 species of annual and perennial herbs and shrubs widely distributed mainly in N temperate regions but also extending to S America and S Africa.

**angustifolius** LAM. Very dwarf and slow-growing with branches densely set with spines and grey, spine-tipped, pinnate leaves. Flowers pea-shaped, white, tinged blue, borne in clusters in May and June. A rock-garden shrub. SE Europe, SW Asia.

**‡†\*ATHEROSPERMA** LABILL.—**Atherospermataceae**—A monotypic genus.

**moschatum** LABILL. An interesting evergreen, Australasian small tree having lanceolate leaves, white downy beneath. The whole plant is very fragrant and yields an essential oil. Cream-coloured, solitary flowers. Tasmania, SE Australia. I 1824. AM 1989.

**ATRAPHAXIS** L.—**Polygonaceae**—The shrubby "Buckwheats" are a small group of interesting, but not spectacular, usually low, spreading plants for dry, sunny positions. About 20 species from N Africa to Greece and SW and C Asia.

**ATRAPHAXIS**—*continued*

**frutescens** (L.) K. KOCH A small shrub with slender, upright, wiry stems, narrow sea-green leaves and clusters of tiny pink and white flowers in late summer. SE Europe and Caucasus to Siberia and Turkestan. I 1770.

**ATRIPLEX** L.—**Chenopodiaceae**—More than 100 species of annual and perennial herbs and shrubs, widely distributed, the following grown for their silvery-grey foliage. They thrive in coastal districts and saline soil as well as inland. The flowers are inconspicuous.

**canescens** (PURSH) NUTT. "Grey Sage Brush". A lax, semi-evergreen bush of medium size; leaves narrow, greyish-white. W North America. Long cultivated.

**halimus** L. "Tree Purslane". A medium-sized semi-evergreen shrub with silvery-grey leaves. S Europe. C since early 17th century.

**\*AUCUBA** THUNB.—**Cornaceae**—Evergreen, shade-loving, dioecious shrubs, forming dense, rounded bushes 2-3m high, thriving in almost any soil or situation, however sunless. Very handsome when well grown, especially the variegated forms (which retain their colour best in an open position), and the berrying (female) clones. 3 species found in the Himalaya and E Asia.

**japonica** THUNB. A medium-sized shrub with green leaves often referred to as *concolor* or *viridis*. Flowers produced in April, small, reddish-purple, the males with conspicuous creamy-white anthers. The male plant is commonest in cultivation. Japan. I 1783. FCC 1864.

**var. borealis** MIYABE & KUDO An extremely hardy dwarf and slow-growing variety from the forests of N Japan.

**'Crassifolia'** A small to medium-sized shrub with thick, broad, deep green leaves, toothed in the upper half. Male.

**'Crotonifolia'** ('Crotonoides') Leaves large, boldly spotted and blotched with gold. The best golden variegated aucuba. Male. AGM 1984.

**'Dentata'** Leaves undulate, coarsely-toothed in the upper half.

**'Fructu-albo'** ('Fructuluteo') Leaves sparingly spotted and blotched pale green and gold. Fruits yellowish-white. FCC 1883.

**'Gold Dust'** Leaves conspicuously speckled and blotched gold. Female.

**'Golden King'** Similar to 'Crotonifolia' but with a more striking variegation. Male. Best in semi-shade.

**'Grandis'** A form with very large elliptic, deep green leaves. Male. FCC 1867.

**'Hillieri'** A noble form with large, lustrous dark green leaves and pointed fruits. Female.

**'Lance Leaf'** A striking form with polished deep green lance-shaped leaves. A male counterpart of 'Longifolia'.

**'Longifolia'** Leaves long, lanceolate and bright green. Female. FCC 1864. AGM 1984.

**'Maculata'** See 'Variegata'.

**'Nana Rotundifolia'** A small, free-berrying form. Leaves small, rich green with an occasional spot, and sharply-toothed in the upper half. Stems an unusual shade of sea-green. Female.

**'Picturata'** Leaves with a conspicuous, central yellow blotch, the broad margin spotted with yellow. Male.

**'Rozannie'** Broad dark green leaves toothed above the middle. Compact and self-pollinating, with large red fruits freely borne. C 1984.

**'Salicifolia'** A free-berrying form differing from 'Longifolia' in its narrower leaves, and sea-green stems. Female.

**'Speckles'** A male counterpart to 'Variegata'.

**'Sulphurea'** See 'Sulphurea Marginata'.

**'Sulphurea Marginata'** A distinct form with sea-green stems. Leaves green with a pale yellow margin. Inclined to revert in shade. Usually grown as 'Sulphurea'. Female. FCC 1865.

**'Variegata'** ('Maculata') Leaves speckled yellow. Female. It is this form which was first introduced from Japan in 1783. FCC 1865.

**AZALEA** See under *Rhododendron*.

**mollis** See *Rhododendron japonicum* and *R. molle*.

**pontica** See *Rhododendron luteum*.

**procumbens** See *Loiseleuria procumbens*.

†\***AZARA** RUIZ & PAV.—**Flacourtiaceae**—About 10 species of evergreen shrubs or small trees, natives of Chile and Argentina. The following all make attractive foliage plants but except in mild areas need to be grown in a sheltered position or against a wall. The leaves often appear paired owing to the prominent stipules. Flowers fragrant, mustard-yellow, with numerous conspicuous stamens.

**dentata** RUIZ & PAV. Medium-sized shrub confused in cultivation with *A. serrata*, differing in its smaller leaves, dark glossy green above, felted beneath. It is also less hardy. Flowers May-June. Chile. I about 1830.

**gilliesii** See *A. petiolaris*.

**integrifolia** RUIZ. & PAV. A tall wall shrub with oval leaves; the chrome-yellow flower clusters are conspicuous in late winter and early spring. Chile, Argentina. I 1832. AM 1934.

**var. browneae** (PHIL.) REICHE This variety has larger, obovate leaves. An excellent wall shrub; flowers yellow.

**'Variegata'** Leaves with pretty pink and cream variegation. Raised at Kew about 1870.

**lanceolata** HOOK. f. A medium-sized or large shrub with attractive, narrow, bright green leaves; bears multitudes of small, mustard-yellow fragrant flowers in April or May. Chile, Argentina. I 1926 by Harold Comber. AM 1931.

**microphylla** HOOK. f. An elegant small tree with large sprays of dainty foliage; flowers yellow, vanilla-scented, appearing on the undersides of the twigs in early spring. The hardiest species. Chile, Argentina. I 1861 by Richard Pearce. FCC 1872.

**'Variegata'** Leaves prettily margined with cream; slow-growing. C 1916.

**petiolaris** (D. DON) JOHNSTON (*A. gilliesii* HOOK. & ARN.) A tall shrub notable for the fragrance of its small yellow flowers, which appear in February and March. Leaves ovate to oblong, comparatively large, leathery, toothed, teeth with sharp points. Has withstood 15°C of frost without injury. Chile. I 1859. AM 1933.

**serrata** RUIZ & PAV. A large shrub for wall or sheltered site, with distinctive, oval, serrate leaves and conspicuous clusters of yellow flowers, produced in July. Small white berries are produced in a hot summer. Hardier than most. Chile. AM 1957 (as *A. dentata*).

**BACCHARIS** L.—**Compositae**—A large genus of some 350 species of dioecious small trees, shrubs and herbs found in North and South America. Flowers in small heads. The following are rapid-growing and useful seaside shrubs.

**halimifolia** L. "Bush Groundsel". A useful and vigorous shrub up to 4m. Variable, stalked, sage-green leaves to 7cm long and large terminal panicles of white groundsel-like flowers in September-October. E North America. I 1683.

\***patagonica** HOOK. & ARN. Medium-sized shrub with red shoots and short, stalkless, evergreen, dark glossy green, polished leaves. Flower heads yellowish-white appearing singly in the upper leaf axils in May. Patagonia.

**BALLOTA** L.—**Labiatae**—About 35 species of herbs and sub-shrubs occurring in Europe, mainly in the Mediterranean region and W Asia, with a few species in N Africa. The following requires a sunny, well drained position.

**acetabulosa** L. Very similar to *B. pseudodictamnus* but with less densely hairy stems and a broader calyx. SE Europe.

**pseudodictamnus** BENTH. A dwarf sub-shrub entirely covered with greyish-white wool. Leaves orbicular-cordate. A most effective foliage plant particularly if pruned back each spring. An excellent addition to the grey garden. Lilac-pink flowers are produced in whorls in July. Mediterranean region. AGM 1984.

**"BAMBOOS"** See p. 655.

†\***BANKSIA** L. f.—**Proteaceae**—An interesting genus of some 70 species of Australian trees and shrubs with handsome foliage and cone-shaped flower heads recalling the "Bottle-brushes". Only suitable for the mildest localities, or worthy of a conservatory.

**BANKSIA**—*continued*

    **integrifolia** L. f. Medium-sized shrub of dense habit. Leathery leaves, olive-green above and white beneath; flowers yellow. E Australia. I 1788.

    **marginata** CAV. Medium-sized shrub. Leaves somewhat spiny, 5cm long, deep green above, snowy-white beneath; flowers lemon-green. SE Australia, Tasmania.

    **serrata** L. f. A tall shrub with long narrow leaves curiously squared at the apex; flowers silvery-grey. Not very lime-tolerant. E Australia.

**"BARBERRY"** See *Berberis*.

**BAROSMA pulchella** See *Agathosma pulchella*.

**†\*BAUERA** BANKS ex ANDREWS—**Baueraceae**—A small genus of 3 species of small, slender-stemmed, tender evergreen shrubs found in E Australia. Leaves opposite, sessile, trifoliolate.

    **rubioides** ANDREWS An attractive, small, late spring-flowering shrub suitable for mild gardens, also making an excellent pot plant for conservatory; flowers eight-petalled, white, with slight pink flush. Tasmania, SE Australia. AM 1941.

**"BAY"** See *Laurus nobilis*.

**"BEAUTY BUSH"** See *Kolkwitzia amabilis*.

**"BEECH"** See *Fagus*.

**"BEECH, SOUTHERN"** See *Nothofagus*.

**BERBERIS** L.—**Berberidaceae**—The "Barberries" are a large genus of more than 600 species widely distributed in N temperate regions, Africa and S America. They are generally of easy cultivation, thriving in sun or shade and in almost any soil that is not water-logged. They vary in habit from dwarf to large shrubs, but except where otherwise stated are of medium size. The flowers vary from pale yellow to orange and appear during spring. The fruits are often very showy and many species give brilliant autumn colour.

    **\*actinacantha** MARTELLI A remarkable, small Chilean evergreen. Fragrant chrome-yellow flowers. Leaves hard and rigid with an occasional spine, varying from orbicular to ovate, 2.5cm across carried on a long stalk, to a tiny elliptic sessile leaf. I about 1830.

    **aggregata** SCHNEID. A dense-habited bush, usually less than 1.5m high. The numerous paniculate clusters of pale yellow flowers are followed in the autumn by masses of red berries, backed by the rich colouration of the dying leaves. A parent of many hybrids. W China. I 1908 by Ernest Wilson. AM 1913.

    **amoena** DUNN (*B. leptoclada* DIELS) A small shrub similar to *B. wilsoniae* var. *stapfiana*. Leaves sea-green, semi-persistent; most striking when displaying its coral-red fruits. China.

    **angulosa** HOOK. f. & THOMS. Small shrub with large, solitary yellow flowers and dark purplish berries. Leaves dark green, whitish beneath, spiny towards the apex. Himalaya. I about 1850.

    **\* × antoniana** AHRENDT (*B. buxifolia* × *B. darwinii*). A small, rounded bush with almost spineless dark green leaves; very pretty when bearing its single, long-stalked, deep yellow flowers, or blue-black berries. Garden origin at the Daisy Hill Nursery, N Ireland.

    **aristata** See *B. chitria* and *B. floribunda*.

    **†\*asiatica** ROXB. A striking, unmistakable and vigorous species. Leaves leathery, obovate, up to 8cm long, sea-green above, white beneath, conspicuously veined. Berries red, finally blue-black. Nepal, Bhutan, Assam. I 1820.

    **\*atrocarpa** SCHNEID. (*B. levis* HORT.) A small shrub with stout shoots and narrow, dark green leaves. Flowers freely borne on elegant arching branches, differing from *B. sargentiana* in its smaller, less prominently veined leaves. W Sichuan, China. I 1909.

    **'Barbarossa'** A vigorous shrub 1.5-2m tall with arching branches weighed down by profuse red berries. C 1942.

**BERBERIS**—*continued*

**\*bergmanniae** SCHNEID. A compact, pyramidal evergreen up to 3m with clusters of large spiny, leathery leaves. Dense clusters of flowers May-June are followed by blue-black berries. W China. I 1908 by Ernest Wilson.

**\*'Blenheim'** (*B. darwinii* × *B. hakeoides*). A large shrub of upright habit with densely clustered, sharply-toothed leaves and deep golden yellow flowers. Originated in our West Hill nursery and was sent to Blenheim Palace as *B. darwinii*.

**'Bountiful'** A spreading bush about 1m tall. Very decorative in the autumn when laden with clusters of coral-red berries on arching branches.

**brachypoda** MAXIM. A rare, medium-sized species with narrow, elongated racemes of yellow flowers in May, followed by bright red, oblong berries. The leaves, young shoots and spines are characteristically downy. C and NW China. I 1907.

**\* × bristolensis** AHRENDT (*B. calliantha* × *B. verruculosa*). A small shrub of dense rounded habit with small prickly leaves, glossy dark green above, white pruinose beneath. An excellent dwarf hedge if clipped. Garden origin.

**'Buccaneer'** An erect branched shrub, notable for the large size of its deep red berries which are carried in large clusters and last until December.

**buxifolia** LAM. (*B. dulcis* SWEET) A S American semi-evergreen species of medium size, with small, dark green, obovate leaves glaucous grey beneath and spiny at the tip; the solitary, deep orange-yellow flowers in April-May are followed by purple-blue grape-like berries. Magellan Straits. I about 1826. AM 1961.

**'Nana'** A slow-growing, dense, evergreen mound about 50cm high with rounded leaves. Virtually thornless and rarely flowers. C 1867.

**cabrerae** JOB (Comber 798) A large shrub remarkable for the large size of its flowers which are yellow and pale orange. Berries black. Some plants grown as *B. montana* belong here. Andes of Argentina. I 1925-7 by Harold Comber.

**\*calliantha** MULLIGAN A small shrub with small holly-like leaves conspicuously glaucous beneath. Young stems crimson. Flowers pale yellow, solitary or in pairs in May, relatively large; fruits blue-black. SE Tibet. I 1924 by Kingdon-Ward. AM 1942.

**\*candidula** SCHNEID. (*B. hypoleuca* HORT.) A dense, dome-shaped bush up to 1m, with small, shining, dark green leaves, silvery-white beneath and single, bright yellow flowers. W China. I 1895 by Père Farges.

**× carminea** AHRENDT (*B. aggregata* × *B. wilsoniae*). A colourful group of hybrids from an original cross made at Wisley. Vigorous, small to medium-sized shrubs of semi-erect or spreading habit, sometimes forming large mounds, glorious in the autumn when fuming with their red, scarlet or pink berries. See also 'Barbarossa', 'Bountiful', 'Buccaneer' and 'Pirate King'.

**× chenaultii** AHRENDT (*B. gagnepainii* × *B. verruculosa*). A dense-growing, small shrub with arching, verrucose stems and ovate-lanceolate leaves which are undulate and spiny at the margin, dull green above, pruinose-grey at first beneath. Raised about 1926.

**chillanensis** (SCHNEID.) SPRAGUE This species is mainly represented in cultivation by the following variety. The typical form differs in its glabrous flower stalks.

**var. hirsutipes** SPRAGUE A large-growing shrub with yellow and orange flowers displayed profusely in May. The small, glossy leaves, borne closely along slender, erect growths, make this an attractive shrub even when not in bloom. Andes of Chile and Argentina. I 1926 by Harold Comber. AM 1932. FCC 1982.

**chinensis** POIR. Large shrub with red-brown stems, oblanceolate leaves, few flowered racemes and dark red berries. SW Russia. C 1808.

**chitria** KER GAWLER (*B. aristata* HORT. in part) Large-growing, large-leaved species with long, drooping bunches of conspicuous dark red, bloomy berries each about 1.5cm long. Himalaya. I 1818.

**\*chrysosphaera** MULLIGAN An evergreen shrub of small to medium size. Leaves narrow, borne in clusters, glossy green above, white beneath. Flowers canary-yellow, strikingly large for a *Berberis*. A Kingdon-Ward introduction from SE Tibet in 1933-34.

**†\*comberi** SPRAGUE A very distinct, small evergreen shrub difficult to establish. Leaves thick, holly-like; flowers solitary, orange-yellow. Discovered in the Argentine Andes by Harold Comber in 1925 and introduced by him.

**BERBERIS**—*continued*

**concinna** HOOK. f. Small shrub of compact habit with shining, dark green leaves which are white beneath. The solitary yellow flowers are followed by large oblong, red berries up to 2cm long. Himalaya. I about 1850 by Sir Joseph Hooker. AM 1918.

**\*congestiflora** C. GAY A large shrub. The flowers are produced in dense clusters at intervals along the stems. Closely related to *B. hakeoides*, but differing in its thinner-textured leaves and shorter pedicels. Chile. I 1925 by Harold Comber.

**\*coxii** SCHNEID. A handsome, medium-sized species. Leaves leathery, 2.5-5cm long, dark green and lustrous above, glaucous beneath. Relatively large, pale yellow flowers in small clusters in May are followed by blue-black berries. Upper Burma. I 1919 by Reginald Farrer and named after E.H.M. Cox, his companion in Burma.

**†\*crispa** C. GAY A small shrub of dense wiry habit, the 1.5cm long, spoon-shaped, green leaves are spiny-toothed and occur in clusters along the stems. Chile. I 1928.

**\*darwinii** HOOK. This early-flowering species is one of the finest of all flowering shrubs. Leaves three-pointed, dark shining green above. Flowers bright orange tinged red, in drooping clusters, borne over a long period in spring. Chile, Chiloe, Argentina. First discovered in 1835 by Charles Darwin on the voyage of the *Beagle*. Introduced by William Lobb in 1849. FCC 1967. AGM 1984.

**'Nana'** See *B.* × *stenophylla* 'Nana'.

**'Prostrata'** See *B.* × *stenophylla* 'Prostrata'.

**diaphana** MAXIM. A shrub 1-2m high with grey-green leaves giving good autumn colour. Flowers in small clusters of up to 5; berries bright red. NW China. I 1872.

**dictyophylla** FRANCH. (*B. dictyophylla* 'Albicaulis') A Chinese shrub to 2m, colouring well in autumn. Young stems red and covered with white bloom; leaves chalk-white beneath. The large, solitary, red berries are also covered with white bloom. W China. I 1916.

**var. approximata** (SPRAGUE) REHD. (*B. approximata* SPRAGUE) A tall spreading shrub, colouring well in autumn. E Sichuan.

**var. epruinosa** SCHNEID. Less bloomy in all its parts. Yunnan. C 1930.

**dielsiana** FEDDE A large vigorous shrub with slightly angled red-brown stems, narrowly elliptic leaves and racemes of yellow flowers followed by red berries. E China. I 1910.

**\*dumicola** SCHNEID. An uncommon species allied to *B. sargentiana*. Its flowers are orange-tinged followed by bloomy black berries. NW Yunnan. I 1914.

**\*empetrifolia** LAM. Dwarf shrub with slender arching stems, narrow leaves and small golden yellow flowers in May. Intolerant of shallow chalk soils. Chile. I 1827.

**floribunda** G. DON (*B. aristata* HORT. in part) A semi-evergreen species from Nepal, ultimately 3m high. Flowers bright yellow, often tinged red, borne in racemes 5-10cm long and followed by red berries covered with bloom. Nepal. I 1818.

**formosana** See *B. kawakamii*.

**forrestii** AHRENDT Large shrub with loosely arching stems, obovate leaves and long racemes of yellow flowers followed by red berries. W China. I about 1910.

**franchetiana** SCHNEID. This species is mainly represented in cultivation by the following form.

**var. macrobotrys** AHRENDT A large shrub with arching stems, yellow flowers and red berries. W China. I 1937.

**francisci-ferdinandii** SCHNEID. Vigorous, large shrub, producing large drooping bunches of sealing-wax-red berries. W China. I 1900 by Ernest Wilson.

**\* × frikartii** SCHNEID. ex VAN DE LAAR (*B. candidula* × *B. verruculosa*). Evergreen shrubs of dense habit with angled shoots and dark glossy green, spiny leaves glaucous beneath. Flowers pale yellow, relatively large, borne singly or in pairs followed by blue-black berries. The original form of this hybrid was raised in Switzerland in 1928 and has been named 'Stäfa'.

**'Amstelveen'** A dense small shrub with attractive drooping shoots and glossy green leaves white beneath. Raised in Holland about 1960.

**'Telstar'** Similar to 'Amstelveen' but taller, to 1.2m, and more compact. Raised in Holland about 1960.

**\*gagnepainii** SCHNEID. A small shrub making a dense growth of erect stems closely set with narrow, undulate leaves. Berries black, covered by a blue bloom. Forms an impenetrable hedge. W China. I about 1904 by Ernest Wilson.

**BERBERIS**—*continued*

**georgei** AHRENDT A rare and attractive shrub of medium height with arching branches. Flowers yellow in hanging, red-stalked racemes in May. The elliptic-obovate, toothed leaves colour well in autumn when the profuse crimson berries in large, pendulous clusters are most conspicuous. Origin unknown. AM 1979. FCC 1985.

**gilgiana** FEDDE A small shrub with red-brown shoots and leaves 2.5-4cm long, grey beneath; berries deep blood-red. China. I 1910 by William Purdom.

**glaucocarpa** STAPF A large, semi-evergreen shrub notable for its profusion of blue-black berries heavily covered with a white bloom, carried in conspicuous clusters. W Himalaya. I 1832. AM 1943 (for fruit). AM 1983 (for flower).

*****'Goldilocks'** (*B. darwinii* × *B. valdiviana*). A vigorous large shrub with upright and arching branches. Leaves dark glossy green, spiny. Deep golden yellow flowers are profusely borne in hanging, red-stalked clusters over a long period during spring. Raised by our propagator Peter Dummer from a cross made in 1978.

**gyalaica** AHRENDT Medium-sized shrub related to *B. sherriffii*. Berries oblong-elliptic, blackish-purple with blue bloom. The leaves turn red in autumn. SE Tibet. I about 1925 by Kingdon-Ward.

*****hakeoides** (HOOK. f.) SCHNEID. A very distinct and quite remarkable Chilean species. It is of loose habit with shoots, often unbranched, up to 3m high. Leaves usually in pairs, rounded and spiny. Flowers golden yellow, produced in clusters all along the shoots, in April and May. I 1861. AM 1901.

**henryana** SCHNEID. A distinct species with long, pear-shaped leaves and elliptic-oblong, red berries. C China.

**heteropoda** SCHRENK This species is most frequently grown in the following form. The typical variety differs in its oblong berries.

**var. sphaerocarpa** (KAR. & KIR.) AHRENDT Medium-sized shrub with few flowered racemes of orange-yellow flowers followed by globose black berries slightly blue bloomy. NW China.

**hispanica** BOISS. & REUT. An open-habited shrub about 2m high. Leaves rather small, elliptic and light green; flowers orange-yellow; berries oval, blue-black. S Spain, N Africa.

*****hookeri** LEM. (*B. wallichiana* HOOK. not DC.) A Himalayan species forming a dense, evergreen, compact shrub not more than 1-1.5m high. Leaves glaucous beneath. Berries green at first then black. Nepal, Sikkim, Bhutan. I 1848.

**var. viridis** SCHNEID. Leaves green beneath. This is the commonest form in cultivation. There are intermediates between this and the typical variety and it is no longer regarded as distinct.

***** × **hybrido-gagnepainii** SURINGAR (*B. candidula* × *B. gagnepainii*). A small shrub of dense growth. Leaves ovate, with revolute, spiny margins, dull green above, green beneath. Ideal as a small hedge or as undercover.

*****hypokerina** AIRY SHAW An outstanding small shrub forming a thicket of purple stems. Leaves as much as 10cm long, holly-like, silvery-white beneath. Berries dark blue, with white bloom. Called "Silver Holly" by its discoverer, Kingdon-Ward,who also introduced it. Does not thrive in thin, chalky soil. Upper Burma. I 1926.

*****ilicifolia** FORST. "Holly-leaved Barberry". A very rare evergreen species of small to medium size. Leaves spiny and dark shining green. Flowers orange-yellow in short dense racemes in May. Chile. I 1843 by Sir Joseph Hooker. For a plant sometimes grown under this name see × *Mahoberberis neubertii*.

**incrassata** See *B. insignis* subsp. *incrassata*.

*****insignis** HOOK. f. & THOMS. (*B. insignis* var. *tongloensis* SCHNEID.) A noble shrub of medium size forming a dense clump of erect, yellowish stems remarkable for their lack of spines. Leaves usually in clusters of three, lanceolate, large, up to 18cm long, with bold teeth, dark polished green above, yellowish-green and glossy beneath. Flowers large, in dense clusters followed by black, ovoid berries. Often regarded as tender but has proved quite hardy here. N India, Nepal, Bhutan. Introduced from Sikkim by Sir Joseph Hooker in 1850.

**subsp. incrassata** (AHRENDT) CHAMBERLAIN & HU (*B. incrassata* AHRENDT) Differs in its rounded berries. NE Upper Burma, SE Tibet. I 1931.

**BERBERIS**—*continued*

**\* × interposita** AHRENDT (*B. hookeri* × *B. verruculosa*). A vigorous, small shrub, developing into a dense rounded mound of arching stems. Leaves 1.5-2cm long, sharply spiny, glossy dark green above, pruinose below often green by autumn.

    **'Wallich's Purple'** A dense, small bush with arching shoots, the leaves bronze-red when young, later glossy green.

**× irwinii** and its cultivars. See under *B. × stenophylla*.

**jamesiana** FORR. & W.W. SM. A large, erect-branched species giving rich autumn tints. Flowers in racemes, followed by pendulous clusters of translucent, coral-red berries. Yunnan. I 1913 by George Forrest. AM 1925.

**\*julianae** SCHNEID. An excellent dense evergreen to 3m with strongly spiny stems and clusters of stiff, narrow, spine-toothed leaves, copper-tinted when young. Flowers yellow, slightly scented, in dense axillary clusters. A good screening or hedging plant. China. I 1900 by Ernest Wilson.

**\*kawakamii** HAYATA (*B. kawakamii* var. *formosana* AHRENDT) (*B. formosana* (AHRENDT) AHRENDT) A short, spiny, evergreen species, densely furnished with short rather broad leaves, copper-tinted when young. Dense clusters of rich yellow flowers in March and April. Taiwan. I about 1919 by Ernest Wilson.

**koreana** PALIB. An attractive species, its large leaves colouring well in autumn; flowers in drooping racemes; the red, waxen, ovoid berries are conspicuous. Korea.

**\*lempergiana** AHRENDT A distinct species, akin to *B. julianae*, but with broader, paler leaves. Berries oval and bloomy, produced in clusters. Zhejiang, China. I 1935 and originally named from a plant raised in our nurseries.

**leptoclada** See *B. amoena*.

**levis** See *B. atrocarpa*.

**liechtensteinii** SCHNEID. A medium-sized, semi-evergreen shrub. Berries ovoid, red, produced in short racemes. W China. I 1908.

**\*linearifolia** PHIL. An erect, medium-sized shrub of rather ungainly habit, with narrow, dark, glossy green, spine-tipped leaves. The orange-red flowers produced early in spring, and sometimes again in the autumn, are the richest coloured of the genus. Introduced from Argentina by Harold Comber in 1927. Native also of Chile. FCC 1931.

    **'Jewel'** A splendid form and possibly the best in the genus for flower. Flowers scarlet in bud opening to bright orange, relatively large. C 1937. AM 1978.

    **'Orange King'** A selected form with larger flowers of a rich orange. AGM 1984.

**\* × lologensis** SANDW. (*B. darwinii* × *B. linearifolia*). A very beautiful, medium-sized, evergreen shrub, offspring of two superb species. Leaves variable in shape, entire and spiny on the same bush; flowers apricot-yellow. A natural hybrid found with the parents in Argentina by Comber in 1927. AM 1931. AGM 1984.

    **'Apricot Queen'** Profuse, large bright orange flowers, habit broadly upright.

    **'Stapehill'** A form with rich orange flowers freely borne.

**\*lycium** ROYLE A semi-evergreen species of medium height. Leaves up to 5cm long, light sea-green; flowers bright yellow in elongated racemes, followed by purple, bloomy berries. Himalaya. I about 1850 by Sir Joseph Hooker.

**× macracantha** SCHRAD. (*B. aristata* × *B. vulgaris*). A tall shrub up to 4m high. The yellow flowers are produced in racemes of 10-20 blooms and are followed by purple berries. Garden origin.

**\*manipurana** AHRENDT (*B. knightii* HORT.) (*B. xanthoxylon* HORT.) (*B. hookeri* var. *latifolia* HORT.) A vigorous species reaching about 3m with large, lustrous leaves, yellow flowers and oblong, blue-black berries. An excellent hedging plant. Manipur. I 1882. AM 1980.

**\* × media** GROOTEND. (*B. × chenaultii* × *B. thunbergii*). This hybrid is represented in gardens by the following forms.

    **'Parkjuweel'** A small shrub of dense prickly habit. Leaves obovate, almost spineless, colouring richly in autumn, occasionally remaining until the following spring. Flowers borne singly or in small clusters of up to 4. Garden origin in Holland about 1956.

    **'Red Jewel'** A dense, small, semi-evergreen shrub similar to 'Parkjuweel' but with somewhat broader leaves becoming deep metallic purple. A sport of 'Parkjuweel'.

    **'Mentorensis'** (*B. julianae* × *B. thunbergii*). A vigorous and very dense, deciduous or semi-evergreen shrub up to 2m with small, obovate leaves which are entire or toothed towards

**BERBERIS 'Mentorensis'**—*continued*

the apex. Flowers pale yellow tinged red followed by dark brown-red berries. Garden origin in the United States in 1924.

**micrantha** AHRENDT Medium-sized shrub of dense habit. Berries dark red in dense racemes. Bhutan. I 1838.

**mitifolia** STAPF A distinct species, a small to medium-sized shrub with spike-like racemes of yellow flowers, pubescent leaves red in autumn and elongated crimson berries. W China. I 1901 by Ernest Wilson.

**montana** C. GAY A stiffly-branched, upright shrub closely related to *B. cabrerae* with which it has been confused. It differs in having only up to 3 flowers in the inflorescence (up to 6 in *B. cabrerae*). Argentina, Chile. I 1925-1927 by Harold Comber. AM 1935.

**morrisonensis** HAYATA "Mt Morrison Barberry". A low, compact, free-flowering shrub with large bright red berries and brilliant autumn tints of scarlet and gold. Taiwan. I 1912.

**mucrifolia** AHRENDT A dwarf shrub of dense, compact habit, with erect slender, spiny stems and small, mucronate leaves. Flowers usually solitary, berries bright red. Nepal. I about 1954.

**oblonga** (REG.) SCHNEID. Medium to large-sized shrub. Flowers in densely packed racemes. Berries purple-black with white bloom. Turkestan. I 1876.

**orthobotrys** AITCH. A medium-sized shrub of vigorous, upright habit bearing large, bright red, oval berries. Bright autumn tints. Kashmir, Afghanistan, Nepal. AM 1919.

　　**var. canescens** AHRENDT (*B.* 'Unique') A form with narrower leaves, pruinose beneath. Kashmir, Nepal.

× **ottawensis** SCHNEID. (*B. thunbergii* × *B. vulgaris*). A medium-sized shrub with green, rounded or oval leaves and red berries in drooping clusters. C 1893.

　　**Purpurea group** (f. *purpurea* (SCHNEID.) REHD.) This name covers all forms with purple leaves. See also under 'Superba'.

　　**'Superba'** A vigorous hybrid of medium to large size. A really first class shrub with rich vinous purple foliage, yellow flowers and red berries. Usually grown as 'Purpurea'. Garden origin. AM 1979. AGM 1984.

**pallens** FRANCH. A large shrub. Berries ovoid, bright red; leaves richly tinted in autumn. W China. I 1929.

**panlanensis** See *B. sanguinea*.

**parisepala** AHRENDT Slow-growing, small-sized shrub related to *B. angulosa*. Leaves often red-tinted in autumn. Berries large, red. SE Tibet, Bhutan, Nepal. I about 1928.

**'Parkjuweel'** See *B.* × *media* 'Parkjuweel'.

**'Pirate King'** A small, dense shrub of vigorous growth, berries fiery orange-red.

**poiretii** SCHNEID. Attractive shrub up to 1.5m with elegant drooping branches and abundant pale-yellow flowers followed by slender, bright red berries. N China, Amurland. I about 1860.

**polyantha** HEMSL. Medium-sized, erect shrub with large and abundant drooping flower panicles, followed by grape-like clusters of red berries. One of the most constant in the vivid red of its autumn colour. W China. I 1904. AM 1917.

**prattii** SCHNEID. Medium-sized to large shrub. Flowers in erect panicles followed by ovoid, bright coral berries. A lovely shrub of great ornamental beauty when heavy with fruits in the autumn. W China. The plant most commonly grown is var. *laxipendula* AHRENDT with drooping panicles. AM 1953.

*****pruinosa** FRANCH. A vigorous Chinese evergreen of medium size with distinct spine-toothed, sea-green foliage, white beneath. The soft yellow flowers are followed by abundant crops of blue-black berries covered with white bloom. Yunnan. I to France in 1894 by Delavay. AM 1924.

　　**var. longifolia** AHRENDT A form with longer, narrower leaves. Possibly a hybrid.

**'Red Jewel'** See *B.* × *media* 'Red Jewel'.

*****replicata** W.W. SM. A graceful, slow-growing evergreen, attaining about 1.5m; leaves narrow, recurved at the edges and glaucous beneath; berries ellipsoid, black-purple. Yunnan. I 1917 by George Forrest. AM 1923.

**'Rubrostilla'** A beautiful, small-sized shrub of garden origin; very showy in autumn with its large, oblong, coral-red berries. Fruits among the largest in the genus. Garden origin, a hybrid of *B. wilsoniae*. FCC 1916. AGM 1984.

**BERBERIS**—*continued*

**\*sanguinea** SCHNEID. (*B. panlanensis* AHRENDT) A charming, medium-sized, compact evergreen of very neat growth. Leaves linear, sea-green and spine-toothed. An ideal hedging plant. W China. I 1908.

    **'Panlanensis'** The commonly grown form described above.

**\*sargentiana** SCHNEID. A hardy species up to 2m. The evergreen leaves are leathery, elliptic-oblong, net-veined and up to 13cm long; berries blue-black. W China. I 1907 by Ernest Wilson. AM 1915. FCC 1916.

**sherriffii** AHRENDT An elegant, medium-sized shrub with elliptic, entire leaves, conspicuous when bearing its large, drooping panicles of bloomy blue-black berries. SE Tibet. I 1938 by Ludlow, Sherriff and Taylor.

**sieboldii** MIQ. A small suckering shrub of compact habit with oval leaves which colour richly in the autumn. Racemes of pale yellow flowers followed by globose, shining orange berries. Japan. I 1892.

**sikkimensis** (SCHNEID.) AHRENDT A small shrub with angled shoots and short racemes of ovoid dark red berries. Sikkim. I about 1924.

**silva-taroucana** SCHNEID. A large shrub of elegant habit, the young growths are attractively tinged reddish-purple. The long racemes of yellow flowers are followed by egg-shaped scarlet berries. China. I 1912.

**\*soulieana** SCHNEID. A sparsely-branched, medium-sized evergreen of stiff habit. Leaves narrow, with pronounced spinose teeth. Flowers yellow borne in clusters in the leaf axils in May. Berries black, covered with a glaucous bloom. C China. I 1897.

**\* × stenophylla** LINDL. (*B. darwinii × B. empetrifolia*). An indispensable evergreen, ultimately a medium-sized graceful shrub, its long arching branches wreathed with yellow flowers in April. C 1860. FCC 1864. AGM 1984.

    **'Autumnalis'** Small shrub of graceful habit producing a second crop of flowers in autumn. C 1929.

    **'Claret Cascade'** Flowers rich orange flushed red outside, young foliage purple-tinged.

    **'Coccinea'** (*B. × irwinii* 'Coccinea') A small shrub with crimson buds opening orange. C 1920. AM 1925.

    **'Corallina'** (*B. × irwinii* 'Corallina') A small shrub of lax habit. Buds coral-red opening yellow. C 1912.

    **'Corallina Compacta'** (*B. × irwinii* 'Corallina Compacta') A dwarf shrub rarely exceeding 30cm. Buds coral-red opening yellow. C 1930. AM 1981. AGM 1984.

    **'Crawley Gem'** A small shrub forming a dense mound of arching stems flooded in spring with orange flowers red-tipped in bud. C 1930.

    **'Cream Showers'** An unusual form with creamy-white flowers.

    **'Etna'** A seedling raised in our nurseries before 1935. A small shrub with shining, dark green leaves. In April the whole bush erupts into flower from red buds and the leaves are hidden by clusters of fiery-orange blossoms.

    **'Gracilis'** (*B. × irwinii* 'Gracilis') A small shrub of lax habit. Leaves bright green. Flowers golden yellow. C 1907.

    **'Gracilis Nana'** (*B. × irwinii* 'Gracilis Nana') A dwarf, slow-growing shrub of dense habit, with golden yellow flowers. C 1909.

    **'Irwinii'** (*B. × irwinii* BYHOUWER) A small, compact shrub; flowers deep yellow. C 1903.

    **'Nana'** (*B. darwinii* 'Nana') Small compact shrub with rich yellow flowers.

    **'Picturata'** (*B. × irwinii* 'Picturata') A small floriferous shrub; flowers deep yellow.

    **'Pink Pearl'** A curious form of chameleon nature. Leaves dark green or mottled and striped pink and cream. Flowers may be creamy yellow, orange, pink or bicoloured on different shoots of the same bush. Unfortunately this unusual form reverts badly.

    **'Prostrata'** (*B. darwinii* 'Prostrata') Attractive low shrub; the orange buds open golden yellow.

    **'Semperflorens'** Small shrub with red buds opening orange, still flowering when the typical form has finished. C 1930.

**†\*sublevis** W.W. SM. Medium-sized shrub with ribbed, strongly spiny stems and narrow spine-edged leaves. Flowers primrose-yellow, fragrant. W China. C 1935.

**\*taliensis** SCHNEID. A rigid, slow-growing, evergreen hummock, scarcely exceeding 1m in height. Its lanceolate leaves are dark, glossy green. Flowers lemon-yellow. Berries blue-black. Yunnan. I 1922 by George Forrest.

**BERBERIS**—*continued*

**taylorii** AHRENDT Medium-sized shrub with dense panicles of greenish-yellow flowers. Berries ovoid, black with blue bloom. SE Tibet. I 1938 by Ludlow, Sherriff and Taylor.

**temolaica** AHRENDT One of the most striking barberries. A vigorous shrub up to 3m with stout erect-spreading branches. Young shoots and leaves conspicuously glaucous, the shoots becoming a dark, bloomy, purple-brown with age. Berries egg-shaped, red, covered with bloom. Introduced from SE Tibet by Kingdon-Ward in 1924.

**thunbergii** DC. An invaluable small shrub, compact in growth and unsurpassed in the brilliance of its autumn foliage and bright red berries. Japan. I about 1864. FCC 1890. AGM 1984.

**Atropurpurea group** (f. *atropurpurea* (CHENAULT) REHD.) Foliage rich, reddish-purple, throughout spring and summer, and increasing in intensity as winter approaches. C 1913. AM 1926.

**'Atropurpurea Nana'** ('Crimson Pygmy', 'Little Favourite') A charming dwarf form of this popular purple-foliaged shrub, suitable for the rock-garden or dwarf hedge. Raised in Holland in 1942. AGM 1984.

**'Aurea'** Leaves bright yellow, becoming pale green by late summer. C 1950.

**'Bagatelle'** Similar to 'Atropurpurea Nana' but much more compact. Raised in Holland in 1971 by crossing 'Atropurpurea Nana' with 'Kobold'.

**'Cheal's Scarlet'** Leaves bronze-tinged during summer turning brilliant scarlet in early autumn.

**'Dart's Red Lady'** Very deep purple leaves turn brilliant red in autumn.

**'Erecta'** A small, compact, fastigiate shrub forming a dense clump; excellent for low hedges. Superb autumn colours.

**'Golden Ring'** Leaves reddish-purple with a narrow gold margin. Similar forms can be found when Atropurpurea is raised from seed. C 1950.

**'Green Carpet'** A low shrub to about 1m with wide-spreading, arching shoots. The rounded leaves turn red in autumn. Selected in Holland about 1956.

**'Harlequin'** Similar to 'Rose Glow' but leaves smaller and more heavily mottled pink. C 1969. AM 1978.

**'Helmond Pillar'** A form of narrow, upright habit with rich purple foliage.

**'Kelleriis'** A compact, spreading bush, the leaves mottled creamy-white. In autumn the white portion of the leaf turns through pink to deep crimson. Raised in Denmark. The more recent 'Silver Beauty' is similar.

**'Kobold'** A dwarf form of very dense, rounded habit. Free-fruiting. Raised in Holland about 1960.

**'Minor'** An interesting, dense-habited, dwarf shrub scarcely exceeding 50cm.

**'Pink Queen'** The best pink variegated form with reddish leaves heavily flecked with grey and white. Raised in Holland before 1958.

**'Red Chief'** A small shrub of upright habit later with arching branches, stems bright red, leaves narrow, deep red-purple. Selected in Holland in 1942. AGM 1984.

**'Red Pillar'** A most attractive form of 'Erecta' with reddish-purple leaves which turn brilliant scarlet in autumn.

**'Rose Glow'** A very striking, small colourful shrub. The leaves of the young shoots are purple, mottled silver-pink and bright rose later becoming purple. Selected in Holland about 1957 but now superseded by other forms. AGM 1984.

**'Silver Beauty'** See under 'Kelleriis'.

**tsangpoensis** AHRENDT A most interesting species, forming a dwarf, wide-spreading mound, the slender yellow stems often extending several feet along the ground. Attractive autumn tints and red berries. SE Tibet. I 1925.

**umbellata** G. DON A medium-sized shrub, semi-evergreen except in severe winters; shoots bright red at first; yellow flowers in long-stalked corymbs followed by red, egg-shaped berries. Nepal. I 1848.

**'Unique'** See *B. orthobotrys* var. *canescens*.

**\*valdiviana** PHIL. A large, stately species, like a smooth-leaved holly, distinct on account of its large, leathery, polished almost spineless leaves. Flowers saffron-yellow in long, drooping racemes. A first class hardy plant deserving wider planting. Chile. I 1902 and again by Clarence Elliott in 1930. AM 1939.

**BERBERIS**—*continued*

**validisepala** AHRENDT A medium-sized species allied to *B. yunnanensis* and differing in its shorter spines and smaller flowers and berries. Yunnan. I about 1930.

**\*veitchii** SCHNEID. (*B. acuminata* VEITCH) An evergreen to about 2m with long, lanceolate, spine-toothed leaves and red young shoots; flowers bronze-yellow, long-stalked in axillary clusters; berries black. C China. I 1900 by Ernest Wilson.

**vernae** SCHNEID. (*B. caroli* var. *hoanghensis* SCHNEID.) A very graceful, medium-sized Chinese shrub; flowers in dense, slender racemes all along the stems; berries globose, salmon-red. I 1910. AM 1926.

**\*verruculosa** HEMSL. & WILS. A very pleasing, compact, slow-growing Chinese shrub 1.5-2m high, with rough, minutely warty, drooping stems densely covered with small, glossy, dark green leaves which are white beneath. Flowers usually solitary, golden yellow. W China. I 1904 by Ernest Wilson. AM 1911. AGM 1984.

**virescens** HOOK. f. & THOMS. A tall, erect-branched shrub with red shoots and brilliant red autumn colour. Berries reddish, bloomy. Sikkim. I 1849.

**virgetorum** SCHNEID. Shrub up to 2m with comparatively large obovate spineless leaves and oblong-elliptic reddish berries. China. I about 1909.

**vulgaris** L. The "Common Barberry", a medium-sized shrub producing pendulous clusters of egg-shaped, bright red, translucent berries. The bark and wood were once used in the treatment of jaundice. Now rarely grown as it is a host to wheat rust. Europe (incl British Isles), N Africa, temperate Asia. Naturalised in North America.

**'Atropurpurea'** "Purple-leaf Barberry". A striking shrub, its deep vinous-purple foliage contrasting with the nodding racemes of yellow flowers. AM 1905.

**wilsoniae** HEMSL. A splendid small shrub forming dense mounds of thorny stems. Leaves small, sea-green turning to attractive autumn shades which blend with the coral of the fruit clusters. W China. I about 1904 by Ernest Wilson and named after his wife. FCC 1907.

**'Globosa'** A dwarf compact globular form.

**var. guhtzunica** (AHRENDT) AHRENDT This variety resembles var. *subcaulialata*, and has attractive, sea-green leaves and reddish-purple young shoots; berries in clusters, translucent white, changing to coral-red. W China. I 1938 by Dr Yu.

**var. stapfiana** (SCHNEID.) SCHNEID. This semi-evergreen shrub with its soft yellow flowers is a little taller and has more glaucous sea-green spathulate leaves and elliptic coral-red berries. W China. I 1896.

**var. subcaulialata** (SCHNEID.) SCHNEID. A taller variety with larger leaves. W China. I 1908.

**\* × wintonensis** AHRENDT A dense, medium-sized shrub, a hybrid of *B. bergmanniae* which it resembles but with very narrow leaves. The flowers appearing in February are exceptionally freely borne and are followed by blue-black, bloomy berries. Raised in our nurseries in about 1935.

**yunnanensis** FRANCH. An attractive, medium-sized shrub of rounded habit with relatively large, golden yellow flowers, brilliant autumn colours and bright red berries. W China. I 1885 by Delavay.

**zabeliana** SCHNEID. A neat, compact bush of medium height with plum-red berries and good autumn colour. Kashmir, Afghanistan.

†**\*BESCHORNERIA** KUNTH—**Agavaceae**—A small genus related to *Agave*. About 10 species, natives of Mexico.

**yuccoides** K. KOCH A striking, Mexican yucca-like plant. The flower stems attain about 2m carrying drooping racemes of bright green flowers with red bracts. This remarkable plant flourished in our Winchester nursery on chalk at the foot of a south-facing wall for more than twenty years. Requires full sun and a well drained position. I before 1859. AM 1933.

**BETULA** L.—**Betulaceae**—The "Birches" comprise about 60 species of deciduous trees and shrubs found in N temperate regions. Male and female catkins are borne on the same tree, the males pendulous and elongating in spring, the females shorter and erect. They include some of the most elegant trees, many of which are noteworthy for their stem colour, and attractive yellow leaves in autumn. They succeed on most soils, both damp and dry, but do not reach maximum size on shallow chalk soils.

**BETULA**—*continued*

**alba** See *B. pendula* and *B. pubescens*.

**albo-sinensis** BURK. Beautiful medium-sized species with glossy green leaves on slightly rough shoots. The attractive peeling bark is pinkish to coppery-red, cream when first exposed. W China. I 1901 by Ernest Wilson.

**var. septentrionalis** SCHNEID. This splendid variety has striking grey-pink bark, coppery-pink on the main branches. It also differs in its matt green leaves. I 1908 by Ernest Wilson.

**alleghaniensis** BRITT. (*B. lutea* MICHX.) A medium-sized tree with smooth, shining, amber coloured or golden brown bark which peels prettily. Leaves ovate-oblong, downy, turning rich yellow in autumn. E North America. I about 1767.

× **aurata** BORKH. (*B. pendula* × *B. pubescens*). A small to medium-sized tree, variable in shape and texture of leaf but generally intermediate between the parents. Frequent with the parents in the wild.

× **caerulea** BLANCH. (*B. caerulea-grandis* BLANCH. ) (*B. cordifolia* × *B. populifolia*). A small tree with creamy white, orange-tinted bark and ovate, sharply-pointed leaves. Occurring with the parents in the wild. I 1905.

**caerulea-grandis** See *B.* × *caerulea*.

**chinensis** MAXIM. Large shrub, occasionally a small tree, without conspicuous bark. An uncommon species of neat habit with small, oval, sharply-toothed leaves on slender, downy shoots. China. I 1906.

**costata** TRAUTV. The true species of this name is a native of NE Asia and is rare in cultivation. Plants grown as *B. costata* are usually a form of *B. ermanii* qv.

**cylindrostachya** LINDL. A rare, small tree which is proving fairly hardy here. Stout, downy, drooping shoots bear large ovate to ovate-oblong, glossy, short-stalked leaves downy on both sides and occasionally to 15cm long. An interesting species with large leaves requiring a sheltered position and happiest in the milder areas of the British Isles. Himalaya.

**davurica** PALL. A medium-sized tree with peculiarly rugged silvery-grey bark, dark brown on the main branches. Leaves dark green with triangular teeth, on very rough shoots. Tends to be early leafing and perhaps more suited for northerly and colder areas. Manchuria, N China, Korea. I 1882.

**ermanii** CHAM. (*B. ermanii* var. *subcordata* (REG.) KOIDZ.) A very graceful, vigorous tree with very rough shoots and bright green often heart-shaped, conspicuously veined leaves. Bark creamy-white and pinkish, fawn when first exposed with numerous pale brown lenticels, brown to red-brown on the branches. NE Asia. AGM 1984. Most plants grown as *B. costata* are a fine form of this species known as 'Grayswood Hill'.

**'Fetisowii'** A hybrid originally from C Asia, forming a graceful, narrow-headed tree notable for its peeling, chalk-white bark extending up the trunk to the branches. Plants grown under this name are probably seedlings of the original.

**glandulifera** (REG.) BUTLER (*B. pumila* var. *glandulifera* REG.) Medium-sized shrub. Leaves small, obovate, sometimes orbicular, gland dotted. Male catkins pink, passing to yellow. North America.

**grossa** SIEB. & ZUCC. "Japanese Cherry Birch". Medium-sized tree with smooth, dark grey bark and hornbeam-like leaves. The twigs have a distinctive smell when bruised. Japan. I 1896.

**humilis** SCHRANK A small to medium-size shrub with hairy and warty twigs and small leaves. Europe and N Asia.

**jacquemontii** See *B. utilis* var. *jacquemontii*.

**'Jermyns'** See *B. utilis* 'Jermyns'.

× **koehnei** SCHNEID. (*B. papyrifera* × *B. pendula*). Medium-sized tree of graceful habit, the lower branches drooping, leaves blue-green, with jagged teeth. Outstanding for its pure white bark on the trunk and larger branches.

**lenta** L. "Cherry Birch". Rarely a tall tree in this country, though attaining 25m in its native land. Trunk smooth, dark, reddish-brown or purple. The young bark is sweet and aromatic. Leaves turn rich yellow in autumn. E North America. I 1759.

**luminifera** WINKL. A remarkable large tree. The large, deep green, lustrous leaves persist until sharp frost in late autumn. W China. I 1901 by Ernest Wilson.

**BETULA**—*continued*

**lutea** See *B. alleghaniensis*.

**lyalliana** See *B. papyrifera* var. *commutata*.

**mandshurica** See *B. platyphylla*.

    **var. szechuanica** See *B. szechuanica*.

**maximowicziana** REG. "Monarch Birch". This, the largest-leaved birch, reaches 30m in its native habitat. As seen in this country it is a fast-growing wide-headed tree of medium height. Trunk orange-brown, finally grey and pinkish, peeling in narrow strips, coppery on the branches. Leaves heart-shaped, up to 15cm long, turning a lovely clear butter-yellow in the autumn. Japan. I 1893.

**medwediewii** REG. A large shrub or small shrubby tree with stout erect branches. Distinct in its large terminal buds and large corrugated leaves which turn yellow in autumn. Transcaucasus. I 1897. AM 1975 (for autumn colour).

**middendorffii** TRAUTV. & MEY. Medium to large shrub with usually resinous-glandular stems and small rounded leaves. Closely related to *B. humilis*. NE Asia. C 1904.

**nana** L. "Dwarf Birch". A small native shrub with tiny, neat, rounded leaves. N temperate regions. Similar species occur in North America and NE Asia.

**neoalaskana** SARG. (*B. papyrifera* var. *humilis* (REG.) FERN. & RAUP) (*B. papyrifera* var. *neoalaskana* (SARG.) RAUP) "Yukon White Birch". A handsome, large tree with white to red-brown, peeling bark. Alaska. I 1905.

**nigra** L. "River Birch" "Red Birch". A beautiful, fast-growing tree remarkable for its pinkish-orange, shaggy bark, becomes brown and ridged on old trees. As its common name suggests, it is one of the finest trees for planting in damp ground. The soft green diamond-shaped leaves are glaucous beneath. C and E United States. Introduced by Peter Collinson in 1736.

    **'Heritage'** An outstanding form found as a seedling in the United States in 1968. A vigorous tree with peeling light brown to creamy bark and dark glossy green leaves.

**papyrifera** MARSH. "Paper Birch" "Canoe Birch". A striking, large tree with white papery bark and yellow autumn foliage. North America. I 1750.

    **var. commutata** (REG.) FERN. (*B. papyrifera* var. *occidentalis* SARG.) (*B. lyalliana* BEAN) An attractive, large tree with white bark and broad, ovate leaves.

    **var. humilis** See *B. neoalaskana*.

    **var. kenaica** (EVANS) HENRY A tree from the coast of Alaska with white bark tinged orange. I 1891.

    **var. minor** (TUCKERM.) S. WATS. "Dwarf White Birch". A shrubby form or occasionally a small bushy tree. NE North America. I 1904.

    **var. neoalaskana** See *B. neoalaskana*.

**pendula** ROTH. (*B. verrucosa* EHRH.) (*B. alba* L. in part) The "Common Silver Birch", aptly described as the "Lady of the Woods". A medium-sized, white-stemmed tree thriving in drier soils than *B. pubescens*, from which it is distinguished by its rough, warty shoots and sharply cut, diamond-shaped leaves. Unlike *B. pubescens* old trees develop rough, black bark at the base. Europe (incl British Isles), N Asia. AGM 1984.

    **'Dalecarlica'** "Swedish Birch". A tall, slender, graceful tree with drooping branchlets and prettily cut leaves. The plant commonly grown under this name should correctly be known as 'Laciniata'; the true 'Dalecarlica' differs in being not as weeping and with more deeply cut leaves. It was originally found in Sweden in 1767 and is rare in cultivation. Forms similar to both occur wild in Sweden. AGM 1984 (to 'Dalecarlica').

    **'Dentata Viscosa'** A small, bushy tree with coarsely-toothed leaves. Young growths sticky. Of no special horticultural merit. C 1912.

    **'Fastigiata'** An erect form of medium size and rather stiff habit. 'Obelisk' is similar but perhaps not becoming as wide. C 1870.

    **'Golden Cloud'** A selection with yellow leaves. Tends to burn badly.

    **'Gracilis'** A small tree with arching branches and slender weeping shoots. Leaves finely and deeply cut.

**BETULA pendula**—*continued*

    **'Obelisk'** See under 'Fastigiata'.

    **'Purpurea'** "Purple Leaf Birch". A slow-growing tree with purple leaves. Rather weak constitution. C 1872. FCC 1874.

    **'Tristis'** A tall graceful tree with slender, pendulous branches, forming a narrow, symmetrical head. A tree of outstanding merit. C 1867. AGM 1984.

    **'Youngii'** "Young's Weeping Birch". Ultimately a beautiful dome-shaped or mushroom-headed, small weeping tree. AGM 1984.

**platyphylla** SUK. (*B. mandshurica* (REG.) NAKAI) A large tree with white bark. Allied to *B. pendula* but differing in its larger leaves. NE Asia. Rare in cultivation.

    **var. japonica** (MIQ.) HARA (*B. mandshurica* var. *japonica* (MIQ.) REHD.) (*B. tauschii* (REG.) KOIDZ.) "Japanese White Birch". A medium-sized tree with white resinous shoots related to *B. pendula* but with larger leaves. Bark pure white. Japan. C 1887.

    **var. rockii** See *B. rockii*.

    **var. szechuanica** See *B. szechuanica*.

**populifolia** MARSH. The "Grey Birch" is the American counterpart of our "Silver Birch". A small tree with ashen-white bark, purplish-brown on the branches, thriving equally well in dry or boggy ground. Leaves bright green, sharply-toothed, on rough shoots. E North America. I 1750.

**pubescens** EHRH. (*B. alba* L. in part) "Common White Birch". This species thrives on a variety of soils and especially in damp localities; it is distinguished from *B. pendula* by the less weeping habit, smooth downy shoots, more rounded leaves and the bark being white to the base. Europe (incl British Isles), N Asia.

    **subsp. carpatica** (WILLD.) ASCH. & GRAEBN. (*B. coriacea* GUNNARSON) A small tree with a wide distribution from Iceland to the Carpathians, forming a densely branched head. An extremely tough hardy tree, ideal for exposed windy situations.

**pumila** L. A small to large shrub of upright habit with downy young shoots and pointed, coarsely-toothed leaves. E North America. I 1762.

**rockii** (REHD.) JANSSON (*B. platyphylla* var. *rockii* (REHD.) REHD.) A small, white-barked tree allied to *B. platyphylla* and *B. szechuanica* introduced by the American collector Joseph Rock from Lake Koko Nor, China. W China.

**szechuanica** (SCHNEID.) JANSSON (*B. platyphylla* var. *szechuanica* (SCHNEID.) REHD. ) (*B. mandschurica* var. *szechuanica* (SCHNEID.) REHD.) A vigorous, medium-sized tree with glossy blue-green leaves and chalk-white bark. W China, SE Tibet. I 1908 by Ernest Wilson.

**tatewakiana** OKHI & WATANABE A small to medium-sized shrub with densely glandular branches downy when young. Leaves leathery, ovate to obovate, serrate in the upper half and downy beneath, 1.5-2.5cm long. A rare species, native of bogs in N Japan.

**'Trost's Dwarf'** A weak-growing small shrub with slender arching branches and small, finely cut leaves. Susceptible to rust.

**utilis** D. DON (*B. bhojpattra* LINDL.) "Himalayan Birch". A widely distributed species occurring throughout the Himalaya from Afghanistan to SW China and very variable in bark colour. The typical form is an attractive medium-sized tree with orange-brown or dark, coppery-brown, peeling bark often bloomed grey-pink and occurs in the eastern half of the range from SW China to Nepal. Introduced by Sir Joseph Hooker in 1849. AGM 1984.

    **var. jacquemontii** (SPACH) WINKLER (*B. jacquemontii* SPACH) Differs from the typical form in its white bark. For grafted plants previously distributed by us under this name see 'Silver Shadow'. N India, C and W Nepal. C 1880.

    **'Jermyns'** A very vigorous form making a medium-sized broadly conical tree, the very fine white bark retained into maturity. Catkins long and showy, up to 17cm. A form of var. *jacquemontii* selected in our nurseries from plants received from Belgium. It has reached 14m in the Hillier Gardens and Arboretum (1990).

    **var. occidentalis** (KITAMURA) K. ASHBURNER & SCHILLING A form from the W Himalaya with pure white peeling bark and densely warty shoots. Buds covered with white resin. Veins 7-10.

**BETULA utilis**—*continued*

    **'Silver Shadow'** One of the loveliest birches, with dazzling white stems. A very distinct form of var. *jacquemontii* making a small to medium sized tree with striking white bark and large, drooping, dark green leaves. The original tree grew for many years in our West Hill Nursery, Winchester. Previously distributed by us as *B. jacquemontii*.

    **verrucosa** See *B. pendula*.

**"BILBERRY"** See *Vaccinium myrtillus*.

**"BIRCH"** See *Betula*.

**"BLACKTHORN"** See *Prunus spinosa*.

**"BLADDER NUT"** See *Staphylea*.

**"BLADDER SENNA"** See *Colutea*.

**BOENNINGHAUSENIA** REICHB. ex MEISSN.—**Rutaceae**—A monotypic genus allied to *Ruta*.

    **albiflora** (HOOK.) REICHB. A late-flowering sub-shrub, in flower and foliage somewhat like a white *Thalictrum*. Flowers during late summer. Good on chalk soils. E Asia.

**"BOTTLEBRUSH"** See *Callistemon*.

†**BOUVARDIA** SALISB.—**Rubiaceae**—A genus of about 20 species of evergreen herbs and shrubs native of Mexico and tropical S America.

    **triphylla** SALISB. A small, showy Mexican plant with glossy green leaves usually in threes and orange-scarlet tubular flowers 5cm long produced late in summer and autumn. Suitable for the conservatory. I 1794.

†\***BOWKERIA** HARVEY—**Scrophulariaceae**—A small genus of some 5 species of tender, evergreen, S African shrubs and small trees.

    **gerardiana** HARVEY A tender, medium-sized, S African shrub, producing white calceolaria-like flowers during summer. Requires conservatory cultivation except in the mildest areas. Natal. I about 1890.

**"BOX"** See *Buxus*.

**"BOX ELDER"** See *Acer negundo*.

†\***BRACHYGLOTTIS** FORST. & FORST. f.—**Compositae**—A genus of 2 species of evergreen New Zealand shrubs closely related to *Senecio*. Some authorities include here the New Zealand shrubby members of *Senecio* such as *S. greyi*, *S. laxifolius* and their allies.

    **repanda** FORST. & FORST. f. A large shrub with very large, soft green leaves white beneath, and mignonette-scented flowers in large panicles. Creates a tropical effect. The leaves were used as primitive postcards by Maori tribes in remote areas of New Zealand. Only for the mildest areas or conservatories.

    **'Purpurea'** Leaves purple above, white beneath. It was found in the Wanganui district of New Zealand. AM 1977.

**"BRAMBLE"** See *Rubus*.

**"BRIDAL WREATH"** See *Spiraea* 'Arguta'.

**"BROOM"** See *Cytisus* and *Genista*.

**"BROOM, BUTCHER'S"** See *Ruscus aculeatus*.

**"BROOM, HEDGEHOG"** See *Erinacea anthyllis*.

**"BROOM, SPANISH"** See *Spartium junceum*.

**BROUSSONETIA** L'HERIT ex VENT.—**Moraceae**—A small genus of dioecious shrubs and trees with about 7 species found in E and SE Asia and Polynesia. The male flowers are produced in catkin-like spikes, the females in globose heads.

    **kazinoki** SIEB. & ZUCC. A large, spreading shrub with ovate leaves variously one to three-lobed and toothed. A rare shrub mainly differing from *B. papyrifera* in its glabrous young shoots and leaves. China, Japan.

    **papyrifera** (L.) VENT. "Paper Mulberry". A large shrub or small tree with variously lobed, hairy leaves. The female is decorative, with its peculiar globular heads of orange-red fruits. In Japan paper is made from its bark. E Asia, naturalised in the United States. I early in the 18th century.

        **'Laciniata'** ('Dissecta') A dwarf form with curious, finely and deeply divided leaves. Raised in France about 1830.

‡\***BRUCKENTHALIA** REICHB.—**Ericaceae**—A monotypic genus related to *Erica*.

    **spiculifolia** (SALISB.) REICHB. A dwarf, heath-like plant up to 25cm high. Terminal racemes of rose-pink bell-shaped flowers in June. E Europe, Asia Minor. I 1888.

† **BRUGMANSIA** PERS. (*Datura* L. in part)—**Solanaceae**—The "Angel's Trumpets" are a genus of 5 species of poisonous shrubs and trees native to S America, particularly the Andes. Grown outside only in the south-west and the Isles of Scilly but suitable for the conservatory. They are conspicuous in their large, hanging, trumpet-shaped flowers. Previously included in *Datura* which is now restricted to annual species with upright flowers.

    × **candida** PERS. (*B. aurea* × *B. versicolor*). This splendid hybrid occurs in the wild in Ecuador where the flowers can be white, yellow or pink. The following form is grown:

        **'Grand Marnier'** A large shrub with large, hanging, trumpet-shaped flowers of a beautiful peach colour, the lobes ending in long, tail-like points.

    **sanguinea** (RUIZ & PAVON) D. DON (*Datura sanguinea* RUIZ & PAVON) Tree-like shrub up to 3m, taller in the Isles of Scilly. Large softly hairy leaves, toothed on young plants and large orange-red trumpets hanging from the branches in May and June. Colombia to N Chile.

    **suaveolens** (HUMB. & BONPL. ex WILLD.) BERCHT. & J. PRESL. (*Datura suaveolens* HUMB. & BONPL. ex WILLD.) A large tree-like shrub with flannel-like, untoothed leaves and large, pendulous, trumpet-shaped, fragrant white flowers from June to August. An excellent conservatory subject. Brazil.

‡\***BRYANTHUS** S. GMELIN—**Ericaceae**—A monotypic genus related to Phyllodoce.

    **gmelinii** D. DON (*B. musciformis* NAKAI) A rare shrublet related to *Phyllodoce*, having prostrate branches, closely set with small linear leaves. Flowers rose-pink borne three or more together upon slender, erect stalks. Japan, Kamchatka. C 1834.

**"BUCKEYE"** See *Aesculus*.

**"BUCKTHORN"** See *Rhamnus*.

**"BUCKTHORN, SEA"** See *Hippophae rhamnoides.*

**BUDDLEJA** L.—**Loganiaceae**—(*Buddleia* L.) About 100 species of mainly shrubs and small trees found in Africa, Asia and in the Americas from the S United States to S America. A genus including several species of the greatest garden value, thriving in almost any soil and revelling in full sun. The flowering period is July to September unless otherwise stated. All have opposite leaves except *B. alternifolia.* Many species almost double their height when grown against a sunny wall.

**albiflora** HEMSL. A large shrub similar in general appearance to *B. davidii* but with stems rounded not four-angled as in the common species. Flowers pale lilac in long slender terminal panicles. Horticulturally inferior to *B. davidii.* China. I 1900.

**alternifolia** MAXIM. A large shrub or occasionally a small tree, with graceful arching branches bearing long, narrow, dark green, alternate leaves and wreathed in June with delicately fragrant, lilac flowers. China. I 1915. AM 1922. AGM 1984.
**'Argentea'** An uncommon form having leaves covered with closely adpressed, silky hairs giving them a silvery sheen.

†\***asiatica** LOUR. A large shrub or small tree with long, lax stems, narrowly lanceolate leaves, white beneath, and terminal and axillary, drooping cylindrical panicles of sweetly scented white flowers during winter. Widely distributed in E Asia from Nepal and China to the Philippines. I 1876. FCC 1906.

†\***auriculata** BENTH. A medium-sized shrub of open habit. Leaves white-felted beneath. Flowers in long, cylindrical panicles, strongly fragrant, creamy-white with yellow throat. Winter. Suitable for a warm wall. S Africa, from Zimbabwe to Cape Province. AM 1923.

†**candida** DUNN A medium-sized shrub distinguished by soft, flannel-like, fawn-grey leaves and small racemes of violet flowers. E Himalaya. I 1928.

**caryopteridifolia** W.W. SM. This seems to be the hardiest of a small group of spring-flowering species. A medium to large shrub with woolly, white leaves and shoots. The fragrant, lilac-coloured flowers are borne in late spring or early autumn. China. I 1913.

**colvilei** HOOK. f. & THOMS. A large shrub or small tree of vigorous growth. Leaves dark green. The large, tubular, deep rose flowers are produced in terminal, drooping panicles in June. While tender as a young plant, mature specimens have withstood zero temperatures at Winchester and survived all winters since 1925. E Himalaya. I 1849. FCC 1896.
**'Kewensis'** A form with rich red flowers. AM 1947.

**crispa** BENTH. (*B. paniculata* HORT.) A medium-sized to large shrub, the deeply toothed leaves and stems covered with a dense white felt. Flowers fragrant, lilac with an orange throat, produced in terminal cylindrical panicles in late summer. N India. I 1850. AM 1961.

**davidii** FRANCH. (*B. variabilis* HEMSL.) This universally grown medium-sized shrub gives the best results when hard pruned in March. The fragrant flowers, in long racemes, are very attractive to butterflies. Does well near the sea. Well naturalised in many towns and cities in the British Isles. C and W China, Japan. C 1890. AM 1898.
**var. alba** REHD. & WILS. White flowers.
**'Amplissima'** Huge panicles, deep mauve. C 1911.
**'Black Knight'** Long trusses of very deep violet. C 1959. AGM 1984.
**'Border Beauty'** Deep crimson-purple; compact habit. C 1962.
**'Charming'** Lavender-pink.
**'Dartmoor'** An unusual form with magenta flowers in compact, short, broad panicles. Found by Mr Hayles near Yelverton on Dartmoor. AM 1973. FCC 1990.
**'Dubonnet'** Strong-growing with massive panicles of deep purple. C 1940.
**'Empire Blue'** Rich violet-blue with orange eye. C 1941. AGM 1984.
**'Fascinating'** ('Fascination') Wide, full panicles of vivid lilac-pink. C 1940.
**'Fortune'** Long cylindrical racemes of soft lilac with orange eye. C 1936.
**'Fromow's Purple'** Deep purple-violet, in large handsome panicles. C 1949.
**'Harlequin'** Leaves conspicuously variegated creamy-white; flowers reddish purple. Lower-growing than most cultivars. 'Variegata' is a similar, but inferior clone. A sport of 'Royal Red'. C 1964.

**BUDDLEJA davidii**—*continued*

**'Ile de France'** Long, elegant racemes of rich violet. C 1930.

**var. magnifica** (WILS.) REHD. & WILS. Bluish-purple. Petal lobes reflexed. I 1900 by Ernest Wilson. AM 1905. FCC 1905.

**var. nanhoensis** (CHITT.) REHD. An elegant, slender-branched variety with narrow leaves and long, narrowly cylindrical panicles of mauve flowers. Introduced by Reginald Farrer from Kansu in 1914.

    **'Alba'** A lovely form with white flowers.

**'Nanho Blue'** Flowers pale blue.

**'Nanho Purple'** Violet-purple with an orange centre. Spreading habit. C 1980.

**'Peace'** Large panicles of white flowers with an orange eye. C 1945. AM 1952.

**'Pink Delight'** See *B.* 'Pink Delight'.

**'Pink Pearl'** Lilac-pink with soft yellow eye, in dense panicles.

**'Royal Red'** Massive panicles of red-purple. C 1941. AM 1950. AGM 1984.

**'Salicifolia'** A low-growing form with linear leaves and slender, narrow racemes.

**'Variegata'** See under 'Harlequin'.

**var. veitchiana** (VEITCH) REHD. Lavender, in large panicles. C 1893. FCC 1902.

**'White Bouquet'** Fragrant white, yellow-eyed flowers in large panicles. C 1942.

**'White Cloud'** Pure white flowers in dense panicles.

**'White Profusion'** Large panicles of pure white, yellow-eyed flowers. C 1945.

**fallowiana** BALF. f. & W.W. SM. Medium-sized to large shrub. Stems and leaves white woolly; flowers very fragrant, pale lavender-blue, in large panicles. Requires a sheltered position. N Burma, SW China. C 1921.

**var. alba** SABOURIN Flowers creamy white, with orange eye. AM 1978. AGM 1984.

†**farreri** BALF. f. & W.W. SM. A noble, tall foliage shrub for a sheltered site in full sun. Leaves hastate, very large, densely woolly-white beneath, velvety above. Flowers fragrant, rose-lilac, appearing in April. China. I 1915.

†**forrestii** DIELS A large shrub, young leaves pubescent beneath. Flowers fragrant, usually pale lilac, produced in cylindrical racemes in late summer to early autumn. Requires a sheltered position. E Himalaya, SW China. I 1903.

**globosa** HOPE The Chilean "Orange Ball Tree". A striking, erect, medium-sized shrub with handsome foliage. In June, laden with orange-yellow, ball-like inflorescences. Andes of Chile, Peru and Argentina. I 1774. AGM 1984.

**'Lemon Ball'** A form with lemon-yellow flowers.

**japonica** HEMSL. (*B. curviflora* HORT. not ANDRE) A medium-sized shrub of arching habit. Shoots four-winged producing drooping, dense terminal panicles of lavender woolly flowers during summer. S Japan. I about 1896.

† × **lewisiana** EVERETT (*B. asiatica* × *B. madagascariensis*). (*B.* × *madagasiatica* PIKE) Hybrids of garden origin between two floriferous species.

**'Margaret Pike'** A large, strong-growing shrub with wand-like, white woolly stems. Flowers of soft yellow carried in long, dense terminal racemes during winter. AM 1953. FCC 1954.

**lindleyana** FORTUNE Medium-sized shrub with long, slender, curved racemes of purple-violet flowers, which are individually strikingly beautiful. China, Japan. I 1843 by Robert Fortune.

**'Lochinch'** (*B. davidii* × *B. fallowiana*). A medium-sized shrub of bushy compact habit with grey pubescent young stems and leaves. Later the leaves become green and glabrous above, remaining white tomentose beneath. Flowers scented, violet-blue with deep orange eye, in dense conical panicles. AGM 1984.

× **madagasiatica** See *B.* × *lewisiana*.

†\***madagascariensis** LAM. Yellow flowers in long panicles during winter. A beautiful tall evergreen for the conservatory. Mountains of Madagascar, widely naturalised in warm regions. I 1827.

**myriantha** DIELS A medium-sized shrub with lanceolate leaves which are white or yellow tomentose beneath. Flowers purple, downy, in slender panicles in late summer. W China, Burma. C 1933.

**nivea** DUTHIE A vigorous, medium-sized shrub with large leaves, the whole plant woolly white with a thick white felted down. Flowers small, lilac-purple in August. China. I 1901.

**BUDDLEJA**—*continued*

†**officinalis** MAXIM. Flowers throughout winter if given cool greenhouse treatment. Leaves clothed beneath with grey wool, semi-evergreen. Delicate mauve, fragrant flowers in panicles. W and C China. I 1908 by Ernest Wilson. AM 1911.

×**pikei** FLETCHER (*B. alternifolia* × *B. caryopteridifolia*). This cross was made in June 1950 by Mr A.V. Pike, then Head Gardener at Hever Castle, Kent.

**'Hever'** A medium-sized hardy shrub with opposite, sometimes alternate leaves. Lilac-mauve, strongly scented flowers with a bright orange throat are borne in terminal panicles 15-30cm. AM 1953.

**'Pink Delight'** (*B. davidii* 'Pink Delight') A recent hybrid involving *B. davidii* 'Fascinating', *B. davidii* var. *nanhoensis* 'Alba' and *B.* 'West Hill'. Long panicles of bright pink flowers. AM 1988.

†**pterocaulis** A.B. JACKS. A rare species from Yunnan and Burma having long pointed leaves and stout spiky lilac inflorescences.

†**salviifolia** (L.) LAM. "South African Sage Wood". A medium-sized shrub, hardy in the south-west of England. Leaves sage-like; flowers fragrant, white or pale lilac with orange eye. South Africa. C 1783.

**sterniana** COTTON A large shrub with very large hastate leaves, densely woolly white beneath, velvety above, making this an attractive foliage plant; flowers produced in spring, pale lavender with a deep orange eye. China. I 1922.

**tibetica** W.W. SM. A medium-sized, attractive shrub with heart-shaped, bullate leaves covered with soft white velvety down which also clothes the shoots. The leaf-stalks are winged. Flowers soft lilac during March and April. Tibet. I 1931.

**'West Hill'** (*B. davidii* × *B. fallowiana*). A medium-sized shrub of spreading habit. The long arching stems are thinly covered with a loose tomentum. The leaves are grey pubescent above, later almost glabrous and green, and white tomentose beneath. Flowers fragrant, pale lavender with an orange eye, produced in large terminal, curved panicles in late summer. This attractive shrub was for many years distributed as *B. fallowiana*.

×**weyeriana** WEYER ex REHD. (*B. davidii* var. *magnifica* × *B. globosa*). An unusual hybrid with ball-shaped heads of orange-yellow, often mauve-tinged, flowers borne in long slender panicles on the young wood in summer. Garden origin.

**'Golden Glow'** Orange-yellow flushed lilac, vigorous. AM 1923. AM 1981.

**'Moonlight'** Creamy yellow flushed lilac-pink. AM 1923.

**'Sungold'** A sport of 'Golden Glow' with deep orange flowers. C 1966.

**BUPLEURUM** L.—**Umbelliferae**—A genus of about 75 species, mostly herbs and sub-shrubs, found in Europe, Asia, N Africa and North America, of which the following is the only woody species normally cultivated in the open in Britain.

*****fruticosum** L. One of the best evergreen shrubs of medium size for exposed places near the sea and for all types of soil. Foliage sea-green; flowers yellow, July to September. S Europe. Long cultivated. AM 1979.

†*****BURSARIA** CAV.—**Pittosporaceae**—A small genus of 3 or 4 species related to *Pittosporum* and found in Australia and Tasmania.

**spinosa** CAV. An Australian and Tasmanian shrub growing to about 2.5m. It has dainty foliage and panicles of small, fragrant white flowers in summer. AM 1928.

**"BUTCHER'S BROOM"** See *Ruscus aculeatus*.

**"BUTTER NUT"** See *Juglans cinerea*.

**"BUTTON BUSH"** See *Cephalanthus occidentalis*.

*****BUXUS** L.—**Buxaceae**—The "Boxes" comprise about 30 species of evergreen shrubs and small trees with opposite, leathery leaves. The small, petalless flowers are produced in clusters in the leaf axils in spring, male and female flowers occurring on the same plant. Widely distributed in the Old World, the W Indies and C America. The following thrive on most soils, in sun or shade. Many are useful for hedging purposes.

**BUXUS**—*continued*

**balearica** LAM. "Balearic Islands Box". A large shrub or small erect-growing tree with large, firm, bright green leathery leaves 4cm long by 2cm broad. Balearic Isles and SW Spain. I before 1780.

**harlandii** HORT. not HANCE A hardy, dwarf shrub of distinct habit, forming a dense, compact dome of bright green, oblanceolate leaves. Probably a form of *B. microphylla* var. *sinica*. The true *B. harlandii* HANCE from C and S China is more tender and has only recently been introduced to cultivation.

**microphylla** SIEB. & ZUCC. A dwarf or small shrub of dense rounded habit. Leaves narrowly oblong, thin in texture, up to 1.5cm long. Of Japanese origin but unknown in the wild. I 1860.

    **'Compacta'** A dwarf clone with tiny leaves, slowly forming a dense compact bun. Suitable for rock garden or trough. C 1928.

    **'Green Pillow'** A slow-growing clone of American origin forming a dense, compact hummock. Leaves larger than those of 'Compacta' and of a brighter green.

    **var. japonica** (MUELL.-ARG.) REHD. & WILS. (*B. japonica* MUELL.-ARG.) A distinct small to medium-sized shrub of open, spreading habit. Leaves broadly obovate of thick leathery texture. Twigs four-angled. Japan. I 1800.

    **var. koreana** NAKAI A dwarf variety differing in its loose, spreading habit and dark green, often bronze-tinted leaves. Korea. I 1919.

    **'Richard'** A dwarf cultivar from the United States. The leaves are obovate, thick and firm with a deep apical notch, and of a bright green.

    **var. sinica** REHD. & WILS. Taller and more spreading, also looser in habit, with slightly larger leaves and pubescent branches. China. I 1900.

**sempervirens** L. "Common Box". A large shrub or small tree producing luxuriant masses of small dark green leaves. Distributed through S Europe, N Africa and W Asia. Naturalised and possibly wild in S England. The "Common Box" has given rise to innumerable forms and variations, many of which are suitable for hedging and topiary. AGM 1984.

    **'Agram'** A selection from the United States of columnar form. Leaves elliptic, emarginate, medium to large, deep shining green.

    **'Arborescens'** A large shrub or occasionally a small tree with medium to large, dark green leaves. Excellent for screening.

    **'Argentea'** A wide-spreading shrub. Leaves dark green shaded grey and margined creamy-white. Tends to revert.

    **'Aurea Maculata'** See 'Aureovariegata'.

    **'Aurea Maculata Pendula'** See 'Aurea Pendula'.

    **'Aurea Marginata'** See 'Marginata'.

    **'Aurea Pendula'** ('Aurea Maculata Pendula') An attractive cultivar forming a large bush or a small tree with weeping branchlets and leaves mottled and blotched creamy-yellow.

    **'Aureovariegata'** ('Aurea Maculata') A medium to large shrub of dense bushy habit. Leaves green, variously striped, splashed and mottled creamy yellow.

    **'Elata'** See 'Longifolia'.

    **'Elegantissima'** A small to medium-sized, slow-growing shrub of dense, compact, dome-shaped habit. Leaves small often mis-shapen, green with irregular creamy white margin. Makes an attractive specimen shrub. The best silver box. AGM 1984.

    **'Gold Tip'** This is one of the most common forms of box in commercial horticulture. The upper leaves of the terminal shoots are often tipped with yellow.

    **'Handsworthensis'** ('Handsworthii') A large shrub, initially of erect habit but spreading in maturity. Leaves thick, leathery, dark green, of rounded or oblong shape. Excellent as a tall hedge or screen. C 1872.

    **'Hardwickensis'** A large strong-growing shrub of stiff habit. The stout shoots are well clothed with leathery leaves more rounded and bullate than those of the related 'Handsworthensis'.

    **'Horizontalis'** See 'Prostrata'.

    **'Japonica Aurea'** See 'Latifolia Maculata'.

    **'Latifolia'** A large shrub of dense but spreading habit. Leaves comparatively large, of a deep shining green.

**BUXUS sempervirens**—*continued*

**'Latifolia Bullata'** Similar in habit to 'Latifolia Macrophylla' but with leaves blistered and puckered.

**'Latifolia Macrophylla'** A medium to large shrub of loose, spreading habit. Leaves large, broadly ovate to rounded, dark shining green.

**'Latifolia Maculata'** ('Japonica Aurea') A small to medium-sized shrub of dense compact habit when young, forming a large mound. The large leaves are irregularly blotched dull yellow. When grown in the open the bright yellow young growths are attractive in spring. Makes an excellent hedge of dense habit.

**'Longifolia'** ('Elata') A large shrub or small tree producing dense sprays of large, narrowly-oblong leaves. An attractive cultivar of elegant habit particularly when grown on a single stem. 'Salicifolia' has been confused with this but is more vigorous with narrower leaves and weeping branches.

**'Marginata'** ('Aurea Marginata') A large-growing cultivar of erect habit. The medium-sized leaves, often puckered and mis-shapen, are green, irregularly splashed and margined yellow. Tends to revert when allowed to grow too freely. A branch sport of 'Hardwickensis'.

**'Myosotifolia'** An erect, slow-growing, small to medium-sized shrub of compact twiggy habit, with small dark green leaves.

**'Myrtifolia'** Usually seen as a small or medium-sized shrub, but in time reaching a large size. Leaves small, narrow, occurring in characteristic dense, flattened sprays, sometimes becoming bronzed in winter.

**'Pendula'** A large shrub of loose, open growth. The branchlets are pendulous and bear masses of dark green leaves. Makes an unusual small tree when trained to a single stem.

**'Prostrata'** ('Horizontalis') A strong-growing, medium-sized shrub with horizontally spreading branches. C 1908.

**'Rosmarinifolia'** ('Thymifolia') A dwarf shrub of neat habit. The small leaves are linear to linear-lanceolate in shape, of a distinct dark sage green and rough to the touch.

**'Rotundifolia'** A small, slow-growing form with rounded leaves.

**'Salicifolia'** See under 'Longifolia'.

**'Suffruticosa'** "Edging Box". A dwarf or small shrub commonly used as an edging to paths and flower beds, particularly those of a formal nature. Leaves, of medium size, ovate, bright shining green. Long cultivated. AGM 1984.

**'Thymifolia'** See 'Rosmarinifolia'.

**'Vardar Valley'** A dwarf geographical form from the Balkans making a low, compact mound. A specimen in the Hillier Gardens and Arboretum is 1.5m tall and 5m across after 25 years (1990).

**wallichiana** BAILL. "Himalayan Box". A rare species in cultivation, usually of open, lax habit and of medium size. Leaves narrowly oblong-lanceolate, to 5cm or more long. Very hardy but subject to injury in our most severe winters. NW Himalaya. I 1850.

**"CABBAGE TREE"** See *Cordyline australis*.

**CAESALPINIA** L.—**Leguminosae**—A genus of about 100 species of trees, shrubs and climbers with showy flowers and bipinnate leaves found throughout tropical and subtropical regions. Spectacular shrubs for sunny, sheltered sites.

†**gilliesii** (HOOK.) BENTH. (*Poinciana gilliesii* HOOK.) A large S American shrub popularly known as "Bird of Paradise". Dainty leaflets, bipinnately arranged. Flowers borne as many as 30-40 together, in long, erect racemes and consisting of rich yellow petals and a cluster of scarlet stamens 5-8cm long; opening in July and August. Requires a hot, sunny wall. Argentina. I 1829. AM 1927.

**japonica** SIEB. & ZUCC. Handsome, large Japanese shrub armed with prominent spines. Flowers 20-30 in a raceme, bright yellow, with scarlet stamens, opening in June. Leaves acacia-like, of a refreshing shade of soft green. I 1881. FCC 1888.

†**tinctoria** DOMB. A strong-growing, scandent shrub with attractively divided leaves and elegant racemes of yellow flowers in summer. Columbia.

†**CALCEOLARIA** L.—**Scrophulariaceae**—A large genus with some 3-400 species of shrubs and herbs distributed from Mexico to S America and including many popular greenhouse plants. The shrubby members are sun-loving evergreen plants having pouch-shaped flowers in terminal panicles. All require a well drained position at the foot of a sunny wall.

*integrifolia* MURR. Handsome small shrub bearing corymbs of large yellow flowers in late summer. Chiloe. I 1822.

**var. angustifolia** LINDL. A variety with narrow leaves. AM 1960.

**violacea** See *Jovellana violacea*.

† ***CALDCLUVIA** D. DON—**Cunoniaceae**—A genus of 11 species, native from tropical SE Asia to Australia and New Zealand with one species in Chile. The following is only suitable for the mildest areas.

**paniculata** (CAV.) D. DON A large, erect-branched evergreen shrub or small tree with somewhat angled and flattened shoots. Leaves opposite, oblong-elliptic, to 13cm long and 4cm wide, glossy green above with serrate margins and conspicuously elevated veins, resembling somewhat those of the sweet chestnut. Small white flowers are borne in axillary corymbs in midsummer. Chile. I 1832 and again by Harold Comber in 1925.

**"CALICO BUSH"** See *Kalmia latifolia*.

**CALLICARPA** L.—**Verbenaceae**—About 140 species of shrubs and small trees found mainly in tropical and subtropical regions. The following are particularly notable for their soft rose-madder autumn colour and conspicuous violet or lilac-purple, small, rounded fruits which are freely produced where several plants are grown together. Flowers in cymes, small, pink.

**bodinieri** LEVL. Medium-sized shrub with long leaves and deep lilac fruits. Foliage deep rose-purple in autumn. C and W China. I about 1845.

**var. giraldii** (REHD.) REHD. (*C. giraldiana* SCHNEID.) A medium-sized to large shrub with long, scurfy pubescent stems and elliptic to lanceolate long-pointed leaves. Flowers lilac, produced during late summer, and followed by masses of small dark lilac or pale violet fruits. E to W China. C 1900. FCC 1924.

**'Profusion'** A free-fruiting selection of var. *giraldii* with bronze-purple young foliage and dense clusters of violet fruits. AGM 1984.

**dichotoma** (LOUR.) K. KOCH (*C. purpurea* JUSS.) (*C. koreana* HORT.) A compact shrub to about 1.5m. Leaves ovate to obovate, coarsely serrated; flowers pink in July, followed by deep lilac fruits. China, Korea, N Taiwan. I 1857. AM 1962.

**giraldiana** See *C. bodinieri* var. *giraldii*.

**japonica** THUNB. An attractive, small shrub of compact growth, with oval leaves, pale pink flowers and violet fruits. Japan. I 1845.

**var. angustata** REHD. (*C. longifolia* HEMSL.) A form with narrow leaves attaining as much as 23cm in length. China, Taiwan. I 1907.

**'Leucocarpa'** An attractive and unusual form with white fruits.

**var. luxurians** REHD. A form with larger leaves and flower clusters. Japan.

**koreana** See *C. dichotoma*

†***CALLISTEMON** R. BR.—**Myrtaceae**—With about 25 species of shrubs and small trees found only in Australia and Tasmania, the "Bottlebrushes" are magnificent sun-loving evergreens, but are only suited to the mildest districts. Flowers are produced during summer in cylindrical spikes, the axis of which grows on to produce more foliage. The long stamens are the colourful part of the flower. Not successful on shallow chalky soils.

**citrinus** (CURT.) SKEELS (*C. lanceolatus* (SM.) DC.) A vigorous spreading shrub of medium size with narrow, rigid leaves, lemon-scented when crushed. Flowers red, in dense spikes during summer. E Australia. I 1788.

**'Splendens'** Flowers brilliant scarlet. A graceful shrub, 1.5-2m in height, flowering throughout summer, and thriving in the open in the milder southern countries. AM 1926.

**CALLISTEMON**—*continued*

**linearis** DC. Small narrow leaves and long cylindrical spikes of scarlet flowers. Hardy in sheltered positions along the South Coast. New South Wales. I 1788. See also *C. subulatus.*

**pallidus** DC. A medium-sized shrub related to *C. salignus.* Leaves narrowly elliptic. Flowers cream-coloured. Tasmania, Victoria. AM 1984.

**rigidus** R. BR. A medium-sized shrub with narrow, rigid leaves up to 13cm long. Flowers dark red, densely crowded in spikes 8-10cm long. E Australia.

**salignus** DC. One of the hardiest of the "Bottlebrush" family, in favourable localities attaining a height and width of about 2.5m. Leaves narrow, willow-like; flowers pale yellow. SE Australia. I 1788. AM 1948.

**sieberi** DC. (*C. pithyoides* MIQ.) "Alpine Bottlebrush". This is the hardiest species having survived many hard winters outside in the Hillier Gardens and Arboretum. A medium-sized shrub with small, narrow leaves densely arranged and pale yellow flowers in short spikes. SE Australia.

**speciosus** DC. A medium-sized shrub with narrow sharp-pointed leaves and deep scarlet flowers. I 1823.

**subulatus** CHEEL A small shrub with sharp-pointed, bright green leaves silky hairy when young. Flowers crimson in late summer. The hardiest red-flowered species which has been confused with *C. linearis.* SE Australia.

‡\***CALLUNA** SALISB.—**Ericaceae**—A genus of a single species, differing from *Erica* in its four-parted corolla and the large four-parted calyx.

**vulgaris** (L.) HULL (*Erica vulgaris* L.) "Heather" "Ling". One of our most familiar native shrublets, covering large tracts of mountain and moorland in northern and western parts of the British Isles, and equally well known on the heaths and commons of the south.

A great number of forms are cultivated in gardens, varying in colour of flower and foliage, time of flowering and habit. All are easily grown plants for lime-free soils even tolerating moist positions. Though tolerant of shade, they are freer-flowering and happier in full sun. One of the most beautiful shrubs, especially the double-flowered forms, for cutting for indoor decoration, the dried flowers retaining their colour indefinitely. Native of Europe and Asia Minor.

Pruning, consisting of the removal of the old inflorescences, may be carried out after flowering. In the case of cultivars with coloured foliage and those with attractive dried inflorescences, pruning is best left until late March.

Flowering times are indicated as follows:—

> Early—July to August
> Mid—August to September
> Late—October to November

**Alba group** (f. *alba* (WEST.) BRAUN-BLANQUET) "White Heather". A white-flowered form. Mid. 50cm. Popularly connected with Scotland but liable to appear wherever the species grows.

**'Alba Aurea'** Bright green foliage with yellow tips; flowers white. Mid. 10cm.

**'Alba Elata'** Dense habit. Flowers white. Mid to late. 60cm.

**'Alba Plena'** ('Alba Flore Pleno') A popular free-flowering cultivar. Flowers white, double. Mid. 50cm. A sport of 'Alba Elegans'. AM 1938. AMT 1960. AGM 1984.

**'Alba Pumila'** Dwarf form of compact habit. Flowers white. Mid. 10cm.

**'Alba Rigida'** An attractive plant with distinctive horizontal branching habit. Flowers white. Mid. 15cm. AMT 1964.

**'Allegro'** Deep red. Mid to late. 50cm.

**'Alportii'** Tall erect growth. Flowers crimson. Mid. 60cm.

**'Alportii Praecox'** Similar to 'Alportii' but a little dwarfer and flowering two to three weeks earlier. Early. 50cm.

**'Anthony Davis'** Profuse white flowers. Silvery-grey foliage. Mid. 45cm.

**'Argentea'** Young shoots of a bright pale green in spring. Flowers mauve. Mid. 30cm.

**'August Beauty'** Free-flowering, white. Mid. 50cm. AMT 1960.

**'Aurea'** An attractive form. Foliage gold-tinted, turning bronze-red in winter. Flowers purple. Mid. 30cm. AMT 1961.

**CALLUNA vulgaris**—*continued*

**'Barnett Anley'** Compact and erect, dark green foliage. Flowers petunia-purple in densely packed racemes. Mid. 50cm. AMT 1960. FCCT 1962.

**'Beoley Crimson'** Deep crimson, upright habit. Mid to late. 60cm.

**'Beoley Gold'** A strong-growing form with bright yellow foliage and short sprays of white flowers. Mid. 50cm. AMT 1968. AGM 1984.

**'Blazeaway'** A startling foliage plant. The green foliage changes to rich red in winter. Flowers lilac-mauve. Mid. 50cm.

**'Boskoop'** Foliage rich gold turning orange-red in winter. Flowers lilac-pink. Mid.

**'Camla'** See 'County Wicklow'.

**'Coccinea'** Grey-green foliage. Flowers dark crimson contrasting with the pale grey young shoots. Mid. 25cm.

**'County Wicklow'** ('Camla') Dwarf and spreading. Flowers shell-pink, double. Mid. 25cm. AMT 1960. FCCT 1961. AGM 1984.

**'Cramond'** Vigorous with dark green foliage and rich pink flowers in long spikes. Mid. 50cm. Raised at Cramond near Edinburgh before 1963. AMT 1970.

**'Cuprea'** An old cultivar with young shoots golden in summer, ruddy-bronze in autumn and winter. Flowers pale mauve. Mid. 30cm. FCC 1873.

**'C.W. Nix'** A choice plant with dark green foliage and long tapered racemes of dark, glowing, crimson flowers. Mid. 60cm. AMT 1961.

**'Darkness'** A dense bush with bright green foliage and deep purplish-pink flowers in short, dense racemes. Mid. 30cm.

**'Drum-ra'** A pretty cultivar with white flowers. Mid. 50cm. AMT 1961.

**'Elsie Purnell'** Flowers of a lively silvery-pink, double, deeper coloured in bud. Mid to late. 60-80cm. AMT 1963. AGM 1984.

**'Fairy'** Clear yellow foliage orange to bronze-red in winter. Flowers pale purplish-pink, profuse. Mid. 30cm. C 1966.

**'Firefly'** Foliage reddish-brown turning deep orange-red in winter. Flowers deep lilac. Mid. 45cm.

**'Flore Pleno'** An old cultivar with flowers lilac-pink, double. Mid. 50cm. AM 1929.

**'Foxii Nana'** Dwarf, forming a dense cushion of green. Flowers, when produced, light purple. Mid. 10cm.

**'Fred J. Chapple'** Compact and vigorous, flowers mallow-purple. 25cm. AMT 1961.

**'Glencoe'** Dark green foliage and double silvery-pink flowers. Mid to late. 45cm.

**'Gold Haze'** Foliage of a bright golden hue. Flowers white. Mid. 50-60cm. AMT 1961. FCCT 1963. AGM 1984.

**'Golden Carpet'** A low-growing plant with orange-yellow foliage and short racemes of purplish-pink flowers. AMT 1971.

**'Golden Feather'** A most attractive clone with golden feathery foliage changing to a gentle orange in winter. 50cm. AMT 1965. FCCT 1967. AGM 1984.

**'Goldsworth Crimson'** A strong-growing plant. Flowers deep crimson. Mid to late. 50-80cm.

**'Hammondii'** A strong-growing cultivar with dark green foliage. Flowers white. Mid. 80cm. Useful as a low hedge.

**'Hammondii Aureifolia'** Tips of young shoots coloured golden yellow in spring. Flowers white. Mid. 50-60cm.

**'Hammondii Rubrifolia'** Similar in habit to 'Hammondii Aureifolia' but tips of young shoots red-tinged in spring. Flowers purple. Mid. 50-60cm.

**'H.E. Beale'** A splendid cultivar producing very long racemes of double, bright rose-pink flowers, excellent for cutting. Mid to late. 60cm. FCC 1943. AGM 1984.

**'Hibernica'** A dwarf clone, extremely free-flowering, the mauve flowers often outnumbering and smothering the leaves. Late. 15cm.

**'Hiemalis'** Erect-growing, flowers of a soft mauve. Mid to late. 50cm.

**var. hirsuta** (WAITZ) S.F. GRAY This variety includes plants with grey hairy leaves and stems. Found occasionally in the wild.

**'Hirsuta Compacta'** See 'Sister Anne'.

**'Hookstone'** Erect-growing; flowers salmon-pink in long racemes. Mid. 50-60cm.

**CALLUNA vulgaris**—*continued*

**'Humpty Dumpty'** An amusing form of compact but uneven habit. Flowers white, not freely produced. Mid. 15cm.

**'Ineke'** Golden foliage, rose-violet flowers. Mid. 30cm.

**'J.H. Hamilton'** A pretty dwarf with large, pink, double flowers. Early. 25cm. Perhaps the finest double heather. AM 1935. AMT 1960. FCCT 1961. AGM 1984.

**'Joan Sparkes'** Flowers mauve, double, occasionally producing single flowers. A sport of 'Alba Plena'. Mid. 25cm. AM 1957.

**'Joy Vanstone'** Golden foliage, deepening to rich orange in winter. Flowers orchid-pink. Mid. 50cm. AMT 1971.

**'Kinlochruel'** Flowers double, white, foliage bright green. A sport of 'County Wicklow'. Mid. 25cm. AM 1980. FCC 1982. AGM 1984.

**'Kirby White'** Dark green foliage tipped gold when young. White flowers. Mid. 30cm.

**'Loch Turret'** Flowers white, foliage emerald-green. Early. 30cm.

**'Mair's Variety'** Tall, flowers white, especially suitable for cutting. Mid. 80cm. AMT 1961. FCCT 1963.

**'Minima'** A dwarf compact form. Flowers when produced are purple. Mid. 80cm.

**'Mousehole'** Dwarf, compact habit. Dark green foliage and pale purple flowers. Found in Cornwall. 10cm.

**'Mrs Ronald Gray'** A charming prostrate mat. Flowers reddish-purple. Mid. 5-8cm.

**'Mullion'** Semi-prostrate, with numerous branches and densely packed racemes of deep pink flowers. Mid. 15-25cm. AMT 1963.

**'Multicolor'** Foliage bright green tipped red in winter, gold and coral in summer. Flowers phlox-purple. 10cm. AMT 1961 (for flower). AMT 1962 (for winter foliage).

**'Nana Compacta'** Low, compact habit, purplish-pink flowers profusely born. Mid. 20cm.

**'Orange Queen'** The young foliage in spring is gold and as the season advances turns to deep orange. Flowers pink. Mid. 60cm.

**'Peter Sparkes'** Flowers deep pink, double, in long racemes. Useful for cutting. Mid to late. 50cm. AM 1958. FCCT 1962. AGM 1984.

**'Pygmaea'** Very dwarf, spreading branchlets, and dark green foliage. Flowers purple, rarely produced. Mid. 8cm. AMT 1962.

**'Radnor'** Very compact with bright green foliage. Flowers double, pale lilac-pink with white inner petals. 25cm.

**'Robert Chapman'** The spring foliage is gold and changes first to orange then finally red. Flowers soft purple. Mid. 30-60cm. AMT 1962. AGM 1984.

**'Rosalind'** Golden foliage and pink flowers. Mid. 30-60cm. AMT 1961.

**'Ruth Sparkes'** Foliage bright yellow-green but inclined to revert. Flowers white, double. Sport of 'Alba Plena'. Mid. 25cm.

**'Serlei'** Erect-growing with dark green foliage. Flowers white, in long racemes. Late. 60cm. AMT 1961. FCCT 1962. AGM 1984.

**'Serlei Aurea'** Similar to 'Serlei' but possesses foliage of a bright golden hue. 60cm. AMT 1961.

**'Serlei Rubra'** ('Serlei Grandiflora') Similar to 'Serlei' but flowers dark reddish-purple. 60cm.

**'Silver Knight'** Upright habit with grey foliage. Flowers mauve-pink. Mid. 30cm.

**'Silver Queen'** A very beautiful plant. Foliage silvery-grey, flowers pale mauve. Mid. 60cm. AGM 1984.

**'Sir John Charrington'** Vigorous, spreading habit. Leaves yellow tinged red in summer, reddish in winter, flowers lilac-pink. Early. 40cm. AMT 1970.

**'Sister Anne'** ('Hirsuta Compacta') Compact mounds of pretty grey foliage; flowers pink. Mid. 8-10cm. AGM 1984.

**'Spitfire'** Golden foliage turning bronze-red in winter. Flowers pink. Mid. 25-30cm.

**'Spring Cream'** Very vigorous with dark green foliage tipped with cream in spring. Long spikes of white flowers. Mid. 50cm.

**'Spring Glow'** Young foliage attractively tipped with pink and red. Flowers lilac. Mid. 50cm.

**'Spring Torch'** Young foliage orange-red. Flowers purplish-pink. Upright habit. Mid. 25cm.

**CALLUNA vulgaris**—*continued*

**'Sunrise'** Golden yellow foliage turns orange-red in winter. Flowers purple. Mid. 30cm. C 1970.

**'Sunset'** Foliage variegated yellow, gold and orange. Flowers pink. Mid. 25-30cm. AMT 1967. FCCT 1968. AGM 1984.

**'Tenuis'** Loose-growing; flowers red-purple in long racemes. Early to mid. 25cm.

**'Tib'** A lovely, floriferous cultivar. Flowers rosy-red, double. Early. 30-60cm. AMT 1960. FCCT 1962. AGM 1984.

**'Tricolorifolia'** Young growths in spring turning from bronze to red, finally deep green. Flowers pink. Mid. 60cm.

**'Underwoodii'** The pale mauve buds remain closed and gradually change to an effective silvery-white colour which lasts well into winter. Mid to late. 30cm. AMT 1960.

**'White Gown'** Long racemes of white flowers. Mid to late. 60-80cm.

**'Wickwar Flame'** Bright orange and yellow summer foliage turns copper and gold in winter. Flowers mauve-pink. 30cm. Raised by George Osmond.

**'Winter Chocolate'** Foliage greenish-yellow and orange, becoming dark chocolate tipped red in winter. Flowers lilac-pink.

**CALOPHACA** FISCHER ex DC.—**Leguminosae**—A small genus of low shrubs and herbs for sunny, well drained positions. About 5 species found from SW to E Asia.

**grandiflora** REGEL Dwarf, often procumbent shrub with pinnate leaves and axillary racemes of bright yellow pea flowers in June or July. Turkestan. I 1880.

**wolgarica** (L.f.) FISCH. A very hardy prostrate shrub bearing yellow, pea flowers in June and July. Leaves pinnate. Needs full sun and good drainage. SE Russia. I 1786.

**CALYCANTHUS** L.—**Calycanthaceae**—The "Allspices" are a small genus of 4 species of deciduous, medium-sized shrubs with opposite leaves and aromatic bark, confined in the wild to North America. They are of easy cultivation, with conspicuous red-brown flowers composed of numerous sepals and petals borne during summer and early autumn.

**fertilis** See *C. floridus* var. *laevigatus*.

**'Purpureus'** See *C. floridus* 'Purpureus'.

**floridus** L. "Carolina Allspice". A dense bushy medium-sized shrub with dark glossy green, aromatic leaves downy beneath. Brownish-red flowers with numerous petals are borne over a long period during summer. SE United States. I 1726.

**var. laevigatus** (WILLD.) TORR. & A. GRAY (*C. fertilis* WALT.) (*C. glaucus* WILLD.) Leaves smooth or only slightly downy beneath. I 1806.

**'Purpureus'** (*C. fertilis* 'Purpureus') Leaves tinged purple beneath. A form of var. *laevigatus*.

**occidentalis** HOOK. & ARN. (*C. macrophyllus* HORT.) A Californian species with larger flowers and leaves than *C. floridus*, differing also in the exposed leaf buds. I 1831 by David Douglas.

**praecox** See *Chimonanthus praecox*.

‡*CAMELLIA** L.—**Theaceae**—More than 200 species of mainly tender evergreen shrubs and trees found in E and SE Asia, concentrated in S China. Camellias are magnificent flowering evergreens, of which the majority in cultivation are as hardy as laurel. They are a little more lime-tolerant than *Rhododendrons*, and thrive in a good acid or neutral peaty soil. A woodland site with light overhead shade is ideal but they can be grown successfully and often flower more freely when planted open to full sun as, for example, when against a south or west-facing wall. In such positions careful attention to watering and mulching is vital, or bud-dropping may result. Damage to open flowers will result from the effects of early morning spring sunshine following frost, so in some areas of the British Isles a north or west-facing site is good unless light overhead shade of trees is available. They are ideal plants for growing in tubs and for a cool greenhouse or conservatory.

**CAMELLIA**—*continued*

**Flowers:**

| | |
|---|---|
| Single | One row of not over eight regular, irregular or loose petals and conspicuous stamens. |
| Semi-double | Two or more rows of regular, irregular or loose petals and conspicuous stamens. |
| Anemone form | One or more rows of large outer petals lying flat or wavy; the centre a convex mass of intermingled petaloids and stamens. |
| Paeony form | A deep rounded flower consisting of a convex mass of petals, petaloids and sometimes stamens. |
| Double | Imbricated petals showing stamens in a concave centre when open. |
| Formal double | Fully imbricated, many rows of petals with no stamens. |

**Flower sizes:**

| | |
|---|---|
| Very large | Over 12.5cm (5in) across |
| Large | 10-12.5 cm (4-5in) across |
| Medium | 5-7.5cm (2-3in) across |
| Small | 5-7.5cm (2-3in) across |

Flower size, form and colour are subject to some variation in certain cultivars; type of soil, aspect and general cultivation all playing a part.

**'Barbara Clark'** (*C. saluenensis* × *C. reticulata* 'Captain Rawes'). Rose-pink, medium, semi-double with notched petals. Vigorous, compact, upright habit. C 1958.

**'Barbara Hillier'** A beautiful large shrub with large, handsome polished leaves and large, single, satin-pink flowers. A first class shrub, a hybrid between *C. japonica* and *C. reticulata* which originated at Embley Park.

**'Candle Glow'** (*C. cuspidata* × *C. japonica*). White with light pink centre, medium, single, compact habit. C 1980.

†**chrysantha** (HU) TUYAMA One of a number of Chinese species with yellow flowers, this remarkable plant is unfortunately very tender. It makes a large shrub with deep yellow flowers composed of 8-10 petals and purple young foliage similar to *C. granthamiana*. Native to Guangxi (S China) and Vietnam. Attempts are currently being made in North America, Australia, Japan and China to cross it with hardier species.

**'Cornish Snow'** (*C. cuspidata* × *C. saluenensis*). A delightful, free-growing medium-sized to large hybrid, bearing multitudes of small, white flowers along the branchlets. Garden origin about 1930. AM 1948.

**'Cornish Snow Michael'** See *C.* 'Michael'.

**'Cornish Snow Winton'** See *C.* 'Winton'.

**'Cornish Spring'** (*C. cuspidata* × *C. japonica* 'Rosea Simplex'). Pink, small, single, vigorous upright habit. C 1972.

**cuspidata** (KOCHS) HORT. ex BEAN A large shrub with small leaves, copper-tinted when young, and small creamy white flowers. Widely distributed in China. I 1900 by Ernest Wilson. AM 1912.

**'Dr Clifford Parks'** (*C. reticulata* 'Crimson Robe' × *C. japonica* 'Kramer's Supreme'). Red with orange cast, very large, semi-double to paeony or anemone form. Vigorous, upright habit. C 1971.

**'Felice Harris'** (*C. sasanqua* 'Narumi-gata' × *C.* 'Buddha'). Very pale pink with deeper veins, medium, semi-double. Dark, slightly glaucous green leaves. Vigorous, upright, compact habit. C 1960. AMT 1979.

**'Francie L.'** (*C. reticulata* 'Buddha' × *C. saluenensis* 'Apple Blossom'). Rose-pink, very large, semi-double with wavy petals. A vigorous shrub good on a wall. AM 1972.

†**granthamiana** SEALY A remarkable species from Hong Kong and Guangdong, SE China, discovered in 1955. A large shrub, having large parchment-white flowers. The leaves are distinct with their conspicuously impressed venation, bronze when unfolding. AM 1974.

**heterophylla** HU The original plant to which this name was given was found in a temple garden in Yunnan. Previously regarded as a hybrid between *C. japonica* and *C. reticulata* it is now considered to be a garden form of the latter. For hybrids previously listed here see individual entries.

**'Inspiration'** (*C. reticulata* × *C. saluenensis*). A medium-sized shrub with large, semi-double flowers of a deep pink. AM 1954. FCCT 1979. AGM 1984.

**CAMELLIA**—*continued*

**japonica** L. "Common Camellia". A large evergreen shrub with characteristically polished leaves. The wild species, a native of Japan and China, was originally introduced in 1739 and was later followed by various cultivars from China and Japan. As the rose has become the plaything of the commercial hybridist so the camellia has become the toy of both the commercial and the amateur gardener. Far too many scarcely separable sports (mutations) have been made separate entities. In fact a single bush may embrace three cultivars. At the present time named cultivars of this species are numbered in thousands and are constantly being added to. The majority are of medium size, the more vigorous clones reaching a large size after many years. In most areas flowers are normally produced from February to early or mid-May, but their size and colour may vary depending on age of plant, growing conditions and season.

**'Abundance'** White; medium, paeony form. Growth slow and upright.

**'Admiral Nimitz'** ('Kishu-tsukasa') Deep rose-pink; large, formal double. Growth vigorous, compact and erect.

**'Adolphe Audusson'** Blood-red, conspicuous stamens; large, semi-double. Growth vigorous, compact. A first class, well proved plant. AM 1934. FCC 1956. AGM 1984.

**'Alba Plena'** ('Alba Grandiflora') White; large, formal double. Growth erect, bushy. Probably the best double white for general planting. AM 1948.

**'Alba Simplex'** White with conspicuous stamens; large, single. The most proven single white. AGM 1984.

**'Althaeiflora'** Dark red; large, paeony form. Large specimens are to be found in old gardens. AM 1950.

**'Anemoniflora'** Dark crimson; medium, anemone form. Growth vigorous and erect.

**'Apollo'** Rose-red, occasionally blotched white; medium, semi-double. Growth vigorous and open. One of the most satisfactory camellias for British gardens. It is often confused with 'Jupiter' from which it differs in its more numerous, deeper coloured petals, also in its longer, pointed leaves which possess a characteristic twisted tip. AM 1956.

**'Apple Blossom'** ('Joy Sander') Pale blush-pink, deepening at margin; medium, semi-double. AM 1933.

**'Are-jishi'** See 'Beni-arajishi'.

**'Augusto Pinto'** ('Augusto Leal de Gouveia Pinto') Light lavender-pink to carmine, each petal bordered white; large, semi-double to double. AM 1958.

**'Australis'** Rose-red, medium, paeony form. Vigorous, compact, upright habit. C 1951.

**'Ballet Dancer'** Cream shading to coral-pink at the margins, medium, full paeony form. Compact, upright habit. C 1960. AM 1976.

**'Beni-arajishi'** Rose-red; medium, paeony form. Growth vigorous and open. Distinct in its thick, coarsely-toothed, tapering leaves. Previously listed as 'Are-jishi'.

**'Benten'** Rose-red, small, single. Leaves with a broad, creamy white margin. Rather tender and weak-growing. C 1930.

**'Berenice Boddy'** Light pink, deeper beneath; medium, semi-double. Growth vigorous and erect.

**'Betty Sheffield'** White, striped and blotched red and pink, medium to large, semi-double to loose paeony form. Leaves tend to burn in exposed situations. This and its forms often produce sports and reversions. C 1949.

**'Betty Sheffield Blush'** Light pink with several darker markings; large, semi-double to loose paeony form. A sport of 'Betty Sheffield'.

**'Betty Sheffield Pink'** Deep pink. A sport of 'Betty Sheffield'.

**'Betty Sheffield Supreme'** White, each petal bordered deep pink to red; large, semi-double to loose paeony form. A sport of 'Betty Sheffield'.

**'Blood of China'** Deep salmon-red; large, semi-double to loose paeony form. Growth vigorous and compact.

**'Bob Hope'** Very dark red, large, semi-double. Compact habit. C 1972.

**'Bob's Tinsie'** Brilliant red, small, anemone form. Compact, upright habit. C 1962.

**'Brushfield's Yellow'** Creamy white with pale primrose centre, medium, anemone form. Compact, upright habit. C 1968.

**'C.M. Hovey'** Carmine; medium, formal double. Growth vigorous and compact. FCC 1879.

**CAMELLIA japonica**—*continued*

**'C.M. Wilson'** Light pink; very large, anemone form. Growth slow, spreading. A sport of 'Elegans'. AM 1956.

**'Carter's Sunburst'** Pale pink striped or marked deeper pink, large or very large, semi-double to paeony form or formal double. Compact habit. C 1958. AM 1977.

**'Cecile Brunazzi'** Light pink, medium, semi-double to loose paeony form with large outer petals and twisted, upright centre petals. Open, upright habit. C 1951.

**'Chandleri Elegans'** See 'Elegans'.

**'Clarise Carleton'** Red, large to very large, semi-double. Vigorous, upright habit. C 1955.

**'Compte de Gomer'** Pale pink, striped and speckled rose-pink; medium, double. Growth medium, compact.

**'Contessa Lavinia Maggi'** See 'Lavinia Maggi'.

**'Coquetti'** Delft-rose; medium, double. Growth slow, compact and erect. AM 1956.

**'Daikagura'** Bright rose-pink blotched white; large, paeony form. Growth slow, compact.

**'Daitairin'** ('Hatsusakura') Light rose-pink; large, single, with mass of petaloids in centre. Growth vigorous, erect. AM 1953.

**'Debutante'** Light pink; medium, paeony form. Growth vigorous, erect.

**'Devonia'** ('Devoniensis') White; medium, single rather cup-shaped. Growth vigorous, erect. AM 1900.

**'Dobreei'** Geranium-lake with darker veins; medium, semi-double. Growth vigorous, erect.

**'Donckelaeri'** Red, often marbled white; large, semi-double. Growth slow and bushy. A first class plant for the open garden. I by Siebold before 1834. AM 1960.

**'Drama Girl'** Deep salmon-rose pink; very large, semi-double. Vigorous, open slightly pendulous growth. AM 1966 (for the cool greenhouse). FCC 1969. AM 1975 (as a hardy flowering shrub).

**'Dr Tinsley'** Pale pink shading to deep pink at margins; medium, semi-double. Compact, upright growth.

**'Elegans'** ('Chandleri Elegans') Deep peach-pink; very large, anemone form. Growth spreading. A well proved cultivar for general cultivation. C 1822. AM 1953. FCC 1958. AGM 1984.

**'Elegans Champagne'** Similar to 'Elegans' but white, the creamy central petaloids sometimes flushed pink. A sport of 'Elegans Splendor'. Good for exhibition but with poor foliage and constitution. C 1975.

**'Extravaganza'** White, vividly marked and striped light red. Large to very large, anemone form. Compact upright habit.

**'Fimbriata Superba'** See 'Fred Sander'.

**'Flora'** White; large, single with waxy petals.

**'Frau Minna Seidel'** See 'Pink Perfection'.

**'Fred Sander'** ('Fimbriata Superba') Crimson with curled, fimbriated petals; medium, semi-double. Growth vigorous, compact and erect. A sport of 'Tricolor'. C 1913. AM 1921.

**'Furoan'** Soft pink; medium, single. AM 1956. AGM 1984.

**'Gauntlettii'** ('Lotus') ('Sode-gashuki') White; very large, semi-double, of water-lily form. This vigorous cultivar with spreading branches is of weak constitution.

**'Geisha Girl'** Light pink with darker stripes and blotches; large, semi-double. Open, upright growth.

**'General Lamorciere'** See 'Marguerite Gouillon'.

**'Gloire de Nantes'** Rose-pink; large, semi-double. Growth medium, compact and erect. A splendid, well proved, early flowering cultivar. AM 1956. AGM 1984.

**'Grand Prix'** Brilliant red, very large, semi-double with irregular petals. Vigorous upright habit. C 1968.

**'Grand Slam'** Brilliant dark red, large to very large, semi-double to anemone form. Vigorous, open, upright habit. C 1962. AM 1975.

**'Guest of Honor'** Salmon-pink; very large, semi-double to loose paeony form. Growth vigorous, compact and erect. Shy flowering in the open and best under glass. AM 1967.

**'Guilio Nuccio'** Coral rose-pink; very large, semi-double. Growth vigorous, erect. AM 1962.

**CAMELLIA japonica**—*continued*

'**Hakurakuten**' White; large, semi-double to loose paeony form with curved and fluted petals. Growth vigorous and erect. AM 1977. AGM 1984.

'**Hanafuki**' Soft pink, sometimes splashed white; large, semi-double cup-shaped flowers. Growth medium and compact. AM 1956.

'**Hatsusakura**' See 'Daitairin'.

'**Hawaii**' Pale pink, medium to large, paeony form with fringed petals. A sport of 'C.M. Wilson'. C 1961.

'**High Hat**' Light pink; large, paeony form. Growth slow, compact. A sport of 'Daikagura'.

'**Imbricata Rubra**' Light red; medium, formal double. Distinct leaves, inclined to curl.

'**James Allan**' Fiery-red; large, variable in form, single, semi-double, paeony or anemone form. Growth medium and open.

'**Jingle Bells**' Red, small, anemone form. Vigorous, upright habit. A sport of 'Tinker Bell'. C 1959.

'**Joseph Pfingstl**' Dark red, medium to large, semi-double to loose paeony form. Vigorous. C 1948.

'**Joshua E. Youtz**' White; large, paeony form. Growth slow, compact.

'**Joy Sander**' See 'Apple Blossom'.

'**Jupiter**' Bright scarlet, sometimes blotched white; medium, single to semi-double with conspicuous bunch of stamens. Growth vigorous, erect. One of the best camellias for general planting. AM 1953. AGM 1984.

'**Kelvingtoniana**' Red with conspicuous white variegations; large, semi-double to loose paeony form. A wide-spreading, sparsely branched, well proved cultivar. FCC 1869.

'**Kimberley**' Carmine, with red stamens; medium, single, cup-shaped flowers. Growth vigorous, compact and erect. AM 1934.

'**Konronkuro**' ('Kouron-jura') Very dark self-red; medium, formal double. One of the darkest of all camellias. Growth medium, semi-erect. AM 1960.

'**Kramer's Supreme**' Red, large to very large, paeony form, slight fragrance. Compact, upright habit. C 1957.

'**Lady Clare**' Deep, clear peach-pink; large, semi-double. Growth vigorous and spreading. Still one of the best of all camellias. AM 1927. AGM 1984.

'**Lady de Saumerez**' Bright red spotted white; medium, semi-double. Growth vigorous, compact. A well proved cultivar for English gardens. A sport of 'Tricolor'.

'**Lady McCulloch**' White blotched crimson; medium, semi-double.

'**Lady Vansittart**' White, striped rose-pink; medium, semi-double, with wavy-edged petals. Growth slow, bushy, leaves undulate. Sometimes produces sports, see 'Yours Truly'. I from Japan in 1887.

'**Lalla Rookh**' ('Laurel Leaf') Pink, marbled white; large, formal double. Growth slow and compact; foliage laurel-like.

'**Lanarth**' Cardinal-red; medium, nearly single. Growth vigorous and erect. AM 1960.

'**Latifolia**' Soft rose-red; medium, semi-double. Growth vigorous and bushy. A broad-leaved, hardy cultivar succeeding well in the open.

'**Laurel Leaf**' See 'Lalla Rookh'.

'**Lavinia Maggi**' ('Contessa Lavinia Maggi') White or pale pink with broad rose-cerise stripes; large, formal double. FCC 1862. AGM 1984.

'**Lotus**' See 'Gauntlettii'.

'**Madame de Bisschop**' ('Madame Victor de Bisschop') White, medium, semi-double. Growth open and vigorous.

'**Magnoliiflora**' Blush-pink, with forward-pointing petals rather like the expanding buds of *Magnolia stellata*: medium, semi-double. Growth medium, compact. AM 1953.

'**Margaret Davis**' White streaked rose-red edged vermilion, medium, paeony form. A sport of 'Aspasia MacArthur'. C 1961. AM 1984.

'**Margherita Coleoni**' Dark red; medium, double to formal double. Growth vigorous, erect.

'**Marguerite Gouillon**' ('General Lamorciere') Delicate pink, slightly striped and flecked deeper pink; medium, full paeony form. Growth vigorous, bushy.

'**Mars**' Turkey-red; large semi-double with conspicuous bunch of stamens. Growth open and loose. Often confused in cultivation with both 'Apollo' and 'Mercury'.

**CAMELLIA japonica**—*continued*

'**Mary Charlotte**' Light pink; medium, anemone form. Growth compact and upright.

'**Mathotiana**' ('Mathotiana Rubra') Crimson; large, double to formal double. Growth compact and upright.

'**Mathotiana Alba**' White, rarely with a pink spot; large, formal double. Not recommended for an exposed position. AGM 1984.

'**Mathotiana Rosea**' Clear pink; large, formal double. Vigorous, compact and erect. A sport of 'Mathotiana Alba'. AM 1954. AGM 1984.

'**Mathotiana Rubra**' See 'Mathotiana'.

'**Mattie Cole**' Rose-carmine, large, single. C 1955.

'**Mercury**' Deep soft crimson with slightly darker veins; large, semi-double. Growth medium, compact. AM 1948.

'**Momiji-gari**' Scarlet, large, single with flared white stamens. One of the Japanese Higo Camellias.

'**Morning Glow**' White; large, formal double. Growth vigorous, compact and erect.

'**Mrs D.W. Davis**' Blush-pink, very large, semi-double. Growth vigorous, compact. Requires shelter but makes an excellent conservatory shrub. AM 1960. FCC 1968.

'**Nagasaki**' ('Lady Buller') Rose-pink, marbled white; large, semi-double. Leaves often mottled yellow. Growth spreading. A well proved cultivar for English gardens. AM 1953.

'**Nobilissima**' White with yellow shading; medium, paeony form. Growth fairly erect. One of the earliest to flower.

'**Nuccio's Gem**' White, medium to large, formal double. Compact, upright habit. C 1970.

'**Nuccio's Jewel**' White flushed orchid-pink, medium paeony form. Bushy habit. C 1977.

'**Nuccio's Pearl**' White flushed orchid-pink, medium, formal double. Compact, upright habit. C 1977.

'**Peach Blossom**' Light pink; medium, semi-double. Growth medium and compact. A shade deeper than 'Magnoliiflora'.

'**Pink Champagne**' Soft pink; large, semi-double to paeony form with irregular petals. Vigorous open growth. AM 1960.

'**Pink Perfection**' ('Frau Minna Seidel') Shell-pink, small, formal double. Growth vigorous and erect.

'**Premier**' Clear rose-red, large, full paeony form. Vigorous upright habit. Best under glass. C 1965.

'**Preston Rose**' ('Duchesse de Rohan') Salmon-pink; medium, paeony form. Growth vigorous.

'**Pride of Descanso**' ('Yuki-botan') White; large, semi-double to loose paeony form with irregular petals. Growth vigorous.

'**Purity**' ('Shiragiku') White; medium, double to formal double. Growth vigorous and upright.

'**Quercifolia**' ('Kingyo-tsubaki') Crimson, large, single, fishtail foliage.

'**R.L. Wheeler**' Rose-pink, large to very large, semi-double to anemone form. Growth vigorous. AM 1959. FCC 1975. AGM 1984.

'**Rogetsu**' White with cream-coloured stamens; medium, single, with rounded petals frilled at the margins.

'**Rubescens Major**' Crimson, with darker veining; large, double. Habit compact and bushy. AM 1959. AGM 1984.

subsp. **rusticana** (HONDA) KITAMURA (*C. rusticana* HONDA) "Snow Camellia". A tough, hardy variety from the mountains of N Japan (Hondo), differing from the typical form in its wide-spreading petals which open out flat, and its shorter stamens which are almost free to the base, not united into a tube as in subsp. *japonica*. Flowers red, comparatively small. I 1954.

'**Shiragiku**' See 'Purity'.

'**Shirodaikagura**' ('Daikagura White') White; medium, loose paeony form. Growth medium, compact and erect.

'**Sieboldii**' See 'Tricolor'.

'**Silver Anniversary**' White, large, semi-double, irregular petals and golden stamens. Vigorous, upright habit. C 1960.

**CAMELLIA japonica**—*continued*

'**Sode-gashuki**' See 'Gauntlettii'.

'**Souvenir de Bahuaud Litou**' Light pink; large, formal double. Growth vigorous and erect. A sport of 'Mathotiana Alba'.

'**Splendens**' Red; large, semi-double.

'**Sylva**' Carmine-red, flecked white; medium single, of cupped form. A sport of 'Kimberley'. AGM 1984.

'**Tammia**' White with pink centre and edge, miniature to small, formal double with incurved petals. Compact, upright habit. C 1971.

'**Tiffany**' Light orchid-pink deeper at margin, large to very large, loose paeony to anemone form. Upright habit. Best under glass. C 1962.

'**Tinker Bell**' White striped red and rose-pink, small, anemone form. Vigorous, upright habit. C 1958.

'**Tinsie**' Red outer petals with white paeony centre, miniature, anemone form. Vigorous upright habit. C 1930.

'**Tomorrow**' Rose; very large. semi-double to paeony form. Vigorous, open, slightly pendulous growth. Best under glass. C 1953. AM 1960.

'**Tomorrow's Dawn**' Deep soft pink to light pink shading to white at margin, with occasional red streaks and white petaloids; very large, semi-double with irregular petals and large petaloids to full paeony form. Vigorous, open growth. A sport of 'Tomorrow'. Best under glass. C 1960.

'**Tricolor**' ('Sieboldii') White, streaked carmine; medium, semi-double. Growth compact. A well proved cultivar for English gardens.

'**Ville de Nantes**' Dark red, usually blotched white; large, semi-double with erect fimbriated petals. Growth slow and bushy. A sport of 'Donckelaeri'.

'**Waiwhetu Beauty**' Light pink; medium, semi-double. Growth vigorous.

'**Yoibijin**' Pale pink; small, single. Growth medium, open.

'**Yours Truly**' Pink, streaked deep pink and bordered white; medium, semi-double. Growth slow, bushy; leaves undulate. A sport of 'Lady Vansittart'. AM 1960.

'**Yuki-botan**' See 'Pride of Descanso'.

'**Julia Hamiter**' Blush-pink to white, medium, semi-double to double. Compact habit. A seedling of *C. × williamsii* 'Donation'. C 1964.

'**Leonard Messel**' (*C. reticulata × C. × williamsii* 'Mary Christian'). A very beautiful, large shrub which originated at Nymans in Sussex, where it proves to be hardy. Flowers large, rich clear pink; semi-double. The dark green leaves incline, like the flower, towards *C. reticulata*. AM 1958. FCC and Cory Cup 1970. AGM 1984.

'**Mary Phoebe Taylor**' Light rose-pink, very large, paeony form. A seedling of *C. saluenensis* raised in New Zealand. C 1975.

'**Michael**' (*C. cuspidata × C. saluenensis*). A beautiful, medium-sized to large shrub similar to 'Cornish Snow' but with larger single, white flowers. The best form of this attractive hybrid.

**oleifera** ABEL A medium-sized to large shrub with elliptic, toothed leaves to 6cm long and small, fragrant, white flowers in spring. This species has grown undamaged in the Hillier Gardens and Arboretum for many years. It has been used by the U.S. National Arboretum, Washington to develop hardy hybrids for the E United States. EC and S China, SE Asia. I 1818.

**reticulata** LINDL. One of the most beautiful of all flowering shrubs. The semi-double form 'Captain Rawes' introduced by Robert Fortune in 1820 was, for a hundred years, regarded in western gardens as the type plant to which Lindley gave the name *C. reticulata*, until that great plant collector George Forrest sent home the single wild form from W China in 1924. This form is generally grown as Wild Type or Wild Form. It makes a large compact shrub of much better constitution than the more popular named cultivars. It is hardy in all but the coldest and most exposed gardens and has been uninjured here since it was planted in 1954. There has been extremely little variation between the hundreds of plants raised from the seed. The handsome, rigid, leathery, net-veined leaves are an excellent foil for the large, single, rose-pink flowers, which are inclined to be trumpet-shaped before finally expanding, and are usually freely produced during late winter and early spring. Yunnan, China. AM 1944. The tender forms of this

**CAMELLIA reticulata**—*continued*

species introduced in 1948 ('Butterfly Wings', 'Crimson Robe', 'Lion Head', 'Noble Pearl', 'Professor Tsai', 'Purple Gown' and 'Shot Silk') suffer badly from virus infection and are now little grown.

The following clones with single or semi-double flowers are large shrubs or small trees and are only suitable for the conservatory, except in mild areas.

**'Arch of Triumph'** Deep pink to wine-red, very large, loose paeony form. Vigorous upright habit. A seedling of *C. reticulata* (Wild Type). C 1970.

†**'Captain Rawes'** ('Semi-plena') Carmine rose-pink; very large, semi-double. The original form, introduced in 1820 by Robert Fortune from Guangzhou (Canton), is a magnificent shrub. FCC 1963.

**'Flore Pleno'** See 'Robert Fortune'.

**'Mary Williams'** Crimson to rose; large, single. A vigorous and hardy shrub raised as a seedling of the Wild Type at Caerhays Castle by that great gardener J.C. Williams. AM 1942. FCC 1964.

**'Miss Tulare'** Bright red to rose-red, large to very large, double to full paeony form. Vigorous upright habit. A seedling of 'Crimson Robe'. C 1975.

**'Pagoda'** See 'Robert Fortune'.

†**'Robert Fortune'** ('Pagoda') ('Flore Pleno') Deep crimson; large, double. Growth compact. I by Robert Fortune about 1850. FCC 1865.

**'Semi-plena'** See 'Captain Rawes'.

**'Trewithen Pink'** Deep rose; large, semi-double. A vigorous, hardy clone selected by G.H. Johnstone who made Trewithen one of the great Cornish gardens, and wrote a standard work on magnolias. AM 1950.

**'William Hertrich'** Deep cherry-red, very large, semi-double with slightly reflexed outer petals and upright, loosely arranged inner petals. A seedling of *C. reticulata* 'Cornelian'. C 1962. AM 1981.

**'Royalty'** (*C. japonica* 'Clarise Carlton' × *C. reticulata* 'Cornelian'). Bright pink, deeper in centre, very large, semi-double with crinkled petals. C 1968. AM 1986.

**rusticana** See *C. japonica* subsp. *rusticana*.

†**saluenensis** STAPF ex BEAN A beautiful medium to large shrub somewhat similar to *C. reticulata* but with smaller leaves and medium-sized flowers, the latter being a lovely soft pink, single, carried in great profusion. Yunnan, W China. I 1924.

**'Salutation'** (*C. reticulata* × *C. saluenensis*). A deliberate cross raised at Borde Hill, Sussex, by Col Stephenson Clarke, possibly the greatest "all round" amateur gardener of this century, who left to posterity one of the most complete arboretums. A splendid hybrid of medium to large size with matt green leaves and semi-double, soft silvery-pink flowers, 13cm across, during late winter and early spring. AM 1936.

**sasanqua** THUNB. An attractive winter and early spring-flowering species producing small but fragrant, usually white flowers. This delightful species with its numerous progeny is worthy of wall protection. As the plants age and mature they withstand our winters with only a little occasional damage, but they are not generally so reliable as forms of *C. japonica* and require the Californian sun to do them justice. Of the following only 'Crimson King' and 'Narumi-gata' are free-flowering outside in this country though others can perform well following very hot summers. Japan. I 1896.

**'Blanchette'** White; single.

**'Briar Rose'** Soft, clear pink; single.

**'Crimson King'** Bright red; single. Proving one of the most reliable and prolific flowering.

**'Duff Allan'** White flushed pink, large, single.

**'Hiryu'** Crimson; single to semi-double.

**'Mine-no-yuki'** White, large, paeony form. AM 1964.

**'Momozono-nishiki'** Rose, shaded white; semi-double with curled petals.

**'Narumi-gata'** Large creamy-white, shaded pink towards the margin; fragrant. One of the most reliable flowering forms of this species. AM 1953 (as *C. oleifera*).

**'Rosea Plena'** Pink; double.

**'Rubra'** Rich red; single.

**'Tricolor'** White, striped pink and red; single.

**'Usubeni'** Soft pink, occasionally marbled white; semi-double.

**CAMELLIA sasanqua**—*continued*

    **'Variegata'** Blush-white. Leaves grey-green, margined white.

    **'Versicolor'** White centre, edged lavender with pink in between; single.

    **'Satan's Robe'** (*C.* 'Satan's Satin' × *C. reticulata* 'Crimson Robe'). Oriental red, large, semi-double. Vigorous upright habit. C 1965. AM 1984.

    **sinensis** (L.) KTZE. (*C. thea* LINK) (*Thea sinensis* L.) The "Tea Plant" of commerce, geographically a variable species in size and shape of leaf. The form we have been growing here for the past forty years has proved a slow-growing, compact, rather small shrub with small, nodding white flowers in November and December. China, widely cultivated for tea production. I 1740.

    **'Spring Festival'** A large shrub of narrow, upright habit, a seedling of *C. cuspidata* raised in California. Flowers pink, fading to light pink, miniature, double. C 1975.

    **†taliensis** (W.W. SM.) MELCHIOR An interesting species related to *C. sinensis*. A large shrub or small tree; leaves bright green, laurel-like; flowers small, axillary, cream with conspicuous yellow stamens. Yunnan, W China. I 1914 by George Forrest.

    **thea** See *C. sinensis*.

    **'Tristrem Carlyon'** (*C. japonica* 'Rosea Simplex' × *C.* 'Salutation'). Rose-pink, medium, paeony form. Vigorous upright habit. C 1972. AM 1977.

    **†tsaii** HU A tender, very graceful large shrub resembling *C. cuspidata*. Flowers white, small but numerous; foliage copper-coloured when young. W China, Burma, N Vietnam. I 1924 by George Forrest. AM 1960. FCC 1985.

    × **vernalis** (MAK.) MAK. (*C. japonica* × *C. sasanqua*). Intermediate between its parents, this hybrid has pure white, slightly fragrant flowers with petals arranged in three rows. Flowering from February to May.

    × **williamsii** W.W. SM. (*C. japonica* × *C. saluenensis*). One of the most valuable hybrid shrubs ever produced and perhaps the best camellia for general planting in the British Isles. The cultivars originating from this cross are invaluable shrubs, exquisitely beautiful, and exceedingly free-flowering over a long period from November to May. In foliage they tend towards the *C. japonica* parent and in flowers towards *C. saluenensis*. First raised by J.C. Williams at Caerhays Castle, Cornwall about 1925.

    **'Anticipation'** Deep rose, large, paeony form. Upright habit. The *C. japonica* parent was 'Leviathan'. C 1962. FCCT 1975. AGM 1984.

    **'Bartley Pink'** Bright cherry-pink; small, single. C 1955. AMT 1985.

    **'Bow Bells'** Bright rose; semi-double carried continuously over a long period.

    **'Bowen Briant'** Deep pink, large, semi-double. Vigorous upright habit. C 1960. AMT 1981.

    **'Brigadoon'** Rose-pink, medium, semi-double. Compact, upright habit. The *C. japonica* parent was 'Princess Baciocchi'. C 1960. AMT 1974. FCCT 1975.

    **'Caerhays'** Lilac-rose; medium, anemone form. Spreading, somewhat pendulous habit gained from its parent *C. japonica* 'Lady Clare'. C 1948. AM 1969.

    **'C.F. Coates'** Deep rose; medium, single; leaves peculiarly three-lobed at the apex, derived from the *C. japonica* parent 'Quercifolia', hence sometimes known as the "Fishtail Camellia". C 1935.

    **'Charles Michael'** Pale pink; large, semi-double with long petals. C 1951.

    **'China Clay'** White, medium, semi-double. Open habit. The *C. japonica* parent was 'Marjorie Magnificent'. C 1972. AM 1976.

    **'Citation'** Silver blush-pink; large, semi-double with irregular petals. Growth vigorous, open and erect. C 1950. AM 1960.

    **'Coppelia'** Carmine-rose; single. C 1950. AMT 1987.

    **'Crinkles'** Rose-pink; large, semi-double with crinkled petals. Growth bushy and erect. C 1955.

    **'Daintiness'** Salmon-pink, large, semi-double. Open habit. The *C. japonica* parent was 'Magnoliiflora'. C 1975. AM 1986.

    **'Debbie'** Clear pink, large, paeony form. The *C. japonica* parent was 'Debutante'. C 1965. AM 1971. AGM 1984.

    **'Donation'** Orchid-pink; large, semi-double. Perhaps the most beautiful camellia raised this century. Growth vigorous, erect. Raised at Borde Hill before 1941. The *C. japonica* parent was 'Donckelaeri'. AM 1941. AM 1952. FCCT 1974. AGM 1984.

**CAMELLIA × williamsii**—*continued*

**'E.G. Waterhouse'** Light pink, medium, formal double. Growth upright. C 1954. AMT 1989.

**'Elegant Beauty'** Deep rose-pink, large, anemone form. Open straggly habit and best with some pruning. C 1962. AMT 1976.

**'Elizabeth Rothschild'** Soft rose-pink; medium, semi-double. C 1950.

**'Elsie Jury'** Clear pink shaded orchid-pink, large, full paeony form. Open, spreading habit. The *C. japonica* parent was 'Pukekura White'. C 1964. FCCT 1975.

**'E.T.R. Carlyon'** (*C. × williamsii* 'J.C. Williams' × *C. japonica* 'Adolphe Audusson'). White, medium, semi-double to rose form double. Vigorous upright habit. C 1972.

**'First Flush'** Apple blossom-pink; medium, semi-double. Free and early flowering.

**'Francis Hanger'** White; single. Growth erect, inclined towards *C. japonica*. Leaves strongly undulate. AM 1953.

**'Glenn's Orbit'** Deep orchid-pink, large, semi-double to loose paeony form. Vigorous upright habit. A seedling of 'Donation'. AM 1962. AMT 1976.

**'Golden Spangles'** Phlox-pink; small, single; leaves with yellow-green central blotch. Found at Wisley in 1957. AMT 1987.

**'Hiraethlyn'** Palest pink; perfect single form. The *C. japonica* parent is said to be 'Flora'. C 1950. AMT 1989.

**'J.C. Williams'** Phlox-pink; medium single. The first clone of *C. × williamsii* to be named, and one of the most beautiful of all camellias. Raised by J.C. Williams at Caerhays. FCC 1942. AMT 1977. AGM 1984.

**'Jermyns'** Clear, self peach-pink, with broad petals. A first class selection raised in our nurseries.

**'Jury's Yellow'** White with wavy petals and central mass of creamy yellow petaloids. Medium, anemone form. Compact, upright habit. C 1976.

**'Lady Gowrie'** Pink; large, semi-double. Growth vigorous and compact. C 1954.

**'Mary Christian'** Clear pink; small, single. AM 1942. FCCT 1977.

**'Mildred Veitch'** Orchid-pink, large, semi-double to anemone form with a loose centre. Compact, upright habit. The *C. japonica* parent was 'Elegans'. C 1962. AM 1967. AMT 1977.

**'November Pink'** Phlox-pink; medium, single. Usually the earliest of the group to flower. AM 1950.

**'Rose Parade'** Deep rose-pink, medium, formal double. Vigorous, compact, upright habit. A cross between 'Donation' and *C. japonica*. C 1969.

**'Rosemary Williams'** Rose-pink, medium, single. Compact, upright habit. C 1961.

**'St Ewe'** Rose-pink; medium, single of cup form. AM 1947. FCCT 1974. AGM 1984.

**'Tiptoe'** (*C. japonica* × *C. × williamsii* 'Farfalla'). Silvery-pink, cherry-pink at the edges, medium, semi-double. Compact, upright, bushy habit. C 1965. AMT 1985.

**'Tregrehan'** Apricot-pink, medium, semi-double to double. Vigorous, upright habit. The *C. japonica* parent was 'Marjorie Magnificent'. Raised by Gillian Carlyon. C 1972.

**'Water Lily'** Lavender flushed bright pink, medium, formal double. Vigorous upright habit. C 1967.

**'Winton'** (*C. cuspidata* × *C. saluenensis*). Similar to 'Cornish Snow' but flowers soft almond-pink.

†\***CAMPHOROSMA** L.—**Chenopodiaceae**—A small genus of about 10 species of aromatic, heath-like shrubs native from the E Mediterranean region to C Asia.

**monspeliaca** L. A small, aromatic shrub with inconspicuous flowers and sage-green leaves. Suitable for sunny, dry positions in coastal areas. N Africa, S Europe to C Asia.

†\***CANTUA** LAM.—**Polemoniaceae**—A small genus of about 6 species of shrubs and trees found in the northern Andes of S America. It is one of the few woody representatives of the family.

**buxifolia** JUSS. (*C. dependens* PERS.) "Magic Tree". A very beautiful small shrub with graceful drooping corymbs of bright cherry-red tubular flowers in April; semi-evergreen in mild localities. Requires a warm, sheltered wall. Andes of Bolivia, Peru and Chile. I 1849. AM 1905.

**"CAPE FIGWORT"** See *Phygelius capensis.*

**CARAGANA** LAM.—**Leguminosae**—About 80 species of usually spiny shrubs or small trees distributed between E Europe and Japan and mainly occurring in C Asia. Leaves even pinnate, the terminal leaflet reduced to a spine but sometimes appear odd pinnate owing to the reduction of one of the leaflets at the base of the spine. The spines are formed from either the leaf rachis, the persistent stipules or both. The pea-like flowers are normally yellow and are borne in early summer. They are good in dry soils.

**arborescens** LAM. A small shrubby tree from Siberia and Manchuria. One of the toughest and most accommodating of all plants, succeeding in the most exposed areas on all types of soil. Flowers yellow. I 1752.

**'Lorbergii'** An extremely graceful, medium-sized shrub with narrow, almost grass-like, leaflets and much smaller flowers. C about 1906.

**'Nana'** A remarkable dwarf shrub; an outstanding "dot plant" for the rock garden.

**'Pendula'** A very attractive weeping form. C 1856.

**'Walker'** Foliage similar to 'Lorbergii' but growth prostrate. Usually top-grafted to produce a weeping standard with hanging branches. Raised in Canada by crossing 'Lorbergii' with 'Pendula'.

**boisii** SCHNEID. A yellow-flowered species from China and Tibet, attaining about 2m. Differs from *C. arborescens* in its downy seed pods. C 1904.

**brevispina** ROYLE A medium-sized spreading shrub of open habit with arching branches and pink-tinged, downy young shoots. Leaves pinnate with usually 8-10 leaflets, softly downy when young, the persistent rachis developing into a spine up to 6cm long. Flowers yellow flushed green, reddish with age, borne in pairs or threes on slender peduncles in June. NW Himalaya. I 1849.

**chamlagu.** See *C. sinica.*

**decorticans** HEMSL. A shrubby or tree-like species from Afghanistan, ultimately 5-5.5m. Leaves with 10-12 leaflets and tiny stipules. Flowers light yellow, about 2.5cm long. I 1879.

**franchetiana** KOMAR. A tall Chinese shrub of open spreading habit. The bright yellow flowers are 2.5cm long, the pinnate leaves have 12-18 leaflets and are bright apple-green. I 1913 by George Forrest.

**frutex** (L.) K. KOCH (*C. frutescens* DC.) A spineless, glabrous shrub up to 3m producing bright yellow flowers in May. Leaves with 4 leaflets. Widely distributed from E Europe to C Asia. I 1752.

**jubata** (PALL.) POIR. A curious small slow-growing shrub of irregular form, thickly covered with coarse brownish-grey hairs and slender spines. Leaves with 12-14 leaflets, the rachis, margin and midrib beneath covered in long, white hairs. Large white pea flowers produced singly in late spring. Siberia, Mongolia. I 1796.

**maximowicziana** KOMAR. A small semi-pendulous species, 1.2-2m high, with spiny branchlets, bearing solitary yellow flowers 2.5cm long. China, Tibet. I 1910 by Ernest Wilson.

**microphylla** LAM. A spreading shrub of medium height from Siberia and N China; flowers bright yellow, usually in pairs. I 1789.

**pygmaea** (L.) DC. A small shrub sometimes prostrate in habit with long slender somewhat pendulous branches. The 2.5cm long yellow flowers hang on drooping stalks beneath the branches in May or June. Leaves with 4 narrow leaflets and a small, terminal spine. China to Siberia. I 1751.

**sinica** (BUC'HOZ) REHD. (*C. chamlagu* LAM.) A rounded bushy, Chinese shrub of medium size, displaying buff-yellow, pea-shaped flowers in May and June. Leaves with 2 pairs of glossy green leaflets on a persistent, spine-tipped rachis. I 1773.

× **sophorifolia** TAUSCH (*C. arborescens* × *C. microphylla*). Intermediate between its parents and of equal garden value. Leaves with 8-10 leaflets.

**tragacanthoides** (PALL.) POIR. A low, spreading, very spiny shrub from Tibet, China and Siberia. The bright yellow flowers produced in June are followed by grey, silky seed-pods. Leaves with 4 obovate, dark blue-green leaflets. I 1816.

**turkestanica** KUM. An uncommon, spiny species of loose habit; yellow flowers.

**CARMICHAELIA** R. BR.—**Leguminosae**—Erect or prostrate broom-like shrubs. Many have distinctive flattened stems which carry out the work normally performed by the leaves. All require a sunny, well drained position. About 40 species mainly in New Zealand, one on Lord Howe Island.

†**australis** R. BR. A small to medium-sized shrub with flattened young stems and tiny pale purple pea flowers during June and July. C 1823. AM 1927.

**enysii** T. KIRK Occasionally forms a hummock up to 20cm with a dense mat of branchlets; flowers small, lilac-pink. I 1892.

†**flagelliformis** COLENSO An erect shrub 1m or more high, with compressed branchlets. Flowers small, blue-purple with darker veining.

**petriei** T. KIRK Distinguished by its stout branchlets and erect growth; fragrant, thickly clustered racemes of violet-purple flowers.

†**williamsii** T. KIRK Distinguished from other cultivated species by its branchlets, being 6-12mm wide, and by its larger flowers which are creamy-yellow; attains about 1.5m. Only for the mildest localities. I 1925.

\***CARPENTERIA** TORR.—**Philadelphaceae**—A monotypic genus for a warm sunny position.

**californica** TORR. "Tree Anemone". A beautiful medium-sized Californian evergreen, producing in July its large white flowers with golden anthers. Needs a sunny site, preferably backed by a wall. I about 1880. FCC 1888.

'**Bodnant**' A large flowered form similar to 'Ladham's Variety' but hardier. Selected at Bodnant in the 1960s by Charles Puddle.

'**Ladham's Variety**' A vigorous free-flowering clone with larger flowers often measuring 8cm across. AM 1924.

**CARPINUS** L.—**Carpinaceae**—The "Hornbeams" are picturesque and easily grown trees, suitable for clay or chalky soils, and very attractive when laden with their hop-like fruit clusters. More than 30 species mainly in China but widely distributed in N temperate regions south to C America.

**betulus** L. "Common Hornbeam". Recommended both for single specimens and for hedging, resembling beech in the latter respect. A medium-sized to large tree with a characteristic grey, fluted trunk and ovate, serrate, ribbed leaves. Europe (incl British Isles), Asia Minor. AGM 1984.

'**Columnaris**' A small columnar tree of dense, compact growth, conical when young. Slower growing and smaller than 'Fastigiata'. C 1891.

'**Fastigiata**' ('Pyramidalis') A medium-sized tree of erect, pyramidal habit. Quite narrow as a young tree but broadening as it matures. C 1883. AGM 1984.

'**Frans Fontaine**' A fastigiate form which retains its habit with age. Selected from a street in Eindhoven, Holland.

'**Incisa**' A form with small, narrow, deeply and usually singly toothed leaves, but inclined to revert. 'Quercifolia' is similar. C 1789.

'**Pendula**' A dwarf, mushroom-headed tree with steeply pendulous branches.

'**Purpurea**' The young leaves have a purple tinge, but soon become green. Only a collector's plant. C 1873.

'**Pyramidalis**' See 'Fastigiata'.

'**Quercifolia**' See under 'Incisa'.

'**Variegata**' A form in which some leaves are splashed creamy white. Often reverts with age. C 1770.

**caroliniana** WALT. (*C. americana* MICHX.) The "American Hornbeam" or "Blue Beech", forms a beautiful small tree with grey fluted bark, but not so tall as our native species. Branches spreading, arching at their tips. Leaves polished apple-green, tinted as autumn approaches. E North America with a variety in Mexico and C America. I 1812.

**cordata** BLUME A slow-growing, small tree with comparatively broad, deeply veined leaves, heart-shaped at the base. Fruits green, in large clusters. Japan, NE Asia, N and W China. I 1879.

**henryana** (WINKLER) WINKLER Medium-sized tree. Leaves ovate lanceolate, up to 9cm long. C and W China. I 1907 by Ernest Wilson.

**CARPINUS**—*continued*

**japonica** BLUME A very beautiful, wide-spreading, small Japanese tree or large shrub, with prominently corrugated leaves and conspicuous fruiting catkins. In general appearance recalls *Alnus firma*. Japan. I 1895.

**laxiflora** (SIEB. & ZUCC.) BLUME Medium-sized tree with rather drooping branches and ovate-oblong, slenderly-pointed leaves and conspicuous, loose clusters of green fruiting "keys". Japan, Korea. I 1914.

    **var. macrostachya** OLIVER Differs in its larger leaves and fruit clusters. Throughout the summer the young growths are bright red. W and C China. I 1900 by Augustine Henry.

**orientalis** MILL. Small, bushy tree or shrub with small, sharply-toothed leaves. SE Europe, SW Asia, Caucasus. I 1735.

**tschonoskii** MAXIM. Small ornamental tree, leaves varying in length from 4-8cm. Japan, Korea. I 1901.

**turczaninowii** HANCE An attractive small, shrubby tree recalling *Nothofagus dombeyi*, with slender stems and small leaves. The young emerging leaves are bright red. N China, Korea, Japan. I 1914 by Reginald Farrer.

    **var. ovalifolia** WINKL. The form most often cultivated with slightly larger serrated leaves. W China. I 1889 by Augustine Henry.

†**CARPODETUS** FORST. & FORST. f.—**Escalloniaceae**—A small genus of 10 species of evergreen trees found in New Zealand and New Guinea.

    \***serratus** FORST. & FORST. f. A graceful, tall New Zealand evergreen with small, dark green leaves. Flowers small, white, in cymose panicles in summer; needs a sheltered site.

**CARRIEREA** FRANCH.—**Flacourtiaceae**—A small genus of 3 species. Small trees from SE Asia.

**calycina** FRANCH. A very rare large shrub or small tree forming a broad head. Leaves glabrous, shining dark green. Flowers cup-shaped, creamy white in terminal candelabra-like racemes in June. Fruit an oblong or spindle-shaped woody capsule. W China. I 1908 by Ernest Wilson.

**CARYA** NUTT.—**Juglandaceae**—The "Hickories" are a genus of about 17 species of fast-growing, stately, large trees allied to the walnuts (*Juglans*) and mainly confined to E North America but also occurring in Mexico and SE Asia. They are distinguished from *Juglans* and *Pterocarya* by lacking the chambered pith found in those genera. The large compound leaves, often over 30cm long, turn a clear yellow before falling in the autumn and the picturesque grey trunks are attractive in winter. Difficult subjects to transplant, they are best planted when small.

**amara** See *C. cordiformis*.

**cordiformis** (WANGENH.) K. KOCH (*C. amara* (MICHX.) NUTT.) "Bitter Nut". Eventually a large tree with thin, brown scaly bark. Characteristic yellow winter buds. Leaves with usually 7, occasionally 5 or 9, lanceolate leaflets. Perhaps the best "Hickory" for general planting. E North America. I 1766. AM 1989.

**glabra** (MILL.) SWEET (*C. porcina* (MICHX. f.) NUTT.) "Pignut". A medium-sized to large tree with smooth, regularly folded bark. Leaves composed of 5-7 taper-pointed leaflets, the terminal one large, obovate, 13-18cm long. E North America. I 1799. AM 1967.

**illinoinensis** (WANGENH.) K. KOCH (*C. pecan* (MARSH.) ENGL. & GRAEBN.) (*C. oliviformis* (MICHX.) NUTT.) "Pecan". A large and valuable nut-bearing tree in North America, but not so successful in the British Isles. Distinct by reason of its numerous leaflets—usually 11-17 on each leaf. SE and SC United States. I about 1760.

**laciniosa** (MICHX. f.) LOUD. (*C. sulcata* NUTT.) "Big Shellbark" "Kingnut". A medium-sized tree in this country, with large handsome leaves, with usually 7, occasionally 9, ovate leaflets, the terminal one larger and obovate. Mature trees with shaggy bark. E United States. I 1804.

**oliviformis** See *C. illinoinensis*.

**ovata** (MILL.) K. KOCH (*C. alba* NUTT. not K. KOCH) "Shagbark Hickory". The most valuable nut-producing species in the United States. A handsome tree of medium to large size. Leaves composed of 5 long-pointed leaflets, the three upper ones large and obovate.

**CARYA ovata**—*continued*

Rich yellow autumn foliage. Can fruit here after hot summers. E North America. C 1629.

**pecan** See *C. illinoinensis*.

**tomentosa** (POIR.) NUTT. (*C. alba* K. KOCH not NUTT.) "Mockernut" "Big-bud Hickory". A medium-sized tree occasionally over 18m with downy young shoots. Leaves over 30cm long composed of 7, sometimes 5 or 9 ovate leaflets, the terminal leaflet larger and obovate. All are downy and glandular beneath and turn rich butter-yellow in autumn. A stately tree easily recognised by its fragrant, ornamental foliage and large winter buds. SE Canada, E United States. I 1766.

**CARYOPTERIS** BUNGE—**Verbenaceae**—Small, showy, late summer flowering shrubs with aromatic leaves, best grown in well drained soil and in full sun. Excellent for chalky soils. About 6 species in E Asia from the Himalaya to Japan.

×**clandonensis** SIMMONDS (*C. incana* × *C. mongolica*). A variable hybrid first raised by Mr Arthur Simmonds when he sowed seed from *C. mongolica* next to which grew *C. incana*.

**'Arthur Simmonds'** This attractive hybrid thrives almost anywhere, producing its bright blue flowers in August and September. An ideal subject for mass effect, and can be kept to a height of about 60cm. Deservedly one of the most popular small hybrid shrubs raised this century. A fitting plant to commemorate its raiser A. Simmonds, perhaps the greatest secretary ever to have served the Royal Horticultural Society in whose garden it was raised before 1933. AM 1933. FCC 1941. AGM 1984.

**'Ferndown'** A seeding selection with slightly darker flowers of a blue-violet shade. AM 1953. AGM 1984.

**'Heavenly Blue'** A clone of American origin. The habit is a little more compact than 'Arthur Simmonds' and the colour perhaps a shade deeper. AGM 1984.

**'Kew Blue'** A seedling of 'Arthur Simmonds' with slightly darker flowers. Raised at Kew in 1945. AGM 1984.

**incana** (HOUTT.) MIQ. (*C. tangutica* MAXIM.) (*C. mastacanthus* SCHAU.) A small shrub covered by a greyish felt-like pubescence. Flowers violet-blue. The dominant parent of *C. × clandonensis*. Japan, Korea, China, Taiwan. I 1844. AM 1899.

**mastacanthus** See *C. incana*.

**mongolica** BUNGE Distinct in its dwarf habit, narrow leaves, and comparatively large, rich blue flowers. A plant of weak constitution. Mongolia, China. C 1844. AM 1928.

**tangutica** See *C. incana*.

**CASSIA corymbosa** See *Senna corymbosa*, *S. × floribunda* and *S. septemtrionalis*.

**obtusa** See under *Senna × floribunda* and *S. septemtrionalis*.

*****CASSINIA** R. BR.—**Compositae**—About 28 species of evergreen, heath-like shrubs found in Australia, New Zealand and S Africa. Those listed are of dense habit and are grown mainly for foliage effect. They are all from New Zealand and pass all but the severest winters more or less unharmed. Best given full sun and good drainage.

**fulvida** HOOK. f. (*Diplopappus chrysophyllus* KOEHNE) "Golden Heather" "Golden Cotton-wood". A small, erect, dense shrub, the small, crowded leaves give a golden effect; flowers white in dense terminal heads in July. Young growths sticky to the touch.

**leptophylla** (FORST. f.) R. BR. Erect, greyish shrub up to 2m with tiny leaves, white or yellowish downy beneath. Flower heads white in terminal corymbs in August and September.

**vauvilliersii** HOOK. f. "Mountain Cottonwood". Similar to *C. fulvida* but taller and more upright with larger leaves, dark green and glabrous above and tawny-yellow or white beneath.

**var. albida** (KIRK) CKN. "Silver Heather". An attractive variety with white hoary stems and leaves.

‡*****CASSIOPE** D. DON—**Ericaceae**—About 10 species of dwarf, attractive shrublets related to *Calluna* and *Erica* with densely overlapping leaves and solitary bell-shaped flowers. Natives of northern arctic and mountain regions they require a moist peaty soil, and conditions simulating open moorlands.

**CASSIOPE**—*continued*

**'Badenoch'** A slender-branched hybrid; probably *C. fastigiata* × *C. lycopodiodes*, forming a loose clump of narrow stems up to 10cm bearing white bells on thread-like pedicels.

**'Bearsden'** (*C. fastigiata* × *C. lycopodioides*). Similar to 'Badenoch' with 4-angled shoots bearing tightly adpressed, pointed leaves and white bell-shaped flowers in April and May. Originated as a chance seedling about 1955. AM 1971.

**'Edinburgh'** (*C. fastigiata* × *C. tetragona*). A chance seedling raised at the Royal Botanic Garden, Edinburgh. Slender, dark green stems up to 18cm high. Flowers white, calyx green edged red; spring. Perhaps the most accommodating of a pernickety genus. AM 1957. AGM 1984.

**fastigiata** (WALL.) D. DON A dwarf shrublet up to 30cm high, with white-margined, adpressed leaves, giving a four-angled effect to the stems. The white bell-shaped flowers are carried on hair-like stalks in April and May. Himalaya. I about 1849. FCC 1863.

**lycopodioides** (PALL.) D. DON A prostrate mat of thread-like branchlets above which little white bells dangle from the slenderest of stalks. NE Asia, NW North America. AM 1937. FCC 1962.

**'Rigida'** (*C. rigida* HORT.) Similar but with comparatively large, white, semi-pendulous flowers. AM 1938.

**mertensiana** (BONG.) D. DON Dwarf shrub 15-30cm in height. Stems erect or spreading, four-angled. Flowers pure white in April. Mountains of W North America. I about 1885. AM 1927.

**subsp. gracilis** PIPER A low-growing form with darker shoots and larger flowers.

**'Muirhead'** (*C. lycopodioides* × *C. wardii*). A tiny shrublet with characteristic, curved, repeatedly forked shoots and small nodding white flowers in spring. AM 1953. FCC 1962. AGM 1984.

**'Randle Cooke'** (*C. fastigiata* × *C. lycopodioides*). A mat-forming shrublet with stems up to 15cm high. The white bell flowers appear along the stems in late April. Garden origin 1957. AM 1964.

**rigida** HORT. See *C. lycopodioides* 'Rigida'.

**tetragona** (L.) D. DON (*Andromeda tetragona* L.) Forms tufts of erect shoots covered with closely imbricated, deep green leaves, from which the nodding white, bell-shaped flowers appear in April and May. North America, Asia, Europe. I 1810.

**wardii** MARQ. A dwarf, erect-branched shrublet with leaves distinctly arranged in 4 rows and edged with fine white hairs. Flowers bell-shaped, white tinged red. E Himalaya. I 1938. AM 1949. FCC 1982.

**CASTANEA** MILLER—**Fagaceae**—The "Chestnuts" are a genus of some 12 species of deciduous trees and shrubs found in the temperate northern hemisphere. The sharply serrate leaves are common to all species and the twigs lack a terminal bud. The tiny yellowish, unisexual flowers are borne in long, slender catkins, some male, some male and female and although individually not conspicuous can be very ornamental *en masse*. They are long-lived, drought-resistant trees thriving on well drained, preferably rather light soils. They are moderately lime-tolerant and may be grown with fair success given deep soils over chalk, but become chlorotic on shallow chalky soils.

**alnifolia** NUTT. "Trailing Chinquapin". A small suckering shrub to 1m tall. Leaves elliptic, edged with shallow, bristle-tipped teeth, to 12cm long, glossy green above, with a tawny pubescence beneath when young becoming glabrous or nearly so. SE United States.

**ashei** See *C. pumila* var. *ashei*.

**crenata** SIEB. & ZUCC. (*C. japonica* BLUME) "Japanese Chestnut". A small tree or large shrub with long bristle-toothed leaves. Japan. I 1895.

**dentata** (MARSH.) BORKH. (*C. americana* RAF.) The "American Sweet Chestnut", rare in cultivation and becoming so in its native haunts owing to the devastating effects of chestnut blight. Differs mainly from the European species in its narrower always glabrous leaves. E North America. C 1800.

**henryi** (SKAN) REHD. & WILS. A native of C and W China, in nature a tree upwards of 20m high. In cultivation in our area a rare and very distinct shrub, making late, unripened growth which is cut back by winter frost. Introduced by E.H. Wilson in 1900.

**CASTANEA**—*continued*

**mollissima** BLUME "Chinese Chestnut". Medium to large-size tree with ovate or oblong, coarsely serrate leaves. China, Korea. I 1908 by Ernest Wilson.

×**neglecta** DODE (*C. ozarkensis* × *C. pumila*). Similar to *C. pumila*, but leaves less white pubescent beneath; fruits a little larger.

**ozarkensis** ASHE (*C. arkansana* SARG.) "Ozark Chestnut". Generally a medium-sized tree with long, coarsely serrate leaves. Closely related to *C. pumila* but with shoots glabrous and leaves nearly so. C United States. I 1891.

**pumila** (L.) MILL. "Chinquapin". A large suckering shrub or small tree with downy young shoots. Leaves white tomentose beneath at least when young. Distinguished from the closely related *C. alnifolia* by its acute not obtuse leaves which are tomentose beneath. E and S United States. I 1699.

**var. ashei** SUDW. (*C. ashei* (SUDW.) SUDW. ex ASHE) "Coastal Chinquapin". This differs from the typical variety in the less densely spiny involucres. Specimens in the Hillier Gardens and Arboretum fruited prolifically after the 1989 summer, the fruits opening to release the nuts before falling. Coastal SE United States.

**sativa** MILL. "Sweet Chestnut" "Spanish Chestnut". A fast-growing tree, a large specimen being extremely ornamental particularly in July when laden with its yellowish-green male and female catkins. Hotter than average summers are required to produce good crops of nuts. A valuable timber tree, and especially useful for coppicing. Native of S Europe, N Africa and Asia Minor. Long cultivated and naturalised in the British Isles, where it is believed to have been introduced by the Romans. AGM 1984.

**'Albomarginata'** Leaves with a creamy white margin. AM 1964.

**'Aureomarginata'** Leaves bordered yellow.

**'Heterophylla'** Leaves variously shaped, sometimes linear with irregular lobed margin. Inclined to revert.

**'Marron de Lyon'** ('Macrocarpa') The best fruiting clone, bearing at a very early age.

**seguinii** DODE Large shrub or small tree with long, coarsely serrate leaves. E and C China. I 1853.

**\*CASTANOPSIS** (D. DON) SPACH—**Fagaceae**—A genus of about 120 species of evergreen trees related to *Quercus* and *Castanea*, differing from the former in their erect male spikes and the latter in having terminal buds and the female flowers on separate spikes. Natives of tropical and subtropical SE Asia, particularly Malaysia.

**chrysophylla** See *Chrysolepis chrysophylla*.

**cuspidata** (THUNB.) SCHOTTKY (*Quercus cuspidata* THUNB.) A large shrub or small bushy tree with glabrous twigs. The leathery, shining, dark green leaves are oval in shape and possess a slenderly drawn out apex. Requires a sheltered position. Japan, Korea. I 1830.

**†\*CASUARINA** L.—**Casuarinaceae**—The "Sheokes" are a genus of evergreen trees and shrubs with about 65 species distributed from the Malay archipelago to the Pacific islands and Australia. An interesting genus with no clear relatives, they show reduction in many features. Once thought to be very primitive they are now considered to be highly evolved. They are all very tender.

**nana** SIEB. "Dwarf Sheoke". Small, densely-branched Australian shrub with slender rush-like stems. Only for the mildest areas.

**CATALPA** SCOP.—**Bignoniaceae**—A small genus of about 11 species of beautiful late summer-flowering trees, mostly of low, wide-spreading habit, natives of North America and China. The foxglove-like flowers, which do not occur in young plants, are borne in conspicuous panicles. When planting avoid exposed areas, where the large leaves would become tattered. Suitable for all types of well drained soils.

**bignonioides** WALT. "Indian Bean Tree". A medium-sized tree. Flowers white with yellow and purple markings in July and August. E United States. I 1726. AM 1933. AGM 1984.

**'Aurea'** "Golden Indian Bean Tree". An outstanding form with large, velvety, soft yellow leaves which are almost green by the time the flowers open. C 1877. AM 1974. AGM 1984.

**CATALPA bignonioides**—*continued*

'**Koehnei**' ('Aureomarginata') Leaves with a broad yellow margin, green in late summer. C 1903.

'**Nana**' A compact rounded bush or a small round-headed tree if grafted as a standard. Originated in France about 1850.

'**Variegata**' Leaves variegated white, or creamy-yellow.

**bungei** C. MEY. A small Chinese tree. Flowers white with purple spots, in clusters of 8-30cm in July but not freely produced. The broadly palmate leaves have slender acuminate lobes. N China. I 1905.

×**erubescens** CARR. (*C. bignonioides* × *C. ovata*). (*C.* × *hybrida* SPAETH) This hybrid first arose before 1869. The following forms are cultivated.

'**J.C. Teas**' A medium-sized tree, intermediate between the parents. Leaves broad ovate, both three-lobed and entire on the same tree, purple when unfolding; flowers in late July, like those of *C. bignonioides*, but smaller and more numerous. Raised in the United States about 1874. Originally listed as *C.* × *erubescens*.

'**Purpurea**' Young leaves and shoots dark purple, almost black, gradually becoming dark green. C 1886. AM 1970.

**fargesii** BUR. One of the best of the midsummer-flowering trees. It is allied to its Chinese neighbour, *C. bungei* and as seen in cultivation it forms a tree of medium size with leaves smaller than those of the "Indian Bean Tree". The conspicuous flowers are of typical form, lilac-pink with red-brown spots and stained with yellow, carried 7-15 together in corymbs. China. I 1901 by Ernest Wilson. AM 1973.

**f. duclouxii** (DODE) GILMOUR (*C. duclouxii* DODE) A tree equal in merit to the typical form and with similar flowers, but differs in the leaves being less pubescent and having more conspicuous acuminate lobes. China. I 1907 by Ernest Wilson. AM 1934.

×**hybrida** See *C.* × *erubescens*.

**ovata** G. DON (*C. kaempferi* SIEB.) A Chinese species, forming a tree 11m or more in height. Leaves usually three-lobed. Small, white flowers with yellow and red markings, produced in many-flowered narrowly pyramidal panicles in July and August. I 1849 by Siebold. AM 1933.

**speciosa** (WARDER ex BARNEY) ENGELM. "Western Catalpa". A tall tree with large heart-shaped leaves. The purple-spotted white flowers, appearing in July, are slightly larger than those of *C. bignonioides*, but are fewer in the panicle. C United States. I 1880. AM 1956.

**CEANOTHUS** L.—**Rhamnaceae**—The "Californian Lilacs" include some 55 species of evergreen and deciduous shrubs and trees widely distributed over the United States, S Canada and Mexico south to Guatemala but occurring mainly in California, where the following species are native unless otherwise stated. They vary from prostrate plants to very vigorous, tall shrubs, but are mostly of medium size and provide us with the best blue-flowered shrubs which can be grown out-of-doors in this country. The Ceanothus require full sun and good drainage; all are to a point lime-tolerant, but only a few give a good account of themselves in a really poor, shallow, chalky soil and some can become chlorotic. Most are excellent for seaside gardens and in colder areas are ideal for growing against a wall. The deciduous kinds may have the laterals cut back to within 8 or 10cm of the previous year's growth in March. The evergreen kinds need little, if any, pruning, but when desirable, light pruning should be carried out immediately after flowering.

**americanus** L. "New Jersey Tea". A small, very hardy shrub bearing dense panicles of dull white flowers in June and July. E and C United States. I 1713. The leaves are said to have been used as a substitute for tea, especially during the American Civil War.

†\***arboreus** GREENE A vigorous, large, spreading shrub or small tree with large, ovate leaves. Flowers deep vivid blue, fragrant, borne abundantly in large panicles in spring.

'**Trewithen Blue**' An improved selection with large panicles of deep blue, slightly scented flowers. Originated at Trewithen Gardens, nr Truro, home of one of the finest collections of trees and shrubs in Cornwall. AM 1967. AGM 1984.

†\*'**A.T. Johnson**' A vigorous and floriferous hybrid, with rich blue flowers in spring and again in autumn. Leaves ovate, glossy green, grey-downy beneath. AM 1934.

**CEANOTHUS**—*continued*

*\*'Autumnal Blue'* Possibly the hardiest evergreen hybrid ceanothus; bears panicles of rich, sky-blue flowers abundantly in late summer, autumn and often spring as well. Leaves broadly ovate, 3-veined, bright glossy green. AM 1930. AGM 1984.

'Blue Mound' A dense, bushy, small to medium-sized shrub with glossy green, wavy-edged leaves and dense clusters of bright blue flowers in May and June and usually again in late summer and autumn. A seedling of *C. griseus* raised in our nurseries, it is a hybrid, possibly with *C. impressus*.

'Brilliant' See *C. × veitchianus*.

†\*'Burkwoodii' (*C.* 'Indigo' × *C. floribundus*). A medium-sized, rounded shrub of dense habit with oval, glossy green leaves. Flowers rich dark blue throughout summer and autumn. AM 1930. AGM 1984.

†\*'Cascade' A lovely hybrid of the evergreen, spring-flowered group, bearing its bright blue flowers in elongated, long-stalked clusters. AM 1946. AGM 1984.

'Ceres' (Pallidus group) Panicles of lilac-pink flowers during summer.

'Charles Detriche' (Delileanus group) A medium-sized shrub with flowers of a rich dark blue during summer.

†coeruleus LAG. "Azure Ceanothus". A medium-sized shrub with semi-evergreen, ovate, dark green leaves and long panicles of sky-blue flowers in summer and autumn. Mexico to Guatemala. I 1818.

*\*'Concha' (*C. impressus* × *C. papillosus* subsp. *roweanus*). A dense, medium-sized shrub with arching branches and narrow, dark green leaves. Clusters of deep blue flowers are profusely borne from red buds.

†\*crassifolius TORR. "Hoaryleaf Ceanothus". Medium-sized shrub with tomentose branches and opposite, thick, leathery, sharply toothed leaves. Flowers white in spring.

†\*cyaneus EASTW. "San Diego Ceanothus". A dense, bushy, medium-sized shrub. Bright green, shiny, and ovate leaves, and intense blue flowers, borne in long-stalked panicles in early summer. I 1925. AM 1934.

*\*'Delight' (*C. papillosus* × *C. rigidus*). A splendid hybrid, and one of the hardiest. Flowers rich blue, in long panicles in spring. AM 1933. AGM 1984.

× delileanus SPACH (*C. americanus* × *C. coeruleus*). (*C. arnouldii* CARR.) A small to medium-sized deciduous shrub producing its panicles of soft blue flowers throughout summer. Many of the popular deciduous hybrids are selected clones of this cross.

†\*dentatus TORREY & A. GRAY "Cropleaf Ceanothus". The true species is a low, spreading shrub with tiny, oblong, glandular leaves and clusters of bright blue flowers in May. I 1848. See also *C. × lobbianus* and *C. × veitchianus* which have been confused with this species.

†\*'Dignity' A beautiful hybrid, somewhat similar to 'Delight', frequently flowering again in autumn.

†\*divergens PARRY "Calistoga Ceanothus". An attractive semi-prostrate evergreen with opposite, spine-toothed, bright green leaves grey beneath. The rigid branches are smothered in spring with racemose inflorescences of deep blue flowers.

†\*'Edinburgh' ('Edinensis') (*C. foliosus* × *C. griseus*). Rich blue flowers and olive-green foliage. An attractive plant. Originated at the Royal Botanic Garden, Edinburgh about 1934.

*fendleri A. GRAY A low, spring flowering, spiny shrub with downy shoots; white or mauve-tinted flowers in terminal clusters. SW United States, Mexico. I 1893.

†\*foliosus PARRY "Wavyleaf Ceanothus". Forms a spreading shrub with small glossy leaves and heads of rich blue flowers in spring.

'Gloire de Plantires' (Delileanus group) A small shrub with panicles of deep blue flowers in summer.

'Gloire de Versailles' (Delileanus group) The most popular deciduous ceanothus. Large panicles of powder-blue flowers in summer and autumn. FCC 1872. AGM 1984.

†\*gloriosus J.T. HOWELL (*C. rigidus* var. *grandifolius* TORR.) "Point Reyes Ceanothus". A remarkable prostrate shrub bearing opposite, dark glossy green, toothed leaves and clusters of lavender-blue flowers in April and May. Here it has formed a flat carpet 4m across.

var. exaltatus J.T. HOWELL "Navarro Ceanothus". A more upright-growing variety.

**CEANOTHUS**—*continued*

**\*griseus** (TREL.) MCMINN (*C. thyrsiflorus* var. *griseus* TREL.) Known in California as the "Carmel Ceanothus". A medium-sized to large shrub resembling *C. thyrsiflorus* with broadly ovate dark green leaves grey beneath. The form cultivated in this country has pale lilac-blue flowers in May.

**var. horizontalis** MCMINN A low-growing form of spreading habit reaching about 1m tall.

**'Yankee Point'** A compact selection of var. *horizontalis* with particularly dark green leaves and deeper blue flowers.

**'Henri Desfosse'** (Delileanus group) A hybrid resembling 'Gloire de Versailles', but with flowers a deeper almost violet-blue, summer. AM 1926.

**\*impressus** TREL. "Santa Barbara Ceanothus". A small to medium-sized shrub very distinct in its small leaves, with deeply impressed veins. Flowers deep blue in spring. Among the hardiest of the evergreen sorts. AM 1944. FCC 1957. AGM 1984.

**'Puget Blue'** See *C.* 'Puget Blue'.

**\*incanus** TORREY & A. GRAY "Coast Whitethorn". A spreading medium-sized shrub with 3-veined, ovate, grey-green leaves and thorny whitish branches. Slightly fragrant, creamy white flowers in April and May.

**†'Indigo'** (Delileanus group) True indigo-blue; summer flowering. AM 1902.

**†integerrimus** HOOK. & ARN. "Deer Bush". Large semi-evergreen shrub. The three-nerved leaves are dull sea-green. Flowers pale blue in large panicles in June. I 1853.

**†\*'Italian Skies'** A vigorous, medium-sized spreading shrub with small dark green leaves and deep blue flowers in May. A seedling of *C. foliosus* raised in 1956 by E.B. Anderson.

**†\*jepsonii** GREENE "Musk Brush". A small spreading shrub with opposite, dark green, holly-like, leathery leaves and rich blue flowers in spring.

**†\* × lobbianus** HOOK. (*C. dentatus × C. griseus*). (*C. dentatus* HORT.) A large shrub, excellent for covering a wall. Leaves small, oblong, 3-veined and edged with small teeth. Bright blue flowers are profusely borne in May and June. Discovered by William Lobb near Monterey in California about 1853 and introduced by him.

**'Russellianus'** This clone is distinguished by its very glossy, small leaves, and long-stalked, bright blue flower-heads.

**'Marie Simon'** (Pallidus group) Pink flowers in panicles on the young growths in summer.

**†\*megacarpus** NUTT. "Bigpod Ceanothus". Medium-sized shrub with small, crowded, wedge-shaped leaves and panicles of white flowers in spring.

**\* × mendocinensis** MCMINN (*C. thyrsiflorus × C. velutinus* var. *laevigatus*). "Mendocino Ceanothus". A small to medium-sized shrub with long, arching shoots and broad ovate, dark glossy green rather sticky leaves. Racemes of pale blue flowers are borne in spring. A naturally occurring hybrid.

**× pallidus** LINDL. (? *C. × delileanus × C. ovatus*). This very hardy, small to medium-sized garden hybrid of European origin has light blue flowers in summer. There are several named clones.

**'Plenus'** (*C.* 'Albus Plenus') An equally hardy summer flowering hybrid with double white flowers, pink in bud.

**†\*papillosus** TORR. & GRAY A distinct species, a large shrub with comparatively long, narrow, viscid leaves. Gives a brilliant display of rich blue flowers in late spring. I 1850 by William Lobb. AM 1980.

**subsp. roweanus** (MCMINN) MUNZ A form with narrower leaves. It has been confused with the typical form.

**'Perle Rose'** (Pallidus group) Bright rose-carmine; summer. AGM 1984.

**'Pinquet-Guindon'** Lavender, suffused pink, a curious colour combination; summer.

**\*prostratus** BENTH. Known in California as "Squaw Carpet", this creeping evergreen makes a dense mat up to 1.5m wide with opposite, leathery, dark green, toothed leaves. Bears quantities of bright blue flowers in spring. AM 1935.

**\*'Puget Blue'** (*C. impressus* 'Puget Blue') A dense, medium-sized shrub producing deep blue flowers over a long period during late spring and early summer. Raised at the University of Washington Arboretum, Seattle before 1945. Originally said to be a form of *C. impressus* but the longer, narrower leaves with glandular papillae above and on the margin indicate that it could be a hybrid with *C. papillosus*. AM 1971. AGM 1984.

**CEANOTHUS**—*continued*

**\*pumilus** GREENE "Siskiyou Mat". A creeping, alpine species. Leaves opposite, narrowly oblong, usually 3-toothed at the apex. Flowers pale blue in spring. Leaves narrower than those of *C. prostratus*.

**†\*purpureus** JEPSON "Hollyleaf Ceanothus". A dwarf spreading shrub with leathery, holly-like, opposite leaves and lavender-purple flower-clusters in late spring.

**†\*rigidus** NUTT. (*C. rigidus* var. *pallens* SPRAGUE) "Monterey Ceanothus". A low, spreading, densely branched shrub with distinctive, dark glossy green, leathery and toothed, wedge-shaped leaves, and purple-blue flowers in spring. Growth compact. I 1847.

**†\*sorediatus** HOOK. & ARN. "Jim Brush". A small to medium-sized shrub with rigid branches and glandular-toothed, three-veined leaves, glossy dark green above. Flowers varying from pale to dark blue in spring.

**\*'Southmead'** A dense-growing shrub of medium size with small oblong leaves, glossy dark green above. Flowers rich blue in May and June. AM 1964. AGM 1984.

**†\*spinosus** NUTT. "Greenbark Ceanothus". A large shrub, only rarely spiny in cultivation. Leaves leathery, glossy green on both surfaces. Flowers rich blue in spring.

**\*thyrsiflorus** ESCHSCH. "Blue Blossom". A large shrub, one of the hardiest evergreen species. Leaves broadly elliptic, dark green and 3-veined. Flowers bright blue in early summer. I 1837. AM 1935.

> **var. repens** MCMINN "Creeping Blue Blossom". A vigorous, mound-forming, hardy form, producing early in its life generous quantities of Cambridge-blue flowers. It is variable in habit. AGM 1984.

**'Topaz'** (Delileanus group) Light indigo-blue; summer flowering. AM 1961. AGM 1984.

**\*×veitchianus** HOOK. (*C. rigidus* × *C. thyrsiflorus*). (*C.* 'Brilliant') (*C. dentatus floribundus* HORT.) A large evergreen shrub with small, glossy green, wedge-shaped leaves and deep blue flowers in May and June. For hardiness, freedom of flowering and richness of colour, this shrub well merits its popularity. A natural hybrid discovered and introduced by William Lobb about 1853.

**\*velutinus var. laevigatus** TORREY & A. GRAY A wide-spreading shrub with large glossy, somewhat viscid, leaves. Flowers grey-white in dense panicles in autumn. Here uninjured for many years by our severest winters. The typical variety is a small shrub with the leaves velvety beneath.

**†\*verrucosus** NUTT. "Wartystem Ceanothus". A vigorous, medium-sized shrub with rigid, verrucose stems and crowded leathery leaves which have a single vein and are sometimes notched at the apex. Flowers white, with darker centres, appearing in spring. AM 1977.

**'Yankee Point'** See *C. griseus* 'Yankee Point'.


**CEDRELA sinensis** See *Toona sinensis*.


**CELTIS** L.—**Ulmaceae**—The "Nettle Trees" or "Hackberries" are elegant, fast-growing, medium-sized trees allied to the Elms. About 60 species in N temperate regions and the tropics.

**australis** L. Small to medium-sized tree with characteristic broad lanceolate leaves, rough to the touch above. S Europe, N Africa, Asia Minor. C in England since the 16th century.

**caucasica** WILLD. "Caucasian Nettle Tree". Medium-sized tree with ovate coarsely-toothed leaves. E Bulgaria, W Asia, Himalaya. I 1885.

**glabrata** PLANCH. Small tree or large shrub forming a rounded head. Distinct in its glabrous leaves which are markedly unequal at the base. W Asia. C 1870.

**jessoensis** KOIDZ. A small to medium-sized tree with narrowly, occasionally broadly ovate leaves, obliquely rounded at base, acuminate at apex, pale green or glaucous beneath. Japan, Korea. I 1892.

**labilis** SCHNEID. Small tree with long acuminate leaves. China. I 1907 by Ernest Wilson.

**laevigata** WILLD (*C. mississippiensis* BOSC) "Mississippi Hackberry". A handsome large tree with lanceolate, entire or few-toothed leaves. SE United States. C 1811.

**occidentalis** L. "Hackberry". Medium-sized tree; mature specimens have rough, warted, corky bark, and produce black fruits in profusion. North America. I 1656.

> **var. cordata** (PERS.) WILLD. (*C. occidentalis* var. *crassifolia* (LAM.) GRAY) A vigorous tree, the arching stems bearing heart-shaped leaves larger than those of the typical form.

**CELTIS**—*continued*

**pumila** (MUHL.) PURSH A large shrub of dense habit or a small tree with ovate leaves downy when young. W United States. I 1876.

**reticulata** TORR. Small to medium-sized tree with ovate, conspicuously reticulate leaves, which may be entire or coarsely toothed in the upper half. Fruits orange-red. SW United States. I 1890.

**sinensis** PERS. A small tree, very striking in the polished surface of its foliage. E China, Korea, Japan. I 1910.

**tournefortii** LAM. A small "Hackberry" from the Orient with polished green leaves and red and yellow fruits. SE Europe, SW Asia. I 1738.

**CEPHALANTHUS** L.—**Rubiaceae**—A small genus of evergreen and deciduous trees and shrubs. About 6 species in N and C America, E Asia and Africa.

**occidentalis** L. The "Button Bush" is an easily cultivated but rarely grown shrub of medium height. Leaves ovate, 5-15cm long; flowers creamy-white, produced during August, in small, globular heads. E and S United States, Mexico, Cuba. I 1735.

**'Angustifolius'** A form with lanceolate or narrow-elliptic leaves, often in whorls of three.

**\*†CERATONIA** L.—**Leguminosae**—A genus of 2 species of evergreen trees native to SW Asia. The following requires a sheltered, sunny position.

**siliqua** L. "Carob Tree" "St. John's Bread". Supposedly the source of "locusts and wild honey". A large shrub with dark green pinnate leaves, extensively planted in the Mediterranean region where it forms a picturesque round-headed tree. Mediterranean region (naturalised), SW Asia.

**CERATOSTIGMA** BUNGE—**Plumbaginaceae**—A small genus of about 8 species found in E Asia and tropical E Africa. The cultivated species are small ornamental shrubs often referred to as "Hardy Plumbago", useful on account of their blue flowers over a long period during early autumn. Suitable for dry, well drained soil, preferably in full sun.

**griffithii** C.B. CLARKE A beautiful Himalayan species with deep blue flowers. Leaves often turn conspicuously red late in autumn and often persist well into the New Year. In our nurseries survived the hard winter of 1963.

**†minus** PRAIN (*C. polhillii* BULLEY) A slender species resembling *C. willmottianum*, but smaller in all its parts. Flowers slate-blue. W China.

**willmottianum** STAPF Forms a shrub of about 1m in height. The rich blue flowers appear in July and continue until autumn. Suitable either for the shrub border or herbaceous border. The foliage is tinted red in the autumn. W China. I 1908 by Ernest Wilson. AM 1917. AGM 1984.

**CERCIDIPHYLLUM** SIEB. & ZUCC.—**Cercidiphyllaceae**—One species, a deciduous tree native to E Asia and grown for its autumn colour. The tiny red flowers emerge with the young leaves, males and females on separate plants. The affinities of this genus, which is the only one in the family, have been disputed. It has been thought to be related to either *Euptelea* or *Liriodendron*.

**japonicum** SIEB. & ZUCC. "Katsura Tree". An attractive Japanese tree with leaves similar to those of the "Judas Tree" (*Cercis siliquastrum*), but opposite and smaller. In this country forms a small to medium-sized tree, assuming pale yellow or smoky-pink autumnal colouring in favourable seasons when, at the same time, a sweetly pungent scent like burnt sugar pervades the air. May be grown in any deep, fertile soil. Japan, China. I 1881. AGM 1984.

**var. magnificum** NAKAI (*C. magnificum* (NAKAI) NAKAI) A rare tree of medium size. Differs in its smoother bark and its larger, more cordate leaves with coarser serrations. Lovely yellow autumn tints. Japan.

**'Pendulum'** A rare and unusual form with long, pendulous branches. Long cultivated in Japan where similar forms occur in the wild and may belong to var. *magnificum* or be hybrids between the two varieties.

**var. sinense** REHD. & WILS. A Chinese form introduced by E.H. Wilson in 1907. Stated to be more tree-like in habit but differing very little from the typical form.

**magnificum** See *C. japonicum* var. *magnificum*.

**CERCIS** L.—**Leguminosae**—A distinct genus of small trees with broad, rounded, heart-shaped leaves and beautiful pea flowers in spring. 6 or 7 species widely distributed in N temperate regions. The apparently simple leaves are derived from the fusion of two leaflets of an evenly pinnate leaf. They require full sun and good drainage.

**canadensis** L. The North American "Redbud". A small tree with a broad, round head, unfortunately not very free-flowering in this country. Flowers pale rose in May and June. It may be distinguished from *C. siliquastrum* by its thinner, brighter green leaves. SE Canada, E United States, NE Mexico. I 1730.

**'Forest Pansy'** A splendid selection with deep reddish-purple foliage. Flowers pink but not conspicuous.

**var. texensis** (S . WATS.) HOPKINS (*C. reniformis* S. WATS.) "Texas Redbud". Differs from the typical form in being more shrubby and in having rich glossy green leaves blunt at the tip and glabrous shoots. Oklahoma, Texas.

**chinensis** BUNGE (*C. japonica* PLANCH.) A Chinese species having glossy-green, heart-shaped leaves up to 12.5cm across; flowers bright pink in May. Not suitable for cold areas.

**occidentalis** A. GRAY "Western Redbud". A deciduous shrub, or occasionally a small tree up to 5m. Leaves rounded or notched at apex, rather leathery; flowers rose-coloured, produced on short stalks in clusters. SW United States.

**racemosa** OLIV. A tree up to 11m high. Flowers pink in drooping racemes, freely produced in May, but not on young trees. Flowered and fruited profusely in the Hillier Gardens and Arboretum in 1990. China. I 1907 by Ernest Wilson. AM 1927.

**reniformis** See *C. canadensis* var. *texensis*.

**siliquastrum** L. "Judas Tree". Clustered, rosy-lilac flowers wreathe the branches in May. The purple-tinted seed pods are often conspicuous from July onwards. E mediterranean region. I 16th century. Legend has it that this is the tree on which Judas hanged himself. AGM 1984.

**'Alba'** Flowers white and foliage a pale green. AM 1972.

**'Bodnant'** A clone with deep purple flowers. FCC 1944.

**\*CERCOCARPUS** KUNTH—**Rosaceae**—About 6 species of evergreen or semi-evergreen small trees or large shrubs from W North America and Mexico known for their hard, heavy wood which has given rise to the common name "Mountain Mahogany". They have little ornamental value here but are sometimes planted in their native lands.

**betuloides** TORR. & GRAY (*C. betulifolius* HOOK.) A large, graceful, lax shrub with small obovate leaves. W United States, Mexico.

**ledifolius** NUTT. Small tree or large shrub with furrowed bark. Leaves narrow lanceolate, thick and leathery. W North America. I 1879.

**montanus** RAF. A medium-sized shrub of open habit, with obovate, prominently-veined leaves coarsely toothed at the apex. In common with other species it has no beauty of flower but the fruits possess a slender, twisted, silky white tail 5-10cm long. W North America. C 1913.

**†\*CESTRUM** L.—**Solanaceae**—A large genus of some 200 species of shrubs and small trees native to C and S America and the West Indies. The cultivated species are showy medium-sized shrubs suitable for warm wall or conservatory.

**aurantiacum** LINDL. Long, tubular flowers, deep orange-yellow in large terminal panicles. Guatemala. I 1840. AM 1961.

**elegans** (BRONGN.) SCHLECHT (*C. purpureum* (LINDL.) STANDLEY) Clusters of bright red flowers over a long period. Mexico. I 1840. AM 1975.

**'Newellii'** A seedling resembling *C. elegans* in habit. Flowers large, orange-red. Garden origin. FCC 1876. AM 1951.

**parqui** L'HERIT. A Chilean species. Flowers yellowish-green, fragrant at night, borne in June and July. Hardy in sunny sheltered places in the south and west. It grows well at Hyde Hall, where it is occasionally cut to the ground in cold winters but quickly recovers. I 1787. AM 1990.

**purpureum** See *C. elegans*.

**CHAENOMELES** L.—**Rosaceae**—Familiarly known as "Japonica" and once listed under *Cydonia*, these ornamental "Quinces" are among the most beautiful and easily cultivated of early spring-flowering shrubs. The saucer-shaped flowers varying in shades of red, orange and white are followed by large yellow quinces. Will thrive in the open border or against a wall even if shaded. When treated as a wall shrub, they may be cut back immediately after flowering. 3 species in E Asia.

× **californica** CLARKE ex WEBER (*C. cathayensis* × *C.* × *superba*). A group of small shrubs with stiff, erect, spiny branches, narrow leaves and pink or rosy-red flowers. Raised by Messrs. Clarke and Co of California.

    **'Enchantress'** Flowers deep rose-pink, freely produced. One of the original cultivars. C 1938. AM 1943.

**cathayensis** (HEMSL.) SCHNEID. (*C. lagenaria* var. *wilsonii* REHD.) A large, sparsely branched shrub with formidable spines, and long, narrow, finely-toothed leaves. Flowers white flushed salmon-pink appearing in spring; fruits very large, occasionally 15cm or more long. C China. I about 1800.

**japonica** (THUNB.) SPACH (*Cydonia japonica* (THUNB.) PERS.) (*Cydonia maulei* T. MOORE) A small shrub, flowers bright orange-flame followed by rounded, yellow, fragrant fruits. Japan. I about 1869. FCC 1890.

    **var. alpina** MAXIM. A dwarf form with ascending branchlets and procumbent stems. Flowers bright orange, fruits smaller.

**lagenaria** See *C. speciosa*.

    **var. wilsonii** See *C. cathayensis*.

**sinensis** See *Pseudocydonia sinensis*.

**speciosa** (SWEET) NAKAI (*C. lagenaria* (LOISEL.) KOIDZ.) (*Cydonia speciosa* SWEET) The well-known, early-flowering "Japonica", a much-branched, spreading shrub of medium size. Seedling-raised plants bear flowers of mixed colours, dominantly red. China. I 1869 by Sir Joseph Banks.

    **'Apple Blossom'** White tinged pale pink and cream. C 1932.

    **'Atrococcinea'** Deep crimson. C 1909.

    **'Brilliant'** Clear scarlet; large. C 1939.

    **'Cardinalis'** Crimson-scarlet. C 1835. AM 1893.

    **'Contorta'** White tinged pink, branches twisted. I from Japan about 1929.

    **'Eximia'** Deep brick-red. C 1880.

    **'Falconnet Charlet'** Double flowers of an attractive salmon-pink. C 1915.

    **'Kermesina Semiplena'** Scarlet; semi-double. C 1887.

    **'Knap Hill Radiance'** Bright red, large. AM 1948.

    **'Moerloosei'** Delicate pink and white, in thick clusters. AM 1957. AGM 1984. C 1856.

    **'Nivalis'** Pure white; large. C 1881.

    **'Phylis Moore'** Clear almond-pink in large clusters; semi-double. AM 1931. C 1930.

    **'Red Ruffles'** Clear red; large, semi-double. C 1950.

    **'Rosea Plena'** Rose-pink; double. C 1878.

    **'Rubra Grandiflora'** Crimson; extra large. Low, spreading habit. C 1867.

    **'Sanguinea Plena'** Red, double. C 1880.

    **'Simonii'** Blood-red; flat, semi-double. Dwarf, spreading habit. An exceptionally beautiful cultivar. AM 1907. C 1882.

    **'Snow'** Pure white; large. C 1945.

    **'Spitfire'** Deep crimson-red; large. Erect habit. C 1949.

    **'Umbilicata'** Deep salmon-pink. I from Japan by Siebold before 1847. AM 1983.

    **'Versicolor Lutescens'** Flowers large, pale creamy-yellow, flushed pink. Low-growing. C 1865.

× **superba** (FRAHM) REHD. (*C. japonica* × *C. speciosa*). Small to medium-sized shrubs of vigorous habit.

    **'Boule de Feu'** Orange-red. C 1913.

    **'Crimson and Gold'** Deep crimson petals and golden anthers. C 1939. AM 1979.

    **'Elly Mossel'** Orange-red; large. Somewhat spreading habit.

    **'Ernst Finken'** Fiery red, produced in abundance. Vigorous in growth. C 1952.

    **'Etna'** (*C. speciosa* 'Simonii' × *C.* × *superba*). Rich vermilion. Small shrub.

**CHAENOMELES × superba**—*continued*

**'Fire Dance'** (*C. speciosa* 'Simonii' × *C.* × *superba*). Glowing signal-red. Spreading habit. C 1953.

**'Hever Castle'** Shrimp-pink. Originated at Hever Castle, Kent before 1940.

**'Incendie'** Orange-red of a distinct shade; semi-double. C 1912.

**'Knap Hill Scarlet'** Bright orange-scarlet, profusely borne throughout spring and early summer. C 1891. AM 1961. AGM 1984.

**'Nicoline'** ('Incendie' × 'Rowallane'). Scarlet-red. Spreading habit. C 1954. AGM 1984.

**'Pink Lady'** Clear rose-pink, darker in bud, profuse and early. Spreading habit. C 1946.

**'Red Chief'** Bright red; large; double. C 1953.

**'Rowallane'** Blood-crimson; large. C 1920. AGM 1984.

**'Vermilion'** Brilliant vermilion. C 1913.

**CHAMAEBATIARIA** (PORTER) MAXIM.—**Rosaceae**—A monotypic genus related to *Sorbaria*.

**millefolium** (TORR.) MAXIM. A small shrub with erect, downy, aromatic stems, sticky when young, and elegant, finely divided leaves. White flowers in terminal panicles in summer. Requires a sunny position. W North America. I 1891.

‡\***CHAMAEDAPHNE** MOENCH (*Cassandra* D. DON)—**Ericaceae**—A monotypic genus related to *Leucothoe*.

**calyculata** (L.) MOENCH "Leather Leaf". A small wiry shrub for a lime-free soil. Flowers heath-like, white, borne all along the arching branches in March and April. E North America, N Europe, N Asia. I 1748.

**'Nana'** A very attractive form of dwarf, compact habit.

**CHAMAEPERICLYMENUM canadense** See *Cornus canadensis*.

†\***CHAMAEROPS** L.—**Palmae**—A monotypic genus, interesting in being a native European palm though many others are commonly planted. The only other palm found wild in Europe is *Phoenix theophrasti* W. GREUTER which is restricted to the coast of Crete.

**excelsus** See *Trachycarpus fortunei*.

**humilis** L. "Dwarf Fan Palm". A most interesting miniature palm from SW Europe and N Africa where it covers mountain sides in coastal areas. Rarely exceeds 1.5m in height, occasionally forms a short trunk. Leaves large, deeply palmately divided into very stiff segments. Hardy in mild localities. I 1731 by Philip Miller.

**"CHASTE TREE"** See *Vitex agnus-castus*.

**"CHERRY"** See *Prunus*.

**"CHERRY, CORNELIAN"** See *Cornus mas*.

**"CHESTNUT, GOLDEN"** See *Chrysolepis chrysophylla*.

**"CHESTNUT, HORSE"** See *Aesculus hippocastanum*.

**"CHESTNUT, SPANISH"** See *Castanea sativa*.

**"CHESTNUT, SWEET"** See *Castanea sativa*.

**"CHILEAN FIRE BUSH"** See *Embothrium coccineum*.

**\*CHILIOTRICHUM** CASS.—**Compositae**—2 species of evergreen shrubs related to *Olearia* and native to S America.

**diffusum** (FORST.) KUNTZE (*C. amelloides* DC.) (*C. rosmarinifolium* LESS.) A small shrub with evergreen linear leaves 2-5cm long, white tomentose beneath becoming brown. Conspicuous white, daisy flowers in summer. A variable species found over a wide area in southern S America. Some forms are hardier than others. I about 1926 by Harold Comber.

**CHIMONANTHUS** LINDL.—**Calycanthaceae**—The "Winter Sweets" consist of 6 species of deciduous and evergreen shrubs found in China, only the following species in general cultivation. A medium-sized, easily grown shrub best planted against a sunny wall to ripen growth. Succeeds in any well drained soil, and excellent on chalk. When treated as a wall shrub, long growths may be cut back immediately after flowering.

**fragrans** See *C. praecox*.

**praecox** (L.) LINK. (*C. fragrans* (LOISEL.) LINDL.) (*Calycanthus praecox* L.) Flowers sweetly scented, pale, waxy-yellow, stained purple at the centre, appearing on the leafless branches during winter but not produced on young plants. China. I 1766.

**'Grandiflorus'** A form with deeper yellow flowers conspicuously stained with red. AM 1928. FCC 1991.

**'Luteus'** Well distinguished by its rather large unstained flowers which are a uniform clear waxy-yellow, and open later than those of the typical form. AM 1948. FCC 1970. AGM 1984.

**CHIONANTHUS** L.—**Oleaceae**—The "Fringe Trees" are a genus with about 120 species of wide distribution in the tropics with 2 hardy species, one from the New and one from the Old World. They are both of easy cultivation, producing during June and July an abundance of white flowers, conspicuous by their 4 or 5 narrow, strap-shaped petals. Flowers not carried by young plants. Best in full sun.

**retusus** LINDL. "Chinese Fringe Tree". Given a continental climate, it is one of the most handsome of large shrubs, bearing a profusion of snow-white flowers in June and July, followed by damson-like fruits. China. I 1845 by Robert Fortune. FCC 1885.

**virginicus** L. The North American "Fringe Tree", ultimately a large shrub with larger and more noteworthy leaves than its Chinese counterpart; flowers white, slightly fragrant. E North America. I 1736. AM 1931.

**CHLORANTHUS brachystachys** See *Sarcandra glabra*.

**\*CHOISYA** KUNTH—**Rutaceae**—A small genus of 7 species of evergreen, aromatic shrubs natives of Mexico and the SW United States.

**†arizonica** STANDL. A small aromatic shrub with warty shoots. Leaves with usually 5 leaflets which are linear and edged with wart-like teeth. Flowers borne singly or in clusters of up to 5 in the leaf axils, white flushed pink outside, slightly fragrant, about 2.5cm across, April to May. Mountains of S Arizona.

**'Aztec Pearl'** (*C. arizonica* × *C. ternata*). This remarkable hybrid, the first in the genus, was raised by our propagator Peter Moore in 1982. An elegant small shrub, the aromatic leaves attractively divided into 3-5 slender, bright green leaflets. Flowers fragrant, like *C. ternata* but larger, pink-flushed in bud, opening white flushed pink on the back of the petals, profusely borne in May and again in late summer in clusters of 3-5 in the leaf axils. AM 1990.

**ternata** KUNTH "Mexican Orange Blossom". A medium-sized shrub of rounded habit. The trifoliolate leaves are shining dark green, aromatic when crushed. Flowers white, sweetly scented, borne in clusters of up to 6 from the leaf axils throughout late spring and early summer, usually flowering again in autumn. A useful shrub for sun or shade. SW Mexico. I 1825. FCC 1880. AGM 1984.

**'Sundance'** A striking form with the young foliage bright yellow.

**"CHOKEBRRY, RED"** See *Aronia arbutifolia*.

**CHORDOSPARTIUM** CHEESEM.—**Leguminosae**—A monotypic genus related to *Carmichaelia*.
  **stevensonii** CHEESEM. "Weeping Broom". A medium-sized, rare broom-like, leafless shrub, bearing racemes of lavender-pink flowers in summer. In habit resembles a miniature weeping willow. New Zealand (S Island) where it is rare in the wild. The stems of young plants appear brown and lifeless for the first 3-4 years. I 1923. AM 1943.

**CHOSENIA arbutifolia** See *Salix arbutifolia*.

*****CHRYSOLEPIS** HJELMQVIST—**Fagaceae**—A genus of 2 species of evergreens closely related to *Castanea* and *Castanopsis*. Both are native to W North America.
  **chrysophylla** (HOOK.) HJELMQVIST (*Castanopsis chrysophylla* (HOOK.) DC.) "Golden Chestnut". A small to medium-sized tree or large shrub. Leaves leathery and pointed, dark green above, yellow beneath. Fruits produced in dense green, prickly clusters. Succeeds best in a well drained acid or neutral soil. W United States. I 1844. AM 1935.
    **'Obovata'** ('Obtusata') A distinct form with obtuse leaves 5cm or more long. Free-fruiting. A small tree in our Chandler's Ford nursery survived the severest winters without any ill effect as have its descendants in the Hillier Gardens and Arboretum where one has reached 4m tall (1990).
  **vacciniifolia** See *Quercus vacciniifolia*.

†*****CINNAMOMUM** SCHAEFFER—**Lauraceae**—A genus of trees and shrubs of mainly economic importance. About 250 species native from E and SE Asia to Australia. The following are suitable for the mildest areas only and have aromatic, three-veined leaves.
  **camphora** (L.) SIEB. "Camphor Tree". A handsome foliage shrub, but too tender for any but the mildest localities. The wood yields the camphor of commerce. Tropical Asia and Malaya to China and Japan. I 1727.
  **daphnoides** SIEB. & ZUCC. A distinct species with leathery, obovate three-veined leaves, rounded at the tip, to 3cm long, closely silvery hairy beneath. A large shrub or small tree in mild areas. S Japan.
  **glanduliferum** (WALL.) MEISSN. A rare Chinese species. Leaves evergreen, broadly ovate, leathery, light green above and white beneath; aromatic when crushed.
  **japonicum** SIEB. ex NAKAI An attractive large bushy shrub or small tree with reddish shoots and petioles. Leaves ovate-lanceolate, acuminate, glossy green above, glabrous and glaucous beneath. Japan, Korea, China.

†**CIONURA** GRISEB.—**Asclepiadaceae**—A monotypic genus related to *Periploca* and previously included in *Marsdenia* which now contains only tropical species. Easily grown in full sun in any well drained soil.
  **erecta** (L.) GRISEB. (*Marsdenia erecta* (L.) R. BR.) An interesting lax shrub up to 2m with attractively marbled, silvery-green, cordate-ovate leaves, and cymes of fragrant, white flowers from May to July. Sap milky white. Requires a warm border or wall. E Mediterranean region. C since the 16th century.

*****CISTUS** L.—**Cistaceae**—The "Sun Roses" consist of about 20 species of evergreen, usually small shrubs found in the wild from the Canary Islands throughout the Mediterranean region to the Caucasus. Numerous hybrids have originated both in the wild and in cultivation. They revel in full sun and are excellent for dry banks, rock-gardens and similar positions. The flowers, though individually short-lived, are very freely produced mainly in June and July, and unless otherwise stated are white. Where no height is given it may be assumed to be about 1m. Native of S Europe and N Africa.
  Most of the Cistus resent severe frost, but are remarkably wind-tolerant and withstand maritime exposure. They do well on chalk.
† × **aguilari** PAU (*C. ladanifer* × *C. populifolius*). A vigorous plant with very large flowers. Spain, Morocco.
    **'Maculatus'** Flowers with a central ring of crimson blotches. A most handsome plant. AM 1936.

**CISTUS**—*continued*

**albidus** L. A small, compact shrub with whitish-hoary leaves. Flowers pale rose-lilac, with a yellow eye. SW Europe and N Africa. C 1640.

**'Anne Palmer'** (*C. crispus* × *C. palhinhae*). A small shrub with sticky shoots bearing long white hairs and wavy-edged leaves. Flowers soft pink, up to 7cm across. Raised by Collingwood Ingram before 1960 and named after Lady Anne Palmer, now Lady Anne Berry, who in 1987 gave her garden Rosemoor in N Devon to the Royal Horticultural Society. Cory Cup 1960. AM 1964. AGM 1984.

**atchleyi** WARBURG A dwarf shrub of compact dome-shaped habit, with green reticulate leaves and racemes of white flowers. Found by W. Ingwersen and S. Atchley in N Greece in 1929.

**'Blanche'** (*C. ladanifer* × *C. palhinhae*). A most attractive hybrid raised by Capt Collingwood Ingram. Leaves glossy green, white beneath, flowers pure white. AM 1967. FCC and Cory Cup 1976.

×**canescens** SWEET (*C. albidus* × *C. creticus*). A naturally occurring hybrid found in the wild with the parents, with grey-green leaves and usually pink flowers.

**'Albus'** A form with white flowers 5cm across.

×**corbariensis** POURR. (*C. populifolius* × *C. salviifolius*). One of the hardiest. Crimson-tinted buds, opening pure white. AGM 1984.

**creticus** L. (*C. villosus* L.) An extremely variable small shrub with often shaggily hairy stems; flowers varying from purple to rose, with yellow centre. Widely distributed in the Mediterranean region. C 1650.

**'Albus'** Flowers white.

**crispus** L. A small spreading shrub of dense habit with wavy-edged, three-veined, grey-green leaves and deep purplish-pink flowers with crumpled petals. W Mediterranean region. I about 1656. AGM 1984. See also *C.* × *pulverulentus*.

×**cyprius** LAM. (*C. ladanifer* × *C. laurifolius*). A hardy, vigorous hybrid about 2m high. Clusters of 8cm wide, white flowers with crimson basal blotches. France, Spain. AMT 1925. AGM 1984.

**'Albiflorus'** Flowers without blotches.

×**dansereaui** PINTO DA SILVA (*C.* × *lusitanicus* MAUND not MILL.) A vigorous small shrub with lance-shaped, dark green, sticky and wavy-edged leaves. Large white flowers with crimson basal blotches. C 1830.

**'Decumbens'** A wide-spreading form, growing 1.2m or more across and 0.6m high.

†**'Elma'** (*C. laurifolius* × *C. palhinhae*). The beautifully formed, extra large, pure white flowers contrast with the deep green, polished, lanceolate leaves glaucous beneath. Sturdy, bushy habit to 2m. AM 1949.

×**florentinus** LAM. (*C. monspeliensis* × *C. salviifolius*). A floriferous, white flowered, natural hybrid, seldom above 0.6m high. S Europe, Algiers. AMT 1925.

**formosus** See *Halimium lasianthum*.

×**glaucus** POURR. (*C. laurifolius* × *C. monspeliensis*). An attractive shrub up to 1.2m high with slender shoots and white flowers 4-5cm across. S France, Pyrenees.

**hirsutus** LAM. A dwarf floriferous species with white flowers stained yellow at base, and conspicuous yellow stamens. Portugal, W Spain. C 1634.

†**ladanifer** L. "Gum Cistus". A tall erect species with lance-shaped dark green leaves. The flowers, up to 10cm across, are white with a chocolate basal stain; petals crumpled. SW Europe and N Africa. C 1629.

**'Albiflorus'** Flowers pure white.

**laurifolius** L. The hardiest species, sometimes exceeding 2m in height. Leaves leathery, dark glaucous green; flowers white with yellow centre. SW Europe to C Italy. I 1731. AGM 1984.

×**laxus** AIT. (*C. hirsutus* × *C. populifolius*). Intermediate in character between its parents. Flowers white with yellow centre. C 1656.

**libanotis** L. (*C. bourgeanus* COSS.) A dwarf, lax shrub. Leaves linear, dark green, up to 5cm long. Flowers small, white. SW Portugal, SW Spain.

×**loretii** ROUY & FOUC. (*C. ladanifer* × *C. monspeliensis*). The large white flowers have crimson basal blotches. Dwarf habit. Occurs in the wild.

**CISTUS**—*continued*

× **lusitanicus** See *C.* × *dansereaui.*

†**monspeliensis** L. "Montpelier Rock Rose". A small shrub distinguished by its linear-oblong, sticky leaves and pure white flowers 2.5cm across. S Europe. C 1634.

† × **obtusifolius** SWEET (*C. hirsutus* × *C. salviifolius*). A dwarf shrub of rounded habit. Flowers 2.5-4cm across, white with a yellow basal stain. Portugal. C 1827.

'**Paladin**' (*C. ladanifer* × *C. palhinhae*). A very attractive plant similar to 'Pat' with glossy green leaves white beneath and large white flowers blotched with maroon. Raised by Capt Collingwood Ingram. AM 1946.

†**palhinhae** INGRAM (*C. ladanifer* f. *latifolius* DAVEAU) This strikingly handsome and distinct species is proving remarkably hardy. Low-growing and compact, with glossy, sticky leaves, the pure white flowers are nearly 10cm across. Collected in SW Portugal in 1939 by Capt Collingwood Ingram and Senhor Palhinha. AM 1944.

†**parviflorus** LAM. Shrub with small, grey-felted leaves and clear pink flowers. Only suitable for the mildest localities. SE Italy to Cyprus and SW Turkey. C 1825.

'**Pat**' (*C. ladanifer* × *C. palhinhae*). (*C.* 'Paladin Pat') A beautiful hardy hybrid reminiscent of *C. ladanifer* in foliage and producing 13cm wide white, maroon-blotched flowers. AM 1955.

'**Peggy Sammons**' (*C. albidus* × *C. laurifolius*). A small to medium-sized shrub of erect habit, with grey-green downy stems and leaves. Flowers of a delicate shade of pink. Raised in 1955 by Mr J.E. Sammons. AGM 1984.

× **platysepalus** SWEET (*C. hirsutus* × *C. monspeliensis*). Intermediate between its parents, flowers white stained yellow at base. Portugal.

**populifolius** L. An erect shrub with small, hairy, poplar-like leaves and flowers white stained yellow at the base. One of the hardiest. SW Europe. C 1634. AM 1930.

    **var. lasiocalyx** WILLK. This variety has larger, wavy flowers with a conspicuous inflated calyx and has proved one of the hardiest. S Spain, S Portugal, Morocco.

† × **pulverulentus** POURR. (*C. albidus* × *C. crispus*). (*C. crispus* HORT.) (*C.* 'Roseus') (*C.* 'Sunset') (*C.* 'Warley Rose') A dwarf shrub of compact habit with sage-green wavy leaves. Flowers vivid cerise. SW Europe. C 1929.

† × **purpureus** LAM. (*C. creticus* × *C. ladanifer*). A small shrub with reddish stems and narrow, rather wavy-edged, dark green leaves. Flowers large, rosy-crimson with conspicuous maroon basal blotches and a contrasting central cluster of yellow stamens. I 1790. AMT 1925. AGM 1984.

'**Roseus**' See *C.* × *pulverulentus.*

†**salviifolius** L. A low shrub with sage-like leaves and white flowers with a yellow basal stain. S Europe. C 1548.

'**Prostratus**' A dwarf form.

'**Silver Pink**' An exceptionally hardy plant. The flowers, of a lovely shade of silver-pink, are carried in long clusters. Originated as chance hybrid, possibly *C. creticus* × *C. laurifolius*, in our nurseries about 1910. AM 1919.

† × **skanbergii** LOJAC. (*C. monspeliensis* × *C. parviflorus*). One of the most beautiful with clear pink flowers. Greece. AGM 1984.

'**Sunset**' See *C.* × *pulverulentus.*

†**symphitifolius** LAM. (*C. vaginatus* AIT.) A very distinct, tall-growing plant for mildest localities with vivid magenta flowers and golden anthers. Canary Isles. I 1799.

× **verguinii** COSTE & SOULIE (*C. ladanifer* × *C. salviifolius*). The large white flowers have maroon blotches.

**villosus** See *C. creticus.*

**CITHAREXYLUM** L.—**Verbenaceae**—About 70 species of trees and shrubs related to *Lantana* and natives of the S United States, the West Indies, Mexico and S America.

†\***spicatum** RUSBY Evergreen shrub with purplish stems and opposite, leathery, dark glossy green, lanceolate leaves. The tiny, fragrant, lilac, verbena-like flowers are produced in drooping spikes during summer. Only suitable for the mildest gardens. Bolivia.

"**CITRANGE**" See × *Citroncirus webberi.*

× **CITRONCIRUS** J. INGRAM & H.E. MOORE—**Rutaceae**—(*Citrus* × *Poncirus*). An intergeneric hybrid of which only the following is known. Another intergeneric hybrid, × *Citrofortunella*, contains citrus fruits such as the limequats and the calamondin.

**webberi** J. INGRAM & H.E. MOORE (*Citrus sinensis* × *Poncirus trifoliata*). "Citrange". A large, semi-evergreen, vigorous shrub with long spines. Leaves large, trifoliolate with narrowly winged petioles; flowers, when produced, large, up to 6cm across, white, fragrant. Fruits the size of a golf ball or larger, orange or yellow. Hardy in the south of England. Garden origin 1897.

†\***CITRONELLA** D. DON—**Icacinaceae**—(*Villaresia* RUIZ & PAVON) About 20 species of evergreen trees and shrubs mainly natives of the tropics.

**mucronata** (RUIZ & PAVON) D. DON (*Villaresia mucronata* RUIZ & PAVON) A large, evergreen shrub attaining tree-size in favoured areas of the south-west. Leaves ovate, leathery, glossy green and spine-toothed, rather holly-like on young trees, becoming smooth and entire on older specimens. The small, fragrant, creamy white flowers are borne in dense panicles in June. The black, egg-shaped fruits, 5-7.5cm long are regularly produced, even on young plants in the nursery. C Chile. I 1840.

†**CITRUS** L.—**Rutaceae**—A genus of about 15 species of partially armed, semi-evergreen trees or shrubs of great economic importance for their fruits. Originally native to SE Asia, they are now extensively cultivated in warm temperate and subtropical regions of the world. A few may be grown against sunny walls in very warm, sheltered gardens, but most are best given conservatory treatment.

**ichangensis** SWINGLE "Ichang Lemon". Small to medium-sized shrub with ovate-elliptic, tapered leaves and conspicuously winged petioles, the wings as broad as the leaf blades. Flowers, when produced, white. Fruits lemon-shaped. This remarkably hardy shrub has grown outside at the Hillier Gardens and Arboretum for nearly 30 years. It can fruit freely on a warm wall. C and SW China. I about 1907.

**japonica** See *Fortunella japonica*.

**'Meyer's Lemon'** A medium-sized to large shrub with short-stalked, large, dark green leaves. Clusters of fragrant white flowers are followed by freely produced, large yellow fruits. AM 1982.

**trifoliata** See *Poncirus trifoliata*.

**CLADOTHAMNUS pyrolifolius** See *Elliottia pyrolifolia*.

**CLADRASTIS** RAF.—**Leguminosae**—A small genus of some 6 species of deciduous trees with pinnate leaves, natives of E Asia with one species in the SE United States. The following are very ornamental trees but the flowers, similar to those of the "False Acacia" (*Robinia pseudoacacia*), do not appear on young trees.

**lutea** K. KOCH (*C. tinctoria* RAF.) "Yellow Wood". A very handsome, medium-sized tree producing, in June, long, drooping, wisteria-like panicles of fragrant white flowers. The leaves turn clear yellow before falling. SE United States. I 1812. AM 1924.

**sinensis** HEMSL. The "Chinese Yellow Wood" is a remarkably beautiful and distinct July-flowering tree of medium size. The compound leaves are soft green above and glaucous beneath, and the pink-tinged, white, slightly fragrant flowers are borne in large panicles. China. I 1901 by Ernest Wilson. AM 1923. AM 1938.

**CLERODENDRUM** L.—**Verbenaceae**—A large genus of some 400 species of trees, shrubs and climbers with opposite leaves and showy flowers found mainly in tropical regions. Apart from the hardy species many are grown for greenhouse decoration.

**bungei** STEUD. (*C. foetidum* BUNGE) A remarkable, semi-woody, suckering shrub of medium height. Stems dark coloured, erect, bearing large heart-shaped leaves and large terminal corymbs of rosy-red fragrant flowers in August and September. China. I 1844 by Robert Fortune. AM 1926.

**CLERODENDRUM**—*continued*

**trichotomum** THUNB. A strong-growing, large shrub valuable for autumn effects. The white, very fragrant flowers enclosed in maroon calyces appear in August and September, and are followed by bright blue berries still with their colourful calyces. China, Japan. C 1880. FCC 1893.

**var. fargesii** (DODE) REHD. Differs in having smooth leaves and stems, and usually fruits with greater freedom. W China. I by Père Farges in 1898. AM 1911.

‡**CLETHRA** L.—**Clethraceae**—About 60 species of deciduous and evergreen shrubs or small trees native to the S United States, C and S America, SE Asia and Madeira. Closely related to the Ericaceae, they require a lime-free soil and produce small, white, fragrant flowers in long racemes or panicles in July or August. Several have peeling bark.

**acuminata** MICHX. "White Alder". A large shrub, with racemes of fragrant, cream coloured flowers; leaves yellow in autumn. SE United States. I 1806.

**alnifolia** L. The "Sweet Pepper Bush", usually not much exceeding 2m in height. Flowers in erect, terminal racemes, white or nearly white, sweetly scented in August. E North America. I 1731.

'**Paniculata**' A superior form with flowers in terminal panicles. I 1770. AM 1956. AGM 1984.

'**Rosea**' A lovely clone with buds and flowers tinged pink. Also distinct in its leaves, which carry a very healthy gloss. I 1906. 'Pink Spire' is similar.

†*‬**arborea** AIT. A magnificent large shrub or small tree with lily-of-the-valley-like flowers produced in large terminal panicles; only suitable for the mildest counties. Madeira. I 1784. AM 1912.

**barbinervis** SIEB. & ZUCC. (*C. canescens* HORT.) A medium-sized handsome Japanese species with long racemes of fragrant flowers. Leaves red and yellow in autumn. Japan. I 1870. AM 1985.

**delavayi** FRANCH. A magnificent large shrub of great beauty, requiring a sheltered site. The long, broad, many-flowered racemes of white lily-of-the-valley-like flowers are horizontally disposed over the whole plant. Injured only by exceptionally severe frost. W China. I 1913. FCC 1927.

**fargesii** FRANCH. (*C. wilsonii*) A very beautiful Chinese species attaining about 2.5m, producing, in July, pure white, fragrant flowers in panicles up to 25cm long. Rich yellow autumn colour. C China. I 1900 by Ernest Wilson. AM 1924.

†**monostachya** REHD. & WILS. A large shrub with long terminal racemes of pure white flowers. One of the most beautiful of late summer-flowering shrubs. W China. I 1903 by Ernest Wilson.

**tomentosa** LAM. A beautiful, medium-sized, summer-flowering shrub resembling *C. alnifolia*, but having greyer foliage and later flowers. SE United States. I 1731.

‡**CLEYERA** THUNB.—**Theaceae**—A small genus of about 18 species of evergreen trees and shrubs mostly of Mexico and C America but with one species in E Asia. They are related to *Eurya*, but differ in their bisexual flowers and normally entire leaves.

**fortunei** See *C. japonica* 'Tricolor'.

**japonica** THUNB. (*C. ochnacea* DC.) (*Eurya ochnacea* (DC.) SZYSZ.) (*Ternstroemia japonica*) A slow-growing shrub up to 3m, distinctive in its habit of growth, the branches rigidly spreading and densely leafy. Leaves entire, leathery, dark, shining green above often turning red in winter. Flowers small, white, very numerous in spring but not conspicuous. Japan, China, Korea, Taiwan. C 1870.

'**Tricolor**' (*C. fortunei* HOOK. f.) (*Eurya fortunei*) (*E. latifolia* 'Variegata') Leaves dark, shining green, marbled grey, with a cream margin which is flushed deep rose when young. A most attractive evergreen for favoured localities where it forms a large shrub. Introduced from Japan in 1861. AM 1963.

**ochnacea** See *C. japonica*.

†**CLIANTHUS** SOLAND. ex LINDL.—**Leguminosae**—A genus of 2 species of shrubs. The following requires a hot sunny position in a well drained soil and makes an excellent conservatory shrub. *C. formosus* G. DON is the spectacular "Sturt's Desert Pea" of Australia.

**puniceus** (G. DON) LINDL. "Parrot's Bill" "Lobster's Claw". A vigorous, semi-evergreen, scandent shrub of medium size with pinnate leaves 8-15cm long composed of 11-25 oblong leaflets. The curious claw-like flowers are brilliant red and carried in pendulous racemes during early summer. When grown outside it succeeds best against a warm south or west-facing wall. New Zealand (N Island) where it is now extremely rare. I 1831. AM 1938.

**'Albus'** Flowers white. AM 1938.

**'Flamingo'** Flowers deep rose-pink.

**'Red Cardinal'** Flowers brilliant scarlet.

**'White Heron'** Pure white flushed with green.

**CNEORUM** L.—**Cneoraceae**—A genus of 3 species of evergreen shrubs found in the Mediterranean region, the Canary Islands and Cuba.

†\***tricoccon** L. A dwarf, evergreen shrub with small yellow flowers and three-sided brownish-red fruits. Sunny well drained position. W Mediterranean region. C 1793.

†\***COLEONEMA** BARTL. & WENDL.—**Rutaceae**—A small genus of 8 species of small, tender, evergreen shrubs, natives of S Africa.

**album** (THUNB.) BARTL. & WENDL. A small dainty, white-flowered, S African shrub for the mildest localities, with aromatic, heath-like foliage. An excellent pot plant.

**COLLETIA** COMM. ex JUSS.—**Rhamnaceae**—A genus of 5 species of spiny shrubs native to S South America. The following are very distinct among cultivated plants being quite or almost leafless and bearing opposite, very prominent spines. The attractive, small, scented flowers are usually produced in summer and autumn.

**armata** See *C. hystrix*.

**cruciata** See *C. paradoxa*.

**hystrix** CLOS (*C. armata* MIERS) This robust shrub, attaining about 2.5m in height, has strong, stout rounded spines. In late summer and autumn the branches are crowded with small, fragrant, pitcher-shaped, white flowers. Chile, N Argentina. I about 1882. AM 1973.

**'Rosea'** (*C. armata* 'Rosea') Flowers pink in bud; a delightful shrub. AM 1972.

**infausta** See *C. spinosissima*.

**paradoxa** (SPRENG.) ESCALENTE (*C. cruciata* GILLIES & HOOK.) (*C. bictoniensis* LINDL.) A remarkable, rather slow-growing shrub, with branchlets transformed into formidable flat, triangular spines, crowded with small, pitcher-shaped white flowers in late summer and autumn. E Argentina, Uruguay, S Brazil. I 1824. AM 1959.

†**spinosissima** GMEL. (*C. infausta* N.E. BR.) Related to and resembling *C. hystrix* but completely glabrous. A spiny shrub of medium size. Flowers white or greenish-white, from March to June. Ecuador to Argentina. I 1823.

†**COLQUHOUNIA** WALL.—**Labiatae**—A genus of about 3 species of evergreen sub-shrubs native to the Himalaya and SE Asia.

**coccinea** WALL. A showy, Himalayan shrub, with large downy leaves and bearing scarlet tubular flowers in autumn. Requires a sunny site, preferably against a wall where it will attain 2.5-3m. Occasionally cut back by sharp frost, but usually shoots again in early summer. I before 1850. AM 1978. AM 1981 to 'Jumbesi' introduced from Nepal by Tony Schilling (Schl. 2098).

**var. vestita** (PRAIN) WALL. (*C. coccinea* var. *mollis* (SCHLECHT) PRAIN) A form with slightly woolier leaves, and orange and yellow flowers. Nepal.

**COLUTEA** L.—**Leguminosae**—Some 25 species of deciduous shrubs with a distribution ranging from S Europe to N Africa and the W Himalaya. They are very distinct on account of their large, inflated seed pods giving the common name "Bladder Sennas". They are easily grown shrubs with pinnate leaves and conspicuous, pea flowers throughout the summer. If encroaching on other plants or getting out of hand they may be hard pruned in March.

**aborescens** L. A vigorous bush up to 4m high; flowers yellow. S Europe, Mediterranean region. Often naturalised on railway embankments. I in the 16th century.

**'Bullata'** A slow-growing, dense-habited form.

**buhsei** (BOISS.) SHAPARENKO A vigorous large shrub of upright habit to 5m, the blue-green, pinnate leaves with 7-9 leaflets. Large, golden-yellow pea flowers in racemes of 2-7 are borne over a long period from June to autumn followed by conspicuous bladders. N Iran and neighbouring USSR. I by Roy Lancaster and Mrs Ala (A. and L. 7) from N Iran in 1972. AM 1987.

×**media** WILLD. (*C. arborescens* × *C. orientalis*). A strong-growing, medium-sized shrub with greyish leaves and rich, bronze-yellow flowers. Garden origin. C 1809.

**'Copper Beauty'** A selected form with blue-green leaves and bright orange flowers freely borne.

**multiflora** SHAPARENKO ex ALI An arching medium-sized shrub with purplish-red shoots and deep blue-green leaves with 11-15 leaflets. Flowers small, crimson in bud opening brick-red and becoming orange, in racemes of up to 14 in July. I by Tony Schilling from Nepal (Schl. 2165).

**orientalis** MILL. Rounded shrub of medium size with attractive glaucous leaves and copper-coloured flowers. Caucasian region. I 1710.

**COMAROSTAPHYLIS diversifolia** See *Arctostaphylos diversifolia.*

‡**COMPTONIA** AITON—**Myricaceae**—A genus of a single species related to and once included under *Myrica.*

**peregrina** (L.) COULT. "Sweet Fern". A small, suckering, aromatic shrub having downy stems and narrow, downy leaves shaped somewhat like the fronds of a small "Spleenwort" fern; small, glistening, brown catkins in spring. Thrives in lime-free soil and, if given sufficient moisture, is best in full sun. E North America. I 1714.

**CONVOLVULUS** L.—**Convolvulaceae**—A large genus of more than 200 species of mainly trailing perennials but including several shrubby species. Widely distributed mainly in temperate regions with many species in the Mediterranean area.

†*****cneorum** L. A good rock-garden shrub with silvery, silky leaves and large pale pink and white, funnel-shaped flowers in May. Full sun and well drained position. SE Europe. C 1640. AM 1977. AGM 1984.

*****COPROSMA** FORST. & FORST. f.—**Rubiaceae**—About 90 species of usually dioecious evergreen shrubs or small trees with opposite leaves mainly found in New Zealand but also occurring in Tasmania, the East Indies, New Guinea and Chile. Flowers small but many species have attractive fruits which, however, are only produced if male and female plants are grown together. In addition to the following are 3 species which are proving very hardy. These are *C. nitida* HOOK. f. from SE Australia introduced by Harold Comber and two species introduced to our nurseries by Sir Harold Hillier from New Zealand, *C. pseudocuneata* W.R.B. OLIV. and *C. tenuifolia* CHEESEM.

**acerosa** A. CUNN. One of the hardiest of the genus. A low, wiry shrub suitable for the rock-garden, with small, linear leaves, female plants with translucent blue berries. New Zealand. *C. brunnea* (KIRK) CKN. ex CHEESEM. is similar, differing in the dark brown colour of the leaves and stems.

**brunnea** See under *C. acerosa.*

†×**cunninghamii** HOOK. f. (*C. propinqua* × *C. robusta*) Medium-sized shrub, a natural hybrid from New Zealand, with linear-lanceolate, leathery leaves about 5cm long. Pale-coloured, translucent berries.

**COPROSMA**—*continued*

†×**kirkii** CHEESEM. (*C. acerosa*×*C. repens*). This hybrid occurs in the wild where the parents meet. Hardier than *C. repens*.

    **'Prostrata'** A dense, wide-spreading low shrub forming an intricately branched mound. Leaves oblong-lanceolate, to 2×0.5cm, glossy green. Excellent ground-cover in mild areas.

    **'Variegata'** A form with the leaves margined with white. AM 1982 (as a cool greenhouse plant).

†**lucida** FORST. & FORST. f. A medium-sized shrub with large, glossy, obovate leaves; fruits, when produced, reddish-orange. New Zealand.

**petriei** CHEESEM. Creeping shrub forming dense mats, quite hardy on a rock-garden. Female plants bear conspicuous blue berries. New Zealand.

**propinqua** A. CUNN. A wiry-stemmed shrub of medium size with small linear leaves; related to *C. acerosa*. Fruits blue. New Zealand.

**"CORAL BERRY"** See *Symphoricarpos orbiculatus*.

**"CORAL TREE"** See *Erythrina crista-galli*.

†*****CORDYLINE** COMM. ex R. BR. (*Dracaena* L. in part)—**Agavaceae**—A small genus of about 15 species of evergreen trees and shrubs native to New Zealand, Australia, India and S America.

**australis** (FORST. f.) HOOK. f. (*Dracaena australis* HOOK. f.) The "Cabbage Tree" of New Zealand. A conspicuous feature of gardens in the south-west. A small tree, usually forming a single trunk and bearing several stout ascending branches. Each branch is crowned by a large dense mass of long sword-like leaves. Flowers small, creamy white and fragrant, produced in large terminal panicles in early summer. I 1823. AM 1953.

    **'Purpurea'** ('Atropurpurea') A form with purple leaves.

**indivisa** (FORST. f.) STEUD. (*Dracaena indivisa* FORST. f.) A tender species differing from *C. australis* in its normally unbranched stem and dense head of much broader leaves. New Zealand. I about 1850. FCC 1860.

**CORIARIA** L.—**Coriariaceae**—An interesting small genus of some 8 species of shrubs and herbs with angled branchlets characterised by the frond-like arrangement of their leaves, and the persistence of their attractive flower petals which become thick and fleshy, enclosing the seeds. Of wide distribution.

**japonica** GRAY A pleasing, small, low-growing Japanese shrub, the arching stems making good ground cover. The red fruits are most conspicuous and the autumun foliage is attractively tinted. I before 1893. AM 1908.

**myrtifolia** L. A graceful shrub to 1.5m, with glistening black fruits. Both leaves and fruits are poisonous. Mediterranean region. I 1629.

†**napalensis** WALL. A small to medium-sized, spreading shrub with black-purple fruits. Foliage attractively tinted in autumn. Himalaya. Upper Burma. *C. sinica* MAXIM. is a hardier relative of this species which was introduced from China in 1907 by Ernest Wilson.

**sinica** See under *C. napalensis*.

**terminalis** HEMSL. An attractive small sub-shrub. The frond-like leaves give rich autumn tints. Conspicuous black fruits. Sikkim, Tibet, China. I 1897. AM 1931.

    **var. fructurubro** HEMSL. A form with very effective translucent currant-red fruits. There seems no record of the origin of this attractive form which links the black-fruited Chinese type with the yellow-fruited Sikkim form.

    **var. xanthocarpa** REHD. Translucent yellow fruits. Sikkim, E Nepal. AM 1904. FCC 1970.

**thymifolia** HUMB. A dwarf, suckering, ground-covering shrub throwing out graceful frond-like stems with pinnate leaves, the whole creating dense fern-like clumps. The insignificant flowers are followed in late summer by racemes of tiny black currant-like fruits. Mexico to Peru.

**"CORNEL"** See *Cornus*.

**CORNUS** L.—**Cornaceae**—The "Dogwoods" or "Cornels" range from creeping shrubs to trees, the majority being from 2-3m high, and comprise some 50 species widely distributed, mainly in temperate regions. They are ornamental in diverse ways, and mostly of easy cultivation. All have opposite leaves excepting *C. alternifolia* and *C. controversa*. Those grown for their attractive coloured stems should be hard pruned every other year in March.

The genus is sometimes split into several genera (here regarded as synonyms of *Cornus*) in which case *Cornus* L. sensu stricto is regarded as containing (of the species listed here) only *C. mas*, *C. officinalis*, and *C. chinensis*. The other genera involved are: *Swida* OPIZ, (*Thelycrania* (DUMORT.) FOURR.), *Chamaepericlymenum* HILL and *Benthamidia* SPACH, (*Benthamia* LINDL., *Cynoxylon* RAF., *Dendrobenthamidia* HUTCH.).

**alba** L. (*Swida alba* (L.) OPIZ) "Red-barked Dogwood". This well-known species, succeeding in wet or dry soils, forms a thicket of stems up to 3m high, the young branches being rich red in winter. Leaves colour well in autumn. Fruits white or tinged blue. Siberia to Manchuria, N Korea. I 1741.

**'Atrosanguinea'** See 'Sibirica'.

**'Aurea'** A charming form, the leaves suffused soft yellow.

**'Elegantissima'** Leaves broadly margined and mottled white. C 1900. AGM 1984. 'Sibirica Variegata' is similar.

**'Gouchaltii'** Similar to 'Spaethii' with which it is often confused but the leaves duller and with a pinkish tinge. C 1888.

**'Hessei'** (*C. hessei* KOEHNE) A remarkable and rare dwarf shrub of dense, spreading habit with crowded, narrow, purple-tinged leaves which turn deep purple in autumn as the white fruits ripen. Flowers profusely borne in dense heads up to 4cm across, purple-tinged in bud opening creamy white. Raised in Germany by Hesse. See also *C. sanguinea* 'Compressa'.

**'Kesselringii'** Stems almost black-purple. Very striking. C 1907.

**'Sibirica'** ('Atrosanguinea') ('Westonbirt') A less robust form with brilliant crimson winter shoots. There is very little of this plant now at Westonbirt. C 1838. AM 1961. AGM 1984.

**'Spaethii'** A superb form with conspicuously golden-variegated leaves. C 1884. FCC 1889. AGM 1984.

**'Variegata'** Leaves greyish-green with an irregular creamy white margin.

**alternifolia** L. f. (*Swida alternifolia* (L. f.) SMALL) A large shrub occasionally a small tree with horizontally spreading branches. Leaves alternate, sometimes giving rich autumn tints. E North America. I 1760.

**'Argentea'** ('Variegata') One of the very best silver-variegated shrubs, forming a dense bush of 2.5-3m. Leaves small with a regular creamy-white margin. C 1900. FCC 1974. AGM 1984.

**amomum** MILL. (*Swida amomum* (MILL.) SMALL) Medium-sized shrub, notable for its rich blue fruits and for its purple winter shoots. E North America. I 1683. AM 1968.

**'Ascona'** (*C. florida* × *C. nuttallii*). A wide-spreading large shrub. Flowerheads freely borne when young, 7.5cm across with 4 pointed, white bracts. The leaves colour well in autumn.

**asperifolia** HORT. See *C. drummondii*.

**baileyi** COULT. & EVANS (*Swida baileyi* (COULT. & EVANS) RYDB.) A vigorous shrub with erect reddish-brown branches up to 3m high. The leaves, which colour brilliantly in the autumn, are glaucous beneath. Fruits white. E North America. I 1892.

**bretschneideri** L. HENRY. A medium-sized shrub with usually reddish shoots and ovate leaves. Flowers creamy white in cymes, followed by bluish-black fruits. N China. I about 1800.

‡**canadensis** L. (*Chamaepericlymenum canadense* (L.) ASCHERS. & GRAEBN.) The "Creeping Dogwood" is not strictly a shrub, the 15cm shoots being renewed from ground level annually. It forms attractive carpets starred in summer with white flowers, succeeded by tight heads of vivid red fruits. Does best in sandy peat or leaf-mould. North America. I 1774. AM 1937. AGM 1984.

**CORNUS**—*continued*

**candidissima** MARSH. See *C. racemosa*.

†\***capitata** WALL. (*Benthamidia capitata* (WALL.) HARA) (*Benthamia fragifera* LINDL.) In the mildest districts this beautiful species is a small tree. Flowerheads surrounded by attractive sulphur-yellow bracts in June and July, followed in October by large strawberry-like fruits. Himalaya, W and C China. I 1825. AM 1922 (for flower), AM 1974 (for fruit).

†**chinensis** WANGER (KW.19300) A large shrub or small tree not to be confused with *C. kousa* var. *chinensis*. Green young stems and large, conspicuously veined leaves. Flowers yellow, produced in large sessile clusters on the naked branches in late winter. Collected by Kingdon-Ward in N Assam in 1950. The species also occurs in W China.

**controversa** HEMSL. (*Swida controversa* (HEMSL.) SOJAK) A magnificent tree-like species with alternate leaves. The sweeping, tabulated branches are clothed during May with broad clusters of cream coloured flowers. In autumn small black fruits are produced and at the same time the foliage often turns to a rich purple-red. Japan, China, Taiwan. I before 1880. AM 1984.

**'Variegata'** A very ornamental small tree, retaining the horizontal branching but slower growing and with striking silver margined leaves. C 1890. AGM 1984.

**drummondii** C.A. MEY. (*C. asperifolia* HORT.) A large shrub or small tree with red-brown twigs. Leaves ovate, slender-pointed; fruits white. E and C United States. C 1836.

**'Eddie's White Wonder'** (*C. florida* × *C. nuttallii*). A superb hardy large shrub or small tree of compact, upright habit producing large white flowerheads in spring. Leaves colouring brilliantly in autumn. Highly praised by its American raisers this splendid plant has proved itself here to be a first rate ornamental. Its hybrid nature is clearly shown by the bracts which only partially enclose the flower buds in winter. AM and Cory Cup 1972. FCC 1977. AGM 1984.

**florida** L. (*Benthamidia florida* SPACH) The beautiful North American "Flowering Dogwood". A large shrub or small bushy tree. Flower buds enclosed by bracts during winter. When open each flowerhead has 4 conspicuous, white, petal-like bracts in May. Foliage richly coloured in autumn. Not successful on poor, shallow, chalk soils. E United States. C 1730. AM 1951.

**'Apple Blossom'** A cultivar of American origin. Flower bracts apple blossom-pink.

**'Cherokee Chief'** An American selection with bracts of a beautiful deep rose-red. C 1958.

**'Cloud Nine'** Large, showy white bracts, free-flowering even when young.

**'Hohmann's Golden'** Similar to 'Rainbow' but of more spreading habit.

**'Pendula'** An unusual form with pendulous branches making a small shrub. C 1880.

**'Rainbow'** A form of dense, upright habit. Leaves margined with deep yellow, turning in autumn to deep red-purple margined scarlet. Bracts large, white. C 1967.

**Rubra group** (f. *rubra* (WEST) SCHELLE) This name covers all forms in which the bracts are pink to red. Our plant is a beautiful form with rosy-pink bracts; young leaves reddish. C 1889. FCC 1927.

**'Spring Song'** An American cultivar with bracts of a bright, deep rose-red. C 1962.

**'Tricolor'** See 'Welchii'.

**'Welchii'** ('Tricolor') Leaves green with an irregular creamy white margin, flushed rose, turning bronze-purple edged rosy-red in autumn. A superb but slow-growing, variegated shrub.

**'White Cloud'** An American selection with bronzed foliage, noted for its freedom of flowering and the whiteness of its large floral bracts. C 1946.

**glabrata** BENTH. (*Swida glabrata* (BENTH.) HELLER) A large shrub of dense habit. Leaves lanceolate, glossy green on both sides. Fruits white or tinged blue. W North America. I 1894.

**hemsleyi** SCHNEID. & WANGER (*Swida hemsleyi* (SCHNEID. & WANGER) SOJAK) A large vigorous shrub with reddish shoots and leaves greyish downy beneath; fruits blue-black. Distinct in the dark brown hairs on the young shoots and leaves. China. I 1908.

**hessei** See *C. alba* 'Hessei'.

**kousa** HANCE (*Benthamia japonica* SIEB. & ZUCC.) (*Benthamidia japonica* (SIEB. & ZUCC.) HARA) A large, elegant shrub. The numerous flowers, of which the white bracts are the conspicuous part, are poised on slender erect stalks covering the spreading branches in

**CORNUS kousa**—*continued*

June. Fruits strawberry-like. Conspicuous tufts of dark coloured down in the axils of the leaf veins beneath. Rich bronze and crimson autumn colour. Not recommended for poor, shallow, chalk soils. Japan, Korea. I 1875. FCC 1892. AM 1958.

**var. chinensis** OSBORN A taller, more open and equally beautiful geographical form. Leaves slightly larger and normally without tufts of down beneath. China. I 1907. FCC 1924. AM 1956. AM 1975 (for foliage). AGM 1984.

**'Gold Star'** Leaves with a large central blotch of golden yellow. In autumn the centre turns red, the margin purple. I from Japan in 1977.

**'Satomi'** A recently introduced Japanese selection with deep pink bracts. The leaves turn deep purple-red in autumn.

**'Snowboy'** Leaves grey-green with a broad white margin. Japanese origin before 1977.

**macrophylla** WALL. (*Swida macrophylla* (WALL.) SOJAK) A small tree or tall shrub with large glossy green leaves making a splendid specimen. Flowers creamy white in heads 10-15cm across in July and August. Fruits blue-black. Himalaya, China, Japan. I 1827. AM 1899.

**mas** L. "Cornelian Cherry". A large shrub or small, densely branched tree producing an abundance of small yellow flowers on the naked twigs in February. Fruits bright red, cherry-like and edible; leaves reddish-purple in autumn. C and S Europe. Long cultivated. AM 1929. AGM 1984.

**'Aurea'** A large shrub; leaves suffused yellow. C 1895.

**'Aurea Elegantissima'** ('Tricolor') A slow-growing, medium-sized bush best shaded from strong sun. Leaves variegated yellow and flushed pink. Originated about 1869. FCC 1872.

**'Hillier's Upright'** A form of broadly upright habit raised in our nurseries.

**'Macrocarpa'** A form with larger fruits.

**'Tricolor'** See 'Aurea Elegantissima'.

**'Variegata'** Leaves conspicuously margined with white, free fruiting. An outstanding variegated shrub or small tree. C 1838. AM 1981. AGM 1984.

**'Norman Hadden'** (*C. kousa* × *C. capitata*). A beautiful small tree of graceful, spreading habit developing peeling bark with age. Flowerheads with 4 taper-pointed, creamy white bracts opening in June, turning in July to deep pink. In autumn, large crops of hanging strawberry-like fruits are borne. Here, some leaves usually persist over winter while others turn soft red in autumn; in milder areas the foliage is retained until spring. A seedling which arose in the garden of Norman Hadden near Porlock, Somerset in the late 1960s and was later moved to Knightshayes Court in Devon where the original plant still grows. AM 1974 (for flower). See also *C.* 'Porlock'.

**nuttallii** AUDUB. (*Benthamidia nuttallii* (AUDUB.) MOLDENKE) A noble, medium-sized tree from W North America. Flowers appearing in May, often a few expanding in autumn, the heads with usually 6 large, white floral bracts sometimes becoming flushed pink. The flowerheads are not enclosed by bracts during the winter. Foliage turns yellow, occasionally red in autumn. Not recommended for poor, shallow chalk soils. A specimen reached 13m in the Hillier Gardens and Arboretum (1990). Many plants in this country have proved to be the hybrid *C. florida* × *C. nuttallii*. I 1835. FCC 1920. AM 1971.

**'Colrigo Giant'** A vigorous form of American origin of upright habit with very large flowerheads up to 15cm across. Found in the Columbia River Gorge after which it is named.

**'Eddiei'** See under 'Gold Spot'.

**'Gold Spot'** An unusual form, the leaves splashed, spotted and mottled yellow. 'Eddiei' is perhaps the same, it sometimes produces many of its flowers in autumn.

**'North Star'** A selected form of strong, vigorous growth with dark purple young shoots and large flowerheads.

**'Portlemouth'** A selected form with large bracts. This plant first came to notice in 1969 when a party from the International Dendrological Society visited the garden of Dr and Mrs Barker at E Portlemouth near Salcombe, Devon. Often gives good, red autumn colour.

**obliqua** RAF. (*C. purpusii* KOEHNE) Very similar to *C. amomum* but usually more loosely branched; the berries are blue or occasionally white. North America. I 1888.

**CORNUS**—*continued*

†\***oblonga** WALL. (*Swida oblonga* (WALL.) SOJAK) A rare evergreen species making a large shrub. Leaves narrowly elliptic, dark glossy green above, grey downy below. Flowers white, slightly fragrant, produced in late autumn or early winter in domed, terminal corymbs. Has lived for many years in a sheltered position in the Hillier Gardens and Arboretum. Himalaya, W China. I 1818.

**officinalis** SIEB. & ZUCC. A small tree or large shrub with attractive peeling bark and clusters of yellow flowers borne on the naked twigs in February. Red fruits and rich autumn tints. Resembles the closely related *C. mas* but coarser growing with exfoliating bark and earlier flowering, the individual flowers with longer pedicels. Japan, Korea. I about 1870. AM 1970.

**'Ormonde'** (*C. florida* × *C. nuttallii*). A large shrub similar to 'Eddie's White Wonder' but of spreading habit. Origin unknown but grown at Kew for many years as *C. nuttallii*.

**paniculata** See *C. racemosa*.

**paucinervis** HANCE (*Swida paucinervis* (HANCE) SOJAK) A slow-growing, narrow-leaved, Chinese shrub, seldom exceeding 2m; useful in producing its creamy white flowers in 8cm wide rounded clusters during July and August; fruits black. I 1907 by Ernest Wilson. AM 1911.

**'Porlock'** A small spreading tree similar to 'Norman Hadden'. Arose in 1958 as a self-sown seedling at Underway, the garden of Norman Hadden in West Porlock, Somerset where the original plant still grows. The parentage was at first thought to be *C. kousa* × *C. nuttallii*. AM 1986 (for fruit).

**pumila** KOEHNE A dense, rounded, bushy hummock. Flowers seldom seen but stated to be in dense, long-stalked cymes in July. Fruits black. Origin unknown. C 1890.

**racemosa** LAM. (*C. paniculata* L'HERIT., *C. candidissima* MARSH, *Swida racemosa* (LAM.) MOLDENKE) A medium-sized shrub. Flowers creamy-white, in panicles borne in June and July. Fruits white with bright rose-coloured stalks. Good autumn colour. E and C United States. I 1758.

**rugosa** LAM. (*Swida rugosa* (LAM.) RYDB.) An erect-growing shrub of medium size from E North America. Distinct roundish leaves densely grey woolly beneath and conspicuous clusters of white flowers in June; fruits pale blue. I 1784.

**sanguinea** L. (*Swida sanguinea* (L.) OPIZ) "Common Dogwood". Our native hedgerow species, greenish, red-flushed stems and rich purple autumn colour. Fruits black, bitter to the taste. Europe.

**'Compressa'** A remarkable dwarf form of narrow, congested, upright habit. Leaves small, to 3.5 × 2.5cm, down-curved and overlapping with deeply impressed veins. Does not flower. Grown on the Continent as *C. hessei*.

**'Winter Beauty'** A striking Dutch selection of compact habit with the shoots bright orange-yellow and red in winter. The leaves turn orange-yellow in winter. C 1987.

**stolonifera** MICHX. (*Swida stolonifera* (MICHX.) RYDB., *C. sericea* L.) A rampant suckering shrub with vigorous shoots up to 2.5m, in suitable situations forming a dense thicket of dark red stems. Fruits white. North America. I 1656.

**'Flaviramea'** Young shoots yellow to olive-green, very effective in winter, particularly when planted with the red-stemmed sorts. Ideal for moist or wet situations. C 1899. AM 1985. AGM 1984.

**'Kelseyi'** ('Kelsey Dwarf') A dwarf form of dense habit with small, crowded leaves. Winter shoots yellowish-green, red towards the tips. C 1939.

**'Nitida'** A form with the young shoots green in winter and somewhat glossy leaves.

**'White Gold'** ('White Spot') Leaves with a white margin, resembling those of *C. alba* 'Elegantissima'.

**walteri** WANGER (*Swida walteri* (WANGER.) SOJAK) An interesting tall shrub, or small tree from C and W China. Leaves oval, slender-pointed; flowers white in 8cm wide corymbs during June; fruit globose, black. C and W China. I 1907 by Ernest Wilson.

†\***COROKIA** A. CUNN.—**Cornaceae**—A small but interesting genus of 3 species of evergreen shrubs or small trees native to New Zealand. In mild areas the cultivated species make interesting medium-sized to large shrubs with small, starry, yellow flowers and often very conspicuous red or orange fruits.

**COROKIA**—*continued*

**buddlejoides** A. CUNN. "Korokio". A medium-sized shrub with slender stems and long, narrow, leathery leaves which are silvery white beneath. The small yellow star-like flowers are followed by dark red fruits. C 1836. N Island.

**var. linearis** CHEESEM. A form with even narrower, linear leaves.

**cotoneaster** RAOUL "Wire-netting Bush". The tortuous tracery of its twiggy branchlets forms a curiously attractive small to medium-sized bush, with tiny yellow flowers and orange fruits. Hardy except in cold areas. I 1875. AM 1934. N and S Islands.

**macrocarpa** T. KIRK. A tall attractive shrub with comparatively large, lanceolate leaves, silvery beneath. Flowers in axillary racemes; large red fruits. Chatham Islands.

× **virgata** TURRILL (*C. buddlejoides* × *C. cotoneaster*). A medium-sized shrub of erect habit, with oblanceolate leaves, white beneath; very small fruits, bright orange. Floriferous and free fruiting. Survives most winters uninjured. Forms complex hybrid swarms in the wild with the parents. The following make excellent and unusual hedges in mild coastal areas of the south and west. I 1907. AM 1934.

**'Cheesemanii'** ('Erecta') A very upright form with densely crowded branchlets. Fruits orange-red. Found in the wild in New Zealand before 1926.

**'Red Wonder'** A form bearing masses of deep red berries. C 1968.

**'Yellow Wonder'** Similar to 'Red Wonder' but more vigorous with larger leaves and equally profuse bright yellow fruits. C 1968.

**CORONILLA** L. —**Leguminosae**—About 55 species of deciduous and evergreen shrubs and herbs with pinnate leaves native to C and S Europe, the Mediterranean region, Africa, N Asia and China. The following are free-flowering shrubs producing umbels of bright yellow, pea flowers throughout the growing season.

**emerus** L. A hardy, medium-sized, elegant shrub with clusters of flowers in the leaf axils; seed pods slender and articulated, like a scorpion's tail. C and S Europe. Long cultivated.

**subsp. emeroides** (BOISS. & SPRUNER) HAYEK. A small shrub, the leaves with 7 instead of 9 leaflets and flowerheads more crowded and longer-stalked. C and SW Europe.

**glauca** See *C. valentina* subsp. *glauca*.

†\***valentina** L. A charming small glaucous shrub producing a mass of rich yellow flowers, with the fragrance of ripe peaches. C Mediterranean region. C 1596. AM 1977.

**subsp. glauca** (L.) BATT. (*C. glauca* L.) A medium-sized shrub for a warm wall. Leaves glaucous with fewer leaflets than the typical form. Most floriferous in April but bloom is produced intermittently throughout the year. S Europe. I 1722. AM 1957. AGM 1984.

**'Citrina'** A form with pale lemon-yellow flowers. AM 1989.

**'Variegata'** Leaves conspicuously and prettily variegated with creamy white. A form of subsp. *glauca*. AGM 1984.

†\***CORREA** ANDREWS—**Rutaceae**—A small genus of about 10 species of evergreen shrubs native to Australia and Tasmania and suitable only for the mildest gardens or for cool greenhouse cultivation. The attractive, showy and usually bell-shaped flowers are regularly and abundantly produced in late winter when under glass.

**alba** ANDREWS A small Australian shrub with oval leaves, grey beneath. Flowers funnel-shaped with reflexed lobes, creamy white. SE Australia, Tasmania. I 1793.

**backhousiana** HOOK. Medium-sized shrub with clusters of drooping, greenish-white flowers. Tasmania. AM 1977.

**decumbens** F. MUELL. A small shrub with narrow, grey-green leaves. Flowers narrowly tubular, crimson, with a greenish tip. The projecting anthers are yellow. S Australia.

× **harrisii** PAXT. (*C. pulchella* × *C. reflexa*). A beautiful, early flowering, small shrub with rose-scarlet flowers about 2.5cm long. AM 1977.

**pulchella** SWEET A small shrub with leaves green beneath. Flowers palest almond-pink, borne throughout the winter. S Australia.

**reflexa** (LABILL.) VENT. (*C. speciosa* J. DONN ex ANDREWS) A small, variable shrub with oval-oblong leaves green and often rough above. Flowers red tipped with green or all green. SE Australia, Tasmania. C 1804.

**CORYLOPSIS** SIEB & ZUCC.—**Hamamelidaceae**—A genus of 7 species of deciduous shrubs natives of the E Himalaya, China and Japan. These easily grown, exquisitely beautiful

**CORYLOPSIS**—*continued*

plants should be much more widely planted. The conspicuous drooping racemes of fragrant primrose-yellow, cup-shaped flowers are regularly carried just before the leaves in early spring. They thrive on acid or neutral soils and with the exception of *C. pauciflora* will survive indefinitely on chalk given 0.6m depth of soil.

**glabrescens** FRANCH. & SAV. A wide-spreading shrub of medium to large size with broadly ovate or orbicular leaves which are glaucescent beneath. Flowers in freely borne, slender tassels; fruits glabrous. Japan. I 1905. AM 1960. FCC 1968.

**var. gotoana** (MAK.) YAMANAKA (*C. gotoana* MAK.) This is very similar to the typical form and sometimes not separated from it. For the plant previously listed as *C. gotoana* see *C. sinensis* var. *calvescens*.

**gotoana** See *C. glabrescens* var. *gotoana* and *C. sinensis* var. *calvescens*.

‡**pauciflora** SIEB. & ZUCC. A densely branched shrub with slender stems, slowly reaching 2m by as much across. The ovate, bristle-toothed leaves, 4-6cm long, are the smallest in the genus, and are pink when young. Flowers primrose-yellow and cowslip-scented, borne in short two to three-flowered racemes opening in March, generally before those of other species; fruits glabrous. Japan; Taiwan. I about 1860 by Robert Fortune. FCC 1983. AGM 1984.

**platypetala** REHD. & WILS. See *C. sinensis* var. *calvescens*.

**sinensis** HEMSL. A large shrub or small tree to 4.5m with young branches both pubescent and with scattered, stalked glands. Leaves obovate, glaucescent and densely pubescent beneath. Flowers lemon-yellow; fruits pubescent. Said to be the commonest species in China. C and W China. I about 1901. AM 1967.

**var. calvescens** REHD. & WILS. (*C. platypetala* REHD. & WILS.) Leaves usually glabrous beneath. Some plants, previously listed as *C. gotoana* have the leaves large, orbicular and slightly convex, bluish-green above and pink-flushed when young, chalk-white beneath. W China. I 1907. AM 1981 (as *C. platypetala*).

**spicata** SIEB. & ZUCC. A spreading, hazel-like shrub of medium size. Young shoots densely pubescent. Leaves broad ovate to rounded, glaucous and softly pubescent beneath. Flowers in rather narrow racemes, to 15cm long, the petals long and bright yellow, anthers dark purple; fruits pubescent. Japan. I about 1860 by Robert Fortune. AM 1897.

**veitchiana** BEAN A very distinct, large, erect growing shrub with characteristic elongated, oblong-elliptic leaves of a bright green, edged with incurved teeth and glaucous beneath, purplish when young. Flowers in large racemes, primrose-yellow with conspicuous brick-red anthers. W China. I 1900 by Ernest Wilson. AM 1912. FCC 1974.

**willmottiae** REHD. & WILS. A medium-sized to large shrub with variable, but generally obovate leaves, often purple or reddish-purple when young, glaucescent and pubescent on the veins beneath. Flowers soft yellow, in dense showy racemes; fruits glabrous. W China. I 1909 by Ernest Wilson. AM 1912. FCC 1965. AGM 1984.

**'Spring Purple'** A selection with most attractive plum-purple young growths. Raised in our nurseries before 1969.

**wilsonii** HEMSL. A large shrub or occasionally a small tree with stellately-pubescent young branches. Leaves ovate to elliptic, glaucous and pubescent beneath, mainly on the veins. Flowers in dense pendulous racemes; fruits glabrous. C and SW China. I 1900.

**CORYLUS** L.—**Corylaceae**—The "Hazels" are a genus of about 10 species of large shrubs or small trees native of temperate regions of the N hemisphere. Flowers borne in catkins, the males pendulous and elongating in late winter or early spring making an attractive feature. Female catkins bud-like with only the bright red stigmas showing. Many are cultivated for their edible nuts.

**americana** WALT. "American Hazel". A medium-sized shrub with rounded heart-shaped leaves. Nuts 1.5cm long, slightly flattened, concealed by the long, downy husks. E North America. I 1798.

**avellana** L. "Hazel". Our native species, a large shrub or small many-stemmed tree, impressive when draped with its long yellow lambs' tails in February. Useful as a tall screening shrub. Leaves yellow in autumn. Europe, W Asia, N Africa.

**'Aurea'** A soft yellow-leaved form, excellent in contrast with the "Purple-leaf Filbert". (see *C. maxima*. 'Purpurea'). C 1864.

**CORYLUS avellana**—*continued*

**'Contorta'** "Corkscrew Hazel" "Harry Lauder's Walking Stick". Curiously twisted branches; slow-growing to about 3m. A winter feature when in catkin. Discovered in a hedgerow in Gloucestershire about 1863. AM 1917.

**'Heterophylla'** ('Laciniata') ('Quercifolia') Leaves smaller and deeply lobed. Not to be confused with *C. heterophylla*, which is the E Asian representative of *C. avellana*. C 1825.

**'Laciniata'** See 'Heterophylla'.

**'Quercifolia'** See 'Heterophylla'.

**'Pendula'** A form with weeping branches. C 1867.

**chinensis** FRANCH. "Chinese Hazel". A large tree with spreading branches, and light coloured, furrowed bark. Allied to *C. colurna*. W China. I 1900 by Ernest Wilson.

**colurna** L. "Turkish Hazel". A remarkable, large tree of very symmetrical, pyramidal form. The striking, corky corrugations of the bark are an attractive feature. SE Europe, W Asia. I 1582.

**cornuta** MARSH. (*C. rostrata* AIT.) "Beaked Hazel". Medium-sized shrub interesting on account of the slender, bristly-hairy, beaked husk which covers the nut. E and C North America. I 1745.

**jacquemontii** DECNE. A medium-sized tree related to *C. colurna*. W Himalaya. C 1898.

**maxima** MILL. "Filbert". A large shrub or small, spreading tree, with large, rounded, heart-shaped leaves. The nuts are larger and longer than those of *C. avellana* and are concealed by a large husk. Long cultivated for its nuts and parent of numerous cultivars. Balkans. I 1759.

**'Purpurea'** ('Atropurpurea') "Purple-leaf Filbert". A large shrub rivalling the purple beech in the intensity of its colouring. AM 1977. AGM 1984.

**sieboldiana** BLUME This species is mainly represented in gardens by the following variety. The typical form is a native of Japan and differs in the rounder leaf base and the shorter beak to the fruit. I 1904.

**var. mandshurica** (MAXIM. & RUPR.) SCHNEID. A large shrub related to *C. cornuta*. Leaves ovate to obovate, coarsely double-toothed and hairy beneath. Fruits in clusters of 2-4, the nut completely enclosed in the husk which is prolonged into a ridged, tubular beak up to 3.5cm long, flushed with red on the outside and divided at the apex into finger-like lobes. The whole involucre is covered in dense, white, bristly hairs. Plants grown from seed collected in Korea by Carl Miller and Sir Harold Hillier in 1976 (M. & H. 308) fruited in the Hillier Gardens and Arboretum in 1990. NE Asia. I 1882.

**tibetica** BATAL. "Tibetan Hazel". A small to medium-sized tree of wide-spreading habit, with usually numerous stems. Distinct in the spiny burr-like husks which enclose the nuts, the whole cluster resembling that of the "Spanish Chestnut" (*Castanea sativa*). C and W China. I 1901 by Ernest Wilson.

**COTINUS** MILL.—**Anacardiaceae**—A genus of 3 species now separated from *Rhus*, the "Smoke Trees" are among the most attractive of the larger summer-flowering shrubs. The leaves give rich autumn tints.

**americanus** See *C. obovatus*.

**coggygria** SCOP. (*Rhus cotinus* L.) "Venetian Sumach" or "Smoke Tree". This species which extends from C and S Europe to the Himalaya and China attains from 2.5-4m. The smooth, rounded, green leaves give good autumn tints. The fawn-coloured, plume-like inflorescences, 15-20cm long, produced in profusion in June and July, are persistent and turn smoky-grey by late summer. C 1656. AGM 1984.

**'Atropurpureus'** See f. *purpureus*.

**'Flame'** See *C.* 'Flame'.

**'Foliis Purpureis'** ('Rubrifolius') The leaves, especially when young, are of a rich plum-purple colour, changing to light red shades towards autumn. AM 1921.

**f. purpureus** (DUPUY-JAMIN) REHD. ('Atropurpureus') "Burning Bush". Leaves green. The large panicles of purplish-grey flowers resemble puffs of pink smoke from a distance. AM 1948. AGM 1984.

**'Royal Purple'** A selected form with deep wine-purple leaves, translucent in sunshine, the colour reddening towards autumn. AGM 1984. 'Notcutt's Variety' is similar.

**COTINUS coggygria**—*continued*

**'Rubrifolius'** See 'Foliis Purpureis'.

**'Velvet Cloak'** Leaves deep red-purple, the colour retained well into autumn, eventually turning red. Found as a seedling in the United States before 1962.

**Dummer Hybrids** In 1978 our propagator Peter Dummer crossed a male plant of *C. obovatus* with *C. coggygria* 'Velvet Cloak'. The following year 5 seedlings were raised as a result of this cross and have been given this collective name. They are all purple-leaved with the leaves intermediate in size between the parents and showing some of the hairs on the underside characteristic of *C. obovatus*. The fruiting plumes are purple. See also *C.* 'Grace'.

**'Flame'** A large shrub resembling *C. coggygria* but more vigorous and tree-like with larger leaves especially when young or on strong-growing shoots. A splendid plant for the rich colour of its autumn leaves which turn brilliant orange-red before falling. Large pink flower clusters are borne in summer. Originally distributed as a form of *C. obovatus* this plant is almost certainly a hybrid between the two species. Leaves on young plants in the nursery are of the same size as those of *C.* 'Grace' but become smaller on old plants. The leaves also bear some of the hairs beneath characteristic of *C. obovatus*.

**'Grace'** (Dummer Hybrids) A vigorous tall shrub with large soft purplish-red leaves turning scarlet in autumn. Large conical purplish-pink flower clusters are borne in summer. This plant, one of the Dummer Hybrids and originally designated as Clone 2, was selected as the best form and named after the raiser's wife. AM 1983. Cory Cup 1984. FCC 1990.

**obovatus** RAF. (*C. americanus* NUTT.) (*Rhus cotinoides* NUTT.) "Chittamwood". A rare American shrub or small tree which, in favourable seasons and situations, is one of the most brilliantly coloured autumn shrubs. Leaves much larger than in *C. coggygria*, turning to shades of orange, red and purple in autumn. SE United States. I 1882. AM 1904. AM 1976.

**COTONEASTER** MEDIKUS—**Rosaceae**—This important genus includes amongst its members some of the most indispensable of hardy ornamental shrubs. Though mainly ranging in height from 2-3m, they vary from prostrate creepers to small trees, and while the majority are deciduous, many are evergreen. The great variation in habit makes them suitable for many purposes from hedging and border plants to specimen and wall shrubs and plants for rock-garden or ground-cover. Brilliant autumn colour, either of leaf or fruit, are their main attributes, and their white or pink-tinged flowers often smother the branches in June, and are very attractive to bees. They are tolerant of almost all soils and conditions but are susceptible to fireblight.

Probably more than 200 species with some estimates putting the number as high as 400, widely distributed in N temperate regions of the Old World. Though often thought of as hybridising freely this probably only applies to a limited number of species and many are apomictic, thus breeding true. Although some plants known only in gardens behave as species and breed true from seed, they may have originated as hybrids in cultivation. The species are much confused in cultivation. We would like to acknowledge the assistance of Jeanette Fryer with the revision of this section.

**acuminatus** LINDL. Large shrub of vigorous, erect habit, related to *C. simonsii*. Leaves ovate-acuminate, fruits large, bright red. Himalaya. I 1820.

**acutifolius** TURCZ. Medium-sized shrub with lax branches, pointed, dull green leaves and ellipsoid red fruits. N China. C 1883.

**var. villosulus** See *C. villosulus*.

**adpressus** BOIS Dwarf, wide-spreading shrub, a gem for rock work, with bright red fruits, and small wavy-edged leaves which turn scarlet in autumn. W China. I 1896.

**var. praecox** See *C. nanshan*.

**affinis** LINDL. A large, vigorous, Himalayan shrub or small tree related to *C. frigidus*, from which it differs in its sub-globose, purple-black fruits and usually more obovate leaves. I 1828.

**var. bacillaris** See *C. bacillaris*.

**'Aldenhamensis'** A medium-sized to large shrub of wide-spreading habit. The long branches are almost fan-like and carry narrow, ribbed leaves and loose clusters of small bright red fruits. A handsome shrub of distinctive habit. AM 1927.

**COTONEASTER**—*continued*

**ambiguus** REHD. & WILS. A medium-sized shrub akin to *C. acutifolius*. Dark purple-red obovoid fruits and good autumn colour. W China. I 1903 by Ernest Wilson.

**amoenus** WILS. A pretty, semi-evergreen shrub resembling *C. franchetii*, but with smaller leaves more like those of *C. pannosus*, and of more compact, bushy habit; fruits bright red. Yunnan. I 1899 by Ernest Wilson. Several recent introductions from China are close to this species.

**apiculatus** REHD. & WILS. A dwarf shrub closely related to *C. adpressus* and often confused with it on the Continent and in North America where it is more frequently grown. It is distinguished from that species by its flat leaves and by having 3 not 2 nutlets in each fruit. China. I 1910 by Ernest Wilson. The identity of another plant grown under this name is not certain.

**applanatus** See *C. dielsianus*.

*\***'Autumn Fire'** (*C. salicifolius* 'Autumn Fire') ['Herbstfeuer']. A small, wide-spreading, semi-evergreen shrub of lax almost pendulous habit with bright glossy green, elliptic, pointed leaves. The small, bright orange-red fruits are produced in large quantities in autumn. C 1930.

**bacillaris** WALL. ex LINDL. (*C. affinis* var. *bacillaris* (WALL. ex LINDL.) SCHNEID.) A vigorous, large, spreading shrub with arching branches related to *C. affinis* but leaves glabrous beneath. The blue-black, bloomy fruits, 9mm across, are borne in large clusters. Himalaya. See also *C. ignotus*.

**boisianus** KLOTZ A medium-sized to large wide-spreading shrub related to *C. sikangensis*. Leaves dark green and deeply veined, broadly elliptic to obovate or nearly rounded, abruptly acuminate. Fruits orange-red, rather pear-shaped. China.

**bullatus** BOIS (*C. bullatus* f. *floribundus* (STAPF) REHD. & WILS.) Large shrub with large, handsome, conspicuously corrugated leaves, which colour richly in autumn, and clusters of large, bright red fruits early in the season. The foliage assumes rich autumnal colourings. One of the finest species in cultivation. W China. I 1898.

**f. floribundus** See *C. bullatus*.

**var. macrophyllus** See *C. rehderi*.

**buxifolius** This species is rare in cultivation. For the plant previously listed under this name see *C. lidjiangensis*.

*\***cashmiriensis** KLOTZ This appears to be the identity of a plant commonly grown as *C. microphyllus* var. *cochleatus*. A dense dwarf shrub with rigid shoots and tiny deep green leaves forming mats up to 60cm. Berries small, bright red. Kashmir.

**cavei** KLOTZ A small semi-evergreen shrub with reddish shoots densely covered with white bristly hairs and red warts. Leaves glossy blackish-green, more or less orbicular, mucronate at the apex and often wavy-edged, to 1.5cm long. Fruits bright red, to 1cm long, long-persistent. Two slightly different forms are grown, one introduced by the Dutch botanist Harry van de Laar, the other by Tony Schilling of Wakehurst Place. Himalaya, W China.

*\***cochleatus** REHD. & WILS. (*C. microphyllus* var. *cochleatus*) (*C. melanotrichus* HORT.) Charming, slow-growing, prostrate shrub related to *C. microphyllus* but with paler, duller green, broader leaves. W China, SE Tibet, E Nepal. AM 1930. AGM 1984. See also *C. cashmiriensis*.

*\***congestus** BAKER (*C. microphyllus* var. *glacialis* HOOK. f.) (*C. pyrenaicus* HORT.) A pretty, dense-habited, creeping evergreen forming a series of molehill-like mounds of small, bluish-green leaves. Fruits red, but not freely borne. Himalaya. A very variable species. The dwarf form described here is often referred to as 'Nanus'. I 1868.

*\***conspicuus** MARQUAND A graceful medium-sized, small-leaved shrub with strongly arching branches, wide-spreading. Flowers white, covering the plant in early summer, followed by equally numerous bright red fruits which often persist well into the following year. SE Tibet. I 1925 by Kingdon-Ward. AM 1933.

**'Decorus'** A low-growing, free fruiting form, excellent for covering banks. As a cultivar this name refers to the plant which was taken as the type. The name used at a varietal level is a synonym of *C. conspicuus*. FCC 1953. AGM 1984.

**COTONEASTER conspicuus**—*continued*

**'Highlight'** (L. S. and E. 13310) A spectacular shrub of medium size forming a dense mound of arching shoots. The masses of white flowers in May are followed by large orange-red fruits. Probably a distinct species.

**cooperi** MARQUAND A medium-sized to large shrub allied to *C. frigidus* with elliptic leaves dark matt green above. Fruits dull red turning to deep purple. N India. I 1914 by R.E. Cooper.

    **var. microcarpus** MARQUAND Differs in its smaller, reddish-purple fruits. Bhutan. Apparently introduced mixed with the typical form.

**\*'Coral Beauty'** A very dense small shrub with arching branches. Leaves ovate-elliptic, to 2cm long, glossy green. Abundant bright orange-red fruits are borne in autumn. Excellent ground-cover. C 1967. 'Royal Beauty' is similar but lower growing with salmon-red fruits. Probably *C. conspicuus* × *C. dammeri*.

**'Cornubia'** A vigorous semi-evergreen growing upwards of 6m high. Among tall-growing kinds its red fruits are perhaps the largest, and, borne in profusion, weigh down the branches. Raised at Exbury in 1930. AM 1933. FCC 1936. AGM 1984.

**\*dammeri** SCHNEID. (*C. humifusus* DUTHIE ex VEITCH) Quite prostrate, with long, trailing shoots studded in autumn with sealing-wax-red fruits. Leaves oval or obovate, prominently veined, 2.5-4cm long. An ideal shrub for covering banks and as ground-cover beneath other shrubs. China. I 1900 by Ernest Wilson. AGM 1984.

    **'Eichholz'** See *C. radicans*.

    **'Oakwood'** See *C. radicans*.

    **var. radicans** See 'Major' and *C. radicans*.

    **'Major'** (*C. dammeri* var. *radicans* HORT. not SCHNEID.) A vigorous and commonly grown form with large leaves up to 3.5cm long.

**dielsianus** PRITZ (*C. applanatus* DUTHIE) An elegant shrub of medium size crowded with sub-globose scarlet fruits and brilliantly tinted, small leaves in autumn. C China. I 1900 by Ernest Wilson. AM 1907.

    **var. elegans** See *C. elegans*.

**distichus** See *C. nitidus*.

    **var. tongolensis** SCHNEID. This is now regarded as a distinct species, *C. sichuanensis* KLOTZ. The plant previously distributed under this name is *C. splendens*.

**divaricatus** REHD. & WILS. A medium-sized shrub; one of the best and most reliable for autumn fruit and foliage. Fruits dark red. Excellent for hedging. W China. I 1904 by Ernest Wilson. FCC 1912.

**\*'Eastleigh'** (*C. prostratus* 'Eastleigh') A large, vigorous, much branched shrub with dark green leaves up to 3 × 2cm and large, deep ox-blood-red fruits in profusion. Raised in our nurseries about 1960 from seed of *C. marginatus* from which it differs in its larger, duller leaves and larger fruits.

**elegans** REHD. & WILS. A medium-sized shrub related to *C. dielsianus* and differing in its smaller, more rounded, nearly glabrous leaves; berries coral-red. China. I 1908 by Ernest Wilson.

**'Exburiensis'** A large shrub with apricot-yellow fruits becoming pink-tinged in winter. Almost identical to *C.* 'Rothschildianus'. Raised at Exbury in 1930.

**'Firebird'** A medium-sized to large shrub of spreading habit. Leaves bullate, shining dark green above, fruits large, orange-red in dense clusters. Once thought to be a hybrid of *C. bullatus* with *C. franchetii* this plant may represent a new species close to *C. sikangensis*.

**\*floccosus** (REHD. & WILS.) FLINCK & HYLMÖ (*C. salicifolius* var. *floccosus* REHD. & WILS.) A medium-sized to large shrub with small, narrow, polished leaves, shining green above, white woolly beneath, poised on slender, drooping, fan-like stems. Masses of tiny red fruits. Some plants grown under this name are *C. salicifolius*. China. I 1908 by Ernest Wilson. AM 1920. AGM 1984.

**foveolatus** REHD. & WILS. A Chinese shrub to 2.5m having comparatively large leaves which are shining, grass-green, turning orange and scarlet in autumn. Flowers pink; fruits black. I 1908 by Ernest Wilson.

**franchetii** BOIS A very graceful, medium-sized, semi-evergreen shrub, with sage-green foliage and ovoid, orange-scarlet fruits. One of the most popular species. China. I 1895 by the Abbé Soulié. AGM 1984.

**COTONEASTER frangchetii**—*continued*

**var. sternianus** See *C. sternianus*.

**frigidus** WALL. A variable, small spreading tree or large shrub, fast-growing, loaded in autumn and throughout the winter with large, heavy clusters of crimson fruits. The true plant with its large, broad elliptic leaves is now seldom seen, hybrid seedlings of the Watereri group being made to do duty for it. Himalaya. I 1824. AM 1966.

**f. fructu-luteo** (BEAN) REHD. ('Fructuluteo') ('Xanthocarpus') Large bunches of creamy yellow fruits. AM 1932.

**\*glabratus** REHD. & WILS. A very distinct medium-sized to large, spreading shrub with glossy purplish arching shoots. Leaves dark glossy green, purple-tinged in winter, elliptic-oblanceolate and taper-pointed, glaucous and reticulate beneath, to 10cm long. Small bright red fruits are profusely borne in broad clusters. W China. I 1906 by Ernest Wilson and later by Roy Lancaster and Keith Rushforth.

**\*glaucophyllus** FRANCH. A large-sized, July-flowering semi-evergreen shrub with oval leaves, correspondingly late in berrying. At all seasons a handsome species. W China. C 1915. AM 1924.

**f. serotinus** See *C. serotinus* and *C. meiophyllus*.

**var. vestitus** See *C. vestitus* and *C. serotinus*.

**glomerulatus** W.W. SM. (*C. nitidifolius* MARQUAND) A medium-sized shrub of graceful habit with slender, lax stems and wavy-edged, shining green leaves. The clusters of white flowers are followed by small crimson fruits. A distinct and attractive species. Often rich crimson autumn colours. SW China. I 1924 by George Forrest.

**\*'Gnom'** (*C. salicifolius* 'Gnom') A dwarf shrub with slender, purplish, arching shoots making a low, wide mound. Leaves lance-shaped, up to 3 × 1cm, dark glossy green, bronze-tinged in winter. Small bright red berries ripen in November but are not usually freely borne. Excellent ground-cover. Raised in Germany about 1938. AGM 1984.

**'Gracia'** See under *C.* 'Valkenburg'.

**\*harrovianus** WILS. A graceful, arching, evergreen attaining about 3m and very conspicuous in bloom. The attractive red fruits are not fully coloured until late December. China. I 1899 by Ernest Wilson. AM 1905.

**harrysmithii** FLINCK & HYLMÖ Small shrub occasionally up to 2m, branchlets horizontally arranged. Closely related to *C. nitens* but less vigorous, and with smaller leaves, flowers and fruits. Collected in W China in 1934 by the Swedish collector Dr Harry Smith. AM 1987.

**hebephyllus** DIELS Medium-sized shrub with long, arching branches, wreathed with white flowers followed by large, dark red, globular fruits. China. I 1910.

**\*henryanus** (SCHNEID.) REHD. & WILS. A large, wide-growing evergreen or semi-evergreen shrub with long, dark green corrugated leaves, downy on both sides at least when young; fruits crimson. Closely related to *C. salicifolius*. The true plant is elusive in cultivation. C China. I 1901 by Ernest Wilson. AM 1920.

**hjelmqvistii** FLINCK & HYLMÖ (*C. horizontalis* 'Robusta') A wide-spreading small shrub with arching branches and broadly obovate to nearly orbicular glossy green leaves up to 2cm long turning red in autumn. Fruits red, to 8mm across. It was found among seedlings of *C. horizontalis* in a Belgian nursery in 1954 and is occasionally seen mixed with that species. Probably a native of W China.

**horizontalis** DECNE. A low-growing shrub of spreading habit, with branches of characteristic "herring-bone" pattern. Invaluable for north or east walls or for covering banks, etc giving rich colour of fruit and leaf in late autumn and winter. W China. I about 1870 by Père David. FCC 1897. AGM 1984.

**var. perpusillus** See *C. perpusillus*.

**'Robusta'** See *C. hjelmqvistii*.

**'Saxatilis'** A flat-growing, prostrate form with distinctive wide-spreading fan-like branches and small leaves. C 1950.

**'Variegatus'** Especially pleasing in autumn when the small, cream margined leaves are suffused with red. C 1922. AGM 1984.

**humifusus.** See *C. dammeri*.

**hummelii** FLINCK & HYLMÖ nom. ined. A medium-sized shrub related to *C. moupinensis* from which it differs in its narrower, longer stalked, long acuminate, glossier and less deeply

**COTONEASTER hummelii**—*continued*

veined leaves, bronze when young, and longer duller fruits to 11mm. It is named after David Hummel (1893-1984), who collected many plants in China. He was the medical doctor of the Swedish expeditions to China 1927-31 and 1933-34. Some plants distributed as *C. moupinensis* belong here. China.

**hupehensis** REHD. & WILS. A medium-sized shrub of dense yet graceful habit. The oval leaves are interspersed with numerous white flowers in May followed by large, solitary bright red fruits on long slender stalks. W China. I 1907 by Ernest Wilson.

*"**Hybridus Pendulus**' A very striking evergreen or semi-evergreen, with glossy leaves, and long, prostrate branches which carry brilliant red fruits in abundance during autumn and winter. When grown on a stem makes an attractive, small, weeping tree. Garden origin. Variously claimed to be a hybrid of *C. dammeri* with either *C. frigidus* or *C. salicifolius*. AM 1953.

**ignavus** WOLF Medium-sized shrub closely related to *C. melanocarpus*, with many-flowered drooping clusters of pink flowers. Fruits purple-black. E Turkestan. I 1880.

**ignotus** KLOTZ A large, upright shrub with arching branches and conspicuously blunt, broadly elliptic to obovate leaves rounded at the shoot tips; striking in flower and when carrying masses of jet-black, bloomy fruits 11mm across. In common with related species the fruit is open at the top exposing the nutlets. Himalaya from Afghanistan to W Nepal. Some plants grown as *C. affinis* var. *bacillaris* belong here.

'**Inchmery**' A large shrub or small tree raised at Exbury and producing bunches of large, salmon-pink fruits yellow at first. In general appearance closely approaching *C. frigidus*.

**insignis** POJARK. A tall, elegant, Himalayan shrub or small tree with long, sweeping branches, reddish-purple when young. The leaves are orbicular to obovate, emarginate and mucronate at the apex, and usually broadly cuneate at the base. Fruits blackish-purple. C Asia. See also *C. lindleyi*.

**integerrimus** MED. (*C. vulgaris* LINDL.) An erect branched shrub, usually less than 2m high, with roundish leaves, pink-tinged flowers and red fruits. Widely distributed from Europe to N Asia. The plant which still survives on Great Orme Head above Llandudno, N Wales, where it was first discovered in 1783 is now regarded as a distinct species which grows nowhere else.

*****integrifolius** (ROXB.) KLOTZ (*C. microphyllus* HORT.) (*C. microphyllus* var. *thymifolius* (LINDL.) KOEHNE not HORT.) Dwarf, glossy-leaved evergreen with extra large, globose, deep pink fruits, much used for draping walls and banks. Extremely tough and hardy. Commonly cultivated as *C. microphyllus*. Himalaya, SW China. I 1824.

'**John Waterer**' See *C. × watereri* 'John Waterer'.

*****lacteus** W.W. SM. A medium-sized shrub distinct in its large, oval, leathery leaves which are grey tomentose beneath. Fruits red, rather small but carried in broad clusters, ripening late in the year and lasting well after Christmas. China. Introduced by George Forrest in 1913. AM 1935. AGM 1984.

**laxiflorus** LINDL. (*C. melanocarpus* var. *laxiflorus* (LINDL.) SCHNEID.) A medium-sized shrub with dark green leaves woolly beneath and pink flowers in large drooping clusters; fruits black; leaves colouring early in the autumn. Siberia. C 1826.

*****lidjiangensis** KLOTZ Dwarf shrub of dense habit with small dull green leaves and small long-persistent red fruits ripening late. Suitable for the rock-garden. Previously listed as *C. buxifolius* which is very rare in cultivation. Yunnan, China.

**lindleyi** STEUD. (*C. nummularius* LINDL. not FISCH. & MEY.) Though often given as a synonym of *C. insignis* plants grown under this name differ from that species in being less vigorous with more orbicular leaves rounded to truncate, sometimes emarginate at the apex which is more distinctly mucronate and with the fruits fleshier and ripening slightly later. NW Himalaya, C Asia. I 1824.

*****linearifolius** (KLOTZ) KLOTZ (*C. microphyllus* var. *thymifolius* HORT. not (BAKER) KOEHNE) A dwarf, dainty shrub with extremely small, narrow, shining, deep green leaves and small, deep pink, persistent berries. A superb rock plant. Nepal. I 1852.

**lucidus** SCHLECHT. An upright-growing, Siberian species of medium height, with pink and white flowers followed by lustrous, black fruits. The dark, glossy leaves give brilliant autumn colour. Altai Mts. I 1840.

**COTONEASTER**—*continued*

**\*marginatus** LINDL. ex SCHLECHT. (*C. prostratus* var. *lanatus*) (*C. buxifolius* BAK. not LINDL.) (*C. wheeleri* HORT.) A medium-sized to large spreading shrub with long arching branches, dark glossy green leaves up to 1.5cm long and crimson-pink berries. Himalaya.

**marquandii** KLOTZ A medium-sized shrub of upright habit related to *C. nitidus* with densely hairy young shoots and small, dark glossy green leaves turning scarlet in autumn. The very conspicuous orange-red fruits persist well into the following year. Originally described from a plant grown at Bodnant under KW 6778. Himalaya, Burma, Bhutan.

**\*meiophyllus** (W.W. SM.) KLOTZ A medium-sized shrub related to *C. glaucophyllus* with pink-tinged young shoots. Leaves ovate-elliptic to 5.5cm long, glabrous and glaucous beneath. Fruits small, ripening very late and long-persistent. Has been confused with *C. serotinus*. China.

**melanocarpus var. laxiflorus** See *C. laxiflorus*.

**\*microphyllus** LINDL. A dwarf, stiffly branched spreading shrub forming a low mound. Leaves elliptic to obovate, to 1cm long, rounded to notched at the apex. Tiny white flowers are followed by small deep reddish-pink fruits. Himalaya. Several plants are grown under this name. AGM 1984. See also *C. integrifolius*.

    **var. cochleatus** See *C. cochleatus* and *C. cashmiriensis*.

    **var. thymifolius** See *C. linearifolius* and *C. integrifolius*.

**monopyrenus** (W.W. SM.) FLINCK & HYLMÖ A large semi-evergreen or deciduous shrub of rounded habit. Leaves elliptic, obtuse to emarginate and mucronate at the apex, sea-green and glabrous above, grey tomentose beneath when young. White flowers with deep pink sepals are profusely borne in small corymbs along the shoots in May. Fruits dark red becoming deep purple, bloomy. Yunnan, China.

**moupinensis** FRANCH. A medium-sized shrub similar to *C. bullatus*, but with fruits dark red, turning glossy black, 7-9mm long. Leaves broad elliptic-ovate, abruptly acuminate, matt green, giving rich autumn tints. W China. I 1907.

**mucronatus** FRANCH. An erect species of medium height with green, slenderly-pointed leaves and clusters of orange-red fruits. China. Closely related to *C. acuminatus*.

**multiflorus** BUNGE A large spreading shrub, as free in flower as hawthorn, but more graceful; fruits large, bright red, ripening in August. NW China. I 1837.

**nanshan** VILM. (*C. adpressus* var. *praecox* (VILM.) BOIS & BERTHAULT) (*C. praecox* VILM.) A vigorous dwarf shrub with arching branches related to *C. adpressus* but with larger leaves and growing up to 1m high and 2m across. Fruits extra large, orange-red. Autumn colour brilliant red. W China. I 1905.

    **'Boer'** Lower growing and wider spreading with glossier, less wavy leaves and brighter coloured, much longer-lasting fruits. Found in Holland in the 1930s.

**newryensis** LEMOINE A rare, erect branched shrub of medium to large size, closely related to *C. franchetii*; conspicuous orange-red fruits. Origin probably China. C 1911.

**nitens** REHD. & WILS. A very graceful shrub up to 2m with slender drooping branches, the polished leaves being disposed in an almost frond-like arrangement and giving brilliant autumn colour; fruits elliptic, black. W China. I 1910 by Ernest Wilson.

**nitidifolius** See *C. glomerulatus*.

**nitidus** JACQUES (*C. distichus* LANGE) (*C. rotundifolius* HORT. not WALL. ex LINDL.) An excellent, slow-growing deciduous or semi-evergreen shrub of medium size, with rigid, wide-spreading branches, small polished leaves and large, bright scarlet, elliptic fruits persisting until spring. Himalaya, SW China. I 1825.

**nummularius** See *C. lindleyi*.

**obscurus** REHD. & WILS. An uncommon species of medium size; leaves yellow-grey beneath; fruits obovoid, dark red. W China. I 1910 by Ernest Wilson.

**orbicularis** See under *C. sherriffii*.

**\*pannosus** FRANCH. A medium-sized shrub with long, slender, arching branches. It resembles *C. franchetii* but has smaller sage-green leaves and small fruits which are rounded, deep red and colour later. W China. I 1888 by the Abbé Delavay.

**perpusillus** (SCHNEID.) FLINCK & HYLMÖ A charming dwarf shrub related to *C. horizontalis* but with smaller leaves. W China. I 1908 by Ernest Wilson. AM 1916.

**'Pink Champagne'** A large, vigorous, dense-growing shrub with slender arching branches and narrow leaves approaching the habit of *C. salicifolius*. Fruits small but plentifully produced, at first yellow becoming pink-tinged.

COTONEASTER—*continued*

**praecox** See *C. nanshan*.

**prostratus** See *C. rotundifolius*.

  **'Eastleigh'** See *C.* 'Eastleigh'.

  **var. lanatus** See *C. marginatus*.

**pyrenaicus** See *C. congestus*.

**racemiflorus** (DESF.) K. KOCH A widely distributed species, characterised by its tall, slender, arching branches and orbicular leaves, grey-white beneath. Fruits brick-red. The combination of the leaves and fruit in a September sun is most arresting. N Africa to W and C Asia. C 1829.

  **var. veitchii** See *C. veitchii*.

**\*radicans** (SCHNEID.) KLOTZ (*C. dammeri* var. *radicans* SCHNEID. not HORT.) (*C. dammeri* 'Oakwood') (*C. dammeri* 'Eichholz') A prostrate shrub related to *C. dammeri* with which it is sometimes confused but with smaller, generally obovate, longer-stalked leaves which lack the deep veins of *C. dammeri* and flowers generally in pairs. W China.

**rehderi** POJARK. (*C. bullatus* var. *macrophyllus* REHD. & WILS.) An extremely handsome medium-sized to large shrub of open habit with large, dark-green deeply veined leaves and profuse deep red berries. W China. AM 1912.

**roseus** EDGEW. A small, loose-growing shrub related to *C. integerrimus*, occasionally reaching about 2m. Leaves oval, mucronate, quite smooth. Flowers pink-tinged in small clusters followed by small, red, obovoid fruits. NW Himalaya, Afghanistan. I 1882.

**'Rothschildianus'** A large shrub possessing a distinctive spreading habit when young. Large clusters of creamy yellow fruits. AGM 1984. 'Exburiensis' is very similar. Both were raised at Exbury, Hants.

**\*rotundifolius** WALL. ex LINDL. (*C. prostratus* BAK.) (*C. microphyllus* var. *uva-ursi* LINDL.) A small, vigorous, semi-prostrate Himalayan species with long arching branches clothed with small glossy leaves; fruits large, rose-red. See also *C. nitidus*. I 1825.

**'Royal Beauty'** See under 'Coral Beauty'.

**rubens** W.W. SM. Small, free-berrying shrub of spreading habit. The solitary flowers have pink-tinged petals followed by red fruits. W China. I 1927. AM 1924.

**\*rugosus** PRITZ. (*C. salicifolius* var. *rugosus* (PRITZ.) REHD. & WILS.) This plant appears to be not in cultivation. The following description is of the plant grown under this name which probably represents a new species. A medium-sized shrub with arching branches related to *C. floccosus* but with broader and darker leaves deeply veined above, white tomentose beneath and with larger flowers, pink in bud and fruits which persist long on the branches. One of the most ornamental species. I 1907 by Ernest Wilson (Wils. 335). AM 1912.

**'Sabrina'** See *C. splendens*.

**'St Monica'** A semi-evergreen hybrid with leaves which colour brightly before falling in late winter. It forms a large shrub and bears heavy crops of bright red fruits. Found in the garden of the St Monica Home for the Aged in Bristol.

**\*salicifolius** FRANCH. An invaluable but variable evergreen, tall and graceful, carrying heavy crops of small, bright red fruits in autumn. A parent of innumerable hybrids. China. I 1908.

  **'Autumn Fire'** See *C.* 'Autumn Fire'

  **'Avondrood'** See 'Repens'.

  **var. floccosus** See *C. floccosus*.

  **'Fructuluteo'** An interesting form with yellow fruits.

  **'Parkteppich'** A scrambling, partially prostrate shrub covered with small red fruits in autumn. C 1950.

  **'Repens'** ('Avondrood') A prostrate shrub with very narrow leaves and small red fruits. An excellent ground-cover. C 1948.

  **var. rugosus** See *C. rugosus*.

**'Salmon Spray'** A medium-sized free-fruiting shrub producing large leafy sprays of salmon-red fruits, akin to *C. henryanus*. Raised in our nurseries before 1940.

**serotinus** HUTCHINS. (*C. glaucophyllus* f. *serotinus* (HUTCHINS.) STAPF) (*C. glaucophyllus* var. *vestitus* HORT. in part not W.W. SM.) A vigorous bush to 5m or more related to *C. glaucophyllus* but with the blue-green leaves larger and tomentose beneath. It flowers

**COTONEASTER serotinus**—*continued*

profusely in July and it is December before the fruits take on their red colour. W China. I from Yunnan, China in 1907 by George Forrest. FCC 1919. See also *C. meiophyllus*.

**sherriffii** KLOTZ (*C. orbicularis* HORT. not SCHLECHT.) A medium-sized to large deciduous or semi-evergreen shrub of spreading habit. Leaves small, broad-elliptic, greyish hairy beneath, turning purplish in autumn. Fruits top-shaped red, singly or in pairs along the secondary twigs. Sometimes grown as *C. conspicuus*. SE Tibet.

**sikangensis** FLINCK & HYLMÖ Medium-sized shrub related to *C. obscurus*, differing in its more upright habit, thicker leaves and its shiny orange-red fruits which are profusely borne. Collected by Dr Harry Smith in W China in 1934.

**simonsii** BAK. A well-known, semi-evergreen, erect growing shrub, much used in plantations and for hedges. Fruits large, scarlet. Himalaya (Nepal to Bhutan). I 1865. AGM 1984.

*'**Skogholm'** A dwarf, evergreen shrub of wide spreading habit. Leaves small; fruits small, obovoid, coral-red in autumn but not freely produced. A hybrid of *C. dammeri* selected in 1941.

**splendens** FLINCK & HYLMÖ A handsome species up to 2m, related to *C. dielsianus*. The arching shoots with small, greyish-green rounded leaves, are studded with large, obovoid, bright orange fruits in autumn. W China. I 1934 by Dr Harry Smith. 'Sabrina' is a seedling which was found in the garden of Mr Norman Hadden in Somerset. It was originally thought to be a hybrid between *C. horizontalis* and *C. franchetii* but appears identical to *C. splendens*. It received an AM in 1950. Plants previously listed as *C. distichus* var. *tongolensis* belong here.

*'**sternianus** (TURRILL) FLINCK & HYLMÖ (*C. franchetii* var. *sternianus* TURRILL) (*C. wardii* HORT. in part) This excellent more or less evergreen shrub, one of the best of all cotoneasters, has, in the past, been widely distributed wrongly under the name of *C. wardii*. Leaves sage-green above and silvery-white beneath. Flowers pink, fruits large, sub-globose, bright orange-red. Produced in great abundance. S Tibet, N Burma. I 1913. AM 1939 (as *C. wardii*).

*'**Streib's Findling'** A prostrate shrub of dense, congested growth with low, arching branches and tiny dark green leaves. Sometimes said to be a hybrid of *C. dammeri* to which it bears no resemblance. C 1960.

**tomentellus** POJARK. A small to medium-sized, spreading shrub with arching branches, young shoots grey-hairy becoming purplish. Leaves broadly elliptic to obovate up to 3.5cm long, rounded and mucronate at the apex, grey-green and hairy on both sides. Fruits bright red contrasting effectively with the foliage. W Sichuan, China. I by Ernest Wilson.

**tomentosus** LINDL. (*C. nebrodensis* (GUSS.) C. KOCH) A rare, erect branched shrub from the European Alps and W Asia. The rounded leaves are white tomentose beneath, and perhaps the woolliest of the genus; flowers pink, fruits large, brick-red, colouring in August. I 1759.

*'**turbinatus** CRAIB An elegant, large, July-flowering shrub of upright habit; leaves elliptic to obovate, deep blue-green above, grey downy beneath; fruits small, bright scarlet, top-shaped, ripening in October. China. I 1910.

**uniflorus** BUNGE Small shrub closely related to *C. integerrimus* but with smaller leaves and usually solitary flowers. C Asia, W China. C 1907.

**'Valkenburg'** (*C. horizontalis* × *C. floccosus*) A small semi-evergreen shrub of dense habit with wide-spreading stems reaching 2m tall; leaves turn orange, scarlet and yellow in autumn. Raised by Broertjes in Holland in 1951. 'Gracia', from the same cross is similar but lower growing, to 60cm with broader, glossier, more deeply veined leaves purplish in autumn.

**veitchii** (REHD. & WILS.) KLOTZ (*C. racemiflorus* var. *veitchii* REHD. & WILS.) A medium-sized to large wide-spreading shrub with purplish shoots grey-hairy when young. Leaves ovate, to 4.5cm long, tomentose beneath. Large crimson berries with a slight bloom like small cherries 1.5cm across ripen early. China. I 1900.

**vestitus** (W.W. SM.) FLINCK & HYLMÖ (*C. glaucophyllus* var. *vestitus* W.W. SM.) A medium-sized shrub similar to *C. glaucophyllus* but with the leaves densely tomentose beneath. W China. See also *C. serotinus*.

# TREES AND SHRUBS

**COTONEASTER**—*continued*

**villosulus** (REHD. & WILS) FLINCK & HYLMÖ (*C. acutifolius* var. *villosulus* REHD. & WILS.) A large shrub with arching branches and dark glossy green, ovate, taper-pointed leaves which turn purple and red in autumn. Fruits blackish-purple covered with brown hairs. W China. I 1900.

**wardii** HORT. not W.W. SM. A stiff, erect branched deciduous shrub of moderate size. Leaves dark, glossy green above, white beneath. Berries bright orange-red, top-shaped. An apparently un-named and probably Chinese species related to *C. franchetii*. The true plant is probably not in cultivation. *C. sternianus* has also been grown under this name.

*×**watereri** EXELL. Variable semi-evergreen hybrids between *C. frigidus*, *C. henryanus* and *C. salicifolius* and their forms. All are completely hardy, medium to large shrubs or occasionally small trees of strong vigorous growth, with long leaves and heavy crops of normally red or orange-red fruits. There are many named clones. AM 1951.

**'John Waterer'** A large, semi-evergreen shrub, its long spreading branches laden with bunches of red fruits in autumn. C 1928. AM 1951. AGM 1984.

**zabelii** SCHNEID. A medium-sized species of arching, spreading growth. Fruits obovoid, dark red in short stalked pendulous clusters. China. I 1907 by Ernest Wilson. AM 1912.

**"COTTONWOOD"** See *Populus deltoides*.

**"CRAB APPLE"** See *Malus*.

**"CRANBERRY"** See *Vaccinium oxycoccos*.

+**CRATAEGOMESPILUS** SIMON-LOUIS ex BELLAIR (*Crataegus* + *Mespilus*)—**Rosaceae**—Interesting graft hybrids (chimaeras) between hawthorn and medlar.

**dardarii** SIMON-LOUIS (*C. monogyna* + *M. germanica*). Both the following originated on the same tree. They are ornamental, wide-spreading, small trees especially attractive for their comparatively large white flowers and yellow and orange autumn tints.

**'Bronvaux'** "Bronvaux Medlar". The original hybrid, consisting of a central core of hawthorn and an outer envelope of medlar. The shoots are occasionally thorny. Leaves like those of the medlar, but smaller. Fruits also medlar-like but smaller and in clusters. Occasional branches revert to either parent. Originated in the garden of Mons Dardar at Bronvaux, near Metz, France, about 1895.

**'Jules d'Asnières'** (+ *C. asniersii*) Occurred at the same time and on the same tree as 'Bronvaux', but in this case the medlar forms the central core and hawthorn the outer envelope. Young shoots woolly; leaves varying from entire to deeply lobed. Fruits similar to those of the hawthorn.

**grandiflora** See × *Crataemespilus grandiflora*.

**CRATAEGUS** L.—**Rosaceae**—The "Thorns" are among the hardiest and most adaptable trees, giving a good account of themselves even in industrial areas, and in windswept coastal districts. When established they are tolerant of both dryness and excessive moisture. Most are wide-spreading, small trees or large shrubs with attractive autumn tints. Except where otherwise stated the flowers are white, and open in May and June, and the fruits are red.

Although more than 1000 species have been described from North America alone many of these are now regarded as hybrids or forms of variable species and the true number is probably more like 200.

**altaica** (LOUD.) LANGE "Altai Mountain Thorn". A small tree from C Asia with strongly lobed, finely toothed leaves, bearing bright yellow fruits 1.5cm in diameter. I 1876.

**arkansana** SARG. A small elegant North American tree with often thornless branches. Fruits bright red, as much as 2.5cm across. Arkansas. I 1902.

**arnoldiana** SARG. A beautiful small tree with shallowly lobed leaves. Fruits large, like red cherries. NE United States. I 1901. AM 1936.

**azarolus** L. "Azarole". A large shrub or small tree, native of N Africa and W Asia which, although introduced in the 17th century, is still rare in cultivation. The comparatively

**CRATAEGUS azarolus**—*continued*

large white flowers, produced in dense clusters, have purple anthers. The edible fruits are usually orange or pale yellow. Leaves rhomboid, wedge-shaped at the base. C 1640. AM 1976.

**calpodendron** See *C. tomentosa*.

**canbyi** SARG. Small bushy tree, leaves glossy green, serrate and shallowly lobed; fruits dark shining crimson, almost as large as cherries. NE United States. I 1901.

× **carrierei** See *C. × lavallei* 'Carrierei'.

**champlainensis** SARG. Small tree related to *C. arnoldiana*, from which it differs in its more heart-shaped leaves. North America. I 1901.

**chlorosarca** MAXIM. A small, normally thornless tree, notable for its pyramidal habit and dark purple-brown shoots. Leaves shallowly lobed, dark and glossy above; flowers white with pink anthers, fruits dark purple-black. Japan. C 1880.

**coccinea** See *C. intricata* and *C. pedicellata*.

**coccinioides** ASHE A small, round-headed tree with large red fruits. The young leaves are tinged red when opening and in the autumn the foliage gives very good colouring. E United States. I 1883.

**collina** CHAPM. Related to *C. punctata*. Leaves nearly glabrous; fruits large and red. C and E United States. C 1889.

**cordata** See *C. phaenopyrum*.

**crus-galli** L. "Cockspur Thorn". A wide-spreading, small glabrous tree, with thorns often up to 8cm long. Attractive in leaf, flower and fruits, the latter often lasting well into the New Year. Often confused with *C. prunifolia*. E and C North America. I 1691.

**var. oblongata** SARG. A horizontally branched small tree with narrow oblong-elliptic leaves and brighter coloured, oblong fruits.

**var. pyracanthifolia** AIT. Forms a small, picturesque, thornless, horizontally branched tree, with narrower leaves. A mature standard specimen makes a perfect umbrella shape.

**dahurica** KOEHNE An uncommon small species from SE Siberia, and one of the earliest to come into growth; fruits orange-red.

× **dippeliana** LANGE (*C. × leeana* (LOUD.) BEAN) A free-flowering, small tree, a hybrid of *C. tanacetifolia*. Fruits light orange-red. Garden origin about 1830.

**douglasii** LINDL. (*C. rivularis* NUTT.) Small tree with slender, often drooping branches and shining, dark green, often rounded leaves. Fruits black and shining. North America. I 1828.

**dsungarica** ZAB. A small tree with spiny branches, large flowers and purplish-black fruits. SE Siberia, Manchuria. AM 1931.

**durobrivensis** SARG. A large shrub, one of the most ornamental of North American thorns. The flowers are possibly the largest in the genus, and the large, red fruits remain until midwinter. New York State. I 1901.

**ellwangeriana** SARG. Small tree with ascending branches and oval leaves. Large bright crimson fruits. North America. C 1900. AM 1922.

**flabellata** (SPACH) K. KOCH A large shrub or small tree with thorny stems and fan-shaped, double toothed leaves. Fruits crimson. SE Canada, NE United States. C 1830.

**flava** AIT. "Yellow Haw". A very distinct small tree with small leaves and conspicuous ellipsoid, orange-yellow fruits. SE United States.

× **grignonensis** MOUILLEF. A small tree, a hybrid of *C. stipulacea*. Late in flowering and ripening its large, bright red fruits. Leaves remain green until winter. Origin about 1873.

**holmesiana** ASHE An outstanding small tree. The large white flowers are followed by conspicuously large, rather oblong red fruits. NE United States. I 1903.

**intricata** LANGE (*C. coccinea* L. in part) Large shrub or small tree with erect or spreading branches. Fruits reddish-brown. E North America. I 1730.

**jackii** SARG. Medium-sized shrub with spiny stems and large, dark red fruits. Canada. I 1903.

**jonesiae** SARG. A small tree particularly noted for its large, bright, glossy, red fruits. NE United States, SE Canada. AM 1977.

**korolkowii** See *C. wattiana*.

**laciniata** UCRIA (*C. orientalis* BIEB.) A beautiful, small oriental tree, distinguished by its deeply cut, downy leaves, dark green above and grey beneath. Fruits large, coral-red or yellowish-red. Orient. I 1810. AM 1933. FCC 1970. AGM 1984.

**CRATAEGUS**—*continued*

**laevigata** (POIR.) DC. (*C. oxyacantha* AUCT. not L., *C. oxyacanthoides* THUILLIER) Less common as a native than *C. monogyna* from which it differs in its less deeply lobed leaves and flowers with usually 2 styles (usually 1 in *C. monogyna*). Many of the following clones are probably hybrids (*C. × media*) between the two species, all making large shrubs or small trees, and are very showy when covered with flowers in May. NW and C Europe (incl British Isles).

**'Aurea'** Fruits yellow. AM 1976.

**'Coccinea Plena'** See 'Paul's Scarlet'.

**'Gireoudii'** Young leaves prettily mottled pink and white. C 1890. AM 1972.

**'Masekii'** Flowers double; pale rose. C 1899.

**'Paul's Scarlet'** ('Coccinea Plena') Flowers double; scarlet. Originated as a sport of 'Rosea Flore Pleno' in a garden in Hertfordshire in 1858. FCC 1867. AGM 1984.

**'Plena'** Flowers double; white. C 1770.

**'Punicea'** Flowers single; scarlet, with a pronounced white eye. C 1828. AM 1990 (as 'Crimson Cloud').

**'Rosea'** Flowers single; pink. C 1796.

**'Rosea Flore Pleno'** Flowers double; pink. AGM 1984.

× **lavallei** HERINCQ ex LAV. (*C. crus-galli × C. stipulacea*). (*C. carrierei* VAUVEL ex CARR.) The plant previously known under this name is now recognised as a cultivar to distinguish it from other hybrids of the same parentage.

**'Carrierei'** A small, dense-headed tree, distinguished by its long, glossy, dark green leaves which often remain until December. Fruits orange-red persisting throughout the winter and very colourful against the dark foliage. Garden origin about 1870. AM 1924. AGM 1984.

× **leeana** See *C. × dippeliana*.

**macracantha** LOUD. A North American tree or shrub up to 5m high. Leaves attractively coloured in autumn. Fruits bright crimson. Has the longest spines of all thorns sometimes up to 10-13cm in length. I 1819.

**maximowiczii** SCHNEID. (*C. sanguinea* var. *villosa* MAXIM.) A tree forming a compact cone with shallowly lobed leaves, distinct in its flower stalks, calyx, and young fruits being bristly-hairy. Fruits smooth when ripe. NE Asia.

× **media** BECHST. (*C. laevigata × C. monogyna*). A large shrub or small tree, intermediate in character between the parents. It is a variable plant found both in the wild and in cultivation. Several of the cultivars listed under *C. laevigata* belong here.

**missouriensis** ASHE A shrub or small tree having distinctive, sharply-toothed, pubescent leaves and orange-red fruits. SE United States. I 1905.

**mollis** (TORR. & GRAY) SCHEELE "Red Haw". One of the best of the American species, forming a wide-spreading tree 10-12m high. Leaves downy; fruits showy, like red cherries, carried in large clusters. C North America. Long cultivated.

**monogyna** JACQ. "Common Hawthorn" "May" "Quick". A familiar native, extensively planted as a hedge throughout the country. A tree in full flower in May is a wonderful sight and is equal to any of the foreign species. In autumn its branches are often laden with red fruits—"haws". The flowers are white and strongly fragrant. Europe, N Africa, W Asia.

**'Biflora'** ('Praecox') The "Glastonbury Thorn" produces leaves earlier than normal and occasionally an early but smaller crop of flowers during winter. C 1770.

**'Compacta'** ('Inermis Compacta') A remarkable dwarf form with stout, stiff, unarmed branches. C 1907.

**'Flexuosa'** ('Tortuosa') A curious and striking form with twisted corkscrew branches. C 1838.

**'Pendula'** "Weeping Thorn". A form with graceful, arching branches; flowers white.

**'Pendula Rosea'** Graceful pendulous branches and pink flowers.

**'Praecox'** See 'Biflora'.

**'Pteridifolia'** A form with deeply lobed and toothed leaves. C 1838.

**'Stricta'** ('Fastigiata') Branches erect. An excellent, small, tough tree for exposed places.

**'Tortuosa'** See 'Flexuosa'.

**'Variegata'** Leaves splashed and mottled creamy white.

**CRATAEGUS**—*continued*

×**mordenensis** BOOM (*C. laevigata* × *C. succulenta*). In the following form, raised in Canada at the Morden Experimental Station, one parent was *C. laevigata* 'Paul's Scarlet'.

**'Toba'** A small tree with deeply lobed and toothed leaves. Flowers produced in May, double, opening white tinged pink becoming pink. A seedling of this with double white flowers has been called 'Snowbird'.

**nitida** SARG. A small tree with spreading, usually thornless, branches and elliptic to oblong, shining leaves which change to orange and red in the autumn. Fruits red. E United States. I 1883.

**orientalis** See *C. laciniata*.

**var. sanguinea** See *C. schraderiana*.

**oxyacantha** See *C. laevigata*.

**pedicellata** SARG. (*C. coccinea* L. in part) "Scarlet Haw". A small tree with wide-spreading head of thorny branches. Leaves with glandular teeth. Large bunches of scarlet fruits and often rich autumn colour. NE North America. I 1683.

**persistens** SARG. A small tree. Leaves remain green during early winter and are accompanied by the long-persistent, red fruits. Possibly a hybrid of *C. crus-galli*.

**phaenopyrum** L. f. (*C. cordata* AIT.) "Washington Thorn". A striking, round-headed species up to 10m and one of the most distinct of the genus, with its glossy, maple-like leaves and profusion of small, dark-crimson fruits. Good autumn tints. SE United States. I 1738.

**pinnatifida** BUNGE A small tree with large, conspicuously lobed leaves; thorns short or absent. Fruits crimson, minutely dotted. NE Asia. C 1860.

**var. major** N.E. BR. The Chinese variety is one of the most ornamental thorns, with its glossy, crimson fruits to nearly 2.5cm across. Among the best of all small trees for its rich red autumn colour. N China. C 1880. FCC 1886.

**prunifolia** (LAM.) PERS. An excellent, small, compact, broad-headed tree, notable for its persistent, showy fruit, and polished, oval leaves. Rich autumn colour. Possibly a hybrid between *C. macracantha* and *C. crus-galli*. C 1797. AGM 1984.

**punctata** JACQ. An attractive tree up to 11m producing great crops of white blossom. Fruits large, dull crimson with pale spots. E North America. I 1746.

**'Aurea'** ('Xanthocarpa') Fruits yellow.

**rivularis** See *C. douglasii*.

**saligna** GREENE A shrub or small tree from Colorado. Fruits lustrous, at first red, finally black. I 1902.

**schraderiana** LEDEB. (*C. orientalis* var. *sanguinea* LOUD.) A small, round-headed tree with deeply-cut, grey-green, downy leaves. The masses of large, dark purple-red fruits can be spectacular after a hot summer. Greece, Crimea.

**stipulacea** LOUD. A small but vigorous, semi-evergreen tree, remarkable as being one of the few Mexican trees hardy in this country. Leaves glossy green above, pubescent beneath, fruits like yellow crab apples, very persistent. I 1824.

**submollis** SARG. A small tree often grown as *C. mollis* but differing in its rather smaller leaves and bright orange-red fruits. NE United States, SE Canada. AM 1953.

**tanacetifolia** (LAM.) PERS. "Tansy-leaved Thorn". A small, usually thornless, slow-growing tree with grey, downy leaves, conspicuous in flower and fruit; the latter appear like small yellow apples. Asia Minor. I 1789. AM 1976.

**tomentosa** L. (*C. calpodendron* (EHRH.) MED.) A North American species forming a small, round-headed tree, very floriferous and bearing orange-red, pear-shaped fruits. I 1765.

**uniflora** MUENCHH. A medium-sized shrub with small rounded leaves and 1-3 flowers in a cluster. Fruits yellow or greenish-yellow. E United States. I 1704.

**wattiana** HEMSL. & LACE (*C. korolkowii* L. HENRY) Small, often thornless tree with sharply-toothed leaves and translucent yellow fruits. C Asia.

**wilsonii** SARG. A small tree or large shrub. Leaves lustrous; fruits deep-red. C China. I 1907 by Ernest Wilson.

×**CRATAEMESPILUS** E.G. CAMUS (*Crataegus* × *Mespilus*)—**Rosaceae**—A natural hybrid between the hawthorn and medlar, bearing clusters of attractive white flowers. Not to be confused with +*Crataegomespilus* which includes graft hybrids between medlar and hawthorn.

× **CRATAEMESPILUS**—*continued*

**grandiflora** (SMITH) E.G. CAMUS (*C. oxyacantha* × *M. germanica*). (*Crataegomespilus grandiflora* (SMITH) BEAN) An apparently sterile hybrid found wild in France, about 1800. A small, broad-headed tree with hairy leaves, occasionally lobed. Flowers in pairs or threes, 2.5cm across; fruits like large, glossy, brownish-orange haws. Orange and yellow autumn tints, particularly striking after a hot summer.

‡†*CRINODENDRON** MOL. (*Tricuspidaria* RUIZ & PAVON)—**Elaeocarpaceae**—Both species of this genus are native of Chile, and are worthy additions to gardens in the milder areas of Great Britain. They require lime-free soil and partial shade.

**hookerianum** GAY (*Tricuspidaria lanceolata* MIQ.) This shrub is one of the gems of the garden. The flowers, like long-stalked crimson lanterns, hang thickly along the branches in May. A large, dense shrub in mild localities, here it survived the hard winters of the 1980s. Introduced by William Lobb in 1848. FCC 1916 (as *Tricuspidaria lanceolata*).

**patagua** MOL. (*Tricuspidaria dependens* RUIZ & PAVON) This is a strong-growing shrub or small tree, bearing its white, bell-shaped flowers in late summer. Requires wall protection in cold districts. I 1901 by H.J. Elwes. AM 1984.

**"CROWBERRY"** See *Empetrum nigrum*.

**"CUCUMBER TREE"** See *Magnolia acuminata*.

†**CUDRANIA** TRECUL—**Moraceae**—A small genus of about 5 species of climbers, shrubs or small trees among cultivated plants most closely related to *Maclura* and *Broussonetia* and found in E Asia, Polynesia and Australia.

**tricuspidata** (CARR.) BUREAU "Chinese Silkworm Thorn". A large shrub or small tree with ovate, entire or three-lobed leaves and stalked axillary clusters of tiny flowers. Rare in cultivation. China, Korea. C 1872.

**"CURRANT, FLOWERING"** See *Ribes sanguineum*.

**"CURRY PLANT"** See *Helichrysum italicum* subsp. *serotinum*.

‡*CYATHODES** LABILL.—**Epacridaceae**—About 15 species of heath-like Australian and New Zealand shrubs, with tiny white pitcher-shaped flowers and very attractive foliage. They require lime-free soil.

**colensoi** (HOOK. f.) HOOK. f. A decumbent species with glaucous foliage; fruits white or red. A very beautiful prostrate shrub. Proving quite hardy. New Zealand. AM 1962.

†**robusta** HOOK. f. Small, erect shrub with white fruits and narrow leaves, glaucous beneath. Chatham Islands.

**CYDONIA** MILLER—**Rosaceae**—A monotypic genus related to *Chaenomeles*.

**japonica** See *Chaenomeles speciosa*.

**maulei** See *Chaenomeles japonica*.

**oblonga** MILLER (*C. vulgaris* PERS.) The "Common Quince". Native of N Iran and Turkestan. A small, unarmed tree occasionally up to 6m high. Flowers white to pale rose; fruit golden-yellow, fragrant. Leaves often turn a rich yellow before falling. This and its named clones selected for their fruit make picturesque specimen trees for lawns. For ornamental "Cydonias" see *Chaenomeles*.

‡**CYRILLA** GARDEN ex L.—**Cyrillaceae**—An interesting genus containing one variable species of wide distribution, sometimes regarded as several species. In the southern parts of its range it is evergreen and tree-like.

**racemiflora** L. "Leatherwood". A small, late summer-flowering deciduous or semi-evergreen shrub. Leaves lanceolate, turning crimson in autumn. Flowers white, borne in whorls of slender, cylindrical racemes at the base of the current year's shoots in late summer to autumn. SE United States, W Indies, Mexico, northern S America. I 1765. AM 1901.

**CYTISUS** DESF.—**Leguminosae**—About 50 species, native mainly to Europe but extending to W Asia and N Africa. The "Brooms" vary from prostrate shrublets to those attaining small tree-size, all having typical pea-shaped flowers, and mostly late spring or early summer-flowering, but there are a few which flower towards autumn. The species are native of Europe and have yellow flowers unless otherwise stated.

The majority of species are lime-tolerant but *C. multiflorus* and *C. scoparius* and their mixed progeny, comprising the bulk of the hardy hybrid brooms, will not succeed for long on poor, shallow, chalky soils, nor strange to relate, in extremely acid soils. They do best in neutral or acid soils, or deep soils over chalk, including stiff clay-loam. They are all sun-loving, light demanders, and attain about 1.2-2m high.

The more vigorous species and hybrids may be pruned immediately after flowering to prevent legginess, taking care not to cut into the old hard wood.

**albus** HACQ. (*C. leucanthus* WALDST. & KIT.) A dwarf shrub with spreading downy stems. Flowers white or cream, borne in terminal heads in June and July. C and SE Europe. I 1806. See also *C. multiflorus*.

**ardoinii** FOURNIER A miniature, mat-forming alpine shrub from the Maritime Alps (S France). Flowers bright yellow, April to May. I 1866. AM 1955. AGM 1984.

**austriacus** L. (*Chamaecytisus austriacus* (L.) LINK) A valuable, late flowering, dwarf shrub producing a succession of heads of bright yellow flowers from July to September. Foliage covered with silky adpressed hairs. C and SE Europe to C Russia. I 1741.

**battandieri** MAIRE A tall shrub. Leaves laburnum-like, grey, with a silky sheen. Flowers in cone-shaped clusters, bright yellow, pineapple-scented, appearing in July. An excellent shrub for a high wall but being very hardy will survive in the open in many places. Morocco. I about 1922. AM 1931. FCC 1934. AGM 1984.

**'Yellow Tail'** A selected form raised in our nurseries before 1975 bearing racemes up to 15cm or more long.

×**beanii** DALLIM. (*C. ardoinii* × *C. purgans*). Charming dwarf shrub up to 35cm in height. Flowers golden yellow, May. Garden origin 1900. FCC 1955. AGM 1984.

**'Boskoop Ruby'** (*C.* × *praecox* × *C.* 'Hollandia'). A small rounded shrub with very profusely borne deep crimson flowers. Raised in Holland, it is one of the most striking red hybrids.

**'Burkwoodii'** A vigorous hybrid with flowers of cerise; wings deep crimson edged yellow. May to June. AMT 1973. AGM 1984.

**candicans** See *C. monspessulanus*.

**capitatus** See *C. supinus*.

**'C.E. Pearson'** Flowers creamy yellow flushed crimson on standard; wings rich flame. May to June.

**'Cottage'** Similar to *C.* × *kewensis* in its profuse pale creamy yellow flowers but of upright habit.

**'Daisy Hill'** Flowers deep rose in bud, opening to cream, flushed rose on standard; wings deep crimson. May to June.

×**dallimorei** ROLFE (*C. multiflorus* × *C. scoparius* 'Andreanus'). Medium-sized shrub raised at Kew in 1900. Flowers deep rose flushed scarlet. A parent of some of the best hybrids. AM 1910.

**decumbens** (DURANDE) SPACH A prostrate, rock-garden shrublet; flowers bright yellow in May and June. S Europe. I 1775.

**demissus** BOISS. A prostrate shrub no more than 10cm high. A gem for the rock garden with exceptionally large yellow flowers with brown keels, May. Found on Mount Olympus in Greece at about 2,300m. AM 1932.

**'Donard Seedling'** Flowers pale yellow with mauve-pink standard; wings flushed red. May to June.

**'Dorothy Walpole'** Flowers dark cerise-red; wings velvety-crimson; May to June. AM 1923.

**'Dukaat'** A small, erect-branched shrub of dense habit with silky hairy young shoots and small, narrow leaves. Flowers small, golden yellow in May. An $F_1$ hybrid from the cross *C.* 'Burkwoodii' × *C.* × *praecox*. C 1965.

**emeriflorus** REICHB. (*C. glabrescens* SART.) A dwarf, compact shrub. Flowers bright golden yellow produced in small clusters in May and June. Switzerland, N Italy. C 1896.

**CYTISUS**—*continued*

**frivaldskyanus** DEGEN. A dwarf shrub often forming a low, compact mound of hairy, leafy stems. Flowers bright yellow in terminal heads in June and July. Balkans.

**glabrescens** See *C. emeriflorus*.

**grandiflorus** (BROT.) DC. (*Sarothamnus grandiflorus* (DC.) WEBB) "Woolly-podded Broom". In its bright yellow flowers, this species from S Spain and Portugal resembles the "Common Yellow Broom", but is well distinguished by its grey-woolly seed pods. It grows 2.5-3m high and is quite hardy. I 1816.

**hirsutus** L. (*Chamaecytisus hirsutus* (L.) LINK) An extremely variable, dwarf or small hairy shrub of loose habit, producing long leafy racemes of yellow or buff stained pea-flowers in May and June. S and C Europe. I during 18th century.

**'Hollandia'** Flowers pale cream, back of standard cerise; wings dark cerise. May to June. AMT 1973.

**ingramii** BLAKELOCK An interesting species discovered in the mountains of NW Spain by Capt Collingwood Ingram. A medium-sized shrub of erect habit. Flowers yellow and cream, in June.

**'Johnson's Crimson'** Flowers clear crimson. A fine hybrid, in habit resembling the "White Spanish Broom". AMT 1972. FCCT 1973. AGM 1984.

×**kewensis** BEAN (*C. ardoinii* × *C. multiflorus*). Sheets of cream coloured flowers in May; growth semi-prostrate. Raised at Kew in 1891. AGM 1984.

**'Niki'** A form with golden yellow flowers. A sport found in Holland in 1984.

**'Killiney Red'** Flowers rich red; wings darker and velvety. May to June.

**'La Coquette'** Standard rose-red, yellow inside, wings deep orange-yellow veined brick-red, keel pale yellow faintly marked with rose-red. May. AMT 1972.

**'Lady Moore'** Flowers large, creamy yellow, flushed rose on standard and flame on wings; larger and richer than those of 'C.E. Pearson'. May to June. AM 1928.

**'Lena'** A vigorous, compact, free-flowering shrub, standard deep red, wings red margined yellow, keel pale yellow. Raised at Kew. FCCT 1974. AGM 1984.

**leucanthus** See *C. albus*.

**'Lord Lambourne'** Standard pale cream; wings dark red. May to June. AM 1927.

**'Luna'** Flowers large, standard broad, pale creamy yellow tinged red on the back and inside; wings rich yellow, keel pale yellow. May. C 1959. AMT 1972. FCCT 1974. AGM 1984.

†\***maderensis var. magnifoliosus** BRIQ. A large shrub with fragrant, bright yellow flowers in racemes in spring and early summer. A conservatory plant, except in very mild localities. Madeira.

**'Maria Burkwood'** A vigorous shrub, the large red flowers with coppery wings. AMT 1972.

**'Minstead'** A charming hybrid derived from *C. multiflorus*, producing multitudes of small flowers which are white, flushed lilac, darker on wings and in bud. May to June. AM 1949.

†**monspessulanus** L. (*Teline monspessulana* (L.) K. KOCH) (*C. candicans* (L.) DC.) "Montpelier Broom". A medium-sized, graceful, semi-evergreen species; clusters of yellow flowers from April to June. Subject to injury by severe frost. S Europe, SW Asia, N Africa. C 1735. AM 1974.

**'Mrs Norman Henry'** Similar in habit to 'Minstead', but flowers with darker coloured wings. May to June. AMT 1972.

‡**multiflorus** (AIT.) SWEET (*C. albus* LINK) "White Spanish Broom". An erect shrub of medium height, its stems studded with small white flowers in May and June. Parent of many hybrids. Spain, Portugal, NW Africa. C 1752. AMT 1974. AGM 1984.

**nigricans** L. (*Lembotropis nigricans* (L.) GRISEB.) A most useful and elegant small, late flowering shrub producing long terminal racemes of yellow flowers continuously during late summer. C and SE Europe to C Russia. I 1730.

**'Palette'** A vigorous shrub with large flowers. Standard shading from cerise-pink at the tip to orange-yellow at the base, wings rich vermilion, keel pink tipped pale yellow. May. C 1959. AMT 1974.

†**'Porlock'** (*C. monspessulanus* × *C.* × *spachianus*). Quickly forms a large, semi-evergreen bush. Flowers in racemes, butter-yellow, very fragrant, appearing in mild weather between autumn and spring. Remarkably hardy given a sunny wall or makes a lovely conservatory shrub. Raised about 1922. AM 1931. FCC 1990.

**CYTISUS**—*continued*

**× praecox** WHEELER ex BEAN (*C. multiflorus × C. purgans*). A group of hybrids popular in gardens for their compact habit and profusely borne flowers. The original form previously listed as *C. × praecox* has been given the cultivar name 'Warminster' q.v.

**'Albus'** Flowers white.

**'Allgold'** An outstanding small shrub with arching sprays of long-lasting yellow flowers. FCCT 1974. AGM 1984.

**'Gold Spear'** ['Goldspeer'], ('Canary Bird') Small deep yellow flowers profusely borne. C 1955. FCCT 1973.

**'Warminster'** "Warminster Broom". A small shrub, a spectacular plant forming, in early May, a tumbling mass of rich cream. Garden origin about 1867. AGM 1984.

**procumbens** (WILLD.) SPRENG. A dwarf shrub with prostrate branches. Flowers borne in the leaf axils in May and June. SE Europe. AM 1948.

**purgans** (L.) SPACH A dense, usually leafless shrub forming a mass of erect branches 1m high. Flowers yellow in April and May, fragrant. SW Europe, N Africa. C mid 18th century.

**purpureus** SCOP. (*Chamaecytisus purpureus* (SCOP.) LINK) "Purple Broom". A pretty, low shrub about 45cm high. Flowers lilac-purple, produced in May. C and SE Europe. I 1792. AM 1980.

**Albus group** (f. *albus* (SWEET) ZAB.) A slightly dwarfer form with white flowers. C 1838.

**'Atropurpureus'** ('Incarnatus') Flowers deep purple. A superb dwarf shrub.

**ratisbonensis** SCHAEFF. (*C. biflorus* L'HERIT.) (*Chamaecytisus ratisbonensis* (SCHAEFF.) ROTHM.) An attractive small shrub of loose habit somewhat resembling *C. hirsutus*. Flowers yellow or with a reddish stain, arranged in long arching, leafy racemes in May and June. C Europe to Caucasus, W Siberia. I about 1800.

**'Red Favourite'** ['Roter Favorit']. Standard and wings deep velvety-red, wings with a narrow gold line at the base, keel light carmine. C 1959.

**'Red Wings'** Vigorous and compact. Flowers profusely borne, deep velvety red with the keel yellow flushed bright red. AMT 1972.

**scoparius** (L.) LINK (*Sarothamnus scoparius* (L.) K. KOCH) "Common Broom". A familar, medium-sized, native shrub, as conspicuous as the gorse but without its spines. Flowers rich butter-yellow in May. A parent of many named clones. See generic description for soil requirements. Europe. Some of the following are probably hybrids.

**'Andreanus'** A form in which the flowers are attractively marked with brown-crimson. Found wild in Normandy in about 1884. FCC 1890. FCCT 1973. AGM 1984.

**'Cornish Cream'** A most attractive form with cream coloured flowers. AM 1923. FCCT 1973. AGM 1984.

**'Dragonfly'** Standard deep yellow; wings deep crimson. Strong-growing. May to June.

**'Firefly'** Standard yellow; wings with a bronze stain. AM 1907.

**'Fulgens'** A late flowering clone of dense, compact habit. Flowers rufous in bud opening orange-yellow; wings deep crimson. June. Raised about 1906.

**'Golden Sunlight'** A strong-growing form with flowers of a rich yellow. C 1929. AMT 1973.

**f. indefessus** MCCLINTOCK A form which continues to flower during summer and autumn. Found in Brittany in 1962 by David McClintock.

**subsp. maritimus** (ROUY) HEYWOOD (*C. scoparius* var. *prostratus* (C. BAILEY) A.B. JACKS.) A dwarf spreading shrub with large, yellow flowers. Found wild on sea cliffs in a few localities in the west of the British Isles. AM 1913.

**var. prostratus** See subsp. *maritimus*.

**f. sulphureus** (GOLDRING) REHD. Flowers cream, tinged red in bud; wings and keel pale sulphur.

**sessilifolius** L. Elegant shrub of medium size, with short racemes of bright yellow flowers in June. Leaves usually sessile on flowering stems. C and S Europe, N Africa. Long cultivated. AM 1919.

**supinus** L. (*C. capitatus* SCOP.) (*Chamaecytisus supinus* (L.) LINK) A compact shrub about 0.6-1m, very variable in the wild. Flowers large, yellow, in terminal clusters from July onwards. C and S Europe. I 1755.

**CYTISUS**—*continued*

**supranubius** (L. f.) O. KUNTZE (*Spartocytisus supranubius* (L. f.) WEBB. & BERTH.) "Tenerife Broom". A medium-sized shrub resembling *Spartium junceum* in habit. Leaves small, trifoliolate. Flowers fragrant, milky-white, tinted rose, carried in May in axillary clusters on the previous year's wood. A pretty shrub when in flower. Theoretically a tender shrub it remained uninjured by snow and wind for several years in our relatively cold area. Canary Isles. C before 1824. AM 1924.

**'Toome's Variety'** A hybrid of *C. multiflorus* with long slender stems covered in May with multitudes of small creamy white flowers, flushed lilac on the inside of the standard.

× **versicolor** (KIRCHN.) DIPP. (*C. hirsutus* × *C. purpureus*). Of dwarf habit; flowers pale buff shaded lilac-pink. May to June. Garden origin about 1850.

**'Hillieri'** (*C. hirsutus* var. *hirsutissimus* × *C.* × *versicolor*). A low shrub with arching branches. The large flowers, yellow flushed pale bronze changing to buff-pink, are borne in May and June. Raised in our nurseries in about 1933.

**'Windlesham Ruby'** Flowers rich mahogany-crimson. Upright habit.

**'Zeelandia'** (*C.* 'Burkwoodii' × *C.* × *praecox*). Standard lilac outside, cream inside; wings pinkish, keel cream. May to June. FCCT 1974. AGM 1984.

‡*DABOECIA D. DON—**Ericaceae**—A small genus of 2 species of low-growing, lime-hating shrubs, related to *Erica*, but distinct on account of the usually large, glandular, deciduous corolla and broader leaves.

†**azorica** TUT. & E. F. WARB. A very pretty plant, less hardy and dwarfer than the "Connemara Heath", flowers also darker coloured, being of a rich crimson shade. Requires a sheltered position. Azores. I 1929 by E.F. Warburg. AM 1932.

**cantabrica** (HUDS.) K. KOCH (*Menziesia polifolia* JUSS.) "Connemara Heath" "St Dabeoc's Heath". One of the most charming and useful of dwarf shrubs producing long racemes of very showy rose-purple, pitcher-shaped flowers from June to November. W Europe (incl Ireland). C 1800.

**'Alba'** Flowers white. AGM 1984.

**'Atropurpurea'** Rose-purple, darker than the type. AGM 1984.

**'Bicolor'** White, rose-purple and striped flowers often on the same raceme.

**'Porter's Variety'** Dwarf, compact form with small, pinched rose-purple flowers.

**'Praegerae'** Dwarf, spreading habit; flowers curiously narrowed, rich pink. Found by Mrs Praeger in Connemara. C 1932. AMT 1970. AGM 1984.

× **scotica** MCCLINTOCK Hybrids between the two species first originated in a Glasgow garden in about 1953. They are hardier than *D. azorica*. AGM 1984.

**'Jack Drake'** Flowers ruby red. 20cm. AGM 1984.

**'Silverwells'** Flowers white. AGM 1984.

**'William Buchanan'** Flowers deep purple. 45cm. AGM 1984.

**"DAISY BUSH"** See *Olearia*.

†*DAMNACANTHUS GAERTN. f.—**Rubiaceae**—A small genus of about 6 species of evergreen, spiny shrubs native to Asia. The following is suitable for sun or shade, and a well drained soil.

**indicus** GAERTN. f. A dainty, spiny, small shrub, suitable for growing in pots. Small, fragrant, funnel-shaped white flowers followed by coral-red berries. China, Taiwan, Japan, Himalaya. I 1868.

*DANAE MEDIKUS—**Ruscaceae**—A monotypic genus closely related to *Ruscus*, differing in its hermaphrodite flowers borne in short terminal racemes. As in *Ruscus*, the 'leaves' are in fact flattened stems (phylloclades).

**racemosa** (L.) MOENCH (*Ruscus racemosus* L.) "Alexandrian Laurel". A charming, small, shade-bearing evergreen with arching sprays of narrow, polished green leaves. Orange-red fruits produced after hot summers. Excellent for cutting. SW Asia to N Iran. I 1713. AM 1933. AGM 1984.

**DAPHNE** L.—**Thymelaeaceae**—A genus of about 50 species of beautiful, deciduous or evergreen, usually fragrant shrubs native to Europe, Asia and N Africa. They are mostly

**DAPHNE**—*continued*

of small size and suitable for the rock garden but vary from prostrate to large shrubs. Good loamy soil, moisture, and good drainage are essential for their success.

**\*acutiloba** REHD. A medium-sized shrub with long leathery leaves and terminal heads of white, normally scentless flowers in July. Fruits large, bright scarlet. W China. I 1908 by Ernest Wilson.

**\*albowiana** WORON. A close relative of *D. pontica* which it resembles but with red fruits. Some plants grown as *D. pontica* appear to belong here. Caucasus.

**alpina** L. A dwarf, deciduous species with grey-green leaves and fragrant white flowers in May and June; fruits orange-red. Mountains of S and C Europe. C 1759.

**altaica** PALL. Small, semi-evergreen shrub of upright habit. Flowers white, slightly fragrant, in terminal clusters in May or June followed by red fruits. Altai Mts, Siberia. I 1796.

**\*arbuscula** CELAK. A dwarf, rounded, alpine shrublet from the Carpathian Mountains in E Czechoslovakia, with crowded, narrow leaves. Flowers rose-pink, fragrant; fruits brownish-yellow. AM 1915. FCC 1973.

**aurantiaca** DIELS "Golden-flowered Daphne". A small, very distinct and rare Chinese species of slow growth with fragrant, rich yellow flowers in May, and ovate-oblong, opposite leaves glaucous beneath. Sichuan, Yunnan. I 1906 by George Forrest. FCC 1927.

**bholua** BUCH.-HAM. ex D. DON A deciduous or semi-evergreen shrub up to 2m with stout, erect branches. Leaves oblanceolate. Flowers large, sweetly scented, deep reddish-mauve in bud, opening white, with reddish-mauve reverse, twenty or more in a terminal cluster, appearing continuously in January and February. Fruits black. Hardiness and leaf retention in winter varies according to altitude. Himalaya. C 1938. AM 1946. AGM 1984.

'**Gurkha**' (T.S.S. 132b) A very hardy deciduous form collected by Major Tom Spring-Smyth at 3,200m in E Nepal in 1962. Flowers richly scented, purplish-pink and white. The introduction of this form greatly increased the popularity of this splendid species. AGM 1984.

**\*'Jacqueline Postill'** This splendid and very hardy form originated as a seedling of 'Gurkha' raised by our propagator Alan Postill in 1982. It is evergreen or semi-evergreen, flowering when in full leaf. The flowers are larger and more showy than those of 'Gurkha' with an equally powerful fragrance. FCC 1991.

**blagayana** FREYER A dwarf shrub with prostrate branches terminating in bunches of oval leaves and clusters of richly scented, creamy white flowers from March to April; fruits whitish. A difficult plant succeeding best in deep leaf mould and half shade. From the mountain forests of SE Europe. I about 1875. FCC 1880.

×**burkwoodii** TURRILL (*D. caucasica* × *D. cneorum*). This group of hybrids includes some of the most popular and easy to grow plants in the genus. For the plant usually listed as *D. × burkwoodii* see 'Albert Burkwood'.

'**Albert Burkwood**' A fast-growing semi-evergreen shrub attaining 1m in height. The pale pink, deliciously fragrant flowers are borne in clusters on short leafy shoots all along the branches in May and June and often again in autumn. Raised in 1931. AM 1935. AGM 1984.

'**Carol Mackie**' Leaves with a golden yellow margin which becomes creamy white. This form is named after the raiser in whose garden in New Jersey, United States, it occurred as a sport in 1962. Similar plants have been raised in this country and Holland. Previously distributed as 'Variegata'.

'**G.K. Argles**' A form with gold margined leaves raised as a sport at the Champernowne nursery, Buckland Monachorum, Devon.

'**Lavenirii**' Spreading habit with pale pink flowers deep pink in the centre. Raised in France about 1920.

'**Somerset**' A sister seedling of 'Albert Burkwood' from which it differs in its slightly larger size, more upright habit and paler flowers. AM 1937. FCC 1980.

'**Variegata**' See under 'Carol Mackie'.

**caucasica** PALL. A small, narrow-leaved, Caucasian shrub. Terminal clusters of fragrant white flowers in May and June, often again in early autumn; fruits yellow. C 1893.

**DAPHNE**—*continued*

**\*cneorum** L. "Garland Flower". A great favourite on account of its fragrance, and the rose-pink flowers which are borne in clusters on prostrate branches during April and May; fruits brownish-yellow. A difficult plant to establish. C and S Europe.

**'Alba'** A rare, white form of var. *pygmaea*. AM 1920. A white-flowered form of the typical variety is also in cultivation.

**'Eximia'** A more prostrate form with larger leaves and flowers. The unopened flower buds are crimson opening to rich rose-pink. AM 1938. FCC 1967. AGM 1984.

**var. pygmaea** STOKER Free-flowering, its branches lying flat on the ground. AM 1983.

**'Ruby Glow'** A form with very deep pink flowers.

**'Variegata'** A vigorous form; leaves attractively margined with cream.

**var. verlotii** (GREN & GODR.) MEISSN. A rare, lax form from the C and S Alps, differing in its more prostrate growth and narrower, pointed leaves. AM 1916.

**\*collina** DICKSON ex J.E. SMITH. A first rate rock-garden shrub. Forms a shapely bush 28-35cm high, each shoot clothed with blunt, deep green leaves and terminating in a cluster of fragrant, rose-purple flowers in May. One of the most rewarding of daphnes. Very close to and now usually included in *D. sericea*. S Italy. C 1752. AM 1938. FCC 1984. AGM 1984.

**var. neapolitana** See *D. × napolitana*.

**dauphinii** See *D. × hybrida*.

**genkwa** SIEB. & ZUCC. There can be few lovelier shrubs than this oriental species, but it is difficult to establish. A small shrub with light green, mostly opposite leaves. Flowers relatively large, clear lilac-blue, carried all along leafless branches in April and May. China, Taiwan. Introduced by Robert Fortune from China in 1843. Long cultivated in Japan. FCC 1885.

**giraldii** NITSCHE An uncommon dwarf, erect shrub to about 0.75m. It bears fragrant yellow flowers in clusters in May or June, followed by bright red fruits. NW China. I 1911 by William Purdom.

**\*gnidium** L. A small, erect, slender shrub with fragrant creamy-white flowers from June to August, and red fruits. S Europe and N Africa. C since the 16th century.

**× houtteana** LINDL. & PAXT. (*D. laureola × D. mezereum*). A small partially evergreen shrub of erect habit with purplish leaves similar to those of *D. laureola* in shape. Flowers dark red-purple in April. Subject to virus and now rare. C 1850.

**\* × hybrida** COLV. ex SWEET (*D. collina × D. odora*). (*D. dauphinii* LOUD.) This charming small shrub with dark glossy green leaves has the beauty and fragrance of *D. odora*, and is hardier. Reddish-purple very fragrant flowers are produced from late autumn through winter. Raised about 1820.

**†\*jasminea** SIBTH. & SM. A dwarf, cushion-forming shrublet with small, narrow glaucous leaves. Flowers rose-pink in bud, opening white, deliciously fragrant. A rare alpine gem growing on cliffs and rocks in Greece. Requires winter protection. An upright form is also in cultivation. I 1954. AM 1968.

**jezoensis** MAXIM. ex REGEL (*D. kamtschatica* var. *jezoensis* (MAXIM. ex REGEL) OHWI A dwarf shrub, the pale green young leaves emerging in autumn, dark blue-green when mature and deciduous in early summer. Dense clusters of fragrant, golden yellow flowers with exserted stamens and a green tube are borne in winter. Best in a moist, but well drained, peaty soil in a bright but not exposed position. Japan. I about 1960. AM 1985.

**\*juliae** KOS.-POL. A rare dwarf, evergreen, mound-forming shrub from S Russia closely resembling and sometimes included under *D. cneorum* but flowerheads more crowded. I 1959.

**\*laureola** L. "Spurge Laurel". A useful, small, shade-bearing native. Flowers fragrant, yellow-green in dense clusters beneath the leathery, polished green leaves. February and March. Fruits black. S and W Europe (incl England).

**subsp. philippi** (GREN.) ROUY Dwarf variety with smaller, obovate leaves and smaller flowers. A very pleasing evergreen for the rock garden. Pyrenees. C 1894.

**longilobata** (LECOMTE) TURRILL A small, erect, deciduous or semi-evergreen shrub up to 2m with slender purplish stems, narrowly elliptic leaves and white flowers during summer followed by red berries. Closely related to *D. acutiloba*. SE Tibet, NW Yunnan. C 1928.

**DAPHNE longilobata**—*continued*

**'Peter Moore'** A striking variegated form with grey-green leaves margined creamy white. A seedling found by our propagator Peter Moore in 1980.

* × **mantensiana** MANTEN ex TAYLOR & VRUGTMAN (*D.* × *burkwoodii* × *D. retusa*). This hybrid is represented by the following clone.

**'Manten'** A dwarf, evergreen shrub of dense, rounded habit with dark glossy green leaves to 3.5cm long. Flowers strongly scented, deep rose-purple outside, deep lilac within, borne in dense terminal clusters in late April and early May and usually again in summer and autumn. Raised in 1941.

**mezereum** L. The well-known, sweet-scented, deciduous "Mezereon". A small shrub flowering in February and March. The purple-red flowers, covering the previous year's shoots, are followed by scarlet poisonous fruits. Unfortunately the foliage is often poor due to virus. Thrives in chalk soils. Europe (incl British Isles), Asia Minor and Siberia. C 1561.

**f. alba** (WEST.) SCHELLE Flowers white; fruits translucent amber; branches more upright.

**var. autumnalis** HORT. ex REHD. Flowers relatively large and beginning to open as early as September. Previously listed as 'Grandiflora'.

**'Bowles' Variety'** ('Bowles' White') A form with white flowers and pure white fruits. AM 1947.

**'Rosea'** A selected form. Large, clear rose-pink flowers.

* × **napolitana** LODD. (*D. collina* var. *neapolitana* (LODD.) LINDL.) A beautiful dwarf, hardy shrub rarely more than 1m high, with blunt, ash-green leaves. Clusters of rose-pink, fragrant flowers are borne profusely from April to early June. Probably a hybrid between *D. collina* and *D. cneorum*. C 1823. AM 1984. AGM 1984.

* **odora** THUNB. (*D. indica* HORT. not L.) This winter and early spring-flowering, small shrub from China and Japan should be given some protection, but is hardy enough to withstand frost of considerable severity. It makes a bush of 1.2-2m in height with dark green leaves and very fragrant reddish-purple flowers. I 1771.

**f. alba** (HEMSL.) HARA (var. *leucantha* MAK.) A form with white flowers.

**'Aureo-marginata'** Leaves with a narrow yellow margin which becomes creamy white with age. Hardier than the green form. AM 1976.

* **oleoides** SCHREB. (*D. buxifolia* VAHL) An uncommon dwarf species with thick leaves, terminating in a bristle-like tip; flowers cream or pale pink, fragrant, in terminal clusters; fruits red. S Europe to the Himalaya.

**var. brachyloba** MEISSN. Differs in its leaves which are rounded not pointed, and adpressed pilose above; also in the shorter lobed white flowers in a lax head.

†* **papyracea** WALL. ex STEUD. Little-known species related to *D. odora*, and recognised by its long oblanceolate leaves. Flowers white, produced during winter; fruits dark red. W Himalaya. C 1881.

* **petraea** LEYB. (*D. rupestris* FACCHINI) An alpine gem only 5-7.5cm high with small linear leaves; flowers fragrant, rosy-pink, produced in terminal clusters in June. A choice gnarled little shrublet suitable for the alpine house or scree. N Italy. C 1880. AM 1906.

**'Grandiflora'** A form with larger flowers. Collected in the wild in 1914. AM 1918. FCC 1924.

* **pontica** L. A small, free-growing, wide spreading shrub which will thrive under drip and in heavy soil. Bright green, glossy leaves and loose clusters of elusively fragrant, spidery, yellow-green flowers in April and May; fruits blue-black. SE Bulgaria, N Iran, N Turkey. I 1752. AM 1977. AGM 1984.

**pseudomezereum** A. GRAY A rare species similar in habit and leaf to *D. mezereum* but with smaller, greenish-yellow, scentless flowers clustered around the tips of the shoots in April. Fruits red. Male and female flowers on separate plants (dioecious). Japan. C 1905.

* **retusa** HEMSL. A slow-growing, dwarf shrub with stout, stiff branches. Clusters of fragrant deep rose-purple flowers in May and June and often again in autumn. W China, Himalaya. Included in the closely related *D. tangutica* by some authorities. I 1901 by Ernest Wilson. AM 1927. AGM 1984.

* **'Rossetii'** (*D. cneorum* × *D. laureola* subsp. *philippi*) A natural hybrid found in the Pyrenees in 1927. It forms a compact, rounded bush usually less than 0.6m. The reddish flowers are rarely seen. The oblanceolate leaves are intermediate between those of its parents.

**rupestris** See *D. petraea*.

**DAPHNE**—*continued*

**\*sericea** VAHL This small shrub differs from *D. collina* in the leaves being narrower, olive-green and the flowers paler pink. Fruits orange-red. SE Europe. AM 1931.

**\*tangutica** MAXIM. A small Chinese species closely related to and resembling *D. retusa*, but distinguishable by its longer, more acute leaves. Flowers in terminal clusters in March or April, and usually again in late summer, fragrant, white, tinged purple on the inside, rose-purple outside. China. Introduced by Ernest Wilson in the early 1900s. AM 1929. AGM 1984.

×**thauma** FARRER (*D. petraea* × *D. striata*). A dwarf, compact shrub forming a low mound, with narrow leaves densely crowding the branchlets. Flowers bright rose-purple, borne in terminal clusters in May and June. A natural hybrid introduced from the S Tyrol in 1911 by Reginald Farrer.

**\*'Valerie Hillier'** (*D. cneorum* × *D. longilobata*). A dwarf evergreen shrub of spreading habit with downy shoots and narrowly oblong-elliptic, glossy green leaves up to 5cm long. Fragrant flowers are borne in terminal clusters on the young growths continuously from May to autumn; purplish-pink in bud opening pale pink, fading nearly to white with pink-edged lobes, the tube pale pink shading to green at the base. A splendid new hybrid raised by our propagator Alan Postill from a cross made in June 1984. It is named here after the wife of John Hillier, one of the sons of Sir Harold Hillier. The hybrid *D. collina* × *D. longilobata* was raised at the same time.

**\*DAPHNIPHYLLUM** BLUME—**Daphniphyllaceae**—A small genus of about 10 species of dioecious, evergreen trees and shrubs native from E and SE Asia to N Australia. These aristocratic-looking shrubs have leaves recalling *Rhododendron decorum* but the flowers are not conspicuous. They thrive in half shade and a neutral loamy soil, but are lime-tolerant.

**humile** MAXIM. A wide-spreading, much-branched, slow-growing shrub of medium size. Leaves shining green above and glaucous beneath. Japan. I 1879 by Charles Maries.

**macropodum** MIQ. (*D. glaucescens* HORT. not BLUME) A large, striking evergreen shrub from China and Japan. Large rhododendron-like leaves pale green above, glaucous beneath. Flowers pungently scented in clusters beneath the leaves in late spring, the males in purplish, mulberry-like clusters. Remarkably hardy. I 1879 by Charles Maries. FCC 1888 (for foliage). FCC 1987 (for fruit and foliage).

**"DATE PLUM"** See *Diospyros lotus*.

**DATURA** See *Brugmansia*.

**DAVIDIA** BAILL.—**Davidiaceae**—Medium-sized trees recalling *Tilia*, the Davidias are perfectly winter hardy and will thrive in every kind of fertile soil. The small inconspicuous flowers are collected into a dense globular head up to 2.5cm across. Each head is attended by an unequal pair of large, conspicuous white bracts which have been fancifully likened to handkerchiefs. The genus contains one species and is the only member of the family.

**involucrata** BAILL. "Pocket-handkerchief Tree" "Dove Tree" "Ghost Tree". This beautiful medium-sized tree is most conspicuous in May when draped with its large, white bracts. Leaves densely hairy beneath but glabrous on young plants. C and W China. First discovered by the French missionary Père David in 1869, introduced by Ernest Wilson in 1904. AM 1972. AGM 1984.

**var. vilmoriniana** (DODE) WANGER The leaves on established trees are glabrous, not silky hairy beneath, and the fruits more elliptic and less russety. Horticulturally both this and the typical form are very similar and of equal merit. Most plants grown as *D. involucrata* belong here. Introduced by Farges from China in 1897. FCC 1911. AGM 1984.

**†DEBREGEASIA** GAUDICH.—**Urticaceae**—A small genus of about 5 species of tender trees and shrubs native to NE Africa and tropical Asia. They are related to the nettles, but unlike them, harmless to the touch.

**DEBREGEASIA**—*continued*

**longifolia** (BURM. f.) WEDD. A medium-sized shrub of which the long, lance-shaped leaves, pale beneath, are the most striking feature. Produces yellow, mulberry-like fruits. SE Asia.

**DECAISNEA** HOOK. f. & THOMSON—**Lardizabalaceae**—A genus of 2 species of deciduous shrubs from W China and the Himalaya. The following hardy species will grow in sun or semi-shade, and moist but well drained soil.

**fargesii** FRANCH. A very distinct W Chinese shrub attaining about 3m. Large, pinnate leaves 0.6-1m long, blue-tinged when young; flowers often unisexual, yellow-green in racemes up to 0.5m long in May, followed by remarkable metallic-blue pods like those of the broad bean in shape. I 1895 by Farges.

†*****DENDROMECON** BENTHAM—**Papaveraceae**—A genus of 2 species related to *Romneya*, but differing in their entire evergreen leaves and smaller, yellow flowers. Both are natives of California.

**rigida** BENTHAM A large shrub, best grown against a warm sunny wall. Leaves narrow, rigid and glaucous. Flowers poppy-like, four-petalled, bright buttercup-yellow, produced intermittently over a long period. California. I about 1854 by William Lobb. AM 1913.

‡†*****DESFONTAINIA** RUIZ & PAVON—**Potaliaceae**—A monotypic genus found in S America, mainly in the Andes. A variable plant sometimes split into several species. Given a sheltered position and half-shade this beautiful evergreen is hardy in the Home Counties. Not successful on shallow chalk soils.

**spinosa** RUIZ & PAVON (*D. hookeri* DUN.) A magnificent late summer-flowering evergreen, slowly attaining 1.8-2m. Leaves small, holly-like; flowers tubular, scarlet with a yellow mouth. Costa Rica to Cape Horn. I about 1843 by William Lobb. AM 1931.

**'Harold Comber'** A form collected by Comber in about 1925 with 5cm long flowers varying in colour from vermilion to orient red. AM 1955.

**DESMODIUM** DESV.—**Leguminosae**—A large genus of some 300 species of mainly tender herbs and shrubs widely distributed in tropical and subtropical regions. They differ from *Lespedeza* in their many-seeded pods, and leaflets with small subulate stipules.

**penduliflorum** See *Lespedeza thunbergii*.

†**praestans** FORR. A large shrub with long scandent stems and large rounded leaves. The dense covering of silky hairs gives the whole plant a silvery appearance. Flowers purple in compact, crowded racemes during late summer. A species requiring a well drained position in the full sun preferably backed by a wall. SW China. I 1914 by George Forrest.

**tiliifolium** (D. DON) G. DON A small to medium-sized, semi-woody shrub with erect stems and trifoliolate leaves. In summer a profusion of pale-lilac, pea flowers in large panicles followed by flattened and lobed pods. Himalaya. I 1879.

**DEUTZIA** THUNB.—**Philadelphaceae**—A genus of about 70 species of deciduous shrubs native to the Himalaya and E and SE Asia. They are mainly easily cultivated shrubs, succeeding in all types of fertile soil. June-flowering and growing from 1.2-2m high, unless otherwise described. Thin out and cut back old flowering shoots to within a few centimetres of the old wood, immediately after flowering. Gardeners are indebted to Lemoine of Nancy, France, for the many attractive hybrid clones.

**'Avalanche'** See *D.* × *maliflora* 'Avalanche'.

× **candelabra** (LEMOINE) REHD. (*D. gracilis* × *D. sieboldiana*). This graceful shrub is similar to *D. gracilis*, but hardier and the flower panicles are broader and denser. Garden origin. C 1907 (Lemoine).

**chunii** HU A very beautiful and remarkable July-blooming species. Flowers 12mm across; petals white or pink, reflexed, exposing the yellow anthers. Panicles to 10cm long, produced all along the branches. Leaves narrow, grey beneath. This plant both in pink

**DEUTZIA chunii**—*continued*

and white flowered forms is sometimes seen in cultivation under the name *D. ningpoensis.* E China. I 1935.

**'Pink Charm'** A pink-flowered form selected in our nurseries.

**compacta** CRAIB This rare, July-blooming Chinese species forms a neat bush. Flowers in 7.5cm wide corymbs, pink in bud, opening to white, strongly resembling hawthorn in size, form, and in their sweet scent. I 1905.

**'Lavender Time'** Flowers lilac at first, turning to pale lavender. A very distinct shrub, collected in the wild by Kingdon-Ward and which may be a new species.

**'Contraste'** See *D.* × *hybrida* 'Contraste'.

**corymbosa** R. BROWN A medium-sized shrub with ovate leaves and corymbs of white flowers in June. Not so good a garden plant as *D. setchuenensis* var. *corymbiflora*, but hardier. W Himalaya. I 1830.

**discolor** HEMSL. An attractive small shrub with ovate leaves producing its clusters of white or pink flowers in May and June. C and W China.

**'Major'** Flowers 2-2.5cm across in corymbose clusters, white, pink-tinted outside. The best form of this handsome Chinese species. I by Ernest Wilson in 1901.

× **elegantissima** (LEMOINE) REHD. (*D. purpurascens* × *D. sieboldiana*). Rose-pink-tinted, fragrant, flowers in paniculate corymbs. Garden origin 1909. AM 1914.

**'Fasciculata'** A very beautiful clone of medium size. Flowers bright rose-pink. C 1911 (Lemoine). AM 1949. FCC 1972.

**'Rosealind'** A lovely clone with flowers of a deep carmine-pink. C 1962. AM 1972. AGM 1984.

**glomeruliflora** FRANCH. A Chinese shrub usually less than 2m high. Leaves grey beneath; flowers large, white, in dense clusters, in May and June. I 1908 by Ernest Wilson.

**gracilis** SIEB. & ZUCC. An elegant, white flowered, Japanese species, a parent of many good hybrids. Needs protection from late spring frosts. Previously much used for forcing. I about 1840. AM 1980.

**'Hillieri'** (*D. longifolia* 'Veitchii' × *D. setchuenensis* var. *corymbiflora*). An attractive shrub of graceful habit raised in our nurseries in 1926. The star-like flowers are purple-tinged in bud opening pink and fading to white. They are carried twenty to thirty together in compact clusters in late June or July.

**hookeriana** (SCHNEID.) AIRY SHAW This rare species with small leaves comes from Sikkim and W China and is closely related to *D. monbeigii.* Dense corymbs of white flowers in late June.

× **hybrida** LEMOINE (*D. discolor* × *D. longifolia*). A variable hybrid of medium size, extremely floriferous. There are a number of named clones.

**'Contraste'** Flowers star-shaped, in loose panicles, soft lilac-pink; outside of petals rich vinous purple. C 1928. AM 1931.

**'Joconde'** A superb, strong-growing shrub, with very large flowers lined and shaded rose-purple outside. AM 1959.

**'Magicien'** Large flowers, mauve-pink edged white and tinted purple on the reverse.

**'Mont Rose'** Flowers rose-pink with darker tints, very freely borne in paniculate clusters. Raised by Lemoine about 1925. AM 1971. AGM 1984.

**'Perle Rose'** A medium-sized shrub with long, ovate-lanceolate leaves and soft rose flowers, borne in long-stalked, corymbose panicles in June. C 1935 (Lemoine).

**'Pink Pompon'** A medium-sized shrub producing dense heads of double flowers, pink at first becoming white.

**'Strawberry Fields'** (*D.* × *magnifica* 'Rubra') A medium-sized shrub, the large flowers deep crimson outside, white flushed pink within.

**hypoglauca** See *D. rubens.*

**'Joconde'** See *D.* × *hybrida* 'Joconde'.

× **kalmiiflora** LEMOINE (*D. parviflora* × *D. purpurascens*). A charming, floriferous shrub, flowers large, white flushed carmine. Leaves purple in autumn. Garden origin 1900. AGM 1984.

**longifolia** FRANCH. A handsome medium-sized shrub with long, narrowly lanceolate leaves and large clusters of white or pink-tinted flowers in June and July. W China. I 1905 by Ernest Wilson. AM 1912.

**DEUTZIA longifolia**—*continued*

 **'Veitchii'** The large clusters of rich lilac-pink-tinted flowers in June and July make this the most aristocratic of a popular group of shrubs. AM 1912. FCC 1978. AGM 1984.

 **'Magicien'** See *D. × hybrida* 'Magicien'.

× **magnifica** (LEMOINE) REHD. (*D. scabra × D. vilmoriniae*). (*D. crenata magnifica* LEMOINE) A vigorous, medium-sized shrub with large panicles of double, white flowers. Garden origin 1909. This and the following forms raised by Lemoine. AM 1916.

 **'Eburnea'** A very beautiful clone. Single white flowers in loose panicles. C 1912.

 **'Latiflora'** Flowers up to 2.5cm across, white, single. C 1910.

 **'Longipetala'** White, long-petalled flowers. One of the best clones of this popular erect branched shrub.

 **'Macrothyrsa'** White flowers in large clusters. C 1918.

× **maliflora** REHD. (*D. × lemoinei × D. purpurascens*). Strong-growing, medium-sized shrub with large corymbs of white, purple-flushed flowers in June. Garden origin 1905.

 **'Avalanche'** The slender erect branches are arched by the weight of the fragrant white flowers. C 1904 (Lemoine).

**mollis** DUTHIE Small to medium-sized shrub with leaves thickly felted beneath. Flowers white, in dense corymbs in June. W China. I 1901 by Ernest Wilson. AM 1931.

**monbeigii** W.W. SM. A very pretty shrub, distinct in its small leaves, white beneath. A profusion of small, glistening, star-like, white flowers; late. China. I 1921 by George Forrest. AM 1936.

**'Mont Rose'** See *D. × hybrida* 'Mont Rose'.

**'Nikko'** A dwarf, compact shrub with narrow, pointed leaves to 6cm long. Flowers small, white but often not freely produced. A selection of *D. crenata* var. *nakaiana* found in Honshu, Japan. C 1975.

**'Perle Rose'** See *D. × hybrida* 'Perle Rose'.

**pulchra** VIDAL A magnificent, hardy shrub of medium size. The racemes of white flowers are like drooping spikes of lily-of-the-valley. Philippines, Taiwan. I 1918 by Ernest Wilson.

**purpurascens** (L. HENRY) REHD. A graceful species of medium height; flowers white tinted rich purplish-crimson, sweetly scented, in early June. Parent of many hybrids. Yunnan. I 1888 by the Abbé Delavay.

× **rosea** (LEMOINE) REHD. (*D. gracilis × D. purpurascens*). This hybrid forms a compact shrub with arching branches and widely bell-shaped pink flowers. Garden origin 1898. This and the following forms were raised by Lemoine.

 **'Campanulata'** An erect clone with white petals contrasting with the purple calyx. C 1899.

 **'Carminea'** Very attractive clone; flowers flushed rose-carmine. C 1900. AGM 1984.

 **'Floribunda'** Flowers pink-tinged, in dense, erect panicles. C 1901.

 **'Grandiflora'** Large white flowers with pink suffusion. C 1899.

 **'Multiflora'** Free-flowering clone with white flowers. C 1903.

 **'Venusta'** This clone leans towards *D. gracilis*, but has larger white flowers. C 1898.

**rubens** REHD. (*D. hypoglauca* REHD.) A graceful, Chinese shrub with arching branches; leaves lanceolate, white on under-surface; flowers numerous, pure white, appearing in June. I 1910 by William Purdom.

**scabra** THUNB. Tall, erect branched shrub to 3-3.5m producing in June and July large paniculate clusters of white flowers. Japan, China. I 1822.

 **'Azaleiflora'** Flowers smaller with reflexed petals.

 **'Candidissima'** Tall shrub; flowers double, pure white. C 1867. AM 1980.

 **'Macrocephala'** Large bell-shaped white flowers.

 **'Plena'** Double, suffused rose-purple outside. I 1861 by Robert Fortune. FCC 1863.

 **'Watereri'** Flowers single, white, tinted carmine. C 1877.

**schneideriana** REHD. A medium-sized shrub producing panicles of white flowers in June or July. W China. I 1907. AM 1938.

 **var. laxiflora** REHD. A variety with somewhat narrower leaves and lax panicles. I 1901.

**setchuenensis** FRANCH. A charming, slow-growing species up to 2m, producing corymbose clusters of innumerable small, white, star-like flowers during July and August. One of

**DEUTZIA setchuenensis**—*continued*

the very best summer-blooming shrubs, but not quite hardy enough for the coldest parts of the British Isles. China. I 1895. AM 1945.

**var. corymbiflora** (LEMOINE) REHD. This equally beautiful and very floriferous form differs in its broader leaves. AM 1945.

**sieboldiana** MAXIM. An elegant shrub of loose habit, with ovate or elliptic leaves and panicles of white flowers produced in early June. Japan. C 1890.

**staminea** R. BR. A Himalayan species of medium height; flowers white in 5cm wide corymbs, produced in June. Requires a warm sheltered position. I 1841.

**vilmoriniae** LEMOINE A rapid-growing, erect-branched, Chinese species, attaining 2.5-3m; flowers white, in broad corymbose panicles. Leaves long lance-shaped, grey beneath. I 1897 by the Abbé Farges. AM 1917.

× **wilsonii** DUTHIE (*D. discolor* × *D. mollis*). A handsome natural hybrid with brown exfoliating bark and panicles of large white flowers in June. W and C China. I about 1901 by Ernest Wilson. AM 1908.

**"DEVIL'S CLUB"** See *Oplopanax horridus*.

**"DEVIL'S WALKING STICK"** See *Aralia spinosa*.

†*DICHOTOMANTHES KURZ—Rosaceae—A monotypic genus closely related to *Cotoneaster*, differing in the dry capsular fruits with persistent enlarged calyces. Suitable for a sheltered wall in any fertile soil.

**tristaniicarpa** KURZ A large, cotoneaster-like Chinese shrub with white woolly stems and dark green oblong-elliptic leaves to 7cm long, reticulate above, tomentose beneath. Flowers white in terminal corymbs during June followed by orange-red cotoneaster-like fruits which only ripen after hot summers. Spring foliage prettily tinted. I 1917 by George Forrest. This rare plant has grown undamaged at the Hillier Gardens and Arboretum for many years.

**DIERVILLA** MILL.—**Caprifoliaceae**—A genus of 3 species of easily-grown, small, summer-flowering shrubs allied to *Lonicera* and native to North America. Frequently confused with *Weigela* but differing in the smaller, yellow, two-lipped flowers.

**lonicera** MILL. (*D. canadensis* WILLD.) A small suckering shrub; flowers pale-yellow, honey-suckle-shaped, opening in June and July. Good autumn leaf colour in exposed positions. North America. I 1720.

**rivularis** GATT. A small shrub with lemon-yellow flowers in July and August, and attractive autumn tints. SE United States. C 1898.

**sessilifolia** BUCKL. Flowers sulphur-yellow, in short panicles, from June to August. SE United States. I 1844.

× **splendens** (CARR.) KIRCHN. (*D. lonicera* × *D. sessilifolia*). A hybrid with short-petioled leaves and sulphur-yellow flowers. Originated about 1850.

**DIOSMA pulchella** See *Agathosma pulchella*.

**DIOSPYROS** L.—**Ebenaceae**—A large genus of nearly 500 species of mainly tropical evergreen and deciduous dioecious trees and shrubs, many of considerable economic importance such as *D. ebenum*, the source of ebony. Few species are hardy.

**armata** HEMSL. A remarkable, large, slow-growing, semi-evergreen, Chinese shrub with spiny spreading branches; leaves lustrous. I 1904 by Ernest Wilson.

**kaki** L. f. (*D. chinensis* BLUME) "Chinese Persimmon". A large shrub or small tree long cultivated in the East for its edible fruits, and in this country for the glorious orange-yellow to orange-red and plum-purple autumn colour of its large, lustrous leaves. The orange-yellow, tomato-like fruits are carried here in the open most late summers. China. I 1796.

**lotus** L. The "Date Plum" is a perfectly hardy small tree with tapered leaves dark polished green above, paler below. The female trees produce purple or yellow fruits like small tomatoes. E Asia. C 1597.

**DIOSPYROS**—*continued*

**virginiana** L. The North American "Persimmon" forms an elegant, wide-spreading tree of medium size, giving good autumn colour. Has rugged, tessellated bark. I 1629.

**DIOSTEA** MIERS—**Verbenaceae**—A genus of 3 species of shrubs or small trees native to Chile and Argentina.

**juncea** (GILL. & HOOK.) MIERS A tall elegant shrub, resembling the "Spanish Broom" in growth, but with opposite leaves. Clusters of pale lilac, verbena-like flowers are borne in June, but seldom with sufficient profusion to be conspicuous. Andes of Chile and Argentina. I 1890.

**DIPELTA** MAXIM.—**Caprifoliaceae**—A small genus of 4 species of tall shrubs, native of China and bearing a general resemblance to *Weigela*. They differ mainly in their showy, winged fruits.

**floribunda** MAXIM. A large shrub of first class garden merit. Fragrant weigela-like flowers produced in great profusion in May, pink, flushed yellow at the throat. C and W China. I 1902 by Ernest Wilson. AM 1927.

**ventricosa** HEMSL. A large, attractive, spring-flowering shrub. The conspicuous lilac-rose flowers have a curiously swollen base. W China. I 1904 by Ernest Wilson.

**yunnanensis** FRANCH. Large shrub; flowers cream-coloured with orange markings. Related to *D. ventricosa* but flowers narrowed at base. W China. I 1910 by George Forrest.

**DIPLACUS** See *Mimulus*.

**DIPTERONIA** OLIV.—**Aceraceae**—Two species in C and S China allied to *Acer* and the only other member of the family. They differ from *Acer* in having the fruit winged all round instead of on one side.

**sinensis** OLIV. A large Chinese shrub with conspicuous, pinnate leaves. The flowers are inconspicuous but are followed, in autumn, by large clusters of pale green changing to red, winged seeds rather like those of the wych elm, but more conspicuous. I about 1900 by Ernest Wilson. AM 1922.

**DIRCA** L.—**Thymelaeaceae**—A genus of only 2 species of deciduous shrubs native to North America and related to *Daphne*, differing botanically in the exserted stamens and style. They thrive in moist soils particularly those of a calcareous nature.

**occidentalis** A. GRAY A rare medium-sized shrub similar to *D. palustris* and differing in its more upright habit, its hairy young leaves and shoots and the broader leaves. The flowers are slightly larger and more distictly lobed than in *D. palustris*. California. First flowered in the Hillier Gardens and Arboretum in March 1981.

**palustris** L. "Leatherwood". An interesting shrub of medium size. Flowers yellow, about 12mm long, produced usually in threes on the leafless branches during March. The strong, flexible stems are used for basketmaking in some parts of the United States. North America. I 1750.

‡**DISANTHUS** MAXIM.—**Hamamelidaceae**—A monotypic genus related to *Liquidambar*.

**cercidifolius** MAXIM. A medium-sized shrub resembling a witch hazel in habit, and Judas tree in leaf, highly valued for its beautiful soft crimson and claret-red autumn tints. The tiny purplish flowers are produced in October. Requires a moist but well drained soil in semi-shade. Japan, SE China. I 1893. AM 1936. FCC 1970.

**DISCARIA** HOOK.—**Rhamnaceae**—About 15 species of spiny trees and shrubs related to *Colletia* and found in S America, New Zealand, Australia and Tasmania. Like *Colletia* they have prominent, opposite spines and small, clustered flowers. They require a sunny, sheltered position and will grow in most well drained soils.

**crenata** (CLOS) REG. A large, spiny shrub or small tree with drooping branches. Leaves up to $4 \times 1.5$cm, elliptic to ovate-lanceolate, crenate-undulate at the margin, emarginate at

**DISCARIA crenata**—*continued*

the apex. Flowers small, white, with 5 lobes, borne in clusters of 2-4 in the leaf axils in June. Previously listed as *D. serratifolia*. C and S Chile, Argentina. C 1842.

**serratifolia** See *D. crenata*.

**toumatou** RAOUL "Wild Irishman". A botanically interesting, small to medium-sized, curious New Zealand shrub allied to *Colletia* but less formidably armed. Flowers small, green-white but numerous; leaves small, in opposite clusters or occasionally absent. Spines in pairs, slender, green, over 2.5cm long. I 1975.

**\*DISTYLIUM** SIEB. & ZUCC.—**Hamamelidaceae**—A small genus of about 12 species of evergreen shrubs and trees related to *Sycopsis* but with flowers in racemes. Native to E and SE Asia and C America. They thrive best in conditions suitable to *Hamamelis*.

**racemosum** SIEB. & ZUCC. A wide-spreading, but slow-growing evergreen shrub reaching tree size in the wild, with glossy, leathery leaves. Its petalless flowers consist of clusters of conspicuous red stamens produced in racemes in April and May. S Japan, Taiwan, Korea, China. I 1876. The plant previously listed as *Sycopsis tutcheri* is now considered to be the Chinese form of this species. It differs from the more commonly grown form in its much more vigorous habit, smaller, glossier leaves and its smaller flower clusters. It has been seen in flower in late winter at the same time as *Sycopsis sinensis* and in midsummer. The racemes produced in winter barely expand and at that time of year this plant more resembles a *Sycopsis*.

**DOCYNIA** DECNE.—**Rosaceae**—A genus of about 5 species of small, evergreen or semi-evergreen trees and shrubs resembling wild pears and allied to *Cydonia* of which the name is an anagram. Natives of the Himalaya, China and SE Asia. Rare in cultivation in this country.

**delavayi** (FRANCH.) SCHNEID. A Chinese tree; leaves 3-5 lobed on young plants becoming lanceolate, glabrous or nearly so beneath, persisting into the winter; flowers in April, white, rose-tinted without; fruits apple-like, yellow. SW China. C 1890.

**indica** (WALL.) DECNE. (*D. rufifolia* (H. LEV.) REHD.) A species similar to *D. delavayi*, but with less persistent leaves, tomentose beneath. Young leaves reddish. E Himalaya, China, SE Asia. I 1903.

**"DOGWOOD"** See *Cornus*.

**DORYCNIUM** VILL.—**Leguminosae**—A small genus of about 12 species of sub-shrubs and herbs, found in the Mediterranean region and the Canary Islands. Leaves usually 5-foliolate, the basal pair of leaflets resembling stipules, flowers in heads. They require a sunny, well drained position in most soils.

**hirsutum** (L.) SER. A charming dwarf sub-shrub with erect annual stems and terminal heads of pink-tinged white pea flowers during late summer and autumn. The whole plant is silvery hairy, a pleasant foil for the red-tinged fruit pods. Requires a position in full sun. Mediterranean region, S Portugal. C 1683.

**"DOVE TREE"** See *Davidia involucrata*.

**DRACAENA australis** See *Cordyline australis*.

**indivisa** See *Cordyline indivisa*.

**†\*DRIMYS** FORST. & FORST. f.—**Winteraceae**—About 9 species of evergreen trees and shrubs, natives of Malaysia, E Australia, New Guinea and C and S America. The cultivated species are handsome plants for favoured localities.

**andina** See *D. winteri* var. *andina*.

**aromatica** See *D. lanceolata*.

**colorata** See *Pseudowintera colorata*.

**lanceolata** (POIR.) BAILL. (*D. aromatica* (R. BR.) F. MUELL.) A medium-sized to large, aromatic shrub of slender, upright habit with purplish-red shoots and dark green leaves green beneath. Attractive copper-tinted young growths, and numerous small, creamy white

**DRIMYS lanceolata**—*continued*
flowers in April and May. Male and female on separate plants. Tasmania, SE Australia. I 1843. AM 1926.

**winteri** FORST. & FORST. f. "Winter's Bark". A very handsome, tall shrub or small tree with large, leathery leaves glaucous beneath. Flowers fragrant, ivory-white, in loose umbels, opening in May. We grow two forms, one with shorter broader leaves than the other. The broad leaved form is sometimes distinguished as var. *latifolia* MIERS. Both these plants are considered to represent var. *chilense* (DC.) A. GRAY. C Chile. I 1827. AM 1971.
**var. andina** REICHE (*D. andina* HORT.) A dwarf, compact, slow-growing variety. It flowers freely at only 30cm tall. Chile, Argentina.

**\*DRYAS** L.—**Rosaceae**—A genus of 2 species of carpeting plants with small evergreen oak-like leaves, dark shining green above, gleaming white beneath. Natives of N temperate and arctic regions. Suitable for screes or wall tops, between paving or on the rock garden, in most soils.

**octopetala** L. "Mountain Avens". A native species. The white, yellow-centred flowers like little dog roses are carried on 7.5cm stalks, and cover the whole plant during May or early June. These are followed by silky tassels which later change to fluffy grey balls of down. North America, Europe (including the British Isles), Asia. C 1750. AM 1955. AGM 1984.
**'Minor'** A charming miniature, smaller in all its parts. C 1930. AGM 1984.

× **suendermannii** KELLERER ex SUENDERM. (*D. drummondii* × *D. octopetala*) An uncommon hybrid similar in most respects to *D. octopetala*, but differing in its slightly larger, rather erect leaves and its nodding, creamy white flower buds, those of the native plant being erect and white; flowering in May or early June. C 1750. AM 1955. AGM 1984.

**ECHINOPANAX** See *Oplopanax*.

**EDGEWORTHIA** MEISSN.—**Thymelaeaceae**—A small genus of 2 species of shrubs related to *Daphne* and native to the Himalaya and China.

**chrysantha** LINDL. (*E. papyrifera* SIEB. & ZUCC.) A Chinese shrub attaining 1.2-1.5m. Dense, nodding terminal clusters of fragrant yellow flowers clothed on the outside with white, silky hairs open in late winter. Used in Japan for the manufacture of a high class paper for currency. I 1845. AM 1961. A form with orange-red flowers is also in cultivation. It received an AM in 1982 as f. *rubra*.

**EDWARDSIA chilensis** See *Sophora macrocarpa*.

**EHRETIA** P. BROWNE—**Ehretiaceae**—About 50 species of evergreen and deciduous trees and shrubs widely distributed in tropical and subtropical regions. Two species are in cultivation and thrive in any fertile soil, including chalk soils. Both are of distinctive appearance having conspicuous leaves and corymbose panicles of small white flowers. Tender when young, ripened growth will withstand our coldest winters, but unripened growth is liable to frost damage.

**dicksonii** HANCE (*E. macrophylla* HORT. not WALL.) An interesting, fast-growing, small sturdy tree with conspicuously large, roughly hairy, lustrous leaves to 23cm long. Broad corymbs of small, fragrant, white flowers in June. China, Taiwan, Ryukyu Isles. I 1897 by Ernest Wilson.

**ovalifolia** HASSKARL (*E. thyrsiflora* (SIEB. & ZUCC.) NAKAI) (*E. acuminata* HORT. not R. BR.) (*E. serrata* HORT. not ROXB.) A small, slow-growing tree; leaves smaller than those of *E. dicksonii* and glabrous, or nearly so, at maturity; flowers later, normally in August. China, Japan, Korea and Taiwan. I 1900.

**thyrsiflora** See *E. ovalifolia*.

**ELAEAGNUS** L.—**Elaeagnaceae**—A genus of 30 or 40 species of deciduous and evergreen, mostly fast-growing shrubs or small trees natives of S Europe and Asia with one species in North America. Excellent wind resisters; valuable for hedges and shelter belts

**ELAEAGNUS**—*continued*

particularly in maritime and exposed areas. The flowers, though small, are pleasantly scented and produced in abundance. They will thrive in any fertile soil except very shallow chalk soil.

**angustifolia** L. (*E. angustifolia* var. *orientalis* (L.) KUNTZE) "Oleaster". A large, spiny shrub or small tree with fragrant flowers in June and silvery-grey, willow-like leaves. Fruits silvery-amber, oval, 12mm long. Easily mistaken for the "Willow-leaved Pear" (*Pyrus salicifolia*). Seedlings and young plants have broader, hairy leaves. Temperate W Asia, widely naturalised in S Europe. Cultivated in England in the 16th century. AM 1978.

**var. caspica** SOSN. A striking form with broader leaves which are very silvery especially when young. Caucasus.

**var. orientalis** See *E. angustifolia*.

**commutata** BERNH. (*E. argentea* PURSH not MOENCH.) "Silver Berry". A medium-sized, stoloniferous shrub, leaves intensely silver, flowers fragrant in May. Fruits small, egg-shaped, silvery. North America. I 1813. AM 1956.

\* × **ebbingei** HORT. (*E. macrophylla* × *E. pungens*). (*E.* × *submacrophylla* SERVETT.) A large, hardy, fast-growing evergreen shrub, splendid for creating shelter, even near the sea. Leaves large, silvery beneath. Flowers in autumn, silvery-scaly and fragrant; fruits orange with silvery freckles in spring. Garden origin 1929.

**'Albert Doorenbos'** One of the original seedlings. Leaves large, up to 12cm long and 6cm across.

**'Gilt Edge'** Leaves margined with golden yellow. C 1961. AM 1971. FCC 1987. AGM 1984.

**'Limelight'** Leaves green above at first with silvery scales, developing a broad, central blotch of deep yellow and pale green, silvery beneath. Liable to revert.

**'The Hague'** Similar to 'Albert Doorenbos' but leaves smaller, to 10 × 5cm. AM 1989.

\***glabra** THUNB. A first class, vigorous, thornless evergreen shrub similar to *E. macrophylla*, but with narrower leaves. Flowers fragrant in autumn; fruits orange with silvery freckles. China, Korea, Japan. C 1888.

\***macrophylla** THUNB. The broad, rotund leaves of this species are silvery on both surfaces, becoming green above as the season advances. Eventually a large spreading shrub. Flowers in autumn, fragrant. Korea, Japan. I 1879 by Charles Maries. AM 1932.

**multiflora** THUNB. (*E. edulis* CARR.) (*E. longipes* A. GRAY) A wide-spreading shrub of medium size with leaves green above, silvery beneath. Most decorative in July when laden with its oblong, edible, ox-blood-red fruits. Flowers fragrant, produced in April and May on the new shoots. Japan, China. I 1862. AM 1976.

**parvifolia** WALL. ex ROYLE (*E. umbellata* var. *parvifolia* (ROYLE) SCHNEID.) A large shrub with arching branches and bronze-scaly shoots silvery when young. Leaves elliptic-lanceolate, scaly above when young becoming bright glossy green. Fragrant creamy white flowers in spring and early summer are followed by red fruits. Himalaya, W China. AM 1985.

\***pungens** THUNB. A vigorous, spreading, rarely spiny evergreen shrub up to 5m. A good shelter-making evergreen. Leaves green and shiny above, dull white speckled with brown scales beneath. Flowers in autumn, fragrant. Japan. I 1830.

**'Dicksonii'** ('Aurea') A rather slow-growing, erect clone, leaves with a wide irregular margin of golden yellow.

**'Frederici'** A slow-growing form, the narrow leaves mainly pale creamy yellow with a narrow, bright green border. C 1888.

**'Goldrim'** A striking form with deep glossy green leaves margined with bright yellow. The margin is brighter than that of 'Variegata' and narrower than that of 'Dicksonii'. Originated as a sport of 'Maculata'.

**'Maculata'** Leaves with a central splash of gold, giving a very bright effect. A very handsome shrub of moderate growth but prone to reversion. FCC 1891. AGM 1984.

**var. reflexa** See *E.* × *reflexa*.

**'Simonii'** A handsome form of erect habit with broad, elliptic-oblong leaves. C 1862.

**'Variegata'** A large vigorous shrub, leaves with a thin creamy yellow margin.

\* × **reflexa** MORR. & DECNE. (*E. glabra* × *E. pungens*). (*E. pungens* var. *reflexa* (MORR. & DECNE.) SCHNEID.) A tall, vigorous nearly spineless evergreen with elongated, reddish-brown, almost scandent branches. Leaves densely clad beneath with brown scales. Japan.

**ELAEAGNUS**—*continued*

**umbellata** THUNB. (*E. crispa* THUNB.) A large, strong-growing, wide-spreading shrub with yellowish-brown shoots and soft green leaves, silvery beneath, giving a unique effect in autumn when heavily laden with its small, rounded pale red fruits speckled with white. Flowers delightfully fragrant in May and June. China, Korea, Japan. I 1830. AM 1933.

**var. parvifolia** See *E. parvifolia*.

†\***ELAEOCARPUS** L.—**Elaeocarpaceae**—A genus of about 60 species of evergreen trees related to *Aristotelia* and distributed from SE Asia to Australia and New Zealand. The following species thrive best in a peaty soil in very mild areas.

**cyaneus** See *E. reticulatus*.

**dentatus** (FORST. & FORST. f.) VAHL An unusual species with purplish-grey fruits, of botanical interest, for sheltered gardens. Tiny yellow-red flowers are borne in April. New Zealand. I 1883.

**reticulatus** SMITH (*E. cyaneus* AIT. ex SIMS) An Australian shrub of medium size, bearing in summer racemes of white, fringed flowers, recalling those of *Chionanthus*, followed by conspicuous, turquoise-blue, marble-like fruits. For mildest localities only. E Australia. I 1803. FCC 1912.

**"ELDER"** See *Sambucus*.

**"ELDER, BOX"** See *Acer negundo*.

**ELEUTHEROCOCCUS** MAXIM. (*Acanthopanax* (DECNE. & PLANCH.) MIQ.)—**Araliaceae**—About 50 species of trees and shrubs, sometimes climbing, related to *Fatsia* and *Aralia*, natives of E and SE Asia. Leaves lobed to palmately compound. Umbels of small flowers are followed by clusters of black fruits.

**henryi** OLIVER (*Acanthopanax henryi* (OLIVER) HARMS) A large shrub with bristly shoots and leaves with 5 leaflets, producing large spherical heads of black fruits resembling giant blackberries. When in flower besieged by insects of many kinds. C China. I 1901.

**sieboldianus** (MAK.) KOIDZ. (*Acanthopanax sieboldianus* MAK., *A. pentaphyllus* (SIEB. & ZUCC.) MARCHAL, *A. spinosus* HORT. not (L. f.) MIQ.) A medium-sized shrub with numerous erect stems and clusters of three to five-parted leaves, each cluster with a small curved prickle at its base. China. I 1874.

**'Variegatus'** Leaflets edged creamy-white.

**simonii** (SCHNEID.) NAKAI (*Acanthopanax simonii* SCHNEID.) A medium-sized shrub with spiny stems and bristly leaves composed of 5 sharply toothed, bristly leaflets. China. I 1901.

‡**ELLIOTTIA** MUEHLENB. ex ELLIOTT—**Ericaceae**—Until recently regarded as monotypic, this genus is now regarded as containing 4 species. They require a moist, lime-free soil and an open sunny position.

**bracteata** (MAXIM.) BENTH. & HOOK. f. (*Tripetaleia bracteata* MAXIM.) A small, slender shrub with reddish-brown, rounded stems and glabrous, entire, obovate leaves. The greenish-white or pink-tinged flowers are borne in erect, terminal racemes in July and August. Japan. I 1893.

**paniculata** (SIEB. & ZUCC.) BENTH. & HOOK. f. (*Tripetaleia paniculata* SIEB. & ZUCC.) A small, erect shrub with reddish-brown, angular stems. Leaves obovate, minutely pubescent beneath. Flowers white or pink-tinged, with usually 3 petals, borne in erect, terminal panicles from July to September. Japan. Introduced by Maries in 1879.

**pyrolifolia** (BONG.) BRIM & STEVENS (*Cladothamnus pyrolifolius* BONG.) An erect, deciduous North American shrub of about 1.2m, so distinct as to be well worthy of inclusion in any collection of ericaceous plants. The curious flowers, borne in June, have 5 spreading petals of terracotta edged with yellow.

**racemosa** ELLIOTT "Georgia Plume". A beautiful medium-sized, erect-branched, enkianthus-like shrub, scarcely known in European gardens. Leaves oblong-elliptic, 5-10cm

**ELLIOTTIA racemosa**—*continued*

long. The four-petalled, white, slightly fragrant flowers are carried in erect terminal racemes or panicles during late summer. SE United States. I 1813.

**"ELM"** See *Ulmus*.

**"ELM, WATER"** See *Planera aquatica*.

**ELSHOLTZIA** WILLD.—**Labiatae**—A small genus of about 30 species of aromatic herbs and sub-shrubs natives of Asia, Europe and Ethiopia. The following are valued for their late flowers. In cold districts or after severe frost the stems are usually cut to the ground in winter but reappear the following spring. Easily grown in any fertile soil, and an open position in full sun.

**fruticosa** (D. DON) REHD. (*E. polystachya* BENTH.) A vigorous, pubescent shrub up to 2m bearing elliptic-oblong to lanceolate leaves and long slender spikes of small white flowers during late summer and autumn. Himalaya, W China. I about 1903.

**stauntonii** BENTH. A small sub-shrub with rounded stems, the leaves lance-shaped, smelling of mint when crushed. Flowers lilac-purple, freely borne in panicles from August to October making a splendid splash of late colour. N China. I 1909.

'**Alba**' Flowers white.

‡\***EMBOTHRIUM** FORST. & FORST. f.—**Proteaceae**—A small genus of about 8 species of evergreen trees or shrubs, natives of the Andes of S America. Ideally sited when growing in a sheltered border or woodland clearing in a deep, moist but well drained lime-free soil. Particularly suitable for gardens in the west and south-west.

**coccineum** FORST. & FORST. f. "Chilean Fire Bush". This glorious species with its profusion of brilliant orange-scarlet flowers in May and early June is one of the most desirable garden treasures. Normally an erect, semi-evergreen, slender, tall shrub or small tree with a measured span of life, but on Valencia Island, SW Ireland, there is a giant of 15m. Chile. I 1846. AM 1928.

**Lanceolatum group** (*E. coccineum* var. *lanceolatum* (RUIZ & PAVON) KUNTZE) This, the least evergreen form with linear-lanceolate leaves, is perfectly hardy. Collected by Harold Comber. AM 1932. FCC 1948 when exhibited as 'Norquinco Form' by the late Lord Aberconway, who pointed out that the flower clusters touch one another, so that the whole branch is clad in scarlet. AGM 1984.

**Longifolium group** Differs in its longer, usually persistent leaves. FCC 1948.

**EMMENOPTERYS** OLIV.—**Rubiaceae**—A small genus of 2 species of deciduous trees, natives of E Asia. The following is the only species in general cultivation and needs a sheltered site.

**henryi** OLIV. A rare small tree or large shrub of spreading habit. Leaves large, ovate, particularly decorative in spring when the bronze-coloured young growths unfold. E.H. Wilson described it as being "one of the most strikingly beautiful trees of the Chinese forests, with its flattish to pyramidal corymbs of white, rather large flowers and still larger white bracts". First flowered in this country at Wakehurst Place, Sussex in late summer 1987. It prefers a moist, deep loam but is chalk-tolerant. China. I 1907 by Ernest Wilson.

‡\***EMPETRUM** L.—**Empetraceae**—Dwarf carpeting shrubs, natives of moors and mountains and wild, windswept places. 4 or 5 species widely distributed.

**atropurpureum** FERN. & WIEG. A wiry-stemmed shrub covered with a white tomentum. Fruits reddish-purple. North America. C 1890.

**hermaphroditum** (LANGE) HAGERUP (*E. nigrum scoticum*) An hermaphrodite species similar to *E. nigrum* but growth more compact. Northerly latitudes of N hemisphere (incl British Isles).

**nigrum** L. The "Crowberry" is a very widely distributed, procumbent evergreen forming wide-spreading dense carpets; inconspicuous purple-red flowers followed by glossy black

**EMPETRUM nigrum**—*continued*

fruits. Requires a moist, lime-free soil. Northerly latitudes of N hemisphere (incl British Isles).

**'Lucia'** A form with the young growths creamy white.

‡**ENKIANTHUS** LOUR.—**Ericaceae**—An outstanding, distinct group of shrubs, requiring lime-free soil. About 10 species native from the Himalaya to Japan. The flowers, produced in May, are drooping, cup or urn-shaped, and prettily veined, while the exquisite colouring of the fading leaves is not excelled in any other genus.

**campanulatus** (MIQ.) NICHOLS. An erect-branched Japanese species attaining 2.5-3m. A splendid shrub with variable yet subtle qualities and one of the easiest to grow of a lovely genus. Flowers cup-shaped, sulphur to rich bronze carried in great profusion and lasting for three weeks; useful for cutting. Autumn foliage of every shade between yellow and red. Japan. I 1880 by Charles Maries. AM 1890. AGM 1984.

**Albiflorus group** (f. *albiflorus* (MAK.) MAK.) Flowers creamy white.

**cernuus** (SIEB. & ZUCC.) MAK. A Japanese species mainly cultivated as the following form.

**var. rubens** (MAXIM.) MAK. The best form of a choice species. A small to medium-sized shrub noteworthy for its deep red, fringed flowers and brilliant autumn colour of deep reddish-purple. AM 1930.

**chinensis** FRANCH. (*E. himalaicus* var. *chinensis* (FRANCH.) DIELS) (*E. sinohimalaicus* CRAIB) A remarkably beautiful small tree or tall narrow shrub, under favourable conditions reaching 6m. Flowers yellow and red with darker veins, carried in many-flowered umbels. Leaves comparatively large, usually with red petioles, giving attractive autumn tints. See also *E. deflexus*. W China, NE Upper Burma. I 1900. AM 1935.

**deflexus** (GRIFF.) SCHNEID. A small tree related to *E. chinensis* differing in the leaves being hairy beneath and in the larger flowers which are cream veined with pink. Some plants distributed as *E. chinensis* belong here. Himalaya, W China. I 1908 by Ernest Wilson.

**perulatus** (MIQ.) SCHNEID. (*E. japonicus* HOOK. f.) A densely leafy, slow-growing, compact Japanese shrub to 2m high. Masses of urn-shaped, white flowers appear with the leaves in spring. One of the most consistently good autumn shrubs for the intensity of its scarlet leaves. Japan. I about 1870. AM 1979. AGM 1984.

†\***ENTELEA** R. BR.—**Tiliaceae**—A monotypic genus requiring a sheltered site or conservatory. Among cultivated plants it is most closely allied to *Sparmannia*.

**arborescens** R. BR. A shrub up to 3m for the mildest localities. Leaves large, heart-shaped and double toothed. Flowers in erect open heads, white, with central bunch of yellow stamens, May. The wood of this plant is one of the lightest known, lighter even than cork. New Zealand. I 1820.

\***EPHEDRA** L.—**Ephedraceae**—A genus of some 40 species of curious shrubs with slender rush-like green stems and leaves reduced to tiny scales. A genus of great botanical interest, providing a link between flowering plants and conifers. They are widely distributed in N and S America and Eurasia.

**andina** C.A. MEY. A dwarf, spreading species from Chile. I 1896.

**distachya** L. "European Shrubby Horsetail". Dwarf shrub with slender, erect stems forming large creeping patches. Fruits, when produced, red. S and E Europe. Cultivated in the 16th century.

**gerardiana** WALL. **var. sikkimensis** STAPF A dwarf shrub with erect, many-branched stems forming extensive patches. Himalaya (E Nepal, Sikkim, Bhutan). I 1915. The typical variety is found in the W Himalaya.

‡\***EPIGAEA** L.—**Ericaceae**—A genus of 3 species of creeping shrubs for peaty soils and semi-shade. A hybrid between the following species (*E.* × *intertexta* MULLIGAN) was raised in 1928. Also in cultivation is *E. gaultherioides* (BOISS. & BAL.) TAKHTADJAN (*Orphanidesia gaultherioides* BOISS. & BAL.) from NE Turkey. It was introduced in 1934.

**asiatica** MAXIM. A dwarf, creeping, mat-forming evergreen for moist, peaty soils. Flowers rose-pink, urn-shaped, produced in terminal and axillary racemes in April. Japan. I about 1930. AM 1931.

**EPIGAEA**—*continued*

    **repens** L. "May Flower". A creeping evergreen of a few centimetres high. Dense terminal heads of fragrant white or rose-tinted flowers in April. E North America. I 1736. AM 1931.

\***ERICA** L.—**Ericaceae**—The "Heaths" are a large genus of more than 500 species ranging in habit from dwarf shrubs to small trees. Natives of Europe, Turkey and Africa with by far the largest number of species in S Africa. In *Erica* it is the corolla which is coloured and conspicuous, not the calyx as in the closely related *Calluna*.

    Heaths are now very numerous, for apart from the species and older cultivars, scores of newly named cultivars are constantly swelling the ranks. Their popularity arises in part from their all-the-year-round effect when different cultivars are planted.

    The seasons of flowering indicate that it is possible to have ericas in flower most months of the year. Those forms with long racemes are ideal for cutting for indoor decoration, and even when dead and brown they are not without beauty. All but tree heaths may be pruned immediately after flowering by removing the old inflorescences. When such species as *E. arborea* and *E. lusitanica* become too large and lanky they may be hard pruned into the old wood during April.

    With few exceptions ericas are lime-hating and thrive best in acid soils, particularly those of a sandy nature. They are generally tolerant of semi-shade but flower best in full sun, combining most effectively with callunas (heathers), daboecias, dwarf rhododendrons and dwarf conifers.

    For soils containing lime, a number of mainly winter-flowering species and their cultivars are the most suitable, viz *Erica carnea, E. erigena, E. terminalis* and also the several cultivars of *E. × darleyensis*.

    ‡**arborea** L. "Tree Heath". A medium to large shrub which occasionally grows to 5m high and through. Fragrant white, globular flowers are produced profusely in early spring. S Europe, Caucasus, N and E Africa. I 1658.

    **'Albert's Gold'** A vigorous, hardy form with bright yellow foliage.

    **var. alpina** DIECK A more hardy form, less tall, but more erect. Foliage brighter green. Mountains of Spain. I 1899. AM 1962. AGM 1984.

    **'Estrella Gold'** A slow-growing, very hardy form with bright yellow young foliage. Found in the mountains east of Coimbra, Portugal in 1972.

    **'Pink Joy'** See *E. × veitchii* 'Pink Joy'.

    ‡**australis** L. "Spanish Heath". Medium-sized shrub with rose-purple flowers during April and May. One of the showiest of "Tree Heaths". Very hardy but not recommended for the coldest areas. Spain, Portugal. I 1769. AM 1935. FCC 1962. AGM 1984.

    **'Mr Robert'** A beautiful white form. Found in the mountains of S Spain in 1912. AM 1929.

    **'Riverslea'** A lovely cultivar with flowers of fuchsia-purple. AM 1946.

    ‡†**canaliculata** ANDR. This beautiful "Tree Heath" has reached a height of 5.5m in Cornwall. Flowers white or pink-tinged, with protruding brown anthers. January and March. Needs a warm sheltered position. S Africa. C about 1802.

    **carnea** L. (*E. herbacea* L.) One of the most widely planted dwarf shrubs in cultivation, forming dense hummocks and mats covered with rosy-red flowers throughout winter. Alps of C Europe.

    There are today innumerable cultivars available in a wide range of shades through the white-pink-purple spectrum. The early cultivars begin flowering in November and the latest in April, but the majority are mid-season January to March. All are lime-tolerant but not recommended for shallow chalk soils. Heights may be taken as 15-23cm unless otherwise stated. Thanks to the efforts of Chris Brickell and David McClintock it now seems certain that the well-known name for this popular plant can be retained. Recently hybrids have been raised in Germany between this species and *E. arborea*.

    **'Adrienne Duncan'** Dark bronze-green foliage, carmine-red flowers. Mid.

    **'Alan Coates'** Low, spreading habit. Leaves dark. Flowers pale pink. Mid. AMT 1965.

    **'Ann Sparkes'** A slow-growing, spreading form with golden foliage and rich purple flowers. Late. AMT 1971.

    **'Atrorubra'** Dark rose-pink. Late.

**ERICA carnea**—*continued*

**'Aurea'** Foliage bright gold during spring and early summer. Flowers deep pink paling to almost white. Mid to late. AMT 1971.

**'Cecilia M. Beale'** A free-flowering, white form with erect shoots holding the flowers well above the ground. Mid. C 1920. AGM 1984.

**'C.J. Backhouse'** Pale pink, deepening with age. Late.

**'December Red'** Deep green foliage and strong spikes of rose-red flowers. Mid to late. AMT 1966. AGM 1984.

**'Eileen Porter'** Low-growing, with rich carmine-red flowers from October to April. The dark corollas and the pale calyces produce a delightful bicoloured effect. C 1934. AM 1956.

**'Foxhollow'** Yellowish-green foliage becoming rich yellow tinged red in winter. Flowers pale pink. Late. C 1970.

**'Gracilis'** Bright rose-pink; compact. Early to mid.

**'Heathwood'** Dark green foliage bronze in winter. Flowers bright rose-purple.

**'James Backhouse'** Large flowers of soft pink. Late. C 1911.

**'King George'** Very similar to 'Winter Beauty' but differs in bud when the sepals are pale green and the corolla pale mauve. AGM 1984.

**'Loughrigg'** Rose-purple; dark green foliage. Mid. AMT 1966.

**'March Seedling'** Foliage dark green, flowers rich rose-purple. Spreading habit.

**'Mrs Samuel Doncaster'** Rose-carmine; somewhat glaucous foliage. Mid to late.

**'Myretoun Ruby'** Deep green foliage and masses of deep rose-pink flowers. An excellent plant raised in 1965 at Myretoun House, Scotland. Late. FCC 1988. AGM 1984.

**'Pink Spangles'** Profuse pink flowers in winter.

**'Praecox Rubra'** Deep rose-red. Early to mid. AMT 1966. FCCT 1968. AGM 1984.

**'Prince of Wales'** Bright rose-pink. Late.

**'Queen Mary'** Deepest rose-red. Early to mid.

**'Queen of Spain'** Pale madder-pink. Late.

**'R.B. Cooke'** Clear pink flowers over a long period. 20cm.

**'Rosy Gem'** Bright pink flowers, neat bushy habit. Late.

**'Rubra'** Flowers rose-red. Mid.

**'Ruby Glow'** Large flowers, rich dark red; foliage bronzed. Late. AMT 1967. AGM 1984.

**'Snow Queen'** Large pure white flowers held well above the foliage. Mid. C 1934.

**'Springwood Pink'** Clear rose-pink flowers. Good habit and foliage. Mid. AMT 1964. AGM 1984.

**'Springwood White'** Still the finest white cultivar, its strong trailing growths packed with long, urn-shaped flowers. Mid. AM 1930. FCCT 1964. AGM 1984.

**'Startler'** Flowers soft coral-pink. Mid.

**'Sunshine Rambler'** Foliage clear yellow, bronze-yellow in winter. Flowers pink. Late. C 1971.

**'Thomas Kingscote'** Pale pink. Late.

**'Urville'** See 'Vivellii'.

**'Vivellii'** ('Urville') Deep, vivid carmine; bronzy-red foliage in winter; a superb cultivar. Mid. C 1919. AMT 1964. FCCT 1965. AGM 1984.

**'Westwood Yellow'** Foliage golden yellow, flowers deep pink. Compact habit.

**'Winter Beauty'** Bright rose-pink, commencing to flower in December. Sepals and corolla red-tinged in bud. See also 'King George' with which this has been confused. AM 1922.

‡**ciliaris** L. "Dorset Heath". A low, spreading species up to 0.3m high. Flowers comparatively large, rosy-red, in short terminal racemes, from July to October. SW Europe (incl British Isles).

**'Corfe Castle'** Leaves bronze in winter. Flowers salmon-pink. 30cm.

**'David McClintock'** Flowers white tipped with mauve-pink. Foliage grey. Found wild in Brittany by David McClintock. AM 1972.

**'Mawiana'** A form with larger, long-lasting flowers borne on stiff erect stems. Found in Portugal in 1872 by George Maw.

**'Mrs C.H. Gill'** Dark green foliage and freely produced clear red flowers. AGM 1984.

**'Stoborough'** Long racemes of white flowers. Found in Dorset. 0.5-0.6m. AGM 1984.

**'Wych'** Flesh-pink flowers in long racemes. Found in Dorset. 0.5m.

**ERICA**—*continued*

‡**cinerea** L. The common native purple "Bell Heather", forming mats of wiry stems, and flowering from June to September. Height 25-30cm unless otherwise stated. W Europe (incl British Isles).

'**Alba Major**' White flowers in short racemes.

'**Alba Minor**' Small and compact, 15cm. White. AMT 1967. FCCT 1968.

'**Atropurpurea**' Bright purple.

'**Atrorubens**' Quite distinct, brilliant red flowers in long sprays. AM 1915.

'**Atrosanguinea Smith's Variety**' Flowers of an intense scarlet; dark foliage. 15cm. C 1852.

'**C.D. Eason**' Glowing deep pink. C 1931. FCCT 1966. AGM 1984.

'**Cevennes**' Lavender-rose, over a long period. AMT 1968.

'**C.G. Best**' Soft salmon-pink. C 1931.

'**Cindy**' Large pure pink flowers, foliage bronze-green.

'**Coccinea**' ('Fulgida') Of dwarf habit. 10cm. Dark scarlet. C 1852.

'**Colligan Bridge**' Long, erect racemes of vivid purple.

'**Domino**' White flowers and ebony coloured calyces, a charming combination. AMT 1970.

'**Eden Valley**' Soft lilac-pink, paler at base. 15cm. C 1926. AM 1933. AGM 1984.

'**Fiddler's Gold**' Compact and vigorous with pale green foliage flushed yellow and red when young. Flowers deep mauve. 25cm. AMT 1970.

'**Foxhollow Mahogany**' Dark green foliage. Flowers deep wine-red, profusely borne. 30cm.

'**Fulgida**' See 'Coccinea'.

'**Golden Drop**' Summer foliage golden copper-coloured turning to rusty-red in winter. Flowers pink, rarely produced. 15cm.

'**Golden Hue**' Golden foliage turning red in winter. A most effective plant. 0.5m.

'**G. Osmond**' Pale mauve, dark calyces. C 1931.

'**Hookstone White**' Large white flowers in long racemes. Foliage bright green. 35cm.

'**Lilacina**' Pale lilac.

'**Mrs Dill**' Very neat, compact and low-growing; bright pink. 10cm.

'**My Love**' Striking mauve-blue flowers contrasting effectively with the foliage. 25-30cm.

'**P.S. Patrick**' Long sprays of bright purple flowers. C 1928. AMT 1967.

'**Pink Ice**' Compact and vigorous with bright dark green foliage. Flowers clear pale pink. AMT 1968. FCCT 1971.

'**Purple Beauty**' Flowers deep rose-purple. Dark green foliage.

'**Romiley**' A smaller version of 'Atrorubens', flowers vivid rose-red. 15-20cm.

'**Rosea**' Bright pink. AMT 1966.

'**Ruby**' Rose-purple.

'**Sea Foam**' Pale mauve.

'**Sherry**' Glossy green foliage and clear dark red flowers profusely borne. 30cm.

'**Startler**' Bright gleaming pink.

'**Stephen Davis**' Compact with dark green foliage. Vivid deep pink. 20cm. FCCT 1971.

'**Velvet Night**' Blackish-purple, a most unusual colour.

'**W.G. Notley**' (× *Ericalluna bealeana* 'W.G. Notley') Purple flowers, the corolla deeply divided.

'**Windlebrooke**' Vigorous with golden yellow foliage, orange-red in winter. Flowers mauve.

× **darleyensis** BEAN (*E. carnea* × *E. erigena*). A most useful hybrid in its several forms, and a natural companion to *E. carnea*. All the following clones average 0.5-0.6m in height and flower throughout the winter. Lime-tolerant, but not recommended for shallow chalk soils. See 'Darley Dale'.

'**Ada S. Collings**' White flowers contrast well with the attractive dark green foliage. 20cm.

'**Alba**' See under 'Silberschmelze'.

'**Archie Graham**' Compact growth, dark foliage and racemes of deep rose flowers.

**ERICA × darleyensis**—*continued*

**'Arthur Johnson'** Long dense sprays of magenta flowers, useful for cutting. AM 1952. AGM 1984.

**'Darley Dale'** Pale pink flowers over a long period. One of the most popular of all ericas. This, the original plant, appeared in the Darley Dale Nurseries, Derbyshire, about 1890. Originally catalogued as *E. × darleyensis*. AM 1905.

**'Furzey'** Vigorous and compact with dark green foliage. Flowers deep rose-pink over a long period. Raised at Furzey Gardens. AMT 1968.

**'George Rendall'** A superb form with rich pink flowers over a long period. AGM 1984.

**'Ghost Hills'** Foliage bright green, tipped with cream in spring. Flowers pink with deeper tips. A sport of 'Darley Dale'.

**'J.W. Porter'** Flowers mauve-pink. Young shoots reddish in spring.

**'Jenny Porter'** Flowers soft pink. Vigorous, upright habit.

**'Jack H. Brummage'** Pale yellow foliage, golden tinged red in winter. Deep pink flowers in short spikes. AMT 1970.

**'Margaret Porter'** Glossy green foliage tipped cream when young. Clear rose flowers in short, curving racemes.

**'Silberschmelze'** ('Molten Silver') Perhaps the best winter white, certainly the most rewarding. Sweetly scented flowers over a long period. Sometimes referred to as *E. × darleyensis* 'Alba'. C 1937. AMT 1968. AGM 1984.

**'White Glow'** Flowers white.

**'White Perfection'** Bright green foliage and white flowers.

**erigena** R. ROSS (*E. mediterranea* HORT. not L.) (*E. hibernica* (HOOK. & ARN.) SYME) A dense shrub of small to medium size, covered from March to May with fragrant rose-red flowers. Lime-tolerant but not recommended for shallow chalk soils. The wild Irish form often referred to as *E. hibernica* differs in no way from the continental form. S France, Spain, W Eire.

**'Alba'** White, free-flowering, up to 1.2m.

**'Brightness'** A low-growing form; buds bronze-red, opening to rose-pink. 0.6-1m. C 1925. AM 1972.

**'Coccinea'** Similar to 'Brightness' but buds and flowers richer coloured. 0.6-1m.

**'Glauca'** An erect-growing form of dense compact growth, foliage slightly glaucous. Flowers a pale flesh colour. 1-1.2m.

**'Golden Lady'** Foliage golden yellow, flowers white. Compact habit. 30 cm.

**'Irish Dusk'** Compact habit with dark green foliage and salmon-pink flowers. 45cm. AGM 1984.

**'Irish Salmon'** Salmon-pink. 1m.

**'Nana'** ('Compacta') A compact form only 0.5m, with silvery-pink flowers.

**'Rubra'** Compact habit, dark foliage and ruby-red flowers.

**'Superba'** A fine pink-flowered form, up to 2m or over. AM 1972.

**'W.T. Rackliff'** A charming cultivar of dense, compact habit, with dark green foliage and pure white flowers with brown anthers. 1-1.2m. AM 1972. AGM 1984.

**herbacea** See *E. carnea*.

**hibernica** See *E. erigena*.

**hybrida** This name refers correctly to various hybrids of S African species, but has erroneously been used for several European hybrids, including *E. × darleyensis*, *E. × stuartii*, *E. × watsonii* and *E. × williamsii*.

‡**lusitanica** RUDOLF (*E. codonodes* LINDL.) "Portugal Heath". A fine "Tree Heath", resembling *E. arborea*, but earlier flowering. Large pale green plumose stems crowded with white tubular, fragrant flowers, pink in bud, borne over a very long period from late autumn to early spring. Portugal. AM 1972. FCC 1977. AGM 1984.

**'George Hunt'** Foliage golden yellow.

‡**mackayana** BAB. (*E. mackaii* HOOK.) A rare, dwarf species with dark green foliage, and rose-crimson flowers in umbels from July to September. 15cm. W Ireland, Spain.

**'Dr Ronald Gray'** Flowers white. 15cm.

**'Lawsoniana'** Dwarf form with small pink flowers. Found in Connemara.

**'Plena'** ('Crawfordii') Double, rose-crimson. Found in W Galway.

**mediterranea** See *E. erigena*.

**ERICA**—*continued*

‡†**pageana** BOLUS A remarkable, small S African species. Erect growth and cylindrical clusters of bell-shaped, rich yellow flowers of a waxy texture in spring. In our area it survives only the mildest winters. AM 1937.

×**praegeri** See *E.* × *stuartii*.

‡**scoparia** L. "Besom Heath". A medium-sized shrub of loose habit. Flowers greenish, appearing in May and June. W Mediterranean region. I 1770.

  **subsp. azorica** (HOCHST.) D.A. WEBB. A taller growing form with smaller flowers. Azores.

  **'Minima'** ('Nana') ('Pumila') A dwarf form not above 0.6m. C 1825.

†**sicula** GUSS. (*Pentapera sicula* (GUSS.) KLOTZSCH) A dwarf shrub with erect, downy stems clothed with linear heath-like leaves arranged in whorls of 4. The pitcher-shaped white or pink flowers are borne in terminal clusters during May and June. Sicily, Malta, E Mediterranean region. I 1849. AM 1951.

  **stricta** See *E. terminalis*.

‡×**stuartii** (MACF.) E.F. LINTON (*E.* × *praegeri* OSTENF. ) (*E. mackayana* × *E. tetralix*). Hybrids between "Mackay's Heath" and the "Cross-leaved Heath" have been found where the parents come into contact in the wild.

  **'Charles Stuart'** (*E.* 'Stuartii') A plant found in Co Galway, Ireland, in 1890. Flowers pinched and narrow, deep rose; June-September. When a plant of this cultivar reverted it was shown to have the same parentage as *E.* × *praegeri*, unfortunately the name *E.* × *stuartii* was published first. 0.3m.

  **'Connemara'** (*E.* × *praegeri* 'Connemara') A dwarf shrub with terminal clusters of pale pink flowers during late summer. 15cm. This is the original plant of *E.* × *praegeri* collected in the wild in Connemara in 1890.

  **'Irish Lemon'** Flowers bright pink, young foliage lemon-yellow in spring.

  **'Irish Orange'** Flowers deep pink, young foliage orange tipped.

  **'Stuartii'** See *E.* × *stuartii* 'Charles Stuart'.

**terminalis** SALISB. (*E. stricta* WILLD.) (*E. corsica* DC.) "Corsican Heath". Bushy, medium-sized shrub with erect branches. The rose coloured flowers, borne in late summer in terminal heads, fade to warm brown and remain throughout winter. Excellent on chalk soils. W Mediterranean region, naturalised in N Ireland. I 1765. AGM 1984.

‡**tetralix** L. "Cross-leaved Heath". A native species growing 0.2-0.5m high. Dense heads of rose coloured flowers are produced from June to October. N and W Europe (incl British Isles).

  **'Alba Mollis'** ('Mollis') Pretty grey foliage and white flowers. AM 1927. AGM 1984.

  **'Alba Praecox'** Grey foliage and white flowers; earlier than 'Alba Mollis'.

  **'Con Underwood'** Grey-green hummocks studded with crimson flower clusters. C 1938. AGM 1984.

  **'Hookstone Pink'** Vigorous with silvery-grey foliage. Flowers pale pink. C 1953.

  **'Lawsoniana'** See *E. mackayana* 'Lawsoniana'.

  **'L.E. Underwood'** Silver-grey mounds; flowers pale pink, a striking terracotta in bud. C 1937.

  **'Mary Grace'** Bright pink flowers set amid silvery foliage.

  **'Mollis'** See 'Alba Mollis'.

  **'Pink Glow'** Grey foliage and bright pink flowers.

  **'Pink Star'** An unusual form in which the lilac-pink flowers are held erect on the stems. Foliage grey-green. Low, spreading habit. Found in the wild in Cornwall.

  **'Rosea'** Flowers rose-coloured.

†**umbellata** L. An attractive species of dwarf habit, proving fairly hardy. Flowers throughout summer, cerise-pink, with chocolate anthers. Lime-tolerant. Spain, Portugal and Morocco. AM 1926.

‡**vagans** L. "Cornish Heath". A dwarf, spreading shrub, producing its flowers in long sprays from July to October. SW Europe (incl British Isles).

  **'Alba'** A compact form, flowers white. 0.6m.

  **'Cornish Cream'** Flowers creamy white in slender racemes. Found in Cornwall. 50cm.

  **'Cream'** White flowers in long racemes, an improvement on 'Alba'. 0.6m. AMT 1968.

  **'Diana Hornibrooke'** Red flowers and dark green foliage. Compact habit. 30cm. AMT 1967.

**ERICA vagans**—*continued*

**'Fiddlestone'** A superb form, throwing up long racemes of rose-cerise flowers over a long period. 0.5-0.6m.

**'Grandiflora'** Very long sprays of rose coloured flowers. 1m.

**'Holden Pink'** Compact, mound-forming with dark green foliage. Flowers white flushed mallow-purple at the tips. 35cm. AMT 1966.

**'Kevernensis'** See 'St Keverne'.

**'Kevernensis Alba'** A compact form with small racemes of white flowers. 0.3m. AMT 1971.

**'Lilacina'** Short racemes of lilac-pink flowers over a long period. 0.5m.

**'Lyonesse'** Pure white, with protruding brown anthers. 0.5-1m. C 1925. AM 1928. AGM 1984.

**'Mrs D.F. Maxwell'** Deep cerise; a superb cultivar. 0.5m. AM 1925. FCCT 1970. AGM 1984.

**'Pyrenees Pink'** Long racemes of pink flowers. 0.5m.

**'Rubra'** Rosy-red. 0.5m.

**'St Keverne'** ('Kevernensis') Flowers clear rose-pink. Found in the wild in Cornwall. 0.5m. AM 1914. FCCT 1971. AGM 1984.

**'Valerie Proudley'** A dwarf, dense bush with bright yellow foliage and white flowers. AMT 1971 (for summer foliage). AMT 1971 (for winter foliage).

‡ × **veitchii** BEAN (*E. arborea* × *E. lusitanica*). A hybrid "Tree Heath" of which the following are the most common clones at present in general cultivation:-

**'Exeter'** A beautiful shrub of medium size, with attractive bright green foliage, and great plumes of fragrant white flowers in spring. Not recommended for the coldest areas. AM 1905. This is the original clone raised by Messrs Veitch at Exeter, before 1900. Originally catalogued as *E.* × *veitchii*. AGM 1984.

**'Gold Tips'** Young foliage bright yellow becoming dark green. AM 1981.

**'Pink Joy'** (*E. arborea* 'Pink Joy') Flowers deep pink in bud opening nearly white. C 1969.

**vulgaris** See *Calluna vulgaris*.

‡ × **watsonii** (BENTH.) BEAN (*E. ciliaris* × *E. tetralix*). Hybrids between 2 native species. The following clones are grown:-

**'Dawn'** A spreading form with young foliage yellow in spring, and terminal clusters of large, rose-pink flowers; July to October, often continuing until November. 23cm. Found in Dorset in 1923.

**'F. White'** Flowers white suffused pink. July to October. 20cm. Found in Dorset before 1931.

**'H. Maxwell'** An attractive clone similar to 'Dawn' but taller and more upright in habit, and flowers slightly paler in colour; July to October. 0.3m.

**'Truro'** Rose-coloured flowers in short racemes; July to October. 23cm. The original clone, found wild in Cornwall in 1839 by H.C. Watson. Originally catalogued as *E.* × *watsonii*.

‡ × **williamsii** DRUCE (*E. tetralix* × *E. vagans*). A variable hybrid of which the following are the most common clones at present in general cultivation:-

**'Gwavas'** A dwarf shrub of compact habit with yellowish-green foliage in spring. Flowers pink; July to October. 0.5-0.6m. C 1924.

**'P.D. Williams'** A pretty, late flowering heath. Young growths tipped yellow in spring, becoming bronze in winter. Flowers rose-pink in umbels; July to September. 0.3-0.6m. This is the original clone found in the wild in Cornwall in 1910. Originally catalogued as *E.* × *williamsii*.

× **ERICALLUNA bealeana** KRUSSMANN Plants once listed here eg 'W.G. Notley' were thought to be hybrids between *Calluna vulgaris* and *Erica cinerea*. They are now treated as cultivars of the latter.

**ERINACEA** ADANS.—**Leguminosae**—A monotypic genus related to *Genista* and *Spartium*.

**anthyllis** LINK (*E. pungens* BOISS.) "Hedgehog Broom" "Blue Broom". A dwarf, slow-growing spiny shrub making a very dense, rigid hummock. Requires a well drained

**ERINACEA anthyllis**—*continued*

position in full sun. Flowers slate-blue, in April and May. A splendid sight in the mountains above Granada. SW Europe, N Africa. I 1759. AM 1922. FCC 1976.

**\*ERIOBOTRYA** LINDL.—**Rosaceae**—A small genus of about 27 species of evergreen trees and shrubs related to *Photinia* and native of the Himalaya and E Asia.

**deflexa** (HEMSL.) NAKAI A large shrub similar to *E. japonica* differing in its oblong rather than oblanceolate leaves with rounded not pointed teeth and soon glabrous beneath (with a persistent pale brown tomentum in *E. japonica*). The leaves are also not of such a deep glossy green and are borne on a longer petiole of up to 5cm (up to 1cm in *E. japonica*). Flowers creamy white in panicles during spring and early summer. Taiwan.

**japonica** (THUNB.) LINDL. "Loquat". An architectural plant normally seen as a large shrub in the British Isles, and best grown against a wall. One of the most striking evergreens on account of its firm, leathery, corrugated leaves often 0.3m. long. The clusters of strongly fragrant, hawthorn-like flowers, produced only after a hot summer, open intermittently from November to April, and are sometimes followed by globular or pear-shaped, yellow fruits 4-5cm across. China, Japan. Commonly cultivated in warmer countries for its edible fruits. I 1787.

**†ERYTHRINA** L.—**Leguminosae**—A large genus of more than 100 species of mainly tropical deciduous trees and shrubs with trifoliolate leaves and often prickly stems. Natives of tropical and subtropical regions in both hemispheres.

**crista-galli** L. "Coral Tree". A very beautiful semi-woody plant from Brazil, with trifoliolate leaves. Flowers like waxen "Sweet-peas", deep scarlet, in large terminal racemes during summer. Needs a warm, sunny wall, and protection for the crown in winter. I 1771. AM 1954. FCC 1987.

**\*ESCALLONIA** MUTIS ex L. f.—**Escalloniaceae**—About 40 species of mainly evergreen shrubs and small trees, all natives of S America, mainly in the Andes. They rank high among flowering evergreens, and are all the more valuable for giving their display during summer and early autumn. Though not all are hardy inland, most can be grown successfully near the sea, and there make perfect hedges and wind-breaks. Unless otherwise stated they average 1.5-2.5m in height. The species are native of S America. With rare exceptions they are lime-tolerant and drought-resistant, thriving in all types of well drained soil. No species have large leaves or large flowers, reference to size being only comparative within the group.

Pruning consisting of cutting back the old flowering growths may be carried out immediately after flowering and large unwieldy plants may be hard pruned at the same time.

**'Alice'** A first class hybrid with large leaves and large, rose-red flowers.

**'Apple Blossom'** A very attractive, slow-growing hybrid with pink and white flowers. AM 1946. AGM 1984.

**bellidifolia** See under *E.* × *stricta* 'Harold Comber'.

**†bifida** LINK & OTTO (*E. montevidensis* (CHAM. & SCHLECHT.) DC.) Handsome large shrub from S Brazil, requiring wall protection. Leaves large, flowers white, carried in large panicles, in late summer and autumn. S Brazil, Uruguay. I 1827. AM 1915.

**'C.F. Ball'** Large leaves aromatic when bruised. Crimson flowers; vigorous-growing up to 3m. Excellent for maritime exposure. A seedling of *E. rubra* var. *macrantha* raised at Glasnevin about 1912. AM 1926.

**'C.H. Beale'** A strong-growing medium-sized shrub with crimson-red flowers borne in profusion.

**'Crimson Spire'** See *E. rubra* 'Crimson Spire'.

**'Donard Beauty'** Rich rose-red, exceedingly free-flowering shrub with large leaves, aromatic when bruised. AM 1930.

**'Donard Brilliance'** Flowers rich rose-red, large. A shrub of graceful habit with arching branches and large leaves. AM 1928.

**'Donard Gem'** Large pink, sweetly-scented flowers; growth compact, leaves small. AM 1927.

# TREES AND SHRUBS

ESCALLONIA—*continued*

**'Donard Radiance'** A magnificent strong-growing shrub of compact habit and medium size. Large, brilliant, soft rose-red, chalice-shaped flowers. Leaves large, shining deep green. AM 1954.

**'Donard Seedling'** (*E.* 'Langleyensis' × *E.* × *virgata*). A vigorous hybrid up to 3m; flowers flesh-pink in bud, opening white, leaves large. AM 1916.

**'Donard Star'** Medium-sized shrub of compact upright habit. Large leaves and large flowers of a lovely rose-pink. AM 1967.

**'Donard White'** Medium-sized shrub of compact, rounded habit with small leaves. Flowers white, pink in bud, produced over a long period.

**'Edinensis'** (*E. rubra* × *E.* × *virgata*). Of neat, bushy habit, 2-2.5m high, leaves small. Flowers carmine in bud opening to clear shell-pink. Raised at Edinburgh Botanic Garden before 1914. AM 1918.

**'E.G. Cheeseman'** A vigorous hybrid of which *E. revoluta* is probably one parent. Flowers deep, bright cherry-red, bell-shaped, 12mm long, nodding, carried in terminal leafy panicles. Leaves large, ovate to rotund obovate, coarsely serrated sage or grey-green. Downy in all its parts.

× **exoniensis** VEITCH (*E. rosea* × *E. rubra*). A vigorous shrub to 4m high with downy, glandular shoots and large leaves; flowers white or blush. AM 1891.

**'Gwendolyn Anley'** A small, very hardy shrub of bushy habit, leaves small, flowers flesh-pink.

**illinita** PRESL. (*E. viscosa* FORBES) A tall, strong-smelling shrub up to 3m with glandular shoots, large glossy green leaves and cylindrical panicles of white flowers. Chile. I 1830.

**'Ingramii'** See *E. rubra* 'Ingramii'.

†**'Iveyi'** (*E. bifida* × *E.* × *exoniensis*). A large, vigorous hybrid with large, handsome, glossy foliage and large panicles of white flowers in autumn. Originally found at Caerhays. AM 1926. AGM 1984.

†**laevis** (VELL.) SLEUM. (*E. organensis* GARDN.) A small Brazilian shrub with large lustrous leaves, aromatic when bruised and large clear pink flowers. I 1844 by William Lobb.

**'Langleyensis'** (*E. rubra* × *E.* × *virgata*). A hardy, graceful shrub up to 2.5m in height with small leaves, the rose-pink flowers wreathing the arching branches. Garden origin 1893. The same cross has occurred in the wild. AM 1897.

**leucantha** REMY. (*E. bellidifolia* PHIL.) A tall graceful shrub recalling *Leptospermum stellatum*, with angular stems and large crowded panicles of white flowers in July. Chile. I 1927 by Harold Comber.

**macrantha** See *E. rubra* var. *macrantha*.

**montana** See under *E. rubra* var. *uniflora*.

**montevidensis** See *E. bifida*.

**'Newryensis'** (*E.* 'Langleyensis' × *E. rosea*). Vigorous, upright growth. Flowers white tinged pink. Leaves large, aromatic when bruised. Makes a good wind-break.

**organensis** See *E. laevis*.

**'Peach Blossom'** Medium-sized shrub, similar in habit to 'Apple Blossom' but with flowers of a clear peach-pink. AGM 1984.

**'Pink Pearl'** Flowers soft pink stained bright rose-pink about 20mm across, when wide open, carried in short dense racemes on arching branches. Rather small obovate leaves.

**'Pride of Donard'** Flowers large, brilliant rose, somewhat bell-shaped, carried in terminal racemes from June onwards. Leaves large, dark polished green above. AGM 1984.

**punctata** See *E. rubra*.

**'Red Elf'** (*E.* 'William Watson' × *E.* 'C.F. Ball'). A vigorous and free-flowering medium-sized shrub with dark glossy green leaves and deep crimson flowers. C 1970. AGM 1984.

†**revoluta** (RUIZ & PAV.) PERS. A large shrub with grey felted shoots and foliage; soft pink to white flowers in terminal racemes from August to September. Chile. I 1887.

**rosea** GRISEB. (*E. pterocladon* HOOK.) Medium-sized shrub with downy angled branches and small leaves. Flowers white, fragrant, in slender racemes. Parent of many hybrids. Patagonia. I 1847 by William Lobb.

**rubra** (RUIZ & PAV.) PERS. (*E. punctata* DC., *E. microphylla* HORT., *E. sanguinea* HORT.) A medium-sized shrub with loose panicles of red flowers in July. Leaves aromatic when bruised. Chile. I 1827.

**ESCALLONIA rubra**—*continued*

**'Crimson Spire'** A strong-growing shrub of erect growth up to 2m. Leaves comparatively large, dark glistening green. Flowers bright crimson. An excellent hedging shrub. AGM 1984.

**'Ingramii'** Flowers deep rose-pink; grows 4m high and makes a good hedge; leaves large, aromatic when bruised. An excellent maritime shrub. C 1833.

**var. macrantha** (HOOK. & ARN.) REICHE (*E. macrantha* HOOK. & ARN.) Flowers rose-crimson, set amidst large, fine, glossy, aromatic leaves. Strong-growing up to 4m, and one of the best hedge plants to withstand sea gales. Parent of many hybrids. Chiloe. I 1848. AGM 1984.

**'Pygmaea'** See 'Woodside'.

**var. uniflora** POEPP. & ENDL. A low, compact, dense-growing shrub with long leaves. Flowers deep red. Originally grown and catalogued as *E. montana*.

**'Woodside'** ('Pygmaea') A small shrub of neat habit, the product of a witches broom in Ireland, suitable for the large rock garden, its branches spreading over a considerable area. Flowers small, crimson.

**'St Keverne'** (*E. kevernensis* HORT.) Medium-sized shrub of arching habit, with small leaves and large, rich, pink flowers; free-flowering.

**'Slieve Donard'** A medium-sized, compact shrub. Leaves small and large panicles of apple-blossom-pink flowers. Very hardy.

× **stricta** REMY. (*E. leucantha* × *E.* × *virgata*). A variable, natural hybrid of which the following clone is grown:-

**'Harold Comber'** One of the hardiest of the family. A dense shrub up to 1.5m, the slender stems crowded with small leaves and small white flowers. Introduced in 1927 by Harold Comber from Chile as *E. bellidifolia* (Comber 988).

†**tucumanensis** HOSSEUS A very distinct and beautiful species making a large shrub with widely arching branches. Leaves rather thin, narrowly elliptic to oblanceolate, to 10cm long, toothed above the middle. Flowers white, 1.5cm long, in drooping panicles in July. NW Argentina. I 1961.

× **virgata** (RUIZ & PAV.) PERS. (*E. philippiana* (A. ENGL.) MAST.) A graceful, small-leaved deciduous shrub with arching branches and white flowers. Not suitable for chalky soils. A hardy species and parent of many hybrids. Chile. I 1866. FCC 1888.

**viscosa** See *E. illinita*.

**'William Watson'** A medium-sized, small-leaved shrub of compact growth. Flowers bright red over a long period.

\***EUCALYPTUS** L'HERIT.—**Myrtaceae**—The "Gum Trees" are a large genus of more than 400 species of fast-growing, evergreen trees, sometimes shrubs, mainly native of Australia with a few species extending to New Guinea, the Phillipines and Java. Not found wild in New Zealand. In common with many other plants of wide distribution, selections from high altitudes usually prove hardier than the same species from lower levels. Several species are hardy or nearly hardy in the British Isles, their lush foliage, unusual multi-stamened flowers (which are white unless otherwise stated) and attractive stems providing an impressive subtropical effect. The leaves of adult trees are often very different from those of young specimens, many providing excellent foliage for floral decoration. The common name refers to the quantity of gum that exudes from their trunks.

Eucalyptus will grow in a great variety of soils and many are tolerant of wet sites but some species tend to become chlorotic in very shallow chalk soils. As yet *E. parvifolia* is the only species which we have proved will grow indefinitely on a chalk soil.

They are best planted as small, pot-grown plants, preferably in the spring. If, due to over-rapid growth, there is a likelihood that a tall, young tree will blow over, we recommend cutting back to about 25-45cm from the ground in the spring and selecting the strongest new growth, removing all other subsidiary shoots, unless a bushy plant with several stems is preferred. Strong cold winds are a greater danger to many eucalypts than hard frosts.

†**amygdalina** LABILL. (*E. salicifolia* CAV. ) "Black Peppermint". A large shrub or medium-sized tree with fibrous bark and long, narrow, aromatic, green leaves. E Tasmania.

**EUCALYPTUS**—*continued*

**camphora** R.T. BAKER (*E. ovata* var. *aquatica* BLAKELY) "Broad-leaved Sally". One of the hardiest species. A small to medium-sized tree with rough bark, forming clumps. Leaves ovate to lanceolate. In its native habitat this species usually grows in wet areas, even in standing water. New South Wales, E Victoria. AM 1977.

†**cinerea** BENTH. "Argyle Apple". A medium-sized tree with silver-grey leaves and fibrous bark. Only hardy in the mildest localities. New South Wales, Victoria.

†**citriodora** HOOK. "Lemon-scented Gum". A large tree in the wild with smooth white bark, adult leaves very slender. Mainly grown in its juvenile stage for its lemon-scented foliage it is only suitable for the mildest areas but worth a place in the conservatory. Widely planted in warm countries. Queensland.

**coccifera** HOOK. f. "Mount Wellington Peppermint". A large Tasmanian tree with striking glaucous leaves and stems, which quality is not apparent in young plants. Passes without injury all but the very severest winters in the Home Counties. Tasmania. I 1840. AM 1953.

†**cordata** LABILL. "Silver Gum". A dense growing species making a small tree with grey-silver sessile leaves and strongly four-angled glaucous-bloomed shoots. The attractive white bark is marked with green or purplish patches. Flowers in winter. It is often seen as a bedding plant grown for its ornamental foliage. E Tasmania. C 1850.

**coriacea** See *E. pauciflora*.

**dalrympleana** MAIDEN "Mountain Gum". A most attractive, very fast-growing species of medium size, proving one of the hardiest. Attractive patchwork bark becoming white and handsome grey-green leaves which are bronze coloured when young. A specimen in the Hillier Gardens and Arboretum was 22m in 1990. New South Wales, Victoria, Tasmania. AM 1953.

†**ficifolia** F. MUELL. "Red-flowering Gum". A superb small tree of lax habit. Leaves broad lanceolate up to 15cm long. Flowers scarlet or flame coloured in large corymbs towards the ends of the branches, very effective against the glossy, green foliage. Very tender, best under glass. Both flowers and foliage are cut and sold in florists' shops. SW Australia. FCC 1907.

†**globulus** LABILL. "Tasmanian Blue Gum". In mild districts this species will make a large noble tree but is more usually seen as a sparsely branched shrub in subtropical bedding schemes. The large leaves are blue-green in colour, almost silvery on young specimens. Tasmania, Victoria. C 1829.

**gunnii** HOOK. f. "Cider Gum". The best known species in cultivation, this fine tree is one of the hardiest. Leaves of adult tree sickle-shaped, sage-green, of young trees rounded and of a startling silver-blue. It will attain large tree size or will make an excellent bush if regularly pruned. Tasmania. C 1853. AM 1950. AGM 1984.

**johnstonii** MAIDEN "Yellow Gum". One of the hardier species. A large tree with reddish peeling bark and bright, glossy, apple-green leaves. A specimen in the Hillier Gardens and Arboretum was 23m in 1990. C 1886. Tasmania. *E. subcrenulata* MAIDEN & BLAKELY is similar but a smaller tree with wavy-edged leaves. It occurs at higher altitudes than *E. johnstonii*.

**mitchelliana** CAMBAGE A small to medium-sized weeping tree or large shrub known as "Weeping Sally" in Australia. Bark smooth and white with age. Leaves narrowly lanceolate, green. Victoria (Mt Buffalo).

**niphophila** See *E. pauciflora* subsp. *niphophila*.

**nitens** MAIDEN "Silver Top". A vigorous, large tree with long, ribbon-like glaucous leaves. Appears to be one of the more hardy species but can be damaged or even killed in the hardest winters. Victoria, New South Wales. AM 1975.

**parvifolia** CAMBAGE An exceptionally hardy species, here making a handsome medium-sized tree with attractively peeling bark and surviving the severest winters. Will even tolerate chalk soils. Mature leaves narrow, blue-green. New South Wales.

**pauciflora** SIEB. ex SPRENG. (*E. coriacea* SCHAUER) "Snow Gum". A small high-mountain tree, and one of the hardiest species. When growing conditions are favourable will withstand up to 15°C of frost. The sickle-shaped leaves are up to 20cm long , the trunk white. C 1880. SE Australia, Tasmania.

**EUCALYPTUS pauciflora**—*continued*

**subsp. niphophila** (MAIDEN & BLAKELY) L. JOHNSON & BLAXELL (*E. niphophila* MAIDEN & BLAKELY) "Snow Gum". A beautiful small tree of comparatively slow growth with large, leathery, grey-green leaves. The trunk is a lovely green, grey and cream patchwork and has been likened to a python's skin. A tree in the Hillier Gardens and Arboretum has sustained no frost damage since it was planted in 1960. AM 1977. AGM 1984.

**pauciflora × amygdalina** A medium-sized tree with attractive bark and long, narrow, sickle-shaped, sage-green leaves. Hardier than *E. pauciflora*.

**perriniana** F. MUELL. ex RODWAY "Spinning Gum". A small silver-leaved tree. Stems white, with dark blotches. Juvenile leaves rounded; mature leaves oblanceolate, glaucous. Victoria, New South Wales, Tasmania. AM 1982.

**†pulverulenta** SIMS "Silver-leaved Mountain Gum". A handsome small tree resembling *E. cordata*, with attractive, bluish, rounded leaves. Hardy in the south-west and similar areas. New South Wales. I 1819.

**salicifolia** See *E. amygdalina*.

**subcrenulata** See under *E. johnstonii*.

**urnigera** HOOK. f. "Urn Gum". Small to medium-sized, fairly hardy, Tasmanian species with greyish, peeling bark and dark green leaves. Distinct in its urn-shaped fruits. C 1860.

**vernicosa** HOOK. f. "Varnished Gum". A very hardy Tasmanian shrub or occasionally a small tree producing dense masses of thick, elliptic-lanceolate, shining green leaves.

**EUCOMMIA** OLIV.—**Eucommiaceae**—A monotypic genus and the only member of the family. The one species is perfectly hardy and thrives in all types of fertile soil.

**ulmoides** OLIV. The only hardy tree known to produce rubber. A vigorous and ornamental Chinese tree up to 9m or more, with rather large, leathery, glossy elm-like leaves. If a leaf is torn gently in half, and the two halves are eased apart, then by holding the stalk the detached lower half will hang seemingly unconnected, but it is in fact attached by fine strands of latex almost invisible to the naked eye. I about 1896 from cultivation in China and not known in the wild.

**‡EUCRYPHIA** CAV.—**Eucryphiaceae**—A small genus of 5 species of highly ornamental shrubs or trees flowering when sufficiently mature from July to September. All have white flowers with conspicuous stamens. They thrive best in sheltered positions and in moist loam, preferably non-calcareous. The roots should be shaded from hot sun.

**billardieri** See *E. lucida*.

**†\*cordifolia** CAV. "Ulmo". A very beautiful large evergreen shrub or, in favoured areas, a broad columnar tree of 9-12m. Leaves oblong, wavy-edged, often heart-shaped at the base; flowers like a white Rose of Sharon. Somewhat lime-tolerant. Chile. I 1851. AM 1936.

**cordifolia × lucida** See *E.* 'Penwith'.

**glutinosa** (POEPP. & ENDL.) BAILL. (*E. pinnatifolia* GAY) One of the most glorious of woody plants. A large erect-branched deciduous shrub or small tree, with pinnate leaves; flowers 6cm across are borne profusely in July and August. Beautiful autumn tints. It is evergreen in the wild. Chile. I 1859. FCC 1880. FCC 1976 (for autumn foliage). AGM 1984.

**Plena group** Flowers double or semi-double. Arises fairly frequently in seed batches.

**†\* × hillieri** IVENS (*E. lucida × E. moorei*). An interesting chance hybrid between an Australian and a Tasmanian species. The following clone is the one in general cultivation but other plants of the same parentage have arisen independently.

**'Penwith'** See *E.* 'Penwith'.

**'Winton'** This interesting hybrid originated as a self-sown seedling in our Chandler's Ford nursery. Its pinnate leaves have fewer leaflets than those of *E. moorei* and it is also considerably hardier. Its beautifully formed, cup-shaped flowers resemble those of *E. lucida*.

**\* × hybrida** BAUSCH (*E. lucida × E. milliganii*). A naturally occurring hybrid intermediate between the parents in leaf and flower size and making a large shrub or small tree.

**EUCRYPHIA** × **hybrida**—*continued*

Cultivated plants have leaves about 2cm long and 1cm wide and flowers 2-2.5cm across. Some plants grown as *E. milliganii* belong here. It was collected in Tasmania by Harold Comber and may also have arisen in cultivation.

**\*** × **intermedia** BAUSCH (*E. glutinosa* × *E. lucida*). A lovely, fast-growing hybrid. Leaves variable both simple and trifoliolate occurring on the same plant, glaucous beneath. Flowers smaller than those of *E. glutinosa*, crowding the branches. This hybrid first occurred at Rostrevor, N Ireland, the garden of the late Sir John Ross of Blandenburg, but other forms are also in cultivation.

**'Rostrevor'** The form in general cultivation. An extremely floriferous, free-growing, small tree of compact, broadly columnar habit. The fragrant, white flowers each 2.5-5cm across the slender branches in August and September. Raised at Rostrevor, Co Down. AM 1936. FCC 1973. AGM 1984. 'Grayswood' is similar.

**\*lucida** (LABILL.) BAILL. (*E. billardieri* SPACH) A delightful species, a large, densely leafy shrub or small tree, with simple, oblong leaves, glaucous beneath. The charming, fragrant, pendulous flowers, up to 5cm across, appear in June and July. Tasmania. I 1820. AM 1936.

**'Pink Cloud'** Flowers pale pink at the margins of the petals shading to white, red at the base. This recently introduced form was discovered as a 20m tree in a remote area of NW Tasmania.

**var. milliganii** See *E. milliganii*.

**\*milliganii** HOOK. f. (*E. lucida* var. *milliganii* (HOOK. f.) SUMMERHAYES) A delightful and very hardy miniature species eventually a small, usually slender, shrubby tree. Leaves tiny, neat, shining dark green, glaucous beneath. Buds exceptionally sticky. Flowers cup-shaped, similar to those of *E. lucida* but smaller. Even as a small shrub it flowers freely. It has reached 6m tall by 1m across in the Hillier Gardens and Arboretum. Tasmania. Introduced by Harold Comber in 1929. AM 1978.

**†\*moorei** F. MUELL. A rare small tree, having pinnate leaves with up to 13 slender leaflets, elegantly poised. The white flowers are rather smaller than those of *E. glutinosa*. Suitable only for the mildest localities. SE Australia. I 1915. AM 1933.

**\*** × **nymansensis** BAUSCH (*E. cordifolia* × *E. glutinosa*). A variable hybrid between 2 superb South American species. The leaves are intermediate between those of the parents, both simple and compound leaves appearing on the same plant.

**'Mount Usher'** Resembling more *E. cordifolia* in general appearance. The flowers are often double. Raised at Mount Usher in Ireland.

**'Nymansay'** A magnificent small to medium-sized tree of rapid growth and dense, columnar habit. Flowers 6cm across, wreathing the branches in August and September. Raised about 1915 at Nymans, Sussex, by James Comber, Head Gardener to the late Lt Col L.C.R. Messel. AM 1924. FCC 1926. AGM 1984.

**†\*'Penwith'** (*E. cordifolia* × *E. lucida*). A large, tall-growing evergreen of vigorous growth. Leaves oblong-lanceolate, leathery, dark shining green above, glaucous beneath. Flowers white. Resembles *E. lucida* in general appearance but differs in its larger flowers and leaves which are wavy-edged, pointed and occasionally toothed. Raised at Trengwainton. In recent years it has been incorrectly distributed as a form of *E.* × *hillieri*.

**\*EUMORPHIA** DC.—**Compositae**—About 4 species of small shrubs, natives of South Africa.

**sericea** WOOD & EVANS A grey-leaved shrub reaching about 1m with smooth yellowish-brown stems grey tomentose when young. Leaves small, opposite, entire or two to three-lobed at the apex, silky hairy on both sides. Solitary white daisy flowerheads 2.5cm across are borne on short peduncles at the tips of the shoots over a long period during summer and autumn. Has proven remarkably hardy in an open position at the Hillier Gardens and Arboretum.

**EUODIA** See *Tetradium*.

**hupehensis** See *Tetradium daniellii*.

**velutina** See *Tetradium daniellii*.

**EUONYMUS** L.—**Celastraceae**—A genus of about 175 species ranging from dwarf shrubs to creepers, climbers and small trees, both evergreen and deciduous, natives mainly of Asia but also occurring in Europe, North America, Africa and Australia. The wide range of forms makes them suitable for a variety of purposes in gardens including valuable hedging and ground-cover plants. They thrive in almost any soil, and are particularly at home on chalk. The flowers, in early summer, are normally green or purplish and of little ornament. The chief attraction is the often very showy, lobed, sometimes winged, fruits which persist into winter and open to reveal the seeds covered by a coloured aril. It is desirable to plant several specimens in close proximity to obtain cross-pollination, as single specimens sometimes never fruit due to imperfect flowers. Many deciduous species give attractive autumn tints.

**alatus** (THUNB.) SIEB. A slow-growing, much-branched shrub of medium size, distinguished by the broad corky wings on the branchlets under favourable conditions. One of the finest and most reliable of all deciduous shrubs for autumn colour, the leaves turning to brilliant crimson-pink. Fruits reddish-purple opening to reveal bright orange-coated seeds. China, Japan. I 1860. AGM 1984.

**var. apterus** REG. An unusual form differing from the typical form in its more lax habit and its scarcely winged or wingless stems. Equally colourful in autumn.

**'Compactus'** A dense compact form colouring equally well; ideal for a low hedge. Raised in the United States before 1928.

**americanus** L. "Strawberry Bush". A medium-sized shrub with four-angled branches and narrowly oval, glossy green leaves sometimes red in autumn. The tiny flowers are succeeded by three to five-lobed, red, warty capsules. E United States. C 1683.

**bungeanus** MAXIM. A large shrub or small tree with slender arching branches and elliptic, slender-pointed leaves. Flowers yellowish-white in June; fruits four-lobed, cream to flesh-pink, only produced after a hot summer. Autumn colour pale straw-yellow. N and NE China. I 1883. AM 1941.

**var. semi-persistens** (REHD.) SCHNEID. A distinct semi-evergreen shrub often retaining its leaves until the New Year. Fruits pink.

**cornutus** HEMSL. A rare small to medium-sized shrub of loose habit. The remarkable pink tinged fruits bear 4 slender, horn-like extensions, giving them the appearance of jesters' caps. W and SW China. I 1908 by Ernest Wilson.

**var. quinquecornutus** (COMBER) BLAKEL. In this form the fruit has 5 or 6 horns.

**europaeus** L. "Spindle". A familiar native hedgerow shrub, particularly on chalk soils. A vigorous green-stemmed shrub occasionally a small tree, producing an abundance of scarlet capsules which open to reveal the orange-coated seeds. Europe, W Asia.

**f. albus** (WEST.) REHD. ('Fructu-albo') A conspicuous white-fruited form, showy in winter.

**'Atropurpureus'** Leaves green at first turning to deep purple in early summer, passing to vivid shades of red in the autumn.

**'Aucubifolius'** Leaves mottled with yellow and white and attractively tinted with pink in autumn.

**'Fructu-coccineo'** Capsules bright red.

**'Red Cascade'** A selected form, the arching branches often pendulous under the weight of the rosy-red fruits. Rich scarlet autumn colour. AM 1949. AGM 1984.

**\*fortunei** HAND-MAZZ. An extremely hardy, trailing evergreen, suitable for ground cover in sun or shade, or as a self-clinging climber, the long stems rooting at intervals. Leaves generally elliptic, up to 6cm long, distinctly veined beneath. Like the English ivy, the creeping and climbing stems are barren and only when adult growths appear are flowers and fruits produced. Flowers small, pale green, produced in loose cymes during summer, followed in autumn by pinkish capsules with orange seeds. Most cultivated plants belong to var. *radicans*. China. I 1907.

**'Carrierei'** A small shrub with larger leaves, reaching 2-2.5m against a wall. This is regarded as the adult form of var. *radicans* and produces both flowers and fruits. C 1881. AM 1936.

**'Coloratus'** A trailing or climbing form reaching 8m with support, leaves beautifully coloured sanguineous-purple throughout winter, especially when the roots are starved or

**EUONYMUS fortunei 'Coloratus'**—*continued*

controlled. An unusual character is that the leaves which are coloured in winter may resume their summer green in spring.

**'Dart's Blanket'** An improvement on 'Coloratus', this was selected in Holland where it is widely planted for ground cover. Leaves deep green turning bronze-red in autumn. C 1969.

**'Emerald Charm'** An adult form of upright habit with glossy green leaves. Fruits yellowish-white, opening to reveal orange-coated seeds. Raised in the United States.

**'Emerald Cushion'** A dwarf, mound-forming shrub of dense habit with rich green leaves. Raised in the United States.

**'Emerald Gaiety'** A small, compact, bushy shrub. Leaves broad, deep green with an irregular white margin which becomes pink-tinged during winter. Raised in the United States. AGM 1984.

**'Emerald 'n' Gold'** A very striking form making a dense, dwarf bush. Leaves deep green with a broad, bright golden margin which becomes cream flushed with pink in winter. Climbs given support. Raised in the United States before 1967. AM 1979. AGM 1984.

**'Gold Tip'** ('Golden Prince') Broadly upright habit, leaves margined golden yellow. C 1972.

**'Gracilis'** See 'Variegatus'.

**'Kewensis'** A dainty form with slender prostrate stems and minute leaves. Suitable for the rock garden where it will form small hummocks or cover rocks. Climbing if support is available. Possibly a sport of var. *radicans*. 'Minimus' is similar but with larger leaves. I 1893.

**'Minimus'** See under 'Kewensis'.

**var. radicans** (MIQ.) REHD. A trailing or climbing shrub with ovate or elliptic, shallowly-toothed leaves up to 3.5cm long, rather leathery in texture. This is the commonest form in cultivation with smaller leaves than the typical form. Propagation of the adult growth has resulted in various shrubby forms such as 'Carrierei'. Japan. I about 1865.

**'Sarcoxie'** Upright habit to 1.8m. Leaves dark glossy green. Large fruits white tinged pink. Raised in the United States in 1950.

**'Sheridan Gold'** A dwarf shrub with upright shoots, the young leaves suffused with yellow, later green. Not very exciting.

**'Silver Pillar'** ('Versicolor Albus') Leaves narrow with a broad marginal white variegation. Habit erect.

**'Silver Queen'** A small shrub of compact habit, attaining 2.5-3m against a wall. The unfolding leaves in spring are a rich creamy-yellow later becoming green with a broad creamy white margin. One of the loveliest of variegated shrubs. A sport of 'Carrierei', producing flowers and fruits. C 1914. AM 1977. AGM 1984.

**'Sunspot'** ('Goldspot') Leaves deep green with an elongated central golden blotch, red-tinged underneath in winter. Stems yellowish. C 1980.

**'Variegatus'** ('Gracilis') A trailing or climbing form, the leaves greyish-green, margined white, often tinged pink. A sport of var. *radicans*. Now superseded by other selections. AM 1977.

**var. vegetus** (REHD.) REHD. A small, bushy, creeping form with both prostrate and erect stems, climbing if support is available. The leaves are quite distinct being broad ovate to orbicular, thick in texture and dull green. Flowers and fruits are normally freely produced. Probably a distinct form of var. *radicans*. Introduced from Japan in 1876.

†\***frigidus** WALL. A rare, tender species of medium size, with small, chocolate-coloured flowers hanging on slender stalks followed by four-winged red fruits opening to show orange-coated seeds. Leaves oblanceolate. E Himalaya, W China. I 1931 by Kingdon-Ward.

**grandiflorus** WALL. An erect, semi-evergreen shrub to 4m high with conspicuous, compara-tively large, straw-yellow flowers and yellow capsules with scarlet seeds. Leaves give rich wine-purple autumn colour. Himalaya, W China. I 1824. AM 1927.

**f. salicifolius** STAPF & F. BALLARD The form most usually grown, with longer, narrower leaves. W China. C 1867. AM 1953.

**hamiltonianus** WALL. A large, deciduous or semi-evergreen shrub or small tree related to *E. europaeus*. Fruits pink with orange or red-coated seeds. A variable species of wide

**EUONYMUS hamiltonianus**—*continued*

distribution in E Asia. The typical variety is native to the Himalaya and may not be in cultivation.

**'Corai Charm'** Leaves pale yellow and green in autumn. Fruits freely borne, pale pink, the seeds with red arils. Habit spreading. Selected in the Hillier Gardens and Arboretum. AM 1981.

**'Coral Chief'** Similar to 'Coral Charm' but of upright habit, the pink fruits opening to show red arils. Selected in the Hillier Gardens and Arboretum.

**'Fiesta'** Leaves blotched with creamy-yellow and pink, turning purple in autumn. Raised from a sport found by our Foreman Alf Alford on a plant grown as *E. yedoensis* in 1967. Shy fruiting.

**var. lanceifolius** (LOES.) BLAKEL. (*E. lanceifolius* LOES.) A deciduous or semi-evergreen small tree or large shrub from China; leaves 7.5-12.5cm long, usually lanceolate-oblong; the pink four-lobed fruits open to disclose the scarlet-coated seeds. Unfortunately this variety fruits too infrequently in cultivation. C and W China. I 1908 by Ernest Wilson. AM 1929.

**var. maackii** (RUPR.) KOMAR. (*E. maackii* RUPR.) Leaves smaller and narrower, more finely toothed. Cultivated plants have beautiful autumn colour and pink fruits with orange-coated seeds. N China, Manchuria, Korea. C 1880.

**'Red Elf'** Upright habit similar to 'Coral Chief' but fruits rich deep pink with red-coated seeds. Selected in the 1970s in the Hillier Gardens and Arboretum from plants grown as *E. hians* and originally named 'Red Cap'. AM 1981.

**subsp. sieboldianus** (BLUME) HARA (*E. hians* KOMAR.) (*E. semiexsertus* KOEHNE) (*E. sieboldianus* BLUME) (*E. yedoensis* KOEHNE) Leaves yellow, pink or red in autumn. Fruits conspicuous, rose-pink, often abundantly produced. Japan, E China, Korea. I 1865. AM 1924.

**hians** See *E. hamiltonianus* subsp. *sieboldianus*.

†**\*ilicifolius** FRANCH. A remarkable Chinese species with thick, spiny, holly-like leaves. Capsules rounded, whitish; seeds orange-coloured. W China. I 1930. Only suitable for the mildest localities and now probably no longer in cultivation.

**\*japonicus** THUNB. A large, densely branched shrub with dark glossy green, leathery leaves. One of the best evergreens for coastal or town planting, and succeeding in sun or shade. AM 1976.

**'Albomarginatus'** Leaves pale green when young becoming blue-green, narrowly margined with white.

**'Aureopictus'** See 'Aureus'.

**'Aureus'** ('Aureopictus') Leaves with golden centre and a broad green margin. Liable to revert.

**'Duc d'Anjou'** ('Viridivariegatus') Leaves pale or yellowish-green with a central splash of dark green.

**'Hibarimasaki'** An unusual and distinct dwarf shrub 10-20cm tall of congested habit with upright shoots. Leaves very small, downcurved and overlapping with a narrow silvery margin. Suitable for a sheltered scree or alpine house.

**'Latifolius Albomarginatus'** ('Macrophyllus Albus') Leaves with a conspicuous broad white margin. The most conspicuous variegated form. AGM 1984.

**'Macrophyllus'** ('Latifolius') Leaves larger than those of the typical form, elliptic. FCC 1866.

**'Macrophyllus Albus'** See 'Latifolius Albomarginatus'.

**'Marieke'** See under 'Ovatus Aureus'.

**'Microphyllus'** ('Myrtifolius') A small, slow-growing form of dense, compact habit with small, narrow leaves. Somewhat resembling "Box" in general appearance.

**'Microphyllus Pulchellus'** ('Microphyllus Aureus') Similar to 'Microphyllus' but leaves suffused with gold.

**'Microphyllus Variegatus'** Small leaves with a white margin.

**'Myrtifolius'** See 'Microphyllus'.

**'Ovatus Aureus'** ('Aureovariegatus') Leaves margined and suffused creamy-yellow, particularly apparent in the young leaves; growth rather slow and compact. Requires a sunny

**EUONYMUS japonicus 'Ovatus Aureus'**—*continued*

site to retain its colour. The most popular golden euonymus. Plants received under the name 'Marieke' appear identical. AGM 1984.

**'Robustus'** A very hardy form with rather thick, round ovate leaves and stiff compact growth. Under favourable conditions the first fruiting form of the species.

**\*kiautschovicus** LOES. (*E. patens* REHD.) Hardy, spreading, evergreen shrub of medium size, producing green-yellow flowers in early autumn, followed by late pink fruits. Akin to *E. japonicus* from which it differs in its wider inflorescence, thinner more pointed leaves and laxer habit. This plant should replace *E. japonicus* in the coldest areas. E and C China. I about 1860. AM 1961.

**lanceifolius** See *E. hamiltonianus* var. *lanceifolius*.

**latifolius** (L.) MILL. A European species growing 3-4.5m high. Has larger, scarlet fruits, and more brilliant autumn foliage than the common " Spindle Tree". It is similar to and has been confused with *E. planipes* but differs in the sharp-edged wings of the fruit. I 1730. AM 1916.

**†\*lucidus** D. DON (*E. pendulus* WALL.) A large, evergreen shrub or small to medium-sized tree suitable only for the mildest localities. In spring the young growths are crimson, passing to coppery-salmon, finally deep green. Confused in gardens with *E. fimbriatus*, which however is a deciduous species. Himalaya. I 1850.

**maackii** See *E. hamiltonianus* var. *maackii*.

**macropterus** RUPR. A medium-sized to large shrub of spreading habit, with oval or obovate leaves and attractive pink, four-winged capsules. NE Asia, Japan. I 1905.

**\*myrianthus** HEMSL. (*E. sargentianus* LOES. & REHD.) A large, slow-growing evergreen shrub with rather long, tough, leathery leaves. Flowers greenish-yellow, in dense rounded heads of up to 7.5cm across. Fruits orange-yellow, splitting to expose the attractive orange-scarlet seeds. W China. I 1908 by Ernest Wilson. AM 1976.

**nanus** BIEB. (*E. farreri* HORT.) (*E. rosmarinifolius* HORT.) A useful, dwarf, semi-evergreen shrub with narrow leaves and tiny, brown-purple flowers. Ideal as a ground cover and for banks. Caucasus to China. I 1830. AM 1920.

**var. turkestanicus** (DIECK) KRISHT. (*E. nanus* var. *koopmannii* KOEHNE) A semi-erect form up to 1m with longer leaves. The commonest form in cultivation. Fruits bright pink with orange seeds. Tian Shan and Altai Mts. C 1883.

**obovatus** NUTT. A prostrate shrub with long trailing stems. Peculiar in its three-lobed crimson fruits which are covered with prickly warts. E North America. I 1820.

**oresbius** W.W. SM. An uncommon shrub to about 2m, with very narrow, linear leaves. The pendulous, rosy-red, scarlet-seeded fruits are seldom seen in cultivation. Yunnan, W China. C 1934.

**oxyphyllus** MIQ. A slow-growing, medium-sized to large shrub; leaves pass to rich shades of red and purple-red in the autumn when at the same time the branches are strung with rich carmine-red capsules. Japan, Korea and China. I 1892.

**patens** See *E. kiautschovicus*.

**pendulus** See *E. lucidus*.

**phellomanus** LOES. A Chinese shrub of large size with shoots conspicuously corky-winged. Leaves oval to obovate, 5-10cm long; the conspicuous, four-lobed, pink fruits are freely carried. N and W China. C 1924. FCC 1924.

**planipes** (KOEHNE) KOEHNE (*E. sachalinensis* HORT.) A large, handsome species similar to *E. latifolius* and equally colourful in autumn. The large and showy scarlet fruits are freely borne. NE Asia. I 1892. *E. sachalinensis* (FR. SCHMIDT) MAXIM. is probably not in cultivation. It is a native of Sakhalin with a variety in Japan. AM 1954. AGM 1984.

**sachalinensis** See *E. planipes*.

**sanguineus** LOES. A medium-sized, occasionally large, Chinese shrub, rare in cultivation. The young shoots and leaves are often flushed purple beneath. The red fruits and tinted leaves are attractive in autumn. C and W China. I 1900 by Ernest Wilson.

**sargentianus** See *E. myrianthus*.

**semiexsertus** See *E. hamiltonianus* subsp. *sieboldianus*.

**sieboldianus** See *E. hamiltonianus* subsp. *sieboldianus*.

**EUONYMUS**—*continued*

**\*tingens** WALL. (L.S. & H. 17559) A large shrub or small tree with elliptic, toothed, dark green leaves. Flowers creamy white conspicuously veined with purple, borne in stalked clusters in May and June. Fruits pink with scarlet-coated seeds, ripening in late autumn. Himalaya, W China. Originally introduced by Sir Joseph Hooker in 1850. Proving hardy in the Hillier Gardens and Arboretum.

**velutinus** (C.A. MEY.) FISCH. & MEY. A medium-sized to large shrub related to *E. europaeus*. Young shoots and the leaves beneath grey pubescent. Small pink-tinged flowers in July are followed by conspicuous rich pink fruits. Autumn colour soft pink. I 1972 by Mrs Ala and Roy Lancaster from the Elburz Mountains of N Iran (A. & L. 2). W Asia.

**verrucosus** SCOP. Medium-sized shrub with densely warty branches. Flowers purple-brown in three to seven-flowered cymes, followed after a hot summer by yellowish-red capsules. Attractive autumn tints. E Europe, W Asia. I 1763.

**\*wilsonii** SPRAGUE A large and striking, Chinese evergreen of lax habit. The lanceolate dark green leaves are 7-15cm long, one third as wide and tapered to a slender point. The four-lobed fruits are set with awl-shaped spines giving a remarkable hedgehog-like appearance. I 1904 by Ernest Wilson.

**yedoensis** See *E. hamiltonianus* subsp. *sieboldianus*.

**EUPATORIUM** L.—**Compositae**—A large genus of 500 or more species of trees, shrubs and herbs widely distributed mainly in tropical America.

**†\*ligustrinum** DC. (*E. micranthum* LESSING) (*E. weinmannianum* REG. & KOERN.) An evergreen Mexican shrub producing large, flat heads of small white flowers in late summer and autumn. In favoured districts grows to 2.5m. I 1867.

**micranthum** See *E. ligustrinum*.

**EUPHORBIA** L.—**Euphorbiaceae**—The "Spurges" make up a very large genus of more than 1500 species of herbs and shrubs of cosmopolitan distribution particularly in subtropical areas. Many species are spiny succulents resembling cacti. Several are commonly grown as indoor or conservatory plants. The species listed here are evergreen sub-shrubs. The individual flowers are not showy but each inflorescence bears showy bracts and often contains conspicuous glands.

**amygdaloides** L. "Wood Spurge". A British native common in woods in the south of the country but better known in gardens as the following variety. There are attractive forms with purple leaves and stems. Europe, SW Asia.

**var. robbiae** (TURRILL) RADCLIFFE-SMITH (*E. robbiae* TURRILL) "Mrs Robb's Bonnet". A dwarf sub-shrub spreading rapidly by underground stems. Leaves obovate, deep glossy green and leathery, borne in dense rosettes at the stem tips. Conspicuous greenish-yellow flowerheads are borne over a long period during late winter and spring. Excellent ground cover in shade. Turkey. I in the early 1890s by Mrs Robb. AM 1968. AMT 1975. AGM 1984.

**\*characias** L. A small sub-shrub bearing erect, unbranched, biennial stems. Leaves linear, downy, bluish-green, borne in dense clusters at the ends of the shoots. Flowers in terminal panicles with conspicuous yellowish-green bracts and reddish-purple glands, attractive for several months during spring and summer. Mediterranean region. AM 1961. AGM 1984.

**subsp. wulfenii** (HOPPE ex KOCH) RADCLIFFE-SMITH (*E. wulfenii* HOPPE ex KOCH) Differs from the typical form in the yellowish-green glands of the inflorescence. SE Europe. C 1837. AM 1905. FCC 1988. AGM 1984.

**'John Tomlinson'** Flowers in large heads with long upper rays making the inflorescence nearly rounded, bracts bright yellow-green. Wild collected in Yugoslavia in 1966 (Mathew & Tomlinson 4005). FCC 1977 (as *E. characias* subsp. *wulfenii*).

**'Lambrook Gold'** Inflorescence columnar, bracts bright golden-green.

**†\*mellifera** AIT. A medium-sized, dense, rounded shrub with stout, glabrous shoots and narrowly oblong leaves up to 20cm long downy only at the base of the midrib beneath. Flowers brown, honey-scented, borne in May followed by warty fruits. Madeira, Canary Islands.

**175**

**EUPTELEA** SIEB. & ZUCC.—**Eupteleaceae**—A small genus of 2 species. Large shrubs or small trees. The flowers lack petals, appear in dense clusters all along the leafless branches in spring and consist of bunches of red-anthered stamens. They succeed in all types of fertile soil.

**franchetii** See *E. pleiosperma*.

**pleiosperma** HOOK. f. & THOMS. (*E. franchetii* VAN TIEGH.) (*E. davidiana* BAILL.) A small, multi-stemmed tree or large shrub with stout erect stems, attracting attention in spring when crowded with clusters of red anthers. Young growths copper-tinted. Autumn leaf colour is sometimes conspicuous. E Himalaya, W China. I 1896.

**polyandra** SIEB. & ZUCC. A large shrub or small tree, differing from *E. pleiosperma* in its coarsely and irregularly toothed leaves; also notable for its pretty red and yellow autumn colours. Japan. C 1877.

**\*EURYA** THUNB.—**Theaceae**—About 70 species of evergreen shrubs and trees related to and often confused with *Cleyera*, but differing in the dioecious flowers and usually toothed leaves. Natives of SE Asia and the Pacific islands.

**†emarginata** (THUNB.) MAK. A small to medium-sized shrub with brown hairy young shoots conspicuously lined with ridges decurrent from the base of the petioles. Leaves obovate, toothed, obtuse to emarginate at the apex, glossy green, reddish-tinged in winter, to 3.5 × 1cm. Small, pale yellow-green flowers are borne in the leaf axils in spring. Coastal areas of S Japan.

'**Microphylla**' A curious form making a small, densely branched shrub recalling *Cotoneaster horizontalis* when young. Leaves arranged in two ranks, obovate or orbicular, notched at the apex, 6-8mm long.

**fortunei** See *Cleyera japonica* 'Tricolor'.

**japonica** THUNB. A small evergreen shrub with bluntly serrate, leathery leaves, dark green and lustrous above, pale green beneath. The inconspicuous greenish-yellow flowers formed in late summer open in spring and possess an objectionable smell. They are followed by purplish-black berries. Japan, Taiwan, Korea. FCC 1861.

'**Variegata**' A charming small, slow-growing shrub, compact in habit. Leaves two ranked, oblanceolate, toothed, pale green with a dark green margin. This name has also been applied to *Cleyera japonica* 'Tricolor'. FCC 1894.

**latifolia 'Variegata'** See *Cleyera japonica* 'Tricolor'.

**ochnacea** See *Cleyera japonica*.

**\*EURYOPS** CASS.—**Compositae**—About 100 species of evergreen shrubs with conspicuous, yellow, daisy flowerheads. Natives mainly of South Africa but extending north to Arabia. The following require a warm sunny position and a well drained soil.

**acraeus** M.D. HENDERSON (*E. evansii* HORT.) A dwarf shrub of rather neat habit, forming a low compact mound of grey stems and small, narrow, silvery-grey leaves. The canary-yellow flowerheads, 2.5cm across, smother the plant during late May and June. Introduced about 1945 from the Drakensburg Mountains, Lesotho. At first confused with *E. evansii*, a related species. Ideal for the rock garden or scree and generally hardy if soil and aspect are suitable. AM 1952.

**hybridus** See under *E. pectinatus*.

**†chrysanthemoides** (DC.) NORDENST. A small shrub with purplish stems, the leaves deeply divided into oblong lobes which become linear towards the base. The solitary, yellow, daisy flowerheads deeper in the centre and 6cm across are borne on long, erect stalks from midsummer onwards. Differs from *E. pectinatus* in the nearly glabrous leaves with fewer, broader lobes. S Africa. AM 1988.

**†pectinatus** CASS. A small shrub with erect, greyish, downy shoots up to 1m. Leaves 5-7.5cm long, deeply lobed (pectinate), grey-downy. Flowerheads rich yellow, 4cm across, borne on long, slender, erect peduncles in late May and June and often again during winter. Plants we have grown under the name *E. hybridus* have proved to be this species. S Africa. I 1731.

**†virgineus** LESS. A small shrub forming a dense clump of erect glabrous shoots 0.6-1m in height. The neat, tiny, green, pectinate leaves densely crowd the stems. Flowers 1.25cm across, produced on slender stalks in the axils of the upper leaves during spring. S Africa. I 1821.

**EVODIA** See *Tetradium*.

**EXOCHORDA** LINDL.—**Rosaceae**—4 or 5 species of beautiful, May-blooming shrubs with long, arching branches festooned with conspicuous racemes of comparatively large paper-white flowers. Generally inclined to become chlorotic on very shallow chalk soils.

**giraldii** HESSE An excellent large free-flowering shrub similar to *E. korolkowii*, but not so erect in habit. NW China. I 1907.

**var. wilsonii** (REHD.) REHD. This variety has the largest flowers in the genus, being 5cm across. C China. I 1907. AM 1931.

**korolkowii** LAV. (*E. albertii* REGEL) A vigorous species from Turkestan, attaining about 4.5m; one of the best for chalky soils. I 1881. AM 1894.

× **macrantha** (LEMOINE) SCHNEIDER (*E. korolkowii* × *E. racemosa*). Large shrub similar in habit to *E. racemosa*. Abundant racemes of large white flowers in late spring. Garden origin about 1900. AM 1917.

**'The Bride'** A small to medium-sized dense bush of weeping habit. Very attractive when the arching branches are wreathed in large white flowers in April or May. C 1938. AM 1973. AGM 1984. FCC 1985.

‡**racemosa** (LINDL.) REHD. (*E. grandiflora* (HOOKER) LINDL.) The best-known species, a large shrub rather spreading in habit. Not suitable for shallow chalk soil. China. I 1849. AM 1979.

**serratifolia** MOORE An extremely free-flowering species which thrives in chalky soils, forming an elegant medium-sized bush.

**var. pubescens** REHD. Leaves pubescent beneath.

\***FABIANA** RUIZ & PAVON—**Solanaceae**—About 25 species of evergreen heath-like shrubs, belonging to the potato family and amongst hardy plants most closely related to *Cestrum*. Natives of S America mainly in temperate regions. One species is in general cultivation. Succeeds best in a sunny position in moist, well drained neutral or acid soil, but is sufficiently lime-tolerant to be well worth growing in all but very shallow soils over chalk.

†**imbricata** RUIZ & PAVON A charming shrub of medium size. In June its branches are transformed into plumes of white tubular flowers. Chile. I 1838. AM 1934.

**'Prostrata'.** A small shrub, hardier than the typical form, forming a dense rounded mound of feathery branchlets which are usually covered with small, pale mauve-tinted flowers in May and June. Ideal for the large rock garden or wall top.

**f. violacea** HORT. Similar to the typical form but with lavender-mauve flowers. FCC 1932.

**FAGUS** L.—**Fagaceae**—The "Beeches" are a small genus containing some of the most noble of trees. About 10 species in north temperate regions. The European species reach their maximum size in deep well drained soils in the British Isles. The Asiatic species are also giving a good account of themselves, but the American Beech is disappointing as seen in cultivation and is less lime-tolerant.

**americana** See *F. grandifolia*.

**crenata** BLUME (*F. sieboldii* A.DC.) A large tree closely allied to the "Common Beech" (*F. sylvatica*) from which it differs in its rather more obovate leaves. Japan. I 1892.

**engleriana** SEEMEN A rare tree of medium size with foliage of a glaucous sea-green hue. C China. I 1907 by Ernest Wilson.

**grandifolia** EHRH. (*F. americana* SWEET) (*F. ferruginea* AIT.) The "American Beech" does not form a large tree in this country. Distinguished from the "Common Beech" by its suckering habit and its longer, narrower leaves, with nearly twice as many veins. E North America. I 1766. FCC 1894.

**f. pubescens** FERN. & REHD. Leaves pubescent beneath.

**japonica** MAXIM. "Japanese Beech". A small, often shrubby tree in British gardens, with ovate to elliptic, bright green leaves. Japan. I 1905.

**lucida** REHD. & WILS. A small tree with ovate leaves which are often shining green on both surfaces. W China. I 1905.

**FAGUS**—*continued*

**orientalis** LIPSKY "Oriental Beech". A large tree differing from the "Common Beech" in its rather larger, obovate leaves, which in autumn turn a rich yellow. E Europe, Asia Minor. I 1904.

**sieboldii** See *F. crenata*.

**sylvatica** L. "Common Beech". Our native beech is undoubtedly the most noble large tree for calcareous soils and is excellent for hedgemaking. The rich golden copper of its autumn foliage is not excelled by any other tree. Given a well drained soil and avoiding heavy clay there is perhaps no other tree which will thrive in such extremes of acidity and alkalinity. Europe. There are many named cultivars. AGM 1984.

**'Albovariegata'** ('Argenteovariegata') Leaves margined and streaked white. C 1770.

**'Ansorgei'** A remarkable form with very narrow lanceolate to almost linear dark purple leaves. Originated about 1891.

**'Aspleniifolia'** "Fern-leaved Beech" "Cut-leaved Beech". Leaves relatively narrow, deeply cut into slender lobes. C 1804. AGM 1984.

**'Atropunicea'** See under Purpurea group.

**'Atropurpurea'** See under 'Riversii'.

**'Atropurpurea Macrophylla'** See under 'Riversii'.

**'Aurea Pendula'** An extremely elegant form of tall slender growth, the branches hanging down almost parallel with the main stem. Leaves golden yellow, but will sometimes scorch in full sun, and in too deep shade lose their rich colour. Originated as a sport about 1900.

**'Aureovariegata'** See 'Luteovariegata'.

**'Cochleata'** A slow-growing, shrubby form with obovate leaves strongly-toothed in the upper half. C 1842.

**'Cockleshell'** A tall columnar form, the leaves small and rounded. A sport of 'Rotundifolia' raised in our nurseries in 1960.

**'Cristata'** "Cock's Comb Beech". A slow-growing eventually large tree, with clustered leaves, deeply lobed and curled. C 1811.

**'Cuprea'** See under Purpurea group.

**'Dawyck'** "Dawyck Beech". A tall columnar tree broadening in maturity. Originated at Dawyck in Scotland before 1850. Sometimes incorrectly known as 'Fastigiata'. AGM 1984.

**'Dawyck Gold'** A columnar tree of dense habit with bright yellow young foliage pale yellow green in summer. A seedling of 'Dawyck' probably pollinated by 'Zlatia' raised by J.R.P. van Hoey-Smith in 1969.

**'Dawyck Purple'** A splendid narrowly columnar tree with deep purple foliage. Originated at the same time as 'Dawyck Gold' but in this case the pollen parent was a purple beech. Narrower than 'Dawyck Gold' and not as dense. AM 1973.

**'Fastigiata'** See under 'Dawyck'.

**'Grandidentata'** A form with leaves coarsely-toothed; branches slender. C 1864.

**Heterophylla group** (var. *heterophylla* LOUD.) As used here this name covers several forms in which the leaves are narrow and variously cut and lobed. The plant previously grown under this name is 'Aspleniifolia' while other forms include 'Incisa', 'Laciniata' and 'Quercifolia'.

**'Incisa'** See under Heterophylla group.

**'Laciniata'** See under Heterophylla group.

**f. latifolia** KIRCHNER (*F. sylvatica* var. *macrophylla* DIPP.) Leaves much larger, often up to 15cm long and 10cm wide. C 1864.

**'Luteovariegata'** ('Aureovariegata') Leaves variegated with yellow.

**var. macrophylla** See f. *latifolia*.

**'Norwegiensis'** See under 'Riversii'.

**'Pendula'** "Weeping Beech". A spectacular large, weeping tree taking on various forms, sometimes the enormous branches hang close to and perpendicular with the main stem like an elephant's trunk while in other specimens some primary branches are almost horizontal and draped with long hanging branchlets. C 1836. AGM 1984.

**'Prince George of Crete'** A striking form with very large leaves. C 1898.

**FAGUS sylvatica**—*continued*

**'Purple Fountain'** A seedling of 'Purpurea Pendula' raised in Holland making a narrowly upright tree with purple leaves and weeping branches. C 1975.

**Purpurea group** (f. *purpurea* (AIT.) SCHNEIDER) "Purple Beech". This name covers purplish-leaved forms which are normally selected from seed-raised plants. They include 'Atropunicea' and 'Cuprea'. See also under 'Riversii'.

**'Purpurea Latifolia'** See under 'Riversii'.

**'Purpurea Pendula'** "Weeping Purple Beech". A superb small weeping tree with dark leaves. Usually top-worked to make a small mushroom-headed tree. C 1865.

**'Purpurea Tricolor'** ('Roseomarginata') An attractive cultivar with purple leaves edged with an irregular pale pink border. Not very constant. C 1888.

**'Riversii'** "Purple Beech". A large tree with large, dark purple leaves. 'Atropurpurea', 'Atropurpurea Macrophylla', 'Norwegiensis' and 'Purpurea Latifolia' are similar clones. C 1880. AGM 1984.

**'Rohan Gold'** Similar to 'Rohanii' but more vigorous, with the leaves yellow when young becoming green. Raised in 1970 by J.R.P. van Hoey-Smith from seed of 'Rohanii' almost certainly pollinated by 'Zlatia'.

**'Rohanii'** A purple-leaved form of the "Fern-leaved Beech". A remarkably beautiful, rather slow-growing tree. C 1894.

**'Roseomarginata'** See 'Purpurea Tricolor'.

**'Rotundifolia'** Unusual cultivar with strongly ascending branches and small rounded leaves. C 1872.

**'Tortuosa'** A low, wide-spreading tree, with twisted and contorted branches which are pendulous at their extremities. C 1861.

**'Zlatia'** A slow-growing tree. Leaves soft yellow at first becoming green in late summer. The original tree grows in Yugoslavia in a native stand of *F. moesiaca*, an intermediate between *F. sylvatica* and *F. orientalis*. C 1890.

†*FASCICULARIA** MEZ.—**Bromeliaceae**—A small genus of about 5 species of stemless plants forming dense clumps of evergreen, strap-shaped, spiny leaves, all natives of Chile. They require a warm, sunny, sheltered position in a well drained soil or rock fissure.

**bicolor** (RUIZ & PAVON) MEZ. (*Rhodostachys bicolor* RUIZ & PAVON) A hardy plant in mild areas and, given winter protection, almost so in colder areas. Leaves long, narrow and spine-toothed, sage-green above, glaucous beneath, produced in dense tufted rosettes. The shorter, central leaves are a rich crimson colour producing a delightful bicolor effect. Flowers tubular, sky-blue gathered in a dense, sessile head in the centre of the rosette. Whilst in bud the flowerhead is surrounded and concealed by conspicuous ivory coloured bracts. I 1851. AM 1949.

* × **FATSHEDERA** GUILLAUM. (*Fatsia* × *Hedera*)—**Araliaceae**—An interesting and very useful evergreen intergeneric hybrid. Splendid shade-bearing plant creating excellent ground cover. Tolerant of atmospheric pollution, maritime exposure and all types of soil. In constant demand as a house plant.

**lizei** GUILLAUM. (*F. japonica* × *H. hibernica*). A small to medium-sized shrub of loose habit with large, leathery palmate leaves. Spherical heads of white flowers are borne in autumn. Said to be a hybrid between the "Irish Ivy" and *Fatsia japonica* 'Moseri'. Garden origin 1910.

**'Annemieke'** Leaves with a conspicuous central blotch of bright yellow-green.

**'Variegata'** Leaves grey-green with an irregular creamy-white margin.

*FATSIA** DECNE. & PLANCH.—**Araliaceae**—A monotypic genus succeeding in all types of well drained soil.

**japonica** (THUNB.) DECNE. & PLANCH. (*Aralia sieboldii* K. KOCH) A handsome medium-sized to large shrub of spreading habit. The very large polished, dark green, palmate leaves give a subtropical effect and are an admirable foil to the panicles of milk-white, globular flowerheads that terminate the stems in October. Succeeds in sun or semi-shade and is excellent for seaside gardens. Japan. I 1838. FCC 1966. AGM 1984.

**'Variegata'** Lobes of leaves white at tips. FCC 1868. AGM 1984.

**179**

†\***FEIJOA** BERG—**Myrtaceae**—2 species of evergreen shrubs with opposite leaves and solitary flowers borne in the leaf axils. Native of S America, they are closely related to the guavas (*Psidium*).

**sellowiana** BERG "Pineapple Guava". A large shrub, fairly hardy given a warm, sheltered position. Leaves grey-green, white-felted beneath; flowers with fleshy crimson and white petals and a central bunch of long crimson stamens. The large egg-shaped berries are sometimes produced after a long hot summer. Both petals and fruits are edible, having a rich, aromatic flavour. Brazil, Uruguay. I 1898. AM 1927.

**'Variegata'** A form with cream and white margined leaves. AM 1969.

†**FENDLERA** ENGELM. & A. GRAY—**Philadelphaceae**—A small genus of 3 species of shrubs with opposite leaves. They require a warm, sunny position in a well drained soil.

**wrightii** HELL. A beautiful but difficult plant to grow, forming a small to medium-sized shrub for a warm sunny position. The small leaves are lanceolate, three-nerved and roughly hairy above. The white or pink-tinted four-petalled flowers are produced singly or in small clusters in the leaf axils during May and June. SW United States. N Mexico. I 1879.

**FICUS** L.—**Moraceae**—The "Figs" are a vast genus probably numbering over 800 species of trees, shrubs and woody vines found throughout tropical and subtropical regions. Only a few species may be grown outside in this country but many are popular as indoor or conservatory plants.

**carica** L. "Common Fig". A very handsome, large shrub, or small spreading tree in suitable districts. Often grown against a warm sunny wall where its handsome, lobed leaves and delicious, edible fruits are an object of interest throughout the year. W Asia. Cultivated in England since early 16th century.

**'Brown Turkey'** The most popular fruit-producing cultivar.

**nipponica** See *F. sagittata*.

†\***pumila** L. (*F. stipulata* THUNB.) A scandent shrub, climbing the trunks of trees like ivy in its native habitat. The juvenile growths bear small, neat ovate or heart-shaped leaves 1.25-2cm long. In time adult growths are formed which produce larger leaves up to 10cm long, also, if conditions are suitable, flowers and fruits. A tender plant for the conservatory where it may be encouraged to cover walls or used in hanging baskets. It may also be grown in a sheltered corner outside in milder districts. Japan, Ryukyus, Taiwan, China. I 1721.

**'Minima'** (*F. stipulata* 'Minima') A very slender creeper, forming close carpets of minute leaves 6mm long. It is an ideal plant for clothing shady rocks and low walls and in such a situation survived outside for over thirty-five years in our Winchester nursery.

**radicans** See *F. sagittata*.

†\***sagittata** VAHL (*F. nipponica* HORT.) (*F. radicans* DESF.) Similar to *F. pumila* in habit but with longer, narrower leaves which end in a long point. Only suitable for the conservatory or for use in hanging baskets though it may survive outside for several years in a warm sheltered position in the milder counties. N India to SE Asia.

**'Variegata'** (*F. radicans* 'Variegata') An attractive form with leaves irregularly margined creamy-white.

**"FIG, COMMON"** See *Ficus carica*.

**"FIRETHORN"** See *Pyracantha*.

†**FIRMIANA** MARSIGLI—**Sterculiaceae**—A small genus of about 8 species of trees with large, lobed leaves. Found from New Guinea to SE Asia and in tropical Africa.

**simplex** (L.) WIGHT (*Sterculia platanifolia* L. f.) A noble foliage tree of medium size for the mildest localities. Large maple-like leaves. China, long cultivated in Japan, Taiwan. I 1757.

**FONTANESIA** LABILL.—**Oleaceae**—A small genus of 2 similar species. Privet-like shrubs closely related to the ash (*Fraxinus*), but with simple leaves.

**fortunei** CARR. A large shrub with lanceolate leaves. The minute, greenish-white flower clusters are produced in May and June. China. I 1845 by Robert Fortune.

**phillyreoides** LABILL. A medium-sized shrub with ovate or elliptic leaves. Flowers greenish-white in June. Sicily, SW Asia. I 1787.

**FORESTIERA** POIR.—**Oleaceae**—A genus of about 15 species of mainly privet-like shrubs succeeding in any ordinary soil. Natives of N and S America and the West Indies. The leaves are opposite and the small unisexual flowers greenish, of little or no ornament.

**acuminata** (MICHX.) POIR. (*Adelia acuminata* MICHX.) "Swamp Privet". A large shrub or small tree. Fruits narrow-oblong, dark purple. SE United States. I 1812.

**neo-mexicana** A. GRAY "Desert Olive". Medium-sized shrub of spreading habit. Flowers inconspicuous, followed by black, egg-shaped fruits covered with a blue bloom. SW United States. C 1913.

**FORSYTHIA** VAHL—**Oleaceae**—The most colourful of early spring-flowering shrubs, all very hardy and easy to grow. About 7 species mainly in E Asia with one in SE Europe. The bell-shaped flowers which wreathe the branches are golden yellow unless otherwise described. Several large-flowered hybrids have been raised by Dr Karl Sax at the Arnold Arboretum.

Thin out and cut back old flowering shoots to within a few centimetres of the old wood, immediately after flowering.

**'Arnold Dwarf'** (*F.* × *intermedia* × *F. japonica* var. *saxatilis*) An interesting hybrid raised at the Arnold Arboretum in 1941. It has value as a low, ground-cover plant attaining a height of only 0.6-1m, but a spread of 1.8-2.1m. Flowers few, yellow-green, of no merit.

**'Beatrix Farrand'** The plant grown under this name is a tetraploid raised at the Arnold Arboretum in 1944. The deep, canary-yellow, nodding flowers are exceptionally large, being considerably more than 2.5cm across when fully expanded. The habit is upright and dense. AM 1961. The original clone was a triploid hybrid between *F.* 'Arnold Giant' and *F. ovata* and is probably no longer in cultivation. Named after the American garden designer who was influenced by Gertrude Jekyll.

**europaea** DEG. & BALD. "European Golden Ball". A medium-sized shrub with long, four-angled branches and ovate-lanceolate, usually entire leaves. Flowers pale yellow appearing in April. Albania, Yugoslavia, Bulgaria. I 1899.

**giraldiana** LINGELSH. A large shrub of loose, graceful habit, the first species to begin flowering, its pale yellow blossoms sometimes appearing in late February. NW China. I 1910.

**'Golden Nugget'** ('Beatrix Farrand' × 'Arnold Giant') A vigorous medium-sized shrub bearing large, golden yellow flowers up to 5cm across. Occasionally flowers with 6 corolla lobes are borne. Raised by our Foreman Alf Alford from a cross made in 1964.

× **intermedia** ZAB. (*F. suspensa* × *F. viridissima*). A vigorous hybrid of medium to large size, intermediate in habit and flower between its parents, flowering during late March and April. Leaves sometimes trifoliolate. C before 1880. AM 1894. There are several named clones.

**'Arnold Giant'** A tetraploid hybrid raised at the Arnold Arboretum in 1939. A robust shrub of medium size with exceptionally large, nodding, rich yellow flowers.

**'Densiflora'** Habit of growth fairly compact. The flowers are carried in such profusion as almost to hide the branches. Garden origin 1899.

**'Karl Sax'** A strong-growing, floriferous hybrid with deep canary-yellow flowers. A few flowers open in autumn when the leaves turn purple. A tetraploid hybrid of 'Arnold Giant' and 'Spectabilis' raised at the Arnold Arboretum in 1944.

**'Lynwood'** A lovely cultivar, found in a cottage garden in Northern Ireland in 1935 as a sport of 'Spectabilis'. The large, broad-petalled, rich yellow flowers are borne profusely all along the branches. This clone together with 'Beatrix Farrand' and 'Karl Sax' is one of the most spectacular of the forsythias. FCC 1966. AGM 1984.

**'Minigold'** Compact, upright habit. Flowers deep yellow, small with broad lobes, profusely borne.

**FORSYTHIA** × **intermedia**—*continued*

**'Primulina'** Flowers pale yellow. A seedling raised in the Arnold Arboretum before 1912.

**'Spectabilis'** One of the most popular of early spring-flowering shrubs. The flowers are so profuse as to create a mass of golden yellow. Garden origin 1906. AM 1915. FCC 1935.

**'Spring Glory'** A sport of 'Primulina' with larger flowers more freely borne. Found in a garden in Mentor, Ohio about 1930.

**'Tremonia'** A small, compact shrub distinct in its very deeply-toothed leaves. Flowers large, pale yellow, the broad petals serrate at the apex, freely borne. A hybrid of 'Beatrix Farrand' raised at the Dortmund Botanic Garden. C 1963.

**'Vitellina'** Strong and erect growth; flowers deep yellow. Garden origin 1899.

**ovata** NAKAI An early flowering Korean species only 1.2-1.5m high. Leaves ovate, flowers amber-yellow in early March. Associates well with heaths and *Rhododendron* 'Praecox'. I 1918. AM 1941. AGM 1984.

**'Tetragold'** A colchicine-induced, tetraploidal form raised in Holland. It is of dense habit with larger flowers borne slightly earler than normal. C 1963.

**'Robusta'** A strong-growing shrub probably of hybrid origin, attaining 1.8-2.7m. Flowers deep yellow. In the past wrongly catalogued as *F. ovata* 'Robusta'.

**suspensa** (THUNB.) VAHL A rambling shrub attaining about 3m but much higher against a wall, with slender interlacing branches. Flowers on slender pedicels produced in late March and early April. Leaves often trifoliolate. China. I 1833. AGM 1984.

**f. atrocaulis** REHD. Young stems almost black-purple, contrasting with the comparatively large, pale lemon-yellow flowers. AM 1934.

**var. fortunei** (LINDL.) REHD. The largest and most vigorous form with stout arching branches. China. I about 1860.

**'Nymans'** A large shrub with bronze-purple branches and large, primrose-yellow flowers. A sport of f. *atrocaulis*. C 1951.

**var. sieboldii** ZAB. A variety with slender, pendent almost prostrate branches. An excellent wall shrub for a north or east aspect, or for covering an unsightly bank. China, long cultivated in Japan. I 1833.

**viridissima** LINDL. Erect, square-stemmed shrub up to 2.4m high, with lanceolate leaves. Normally the last forsythia to flower, commencing in April, some time after *F. suspensa*. China. I 1844 by Robert Fortune.

**'Bronxensis'** A dense and compact dwarf form with masses of twiggy branchlets. Garden origin 1928. AM 1958.

**'Volunteer'** (*F. ovata* × *F. suspensa*). A vigorous shrub of medium size, with dark coloured young shoots and thickly clustered, deep yellow flowers. An interesting hybrid which originated in the garden of the late Mr Arthur Simmonds VMH, at Clandon in Surrey.

**FORTUNEARIA** REHD. & WILS.—**Hamamelidaceae**—A monotypic genus differing from *Hamamelis* in its five-parted flowers, and from *Corylopsis* in its tiny, narrow petals.

**sinensis** REHD. & WILS. A large, rather slow-growing shrub. Similar in general appearance to *Hamamelis*, but with tiny green flowers borne in terminal racemes during winter. Moderately lime-tolerant but grows better in neutral or acid soil. W China. I 1907 by Ernest Wilson.

†**\*FORTUNELLA** SWINGLE—**Rutaceae**—A small genus of 4 or 5 species of evergreen shrubs or small trees formerly included under *Citrus*. Natives of SE Asia. Suitable only for the conservatory.

**japonica** (THUNB.) SWINGLE (*Citrus japonica* THUNB.) "Round Kumquat". A large shrub with spiny green branches and ovate leaves. Flowers white; fruits the size of a cherry, golden yellow. Only known in cultivation but probably native to S China. AM 1905.

‡**FOTHERGILLA** MURR.—**Hamamelidaceae**—The "Witch Alders" are a genus of 2 species of shrubs native to the SE United States. Conspicuous in spring with their bottle brush-like flower spikes and again in autumn for the rich colouring of their leaves. They require lime-free soil.

**FOTHERGILLA**—*continued*

**gardenii** MURR. (*F. alnifolia* L. f.) (*F. carolina* BRITTON) Pretty shrub usually less than 1m high, conspicuous in April and May with its erect, fragrant inflorescences, composed of clusters of white stamens. SE United States. I 1765.

**major** LODD. (*F. monticola* ASHE) A slow-growing shrub of medium size. Conspicuous, white flower clusters emerge before the leaves. Leaves glaucous beneath. Brilliant autumn colours. Alleghany Mts (United States). I 1780. AM 1927. AM 1937 (as *F. monticola*). FCC 1969. FCC 1971 (as *F. monticola*). AGM 1984.

**monticola** See *F. major*.

**FRANGULA** See under *Rhamnus*.

‡**FRANKLINIA** MARSH.—**Theaceae**—A monotypic genus allied to *Gordonia* and sometimes included in it. A gorgeous autumn-flowering shrub given a hot continental summer, when its ripened growths will withstand a zero winter. Not a plant for our insular climate.

**alatamaha** MARSH. (*Gordonia alatamaha* (MARSH.) SARG.) (*G. pubescens* L'HERIT.) A remarkable and rare shrub or small tree from Georgia, United States but not found in a wild state since the 18th century. Large, lustrous, green, oblong leaves, turning crimson in autumn. The large Stuartia-like, cup-shaped, snow-white flowers only open during a hot, late summer. Perhaps last seen in the wild by the American collector, Lyon, in 1803. I 1770.

**FRAXINUS** L.—**Oleaceae**—The "Ashes" are an extensive genus of about 65 species of mainly hardy, fast-growing trees, which thrive in almost any soil. Tolerant of windswept and coastal localities, and smoke-polluted areas. Leaves pinnate. Those of Sect. Ornus are attractive flowering trees.

**americana** L. (*F. alba* MARSH.) "White Ash". A large species soon forming a noble shade tree. One of the fastest-growing of American hardwoods. Winter buds brown. E North America. I 1724.

**'Autumn Purple'** An American selection of broadly conical habit with dark green leaves reddish-purple in autumn.

**'Rosehill'** Leaves dark green, bronze-red in autumn.

**angustifolia** VAHL. A large, elegant, fast-growing tree with perfectly glabrous, slender pointed leaflets. Winter buds brown. S Europe, N Africa. C 1800.

**var. australis** (GAY) SCHNEID. A geographical form with undersides of leaves slightly hairy. S Europe, N Africa. C 1890.

**var. lentiscifolia** HENRY. A beautiful variety with small, graceful and semi-pendulous branches.

**subsp. oxycarpa** (M. BIEB. ex WILLD.) FRANCO & ROCHA ALFONSO (*F. oxycarpa* M. BIEB. ex WILLD.) A graceful, small-leaved tree akin to *F. angustifolia* from which it is doubtfully distinct. Winter buds dark brown. SE Europe to SW Asia. Mainly represented in gardens by 'Raywood'. I 1815.

**'Pendula'** A handsome tree with slender pendulous branches.

**'Raywood'** (*F. oxycarpa* 'Raywood') A fast-growing tree of dense, fairly upright habit. This form is especially attractive in the autumn when its dark green leaves turn plum-purple. An excellent tree of relatively compact habit. C 1928. AM 1978. AGM 1984.

**subsp. syriaca** (BOISS.) YALTRIK (*F. syriaca* BOISS.) "Syrian Ash". A rare small tree with crowded, whorled leaves of a bright apple-green. Winter buds brown. W and C Asia. C 1880.

**bungeana** DC. (Sect. Ornus) A large shrub or small tree. Twigs and petioles downy but leaflets glabrous, 5-7 in number. Flowers produced in terminal panicles in May. Winter buds black. N China. I 1881.

**chinensis** ROXB. (Sect. Ornus) "Chinese Ash". A free-growing, medium-sized tree with attractive leaves which sometimes give wine-purple autumn colours. Winter buds a conspicuous grey. Flowers sweetly scented. China. I 1891.

**FRAXINUS chinensis**—*continued*

**var. acuminata** LINGELSH. A variety having leaflets with longer tapering points. China. I 1910.

**subsp. rhyncophylla** (HANCE) E. MURR. An outstanding, tall, Chinese variety; grows well in this country and is notable for the large size of its terminal leaflets. NE Asia. I 1881.

†**dipetala** HOOK. & ARN. A medium-sized to large shrub with four-angled branches; leaves varying in number of leaflets, usually 5. This species is particularly useful for the creamy-white flowers which are produced in conspicuous panicles on the previous year's growth in late spring. Requires a warm sheltered position as the young growths are subject to damage by late frosts. California, Mexico. I 1878.

**excelsior** L. "Common Ash". A large, magnificent tree and one of the most valuable for timber. Winter buds black. Europe (incl British Isles), Caucasus. There are several named clones. Forms selected in the 1940s in Holland for their suitability as street trees include 'Altena', 'Atlas' and 'Eureka'. See also 'Westhof's Glorie'.

**'Aurea'** See under 'Jaspidea'.

**'Aurea Pendula'** A small tree of rather weak constitution, the young shoots yellow and drooping, forming an umbrella-shaped crown.

**'Crispa'** Slow-growing, shrubby form of stiff, upright growth. Leaves small, shining, dark green with curled and twisted leaflets.

**'Diversifolia'** ('Monophylla') "One-leaved Ash". A vigorous tree, with leaves simple or sometimes three-parted and usually jaggedly toothed. C 1789.

**'Erosa'** A small tree with very narrow, deeply cut leaflets. C 1806.

**'Jaspidea'** A vigorous clone, the young shoots golden yellow, branches yellowish, conspicuous in winter. Leaves clear yellow in autumn. Often found in cultivation under the name 'Aurea' which is a dwarf, slow-growing tree. C 1873.

**'Monophylla'** See 'Diversifolia'.

**'Nana'** A densely branched small rounded bush.

**'Pendula'** "Weeping Ash". A strong-growing tree, forming an attractive wide-spreading mound of divergent, weeping branches. AGM 1984.

**'Westhof's Glorie'** A vigorous tree, narrowly upright when young, later spreading. Leaves dark green, opening late. A common street tree on the Continent. C 1947.

**floribunda** WALL. (Sect. Ornus) Striking small tree with purplish young wood. The large leaves bear a conspicuous polished sheen. Flowers white, in large terminal panicles. Proving hardy in the Hillier Gardens and Arboretum. Himalaya. I 1822.

†**griffithii** C.B. CLARKE (*F. bracteata* HEMSL.) A nearly evergreen species with quadran-gular green shoots and leathery, dark green and glabrous, entire leaflets. Flowers in large, loose panicles. Requires shelter in all but the mildest areas. N India to SE Asia. I 1900 by Ernest Wilson.

**holotricha** KOEHNE A small tree with downy young growths. Leaflets many, narrow, decidedly greyish. Balkan peninsula. C 1870.

**latifolia** BENTH. (*F. oregona* NUTT.) "Oregon Ash". A medium-sized, fast-growing tree with large leaves. Winter buds brown. W North America. C 1870.

**mandshurica** RUPR. "Manchurian Ash". A large tree showing kinship with our native species. Winter buds dark brown. The leaves often turn red and yellow in autumn. NE Asia. I 1882.

**mariesii** HOOK. f. (Sect. Ornus) The most beautiful "Flowering Ash". A small tree with creamy-white flowers in handsome panicles during June. C China. I 1878 by Charles Maries. AM 1962.

**nigra** MARSH. "Black Ash". A small to medium-sized tree which in the wild is said to grow in wet situations. Winter buds dark brown; leaves with 7-11 slender pointed leaflets. Not one of the best species in cultivation. E North America. I 1800.

**oregona** See *F. latifolia*.

**ornus** L. (Sect. Ornus) "Manna Ash". A pretty tree of medium size, flowering abundantly in May. This is the type species of Section Ornus, popularly known as "Flowering Ashes". S Europe, SW Asia. I before 1700. AGM 1984.

**oxycarpa** See *F. angustifolia* subsp. *oxycarpa*.

**'Raywood'** See *F. angustifolia* 'Raywood'.

**FRAXINUS**—*continued*

**paxiana** LINGELSH. (Sect. Ornus) A remarkable tree of medium size with glabrous twigs and large terminal winter buds coated with brownish down. Leaves about 30cm long composed of 7-9 lanceolate, toothed, slender pointed leaflets, the lowest pair much smaller than the rest. Petioles often enlarged at the base. Flowers white, produced in large panicles during May and June. Himalaya, W and C China. I 1901 by Ernest Wilson.

**pennsylvanica** MARSH. (*F. pubescens* LAM.) (*F. pennsylvanica* var. *lanceolata* (BORKH.) SARG.) "Green Ash" "Red Ash". A fast-growing, shade-giving tree of medium size, with downy shoots and large leaves. Winter buds brown. E North America. I 1783.

**'Aucubifolia'** Leaves mottled golden yellow.

**'Summit'** An American selection of broadly conical habit with glossy leaves turning golden yellow in autumn.

**'Variegata'** A brightly variegated tree; leaves silver-grey, margined and mottled cream-white.

**platypoda** OLIV. A medium-sized tree, the leaves with 7-11 sessile, finely-toothed leaflets and a conspicuously enlarged and swollen petiole base. W and C China. I 1909.

**potamophila** See *F. sogdiana*.

**quadrangulata** MICHX. "Blue Ash". Small tree with distinctly four-winged, square branchlets. Leaves with 7-11 short-stalked leaflets. C and E United States. I 1823.

**sieboldiana** BLUME (*F. longicuspis* var. *sieboldiana* (BLUME) LINGELSH.) (Sect. Ornus) A medium-sized tree. Leaflets 5, rarely 7, often giving autumn tints. Flowers white in terminal panicles in May. Japan, Korea. I 1894.

**sogdiana** BUNGE ( *F. potamophila* HERDER) A small tree with greenish, glabrous shoots; leaves with 7-11 lanceolate, glabrous leaflets conspicuously toothed, sessile or almost so. Turkestan. C 1890.

**spaethiana** LINGELSH. A small to medium-sized tree with conspicuously large leaves, remarkable for the large, swollen, often red-brown base of its petioles. Large panicles of flowers. Japan. C 1873.

**syriaca** See *F. angustifolia* subsp. *syriaca*.

**tomentosa** MICHX. f. "Pumpkin Ash". A medium-sized tree with downy young shoots and petioles. Leaves large, with usually 9 stalked leaflets, downy beneath. E United States. C 1912.

**velutina** TORR. "Arizona Ash". A neat and pretty tree of 9-12m. Remarkable for its leaves and shoots which are densely clothed with grey, velvety down. Winter buds brown. SW United States, N Mexico. I 1891.

**var. coriacea** (S. WATS.) REHD. A form with leaflets more leathery and less downy. California. C 1900.

**var. glabra** REHD. Leaves with 3-7 leaflets which are glabrous like the branches.

**var. toumeyi** REHD. A distinct variety of dense habit. Leaves smaller with 3-5 downy leaflets. Arizona, New Mexico, Mexico. I 1891.

**xanthoxyloides** DC. The "Afghan Ash" is a small tree or large shrub of unusual appearance, with small, rounded, close-set leaflets on a winged petiole. Winter buds brown. Himalaya to Afghanistan. C 1870.

**var. dimorpha** (COSS. & DUR.) WENZ. "Algerian Ash". A geographical form from N Africa differing in leaf shape and other minor characters. N Africa. I about 1855.

**var. dumosa** CARR. A curious small bush with interlacing branches and tiny leaflets. C 1865.

†*FREMONTODENDRON COV. (*Fremontia* TORR.)—**Sterculiaceae**—A genus of 2 species of tall evergreen shrubs best grown on a sunny wall in all but the milder parts of the British Isles. The flowers have no petals but possess a large, coloured calyx. Requires full sun and good drainage, excellent on chalk soils.

**'California Glory'** (*F. californicum* × *F. mexicanum*). A floriferous hybrid of vigorous growth which originated in California in 1952. Flowers yellow, up to 6cm across borne over a long period. FCC 1967. AGM 1984.

**californicum** (TORR.) COV. A beautiful large, semi-evergreen shrub with usually three-lobed leaves, and large yellow flowers borne freely throughout the summer and autumn. California, Arizona. I 1851. FCC 1866.

**185**

**FREMONTODENDRON**—*continued*

**mexicanum** DAVIDSON Similar to, but differing from *F. californicum* in its generally five-lobed leaves which are often shiny above. Flowers with slightly narrower sepals, giving a star-like appearance. California, Mexico. I 1926. AM 1927.

**'Pacific Sunset'** Similar to 'California Glory' but with the leaves more angularly lobed and the calyx brighter yellow, the lobes ending in conspicuous tail-like points. C 1984.

†\***FREYLINIA** COLLA—**Scrophulariaceae**—A small genus of about 4 species of evergreen shrubs native of tropical and South Africa.

**lanceolata** (L. f.) G. DON (*F. cestroides* COLLA) A pretty medium-sized shrub for the mildest localities. Panicles of fragrant, creamy-white or yellow flowers in late summer. S Africa. I 1774.

**"FRINGE TREE"** See *Chionanthus*.

**FUCHSIA** L.—**Onagraceae**—Some 100 species of shrubs, small trees and climbers, natives mainly of C and S America but also occurring in Tahiti and New Zealand. Flowers mostly pendulous with a showy calyx and corolla.

Most of the kinds listed below have passed successfully many winters out-of-doors in our nurseries. Although the tender sorts may be cut to ground level, they usually shoot up strongly again in spring. All have red sepals except where otherwise stated, and flower freely throughout summer and autumn. Remarkable in thriving alike in sun or shade in any well drained soil.

**'Alice Hoffman'** A small shrub with small purple-tinged leaves in dense clusters. Flowers small, calyx scarlet, petals white.

† × **bacillaris** LINDL. (*F. microphylla* × *F. thymifolia*). A beautiful shrub with small flowers; calyx glowing crimson, petals reflexed, coral-red. This plant was originally wrongly catalogued as *F. parviflora*.

**'Cottinghamii'** A charming shrub taller than the above described, the flowers similar in colour and shape but smaller, and succeeded by glossy, purple-brown, bead-like fruits.

**'Blue Gown'** A dwarf floriferous shrub of compact habit. Flowers double, corolla deep purple, calyx scarlet.

†**'Brilliant'** A small shrub with large flowers. Calyx rose-scarlet; petals broad, rose-purple. AMT 1962.

**'Chillerton Beauty'** A beautiful, small shrub with medium-sized flowers; calyx white, flushed deep rose, petals clear soft violet. AMT 1977. AGM 1984.

**'Corallina'** A strong, robust shrub with large, deep green leaves and scarlet and violet flowers. Raised about 1914. Originally catalogued as *F.* 'Exoniensis' which is probably no longer in cultivation. AGM 1984.

**'Cottinghamii'** See *F.* × *bacillaris* 'Cottinghamii'.

†**'Display'** A small shrub with large flowers. Calyx carmine; petals and long protruding stamens rose-pink.

**'Dunrobin Bedder'** Small shrub of spreading habit. Flowers similar to *F. magellanica*, scarlet and violet. AM 1890.

†**'Elsa'** Small shrub with large flowers. Calyx white flushed pink; petals doubled, violet-rose.

†**excorticata** (FORST. & FORST. f.) L. f. The largest of the three New Zealand species, making a very large tree-like shrub in the mildest localities, but here never more than a medium-sized bush. Flowers 2.5cm long, resembling *F. procumbens* in colour, appearing in spring. I 1824.

**'Garden News'** A vigorous and very hardy shrub of upright habit. Flowers large, double, calyx and tube pale pink, corolla magenta-rose. C 1978.

**'Genii'** A dwarf upright shrub with red shoots and attractive lime-yellow leaves. Flowers small with a violet then reddish-purple corolla and cerise calyx. Leaf colour develops best in full sun. C 1951.

**gracilis** See *F. magellanica* var. *gracilis*.

**'Variegata'** See *F. magellanica* 'Variegata'.

**'Graf Witte'** A small shrub with profusely borne, small, single flowers. Calyx carmine, corolla purple shaded rosy-mauve. C 1899. AMT 1978.

**FUCHSIA**—*continued*

**'Lady Thumb'** A bushy dwarf shrub with profusely borne, semi-double flowers; calyx light red, corolla white with red veins. C 1966. FCCT 1977. AGM 1984.

**'Lena'** Flowers semi-double, calyx pale pink, corolla rosy-magenta flushed pink; good for training. C 1862. AMT 1962. AGM 1984.

†**'Madame Cornelissen'** A large-flowered hybrid of *F. magellanica*, with red calyx and white petals. AM 1941. AMT 1965. FCCT 1978. AGM 1984.

**magellanica** LAM. A graceful South American shrub of medium size with long, slender flowers; calyx scarlet, petals violet. Leaves generally in whorls of three. I 1823.

**'Alba'** See *F. magellanica* var. *molinae*.

**var. gracilis** (LINDL.) BAILEY A beautiful, floriferous shrub of slender habit, with leaves generally in pairs. Flowers small, scarlet and violet. 1930. AMT 1978. AGM 1984.

**var. molinae** ESPINOZA ('Alba') Flowers shorter, white, faintly tinged mauve. AM 1932.

**'Pumila'** A charming dwarf shrub with small, narrow and tiny flowers of scarlet and deep violet. AGM 1984.

**'Riccartonii'** See *F.* 'Riccartonii'.

**'Sharpitor'** A form of var. *molinae* in which the leaves are grey-green margined with white. Originated at the National Trust garden of Sharpitor in Devon about 1973.

**'Tricolor'** See 'Versicolor'.

**'Variegata'** (*F. gracilis* 'Variegata') A striking, variegated form. Leaves green, margined creamy-yellow flushed pink, against which the small scarlet and purple flowers appear most effectively. Less hardy than the green form. AMT 1975. AGM 1984.

**'Versicolor'** ('Tricolor') A small shrub of spreading habit. The slender stems sport leaves of a striking grey-green which are rose-tinted when young and irregularly variegated creamy-white when mature. A lovely foliage shrub. AMT 1965. AGM 1984.

**'Margaret'** A vigorous shrub producing an abundance of crimson and violet-purple, semi-double flowers. AMT 1965.

**'Margaret Brown'** A dwarf shrub of erect, compact habit with large flowers; calyx crimson, petals magenta.

**'Mrs Popple'** A small, large-flowered, hardy hybrid with spreading scarlet sepals, violet petals, and long protruding crimson stamens and style. AM 1934. AMT 1962. AGM 1984.

**'Mrs W.P. Wood'** Flowers single, very freely borne, calyx pale pink with slender, upturned sepals, corolla white. C 1949. AGM 1984.

**parviflora** See under *F.* × *bacillaris*.

**'Peter Pan'** A dwarf shrub producing an abundance of small red and purple flowers.

**'Pixie'** A sport of 'Graf Witte' making an upright shrub to about 90cm with yellowish-green foliage. Flowers single with carmine tube and sepals and mauve-purple corolla veined with carmine.

†**procumbens** A. CUNN. A trailing, small-leaved New Zealand species. Flowers small, erect; calyx tube yellow, sepals violet and green, stamens red and blue, petals absent. Fruits comparatively large, magenta. I about 1854. AM 1980.

**'Prosperity'** A beautiful small shrub of upright habit and vigorous growth with large, double flowers. Corolla white veined pink, calyx deep rose-pink. One of the most spectacular hardy fuchsias.

†**'Reflexa'** A small shrub with tiny leaves and small, bright cerise flowers darkening with age; fruits black. Regarded by some authorities as a form of *F. thymifolia*, whilst others suggest it may belong to *F.* × *bacillaris*.

**'Riccartonii'** (*F. magellanica* 'Riccartonii') This common, hardy shrub attains a large size, and is often used as a hedging plant in mild districts. Differing from *F. magellanica* in its deeper coloured calyx and broader sepals. AMT 1966. FCCT 1977. AGM 1984.

**'Rose of Castille Improved'** A vigorous small shrub with large flowers. Corolla deep violet-purple, calyx spreading, white tinged pink inside, tipped with green. C 1871.

**'Snowcap'** A dwarf shrub, flowers 5cm long with red sepals and tube, the petals white veined with red. AMT 1966 (for summer bedding).

**'Tennessee Waltz'** A low shrub of arching habit. Corolla rich purple-violet, calyx deep glossy scarlet. C 1950. AMT 1978.

**FUCHSIA**—*continued*

'**Tom Thumb**' A very free-flowering dwarf shrub; calyx rose-scarlet; petals violet. AMT 1938. FCCT 1962. AGM 1984.

"**FURZE**" See *Ulex*.

"**FURZE, NEEDLE**" See *Genista anglica*.

\***GARRYA** DOUGL. ex LINDL.—**Garryaceae**—About 13 species of evergreen, dioecious shrubs with opposite, leathery leaves. Natives of the SW United States, Mexico and the West Indies. Flowers are borne in long, slender, conspicuous catkins. Excellent both in maritime exposure and atmospheric pollution and useful for furnishing north or east-facing walls. They succeed in all types of well drained soil, but require protection in cold areas.

**congdonii** EASTW. A shrub up to 1.8m with narrowly oval leaves, rounded on juvenile plants. Male catkins up to 7.5cm long in late spring. California.

**elliptica** DOUGL. ex LINDL. The male plant of this species is a magnificent evergreen, draped, during January and February, with long, greyish-green catkins. The female plant is scarcely less effective, with its long clusters of deep purple-brown fruits. California, Oregon. I 1828 by David Douglas. AM 1931. AM 1975 (for fruit). AGM 1984 (male plants only).

'**James Roof**' A strong, vigorous male with large leathery leaves and extra long catkins to 20cm. Originated as a seedling in California before 1950. AM 1974. AGM 1984.

†**flavescens** WATS. An erect, medium-sized shrub with leathery, elliptic, sharply-pointed leaves. Flowers in stout, pendulous catkins during spring. A variable species, the typical form has leaves and young stems clothed with yellowish hairs but in their sage-green and greyish-green appearance our plants approach the variety *pallida*. California.

× **issaquahensis** TALBOT DE MALAHIDE ex NELSON (*G. elliptica* × *G. fremontii*). A large shrub intermediate between the parents. Leaves dark glossy green above, green and glaucous green and only slightly hairy beneath, flat or slightly undulate. First raised in Seattle in about 1957, the cross later occurred accidentally in the garden of Mrs Pat Ballard at Issaquah, Washington in 1960. The following clone was raised at Malahide Castle.

'**Pat Ballard**' A male selection with reddish-purple shoots and petioles. Catkins to 22cm long in midwinter, purple-tinged at first becoming green tinged red. AM 1971.

†**laurifolia** BENTH. A tender species of which the following form is cultivated.

**subsp. macrophylla** (BENTH.) G.V. DAHLING (*G. fadyenii* HORT. not HOOK.) A vigorous, medium-sized to large shrub with large leaves up to 15cm long. Catkins less spectacular than those of *G. elliptica*, appearing in late spring. Mexico. I 1846.

× **thuretii** CARR. (*G. elliptica* × *G. laurifolia* subsp. *macrophylla*). A vigorous hybrid, rapidly attaining 5.5m and making a solid green wall. Leaves dark green, glossy, about 14cm long. An excellent wind resister. Garden origin about 1862.

**wrightii** TORR. A medium-sized shrub with slender, 5cm catkins in summer. Leaves elliptic, firm and leathery with a sharp mucro-point, sage-green and conspicuously veined. SW United States. I 1901.

‡\* × **GAULNETTYA** MARCHANT (*Gaultheria* × *Pernettya*). (× *Gaulthettya* CAMP)—**Ericaceae**—Hybrids between these two closely related genera are known to occur in the wild both in New Zealand and in C and S America. The following are of garden origin and are all *G. shallon* × *P. mucronata*.

**wisleyensis** See *G.* 'Wisley Pearl'.

'**Pink Pixie**' A dwarf suckering shrub with white tinged pink flowers in May followed by purplish-red fruits. Raised by our propagator Peter Dummer by back-crossing 'Wisley Pearl' with *Gaultheria shallon* in 1965. AM 1976.

'**Ruby**' A small shrub of vigorous habit forming a dense evergreen thicket. Leaves up to 2.5cm long, dark green and leathery; flowers white, produced in late May and early June in dense terminal and axillary racemes. The fruits, ripening in late autumn and winter, are ruby-red, each crowned by a similarly coloured swollen calyx like a tiny elf's cap.

×**GAULNETTYA**—*continued*

**'Wisley Pearl'** A small shrub with dull, dark green leaves 3.8cm or more long and half as wide. The branches are laden during autumn and winter with short but crowded bunches of large ox-blood-red fruits. An interesting hybrid which originated at Wisley about 1929. This is the original selected clone usually distributed as ×*Gaulnettya wisleyensis*. AM 1939.

‡***GAULTHERIA** L.—**Ericaceae**—An interesting genus of some 150 species, related to *Vaccinium*, differing in the superior ovary; thriving in moist, lime-free, preferably peaty soil, and a shady position. Natives mainly of the Andes but also occurring in North America, E Asia and Australasia. They are mainly tufted shrubs, spreading by underground stems. In the majority of species the calyx enlarges after flowering, becomes fleshy and coloured and encloses the true fruit. The white urn-shaped flowers are normally borne in late spring or early summer.

**adenothrix** (MIQ.) MAXIM. A dainty dwarf creeping shrub forming a low carpet of zig-zag red-brown hairy stems furnished with small leathery dark green leaves. Flowers white suffused pink borne from May to July and followed by hairy crimson fruits. Japan. I 1915.

**antipoda** FORST. f. An interesting New Zealand species, varying in habit between a prostrate shrub and an erect bush of 1.2m. Fruits red or white, globose, about 1.25cm across. I 1820.

**caudata** STAPF A low-growing, wide-spreading shrub forming a dense mound. A specimen in the Hillier Gardens and Arboretum reached 0.75m high and 2.5m across. The narrowly elliptic to elliptic-oblong, sharply serrulate leaves which are reticulate and punctate beneath are widely spaced along the attractively arching, reddish shoots. Flowering in axillary racemes. Yunnan.

**cuneata** (REHD. & WILSON) BEAN A dwarf shrub of compact habit. Leaves narrowly oblanceolate. Fruits white, smelling of Germolene when crushed. A delightful species. W China. I 1909 by Ernest Wilson. AM 1924.

**forrestii** DIELS An attractive, spreading, Chinese shrub having conspicuous, white-stalked axillary racemes of white, waxy, fragrant flowers, followed by blue fruits. I about 1908. AM 1927. AM 1937.

**fragrantissima** WALL. A medium-sized species with narrowly elliptic, toothed, subglabrous leaves; flowers in racemes from the leaf axils, fragrant; fruits bright blue. Himalaya, Mts of Burma, India and Sri Lanka. I about 1850.

**hispida** R. BR. Small shrub with bristly young shoots. Leaves oblong, up to 6.3cm long. Flowers white, in terminal panicles followed by succulent, berry-like white fruits. Australia, Tasmania. C 1927. AM 1927.

**hookeri** C.B. CLARKE (*G. veitchiana* CRAIB) A dwarf, densely spreading shrub with bristly arching stems. Leaves leathery and glandular toothed, elliptic to obovate 5-7.5cm long. Flowers white in dense, axillary terminal clusters in May; fruits blue. Himalaya, W China. I 1907 by Ernest Wilson. AM 1943. FCC 1945.

**humifusa** (GRAHAM) RYBD. (*G. myrsinites* HOOK.) A dwarf shrub of dense compact habit and only a few centimetres high, bearing small, rounded, wavy leaves. The small, pink-tinged, bell-shaped flowers in summer are followed by small red fruits. NW North America. C 1830.

**itoana** HAYATA A rare, creeping species forming close mats of bright green, pernettya-like foliage. Fruits white. Taiwan. I shortly before 1936. AM 1982.

**miqueliana** TAKEDA A neat, dwarf, Japanese shrub, usually not above 30cm high, with shining green, oblong leaves. The short racemes are conspicuous in June, and are followed by white or pink edible fruits. I 1892. AM 1948.

†**nummularioides** D. DON A neat, creeping, Himalayan species with small, broadly ovate, bristly leaves arranged in two ranks; fruits blue-black. Suitable for a sheltered shady bank. I about 1850.

**oppositifolia** HOOK. f. A small, densely branched shrub of spreading habit with arching, usually glabrous shoots. Leaves normally opposite, ovate to oblong, dark glossy green above and strongly reticulate. The white, bell-shaped flowers are borne in conspicuous terminal panicles during May and June. Fruits white. An extremely ornamental New

**GAULTHERIA oppositifolia**—*continued*

Zealand species easily recognised by its opposite leaves. It requires a sheltered position. AM 1927.

**procumbens** L. "Checkerberry". A North American creeping evergreen, forming carpets of dark green leaves amongst which, in autumn and winter, the bright red fruits are freely intermixed. I before 1762. AM 1982.

**pyroloides** MIQ. emend TAKEDA (*G. pyrolifolia* C.B. CLARKE) A dwarf creeping shrub forming mats of short stems and bright green, obovate or rounded, reticulately-veined leaves, 2.5cm long. The pink-tinged urn-shaped flowers are borne in short leafy racemes from mid May often to July. Fruits blue-black. An interesting little plant recalling *Salix reticulata* in leaf. Himalaya. C 1933.

**semi-infera** (C.B. CLARKE) AIRY SHAW A dwarf shrub with hispid shoots and obovate to oblanceolate leaves 5-8cm long, glossy green above. Flowers white, occasionally blush, followed by obovoid fruits variable in colour, often indigo-blue. Himalaya. AM 1950.

**shallon** PURSH A vigorous species forming thickets up to 1.8m high, and ideal undergrowth for game coverts, etc. Leaves broad and leathery; flowers pinkish-white, fruits dark purple, in large clusters. W North America. I 1826.

**stapfiana** AIRY SHAW A dwarf shrub with arching and erect stems and elliptic to oblanceolate leaves. Flowers white followed by bright blue fruits. Closely related to *G. hookeri* under which name it is often found in gardens. It mainly differs from this species in its usually more erect, glabrous or adpressed bristly stems. W China.

**tetramera** W.W. SM. A dwarf shrub of compact habit forming a wide mound of arching stems. Leaves broadly oval to lanceolate-elliptic, reticulate and dark green above. Flowers white, borne in May and June and followed by blue or violet coloured fruits. W China. C 1933. AM 1950.

**trichophylla** ROYLE A charming shrublet of tufted habit. Flowers pink followed by conspicuous large blue fruits. Himalaya, W China. I 1897. AM 1918.

**veitchiana**. See *G. hookeri*.

**wardii** MARQUAND & SHAW A Kingdon-Ward introduction from SE Tibet, distinct in its bristly nature and leathery, lanceolate leaves with deeply impressed veins. May or June-blooming; flowers in racemes, white; fruits milky-blue. C 1933. AM 1933.

‡**GAYLUSSACIA** KUNTH—**Ericaceae**—The "Huckleberries" are evergreen or deciduous shrubs closely resembling *Vaccinium*, and requiring similar conditions. There are some 40-50 species in N and S America.

**baccata** (WANGENH.) K. KOCH "Black Huckleberry". A small shrub of erect habit. Leaves resinous beneath; flowers in May, dull red, in short dense racemes; fruits lustrous black, edible. Autumn tints of a soft crimson. E North America. I 1772.

*****brachycera** (MICHX.) A. GRAY. "Box Huckleberry". Dwarf shrub with thick, leathery, glossy green leaves. Flowers white, produced in May and June. E United States. I 1796. AM 1940.

"**GEAN**" See *Prunus avium*.

**GENISTA** L.—**Leguminosae**—About 80 species of shrubs native to Europe, W Asia and N Africa, allied to *Cytisus* and requiring similar treatment. They range in habit from prostrate to almost tree-like. Some of the dwarf species are indispensable alpines, while the taller ones include some invaluable summer-flowering shrubs. They associate well with the heathers. All succeeded in acid or neutral soil and are lime-tolerant. All have yellow flowers unless otherwise described.

**aetnensis** (BIVONA) DC. "Mount Etna Broom". A large, elegant shrub or small tree with slender, green leafless shoots. Fragrant flowers are profusely borne in July and August. Sardinia and Sicily. FCC 1938. AGM 1984.

**anglica** L. "Needle Furze" "Petty Whin". A dwarf, spiny, native shrub. Showy yellow flowers from May to July. W Europe.

**cinerea** (VILL.) DC. A medium-sized shrub with slender silky shoots and clusters of golden yellow flowers during June and July. SW Europe, N Africa. For the plant usually grown under this name see *G. tenera* 'Golden Shower'. AM 1924.

**GENISTA**—*continued*

**delphinensis** VILL. This tiny decumbent shrub is one of the best species for the rock garden. Deep yellow flowers in terminal or axillary clusters in July to August. Like a miniature *G. sagittalis*. S France.

†**ephedroides** DC. An unusual, small, erect-branched shrub with very small leaves which soon fall, leaving the slender stems quite naked. The solitary, fragrant, yellow flowers are borne towards the end of the shoots in May and June. Sardinia, Sicily and S Italy.

†**falcata** BROT. A small gorse-like shrub. Slender branches, with spiny lateral shoots; flowers deep golden yellow in long panicles in May. Portugal, W Spain.

†**fasselata** DECNE. (*G. sphacelata* SPACH) A curious, small, rather gorse-like, spiny shrub with typical yellow flowers, from the E Mediterranean region.

**germanica** L. A dwarf, spiny shrub covered with short racemes of yellow flowers in June. C and W Europe to C Russia. C 1588.

**hispanica** L. "Spanish Gorse". One of the best plants for sunny sites, dry banks, etc forming 0.6m high dense, prickly mounds covered unfailingly in May and June with masses of yellow flowers. SW Europe. I 1759. AGM 1984.

**horrida** (VAHL) DC. (*Echinospartium horridum* (VAHL) ROTHM.) A dwarf, rigid, spiny shrub of silvery-grey hue. Flowers in small terminal heads from July to September. SW Europe. I 1821.

**januensis** VIV. (*G. triquetra* WALDST. & KIT.) "Genoa Broom". A rare, procumbent shrub with somewhat winged branches. Flowers bright yellow in May. SE Europe. I about 1840. AM 1932.

**lydia** BOISS. (*G. spathulata* SPACH) An outstanding dwarf shrub. Slender pendulous branchlets are smothered in golden yellow flowers in May and June. E Balkans. I 1926. AM 1937. FCC 1957. AGM 1984.

†**monosperma** (L.) LAM. (*Lygos monosperma* (L.) HEYWOOD) An unusual species up to 1.8m with long, slender, rush-like stems. The young growths give the plant a silvery appearance. Flowers milky-white, fragrant. S Europe and N Africa. I 1690.

**pilosa** L. A dwarf, native shrub, producing cascades of golden-yellow flowers in May. W and C Europe (incl British Isles). The forms named 'Lemon Spreader' and 'Vancouver Gold' seem to differ little from the typical plant as grown here.

'**Goldilocks**' A vigorous Dutch selection with ascending branches reaching 60cm. Golden yellow flowers are profusely borne over a long period. C 1970.

**radiata** (L.) SCOP. A slow-growing species, forming a dense shrub about 1m high. Flowers in June, deep yellow. C and SE Europe. I 1758.

**sagittalis** L. (*Chamaespartium sagittale* (L.) P. GIBBS) A dwarf shrub with broadly winged, prostrate branches, giving an evergreen appearance; flowers in June. Useful for dry walls etc. C and S Europe. C 1588.

**scorpius** (L.) DC. A rare species, which has here reached a height of 1.8m. Branches spiny, like gorse but grey; flowers in bright yellow masses in April and May. SW Europe.

**sylvestris** SCOP. (*G. dalmatica* BARTL.) "Dalmatian Broom". A decumbent shrub forming hummocks 15-23cm high, covered with terminal racemes of yellow flowers in June and July. An excellent plant for a well drained ledge in the rock garden. W Balkans, C and S Italy. I 1893.

**tenera** (JACQ.) O. KUNTZE (*G. virgata* (AIT.) LINK) A beautiful, hardy shrub attaining 3.5m and as much through, flowering in June and July. Resembles *G. cinerea*. Madeira, Tenerife. I 1777.

'**Golden Shower**' A vigorous, large, arching shrub bearing masses of brilliant yellow fragrant flowers in June. Long grown incorrectly as *G. cinerea*. AGM 1984.

**tinctoria** L. "Dyer's Greenweed". A late flowering native shrub of about 0.6m with bright yellow flowers in long terminal racemes from June to September. Europe.

**var. anxantica** (TEN.) FIORI A glabrous, dwarf form. Italy. I 1818.

**var. humilior** (BERTOL.) SCHNEID. (*G. mantica* POLL.) A distinct, downy, erect variety with purple stems and deep yellow flowers. Italy. I 1816.

'**Golden Plate**' A low-growing form of spreading habit up to 30cm tall, suitable for ground cover. Found on the island of Texel in the Waddenzee off the north-west coast of Holland.

**GENISTA tinctoria**—*continued*

**'Plena'** Floriferous dwarf, semi-prostrate form with double flowers. A superb dwarf shrub for the rock garden. AGM 1984.

**'Royal Gold'** A small, free-flowering shrub, the stems thickly covered with rich yellow flowers through summer.

**var. virgata** KOCH (*G. virgata* WILLD.) Habit upright, to 2m tall. SE Europe.

**villarsii** CLEMENTI (*G. pulchella* GREN. & GODR.) A miniature rock garden shrub 7.5-10cm high. Young shoots grey, hairy; flowers bright yellow, solitary in the axils of the terminal leaves in May. SE France, W Balkans.

**virgata** See *G. tenera* and *G. tinctoria* var. *virgata*.

‡†*GEVUINA MOL.—**Proteaceae**—A monotypic genus related to *Grevillea*.

**avellana** MOL. "Chilean Hazel". An interesting species making, in favourable localities, a large shrub or small tree. The long branches are held rather loosely and carry handsome polished pinnate leaves. Flowers white in panicles followed by bright red, cherry-like fruits, rarely produced in this country. It grows best in sheltered woodlands. S Chile, Argentina. I 1826. AM 1983.

**"GHOST TREE"** See *Davidia involucrata*.

**GLEDITSIA** L. (GLEDITSCHIA SCOP.)—**Leguminosae**—A genus of about 12 species of deciduous spiny trees, natives of North America and Asia, one species in Argentina. Valuable in gardens for their extremely beautiful foliage. Mature trunks often formidably armed with long thorns. Leaves pinnate or bipinnate. Flowers greenish and insignificant. Seeds produced in flattened pods of varying length. Succeed in all types of well drained soils and tolerant of atmospheric pollution.

**aquatica** MARSH. "Water Locust". Small, shrubby tree with large branched spines and simply or doubly pinnate leaves. Pods, when produced, short, less than 5cm long containing a solitary seed. SE United States. I 1723.

**caspica** DESF. "Caspian Locust". A small tree, old specimens with trunks formidably armed with numerous spines 15cm or more long. Leaflets larger than in most species. Transcaucasus, N Iran. I 1822.

**delavayi** FRANCH. A Chinese tree of medium height, with dark green, lustrous leaves, coppery-red young growths and enormous spines. Unripened growths are cut back in very cold winters. I 1900 by Ernest Wilson.

**horrida** See *G. japonica* and *G. sinensis*.

**japonica** MIQ. (*G. horrida* (THUNB.) MAK.) A graceful, medium-sized Japanese tree of somewhat pyramidal habit, its trunk being armed with branched spines. The fern-like leaves are composed of up to thirty small leaflets. Quite hardy even in a young state. I 1894.

**macracantha** DESF. A tall, medium-sized, spiny tree from C China, particularly notable for the variable size of its leaflets; flowers in downy racemes followed by long seed pods. C 1800.

**sinensis** LAM. (*G. horrida* WILLD.) "Chinese Honey Locust". A handsome medium-sized tree with branched spines and fern-like foliage. China. I 1774.

×**texana** SARG. (*G. aquatica* × *G. triacanthos*). A natural hybrid making eventually a large tree with smooth bark and spineless branches. Similar in general appearance to *G. triacanthos*. Only found in one locality in Texas. I 1900.

**triacanthos** L. "Honey Locust". This elegant large-sized tree, with frond-like leaves, is very tolerant of industrially polluted atmosphere. A large specimen is quite effective when strung with its long, shining-brown seed pods. C and E United States. I 1700.

**'Bujotii'** ('Pendula') A shrubby form or occasionally small tree, with narrower leaflets and slender pendulous branchlets. C 1845.

**'Elegantissima'** A beautiful, slow-growing shrub of dense, bushy habit, attaining 3.5-4.5m with attractive, fern-like foliage. Raised about 1880.

**f. inermis** (L.) ZAB. A form which bears no thorns.

**'Inermis Aurea'** See 'Sunburst'.

**'Pendula'** See 'Bujotii'.

**GLEDITSIA triacanthos**—*continued*

**'Ruby Lace'** An American selection with deep bronze-red young foliage. C 1961.

**'Shademaster'** A vigorous, thornless form with ascending branches and dark green, long-persistent leaves. C 1954.

**'Sunburst'** ('Inermis Aurea') A striking, medium-sized tree, having thornless stems and bright yellow young leaves which contrast effectively with the older dark green foliage. C 1953. AGM 1984.

†**GLOCHIDION** FORST. & FORST. f.—**Euphorbiaceae**—A large genus of some 300 species of trees and shrubs distributed throughout tropical areas but found mainly between tropical Asia, Polynesia and Queensland.

**sinicum** HOOK. & ARN. (*G. fortunei* HANCE) A rare and interesting, shrubby Chinese member of the *Euphorbia* family, with slender, reddish shoots and ovate-lanceolate, glabrous leaves up to 9 × 3cm, dark glossy green above, glaucous beneath, reddish in autumn. Tiny green flowers similar to those of *Securinega suffruticosa* hang on slender stalks in clusters of 1-3 from the leaf axils in autumn.

**"GOLDEN RAIN"** See *Laburnum*.

‡†*****GORDONIA** ELLIS—**Theaceae**—About 70 species of camellia-like trees and shrubs, found in the warmer parts of the S United States and SE Asia. They are conspicuous both in leaf and flower and require a lime-free soil.

**alatamaha** See *Franklinia alatamaha*.

**axillaris** (KER-GAWL.) ENDL. (*G. anomala* SPRENG.) A rare evergreen, large shrub or small tree. Large, leathery, dark, glossy green leaves; flowers 7.5-15cm across, creamy-white, appearing from November to May. China and Taiwan. I 1818. AM 1929.

**chrysandra** COWAN A large, Chinese shrub. Flowers creamy-white, fragrant, 5cm across during late winter. Yunnan. I 1917 by George Forrest.

**lasianthus** (L.) ELLIS "Loblolly Bay". A beautiful, but tender, magnolia-like species attaining small tree size in this country. Flowers white, 7.5cm across, in July and August. SE United States. I 1768.

**"GORSE, COMMON"** See *Ulex europaeus*.

**"GORSE, SPANISH"** See *Genista hispanica*.

‡†*****GREVILLEA** R. BR.—**Proteaceae**—A genus of some 250 species of beautiful, evergreen trees and shrubs almost all of which are natives of Australia or Tasmania with a few species in New Caledonia and Sulawesi (the Celebes). The flowers, superficially like those of honeysuckle, but smaller, with showy, exserted styles, are produced over a long period. Good drainage essential and avoid overhead shade and chalk soils.

**alpina** LINDL. A charming, compact, low shrub for the mildest parts, freely producing its curious, red and cream flowers over a long season. Grey-green, needle-like leaves. An excellent pot plant. SE Australia. I before 1857. AM 1936. See also *G. rosmarinifolia*.

**glabrata** (LINDL.) MEISSN. An erect glabrous shrub with attractive lobed leaves and long, pyramidal panicles of white flowers with pink stigmas in spring. A conservatory plant except in the mildest localities. W Australia.

**juniperina** R. BR. A beautiful, medium-sized shrub for mild districts. Terminal racemes of bright red flowers in summer. Bright green needle-like leaves. SE Australia (New South Wales). Mainly cultivated in the following form.

**'Sulphurea'** (*G. sulphurea* (CUNN.) BENTH.) Flowers bright yellow. AM 1974.

**ornithopoda** MEISSN. A medium-sized to large shrub for the conservatory. The pendulous branches carry long, flat, pale green, trifid leaves. The thick clusters of creamy-white flowers cascade down the stems in April. W Australia. I 1850.

**rosmarinifolia** CUNN. A beautiful shrub for mild districts, where it will attain 1.8m. The conspicuous, crimson flowers are produced in long terminal racemes during summer. Deep green, needle-like leaves. SE Australia. Cultivated plants may be hybrids with *G. lanigera*. I about 1822. AM 1932. Some plants grown as *G. alpina* belong here.

**GREVILLEA**—*continued*

× **semperflorens** MULLIGAN (*G. juniperina* 'Sulphurea' × *G. thelmanniana*). An interesting and beautiful hybrid of garden origin. The flowers are a combination of yellow suffused rose-pink and tipped at the apex with green during summer. Leaves needle-like. Attains about 1.8m in sheltered areas of SW England. Raised by Miss F.E. Briggs of Plymouth in 1926.

**sulphurea** See *G. juniperina* 'Sulphurea'.

**GREWIA** L.—**Tiliaceae**—A large genus of more than 150 species of trees and shrubs found in Asia and Africa, mainly in tropical and subtropical regions.

†**occidentalis** L. A little-known South African shrub or small tree allied to the "Lime". Leaves oval; flowers in stalked clusters, pink. I 1690.

†**GRINDELIA** WILLD.—**Compositae**—A small genus of about 60 species of sub-shrubs and herbaceous plants. Natives of W North America and S America.

*****chiloensis** (CORNELISSEN) CABRERA (*G. speciosa* HOOK. & ARN.) This surprisingly hardy, small evergreen sub-shrub is a really handsome plant. The narrow leaves with undulate, toothed margins are hoary, affording a harmonious contrast with the large, rich cornflower-like yellow flowers, which appear from June to October, carried singly on stout tall stems. Buds covered with a milk-white, sticky varnish. Requires full sun and acute drainage. Argentina. I about 1850. AM 1931.

†*****GRISELINIA** FORST. f.—**Cornaceae**—A small genus of about 6 species of trees and shrubs, native of New Zealand, Chile and SE Brazil. Flowers inconspicuous, male and female on separate plants.

**littoralis** RAOUL "Broadleaf". This densely leafy, large, evergreen shrub, which is tree-like in mild localities, is an excellent hedge plant for maritime exposure. Leaves leathery, apple-green. Succeeds in all types of fertile soil. Liable to frost damage in cold inland areas. New Zealand. I about 1850. AGM 1984.

**'Dixon's Cream'** An attractive form with leaves splashed and marked creamy-white. Occurred as a sport of 'Variegata' in the garden of Major W.G.M. Dixon in Jersey. Forms similar to this include 'Luscombe's Gold' which occurred as a sport of 'Variegata' in Luscombe's Nursery, Torquay in 1970 and 'Bantry Bay'. Similar sports have also occurred in New Zealand.

**'Variegata'** Conspicuous white variegated foliage. AM 1978.

**lucida** FORST. f. A very handsome, tender species with large leaves which have a noticeably oblique base and an almost varnished upper surface. Usually epiphytic in the wild. New Zealand.

**"GUELDER ROSE"** See *Viburnum opulus*.

**"GUM TREE"** See *Eucalyptus*.

**GYMNOCLADUS** LAM.—**Leguminosae**—A genus of deciduous trees with a single species in North America and 3 species in E Asia. They are related to *Gleditsia*, with bipinnate leaves, inconspicuous flowers and seeds borne in pods.

**dioica** (L.) K. KOCH (*G. canadensis* LAM.) "Kentucky Coffee Tree". This medium-sized, slow-growing tree is one of the most handsome of all hardy trees. Young twigs light grey, almost white, specially noticeable in winter. The large compound leaves are pink-tinted when unfolding, and turn clear yellow before falling. The seeds were used as a substitute for coffee by the early settlers in North America. E and C United States. I before 1748.

**'Variegata'** Leaflets with a creamy-white variegation.

**"HACKBERRY"** See *Celtis*.

**\*HAKEA** SCHRAD.—**Proteaceae**—A remarkable genus of about 100 species of evergreen shrubs or small trees native to Australia and Tasmania, some suggesting kinship with the conifers. A few species are hardy and make excellent subjects for sunny, arid positions. Not good on chalk soils.

**acicularis** See *H. sericea*.

**lissosperma** R. BR. A tall, erect-branched, columnar shrub creating an effect which might be associated with the desert. The rigid, grey-green, needle-like, sharply-pointed leaves 2.5-7.5cm long are narrowed at the base and held more or less erect on the shoots. Showy white flowers are produced in clusters in the leaf axils from April to May. Previously listed as *H. sericea*. This splendid plant has proved perfectly hardy at the Hillier Gardens and Arboretum where it has reached 5.5m tall (1990). SE Australia, Tasmania.

**microcarpa** R. BR. An interesting medium to large-sized shrub of dense rounded habit. The fragrant, creamy-white flowers are produced in clusters in the axils of needle-like leaves in May and are followed by chestnut-brown seed capsules. SE Australia, Tasmania.

**sericea** SCHRAD. (*H. acicularis* (SM. ex VENT.) KNIGHT) A medium-sized to large shrub similar to *H. lissosperma* but differing in the more slender, longer-pointed, shorter, bright green leaves which are not narrowed at the base and are more spreading on the shoot. In a form we sent to the Ventnor Botanic Garden the flowers were deep pink in bud opening white flushed pink at the tips of the perianth segments. The plant previously listed under this name is *H. lissosperma* q.v. SE Australia, Tasmania. C 1796.

**‡HALESIA** L.—**Styracaceae**—The "Snowdrop Trees" or "Silverbells" are a small genus of 5 species of very beautiful shrubs or small trees allied to *Styrax* and natives of the SE United States with one species in E China. The pendulous, snowdrop-like flowers are produced in clusters along naked branches in May followed by small, green, winged fruits. They thrive in a moist but well drained, lime-free soil in sun or semi-shade.

**carolina** L. (*H. tetraptera* ELLIS) "Snowdrop Tree". A large shrub or occasionally small, spreading tree, very beautiful in spring when the branches are draped with white, nodding, bell-shaped flowers in clusters of 3 or 5. Fruits pear-shaped, four-winged. SE United States. I 1756. AM 1954. FCC 1980.

**diptera** ELLIS This species is similar to *H. carolina*, but is more shrubby in habit and less free-flowering. It is also distinguished by its broader leaves and two-winged fruits. SE United States. I 1758. AM 1948.

**var. magniflora** GODFREY A wide-spreading large shrub of bushy habit differing from the typical form in its larger flowers, 2-3cm long. The best form of the species. AM 1970.

**monticola** (REHD.) SARG. "Mountain Snowdrop Tree". A magnificent small spreading tree differing from *H. carolina* in its greater size and its larger flowers and fruits, the latter up to 5cm long. Mts of SE United States. I about 1897. AM 1930. AGM 1984 (to the species and its variants).

**‘Rosea’** Flowers very pale pink. FCC 1984.

**var. vestita** SARG. A magnificent variety which in gardens produces larger flowers up to 3cm across, white sometimes tinged rose. Leaves more or less downy beneath at first, becoming glabrous. AM 1958.

**tetraptera** See *H. carolina*.

**\* × HALIMIOCISTUS** JANCHEN (*Halimium × Cistus*)—**Cistaceae**—Pretty and interesting hybrids surviving, when given full sun and good drainage, all but the coldest winters. See also *Cistus, Halimium* and *Helianthemum*.

**‘Ingwersenii’** (*Helianthemum clusii*) Discovered in Portugal, and believed to be *H. umbellatum × C. hirsutus*. A free-growing, dwarf, spreading shrub, with pure white flowers borne over a long period and linear, dark green, conspicuously hairy leaves. I about 1929.

**revolii** (COSTE & SOULIE) DANSEREAU A beautiful low evergreen producing a long succession of white, yellow-centred flowers. Found in France in 1914.

**sahucii** (COSTE & SOULIE) JANCHEN (*H. umbellatum × C. salviifolius*). A dwarf spreading shrub with linear leaves and pure white flowers from May to September. S France. I about 1929. AGM 1984.

× **HALIMIOCISTUS**—*continued*

†**wintonensis** O. & E.F. WARB. This beautiful hybrid originated in our nurseries, and is believed to be *H. ocymoides* × *C. salviifolius*. Flowers 5cm across, pearly white with a feathered and pencilled zone of crimson-maroon, contrasting with yellow stains at the base of the petals; May to June. An attractive dwarf grey-foliaged shrub. I about 1910. AM 1926 (as *Cistus wintonensis*). AGM 1984.

'**Merrist Wood Cream**' In this attractive form the base colour of the flower is pale creamy-yellow. A sport found at Merrist Wood Agricultural College in 1978.

***HALIMIUM** (DUNAL) SPACH—**Cistaceae**—A small genus of about 7 species, natives of the Mediterranean region and W Asia. Mostly low, spreading shrubs, akin to *Helianthemum*. They require full sun, and are subject to injury by severe frost. See also *Cistus*, × *Halimiocistus* and *Helianthemum*.

†**atriplicifolium** (LAM.) SPACH A very beautiful but tender small, silver shrub of spreading habit. Flowers golden yellow, up to 4cm across in June; leaves broad, silvery-grey. Requires a sheltered sunny site. C and S Spain. C in the mid 17th century.

**commutatum** PAU (*H. libanotis* LANGE in part) (*H. rosmarinifolium*) Dwarf shrub of semi-erect habit with linear leaves and golden yellow flowers 2.5cm across; June. Mediterranean region.

†**halimifolium** (L.) WILLK. & LANGE A small, erect shrub with narrow grey leaves. From May onwards the bright yellow flowers, up to 4cm across, appear in erect, few-flowered panicles. Each petal has a dark spot at its base. Mediterranean region. C since middle of 17th century.

**lasianthum** SPACH (*Cistus formosus*) A low, spreading shrub, ultimately 0.6-1m high, with greyish leaves, and golden yellow flowers with a dark blotch at the base of each petal; May. S Portugal, S Spain. I 1780. AM 1951. Plants in cultivation belong to subsp. *formosum* (CURT.) HEYWOOD.

'**Concolor**' Petals without blotches.

'**Sandling**' A form with large crescent-shaped maroon blotches on the petals.

**libanotis** See *H. commutatum*.

**ocymoides** (LAM.) WILLK. & LANGE. (*Helianthemum algarvense* (SIMS) DUN.) Charming, compact shrub of 0.6-1m with small, grey leaves and bright yellow flowers, with blackish-brown basal markings. Portugal and Spain. C 1800. AGM 1984.

'**Susan**' A more compact form with relatively broad leaves.

**umbellatum** (L.) SPACH A dwarf species, very similar to *H. commutatum*, from which it differs in its white flowers; June. Mediterranean region. I 1731.

**HALIMODENDRON** FISCH. ex DC.—**Leguminosae**—A monotypic genus allied to *Caragana*. Succeeds in any well drained, open site.

**halodendron** (PALL.) VOSS (*H. argenteum* (LAM.) DC.) "Salt Tree". An attractive, spiny, silvery-leaved shrub up to 1.8m. Leaves with 2-3 pairs of oblanceolate, grey tomentose leaflets and a terminal spine. Masses of purplish pink pea flowers in June and July. An excellent seaside plant. Grows in dry saltfields in Siberia. SE Russia, C and SW Asia. I 1779.

**HAMAMELIS** L.—**Hamamelidaceae**—The "Witch Hazels" are a most distinct and beautiful genus of mainly winter-flowering shrubs or small trees with 5 or 6 species in E North America and E Asia. In the majority, the spider-like yellow or reddish flowers appear on the normally leafless branches from December to March. The curious strap-shaped petals withstand the severest weather without injury, and the hazel-like foliage usually gives attractive autumn colour.

Size of flower $\begin{cases} \text{Large—over 3cm (1}\frac{1}{4}\text{in) across} \\ \text{Medium—2-3cm (}\frac{3}{4}\text{-1}\frac{1}{4}\text{in) across} \\ \text{Small—up to 2cm (}\frac{3}{4}\text{in) across} \end{cases}$

× **intermedia** REHD. (*H. japonica* × *H. mollis*). Large shrubs of variable nature generally intermediate between the parents. Leaves often large particularly on vigorous shoots. Flowers medium to large, rarely strongly scented, with petals somewhat folded and

**HAMAMELIS × intermedia**—*continued*

crimpled, appearing from December to March. All the following clones have arisen in cultivation.

**'Adonis'** See 'Ruby Glow'.

**'Advent'** A large shrub with ascending branches. Medium-sized, fragrant, bright yellow flowers, the petals red-tinged at the base with purplish-red calyces are abundantly produced from mid December. Selected from plants of *H. × intermedia* in the Hillier Gardens and Arboretum in 1979.

**'Allgold'** Leaves varying from elliptic to obovate-orbicular. Flowers deep yellow with reddish calyces, forming thick clusters on the ascending branches. Autumn colour yellow.

**'Arnold Promise'** A vigorous, large, wide-spreading bush. Flowers large, bright yellow, very freely borne. One of the original seedlings raised at the Arnold Arboretum in 1928 from seed of *H. mollis*.

**'Carmine Red'** (*H. japonica* 'Carmine Red') A strong-growing clone of somewhat spreading habit, raised in our nurseries. Leaves large, almost round in shape with strongly oblique base, and dark shining green above. Flowers large, pale bronze, suffused copper at tips, appearing red. Autumn colour yellow.

**'Copper Beauty'** See 'Jelena'.

**'Diane'** Claimed by its raiser to be one of the best red-flowered seedlings yet raised, and superior in this respect to 'Ruby Glow'. The large leaves colour richly in autumn. Originated in the Kalmthout Arboretum, Belgium. AM 1969. AGM 1984.

**'Feuerzauber'** See 'Magic Fire'.

**'Hiltingbury'** (*H. japonica* 'Hiltingbury') A large shrub of spreading habit, raised in our nurseries. The large leaves give brilliant autumn tints of orange, scarlet and red. Flowers medium to large, pale copper, suffused red.

**'Jelena'** ('Copper Beauty') A superb clone of vigorous spreading habit. Leaves large, broad and softly hairy. Flowers large, in dense clusters, yellow suffused a rich coppery-red, appearing orange. Lovely autumn colours of orange, red and scarlet. Raised at Kalmthout Arboretum, Belgium before 1935, and named after a great gardener, Jelena de Belder. AM 1955. AGM 1984.

**'Magic Fire'** ['Feuerzauber'] A vigorous clone with strong ascending branches, and large rounded leaves. Flowers medium to large, bright coppery-orange suffused red. C 1935.

**'Moonlight'** A large shrub with ascending branches. Flowers medium to large, petals folded and crimpled, pale sulphur-yellow with a claret-red tinge at base; scent strong and sweet. As effective a shrub as *H. mollis* 'Pallida', but differing from this clone in its narrower, more crimpled and paler petals. Autumn colour yellow.

**'Primavera'** A Dutch selection of broadly upright habit. Petals bright yellow tinged purplish-red at the base.

**'Ruby Glow'** (*H. japonica* 'Rubra Superba') ('Adonis') A strong-growing cultivar of somewhat erect habit. Flowers coppery-red. Rich autumn colour. C 1935.

**'Sunburst'** (*H. mollis* 'Sunburst') Flowers large, very pale yellow, faintly scented, autumn colour yellow. Habit upright. An improvement on 'Moonlight'.

**'Winter Beauty'** Flowers large with orange-yellow petals, deeper and reddish-tinged towards the base. Originated in Japan before 1962.

**japonica** SIEB. & ZUCC. "Japanese Witch Hazel". A variable species, commonly a large spreading shrub. Leaves generally obovate or somewhat diamond-shaped, smaller than those of *H. mollis* and becoming glabrous and shining. Flowers small to medium with much-twisted and crimpled petals, appearing from December to March. Rich autumn colour. Japan. I 1862.

**'Arborea'** A tall-growing form occasionally making a small wide-spreading tree. The almost horizontal arrangement of the branches is most characteristic. Flowers normally small but plentifully produced in dense clusters, rich deep yellow with red calyces; sweet scent but faint. Autumn colour yellow. I 1862 by Siebold. FCC 1881.

**var. flavopurpurascens** (MAK.) REHD. A large shrub developing in time a spreading habit similar to *H. japonica* 'Arborea'. Flowers small to medium, sulphur-yellow suffused red at base. Autumn colour yellow. Japan. C 1919.

**'Sulphurea'** A large, spreading shrub with ascending branches. Flowers small to medium, petals much crimpled and curved, pale sulphur-yellow; scent sweet but faint. Autumn colour yellow. AM 1958.

**HAMAMELIS japonica**—*continued*

    **'Zuccariniana'** A large shrub distinctly erect in growth, at least in the young stage, but flattening out later. Flowers small, pale sulphur-yellow, with greenish-brown calyces; scent variously described as sweet to pungent. One of the latest witch hazels to flower, usually in March. Autumn colour yellow. FCC 1891.

    **macrophylla** PURSH A rare species closely allied to *H. virginiana* of which it is sometimes regarded as a variety. A large shrub or small tree. Leaves obovate, sinuately lobed in the upper half, bright green, turning a startling butter-yellow in autumn. Flowers small to medium, with narrow, crimpled, pale yellow petals, normally opening in December or January, or earlier if the weather permits. SE United States. I 1828.

    **mollis** OLIV. "Chinese Witch Hazel". Perhaps the handsomest of all witch hazels and certainly the most popular. A large shrub with large, softly hairy, rounded leaves and clusters of large, sweetly fragrant, golden yellow, broad-petalled flowers from December to March. Autumn colour yellow. China. First introduced by C. Maries in 1879 (see 'Coombe Wood') and much later by E.H. Wilson. FCC 1918. AGM 1984.

    **'Brevipetala'** ('Aurantiaca') An upright form with rounded, softly hairy leaves which are characteristically glaucous beneath, and thick clusters of deep yellow, short-petalled flowers, appearing orange from a distance. Scent heavy and sweet. Autumn colour yellow. AM 1960.

    **'Coombe Wood'** A choice form more spreading in habit than the type and with slightly larger flowers. Scent strong and sweet. Autumn colour yellow. The original form introduced by C. Maries in 1879.

    **'Goldcrest'** A selected form with large flowers of a rich golden yellow suffused claret-red at base. The red suffusion occurs also on the backs of the rolled petals in bud creating a characteristic orange cluster effect. Scent strong and sweet. Generally later flowering than other *H. mollis* clones. Autumn colour yellow. AM 1961.

    **'Pallida'** Deservedly one of the most popular witch hazels. The large, sulphur-yellow flowers are borne in densely crowded clusters along the naked stems. Scent strong and sweet, but delicate. Autumn colour yellow. AM 1932. FCC 1958. AGM 1984.

    **vernalis** SARG. "Ozark Witch Hazel". A medium-sized to large shrub producing tall, erect stems. The flowers though very small are produced in large quantities during January and February, varying in colour from pale yellow to red, but generally of a pale orange or copper. The scent is heavy and pungent, but not unpleasant. Autumn tints usually butter-yellow. C United States. I 1908.

    **'Red Imp'** A selection with petals claret-red at base, paling to copper at tips. Calyces claret-red. Originated in our nurseries in 1966.

    **'Sandra'** Young unfolding leaves suffused plum-purple, becoming green and purple flushed on undersides. In autumn the whole bush ignites into orange, scarlet and red. Flower petals cadmium-yellow. Originated in our nurseries in 1962. AM 1976.

    **'Squib'** A selection with petals of cadmium-yellow; calyces green. Originated in our nurseries in 1966.

    **f. tomentella** REHD. Leaves glaucescent and pubescent beneath.

    **virginiana** L. The commercial source of Witch-Hazel. A large shrub, occasionally a small broad-crowned tree. Often used as an understock for the larger flowered witch hazels but produces lovely golden yellow autumn tints and myriads of small to medium-sized yellow flowers from September to November. Scent sweet but faint. E North America. I 1736.

**"HAWTHORN"** See *Crataegus monogyna* and *C. laevigata*.

**"HAZEL"** See *Corylus*.

**"HEATH"** See *Erica*.

**"HEATH, CONNEMARA"** See *Daboecia cantabrica*.

**"HEATHER"** See *Calluna vulgaris*.

**"HEATHER, BELL"** See *Erica cinerea*.

**"HEATHER, GOLDEN"** See *Cassinia fulvida*.

**"HEATHER, SILVER"** See *Cassinia vauvilliersii* var. *albida*.

**\*HEBE** COMM. ex JUSS. (*Veronica* L. in part)—**Scrophulariaceae**—100 or more species of evergreen shrubs, occasionally trees, formerly included under *Veronica*. Most are natives of New Zealand, with a few species in Australia and S South America. They are ornamental spring to autumn-flowering shrubs and are invaluable for seaside and industrial planting. Most of those which do not thrive inland may be safely planted along the south and west coasts, even in exposed places where few other shrubs will survive. They will succeed in all types of well drained soil. Flowers white unless otherwise stated.

    **albicans** (PETRIE) CKN. A very splendid, dwarf, dense, rounded, glaucous shrub. White flowers in dense spikes during summer. Perfectly hardy and very ornamental. New Zealand (S Island). I about 1880. AGM 1984.

      **'Pewter Dome'** See *H*. 'Pewter Dome'.

      **'Red Edge'** See *H*. 'Red Edge'.

    †**'Alicia Amherst'** (*H*. 'Veitchii') (*H*. 'Royal Purple') A magnificent *H. speciosa* hybrid. A small shrub with long racemes of deep purple-blue flowers in late summer. Raised by Veitch in 1911. AGM 1984.

    †**'Amy'** A small, rounded shrub of compact, upright habit, the purplish young foliage effective over a long period. Leaves to 7.5cm long, becoming dark glossy green. Racemes of violet-purple flowers are borne during summer. Raised in Dublin and named after Lady Amy Ardilaun.

    † × **andersonii** (LINDL. & PAXT.) CKN. (*H. salicifolia* × *H. speciosa*). A vigorous shrub to 1.8m. Leaves about 10cm long. Long racemes of soft lavender-blue flowers, fading to white; August to September. Raised by Isaac Anderson-Henry before 1849.

      **'Variegata'** A very attractive form with leaves broadly margined and splashed creamy-white. C 1887. AGM 1984.

    **anomala** See *H. odora*.

    **'Aoira'** See *H. recurva*.

    **armstrongii** (J.B. ARMSTR.) CKN. & ALLAN A dwarf "whipcord" species with erect densely branched stems of an olive-green colour, sometimes yellow-tinged at tips. Flowers appearing in July and August. The plant commonly grown under this name in gardens is *H. ochracea*. AM 1925 (possibly to *H. ochracea*). Mountains of S Island, where it is rare.

    **'Autumn Glory'** (*H. pimeleoides* × *H.* ×*franciscana* 'Blue Gem'). A small shrub of loose habit. Flowers intense violet, borne continuously in short dense racemes in late summer and autumn. C 1900. AGM 1984.

    **'Balfouriana'** A dwarf shrub of compact growth with small, obovate, pointed, yellowish-green leaves, purple-edged in bud, densely crowding the dark coloured stems. Flowers purplish-blue during summer. Raised at Edinburgh Botanic Garden from New Zealand seed before 1894. It is believed to be a hybrid of *H. vernicosa* with perhaps *H. pimeleoides*.

    **'Blue Clouds'** A small shrub with dark glossy green leaves purplish in winter. Long spikes of wisteria-blue flowers are borne over a long period during summer and autumn. A seedling of 'Mrs Winder'.

    **'Bowles' Hybrid'** A charming, dwarf shrub for the rock garden. The flowers, both in spring and summer, crowd the short branches in pretty, mauve-coloured racemes. Moderately hardy. Possibly *H. diosmifolia* × *H. parviflora*.

    **brachysiphon** SUMMERHAYES (*H. traversii* HORT. not (HOOK. f.) CKN. & ALLAN) A popular shrub growing 1.5m high or sometimes considerably more, and flowering profusely in June or July. S Island. I 1868.

      **'White Gem'** See *H*. 'White Gem'.

    **buchananii** (HOOK. f.) CKN. & ALLAN A dwarf shrub with tiny, rounded, leathery, closely imbricated leaves. Flowers June and July. Suitable for the rock garden. Mountains of S Island. AMT 1982.

**HEBE**—*continued*

**buxifolia** See *H. odora*.

**canterburiensis** (J.B. ARMSTR.) L.B. MOORE A dwarf shrub forming a neat, rounded hummock covered by short racemes of white flowers in June to July. Mountains of N and S Islands. I 1910.

**'Carl Teschner'** See *H.* 'Youngii'.

†**'Carnea'** An attractive shrub growing about 1.2m high, with long racemes of rose-pink flowers which fade to white, produced plentifully from May to late summer. C 1881. AM 1925.

†**'Carnea Variegata'** Similar to 'Carnea' but the leaves grey-green margined with creamy-white. C 1945.

**carnosula** (HOOK. f.) CKN. Dwarf to prostrate in habit; leaves small, glaucous, shell-like. Flowers white; July to August. Suitable for the rock garden and excellent ground cover. Possibly of hybrid origin. Found in the mountains of S Island.

**ciliolata** (HOOK. f.) CKN. & ALLAN A miniature shrublet with congested, greyish-green stems and closely imbricated leaves. Mountains of S Island.

**colensoi** (HOOK. f.) CKN. A dwarf bushy shrub with dark glossy green leaves glaucous when young. Flowers white in dense, short racemes during summer. N Island.

  **'Glauca'** A dense-habited shrub with attractive glaucous-blue foliage; height 0.6-1m. Flowers July to August.

**cookiana** See *H. stricta* 'Cookiana'.

**'County Park'** A dwarf shrub of spreading habit suitable for ground cover. Leaves grey-green margined red, flushed pink in winter. Flowers violet in short racemes during summer. A seedling of *H. pimeleoides* 'Glauco-caerulea' raised at County Park Nursery, Essex.

**cupressoides** (HOOK. f.) CKN. & ALLAN Normally a small shrub, but occasionally reaching as much as 2m, of very distinct appearance. The long, slender, green or grey branches are remarkably like those of a *Cupressus*. Flowers small, pale blue, produced quite freely in June and July. Mountains of S Island. FCC 1894.

  **'Boughton Dome'** A dwarf form of dense habit making a very compact, rounded bush. FCCT 1982. AGM 1984.

**darwiniana** See *H. glaucophylla*.

†**dieffenbachii** (BENTH.) CKN. & ALLAN A small, wide-spreading, irregular shrub with long, lance-shaped leaves distinctly tiered. Flowers lilac-purple, in long showy racemes in September. Chatham Islands.

×**divergens** (CHEESEM.) CKN. (possibly *H. elliptica* × *H. gracillima*). Forms a neat, rounded shrub to 1.2m, well characterised by its short, elliptic-oblong, flat-spreading leaves, and dense racemes of white or pale lilac flowers with violet anthers. S Island.

**'Edinensis'** (*H. muscoidea* HORT.) (possibly *H. hectoris* × *H. odora*). A charming, dwarf shrub suitable for the rock garden. Leaves tiny, bright green, imbricated. Originated in 1904 at the Edinburgh Botanic Garden.

**elliptica** (FORST. f.) PENNELL (*Veronica decussata* SOL.) (*H. magellanica* GMELIN) A rare, small to medium-sized shrub with oval or obovate, pale green leaves, downy at the margins. Flowers comparatively large, white, fragrant, borne in racemes. New Zealand (N, S and other islands), Chile, Tierra del Fuego, Falkland Isles. I 1776.

**'Emerald Green'** ('Green Globe') A dwarf bun-shaped shrub of compact habit up to 30cm tall with upright green shoots and tiny, densely arranged glossy leaves. Small white flowers are borne in summer. It was found in 1970 in the Ruahine Mts, North Island, New Zealand and is possibly a hybrid between *H. odora* and *H. subsimilis*.

**epacridea** (HOOK. f.) CKN. & ALLAN A tiny, conifer-like shrublet, densely clothed with recurved scale-like leaves. Flowers white in short terminal racemes in July. A miniature carpeting evergreen suitable for the rock garden or scree. Mountains of S Island. I 1860.

**'Ettrick Shepherd'** A small, moderately hardy hybrid with violet-coloured flowers in long racemes.

×**franciscana** (EASTW.) SOUSTER (*H. elliptica* × *H. speciosa*). (*Veronica lobelioides* ANDERSON-HENRY) A first rate and most popular hybrid originally raised before 1859.

  **'Blue Gem'** A small, compact dome-shaped shrub producing dense racemes of bright blue flowers. One of the hardiest hebes and resistant to salt-laden winds. This is perhaps

**HEBE** × **franciscana 'Blue Gem'**—*continued*

the most commonly planted hebe and is hardy anywhere along the English coast, except in the very coldest areas. Excellent for low hedges. Raised by a Salisbury nurseryman about 1868. FCC 1869. AGM 1984.

'**Variegata**' Leaves broadly edged with creamy-white. Commonly seen in London window-boxes.

**gibbsii** (T. KIRK) CKN. & ALLAN A dwarf shrub, the stout branches almost hidden by the comparatively large, glaucous, reflexed leaves which are noticeably ciliate and densely arranged in four ranks. Flowers white, produced in short, dense racemes during late summer. An easily recognised species, rare both in the wild and in cultivation. Mountains of S Island.

**glaucophylla** (CKN.) CKN. (*H. darwiniana* HORT. not (COL.) CKN.) A small, bushy shrub with slender branches bearing small, narrow, greyish-green leaves. Flowers white, borne in slender racemes towards the ends of the branches in July and August. Often found in gardens under the synonym. S Island.

'**Variegata**' (*H. darwiniana* 'Variegata') A small, neat-habited shrub with slender wiry shoots. Leaves greyish-green, margined creamy-white. A most attractive form. AMT 1982.

†'**Gloriosa**' (*H.* 'Pink Pearl') A most attractive *H. speciosa* hybrid. A small, compact shrub with bright pink flowers carried in conspicuous long racemes.

'**Great Orme**' A compact bush to 1m high. Leaves lance-shaped, 5-7.5cm long. Flowers bright pink in long tapering racemes. A seedling of 'Carnea'. Reasonably hardy. AGM 1984.

**haastii** (HOOK. f.) CKN. & ALLAN A very hardy, dwarf species, its stems densely covered with small overlapping leaves. Flowers forming a terminal head; July to August. Mountains of S Island.

'**Hagley Park**' (*H.* 'Hagleyensis') (*H. hulkeana* × *H. raoulii*). A dwarf upright shrub with glossy green, red margined and bluntly-toothed leaves. Flowers rose-purple, in large panicles in early summer. Raised in the Christchurch Botanic Gardens, New Zealand. AM 1976.

†'**Headfortii**' An attractive, purple-blue flowered *H. speciosa* hybrid, growing about 0.6-1m high.

**hectoris** (HOOK. f.) CKN. & ALLAN An interesting hardy, dwarf shrub of erect habit, having thick, rounded, stiffly cord-like branches thickly covered by yellowish-green closely adpressed leaves. Flowers white or pale pink in a crowded terminal head in July. Mountains of S Island.

'**Hielan Lassie**' A moderately hardy, compact, narrow-leaved shrub. Flowers rich blue-violet, in racemes 5-7.5cm long, from July to September.

**hulkeana** (F. MUELL.) CKN. & ALLAN Perhaps the most beautiful species of hebe in cultivation. A small shrub of loose habit occasionally reaching 1.8m against a sheltered wall. Glossy green, toothed, ovate leaves and large panicles of delicate lavender-blue flowers in May and June. It survived uninjured at Winchester the severe winter of 1962-63. Prune lightly to remove heads after flowering. S Island. I about 1860. FCC 1882.

†**insularis** (CHEESEM.) CKN. & ALLAN Dwarf shrub, resembling *H. diosmifolia*, but differing in its rather broader, somewhat oblong leaves, and less densely branched inflorescence. Flowers pale lavender-blue in June and July. Cliffs on Three Kings Islands.

'**James Stirling**' See *H. ochracea* 'James Stirling'.

× **kirkii** (J.B. ARMSTR.) CKN. & ALLAN (*Veronica salicifolia* var. *kirkii* (J.B. ARMSTR.) CHEESEM.) One of the hardiest of large-flowered hebes, similar to *H. salicifolia* but with shorter leaves. A hybrid of *H. salicifolia*, possibly with *H. rakaiensis*. S Island. I about 1870.

†'**La Seduisante**' (*H.* 'Diamant') A very attractive *H. speciosa* hybrid. A small shrub with large bright crimson racemes of flowers and dark glossy green leaves purple-tinged when young. AM 1897.

†**lavaudiana** (RAOUL) CKN. & ALLAN A small shrublet closely related to *H. hulkeana* but with smaller leaves. Inflorescence a compact corymb of spikes. Flowers lilac-pink in May. I 1880. Banks Peninsula, S Island.

**HEBE**—*continued*

    **leiophylla** CKN. & ALLAN One of the hardiest of the New Zealand species forming a shrub about 1.2m high. Leaves narrow, resembling those of *H. parviflora*. Flowers in 10cm long racemes in July and August. Possibly a naturally occurring hybrid. S Island.

    × **lewisii** (J.B. ARMSTR.) CKN. & ALLAN A naturally occurring hybrid, possibly *H. elliptica* × *H. salicifolia*. A small to medium-sized shrub of erect habit. Pale blue flowers are borne in 5-6.5cm racemes at the end of the stems; July and August. Named after a New Zealand nurseryman. S Island.

    **'Lindsayi'** (*H. amplexicaulis* × *H. pimeleoides*). A very hardy shrub to about 1m high and of equal width. Leaves rather rotund; flowers pink in short conspicuous racemes.

    **loganioides** (J.B. ARMST.) WALL (*H. selaginoides* HORT.) A dwarf shrublet only a few inches high, its slender stems clothed with tiny, spreading, scale-like leaves. Flowers white, borne in short terminal racemes during summer. A peculiar, almost conifer-like plant which may well be of hybrid origin. Found in New Zealand in 1869. S Island.

    **lycopodioides** (HOOK. f.) CKN. & ALLAN A dwarf shrub with slender, erect four-sided stems of a yellow-green colour. Leaves scale-like, with a sharp horn-like point, densely clothing the branches. Flowers white in July. S Island. FCC 1894.

    **'MacEwanii'** A dwarf shrub with glaucous foliage and blue flowers. A hybrid of *H. pimeleoides*.

    †**macrantha** (HOOK. f.) CKN. & ALLAN A very valuable dwarf shrub, noteworthy on account of its leathery, toothed leaves, and its pure white flowers which are as much as 2cm across. Mountains of S Island. AM 1952.

    **macroura** See *H. stricta* var. *macroura*.

    **'Marjorie'** A shrub of remarkable hardiness for a hebe. Forms a neat bush about 1m high, and produces racemes 5-7.5cm long of light violet and white flowers from July to September.

    **matthewsii** (CHEESEM.) CKN. An erect-growing shrub to 1.2m. Leaves thick, and leathery, oblong or oval; flowers white or pale purple in July, in racemes 5-10cm long. S Island. AM 1927.

    **'Midsummer Beauty'** (*H.* 'Miss E. Fittall' × *H. speciosa*) A handsome small shrub with conspicuous reddish undersides to the leaves. Flowers in long lavender racemes throughout summer. Moderately hardy. AM 1960. FCC 1975. AGM 1984.

    **'Mrs E. Tennant'** A comparatively hardy small shrub. Flowers light violet, in racemes 7.5-12.5cm long, from July to September.

    **'Mrs Winder'** A small to medium-sized, moderately hardy hybrid with purple foliage and bright blue flowers. AM 1978. AMT 1982. AGM 1984.

    **muscoidea** See *H.* 'Edinensis'.

    **ochracea** M.B. ASHWIN A dwarf, densely branched shrub with erect, glossy cord-like stems of a characteristic ochre or old gold colour. Flowers appearing in July and August. This plant is commonly found in gardens under the name *H. armstrongii* which differs in its greener branches and its sharply keeled and pointed leaves. Mountains of S Island. AMT 1982. AGM 1984.

        **'James Stirling'** A dwarf form with stouter branches and bright ochre-gold foliage, which, however, lacks the grace of the typical form. AMT 1982. AGM 1984.

    **odora** (HOOK. f.) CKN. (*H. anomala* (J.F. ARMSTR.) CKN.) (*H. buxifolia* (BENTH.) CKN. & ALLAN) A small to medium-sized very hardy shrub with crowded leaves and white flowers during summer. Extremely variable. Mountains of N, S and Stewart Islands.

        **'New Zealand Gold'** A form with the young growths tipped bright yellow. I from Arthur's Pass in New Zealand by Kenneth Beckett.

    †**parviflora** (VAHL) CKN. & ALLAN A variable species in the wild mainly represented in cultivation by the following.

        **var. angustifolia** (HOOK. f.) L.B. MOORE A variety with linear, grass-like leaves and purple-brown stems. S Island. I about 1868.

        **var. arborea** (BUCHAN.) L.B. MOORE (*Veronica arborea* BUCHAN.) An erect-branched shrub to about 1.5m, but considerably taller and tree-like in its native habitat. Leaves long and narrow; flowers white, tinged lilac-pink in July and August. N Island. I 1822.

    **'Pewter Dome'** (*H. albicans* 'Pewter Dome') A low-growing shrub making a dense, dome-shaped bush with grey-green leaves and short spikes of white flowers in early summer. A hybrid of *H. albicans*. AGM 1984.

**HEBE**—*continued*

**pimeleoides** (HOOK. f.) CKN. & ALLAN A distinct but variable species making a dwarf or almost prostrate shrub with purplish shoots and glaucous rather red-edged leaves. Flowers blue to purple, borne in racemes during summer. Mountains of S Island.

**'Glauco-caerulea'** A form with upright shoots, small, glaucous-blue leaves and violet-blue flowers; June and July.

**var. minor** (HOOK. f.) CKN. & ALLAN A minute shrub forming loose mounds 5-7.5cm high, the slender stems clothed with narrow glaucous leaves 5mm long. A choice little plant for the scree or trough.

**'Quicksilver'** A dwarf, spreading shrub with tiny, silvery-blue leaves contrasting with the very dark shoots. Flowers pale lilac.

**pinguifolia** (HOOK. f.) CKN. & ALLAN A dwarf shrub with purplish nodes and small, glaucous, often red-margined leaves. Flowers white, in dense spikes during summer. Mountains of S Island. I about 1864.

**'Pagei'** (*Veronica pageana* HORT.) Wide mats of small, glaucous-grey leaves which are attractive throughout the year. The small white flowers are borne in quantity in May. Excellent ground cover or rock garden plant. AM 1958. AMT 1982. AGM 1984.

**'Sutherlandii'** Differs from 'Pagei' in its much denser, more upright habit making a compact, rounded, dwarf bush with grey-green foliage.

**propinqua** (CHEESEM.) CKN. & ALLAN A dwarf many-branched shrublet forming a low mound of rounded, green or yellowish-green, thread-like stems. Mountains of S Island. Sometimes found in gardens, quite wrongly, under the names *H. armstrongii* 'Compacta' and *H. salicornioides* 'Aurea'.

†**'Purple Queen'** An outstanding *H. speciosa* hybrid. A small shrub with large racemes of purple flowers. AM 1893.

†**'Purple Tips'** (*H. speciosa* 'Tricolor') A small shrub, a sport of 'La Seduisante'. Leaves rose-purple on the back when young opening grey-green with deep green veins, broadly margined creamy-white and becoming rose-tinted during winter. Flowers magenta-purple fading to white, in long racemes. Rather tender. C 1926.

**rakaiensis** (J.B. ARMSTR.) CKN. (*H. subalpina* HORT. not CKN. & ALLAN) A dwarf, very hardy shrub forming dense, compact mounds of crowded stems bearing small, neat, pale green leaves. Flowers white, borne in short, crowded racemes in June and July. A splendid ground cover in full sun. Sometimes found in gardens wrongly as *H. subalpina*. S Island. AMT 1982. AGM 1984.

**raoulii** (HOOK. f.) CKN. & ALLAN A dwarf shrub with spathulate leaves which are toothed and often reddish at the margins. Flowers lavender or almost white, borne in crowded terminal spikes during summer. S Island.

**recurva** SIMP. & THOMS. A small, slender-branched shrub of open, rounded habit up to 1m. Leaves narrow, lanceolate, glaucous above. Flowers white, in slender racemes. The clone in general cultivation is known as 'Aoira'. S Island. I 1923. AM 1972.

**'Boughton Silver'** A compact form with very silvery-blue leaves.

**'Red Edge'** (*H. albicans* 'Red Edge') A dwarf shrub with blue-grey leaves densely arranged, narrowly margined with red particularly in winter. Flowers in summer, lilac becoming white. Possible *H. albicans* × *H. pimeleoides*.

**salicifolia** (FORST. f.) PENNELL A medium-sized shrub for maritime districts. Leaves lanceolate, bright green; flowers white, or lilac-tinged in long racemes; June to August. Withstands most winters with only superficial injury. A parent of many hybrids. S and Stewart Islands, S Chile. AMT 1982.

**'Spender's Seedling'** See *H.* 'Spender 's Seedling'.

**'Variegata'** Leaves with creamy-white margins.

†**'Simon Delaux'** Small rounded shrub with rich crimson flowers in large racemes. One of the best of the *H. speciosa* hybrids. AGM 1984.

†**speciosa** (A. CUNN.) CKN. & ALLAN A small shrub of dense rounded habit with handsome leathery leaves and dark, reddish-purple flowers. Represented in cultivation by innumerable colourful hybrids and cultivars, many of which are only suitable for seaside gardens. N and S Islands.

**'Tricolor'** See *H.* 'Purple Tips'.

# TREES AND SHRUBS

**HEBE**—*continued*

**'Spender's Seedling'** (*H. salicifolia* 'Spender's Seedling') A small, very hardy, free-flowering shrub. Its fragrant white flowers are produced over a long period. AM 1954. AMT 1982.

†**stricta** (BENTH.) L.B. MOORE A variable, often large shrub related to *H. salicifolia*. The typical form is confined to N Island.

**var. macroura** (BENTH.) L.B . MOORE. Small shrub to 1.2m with long, dense racemes of white flowers; leaves long, elliptic-lanceolate. N Island.

**'Cookiana'** (*H. cookiana* (COL.) CKN. & ALLAN Small, dense floriferous shrub with elliptic fleshy leaves and long dense racemes of white, mauve-tinged, flowers from August to October.

**subalpina** (CKN.) CKN. & ALLAN A small, very hardy shrub of dense, rounded habit. Similar to *H. rakaiensis* and confused with it in cultivation. It differs in its longer leaves to 3cm or more (2cm in *H. rakaiensis*) and its glabrous capsules. S Island. See also under *H. rakaiensis*.

**subsimilis** (COL.) M.B. ASHWIN A dwarf "whipcord" shrub of upright habit reaching about 25cm. Leaves tiny, green. Flowers white in small spikes during summer. N and S Islands.

**var. astonii** (PETRIE) M.B. ASHWIN Miniature, much branched shrublet forming a compact hummock of thin, rounded, green stems. N Island.

**tetrasticha** (HOOK. f.) CKN. & ALLAN A miniature shrublet forming tiny patches of green, four-sided stems, thickly clothed with the closely adpressed scale-like leaves. Mountains of S Island.

**traversii** HORT. See *H. brachysiphon*.

**venustula** (COL.) L.B. MOORE (*H. laevis* (BENTH.) CKN. & ALLAN) Dwarf or small shrub forming a rounded hummock. The small 1.25cm long, yellowish-green leaves have a thin yellowish margin. Flowers white in short racemes crowding the branches in summer. Mountains of N and S Islands.

**vernicosa** (HOOK. f.) CKN. & ALLAN A very hardy dwarf shrub of spreading habit with small, bright glossy green leaves. Flowers white or pale lilac at first, in slender racemes up to 5cm long in late spring. S Island.

**'Waikiki'** A moderately hardy shrub of medium size with bluish flowers. The young growths are bronze-tinted. AMT 1982.

**'White Gem'** (*H. brachysiphon* 'White Gem') A dwarf, compact, hardy shrub rarely over 0.5m producing a profusion of white flowers in June. It differs from *H. brachysiphon* in its dwarfer habit, smaller, paler leaves and earlier flowering with shorter racemes. Possibly *H. brachysiphon* × *H. pinguifolia*. C 1964.

**'Wingletye'** A prostrate shrub of compact habit suitable for the rock garden with small, glaucous leaves. Ascending shoots bear racemes of deep mauve flowers in early summer. A seedling of *H. pimeleoides* 'Glauco-caerulea' raised at County Park Nursery.

**'Youngii'** (*H.* 'Carl Teschner') (*H. elliptica* × *H. pimeleoides*). A hardy, dwarf, summer-flowering shrub of compact habit with small leaves and abundantly produced, short racemes of violet flowers with a white throat; June to July. A splendid free-growing ground cover. Garden origin. Raised in New Zealand and long known under this name, it was re-christened 'Carl Teschner' in England after the New Zealand nurseryman who sent it, un-named, to this country. AM 1964. AGM 1984.

**HEDYSARUM** L.—**Leguminosae**—A large genus of about 100 species of perennials and shrubs found throughout N temperate regions. The following is easily cultivated given full sun.

**multijugum** MAXIM. A small Mongolian shrub of lax habit with sea-green pinnate leaves and producing long racemes of rose-purple, pea-flowers throughout summer. Plants in cultivation belong to var. *apiculatum* SPRAGUE. I 1883. AM 1898.

**HEIMIA** LINK—**Lythraceae**—A small genus of 3 species of shrubs related to the familiar "Loosestrife"and natives of N and S America.

**salicifolia** (H.B.K.) LINK An interesting shrub attaining 1.2m. Leaves narrow; flowers yellow, 1.25cm across, produced in the leaf axils from July to September. C and S America. I 1821.

**\*HELIANTHEMUM** MILLER—**Cistaceae**—The "Rock Roses" or "Sun Roses" consist of more than 100 species of mainly dwarf evergreen shrubs natives of Europe, N Africa, W and C Asia and N and S America. The following are excellent for dry, sunny situations, producing multitudes of flowers in brilliant colours throughout summer.

204

**HELIANTHEMUM**—*continued*

**algarvense** See *Halimium ocymoides.*

**alpestre** See *H. oelandicum* subsp. *alpestre.*

**apenninum** (L.) MILLER "White Rockrose". A dwarf shrublet forming mats of slender, spreading shoots crowded with narrow, grey leaves. Flowers white with a yellow eye, borne in profusion from May to July. W and S Europe. A rare native species found only in two localities, one in Devon another in Somerset. C 1768.

    **var. roseum** (JACQ.) SCHNEIDER (*H. rhodanthum* DUN.) An attractive dwarf form with hoary foliage and silvery-rose flowers.

**canadense** (L.) MICHX. (*Crocanthemum canadense* (L.) BRITT. & A. BR.) A rare dwarf shrublet with downy stems and small, alternate leaves, greyish-tomentose beneath. Flowers bright yellow, usually solitary in the leaf axils during early summer. We are indebted to Dr Henry Skinner of the National Arboretum, Washington, for locating this plant in the wild and sending us seeds. E United States. C 1825.

**chamaecistus** See *H. nummularium.*

**lunulatum** (ALL.) DC. A dainty, cushion-like alpine with yellow flowers having a small orange spot at the base of each petal; June to July. NW Italy.

**nummularium** (L.) MILLER (*H. chamaecistus* MILLER) (*H. vulgare* GAERTN.) "Common Sun Rose". A dwarf, spreading shrublet with ascending or prostrate stems. Leaves green above, grey or white beneath in the typical form. Most forms usually listed here are hybrids. Splendid ground cover plants for full sun and poor dry soil. Europe (incl British Isles).

    **'Amy Baring'** Deep buttercup-yellow; dwarf, compact habit; foliage green. Found in the French Pyrenees by Mrs Amy Doncaster and named after her by the nurseryman A.K. Bulley.

**oelandicum** (L.) DC. A variable and widely distributed species mainly represented in gardens by the following.

    **subsp. alpestre** (JACQ.) BREITST. (*H. alpestre* (JACQ.) DC.) A very dwarf shrub with grey-green foliage and bright yellow flowers in June and July. Mts. of S and C Europe. I 1818. AMT 1925.

## HYBRIDS

The many colourful plants generally seen in cultivation are mainly hybrids of a group of 3 species—*H. apenninum, H. nummularium* and *H. croceum.* Between them they have produced a great variety of silver and green leaved plants with flowers ranging in colour from orange, yellow or white, to rose, red and scarlet, both single and double.

**'Afflick'** Bright deep orange-bronze, with bronze-copper centre; foliage green.

**'Ben Dearg'** Deep copper-orange, with darker centre; foliage green.

**'Ben Fhada'** Golden yellow, with orange centre; foliage grey-green.

**'Ben Hope'** Carmine, with deep orange centre; foliage light grey-green.

**'Ben Ledi'** Bright, deep tyrian-rose; foliage dark green.

**'Ben More'** Bright, rich orange, with darker centre; foliage dark green.

**'Ben Nevis'** Deep buttercup-yellow, with conspicuous bronze-crimson central zone; foliage green. AM 1924. AMT 1924.

**'Cerise Queen'** Scarlet, double. Foliage green.

**'Coppernob'** Deep glowing copper, with bronze-crimson centre, foliage grey-green.

**'Fire Dragon'** Bright orange-scarlet. Foliage grey-green. AGM 1984.

**'Golden Queen'** Bright golden yellow; foliage green.

**'Henfield Brilliant'** Bright orange; foliage grey-green.

**'Jock Scott'** Bright, deep rose-cerise, with darker centre; foliage green.

**'Jubilee'** Drooping, primrose-yellow, double; foliage green. AMT 1970. AGM 1984.

**'Mrs Croft'** Pink, suffused orange; foliage silver-grey.

**'Mrs C.W. Earle'** Scarlet, with yellow basal flush, double; foliage dark green. AGM 1984.

**'Praecox'** Lemon-yellow. Dense habit with grey foliage.

**'Raspberry Ripple'** Deep reddish-pink with white-tipped petals; foliage dark green.

**'Red Dragon'** Scarlet, with yellow centre; foliage green.

**'Red Orient'** See 'Supreme'.

**'Rhodanthe Carneum'** Pale rhodamine-pink, with orange centre; foliage silver-grey.

**HELIANTHEMUM**—*continued*

**'Rose of Leeswood'** Rose-pink, double; foliage green.

**'Snowball'** Creamy-white, with pale yellow centre; double; foliage green.

**'Sudbury Gem'** Deep pink with a flame centre. Grey-green foliage.

**'Supreme'** ('Red Orient') Crimson; foliage grey-green.

**'The Bride'** Creamy-white, with bright yellow centre; foliage silver-grey. AM 1924. AMT 1924. AGM 1984.

**'Watergate Rose'** Rose-crimson, with orange-tinged centre; foliage grey-green. AMT 1932.

**'Wisley Pink'** Soft pink, grey foliage. AGM 1984.

**'Wisley Primrose'** Primrose-yellow, with deeper yellow centre; foliage light grey-green. AMT 1970. AGM 1984.

**'Wisley White'** Pure white, single with a centre of golden anthers. Narrow grey leaves.

**\*HELICHRYSUM** MILLER—**Compositae**—A large genus of some 500 species of herbs and shrubs widely distributed in the Old World, particularly in S Africa and Australia. The shrubby members provide some interesting, mainly low-growing, often aromatic plants with attractive foliage. Most are reasonably hardy given full sun and well drained poor soil. Many of the shrubby species native to New Zealand and Australia and often listed here are treated under *Ozothamnus*.

**angustifolium** See *H. italicum*.

**antennarium** See *Ozothamnus antennaria*.

**diosmifolium** See *Ozothamnus thyrsoideus*.

**ericeteum** See under *Ozothamnus pupurascens*.

**italicum** (ROTH.) G. DON (*H. angustifolium* (LAM.) DC.) (*H. rupestre* HORT.) A variable species. A superb, dwarf shrub with long, narrow grey leaves and terminal, long-stalked clusters of bright yellow flowerheads during summer. One of the best of all silvery-grey shrubs. Mediterranean region. Plants received under the name *H. rupestre* belong here.

    **subsp. serotinum** (BOISS.) P. FOURN. (*H. serotinum* BOISS.) "Curry Plant". Dense, dwarf shrub with narrow, sage-green leaves with a strong curry-like smell. Heads of yellow flowers in midsummer. S Europe. AGM 1984.

**ledifolium** See *Ozothamnus ledifolius*.

**microphyllum** HORT. See *Plecostachys serpyllifolia*.

**†petiolare** HILLIARD & B.L. BURTT (*H. petiolatum* HORT. not (L.) DC.) A dwarf, often trailing shrublet with white woolly stems and long-stalked, ovate, grey, woolly leaves. Flowers yellow in late summer. Normally a tender species but may overwinter in the milder areas if given good drainage and overhead protection. S Africa. AM 1987.

**petiolatum** See *H. petiolare*.

**†plicatum** (FISCH. & MEY.) DC. An attractive, dwarf, silvery-white shrub, with long, narrow, downy leaves and terminal clusters of bright yellow flowers in July. SE Europe. I 1877.

**rosmarinifolium** See *Ozothamnus rosmarinifolius*.

**scutellifolium** See *Ozothamnus scutellifolius*.

**selago** See *Ozothamnus selago*.

**serotinum** See *H. italicum* subsp. *serotinum*.

**splendidum** (THUNB.) LESS. (*H. triliniatum* HORT. not DC.) (*H. aveolatum* HORT. not DC.) A small, globular shrub to about 1m. Leaves silvery-grey, with 3 longitudinal ridges. The everlasting flowers remain a good yellow into the New Year. One of the very few South African plants hardy in the Home Counties. AGM 1984.

**†stoechas** (L.) MOENCH "Goldilocks". A dwarf shrub. Leaves silvery-white; flowers bright yellow, in corymbs during summer. S Europe. C 1629.

**thyrsoideum** See *Ozothamnus thyrsoideus*.

**triliniatum** HORT. See *H. splendidum*.

**HELWINGIA** WILLD.—**Cornaceae**—A small genus of 3 species, interesting on account of the peculiar position of the insignificant flowers which, due to the fusion of the pedicel with the petiole and leaf midrib, appear on the upper surface of the leaf. Native to E Asia from the Himalaya to Japan.

**HELWINGIA**—*continued*

**japonica** (THUNB.) F.G. DIETR. (*H. rusciflora* WILLD.) A small shrub, bearing its pale green flowers, and later its black berries, upon the upper surface of the leaves. Japan. I 1830.

**HEMIPTELEA** PLANCH.—**Ulmaceae**—A monotypic genus closely related to *Zelkova* and sometimes included in it but differing in its spiny branches and winged fruits.

**davidii** (HANCE) PLANCH. (*Zelkova davidii* (HANCE) HEMSL.) A small, dense, shrubby tree with spine-tipped branchlets and oval, toothed leaves. China, Korea. I 1908.

**HEPTACODIUM** REHD.—**Caprifoliaceae**—A genus of 2 species of deciduous Chinese shrubs related to *Abelia*.

**jasminoides** AIRY SHAW "Seven Son Flower of Zhejiang". A vigorous and very hardy large deciduous shrub of upright habit with peeling bark. Bold, conspicuously three-veined leaves are retained until late autumn or early winter. Small, fragrant, white flowers are borne in whorls at the ends of the shoots in late summer and autumn. Given good weather the calyx enlarges and turns bright red after flowering. E China (Zhejiang). I to the Hillier Gardens and Arboretum in 1981.

**"HERCULES' CLUB"** See *Oplopanax horridus*.

†\***HESPERALOE** ENGELM.—**Agavaceae**—A genus of 3 species of stemless, evergreen herbs related to *Yucca*, natives of the SW United States.

**parviflora** (TORR.) COULT. An evergreen, spreading shrub having thick, leathery, linear leaves 2.5cm wide and up to 1.2m long. bright green with white threads hanging from the margins. The aloe-like, tomato-red flowers, golden within, are produced in slender panicles up to 1.2m long in July. Texas. I 1822.

**var. engelmannii** (KRAUSK.) TREL. Flowers more bell-shaped.

**HESPEROYUCCA whipplei** See *Yucca whipplei*.

†\***HETEROMELES** M. ROEM.—**Rosaceae**—A monotypic genus formerly included in *Photinia*.

**arbutifolia** (LINDL.) M. ROEM. (*Photinia arbutifolia* LINDL.) "Christmas Berry" "Tollon" "Toyon". A large shrub in favoured areas. Leaves thick and leathery, lanceolate to obovate, sharply-toothed, 5-10cm long. Flowers white, produced in flattened terminal panicles in late summer. Fruits bright red, like haws. California. I 1796.

**HIBISCUS** L.—**Malvaceae**—A large genus of some 200 species of herbs, shrubs and trees widely distributed in tropical and subtropical regions. Of this extensive genus, few are hardy in our climate, but of these the following provide us with some of the most effective late summer and early autumn flowering shrubs. They need full sun.

**hamabo** See under *H. syriacus* 'Hamabo'.

**sinosyriacus** L.H. BAILEY A very handsome and hardy, vigorous species making a medium-sized shrub more spreading in habit than *H. syriacus*. The leaves are broader than those of *H. syriacus* and are sage-green in colour. The flowers, too, are slightly larger, and the petals thicker, appearing in late summer and autumn. It enjoys similar conditions to *H. syriacus* and is equally hardy. C China. Introduced by us in 1936 when we received seed from the Lushan Botanic Garden from which we raised the following clones:

**'Autumn Surprise'** Petals white with attractively feathered cerise base.

**'Lilac Queen'** Petals lilac with garnet-red base.

**'Ruby Glow'** Petals white with a cerise base.

**syriacus** L. Given a position in full sun and a favourable season, no late flowering shrub is more beautiful than this shrubby "Mallow". The large, trumpet-shaped flowers open in succession between July and October according to the season. It is generally seen as a medium to large-sized shrub of upright habit, occasionally a small tree. E Asia. It is not known when this species was introduced into cultivation but it existed in England in the late 16th century.

**HIBISCUS syriacus**—*continued*

**'Ardens'** Pale rosy-purple with maroon blotch at base; double, large. Erect, compact habit, spreading later. 'Caeruleus Plenus' is a similar clone. C 1873.

**'Blue Bird'** ['Oiseau Bleu'] Violet-blue with a darker eye; single. The best single blue, an improvement on 'Coelestis'. AM 1965. AGM 1984.

**'Coelestis'** Light violet-blue with reddish base; single. AM 1897.

**'Diana'** Pure white, single, large with crimped petals, occasionally with a few small petaloids in the centre. The best white, raised at the U.S. National Arboretum, Washington in 1963. AGM 1984.

**'Dorothy Crane'** Flowers large, white, with a feathered red centre. Raised by Notcutts before 1935.

**'Duc de Brabant'** Deep rose-purple; double. C 1872.

**'Elegantissimus'** See 'Lady Stanley'.

**'Hamabo'** Pale blush with crimson eye; single, large. One of the best of the cultivars. Not to be confused with *H. hamabo* SIEB. & ZUCC., a tender species with yellow, red-centred flowers.

**'Helene'** Flowers large, 9cm across, often semi-double, white, flushed pink when opening, the outer petals streaked with deep pink with attractively feathered deep maroon blotches at the base and white petaloid stamens in the centre. A sister seedling of 'Diana'.

**'Hinomaru'** Flowers pink with deep cerise anemone centre.

**'Jeanne d'Arc'** White; semi-double. C 1894.

**'Lady Stanley'** ('Elegantissimus') White, shaded blush-pink with maroon base; almost double. C 1875.

**'Meehanii'** Lilac-mauve with maroon eye; single. Leaves with an irregular creamy-white margin.

**'Monstrosus'** White with maroon centre; single. C 1873.

**'Monstrosus Plenus'** Similar in colour to 'Monstrosus' but double.

**'Pink Giant'** Clear pink with a deep red eye. Raised by crossing 'Red Heart' with 'Woodbridge'. It differs from the latter in the larger flowers, the basal blotches with a dark band near the apex and distinctly feathered.

**'Puniceus Plenus'** See under 'Violet Clair Double'.

**'Red Heart'** Large, white with a conspicuous red eye. AGM 1984.

**'Roseus Plenus'** See under 'Violet Clair Double'.

**'Russian Violet'** Large, lilac-pink with a deep red centre. Raised by crossing 'Blue Bird' with 'Red Heart'.

**'Snowdrift'** White; single. Large and early flowering. AM 1911. 'Totus Albus' is scarcely different.

**'Totus Albus'** See under 'Snowdrift'.

**'Violet Clair Double'** ('Violaceus Plenus') Wine-purple, deep reddish-purple at base within; double. 'Puniceus Plenus' and 'Roseus Plenus' are scarcely different.

**'William R. Smith'** Pure white; single, large. C 1916.

**'Woodbridge'** Rich rose-pink with carmine centre; single, large. Basal blotches concolorous, not feathered. An improvement on 'Rubis'. AM 1937. AGM 1984.

**"HICKORY"** See *Carya*.

**HIPPOPHAE** L.—**Elaeagnaceae**—A genus of 3 species of hardy shrubs or small trees with slender, willow-like, silvery or sage-green leaves. Natives of Eurasia. Attractive orange berries are produced on female plants. Excellent wind resisters for maritime exposure.

**rhamnoides** L. "Sea Buckthorn". A tall shrub, sometimes a small tree, succeeding in almost any soil. Attractive in summer with its narrow, silvery leaves, and in winter with its orange-yellow berries which contain an intensely acrid yellow juice and which are normally avoided by birds, although pheasants are said to eat them. Plant in groups to contain both sexes. Europe (incl British Isles), temperate Asia. AM 1944. AGM 1984.

**salicifolia** D. DON A rare species making a small to medium-sized tree. Differing from *H. rhamnoides* in its taller habit, pendulous branches which are less spiny and its sage-green leaves. Himalaya. I 1822.

# TREES AND SHRUBS

**HOHERIA** A. CUNN.—**Malvaceae**—A genus of beautiful, floriferous, mid to late summer-flowering shrubs or small trees belonging to the mallow family. 5 species native to New Zealand. All have white flowers. The evergreen species need a specially selected site, or wall protection except in mild districts. The leaves of juvenile plants are often deeply toothed and lobed and are smaller than those of adult plants.

**\*angustifolia** RAOUL An elegant small tree of columnar habit with roundish to narrowly lanceolate leaves up to 5cm long. Juvenile plants are dense and bushy with slender interlacing branches and minute, obovate, shallowly-toothed leaves. Masses of small white flowers 1.25cm across cover the plant in July. AM 1967.

**glabrata** SPRAGUE & SUMMERH. "Mountain Ribbonwood". A magnificent large shrub or small tree, possibly a little hardier than *H. lyallii*. In June and July its flexible branches are bent with the weight of masses of fragrant, almost translucent, white flowers. C 1871. AM 1911. FCC 1946. AGM 1984.

**'Glory of Amlwch'** (*H. glabrata* × *H. sexstylosa*). A large shrub or small tree, retaining its foliage during mild winters. Flowers of pure white, 3.75cm across, densely crowded on the stems. Originated in the garden of Dr Jones, Amlwch, Anglesey. AM 1960.

**lyallii** HOOK. f. "Mountain Ribbonwood". A beautiful but variable large shrub or small tree. The more or less glabrous juvenile leaves change to grey tomentose adult foliage. Clusters of cherry-like, white flowers crowd the branches in July, normally later than *H. glabrata*. AM 1955. FCC 1964. AGM 1984.

**†\*populnea** A. CUNN. "Lacebark". Beautiful large shrub or small tree with broadly ovate leaves; blooming in late summer or autumn. Flowers about 2cm across, in dense clusters. AM 1912.

**'Alba Variegata'** Leaves with a broad creamy-white margin, often pink-tinged when young. A sport of 'Variegata' raised in New Zealand. AM 1976.

**'Foliis Purpureis'** Leaves plum-purple on the lower surface. AM 1977.

**var. lanceolata** See *H. sexstylosa*.

**'Osbornei'** Flowers with blue stamens. Leaves purple-tinged beneath. Named after the Osborne family on whose property on Great Barrier Island it was found in about 1910.

**'Variegata'** Leaves yellow-green, edged deep green. C 1926.

**†\*sexstylosa** COL. (*H. populnea* var. *lanceolata* HOOK. f.) "Lacebark". This splendid floriferous, tall vigorous shrub or small tree differs from *H. populnea* in its greater hardiness, more upright growth and narrower adult leaves. Those of young trees are extremely variable. FCC 1924 (under the synonym). AM 1964. AGM 1984.

**'Crataegifolia'** The juvenile form with small, coarsely-toothed leaves, maintained as a bush by vegetative propagation.

**"HOLLY"** See *Ilex*.

**HOLODISCUS** (K. KOCH) MAXIM.—**Rosaceae**—A small genus of about 8 species of hardy spiraea-like shrubs native from W North America to Colombia.

**discolor** (PURSH) MAXIM. (*Spiraea discolor* PURSH) "Ocean Spray". A handsome and elegant shrub to 3.5m high, blooming in July when its long, drooping, feathery panicles of creamy-white flowers are most conspicuous. Leaves greyish-white tomentose beneath. W North America. Introduced by David Douglas in 1927. AM 1978.

**"HONEY LOCUST"** See *Gleditsia triacanthos*.

**"HONEYSUCKLE"** See *Lonicera*.

**"HOP HORNBEAM"** See *Ostrya carpinifolia*.

**"HOP TREE"** See *Ptelea trifoliata*.

**"HORNBEAM"** See *Carpinus*.

**"HORSE CHESTNUT"** See *Aesculus hippocastanum*.

**HOVENIA** THUNB.—**Rhamnaceae**—A small genus of 2 species of trees and shrubs native of E Asia.

    **dulcis** THUNB. "Japanese Raisin Tree". A large shrub or small tree, native of China and the Himalaya, grown for its handsome, polished foliage. The fleshy, reddish branches of the inflorescences are edible. China. Cultivated in Japan and India. I 1912.

**HYDRANGEA** L.—**Hydrangeaceae**—About 23 species of shrubs, small trees and climbers natives of E Asia and N and S America. The cultivated members of this genus are easily grown, but all require generous treatment and resent dryness at the roots. For the larger leaved species some shade is essential. Summer and autumn is the flowering period unless otherwise stated.

    The majority of species and their forms produce flowers in a flattened or dome-shaped terminal head. These heads are composed of flowers of two kinds. The majority are fertile and though coloured are rather small and often insignificant. The second type are sterile but possess rather large, conspicuous, coloured sepals. These sterile flowers or ray-florets occur on the outside of the head and in some instances completely surround the fertile flowers, hence the popular name "Lacecap". Some hydrangeas, in particular the Hortensia group of *H. macrophylla*, have flowerheads which are composed entirely of ray-florets.

    **acuminata** See under *H. serrata* 'Bluebird'.

    **arborescens** L. A small shrub of loose bushy growth, with ovate, slender pointed, serrated leaves. Flowers in corymbs up to 15cm across, bearing several long-stalked, creamy-white marginal ray-florets. They are borne in succession from July to September. Leaves usually glabrous. E United States. I 1736.

    **'Annabelle'** A spectacular form with huge, rounded heads of white, sterile flowers up to 30cm across. AM 1978.

    **subsp. discolor** (SER.) MCCLINTOCK (*H. cinerea* SMALL) Leaves grey tomentose beneath; flowers with a few white ray-florets. I 1908.

    **'Grandiflora'** The commonly cultivated form with large globular heads of creamy-white sterile florets. I 1907. AM 1907. AGM 1984.

    **subsp. radiata** (WALT.) MCCLINTOCK (*H. radiata* WALT.) (*H. nivea* MICHX.) An erect shrub up to 1.8m, remarkable for the snow-white under-surfaces of the leaves. Flowers creamy-white, sweetly scented, produced in broad corymbs in July. Carolina (United States). I 1786.

    **'Sterilis'** A form of subsp. *discolor* with globular heads of sterile creamy-white florets. Originated before 1908. AGM 1984.

    **aspera** D. DON. A magnificent, but variable, large-leaved species of medium size covered in June and July with large heads of pale porcelain-blue flowers, with a ring of lilac-pink or white ray-florets. Himalaya, W and C China, Taiwan.

    **'Macrophylla'** A form with very large leaves and flowerheads. AGM 1984.

    **subsp. sargentiana** (REHD.) MCCLINTOCK (*H. sargentiana* REHD.) A noble shrub of medium size. The shoots are thickly clothed with a curious moss-like covering of hairs and bristles. Leaves very large and velvety. The large inflorescences in July and August are bluish, with white ray-florets. Suitable for a sheltered shrub border or woodland. Winter hardy, but requires shade and wind protection. China. I 1908 by Ernest Wilson. AM 1912. AGM 1984.

    **subsp. strigosa** (REHD.) MCCLINTOCK (*H. strigosa* REHD.) A striking, rare, slow-growing, medium-sized shrub. The lilac and white flowers appear in the autumn after all the other hydrangeas are over. Leaves lance-shaped, conspicuously adpressed hairy, as are the shoots. Subject to damage by late spring frosts. C China. I 1907 by Ernest Wilson.

    **Villosa group** (*H. villosa* REHD.) Close to the typical form but differing in its less coarse habit and smaller leaves and flowerheads. It is one of the loveliest of late summer flowering hydrangeas. A medium-sized shrub of spreading habit, with stems, leaf and flower stalks densely villous. The large inflorescences are lilac-blue with prettily-toothed marginal sepals. Requires half-shade. W China. I 1908. AM 1950. AGM 1984.

    **'Ayesha'** ('Silver Slipper') A most distinct and unusual hydrangea of puzzling origin. It is usually placed in the Hortensia group of *H. macrophylla* but its appearance is very

**HYDRANGEA 'Ayesha'**—*continued*

different from the usual "mop-headed" hydrangea. The leaves are bold and glossy green above. The rather flattened dense heads are composed of thick-petalled, cup-shaped florets resembling those of a large lilac. They possess a faint but distinct fragrance and in colour are greyish-lilac or pink. AM 1974. AGM 1984.

**bretschneideri** See *H. heteromalla* 'Bretschneideri'.

**chinensis** MAXIM. A rare, small shrub with oval or lanceolate-oblong, denticulate leaves. Flowers produced in corymbs, composed of bluish fertile flowers and a few slender-stalked white ray-florets. Requires a sheltered position. SE China, Taiwan. C 1934.

**cinerea** See *H. arborescens* subsp. *discolor*.

   **'Sterilis'** See *H. arborescens* 'Sterilis'.

**dumicola** See *H. heteromalla*.

**heteromalla** D. DON (*H. dumicola* W.W. SM.) (*H. xanthoneura* DIELS) A very variable, medium-sized to large shrub or small tree. The leaves are dark green above and whitish beneath. Flowers in broad corymbs, white, with conspicuous marginal ray-florets. Himalaya, N and W China. I 1821. AM 1978.

   **'Bretschneideri'** (*H. bretschneideri* DIPP.) A medium-sized July blooming shrub, with broad, flattened white lacecaps. Bark chestnut brown, exfoliating. Hardy in full exposure. I about 1882 from China. AGM 1984.

   **'Snowcap'** A superb shrub of stately habit with large heart-shaped leaves and white flowers in large flattened corymbs 20-25cm across. A hardy shrub, tolerant of wind, sun and drought. For many years this plant was grown by us under the name *H. robusta*, which species is now regarded as a subsp. of *H. aspera*. Collected in the Himalaya, our plant is sufficiently distinct and ornamental to deserve the above clonal name.

**hirta** (THUNB.) SIEB. A small, much-branched shrub with dark-coloured stems and ovate, deeply-toothed leaves. Dense compact corymbs of blue-purple fertile flowers. Ray-florets absent. Japan.

**involucrata** SIEB. A pretty dwarf species. Flowers blue or rosy-lilac, surrounded by white or variously tinted ray-florets. Japan, Taiwan. C 1864.

   **'Hortensis'** A remarkable and attractive form with double, creamy-white, florets which become rose-tinted in the open. AM 1956.

**longipes** FRANCH. A medium-sized, spreading shrub of loose habit, remarkable in the genus for the length of the leaf-stalks. Flowers white, the outer ray-florets as much as 4cm across. W China. I 1901.

**macrophylla** (THUNB.) SER. This name covers a large and varied group of hydrangeas, many of which are possibly of hybrid origin, and may be divided into two groups, namely the **Hortensias** and the **Lacecaps** (see below).

   **var. acuminata** See under *H. serrata* 'Bluebird'.

   **var. normalis** WILS. (*H. maritima* HOWARTH-BOOTH) A small to medium-sized shrub producing flat corymbs of fertile flowers with a few pink, marginal ray-florets. The wild form, a native of the coastal regions of C Japan, first introduced by E.H. Wilson in 1917. See also 'Seafoam' under Lacecaps below.

   **subsp. serrata** See *H. serrata*.

## HORTENSIAS

The familiar mop-headed hydrangeas. Their average height in most gardens ranges from 1.2-1.8m (4-6ft), but in sheltered gardens and woodlands in mild localities some cultivars will reach as much as 3.5m (10ft). They are admirable for seaside planting and many are seen at their best in coastal gardens.

The florets are sterile, forming large globular heads of white, pink, red, blue or a combination of these colours which in some cultivars give a wonderful almost metallic lustre which creates, when dead, marvellous everlasting flowers for the floral artist.

In very shallow chalk soils *H. macrophylla* and its forms may become chlorotic; this can be counteracted by generous mulching and feeding. In all alkaline soils it is impossible to retain the blue shades of colour without treatment. By treatment it is comparatively easy to control the colour of container-grown plants and plants in soils which are only slightly alkaline. Where its use is desirable Blueing Powder should be applied every seven

**HYDRANGEA macrophylia**—*continued*

or fourteen days during the growing season at the rate of 85g (3oz) being dissolved in 13.5 litres (3 gallons) of water.

Thin out and cut back immediately after flowering (except in cold areas) old flowering shoots to within a few centimetres of the old wood.

**'Alpenglühen'** Large heads of crimson florets. C 1950.

**'Altona'** Rose coloured; large florets. Blues well when treated. Best in shade. AM 1957. AGM 1984.

**'Ami Pasquier'** Deep red; dwarf habit. AM 1953. AGM 1984.

**'Ayesha'** See *H*. 'Ayesha'.

**'Baardse's Favourite'** Rich pink; dwarf.

**'Blue Prince'** ['Blauer Prinz'] Rose-red; cornflower-blue when treated.

**'Bodensee'** Pink, blues well when treated.

**'Deutschland'** Deep pink; attractive autumn tints. AM 1927.

**'Domotoi'** Loose irregular heads of large double, pale pink or blue florets.

**'Europa'** Deep pink; large florets.

**'Garten-Baudirektor Kuhnert'** Rose coloured; vivid blue if treated.

**'Générale Vicomtesse de Vibraye'** Vivid rose; good blue when treated. AM 1947. AGM 1984.

**'Gertrude Glahn'** Deep pink to purple.

**'Goliath'** Deep pink or purplish-blue, very large florets in small heads. One of the finest cultivars for seaside gardens.

**'Hamburg'** Deep rose or purplish; large florets. AGM 1984.

**'Heinrich Seidel'** Glowing red to purple; large, fringed florets. Best in semi-shade.

**'Holstein'** Pink; sky-blue in acid soils. Free-flowering, large florets with serrated sepals. C 1928.

**'Joseph Banks'** A medium-sized shrub of vigorous growth, of particular value for coastal planting. Very large heads which are cream at first, passing to pale pink or pale hyacinth-blue. Said to be a branch sport of the wild Japanese type. Introduced via China in 1789.

**'King George'** Rose-pink; large florets with serrated sepals. AM 1927.

**'La France'** Phlox-pink to mid-blue in huge heads.

**'La Marne'** Pale pink or blue in enormous heads, sepals prettily feathered. Excellent by the sea.

**'Loreley'** Carmine to deep blue, free-flowering.

**'Madame Emile Mouillère'** Florets large, with serrated sepals; white, with pink or blue eyes. Perhaps the best white cultivar and certainly one of the most popular. AM 1910. AGM 1984.

**'Mandshurica'** See 'Nigra'.

**'Maréchal Foch'** Rich rosy-pink, purple to vivid deep gentian-blue in an acid soil. Very free flowering. AM 1923.

**'Masja'** Compact habit with red flowers. A sport of 'Alpenglühen'. C 1977.

**'Miss Belgium'** Rosy-red; dwarf.

**'Münster'** Florets violet, crimson or deep blue turning to bright autumn tints of red and scarlet; dwarf.

**'Niedersachsen'** Pale pink; good blue when treated. AM 1968.

**'Nigra'** ('Mandshurica') A distinct cultivar with stems black or almost so; florets rose or occasionally blue. C 1870. FCC 1895.

**'Pia'** A slow-growing dwarf, with long-lasting heads of purplish-red florets on any soil.

**'Queen Elizabeth'** A lovely shade of rose-pink. A cultivar which lends itself readily to blueing.

**'Queen Emma'** Large heads of crimson.

**'Silver Slipper'** See *H*. 'Ayesha'.

**'Soeur Thérèse'** Rather flattened heads of large, white florets. C 1950.

**'Souvenir de Madame E. Chautard'** Clear pale pink, mauve or blue; dwarf, early flowering.

**'Souvenir de Président Doumer'** Dark velvety-red, purple to dark blue. Dwarf habit.

**'Strafford'** Light red.

**'Westfalen'** Vivid crimson or violet. AM 1958. AGM 1984.

**HYDRANGEA macrophylia**—*continued*

### LACECAPS

A smaller group than the Hortensias, but similar in growth and requirements. Producing large, flattened corymbs of fertile flowers around which are borne a ring of coloured ray-florets.

**'Blaumeise'** A broad shrub to 1m; heads rather flattened with up to 15 large, lilac-blue florets. C 1979.

**'Blue Wave'** A strong-growing shrub of medium size producing beautifully shaped heads of blue fertile flowers surrounded by numerous large ray-florets, varying in colour from pink to blue. In suitable soils the colour is a lovely gentian-blue. Best in semi-shade. Raised by Messrs Lemoine from seed of 'Mariesii' about 1900. AM 1956. FCC 1965. AGM 1984.

**'Geoffrey Chadbund'** Flowers brick-red on alkaline or neutral soils. AGM 1984.

**'Lanarth White'** Compact growing, and with large flattened heads of bright blue or pink fertile flowers surrounded by a ring of white ray-florets. A superb cultivar. AM 1949. AGM 1984.

**'Libelle'** A very fine selection, the heads with large, pure white sterile florets, fertile flowers blue. C 1964.

**'Maculata'** ('Variegata') A medium-sized shrub of erect habit; flowerheads with a few small white ray-florets. Grown for its attractive leaves which have a broad creamy-white margin.

**'Mariesii'** Wide flat corymbs of rosy-pink flowers, the ray-florets very large. When grown in suitable soil the flowers turn a very rich blue. Introduced by Maries from Japan in 1879. FCC 1881.

**'Mariesii Alba'** See 'White Wave'.

**'Miranda'** Dwarf habit with deep blue flowers.

**'Quadricolor'** Leaves variegated dark green, pale green, cream and deep yellow. Flowers pale pink.

**'Sea Foam'** (*H. maritima* 'Seafoam') A small to medium-sized shrub with blue fertile flowers surrounded by white ray-florets. A handsome shrub succeeding best in seaside and sheltered gardens. Said to be a clone of the wild coastal hydrangea *H. macrophylla* var. *normalis* and to have arisen as a reversion on the Hortensia 'Joseph Banks'.

**'Tricolor'** A choice, strong-growing cultivar with leaves which are most attractively variegated green, grey and pale yellow. Flowers pale pink to white, large, freely produced. Said to be a branch sport of 'Mariesii'. C 1860. FCC 1882.

**'Veitchii'** A medium-sized shrub with rich, dark green leaves, growing best in semi-shade. Flowers in flattened corymbs, the sterile outer florets white fading to pink. Very hardy and very lime-tolerant. Introduced from Japan about 1880. AM 1974. AGM 1984.

**'White Wave'** ('Mariesii Alba') ('Mariesii Grandiflora') A small shrub which originated in the nursery of Messrs Lemoine of Nancy as a seedling of 'Mariesii', about 1902. It is a strong-growing clone with flattened heads of bluish or pinkish, fertile flowers margined by large, beautifully formed, pearly-white ray-florets. Free-flowering in an open position. AM 1948.

**maritima** See *H. macrophylla* var. *normalis*.

**'Seafoam'** See under Lacecaps.

**paniculata** SIEB. A medium-sized to large shrub with both fertile and large, creamy-white sterile florets in dense terminal panicles in late summer and autumn. For large panicles, the laterals should be cut back to within 5 or 7.5cm of the previous year's growth in early spring (except for 'Praecox'). Japan, China, Taiwan. I 1861. AM 1964.

**'Everest'** A splendid form with handsome dark green foliage and large very dense heads of fully sterile florets, white at first turning to pink. AM 1990.

**'Floribunda'** Long, narrow panicles with numerous ray-florets. Flowering from late July. C 1867. AM 1953.

**'Grandiflora'** One of the showiest of hardy large shrubs. The massive panicles of numerous small, white, sterile florets, appearing in summer and autumn, become deep pink. When cut make excellent winter decoration. Introduced by Siebold from Japan about 1867. FCC 1869. AGM 1984.

**HYDRANGEA paniculata**—*continued*

    **'Greenspire'** Similar to 'Kyushu' but with green sterile flowers becoming tinged with pink.

    **'Kyushu'** Upright habit with dark glossy green, taper-pointed leaves and panicles liberally sprinkled with sterile flowers. A selection of the Collingwood Ingram introduction from Kyushu, Japan. AM 1964.

    **'Pink Diamond'** Large heads of sterile florets similar to but larger than 'Unique', white becoming pink. AM 1990.

    **'Praecox'** A form with smaller panicles of toothed ray-florets, the earliest form, flowering generally in early July and hardy in the coldest areas of Europe. Hard pruning early in the year will prevent flowering. Raised at the Arnold Arboretum from Japanese seed collected by Sargent in 1893. AM 1956. FCC 1973. AGM 1984.

    **'Tardiva'** Late flowering, from late August or September, the large heads with numerous ray-florets. AM 1966. AGM 1984.

    **'Unique'** Similar to 'Grandiflora' but with even larger flowerheads. AM 1990.

**'Preziosa'** See *H. serrata* 'Preziosa'.

**quercifolia** BARTR. The value of this medium-sized, white-flowered shrub lies in the magnificent autumnal tints of its large, strongly lobed leaves. Conical heads are borne in late summer with large white, sterile flowers. SE United States. I 1803. AM 1928. AGM 1984.

    **'Snowflake'** A striking form in which several series of bracts are produced in each flower creating a doubled appearance.

**radiata** See *H. arborescens* subsp. *radiata*.

**robusta** HORT. See under *H. heteromalla* 'Snowcap'.

**sargentiana** See *H. aspera* subsp. *sargentiana*.

**serrata** (THUNB.) SER. (*H. macrophylla* subsp. *serrata* (THUNB.) MAK.) A charming dwarf shrub rarely exceeding 1m. Flattened corymbs of blue or white flowers surrounded by a pretty circle of white, pink, or bluish ray-florets often deepening to crimson in autumn. A variable species. Japan, Korea. I 1843.

    **f. acuminata** See under 'Bluebird'.

    **'Blue Deckle'** Compact and slow-growing, lacecap type, with clear blue to pink, toothed ray-florets. Raised by Michael Haworth-Booth.

    **'Bluebird'** (*H. acuminata* 'Bluebird') A small, robust shrub with stout shoots and abruptly acuminate leaves. The blue fertile flowers are borne in slightly dome-shaped corymbs surrounded by large ray-florets which are reddish-purple on chalk soils, and a lovely sea-blue on acid soils. Reputedly a selected form of *H. serrata* f. *acuminata*, but in our experience the two are identical. Plants seen under either name would suggest by their robust nature a hybrid origin with *H. macrophylla* as one parent. AM 1960. AGM 1984.

    **'Chinensis'** A charming, dwarf shrub of dense habit with rather wiry branches and short-stalked downy leaves. Flowers in flattened corymbs, ray-florets lilac-blue on chalk soils, powder-blue on acid soils. The origin and botanical status of this shrub is something of a conundrum. It has every appearance of being a wild species though it does not fit any available description. It is sometimes found in cultivation under the name *H. chinensis acuminata*, but bears no resemblance to the plants generally grown in gardens as *H. serrata acuminata*. Our stock plant only attained 30 × 60cm after many years. See also 'Koreana'.

    **'Diadem'** A very hardy, compact shrub; flowers vivid blue or pink. Leaves reddening in full sun. AM 1963.

    **'Grayswood'** An attractive small shrub. Flattened corymbs of blue fertile flowers surrounded by a ring of ray-florets which are white at first, changing to rose and finally deep crimson. AM 1948. AGM 1984.

    **'Intermedia'** Small shrub with flat corymbs of pinkish fertile flowers surrounded by a ring of ray-florets which are white at first turning to shades of crimson.

    **'Koreana'** A delightful dwarf shrub, with slender branches and slender, acuminate, almost sessile leaves. Ray-florets lilac on chalk soils, sky-blue on acid soils. Similar in habit to 'Chinensis' but even smaller with longer, smoother, thicker-textured leaves. Our stock plant only attained 30 × 30cm after many years. Origin unknown, possibly Korea.

**HYDRANGEA serrata**—*continued*

    **'Preziosa'** A handsome shrub with purplish-red stems up to 1.5m high. Leaves purple-tinged when young. Attractive globular heads of large rose-pink florets deepening to reddish-purple in autumn. A hybrid between *H. macrophylla* and *H. serrata*. Garden origin. AM 1963. FCC 1964. AGM 1984.

    **'Rosalba'** A small shrub distinguished by its larger leaves, and ray-florets which are white at first, quickly turning to crimson. AM 1939. AGM 1984.

  **strigosa** See *H. aspera* subsp. *strigosa*.

  **villosa** See *H. aspera* Villosa group.

  **xanthoneura** See *H. heteromalla*.

**\*HYMENANTHERA** R. BR.—**Violaceae**—A small genus of about 5 species of evergreen or semi-evergreen shrubs of rigid habit, related to the "Pansy" and "Violet" but completely different in appearance. Natives of Australia, New Zealand and Tasmania.

  **angustifolia** R. BR. ex DC. (*H. dentata* var. *angustifolia* (R. BR.) BENTH.) A small, erect-growing shrub with smooth, oblanceolate leaves. Flowers small, yellow, often unisexual; berries white with purple markings. Tasmania, SE Australia, New Zealand. I 1820.

  **crassifolia** HOOK. f. A semi-evergreen New Zealand shrub of spreading habit, usually less than 1.5m high. Leaves obovate. Bears quantities of white berries on the underside of the branches. C about 1875. FCC 1892.

  **obovata** T. KIRK An erect, medium-sized, New Zealand species, with obovate, occasionally toothed, leathery leaves up to 5cm long; berries purplish.

**HYPERICUM** L.—**Guttiferae**—A genus of about 370 species of herbs, shrubs and trees widely distributed. The shrubby hypericums will thrive in almost any well-drained soil. They are very desirable summer and autumn blooming shrubs, producing their conspicuous bright yellow flowers in great abundance. They are happy in full sun or semi-shade.

Many of the Asiatic species have been mixed or mis-named in cultivation. The species described below are treated in accordance with research carried out by Dr N. K. B. Robson of the Natural History Museum.

  **acmosepalum** ROBSON (*H. oblongifolium* HORT. not CHOISY) (*H. kouytchense* HORT. not LEVL.) A splendid, very hardy, small, semi-evergreen shrub of erect habit, distinguished by its close-set, narrowly oblong leaves which often turn orange or scarlet in late autumn and winter. Flowers 5cm across, golden yellow, freely borne from June to October, followed by bright red capsules. SW China.

  **addingtonii** ROBSON A splendid semi-evergreen shrub of upright habit and medium size. Leaves short-stalked, ovate-oblong. The large, rich yellow flowers, 6-7.5cm across, are borne singly or in clusters at the ends of the shoots. Previously listed as *H. leschenaultii*. China (NW Yunnan). Possibly introduced by Forrest.

  **androsaemum** L. "Tutsan". A good shade-bearing shrub, seldom above 0.75m high, continuous and free-flowering. Flowers rather small but with conspicuous anthers, followed in autumn by erect, red, finally black, berry-like capsules. W and S Europe (incl British Isles), N Africa, W Asia. C before 1600.

    **'Gladys Brabazon'** A poor variegated form which originated in Ireland. Leaves irregularly blotched with white.

  **augustinii** ROBSON A rare, small, densely branched shrub with arching branches and sessile, ovate to oblong-lanceolate leathery leaves, the upper leaves amplexicaule. Flowers golden yellow, 4-6cm across, clustered at the ends of the branches during autumn. Named in honour of Augustine Henry who first discovered this species. China (S Yunnan).

  **aureum** See *H. frondosum*.

  **†\*balearicum** L. A dwarf, erect-branched shrub with very distinctive winged stems and small, curiously warted leaves. Flowers small, yellow, fragrant, borne from June to September. Balearic Isles. I 1714.

  **beanii** ROBSON (*H. patulum* var. *henryi* VEITCH ex BEAN) A small shrub related to *H. patulum*. Branches gracefully arching, producing slightly drooping flowers up to 6cm across. Named in honour of W.J. Bean who first described it. China (Yunnan and Guizhou). AM 1904.

    **'Gold Cup'** See *H. × cyathiflorum* 'Gold Cup'.

**HYPERICUM**—*continued*

**bellum** LI (L.S. & E. 15737) A small, elegant, densely branched shrub with broadly ovate to orbicular, wavy-edged leaves and deep yellow, slightly cup-shaped flowers 3.5cm across. Capsules puckered. A rare species related to *H. forrestii*. W China, E Himalaya. I about 1908.

**'Buttercup'** See *H. uralum*.

**\*calycinum** L. "Rose of Sharon". A dwarf, evergreen shrub with large leaves and large golden flowers. Excellent as a ground cover in dry and shaded places, but if left unchecked can become a weed. Occasionally naturalised. Suffers badly from rust. SE Bulgaria, N Turkey. I 1676. AM 1978. AGM 1984.

**chinense** See *H. monogynum*.

**choisyanum** WALL. ex ROBSON (B.L. & M. 147) A small to medium-sized shrub with slender, arching, reddish shoots. Leaves lanceolate, short-stalked, up to 8cm long and 3cm across, purple-tinged when young. Deep yellow, cup-shaped flowers about 4cm across are borne in summer. SW China, Himalaya, NE India. I 1971.

**\*coris** L. A dwarf or prostrate evergreen shrublet with slender stems and linear leaves, arranged in whorls of 3-6. The golden yellow flowers, 1.25-2cm across, are borne in terminal panicles up to 12cm long during summer. Ideal for the rock garden, scree or dry wall. C and S Europe. C 1640.

× **cyathiflorum** ROBSON (*H. addingtonii* × *H. hookerianum*). This hybrid only occurs in gardens where it is represented by the following form.

**'Gold Cup'** (*H. beanii* 'Gold Cup') A graceful small shrub with attractive lanceolate leaves arranged along the arching branches in two opposite rows. Flowers deep yellow, cup-shaped, 6cm across.

**densiflorum** PURSH A small, densely branched shrub with linear-oblong leaves and corymbs of small, abundantly produced deep yellow flowers in July and August. E United States. I 1889.

× **dummeri** ROBSON (*H. forrestii* × *H. calycinum*). The following plant was raised in 1975 by our propagator Peter Dummer at the suggestion of Dr Norman Robson in an attempt to determine the parentage of 'Hidcote'.

**'Peter Dummer'** A dwarf, mound-forming shrub reaching 80cm tall, with arching reddish shoots and ovate leaves bronze-red when young and somewhat red or purplish-tinged in winter. Large golden yellow flowers with orange anthers are borne in summer and autumn from deep orange flushed buds and are followed by red-tinged fruits.

**'Eastleigh Gold'** A small semi-evergreen shrub of loose, spreading habit with drooping, reddish-brown branchlets. Leaves elliptic, slightly leathery, dark shining green above, 4-5cm long. Flowers 6cm across, slightly cup-shaped, golden yellow with comparatively short stamens, freely borne from late June to October. Capsules puckered. This plant occurred as a seedling in our nurseries about 1964. It is probably a hybrid but the parentage is uncertain.

**elatum** See *H.* × *inodorum* MILL.

**'Elstead'** See *H.* × *inodorum* 'Elstead'.

**\*empetrifolium** WILLD. A dwarf evergreen shrublet with slender stems and small linear leaves. Flowers golden yellow, 1.25-2cm across, borne in small, erect panicles during summer. Requires a warm, sunny, well drained position on the rock garden or scree. Greece. I 1788. AM 1937.

**var. oliganthum** RECH. f. A prostrate form found in the mountains of Crete.

**forrestii** (CHITTENDEN) ROBSON (*H. patulum* var. *forrestii* CHITTENDEN) (*H. calcaratum* HORT.) (*H. patulum* var. *henryi* HORT.) A hardy shrub of neat habit usually attaining 1-1.2m in height. Leaves persist into the early winter giving rich autumn tints. The saucer-shaped, golden yellow flowers, 5-6cm across, rounded in bud, are profusely borne throughout summer and autumn. SW China, NE Burma. Introduced by George Forrest in 1906. AM 1922. AGM 1984.

**fragile** HORT. See *H. olympicum* f. *minus*.

**frondosum** MICHX. An attractive North American shrub up to 1.2m high, often giving the effect of a miniature tree with flaking bark. Leaves sea-green; flowers in clusters, bright yellow with a large boss of stamens, appearing in July and August. The sepals are large and leaf-like. A beautiful and unmistakable species. SE and S United States.

**HYPERICUM**—*continued*

**'Hidcote'** (*H. patulum* 'Hidcote') (*H.* 'Hidcote Gold') (*H.* × *cyathiflorum* 'Gold Cup' × *H. calycinum*). A superb hardy, semi-evergreen shrub of compact habit, attaining approximately 2m in height and 2m to 2.5m spread. The golden yellow saucer-shaped flowers, which are among the largest of any hardy *Hypericum*, are produced with gay abandon from July to October. The origin of this plant is uncertain but it probably originated at Hidcote Manor. Whatever its history it is now one of the most popular of all flowering shrubs. AM 1954.

**'Hidcote Variegated'** Leaves rather narrow, dark green with a white margin. A poor plant that tends to revert.

**hircinum** L. A compact shrub to about 1m. Leaves emitting a strong, pungent odour when bruised. Flowers 2.5cm across, bright yellow with conspicuous stamens, borne freely from July to September. A variable species. The most commonly grown form is subsp. *majus* (AIT.) ROBSON which differs from the typical form (a native of Corsica and Sardinia) in its narrower leaves. S Europe, SW Asia. Naturalised in the British Isles. I 1640.

**hookerianum** WIGHT & ARN. A small semi-evergreen shrub, distinguished by its leathery, ovate-oblong, sea-green leaves on pale green, stout, rounded branchlets, and clusters of large cup-shaped, pale yellow flowers from August to October. These are followed by puckered fruits. Nepal to Burma and Thailand, Yunnan, S India. I before 1853. AM 1890.

× **inodorum** MILL. (*H. androsaemum* × *H. hircinum*). (*H. elatum* AIT.) (*H. multiflorum* HORT.) (*H. persistens* I.F. SCHNEID.) An erect-growing shrub up to 1.5m. Leaves ovate to ovate-oblong. The small, pale yellow flowers are produced in terminal cymes and are followed by attractive red fruits. A variable hybrid, some forms tending more to one parent than the other. SW Europe, naturalised in the British Isles. C 1850.

**'Albury Purple'** Leaves purple but subject to mildew.

**'Elstead'** (*H. elatum* 'Elstead') A selected form with brilliant salmon-red fruits. Suffers badly from rust. AM 1933.

**'Summergold'** Young foliage golden yellow, burns badly in sun. 'Ysella' is similar.

**kalmianum** L. A slender-branched shrub of dense, compact habit up to 1m high. Main stems often gnarled, with pale brown, flaky bark. Leaves narrow, 2.5-5cm long, sea-green when young. Flowers 1.25-2cm across, bright yellow produced in the axils of the terminal leaves. NE United States, E Canada. I 1759.

**kouytchense** LEVL. (*H. penduliflorum* HORT.) (*H. patulum* var. *grandiflorum* HORT.) (*H. patulum* 'Sungold') A small, semi-evergreen shrub of rounded, compact habit. Leaves ovate. Flowers up to 6cm across, golden yellow, with conspicuous long stamens, freely borne from late June to October. The bright red, long-styled capsules resemble colourful upturned stork's heads. China (Guizhou). AGM 1984.

**lancasteri** N. ROBSON An attractive small shrub of graceful habit related to *H. stellatum* with bloomy young shoots flushed reddish on the exposed side and purple-tinged when young. Leaves ovate, sea-green. Flowers golden yellow, up to nearly 6cm across; calyx star-like, the red-margined sepals creating an attractive effect before the flowers open. Capsules attractively red-tinged. A delightful recently named species, first collected by George Forrest in 1906, introduced in 1980 by both Roy Lancaster and Keith Rushforth. N Yunnan and S Sichuan, China.

†\***leschenaultii** CHOISY A beautiful but tender shrub rarely cultivated. For the plant previously grown under this name see *H. addingtonii*. Indonesia. I 1853.

**lysimachioides** HORT. See *H. stellatum*.

**monogynum** L. (*H. chinense* L.) A pretty, semi-evergreen shrub, not above 1m high, with oblong-oval leaves and 6cm wide golden flowers with conspicuous stamens. A choice shrub for mild localities. China, Taiwan. I 1753.

× **moserianum** ANDRE (*H. calycinum* × *H. patulum*). A first-rate, dwarf shrub, usually not more than 0.5m high, making excellent ground cover. Stems arching, reddish. Flowers 5-6cm across with conspicuous reddish anthers, borne from July to October. Garden origin about 1887. FCC 1891. AGM 1984.

**'Tricolor'** Leaves prettily variegated white, pink and green. Succeeds best in a sheltered position. AM 1896.

**HYPERICUM**—*continued*

×**nothum** REHD. (*H. densiflorum* × *H. kalmianum*). A curious small shrub distinguished by its slender, interlacing stems with brown peeling bark, narrow leaves and numerous small flowers in late summer. Raised at the Arnold Arboretum in 1903.

**olympicum** L. A dwarf, erect or hummock-forming sub-shrub with small, glaucous-green leaves. Flowers bright yellow borne in clusters at the ends of the shoots in summer. Balkan peninsula, Turkey. I 1675. AGM 1984.

    **f. uniflorum** D. JORD. & KOZ. More commonly cultivated than the typical form this has rather broadly elliptic to obovate leaves. NE Greece, S Bulgaria, NW Turkey.

    **'Citrinum'** Flowers pale sulphur-yellow, 3.5cm across. Habit upright. AGM 1984.

    **'Sunburst'** Flowers large, 6cm across, golden yellow. Habit upright.

    **f. minus** (*H. polyphyllum* HORT. not BOISS. & BAL.) (*H. fragile* HORT. not. HELDR. & SART.) Leaves narrowly elliptic, prostrate or erect. C and S Greece.

    **'Sulphureum'** Flowers large, pale yellow.

**patulum** THUNB. ex MURRAY The true species of this name is a tender plant from SW China and is rare in cultivation in the British Isles. It was originally introduced from Japan (where it was widely cultivated) by Richard Oldham in 1862, and became popular in European gardens. The subsequent introduction of closely related, but hardier species from China, such as *H. beanii, H. forrestii* and *H. pseudohenryi* saw its gradual replacement.

**penduliflorum** See *H. kouytchense* LEVL.

**polyphyllum** HORT. See *H. olympicum* f. *minus*.

**prolificum** L. A small, densely branched shrub of rounded bushy habit. Main stems often gnarled, with attractive grey and brown peeling bark. Leaves narrow, 2.5-5cm long, shining above. Flowers 1.25-2cm across, bright yellow, borne in terminal clusters from July to September. E and C United States. I about 1750.

**pseudohenryi** ROBSON (*H. patulum henryi* HORT.) A small, mound-forming shrub with arching stems and narrowly ovate to lanceolate-oblong leaves. Flowers 3-5cm across, with spreading petals and conspicuous stamens, abundantly produced in July and August. First introduced by Ernest Wilson in 1908. China (Yunnan, Sichuan). Often grown under the name *H. patulum* var. *henryi*. See also *H. beanii* and *H. forrestii*.

**reptans** HOOK. f & THOM. A slender shrublet with prostrate stems rooting at intervals and forming small mats. Leaves 0.6-2cm long, crowding the stems. Flowers terminal, solitary, rich golden yellow, 4.5cm across, borne from June to September. A choice alpine species for the rock garden or scree. Himalaya. C 1881.

†**'Rowallane'** (*H. hookerianum* 'Charles Rogers' × *H. leschenaultii*). This magnificent, semi-evergreen plant is the finest of the genus, but needs a sheltered site. The 5-7.5cm wide, bowl-shaped flowers are of an intensely rich golden-yellow colour, of firm texture, and beautifully moulded. Graceful in habit, and as much as 2m high in mild districts. AM 1943. AGM 1984. Has been wrongly grown under the name *H. rogersii*.

**stellatum** ROBSON (*H. dyeri* HORT. not REHD.) (*H. lysimachioides* HORT.) An elegant, semi-evergreen species of semi-pendulous habit 1-1.2m in height and greater in width. Flowers 4cm across. The slender pointed sepals give the prettily red-tinted calyces a delightful star-like effect, hence the name. The young growths are similarly tinted. Capsules puckered. China (NE Sichuan). I 1894.

**tenuicaule** HOOK. f. & THOMS. ex DYER (B.L. & M. 238) A small to medium-sized elegant shrub with slender, strongly arching shoots bloomy when young. Leaves lanceolate, purplish at first, glaucous and gland dotted beneath, up to 6×2cm. Yellow cup-shaped flowers are borne in terminal clusters. E Nepal, Sikkim. I 1971.

**uralum** BUCH.- HAM. ex D. DON (*H.* 'Buttercup') A delightful, hardy, semi-evergreen shrub attaining 0.6-1m, with arching stems and ovate or oval, often wavy-edged leaves, 2.5-4cm long, smelling faintly of oranges when crushed. The golden yellow flowers, 2.5cm across, are borne in terminal cymes during August and September. Himalaya, Tibet. I 1820.

**wilsonii** ROBSON A small shrub with spreading branches and ovate to ovate lanceolate leaves. Flowers 4-5cm across, golden yellow, with spreading petals and conspicuous stamens. Discovered by Ernest Wilson in 1907. China (Hubei, Sichuan).

**HYPERICUM**—*continued*

**xylosteifolium** (SPACH) ROBSON (*H. inodorum* WILLD. not MILL.) A small suckering shrub, forming a dense thicket of erect, slender, usually unbranched stems 1-1.2m high. Leaves ovate or oblong, 2.5-5cm long. Flowers rather small, 2-2.5cm across, solitary or in terminal clusters at the ends of the shoots opening intermittently from July to September. Caucasus (Georgia), NE Turkey. C 1870.

**IDESIA** MAXIM.—**Flacourtiaceae**—A monotypic genus related to *Azara*. It succeeds best in a deep neutral or somewhat acid soil, but may be grown quite well given 75cm of loam over chalk. Some geographical forms are subject to damage in severe weather whilst others seem quite hardy.

**polycarpa** MAXIM. An ornamental, medium-sized, sometimes dioecious tree with large, ovate, long-stalked leaves, glaucous beneath, recalling those of *Populus wilsonii*. The tiny yellowish-green flowers are borne in large terminal panicles in summer, but not on young trees. Large bunches of pea-like, bright red berries are borne on female trees in autumn. Japan, China. I about 1864 by Richard Oldham. AM 1934.

**var. vestita** DIELS A particularly hardy, Chinese form with leaves tomentose beneath. W China. I 1908 by Ernest Wilson.

**ILEX** L.—**Aquifoliaceae**—The "Hollies" are a large genus of about 400 species of evergreen and deciduous trees and shrubs, rarely climbers, occurring in temperate and tropical regions of both hemispheres. The evergreen species and their forms provide some of the handsomest specimen trees hardy in our climate. The European and Asiatic species are adaptable to most soils and are indifferent to sun or shade, but most of the North American species require a neutral or preferably an acid soil. For assistance with this account we are indebted to Susyn Andrews of the Royal Botanic Gardens, Kew, who, in recent years, has carried out a great deal of work on the cultivated hollies.

Certain species are invaluable for hedgemaking and will withstand polluted atmosphere and maritime exposure. As a group they display a great variety of form and colour of leaf excelled by few other genera. Male and female flowers are borne usually on separate plants, and in a favourable season female plants fruit abundantly. Well rooted and balled nursery stock may be moved throughout the dormant season. In a damp spring evergreen hollies move well in May. Reversions which occur on variegated hollies should be cut out.

* × **altaclerensis** (HORT. ex LOUD.) DALLIM. This name was originally used to describe the "Highclere Holly" which was said to be the result of a cross between *I. aquifolium* (*I. balearica* DESF.) and *I. perado* (*I. maderensis* LAM.). The name is now used to cover a number of similar but variable hybrids in which *I. perado* subsp. *platyphylla* also played a part. Most are large shrubs or small to medium-sized trees of vigorous growth, with handsome, normally large leaves. The majority are excellent for tall hedges or screens. They are quite tolerant of industrial conditions and seaside exposure. The name derives from *Alta Clera*, the medieval Latin name for Highclere.

'**Atkinsonii**' A green-stemmed clone with large, handsome, rugose leaves, glossy dark green above and with regular spiny serrations. A bold holly with leaves amongst the finest in the group. Male.

'**Balearica**' (*I. balearica* HORT. not DESF.) (*I. aquifolium* var. *balearica* HORT. not (DESF.) LOES.) A hardy, vigorous, medium-sized tree of erect, somewhat conical habit when young. Leaves ovate to broadly ovate, flat, leathery, shining green, entire or spiny, always spine-tipped. Free fruiting. Both this plant and 'Maderensis' are clones of hybrid origin despite their geographical attributions. Not to be confused with *I. aquifolium* (*I. balearica* DESF.). See also 'Belgica'.

'**Belgica**' A strong-growing conical tree with stout green to yellow-green shoots. Leaves elliptic-lanceolate, dark glossy green, usually spineless to few spined. Large, orange-red fruits are profusely borne. Some plants distributed as 'Balearica' belong here. C 1874.

'**Belgica Aurea**' ('Silver Sentinel') (*I. perado* 'Aurea') One of the handsomest variegated hollies. A vigorous, erect-growing, female clone. The firm, flat, sparsely spiny leaves are often 8.25-10cm long, and in colour deep green with pale green and grey mottling, and

**ILEX × altaclerensis 'Belgica Aurea'**—*continued*

an irregular, but conspicuous creamy-white or creamy-yellow margin. It is probably a sport of the clone 'Belgica' which it resembles in habit and leaf shape. AM 1985.

**'Camelliifolia'** A beautiful large-fruiting clone of pyramidal habit, and with purple stems. The long, large, mainly spineless leaves are a lovely shining dark green, reddish-purple when young. C 1865. AGM 1984.

**'Camelliifolia Variegata'** Leaves dark polished green, marbled paler green and margined gold. Sometimes half or complete leaves are gold. Slow-growing to about 5m. C 1865.

**'Golden King'** One of the best golden-variegated hollies and one of the few plants to have received two awards in the same year. The broad, almost spineless leaves are green, with a bright yellow margin. A sport of 'Hendersonii' found in Edinburgh in 1884. Female. AM and FCC 1898. AGM 1984.

**'Hendersonii'** Vigorous in growth, the comparatively dull green leaves are generally entire though occasionally shortly spiny. A female clone, producing often heavy crops of large brown-red fruits. Raised in the early 1800s by Edward Hodgins of Co Wicklow.

**'Hodginsii'** ('Nobilis') ('Shepherdii') A strong, vigorous, male clone with purple stems. The large, dark green rounded or oval leaves are variably armed, some boldly spiny others few spined, the latter more prevalent on older specimens. It forms a noble specimen tree for a lawn and is especially suitable for coastal and industrial areas. There is also a female form. AGM 1984.

**'Howick'** A sport of 'Hendersonii' with dark green leaves narrowly margined creamy-white. A vigorous female tree with red berries.

**'Jermyns'** A strong-growing, green-stemmed clone with polished green, almost spineless leaves. Male. Ideal for hedging. A tree growing in the grounds of Jermyns House when Harold Hillier moved there in 1952.

**'Lawsoniana'** A very colourful branch sport of 'Hendersonii' with large, generally spineless leaves splashed yellow in the centre. Female. Reverting shoots should be removed. FCC 1894. AGM 1984.

**'Maderensis'** (*I. maderensis* HORT.) A vigorous, medium-sized tree with dark stems and regularly spined, flat leaves. A male clone which probably originated in a similar way to 'Balearica'. *I. maderensis* LAM. is a synonym of *I. perado*.

**'Maderensis Variegata'** See *I. aquifolium* 'Maderensis Variegata'.

**'Moorei'** A vigorous large-leaved clone with stems green, tinged reddish-purple. Leaves large, approaching those of 'Wilsonii', but rather longer in outline, polished dark green above, boldly and regularly spined. Male.

**'Mundyi'** A most pleasing green-stemmed clone. Leaves large, broadly oval, concave, regularly spiny and with a prominent venation. Male. One of the most magnificent of this group. Named after Mr Mundy of Shipley Hall, Derby. C 1898.

**'N.F. Barnes'** (*I. aquifolium* 'N.F. Barnes') Distinct purple shoots and large, dark, shining green leaves. Female.

**'Purple Shaft'** A striking cultivar with strong, dark purple, young shoots and abundant fruit. Fast-growing and making a fine specimen tree. A sport of 'Balearica'.

**'Silver Sentinel'** See 'Belgica Aurea'.

**'W.J. Bean'** (*I. aquifolium* 'W.J. Bean') A compact-growing clone with large, spiny, dark green leaves and bright red fruits.

**'Wilsonii'** A compact, dome-shaped clone with green stems and large, evenly spiny, prominently veined leaves. Female, with large, scarlet fruits. A seedling raised by Fisher, Son and Sibray in the early 1890s. Deservedly one of the most popular of this group. FCC 1899.

**\*aquifolium** L. "Common Holly". There is no more beautiful or useful evergreen for this climate. It is usually seen as a small tree or large bush, but in favourable positions may reach 18-21m or more. It is native over a wide area from W and S Europe (incl the British Isles), North Africa and W Asia. Cultivated since ancient times. AGM 1984.

Innumerable cultivars have arisen with variously shaped and coloured leaves, of different habits and with different coloured fruits. Unless otherwise stated all will eventually make large shrubs or small trees. Both the typical form and many of its cultivars are excellent for hedgemaking and are excellent both in industrial and coastal areas.

**ILEX aquifolium**—*continued*

**'Amber'** An interesting clone, selected in our nurseries before 1955; attractive, large bronze-yellow fruits. FCC 1985.

**'Angustifolia'** A slow-growing cultivar of neat pyramidal habit when young. Stems purple; leaves varying to 3.75cm long by 1.25cm wide, long pointed and with 10-16 slender marginal spines. Female. 'Serratifolia', 'Hascombensis' and 'Pernettyifolia' are similar clones.

**'Angustimarginata Aurea'** Dark purple stems and strongly spined narrow leaves about 5cm long, dark mottled green with a narrow deep yellow margin. Male.

**'Argentea Marginata'** "Broad-leaved Silver Holly". A handsome free-fruiting female tree with green stems and white margined leaves. Young growth pink. AGM 1984.

**'Argentea Marginata Pendula'** "Perry's Silver Weeping Holly". A small, graceful tree with strongly weeping branches, forming in time a compact mushroom of white margined leaves. It is a female clone and fruits freely.

**'Argentea Regina'** See 'Silver Queen'.

**'Aurea Marginata'** A small bushy tree. Leaves spiny, margined with yellow.

**'Aurea Marginata Ovata'** See 'Ovata Aurea'.

**'Aurifodina'** ('Muricata') ('Bicolor') An effective green-stemmed clone. Leaves flattened, dark green with a dark old gold margin. Female, free fruiting with scarlet berries.

**'Bacciflava'** "Yellow-fruited Holly". A handsome cultivar with heavy crops of bright yellow fruits. 'Fructu Luteo' is similar. AM 1984.

**var. chinensis** LOES. A synonym of *I. centrochinensis* for which see under *I. corallina*.

**'Crassifolia'** A curious slow-growing clone with very thick, curved, strongly spine-edged leaves, and purple young shoots. Male. Cultivated since the mid 1700s.

**'Crispa'** ('Tortuosa') ('Calamistrata') A peculiar clone with twisted and curled, thick leathery leaves, tipped with a sharp, decurved spine. A sport of 'Scotica'. Male.

**'Crispa Aurea Picta'** Similar to 'Crispa' but the dark green leaves have a central splash of yellow and pale green. Tends to revert. Male.

**'Donningtonensis'** Dark blackish-purple stems and purple-flushed, spiny young leaves. Male.

**'Elegantissima'** (Argentea Marginata group) A green-stemmed clone with boldly spined, wavy-edged leaves, green with faint marbling and creamy-white margins. Young leaves pink. Male.

**'Ferox'** "Hedgehog Holly". A distinctive clone with small leaves, the upper surfaces of which are puckered and furnished with short, sharp spines. Male. Lower and slower-growing than most, making an excellent hedge. This is said to be the oldest identifiable cultivar of holly still in cultivation, having been known at least since the early 17th century.

**'Ferox Argentea'** "Silver Hedgehog Holly". Rich purple twigs, the leaves with creamy-white margin and spines. A very effective combination. Male. C 1662. AGM 1984. AM 1988.

**'Ferox Aurea'** "Gold Hedgehog Holly". Leaves with a central deep gold or yellow-green blotch. Male.

**'Flavescens'** ('Clouded Gold') "Moonlight Holly". Leaves suffused canary-yellow, shaded old gold. Particularly effective on a dull winter afternoon or in spring when the young leaves appear. Best in full sun. Female.

**'Foxii'** A purple-stemmed clone with shining green, ovate leaves bearing evenly spaced marginal spines. Resembles a long spined 'Ovata'. Male.

**'Fructu Luteo'** See under 'Bacciflava'.

**'Golden Milkmaid'** Similar to 'Golden Milkboy' but female with red berries.

**'Golden Milkboy'** A striking and most ornamental holly with large flattened, spine-edged leaves which are green with a large splash of gold in the centre. Reverting shoots should be removed. Male.

**'Golden Queen'** ('Aurea Regina') A striking cultivar, young shoots green. Leaves broad, spiny, dark green with pale green and grey shading and a broad yellow margin. Male. AGM 1984.

**'Golden van Tol'** A sport of 'J.C. van Tol' with attractive golden-margined leaves.

**'Grandis'** See under 'Silver Queen'.

**ILEX aquifolium**—*continued*

**'Green Pillar'** An erect-growing form of narrow habit with upright branches and dark green, spiny leaves. Female. An excellent specimen or screening tree and suitable for growing in tubs.

**'Handsworthensis'** A green or dusky-stemmed cultivar of compact habit, with small, regularly and sharply spined leaves. Male.

**'Handsworth New Silver'** (Argentea Marginata group) An attractive purple-stemmed clone, distinguished by its comparatively long leaves which are deep green mottled grey, with a broad, creamy-white margin. Female, free fruiting. AGM 1984.

**'Hastata'** ('Latispina Minor') A remarkable, dense, slow-growing cultivar with deep purple shoots and small, rigid, undulating leaves with an occasional stout spine towards the base. Male.

**f. heterophylla** (AIT.) LOES. A name previously used to cover plants bearing both entire and spiny leaves, now regarded as a synonym of *I. aquifolium*. The plant previously distributed by us under this name is 'Pyramidalis'.

**'Heterophylla Aureomarginata'** See under 'Pyramidalis Aurea Marginata'.

**'Ingramii'** Shoots deep purple, leaves sharply spiny, flecked and margined creamy-white. Young growth pinky-mauve. Male.

**'J.C. van Tol'** ('Polycarpa') ('Polycarpa Laevigata') A superb cultivar with dark, shining, almost spineless green leaves, and producing large, regular crops of red fruits. Self pollinating. AGM 1984.

**'Laurifolia'** A striking cultivar with glossy, usually spineless leaves and deep purple shoots. Male.

**'Laurifolia Aurea'** ('Laurifolia Variegata') Dark green leaves thinly edged yellow. Very effective with the deep purple twigs. Male. FCC 1883.

**'Lichtenthalii'** A curious form making a low, spreading bush. Leaves long, twisted and irregularly spiny with a prominent pale green midrib. Of unknown origin. Female.

**'Madame Briot'** (Aureomarginata group) An attractive purple-stemmed clone with large, strongly spiny leaves which are green, mottled and margined dark yellow. Female. AGM 1984.

**'Maderensis Variegata'** (*I. × altaclerensis* 'Maderensis Variegata') A striking clone with reddish-purple stems. Leaves dark green, with a bold, irregular central splash of yellow and pale green. Tends to revert. Female.

**'Monstrosa'** ('Latispina Major') An easily-recognised cultivar of dense habit with bright green stems and broad, viciously spiny leaves. Male.

**'Muricata'** See 'Aurifodina'.

**'Myrtifolia'** A neat-growing cultivar with purple shoots; leaves small, dark green, variably edged with sharp spines or entire. Male.

**'Myrtifolia Aurea'** ('Myrtifolia Variegata') Purple stems. Leaves ovate-lanceolate, to 4cm long, dark glossy green with golden yellow margins. Male. Dense habit to about 4m.

**'Myrtifolia Aureomaculata'** A dense compact form with small, evenly spined leaves. In colour they are dark green with a pale green shading and an irregular central splash of gold. Male. AGM 1984.

**'N.F. Barnes'** See *I. × altaclerensis* 'N.F. Barnes'.

**'Ovata'** A slow-growing cultivar with purple shoots and distinct, neat, ovate leaves, shallowly scalloped along the margin. Male.

**'Ovata Aurea'** ('Aurea Marginata Ovata') A strong-growing clone. The thick, short-spined leaves are margined gold, and contrast beautifully with the deep purple twigs. One of the brightest and neatest of variegated hollies. Male.

**'Pendula'** An elegant, free fruiting, small tree forming a dense mound of weeping stems thickly clothed with dark green, spiny leaves. Female.

**'Polycarpa'** See 'J.C. van Tol'.

**'Pyramidalis'** A handsome, free fruiting clone with green stems and bright green, variously spined leaves. Conical in habit when young, broadening in maturity. AM 1989. AGM 1984.

**'Pyramidalis Aurea Marginata'** A strong-growing, green-stemmed clone. Leaves deep shining green with an irregular but conspicuous golden margin. Female. Plants grown by us as 'Heterophylla Aureomarginata' belong here.

**ILEX aquifolium**—*continued*

**'Pyramidalis Fructu Luteo'** Similar to 'Pyramidalis' in habit, but with profuse bright yellow fruits. AM 1985. AGM 1984.

**'Recurva'** A slow-growing clone of dense habit with purplish twigs and strongly spined, recurved leaves, 2.5-3.75cm long. Male.

**'Scotica'** A distinct cultivar with thick, leathery deep green leaves which are spineless and slightly twisted, with a cup-shaped depression below the apex. Female.

**'Silver Milkboy'** See 'Silver Milkmaid'.

**'Silver Milkmaid'** ('Silver Milkboy') ('Argentea Mediopicta') An old, attractive cultivar with strongly spiny leaves which are dark green with a central blotch of creamy-white. Female. Plants previously grown as 'Silver Milkboy' have proven to be female. Reverting shoots should be removed. AGM 1984. FCC 1985.

**'Silver Queen'** ('Argentea Regina') A striking clone with blackish-purple young shoots and broadly ovate dark green leaves faintly marbled grey and bordered creamy-white. Young leaves shrimp-pink. Male. AGM 1984.

**'Silver van Tol'** A sport of 'J.C. van Tol' with the leaves margined creamy-white.

**'Smithiana'** ('Smithii') A dense-growing clone with purplish twigs and narrow, often spineless leaves. Male.

**'Tortuosa'** See 'Crispa'.

**'W.J. Bean'** See *I. × altaclerensis* 'W.J. Bean'.

**'Watereriana'** ('Waterer's Gold') (Aureomarginata group) Dense, compact, slow-growing shrub with green stems striped greenish-yellow. The small, rounded, generally spineless leaves are mottled yellow-green and grey, with an irregular yellow margin. Male.

**'Weeping Golden Milkmaid'** An attractive shrub with stiffly pendulous branches and dark green leaves blotched in the centre with bright green and golden yellow. A female form with red berries.

* × **aquipernyi** GABLE ex W. CLARKE (*I. aquifolium × I. pernyi*). A group of hybrids first raised in North America where they are hardier than *I. aquifolium*.

**'Aquipern'** The first form raised. A large, densely branched conical shrub or small tree intermediate between the parents. Leaves similar to those of *I. pernyi* but larger, usually with 5-7 prominent spines, the terminal one long and deflexed. Male. Raised in the United States in 1933.

* × **attenuata** ASHE (*I. cassine × I. opaca*). (*I. × topelii*) "Topal Holly". A tall, slender shrub or small tree of rather conical habit, with narrow, normally entire leaves 5-10cm long, and clusters of red fruits. A natural hybrid found with the parents in S United States. Not suitable for chalky soils.

**'East Palatka'** A female clone of upright conical habit. Leaves pale glossy green, obovate, entire except for a sharp terminal point and an occasional spine.

**Foster group** This name covers a number of clones of the parentage *I. cassine* var. *angustifolia × I. opaca* with narrow, variously spined, glossy-green leaves bronze when young.

**'Sunny Foster'** A slow-growing form with narrow, golden yellow leaves. Particularly attractive during winter. A sport of 'Foster no. 2' which occurred at the United States National Arboretum in Washington. AM 1989.

**balearica** See *I. × altaclerensis* 'Balearica' and *I. aquifolium*.

* × **beanii** REHD. (*I. aquifolium × I. dipyrena*). A variable hybrid with leaves generally of a matt green. Superficially closer to the *aquifolium* parent. C early 1900s.

* **bioritsensis** HAYATA An evergreen shrub closely related to *I. pernyi* var. *veitchii*. Leaves 3-6cm × 1.5-4cm, ovate-rhomboid with a prolonged apex and sporadic spines. Fruits red. It has been wrongly distributed in the United States as *I. ficoidea* HEMSL. Burma, SW China, Taiwan.

‡* **cassine** L. not WALT. "Dahoon Holly". An extremely variable species making a large shrub, or rarely a small tree. The lanceolate leaves are occasionally 10cm long. Fruits red. SE United States. Not suitable for chalky soils. I 1726.

**var. angustifolia** AIT. A form with smaller, narrower leaves .

**centrochinensis** See under *I. corallina*.

**chinensis** See *I. purpurea*.

**ILEX**—*continued*

**\*ciliospinosa** LOES. Large shrub bearing small, neat, leathery, weakly spined leaves up to 5.5cm long. Fruits egg-shaped, red. Related to *I. dipyrena*, but differs in its smaller, more regularly spiny leaves and rounded shoots. W China. I 1908.

**\*colchica** POJARK. A large shrub closely related to *I. aquifolium* but with narrower, often less undulate, shorter-stalked leaves with fewer, more forward-pointing teeth. Some of the plants of this species in the Hillier Gardens and Arboretum derive from introductions made by Sir Harold Hillier. N Turkey, Caucasus.

**collina** ALEX. (*Nemopanthus collinus* (ALEX.) CLARK) A large deciduous shrub or small tree with elliptic to obovate, serrate leaves. Fruits bright red. Virginia and W Virginia. C 1930s. Has been distributed by us as *Nemopanthus mucronatus* (L.) TRELEASE.

**†\*corallina** FRANCH. (*I. corallina* var. *pubescens* S.Y. HU) A small, variable, graceful tree with slender stems and narrowly elliptic to elliptic-lanceolate, slender pointed and serrated leaves. Small red fruits produced in axillary clusters. The juvenile form with slender purple twigs and shining deep green, oblong-lanceolate, strongly spiny leaves was previously listed as *I. centrochinensis* (*I. aquifolium* var. *chinensis* LOES.) which is not in cultivation. W and SW China. I about 1900.

    **var. pubescens** See *I. corallina*.

**\*cornuta** LINDL. & PAXT. (*I. furcata* LINDL.) A dense, slow-growing species, rarely 2.4m high. Leaves of a peculiar, rectangular form, mainly five-spined. The large red fruits are rarely abundant. China, Korea. I 1846.

    **'Burfordii'** A very free fruiting shrub of compact growth with shining green, leathery leaves which, except for a short terminal spine, are entire. Extensively planted in the United States as an evergreen hedge where it can reach 4m. Female.

    **'Burford Variegated'** Leaves pale green with a broad, bright yellow margin.

    **'Dazzler'** A compact bush with rich glossy green leaves and large, bright red berries.

    **'D'Or'** Leaves entire or nearly so, fruits yellow.

    **'Dwarf Burford'** ('Burfordii Nana') A dwarf female form of slow growth and dense, compact habit. Leaves varying from entire to spiny. Fruits dark red.

    **'Kingsville Special'** A strong-growing shrub with large, leathery, almost spineless leaves.

    **'O' Spring'** Leaves spiny, green and grey-green in the centre margined with dull golden yellow. Shoots deep purple above. A sport of 'Rotunda'. Female.

    **'Rotunda'** Dwarf selection with compact, rounded habit, and strongly spined, oblong leaves. Female.

**\*crenata** THUNB. "Japanese Holly". A tiny-leaved holly of slow growth reaching 4-6m. Fruits small, shining black. A variable species particularly in cultivation. Excellent as a dwarf clipped hedge. Sakhalin Is, Korea, Japan. I about 1864.

    **'Aureovariegata'** See 'Variegata'.

    **'Convexa'** ('Bullata') A free-fruiting, small, bushy shrub, with glossy bullate or convex leaves. A superb low hedge. C 1919.

    **var. fukasawana** MAK. A distinct, comparatively large-leaved variety of dense, erect habit with strong, angular shoots and lanceolate or narrowly-elliptic, blunt-toothed leaves up to 5cm long, bright or yellowish-green when young. Japan.

    **'Golden Gem'** A small, compact shrub with flattened top and yellow leaves, particularly attractive during winter and spring. Female but very shy flowering.

    **'Helleri'** Perhaps the most attractive dwarf, small-leaved form, making a low, dense, flattened hummock. Originated in the United States in 1925. Female.

    **'Hetzii'** A vigorous form of broad, bushy habit with oblong-elliptic leaves to 3.5cm long. C 1943.

    **'Latifolia'** (*I. crenata* f. *latifolia* (GOLDRING) REHD.) A strong-growing form with larger elliptic leaves 2-3cm long. I 1860.

    **'Mariesii'** (*I. mariesii*) (*I. crenata* var. *nummularioides* (FRANCH. & SAV.) YATABE) A dwarf, most unholly-like clone of very slow growth, with crowded, tiny, round leaves. Ideal for troughs or Bonsai culture. Eventually makes a stiffly upright shrub of about 2m most attractive when covered with its black berries in winter. Female. Introduced by Maries in 1879. A male plant with larger leaves and of faster growth has also been grown under this name. It is similar to 'Nakada', named in the United States.

**ILEX crenata**—*continued*

**var.paludosa** (NAKAI) HARA (*I. radicans* NAKAI) A low-growing, spreading variety of dense habit with broad elliptic leaves, eventually reaching 1.5m tall and twice as much across. Found in damp places in Japan.

'**Stokes**' A dwarf shrub, forming a dense, compact mound of tiny leaves. Male. C 1949.

'**Variegata**' ('Aureovariegata') ('Luteovariegata') Leaves irregularly blotched with gold.

†\***cyrtura** MERRILL A rare and tender species making a medium-sized tree in mild areas. Leaves leathery and toothed, with a long, slender tip. Female plants bear bright red fruits. A plant in the Hillier Gardens and Arboretum has survived for many years and derives from the trees at Trewithen, Cornwall which were probably raised from seed collected by George Forrest. SW China (Yunnan), Upper Burma.

‡**decidua** WALT. "Possum Haw Holly" "Winterberry". A medium-sized to large shrub with slender stems and obovate to oblanceolate, crenately-toothed leaves. Fruits bright orange or red, lasting well into winter, but not very prolific on young plants. Not suitable for chalky soils. SE United States. I 1760.

†\***dimorphophylla** KOIDZ. A small shrub of upright habit proving fairly hardy given shelter. Juvenile foliage very spiny, adult leaves dark green, to 3cm long, entire except for the apical spine. Liukiu Islands. C 1976.

\***dipyrena** WALL. "Himalayan Holly'. A large shrub or small to medium-sized tree, conical in outline, with angled young shoots. Leaves dark green, with a short purplish petiole; juvenile foliage very spiny. Fruits deep red, slightly two-lobed. E Himalaya, W China. I 1840.

\*'**Dr Kassob**' (*I. cornuta* × *I. pernyi*). A neat-growing large shrub with conspicuous, ridged, yellow-green stems and very dark green, often somewhat convex, oblong, five-spined leaves up to 4 × 3cm. Female.

\***fargesii** FRANCH. (*I. franchetiana* LOES.) A large shrub or occasionally a small tree, easily recognised by its narrow, oblong or oblanceolate leaves up to 12.5cm long. Fruits small, red. SW China. I 1911. AM 1926.

**var. brevifolia** S. ANDREWS A shrubby form with smaller leaves up to about 7cm long. Belongs to the typical subspecies. Some plants previously distributed as *I. fargesii* may belong here. China (W Hubei). I 1900s.

**subsp. melanotricha** (MERRILL) S. ANDREWS (*I. melanotricha* MERRILL) Differs from the typical subspecies in the pubescent pedicels. Makes a graceful large shrub with slender shoots and profuse, orange-red fruits. China (Yunnan), N Burma, SE Tibet. The plant previously listed as *I. fargesii* var. *sclerophylla* is a form of this with purple shoots and petioles and smaller deep red fruits.

**var. sclerophylla** HORT. See under subsp. *melanotricha*.

**fragilis** HOOK. f. Plants previously listed under this name are *Myrsine semiserrata* (Myrsinaceae).

**franchetiana** See *I. fargesii*.

**geniculata** MAXIM. A large, deciduous shrub or small tree, with slender, greyish branches. Leaves ovate to elliptic, shallowly-toothed and thin in texture. Fruits red, on jointed pedicels. Japan. I 1926.

†\***georgei** COMBER A rare species allied to *I. pernyi* making a medium-sized to large shrub of compact habit. Leaves elliptic-lanceolate, up to 5cm long, thick and weakly spinose. Fruits small, sealing-wax red. Not hardy in the Home Counties. Discovered by George Forrest in SW China. I 1900s.

‡\***glabra** (L.) A. GRAY "Inkberry". A small to medium-sized shrub forming a dense rounded bush. Leaves small, dark shining green, in some forms turning purple in winter. Fruits small, black. Not suitable for chalky soils. E North America. I 1759.

**f. leucocarpa** F.W. WOODS An unusual form with white fruits.

\***hookeri** KING This species is not in cultivation. Plants previously grown by us under this name have been *I. kingiana* or *I. dipyrena*. All 3 species have very spiny juvenile foliage.

\***integra** THUNB. A medium-sized to large shrub, tender when young. Leaves obovate to broad elliptic, spineless and leathery. Fruit 1.25cm long, red. Japan, Ryukyu Is, Korea, Taiwan. I 1864.

\*'**Jermyns Dwarf**' A dwarf shrub with arching stems forming a low, dense mound, eventually forming a leader and reaching about 2m. Leaves polished dark green, strongly spine-toothed. Of hybrid origin, or a seedling of *I. pernyi*. Female, with red fruits.

ILEX—*continued*

*'**John T. Morris'** (*I. cornuta* × *I. pernyi*). A medium-sized to large shrub of dense, compact habit. Leaves oblong, glossy green, up to 5 × 4cm, with 5 triangular lobes tipped with sharp spines. Male.

*****kingiana** COCKERELL (*I. insignis* HOOK. f. not HEER) (*I. nobilis* GUMBLETON) A remarkable species with stout shoots and elliptic-lanceolate, leathery, few-toothed leaves 12-20cm long. Fruits large, red. Leaves of juvenile plants and suckers are smaller and markedly spiny. We have long grown two forms, one of which is very hardy while the other is damaged in very cold winters. It makes a small tree or large shrub. Some plants previously listed by us as *I. hookeri* belong here. E Himalaya, Yunnan. I 1880. AM 1964.

* × **koehneana** LOES. (*I. aquifolium* × *I. latifolia*). An interesting evergreen hybrid first reported in Florence. A large shrub or small tree with purple-flushed young shoots. Leaves elliptic to oblong-lanceolate, slightly undulate, dark polished green above and evenly spiny throughout. Female plants bear large red fruits. I 1890s or earlier.

'**Chestnut Leaf'** (*castaneifolia* HORT.) A robust clone of French origin. The thick, leathery, yellowish-green leaves are boldly margined with strong, spiny teeth.

*****latifolia** THUNB. "Tarajo". A magnificent species, in this country usually making a small tree or large shrub up to 7m. Leaves nearly equal in size to those of *Magnolia grandiflora*, dark glossy green, leathery, oblong with serrated margins. Although quite hardy it is tender when young and succeeds best in a sheltered position. Orange-red fruits often abundantly produced. Japan, China. I 1840. AM 1952. AM 1977.

*'**Lydia Morris'** (*I. cornuta* 'Burfordii' × *I. pernyi*). A medium-sized, compact, pyramidal shrub up to 2.5m with polished green, strongly spiny leaves, a little smaller than those of *I. cornuta*. Large red fruits. A female counterpart to *I.* 'John T. Morris'.

**macrocarpa** OLIV. A small to medium-sized, deciduous tree with spur-like branches and ovate, serrated leaves up to 15cm long. Remarkable on account of the size of its fruits, which resemble small black cherries. S and SW China. I 1907.

**macropoda** MIQ. A large shrub or small tree with ovate to broad elliptic, serrated leaves. Fruits red. Related to and resembling the American *I. montana*. China, Japan, Korea. I 1894.

**maderensis** HORT. See *I.* × *altaclerensis* 'Maderensis'.

**maderensis** LAM. See *I. perado*.

* × **makinoi** HARA (*I. leucoclada* × *I. rugosa*). A dwarf evergreen shrub similar in general appearance to *I. rugosa* but larger in all its parts. Leaves narrowly oblong, less conspicuously veined. Fruits red. Japan. I early 1900s.

**melanotricha** See *I. fargesii* subsp. *melanotricha*.

* × **meserveae** S.Y. HU "Blue Hollies". (*I. aquifolium* × *I. rugosa*). This group of hybrids was originally raised by Mrs Kathleen Meserve of New York in an attempt to produce an ornamental holly for the eastern half of North America where *I. aquifolium* is not hardy. They are bushy, small to medium-sized shrubs up to 2m with angled, purplish shoots and softly spiny, dark glossy blue-green leaves. They are best given a continental climate. Forms in cultivation include 'Blue Angel', 'Blue Girl', and 'Blue Princess' (female), 'Blue Boy' and 'Blue Prince' (male).

‡*****myrtifolia** WALT. (*I. cassine* var. *myrtifolia* (WALT.) SARG.) A medium-sized to large, evergreen shrub with narrow leaves, 2.5-5cm long. Fruits normally red. Not suitable for chalky soils. SE United States. I 1700s.

*'**Nellie R. Stevens'** (*I. aquifolium* × *I. cornuta*). An ornamental small tree with green shoots and oblong-elliptic, blackish-green, often bullate leaves up to 7.5cm long which are spine-tipped with usually 2 spines on each side. Female, bearing profuse and long-persistent orange-red fruits.

†*****nothofagifolia** KINGDON-WARD A very distinct and unusual large shrub or small tree of spreading habit. Shoots lined with longitudinal ridges of warts. Leaves glossy dark green, resembling those of *Nothofagus antarctica*, densely clustered, up to 2cm long, broadly ovate and margined with short, slender spines. Fruit scarlet. NE Upper Burma, Yunnan, Assam. I about 1919 and again in 1963.

‡*****opaca** AIT. "American Holly". In this country, a large shrub or small tree. Leaves variously spiny, of a distinctive soft, matt olive-green or yellow-green. Not suitable for chalky soils

**ILEX opaca**—*continued*

and best in a continental climate. Fruits red. Numerous cultivars are grown in North America. E and C United States. I 1744.

**'Natalie Webster'** Leaves darker and glossier than normal. Female. The original plant was found on Fire Island, off Long Island, New York in the early 1930s by Charles Webster. I to our nursery in 1964.

**f. xanthocarpa** REHD. Fruits yellow. I 1811.

‡\***pedunculosa** MIQ. (*I. pedunculosa* f. *continentalis* LOES.) An attractive large shrub or small tree with dark, glossy green, entire, wavy-edged leaves. Fruits bright red, carried on slender stalks 2.5-3.75cm long. Not suitable for chalky soils. China, Japan, Taiwan. I 1893 by Charles Sargent.

**f. continentalis** See *I. pedunculosa*.

†\***perado** AIT. (*I. maderensis* LAM.) A small to medium-sized tree which is one parent of many of the *I. × altaclerensis* hybrids. It is distinguished from our native holly mainly by its distinctly winged leaf stalks and flatter leaves which are variously short-spined when young, occasionally entire, and rounded at the tip. Rather tender except in sheltered gardens and mild districts. Madeira. I 1760. Subsp. *azorica* (LOES.) TUTIN occurs in the Azores.

**subsp. platyphylla** (WEBB & BERTH.) TUTIN (*I. platyphylla* WEBB & BERTH.) "Canary Island Holly". A handsome and relatively hardy form of bushy habit making a small tree in mild districts. The leaves are large and broad, occasionally 12.5-15cm long by half as wide or more. They are dark green, leathery, short-stalked and short-toothed. The fruits are deep red. This remarkable plant has survived undamaged here for many years. Canary Isles (Tenerife, Gomera). I 1842.

\***pernyi** FRANCH. A distinguished large shrub or small tree with small, peculiarly spined leaves, almost triangular in shape. Fruits small, bright red. C and W China. I 1900. FCC 1908.

**var. veitchii** BEAN Similar in general appearance but with larger leaves with 3-5 spines per side. Fruits small, red. W China. I 1912. AM 1930.

**platyphylla** See *I. perado* subsp. *platyphylla*.

†\***purpurea** HASSK. (*I. chinensis* SIMS) A small tree remarkable for its bright pink young foliage. Leaves rather thin, elliptic-lanceolate, shallowly-toothed at the margin and taper-pointed at the apex, up to 13cm long. Flowers said to be lilac or red followed on female plants by glossy, scarlet fruits. Has reached 4m in the Hillier Gardens and Arboretum in spite of defoliation in very severe winters. China.

†\***rotunda** THUNB. A small tree with ovate or broad elliptic, entire leaves up to 10cm long, recalling those of *Ligustrum japonicum*. Fruits small, red, borne in clusters on the current year's growth. Ryukyu Is, Korea, China, Taiwan. I 1848.

‡\***rugosa** F. SCHMIDT A dwarf, prostrate shrub, forming a dense low mound. Young stems sharply angled almost quadrangular; leaves elliptic to lanceolate, acute and toothed, slightly rugose above. Fruits red. Not suitable for chalky soils. It is best known as one of the parents of the "Blue Hollies" (*I. × meserveae*). Japan, Sakhalin Is, Kurile Is. I 1895.

\***'San Jose'** An attractive, vigorous, small tree or large shrub of American origin, reputedly a hybrid between *I. × altaclerensis* 'Wilsonii' and *I. sikkimensis*. Young shoots purple-flushed; leaves elliptic to ovate-lanceolate, dark polished green above, paler beneath, conspicuously and evenly spined.

‡**serrata** THUNB. (*I. sieboldii* MIQ.) A deciduous, slow-growing, small to medium-sized shrub of dense twiggy habit. Leaves small and thin, attractively tinted in autumn. Flowers pink. The tiny red fruits of the female plants are produced in abundance and last throughout the winter or until eaten by birds. Not recommended for chalky soils. Japan, China. I 1893.

**'Leucocarpa'** A form with pale creamy-yellowish-white berries.

**sieboldii** See *I. serrata*.

**'Sparkleberry'** (*I. serrata × I. verticillata*). A medium-sized to large shrub with ovate, long-acuminate leaves attractively purple-tinted in spring. The small, bright scarlet berries are profusely borne. 'Apollo' is a male plant of the same parentage.

ILEX—*continued*

**\*spinigera** (LOES.) LOES. A large shrub or small tree close to *I. colchica* but with leaves strongly undulate and deeply spined and pubescent branches. Spines usually 3-4 on each side, the terminal one strongly deflexed. Berries orange-red. N Iran and neighbouring Russia.

**\*sugerokii** MAXIM. A rare, small to medium-sized shrub of dense, compact, upright habit. Leaves elliptic, 2.5-3.75cm long, shallowly-toothed in upper half, leathery and glossy dark green. Fruits red, solitary in the leaf axils of the current year's growths. Closely related to *I. yunnanensis*, differing in its generally glabrous shoots and few-toothed leaves. In the wild it is often found with *I. crenata*, and like that species is suitable as a dense hedge. Japan. I 1914.

**‡verticillata** (L.) A. GRAY (*Prinos verticillatus* L.) "Winterberry". A deciduous large shrub with leaves turning yellow in the autumn. Fruits bright red and long persisting. Not suitable for chalky soils. E North America. I 1736. AM 1962.

**f. aurantiaca** (MOLDENKE) REHD. Fruits orange.

**'Xmas Cheer'** A selected female clone of American origin bearing masses of bright red fruits which normally last through the winter months.

**†\*vomitoria** AIT. "Yaupon". A large evergreen shrub or small tree to 6m with ovate or elliptic leaves up to 4.5cm long, often purple-tinged when young, becoming dark glossy green. Fruit bright red, or in some forms yellow, profusely borne and long persistent. SE United States. Tender and little planted in this country it is very popular in the S United States where many selections have been made. An infusion of the leaves was used as a drink by the North American Indians. SE United States, Mexico, naturalised in Bermuda. I before 1700.

**\* × wandoensis** T.R. DUDLEY (*I. cornuta × I. integra*). A naturally occurring very variable hybrid. Generally tends towards *I. cornuta*. Korea. I about 1980.

**\*yunnanensis** FRANCH. (*I. yunnanensis* f. *gentilis* LOES.) A medium-sized to large shrub of bushy habit. Leaves small; ovate to ovate-lanceolate, acute or obtuse, crenately-toothed, glossy green above, neatly arranged on the slender, densely pubescent twigs. The small, slender-stalked, bright red fruits are conspicuous on female plants. W China. I 1901 by Ernest Wilson.

**f. gentilis** See *I. yunnanensis*.

**\*ILLICIUM** L.—**Illiciaceae**—A genus of about 40 species of aromatic evergreen shrubs and trees natives of E and SE Asia and warm parts of America. The only genus in the family, they are allied to *Magnolia* and thrive under conditions congenial to *Rhododendron*, though tolerant of a little lime. A small group of outstanding evergreens with unusual, many-petalled flowers.

**anisatum** L. (*I. religiosum* SIEB. & ZUCC.) A medium-sized to large aromatic shrub of slow growth. Leaves obovate or oval, abruptly pointed, thick and fleshy, glossy deep green. Flowers pale yellow, about 2.5cm across, in spring, carried even on young plants. Japan, China. I 1790. AM 1930.

**floridanum** ELLIS A medium-sized, aromatic shrub with deep green, broadly oval, leathery leaves; flowers maroon-purple in May and June. S United States. I 1771.

**henryi** DIELS A medium-sized shrub with glossy, leathery leaves and flowers of a bright rose. W China.

**"INDIAN BEAN TREE"** See *Catalpa bignonioides*.

**INDIGOFERA** L.—**Leguminosae**—A very large genus of some 700 or more species of shrubs and herbs found mainly in tropical and subtropical regions. The following are a very attractive group of shrubs which, owing to their racemes being produced from leaf-axils of growing shoots, flower continuously throughout summer and autumn. All have elegant, pinnate leaves and require full sun. They thrive in all types of soil and are especially good on dry sites. Some species may be cut back during severe winters but these usually throw up a thicket of strong shoots the following spring. Old, poorly shaped specimens may also be hard pruned to achieve the same effect.

**INDIGOFERA**—*continued*

**amblyantha** CRAIB Similar to and with all the good qualities of *I. potaninii*. In our experience they are, for garden purposes, identical. Flowers a delightful shrimp-pink. China. I 1908 by William Purdom.

**decora** LINDL. (*I. incarnata* (WILLD.) NAKAI) A rare and pretty, dwarf shrub from China and Japan, producing long racemes of pink pea-flowers. I 1846. AM 1933.

**f. alba** SARG. An attractive form with white flowers. I about 1878. AM 1939.

**hebepetala** BENTH. A medium-sized, wide-spreading shrub with flowers of distinct colouring, being rose with a deep crimson standard. NW Himalaya. C 1881.

**heterantha** WALL. ex BRANDIS (*I. gerardiana* WALL. ex BAKER) Flowers bright purplish-rose, foliage very elegant. Grows 0.9-1.2m in the open, but much higher against a wall. Plants we have received under the name *I. divaricata* are almost identical with this species and it is perhaps merely a geographical form. NW Himalaya. C 1840. AM 1977. AGM 1984.

**incarnata** See *I. decora*.

**kirilowii** PALIB. (*I. macrostachya* BUNGE) A small shrub with flowers of bright almond-pink in long, dense racemes, but rather hidden by the leaves. N China. Korea. I 1899.

**potaninii** CRAIB A splendid, medium-sized shrub. Flowers clear pink in racemes 12-20cm long produced continuously from June to September. NW China. C 1925.

**pseudotinctoria** MATSUM. A vigorous species from China and Japan, attaining about 1.5m. Related to *I. amblyantha*, it has pink flowers in dense racemes up to 10cm long. I 1897 by Augustine Henry. AM 1965.

†**pulchella** ROXB. (*I. rubra*) (*I. violacea*) A small shrub bearing long, axillary racemes of purple-red flowers. Only for the mildest areas or conservatory. East Indies. I 1819.

**"IRONWOOD"** See *Ostrya virginiana*.

**ITEA** L.—**Grossulariaceae**—A small genus of about 10 species of deciduous and evergreen shrubs and small trees native of E Asia from the Himalaya to the Philippines with one species in E North America. The following make attractive and unusual, summer-flowering shrubs thriving in half shade. The evergreen species will take full sun against a south or west wall, providing the soil is not too dry.

*****ilicifolia** OLIV. A lax, evergreen, holly-like shrub up to 3m or more in height, charming in appearance when, in late summer, it is laden with long, drooping, catkin-like racemes of fragrant greenish-white flowers. C China. I before 1895 by Augustine Henry. AM 1911. AGM 1984. FCC 1988.

‡**virginica** L. An attractive, small, erect-branched, deciduous shrub, producing upright cylindrical racemes of fragrant, creamy-white flowers in July. Foliage often colours well in the autumn. E United States. I 1744. AM 1972.

†*****yunnanensis** FRANCH. Closely resembles *I. ilicifolia*, but has longer leaves. Flowers white in racemes 15-18cm long. Yunnan, China. I about 1918 by George Forrest.

**JAMESIA** TORREY & A. GRAY—**Philadelphaceae**—A monotypic genus related to *Fendlera* and *Carpenteria*. Suitable for any ordinary soil in full sun.

**americana** TORREY & A. GRAY A small to medium-sized erect shrub, with greyish leaves and slightly fragrant, white flowers produced in cymose clusters during May and June. W North America. I 1862.

**"JASMINE"** See *Jasminum*.

**"JASMINE, WINTER"** See *Jasminum nudiflorum*.

**JASMINUM** L.—**Oleaceae**—The "Jasmines" or "Jessamines" consist of more than 200 species of evergreen and deciduous shrubs and climbers natives of tropical and temperate regions of the Old World. They are popular as climbing plants but too little planted as self-supporting shrubs. All the hardy shrubby species have yellow flowers and are more or less deciduous in a hard winter but their usually green stems create an evergreen effect. Their soil requirements are cosmopolitan. For climbing species see under CLIMBERS at end of Manual.

**JASMINUM**—*continued*

    **fruticans** L. A small to medium-sized, semi-evergreen shrub with erect stems. Leaves normally trifoliolate; flowers yellow, in clusters at the end of the stems from June to September. Fruits black. Mediterranean region. C 1517.

    **humile** L. "Italian Jasmine". A small to medium-sized, semi-scandent, half evergreen shrub, leaves with normally 3-7 leaflets. Flowers bright yellow, in terminal clusters in June or July. This extremely variable species is distributed over a wide area from Afghanistan to Yunnan and Sichuan, China. C 1656.

        **var. glabrum** See f. *wallichianum*.

        *\**'Revolutum'** (*J. revolutum* SIMS) A quite remarkable and beautiful medium-sized shrub with deep green persistent leaves of good texture, composed of usually 5-7 leaflets. These create a splendid setting for the comparatively large deep yellow, slightly fragrant flowers in cymbose clusters during summer. Originally introduced from China in 1814. AM 1976.

        **f. wallichianum** (LINDL.) P.S. GREEN (*J. humile* var. *glabrum* (DC.) KOBUSKI) A form of tall, scandent growth, the leaves with normally 7-11 leaflets, the terminal one long and acuminate. Flowers yellow, in pendant clusters. NE Nepal. I 1812.

    **nudiflorum** LINDL. "Winter Jasmine". One of the most tolerant and beautiful of winter-flowering shrubs. Flowers bright yellow appearing on the naked green branches from November to February. Makes strong, angular growths up to 4.5m long. Excellent for covering unsightly walls and banks. When grown as a wall shrub, long growths may be cut back immediately after flowering. W China. Introduced by Robert Fortune in 1844. AGM 1984.

        **'Aureum'** Leaves blotched with or almost entirely yellow. C 1889.

    **parkeri** DUNN A dwarf or prostrate shrub normally forming a low mound of densely crowded, greenish stems; bearing small, pinnate leaves and tiny yellow flowers in summer. Suitable for the rock garden. W Himalaya. Discovered and introduced by R.N. Parker in 1923. AM 1933.

    **revolutum** See *J. humile* 'Revolutum'.

**"JERUSALEM SAGE"** See *Phlomis fruticosa*.

†**JOVELLANA** RUIZ & PAVON—**Scrophulariaceae**—About 6 species of herbs and sub-shrubs native to New Zealand and Chile. Related to *Calceolaria*, but their flowers lack the pouched lip of the latter.

    **sinclairii** (HOOK.) KRANZL. A very distinct New Zealand species of dwarf habit, suitable for a rock garden in a mild locality, with white or pale lavender, purple spotted flowers in June. I 1881.

    *\**violacea** (CAV.) G. DON (*Calceolaria violacea* CAV.) A charming, small, Chilean shrub with erect branches and small neat leaves. Flowers pale violet with darker markings, produced in June and July. I 1853. AM 1930.

**"JUDAS TREE"** See *Cercis siliquastrum*.

**JUGLANS** L.—**Juglandaceae**—The "Walnuts" are a genus of some 20 species of deciduous trees, native to N and S America and from SE Europe to SE Asia. They are mostly fast-growing, ornamental trees which are not particular as to soil, but should not be planted in sites subject to late frosts. Their leaves are pinnate, like those of the ash and, in some species, are large and ornamental. Distinguished from *Carya* by the chambered pith.

    **ailantifolia** CARR. (*J. sieboldiana* MAXIM.) An erect-growing tree of medium size with large, handsome leaves often as much as 1m long. Japan. I 1860.

        **var. cordiformis** (MAXIM.) REHD. A form differing only in the shape of its fruits.

    **californica** S. WATS. A distinct, large shrub or small tree, with attractive leaves composed of 11-15 oblong-lanceolate leaflets. S California. C 1889.

    **cathayensis** See *J. mandshurica*.

**JUGLANS**—*continued*

**cinerea** L. "Butternut". A handsome, fast-growing species of medium size with shoots sticky to the touch, and large, hairy leaves and exceptionally large fruits. E North America. C 1633.

**elaeopyren** DODE (*J. major* (TORR.) HELLER) (*J. microcarpa* var. *major* (TORR.) BENSON) A very handsome, medium-sized tree differing from *J. microcarpa* in its larger size, generally larger, more coarsely-toothed leaflets and larger fruits. The leaves turn butter-yellow in autumn. New Mexico to Arizona, NW Mexico. Some plants grown as *J. microcarpa* belong here. I about 1894.

**hindsii** (JEPS.) R.E. SMITH Medium-sized tree with handsome foliage. C California. C 1878.

× **intermedia** CARR. (*J. nigra* × *J. regia*). A vigorous tree intermediate between the parents. Leaves usually with 5 or 6 pairs of leaflets, the terminal one often missing as in *J. nigra*. Leaflets oblong, crenate at the margin, glabrous apart from axillary tufts beneath.

**major** See *J. elaeopyren*.

**mandshurica** MAXIM. (*J. cathayensis* DODE) Medium-sized tree with stout, glandular hairy young shoots. Leaves up to 0.6m long, sometimes longer on young trees, composed of 11-19 taper-pointed leaflets. NE USSR, NE China, Korea. I 1859.

**microcarpa** BERL. (*J. rupestris* TORR.) "Texan Walnut". A very graceful, small, shrubby tree similar to *J. californica*, but with numerous small, thin, narrow leaflets. Some plants grown under this name are *J. elaeopyren*. Texas, New Mexico. C 1868.

    **var. major** See *J. elaeopyren*.

**nigra** L. "Black Walnut". A large, noble, fast-growing tree, with deeply furrowed bark and large leaves. Fruits large and round, generally in pairs. E and C United States. C 1686. AGM 1984.

**regia** L. "Common Walnut". (*J. sinensis* (DC.) DODE) A slow-growing, medium-sized to large tree with a characteristic rounded head. SE Europe, Himalaya and China. Cultivated in England for many centuries. The timber is highly prized and very valuable. Normally grown from seed, selected clones, propagated vegetatively, such as 'Broadview' and 'Buccaneer', are grown for their early fruiting and the quality of their nuts.

    **'Laciniata'** "Cut-leaved Walnut". A form with somewhat pendulous branchlets and deeply cut leaflets. A tree on the site of our West Hill nursery in Winchester has reached 16m (1990). AM 1960.

**rupestris** See *J. microcarpa*.

**sieboldiana** See *J. ailantifolia*.

**sinensis** See *J. regia*.

**"JUNE BERRY"** See *Amelanchier*.

‡**KALMIA** L.—**Ericaceae**—A genus of 7 species of mainly evergreen shrubs natives of North America with one species in Cuba. Charming spring and early summer-flowering shrubs luxuriating under conditions similar to those required by *Rhododendron*. The conspicuous flowers are saucer-shaped; for maximum flowering, plant in full sun and moist soil.

\***angustifolia** L. "Sheep Laurel". A low-growing shrub up to 1m high, slowly spreading and forming thickets. Leaves variable in shape, normally ovate-oblong, in pairs or threes. Flowers rosy-red; June. A very poisonous plant. E North America. I 1736.

    **var. carolina** (SMALL) FERN. (*K. carolina* SMALL) "Southern Sheep Laurel". Leaves grey-downy underneath. Flowers purple-rose. SE United States. I 1906.

    **var. ovata** PURSH A form with broader, ovate leaves of a bright green.

    **'Rubra'** Foliage deep green; flowers deep rosy-red, carried over a long period.

    **'Rubra Nana'** A dwarf form with flowers of a rich garnet-red.

**carolina** See *K. angustifolia* var. *carolina*.

**cuneata** MICHX. "White Wicky". A small, deciduous or semi-evergreen shrub rarely above 1m high. The small, alternate, dark green leaves are sessile or nearly so; flowers white, cup-shaped in clusters among the stems during summer. Marshy places in N and S Carolina, very rare. I 1820.

\***latifolia** L. "Calico Bush" "Mountain Laurel". A magnificent rhododendron-like shrub of medium size. Apart from roses and rhododendrons possibly the best June flowering shrub for acid soils. The glossy, alternate leaves 5-13cm long make a pleasing setting for

**KALMIA latifolia**—*continued*

the clusters of bright pink, saucer-shaped flowers which open in June, giving the impression of sugar-icing when in bud. E North America. I 1734. AGM 1984.

**'Alba'** Plants seen under this name have the flowers pale pink in bud opening white flushed pink. There seems to be a relationship between the flower colour and the number of glands in the inflorescence, the pale coloured forms being the most glandular.

**'Clementine Churchill'** Flowers deep pink in bud opening rich pink. A lovely clone. AM 1952.

**'Elf'** A selection of f. *myrtifolia*. Compact habit with small leaves, young shoots purplish-red on the exposed side. Flowers pale pink in bud opening nearly white. C 1982.

**'Goodrich'** Corolla deep red inside with a narrow white border. Selected from wild plants in Connecticut, United States in 1972.

**f. myrtifolia** (JAGER) K. KOCH A very slow-growing, small bush of compact habit, with smaller leaves and flowers. C 1840. AM 1965.

**'Nipmuck'** Bright deep red in bud, nearly white when open; pale green foliage. Raised in 1963.

**'Olympic Fire'** A seedling of 'Ostbo Red' on which it is said to be an improvement. Large red buds open pink. Leaves wavy-edged. Selected in 1971.

**'Ostbo Red'** Flowers bright red in bud opening to pale pink. The first red-budded kalmia. Selected in the United States in the 1940s.

**'Pink Charm'** Deep pink to red buds open rich pink with a deep maroon band inside. Selected in 1974.

**'Shooting Star'** An unusual form in which the corolla is divided into 5 lobes which reflex as the flower opens. Flowers slightly later than normal. Selected from wild plants in North Carolina in 1972.

**'Silver Dollar'** Very large flowers up to 4cm across, white with red anther pockets and basal ring. Selected in 1952.

**\*polifolia** WANGENH. (*K. glauca* AIT.) "Eastern Bog Laurel". A small, wiry shrub 0.3-0.6m high with narrow leaves, dark shining green above, glaucous beneath, in pairs or threes. Flowers in large terminal clusters, bright rose-purple, opening in April. In its native land this species grows in swamps and boggy places. E North America. I 1767.

**\*KALMIOPSIS** REHD.—**Ericaceae**—A monotypic genus related to *Rhodothamnus*.

**leachiana** (HENDERSON) REHD. A choice and rare, dwarf shrub of considerable beauty. Pink kalmia-like blooms in terminal, leafy racemes from March to May. Quite hardy. A protected plant in SW Oregon. I 1931. AM 1937. FCC 1987.

**KALOPANAX** MIQ.—**Araliaceae**—A monotypic genus differing from *Eleutherococcus* in its lobed but not compound leaves.

**pictus** (THUNB.) NAKAI (*K. septemlobus* (THUNB.) KOIDZ.) (*Acanthopanax ricinifolium* (SIEB. & ZUCC.) SEEM.) A small to medium-sized tree in cultivation, superficially resembling an *Acer*. The branches and sucker growths bear scattered, stout prickles. Leaves 5-7-lobed, in young plants over 30cm across. The small clusters of white flowers are borne in large, flattish heads 30-60cm across in autumn. Japan, E Russia, Korea, China. I 1865.

**var. maximowiczii** (VAN HOUTTE) LI Leaves deeply lobed.

**"KENTUCKY COFFEE TREE"** See *Gymnocladus dioica*.

**KERRIA** DC.—**Rosaceae**—A monotypic genus differing from *Rhodotypos* in its alternate leaves and yellow flowers. A suckering shrub which has adorned our gardens since Victorian days. May be thinned and pruned immediately after flowering.

**japonica** (L.) DC. A graceful shrub up to 1.8m high, or more against a wall. In April and May, or earlier given mild weather, its arching branches are wreathed with rich yellow flowers, like large buttercups. Its green stems are most effective in winter. China, long cultivated in Japan. I 1834. AGM 1984.

**'Golden Guinea'** A form with very large, single flowers.

**'Picta'** See 'Variegata'.

**KERRIA japonica**—*continued*

**'Picta'** See 'Variegata'.

**'Pleniflora'** ('Flore Pleno') The well-known double flowered form. Taller and more vigorous and erect than the single-flowered form. Introduced from China by William Kerr in 1804. AM 1978. AGM 1984.

**'Variegata'** ('Picta') A pleasing and elegant creamy-white, variegated form of lower spreading habit, up to 1.5m in height. C 1844.

**KOELREUTERIA** LAXM.—**Sapindaceae**—3 species of deciduous trees, natives of China and Taiwan, only the following widely grown. Of easy cultivation on all soils. Flowering and fruiting best in hot, dry summers.

**paniculata** LAXM. (*K. paniculata* var. *apiculata* (REHD. & WILS.) REHD.) The best-known species, given such names as "Pride of India", "China-tree" and "Goldenrain-tree". A very attractive, broad-headed tree 9-12m high, with pinnate leaves comprising 9-15 ovate leaflets. The large panicles of small yellow flowers in July and August are followed by conspicuous bladder-like fruits. The leaves turn yellow in autumn. China. I 1763. AM 1932.

**var. apiculata** See *K. paniculata*.

**'Fastigiata'** A rare and remarkable, slow-growing form of narrowly columnar habit, attaining 8m high by 1m wide. Raised at Kew in 1888.

**'September Gold'** An American selection raised about 1965. Flowers one month later than normal in September and October. Young pods red-tinged.

**KOLKWITZIA** GRAEBN.—**Caprifoliaceae**—A monotypic genus related to *Abelia*.

**amabilis** GRAEBN. "Beauty Bush". This lovely and graceful, very hardy and adaptable, medium-sized shrub forms a dense, twiggy bush. In May and June its drooping branches are draped with masses of bell-shaped flowers, soft pink with a yellow throat. The calyces and pedicels are conspicuously hairy. One of the many lovely shrubs introduced by Ernest Wilson. W China. I 1901. AM 1923.

**'Pink Cloud'** A lovely pink flowered seedling selected and raised at Wisley in 1946. FCC 1963. AGM 1984. 'Rosea' is a similar clone.

+**LABURNOCYTISUS** SCHNEID. (*Laburnum* + *Cytisus*)—**Leguminosae**—A graft hybrid between *Cytisus* and *Laburnum*. Only the following form is known.

**adamii** (POITEAU) SCHNEID. (*Laburnum anagyroides* + *Cytisus purpureus*). A remarkable small tree, a graft hybrid (chimaera) with laburnum forming the core and broom the outer envelope. Some branches bear the yellow flowers of the laburnum, whilst other branches bear dense, congested clusters of the purple-flowered broom. To add to the "confusion" most branches produce intermediate flowers of a striking, coppery-pink shade. Originated in the nursery of M. Adam near Paris in 1825.

**LABURNUM** MEDIKUS—**Leguminosae**—"Golden Rain". A genus of 2 species of small, ornamental trees of easy cultivation, suitable for almost all types of soil. The yellow pea-flowers are produced in drooping racemes during late spring and early summer. All parts of the plant are poisonous, particularly the seeds.

**alpinum** (MILL.) BERCHT. & PRESL. "Scotch Laburnum". A small, broad-headed tree producing long, drooping racemes of fragrant flowers in early June. Leaves trifoliolate, deep shining green above, paler and with a few hairs beneath. Pods flattened, glabrous and shining. C and S Europe. C 1596.

**'Pendulum'** A slow-growing form developing a low, dome-shaped head of stiffly weeping branches.

**'Pyramidale'** A form with erect branches.

**anagyroides** MEDIKUS (*L. vulgare* BERCHT. & PRESL.) "Common Laburnum". A small tree flowering in late May or early June, the drooping racemes crowded along the branches. This species differs from *L. alpinum* in its earlier flowering, shorter racemes, smaller, dull green leaves which are grey-green and densely adpressed hairy beneath and in its rounder, adpressed hairy pods. C and S Europe. C 1560.

**LABURNUM anagyroides**—*continued*

    **'Aureum'** "Golden-leaved Laburnum". Leaves soft yellow during summer; sometimes liable to revert. FCC 1875.

    **'Autumnale'** ('Semperflorens') A form which frequently flowers for a second time in the autumn.

    **'Erect'** An excellent small tree with stiffly ascending branches. Originated as a seedling in our nurseries and found by our Foreman Alf Alford in 1964.

    **'Pendulum'** A low, elegant tree with long, slender, drooping branches.

    **'Quercifolium'** A curious, small tree with leaflets deeply lobed.

  ×**watereri** (WETTST.) DIPP. (*L. alpinum* × *L. anagyroides*). A small tree with glossy leaves and long, slender racemes in June. Resembles *L. alpinum* in general habit, but leaves and pods slightly more hairy, the latter usually only partially developed.

    **'Alford's Weeping'** A vigorous, small tree with a wide-spreading head of long, drooping branches. Originated as a seedling in our nurseries and found by our Foreman Alf Alford in 1965.

    **'Vossii'** (*L.* × *vossii* HORT.) A lovely form, very free-flowering, with long racemes. AGM 1984.

**"LABURNUM, EVERGREEN"** See *Piptanthus nepalensis*.

†**LAGERSTROEMIA** L.—**Lythraceae**—A genus of some 50 species of evergreen and deciduous trees and shrubs often with exotic flowers. Natives of warm parts of Asia, the Pacific Islands and Australia.

  **indica** L. "Crape Myrtle". A beautiful, large shrub or small tree requiring more hot sun than we can anticipate in our insular climate. The main stem is attractively mottled grey, pink and cinnamon. Flowers usually lilac-pink with crinkled petals, borne in terminal panicles in autumn, only opening outside after a warm, late summer. Best planted against a south-facing wall. China, Korea. I 1759. AM 1924.

    **'Rosea'** Flowers deep rose.

**"LAUREL, ALEXANDRIAN"** See *Danae racemosa*.

**"LAUREL, CALIFORNIAN"** See *Umbellularia californica*.

**"LAUREL, COMMON"** or **"CHERRY"** See *Prunus laurocerasus*.

**"LAUREL, MOUNTAIN"** See *Kalmia latifolia*.

**"LAUREL, PORTUGAL"** See *Prunus lusitanica*.

†*****LAURELIA** JUSS.—**Atherospermataceae**—A small genus of 3 species of evergreen trees with opposite leaves, natives of Chile, Argentina and New Zealand.

  **sempervirens** (RUIZ & PAVON) TULASNE (*L. serrata* BERTERO) (*L. aromatica* JUSS. ex POIR.) "Chilean Laurel". A handsome, large evergreen shrub or small to medium-sized, lime-tolerant tree. The leathery, serrated leaves are of a bright green and are strongly aromatic. Proving remarkably hardy given reasonable shelter. Chile. I before 1868.

  **serrata** See *L. sempervirens*.

*****LAURUS** L.—**Lauraceae**—The true "Laurels" are a genus of only 2 species of dioecious, evergreen shrubs or small trees. The small, yellowish-green flowers cluster the branches in April or earlier in mild weather and are followed, on female trees, by shining black fruits. Suitable for all types of well drained soil.

  †**azorica** (SEUB.) FRANCO (*L. canariensis* WEBB & BERTH.) "Canary Island Laurel". In this country a large, evergreen shrub. A handsome species, differing from *L. nobilis* in its larger, broader leaves and its downy young twigs; leaves of older trees become narrower. Suitable only for the mildest gardens. There appear to be 2 forms in cultivation; one

**LAURUS azorica**—*continued*
with hairy leaves and another with glabrous leaves, the latter being more tender. Canary Islands, Azores.

**nobilis** L. "Bay Laurel". The "Laurel" of the ancients, now grown for its aromatic foliage and for its usefulness as a dense, pyramidal evergreen shrub or tree. Stands clipping well, and thrives in coastal regions where it will form good hedges. Subject to frost damage in cold areas. Mediterranean region. C 1562. AGM 1984.

**'Angustifolia'** ('Salicifolia') "Willow-leaf Bay". A remarkably hardy form with long narrow, pale green, leathery, wavy-edged leaves.

**'Aurea'** Leaves golden yellow, particularly attractive in winter and spring.

**"LAURUSTINUS"** See *Viburnum tinus*.

**\*LAVANDULA** L.—**Labiatae**—About 20 species of aromatic shrubs and herbs natives of the Mediterranean region, W Asia, India and NE Africa. Lavender is perhaps the most highly prized of all aromatic shrubs. It is a favourite for dwarf hedges, associating well with stonework or rose beds, and as a component of grey or blue borders. It succeeds in all types of well drained soil preferably in full sun. An excellent maritime plant.

**angustifolia** MILL. (*L. spica* L. in part) (*L. officinalis* CHAIX) "Old English Lavender". It has been pointed out by various authorities that most of the clones generally grown in gardens under this name are hybrids between *L. angustifolia* and *L. latifolia*. Both species are native of the Mediterranean region and have been cultivated since the mid 16th century. The flowers are borne in dense spikes on long slender stems. AMT 1962.

**'Alba'** A robust form with long, narrow, grey-green leaves producing erect stems from 0.9-1.2m high. Flowers white, opening in late July.

**'Folgate'** A compact form with narrow, grey-green leaves and stems from 0.6-0.75m high. Flowers lavender-blue, opening in early July. C 1933. AMT 1963.

**'Grappenhall'** A robust form with comparatively broad, grey-green leaves and strong stems from 0.9-1.2m high. Flowers lavender-blue, opening in late July.

**'Hidcote'** A compact form with narrow, grey-green leaves and stems from 0.6-0.8m high. Flowers violet in dense spikes, opening in early July. One of the best and most popular cultivars. AM 1950. FCCT 1963. AGM 1984. 'Nana Atropurpurea' is a similar, though older clone.

**'Hidcote Giant'** Similar in habit and appearance to 'Grappenhall', but flowers a little darker in colour. C 1950. AGM 1984.

**'Hidcote Pink'** Compact habit to 0.6m with grey-green leaves, similar to 'Hidcote' but flowers pale pink. C 1962.

**'Loddon Pink'** A compact form with narrow grey-green leaves and stems from 0.6-0.75m high. Flowers pale pink opening in early July. C 1950. AMT 1963.

**'Munstead'** A compact form with narrow, green leaves and stems from 0.6-0.75m high. Flowers lavender-blue, bluer than in most, opening in early July. C 1916. AMT 1963.

**'Nana Alba'** A dwarf, compact form with comparatively broad, grey-green leaves and stems up to 0.3m. Flowers white, opening in early July.

**'Rosea'** A compact form with narrow leaves, greener than those of 'Loddon Pink'. Stems 0.6-0.75m high, bearing lavender-pink flowers in early to mid July. C 1949.

**'Twickel Purple'** A compact form with comparatively broad, grey-green leaves and stems from 0.6-0.75m high. Flowers lavender-blue, opening in early July. AMT 1961. AGM 1984.

**'Vera'** A robust form with comparatively broad, grey leaves and stems from 1-1.2m high. Flowers lavender-blue, opening in late July. Usually referred to in cultivation as "Dutch Lavender". AMT 1962.

†**dentata** L. A dwarf aromatic shrub with oblong leaves, each one divided like the pinnae of a fern. The powdery-blue flowers are borne in dense, short spikes in late summer. S and E Spain, Balearic Islands. C 1597.

† **lanata** BOISS. A small white-woolly shrub producing long-stalked spikes of fragrant, bright violet flowers from July to September. Spain.

**pedunculata** See *L. stoechas* subsp. *pedunculata*.

**LAVANDULA**—*continued*

**spica** See *L. angustifolia*.

**stoechas** L. "French Lavender". A dwarf, intensely aromatic shrublet with narrow leaves. Flowers dark purple borne in dense, congested terminal heads during summer. It requires a warm, dry, sunny position. Mediterranean region, with subspecies in Turkey and N Africa. Cultivated since mid 16th century. AM 1960.

**var. albiflora** See var. *leucantha*.

**var. leucantha** LASSARAZ (var. *albiflora* BEAN) Flowers and bracts white.

**subsp. pedunculata** (MILL.) ROZEIRA Flower spikes shorter, on long peduncles. Spain, Portugal. AM 1981.

**LAVATERA** L.—**Malvaceae**—A genus of some 25 species of herbs and shrubs, natives of Europe, W Asia, Australia and California. The shrubby mallows have typical mallow flowers and palmate leaves. Succeeding in all types of soil preferably in full sun. Excellent for maritime exposure.

**bicolor** See under *L. maritima*.

†**maritima** GOUAN An elegant species attaining 1.5-1.8m against a sunny wall. Both the stems and the palmate leaves are greyish and downy. Flowers large, saucer-shaped, pale lilac with purple veins and eye, produced continuously from midsummer to late autumn. Needs a warm, sheltered position. SW Europe, N Africa. The plant described here was originally known as *L. bicolor*.

**olbia** See under *L. thuringiaca*.

**thuringiaca** L. (*L. olbia* HORT. not L.) A vigorous subshrub up to 2.5m high, the whole plant conspicuously and softly grey downy. Large, pink or reddish-pink flowers throughout summer. Best in a warm, sunny position. C and S Europe to the W Himalaya. AM 1912. The closely related *L. olbia* L., a native of SW Europe, is rarely grown.

**'Barnsley'** Flowers very pale, nearly white with a red eye. It has now been shown that this splendid form is a periclinal chimaera which originated as a sport of 'Rosea'. Any reversions should be removed. AM 1986.

**'Burgundy Wine'** Deep purplish-pink.

**'Candy Floss'** Very pale pink.

**'Ice Cool'** Flowers white.

**'Kew Rose'** More vigorous than 'Rosea' with darker, purplish stems and larger, bright pink flowers. Previously grown as *Lavatera olbia*. AM 1988.

**'Rosea'** (*L. olbia* 'Rosea') Flowers pale pink. AM 1920. AGM 1984.

**"LAVENDER"** See *Lavandula*.

**"LEATHERWOOD"** See *Cyrilla racemiflora* and *Dirca palustris*.

‡\***LEDUM** L.—**Ericaceae**—A small genus of about 4 species of low-growing, evergreen shrubs, inhabitants of swamp moors in northern latitudes. All have neat foliage, usually covered below with a white or rust coloured woolly tomentum, and terminal clusters of white flowers. They require a lime-free soil.

**buxifolium** See *Leiophyllum buxifolium*.

**glandulosum** NUTT. A useful, dwarf species, occasionally up to 1m. Leaves oblong, oval or ovate, glandular and scaly beneath; flowers in terminal clusters 2.5-5cm across in May. W North America.

**groenlandicum** OED. (*L. latifolium* JACQ.) "Labrador Tea". The best known of the genus, a dwarf, upright evergreen occasionally to 1m. Flowers white, produced from April to June in conspicuous terminal clusters. North America, Greenland. I 1763.

**'Compactum'** A compact form developing into a neat shrub 0.3-0.45m high, with broader leaves on shorter branches, and smaller flower clusters than in the typical form. AM 1980.

**latifolium** See *L. groenlandicum*.

**minus** HORT. A dwarf shrub possibly only a form of *L. palustre*. Narrow leaves and clusters of white flowers in May. NE Asia.

**LEDUM**—*continued*

**palustre** L. "Wild Rosemary". A variable species up to 1m high, closely related to *L. groenlandicum*, producing terminal clusters of white flowers in April and May. Arctic regions of Europe, Asia and America. I 1762.

**f. dilatatum** (WAHLENB.) O. FEDTSCH. A form with slightly broader leaves. Japan, Korea, E Siberia. C 1902. AM 1938.

‡*LEIOPHYLLUM** HEDWIG f.—**Ericaceae**—A monotypic genus requiring the same conditions as *Ledum* from which it differs in the small, glabrous, box-like leaves.

**buxifolium** (BERGIUS) ELL. (*Ledum buxifolium* BERGIUS) "Sand Myrtle". A dwarf shrub of neat, compact, rounded habit, producing in May and June clusters of white flowers, pink in bud. Leaves opposite and alternate. An attractive species requiring lime-free soil. E North America. I by Peter Collinson in 1736. AM 1955.

**var. hugeri** (SMALL) SCHNEID. Leaves mostly alternate, longer than in the typical form.

**var. prostratum** (LOUD) A. GRAY A very dainty, prostrate or loosely spreading, dwarf shrub. Leaves mostly opposite. AM 1945.

‡**LEITNERIA** CHAPMAN—**Leitneriaceae**—A monotypic genus and the only member of the family, most closely related to *Myrica*, *Populus* and *Salix* but very different in general appearance. It requires a moist, lime-free soil.

**floridana** CHAPMAN "Corkwood". A rare and botanically interesting medium-sized to large, suckering shrub, occasionally a small tree. Leaves narrow-elliptic to elliptic-lanceolate, 12-20cm long. Flowers small, appearing in slender greyish catkins in spring, male and female borne on separate plants. SE United States. I 1894.

**"LEMON VERBENA"** See *Aloysia triphylla*.

†**LEONOTIS** (PERS.) R. BR.—**Labiatae**—About 15 species of annuals, perennials and shrubs native to tropical and S Africa. The following is an easily grown shrub in all types of soil but only suitable for a sunny wall in very mild localities. Excellent for the conservatory.

**leonurus** (L.) R. BR. "Lion's Ear". A small, square-stemmed shrub with downy, lanceolate, opposite leaves and dense axillary whorls of 5cm long, downy, bright orange-scarlet, two-lipped flowers in late autumn. S Africa. I 1712. AM 1982.

†**LEPTODERMIS** WALL.—**Rubiaceae**—About 30 species of deciduous shrubs, natives of the Himalaya and E Asia. The following are interesting and subtly attractive small to medium-sized shrubs for all soils in moderately sheltered gardens.

**kumaonensis** PARKER An uncommon small shrub with downy leaves. Flowers small, trumpet-shaped, white becoming lilac or purplish, borne in clusters in the leaf axils from July to October. NW Himalaya. I 1923.

**pilosa** DIELS (*Hamiltonia pilosa* FRANCH.) A medium-sized shrub with smaller leaves than *L. kumaonensis*. Flowers lavender, produced from July to September. Yunnan. I 1904 by George Forrest.

*LEPTOSPERMUM** FORST. & FORST. f.—**Myrtaceae**—A genus of some 30 species of attractive, small-leaved, evergreen shrubs or small trees mainly natives of Australia, a few found in New Zealand, New Caledonia and Malaysia. They are related to the myrtles and of about equal merit to the tree heaths. In warm maritime and mild localities many form large shrubs up to 4.6m high, but elsewhere most require the protection of a wall. They succeed best in full sun in well drained acid or neutral soils. Flowers white unless otherwise stated, and borne in May and June.

**cunninghamii** See *L. lanigerum*.

**humifusum** SCHAU. (*L. rupestre* HOOK. f.) (*L. scoparium* var. *prostratum* HORT. not HOOK. f.) An extremely hardy, prostrate shrub, forming an extensive carpet of reddish stems and small, blunt, leathery leaves which turn bronze-purple in very cold weather. Small, white flowers stud the branches of mature specimens in early summer. A splendid specimen in

**LEPTOSPERMUM humifusum**—*continued*

the Hillier Gardens and Arboretum has reached 1m tall and 5m across. Tasmania. Introduced by H. Comber in 1930.

†**laevigatum** F. MUELL. A vigorous species with comparatively large, glossy, glabrous leaves and flowers 2cm across. Australia, Tasmania. AM 1927.

**lanigerum** (AIT.) SMITH (*L. pubescens* LAM.) (*L. cunninghamii* SCHAU.) A beautiful medium-sized shrub with long, silvery leaves, often bronzed towards autumn, flowering in early summer. In the southern counties there are bushes which have grown splendidly in open borders for more than twenty years. Australia, Tasmania. I 1774. AGM 1984.

'**Silver Sheen**' A selection from the plants previously grown as *L. cunninghamii*. Attractive silvery-grey leaves and reddish stems. Flowering in July, several weeks later than those of typical *L. lanigerum*. Exceptionally hardy.

**liversidgei** R.T. BAKER & H.G. SMITH An Australian species with numerous small, crowded leaves, lemon-scented when crushed. Flowers white in graceful sprays. One of the hardier species which has here survived many winters in the open.

†**rodwayanum** SUMMERHAYES & COMBER Tasmanian species bearing flowers as much as 3cm across, the largest of the genus, borne in late summer. Introduced by Harold Comber in 1930.

†**scoparium** FORST. & FORST. f. The common "Manuka" or "Tea-tree" of New Zealand. A variable species which has given rise to numerous forms. Flowers white. Australia, Tasmania, New Zealand. I 1772. AM 1972.

'**Album Flore Pleno**' Flowers white, double; habit compact and erect. C 1926.

'**Boscawenii**' Flowers up to 2.5cm across, rich pink in bud opening white with reddish centre. Compact habit. Raised in 1909. AM 1912.

'**Chapmanii**' Leaves brownish green, flowers bright rose. Found as a seedling near Dunedin, New Zealand in 1890.

'**Decumbens**' A semi-prostrate form, with pale pink, long-lasting flowers, freely produced.

'**Keatleyi**' An outstanding cultivar with large, waxy-petalled flowers of a soft pink. Young shoots and leaves crimson and silky. Found in the wild in New Zealand by Captain Keatley before 1926. AM 1961. AGM 1984.

'**Kiwi**' A dwarf form of dense habit with freely produced deep pink flowers and bronze foliage. A seedling of 'Nanum' raised in New Zealand.

'**Nanum**' A charming, dwarf form, attaining about 0.3m; rose-pink flowers produced with great freedom. An excellent alpine-house shrub. Raised in New Zealand before 1940. AM 1952.

'**Nichollsii**' Flowers carmine-red; foliage dark purplish-bronze. Seed raised from a plant found in New Zealand in 1898 and brought into cultivation there by William Nicholls in 1904. FCC 1912. AM 1953.

'**Nichollsii Grandiflorum**' A selected form of 'Nichollsii' with larger flowers.

**var. prostratum** See *L. humifusum*.

'**Red Damask**' Very double, deep red, long-lasting flowers. An $F_2$ hybrid from a cross between 'Nichollsii' and a double pink flowered plant. Raised in California in 1944. AM 1955. AGM 1984.

'**Roseum Multipetalum**' Double, rose-pink flowers in profusion. AM 1928.

**sericeum** LABILL. A moderately hardy Tasmanian shrub of medium height. Leaves small, bright green, pointed; flowers white; young stems red.

**stellatum** CAV. A medium-sized shrub; leaves bright green; only injured by the severest weather. Australia.

**LESPEDEZA** MICHX.—**Leguminosae**—The "Bush Clovers" contain about 40 species of herbs and shrubs, natives of North America, E Asia and Australia. The cultivated species of this extensive genus are very useful, late flowering shrubs, their racemes of small, pea-flowers being borne profusely and continuously along the shoots which are bowed by their weight. All have trifoliolate leaves and given full sun are of the easiest cultivation.

**bicolor** TURCZ. A medium-sized shrub of semi-erect habit. The bright rose-purple flowers are borne in racemose inflorescences in late summer. Korea, Manchuria, China, Japan. Introduced by Maximowicz in 1856.

**LESPEDEZA bicolor**—*continued*

**'Yakushima'** A low-growing, almost prostrate form with short, upright shoots to about 20cm tall and very small leaves and flowers.

**buergeri** MIQ. A medium-sized shrub of spreading habit. Flowers purple and white in dense racemes. Japan, China.

**cyrtobotrya** MIQ. A small shrub throwing up erect, woody stems annually. In late summer rose-purple pea-flowers crowd the ends of each shoot. Japan, Korea. I 1899.

**kiusiana** NAKAI Of uncertain identity, but a distinct and very attractive small shrub with soft green, clover-like leaves, and light rose-purple flowers in large compound leafy panicles.

**thunbergii** (DC.) NAKAI (*L. sieboldii* MIQ.) (*Desmodium penduliflorum* OUDEMANS) One of the best autumn-flowering shrubs. The arching 1.2-1.5m stems are bowed to the ground in September by the weight of the huge terminal panicles of rose-purple pea-flowers. Japan, China. I about 1837. FCC 1871. FCC 1987.

‡***LEUCOPOGON** R. BR.—**Epacridaceae**—A large genus of about 150 species of evergreen shrubs and trees natives mainly of Australia and New Zealand with a few species in Malaysia and the Pacific Islands. They require the same conditions as *Erica*.

**fraseri** A. CUNN. A dwarf, New Zealand shrublet related to *Cyathodes* and requiring similar treatment. The decumbent branchlets are clothed with close-set, imbricated, shining green leaves. Flowers small, white or lavender, tubular, fruits orange-yellow. C 1911.

‡**LEUCOTHOE** D. DON—**Ericaceae**—An attractive and useful genus of shade-bearing shrubs for lime-free soils. They are natives of North America and Japan.

**catesbaei** See *L. fontanesiana*.

*__davisiae__ TORR. (*Andromeda davisiae* SCHNEID.) A pretty shrub, usually less than 1m high, with dark green, glossy leaves and erect panicles of pure white flowers in June. California. Introduced by William Lobb in 1853. FCC 1883.

*__fontanesiana__ SLEUM. (*L. catesbaei* HORT. not (WALT.) A. GRAY) A small to medium-sized shrub of elegant habit. An excellent ground cover for acid soils. The graceful arching stems carry lanceolate, leathery, green leaves which, in autumn and winter, especially in exposed positions, become tinged a rich beetroot-red or bronze-purple. The short, pendent racemes of white, pitcher-shaped flowers, appear all along the stems in May. SE United States. I 1793. AM 1972. For many years this plant has been grown as *L. catesbaei* which name rightly belongs to another, closely related, species (*L. axillaris*).

**'Nana'** A lower growing, more compact form.

**'Rainbow'** Leaves variegated with cream, yellow and pink. This plant arose as a seedling in our Chandler's Ford nursery. The American-raised 'Girard's Rainbow' is the same or very similar.

**'Rollissonii'** A selection with narrower leaves. AM 1981.

**grayana** MAXIM. A remarkable, small semi-evergreen shrub with stout, green, ascending stems becoming an attractive, deep polished red in winter, and large, broadly oval leaves usually turning bronze-yellow tinted purple in autumn. Flowers pale green, produced in July and August in ascending one-sided racemes. Japan. I 1890.

**var. oblongifolia** (MIQ.) OHWI A slightly dwarfer variety of stiffer, more upright habit; stems dark polished reddish-purple in winter. Leaves markedly oblong, smaller and darker than those of the typical form, turning to yellow and flame in the autumn. Japan.

*__keiskei__ MIQ. A small, glabrous, evergreen shrub with arching red-tinged shoots. Leaves ovate to ovate-elliptic, slender pointed, glossy green above, and 5-10cm long. The comparatively large, cylindrical, white flowers are borne in nodding, terminal and axillary racemes in July. Japan. I 1915 by Ernest Wilson. AM 1933.

**populifolia** See *Agarista populifolia*.

**racemosa** (L.) A. GRAY "Fetter-bush". A small to medium-sized, deciduous or semi-evergreen shrub with narrow elliptic to ovate leaves. White urn-shaped flowers are borne in one-sided, often curved racemes in June. SE United States.

**LEYCESTERIA** WALL.—**Caprifoliaceae**—A small genus of 6 species of hollow-stemmed shrubs, natives of the Himalaya and China. Suitable for any reasonably fertile soil.

**LEYCESTERIA**—*continued*

†**crocothyrsos** AIRY SHAW An interesting and attractive, medium-sized shrub, unfortunately suitable only for mild districts. Leaves large, slender pointed, glossy green and prominently veined. The showy yellow flowers are borne in terminal racemes in April and are followed by small, gooseberry-like, green fruits. Assam. Introduced by Kingdon-Ward in 1928. AM 1960.

**formosa** WALL. A medium-sized erect shrub with stout, hollow, sea-green shoots covered at first with a glaucous bloom. Flowers white, carried in dense, terminal, drooping panicles of claret coloured bracts, appearing from June to September. These are followed by large, shining, reddish-purple berries which are attractive to pheasants. Himalaya. I 1824.

**LIGUSTRUM** L.—**Oleaceae**—The "Privets" consist of some 50 species of deciduous and evergreen shrubs or trees natives of the Himalaya and E and SE Asia to Australia with one species in Europe and N Africa. They are mostly fast-growing, not particular as to soil and shade-tolerant. Many produce conspicuous flowerheads and fruits.

**acutissimum** KOEHNE A Chinese shrub of medium height akin to *L. obtusifolium*. I about 1900.

**amurense** CARR. "Amur Privet". A large shrub of tough constitution. Similar in most respects to *L. ovalifolium*, but with twigs and leaves below, pubescent. N China. C 1860.

**chenaultii** HICKEL A remarkable semi-evergreen small tree or large shrub worthy of a place in every large garden. Leaves conspicuously long, lance-shaped and slender, up to 15cm long and 6cm across, sometimes with a few small teeth at the margin. Flowers white in large lilac-like panicles in late summer. SW China. I 1908 by Ducloux.

**compactum** BRANDIS (*L. yunnanense* HENRY) A striking, large, semi-evergreen shrub or small tree with glossy, bright green, lanceolate leaves up to 12.5cm long. Bears large panicles of white flowers in June and July followed by blue-black fruits. Himalaya, SW China. I 1874.

†**confusum** DECNE. A conspicuous, but rather tender, Himalayan species, forming a large shrub in mild districts. Flowers white, very freely borne in wide panicles in June and July. The clusters of bloomy black fruits are very striking. I 1919.

\***delavayanum** HARIOT (*L. ionandrum* DIELS) (*L. prattii* KOEHNE) A rather variable, small-leaved, evergreen, spreading shrub of medium size. Flowers in dense panicles, white with violet anthers, fruits black. A good hedging plant but not for the colder counties. Yunnan. I 1890 by the Abbé Delavay.

\***henryi** HEMSL. A medium-sized to large shrub of compact growth. Leaves small, roundish, dark almost black-green and glossy. Flowers in August. C China. I 1901 by Ernest Wilson. AM 1910.

**ibota** SIEB. & ZUCC. Small to medium-sized shrub of spreading habit, similar to but more elegant than *L. ovalifolium*. Japan. I 1860.

**ionandrum** See *L. delavayanum*.

\***japonicum** THUNB. "Japanese Privet". A compact, medium-sized, very dense evergreen shrub with camellia-like foliage, of a shining olive-green. Bears large panicles of white flowers in late summer. An excellent evergreen for screening or hedging. N China, Korea, Taiwan, Japan. Introduced by Siebold in 1845. AGM 1984.

'**Macrophyllum**' A splendid form with broad, glossy, black-green, camellia-like leaves. Sometimes wrongly referred to as a form of *L. lucidum*. An outstanding evergreen.

'**Rotundifolium**' ('Coriaceum') A very slow-growing, rigid, compact form with round, leathery, black-green leaves. Introduced from cultivation in Japan by Robert Fortune in 1860.

\***lucidum** AIT. f. A large, evergreen shrub or small to medium-sized tree with large, glossy green, long pointed leaves and large, handsome panicles of white flowers in autumn. Occasionally seen as a beautiful, symmetrical tree up to 12m or more high with an attractive fluted trunk. A worthy street tree for restricted areas. China. I 1794. AM 1965. AGM 1984.

'**Excelsum Superbum**' A very striking, variegated form, the leaves being bright green marked with pale green, edged with yellow or greenish yellow. AGM 1984.

'**Latifolium**' A conspicuous form with large, camellia-like leaves.

**LIGUSTRUM lucidum**—*continued*

**'Tricolor'** Leaves rather narrow, deep green, prominently marked with grey-green, edged with pale creamy-yellow or nearly white, tinged pink when young. It has reached 9m on the site of our West Hill nursery (1990). C 1895.

**obtusifolium** SIEB. & ZUCC. A vigorous, medium-sized to large deciduous shrub with dark green, elliptic-obovate leaves often purplish in autumn. Profuse flowers in nodding panicles are borne in July followed by blue-black fruits bloomy at first. Japan. I 1860.

**var. regelianum** REHD. A low-growing form with horizontally spreading branches. White flowers in terminal, nodding clusters, very freely produced in July; leaves rose-madder in autumn persisting for several weeks. C 1885.

**\*ovalifolium** HASSK. "Oval-leaf Privet". The ubiquitous "Privet" is one of the commonest of cultivated shrubs, much used for hedging, but when unpruned will reach a large size. It tolerates most soils and aspects, only losing its leaves in cold districts. Useful for game coverts. Japan. C 1885.

**'Argenteum'** Leaves with creamy-white margin.

**'Aureum'** "Golden Privet". A brightly coloured shrub with rich yellow, green-centred leaves, often completely yellow. C 1862. AM 1977. AGM 1984.

**pekinensis** See *Syringa pekinensis*.

**quihoui** CARR. A medium-sized shrub of elegant habit. Florally, this Chinese species is one of the best of the genus, producing, in August and September, panicles up to 0.5m long. China. I about 1862. AM 1980. AGM 1984.

**sempervirens** See *Parasyringa sempervirens*.

**sinense** LOUR. This free-flowering, Chinese species is perhaps the most floriferous of deciduous privets. A large shrub of spreading habit with downy stems; leaves oval; flowers white, produced in long, dense sprays in July, followed by equally numerous black-purple fruits. I about 1852 by Robert Fortune.

**'Pendulum'** A medium-sized to large shrub with pendulous branches.

**'Variegatum'** An attractive form. The soft grey-green, white-margined leaves combining with the sprays of white flowers will lighten the dullest corner.

**\*strongylophyllum** HEMSL. Large shrub or small tree with small, rounded or ovate-lanceolate leaves and loose panicles of white flowers in late summer. C China. I 1879 by Charles Maries.

**tschonoskii** DECNE. (*L. acuminatum* KOEHNE) Medium-sized shrub of upright habit with large, slender-pointed leaves. Flowers white in June followed by lustrous black fruits. Japan. I 1888.

**'Vicaryi'** Medium-sized semi-evergreen shrub with leaves suffused golden yellow turning bronze-purple in winter. Said to be a hybrid between *L. ovalifolium* 'Aureum' and *L. vulgare*. Garden origin. C about 1920.

**vulgare** L. The partially evergreen "Common Privet" is a familiar native of our hedgerows and woodlands particularly in chalk areas. Leaves lanceolate, dark green. Its long clusters of shining black fruits are conspicuous during autumn. Europe, N Africa, SW Asia.

**'Aureum'** A form with dull yellow leaves. C 1884.

**'Chlorocarpum'** Mature fruits yellowish-green.

**'Glaucum'** Leaves a metallic blue-green. C 1838.

**'Insulense'** Leaves longer; inflorescences and fruits larger. C 1883.

**var. italicum** (MILL.) VAHL ('Sempervirens') (*L. vulgare* var. *sempervirens* LOUD.) Leaves almost evergreen.

**'Pyramidale'** ('Fastigiatum') A form of dense habit with erect branches. C 1893.

**'Sempervirens'** See var. *italicum*.

**'Xanthocarpum'** A form with yellow fruits. C 1811.

**yunnanense** See *L. compactum*.

**"LILAC"** See *Syringa*.

**"LIME"** See *Tilia*.

**‡LINDERA** THUNB.—**Lauraceae**—A genus of about 80 species of deciduous and evergreen aromatic trees and shrubs related to the bay (*Laurus nobilis*), requiring lime-free soil.

**LINDERA**—*continued*

Natives mainly of S and E Asia with 2 species in E North America. Flowers unisexual, small but sometimes conspicuous in the mass. Grown primarily for their attractive, variably shaped leaves which in the deciduous species give rich autumn tints. Fruit a berry.

**benzoin** (L.) BLUME (*Benzoin aestivale* NEES) "Spice Bush". A medium-sized to large shrub with large obovate leaves turning clear yellow in the fall. The small, greenish-yellow flowers in spring are followed, on female plants, by red berries. SE United States. I 1683.

**cercidifolia** See *L. obtusiloba* and *L. praetermissa*.

**glauca** (SIEB. & ZUCC.) BLUME A large shrub with narrow-elliptic leaves, glaucous beneath and turning to purple, orange and red in November. In China this and several other species are used in the manufacture of incense-sticks (joss-sticks). Japan, China, Korea, Taiwan.

**\*megaphylla** HEMSL. A large, handsome, evergreen shrub or small tree recalling *Daphniphyllum*. Leaves up to 22cm long by 6.5cm wide, dark, shining green above, glaucous beneath. Flowers dioecious, the females producing plum-like fruits. Proving remarkably hardy in the Hillier Gardens and Arboretum where a specimen has reached 9.5m (1990). S China, Taiwan. I 1900 by Ernest Wilson.

**obtusiloba** BLUME (*L. cercidifolia* HEMSL.) A magnificent, medium-sized to large shrub of erect or compact habit. The large, three-nerved, broadly ovate to obovate leaves are entire or three-lobed at the tip, turning in autumn from their bright summer green to a glorious butter-yellow, with rich pink tints. The flowers, in early spring, are the colour of newly-made mustard. Japan, China, Korea. I 1880. AM 1952 (as *L. triloba*).

**praecox** (SIEB. & ZUCC.) BLUME (*Parabenzoin praecox* (SIEB. & ZUCC.) NAKAI) A large shrub or small tree of upright habit. Leaves light green turning glorious yellow in autumn. The greenish-yellow flowers occur in short-stalked clusters along the bare twigs in March or early April. Japan. I 1891.

**praetermissa** GRIERSON & LONG (*L. cercidifolia* HORT. not HEMSL.) A large shrub or small tree with ovate or rounded, entire leaves bronze when young. Flowers sulphur-yellow, in clusters on the leafless stems in March. Berries red. Leaves turn yellow in autumn. Assam, SE Tibet, Upper Burma, Yunnan. I by George Forrest.

†**rubronervia** GAMBLE A handsome, medium-sized shrub with oblong-elliptic leaves which are shining green above, paler or glaucous below, turning orange and red in late autumn. SW China.

**umbellata** THUNB. A semi-erect-growing, medium-sized shrub with slender branches and elliptic to obovate, thin-textured leaves 6.5-14cm long, glaucescent beneath. Flowers appearing with the leaves, yellow, in short umbels. Yellow is the dominant autumn colour. Japan, C and W China. I 1892.

**"LING"** See *Calluna vulgaris*.

‡**\*LINNAEA** L.—**Caprifoliaceae**—A monotypic genus named in honour of Linnaeus. It requires a peaty woodland soil.

**borealis** L. "Twinflower". A charming little shrublet, its slender stems carpeting the ground, in moist acid soils forming extensive colonies. The small, delicate, nodding, pinkish, bell-like flowers are carried in pairs on thread-like stems from June to early August. A large patch in full flower in a Scottish woodland, a slight breeze wafting through the pink bells is an unforgettable sight. Throughout the N hemisphere (incl British Isles). C 1762.

**LINUM** L.—**Linaceae**—About 200 species of annual and perennial herbs and small shrubs native mainly of S Europe and W Asia but widely distributed throughout temperate and tropical regions. Attractive plants many of which are suitable for the rock garden. The following require full sun and good drainage.

**\*arboreum** L. "Tree Flax". Dwarf, spreading shrub with narrow, glaucous leaves. Flowers golden yellow, in loose terminal clusters during summer. E Mediterranean region. C 1788. AGM 1984.

**campanulatum** L. A dwarf shrub with erect stems and glaucous, slender pointed leaves. Flowers yellow in terminal corymbs during summer. S Europe. C 1795. FCC 1871.

**LIPPIA citriodora** See *Aloysia triphylla*.

‡**LIQUIDAMBAR** L.—**Hamamelidaceae**—A small genus of 4 species of deciduous trees with maple-like, alternate leaves, which usually colour well in autumn. Not suitable for shallow chalky soil. The leaves of juvenile and adult trees are sometimes variable.

**formosana** HANCE A beautiful tree surviving, uninjured, all but our severest winters. The leaves are attractively red-tinted in spring and again in autumn. Differing from *L. styraciflua* in its duller, green, three to five-lobed leaves which are hairy beneath, and its normally hairy shoots. S China, Taiwan. I 1884.

**Monticola group** (var. *monticola* REHD. & WILS.) This Chinese form, discovered by E.H. Wilson, is perfectly hardy. It has remarkably large, normally three-lobed, glabrous leaves which colour richly in autumn. I 1908. AM 1958.

**orientalis** MILL. A slow-growing, large bush or small bushy tree. Leaves small, glabrous, deeply five-lobed, attractively tinted in autumn. In warmer, drier climates it attains large tree size. Asia Minor. I about 1750.

**styraciflua** L. A beautiful, large tree, conspicuous at all times, especially in autumn when, if happily placed, the deeply five to seven-lobed, shining green, maple-like leaves assume their gorgeous crimson colouring. In winter, the corky bark of the older twigs is often a feature. It is occasionally confused with the maples (*Acer*), but its alternate leaves easily identify it. Autumn colour is variable on seed-raised plants. E United States. I in the 17th century. AM 1952. FCCT 1975. AGM 1984.

**'Aurea'** See 'Variegata'.

**'Golden Treasure'** Leaves with a conspicuous deep yellow margin turning reddish-purple edged yellow in autumn. Slow growing.

**'Gum Ball'** A remarkable form of dense, shrubby habit with long persistent leaves turning orange-red and purple in winter. Colours best in an open position. It was found in Tennessee.

**'Lane Roberts'** A selected clone and one of the most reliable for its autumn colour which is a rich black crimson-red. Bark comparatively smooth. AGM 1984.

**'Moonbeam'** Leaves pale creamy-yellow, eventually green turning red, yellow and purple in autumn.

**'Silver King'** Leaves attractively margined creamy-white, flushed rose in late summer and autumn. Previously listed as 'Variegata'.

**'Variegata'** Leaves striped and mottled yellow. Previously listed as 'Aurea'. See also 'Silver King'.

**'Worplesdon'** Leaves with long, narrow lobes, orange and yellow in autumn. AGM 1984. AM 1987.

**LIRIODENDRON** L.—**Magnoliaceae**—The North American "Tulip Tree" was considered monotypic until, at the beginning of this century, a second and very similar species was discovered in China. Fast-growing trees succeeding in all types of fertile soil, they are made conspicuous by their curiously shaped, fore-shortened, three-lobed leaves, which turn clear yellow in autumn. Hybrids between the 2 species are also in cultivation from a cross made in the United States in 1970.

**chinense** (HEMSL.) SARG. A rare tree of medium size, similar to *L. tulipifera*, but leaves more glaucous beneath and narrower waisted. Flowers smaller, green without, green with yellowish veins within. China, N Vietnam. Introduced by Wilson in 1901. AM 1980.

**tulipifera** L. "Tulip Tree". A beautiful, large tree characterised by its distinctive, oddly shaped leaves which turn a rich butter-yellow in autumn. The peculiar flowers, appearing in June and July, are tulip-shaped, yellow-green banded with orange at the base of the petals but are not produced on young trees. E North America. C 1688. AM 1970. AGM 1984.

**'Aureomarginatum'** A striking tree, the leaves bordered with bright yellow, turning greenish-yellow by late summer. C 1903. AM 1974. AGM 1984.

**'Cortortum'** A form with somewhat contorted, undulating leaves.

**'Fastigiatum'** ('Pyramidale') An erect tree of broadly columnar habit. A magnificent medium-sized tree where height is required and space confined.

**'Integrifolium'** An unusual form, the leaves without side lobes. C 1864.

‡*LITHOCARPUS BLUME—**Fagaceae**—A large genus of nearly 300 species of evergreen trees and shrubs, all but one native of E and S Asia. Differing from *Quercus* in the erect male spikes. They require a lime-free soil.

†**densiflorus** (HOOK. & ARN.) REHD. (*Quercus densiflora* HOOK. & ARN.) "Tanbark Oak". A small, evergreen tree native of California and Oregon. The shoots and the sharply-toothed, oblong, leathery leaves are covered with milk-white down when young, the leaves becoming dark shining green above and whitish or tawny downy below, finally glabrous. The bark of this tree is a source of tannin. Only for the most sheltered gardens in the south and west. I 1874.

**var. echinoides** (R. BR.) ABRAMS (*Quercus echinoides* R. BR.) "Dwarf Tanbark". A small to medium-sized, comparatively hardy shrub of open habit with glabrous, greyish-brown twigs. Leaves leathery, entire, ovate-elliptic to oblong-elliptic, 1.25-4cm in length, green above, paler below, petioles yellow. California, Oregon.

**edulis** (MAK.) NAKAI (*Quercus edulis* MAK.) (*Pasania edulis* MAK.) A small bushy tree or large shrub with glabrous young shoots. Leaves glabrous, leathery, tapered at both ends, yellowish-green above, scaly when young. Proving hardy and free-fruiting given reasonable shelter. Japan. I early 19th century.

**henryi** (SEEM.) REHD. & WILS. (*Quercus henryi* SEEM.) An outstanding, small, evergreen tree with very long, lanceolate, slender-pointed leaves. Fruits when produced, in dense heads. This remarkable evergreen has grown slowly but successfully here for the past forty years. C China. I 1901 by Ernest Wilson.

†**pachyphyllus** (KURZ) REHD. (*Quercus pachyphylla* KURZ) A small tree with a low, spreading head of branches. Leaves elliptic to elliptic-lanceolate 10-20cm long, abruptly acuminate, dark glossy green above, pale metallic silvery-green beneath. A rare species only suitable for the milder counties. A fine tree at Caerhays, Cornwall, produces shillalah-like clusters of strangely contorted fruits which appear to be infertile. E Himalaya, W China.

*LITHODORA GRISEB. (*Lithospermum* L. in part)—**Boraginaceae**—A genus of 7 species of dwarf shrubs, natives of Europe and SW Asia. The following are delightful, low-growing, blue-flowered plants particularly when associated with the rock garden. With the exception of *L. diffusa* all are lime-tolerant.

‡**diffusa** (LAG.) I.M. JOHNST. (*Lithospermum diffusum* LAG.) (*Lithospermum prostratum* LOISEL.) A prostrate shrub, forming large mats covered with lovely blue flowers in late spring and early summer. Not recommended for shallow chalky soils. SW Europe. I 1825.

**'Alba'** Flowers white.

**'Grace Ward'** A form with larger flowers. AM 1938. AGM 1984.

**'Heavenly Blue'** The most common form in general cultivation. The name is self-explanatory. AM 1909.

**oleifolia** (LAPEYR.) GRISEB. (*Lithospermum oleifolium* LAPEYR.) A choice and rare, evergreen, semi-prostrate shrub for sheltered rock garden or alpine-house; beautiful, azure-blue, bell-shaped flowers from June to September. Spain (E Pyrenees). I about 1900. AM 1938. AGM 1984.

†**rosmarinifolia** (TENORE) I.M. JOHNST. (*Lithospermum rosmarinifolium* TENORE) A lovely dwarf, erect, rosemary-like shrub with narrow leaves and bright blue flowers, during winter and early spring. A rock garden shrub for the milder counties, otherwise an excellent plant for the alpine-house. S Italy, Sicily.

**LITHOSPERMUM** See *Lithodora*.
**petraeum** See *Moltkia petraea*.

**LITSEA glauca** See *Neolitsea sericea*.

**"LOBSTER'S CLAW"** See *Clianthus puniceus*.

244

‡***LOISELEURIA** DESV.—**Ericaceae**—A monotypic genus related to *Rhododendron*.

    **procumbens** (L.) DESV. (*Azalea procumbens* L.) "Mountain Azalea". A charming, prostrate, native shrub, forming large mats or low mounds of procumbent stems and tiny leaves, studded in May with clusters of small, pink flowers. Requires moist, peaty conditions, best in full exposure. Alpine and arctic regions of the northern hemisphere (incl Scotland). C 1800.

‡***LOMATIA** R. BR.—**Proteaceae**—A small genus about 12 species of striking Australian and S American evergreen trees and shrubs. Attractive both in foliage and flower, they should be better known and more widely planted. Whilst hardy or near hardy in all but the coolest areas they cannot be recommended for shallow, chalky soils and succeed best in partial shade. A splendid group of plants for the flower arranger though some are a little too slow in growth for cutting.

    †**dentata** (RUIZ & PAVON) R. BR. A medium-sized to large shrub in cultivation with elliptic to obovate, holly-like leaves, coarsely-toothed except at the base, shining dark green above, pale green or glaucescent beneath. Flowers greenish-white. Chile, Argentina. Introduced by Harold Comber. Reintroduced in 1963.

    †**ferruginea** (CAV.) R. BR. A magnificent foliage plant. A large shrub or small, erect tree with large, deep green, much divided, fern-like leaves and red-brown, velvety stems. Flowers buff and scarlet in short racemes. Hardy only in mild localities. Chile, Argentina. I about 1846 by William Lobb. AM 1927.

    **hirsuta** (LAM.) DIELS (*L. obliqua* (RUIZ & PAVON) R. BR.) A little-known Chilean species, here proving hardy in a sheltered woodland. It is a remarkable, large shrub, with rather large, leathery, broadly and obliquely ovate leaves. The cream flowers are borne in May. W South America. I 1902 by H.J. Elwes. AM 1956.

    **longifolia** See *L. myricoides*.

    **myricoides** (GAERTN.) DOMIN (*L. longifolia* R. BR.) This species has proved hardy and long-lived here, making a well-furnished, wide-spreading shrub 1.8-2.4m high. Leaves long and narrow, distantly-toothed. Flowers white, grevillea-like, very fragrant, borne freely in July. An excellent evergreen for the flower arranger. SE Australia. I 1816. AM 1955.

    **obliqua** See *L. hirsuta*.

    **silaifolia** (SM.) R. BR. A small, wide-spreading shrub with ascending stems, finely divided leaves and large panicles of creamy-white flowers in July. Leaves less finely divided than those of the very similar *L. tinctoria*. Both species have lived outside here for many years. E Australia. I 1792.

    **tinctoria** (LABILL.) R. BR. Small, suckering shrub forming in time a dense thicket. Leaves pinnate or double pinnate with long, narrow segments. Flowers sulphur-yellow in bud changing to creamy-white, in long spreading racemes at the ends of the shoots. Tasmania. I 1822. AM 1948.

**"LOMBARDY POPLAR"** See *Populus nigra* 'Italica'.

**"LONDON PLANE"** See *Platanus* × *hispanica*.

**LONICERA** L.—**Caprifoliaceae**—A genus of some 180 species of deciduous and evergreen shrubs and climbers widely distributed in the northern hemisphere, mainly in temperate regions. The shrubby honeysuckles are very different in appearance from the climbing species to which their colloquial name properly belongs. Their flowers are borne in pairs normally on slender peduncles and are followed by partially or completely fused berries. All are of easy cultivation in any ordinary soil. Thin out and cut back immediately after flowering, old flowering shoots to within a few centimetres of the old wood. For climbing species see CLIMBERS at end of Manual.

    **albertii** REG. (*L. spinosa* var. *albertii* (REG.) REHD.) A low-growing shrub of spreading habit attaining 0.9-1.2m with slender, arching branches. Leaves linear, glaucous; flowers relatively large and showy, fragrant, lilac-pink in May. Berries purplish-red. Turkestan. I about 1880.

**LONICERA**—*continued*

**alpigena** L. Erect, medium-sized shrub of dense habit. Leaves oval, oblong or obovate, 5-10cm long, half as wide. Flowers in pairs, yellow, tinged red, produced in May. Berries red, drooping, cherry-like. C Europe. C since the 16th century.

×**amoena** ZAB. (*L. korolkowii* × *L. tatarica*). A vigorous floriferous shrub with grey-green leaves.

    **'Rosea'** An attractive, medium-sized shrub producing an abundance of fragrant, pink flowers in May and June. Garden origin before 1895.

**angustifolia** WALL. An elegant, narrow leaved, Himalayan species of medium size. The small, fragrant, pale pink flowers produced in April and May are followed by red, edible berries. I about 1849 by Sir Joseph Hooker.

**caerulea** L. A variable species, typically a stiff, compact shrub attaining about 1.5m with orbicular-ovate, sea-green leaves, yellowish-white flowers and conspicuous, dark blue berries. N and C Europe, N Asia, Japan. Long cultivated.

**chaetocarpa** (BATAL. ex REHD.) REHD. A pretty, erect-growing shrub 1.8-2.1m in height with bristly stems and leaves. Flowers primrose-yellow, comparatively large, subtended by 2 large, conspicuous bracts; May and June. Berries bright red. A shrub of quality and interest for every well-stocked garden. W China. I 1904 by Ernest Wilson.

**chrysantha** TURCZ. A tall, hardy shrub up to 3.7m, blooming in May and June; flowers cream, becoming yellow. Berries coral-red. NE Asia. C 1880.

**'Clavey's Dwarf'** A small shrub of dense habit up to 1m, possibly a hybrid of *L. xylosteum* and *L. tatarica*. Flowers creamy-white; berries large, translucent red. C 1955.

**discolor** LINDL. A medium-sized shrub with elliptic leaves, dark green above, glaucous beneath. Flowers yellowish-white or tinged rose. Kashmir to Afghanistan. C 1847.

**fragrantissima** LINDL. & PAXT. A partially evergreen shrub of medium size, producing its sweetly fragrant, cream-coloured flowers during late winter and spring. Red berries in May. Introduced by Robert Fortune from China in 1845 but not known in the wild.

**gracilipes** MIQ. (*L. tenuipes* NAKAI) An attractive small shrub with reddish-tinged young shoots densely covered in red-tipped glandular hairs. Leaves ovate, short-stalked and densely pilose. Flowers deep pink with conspicuous yellow anthers, borne singly or in pairs on a long, slender, glandular hairy peduncle. Fruit oblong, scarlet, glandular, hairy. Japan.

**iberica** BIEB. Densely-branched shrub up to 3m high. Flowers cream, borne on short stalks and enclosed by the cup-shaped, united bracts. Its unusual orbicular leaves make this a distinctive species. Caucasus, Persia. I 1824.

    **'Microphylla'** A looser-growing form with smaller leaves.

**involucrata** (RICHARDSON) SPRENG. A vigorous, spreading, distinct shrub of medium size, blooming in June. Flowers yellow subtended by 2 conspicuous red bracts, which persist during fruiting; berries shining black. A robust, adaptable species growing equally well in seaside gardens and industrial areas. W North America. I 1824.

    **var. ledebourii** (ESCHS.) ZAB. (*L. ledebourii* ESCHS.) Corolla orange-yellow tinged red, leaves more hairy beneath. Coastal regions of California. I 1838.

**korolkowii** STAPF A very attractive, vigorous, large shrub of graceful, arching habit, the downy shoots and pale, sea-green, downy leaves giving the shrub a striking grey-blue hue. Pink flowers are produced in June and are followed by red berries. Turkestan. C 1880.

    **var. zabelii** (REHD.) REHD. Leaves usually glabrous and broader than those of the typical form. See also *L. tatarica* 'Zabelii'.

**ledebourii** See *L. involucrata* var. *ledebourii*.

**ligustrina var. yunnanensis**. See under *L. nitida* 'Fertilis'.

**maackii** (RUPR.) MAXIM. A large shrub bearing fragrant, white flowers which turn yellow as they age. Berries dark red, long-lasting. Manchuria, Korea. I 1880.

    **f. podocarpa** REHD. A tall, graceful, wide-spreading shrub, attaining 3m, beautiful when bearing its white to yellow flowers, or loaded with red berries. This form is considered superior to the typical one. I 1900 by Ernest Wilson. AM 1907.

**maximowiczii** (RUPR.) MAXIM. A vigorous, upright, medium-sized shrub with reddish shoots and dark green, pointed leaves. Flowers violet-red in May-June followed by red berries. Manchuria, Korea. C 1878.

## LONICERA maximowiczii—*continued*

**var. sachalinensis** FR. SCHMIDT (*L. sachalinensis* (FR. SCHMIDT) NAKAI) A medium-sized shrub of erect habit. Flowers dark violet-purple in May and June, followed by dark purple berries. Japan, Sakhalin, N Korea, Manchuria, Ussuri. C 1917.

**microphylla** ROEM. & SCHULT. A small shrub of stiff habit with purplish young shoots and small, glaucous leaves, producing pale yellow flowers in pairs in spring, best after a hot summer, followed by bright red berries. C Asia. I 1818.

**morrowii** A. GRAY A vigorous, medium-sized shrub of spreading habit; leaves grey-green, those at the tips of the shoots purplish in late summer and autumn; flowers in early summer, creamy-white changing to yellow followed by dark red berries. Japan. I 1875.

**myrtilloides** PURPUS A small, slender-branched shrub with reddish young shoots. Leaves lanceolate, to 2.5cm long. Flowers urn-shaped with small, spreading lobes, white flushed purplish-pink, 5mm long, in May and June followed by translucent bright red fruits. E Himalaya. C 1907.

**myrtillus** HOOK. f. & THOMS. In general appearance this remarkable Himalayan species resembles a *Ledum*. A dense, rounded shrub about 1m high with small, conspicuously veined, ovate leaves glaucous beneath and small, fragrant, pitcher-shaped, creamy-white flowers produced in pairs in May. Berries orange-red. Himalaya, Afghanistan.

**nigra** L. A small to medium-sized shrub of stiff upright habit with deep purplish young shoots. Leaves ovate, short-stalked, downy beneath. The small pink flowers in May are followed by green berries which turn purplish-black. Mountains of C and S Europe. I in the 16th century.

**\*nitida** WILS. This dense-habited, small-leaved evergreen reaching a height of 1.5-1.8m, has long been used extensively for hedging, being quick in growth and responding well to clipping. W China. I 1908 by Ernest Wilson.

**'Baggesen's Gold'** A form with yellow leaves during summer, turning yellow-green in autumn. C 1967. AM 1988. AGM 1984.

**'Elegant'** A small, dense, spreading shrub with arching branches bearing small, ovate, matt green leaves. A form grown in Germany since 1935 as *L. pileata yunnanensis*. It is now regarded as a hybrid between *L. nitida* and *L. pileata*.

**'Ernest Wilson'** This, the commonest form, has been the one most extensively used for hedging and is the "nitida" of the trade. Its habit is rather spreading with arching or drooping branches and tiny, ovate leaves. Flowers and fruits poorly produced in the British Isles. AM 1911 (as *L. nitida*).

**'Fertilis'** A strong-growing clone of erect habit, with long arching branchlets and ovate or elliptic leaves. It differs from 'Ernest Wilson' in its more erect habit, larger, narrower-based leaves, fragrant flowers and rather more freely produced translucent violet fruits. It has in the past been catalogued under the names *L. pileata yunnanensis* and *L. ligustrina* var. *yunnanensis*. AM 1924.

**'Maigrün'** A small bush of dense spreading habit, the pale green young leaves in spring contrasting with the dark green older foliage.

**'Yunnan'** Similar to 'Ernest Wilson', but stouter and more erect in habit. Its leaves are also slightly larger and it rather more freely produces both flowers and fruits. It has in the past been distributed under the name *L. yunnanensis* which, correctly, applies to an unrelated species. Excellent for hedging.

**pileata** OLIV. A dwarf, semi-evergreen, horizontally-branched shrub, occasionally 1.5m high, most suitable for under-planting and ground cover particularly in shade. Leaves small, elliptic, bright green; berries in clusters, translucent violet. Very pretty in spring when the bright green young leaves appear among the dark green old leaves. China. I 1900 by Ernest Wilson. AM 1910.

**yunnanensis** See under *L. nitida* 'Fertilis'.

**× purpusii** REHD. (*L. fragrantissima × L. standishii*). A vigorous hybrid of medium size, producing its very fragrant, cream-coloured flowers in winter. AM 1971. AGM 1984.

**'Winter Beauty'** A backcross of *L. × purpusii* with *L. standishii*. A very free-flowering form raised by our Foreman Alf Alford from a cross made in 1966. Flowers when young, often from early December to early April. AGM 1984.

**pyrenaica** L. This is perhaps the choicest shrubby honeysuckle, attaining about 1m. Small, sea-green leaves and nodding, comparatively large, funnel-shaped, cream and pink

**LONICERA pyrenaica**—*continued*

flowers in May and June, followed by orange-red berries. C and E Pyrenees, Balearic Isles. Perhaps the least easy shrubby honeysuckle to propagate. I 1739. AM 1928.

**quinquelocularis** HARDW. A large shrub with oval leaves. Flowers white, changing to yellow, freely borne from the leaf axils in June and followed by translucent white berries. Himalaya, China. C 1840.

**f. translucens** (CARR.) ZAB. Leaves longer, heart-shaped at base. Flowers with distinctly gibbous corolla tube. C 1870.

**rupicola** HOOK. f. & THOMS. A low, dense, globular shrub with interlacing branches. Flowers fragrant, lilac-pink in May and June. Related to *L. syringantha*. Himalaya, Tibet, W China. C 1850.

**ruprechtiana** REG. A vigorous species forming a shapely bush of 2.4m or more. The oblong-ovate to lanceolate leaves are downy beneath; flowers in axillary pairs, white changing to yellow, May and June. NE Asia. I about 1860.

**sachalinensis** See *L. maximowiczii* var. *sachalinensis*.

**setifera** FRANCH. (Rock 13520) A rare and beautiful shrub of medium size. The erect stems are densely bristly. The tubular, sweetly scented, daphne-like white and pink flowers appear in short clusters on the naked stems during late winter and early spring, earlier in mild weather. Berries red, bristly. Himalaya, China. This species, originally introduced by Kingdon-Ward in 1924, has recently been reintroduced. AM 1980.

**spinosa var. albertii**. See *L. albertii*.

**standishii** JACQUES A charming, deciduous or semi-evergreen, medium-sized, fragrant, winter-flowering species, resembling *L. fragrantissima*, differing in its bristly stems and more elliptic hairy leaves. Flowers white tinged pink with conspicuous yellow anthers. Bears red berries in June. China. Introduced by Robert Fortune in 1845.

**var. lancifolia** REHD. A narrow-leaved form of more distinct appearance. China. I 1908 by Ernest Wilson.

**syringantha** MAXIM. A graceful, intricately-branched shrub of rounded habit 1.2-1.8m in height. Leaves small, sea-green, borne in threes on strong shoots. Flowers tubular, soft lilac, fragrant, appearing in May and June. Berries red. China, Tibet. I about 1890. AM 1984.

**tatarica** L. A vigorous, variable shrub up to 3m, producing multitudes of pink flowers in May and June. Berries red. C Asia to Russia. I 1752.

**'Alba'** A form with white flowers. C 1801.

**'Arnold Red'** Flowers rose-pink; berries larger. This cultivar originated as a seedling of 'Latifolia' in the Arnold Arboretum in 1945.

**'Hack's Red'** A first class selection with rose-pink flowers.

**f. sibirica** (PERS.) REHD. Flowers rosy-pink. AM 1947. The forms *punicea*, *pulcherrima* and *rubra* are very similar. C 1882.

**'Zabelii'** Flowers bright pink, not as deep as either 'Arnold Red' or 'Hack's Red'. This has been distributed as *L. korolkowii* var. *zabelii*.

**tenuipes** See *L. gracilipes*.

**thibetica** BUR. & FRANCH. A vigorous species up to 1.8m high, resembling *L. syringantha* in its lilac-pink, fragrant flowers, but differing in its leaves being dark glossy green above, white-tomentose beneath. Flowering in May and June. Berries red. Tibet. I 1897.

**tomentella** HOOK. f. & THOMS. An elegant, small to medium-sized shrub with small, neat leaves and tubular, white, pink-tinged flowers in June. Berries small, black with a blue bloom. Sikkim. I 1849 by Sir Joseph Hooker.

**trichosantha** BUR. & FRANCH. A medium-sized, spreading Chinese shrub. The pale yellow flowers produced in axillary pairs are followed by dark red berries. W China. I about 1908 by Ernest Wilson.

× **vilmorinii** REHD. (*L. deflexicalyx* × *L. quinquelocularis*). A floriferous small-flowered hybrid attaining 2.7m. Flowers yellow, berries pink suffused yellow, minutely speckled red. Garden origin about 1900.

**xylosteum** L. "Fly Honeysuckle". A presumed native shrub attaining about 3m; flowers yellowish-white; attractive when bearing its red berries in late summer. Europe (incl SE England), W Siberia.

**yunnanensis** See under *L. nitida* 'Yunnan'.

**LOPHOMYRTUS bullata** See *Myrtus bullata*.
**obcordata** See *Myrtus obcordata*.

**"LOQUAT"** See *Eriobotrya japonica*.

†*LOROPETALUM** R. BR. ex REICHB.—**Hamamelidaceae**—A genus of 1 or 2 species, differing from *Hamamelis* in their evergreen leaves, inferior ovary and white petals. Unsuitable for shallow chalky soils.
  **chinense** (R. BR.) OLIV. A distinct evergreen shrub attaining 1.5-2m and recalling *Sycopsis*. The white, witch-hazel-like flowers are freely produced during February and March. An interesting and attractive shrub in mild localities. China, Japan. Introduced by Charles Maries in 1880. FCC 1894.

†*LUCULIA** SWEET—**Rubiaceae**—A small genus of 5 species of very beautiful evergreen shrubs or small trees from the temperate Himalaya and SW China. They are mainly suitable as winter-flowering shrubs for the conservatory or the mildest gardens out-of-doors.
  **grandifolia** GHOSE A beautiful shrub to 2m from Bhutan, where it was discovered by Kingdon-Ward growing at an altitude of 2,500m indicating its probable greater hardiness than others of the genus. Fragrant trusses of snow-white flowers in June or July, and large, prominently veined leaves which give rich autumn colours. AM 1955.
  **gratissima** (WALL.) SWEET A semi-evergreen, free-growing shrub producing sweetly fragrant, almond-pink flowers in winter. Himalaya. I 1816. AM 1938.
  **pinceana** HOOK. A beautiful semi-evergreen plant with deliciously-scented almond-pink flowers from May to September. Leaves narrower and flowers larger than those of *L. gratissima*. Khasia Hills (Assam). I 1843. AM 1930. FCC 1935.

*LUETKEA** BONG.—**Rosaceae**—A rare monotypic genus differing from the closely related *Spiraea* in its dissected leaves.
  **pectinata** (PURSH) KUNTZE (*Spiraea pectinata* (PURSH) TORR. & A. GRAY) A dwarf, evergreen, mat-forming shrublet with tiny pectinate leaves and small racemes of white flowers in May and June. A choice little shrublet resembling a mossy saxifrage (*Saxifraga hypnoides*). Suitable for a cool moist pocket on the rock or peat garden. W North America. C 1890.

**LUPINUS** L.—**Leguminosae**—The "Lupins" are a genus of some 200 or more species of annual and perennial herbs and shrubs mainly found in W North America but also in N and S America and the Mediterranean region. The majority are herbaceous in nature, but amongst the shrubby species are several worthy garden plants.
  ***arboreus** SIMS. "Yellow Tree Lupin". A comparatively short-lived, more or less evergreen, fast-growing shrub up to 2m. Flowers normally yellow, but variable from seed and sometimes blue, delicately scented, produced in dense racemes continuously throughout summer. Thrives in full sun in a well drained position and easily naturalises in sandy soils, particularly by the sea. California. C 1793. AGM 1984.
    **'Golden Spire'** A form with deeper yellow flowers.
    **'Snow Queen'** Flowers white. AM 1899.
  **chamissonis** ESCHS. A densely-branched silvery lupin up to 1m. Ideal for "grey" borders; flowers clouded purple-blue, borne during early summer. Requires a sunny, preferably well drained position. Coastal regions of California. I about 1826.

†*LUZURIAGA** RUIZ & PAVON—**Philesiaceae**—A small genus of 2 or 3 species of half-hardy plants natives of S America and New Zealand.
  **radicans** RUIZ & PAVON A shrubby evergreen of creeping habit and but a few cm high. Leaves ovate, flowers star-shaped, glistening white, with prominent yellow anthers; summer; berries bright orange. Requires shade and moist conditions. Native of Chile and Argentina where it is often found growing on the trunks of forest trees. I before 1850.

**LYCIUM** L.—**Solanaceae**—About 100 species of often spiny, rambling shrubs widely distributed throughout the world. Excellent for maritime exposure and for fixing sandy banks. Flowers small, usually violet, followed by conspicuous berries.

**barbarum** L. (*L. halimifolium* MILL.) (*L. chinense* MILL.) (*L. europaeum* HORT. not L.) "Duke of Argyll's Tea Tree". A vigorous, medium-sized shrub with long, often spiny, scrambling, arching stems. Flowers funnel-shaped, purple, in clusters in the leaf axils from June to September followed by small, egg-shaped orange or scarlet berries. We have also grown 'Carnosum', with pink flowers. Excellent by the sea. Long cultivated, since about 1700. China; extensively naturalised in Europe and W Asia. I about 1700.

**chilense** BERT. (*L. grevilleanum* MIERS) A medium-sized, lax shrub with spineless, spreading branches, slender, almost linear, fleshy leaves and yellowish-white and purple, funnel-shaped flowers from June to August. Chile, Argentina.

**chinense** See *L. barbarum.*

**europaeum** HORT. See *L. barbarum.*

**halimifolium** See *L. barbarum.*

‡**LYONIA** NUTT.—**Ericaceae**—Attractive shrubs or occasionally small trees, closely related to *Pieris*, and requiring lime-free soil. About 35 species in E Asia, the Malay peninsula, North America, the Greater Antilles and Mexico.

**ligustrina** (L.) DC. "Male Berry". A deciduous, small to medium-sized shrub with oval or obovate leaves. Flowers pitcher-shaped, white, carried in panicles during July and August. Thrives in a moist, peaty or sandy loam. E United States. I 1748.

**var. foliosiflora** (MICHX.) FERN. An unusual variety with leafy bracts in the flower panicles. SE United States.

*****lucida** (LAM.) K. KOCH (*Andromeda lucida* LAM.) (*Pieris lucida* LAM.) REHD.) "Fetter Bush". Small to medium-sized shrub with rather lax, sharply angled stems. Leaves broadly elliptic to ovate, entire, leathery and shining dark green above. Flowers white to pink, in axillary clusters in May and June. SE United States. I 1765.

**mariana** (L.) D. DON "Stagger Bush". A small shrub somewhat resembling *Gaultheria shallon.* Stems erect, flexuous and shiny; leaves oval, dark green and leathery. Flowers white or pink-tinged, nodding, borne in axillary panicles in May or early June. E United States. I before 1736.

**ovalifolia** (WALL.) DRUDE A medium-sized to large semi-evergreen shrub widely distributed in E and SE Asia of which we have grown the following form:

**var. elliptica** (SIEB. & ZUCC.) HAND.-MAZZ. Medium-sized to large shrub with slender, reddish shoots and elliptic, slender-pointed leaves, bronze when unfolding. Flowers small, white, occurring in axillary racemes in June and July. Japan, Taiwan. I 1829.

‡†*****LYONOTHAMNUS** A. GRAY—**Rosaceae**—A monotypic genus.

**floribundus** A. GRAY "Catalina Ironwood". This species is represented in cultivation by the following form. The typical form differs in its simple, entire to toothed leaves. Santa Catalina Island (California).

**subsp. aspleniifolius** (GREENE) RAVEN A small, graceful, fast-growing evergreen tree of slender habit soon forming a remarkable slender trunk, like a miniature redwood, with attractive chestnut-brown and grey shreddy bark. Leaves fern-like, pinnate, the leaflets divided to the base into oblong lobes, glossy green above, grey hairy below. Flowers creamy-white in slender, spiraea-like panicles in early summer. Except in the milder counties needs the shelter of a warm, sunny wall. San Clemente, Santa Rosa and Santa Cruz Islands (California). I 1900.

**MAACKIA** RUPR.—**Leguminosae**—A small genus of about 8 species of very hardy, attractive, small, slow-growing deciduous trees related to *Cladrastis* but differing in the solitary, exposed leaf buds, opposite leaflets and densely packed, more or less erect racemes. They are natives of E Asia. All the species succeed in most soils including deep soil over chalk.

**MAACKIA**—*continued*

**amurensis** (RUPR. & MAXIM.) K. KOCH (*Cladrastis amurensis* RUPR. & MAXIM.) A small tree with pinnate leaves; flowers white, tinged palest slate-blue, in erect racemes, appearing in July and August, even on young plants. Manchuria. I 1864.

**var. buergeri** (MAXIM.) SCHNEID. A variety with obtuse leaflets, usually pubescent beneath. Japan. I 1892.

**chinensis** TAK. (*M. hupehensis* TAK.) A small, broad-headed tree producing downy terminal panicles of dull white pea-flowers in July and August. The dark bluish young shoots which, like the young leaves, are densely covered with silvery-silky down, are particularly outstanding in late spring. China. Introduced by Ernest Wilson in 1908.

**MACHILUS ichangensis** See *Persea ichangensis*.

**\* × MACLUDRANIA** ANDRE (*Cudrania × Maclura*)—**Moraceae**—An interesting intergeneric hybrid for a mild locality and a sunny sheltered site on any well drained, fertile soil.

**hybrida** ANDRE (*Cudrania tricuspidata × Maclura pomifera*). Small to medium-sized tree with spiny branches and long, taper-pointed leaves. The inconspicuous flowers are followed by large, orange-like fruits. Garden origin in France before 1905.

**MACLURA** NUTT.—**Moraceae**—A monotypic genus. Male and female flowers are borne in spherical clusters on separate trees. The fruit is a multiple fruit derived from many flowers.

**pomifera** (RAF.) SCHNEID. (*M. aurantiaca* NUTT.) "Osage Orange". A hardy, free-growing small to medium-sized tree with thorny branches and fleshy yellow roots. Remarkable for its large, pale yellow, orange-like fruits which are borne on mature trees. Yellow autumn leaf colour. Used as an impenetrable hedge in the United States. Any well drained soil; excellent on chalky soils. S and C United States. I 1818.

**MADDENIA** HOOK. f. & THOMS.—**Rosaceae**—A small, botanically interesting genus of 4 species of small trees and shrubs from the Himalaya and China, related to *Prunus*, but differing in the flowers having small petals similar to the calyx lobes, borne in short, dense, terminal racemes as the leaves emerge. Any fertile soil.

**hypoleuca** KOEHNE An unusual shrub or small tree, with cherry-like leaves, bronze-tinged when young, glaucous and nearly glabrous beneath, and small black fruits. The numerous exserted, yellowish stamens make an attractive feature as the flowers open in small clusters with pink-tinged sepals and petals in early spring. Desmond Clarke, in the supplement to Bean, *Trees and Shrubs Hardy in the British Isles*, attributes to our nursery the survival of this rare plant in gardens. W Hubei, China. I 1907 by Ernest Wilson.

**wilsonii** KOEHNE This differs from *M. hypoleuca* in the following respects: leaves emerging green, softly hairy beneath on the veins, young shoots densely hairy, sepals and petals green. W Sichuan, China.

**"MADRONA"** See *Arbutus menziesii*.

**MAGNOLIA** L.—**Magnoliaceae**—A genus of some 125 species of deciduous and evergreen trees and shrubs natives of the Himalaya to E and SE Asia and the New World from North America to Venezuela. The magnolias embrace the most magnificent of flowering trees hardy in the temperate regions. On the whole their cultural requirements are not difficult to provide; they need a reasonable depth of good soil, and respond to rich living, good drainage and plenty of moisture. The early flowering kinds need a sheltered site giving protection from spring frosts and cold winds; those with large leaves should be given shelter from gales, while partial shade provided by woodland or similar sites is beneficial to many species. The petals and sepals are usually similar and are collectively termed 'tepals'.

With the exception of *M. salicifolia*, the larger tree magnolias do not flower when small, and unless otherwise stated the flowers of the deciduous species appear before the leaves. The fruit-clusters of some species are colourful in autumn.

**MAGNOLIA**—*continued*

Magnolias are very tolerant of heavy clay soils and atmospheric pollution. The most lime-tolerant are *MM. acuminata, delavayi, kobus,* × *loebneri* and *wilsonii.* In 1987 our propagator, Peter Dummer, made several crosses using *M. campbellii* as the male parent. As this species flowers much earlier than most others the pollen was collected, dried and stored until required for use. Crosses were carried out using *M. cylindrica, M denudata* 'Purple Eye', *M.* × *soulangeana* 'Picture' and *M.* 'Sayonara' as female parents. The resulting seedlings all appear to be very vigorous in growth and have been distributed to several gardens including the Hillier Gardens and Arboretum.

**acuminata** L. "Cucumber Tree". A vigorous species rapidly growing into a large, spreading tree, conical when young. Flowers with the leaves (not produced on young trees) greenish, metallic-blue and yellow, in May and June. The popular name refers to the shape and colour of the young fruit-clusters. E United States, SE Canada. I 1736.

**var. cordata** See var. *subcordata.*

**var. subcordata** (SPACH) DANDY (*M. cordata* MICHX.) (*M. acuminata* var. *cordata* (MICHX.) SARG.) Usually a smaller, compact, round-headed tree or large shrub. Flowers soft canary-yellow, borne with the leaves in summer and again in early autumn, even on young plants. SE United States. I 1801.

**ashei** WEATHERBY (*M. macrophylla* subsp. *ashei* (WEATHERBY) SPONGBERG) A large shrub, in all respects a miniature *M. macrophylla*, but flowers appearing with the leaves and produced even on young specimens. Outer 3 tepals blotched with maroon at the base. It is strange that a plant of this quality growing in a country enjoying western civilisation was not recorded in cultivation until 1933. Florida.

**auriculata** See *M. fraseri.*

‡**'Betty'** (Kosar Hybrids) (*M. liliiflora* 'Nigra' × *M. stellata* 'Rosea'). A vigorous, medium-sized shrub. Flowers large, to 20cm across with up to 19 tepals, purplish-red outside, white inside.

‡**'Caerhays Belle'** (*M. sargentiana* var. *robusta* × *M. sprengeri* 'Diva'). A magnificent medium-sized tree raised at Caerhays in 1951. Very large, salmon-pink flowers with 12 broad tepals are freely borne before the leaves.

‡**campbellii** HOOK. f. & THOMS. The giant Himalayan "Pink Tulip Tree" attains its greatest dimensions in the warmer counties. The very large flowers, opening in February and continuing into March, are goblet-shaped at first, later spreading wide, like water lilies; tepals usually pink within, deep rose-pink without. Flowers are not normally produced until the tree is between twenty and thirty years old. A large tree carrying many hundreds of blooms is an unforgettable sight. When raised from seed the flowers are usually pink, but many vary between white and deep rose-purple. There is also considerable variation in the degree of hardiness, the deeper coloured forms being usually the least hardy. E Nepal, Sikkim, Bhutan, SW China. I about 1865. FCC 1903. AGM 1984 (to selected vegetatively propagated forms only).

**Alba group** (f. *alba* HORT.) Flowers white. This is the form most common in the wild and would have become the type had not the pink-flowered form been discovered first. First planted in western gardens by J.C. Williams, and now the most glorious tree when in flower in the great garden he made at Caerhays Castle, Cornwall. C 1925. FCC 1951.

**'Charles Raffill'** A vigorous hybrid between the typical form and subsp. *mollicomata*, inheriting the early flowering habit of the latter. The large flowers are deep rose-pink in bud and when expanded are rose-purple on the outside, white with a pinkish-purple marginal flush on the inside. Grown at Windsor, and one of the original seedlings raised by Charles Raffill at Kew in 1946. The same cross had also arisen many years earlier in the garden of the late Sir Charles Cave, Bart. See 'Sidbury'. AM and Cory Cup 1963. FCC 1966.

**'Darjeeling'** A superb clone with flowers of the darkest rose. Our stock was vegetatively propagated from the original tree in Darjeeling Botanic Garden, India.

**'Ethel Hillier'** A vigorous, hardy form raised in our nurseries from wild collected seed, with very large flowers; tepals white with a faint pink flush at the base on the outside.

**'Kew's Surprise'** One of Charles Raffill's seedlings, grown at Caerhays, Cornwall. The magnificent flowers are larger than those of 'Charles Raffill' and the outside of the tepals of a richer pink colouring. FCC and Cory Cup 1967.

**MAGNOLIA campbellii**—*continued*

**'Lanarth'** A striking form of subsp. *mollicomata* raised at Lanarth from seed collected by Forrest (F.25655) in 1924. Flowers very large, of cyclamen-purple with even darker stamens. FCC 1947.

**subsp. mollicomata** (W.W. SM.) JOHNSTONE (*M. mollicomata* W.W. SM.) Similar in many respects to the typical form, but hardier and more dependable in this climate, also flowering at an earlier age, sometimes within ten to fifteen years. The flowers are like large, pink to rose-purple water lilies. Differing from subsp. *campbellii* in the hairy internodes on the peduncles (those of the type being glabrous) and often more hairy leaves. SE Tibet, N Burma, Yunnan. I 1924 by George Forrest. FCC 1939.

**'Princess Margaret'** Large flowers, red-purple outside, cream inside. A seedling of *M. campbellii* Alba group from Caerhays raised in 1957 and grown at Windsor Great Park. FCC 1973.

**'Sidbury'** A medium-sized to large tree of vigorous habit, flowering earlier in life than *M. campbellii*, and equally spectacular in flower. This cross between subsp. *campbellii* and subsp. *mollicomata* was raised some years prior to 1946 at Sidbury Manor, Devon, the home of the late Sir Charles Cave, Bart. It therefore precedes those made by Charles Raffill at Kew.

**'Wakehurst'** A magnificent hybrid differing from 'Charles Raffill' in its darker coloured flowers.

**'Werrington'** A form of subsp. *mollicomata* originating from the same Forrest collection as 'Lanarth' and of similar garden merit.

‡**'Charles Coates'** (*M. sieboldii* × *M. tripetala*). (*M. coatesii* HORT.) A distinct and interesting hybrid making a large bush or small, spreading tree. Flowers fragrant, creamy-white with a conspicuous centre of reddish anthers, resembling those of *M. tripetala*, and produced with the leaves in May and June. Selected from seedlings found by Charles Coates at Kew in about 1946. AM 1973.

†*coco (LOUR.) DC. (*M. pumila* ANDRE) (*Talauma coco*) A small, evergreen or semi-evergreen shrub with smooth, net-veined leaves and nodding creamy-white, fragrant (particularly at night) flowers, produced intermittently during summer. Requires conservatory treatment except in the mildest localities. Java. I 1786.

**conspicua** See *M. denudata*.

**cordata** See *M. acuminata* var. *subcordata*.

‡**cylindrica** WILS. A very rare small tree or large shrub. The white flowers are very similar to those of *M. denudata* but more elegant, appearing on the naked stems in April. The name refers to its cylindrical fruits. We believe we were the first to introduce this species to Britain via the United States. E China. C 1936. AM 1963.

‡**dawsoniana** REHD. & WILS. A rare and magnificent species from W China, attaining a small to medium-sized tree or large shrub. Leaves nearly 15cm long, leathery, bright green above, rather glaucous beneath; flowers in spring, large, pale rose, suffused purple without, held horizontally, not produced on young trees. E Sikang, China. Introduced in 1908 by E.H. Wilson, perhaps the greatest-ever plant collector. AM 1939.

**'Chyverton'** Flowers bright crimson outside, white within with crimson anthers and styles. A seedling raised at Caerhays and planted at Chyverton in 1944. AM 1974.

‡**dealbata** ZUCC. A close relative of *M. macrophylla* and *M. ashei*, this differs in having the fruit follicles beaked and in never having the tepals blotched with maroon at the base. A native of Mexico it was collected by Sir Harold Hillier and introduced to our nursery in 1980.

†*delavayi FRANCH. With the exception of *Rhododendron sinogrande* and *Trachycarpus fortunei* and its allies, this magnificent species has probably the largest leaves of any evergreen tree or shrub grown out-of-doors in this country. A large shrub or bushy tree up to 14m, leaves sea-green, matt above, glaucous beneath. The parchment-coloured, creamy-white, slightly fragrant flowers in late summer and early autumn are 18-20cm across, but the individual blossom seldom survives for more than 2 days. Requires wall protection except in favoured localities. Does well in soils over chalk. China (Yunnan, Sichuan). Introduced by E.H. Wilson in 1899. FCC 1913.

‡**denudata** DESROUSS. (*M. conspicua* SALISB.) "Yulan" "Lily Tree". A large shrub or small rounded tree usually below 9m high. The fragrant, pure white, cup-shaped flowers open

**MAGNOLIA denudata**—*continued*

in early spring. The broad tepals are thick and fleshy. E China. I 1789. FCC 1968. AGM 1984.

**'Purple Eye'** ('Veitch's Var.') A large, wide-spreading shrub, one of the most beautiful of this aristocratic family. Flowers large, fragrant, pure white with a purple stain at the base of the inner tepals. Probably of hybrid origin. AM 1926.

‡**'Elizabeth'** (*M. acuminata* × *M. denudata*). A remarkable small conical tree raised by Eva Maria Sperbes at the Brooklyn Botanic Garden and selected in 1978. It is named after Elizabeth Scholz, then Director. The clear, pale primrose-yellow, fragrant, cup-shaped flowers open before the leaves in April or May.

‡**fraseri** WALT. (*M. auriculata* BARTR.) A rare, medium-sized tree allied to *M. macrophylla*. Leaves up to 40cm long, with 2 distinct auricles at the base, clustered at the ends of the branches. Flowers with the leaves, large, parchment-coloured, slightly fragrant, produced in May and June, and followed by attractive rose coloured fruit-clusters. Mts of SE United States. I 1786. AM 1948.

**var. pyramidata** (BARTR.) PAMP. (*M. pyramidata* BARTR.) A very rare, small tree, differing in its smaller, thinner leaves and smaller flowers in June. SE United States. C 1825.

*****'Freeman'** (*M. grandiflora* × *M. virginiana*). A large evergreen shrub or small tree of dense, columnar habit with glossy green leaves similar to but smaller than those of *M. grandiflora*, up to 20cm long and 6cm wide, thinly felted beneath. White, fragrant, globular flowers are borne in summer but rarely open fully. Raised by Oliver Freeman of the U.S. National Arboretum, Washington from a cross made in 1931.

**fuscata** See *Michelia figo*.

**glauca** See *M. virginiana*.

**globosa** HOOK. f. & THOMS. (*M. tsarongensis* W.W. SM.) A large shrub, or rarely a small tree, with rusty-felted young shoots and buds. The nodding creamy-white, rather globular, fragrant flowers are produced on stout brown-felted stalks during June. The leaves differ from those of the related *M. wilsonii* and *M. sinensis* on account of the red-brown pubescence beneath. Requires a protected site in colder areas. 2 forms of this species, Indian and Chinese, are in cultivation; the Indian form is the hardier of the two. E Himalaya to W China. I 1919 by George Forrest. AM 1931.

**var. sinensis** See *M. sinensis*.

*****grandiflora** L. One of the most magnificent evergreens, generally grown as a wall shrub, for which purpose it is admirably suited. It is, however, hardy in the open if given shelter and full sun, making a massive round-headed shrub or short-stemmed tree. Leaves leathery, glossy green above, often reddish-brown beneath, at least when young. The delightfully fragrant, creamy-white flowers are sometimes up to 25cm across, and are produced throughout summer and early autumn. Lime-tolerant if given a good depth of rich loam. SE United States. I 1734.

**'Angustifolia'** Leaves lanceolate to oblanceolate, 15-20cm long by 3.5-5cm wide, glossy green above, cinnamon pubescent beneath, becoming glabrous. Flowers typical.

**'Charles Dickens'** An American selection with broad leaves and, in the United States, large bright red fruits.

**'Edith Bogue'** A clone of American origin said to be very hardy. C 1920.

**'Exmouth'** ('Exoniensis') ('Lanceolata') A splendid clone with elliptic to elliptic-obovate leaves, polished, soft green above, reddish-brown-felted beneath, becoming glabrous. Flowers very large, and richly fragrant, appearing at an early age. C 1768. AGM 1984.

**'Ferruginea'** A form of erect, compact habit with typical flowers. Leaves elliptic-obovate, dark shining green above, richly ferruginous tomentose beneath, becoming glabrous, veins indistinct. C 1804.

**'Gallissonnière'** A particularly hardy form with very large flowers and the leaves reddish-brown beneath. I to France before 1750.

**'Goliath'** A form with shorter, broader leaves than the type, dark glossy green above; green beneath, or thinly pubescent when very young. Flowers globular, very large, produced at an early age. Selected in Guernsey before 1910. AM 1931. FCC 1951. AGM 1984.

**'Lanceolata'** See 'Exmouth'.

**MAGNOLIA grandiflora**—*continued*

**'Little Gem'** A form of American origin which makes a compact small tree of narrowly columnar habit. Flowers and leaves smaller than usual, the latter dark glossy green above with a deep brown felt beneath. Selected in 1952.

**'Samuel Sommer'** Dark glossy green leaves with a deep brown felt beneath. Huge flowers up to 35cm across borne from an early age. Very hardy and wind resistant, good for planting away from walls. C 1952.

**'Undulata'** A distinct form with typical flowers. Leaves elliptic-oblong to oblong-obovate, margins strongly undulate, distinctly veined; glossy green above and green beneath, even when young. Selected in France about 1850.

**grandiflora × virginiana** See 'Freeman' and 'Maryland'.

‡**Gresham Hybrids** In 1955 Dr Todd Gresham, a noted magnolia enthusiast of Santa Cruz, California, made a series of crosses involving *M. × veitchii* with *M. liliiflora* on the one hand and *M. × soulangeana* 'Lennei Alba' on the other. Of the hundred or so seedlings produced, 24 of each cross were selected and grown on. All proved vigorous in growth, developing into strong trees in the manner of *M. × veitchii*. We are indebted to Dr Gresham for several of his named clones including 'Peppermint Stick', 'Raspberry Ice' and 'Royal Crown', all *M. liliiflora × M. × veitchii*, and 'Crimson Stipple', 'Delicatissima', 'Rouged Albaster' and 'Sayonara', which are *M. × soulangeana* 'Lennei Alba' × *M. × veitchii*.

‡**'Heaven Scent'** (Gresham Hybrids) (*M. × veitchii × M. liliiflora* 'Nigra'). A magnificent, small to medium-sized tree. Flowers April-May, richly scented, narrowly cup-shaped, tepals pale pink, heavily flushed deep pink towards the base with a distinct magenta-pink stripe on the back.

× **highdownensis** See *M. wilsonii*.

‡**hypoleuca** SIEB. & ZUCC. (*M. obovata* THUNB.) A handsome, strong-growing, medium-sized tree with often purple-tinged young shoots, and very large, obovate leaves held in whorls at the ends of the shoots. The creamy-white, very strongly fragrant flowers, borne in May and June, are 20cm across, and have a central ring of crimson stamens; fruit-clusters attractive and large. Japan. I about 1880. FCC 1893.

‡**'Iolanthe'** (*M. × soulangeana* 'Lennei' × *M.* 'Mark Jury'). A vigorous, upright, small to medium-sized tree raised in New Zealand. Flowers large, cup-shaped, rose-pink, creamy-white inside, borne at an early age.

‡**'Jane'** (Kosar Hybrids) (*M. liliiflora* 'Reflorescens' × *M. stellata* 'Water Lily'). A medium-sized upright shrub of compact habit. Fragrant, cup-shaped flowers open from narrow, erect, red-purple buds. Tepals red-purple outside, white within.

**'Kewensis'** (*M. kobus × M. salicifolia*). A small, slender, broadly conical tree, intermediate in habit and appearance between its parents. Flowers white, fragrant, 6cm long, very freely borne in April before the leaves. Originated at Kew about 1938. AM 1952.

**kobus** DC. A very hardy Japanese small tree or large shrub which does not produce its slightly fragrant, white flowers until it has attained an age of about twelve to fifteen years, when they are regularly borne with magnificent freedom during April. Excellent for all types of soil including chalky soils. According to some authorities the correct name for this species is *M. praecocissima* KOIDZ. I 1865. AM 1942.

**var. borealis** SARG. The largest tree form of the species, chiefly renowned for taking many years to flower. AM 1948.

**var. loebneri** See *M. × loebneri*.

**var. stellata** See *M. stellata*.

× **lennei** See *M. × soulangeana* 'Lennei'.

‡**liliiflora** DESROUSS. (*M. discolor* VENTEN.) (*M. purpurea* CURTIS) A wide-spreading medium-sized shrub, occasionally to 4m, with obovate to broad elliptic leaves of a shining dark green above. Flowers erect, like slender tulips, gradually opening wide; purple flushed on the outside, creamy-white within, appearing in late April and continuing until early June, and intermittently during the summer. One of the best species for the smaller garden, thriving in all but chalky soils. C China, long cultivated in Japan. I 1790.

**'Nigra'** (*M. × soulangeana* 'Nigra') A more compact form with slightly larger flowers, deep vinous purple outside, creamy-white stained purple inside, borne freely over a long

**MAGNOLIA liliflora 'Nigra'**—*continued*
period from spring to summer. Introduced from Japan in 1861 by J.G. Veitch. AM 1907. FCC 1981. AGM 1984.

‡**liliiflora × stellata** We are grateful to the U.S. National Arboretum, Washington, for 8 named clones of the above parentage. Raised at the arboretum in 1955/56 by Dr Francis de Vos and William F. Kosar, they were said to be superior to their parents in size, colour, fragrance and abundance of flower. The original plants were described as being multiple-stemmed, rounded or conical, erect-growing and 2-3m in height. Having grown these clones we have found them to be very floriferous and while they will not replace their parents they have managed to combine the best qualities of them, inheriting the narrow tepals and profuse flowers of *M. stellata* and the colouring and long flowering period of *M. liliiflora*. The clones received are as follows:- 'Ann', 'Judy', 'Randy' and 'Ricki' (De Vos Hybrids) and 'Betty', 'Jane', 'Pinkie' and 'Susan' (Kosar Hybrids).

× **loebneri** KACHE (*M. kobus × M. stellata*). (*M. kobus* var. *loebneri* (KACHE) SPONGBERG) A variable hybrid uniting the best qualities of its 2 distinguished parents, and making a small tree or large shrub, flowering with profusion even on small plants. Flowers with numerous white, strap-shaped tepals, fragrant, appearing in April. Succeeds well on all types of soil including chalk soil. Garden origin prior to 1910.

**'Leonard Messel'** A magnificent tall shrub or small tree; flowers lilac-pink, deeper in bud. A chance hybrid between an unusual *M. kobus* which has a pale purple line along the centre of its tepals, and *M. stellata* 'Rosea'. Originated at Nymans, Sussex, a great garden made by the late Col Messel. AM 1955. FCC 1969. AGM 1984.

**'Merrill'** An outstanding selection. A vigorous small tree with large, white, fragrant flowers, freely produced. Named after Prof Elmer Merrill, a former Director of the Arnold Arboretum where it was raised in 1939 by Dr Karl Sax. FCC 1979. AGM 1984.

**'Neil McEacharn'** A vigorous small tree with pink-flushed flowers. A cross between *M. kobus* and *M. stellata* 'Rosea' raised at Windsor from seed received from Neil McEacharn of the Villa Taranto. AM 1968.

**'Snowdrift'** We adopted this name for a clone descended from one of the seedlings from the original cross made in Germany in about 1910. It has larger flowers than *M. stellata* with about twelve tepals; leaves also a little larger.

‡**macrophylla** MICHX. An awe-inspiring small tree when seen alone in its grandeur ideally placed in a site sheltered from the prevailing wind, but open to the sun and backed by dark evergreens. It has perhaps larger leaves and flowers than any other deciduous tree or shrub hardy in the British Isles. The leaves are of rather thin texture, glaucous beneath and sometimes exceed 0.6m in length. The very large, fragrant flowers are parchment coloured with purple markings in the centre and appear in early summer. SE United States. I 1800. FCC 1900.

**subsp. ashei** See *M. ashei*.

**'Manchu Fan'** (Gresham Hybrids) (*M. × veitchii × M. × soulangeana* 'Lennei Alba'). A splendid small to medium-sized tree. The large, goblet-shaped flowers have 9 broad, creamy-white tepals, the inner ones flushed purplish-pink at the base. Similar to 'Sayonara' but flowers less goblet-shaped and less green-flushed at the base with the inner tepals flushed pink only on the basal third.

*'Maryland'* A large shrub or small tree similar to *M.* 'Freeman', differing in its more open habit, larger leaves and flowers that open more widely. Origin as 'Freeman'.

‡**'Michael Rosse'** (*M. campbellii* Alba group × *M. sargentiana* var. *robusta*). A beautiful tree raised at Caerhays and grown at Nymans, Sussex, having large soft purple flowers. AM 1968.

**mollicomata** See *M. campbellii* subsp. *mollicomata*.

**nicholsoniana** HORT. See *M. sinensis*.

**nicholsoniana** REHD. & WILS. See *M. wilsonii*.

‡†*nitida* W.W. SM. An evergreen shrub or small tree of dense habit with leathery leaves dark shining green above. Flowers creamy-white, scented, 5-7.5cm across, borne in late spring or early summer. The young growths have an almost metallic lustre. A charming but tender species, only suitable for the mildest localities. One of the finest specimens is growing in the woods at Caerhays, Cornwall. SW China, SE Tibet. AM 1966.

**'Norman Gould'** See *M. stellata* 'Norman Gould'.

**MAGNOLIA**—*continued*

**obovata** See *M. hypoleuca.*

‡**officinalis** REHD. & WILS. A small to medium-sized tree, closely related to *M. hypoleuca*, with usually yellowish-grey young shoots, and large obovate leaves up to 0.5m long. The large, saucer-shaped flowers are white and fragrant, appearing at the end of leafy young growths in early summer. China but only known in cultivation. I 1900 by Ernest Wilson.
  **var. biloba** REHD. & WILS. A very rare and distinct Chinese tree, introduced by us to British gardens from the Botanic Garden, Lushan in 1936. Its large, obovate leaves are pale green above, glaucous and finely downy beneath; deeply notched at the apex. Flowers cup-shaped, 15-20cm across, parchment coloured with maroon centre, fragrant. AM 1975.

**parviflora** See *M. sieboldii.*

‡'**Peppermint Stick**' (Gresham Hybrids) (*M. liliiflora* × *M.* × *veitchii*). A strong-growing, medium-sized, conical tree with distinctive, narrowly columnar flower buds to 11cm long. Tepals 9, creamy-white flushed pink at the base with a central deep pink line, outer tepals spreading with age. Inner tepals erect, heavily flushed deep pink towards the base.

‡'**Pinkie**' (Kosar Hybrids) (*M. liliiflora* 'Reflorescens' × *M. stellata* 'Rosea'). A medium-sized shrub bearing cup-shaped flowers up to 18cm across with 9-12 tepals, pale red-purple becoming pink outside, white within.

‡ × **proctoriana** REHD. (*M. salicifolia* × *M. stellata*). A large, very floriferous shrub or small tree with shortly pubescent leaf buds, and leaves which are green beneath. Flowers white, with 6-12 tepals, appearing in April. Garden origin 1928. It occurs rarely in the wild with the parents.

**pumila** See *M. coco.*

**purpurea** See *M. liliiflora.*

**pyramidata** See *M. fraseri* var. *pyramidata.*

‡'**Ricki**' (De Vos Hybrids) (*M. liliiflora* 'Nigra' × *M. stellata*). A medium-sized shrub. Flowers large, deep purplish-pink in bud, up to 15cm across when open. Tepals about 15, rather narrow, pink to deep rose-purple at the base outside.

‡‡**rostrata** W.W. SM. A rare, medium-sized, gaunt tree for woodland shelter, with broad, obovate, conspicuously veined leaves up to 0.5m. long. Young foliage and buds clothed with tawny, velvety hairs. Flowers appearing with the leaves in June; tepals fleshy, creamy-white or pink, followed by conspicuous pink cone-like fruits. Yunnan, SE Tibet, Upper Burma. AM 1974 (for foliage).

‡'**Royal Crown**' (Gresham Hybrids) (*M. liliiflora* × *M.* × *veitchii*). A small tree, the large flowers with 12 tepals open before the leaves, deep purplish-pink in bud, fading to white at the tips when open, white inside.

‡**salicifolia** (SIEB. & ZUCC.) MAXIM. A small, broadly conical tree or large shrub with slender branches. Leaves usually narrow and willow-like, occasionally ovate, normally slightly glaucous beneath; flowers, usually produced on young plants, white, fragrant, with mostly 6 narrow tepals, produced on the leafless stems in April. The leaves, bark and wood are pleasantly lemon-scented when bruised. Japan. I 1892. AM 1927. AGM 1984. FCC 1962.
  '**Jermyns**' A slow-growing shrubby form, with broader leaves conspicuously glaucous beneath and larger flowers appearing later. One of the best flowering clones of this beautiful magnolia.

‡**sargentiana** REHD. & WILS. A noble, medium-sized tree from W China. Flowers like enormous water lilies, rose-pink without, paler within, produced on mature specimens in April and May in advance of the leathery, obovate leaves. Introduced by E.H. Wilson in 1908. FCC 1935.
  **var. robusta** REHD. & WILS. This magnificent variety has longer, narrower leaves and larger flowers and fruits. Flowers 23cm in diameter, rosy-crimson without, paler within, and usually with more tepals than the type, but not produced until tree size is attained. W Sichuan, China. I 1908 by Ernest Wilson. FCC 1947.

‡'**Sayonara**' (Gresham Hybrids) (*M.* × *soulangeana* 'Lennei Alba' × *M.* × *veitchii* 'Rubra'). A small tree bearing profuse, white goblet-shaped flowers 10cm long, tepals 9, slightly pink and green flushed at the base, the inner tepals heavily flushed pink to above the middle. AM 1990.

**MAGNOLIA**—*continued*

‡**sieboldii** K. KOCH (*M. parviflora* SIEB. & ZUCC.) A large, wide-spreading shrub with ovate to obovate leaves, glaucous and hairy beneath. The nodding flowers in bud are egg-shaped, but turn outwards as the tepals expand; flowers white and fragrant, appearing intermittently with the leaves from May to August. The crimson fruit-clusters are spectacular. Japan, Korea. I 1865. FCC 1894. AGM 1984.

**sinensis** STAPF (*M. globosa* var. *sinensis* REHD. & WILS.) (*M. nicholsoniana* HORT.) A large, wide-spreading shrub resembling *M. wilsonii*, but easily distinguished by its broader, obovate leaves, tomentose beneath, and wider, more strongly lemon-scented, white, nodding flowers, 10-13cm wide, which appear with the leaves, in June. The paper-white, fragrant flowers contrast with the central red staminal cone. Before 1930 this plant was distributed by Chenault of Orleans, France as *M. nicholsoniana*. W China. I 1908 by Ernest Wilson. AM 1927. FCC 1931.

‡ × **soulangeana** SOULANGE-BODIN (*M. denudata* × *M. liliiflora*). In its numerous forms, the best and most popular magnolia for general planting. Usually seen as a large shrub with several wide-spreading stems. Flowers, before the leaves, large, tulip-shaped, white, stained rose-purple at the base, appearing during April to early May. The best magnolia for tolerating indifferent clay soils and atmospheric pollution, but only moderately lime-tolerant, and no good for shallow chalk soils. Raised by Mons Soulange-Bodin at Fromont, near Paris, early in the 19th century but forms may have originated in Japan long before this. There are a number of named clones all of which have the useful habit of flowering when young. For the plant usually grown under this name see 'Etienne Soulange-Bodin'.

**'Alba'** See 'Alba Superba' and 'Amabilis'.

**'Alba Superba'** ('Alba') One of the first of the group to produce its white, scented flowers, closely resembling those of *M. denudata*. C 1835.

**'Alexandrina'** One of the most popular clones, vigorous, erect and free-flowering; the large, erect flowers are white, flushed purple at the base. C 1831.

**'Amabilis'** ('Alba') A superb clone resembling *M. denudata* in general habit and flowers. The faint purplish flush at the base of the inner tepals is generally quite concealed and the beautifully formed flowers appear ivory-white. C 1865.

**'Brozzonii'** The aristocrat of the "Soulangeanas". Large, elongated, white flowers, shaded purple at the base. One of the largest-flowered and latest of the group. C 1873. FCC 1929. AGM 1984.

**'Etienne Soulange-Bodin'** The typical form described above and usually grown as *M.* × *soulangeana*. AGM 1984.

**'Lennei'** (*M.* × *lennei* HORT.) One of the first clones. A vigorous, spreading, multi-stemmed shrub with large, broadly obovate leaves up to 25cm long. The flowers, like enormous goblets, have thick fleshy tepals which are rose-purple outside and creamy-white, stained soft purple inside, and appear during April and May, and sometimes again in the autumn. Said to have originated in a garden in Lombardy, Italy, sometime before 1850. FCC 1863. AGM 1984.

**'Lennei Alba'** Flowers ivory-white, very like those of *M. denudata*. C 1905. AGM 1984.

**'Nigra'** See *M. liliiflora* 'Nigra'.

**'Norbertii'** A free-flowering clone with white flowers, flushed purple on the outside. Similar to 'Alexandrina', but flowers slightly smaller. C 1835.

**'Picture'** A vigorous, erect-branched clone of Japanese origin, with large leaves and long, erect flowers, vinous-purple on the outside, white on the inside. Flowers when quite young, and said to be *M. denudata* × *M. liliiflora* 'Nigra'. An excellent magnolia found in a Japanese garden in about 1930. AM 1984. AGM 1984.

**'Rubra'** See 'Rustica Rubra'.

**'Rustica Rubra'** ('Rubra') A vigorous clone, one of the best for general planting, with oval leaves and cup-shaped flowers of a rich rosy-red. A seedling of 'Lennei'. AM 1960. AGM 1984.

**'San Jose'** A vigorous large shrub, flowers large, deep pink outside, creamy-white inside. Raised in California about 1938. AM 1986.

**'Speciosa'** A clone with leaves smaller than those of the type, and nearly white flowers abundantly produced. C 1825.

**MAGNOLIA** ×**soulangeana**—*continued*

'Sundew' Large creamy-white flowers flushed pink at the base. C 1966.

'Triumphans' Flowers white within, reddish-purple without, paling towards the tips.

'Verbanica' Tepals pink on the outside. One of the last of the group to flower. C 1873.

‡**sprengeri** PAMPAN. (*M. sprengeri* var. *diva* STAPF ex JOHNST.) (*M. denudata* var. *purpurascens* (MAXIM.) REHD. & WILS.) A small to medium-sized tree occasionally up to 13m, bearing in April fragrant, pink flowers resembling, and as rich as, those of *M. campbellii* but smaller. Leaves up to 18cm long, obovate with a wedge-shaped base. C and W China. Introduced by E.H. Wilson from W Hubei in 1900.

'Claret Cup' Flowers purplish-pink outside, white flushed pink inside. A seedling of 'Diva'. AM 1963.

'Diva' Flowers rose-carmine. Derives from a tree at Caerhays, Cornwall which is the only Wilson seedling of the typical variety to survive. AM 1942.

**var. diva** See *M. sprengeri*.

**var. elongata** (REHD. & WILS.) JOHNSTONE Small bushy tree or large shrub. Flowers pure white, with narrower tepals. Hubei, Sichuan, China. I 1900 by Ernest Wilson. AM 1955.

**stellata** (SIEB. & ZUCC.) MAXIM. (*M. halliana* PARSONS) (*M. kobus* var. *stellata* (SIEB. & ZUCC.) BLACKBURN) A distinct and charming, slow-growing, Japanese shrub, forming a compact, rounded specimen usually wider than high, seldom exceeding a height of 3m. Winter buds grey-hairy. The white, fragrant, many-tepalled flowers are profusely borne in March and April. A rare species restricted in the wild to a small area in the western Tokai district of Japan. The correct name for this plant is considered by some authorities to be *M. tomentosa* THUNB. I 1862. FCC 1878. AGM 1984.

'Dawn' Flowers with numerous narrow tepals, pale pink in bud opening white banded with pink on the outside.

'Norman Gould' (*M.* 'Norman Gould') A very distinct form making a small tree. Flowers opening early with usually 6-9 obovate tepals faintly streaked with pink outside towards the base, and up to 3 small, sepal-like tepals. A colchicine-induced polyploidal form raised in the R.H.S. Gardens at Wisley. Norman Gould was a Wisley botanist who died in 1960. FCC 1967.

'Rosea' Flowers flushed pink, deeper in bud. AM 1893.

'Royal Star' Very large flowers produced later than most other forms, pink-tinged in bud opening white, with numerous tepals. Raised on Long Island in 1947.

'Rubra' Flowers similar to those of 'Rosea', but slightly deeper in colouring. AM 1948.

'Water Lily' An outstanding form of Japanese origin, with larger flowers and more numerous tepals. AGM 1984.

‡'Susan' (Kosar Hybrids) (*M. liliiflora* 'Nigra' × *M. stellata* 'Rosea'). A medium-sized shrub of upright habit. Flowers deep red-purple in bud, red-purple when open, paler within, with up to 6 tepals.

×**thompsoniana** (LOUDON) C. DE VOS (*M. tripetala* × *M. virginiana*). A large, wide-spreading shrub resembling *M. virginiana*, but with larger leaves, up to 25cm long, which persist into early winter. The large, fragrant, parchment-coloured flowers are carried intermittently throughout the summer even on young plants. Garden origin about 1808; raised by Archibald Thompson in London probably from American seed. AM 1958.

‡**tripetala** L. "Umbrella Tree". A very hardy North American tree sometimes attaining 9-12m, with an open head. Leaves large, 30-50cm long and 15-25cm wide. The cream-coloured flowers, 18-25cm across, in May and June are strongly and pungently scented. They are followed by attractive, red, cone-shaped fruit-clusters. E United States. I 1752.

**tsarongensis** See *M. globosa*.

‡ × **veitchii** BEAN (*M. campbellii* × *M. denudata*). A very vigorous, medium-sized to large tree, hardy and attractive both in leaf and flower. The following cultivars are grown, both selected from the 6 seedlings raised by Peter Veitch who made the cross in 1907.

'Isca' Flowers white in April.

'Peter Veitch' A first class hardy magnolia with white, flushed purple-pink goblets produced on the naked branches in April, as soon as it attains small tree size. We are indebted to Veitch's nursery of Exeter for this splendid magnolia. FCC 1921.

**virginiana** L. (*M. glauca* L.) "Sweet Bay" "Swamp Bay". A partially evergreen shrub or small tree. The fragrant, creamy-white, rather small, globular flowers are produced from

**MAGNOLIA virginiana**—*continued*

June to September. Leaves up to 13cm long, glossy above, blue-white beneath. E United States. Probably the first magnolia to be grown in England. C late 17th century.

**'Wada's Memory'** A selected clone out of a number of seed-raised plants supplied in 1940 to the University of Washington Arboretum, Seattle, by Mr K. Wada of Yokohama, Japan. A small tree. The fragrant white flowers are larger than those of *M. kobus* and are borne in abundance. In our opinion it belongs to the same parentage as *M.* 'Kewensis' (*M. kobus* × *M. salicifolia*). It has reached 9m tall and 6.5m across at the Hillier Gardens and Arboretum (1990). FCC 1986.

× **watsonii** See *M.* × *wieseneri*.

× **wieseneri** CARR. (*M.* × *watsonii* HOOK. f.) (*M. hypoleuca* × *M. sieboldii*). A splendid rare shrub or small bushy tree with leathery, obovate leaves. Flowers open in June and July from rounded white buds, upward facing, creamy-white with prominent, rosy-crimson anthers and pink sepals, saucer-shaped, 13cm wide, and with a fragrance almost overpowering. Garden origin in Japan. C 1889. AM 1917. FCC 1975.

**wilsonii** REHD. (*M. nicholsoniana* REHD. & WILS.) (*M.* × *highdownensis* DANDY) A large, wide-spreading shrub with elliptic-lanceolate leaves, pointed at the apex. In May and June, flowers pendulous, saucer-shaped, white with crimson stamens. A lovely species differing from *M. sinensis* in its narrower leaves and rather smaller flowers. Best in a partially shaded position. W China. I 1908 by Ernest Wilson. AM 1932. FCC 1971. AGM 1984.

\* × **MAHOBERBERIS** SCHNEID. (*Mahonia* × *Berberis*)—**Berberidaceae**—Hybrids of botanical interest and some of horticultural merit between 2 closely related genera. In each case the *Mahonia* is the mother parent. Any soil and any exposure.

**aquicandidula** KRUSSMANN (*M. aquifolium* × *B. candidula*). A dwarf, slow-growing, unhappy-looking shrublet of weak growth. The densely clustered leaves are ovate to ovate-elliptic, varying in size from 1-4cm long, lustrous, dark green above and at first pruinose beneath, entire or spine toothed; many are compound, with 2 small leaflets at their base. Flowers yellow. Garden origin in Sweden, 1943.

**aquisargentii** KRUSSMANN (*M. aquifolium* × *B. sargentiana*). A really splendid and remarkable, medium-sized, evergreen shrub of dense, upright habit. Leaves varying in shape, either slender-stalked, elliptic-lanceolate, up to 21cm long, and regularly spine-toothed or short-stalked, ovate-lanceolate and margined with 2cm long, vicious spines. Some leaves are compound, with 2 leaflets at their base. All are shining dark green above, paler beneath. Flowers soft yellow, in terminal clusters, followed by black berries. Garden origin in Sweden. × *M. miethkeana* MELANDER & EADE (*B.* ? *julianae* × *M. aquifolium*) is a similar hybrid raised in the State of Washington, United States, in 1940.

**miethkeana** See under × *M. aquisargentii*.

**neubertii** (BAUMANN) SCHNEID. (*M. aquifolium* × *B. vulgaris*) (*B. ilicifolia* HORT.) A small, loose-habited shrub forming a rounded bush. Leaves both simple and compound, either obovate and finely-toothed as in the *Berberis* parent or ovate, acute and coarsely-toothed. The young foliage is an attractive sea-green, becoming bronze or purple-tinged. Originated in the nursery of Mons Baumann, at Bolwiller in Alsace, France, in 1854.

\***MAHONIA** NUTT.—**Berberidaceae**—About 70 species of evergreen shrubs natives of the Himalaya, E and SE Asia and N and C America. They are distinguished from the closely related *Berberis* by their pinnate leaves and spineless stems. Grown for their attractive evergreen foliage and yellow flowers in winter or spring, followed by usually blue-black berries, they thrive in most types of well drained soils, including chalk soil.

**acanthifolia** See *M. napaulensis*.

**'Aldenhamensis'** See *M.* × *wagneri* 'Aldenhamensis'.

**aquifolium** (PURSH) NUTT. "Oregon Grape". A small shrub, valuable for under-planting or for game covers, in sun or shade. Leaves pinnate, polished green sometimes turning red in winter. Flowers rich yellow, in dense racemes, borne in terminal clusters, opening in early spring; berries blue-black, very decorative. Parent of many hybrids and very variable. W North America. I 1823. AGM 1984.

**'Apollo'** A splendid form of vigorous habit making a dense, low-growing, spreading bush. Leaves deep green with reddish stalks. Flowers bright yellow in large, dense clusters.

**MAHONIA aquifolium**—*continued*

**'Atropurpurea'** A selected form in which the leaves are a rich reddish-purple during winter and early spring. C 1915.

**'Heterophylla'** See *M.* 'Heterophylla'.

**'Moseri'** A small shrub with attractive bronze-red young leaves turning to apple-green and finally dark green. C 1895.

**'Smaragd'** A small, spreading shrub with dark glossy green leaves bronze when young and large, dense clusters of bright yellow flowers. C 1979.

**bealei** See *M. japonica* 'Bealei'.

**confusa** SPRAGUE A small shrub related to *M. fortunei*, the leaves with about 20 narrow, sea-green, spine-toothed leaflets on a purplish rachis. Slender, spike-like upright racemes of small, pale yellow flowers open in early autumn. Berries blue-black, bloomy, ripe by spring. A form with pale green foliage is also cultivated. China. Introduced by Roy Lancaster in 1980.

**eutriphylla** See *M. trifolia*.

**fascicularis** See *M. pinnata*.

**fortunei** (LINDL.) FEDDE A slender, erect shrub, slowly attaining 1.8-2m, with distinctive matt green, linear-lanceolate leaflets. Flowers bright yellow, in erect narrow terminal racemes, from September to November. China. I 1846 by Robert Fortune.

**fremontii** (TORR.) FEDDE A very beautiful blue-green, small to medium-sized shrub, for a well drained site in full sun. The pinnate leaves are composed of small glaucous, crisped and spiny leaflets. Small clusters of flowers in May and June are followed by inflated, dry, yellowish or red berries. SW United States.

†**haematocarpa** (WOOTON) FEDDE An attractive species related to *M. fremontii*, but with smaller plum-coloured berries and longer, narrower, greener leaflets. Requires a sunny site. SW United States, N Mexico. I 1916.

**'Heterophylla'** (*M. aquifolium* var. *heterophylla* HORT.) (*M. toluacensis* BEAN not J.J.) A small shrub of loose, open habit with leaves composed of 5-9 long, narrow, glossy green, wavy-edged leaflets which often turn reddish-purple during winter. Flowers in racemes, clustered at the tips of the shoots in spring. Origin uncertain, but most likely a seedling of the original *M. toluacensis* J.J.

**japonica** (THUNB.) DC. This beautiful species is deservedly one of the most popular and ornamental of all evergreen shrubs. Magnificent deep green, pinnate leaves and terminal clusters of long, pendulous, or laxly held, racemes of fragrant, lemon-yellow flowers from late autumn to early spring. China, long cultivated in Japan. AM 1916. AGM 1984.

**'Bealei'** (*M. bealei* (FORT.) CARR.) Differs mainly in its stiffer, shorter, erect racemes, and its broad-based often overlapping leaflets. Now much rarer in cultivation than the typical form. I about 1849 by Robert Fortune. AM 1916.

**trifurca** See under *M. japonica* × *napaulensis*.

**japonica × napaulensis** An attractive hybrid with good foliage and erect racemes of yellow flowers in late winter. A plant grown as *M. japonica trifurca* was considered to be *M. japonica* 'Bealei' × *M. napaulensis*. It made a distinct shrub of upright habit, bearing large ruffs of pinnate leaves and erect, clustered racemes of yellow flowers in late winter.

× **lindsayae** P.F. YEO (*M. japonica* × *M. siamensis*). This hybrid was raised in 1959 at the University Botanic Garden, Cambridge, from seed of the tender *M. siamensis* TAKEDA collected at Serre de la Madone, Menton, the garden of the late Major Lawrence Johnston. It was named after Nancy Lindsay who inherited the Serre in 1958.

**'Cantab'** A medium-sized shrub of lax habit, broader than tall. Leaves rich green, long and drooping with up to 15 widely spaced leaflets each bearing up to 6 sharp spines on each side, often red-tinged in cold weather, on a reddish rachis. Flowers lemon-yellow in late autumn and winter in spreading or pendulous racemes, relatively large and strongly fragrant. Proving hardy.

†**lomariifolia** TAKEDA A very imposing species, but only sufficiently hardy for gardens in the milder counties. A large shrub, branches erect, stout, closely beset with long leaves composed of 15-19 pairs of rigid, narrow leaflets. Flowers deep yellow, borne during winter in dense terminal clusters of erect racemes 15-25cm long, each raceme carrying as many as 250 small flowers. W China, Burma. I 1931. AM 1938. FCC 1939.

**MAHONIA**—*continued*

×**media** C.D. BRICKELL (*M. japonica* × *M. lomariifolia*). A vigorous shrub of medium to large size, with ruffs of handsome pinnate leaves and terminal clusters of long, lax racemes in late autumn and early winter. This magnificent hybrid has been independently raised in several places and a number of clones have been named. The flowers are generally only slightly fragrant. AGM 1984.

    **'Arthur Menzies'** (*M. japonica* 'Bealei' × *M. lomariifolia*). A compact medium-sized shrub of upright habit with glaucous-bloomed young shoots. Leaves to 45cm long with up to 19 deep blue-green leaflets, each with 3-4 spines on each side. Flowers lemon-yellow, borne in late autumn to early winter in upright unbranched racemes, spreading as they open. Selected in 1964 at the University of Washington Arboretum and named after the Supervisor of Plant Accessions at the Strybing Arboretum, San Francisco, in whose garden the cross occurred.

    **'Buckland'** A handsome clone raised from a deliberate cross made by Mr Lionel Fortescue at the Garden House, Buckland Monachorum, Devon. In leaf it tends towards *M. japonica*; the racemes are long and spreading. AGM 1984.

    **'Charity'** A superb medium-sized to large shrub of upright, stately habit. Leaves 0.5-0.6m long, bearing two-ranked long, spiny leaflets. The slightly fragrant, deep yellow flowers are borne in long spreading and ascending racemes, in large terminal clusters during autumn and early winter. Selected by Sir Eric Savill and Mr Hope Findlay at the Savill Garden from seedlings raised by the Slieve Donard Nursery in about 1950. AM 1959. FCC 1962. AGM 1984.

    **'Lionel Fortescue'** Flowers bright yellow in numerous, long, upright racemes. Originated in the same batch of seedlings as 'Buckland'. AM and Cory Cup 1975. AGM 1984.

    **'Underway'** Relatively compact, the leaves with 17-21 leaflets. Flowers bright yellow in long, upright racemes.

    **'Winter Sun'** A selected form raised by the Slieve Donard Nursery, N Ireland. Racemes erect, densely packed with fragrant yellow flowers. AGM 1984.

**'Moseri'** See *M. aquifolium* 'Moseri'.

†**napaulensis** DC. (*M. acanthifolia* G. DON) A magnificent large shrub, or small tree in mild areas, of erect habit. The enormous, pinnate leaves are arranged in dense collars at the summit of each stem, ideal backing for the bunches of long, spreading racemes of mimosa-yellow, faintly scented flowers which appear in the autumn and continue into winter. Nepal, Sikkim, Assam. I 1858. AM 1953. AM 1974. FCC 1958 (the last two as *M. acanthifolia*).

    **'Maharajah'** Flowers deep yellow. The best form of the species.

**nervosa** (PURSH) NUTT. A dwarf, suckering species, with lustrous leaves which often turn red in winter. Racemes 15-20cm long in May and June; berries blackish-blue. Not the best of mahonias on chalk. W North America. I 1822.

†**nevinii** (A. GRAY) FEDDE A small shrub with small, pinnate leaves. Leaflets 5, flattened, grey-green above and attractively veined, pruinose beneath. Flowers in small clusters followed by small red berries. S California. I 1928.

**pinnata** (LAG.) FEDDE (*M. fascicularis* DC.) A strong-growing shrub of medium size. Leaves short-stalked, leaflets prickly and sea-green. The rich yellow racemes appear in clusters along the stems during late winter. California. AM 1948. The true plant is rare in cultivation; for the plant often grown under this name see *M.* × *wagneri* 'Pinnacle'. I before 1838.

**pumila** (GREENE) FEDDE A rare, dwarf shrub of neat habit. Leaves with 5-7, flattened, spine-edged, sea-green, somewhat glaucous leaflets; flowers in spring; fruits bloomy-black in large clusters. SW Oregon and California.

**repens** (LINDL.) G. DON A dwarf suckering shrub, in time making small colonies. Leaflets matt green; flowers in terminal clusters followed by bloomy-black berries. W North America. I 1822.

    **'Rotundifolia'** A small shrub of distinct appearance. Leaves ovate or rounded, sea-green, spineless; large plumes of rich yellow flowers borne in May, followed by black, bloomy berries. Probably a hybrid between *M. aquifolium* and *M. repens*. C 1875.

**MAHONIA**—*continued*

†**swaseyi** (BUCKLAND) FEDDE Medium-sized shrub related to *M. fremontii*, differing in its leaflets, which are pruinose beneath and closely reticulate, also in its small leaf-like bracts. Berries yellowish-red. Texas (United States).

**toluacensis** See *M.* 'Heterophylla'.

**trifolia** CHAM. & SCHLECHT. (*M. schiedeana* SCHLECHT.) (*M. eutriphylla* HORT. not FEDDE) (E.K. Balls 4618) A rare, small to medium-sized , slow-growing shrub. Leaves small, with 3-5 thick, rigidly spiny, dark green leaflets, turning plum-purple in cold winters. Dense clusters of yellow flowers in spring are followed by bloomy, black berries. C Mexico. Collected by E. K. Balls to whom we are indebted for this plant. It has reached 3m at the Hillier Gardens and Arboretum.

**trifoliolata** (MORICAND) FEDDE Mainly grown as the following variety, the typical form is a native of SE Texas and differs in its green leaflets.

    **var. glauca** I. M. JOHNSTON An attractive, medium-sized evergreen for a well drained sunny position against a warm sunny wall, where it will attain up to 4-5m. Leaves composed of 3 spiny, conspicuously veined, glaucous leaflets. Clusters of flowers in spring followed by redcurrant-like berries. W Texas to Arizona, N Mexico. I 1839.

**'Undulata'** See *M.* × *wagneri* 'Undulata'.

× **wagneri** (JOUIN) REHD. (*M. aquifolium* × *M. pinnata*). A variable small shrub resembling *M. aquifolium*, producing its racemes of flowers in spring.

    **'Aldenhamensis'** A splendid, strong-growing, medium-sized erect shrub, with distinctive sea-green pinnate leaves and fascicles of rich yellow flowers along the stems in late winter.

    **'Hasting's Elegant'** A small shub of compact, upright habit with bright green leaves. Flowers bright yellow in dense clusters.

    **'Pinnacle'** A vigorous, upright form with bright green leaves bronze when young and showy clusters of bright yellow flowers. A selection from plants previously grown as *M. pinnata*. AGM 1984.

    **'Undulata'** An ornamental medium-sized shrub, taller than *M. aquifolium*, with lustrous dark green leaves, the leaflets with undulate margins. Flowers deep yellow in spring. C 1930. AM 1971. AGM 1984.

**"MAIDENHAIR TREE"** See *Ginkgo biloba* under CONIFERS.

†**MALLOTUS** LOUR.—**Euphorbiaceae**—About 140 species of interesting shrubs or small trees, natives of warm areas of the Old World. The following is lime-tolerant, requiring full sun and a well drained soil. Only suitable for mild areas of the British Isles.

**japonicus** (THUNB.) MUELL.-ARG. A large shrub or small tree with large, handsome, roundish leaves. Flowers small, in large pyramidal panicles; male and female on different plants. A plant grown from seed collected by Kenneth Ashburner in N Honshu, Japan is proving hardy and flowered in the Hillier Gardens and Arboretum in September 1989. Japan, Taiwan, China, Korea.

**MALUS** MILL.—**Rosaceae**—The "Flowering Crabs" comprise a genus of some 25 species of deciduous trees found throughout N temperate regions and may be included with the ornamental cherries as together being unexcelled in floral charm by any other trees. With few exceptions they are easily grown, small to medium-sized trees, and their flowering season is April and May, the flowers having 5 styles as against the solitary ones of *Prunus*. Many bear very attractive fruits in autumn, persisting in several sorts late into winter. Unless otherwise stated, all are small trees, thriving in all types of fertile soil. Straggly or untidy specimens may be hard pruned immediately after flowering.

    E indicates crabs with edible fruits most suitable for using in preserves.

**'Aldenhamensis'** (Purpurea Group) A small tree or tall shrub of loose growth. Leaves purplish becoming bronze-green in late summer. Flowers single or semi-double, deep vinous-red followed by reddish-purple fruits. Resembles *M.* × *purpurea*, but flowering about a fortnight later. AM 1916.

**'Almey'** An early, free-flowering small tree of broad, rounded habit. Young leaves reddish-bronze. Flowers large, soft red with white centre; fruits orange-red with a crimson flush,

**MALUS 'Almey'**—*continued*

persisting into winter. A seedling from the hybrid *M. baccata* × *M. niedzwetzkyana*. C 1945.

**'American Beauty'** A vigorous tree with bronze-red later bronze-green leaves. Flowers double, deep red. Said to be scab resistant. C 1978.

**angustifolia** (AIT.) MICHX. An uncommon tree up to 10m related to *M. coronaria*. The leaves on vigorous shoots are ovate and sharply lobed; on mature shoots, narrow and toothed. Flowers salmon-pink, violet-scented; fruits yellowish-green. E United States. I 1750.

× **arnoldiana** SARG. (*M. baccata* × *M. floribunda*). An extremely floriferous small round-headed tree or large shrub with somewhat drooping branches. Flowers large, fragrant, red in bud, opening pale pink inside, deep pink outside with a red calyx, in umbellate clusters; fruits yellow, with reddish flush. Originated in the Arnold Arboretum, United States in 1883.

× **atrosanguinea** (SPATH) SCHNEID. (*M. halliana* × *M. sieboldii*). A small, mushroom-shaped tree with glossy green leaves. Flowers crimson in bud opening rose. Fruits yellow with a red cheek. Similar to *M. floribunda* but with darker flowers. C 1898.

**baccata** (L.) BORKH. The true "Siberian Crab" is a small to medium-sized tree of rounded habit. Flowers white, fragrant, followed by small red or yellow, berry-like fruits. Widely distributed throughout Asia. I 1784.

**var. mandshurica** (MAXIM.) SCHNEID. An extremely hardy, round-headed tree up to 12m. Flowers early, during late April and May, white, fragrant; fruits slightly larger than those of the type. NE Asia. I 1824. AM 1962. FCC 1969.

**'Butterball'** A small spreading tree with slightly drooping branches. Flowers pink in bud opening white flushed with pink. Fruits yellow with an orange flush, 2-3cm across. A seedling of *M.* × *zumi* 'Calocarpa' raised in North America. C 1961.

**'Cashmere'** A beautiful small hybrid tree having pale pink flowers followed by yellow fruits in abundance.

**'Chilko'** A small tree of Canadian origin, a seedling of *M. niedzwetzkyana* developing a spreading head with large, purplish-red flowers up to 4.5cm across. Fruits ovoid, 4cm long, brilliant crimson with a shiny skin. E. C 1920. AM 1967.

**coronaria** (L.) MILL. A beautiful, strong-growing, American crab up to 10m. Large fragrant flowers of a delightful shade of shell-pink, produced with the foliage towards the latter end of May. Fruits green. Leaves often richly tinted in autumn. E North America. I 1724.

**'Charlottae'** ('Flore Pleno') A most excellent small tree with large, lobed leaves which colour richly in the autumn. Flowers large, semi-double, shell-pink and violet-scented during late May and early June. Can fruit profusely after a hot summer. Originated about 1902.

**'Cowichan'** A vigorous tree up to 9m or more with large, light red flowers. The large, reddish-purple fruits are accompanied by red-tinted foliage. A seedling of *M. niedzwetzkyana*. C 1920.

**crataegifolia** See *M. florentina*.

**'Crittenden'** An excellent small, compact tree with attractive pale pink flowers. Particularly notable for its heavy crops of bright scarlet fruits which persist throughout autumn and winter. E. AM 1961. FCC 1971. AGM 1984.

**'Dartmouth'** An attractive hybrid producing abundant, white flowers and equally plentiful reddish-purple, bloomy fruits. E. Raised before 1883.

**diversifolia** See *M. fusca*.

**domestica** BORKH. "Orchard Apple". A familiar tree of hybrid origin probably derived from *M. dasycarpa*, *M. praecox* and *M. sylvestris*, as well as several Asiatic species. It is cultivated for its fruit throughout the temperate regions of the world. Forms are often found naturalised or as garden escapes in wild situations, but they may always be distinguished from our native wild crab (*M. sylvestris*) by their larger, often sweet fruits. There are said to be over a thousand cultivars.

**'Dorothea'** A small tree, raised at the Arnold Arboretum, and possibly a hybrid between *M.* × *arnoldiana* and *M. halliana* 'Parkmanii'. Flowers semi-double, 4-5cm across, pale crimson, darker in bud; fruits golden yellow. C 1943.

**MALUS**—*continued*

**'Echtermeyer'** (*M*. 'Exzellenz Thiel' × *M. niedzwetzkyana*). (*M*. 'Oekonomierat Echtermeyer') (*M*. × *purpurea* 'Pendula') A graceful, low, wide-spreading tree with weeping branches and purplish or bronze-green leaves. Flowers rose-crimson, deeper in bud, followed by reddish-purple fruits. Prone to mildew. C 1914.

**'Eleyi'** Resembles *M*. × *purpurea* in leaf and flower, but slightly darker in both, the flowers opening slightly later. Carries very decorative purplish-red fruits in autumn. Garden origin before 1920. AM 1922. FCC 1922. See also *M*. 'Profusion', a more recent cultivar.

**'Elise Rathke'** (*M. pumila* 'Pendula') A small tree with stiffly pendulous branches. Flowers large, pink in bud opening white, followed by large, sweet, yellow fruits. C 1885. E.

**'Evereste'** A conical tree with dark green, often somewhat lobed leaves. Flowers freely borne, 5cm across, red in bud later white. Fruits to 2.5cm across, orange to orange-yellow. C 1980.

**'Exzellenz Thiel'** A small, weeping tree or shrub raised by Spaeth about 1909. Flowers semi-double, pink in bud, opening white. Possibly *M. floribunda* × *M. prunifolia* 'Pendula'. C 1909.

**florentina** (ZUCCAGNI) SCHNEID. (*M. crataegifolia* KOEHNE) ( × *Malosorbus florentina* (ZUCCAGNI) BROWICZ) A small, round-headed tree with hawthorn-like foliage, white tomentose beneath, which turns orange and scarlet in autumn. Flowers white, fruits small, red. It has been suggested that this tree is a hybrid between *Malus sylvestris* and the "Wild Service Tree", *Sorbus torminalis*. Italy, S Yugoslavia, N Greece, N Turkey. C 1877. AM 1956.

**floribunda** SIEB. ex VAN HOUTTE "Japanese Crab". A most popular flowering small tree or large shrub with long arching branches. Remarkably beautiful when in flower, the crimson buds opening to white or pale blush. Fruits small, red and yellow. One of the earliest crabs to flower. Introduced from Japan in 1862. AGM 1984.

**fusca** (RAF.) SCHNEID. (*M. diversifolia* ROEM.) (*M. rivularis* (HOOK.) ROEM.) "Oregon Crab". A small tree or large shrub of dense, vigorous growth. Leaves serrate, often three-lobed; flowers like apple blossom, fruits red or yellow. W North America. I 1836.

**'Gibbs' Golden Gage'** A small tree of unusual charm when carrying masses of medium-sized, waxy, almost translucent yellow fruits. C before 1923.

**glaucescens** REHD. A distinct small, round-headed tree with branches sometimes spiny, and lobed leaves, glaucous beneath, turning yellow and purple in autumn. Flowers pink; fruits waxy, green to yellow. North America. C 1902.

**'Golden Hornet'** A small tree producing white flowers followed by large crops of bright yellow fruits which are retained until late in the year. One of the best fruiting crabs for general planting. Probably a seedling of *M*. × *zumi* 'Calocarpa'. C before 1949. AM 1949. FCC 1961. AGM 1984.

**halliana** KOEHNE A small tree up to 5m. Leaves narrow, dark, glossy green; flowers carmine in bud, opening shell-pink; small purple fruits. Originated in China where it is known only in cultivation. Introduced via Japan in 1863. AM 1935.

    **'Parkmanii'** A lovely form with pendulous clusters of partly semi-double flowers, rose-red in bud, opening shell-pink, borne on deep crimson pedicels. I 1861.

× **hartwigii** KOEHNE (*M. baccata* × *M. halliana*). A delightful small tree, intermediate between the parents. Flowers almost semi-double up to 5cm across, pink in bud opening white.

**'Hillieri'** (Scheideckeri Group) A very attractive, late flowering tree, like *M*. × *scheideckeri*, but of better constitution. Flowers semi-double, crimson in bud, opening bright pink, wreathing the arching stems in clusters of 5 to 8. C before 1928.

**'Hopa'** A hybrid between *M. baccata* and *M. niedzwetzkyana*, up to 10m, with large, purple-red flowers, followed by orange and red fruits. E. C 1920.

**hupehensis** (PAMPAN) REHD. (*M. theifera* REHD.) A free-growing small tree with stiff, ascending branches. Flowers fragrant, soft pink in bud, opening white, produced in great abundance during May and June. Fruits small, usually deep red on cultivated plants. China, Japan. Introduced by E.H. Wilson in 1900. AM 1928. AGM 1984.

    **'Rosea'** Differs in its pale pink flowers and rather more spreading branches. A lovely tree in full bloom. AM 1938.

**'Hyslop'** An openly branched, small tree with white flowers 1-4cm across, followed by relatively large red-cheeked fruits 5-8cm across. C 1869. E.

**MALUS** *continued*

†**loensis** BRITT. The "Prairie Crab" is a very attractive North American species closely allied to *M. coronaria*, developing ornamental peeling bark with age. Branches downy, and leaves persistently woolly beneath, turning orange-red in autumn; flowers fragrant, 4-5cm across, white usually flushed pink, in corymbs of 4 to 6. Fruits green. C United States.

   **'Plena'** "Bechtel's Crab". Large, semi-double soft pink, fragrant flowers. At its best perhaps the most beautiful flowering crab apple, but a tree of weak constitution and unsuitable for chalk soils. C 1888. AM 1940. FCC 1950.

**'Jay Darling'** (*M. baccata* × *M. niedzwetzkyana*). A most ornamental tree. Large wine-red flowers produced before or with the crimson-tinted foliage; fruits purplish-red. C 1904.

**'John Downie'** Perhaps the best fruiting crab. Flowers white; fruit comparatively large, conical, bright orange and red, of refreshing flavour. E. Raised in 1875. AM 1895. AGM 1984.

**'Kaido'** See *M.* × *micromalus*.

**kansuensis** (BATAL.) SCHNEID. A large shrub or small tree with ovate, usually three-lobed leaves. Flowers small, creamy-white; fruits elongated, red and yellow. Good autumn colour. W China. I 1904. AM 1933.

**'Katherine'** (Hartwigii Group) A small tree with a regular, densely-branched, globular head. Deep pink buds open to semi-double pink flowers over 5cm in diameter which gradually fade white. Even though the flowers are many-petalled they are followed by bright red fruits flushed yellow. C about 1928. AM 1967.

**'Lady Northcliffe'** An attractive, small, densely-branched, broad-headed tree with flowers carmine-red in bud opening blush then white. Very free-flowering. Fruits small and round, yellow. A most ornamental tree for a small garden. C before 1929.

**lancifolia** REHD. A small tree with variously shaped leaves, those of the flowering shoots lanceolate. Flowers shell-pink followed by round, green fruits 2.5cm across. United States. I 1912.

**'Lemoinei'** (Purpurea Group) This fine hybrid is more erect in growth than typical *M.* × *purpurea*, and has larger, but fewer flowers, deep wine-red in colour. Garden origin 1922. AM 1928.

**'Liset'** (*M.* 'Lemoinei' × *M. sieboldii*). A small tree of dense, rounded habit with purplish young foliage. Flowers rose-red, opening from deep crimson buds followed by glossy crimson fruits. Raised in Holland before 1935.

**'Magdeburgensis'** A small, broad-headed tree like the domestic apple, with somewhat spreading branches and beautiful, large, semi-double flowers which are deep red in bud opening to purplish-pink clouded white. Fruits light green to yellow. AM 1933.

× **micromalus** MAK. (*M. baccata* × *M. spectabilis*). (*M.* 'Kaido') A small, erect-branched tree with clear, deep pink flowers, very showy in the mass. Fruits small, red or yellow. Introduced from Japan before 1856.

**'Montreal Beauty'** A small tree of erect, open habit. Flowers white, slightly fragrant, freely borne along the branches and followed by comparatively large, conical, yellow to orange, scarlet-flushed fruits. E.

**'Neville Copeman'** (Purpurea Group) A seedling from *M.* 'Eleyi', developing into a small tree with green leaves shaded purple throughout summer. Flowers light purple followed by conical orange-red fruits. AM 1953.

**niedzwetzkyana** DIECK (*M. pumila* var. *niedzwetzkyana* (DIECK) SCHNEID.) A small tree with red young growths. Flowers purple-red in clusters followed by large conical, dark red fruits covered with a plum-purple bloom. Parent of many notable hybrids. SW Siberia, Turkestan. I about 1891.

**orthocarpa** LAV. A large shrub or small tree with pale pink flowers followed by orange and scarlet fruits. China.

× **platycarpa** REHD. (*M. coronaria* × *M. domestica*). A low-spreading tree. Flowers large, soft pink followed by large, fragrant, flattened, pale yellow fruits. North America. I 1912.

**prattii** (HEMSL.) SCHNEID. A distinct Chinese tree up to 10m, with very pleasing, large, red-veined leaves which give good autumn colour. Flowers white, followed by red or yellow fruits. China. I 1904 by Ernest Wilson.

**MALUS**—*continued*

**'Prince George's'** Originating in the Arnold Arboretum, this slow-growing tree is probably a hybrid between *M. angustifolia* and *M. ioensis* 'Plena'. The scented, late flowers are fully double, 5cm in diameter, and light pink in colour. C 1919.

**'Professor Sprenger'** (Zumi Group) A small, dense-headed tree flowering in great profusion. Flowers pink in bud, opening white, followed by large quantities of shining, amber coloured fruits which usually remain until late December. Introduced by Mr Doorenbos of The Hague, Holland in 1950.

**'Profusion'** (*M.* 'Lemoinei' × *M. sieboldii*). A first class hybrid flowering a little later than *M.* 'Lemoinei'. Flowers in great profusion, wine-red, slightly fragrant, about 4cm across, borne in clusters of 6 or 7. Fruits small, ox-blood-red. Young leaves coppery-crimson. A tree of good constitution and probably the best of all the crabs with wine-red flowers and red young growths. C 1938. AGM 1984.

**prunifolia** ( WILLD.) BORKH. A small tree with oval, unequally toothed leaves. Flowers rose-crimson in bud opening white flushed pink, produced in April and followed by red conical fruits which retain their calyces. NE Asia. C 1758.

    **'Fastigiata'** Branches ascending, forming a columnar head, becoming spreading with age. Fruits yellow and red. C 1906.

    **'Pendula'** A form with pendulous branches.

    **var. rinki** (KOIDZ.) REHD. (*M. ringo* SIEB.) A variety with almond-pink flowers; fruits bright yellow. W China. I 1850. AM 1984.

**pumila** MILL. This name which correctly belongs to the "Paradise Apple" of gardens has long been used to cover several apples including *M. dasyphylla, M. domestica* and *M. sylvestris*. The latter is the wild crab of the British Isles whilst *M. domestica* is the orchard apple.

    **var. niedzwetzkyana** See *M. niedzwetzkyana*.

    **'Pendula'** See *M.* 'Elise Rathke'.

× **purpurea** (BARBIER) REHD. (*M.* × *atrosanguinea* × *M. niedzwetzkyana*). A beautiful hybrid, producing a wealth of rosy-crimson flowers and dark purplish-green shoots and leaves. Fruits light crimson-purple. Many clones have been named. Garden origin before 1900. We regard *M.* 'Profusion' as a tree of better constitution. AM 1914.

    **'Pendula'** See *M.* 'Echtermeyer'.

**'Red Jade'** A lovely, small tree or shrub with weeping branches. Young leaves bright green; flowers white and pink; fruits red, the size of cherries, long persistent. A seedling of 'Exzellenz Thiel' raised in 1935.

**'Red Sentinel'** An excellent fruiting tree with white flowers and large clusters of deep red fruits which remain on the branches throughout winter. AM 1959. AGM 1984.

**'Red Silver'** A small tree with silvery-grey-hairy young leaves becoming purplish red then dark green. Dark red-purple flowers are followed by small, purplish fruits. Raised in 1928.

**'Red Tip'** (*M. coronaria* 'Elk River' × *M. niedzwetzkyana*). An exciting hybrid worthy of inclusion in every representative group of crabs. Flowers red-purple, leaves broad, slightly lobed, young foliage bright red, fruits red-flushed. C 1919.

**ringo** See *M. prunifolia* var. *rinki*.

× **robusta** (CARR.) REHD. (*M. baccata* × *M. prunifolia*). Popularly, though incorrectly, known as "Siberian Crab", the clones of this variable hybrid have white or pinkish flowers and more or less globular, cherry-like red or yellow fruits without calyces. C about 1815. AM 1957. AGM 1984.

    **'Red Siberian'** Fruits red. AGM 1984.

    **'Yellow Siberian'** Fruits yellow. AGM 1984.

**'Royal Beauty'** A small weeping tree with slender, hanging, reddish-purple stems; leaves reddish-purple when young becoming dark green, purplish beneath. Deep red-purple flowers are followed by small, dark red fruits. C 1980.

**'Royalty'** A small tree of rather upright habit with attractive taper-pointed, glossy dark purple leaves turning red in autumn. Large purplish-crimson flowers rather hidden in the foliage are followed by dark red fruits. Raised in Canada in 1953.

**'Rudolph'** A small tree of upright habit with bronze-red later dark bronze-green leaves. Flowers rose-red, deeper in bud, 4.5cm across followed by long-persistent, orange-yellow, oblong fruits to 18mm long. Raised in Canada in 1954.

**MALUS**—*continued*

**sargentii** REHD. A delightful shrubby species up to 2.8m high, with leaves often three-lobed. Smothered in spring with pure white flowers with golden anthers, and in autumn with small, bright red, cherry-like fruits. Closely related to *M. sieboldii* of which it is by some authorities regarded as a form. Japan. I 1892. AM 1915.

**'Rosea'** Flowers blush, rose in bud; slightly more vigorous. C 1921.

× **scheideckeri** ZAB. (*M. floribunda* × *M. prunifolia*). A very free-flowering, slow-growing shrub or miniature tree with masses of slightly fragrant, semi-double, pink and white blossoms. Not suitable for shallow, chalky soils. C 1888. AM 1896.

**sieboldii** (REG.) REHD. (*M. toringo* SIEB. ex MIQ.) A small, picturesque, semi-weeping, Japanese crab, rarely more than 3m high. Leaves simple or variously lobed. Flowers pink in bud, fading to white, smaller than those of *M. floribunda*; fruits small, red or yellowish. Japan. I 1856.

**sikkimensis** (WENZIG) SCHNEID. A distinct, small, erect-branched tree from the Himalaya. Flowers white, followed by somewhat pear-shaped, dark red fruits. Easily recognised by the excessive development of stout, branching spurs on the trunk around the base of the branches. I 1849 by Sir Joseph Hooker.

**'Simcoe'** (*M. baccata* × *M. niedzwetzkyana*). A small but strong-growing tree of Canadian origin. Young growths copper-tinted. Flowers comparatively large, light purplish-pink produced in large quantities, followed by purplish-red fruits. Best in a continental climate. C 1920. AM 1940 (for flower). AM 1945 (for fruit).

**'Snowcloud'** (*M.* 'Almey' × *M.* 'Katherine'). A small tree of upright habit, the young leaves bronze-green becoming dark green. Flowers pale pink in bud opening white, semi-double to double, 4cm across, long-lasting. Fruits yellow, sparse. Raised in the United States before 1978.

× **soulardii** (BAILEY) BRITT. (*M. domestica* × *M. ioensis*). A very beautiful hybrid with large, clear, almond-pink flowers and yellow, red-flushed fruits. C 1868.

**spectabilis** (AIT.) BORKH. A small tree with upright branches. The flowers are deep rose-red in bud, opening to blush, 5cm wide. One of the loveliest flowering crabs, at its best during late April and early May. China, but not known in the wild. C 1780.

**'Albiplena'** Large, semi-double, white, delicately violet-scented flowers. Probably of hybrid origin, although some authorities regard it as a form of *M. sylvestris*.

**'Riversii'** ('Rosea Plena') A tree with upright branches. The semi-double flowers are deep rose-red in bud, opening to rosy-pink. Raised by the English nurseryman, Thomas Rivers, before 1864.

× **sublobata** REHD. (*M. prunifolia* × *M. sieboldii*). A small, pyramidal tree. Leaves narrow-elliptic with an occasional lobe. Flowers pale pink; fruits yellow. Raised in the Arnold Arboretum from Japanese seed collected by Sargent in about 1892.

**sylvestris** (L.) MILL. (*M. pumila* HORT. in part) (*M. acerba* MERAT) "Common Crab Apple". A small tree or a large shrub, often with spurs. Leaves ovate to broad elliptic, shallowly-toothed, glabrous at maturity. Flowers white or suffused pink followed by yellowish-green or red-flushed fruits, crowned by the persistent calyx and measuring 2-4cm across. A parent of the orchard apple (*M. domestica*), also of several ornamental crabs. Sometimes wrongly referred to in cultivation as *M. pumila*, which name rightly belongs to the "Paradise Apple" of gardens. Europe. The true species is wild in most parts of the British Isles, but is less frequent than the forms of *M. domestica* which are commonly planted and naturalised.

**theifera** See *M. hupehensis*.

**toringo** See *M. sieboldii*.

**toringoides** (REHD.) HUGHES A very beautiful, small, shrubby tree with graceful, slender, wide-spreading branches and deeply lobed leaves. Flowers creamy-white, slightly fragrant, in May, followed by rounded or pear-shaped red and yellow fruits which are particularly conspicuous. Attractive autumn tints. W China. I 1904 by Ernest Wilson. AM 1919.

**transitoria** (BATAL.) SCHNEID. A slender, small tree resembling *M. toringoides* but more elegant, differing in its leaves being usually smaller, more narrowly lobed and more pubescent. Fruits smaller, rounded, yellow. Very beautiful in autumn colour. NW China. I 1911 by William Purdom.

**MALUS**—*continued*

**trilobata** (LABILL.) SCHNEID. A comparatively rare, erect-branched tree to about 13m, so distinct that it is sometimes listed in a separate genus (*Eriolobus*). Leaves maple-like, deeply three-lobed, the lobes themselves often sharply-lobed and toothed, attractively tinted red in autumn. Flowers large, white; fruits green, sometimes with a red flush, most frequent after hot summers. This little-known tree is worthy of more extensive public planting, particularly where space is confined. E Mediterranean region, NE Greece. C 1877.

**tschonoskii** (MAXIM.) SCHNEID. An attractive, strong-growing tree up to 12m of erect, conical habit, and with ovate, irregularly incised leaves. Flowers white, tinged pink; fruits globose, yellowish-green, tinged reddish-purple. One of the best trees for autumn colour, with its bold foliage of yellow, orange, purple and scarlet. A splendid tree for public planting in confined spaces. Japan. Introduced by Sargent in 1897. AM 1962. FCC 1983 (for autumn colour). AGM 1984.

**'Van Eseltine'** (*M.* × *arnoldiana* × *M. spectabilis*). A small tree of distinctive columnar habit, the branches stiffly erect. The semi-double flowers, 3.5-5cm across, are rose-scarlet in bud opening shell-pink, clouded white on the inner petals; fruits yellow. An excellent crab for a small garden. C 1930.

**'Veitch's Scarlet'** (*M.* 'Red Pippins' × *M.* × *robusta* 'Red Siberian'). An outstanding crab with white flowers followed by conspicuous bright red fruits. E. AM 1904. AM 1955.

**'Wintergold'** A shapely, small, round-headed tree with white, pink-budded flowers and an abundance of clear yellow fruits which are carried well into winter. A hybrid of *M. sieboldii*. C 1946.

**'Wisley'** A vigorous seedling of *M. niedzwetzkyana*. Leaves bronzy-red; flowers large, vinous-red, slightly scented, followed by large, purple-red fruits. AM 1924.

**yunnanensis** (FRANCH.) SCHNEID. A notable tree of small to medium size, with ovate, occasionally lobed leaves, turning crimson and orange in autumn. Flowers white; fruits deep red. W China. I 1900 by Ernest Wilson.

**var. veitchii** REHD. A comparatively tall, erect-branched variety, distinguished by its cordate, lobulate leaves and more brightly coloured fruits. C China. I 1901 by Ernest Wilson. AM 1912.

× **zumi** (MATSUM.) REHD. (*M. baccata* var. *mandshurica* × *M. sieboldii*). A small pyramidal tree resembling, and often included as a variety of, *M. sieboldii*, but differing in its rarely lobed leaves, and larger flowers and fruits. Flowers pink in bud, opening white, fragrant; fruits bright red. Japan. I 1892 by Charles Sargent. AM 1933.

**'Calocarpa'** A form of spreading habit and with smaller leaves and flowers. Bright red fruits persist throughout the winter. Japan. I 1890.

‡†*****MANGLIETIA** BLUME—**Magnoliaceae**—A small genus of about 25 species of evergreen trees closely related to *Magnolia* and natives of the Himalaya and SE Asia. They require a moist, lime-free soil and are only suitable for the mildest localities.

**insignis** (WALL.) BLUME A small tree with stout twigs and leathery, oblanceolate to narrowly oval leaves to 10-20cm long, dark glossy green above, pale green or slightly glaucous beneath. The erect, solitary, creamy-white, tinged pink or deep rose, magnolia-like flowers 7.5cm across are borne during May. Himalaya, Burma, W China. I about 1912.

**"MANUKA"** See *Leptospermum scoparium*.

**"MAPLE"** See *Acer*.

*****MARGYRICARPUS** RUIZ & PAVON—**Rosaceae**—A monotypic genus related to *Acaena* and *Alchemilla*. Any well drained soil.

**pinnatus** (LAM.) KUNTZE (*M. setosus* RUIZ & PAVON) "Pearl Berry". A charming, prostrate or slightly erect, white-berrying shrub from the Chilean Andes. Leaves evergreen, deep green and finely cut. Suitable for the rock garden. I 1829.

**MARSDENIA erecta** See *Cionura erecta*.

**"MAY"** See *Crataegus monogyna*.

**"MAY FLOWER"** See *Epigaea repens*.

**\*MAYTENUS** MOL.—**Celastraceae**—A large genus of more than 200 species of evergreen trees and shrubs native to the Americas, from the S United States to southern S America and tropical Africa. Only 1 or 2 species are hardy in most parts of the British Isles. Any well drained soil, acid or alkaline.

  **boaria** MOL. (*M. chilensis* DC.) A large, evergreen shrub or small tree, recalling *Phillyrea latifolia* but more graceful, with slender branches and narrow elliptic, finely-toothed leaves. The flowers are small and insignificant. An unusual species with pleasant, shining green foliage which is proving perfectly hardy. Chile. I 1829.

  **magellanica** (LAM.) HOOK. f. This species is proving hardy but slow-growing. It has leathery, elliptic, toothed leaves and small crimson flowers, scented strongly of orange peel, which are produced in clusters in the leaf axils in winter or early spring. S Chile. I 1938 by Captain Collingwood Ingram.

**"MAZZARD"** See *Prunus avium*.

**MEDICAGO** L.—**Leguminosae**—"Medick". A genus of more than 50 species of mainly annual and perennial, clover-like herbs with trifoliolate leaves. Natives of Europe, W Asia and Africa. Any well drained soil; full sun. The cultivated "Alfalfa" or "Lucerne" is *M. sativa*.

  **†\*arborea** L. "Moon Trefoil" "Tree Medick". A small, semi-evergreen shrub with clusters of yellow pea-flowers produced continuously, though often sparsely, from May to September; seed pods resembling snail shells. Excellent for maritime exposure; elsewhere it requires the shelter of a warm wall. Mediterranean region. I 1596.

**"MEDLAR"** See *Mespilus germanica*.

**†\*MELALEUCA** L.—**Myrtaceae**—About 150 species related to and resembling *Callistemon* and natives of Australia to SE Asia. Elegant shrubs as cultivated in this country but some attain tree size in their native haunts. Even given protection they are only suitable for the mildest localities, and need full sun but are wind resistant. Not tolerant of chalk soils.

  **gibbosa** LABILL. A small to medium-sized, wiry shrub, with small, crowded, opposite leaves. Flowers light purple in short dense terminal "bottlebrushes" during summer. Tasmania, S and SE Australia.

  **hypericifolia** (SALISB.) SMITH Large shrub of graceful habit. Leaves small, aptly described by the specific epithet. Flowers bright red in summer. SE Australia. I 1792.

  **squamea** LABILL. Small to medium-sized, erect shrub with narrow, alternate leaves crowded along the branches. Flowers variable in colour, usually purplish, in dense terminal heads in late spring. Tasmania, S and SE Australia. I 1805.

  **squarrosa** DONN ex SMITH An erect, rigid shrub. Leaves ovate-lanceolate to ovate, sharply-pointed; flowers pale yellow in crowded, oblong spikes during summer. Tasmania, S and SE Australia. I 1794.

  **wilsonii** F. MUELL. An elegant shrub up to 2m, with linear-lanceolate leaves and conspicuous red or pink flowers in clusters along the shoots during late spring or summer. W Australia. I 1861.

**†MELIA** L.—**Meliaceae**—A small genus of 3 species of sun-loving, deciduous, small trees or large shrubs natives of Asia and Australia of which the following species is the only one which sometimes succeeds in the mildest parts of the British Isles. Its bead-like seeds are used in necklaces, etc.

  **azedarach** L. "Bead Tree". A small tree or large shrub best grown against a warm sheltered wall or in a conservatory. Large, elegant, doubly pinnate leaves and small fragrant lilac flowers in loose panicles during summer. In warm countries clusters of rounded, yellow,

**MELIA azedarach**—*continued*

bead-like fruits are produced in autumn which remain long after the leaves have fallen. Commonly planted as a street tree in warmer countries, particularly in the Mediterranean region. It requires hot sun to ripen growth. Asia to Australia. C in England since the 16th century.

†\***MELIANTHUS** L.—**Melianthaceae**—-A small genus of about 6 species of sun-loving evergreen sub-shrubs, natives of S Africa, with attractive foliage and unusual flowers. Only suitable for the mildest parts of the British Isles, it can be herbaceous in colder areas.

**major** L. A handsome, evergreen sub-shrub with spreading, hollow stems. Its glaucous, deeply-toothed, pinnate leaves, 30-45cm long, give a striking subtropical effect. The tubular flowers are tawny-crimson, in dense, erect terminal racemes up to 15cm long in summer. Hardy in Cornwall and S Ireland and similar favoured areas, where it will attain 2m or more. Occasionally used in subtropical bedding. S Africa. I 1688. FCC 1975.

†**MELICOPE** FORST. & FORST. f.—**Rutaceae**—A genus of about 20 species of small trees and shrubs native of Australasia, the Pacific isles and tropical Asia. One species is occasionally grown in the mildest parts of the British Isles.

**ternata** FORST. & FORST. f. A large, semi-evergreen shrub for the mildest localities. Leaves trifoliolate. Flowers greenish-white in cymose inflorescences in autumn. New Zealand. I 1822.

†\***MELICYTUS** FORST. & FORST. f.—**Violaceae**—A small genus of 4 species of dioecious trees and shrubs, natives of New Zealand and the S Pacific Islands, bearing small, clustered flowers.

**ramiflorus** FORST. & FORST. f. "Whiteywood". As seen in this country a large shrub with lanceolate-oblong or narrow elliptic, coarsely-toothed leaves. The clusters of tiny greenish-yellow flowers are followed by violet or dark blue berries. New Zealand, Tonga, Fiji. AM 1925.

**MELIOSMA** BLUME—**Sabiaceae**—A genus of 20-25 species of evergreen and deciduous trees and shrubs, natives of SE Asia and C and S America. The following are handsome in leaf, which may be simple or compound, and produce spiraea-like, paniculate inflorescences, crowded with small, white flowers in summer. Although lime-tolerant, they succeed best in a deep neutral soil.

**cuneifolia** See *M. dilleniifolia* subsp. *cuneifolia*.

**dilleniifolia** (WALL. ex WIGHT & ARN.) WALP. A large shrub or small tree with stout, rusty hairy shoots. The large, prominently veined obovate leaves up to 20cm long and 12cm wide, are rusty hairy on the midrib above, grey hairy beneath. Flowers in large, upright panicles in summer. Himalaya, N Burma.

**subsp. cuneifolia** (FRANCH.) BEUS. (*M. cuneifolia* FRANCH.) A large shrub with simple, obovate, bristle-toothed leaves 8-18cm long, bearing spiraea-like plumes of creamy-white flowers with hawthorn-like fragrance in July. Fruit globose, about the size of a peppercorn, black. W China. I 1901 by Ernest Wilson.

**subsp. flexuosa** (PAMP.) BEUS. (*M. pendens* REHD. & WILS.) A large shrub with simple, obovate, bristle-toothed leaves, up to 15cm long. Flowers fragrant, white, in pendulous, terminal panicles in July. East C China. I 1907 by Ernest Wilson.

**subsp. tenuis** (MAXIM.) BEUS. (*M. tenuis* MAXIM.) A large shrub with slender, dark brown stems and coarsely-toothed, obovate leaves to 15cm long. The tiny, creamy-yellow flowers are carried in pyramidal, nodding panicles in May and June. Japan. I 1915.

**meliantha** See under *M. myriantha*.

**myriantha** SIEB. & ZUCC. In its typical state this is a native of Japan, E China and S Korea and differs from the form described below in the fewer veins of the leaf. I 1879 by Charles Maries.

**subsp. pilosa** (LECOMTE) BEUS. The plants grown under this name were raised from seed received from China. A spreading shrub 1.5-2m high and more across, with downy

**MELIOSMA myriantha subsp. pilosa**—*continued*
young shoots and narrow elliptic leaves sharply-toothed in the upper half to 16cm long. Wide panicles of creamy white flowers are borne at the tips of short, lateral branches in July. Our plants belong to var. *stewardii* (MERR.) BEUS. (*M. stewardii* MERR.) and were previously listed as *M. meliantha*. E and C China.

**oldhamii** See *M. pinnata* var. *oldhamii*.

**parviflora** LECOMTE Medium-sized shrub of semi-erect habit with small, obovate, glossy green, denticulate leaves. So far proving hardy in our nurseries. China. I 1936.

**pendens** See *M. dilleniifolia* subsp. *flexuosa*.

**pinnata** (ROXB.) WALP. A variable species covering a wide area from the Himalaya to E and SE Asia and New Guinea. Cultivated in the following form.

> **var. oldhamii** (MAXIM.) BEUS. (*M. oldhamii* MAXIM.) A rare, small tree with handsome pinnate, ash-like leaves up to 0.5m long. Flowers white in large erect terminal panicles in June. China, Korea. I 1900 by Ernest Wilson.

†**pungens** WALP. Medium-sized, semi-evergreen shrub with greyish stems and rather leathery, oblanceolate leaves conspicuously toothed in the upper half and with a tail-like apex, decurrent at the base.

**stewardii** See under *M. myriantha* subsp. *pilosa*.

**tenuis** See *M. dilleniifolia* subsp. *tenuis*.

**veitchiorum** HEMSL. A rare, small tree of architectural quality, remarkable for its very large, pinnate, red-stalked leaves, stout, rigid branches and prominent winter buds. Flowers creamy-white, fragrant, in 30-45cm long panicles, in May; fruits violet. W and C China. I 1901 by Ernest Wilson.

‡**MENZIESIA** SM.—**Ericaceae**—A genus of about 7 species, natives of North America and E Asia. Small, slow-growing, deciduous shrubs recalling *Enkianthus*, requiring lime-free soil and, if possible, protection from late frosts. Flowers in terminal clusters, resembling *Daboecia*, but waxy in texture. This small genus embracing at least 3 exquisite shrubs of top quality deserves greater recognition.

**ciliicalyx** (MIQ.) MAXIM. A beautiful, small shrub with oval or obovate, ciliate leaves and clusters of nodding, pitcher-shaped flowers in May, varying in colour from cream to soft purple. Japan. I 1915. AM 1938.

> **var. multiflora** See *M. multiflora*.

> **var. purpurea** MAK. (*M. purpurea* HORT. not MAXIM.) A superb, slow-growing variety with obovate, mucronate leaves. The striking, rose-purple flowers are larger than those of the type and appear slightly later. Usually grown in gardens wrongly as *M. purpurea* which is doubtfully in cultivation. Japan.

**ferruginea** SM. A small to medium-sized shrub with peeling bark. The small, cylindrical, pink-tinged flowers are borne in nodding clusters during May. W North America.

**glabella** A. GRAY A small shrub with obovate leaves and clusters of small, orange-flushed, pitcher-shaped flowers in late May and June. North America. I about 1885.

**multiflora** MAXIM. (*M. ciliicalyx* var. *multiflora*) A small shrub similar to *M. ciliicalyx*, but with shorter, more urn-shaped corollas, the colour varying from pale purple to near white, with deeper coloured lobes. Japan.

**pilosa** (MICHX.) JUSS. A small shrub of erect habit and modest charm. Young shoots and leaves glandular downy. The pendulous, urn-shaped flowers are 6mm long, creamy-yellow, flushed red and are carried in glandular-stalked, nodding clusters during May. E United States. I 1806.

**purpurea** See *M. ciliicalyx* var. *purpurea*.

**MESPILUS** L.—**Rosaceae**—A monotypic genus related to *Crataegus* but differing in its solitary flowers.

**germanica** L. "Medlar". A small, thorny, picturesque, wide-spreading tree rivalling the "Black Mulberry" as an isolated specimen for an architectural feature. The large, hairy leaves turn a warm russet in the autumn. Large white flowers are produced singly in May and June, followed by brown fruits, 2-3cm across. SE Europe to C Asia. Long cultivated in England and naturalised in some counties. Named clones selected for their

**MESPILUS germanica**—*continued*

fruits, such as 'Nottingham', are less thorny, with much larger leaves, flowers and fruits than wild plants.

**"MESPILUS, SNOWY"** See *Amelanchier*.

†\***METROSIDEROS** BANKS ex GAERTN.—**Myrtaceae**—A genus of about 50 species of handsome, evergreen trees, shrubs and aerial-rooted climbers related to *Callistemon*, natives of Australasia, Malaysia and S Africa. The brilliantly coloured "bottlebrush" flowers, composed largely of stamens, are often spectacular. All require protection and can only be grown outside in the mildest areas of the British Isles. Moderately lime-tolerant but not suitable for shallow chalk soils.

**diffusa** (FORST. f.) SMITH In cultivation in this country an exceedingly slow-growing small to medium-sized, lax or scandent shrub with cymes of pink-petalled flowers with long pinkish stamens in April and May. New Zealand. I 1910. AM 1931.

**excelsa** SOL. ex GAERTN. (*M. tomentosa* A. RICH.) Called the "Christmas Tree" in New Zealand, where it is abundant in parts of North Island and described as a "noble and picturesque tree". Its large "bottlebrush" flowers are brilliant crimson and smother the branches in summer. The finest examples in the British Isles are to be found in the Tresco Abbey Gardens. Elsewhere it is more usually a conservatory plant. I 1840.

**hypericifolia** HORT. Under this name we have grown a small, slender-branched shrub with angular reddish-brown shoots, small, ovate-oblong leaves and clusters of red flowers.

**kermadecensis** W.R.B. OLIVER (*M. villosa* KIRK not SMITH) Resembling *M. excelsa*, but a little smaller in all its parts; flowers scarlet. Suitable only for the very mildest areas. New Zealand (Kermadec Islands).

'**Variegata**' Leaves with a broad, creamy-white margin. It was originally thought to belong to *M. excelsa*. AM 1981.

**lucida** See *M. umbellata*.

**robusta** A. CUNN. The "Rata" of New Zealand. A magnificent, small to medium-sized, evergreen tree, for mild, maritime districts. Leaves dark green, thick and rounded, narrower on juvenile plants. Flowers coppery-scarlet appearing in late summer. Flowering at an earlier state than *M. umbellata*, but less hardy. AM 1959.

**tomentosa** See *M. excelsa*.

**umbellata** CAV. (*M. lucida* (FORST. f.) A. RICH.) "Southern Rata". One of the hardiest species, thriving in Cornwall and similarly favoured districts where it forms a large shrub or small tree of dense bushy habit. The small, polished, myrtle-like leaves are coppery when young. On mature specimens the clusters of .bright crimson-stamened flowers are produced in late summer illuminating the dark green foliage. New Zealand.

**villosa** See *M. kermadecensis*.

**"MEXICAN ORANGE BLOSSOM"** See *Choisya ternata*.

**"MEYER'S LEMON"** See *Citrus* 'Meyer's Lemon'.

**"MEZEREON"** See *Daphne mezereum*.

‡\***MICHELIA** L.—**Magnoliaceae**—About 45 species of evergreen trees or shrubs closely related to *Magnolia*, but differing most noticeably in the flowers being borne in the axils of the leaves. Natives of tropical and subtropical SE Asia. Only suitable for the milder lime-free areas.

**compressa** (MAXIM.) SARG. A rare, slow-growing shrub or occasionally a small tree with ovate to obovate, glossy green, leathery leaves, 5cm long. Flowers fragrant, pale yellow or whitish, with a purplish-red centre, opening during late spring. Most often seen growing against a south or west wall or in the sheltered corner of a house. Uninjured by the long severe winter of 1962/63. Japan, Ryukyus, I 1894.

†**doltsopa** BUCH.-HAM. ex DC. A magnificent small to medium-sized, semi-evergreen tree in the South West. Leaves 15-18cm long, leathery, glaucous beneath; flowers formed in autumn,

**MICHELIA doltsopa**—*continued*

opening in spring, multipetalled, white and heavily scented. W Yunnan, Tibet, E Himalaya. I about 1918 by George Forrest. AM 1961.

†**figo** (LOUR.) SPRENG. (*M. fuscata* (ANDR.) WALL.) (*Magnolia fuscata* ANDR.) A medium-sized to large shrub, best treated as a greenhouse plant. Leaves small, dark, glossy green; flowers small, brown-purple and strongly scented of pear drops, produced in a long succession during spring and summer. SE China. I 1789.

**MICROGLOSSA albescens** See *Aster albescens*.

**"MIMOSA"** See *Acacia dealbata*.

**MIMULUS** L. (*Diplacus* NUTT.)—**Scrophulariaceae**—A large genus of about 150 species of mainly annual and perennial herbs, but embracing 1 or 2 woody plants suitable for favoured sunny positions. Natives mainly of W North America but also occurring in S Africa, Asia, Australia and S America. Lime-tolerant.

†*****aurantiacus** CURT. (*M. glutinosus* WENDL.) The "Shrubby Musk" is a pretty shrub for mild localities, especially near the sea, growing about 1.2m high. Stems sticky to the touch. Flowers orange or salmon-yellow, borne throughout summer and autumn. California, Oregon. I in the late 18th century. AM 1938.

**var . puniceus** (NUTT.) A. GRAY (*M. puniceus* (NUTT.) STEUD.) A form differing mainly in its smaller, brick-red or orange-red flowers. California.

**glutinosus** See *M. aurantiacus*.

**puniceus** See *M. aurantiacus* var. *puniceus*.

‡*****MITCHELLA** L.—**Rubiaceae**—A genus of only 2 species of evergreen, creeping plants suitable for a cool spot on the rock garden, or as ground cover in shade. They require a lime-free soil.

**repens** L. "Partridge Berry". A charming mat-forming sub-shrub with procumbent rooting stems. The tiny, ovate or rounded leaves are dark glossy green and borne in pairs. The small, fragrant, white or pink flowers are borne in terminal pairs in June and July. Fruits scarlet, 12mm across. E and C North America. I about 1761. AM 1951.

†*****MITRARIA** CAV.—**Gesneriaceae**—A monotypic genus.

**coccinea** CAV. A low, spreading evergreen with small, glossy, leathery leaves and large, bright orange-scarlet tubular flowers borne singly in the leaf-axils from late spring through summer. A charming plant for a partially shaded, sheltered position. Unsuitable for shallow chalk soils. Chile, Chiloe. I 1846 by William Lobb. AM 1927.

**"MOCKERNUT"** See *Carya tomentosa*.

**"MOCK ORANGE"** See *Philadelphus*.

**MOLTKIA** LEHM.—**Boraginaceae**—A small genus of 6 species of herbaceous perennials and sub-shrubs related to *Lithodora*, differing in the exserted style. Natives of S Europe to SW Asia. A well drained site in full sun on scree or rock garden.

**petraea** (TRATT.) GRISEB. (*Lithospermum petraeum* (TRATT.) DC.) A lovely sub-shrub forming a neat bush 30-45cm high. Flowers tubular, pink in bud opening to violet-blue, in June and July. Balkan peninsula. I about 1840. FCC 1871.

**MORUS** L.—**Moraceae**—The "Mulberries" contain some 7 species of deciduous trees and shrubs natives of North and South America, Africa and Asia and generally form small to medium-sized picturesque trees. Although succeeding in any well drained soil, they respond to liberal treatment and are particularly suitable for town or coastal gardens. In winter the twigs may be recognised by the absence of a terminal bud. The brittle fleshy roots call for special care in planting.

**MORUS**—*continued*

**alba** L. "White Mulberry". A small to medium-sized tree of rugged appearance. Leaves heart-shaped, or ovate-lanceolate, often up to 15cm wide. Fruits whitish changing to reddish-pink or nearly black in some forms, sweet and edible. Silkworms are traditionally fed on the leaves of this tree. C Asia to China. Said to have been introduced into England in 1596.

**'Laciniata'** ('Skeletoniana') A curious form, the leaves deeply divided into narrow, long-pointed lobes.

**'Macrophylla'** A remarkable form with large, often lobed, leaves 18-22cm long, recalling those of a fig. C 1836.

**'Nana'** A small shrubby form of compact habit.

**'Pendula'** A striking, small, weeping tree with closely packed, perpendicularly falling branches. Very ornamental when in full fruit. AM 1897.

**'Pyramidalis'** An erect-branched form, resembling a Lombardy Poplar in habit.

**'Skeletoniana'** See 'Laciniata'.

**var. tatarica** (PALL.) SER. A small, bushy-headed geographical variety with smaller leaves and fruits. Withstands very low temperatures.

**'Venosa'** Leaves slenderly tapered at both ends, green with conspicuous, pale veins.

**australis** POIR. (*M. acidosa* GRIFF.) A small bushy tree or large shrub with variously shaped leaves. Fruits dark red, sweet. China, Japan, Korea, Taiwan. I 1907 by Ernest Wilson.

**bombycis** KOIDZ . (*M. kagayamae* KOIDZ.) A large shrub or small tree with ovate, irregularly toothed leaves 10-20cm long. Fruits purplish-black. The leaves are much used for feeding silkworms. Closely related to and possibly only a form of *M. alba*. Japan, Korea, Sakhalin.

**cathayana** HEMSL. A remarkable, small tree with large, heart-shaped, slenderly-pointed leaves and black, red or white fruits 2.5cm long. C and E China. I 1907 by Ernest Wilson.

**kagayamae** See *M. bombycis*.

**†microphylla** BUCKL. In cultivation a very slow-growing bushy shrub, differing from *M. rubra* in its tiny leaves, also smaller catkins and fruits. This distinct species has not succeeded out-of-doors in our nurseries. S United States and Mexico. I 1926.

**nigra** L. "Black Mulberry". A small, very long-lived architectural tree with wide-spreading head, becoming gnarled and picturesque with age. Leaves heart-shaped, rough above, downy below. Fruits dark almost black-red, with an agreeable taste. W Asia. Said to have first been grown in England early in the 16th century. AGM 1984.

**rubra** L. "Red Mulberry". A rare species in cultivation. A small to medium-sized tree with rounded downy leaves, turning bright yellow in autumn. Very like the "White Mulberry". Fruit red. E and C United States. I 1629.

**'Nana'** A dwarf, slow-growing form of compact habit, broader than high. Leaves smaller and prominently three to five-lobed.

**"MOUNTAIN ASH"** See *Sorbus aucuparia*.

**"MULBERRY"** See *Morus*.

**"MULBERRY, PAPER"** See *Broussonetia papyrifera*.

**†\*MUSA** L.—**Musaceae**—The "Bananas" make up a genus of some 35 species of large, often tree-like herbs natives of tropical Asia. The commonly eaten bananas come from forms of *M. acuminata*, native of SE Asia but widely grown in warm regions of the world.

**basjoo** SIEB. & ZUCC. ex IINUMA A large evergreen herb reaching about 3m which although of tree-like habit is not woody. Closely related to the edible banana and similar to it with very large leaves. Flowers creamy-yellow in summer followed by inedible green fruits. A handsome plant for tropical effects but will thrive only in sheltered places in the South West. Ryukyu Islands. I about 1881 by Charles Maries.

**†\*MYOPORUM** BANKS & SOL. ex FORST. f.—**Myoporaceae**—A genus of about 30 species of evergreen trees and shrubs, native mainly of Australia but extending to New Zealand,

**275**

**MYOPORUM**—*continued*

the Pacific Islands and SE Asia. Only for the mildest localities. Lime-tolerant. *M. tenuifolium* G. FORST. is commonly planted and naturalised in S Spain. It has white flowers in spring and purple fruits in summer.

**laetum** FORST. f. (*M. perforatum* HORT.) "Ngaio". An evergreen shrub or small tree notable for its dark, sticky buds and its lanceolate leaves, conspicuously studded with pellucid glands. Flowers small, white, purple-spotted. Will survive only in the mildest parts of the British Isles. Excellent for maritime exposure. New Zealand.

‡**MYRICA** L.—**Myricaceae**—A genus of about 50 species of interesting aromatic shrubs widely distributed throughout the world. Embracing species tolerant of dry sterile soil and those which delight in an acid bog. Flowers unisexual, in small catkins.

*****californica** CHAM. & SCHLECT. "Californian Bayberry". A glossy-leaved, hardy, evergreen shrub of medium to large size, occasionally a small tree. The oblanceolate, serrated leaves are polished apple-green on both surfaces, less aromatic than in other species. Fruits dark purple, clustered like small blackberries on short spurs and persisting until midwinter. Tolerant of both moist and acid conditions. W United States. I 1848.

*****cerifera** L. (*M. caroliniensis* MILL.) "Candleberry" "Wax Myrtle". A North American evergreen shrub or small tree, with narrow obovate or oblanceolate leaves. A pleasing subject for a damp site. The glaucous wax which covers the fruits is made into fragrantly burning candles. E United States. I 1669.

**var. pumila** MICHX. A dwarf form spreading by underground stems and making a low hummock.

**gale** L. "Sweet Gale" "Bog Myrtle". A small, native, deciduous shrub of dense habit. Male and female catkins, of a warm golden brown colour, which glisten in the sunlight are produced on separate plants during April and May. The whole plant is strongly aromatic and may be grown in acid, boggy swamps where few other plants will exist. Europe to NE Asia, North America. C 1750.

**pensylvanica** LOIS. "Bayberry". A hardy, valuable plant for acid soils. The oblong or obovate aromatic leaves fall late in autumn. Conspicuous in winter with its tiny grey-white fruits. An excellent maritime plant, good for dry arid conditions. E North America. I 1727.

**MYRICARIA** DESV.—**Tamaricaceae**—A small genus of about 10 species distributed from Europe to E Asia. Closely related to, and requiring the same conditions as, *Tamarix*, but differing in the flowers which have more numerous stamens, united in the lower half.

**germanica** (L.) DESV. (*Tamarix germanica* L.) Wand-like stems 1.2-2m high carry feathery, blue-green foliage and light pink, fluffy flowers throughout the summer. Succeeds best in neutral or acid soil but is lime-tolerant. C and S Europe, W Asia. C 1582.

**"MYROBALAN"** See *Prunus cerasifera.*

†*****MYRSINE** L.—**Myrsinaceae**—A small genus of 5 species of chiefly tropical trees and shrubs primarily of botanical interest; the females sometimes produce attractive fruits. Moderately lime-tolerant, but not recommended for a shallow, chalky soil.

**africana** L. A small shrub with aromatic myrtle-like leaves and axillary clusters of tiny reddish-brown flowers. On female plants blue-black, pea-like fruits are produced. Resembling in general appearance *Paxistima myrtifolia*, differing in its alternate leaves and dioecious flowers. Perfectly hardy given reasonable shelter. Himalaya, China, Azores, Taiwan, Mts of E and S Africa. I 1691. AM 1927.

**var. retusa** (AIT.) DC. A variety with more rounded-obovate leaves.

†**australis** (A. RICH.) ALLAN (*Suttonia australis* A. RICH.) "Mapau". A small to medium-sized shrub with slender orange-red branchlets and oblong or elliptic leaves with strongly undulate margins. For a sheltered position in mild gardens. New Zealand.

**nummularia** HOOK. f. (*Suttonia nummularia* (HOOK. f.) MEZ) A prostrate, evergreen shrub with wiry stems and densely-set, small, orbicular, brownish-green leaves. On female plants small blue-purple fruits are produced. New Zealand.

**MYRSINE**—*continued*

†**semiserrata** WALL. A large shrub or occasionally a small tree with thinly textured, elliptic-ovate, slender-pointed, serrated leaves up to 12cm long which are prettily tinted when young. Flowers in axillary clusters, reddish to white, followed by blue to reddish-purple berries. Previously listed as *Ilex fragilis*. Only for the mildest areas. E Himalaya, W and C China.

**"MYRTLE"** See *Myrtus*.

*****MYRTUS** L.—**Myrtaceae**—The "Myrtles" are an easily cultivated and effective group of mostly white-flowered, aromatic evergreens for mild climates. They succeed best in full sun on any well drained soil, including chalk soils, and are excellent for maritime exposure.

**apiculata** See *M. luma*.

†**bidevillei** BENTH. A small, erect shrub with dainty leaves rather like those of *Lonicera nitida* in shape and size. Australia.

†**bullata** A. CUNN. not SALISB. (*Lophomyrtus bullata* (A. CUNN.) BURRET) The New Zealand "Rama rama". A large bush or small tree, with distinct round, leathery, coppery-green or reddish-brown, bullate leaves. Flowers white followed by blackish-red berries; suitable only for the mildest localities. C 1854.

†**chequen** (MOL.) SPRENG. A Chilean myrtle proving to be one of the hardiest, and ultimately forming a small, densely leafy tree, flowering in summer and autumn. Leaves aromatic, bright green, undulate. I 1847 by William Lobb.

†**communis** L. The "Common Myrtle", hardy in many localities, particularly by the sea. An aromatic, densely leafy shrub, attaining 3-4.5m against a sunny wall. The white flowers are borne profusely in July and August, followed by purple-black berries. Mediterranean region, SW Europe, W Asia; thoroughly naturalised in S Europe particularly in the Mediterranean region. Cultivated in England in the 16th century. AM 1972. AGM 1984.

'**Flore Pleno**' An uncommon form with double flowers.

'**Microphylla**' An attractive form, smaller in all its parts.

**subsp. tarentina** (L.) NYMAN ('Jenny Reitenbach') A very pretty, compact, free-flowering form with small narrow leaves and white berries. Flowers in autumn with pink-tinged petals. Mediterranean region. AM 1977. AGM 1984.

'**Variegata**' Leaves grey-green, narrowly margined creamy-white. A pretty plant. A variegated form of subsp. *tarentina* is also in cultivation.

†**lechleriana** (MIQ.) SEALY A large shrub or small tree of dense habit, well furnished to the ground. Leaves recalling those of *Vaccinium ovatum*, strikingly copper-coloured when young, ovate, dark polished green with reddish stalks. The clusters of fragrant blossoms appear in May; berries red then black, edible. Chile. I 1927 by Harold Comber. AM 1945.

†**luma** MOL. (*M. apiculata* HORT.) A lovely species attaining small tree size in mild localities. The cinnamon-coloured outer bark of even quite young trees peels off in patches, exposing the beautiful, cream-coloured inner surface. Leaves dark, dull green, oval, ending in a short abrupt point. The solitary, white flowers bedeck the branches during late summer and early autumn. The red and black fruits, when produced, are edible and sweet. In some southern Irish gardens it has become naturalised and reproduction is prolific. Chile. I 1843. AM 1978.

'**Glanleam Gold**' Leaves with a conspicuous creamy-yellow margin, pink-tinged when young. Originated as a seedling at Glanleam House, Valentia Island, Co Kerry before 1970.

'**Penwith**' Leaves deep blue-green and grey-green, margined with creamy-white, strongly pink-tinged in winter and when young. A seedling found in Penlee Memorial Park, Penzance in 1972 by Mr E.M. Cock.

**nummularia** POIR. The hardiest myrtle is a tiny prostrate shrublet with wiry, reddish stems. The tiny, neat, rounded leaves are borne in 2 opposite ranks. Flowers white, borne at the end of the stems in May or June followed by pink berries. S Argentina, S Chile, Falkland Isles. I before 1927. AM 1967.

# TREES AND SHRUBS

**MYRTUS**—*continued*

†**obcordata** (RAOUL) HOOK. f. (*Lophomyrtus obcordata* (RAOUL) BURRET) "Rohutu". A graceful, medium-sized to large shrub, the thin branches clothed with small, notched leaves. Berries dark red or violet. New Zealand.

†×**ralphii** HOOK. f. (*M. bullata* × *M. obcordata*). (*Lophomyrtus* × *ralphii* (HOOK. f.) BURRET) A medium-sized to large shrub, occasionally a small tree, with ovate or rounded, puckered leaves. Flowers almond-pink, solitary in the axils of the leaves; berries dark red. A variable hybrid ranging in character between the parents. There are numerous variegated and purple-leaved forms. New Zealand.

†**ugni** MOL. (*Eugenia ugni* (MOL.) HOOK. f.) "Chilean Guava". A slow-growing, small to medium-sized, leathery-leaved shrub, rather stiff and erect in habit, bearing nodding, waxy, pink bells followed by edible and delicious, aromatic, mahogany-red berries. Chile. I 1844 by William Lobb. AM 1925.

**'Variegata'** Leaves green shaded grey, with creamy-yellow margin.

---

\***NANDINA** THUNB.—**Berberidaceae**—A curious monotypic genus looking somewhat like a bamboo, but related to *Berberis*. Should be given a sheltered position in full sun in any well drained soil.

**domestica** THUNB. "Sacred Bamboo". An extremely decorative, bamboo-like shrub of medium size, with long, erect, unbranched stems. The large, compound, green leaves are attractively tinged purplish-red in spring and autumn. Flowers small, white, in large terminal panicles during summer. Berries red but rarely produced in this country except after very hot summers. Hardy in all but the coldest districts. C China, Japan. I 1804. AM 1897.

**'Firepower'** Similar to 'Nana Purpurea' but foliage yellow-green in summer, orange-red in winter.

**'Nana Purpurea'** A small shrub of more compact habit, with less compound leaves and broader leaflets. The young foliage reddish-purple throughout the season.

---

**NEILLIA** D. DON—**Rosaceae**—A small genus of about 10 species of deciduous shrubs related to *Spiraea* and, like them, of the easiest cultivation in all but very dry soils. Natives of China and the Himalaya.

**longiracemosa** See *N. thibetica*.

**malvacea** See *Physocarpus malvaceus*.

**ribesoides** See *N. sinensis* var. *ribesoides*.

**sinensis** OLIVER A medium-sized shrub with glabrous shoots and bronze-purple young foliage. Leaves lobed and toothed. Flowers in short terminal racemes in June, petals and calyx white. C China. I by Ernest Wilson in 1901.

**var. ribesoides** (REHD.) VIDAL (*N. ribesoides* REHD.) Medium-sized shrub closely related to *N. thibetica*. Leaves deeply and incisely-toothed. Flowers pink, borne in dense racemes in early summer. W China. C 1930.

**thibetica** BUR. & FRANCH. (*N. longiracemosa* HEMSL.) A very attractive medium-sized shrub with erect, downy stems bearing ovate, slender-pointed, often three-lobed leaves and slender terminal racemes of pink, tubular flowers in May and June. W China. Introduced by E.H. Wilson in 1904. AM 1931.

**thyrsiflora** D. DON Small to medium-sized shrub of spreading habit with long, arching stems. Leaves three-lobed, slender-pointed and sharply-toothed. The small, white flowers are borne on branched racemes at the ends of the shoots during summer. E Himalaya.

**torreyi** See *Physocarpus malvaceus*.

---

†\***NEOLITSEA** (BENTH.) MERRILL—**Lauraceae**—A genus of some 60 species of evergreen aromatic trees and shrubs with attractive foliage; mainly native of tropical Asia. Flowers dioecious. A few species succeed in the mildest parts of the British Isles. Not recommended for shallow chalk soil.

**sericea** (BLUME) KOIDZ. (*N. glauca* (SIEB.) KOIDZ.) (*Litsea glauca* SIEB.) A rare and distinguished member of the Lauraceae, forming a medium to large shrub. This remarkable shrub has succeeded here in a sheltered position for the past 25 years with but little frost

**NEOLITSIA sericea**—*continued*

damage. The unfolding fawn-brown leaves are most attractive in colour and texture, like soft suede above and white silk beneath, becoming with age leathery and dark glossy green above, glaucous beneath; aromatic when crushed. Flowers greenish-yellow in dense clusters in October. Japan, China, Taiwan, Korea.

†\***NERIUM** L.—**Apocynaceae**—A small genus of 2 species of tender, ornamental, sun-loving evergreens related to, but very different from, the periwinkle. Lime-tolerant, but not recommended for shallow chalk soil. The foliage is poisonous. The other species, *N. indicum* MILL., is native from SW Asia to China.

**oleander** L. "Oleander". A superb evergreen along the Mediterranean seaboard of S Europe where it rivals *Camellia japonica* of more northern gardens. An erect-branched evergreen shrub of medium to large size with pairs or whorls of leathery, long, lance-shaped leaves. Flowers like large periwinkles. Numerous forms are grown with white, yellow, buff or pink flowers, single, double or semi-double, appearing from June to October, as well as forms with variegated leaves. In the British Isles the oleander is one of the best evergreens for tub culture standing out of doors in full sun in the summer and protected in the conservatory during winter. Mediterranean region to SW Asia. I 1596.

**"NETTLE TREE"** See *Celtis*.

**NEVIUSIA** A. GRAY—**Rosaceae**—A monotypic genus, mainly of botanical interest, related to *Kerria*. The petals are absent, but the white stamens are so numerous as to be conspicuous. Any well drained soil.

**alabamensis** GRAY. "Alabama Snow Wreath". A spiraea-like shrub up to 2m with arching branches, covered during April and May with clusters of fluffy white flowerheads composed of numerous stamens. Enjoys a sunny position. Alabama (United States), rare in the wild. I about 1860.

**"NEW ZEALAND FLAX"** See *Phormium tenax*.

**"NORWAY MAPLE"** See *Acer platonoides*.

**NOTELAEA excelsa** See *Picconia excelsa*.

‡**NOTHOFAGUS** BLUME—**Fagaceae**—The "Southern Beeches" are a small genus of very ornamental, fast-growing evergreen and deciduous trees or large shrubs; about 20 species from S America and Australasia. Related to *Fagus*, but differing in the normally small leaves, closely spaced along the branchlets, and in the male and female flowers appearing singly or in clusters of 3. They vary in degree of hardiness and many are of rapid growth but are poor wind-resisters. They do not survive on chalk soils.

× **alpina** (POEPP. & ENDL.) OERST. (*N. nervosa* × *N. obliqua*). This hybrid which is intermediate between the parents was originally described from Chile where it occurs in the wild with the parents. It has since arisen in cultivation where seed has been collected from the parents when they are grown together. At one time regarded as the correct name for *N. nervosa* and some plants grown under this name may be that species.

**antarctica** (FORST. f.) OERST. "Antarctic Beech". An elegant, fast-growing tree of medium size. Leaves small, rounded and heart-shaped, irregularly toothed, dark green and glossy, turning yellow in autumn. Trunk and primary branches often curiously twisted. Chile. I 1830. AGM 1984.

**'Benmore'** ('Prostrata') A low spreading form growing into a dense mound of interlacing branches.

**var. uliginosa** A. DC. A variety with rather larger, somewhat pubescent leaves. Chile.

\***betuloides** (MIRBEL) BLUME A medium-sized to large, densely leafy, evergreen tree, of columnar habit at least when young. Leaves ovate or roundish, usually less than 2.5cm long, dark shining green and toothed, closely arranged on the branchlets. Chile, Argentina. I 1830.

**NOTHOFAGUS**—*continued*

**cliffortioides** See *N. solanderi* var. *cliffortioides*.

†**cunninghamii** (HOOK.) OERST. A rare, small evergreen tree in mild gardens. The wiry shoots are clothed with tiny, almost diamond-shaped, closely set, glabrous leaves which are bluntly-toothed in the upper half. C 1860. Tasmania.

*****dombeyi** (MIRBEL) BLUME A medium to large evergreen tree of vigorous habit. Leaves 2.5-4cm long, doubly-toothed, dark shining green. A fairly hardy tree which may lose its leaves in cold winters. In leaf very like *N. betuloides* but usually a faster-growing, wider-spreading tree with a more loosely open arrangement of its branches. Chile, Argentina. I 1916. AGM 1984.

*****fusca** (HOOK. f.) OERST. "Red Beech". Somewhat tender when young but developing into a beautiful, hardy, small to medium-sized evergreen tree. The rounded or oval, coarsely-toothed leaves, 2.5-4cm long, often turn copper in the autumn. The bark on old trees becomes flaky. New Zealand.

**glauca** (PHIL.) KRASSER A large tree in the wild related to *N. obliqua* but not adapting well to cultivation in this country. Juvenile trees bear large leaves which are shallowly lobed and toothed and rough on both sides. As the tree matures these are replaced by adult foliage in which the leaves are similar to those of *N. obliqua* but relatively broader. The bark is very distinct and ornamental, even on young trees, being pale orange-brown and peeling in thin flakes. It has reached about 5m in the Hillier Gardens and Arboretum in ten years. C Chile.

†*****menziesii** (HOOK. f.) OERST. "Silver Beech". A graceful, small to medium-sized evergreen tree akin to *N. cunninghamii*. Leaves up to 12mm long, rotund-ovate, dark-green, double-toothed. Hardy in the southern counties if well sited. Bark of young wood cherry-like. New Zealand.

†*****moorei** (F. MUELL.) KRASSER "Australian Beech". A small to medium-sized, evergreen tree with comparatively large, hard, leathery, dark green leaves, 4-8cm long, which are an attractive copper colour when young. Not hardy here and only suitable for the mildest localities. New South Wales, Queensland. I 1892.

**nervosa** (PHIL.) DIM. & MIL. (*N. procera* (POEPP. & ENDL.) OERST.) A fast-growing tree of large size, distinguished by its comparatively large, prominently veined leaves 4-10cm long, resembling those of the hornbeam. Usually gives rich autumn tints. Chile, Argentina. I 1913. AGM 1984.

**obliqua** (MIRBEL) BLUME "Roble Beech". A large, elegant, very fast-growing tree, forming a handsome specimen in a few years. Leaves broadly ovate or oblong, 5-8cm long, irregularly toothed, glabrous. Introduced from Chile by H.J. Elwes in 1902. Chile, Argentina. AGM 1984.

**procera** See *N. nervosa*.

**pumilio** (POEPP. & ENDL.) KRASSER "Lenga". A variable plant in the wild, ranging from a shrub to a tree larger than *N. antarctica* to which it is related. Plants in the Hillier Gardens and Arboretum are making small trees or large shrubs with several upright branches. Leaves ovate, to 3 × 2cm, oblique at the base, dark matt green above, margined with blunt teeth. S Chile, S Argentina. I about 1960.

*****solanderi** (HOOK. f.) OERST. "Black Beech". A tall, slender, medium-sized evergreen tree with ascending fan-like branches. Branchlets wiry, bearing neatly arranged, tiny, oblong or elliptic, entire leaves. C 1917. New Zealand.

**var. cliffortioides** (HOOK. f.) POOLE (*N. cliffortioides* (HOOK. f.) OERST.) "Mountain Beech". An elegant, small to medium-sized, fast-growing tree, differing in its generally smaller, ovate leaves with curled edges and raised tip. New Zealand.

**NOTHOPANAX arboreum** See *Pseudopanax arboreus*.

**davidii** See *Pseudopanax davidii*.

**laetum** See *Pseudopanax laetus*.

**NOTOSPARTIUM** HOOK. f.—**Leguminosae**—A small genus of 3 species embracing some moderately hardy, sun-loving, broom-like shrubs from the South Island of New Zealand. They succeed in full sun in any well drained soil.

**NOTOSPARTIUM**—*continued*

    **carmichaeliae** HOOK. f. The "Pink Broom" of New Zealand is a charming, medium-sized shrub of graceful habit, its arching, leafless stems wreathed in July with lilac-pink pea-flowers. Only injured in the coldest winters. I 1883. FCC 1889.

    **glabrescens** PETRIE A large shrub, a tree in its native habitat. Branches long and whippy; flowers rose, carried in loose racemes during May and June. I 1930.

**NUTTALLIA cerasiformis** See *Oemleria cerasiformis*.

‡**NYSSA** L.—**Nyssaceae**—A small genus of about 5 species of deciduous trees noted for their rich autumn tints. Flowers insignificant followed by equally inconspicuous blue-black fruits. They require moist, lime-free soil, and are best planted when small as they resent disturbance.

    **aquatica** L. (*N. uniflora* WANGENH.) "Water Tupelo". A rare, small tree with ovate-oblong leaves, downy beneath as are the young shoots. SE United States. I 1735.

    **sinensis** OLIV. A rare, large shrub or small tree of spreading habit proving perfectly hardy here. Leaves narrowly ovate up to 15cm long. A magnificent introduction. The young growths are red throughout the growing season and in autumn the leaves change to every shade of red. China. C 1902. FCC 1976. AGM 1984.

    **sylvatica** MARSH. (*N. multiflora* WANGENH.) "Tupelo". A handsome, slow-growing, medium-sized to large tree of broadly columnar outline. Leaves variable in shape generally obovate or oval, pointed, up to 15cm long, dark glossy green, occasionally dull green above. A dense-headed tree with handsome foliage turning rich scarlet, orange and yellow in the autumn. S Canada, E United States, C and S Mexico. I 1750. AM 1951. FCC 1968. AGM 1969.

    **var. biflora** (WALT.) SARG. "Swamp Tupelo". A variety with usually narrower leaves and bearing the female flowers in pairs. SE United States.

    **'Jermyns Flame'** A form selected from plants in the Hillier Gardens and Arboretum by John Hillier in 1985. Leaves relatively large with striking autumn colours of red, yellow and orange.

    **'Sheffield Park'** Selected from one of the many plants of this species raised by Arthur Soames of the National Trust gardens at Sheffield Park. The brilliant orange-red colouring starts 2 or 3 weeks before most other tupelos. AGM 1984.

**"OAK"** See *Quercus*.

**OCHNA** L.—**Ochnaceae**—A large genus of more than 80 species of evergreen and deciduous trees and shrubs natives of warm temperate and tropical regions of the Old World. The following is the only species occasionally met with in cultivation, requiring conservatory treatment.

    *****serrulata** (HOCHST.) WALP. (*O. multiflora* HORT. not DC.) A small shrub for the conservatory. Flowers yellow followed by curious, pendant, black, pea-like fruits, beautifully set-off by the bright crimson, waxy calyces. Natal (S Africa). I 1860. FCC 1879.

**OEMLERIA** REICHB.—**Rosaceae**—A monotypic genus related to, but superficially very different from, *Prunus*, with male and female flowers usually on different plants. Easily cultivated in all types of fertile soil, but sometimes inclined to become chlorotic in very poor shallow chalk soils.

    **cerasiformis** (HOOK. & ARN.) LANDON (*Osmaronia cerasiformis* (TORR. & A. GRAY) GREENE) (*Nuttallia cerasiformis* TORR. & A. GRAY) "Oso Berry". A suckering shrub, forming a thicket of erect stems 2-2.5m or more high; producing its pendent racemes of fragrant, white, ribes-like flowers in February and March. Fruits plum-like, brown at first, purple when ripe. Leaves sea-green, conspicuous on vigorous young growths, emerging very early as the flowers open. California. I 1848. AM 1927 (as *Nuttallia cerasiformis*).

†*****OLEA** L.—**Oleaceae**—A genus of about 20 species of tender evergreen trees and shrubs with opposite, leathery leaves. Natives of warm regions of the Old World. 1 or 2 species survive in the mildest localities. Any well drained soil.

**OLEA**—*continued*

**europaea** L. The "Olive" is only hardy in the mildest areas of the British Isles where it forms a large shrub or small tree, with grey-green, leathery leaves, glaucous beneath, and axillary racemes of fragrant, small white flowers in late summer. The olive oil of commerce is extracted from the fruits. Mediterranean region, widely naturalised in warm temperate countries. Cultivated from time immemorial.

**verrucosa** LINK A small tree or large shrub with greyish, warty shoots and linear-lanceolate leaves. S Africa. I 1814.

**"OLEANDER"** See *Nerium oleander.*

**\*OLEARIA** MOENCH—**Compositae**—The "Daisy Bushes" or "Tree Daisies" are of Australasian origin, with about 130 species. As a genus they are attractive, evergreen, easy to grow, wind-resistant and sun-loving shrubs. They include some of the finest of all evergreens for maritime exposure. All have daisy-like flowerheads, which are white or creamy-white (unless otherwise stated), and the average height attained in this country is 1.2-2.5m. Straggly or untidy specimens may be hard pruned in April. Some species are very tolerant of atmospheric pollution. They will succeed in any well drained soil and are especially recommended for chalky soils.

†**albida** HOOK. f. (*O. albiflora* HORT.) A medium-sized shrub of upright habit with oblong-elliptic, undulate, pale green leaves, white beneath. A tender species, hardy plants in cultivation under this name being referable to *O.* 'Talbot de Malahide', a hybrid of *O. avicenniifolia.* New Zealand.

†**arborescens** (FORST. f.) CKN. & LAING (*O. nitida* (HOOK. f.) HOOK. f.) A vigorous large shrub or small tree up to 4m. Broadly ovate leaves, shining dark green above, with a silvery, satiny sheen beneath, slightly toothed. Flowerheads in large corymbs in May or June. New Zealand.

†**argophylla** (LABILL.) BENTH. A medium-sized to large shrub with grey tomentose shoots. Leaves elliptic, to 10cm long, spiny at the margins, dark glossy green above with a thin silvery tomentum beneath. Small four to six-rayed flowers with yellow centres are borne in large corymbs during autumn and winter. SE Australia, Tasmania.

**avicenniifolia** (RAOUL) HOOK. f. A medium-sized to large shrub with pointed leaves, whitish or buff beneath. Flowerheads sweetly fragrant, borne in wide corymbs, in August and September. The leaves bear a distinct resemblance to those of the "White Mangrove", *Avicennia alba.* A plant often erroneously grown in gardens as *O. albida* is thought to be a hybrid of this species and has been named *O.* 'Talbot de Malahide'. A good dense hedgemaking shrub, especially in maritime exposure or industrial areas. New Zealand.

**'White Confusion'** A form with larger, slightly wavy leaves, and masses of white flowerheads in summer.

**capillaris** BUCHAN. (*O. arborescens* var. *capillaris* (BUCHAN.) KIRK) A small, compact, rounded and very hardy shrub up to 1.2m, with leaves similar to those of *O. arborescens*, but much smaller and entire or minutely toothed. Flowerheads in corymbs in June. New Zealand.

†**chathamica** KIRK. A beautiful, small shrub up to 1.2m resembling *O. semidentata*, but with broader, green leaves inclined to be obovate, three-veined beneath. Flowerheads up to 5cm across, solitary on long stalks, pale violet with purple centres in June. Chatham Isles. I 1910. AM 1938.

†**colensoi** HOOK. f. A large shrub with obovate or oblong-obovate, leathery leaves, shining green above, white woolly beneath; flowerheads brownish-purple in July. Makes an excellent tall, evergreen shrub in favoured localities. New Zealand.

**cymbifolia** See *O. nummulariifolia* var. *cymbifolia.*

**dentata** See *O. macrodonta* and *O. rotundifolia.*

†**erubescens** (DC.) DIPP. A small, spreading shrub with reddish shoots and conspicuously toothed, shining dark green leaves; flowering in May or June. Tasmania. C 1840.

**var. ilicifolia** (DC.) BEAN A form with larger leaves occasionally 7.5cm long by 2.5cm wide. Flowerheads also larger. SE Australia.

**OLEARIA**—*continued*

†×**excorticata** BUCHAN. (*O. arborescens*×*O. lacunosa*). A remarkable shrub up to 3m with narrow, leathery leaves up to 10cm long; shining dark green above, thickly buff-felted beneath. New Zealand.

†**floribunda** (HOOK. f.) BENTH. A slender, Tasmanian species up to 2m, having the appearance of a tree heath. The branches are crowded with minute, deep green leaves and in June are wreathed with small, white flowerheads. Tasmania, S and SE Australia. AM 1935.

**forsteri** See *O. paniculata.*

†**frostii** (F. MUELL.) J.H. WILLIS A small, downy shrub with sage-green, shallowly-toothed leaves. Flowerheads solitary on long peduncles, large, double, mauve, recalling the best forms of the modern michaelmas daisy. Has been wrongly cultivated as *O. gravis.* SE Australia.

†**furfuracea** (A. RICH.) HOOK. f. A large shrub or small tree with attractive, glossy, leathery leaves 5-10cm long, grey-white beneath. Flowerheads borne in wide corymbs in August. New Zealand.

**gunniana** See *O. phlogopappa.*

†**glandulosa** (LABILL.) BENTH. A distinct, small to medium-sized aromatic shrub with green shoots and narrowly linear, dark glossy green leaves edged with curious, small, wart-like glands. Small white flowers are borne in open corymbs in late summer and autumn. SE Australia.

×**haastii** HOOK. f. (*O. avicenniifolia*×*O. moschata*). A rounded bush of medium size with small, entire leaves, white-felted beneath, and smothered with fragrant, white flowerheads in July and August. Hardy almost everywhere in the British Isles, and tolerant of town conditions. An excellent, well-proven hedging plant. New Zealand. I 1858. FCC 1873.

†**'Henry Travers'** (*O. semidentata* HORT. not DECNE. ex HOOK. f.) One of the loveliest of all shrubs for the more favoured coastal gardens. A medium-sized shrub with lanceolate grey-green leaves, silvery beneath. The large, pendent, aster-like flowerheads are lilac, with a purple centre and appear in June. I to Dublin in 1908 and possibly the hybrid *O. chathamica*×*O. semidentata* which occurs in the wild in the Chatham Islands.

**ilicifolia** HOOK. f. A dense, medium-sized shrub with thick, leathery, linear-oblong, grey-green leaves which are sharply and coarsely-toothed and whitish-felted beneath. Flower-heads fragrant in June. The whole plant possesses a musky odour. One of the best of the hardier species. New Zealand. AM 1972.

**insignis** See *Pachystegia insignis.*

†**lacunosa** A very distinct medium-sized to large, slow-growing shrub with stout white tomentose stems. Leaves rigid, long and narrow, tapering from just above the base to a sharp point, up to 17cm long by 1cm across, loosely white floccose above at first becoming dark green with a conspicuous pale midrib; undersurface with a persistent silvery tomentum; margins revolute and not or only slightly toothed. Flowers small, in clusters of terminal panicles but rarely produced out-of-doors in this country. New Zealand.

**macrodonta** BAKER (*O. dentata* HOOK. f.) "New Zealand Holly". A strong-growing, medium-sized shrub up to 3m or more, with sage-green, holly-like leaves 6-9cm long, silvery-white beneath. Flowerheads fragrant, in broad panicles in June. One of the best screening or hedging shrubs for exposed coastal gardens. The whole plant possesses a musky odour. New Zealand. FCC 1895. AGM 1984.

**'Major'** A form with larger leaves and flower corymbs.

**'Minor'** A dwarf form, smaller in all its parts.

†**megalophylla** (F. MUELL.) F. MUELL. ex BENTH. A small shrub with angular pale brown tomentose young shoots. Leaves opposite, lanceolate, up to 14cm long, dark glossy green, glabrous and reticulate above, densely pale brown tomentose beneath. The young growth is tinged with red in some forms. Flowers in compound corymbs. SE Australia. I 1952. AM 1977.

×**mollis** HORT. not (KIRK) CKN. (*O. ilicifolia*×*O. moschata*). A small shrub of rounded, compact habit, with wavy-edged, silvery-grey, slightly-toothed leaves, up to 4cm long. Flowerheads in large corymbs in May. One of the hardiest of the genus. See also *O.* 'Zennorensis'.

**moschata** HOOK. f. A slow-growing, small to medium-sized shrub with small, flat, entire,

**OLEARIA moschata**—*continued*

grey-green leaves 2cm long, white felted beneath. Flowers in July. The whole plant possesses a musky odour. New Zealand.

†**nernstii** (F. MUELL.) F. MUELL ex BENTH. Both the stems and the long, narrow, shining green leaves are clammy to the touch. A plant of botanical interest. SE Australia.

**nitida** See *O. arborescens*.

**nummulariifolia** (HOOK. f.) HOOK. f. One of the hardiest species. A medium-sized, stiffly-branched shrub of unusual appearance, with small, thick, yellow-green leaves, thickly crowding the stems. Flowerheads small, solitary in the axils of the leaves in July, fragrant. Some plants grown under this name are hybrids. New Zealand.

**var. cymbifolia** HOOK. f. (*O. cymbifolia* (HOOK. f.) CHEESEM.) A form with rather sticky young shoots and leaves with strongly revolute margins. New Zealand.

**odorata** PETRIE An elegant, medium-sized, hardy shrub of loose habit, with long, wiry, arching stems and narrow-obovate leaves. Of no floral beauty, but worth growing for its fragrance in July. New Zealand. I 1908.

× **oleifolia** KIRK (*O. avicenniifolia* × *O. odorata*). A slow-growing, medium-sized shrub of compact habit, suitable for windswept coastal gardens. Leaves ovate-elliptic, matt sea-green above, white tomentose beneath, the blade to 5 by 1.5cm, petiole about 5mm. New Zealand.

**'Waikariensis'** (*O. 'Waikariensis'*) A small, attractive shrub with lanceolate leaves, the blade to 6.5 by 1.5cm, glossy green above and white beneath with a buff midrib, petiole about 12mm. White flowerheads produced in axillary clusters. Origin unknown, probably New Zealand from where it was introduced in the early 1930s.

†**pachyphylla** CHEESEM. Medium-sized shrub with large, entire, wavy-edged leaves, brown or silvery beneath. Flowerheads in large corymbs in July. New Zealand.

†**paniculata** (FORST. & FORST. f.) DRUCE (*O. forsteri* (HOOK. f.) HOOK. f.) Large shrub or small tree. A distinct and pleasing species with bright olive-green, undulate leaves, reminding one of *Pittosporum tenuifolium*; flowerheads inconspicuous, but fragrant in November and December. Used for hedgemaking especially in favoured maritime districts. New Zealand. I 1816.

†**phlogopappa** (LABILL.) DC. (*O. gunniana* (DC.) HOOK. f. ex HOOK.) (*O. stellulata* HORT. not (LABILL.) DC.) The popular May-flowering Tasmanian "Daisy Bush". An extremely variable shrub in the wild. Of medium size; leaves aromatic, toothed and narrow, 1-3.5cm long, thickly crowding the erect stems. Flowerheads 2cm across produced in crowded panicles along the stems. Tasmania, SE Australia. I 1848. FCC 1885.

**Splendens group** (*O. stellulata* 'Splendens') We owe a debt to the late Harold Comber for the introduction of several good garden plants including this lovely form with flowerheads resembling michaelmas daisies. Introduced from Tasmania in 1930. For many years we have grown forms of this with blue, lavender and rose flowers.

**var. subrepanda** (DC.) J.H. WILLIS Differs in its smaller, narrower, grey tomentose leaves and denser habit.

†**ramulosa** (LABILL.) BENTH. Small, twiggy shrub with slender, arching stems and small linear leaves. Flowerheads small, crowding the stems in August. Tasmania, S Australia. C 1822. AM 1927.

†**rani** HORT. not (A. CUNN.) DRUCE A medium-sized shrub with narrow leaves dark green above, covered with a buff or whitish tomentum beneath. Flowerheads fragrant, in large branched corymbs, in May. Possibly *O. macrodonta* × *O. moschata*.

†**rotundifolia** (LESS.) DC. (*O. dentata* HORT.) (*O. tomentosa* HORT.) An uncommon tender species usually less than 1m, of special interest on account of its large, mauve, aster-like flowerheads, borne singly and continuously over a long period. Leaves oval, leathery, dark green and serrated. It seldom survives a winter in our area. SE Australia. I 1793.

†**'Rossii'** (*O. argophylla* × *O. macrodonta*). A strong-growing shrub of medium size. Leaves elliptic, green above silvery downy beneath. Garden origin, in Ireland.

† × **scilloniensis** DORRIEN-SMITH (*O. lyrata* × *O. phlogopappa*). A compact, rounded, grey-leaved shrub up to 2.5m. An exceedingly free-flowering hybrid, the plant being literally covered with bloom in May. Garden origin, Tresco (Isles of Scilly). AM 1951. AM 1982. AGM 1984.

**semidentata** See under *O. 'Henry Travers'*.

**OLEARIA**—*continued*

†**solanderi** (HOOK. f.) HOOK. f. A dense, heath-like shrub of medium size giving a yellowish effect, rather like *Cassinia fulvida*. Leaves linear, 6mm long in clusters. Flowerheads small, sweetly scented in August. Requires wall protection except in mild localities. New Zealand.

†**speciosa** HUTCH. A small shrub with brown woolly shoots and thick, leathery, glossy dark green leaves, thickly pale brown-felted beneath. Flowerheads large, white or blue during summer. SE Australia. I before 1883.

†**stellulata** DC. A variable, rather lax, small to medium-sized shrub recalling *O. phlogopappa* but taller and less compact, and with rather longer leaves. Flowerheads white, borne in panicles in May. Tasmania. AM 1893.

'**Splendens**' See *O. phlogopappa* Splendens group.

**tomentosa** See *O. rotundifolia*.

†**traversii** (F. MUELL.) HOOK. f. Considered to be one of the best and fastest growing evergreens for wind-breaks in Cornwall and similar maritime localities, growing to 6m high even in exposed positions on poor sandy soils. Shoots four-angled, covered, as are the leaf-undersurfaces, in a dense white felt. Leaves broad, leathery, opposite, polished green above, silvery-white beneath. Flowerheads insignificant, in summer. Chatham Isles. I 1887.

**virgata** (HOOK. f.) HOOK. f. (*Eurybia virgata* HOOK. f.) A variable, medium-sized to large, hardy shrub of dense habit with long, wiry, four-angled stems. Leaves 1-2cm long, narrowly obovate to linear, arranged in pairs or in small clusters. Flowers in June, small and of little ornamental value. New Zealand.

var. **lineata** KIRK (*O. lineata* (KIRK) CKN.) A large, very graceful shrub of loose habit, with long, slender, angular, pendulous branches. Leaves narrowly linear. New Zealand.

**viscosa** (LABILL.) BENTH. Small shrub up to 2m with sticky young shoots and shiny green lanceolate leaves, silvery-white beneath. Broad corymbs of white flowers in July and August. Tasmania, SE Australia. An extremely floriferous form introduced by Sir Harold Hillier in 1977 is proving very hardy.

'**Waikariensis**' See *O.* × *oleifolia* 'Waikariensis'.

†'**Zennorensis**' (*O. ilicifolia* × *O. lacunosa*). A striking foliage plant up to 2m, with narrow, pointed, sharply-toothed leaves about 10cm long and 12mm wide, dark olive-green above and white beneath. Young stems and leaf stalks heavily coated with pale brown tomentum. Originated in the garden of that splendid gardener Arnold Foster at Zennor, Cornwall. A first class shrub for the less cold garden. Excellent in maritime exposure. It is a form of the true *O.* × *mollis*.

"**OLEASTER**" See *Elaeagnus angustifolia*.

"**OLIVE**" See *Olea europaea*.

**ONONIS** L.—**Leguminosae**—About 75 species of often spiny herbs and shrubs, natives of Europe, the Canary Islands, N Africa and W Asia. The shrubby members come from S and C Europe, and make useful dwarf subjects for border or rock garden. All have trifoliolate leaves and pea-shaped flowers. They require full sun and succeed in any well drained soil including shallow chalk soils.

**arvensis** L. (*O. hircina* JACQ.) A small, moderately hardy, sub-shrub producing in summer dense leafy racemes of pink flowers. Europe.

**fruticosa** L. A splendid small shrub forming a compact mound to 1m high. Flowers bright rose-pink, borne in small clusters throughout summer. Leaflets narrow. W Mediterranean region. C 1680. AM 1926.

**rotundifolia** L. A vigorous but none-too-persistent, sub-shrubby species, rather dwarfer than *O. fruticosa*, and with larger, rounded leaflets. Flowers bright rose-pink, continuous during summer. C and S Europe. Cultivated in England since the 17th century.

**OPLOPANAX** (TORR. & A. GRAY) MIQ. (*Echinopanax* DECNE. & PLANCH.)—**Araliaceae**—A genus of only 3 species, differing from *Eleutherococcus* (*Acanthopanax*) in the simple leaves. Natives of W North America, Korea and Japan.

**OPLOPANAX**—*continued*

**horridus** (SM.) MIQ. (*Echinopanax horridus* (SM.) J.G. COOPER) "Devil's Club". A small to medium-sized shrub with stout spiny stems and broad, palmate, maple-like leaves which are prickly along the veins beneath. Flowers greenish-white, in panicles, followed by scarlet fruits. W North America. I 1828.

**ORIXA** THUNB.—**Rutaceae**—A monotypic genus. Any well drained soil.

**japonica** THUNB. A pungently aromatic, dioecious, medium-sized shrub, with bright green leaves which change to palest lemon or white in autumn, contrasting with the more prevalent reds and purples of that season. Japan, China, Korea. I 1870.

'Variegata' Leaves puckered, shaded silvery-grey, with a broad, creamy-white margin. Particularly attractive when the small, greenish, pungently scented flowers are profusely borne in panicles from the old wood as the leaves emerge. We are indebted to Mons Robert de Belder for this interesting and rare form.

**"OSAGE ORANGE"** See *Maclura pomifera*.

**"OSIER, COMMON"** See *Salix viminalis*.

**\*OSMANTHUS** LOUR.—**Oleaceae**—A genus of about 15 species of evergreen shrubs and trees, natives of the S United States, Asia and the Pacific islands. The following are attractive and useful, often somewhat holly-like shrubs, doing well in almost all soils. Flowers small, white or cream, usually fragrant.

†**americanus** (L.) A. GRAY "Devil Wood". A large shrub or small tree with obovate to oblanceolate, leathery, glossy green, entire leaves up to 15cm long. The fragrant white flowers are borne in short axillary panicles in spring. Fruits dark blue. Requires a warm sheltered position or conservatory. SE United States. C 1758.

**aquifolium** See *O. heterophyllus*.

**armatus** DIELS A handsome, large shrub of dense habit. Leaves elliptic or oblong-lanceolate, thick and rigid, up to 18cm long, edged with stout, often hooked, spiny teeth. Flowers in autumn, sweetly scented. Thrives in sun or shade. A splendid evergreen worthy of more extensive planting. W China. Introduced by E.H. Wilson in 1902.

×**burkwoodii** (BURKW. & SKIPW.) P.S. GREEN (×*Osmarea burkwoodii* BURKW. & SKIPW.) (*O. delavayi* × *O. decorus*). This is a first class, hardy shrub of compact growth, slowly attaining 2.5-3m. Leaves oval 2.5-5cm long, dark shining green, leathery and toothed. The very fragrant white flowers are profusely borne in April or May. Raised by Burkwood and Skipwith about 1930. AM 1978. AGM 1984.

**decorus** (BOISS. & BAL.) KASAPL. (*Phillyrea decora* BOISS. & BAL.) (*Phillyrea decora* 'Latifolia') A dome-shaped bush up to 3m, usually wider than high, with comparatively large, leathery leaves which are more or less entire, glossy green above. The clusters of small, fragrant, white flowers are borne freely in spring and followed by purplish-black fruits like miniature plums. A very distinct, tough evergreen worthy of more extensive planting. W Asia. I 1866. FCC 1888.

'Baki Kasapligil' A form with narrow leaves. Previously distributed as *Phillyrea decora*.

**delavayi** FRANCH. (*Siphonosmanthus delavayi* (FRANCH.) STAPF) One of China's gems; a very beautiful, small-leaved species, slowly growing to 2m high and more in diameter, and bearing its fragrant, white, jessamine-like flowers profusely in April. Yunnan. Introduced by the Abbé Delavay in 1890. AM 1914. FCC 1931. AGM 1984.

'Latifolius' A distinct, taller-growing form with broader, more rotund leaves.

**forrestii** See *O. yunnanensis*.

×**fortunei** CARR. (*O. fragrans* × *O. heterophyllus*). A large, comparatively vigorous evergreen shrub of dense habit. Leaves large, broad ovate, dark polished green and conspicuously veined above, edged with spiny teeth, giving them a holly-like appearance, often becoming entire on mature plants. Flowers delightfully fragrant, produced during autumn. Japan. I 1862 by Robert Fortune.

'Variegatus' See *O. heterophyllus* 'Latifolius Variegatus'.

†**fragrans** LOUR. (*Olea fragrans* THUNB.) A large shrub or small tree with large oblong-lanceolate, finely-toothed leaves. Flowers deliciously and strongly fragrant; summer. A

**OSMANTHUS fragrans**—*continued*

wall shrub for the mildest localities, this plant will not survive our average winter here. China, Japan. I 1771.

**f. aurantiacus** (MAK.) P.S. GREEN An unusual form with yellowish-orange flowers.

**heterophyllus** (G. DON) P.S. GREEN (*O. aquifolium* SIEB.) (*O. ilicifolius* (HASSK.) CARR.) A rather slow-growing, holly-like shrub, occasionally a small tree. Leaves almost as variable as in the common holly, entire or coarsely spine-toothed, dark, shining green. Flowers sweetly scented, in autumn. Often mistaken for a holly but readily distinguished by its opposite leaves. Makes a useful dense hedge. Japan. Introduced by Thomas Lobb in 1856. FCC 1859.

**'Argenteomarginatus'** See 'Variegatus'.

**'Aureomarginatus'** ('Aureovariegatus') ('Aureus') Leaves margined deep yellow. C 1877.

**'Goshiki'** A striking form in which the leaves are conspicuously mottled with yellow, bronze-tinged when young. The name means five-coloured.

**'Gulftide'** Leaves somewhat lobed or twisted and strongly spiny; of dense habit. A remarkable and well worthwhile shrub.

**'Latifolius Variegatus'** (*O.* × *fortunei* 'Variegatus') Similar to 'Variegatus' but leaves broader and less deeply toothed. It appears to belong here and not to *O.* × *fortunei*.

**'Myrtifolius'** A neat, slow-growing, compact form with small, spineless leaves. C 1894.

**'Purpureus'** Growths at first deep purple, later green, slightly tinged purple. Raised at Kew in 1860.

**'Rotundifolius'** A curious, slow-growing form of neat, compact habit, with short, thick, black-green, leathery leaves which are spineless but bluntly-toothed and occasionally twisted. C 1866.

**'Sasaba'** A remarkable form of Japanese origin, the leaves deeply cut into numerous spine-tipped lobes. The name means bamboo-leaf.

**'Variegatus'** ('Argenteomarginatus') Leaves bordered with creamy-white. C 1861. AGM 1984.

**ilicifolius** See *O. heterophyllus*.

**serrulatus** REHD. A medium-sized, slow-growing shrub of compact, rounded habit. Leaves large, ovate-lanceolate, sharply-toothed or entire, glossy dark green. The clusters of white, fragrant flowers are borne in the leaf axils in spring. Himalaya. I 1910.

**suavis** C.B. CLARKE (*Siphonosmanthus suavis*) An erect-growing shrub up to 4m, related to *O. delavayi*, but differing in its 8cm long, oblong-lanceolate, sharply-toothed, shining green leaves. Flowers fragrant, in spring. This species has grown well here for many years given a sheltered position. Himalaya.

**yunnanensis** (FRANCH.) P.S. GREEN (*O. forrestii* REHD.) A remarkable large shrub or small tree. Leaves lanceolate, dark olive-green, up to 15cm long, varying from undulate and coarsely-toothed to flat and entire, both on the same plant. Flowers ivory-white, fragrant, produced during late winter. This splendid plant has proven hardy here given shelter. If you belong to the old school of gardeners, 1920-30 vintage, it is the "done thing" to "sniff" at this plant because its magnificent leaves conjure up thoughts of spectacular flowers which fail to materialise. China (Yunnan, Sichuan). Introduced by George Forrest in 1923. AM 1967.

× **OSMAREA burkwoodii** See *Osmanthus* × *burkwoodii*.

**OSMARONIA cerasiformis** See *Oemleria cerasiformis*.

†\***OSTEOMELES** LINDL.—**Rosaceae**—A genus of probably 3 species of small to medium-sized, evergreen shrubs, natives of E Asia and the Pacific islands. Pinnate leaves with tiny leaflets and corymbs of small, white flowers followed by small fruits. They need the protection of a sunny wall, when they will succeed in any well drained soil.

**subrotunda** K. KOCH A pretty, small to medium-sized, slow-growing shrub with slender arching shoots and dainty, pinnate, fern-like leaves composed of small, glossy green leaflets. Flowers hawthorn-like appearing in June. Fruits reddish. Requires wall protection in cold districts. The plant described may be a form of the similar and very variable *O. schweriniae*. E China. I 1894.

**OSTRYA** SCOP.—**Carpinaceae**—A small genus of medium-sized to large deciduous trees, resembling the hornbeam and notable in autumn when arrayed with their hop-like fruits. About 10 species, natives of the northern hemisphere south to C America. The following are of easy cultivation in any fertile soil.

**carpinifolia** SCOP. (*O. vulgaris* WILLD.) "Hop Hornbeam". A round-headed tree of medium size, with ovate, double-toothed leaves 8-13cm long, which give clear yellow autumn tints. Fruits 3.5-5cm long, each nutlet contained in a flat, bladder-like husk. Enchanting in spring when the many branches are strung with numerous long, drooping male catkins. S Europe, W Asia. I 1724. AM 1976.

**japonica** SARG. "Japanese Hop Hornbeam". A small to medium-sized tree with ovate to ovate-oblong leaves 7-13cm long, velvety hairy beneath. Conspicuous when bearing its multitudes of green, hop-like fruits 4-5cm long. Japan, Korea, China. I 1888.

**virginiana** (MILL.) K. KOCH "Ironwood". A rare and attractive, small tree of elegant, rounded or pyramidal habit, differing from *O. carpinifolia* in its glandular-hairy shoots and fewer-veined leaves. Rich, warm yellow autumn tints. E North America. I 1692.

**OSTRYOPSIS** DECNE.—**Carpinaceae**—A rare genus of 2 species of medium to large shrubs of botanical interest, natives of China and Mongolia, differing from *Ostrya* in the clustered, not racemose, fruits. Any fertile soil.

**davidiana** (BAILL.) DECNE. A medium-sized, somewhat suckering shrub with the general appearance of the common hazel but with sessile red glands on the under-surface of the leaves and long-stalked fruit clusters. N and W China. I about 1865.

†**OTHONNA** L.—**Compositae**—A genus of about 150 species of shrubs and herbs, natives mainly of tropical and S Africa. The following needs a warm position in full sun and a well drained soil.

*****cheirifolia** L. (*Othonnopsis cheirifolia* (L.) BENTH. & HOOK.) A dwarf shrub with spreading stems and short ascending branches clothed with distinctive, paddle-shaped, grey-green leaves. The golden yellow flower heads are borne singly at the ends of the shoots in spring and summer and intermittently through autumn and winter. Algeria, Tunisia. I 1752.

**OTHONNOPSIS cheirifolia** See *Othonna cheirifolia*.

**OXYCOCCUS macrocarpus** See *Vaccinium macrocarpum*.
**palustris** See *Vaccinium oxycoccos*.

‡**OXYDENDRUM** DC.—**Ericaceae**—A monotypic genus succeeding in shade or sun given a lime-free soil.

**arboreum** (L.) DC. (*Andromeda arborea* L.) "Sorrel Tree". A beautiful large shrub or small tree grown chiefly for its exquisite crimson and yellow autumn colouring. The white flowers in slender, drooping racemes are produced in clusters from the tips of the shoots in July and August. The leaves possess a pleasant acid flavour. Thrives under conditions suitable for rhododendrons. E United States. I 1752. AM 1951 (for autumn colour). AM 1957 (for flowers). FCC 1972 (for autumn foliage).

†*****OXYLOBUS** (DC.) A. GRAY—**Compositae**—A genus of 5 species succeeding in any well drained soil but only in mild gardens. They are all native to Mexico.

**arbutifolius** A. GRAY A small shrublet with roughly glandular-hairy shoots. Flowerheads white, borne in erect, slender-stalked corymbs from June onwards. Mexico.

**OXYPETALUM caeruleum** See under CLIMBERS.

*****OZOTHAMNUS** R. BR.—**Compositae**—Evergreen, summer-flowering shrubs related to *Helichrysum* under which name they are sometimes found. They require full sun and a well drained position.

**OZOTHAMNUS**—*continued*

†**antennaria** (DC.) HOOK. f. (*Helichrysum antennaria* (DC.) F. MUELL. ex BENTH.) A small to medium-sized, dense-growing evergreen with narrowly obovate or spathulate, leathery leaves, grey beneath, glossy green above. Flowerheads white, in dense terminal clusters opening in June. Tasmania. I before 1880.

**ericifolius** See under *O. purpurascens*.

**ledifolius** (DC.) HOOK. f. (*Helichrysum ledifolium* (DC.) BENTH.) A small, globular, dense, aromatic shrub. Leaves broadly linear with recurved margins, yellow-backed; flowers comparatively large, their inner bracts with conspicuous white, spreading tips, reddish in bud. Seed heads emit a sweet honey-like aroma. A superb shrub displaying its incurved terminal yellow leaves. Uninjured by the severe winters of 1962/63 and the 1980s. Tasmania. I 1930.

†**purpurascens** DC. An erect, pleasantly aromatic shrub of medium size. Leaves narrow like those of a rosemary, sticky to the touch; flowers white, tinged with purple in bud, in terminal heads. Tasmania. Originally listed as *O. ericifolius*.

**rosmarinifolius** (LABILL.) DC. (*Helichrysum rosmarinifolium* (LABILL.) STEUD. ex BENTH.) A medium-sized shrub with white-woolly stems and dark green, linear, verrucose leaves. The dense corymbs of red buds are spectacular for ten days or more before they open to white, scented flowers. One of the hardiest species, given hot sun and a well drained soil it can survive for many years. Tasmania, SE Australia. I 1827. AM 1968.

'**Silver Jubilee**' A form with silvery-grey leaves.

**scutellifolius** (HOOK. f.) BENTH. (*Helichrysum scutellifolium* (HOOK. f.) BENTH.) A curious dwarf, Tasmanian species reaching 120cm in the wild. Slender, antler-like shoots clothed with white down through which the circular, grey-green, adpressed leaves peep. Flowers yellow in terminal clusters. A plant for the rock garden.

**selago** HOOK. f. (*Helichrysum selago* (HOOK. f.) BENTH. & HOOK. f.) A dwarf shrublet of variable growth. The slender, erect or ascending stems are rather stiffly held and much-branched. The tiny, green, scale-like leaves are closely adpressed to the stems. They are smooth on the outside, but coated white on the inside, and give the stems a chequered appearance. Small creamy-yellow flowerheads are borne at the tips of the shoots in June. New Zealand. A plant for the rock garden or alpine-house.

'**Major**' A more robust selection with thicker stems and larger leaves. AM 1987.

†**thyrsoideus** DC. (*O. rosmarinifolius* HORT.) (*Helichrysum thyrsoideum* (DC.) WILLIS & MORRIS) (*H. diosmifolium* HORT.) "Snow in Summer". This delightful plant was well known to our grandparents long before the related and somewhat similar species were introduced from Tasmania by Harold Comber. A medium-sized shrub with slender, spreading, angular branches and spreading linear leaves. Flowerheads white, in large terminal corymbs during summer. Australia, Tasmania. AM 1925.

**PACHISTIMA** See *Paxistima*.

**PACHYSANDRA** MICHX.—**Buxaceae**—A small genus of 4 or 5 species of dwarf shrubs or sub-shrubs, with monoecious flowers, natives of North America and E Asia. Suitable for ground cover in moist, shaded sites. They do not luxuriate in shallow chalk soils.

\***axillaris** FRANCH. A dwarf, tufted, evergreen shrublet, with comparatively large leaves. Less spreading than *P. terminalis*. Flowers white, produced in short axillary spikes in April. China. I 1901 by Ernest Wilson.

**procumbens** MICHX. A dwarf, creeping, semi-evergreen sub-shrub bearing terminal clusters of ovate to obovate leaves. Flowers with conspicuous pale stamens, borne in crowded cylindrical spikes on the lower halves of the shoots during spring. SE United States. I 1800.

\***terminalis** SIEB. & ZUCC. A very useful dwarf evergreen, carpeting shrublet for covering bare places under trees. Leaves clustered at the ends of the stems, rather diamond-shaped and toothed in the upper half. Spikes of greenish-white flowers are produced at the ends of the previous year's shoots in February and March. Japan. I 1882. AGM 1984.

'**Variegata**' Leaves attractively variegated white. AGM 1984.

†\***PACHYSTEGIA** CHEESEM.—**Compositae**—A monotypic New Zealand genus sometimes united with *Olearia*.

    **insignis** (HOOK. f.) CHEESEM. (*Olearia insignis* HOOK. f.) "Marlborough Rock Daisy". A dwarf shrub of remarkably distinct appearance, suitable for mild districts, and especially for maritime exposures where it will take the full blast of sea winds. Leaves obovate, up to 15cm long, dark green, white-felted beneath. The large, white, yellow-centred, aster-like flowers are carried singly on stiff, erect, white-tomentose stems during late summer. I 1850. AM 1915.

    **var. minor** CHEESEM. Smaller in all its parts and less tomentose. Suitable for the rock garden, in a sunny, well drained position. A distinct and interesting form.

**PACHYSTIMA** See *Paxistima*.

**PAEONIA** L.—**Paeoniaceae**—The "Paeonies" consist of 30 or so species of mainly herbaceous perennials natives of the north temperate regions of Europe, Asia and W North America. The shrubby members or "Tree Paeonies" come from W China and SE Tibet and are represented in gardens by a few species and their varieties and hybrids, but the term is most commonly applied to those which have originated from *P. suffruticosa*. These are amongst the most gorgeously coloured of all shrubs. They pass uninjured our severest winters, but on account of their early growth they should be protected against spring frosts. Such species as *P. delavayi* and *P. lutea* have splendid foliage of architectural quality. Given full sun and a sheltered site they will thrive in any well drained soil.

    **arborea** See *P. suffruticosa*.

    **delavayi** FRANCH. A handsome, suckering shrub, attaining 2m. Flowers, in May, deepest crimson with golden anthers, followed by large, black-seeded fruits surrounded by conspicuously coloured, persistent sepals. The large, deeply cut leaves place this plant in the category of shrubs grown for the quality of their leaves. An excellent shrub for chalky soils. W China. I 1908. AM 1934.

    **var. angustiloba** See *P. potaninii*.

  × **lemoinei** REHD. (*P. lutea* × *P. suffruticosa*). By this cross tree paeonies with enormous yellow flowers have been produced and also cultivars showing gorgeous colour combinations. Most will reach 1.5-2m in height and flower in May or June. They appreciate a rich soil and do well on chalk. First raised by Messrs Lemoine about 1909.

    **'Alice Harding'** Flowers large, fully double, canary-yellow. AMT 1960.

    **'Argosy'** Flowers semi-double, pale yellow streaked carmine at the base. AM 1937. FCC 1956.

    **'Chromatella'** Flowers large, double, sulphur-yellow. A sport of 'Souvenir de Maxime Cornu'.

    **'Souvenir de Maxime Cornu'** Flowers fragrant, very large, double, bright yellow edged with carmine.

    **lutea** FRANCH. A bold shrub of about 2m, possessing the foliage qualities of *P. delavayi*, in fact from leaf only they are difficult to tell apart. Flowers, borne in May or June are cup-shaped, 6cm across, resembling those of the King Cup or Marsh Marigold (*Caltha palustris*). Yunnan. I 1886. FCC 1903.

    **var. ludlowii** STERN & TAYLOR ('Sherriff's Variety') This splendid variety, first collected by Kingdon-Ward and subsequently by Ludlow and Sherriff in SE Tibet, has larger golden yellow, saucer-shaped flowers, opening as the large and conspicuous leaves are beginning to expand. AM 1954. AGM 1984.

    **moutan** See *P. suffruticosa*.

    **potaninii** KOMAR. (*P. delavayi* var. *angustiloba* REHD. & WILS.) A suckering shrub up to 0.6m, forming small patches of glabrous stems and deeply divided, narrowly-lobed leaves. Flowers deep maroon, 5-6cm across, nodding, appearing in May. W China. I 1904.

    **f. alba** STERN A form with creamy-white flowers.

    **var. trollioides** (STAPF ex STERN) STERN Habit more upright, reaching 1m. Flowers yellow, like *Trollius*. I 1914 by George Forrest from Yunnan. AM 1980.

    **suffruticosa** ANDR. (*P. moutan* SIMS) (*P. arborea* DONN ex K. KOCH) "Moutan Peony". A branching shrub up to 2m with large flowers 15cm or more across in May. In 1943 an

**PAEONIA suffruticosa**—*continued*

FCC was given to 'Rock's Variety' a beautiful form introduced by Joseph Rock, with large, single, palest flesh-pink flowers passing to silver-white marked at the base of each petal with a maroon splash. We are indebted to this untiring American collector for the introduction of several new species and many good hardy forms of hitherto tender subjects.

The following is only a selection of the numerous cultivars of this species.

**'Godaishu'** White with yellow centre; semi-double to double.

**'Goshazaki'** Lustrous pink.

**'Hanakishoi'** Deep cherry-red; double, large.

**'Higurashi'** Vivid crimson; semi-double, large.

**'Hodai'** Rosy-red; double, large.

**'Jitsugetsu Nishiki'** Bright scarlet with deeper sheen; semi-double to double.

**'Kumagai'** Deep pink turning to magenta; double.

**'Renkaku'** Pure white, irregularly cut petals; double, large.

**'Rock's Variety''** See above under *P. suffruticosa*.

**'Sakurajishi'** Lustrous pink, irregularly cut petals; double, large.

**'Shichi Fukigin'** Bright crimson, soft pink margin.

**'Shunkoden'** Rosy-violet; semi-double.

**'Taiyo'** Brilliant red with satin sheen of maroon; semi-double.

**'Yachiyo-tsubaki'** Phlox-pink, shading to soft neyron-rose tips, long petals ruffled and fringed at edges; semi-double to double.

## CULTURAL NOTES

Whilst the above are winter hardy, the young growth is susceptible to damage by night frost in the spring and it is wise to provide artificial protection at this time. A sacking screen may be erected on a tripod of bamboos, the covering being positioned nightly during periods of frost, and removed after frost has gone off in the morning. Once growth has been hardened the screen may be removed entirely.

**"PAGODA TREE"** See *Sophora japonica*.

**PALIURUS** MILL.—**Rhamnaceae**—A small genus of about 8 species of deciduous, spiny trees and shrubs, requiring plenty of sun and good drainage. Natives from S Europe to E Asia. *P. spina-christi* is one of the plants from which the "Crown of Thorns" is said to have been made. Any fertile soil.

**spina-christi** MILL. (*P. aculeatus* LAM.) "Christ's Thorn". A medium-sized to large straggling shrub, the long thin stems armed with innumerable pairs of unequal thorns. The ovate leaves turn yellow in autumn. Flowers small, greenish-yellow in late summer. The curious fruits are circular, and remind one of miniature cardinal's hats. S Europe to Himalaya, and N China. C 1597.

**"PALM, HARDY"** See *Chamaerops* and *Trachycarpus*.

**PARABENZOIN praecox** See *Lindera praecox*.

**PARAHEBE** W.R.B. OLIVER—**Scrophulariaceae**—A small genus of about 30 species of semi-woody, dwarf plants intermediate between *Hebe* and *Veronica*, formerly included under the latter. Natives of New Zealand. Suitable for the rock garden in all types of soil.

**catarractae** (FORST. f.) W.R.B. OLIVER (*Veronica catarractae* FORST. f.) A dwarf plant forming low-spreading mounds, making excellent ground cover in full sun. Leaves small, ovate or lanceolate, acute, coarsely-serrate. Flowers white to rose-purple with a central zone of crimson, in slender, erect racemes during late summer. New Zealand. Blue-flowered forms are often cultivated. AGM 1984.

**'Delight'** Flowers white veined heliotrope, profusely borne over a long period. AGM 1984.

**'Diffusa'** A smaller-leaved clone, forming dense mats. Flowers white, veined rose-pink.

**'Miss Willmott'** Flowers veined with mauve.

**PARAHEBE**—*continued*

**decora** M.B. ASHWIN Creeping sub-shrub forming low hummocks and patches. Leaves tiny, ovate or rounded, with 1 or 2 pairs of teeth. Flowers white or pink, borne in long-stalked racemes during summer. New Zealand (S Island). Sometimes grown as *P. × bidwilli*, which is a hybrid between *P. decora* and *P. lyallii*.

**lyallii** (HOOK. f.) W.R.B. OLIVER (*Veronica lyallii* HOOK. f.) A low, prostrate shrublet with small, rounded or ovate leaves which are leathery and slightly crenate. Flowers white, prettily veined pink, anthers blue, appearing in slender racemes from July to August. New Zealand (S Island). I 1870.

**'Mervyn'** A dwarf, spreading shrub with small, red-edged leaves and racemes of lilac-blue flowers in summer. Probably a hybrid of *P. lyallii*.

**†perfoliata** (R. BR.) E. BRIGGS & EHREND. (*Veronica perfoliata* R. BR.) "Digger's Speedwell". A dwarf sub-shrub, herbaceous in most areas, with erect stems usually about 30-45cm. Leaves perfoliate, greyish-green. Flowers violet-blue, borne in long axillary racemes in late summer. An unusual plant for a sunny, well drained spot in mild areas. Australia. I 1834.

**\*PARASYRINGA** W.W. SM.—**Oleaceae**—A monotypic genus related to *Ligustrum* and *Syringa*. It resembles the former in habit and flower, also in the fruit which is fleshy at first, later becoming a dry capsule as in *Syringa*.

**sempervirens** (FRANCH.) W.W.SM. (*Ligustrum sempervirens* (FRANCH.) LINGELSH.) A striking, evergreen shrub of small to medium size with dark green, leathery, rounded leaves. The small, white flowers are produced in conspicuous, dense panicles in August and September. W China. I 1913. AM 1930. Recently reintroduced from China.

**PARROTIA** C.A. MEY.—**Hamamelidaceae**—A monotypic genus, remarkably lime-tolerant for the *Hamamelis* family.

**jacquemontiana** See *Parrotiopsis jacquemontiana*.

**persica** (DC.) C.A. MEY. A large shrub or small tree of wide-spreading habit. Bark of older stems delightfully flaking like that of the London Plane. Leaves turning crimson and gold in autumn. Flowers consisting of clusters of crimson stamens, appearing in late winter and early spring. One of the finest small trees for autumn colour, even on chalk. N Iran to the Caucasus. C 1840. FCC 1884. AGM 1984.

**'Pendula'** A form with pendulous branches, slowly developing into a dome-shaped mound 1.8-3m high. Becoming a richly coloured pile in autumn.

**PARROTIOPSIS** (NIED.) SCHNEID.—**Hamamelidaceae**—A monotypic genus best in an acid or neutral soil, but moderately lime-tolerant. May be grown over chalk given 0.6m of good soil.

**jacquemontiana** (DECNE.) REHD. (*Parrotia jacquemontiana* DECNE.) A large shrub of erect habit. Leaves rounded or broadly ovate, usually turning yellow in autumn. The flower clusters, which remind one of *Cornus florida*, being subtended by conspicuous white bracts, are produced during April and May and intermittently throughout summer. W Himalaya. I 1879.

**"PARTRIDGE BERRY"** See *Mitchella repens*.

**PAULOWNIA** SIEB. & ZUCC.—**Scrophulariaceae**—A small genus of about 6 species of E Asian trees. The species here listed are amongst the grandest of ornamental flowering trees. Their foxglove-shaped flowers, which are not borne on very young trees, are carried in erect panicles and, though formed in autumn, do not open until the following spring. The leaves of mature trees are large, whilst on vigorous, pruned plants they are enormous. Owing to the colour of their flowers, these trees are best planted where they can be viewed from above; the sites should be in full sun, but sheltered from gales. All types of deep, well drained soil.

**PAULOWNIA**—*continued*

**fargesii** FRANCH. A magnificent tree of 18-21m which, though more recently introduced, seems to be better adapted to our climate than the better known *P. tomentosa*, and flowers at a comparatively early age. Flowers fragrant, heliotrope, freely speckled dark purple in the throat and with a creamy basal stain. W China. I about 1896.

**fargesii** HORT. See *P. lilacina*.

**fortunei** (SEEM.) HEMSL. A rare, small tree, similar in habit to *P. tomentosa*. Flowers fragrant, creamy-white, heavily marked with deep purple on the inside, flushed lilac on the outside. China, Taiwan.

**imperialis** See *P. tomentosa*.

**lilacina** SPRAGUE (*P. fargesii* HORT. not FRANCH.) Closely related to *P. tomentosa* this species differs mainly in its unlobed leaves and lilac flowers, pale yellow in the throat, in June. China. C about 1908. FCC 1944.

**tomentosa** (THUNB.) STEUD. (*P. imperialis* SIEB. & ZUCC.) This well-known species forms a round-topped tree 9-12m high. The flowers are heliotrope, slightly darker than those of *P. fargesii*, and providing they come through the winter and escape a late frost, give a wonderful display in May. Alternatively, young plants may be pruned to the ground in spring and the resultant suckers thinned to a single shoot. Such is its vigour the shoot will reach 2.5-3m in a single season and clothe itself with huge leaves up to 0.6m or more across. China. Introduced via Japan in 1834. AM 1934.

**"PAWPAW"** See *Asimina triloba*.

**\*PAXISTIMA** RAF. (*Pachistima*) (*Pachystima*)—**Celastraceae**—A genus of 2 species of interesting, but not conspicuous dwarf, evergreen shrubs of neat habit, with tiny leaves and quadrangular stems. Not recommended for shallow chalk soils. They do best in a moist shady position.

**canbyi** A. GRAY Leaves narrow, small greenish flowers during summer. Fruits white. Makes an unusual dwarf hedge or ground cover. E United States. C 1800.

**myrsinites** See *P. myrtifolia*.

**myrtifolia** (NUTT.) WHEELER (*P. myrsinites* (PURSH) RAF.) Leaves small, leathery, toothed in upper half; opposite. Flowers tiny, four-petalled, red, produced in March. W North America, N Mexico. C 1879.

**"PEACH"** See *Prunus persica*.

**"PEAR"** See *Pyrus*.

**"PEARL BERRY"** See *Margyricarpus pinnatus*.

**PENSTEMON** SCHMIDEL (*Pentstemon*)—**Scrophulariaceae**—A large genus of some 250 species mostly sub-shrubs and herbaceous plants, mainly from NW America and Mexico. The tender species require the shelter of a sunny wall while the hardy members make excellent rock garden plants. Full sun and good drainage.

†**cordifolius** BENTH. A slender-branched, semi-evergreen shrub up to 2m high against a wall. Leaves heart-shaped, coarsely-toothed, dark glossy green. Flowers in panicles, orange-scarlet, from June to August. California. Discovered by David Douglas in 1831; introduced by Hartweg in 1848.

†**corymbosus** BENTH. A small, semi-evergreen shrub, closely related to *P. cordifolius*, differing in its smaller stature, its ovate leaves and its shorter flowers in flattened racemes. California.

\***davidsonii** GREENE (*P. menziesii* HOOK.) A dwarf or prostrate, evergreen shrublet for the rock garden with shortly-stalked, shallowly-toothed leaves and erect racemes of large, tubular, purple flowers in May and June. NW North America. C 1902.

**PENSTEMON**—*continued*

    **fruticosus** (PURSH) GREENE This species is mainly represented in gardens by the following variety.

        **var. scouleri** (LINDL.) CRONQUIST (*P. scouleri* LINDL.) A charming, dwarf sub-shrub with narrow, lanceolate leaves and large, lilac-coloured blossoms, arranged in erect racemes in June. Suitable for the rock garden. W North America. I 1828. AM 1951. AGM 1984.

        **'Albus'** A form with white flowers. AGM 1984.

    **heterophyllus** LINDL. A dwarf, erect shrublet with long, narrow leaves. California. I 1828 by David Douglas.

        **'Blue Gem'** Lovely azure-blue, tubular flowers in long racemes during summer.

    **menziesii** See *P. davidsonii*.

    **\*newberryi** A. GRAY Plants under this name belong mainly to the following form.

        **f. humilior** SEALY (*P. roezlii* HORT.) A dwarf shrub suitable for the rock garden similar to *P. davidsonii*, but with longer, pointed leaves and scarlet flowers in profusion in June. W United States. AGM 1984.

    **scouleri** See *P. fruticosus* var. *scouleri*.

‡\***PENTACHONDRA** R. BR.—**Epacridaceae**—A small genus of 3 species of low-growing, evergreen shrubs for lime-free soils.

    **pumila** (FORST. & FORST. f.) R. BR. A tiny shrublet, a few centimetres high. Stems procumbent; leaves bronze-tinted, very small; crowded on the stems. The small, cylindrical, white flowers are produced singly in the axils of the uppermost leaves in summer and are followed by red fruits. Tasmania, SE Australia, New Zealand.

**PENTAPERA sicula** See *Erica sicula*.

**PENTAPTERYGIUM** See *Agapetes*.

‡**PERAPHYLLUM** NUTT. ex TORR. & A. GRAY—**Rosaceae**—A monotypic genus related to *Amelanchier*, but differing in its narrow leaves, long calyx tube and rounded petals. It is hardy and grows best in a hot, sunny position. Not recommended for chalk soils.

    **ramosissimum** NUTT. A small to medium-sized shrub with clusters of narrowly oblanceolate leaves, which are obscurely toothed in their upper halves, and umbels of pink and white flowers in April and May. The cherry-like fruits are rarely produced in this country. W North America. I 1870.

**"PERIWINKLE"** See *Vinca*.

‡\***PERNETTYA** GAUDICH.—**Ericaceae**—A genus of about 20 species closely related to *Gaultheria*. They extend from Mexico to the Magellan region, at the southern end of S America, with representatives in Tasmania and New Zealand. The following are very attractive, mostly hardy, ornamental evergreens of dense habit for a lime-free soil. Though small in flower, they are so very floriferous as to be conspicuous. The masses of pure white or vividly coloured, marble-like berries are some of the showiest fruits of the plant world and in some species last the whole winter. Whilst tolerant of shade they fruit best in full sun and when planted in groups to ensure cross-pollination. Some plants are hermaphrodite, whilst others are unisexual. Most Pernettyas make splendid ground cover.

    **buxifolia** See *P. ciliata*.

    **ciliata** (CHAM. & SCHLECHT.) SMALL (*P. buxifolia* MART. & GAL.) A dwarf shrub with slender but rigidly arching, sparsely bristly and downy stems forming low mounds. Leaves elliptic-lanceolate, dark glossy green and toothed, borne in 2 ranks. Flowers pitcher-shaped, white, produced in May and June and followed by large white, pink or lavender-flushed berries. Plants with large berries originally listed as *P. buxifolia* and deriving from E.K. Balls 4868 belong here. Mexico.

    **empetrifolia** See *P. pumila*.

    **leucocarpa** DC. A dwarf shrub of compact habit. The small, neat, leathery leaves are densely arranged on the erect, wiry stems. Berries white, edible and sweet. Some plants under this name deriving from Comber introductions may be hybrids with *P. prostrata* subsp. *pentlandii*. S Chile. I 1926. AM 1929.

**PERNETTYA leucocarpa**—*continued*

   **'Harold Comber'** A selection with comparatively large, attractive, deep rose berries. Originally collected by Harold Comber in the Chilean Andes.

  **mucronata** (L. f.) GAUD. The showiest of all dwarf evergreens in fruit and one of the hardiest of S American shrubs. Forms dense thickets of wiry stems about 60-90cm high or occasionally more. The myriads of small, white, heath-like flowers in May to June are followed by dense clusters of long-persistent, marble-like berries, ranging from pure white to mulberry-purple. Though not strictly dioecious it is best to plant in groups of 3 or more and to ensure berry-production include a proven male form. A marvellous plant which should be mass planted for ground cover. Chile to Magellan region. I 1828. AM 1961. AGM 1984.

   **'Alba'** Berries medium-sized, white with a faint pink tinge, which deepens with age. FCC 1882.

   **'Atrococcinea'** Berries large, deep, shining ruby-red.

   **'Bell's Seedling'** A hermaphrodite form with reddish young stems and dark, shining green leaves; berries large, dark red. AM 1928.

   **'Cherry Ripe'** Similar in general appearance to 'Bell's Seedling', but berries medium to large, of a bright cherry-red. AM 1985.

   **'Crimsonia'** Very large crimson fruits. C 1968. AM 1985.

   **Davis's Hybrids** A first rate selection of large berried forms in a mixture of colours.

   **'Edward Balls'** A very distinct male form of erect habit. Shoots stout and stiff, reddish and shortly hispid. Leaves broadly ovate or rounded. Collected in the wild by E.K. Balls.

   **'Lilacina'** A free-berrying form; berries medium-sized, reddish-lilac. FCC 1878.

   **'Lilian'** Berries very large, lilac-pink. C 1968. AM 1985.

   **'Mulberry Wine'** Young stems green; berries large, magenta ripening to deep purple.

   **'Pink Pearl'** Berries medium-sized, lilac-pink.

   **'Rosalind'** Large carmine-pink berries.

   **'Rosie'** Young stems red, leaves dark sea-green; berries large, pink with a deep rose flush.

   **var. rupicola** (PHIL.) REICHE A distinct wild variety of loose habit with relatively narrow, obscurely toothed leaves and medium-sized berries, variably coloured. Chile, Argentina.

   **'Sea Shell'** Berries medium to large, shell-pink, ripening to rose.

   **'Thymifolia'** A charming, small, male form of neat habit. Leaves smaller than in the type; smothered in white flowers during late May and early June.

   **'White Pearl'** A selection of 'Alba', with medium to large berries of a gleaming white.

   **'Wintertime'** Large pure white berries.

  **prostrata** (CAV.) SLEUMER A dwarf or prostrate shrub forming low mounds of arching downy and sparsely bristly stems, and narrow, glossy, bright green leaves. Flowers produced singly or in small racemes in May and June; pitcher-shaped, white, followed by usually black berries. Venezuela to Chile. I about 1870.

   **subsp. pentlandii** (DC.) B.L. BURTT A variety of more vigorous growth with strong, bristly young shoots and bold leathery elliptic or oblong-elliptic leaves up to 2.5cm long. Berries black, slightly larger. AM 1957.

  **pumila** (L. f.) HOOK. (*P. empetrifolia* (LAM.) GAUD.) A dwarf, almost prostrate species with slender wiry stems and tiny leaves. Berries white or pink-tinged. Magellan Straits, Falkland Isles.

  **tasmanica** HOOK. f. A slender, fragile dwarf shrub a few centimetres high, often prostrate. Leaves very small and leathery. Berries up to 1cm, solitary, normally red, produced in the axils of the upper leaves. Tasmania. AM 1971.


**PEROVSKIA** KARELIN—**Labiatae**—A small genus of 7 species of late flowering, aromatic sub-shrubs with deeply-toothed or finely-cut leaves, native from C Asia to the Himalaya. They associate well with lavender for the blue and grey border, and succeed in a sunny position in all types of well drained soil.

  **abrotanoides** KARELIN Small shrub with grey-hairy branching stems and deeply-cut, grey-green leaves. Flowers violet-blue in terminal panicles during late summer and autumn. Afghanistan to W Himalaya. C 1935.

**PEROVSKIA**—*continued*

**atriplicifolia** BENTH. A beautiful, small, Himalayan shrub for the grey or blue border, the long, narrow panicles of lavender-blue flowers, produced in late summer, blending perfectly with the grey foliage and whitish stems. Afghanistan, W Himalaya to Tibet. C 1904. AM 1928.

**'Blue Spire'** A beautiful selection with deeply cut leaves and even larger panicles of lavender-blue flowers. AM 1962. AGM 1984.

**'Hybrida'** (*P. abrotanoides* × *P. atriplicifolia*). An admirable plant for late summer effect, having deeply cut, grey-green leaves and very long panicles of deep lavender-blue flowers. Originated in our nurseries before 1937.

†*****PERSEA** MILLER—**Lauraceae**—A large genus of some 150 species of shrubs and trees widely distributed through tropical and warm temperate regions. *P. americana* MILLER, the "Avocado Pear", native to C America is the most commonly grown species.

**borbonia** (L.) SPRENG. (*P. carolinensis* NEES) "Red Bay". A handsome, small, evergreen tree with leaves glossy above and glaucous beneath, fruits dark blue on red stalks. The wood is used in cabinetmaking. Only possible to grow in the mildest areas. SE United States. I 1739.

**ichangensis** (REHD. & WILS.) KOSTERMANS (*Machilus ichangensis* REHD. & WILS.) A small tree, semi-evergreen in this country. Leaves oblong-lanceolate to lanceolate, long-pointed, 10-20cm long, leathery, of an attractive coppery colour when young. Flowers small, white, produced in short axillary panicles in late spring or early summer, followed by small shining black fruits. A rare species from C and SW China, introduced by E.H. Wilson about 1901.

**PERSICARIA** MILL.—**Polygonaceae**—A genus of mainly herbaceous perennials which contains several garden favourites previously listed under *Polygonum*. The following is the best-known shrubby species.

**vacciniifolia** (WALL. ex MEISSN.) R. DECR. (*Polygonum vacciniifolium* WALL. ex MEISSN.) A prostrate, mat-forming shrub with slender stems and small glossy green leaves glaucous beneath. Flowers bright rose-pink, in slender erect spikes in late summer and autumn. Himalaya. I 1845. AGM 1984.

**"PERSIMMON, CHINESE"** See *Diospyros kaki.*

**PERTYA** SCHULTZ-BIP.—**Compositae**—A small genus of about 16 species of shrubs and herbs native from Afghanistan to Japan. The following is hardy and succeeds in all types of soil.

**sinensis** OLIV. A Chinese shrub up to 1.5m high. Leaves, bitter to the taste, 2.5-7.5cm long, taper-pointed and borne in rosettes. Flowerheads purplish-pink, daisy-like, about 12mm across, produced in June and July. Hubei. I 1901 by Ernest Wilson.

**PETTERIA** C. PRESL—**Leguminosae**—A monotypic genus of restricted distribution. In the wild it seldom exceeds 1.2-1.5m. It succeeds in full sun in all types of well drained soil.

**ramentacea** C. PRESL "Dalmatian Laburnum". An unusual shrub of upright habit with trifoliolate leaves attaining about 1.8-2.5m. May be likened to a shrubby, erect-flowered laburnum, producing its racemes of fragrant yellow flowers in May and June. W Yugoslavia, N Albania. I 1838. AM 1976.

†*****PEUMUS** MOLINA—**Monimiaceae**—A monotypic genus of economic importance in S America. It will succeed in all well drained soils, but only in the mildest gardens.

**boldus** MOLINA "Boldo". A small, dioecious evergreen tree with leathery leaves and white flowers in terminal cymes in summer. The bark is used in tanning and dyeing; the leaves make an interesting tea which is taken medicinally to aid digestion and the fruits are sweet and edible. Chile. I 1844.

**PHELLODENDRON** RUPR.—**Rutaceae**— A small genus of about 10 species of small to medium-sized, wide-spreading trees native to E Asia and resembling *Ailanthus* in their large, handsome, pinnate leaves and graceful habit. Related to *Tetradium* (*Euodia*), but differing in the enclosed winter buds and the fruit which is a drupe. They grow well on chalky soil, their attractive, aromatic leaves usually turning clear yellow before falling. Flowers yellow-green, small, in cymes, followed by small black, viscid fruits.

**amurense** RUPR. The "Amur Cork Tree", so called on account of the corky bark of older trees. Leaves 25-38cm long with 5-11 leaflets. Distinguished by its bright green leaves and silvery-hairy, winter buds. NE Asia. I 1885.

> **var. japonicum** See *P. japonicum*.

> **var. lavallei** (DODE) SPRAGUE Bark less corky, leaves downier beneath with 7-11 leaflets. Japan. I 1866.

> **var. sachalinense** F. SCHMIDT (*P. sachalinense* (F. SCHMIDT) SARG.) A very hardy, Japanese variety with 7-11 leaflets, and without corky bark.

**chinense** SCHNEID. A handsome tree with leaves up to 38cm long, composed of 7-13 acuminate, glossy leaflets, downy beneath, and densely packed fruiting clusters. C China. I 1907 by Ernest Wilson.

> **var. glabriusculum** SCHNEID. A variety differing in its almost glabrous leaflets. C and W China. I 1907.

**japonicum** MAXIM. (*P. amurense* var. *japonicum* (MAXIM.) OHWI) A small tree related to *P. amurense* but with the leaves softly downy beneath with 9-15 leaflets. The black fruits are most attractive after a warm summer. Japan. I 1863.

**sachalinense** See *P. amurense* var. *sachalinense*.


**PHILADELPHUS** L.—**Philadelphaceae**—The "Mock Oranges", often erroneously called "Syringa", are an indispensable genus of shrubs, comprising some 65 species in N temperate regions, giving a good display even on the poorest chalk soils. The flowers, produced in June and July, are fragrant in most and are pure white unless otherwise described. To prune, thin out and cut back, immediately after flowering, old flowering shoots to within a few centimetres of the old wood. Many of the finest hybrids and cultivars were raised by the French nursery firm Lemoine during the early years of the present century. Unless otherwise stated the cultivars reach a height of 1.8-2.4m.

**'Albâtre'** (Cymosus Group) A small shrub with double white, slightly fragrant flowers in large racemes. C 1912 (Lemoine).

**'Amalthée'** (Cymosus Group) A medium-sized shrub with long branches and single, sweetly-scented, rose-stained flowers. C 1923 (Lemoine).

**argyrocalyx** WOOTON. A very beautiful, distinct and graceful shrub, 1.5-1.8m in height, related to *P. microphyllus*. The fragrant, evenly-spaced flowers are 3.5-4cm across, and have large, silky-pubescent calyces. New Mexico (United States). I 1916.

**'Atlas'** A medium-sized shrub of loose habit with long arching branches. Flowers large, 5-6cm across, single, white, slightly scented. Leaves often with faint yellow mottling. C 1923 (Lemoine). AM 1927.

**'Avalanche'** (Lemoinei Group) A small, semi-erect shrub with small leaves. In summer the masses of small single, richly fragrant flowers weigh down the slender branches. C 1896 (Lemoine).

**'Beauclerk'** (Purpureo-maculatus Group) A splendid medium-sized shrub raised by the Hon Lewis Palmer in 1938, with single broad-petalled flowers, 6cm across, milk-white with a zone of light cerise around the stamens. A cross between 'Burfordensis' and 'Sybille'. AM 1947. FCC 1951. AGM 1984.

**'Belle Etoile'** A beautiful compact shrub up to 2m. The single, 5cm wide flowers are flushed maroon at the centre, and are delightfully fragrant. A triploid hybrid. C 1930 (Lemoine). AM 1930. AGM 1984.

**'Bicolore'** Small shrub. The single, cup-shaped flowers are creamy-white with a purple basal stain. A triploid hybrid. C 1918 (Lemoine).

**'Boule d'Argent'** (Polyanthus Group) A small shrub with large, double, pure white flowers freely produced in dense clusters, slightly fragrant. C 1893 (Lemoine). FCC 1895.

**PHILADELPHUS**—*continued*

**'Bouquet Blanc'** (Cymosus Group) Small shrub with double, orange-scented flowers in large crowded clusters. C 1903 (Lemoine). AM 1912.

**brachybotrys** KOEHNE (*P. pekinensis* var. *brachybotrys* (KOEHNE) KOEHNE) An elegant, medium-sized to large Chinese shrub with delicately fragrant, creamy-white flowers. I 1892.

**'Buckley's Quill'** ('Bouquet Blanc' × 'Frosty Morn'). A broadly upright shrub to 2m. The large, double, white flowers each have about 30 quilled petals. Raised in Canada.

**'Burfordensis'** (Virginalis Group) A magnificent, erect-branched, medium-sized shrub raised by Sir William Lawrence. The large, single flowers are cup-shaped and have conspicuous yellow stamens. Originated in 1920 as a sport of 'Virginal'. AM 1921. FCC 1969.

**'Burkwoodii'** ('Etoile Rose' × 'Virginal'). A slender, medium-sized shrub with single, fragrant flowers. The long narrow petals are arranged in windmill fashion, white, with a purple basal stain. C 1929.

**californicus** BENTH. A vigorous, medium-sized shrub attaining 3m. Fragrant flowers, 2.5cm across, are produced in large panicles. California. I 1885.

**'Conquete'** (Cymosus Group) A small shrub with slender, arching branches carrying clusters of large, fragrant, single and semi-double, pure white flowers with long, narrow petals intermixed with shorter petaloid stamens. C 1903 (Lemoine).

**coronarius** L. A strong-growing, medium-sized shrub with creamy-white, richly scented flowers. The most commonly cultivated species, particularly suitable for very dry soils. Origin obscure, perhaps wild in N and C Italy, Austria and C Romania. Long cultivated.

  **'Aureus'** (*P. caucasicus* 'Aureus') Leaves bright yellow when young, becoming greenish-yellow. AM 1983. AGM 1984.

  **'Variegatus'** (*P. caucasicus* 'Variegatus') Leaves with a creamy-white margin. C 1770. AGM 1984.

**'Coupe d'Argent'** (Lemoinei Group) A rather frail aristocrat, and a small shrub of superb quality. The large, single, fragrant flowers have a very slight stain at the base of the petals. They are rather square in outline and beautifully poised at regular intervals. AM 1922. C 1915 (Lemoine).

× **cymosus** REHD. (*P. floribundus* SCHRAD.) A group of variable hybrids with flowers in cyme-like racemes. There are numerous named clones. See 'Albâtre', 'Amalthée', 'Bouquet Blanc', 'Conquete', 'Monster', 'Velleda' and 'Voie Lactée'.

**delavayi** L. HENRY A large vigorous shrub with large leaves, grey-felted beneath. Flowers heavily scented, 3-4cm across, in dense racemes. China, Tibet, Upper Burma. Discovered and introduced by the Abbé Delavay in 1887.

  **var. calvescens** REHD. Leaves less hairy beneath.

  **f. melanocalyx** (L. HENRY) REHD. A delightful form with purple calyces. Often grown as var. *calvescens*.

  **'Nymans Variety'** The best form of f. *melanocalyx* with the calyx deep purple. AM 1935.

**'Enchantment'** (Virginalis Group) A small to medium-sized shrub, producing terminal clusters of double, sweetly scented flowers in profusion. C 1923 (Lemoine). AM 1966.

**'Erectus'** (Lemoinei Group) A small shrub of erect habit, with small leaves and flowers, extremely floriferous and richly scented. AGM 1984. C 1890 (Lemoine).

**'Etoile Rose'** (Purpureo-maculatus Group) Flowers large, fragrant, single, the petals elongated, white with a carmine-rose blotch at base. C 1908 (Lemoine).

**'Falconeri'** (*P. × falconeri* SARG.) A large shrub. The slightly fragrant white flowers, 3-4cm across, are very distinct on account of their narrow, lance-shaped petals. Origin uncertain. C 1881.

**'Favourite'** (Polyanthus Group) An attractive cultivar up to 2m. Single, very large, cup-shaped flowers, pure white with serrated petals and a central cluster of yellow stamens. C 1916 (Lemoine).

**floribundus** See *P. × cymosus*.

**'Frosty Morn'** A small shrub with fragrant, double flowers. C 1953.

**'Girandole'** (Virginalis Group) A showy shrub with clusters of very double, fragrant flowers. AM 1921. C 1915 (Lemoine).

**'Glacier'** (Virginalis Group) A small, late flowering shrub, bearing crowded clusters of very double, fragrant flowers. C 1913 (Lemoine).

**PHILADELPHUS**—*continued*

**incanus** KOEHNE A medium-sized to large shrub, well distinguished by its hairy leaves and late blossoming. Flowers fragrant, in late July. C China. I 1904 by Ernest Wilson.

**'Innocence'** (Lemoinei Group) Flowers single, fragrant, borne with extraordinary freedom. Leaves often with creamy-white variegation. C 1927 (Lemoine).

**insignis** CARR. A vigorous shrub 3-3.6m high. Flowers about 3cm wide, rather cup-shaped, scented, produced in panicles of 15-20. One of the last to flower, the blossoms remaining until mid-July. California. AM 1929.

**intectus** BEADLE (*P. pubescens* var. *intectus* (BEADLE) A.H. MOORE) A very vigorous shrub, growing 4.5m or more high. Outstanding when laden with masses of slightly fragrant flowers. SE United States. C before 1890.

×**lemoinei** LEMOINE (*P. coronarius* × *P. microphyllus*). Raised in 1884 by M. Lemoine, this was the original hybrid of which there are now numerous named clones. A small shrub; flowers very fragrant 2.5cm wide, produced in clusters of 3-7 on short side branches. AM 1898. See 'Avalanche', 'Coupe d'Argent', 'Erectus', 'Innocence' and 'Manteau d'Hermine'.

**lewisii** PURSH A medium-sized to large shrub of erect habit with racemes of white flowers. W North America. I 1823.

**maculatus** See under *P. mexicanus* 'Rose Syringa'.

**'Manteau d'Hermine'** (Lemoinei Group) A popular dwarf, compact shrub attaining about 0.75-1.2m; flowers fragrant, creamy-white, double. AM 1956. AGM 1984. C 1899 (Lemoine).

†**mexicanus** SCHLECHT. A tender species native to Mexico of which the following form is the most commonly cultivated.

   **'Rose Syringa'** (*P. maculatus* HORT. not (HITCHC.) HU) A beautiful medium-sized shrub with richly fragrant flowers which are white, with a purple blotch in the centre. Sometimes wrongly grown in gardens under the name *P. coulteri*, which differs in its exposed buds and pure white flowers. A parent of many fine hybrids. AM 1961.

**microphyllus** A. GRAY A very dainty, small-leaved species, forming a twiggy bush about 1-1.2m high. Flowers richly fragrant. SW United States. I 1883. FCC 1890. AGM 1984.

**'Minnesota Snowflake'** (Virginalis Group) An American cultivar, 1.5-1.8m high, with arching branches bowed by the weight of the double, fragrant flowers. C 1935.

**'Monster'** (Cymosus Group) A vigorous, large shrub, quickly attaining 4.5m. Flowers nearly 5cm across.

**'Norma'** (Polyanthus Group) Flowers single, 5cm across, slightly fragrant, on long slender branches. C 1910 (Lemoine). AM 1913.

**pekinensis var. brachybotrys** See *P. brachybotrys*.

×**pendulifolius** CARR. Medium-sized shrub with racemes of cup-shaped flowers. Probably a hybrid of *P. pubescens*.

×**polyanthus** REHD. A variable group of erect shrubs of which there are several named clones. See 'Favourite' and 'Norma'.

**pubescens** LOISEL. (*P. pubescens* var. *verrucosus* (SCHRAD.) HU) (*P. verrucosus* SCHRAD.) A vigorous shrub up to 3m high. Flowers about 3-4cm across, slightly fragrant, in racemes of 5-7. SE United States.

   **var. intectus** See *P. intectus*.

   **var. verrucosus** See *P. pubescens*.

**purpurascens** (KOEHNE) REHD. A small-leaved species making a medium-sized shrub, with spreading and arching branches, wreathed with sweet-scented flowers, the white petals contrasting with the purple calyces. W China. I 1911.

**'Purpureo-maculatus'** (*P.* × *lemoinei* × *P. mexicanus* 'Rose Syringa'). A small to medium-sized shrub. The arching stems are weighted with white, purple-stained, scented blossoms. See also 'Beauclerk', 'Etoile Rose', and 'Sybille'.

**'Pyramidal'** (Virginalis Group) Strong-growing shrub with semi-double, fragrant flowers. C 1916 (Lemoine).

**'Rosace'** (Cymosus Group) Large, semi-double, fragrant flowers in large sprays. C 1904 (Lemoine). AM 1908.

**satsumanus** See *P. satsumi*.

**PHILADELPHUS**—*continued*

**satsumi** LINDL. & PAXT. (*P. satsumanus* SIEB. & ZUCC.) (*P. acuminatus* LANGE) A slender, erect shrub with rather small, slightly scented flowers in racemes of 5-11. Japan. I 1851.

**schrenkii** RUPR. A large shrub of upright habit akin to *P. coronarius*. Flowers very fragrant. E Siberia, Manchuria, Korea. I 1874.

**sericanthus** KOEHNE A spreading shrub of medium to large size. Late flowering, with racemes of small cupped flowers. C China. Introduced by Paul Farges in 1897.

**'Silberregen'** ('Silver Showers') A dense small shrub with small, pointed leaves and profusely borne, single white, fragrant flowers.

**'Snowbelle'** ('Manteau d'Hermine' × 'Virginal'). A small shrub with double bell-shaped white flowers each with up to 15 petals.

**'Splendens'** (*P.* × *splendens* REHD.) A large, spreading shrub forming a wide mound of arching branches. Flowers large in crowded clusters, white, filled with bright yellow anthers. Origin unknown, possibly *P. lewisii* var. *gordonianus* × *P. grandiflorus*.

**subcanus** KOEHNE (*P. wilsonii* KOEHNE) A large shrub producing long racemes of fragrant, somewhat bell-shaped flowers. C and W China. I 1908 by Ernest Wilson.

**'Sybille'** (Purpureo-maculatus Group) A superb small shrub with arching branches bearing single, about square, purple-stained, orange-scented flowers. A triploid hybrid. C 1913 (Lemoine). AM 1954. AGM 1984.

**tomentosus** G. DON A medium-sized shrub with slender-pointed, hairy leaves, grey-felted beneath. Flowers fragrant, 2.5-3.5cm across, borne in slender racemes in June. Himalaya. I 1822.

**'Velleda'** (Cymosus Group) A pretty cultivar with single, perfectly shaped, fragrant flowers about 3-4cm across, petals crimped at the edges. C 1922 (Lemoine).

**verrucosus** See *P. pubescens*.

**'Virginal'** (Virginal Group) A strong-growing, erect-branched shrub to 3m, with flowers 2.5-3.5cm across, richly fragrant. Still probably the best double flowered cultivar. FCC 1911. AGM 1984.

× **virginalis** REHD. A group of hybrids with double flowers of which the type is 'Virginal'. See 'Burfordensis', 'Enchantment', 'Glacier', 'Minnesota Snowflake' and 'Pyramidal'.

**'Voie Lactée'** (Cymosus Group) Flowers single, 5cm across, their broad petals having slightly reflexed edges. C 1905 (Lemoine). AM 1912.

**wilsonii** See *P. subcanus*.

‡†* × **PHILAGERIA** MAST. (*Lapageria* × *Philesia*)—**Philesiaceae**—An exceedingly rare intergeneric hybrid for a cool, moist, peaty soil in a mild garden or conservatory. A difficult plant to establish.

**veitchii** MAST. (*Lapageria rosea* × *Philesia magellanica*). A small scrambling shrub with wiry branches and small, narrow, leathery leaves. Flowers solitary in the axils of the leaves, drooping, pale rose-purple outside, bright rose inside, appearing in late summer and autumn. Raised by Messrs Veitch in 1872, *Lapageria* being the mother parent.

‡†* **PHILESIA** COMM. ex JUSS.—**Philesiaceae**—A monotypic genus related to *Lapageria*.

**magellanica** GMEL. (*P. buxifolia* LAM.) One of the choicest, most remarkable and beautiful of dwarf, suckering, evergreen shrubs, forming wide thickets of wiry stems and narrow, rigid leaves which are green above, glaucous beneath; producing crimson, tubular flowers, 5cm long, in summer and autumn. Requires a moist, peaty, half shady site, well drained soil and a sheltered position. S Chile. Introduced by William Lobb in 1847. AM 1937.

**'Rosea'** Flowers paler, almost rose-red.

***PHILLYREA** L.—**Oleaceae**—Handsome evergreen shrubs or small trees allied to *Osmanthus*, and sometimes mistaken for the Holm Oak. 4 species in Madeira, the Mediterranean region and SW Asia. The growths of the smaller-leaved kinds develop, at maturity, into elegant plumose masses of foliage. Succeed in all types of soil.

**angustifolia** L. A compact, rounded bush of medium size. Leaves narrow, normally entire, dark green and glabrous. Flowers small, fragrant, creamy-yellow, in axillary clusters in May and June. Excellent for maritime exposure. N Africa, S Europe. C before 1597.

**PHILLYREA angustifolia**—*continued*

**f. rosmarinifolia** (MILLER) SCHELLE A most attractive, neat, compact form with even narrower leaves.

**decora** See *Osmanthus decorus*.

**latifolia** L. An elegant, olive-like small tree or large shrub suitable for planting where the Holm Oak would grow too large. Its branches are bowed by the weight of luxuriant masses of small, glossy, dark green, opposite leaves. Flowers dull white in late spring, followed by tiny, blue-black fruits which are seldom produced in this country. S Europe, Asia Minor. C 1597.

**'Rotundifolia'** Leaves broadly ovate or rotund.

**f. spinosa** (MILLER) REHD. (*P. latifolia* var. *ilicifolia* DC.) Narrow, serrated leaves.

**\*PHLOMIS** L.—**Labiatae**—A valuable genus of about 100 species of mainly low-growing shrubs, sub-shrubs and herbs, usually densely hairy or woolly and producing attractive flowers in axillary whorls. Widely distributed in Europe and Asia. They require full sun and good drainage.

**chrysophylla** BOISS. A pleasing, small shrub, differing from *P. fruticosa* in its sage-like foliage which assumes a golden yellow tinge after midsummer. Flowers golden yellow in June, best in hot summers. Lebanon. AGM 1984.

**'Edward Bowles'** An attractive, small to medium-sized sub-shrub, with large, hoary, heart-shaped leaves, and whorls of sulphur-yellow flowers with a distinctly paler upper lip, in late summer and autumn. Appears to be intermediate between *P. fruticosa* and the herbaceous *P. russeliana*.

**fruticosa** L. "Jerusalem Sage". A small, grey-green shrub, hardy in all but the coldest districts. Its whorls of bright yellow flowers are attractive in summer. A good plant for a sunny bank. Mediterranean region. C 1596. AM 1925. AGM 1984.

**†italica** L. A very desirable dwarf shrub from the Balearic Isles. Stems and leaves white-hairy, flowers pale lilac in terminal spikes in summer. C 1750.

**lanata** WILLD. A dense, dwarf, mound-forming shrub with yellow-woolly shoots and small, sage-green and scurfy, ovate leaves to 3cm long, the veins deeply impressed above. Flowers golden yellow with brownish hairs, borne in whorls in summer. Crete.

**longifolia** BOISS. & BL. A very attractive small shrub proving hardy, with white-woolly young stems and bright green, deeply veined, ovate-triangular leaves heart-shaped at the base. Terminal clusters of deep golden yellow flowers are borne in summer. SW Asia.

**var. bailanica** (VIEH.) HUB.-MOR. A form with broader, darker green and more conspicuously veined leaves.

**\*PHORMIUM** FORST. & FORST. f.—**Phormiaceae**—2 species of New Zealand evergreens with handsome, sword-like leaves. They have much the same garden value as the yuccas and associate well with them. They thrive in a variety of soils and are good plants for maritime exposure and for industrial areas. They are more or less hardy in all but the coldest areas. Many of the more recent forms are hybrids between the 2 species.

**'Apricot Queen'** Low, weeping habit, leaves soft yellow flushed apricot, margined with dark green and bronze.

**'Bronze Baby'** Leaves bronze, drooping at the tips.

**cookianum** LE JOLIS (*P. colensoi* HOOK. f.) Differs from *P. tenax* in its smaller stature and its thinner, greener leaves which are laxer and more flexible. Flowers yellowish, in panicles up to 1m during summer. I 1848. FCC 1868. AGM 1984.

**'Cream Delight'** Leaves with a broad cream central band and narrower stripes of cream towards the margin. Raised in New Zealand before 1978. AGM 1984.

**'Tricolor'** Leaves conspicuously edged with creamy-yellow, narrowly margined with red. Found in New Zealand in the 1880s. AGM 1984.

**'Dark Delight'** Up to 1m. Broad, upright, dark bronze-purple leaves with a reddish midrib, drooping at the tips.

**'Dazzler'** A striking plant to 1m with leaves deep red-purple striped with rose-red in the centre.

**'Maori Chief'** Leaves upright, drooping at the tips, variegated with scarlet, crimson and bronze.

**PHORMIUM**—*continued*
  **'Maori Maiden'** Leaves to 90cm, drooping at the tips, bronze-green striped rose-red.
  **'Maori Queen'** Leaves upright with drooping tips, bronze green with rose-red stripes.
  **'Maori Sunrise'** Low-growing with slender, arching leaves, pale red to pink, margined bronze.
  **'Pink Panther'** Ruby-red with pink margins.
  **tenax** FORST. & FORST. f. The "New Zealand Flax" is a striking evergreen for foliage effect, forming clumps of rigid, leathery, somewhat glaucous, sword-like leaves, varying from 1-3m in length. Flowers bronzy-red in panicles up to 4.5m high in summer. A superb architectural plant for creating contrasting and diverse effects. It possesses something of the subtropical, the arid desert, and the waterside. It may be grown in all types of fertile soil and in all aspects. It is tolerant of sea wind and industrial pollution. Its leaves contain one of the finest fibres known. New Zealand. Often found naturalised in the west of Ireland. I 1789. AGM 1984.
  **'Purpureum'** Leaves bronzy-purple to 2m long. A striking plant contrasting with grey foliage subjects. AGM 1984.
  **'Sundowner'** Leaves bronze-green with a deep rose-red margin, to 1.5m long. AM 1978.
  **'Variegatum'** Leaves with a creamy-white margin. FCC 1864. AGM 1984.
  **'Veitchii'** Leaves striped creamy-yellow in the centre.
  **'Yellow Wave'** Leaves to 1m long, drooping, the yellowish-green central band variously striped with green. Raised in New Zealand about 1967. AM 1977.

**PHOTINIA** LINDLEY (*Stranvaesia* LINDLEY) (× *Stranvinia* HILLIER)—**Rosaceae**—A genus of large, mainly evergreen shrubs or small trees allied to *Crataegus* and comprising about 40 species native from the Himalaya to E and SE Asia. The flowers are white, produced usually in spring in corymbose clusters, followed in autumn by red fruits. The foliage of some deciduous species colours well before falling, and in some evergreen sorts the bronze-red unfolding leaves rival Forrest's *Pieris*. The deciduous species are inclined to be calcifuge, whilst the evergreens are lime-tolerant. Unfortunately, with the exception of *P. davidiana* the evergreen species seldom flower or fruit with any sort of freedom due presumably to lack of sun and warmth.
  **arbutifolia** See *Heteromeles arbutifolia*.
  **beauverdiana** SCHNEID. This Chinese species has proved to be a very desirable small tree up to 6m high, conspicuous in late May or early June when covered with corymbs of hawthorn-like flowers, and in autumn when bedecked with dark red fruits and richly tinted leaves. Moderately lime-tolerant. W China. I 1900 by Ernest Wilson.
    **var. notabilis** (SCHNEID.) REHD. & WILS. Distinguished by its larger leaves, up to 12.5cm long, broader corymbs and taller habit. Excellent in autumn when its leaves colour before falling, leaving clusters of orange-red fruits. C and W China. I 1908 by Ernest Wilson. AM 1960.
  **benthamiana** HANCE This deciduous species related to *P. villosa* appears to be not in cultivation. Plants grown under this name are *P. glabra*. China and Vietnam.
  **\*davidiana** (DECNE.) CARDOT (*Stranvaesia davidiana* DECNE.) An extremely vigorous, large shrub or small tree with erect branches and dark green, lanceolate or oblanceolate, leathery, entire leaves. The globular, brilliant crimson fruits are carried in conspicuous, pendent bunches all along the branches. In established specimens the oldest leaves turn bright red in autumn contrasting effectively with the still green younger leaves. Unfortunately susceptible to fireblight. W China. First discovered by Père Armand David in 1869. Introduced in its typical form by George Forrest in 1917. AM 1928. AGM 1984. In 1967 our propagator Peter Dummer raised a hybrid between this and *Pyracantha atalantioides*.
  **'Fructuluteo'** (Undulata Group) A selected form with bright yellow fruits. AM 1986.
  **'Palette'** A slow-growing form, the leaves conspicuously blotched and streaked with creamy-white, pink-tinged when young. Admired by some, hated by others. Raised in Holland before 1980.
  **'Prostrata'** (Undulata Group) A low-growing, more or less prostrate form.
  **Salicifolia group** (*Stranvaesia davidiana* var. *salicifolia* (HUTCH.) REHD.) (*S. salicifolia* HUTCH.) The most commonly cultivated form differing little from the typical form. The

**PHOTINIA davidiana Salicifolia group**—*continued*
leaves tend to narrow oblong or narrow lanceolate and are more numerously veined. W
China. Introduced by E.H. Wilson in 1907.

**Undulata Group** (*Stranvaesia davidiana* var. *undulata* (DECNE.) REHD. & WILS.) (*S. undulata*
DECNE.) Less vigorous and usually seen as a shrub of medium size with wide-spreading
branches, often twice as wide as high. Leaves generally wavy at the margin. W China.
Introduced by E.H. Wilson in 1901. AM 1922.

**\*davidsoniae** REHD. & WILS. A small to medium-sized thorny tree with reddish, downy shoots
and oblanceolate, dark glossy green, taper-pointed leaves up to 15cm long. Heads of
white flowers in spring are followed by orange-red fruits. The plant previously listed
under this name is a form of *Photinia nussia*. W Hubei, China. I 1900 by Ernest Wilson.

**\* × fraseri** DRESS (*P. glabra* × *P. serratifolia*). A variable hybrid, a large vigorous, evergreen
shrub with dark glossy green, leathery leaves and attractive coppery young growths. The
forms of this hybrid have proven very hardy.

**'Birmingham'** An American-raised clone with generally obovate, abruptly-pointed leaves,
bright coppery-red when young. Tending towards the *P. glabra* parent. C 1940.

**'Red Robin'** (*P. glabra* 'Red Robin') A most spectacular clone raised in New Zealand,
with sharply-toothed, glossy green leaves and brilliant red, young growths, equal to the
best forms of *Pieris formosa*. AM 1977. AGM 1984.

**'Robusta'** (*P. glabra* 'Robusta') A strong-growing clone tending toward the *P. serratifolia*
parent with its thick, leathery oblong to obovate leaves. Young growths brilliant coppery-
red. This is proving the hardiest clone. A seedling raised in Hazelwood's Nursery,
Sydney, Australia. AM 1974 (for foliage). AGM 1984. AM 1990 (for flower).

**\*glabra** (THUNB.) MAXIM. A medium-sized to large shrub with oblong to obovate, dark green,
minutely serrulate, leathery leaves and bronze young growths. Flowers in May or June
followed by red fruits. Japan, China. C about 1903.

**'Parfait'** ('Pink Lady') ('Roseomarginata') ('Variegata') Young leaves bronze margined
pink becoming green flecked with grey-green with a narrow creamy-white margin.

**'Rubens'** A choice cultivar, the young leaves of a brilliant sealing-wax-red. AM 1972.

**'Roseomarginata'** See 'Parfait'.

**†glomerata** REHD. & WILS. A tender, medium-sized to large shrub with lanceolate leaves up
to 12.5cm long. Young foliage bright red. Yunnan.

**†\*integrifolia** LINDL. Medium-sized shrub with slender-pointed, entire, leathery, oblanceolate
leaves up to 15cm long. It is sad that this outstanding evergreen is too tender for our
area. It is lime-tolerant. Himalaya, China, Vietnam.

**koreana** See *P. villosa* f. *maximowicziana*.

**†\*nussia** (D. DON) KALKMANN (*Stranvaesia nussia* (D. DON) DECNE.) (*S. glaucescens* LINDL.) A
large shrub or, in mild localities, a small tree, with oblanceolate to obovate, leathery
leaves up to 10cm long which are dark glossy green and finely-toothed. Flowers appearing
in flattish, tomentose clusters in July, followed by downy orange fruits. Himalaya, SE
Asia. I 1828.

**†\*prionophylla** (FRANCH.) SCHNEID. (*Eriobotrya prionophylla* FRANCH.) A stiff-habited, medium-
sized evergreen from China, with hard, leathery, obovate leaves with prickly margins.
The white flowers appearing in July are borne in corymbs 5-7.5cm across; fruits crimson.
Not hardy in our area. W China. I 1916 by George Forrest.

**\*prunifolia** (HOOK. & ARN.) LINDL. Some plants previously grown as *P. glabra* belong here. It
can be distinguished by the numerous small black spots on the underside of the leaf and
judging by cultivated plants has larger flowers than *P. glabra*. China, Vietnam.

**\*'Redstart'** ( × *Stranvinia* 'Redstart') (*P. davidiana* 'Fructuluteo' × *P. × fraseri* 'Robusta'). A
vigorous large shrub or small tree with bright red young foliage. Leaves dark green,
oblong-elliptic, to 11cm long, finely and sparsely-toothed above the middle, veins in up
to 14 pairs, not or only slightly raised beneath. Flowers white in June in dense,
hemispherical corymbs with reddish-purple calyces and pedicels. Fruits orange-red
flushed yellow. Raised by our propagator Peter Dummer from a cross made in 1969.

**\*serratifolia** (DESF.) KALKMAN (*P. serrulata* LINDL.) A very handsome, large, evergreen shrub
or small tree. Leaves oblong, up to 15cm long, shining dark green and leathery with
coarsely-toothed margins. The young leaves throughout the whole of its long growing
season are bright, coppery-red. Flowers in large corymbs during April and May, best

**303**

**PHOTINIA serratafolia**—*continued*

following hot summers, they were particularly spectacular in 1990; fruits red, the size of haws. One of the most splendid lime-tolerant evergreens. It is remarkable how the young growths withstand spring frost. China, Taiwan. I 1804. The plant previously distributed by us as *P. serrulata* Formosan form is very distinct, with densely white tomentose young stems and petioles and conspicuous red bud scales and stipules. Young foliage rich bronze.

**serrulata** See *P. serratifolia*.

**villosa** (THUNB.) DC. (*P. variabilis* HEMSL.) (*Pourthiaea villosa* (THUNB.) DECNE.) A deciduous species forming a large shrub or small, broad-headed tree, with obovate, shortly acuminate leaves. It bears hawthorn-like flowers in May, followed by small, egg-shaped, bright red fruits, and is one of the most effective autumn-colouring subjects, the leaves turning to scarlet and gold. It does not thrive on shallow, chalky soil. Japan, Korea, China. I about 1865 by Siebold. AM 1932. AGM 1969.

**var. laevis** (THUNB.) DIPP. The most commonly grown form with glabrous, finely-toothed leaves attractively margined with bronze when young, brilliant orange and red in autumn. Unlike other forms of this variable species it tends to make a tree, with spreading rather than arching branches.

**f. maximowicziana** (LEVL.) REHD. (*P. koreana* LANCASTER) Leaves almost sessile, obovate, pale green, rather leathery in texture, the veins strongly impressed above giving the leaf a bullate appearance. Autumn colour rich golden yellow. Originally wrongly catalogued and distributed by us as *P. amphidoxa*. Korea (Quelpaert). Introduced via Japan in 1897.

**var. sinica** REHD. & WILS. A small tree or occasionally a large shrub, differing in its more spreading habit, elliptic or elliptic-oblong leaves and its larger almost cherry-like fruits in pendulous clusters. C China. I about 1901 by Ernest Wilson.

*"Winchester'** A selection from the same cross as 'Redstart'. It differs in its thinner leaves which are elliptic-oblanceolate, to 13.5cm long, veins in up to 18 pairs, distinctly raised beneath. Fruits orange-red flushed yellow at the apex.

**\*PHYGELIUS** E. MEYER ex BENTH.—**Scrophulariaceae**—2 species of attractive, evergreen or semi-evergreen, penstemon-like sub-shrubs from S Africa. *P. capensis* is remarkable as being one of the very few S African shrubs hardy in the British Isles. They reach their greatest height against a sunny wall, but look well towards the front of the shrub or herbaceous border. They succeed in full sun in all types of well drained but not too dry soil.

**aequalis** HIERN A small sub-shrub up to 1m, with four-angled stems. Flowers tubular, 2.5-4cm long, corolla slightly down-curved, regular at the mouth with spreading lobes, pale dusky-pink to red, with a yellow throat, produced in compact, one-sided panicles in late summer and early autumn. Not so hardy as *P. capensis* and requires wall protection. AM 1936.

**'Yellow Trumpet'** A striking form with pale creamy-yellow flowers and broad light green leaves. It was discovered in the wild in SW Natal and introduced to this country from cultivation in S Africa independently by B.L. Burtt and Sir Harold Hillier in 1973. AM 1984. AGM 1984.

**capensis** BENTH. "Cape Figwort". A small shrub, occasionally up to 2m in mild areas. Flowers tubular, nodding and turning back towards the stem when open, irregular at the mouth with reflexed lobes, orange-red to deep red with a yellow throat, elegantly borne on all sides of the stem in tall, open panicles during summer and autumn. C 1855. AGM 1969. AM 1978.

**'Coccineus'** As originally described this form had rich red flowers but may no longer be in cultivation. Plants now grown under this name have large, rich orange-red flowers. AM 1926. AGM 1984.

×**rectus** COOMBES (*P. aequalis* × *P. capensis*). A group of hybrids intermediate between the parents in the shape of the corolla tube. The F$_1$ hybrids have pendulous flowers with a more or less straight tube whereas back-crosses tend more to one of the parents. Several forms have now been raised in various colours. Unless stated they reach about 1-1.5m.

**PHYGELIUS × rectus**—*continued*

**'African Queen'** ('Indian Chief') An F₁ hybrid with pale red flowers. This was the first hybrid, raised by John May at the Wimborne Botanic Garden in 1969.

**'Devil's Tears'** A back-cross between 'Winchester Fanfare' and *P. capensis* 'Coccineus' raised by our propagator Peter Dummer in 1985. Flowers deep reddish-pink, deeper in bud with orange-red lobes. The tall, open inflorescence tends to *P. capensis*.

**'Indian Chief'** See 'African Queen'.

**'Moonraker'** A back-cross between 'Winchester Fanfare' and *P. aequalis* 'Yellow Trumpet' raised by our propagator Peter Dummer in 1985. Resembles 'Yellow Trumpet' but flowers borne on all sides of the inflorescence with a nearly straight corolla tube.

**'Pink Elf'** This very distinct form is a back-cross between 'Winchester Fanfare' and *P. aequalis* 'Yellow Trumpet' raised by our propagator Peter Dummer in 1985. A compact dwarf form with narrow leaves reaching about 75cm. Flowers very slender, pale pink with deep crimson lobes, borne on all sides of the inflorescence and spreading, not pendulous.

**'Salmon Leap'** A back-cross between 'Winchester Fanfare' and *P. capensis* 'Coccineus' raised by our propagator Peter Dummer in 1985. It resembles 'Devil's Tears' but has orange flowers with deeper lobes.

**'Winchester Fanfare'** (*P. aequalis* 'Yellow Trumpet' × *P. capensis* 'Coccineus'). Flowers pendulous with a straight corolla tube, dusky reddish-pink with scarlet lobes. It most resembles 'African Queen' but differs in its flower colour and the broader leaves inherited from 'Yellow Trumpet'. Raised by our propagator Peter Dummer in 1974.

†\***PHYLICA** L.—**Rhamnaceae**—A large genus of about 150 species of evergreen shrubs mainly found in S Africa. Only suitable for sunny positions in the mildest areas.

**arborea** THOUARS (*P. superba* HORT.) A remarkable, small, helichrysum-like shrub with crowded, small, silver-green leaves. Inflorescences, composed of tiny, green-white flowers, open in late autumn, emitting a strong fragrance like Meadow-sweet. Only suitable for the mildest areas, but makes an attractive conservatory shrub. Lime-tolerant. Islands of S Atlantic and Indian Oceans.

**superba** See *P. arborea*.

‡\* × **PHYLLIOPSIS** CULLEN & LANCASTER (*Kalmiopsis* × *Phyllodoce*)—**Ericaceae**—An interesting intergeneric hybrid described from a plant which originated in our nursery.

**hillieri** CULLEN & LANCASTER (*Kalmiopsis leachiana* × *Phyllodoce breweri*). The following is the first hybrid to be recorded between these genera. It was noticed in our nursery in 1960.

**'Pinocchio'** A dwarf shrub with glossy green, oblong-obovate leaves up to 2cm long. Flowers deep pink, bell-shaped, about 1cm across, freely borne in long, slender racemes over a long period in spring and again in autumn. AM 1976. FCC 1984.

‡\***PHYLLODOCE** SALISB.—**Ericaceae**—A genus of about 6 species of dainty, dwarf, heath-like shrubs natives of N temperate and Arctic regions and thriving in cool, moist, moorland conditions, and in lime-free soil. April to July flowering.

**aleutica** (SPRENG.) HELLER A dwarf, carpeting shrublet, 15-23cm high. Flowers pitcher-shaped (urceolate), creamy-white, or pale yellow, in terminal umbels during May and June. S Alaska, Aleutian Isles, Kamtchatka, N Japan. I 1915. AM 1939.

**subsp. glanduliflora** (HOOK.) HULT. (*P. glanduliflora* HOOK.) Corolla densely covered in glandular hairs. Oregon to Alaska. AM 1978.

**breweri** (A. GRAY) HELLER A dwarf, tufted species, 23-30cm high. Flowers comparatively large, saucer-shaped, of a delightful rose-purple, produced in long terminal racemes in May and June. California. I 1896. AM 1956.

**caerulea** (L.) BAB. (*P. taxifolia* SALISB.) A rare, native alpine found wild in Perthshire. A dwarf cushion-forming shrublet up to 15cm; flowers pitcher-shaped, bluish-purple, borne in delicate terminal umbels in May and June. Alpine-Arctic regions of N Europe, North America, N Asia. C 1800. AM 1938.

**PHYLLODOCE**—*continued*

**empetriformis** (SM.) D. DON A dwarf, tufted shrublet, 15-25cm high. Flowers bell-shaped, bright reddish-purple, produced in umbels during April and May. W North America. C 1830.

**glanduliflora** See *P. aleutica* subsp. *glanduliflora*.

× **intermedia** (HOOK.) RYDB. (*P. empetriformis* × *P. aleutica* subsp. *glanduliflora*) (*P. hybrida* RYDB.) A variable dwarf hybrid of vigorous growth, soon forming large mats up to 30cm high and four times as much wide. Often wrongly grown in gardens as *P. empetriformis*, from which it differs in its pitcher-shaped flowers, puckered at the mouth. W North America. AM 1936.

'**Fred Stoker**' (*P. pseudoempetriformis* HORT.) This is the form in general cultivation. Named after that keen amateur gardener the late Dr Fred Stoker. AM 1941.

**nipponica** MAK. One of the most perfect rock garden shrublets for peaty soils. A dwarf, erect-growing species of neat, compact habit, 15-23cm high. Flowers bell-shaped, white or pink-tinged, appearing in terminal umbels in May. N Japan. I 1915. AM 1938. FCC 1946.

\* × **PHYLLOTHAMNUS** SCHNEID. (*Phyllodoce* × *Rhodothamnus*)—**Ericaceae**—An interesting intergeneric hybrid raised by Cunningham and Fraser, nurserymen of Edinburgh in about 1845. Suitable for a lime-free, moist, peaty or leafy soil.

**erectus** (LINDL.) SCHNEID. (*P. empetriformis* × *R. chamaecistus*). A dwarf shrublet, 30-45cm in height, its stems crowded with narrow leaves. Flowers shallowly funnel-shaped of a delicate rose, produced in terminal umbels in April and May. AM 1958. FCC 1969.

**PHYSOCARPUS** MAXIM.—**Rosaceae**—A small genus of about 10 species of tall shrubs related to *Neillia*, and, like them, thriving in open moist positions. Natives of North America, Mexico and NE Asia. Tend to become chlorotic on a dry, shallow, chalk soil.

**amurensis** (MAXIM.) MAXIM. Medium-sized shrub of compact habit with rounded, three to five-lobed leaves. Flowers white, with reddish-purple anthers, in clusters in summer. Manchuria, Korea.

**capitatus** (PURSH) GREENE Medium-sized shrub with three-lobed, double-toothed leaves and clusters of white flowers in summer. W North America. I 1827.

**malvaceus** (GREENE) KUNTZE (*Neillia torreyi* S. WATS.) (*Neillia malvacea* GREENE) An elegant, spiraea-like shrub of medium size, bearing umbels of white flowers in June. W North America. I 1896.

**monogynus** (TORR.) COULT. Small shrub with small, ovate, three to five-lobed leaves and clusters of white or pink-tinged flowers in summer. C United States. I 1879.

**opulifolius** (L.) MAXIM. (*Spiraea opulifolia* L.) "Nine Bark". A vigorous, medium-sized shrub, thriving almost anywhere. Leaves three-lobed; flowers white, tinged pink, produced in dense clusters along the stems in June. E North America. I 1687.

'**Dart's Gold**' A small, compact shrub, an improvement on 'Luteus' with foliage of a brighter, longer-lasting yellow. AGM 1984.

'**Luteus**' Young growths of a clear yellow, very effective when planted with purple-leaved shrubs. C 1969.

**PHYTOLACCA** L.—**Phytolaccaceae**—A small genus of about 25 species of herbs, shrubs and trees, natives of tropical and warm temperate regions. It is best known in gardens for *P. americana*, the pokeweed from the S United States and Mexico, and *P. clavigera* from China.

†**dioica** L. (*P. arborea* MOQUIN) A large, dioecious semi-evergreen shrub of vigorous growth, making a small, heavy-limbed tree in its native habitat and the Mediterranean region where it is often planted. Leaves poplar-like, up to 15cm long. Flowers greenish, in racemes 5-7.5cm long, followed by dark purple, berry-like fruits. A conservatory shrub, only growing outside in the mildest areas. There is or was a thick-trunked tree in the public gardens at Gibraltar. Native of S America.

†**\*PICCONIA** DC.—**Oleaceae**—2 species of large evergreen shrubs or small trees related to the olive and natives of Madeira, the Canary Islands and the Azores. Only suitable for the milder areas of the British Isles.

**excelsa** (AIT.) DC. (*Notelaea excelsa* (AIT.) WEBB. & BERTH.) (*Olea excelsa* AIT.) A large shrub or small tree with glabrous, grey, flattened shoots. Leaves opposite, elliptic to elliptic-lanceolate, 7.5-12.5cm, long. Flowers fragrant, white, borne in short terminal or axillary racemes during spring or summer. A splendid tree like a small evergreen oak (*Quercus ilex*) grows in the Abbotsbury Subtropical Gardens near Weymouth. With us it grows slowly and survives uninjured all but the coldest winters. The wood is extremely hard and heavy. Canary Isles, Madeira. I 1784.

**PICRASMA** BLUME—**Simaroubaceae**—A genus of 6 species of trees and shrubs related to *Ailanthus*, natives of tropical America, E and SE Asia. Succeeding in a cool, well drained loam, in sun or semi-shade.

**quassioides** (D. DON) BENNETT (*P. ailanthoides* PLANCH.) A very ornamental, small hardy tree with attractive, pinnate leaves 15-25cm long, turning brilliant orange and scarlet in the autumn. All parts are bitter to the taste. Flowers tiny, yellow-green, in axillary corymbs in May and June, followed by red, pea-like fruits. Lime-tolerant but succeeding best in neutral or acid soils. Japan, Taiwan, China, Korea, India.

‡**\*PIERIS** D. DON—**Ericaceae**—Highly ornamental, dense-growing evergreen shrubs requiring similar treatment to rhododendrons. The flower panicles are formed in autumn, and those with red-tinged buds are attractive throughout winter. The flowers eventually open during April and May. They are white and pitcher-shaped, rather like lily-of-the-valley. Several have very attractive red or bronze young growth which is vulnerable to late spring frost and, for that reason, light overhead shade and protection on the north and east sides is desirable for *P. formosa* in all its forms.

**'Bert Chandler'** (*P. japonica* 'Bert Chandler') (*P. japonica* 'Chandleri') An unusual small shrub of Australian origin reaching about 1.5m. The young foliage is bright salmon-pink changing to creamy-yellow then white, finally green. Given an open position the leaves are an attractive creamy-yellow throughout winter. Flowers rarely produced. Raised in Chandler's Nurseries in Victoria, Australia about 1936. AM 1977.

**'Firecrest'** (*P. formosa* Forr. 8945 × *P. japonica*). A vigorous large shrub similar to *P.* 'Forest Flame' with bright red young foliage but leaves broader and more deeply veined. Large white flowers are borne in dense panicles. AM 1973 (for foliage). AM 1981 (for flower). AGM 1984.

**'Flaming Silver'** A small shrub with bright red young leaves which show no variegation when young but soon develop a striking silvery-white margin, pink at first. Flowers creamy-white. A sport of 'Forest Flame' raised in Holland. The same or very similar sport has occurred in several places at about the same time, including one in our nurseries. Of these, at least the Dutch 'Havila' appears to be distinct, with narrower leaves and a broader margin.

**floribunda** (PURSH) BENTH. & HOOK. (*Andromeda floribunda* PURSH ex SIMS) "Fetter Bush". A very hardy, slow-growing shrub forming a dense, rounded mound 1.2-2m high. Flowers produced in numerous erect, terminal panicles during March and April. The greenish-white buds are attractive during winter before they open. SE United States. I 1800.

**'Elongata'** ('Grandiflora') A distinct form with longer panicles, also flowering later. Garden origin about 1935. AM 1938.

**'Forest Flame'** (*P. formosa* 'Wakehurst' × *P. japonica*). A superb large shrub, combining the hardiness of *P. japonica* with the brilliant red young growths of 'Wakehurst'. The leaves pass from red, through pink and creamy-white to green. Flowers in large terminal, drooping panicles. Originated as a chance seedling in Sunningdale Nurseries about 1946. AM 1973. AGM 1984.

**formosa** (WALL.) D. DON (*Andromeda formosa* WALL.) A magnificent large evergreen shrub for mild climates. The large leaves are leathery, finely-toothed and of a dark glossy

**PIERIS formosa**—*continued*

green. The clustered flower panicles are produced in May. Young growths copper-tinged. E Himalaya, Upper Burma, SW and C China. C 1858. AM 1894. FCC 1969.

**'Charles Michael'** (Forr. 27765) A striking form raised at Caerhays Castle from Forrest's seed and named after the Head Gardener there. The individual flowers are the largest of any form and occur in large panicles. AM 1965.

**Forrestii Group** (*Pieris formosa* var. *forrestii* (HARROW) AIRY SHAW) In its best forms this is one of the most beautiful of all shrubs, the young growths brilliant red, and the large, slightly fragrant flowers borne in long, conical panicles. A handsome-foliaged shrub 2.5m or more high, blooming in April. Forms placed here come from SW China, NE Upper Burma and represent one extreme of a variable species. Introduced by George Forrest about 1905. AM 1924.

**'Henry Price'** (Forr. 8945) A splendid selection from Wakehurst Place. Leaves broad, very dark green and deeply veined, deep red when young. Flowers large in upright panicles. AM 1957.

**'Jermyns'** A superb clone, selected in our nursery. Young leaves deep vinous-red becoming dark glossy green. Panicles long and drooping, an attractive red over a long period in winter. The whole inflorescence, including the sepals, is of the same rich colouring as the young stems and contrasts strikingly with the white flowers. AM 1959.

**'Wakehurst'** A lovely selection, strong and vigorous, with relatively short, broad leaves. The vivid red young foliage contrasts beautifully with the glistening white flowers. FCC 1930. AGM 1984.

**'Havila'** See under 'Flaming Silver'.

**japonica** (THUNB.) D. DON (*Andromeda japonica* THUNB.) A medium-sized shrub with attractive, glossy foliage, coppery when young and white, waxy flowers borne in drooping panicles during March and April. Japan, E China, Taiwan. C 1870. FCC 1882. AGM 1984.

**'Bert Chandler'** See *P*. 'Bert Chandler'.

**'Blush'** A beautiful form with dark glossy green leaves and the inflorescences deep purplish-pink before they open. Flowers rose in bud, opening white streaked with pink towards the apex, eventually fading to white, contrasting with the red calyx. This form, the first of the pinks, remains one of the best. AGM 1984.

**'Christmas Cheer'** An exceedingly hardy form from Japan. The flowers are flushed with deep rose at the tip, creating a delightful bicolor effect. Corolla with convex lobes, appearing crimped. Abundantly produced even on young plants and often appear during winter. The pedicels are also deep rose.

**'Crispa'** (*P. taiwanensis* 'Crispa') A small shrub of slow growth with matt leaves strongly curled or wavy-edged. Flowers in large, lax racemes which cover the whole bush. Young growths an attractive copper.

**'Daisen'** ('Rosea Daisen Form') A selection from Mount Daisen in Japan. Flowers pink, deeper in bud. An improvement on 'Rosea'. C 1967.

**'Debutante'** An unusual low-growing form making a compact mound. White flowers are borne in dense, strictly upright panicles. Collected in the wild on the Island of Yakushima by Mr and Mrs de Belder.

**'Dorothy Wyckoff'** Leaves dark green, deeply veined, bronzing in cold weather. Inflorescence rich purplish-red during winter. Corolla pale pink in bud opening white contrasting with the deep red calyx. Raised in the United States about 1960. AM 1984.

**'Flamingo'** Flowers deep red in bud in large panicles, opening deep pink fading to rose-pink, eventually striped with white, nearly white at the mouth and base. Calyx pale green, red at the base. Raised in the United States about 1961. AM 1981.

**'Grayswood'** A very distinct form making a compact small shrub with narrow dark green leaves. Panicles with long, spreading and drooping branches bearing numerous, densely packed small white flowers. AM 1981.

**'Little Heath'** Similar to 'Variegata' but more compact with smaller leaves. Flowers sparse but can be freely borne when grown in a light position, buds pink. Occasionally sports to 'Little Heath Green'.

**'Little Heath Green'** A compact dwarf shrub of mound-forming habit with small, dark green leaves bronze-red when young and in winter on red stems. Rarely if ever flowers.

**PIERIS japonica**—*continued*

**'Mountain Fire'** Young leaves red, turning to deep glossy chestnut brown. Flowers white.

**'Pink Delight'** Long drooping panicles, flowers pale pink, white at the base, fading to white.

**'Purity'** A selected seedling from Japan making a small shrub of compact habit and bearing trusses of comparatively large snow-white flowers in clustered, rather upright racemes. Young foliage pale green. AM 1977. AGM 1984.

**'Pygmaea'** A curious dwarf form of slow growth reaching about 1m tall and across, almost unrecognizable as a *Pieris*, with leaves 1.2-2.5cm long, linear-lanceolate, shallowly-toothed. Resembling a rather loose-leaved *Phyllodoce*. Flowers white, in simple racemes but very sparsely produced.

**'Red Mill'** A very hardy North American selection with dark green leaves bronze-red when young and drooping panicles of white flowers.

**'Scarlett O'Hara'** Pure white flowers opening early and profusely borne in dense, hanging clusters. Young growths bronze.

**Taiwanensis Group** (*P. taiwanensis* HAYATA) There is no absolute distinction between the plants from Japan and Taiwan but the latter tend to have matt green, more leathery leaves with fewer teeth and the panicles are less drooping, being spreading or somewhat upright. Young growths bronze or bronze-red. Introduced from Taiwan by E.H. Wilson in 1918. AM 1922. FCC 1923.

**'Valley Rose'** Flowers deep pink in bud opening rose-pink and conspicuously streaked, white at the base, fading to white, freely borne in large hanging clusters. Rather like 'Blush' in flower but slightly deeper pink and lacking the attractively coloured young inflorescence. Young foliage pale green.

**'Valley Valentine'** Flowers deep dusky-red, hardly fading, white at the base of the corolla, in large drooping clusters. Calyx lobes pale green marked with deep red at the centre and base.

**'Variegata'** A slow-growing form of medium size. The leaves are prettily variegated with creamy-white, flushed pink when young. One of the most attractive of all silver variegated shrubs. AGM 1984.

**'White Cascade'** Profuse white flowers densely borne in long racemes. Raised in the United States about 1961.

**'White Pearl'** Low, spreading habit with white flowers in upright clusters, freely borne even when young. A seedling selected in Holland. C 1982.

**nana** (MAXIM.) MAK. (*Arcterica nana* (MAXIM.) MAK.) A prostrate shrublet only a few inches in height. Leaves in pairs or whorls of 3. The fragrant, white, urn-shaped flowers are produced in terminal clusters in April and May. Japan, Kamtchatka. I 1915. AM 1924. AM 1983.

**'Redshank'** A form in which the young growth, calyx and pedicels are red. AM 1974.

**taiwanensis** See *P. japonica* Taiwanensis Group.

**\*PIMELEA** BANKS & SOL. ex GAERTN.—**Thymelaeaceae**—A genus of some 80 species of shrubs, natives of Australasia. Attractive, small-leaved evergreens closely allied to *Daphne*, and requiring similar cultural treatment. Not recommended for shallow chalk soils.

**†drupacea** LABILL. A small, erect shrub with ovate or narrow leaves 2.5-5cm long. Terminal clusters of white flowers in summer, followed by black fruits. SE Australia, Tasmania. I 1817.

**†ferruginea** LABILL. A dwarf, erect shrub of excellent quality, flowering in late spring and early summer. The heads of clear deep peach-pink flowers are borne at the tips of the branchlets, which are continuously produced. Leaves in rows, small and neat, shining green. W Australia. I 1824. AM 1959.

**prostrata** (FORST. & FORST. f.) WILLD. (*P. laevigata* GAERTN.) A pretty and interesting carpeting species having prostrate or sub-erect branches clothed with small, glabrous, grey-green leaves. The fragrant white flowers produced in clusters in summer are followed by fleshy, white fruits. An excellent scree plant which succeeded here for many years. New Zealand. AM 1955.

**PIPTANTHUS** SWEET—**Leguminosae**—A small genus of 2 species of deciduous and evergreen, large shrubs with trifoliolate leaves and comparatively large, showy, yellow, pea-flowers. They succeed in any well drained soil, including chalk soils.

**laburnifolius** See *P. nepalensis.*

**\*nepalensis** (HOOK.) SWEET (*P. laburnifolius* (D. DON) STAPF) "Evergreen Laburnum". An attractive, nearly evergreen Himalayan shrub 2.4-3.5m high, with large, bright yellow, laburnum-like flowers, opening in May. Deciduous in severe winters. May be grown in the open but an excellent wall plant. I 1821. AM 1960. A slightly more tender form collected by Ludlow and Sherriff in Bhutan (L. & S. 17394) had greyish-green, silky leaves and clusters of attractive yellow flowers during April and May.

**"PISTACHIO"** See *Pistacia vera.*

**PISTACIA** L.—**Anacardiaceae**—A small genus of 9 species of evergreen and deciduous shrubs, or occasionally small trees, related to *Rhus*, differing in the petalless flowers. Widely distributed in warm temperate regions of the N hemisphere. *P. chinensis* is the only fully hardy species. Best in sun, they will succeed in all types of soil.

**chinensis** BUNGE "Chinese Pistachio". A hardy, large shrub with elegant, glossy green, pinnate leaves assuming gorgeous colours in autumn. Flowers unisexual, in dense terminal clusters; fruits seldom appearing, small, reddish at first then blue. C and W China. I 1897.

†**\*lentiscus** L. "Mastic Tree". A large shrub or small tree, the pinnate leaves with 8-10 ovate, glossy green leaflets on a winged rachis. Mediterranean region. C 1664.

†**terebinthus** L. "Chian Turpentine Tree". A small tree or large shrub with aromatic, dark glossy green, pinnate leaves. The unisexual flowers are greenish; fruits small, reddish, turning purplish-brown. Asia Minor, Mediterranean region. C 1656.

†**vera** L. "Pistachio". A small tree with pinnate leaves, the leaflets large and downy. The dense panicles of inconspicuous flowers are followed by small, reddish fruits—the pistachio-nuts of commerce, which are rarely developed outside in this country. Requires a hot, dry, sheltered position, or greenhouse. W Asia, long cultivated. Introduced to England in 1770.

**\*PITTOSPORUM** BANKS ex GAERTN.—**Pittosporaceae**—A large genus of some 200 species of evergreen shrubs or small trees, the majority only suitable for mild districts, where they will thrive especially well near the sea. Natives from Australasia to E and SE Asia, tropical and S Africa. Several have small, fragrant flowers, but they are chiefly grown for their foliage which is useful for cutting. All types of well drained soil. *P. dallii* is the only species which has never been injured outside here during its stay of more than 40 years.

†**adaphniphylloides** HU & WANG (*P. daphniphylloides* sens. REHD. & WILS. not HAYATA) A remarkable large shrub or small tree, with large, dark green, obovate or oblanceolate leaves, up to 23cm long. Flowers cream, deliciously scented, in large terminal clusters from April to July. Fruits small, red. Proving hardy given shelter. There are large specimens in Cornwall. W China. Introduced by E.H. Wilson in 1904.

†**bicolor** HOOK. A large shrub or small tree of erect habit with narrow, revolute, entire leaves which are dark green above, white becoming brownish tomentose beneath. Flowers bell-shaped, maroon and yellow in clusters during spring. A useful tall hedge in mild areas. Tasmania, SE Australia. C 1854.

**chinense** See *P. tobira.*

†**colensoi** HOOK. f. A medium-sized to large shrub closely related to *P. tenuifolium*, excellent in maritime districts. Leaves 3.5-10cm long, oblong or oval, leathery and dark glossy green above. Flowers dark red, comparatively large, appearing in April. New Zealand.

†**cornifolium** A. CUNN. A distinct New Zealand species to 1.8m high; leaves 5-7.5cm long, whorled. Flowers purple, musk-scented in terminal umbels of 2-5, in February and March. Normally epiphytic on tree trunks in its native habitat, but succeeds in ordinary, well drained soil in favoured areas of the British Isles.

**crassifolium** A. CUNN. The New Zealand "Karo", one of the hardiest species, passing many years here uninjured. Leaves 5-7.5cm long, oval or obovate, thick and leathery, deep

310

**PITTOSPORUM crassifolium**—*continued*

green above, white-felted beneath. Flowers deep purple, in terminal clusters. An excellent dense-growing screen or shelter-belt in coastal areas. Kermadec and N Islands.

'**Variegatum**' Leaves grey-green, attractively margined creamy-white. AM 1977.

**dallii** CHEESEM. A perfectly hardy, large, spreading New Zealand shrub or rarely a small tree of rounded shape. Shoots and petioles dark reddish-purple. Leaves elliptic to elliptic-lanceolate, leathery and jaggedly-toothed or occasionally entire, matt green. The fragrant, creamy-white flowers with exserted stamens are borne in small, terminal clusters during summer. It flowered at the Hillier Gardens and Arboretum for the first time in August 1988 and it has reached 4 × 6.5m. New Zealand (S Island), rare in the wild.

**daphniphylloides** See *P. adaphniphylloides*.

**divaricatum** CKN. A small to medium-sized shrub with rigid, wiry branches forming a dense, tangled mass. Leaves variable, 12-20mm long, those of juvenile plants deeply-toothed, leaves of adult plants entire to deeply-toothed or lobed. The small, dark maroon flowers are produced at the ends of the shoots, in May. A curious species reminding one of *Corokia cotoneaster* in habit. Proving hardy. New Zealand.

†**eugenioides** A. CUNN. "Tarata". A large shrub or small tree with dark twigs and oval or oblong, glossy green, undulate leaves 5-10cm long, and pleasantly aromatic. Flowers pale yellow, honey-scented, produced in terminal clusters in spring. New Zealand.

'**Variegatum**' One of the prettiest and most elegant of variegated shrubs for very mild climates. Leaves margined creamy-white. C 1882.

'**Garnettii**' (*P. tenuifolium* 'Garnettii') (*P. ralphii* × *P. tenuifolium*). A large, conical to broadly columnar shrub with grey-green leaves irregularly margined with creamy-white and marked or spotted pink to red during winter. Arose in a New Zealand nursery before 1957 and named after its discoverer, Mr Arthur Garnett. A seedling of this is 'Saundersii' which is virtually identical. AGM 1984.

**mayi** See *P. tenuifolium*.

**nigricans** See *P. tenuifolium*.

**patulum** HOOK. A large slender, sparsely-branched, hardy shrub or small erect tree to 4.5m. Leaves variable, those of juvenile plants are 2.5-5cm long, narrow and conspicuously lobed, those of adult plants 12mm long, toothed or entire. Flowers bell-shaped, fragrant, dark crimson with yellow anthers, in terminal clusters during May. New Zealand (S Island).

†**ralphii** T. KIRK This medium-sized to large shrub, though not fully hardy, stood many years uninjured here in our nursery. Related to *P. crassifolium* from which it differs in its larger, more oblong, less obovate leaves which are flat, not recurved, at the margins. Flowers dark crimson with yellow anthers. New Zealand (N Island).

'**Variegatum**' Leaves broadly margined with creamy-white. C 1957. AM 1979.

'**Saundersii**' See under *P.* 'Garnettii'.

**tenuifolium** GAERTN. (*P. nigricans* HORT.) (*P. mayi* HORT.) A charming large shrub or small tree of columnar habit, with bright, pale green, undulate leaves, prettily set on black twigs. One of the hardier species, extensively used as a cut evergreen for floristry. A good hedging plant for mild localities. Flowers small, chocolate-purple, honey-scented, appearing in spring. New Zealand. AM 1931. AGM 1984.

'**Abbotsbury Gold**' A variegated form similar to 'Eila Keightley' but the variegation most apparent on the young foliage, becoming indistinct on mature leaves. Arose as a sport at the Abbotsbury Subtropical Gardens in about 1970.

'**Eila Keightley**' ('Sunburst') Leaves conspicuously blotched in the centre with bright greenish-yellow, the variegation most conspicuous on the older foliage. Discovered in 1964 as a sport of a form with white-margined leaves known as 'Rotundifolium'.

'**Garnettii**' See *P.* 'Garnettii'.

'**Irene Paterson**' A very attractive, slow-growing form eventually reaching about 2.5m. Young leaves emerging creamy-white, becoming deep green marbled with white, developing a pink tinge in winter. Later growth in summer is pale green. Found in the wild near Christchurch, New Zealand by Mr G. Paterson now Parks Director in Dunedin and named after his wife. C 1970.

**PITTOSPORUM tenuifolium**—*continued*

**'James Stirling'** A charming form with small, dainty, silvery-green, rounded or oval leaves crowding the slender, blackish-purple branchlets. It was seed-raised from a plant found by Mr James Stirling of the Government Gardens, Wellington, New Zealand.

**'Purpureum'** An attractive selection in which the pale green leaves gradually change to deep bronze-purple. More tender than the green form.

**'Saundersii'** See under *P.* 'Garnettii'.

**'Silver Queen'** Leaves suffused silvery-grey, narrowly margined with white. Forms a neat and handsome specimen shrub. AM 1914. AGM 1984.

**'Stirling Gold'** A sport of 'James Stirling' raised in New Zealand. The tiny leaves are conspicuously blotched in the centre with bright yellow.

**'Tom Thumb'** A dwarf shrub of dense, rounded habit. Leaves green when young becoming deep reddish-purple. The colour is brighter and redder than 'Purpureum'. A seedling of 'Purpureum' raised in New Zealand about 1960.

**'Variegatum'** Leaves margined creamy-white. Possibly a hybrid.

**'Warnham Gold'** Young leaves greenish-yellow, maturing to golden yellow, particularly attractive during autumn and winter. A selected seedling raised at Warnham Court, Sussex, in 1959.

**'Saundersii'** See under *P.* 'Garnettii'.

†**tobira** AIT. (*P. chinense* DONN) A rather slow-growing species from Japan and China eventually a large shrub with obovate, bright, glossy green leaves in whorls amidst which are set in summer the conspicuous, orange-blossom-scented flowers which are creamy-white at first turning to yellow. An excellent wall shrub. Used extensively in S Europe for hedging, very drought-resistant. China, Taiwan, Japan. I 1804. AM 1984. AGM 1984.

**'Variegatum'** Leaves grey-green with an irregular, but conspicuous creamy-white margin. Plants under glass often flower during winter.

**turneri** PETRIE A large shrub or small tree of erect habit. Leaves 2.5-4cm long, obovate; flowers in terminal clusters pink or purple in May and June. On juvenile plants the slender, tortuous branches are formed in a dense tangled mass. One of the hardier species, it has reached 5.5m in the Hillier Gardens and Arboretum. New Zealand (N Island).

†**undulatum** VENT. A large shrub with dark, shining green, wavy-edged leaves 7.5-15cm in length. Flowers creamy-white, fragrant, produced in terminal clusters in May and June even on young plants. Only suitable for the mildest localities. Australia. I 1789.

**'Variegatum'** A very beautiful silver-variegated form.

**PLAGIANTHUS** FORST. & FORST. f.—**Malvaceae**—A genus of 2 species of graceful trees or shrubs, natives of New Zealand where they hybridise in the wild. They succeed in the South and South West, in all types of fertile soil. The flowers are very small and normally unisexual.

**betulinus** See *P. regius*.

**divaricatus** FORST. & FORST. f. An interesting shrub forming a densely-branched bush 2m high. Leaves of young plants linear or spathulate, 2-3.5cm long, of adult plants spathulate or narrow obovate, 6-20mm long. Flowers small, yellow-white, solitary or in short clusters in May. New Zealand. I 1820.

**lyallii** See *Hoheria glabrata* and *H. lyallii*.

**regius** (POIT.) HOCHR. (*P. betulinus* A. CUNN.) "Ribbonwood". A graceful, slender, small to medium-sized tree. Leaves ovate to ovate-lanceolate, up to 7.5cm long, toothed. Flowers inconspicuous, white, in large panicles during May. Juvenile plants present a dense bush of slender, interlacing branches with short-stalked leaves 1-4cm long, toothed or lobed. A curious tree passing through several stages of growth. New Zealand. I 1870.

**"PLANE"** See *Platanus*.

**PLANERA** GMEL.—**Ulmaceae**—A rare monotypic genus, of easy cultivation in all types of soil; related to *Ulmus*, but differs in its warty, nut-like fruits.

**aquatica** (WALT.) GMEL. (*P. ulmifolia* MICHX.) "Water Elm". A small to medium-sized, wide-spreading tree with oval, simply or doubly serrate leaves which are from 2.5-7.5cm in

**PLANERA aquatica**—*continued*

length and slightly rough to the touch. Flowers monoecious, inconspicuous. A native of swampy forests in the SE United States. I 1816.

**PLANTAGO** L.—**Plantaginaceae**—The "Plantains" contain more than 250 species, nearly all herbaceous, of cosmopolitan distribution. The following is interesting on account of its shrubby nature.

**\*sempervirens** CRANTZ (*P. cynops* L.) "Shrubby Plantain". A dwarf shrub with slender, erect stems reddish-purple when young. Leaves opposite, linear, rough on the margins. The tiny flowers with exserted cream anthers are borne in dense, small heads on short stalks during summer. SW Europe. C 1596.

**PLATANUS** L.—**Platanaceae**—A small genus of about 6 species of magnificent, large, maple-like trees with alternate leaves and attractive flaking bark. Natives of North America and Mexico apart from *P. orientalis* and one species in SE Asia. They may be grown in all types of fertile soil, but will not reach their maximum proportions in chalky soil and may become chlorotic in very shallow chalk soils.

× **acerifolia** See *P.* × *hispanica*.

**'Augustine Henry'** (*P. californica* HORT.) A large tree similar to the London Plane but with drooping lower branches and more conspicuously flaking bark. Leaves large, five-lobed.

× **hispanica** MILL. ex MUENCHH. (*P.* × *acerifolia* (AIT) WILLD.) (*P.* × *hybrida* BROT.) "London Plane". A large, noble, park tree with attractive mottled or patchwork flaking bark, and large, palmate leaves. The rounded, burr-like, fruit-clusters are produced in strings of 2-6 and hang like baubles on the branches, from early summer through to the following spring. Extensively planted as a street tree owing to its tolerance of atmospheric pollution and severe pruning. First recorded about 1663. It has long been considered a hybrid between *P. occidentalis* and *P. orientalis*, though some opinion suggests that it may be a form of the latter. AGM 1984.

**'Pyramidalis'** A large, erect-growing form, making an excellent tree for a broad thoroughfare. C 1850.

**'Suttneri'** A striking form with large leaves boldly variegated creamy-white. C 1896.

**'Tremonia'** A vigorous tree of narrowly conical habit selected in the Dortmund Botanic Garden in 1951.

**occidentalis** L. The "Buttonwood" or "American Sycamore" is a difficult tree to cultivate successfully in this country. It differs from *P.* × *hispanica* in its shallowly lobed leaves and its smoother fruit-clusters which are normally produced singly on long stalks. S Ontario (Canada), E United States, NE Mexico. In spite of several attempts it has proved impossible to establish any of the American species here. I 1636.

**orientalis** L. "Oriental Plane" "Chennar Tree". A large, stately, long-lived tree developing a wide-spreading head of branches. Bark attractively dappled and flaking; leaves deeply five-lobed, the lobes reaching half-way or more to the base. Fruit-clusters bristly, 2-6 on a stalk. One of the most magnificent of all large trees and attaining a great age. SE Europe. Cultivated in England in the early 16th century. AM 1966. AGM 1984.

**'Digitata'** (*P. orientalis laciniata* HORT.) Leaves deeply divided into 3-5 finger-like lobes.

**var. insularis** A. DC. (*P. cretica* DODE) (*P. cyprius* HORT.) "Cyprian Plane". A small tree with smaller leaves of variable shape, usually deeply divided, with narrow lobes and cuneate at the base.

†**racemosa** NUTT. (*P. californica* BENTH.) A rare species, attaining a large size in California but much smaller in England. Leaves three or five-lobed to below the middle, tomentose beneath. Fruit-clusters sessile, 2-7 on each stalk. California, NW Mexico. I 1870.

**PLATYCARYA** SIEB. & ZUCC.—**Juglandaceae**—A monotypic genus related to *Pterocarya*, differing in the erect inflorescences and twigs with a solid pith.

**strobilacea** SIEB. & ZUCC. (*Fortunaea chinensis* LINDL.) A beautiful small tree with pinnate leaves composed of 7-15 sessile, lanceolate toothed leaflets. Flowers small, the males in cylindrical catkins, the females in erect, green, cone-like clusters at the end of the current year's growth in July or August. The distinctive cone-like fruits are conspicuous. It has

**PLATYCARYA strobilacea**—*continued*
reached 9m in the Hillier Gardens and Arboretum (1990). China, Japan, Korea, Taiwan. I 1845 by Robert Fortune.

†\***PLECOSTACHYS** HILLIARD & BURTT—**Compositae**—2 species of intricately branched shrubs allied to *Helichrysum* and natives of S Africa.
**serpyllifolia** (BERG.) HILLIARD & BURTT (*Helichrysum microphyllum* HORT. not BENTH. & HOOK.) A dwarf, spreading, aromatic, stiffly branched shrub with white tomentose stems. Leaves small, sessile, recurved at the apex, white tomentose on both sides. Flowerheads tiny, white, tinged pink, borne in terminal clusters in winter and spring. Commonly grown for summer bedding and hanging baskets and hardy only in mild areas.

**"PLUMBAGO, HARDY"** See *Ceratostigma willmottianum*.

**"POCKET HANDKERCHIEF TREE"** See *Davidia involucrata*.

**POLIOTHYRSIS** OLIVER—**Flacourtiaceae**—A monotypic genus related to *Idesia*, differing in the capsular fruits. It is quite hardy and succeeds in all types of fertile soil.
**sinensis** OLIV. An interesting, small, hardy tree or large shrub with ovate, slender-pointed leaves 10-15cm long, red-tinged and downy on both sides when young becoming dark green and smooth, red-stalked. Flowers unisexual, fragrant, whitish in bud opening creamy-yellow, borne in terminal, conical panicles to 25cm long in July or August, best in hot summers. China. I 1908 by Ernest Wilson. AM 1960.

\***POLYGALA** L.—**Polygalaceae**—A large genus of more than 500 species of annual or perennial herbs and shrubs with colourful pea-flowers; widely distributed. The woody species thrive in most types of soil, but are not recommended for shallow chalk soils.
‡**chamaebuxus** L. A dwarf, evergreen, alpine shrublet forming large tufts a few centimetres high. Flowers creamy-white tipped bright yellow, appearing in profusion from April to June. Suitable for a cool, moist position on the rock garden or in the peat garden. Mts of C Europe; a common plant in the Alps. C 1658.
**'Angustifolia'** A form with narrow leaves up to 2.5cm long by 3mm across. Flowers purple, tipped yellow.
**var. grandiflora** GAUD. (*P. chamaebuxus* var. *purpurea* NEILR.) (*P. chamaebuxus* var. *rhodoptera* BALL) A very beautiful form with purple wing-petals and yellow keel. AM 1896.
**var. rhodoptera** See var. *grandiflora*.
†**'Dalmaisiana'** (*P. myrtifolia* × *P. oppositifolia*) (*P. myrtifolia* var. *grandifolia* HORT.) A small, almost continuously flowering shrub for the conservatory, with bright purple pea-flowers. Both parents are natives of S Africa.
‡**vayredae** COSTA A choice, creeping alpine shrublet, somewhat resembling *P. chamaebuxus*, but with narrower leaves. Flowers reddish-purple, tipped bright yellow in March and April. Suitable for a cool, moist position on the rock garden or in the peat garden. Pyrenees of Spain. C 1923.
†**virgata** THUNB. An erect-growing shrub to 2m with reed-like stems and narrow leaves. Flowers purple, very conspicuous, in long racemes. Suitable for the conservatory. S Africa. I 1814. AM 1977.

**POLYGONUM** L.—**Polygonaceae**—With the splitting of this genus now generally accepted, the following is the only species of garden note that remains. Most of the herbaceous species belong to *Persicaria*. See also *Fallopia* under CLIMBERS.
**equisetiforme** See under *P. scoparium*.
**scoparium** REQ. ex LOISEL. (*P. equisetiforme* HORT. not SIBTH. & SM.) A small sub-shrub of interesting and unusual growth. The long, slender, reed-like stems are usually devoid of leaves and bear a remarkable resemblance to those of a horsetail (*Equisetum* sp.). The small, creamy-white flowers are borne in numerous, axillary clusters during late summer

**POLYGONUM scoparium**—*continued*

and autumn. Requires a warm, sunny, well drained position. Usually cut back during a severe winter. Corsica, Sardinia. *P. equisetiforme*, a native of the Mediterranean region and Middle East, is prostrate and rarely grown.

**vacciniifolium** See *Persicaria vacciniifolia*.

**POLYLEPIS** RUIZ & PAVON—**Rosaceae**—A genus of 15 species of trees and shrubs related to *Margyricarpus* and *Acaena* and natives of the Andes, often at very high altitudes. The generic name refers to the peeling bark.

**australis** BITT. An unusual semi-evergreen shrub of medium size, reaching 10m in the wild, with attractive, pale brown, flaking bark. Leaves congested at the ends of the shoots, pinnate, with five to seven-toothed, short-stalked leaflets, oblique at the base, some turning yellow in autumn. Flowers small, green, with reddish-purple stamens, borne in long, drooping racemes in May. Proving hardy at the Hillier Gardens and Arboretum where it has reached 3 × 4m. N Argentina.

†\***POMADERRIS** LABILL.—**Rhamnaceae**—A genus of about 40 species of evergreen, small trees and shrubs, natives of Australasia. All require a warm, sheltered position or conservatory treatment. They succeed in all types of well drained soil, but are not recommended for very shallow chalk soils.

**apetala** LABILL. A large shrub with oblong-lanceolate, toothed leaves, wrinkled above, densely tomentose beneath; flowers small, mustard-yellow in large panicles in summer. SE Australia, Tasmania, New Zealand. I 1803.

**phylicifolia** LODD. ex LINK A small heath-like shrub having densely woolly shoots, small, narrow leaves, and cream-coloured flowers borne very abundantly in April. SE Australia, Tasmania, New Zealand. I 1819.

**"POMEGRANATE"** See *Punica granatum*.

**PONCIRUS** RAF.—**Rutaceae**—A monotypic genus related to *Citrus*. It is hardy and will succeed in all types of well drained soil, preferably in full sun.

**trifoliata** (L.) RAF. (*Aegle sepiaria* DC.) (*Citrus trifoliata* L.) "Japanese Bitter Orange". A stout, slow-growing, medium-sized shrub with green stems armed with stout spines and trifoliolate leaves. Beautiful in spring when carrying its white, sweetly-scented flowers, like orange blossom. The individual flowers are almost as large as those of *Clematis montana*. Fruits globular, like miniature oranges, 3.5-5cm across, green ripening to yellow. N China. I 1850.

**"POPLAR"** See *Populus*.

**POPULUS** L.—**Salicaceae**—The "Poplars" are a genus of about 35 species of trees, distributed throughout N temperate regions. They include some of the fastest-growing of all trees. Many are well adapted for quickly forming an effective, tall windbreak, but by reason of their rapid growth and surface-rooting they are unsuitable for small gardens, and should not be planted near buildings as problems can be caused by the roots invading drains. Most thrive in all types of soil, even when wet or boggy, but in wet sites mound planting is desirable. With a few exceptions poplars do not thrive on shallow chalky soils and most of the Black Poplars tend to become chlorotic and even die within thirty years. Many are tolerant of atmospheric pollution and several are excellent in maritime exposure. Some of the poplars, especially the newer hybrids, are valuable for timber production and give comparatively quick returns. The Balsam poplars have pleasantly aromatic young leaves, whilst many of the Black Poplars have attractive, copper-coloured growths in spring. The catkins of certain species are long, and drape the bare branches in spring, male and female catkins appearing on separate trees (dioecious). Some species and their hybrids are prone to canker.

× **acuminata** RYBD. (*P. angustifolia* × *P. sargentii*). A medium-sized balsam poplar with rounded twigs and ovate to rhomboid, acuminate, shining green leaves, aromatic when unfolding. W North America. I 1898.

**POPULUS**—*continued*

**alba** L. "White Poplar" "Abele". A large, suckering tree, conspicuous on account of the white-woolly undersurfaces of the leaves which are particularly noticeable when ruffled by the wind. The leaves are variable in shape, some ovate or irregularly lobed or toothed, others larger and distinctly three to five-lobed like a maple. Autumn colour yellow. An excellent tree in exposed sites, particularly in coastal areas where if cut severely and retained as a shrub it is effective with similarly pruned red and yellow-stemmed willows and *Spartium junceum*. Grows well on chalky soil. C and SE Europe to C Asia. Long cultivated and naturalised in the British Isles.

**'Bolleana'** See 'Pyramidalis'.

**'Paletzkyana'** A form with deeply lobed and toothed leaves.

**'Pyramidalis'** ('Bolleana') A large tree with erect branches, resembling in habit the Lombardy Poplar, but slightly broader in relation to height. C 1841.

**'Raket'** A very narrow tree with upright branches. Raised in Holland before 1956.

**'Richardii'** A smaller-growing, less vigorous tree with leaves bright golden yellow above, white beneath. A delightful form, very effective at a distance. C 1910. AM 1912.

**'Andover'** (*P. nigra* var. *betulifolia* × *P. trichocarpa*). A robust, slow-growing, large tree of American origin; a hybrid between a black poplar and a balsam poplar.

**'Androscoggin'** (*P. maximowiczii* × *P. trichocarpa*). A large, extremely vigorous male hybrid of American origin. Specimens growing in the Quantock Forest in Somerset have attained 30m in seventeen years.

**angulata** See *P. deltoides* 'Carolin'.

**'Balsam Spire'** (*P.* 'T.T. 32') (*P.* 'Tacatricho 32') (*P. balsamifera* × *P. trichocarpa*). A large, narrow, female tree of extremely fast growth, with white-backed leaves and fragrant buds.

**balsamifera** L. (*P. tacamahacca* MILL.) "Balsam Poplar". A large, erect-branched tree, grown mainly for the balsamic odour of its unfolding leaves. Twigs rounded, glabrous; buds large and sticky. Leaves ovate to ovate-lanceolate, whitish and reticulate beneath. The sticky buds and balsamic odour is possessed by a number of poplars notably *P.* × *candicans*. North America. Introduced before 1689.

   **var. michauxii** (DODE) HENRY A minor form with petioles and veins of leaf beneath minutely hairy.

**balsamifera** × **trichocarpa** See *P.* 'Balsam Spire'.

× **berolinensis** DIPP. (*P. laurifolia* × *P. nigra* 'Italica'). "Berlin Poplar". A large, broadly columnar tree with slightly angled, downy twigs and ovate to rhomboid, acuminate leaves, pale beneath. Much used for street planting on the Continent and for windbreaks on the North American prairies. A male clone.

   **'Petrowskyana'** (*P.* × *petrowskyana* SCHNEID.) A very hardy hybrid. Branches angled and pubescent, leaves ovate, pale beneath. Raised in Russia about 1880.

   **'Rumford'** A moderately vigorous tree of American origin.

× **canadensis** MOENCH (*P.* × *euramericana* GUINIER) A large group of hybrids between the American *P. deltoides* and forms of the European *P. nigra*. They are known collectively as Hybrid Black Poplars. All are vigorous trees and are excellent for screening purposes. The wood of several clones is used in the match industry. The first clone originated possibly in France about 1750.

   **'Carriereana'** A large, erect tree of vigorous growth. Proving lime-tolerant.

   **'Eugenei'** A narrow male tree with short, ascending branches; young leaves coppery in colour. Among the best poplars to grow commercially in this country. A hybrid between *P. nigra* 'Italica' and *P.* 'Regenerata'. Ours is a canker-resistant form introduced by the late Lt Col Pratt, from Simon Louis' nursery in France.

   **'Gelrica'** A vigorous male tree of Continental origin, with whitish bark and coppery young growths. A hybrid between 'Marilandica' and 'Serotina', usually breaking into leaf after the former and before the latter.

   **'Henryana'** A large tree with wide-spreading, rounded head of branches. A male clone. Origin unknown.

   **'Lloydii'** (*P.* 'Lloydii') A large spreading, female tree of moderate growth, a hybrid between *P. deltoides* and *P. nigra* var. *betulifolia*.

   **'Marilandica'** A large densely-branched female tree, with a wide head. Resembles 'Serotina', but usually earlier leafing and its young leaves green. One of the best poplars for chalk soils. Probably *P. nigra* × 'Serotina'.

**POPULUS** × **canadensis**—*continued*

**'Pacheri'** A fast-growing large tree.

**'Regenerata'** ('Marilandica' × 'Serotina'). A large, female tree with twiggy branches arching outwards. Branchlets slender; young leaves green, appearing about a fortnight earlier than those of 'Serotina'. Originated in a nursery near Paris in 1814 and now universally planted in industrial areas.

**'Robusta'** A large, vigorous, male tree forming an open crown with a straight bole to summit. Young twigs minutely downy; young leaves an attractive coppery-red. A hybrid between *P. deltoides* 'Cordata' and *P. nigra* 'Plantierensis' raised by Messrs Simon-Louis at Plantières, near Metz (France) in 1895.

**'Serotina'** A very vigorous, large, openly branched male tree with a usually uneven crown and glabrous twigs. Leaves late in appearing, copper-red when young. Catkins 7.5-10cm long, with conspicuous red anthers. This commonly planted tree is said to have originated in France early in the 18th century.

**'Serotina Aurea'** ('Van Geertii') "Golden Poplar". Leaves clear golden yellow in spring and early summer, becoming yellowish-green later then golden yellow in autumn. Originated as a sport in Van Geert's nursery at Ghent in 1871. AGM 1984.

**'Serotina de Selys'** ('Serotina Erecta'). A large, columnar form raised in Belgium before 1818.

× **candicans** AIT. (*P. balsamifera* × *P. deltoides* var. *missouriensis*). "Ontario Poplar" "Balm of Gilead Poplar". A medium-sized, broad-headed tree with stout, angled, downy twigs and broad ovate leaves which are greyish-white beneath, strongly balsam-scented when unfolding. Origin uncertain, probably North American. Only the female tree is known. C 1773.

**'Aurora'** A conspicuously variegated form. The leaves, especially when young, are creamy-white, often pink-tinged. Older leaves green. To obtain the best results, hard prune the shoots in late winter. Often does not show variegation the first year after transplanting. AM 1954.

× **canescens** (AIT.) SM. (*P. alba* × *P. tremula*). "Grey Poplar". A medium-sized to large, suckering tree sometimes forming thickets. Mature specimens develop an attractive creamy-grey trunk. Leaves variable in shape, rounded or deltoid, dentate and slightly toothed, more or less grey tomentose beneath. One of the best poplars for chalk soils, giving attractive yellow and sometimes red autumn colour. The male catkins in late winter are most decorative, being woolly and crimson, up to 10cm long. Female trees are rare in this country. W, C and S Europe (including England). Extensively planted and naturalised.

**'De Moffart'** A male selection from Belgium with a dense, conical crown and large leaves which open early. C 1977.

**'Macrophylla'** "Picart's Poplar". A large-leaved form, very vigorous in growth.

**'Carriereana'** See *P.* × *canadensis* 'Carriereana'.

**cathayana** REHD. A rare balsam poplar of vigorous growth. A medium-sized to large tree. The upright branches with rounded twigs carry large, white-backed leaves. It has already reached 26m in the Hillier Gardens and Arboretum (1990). NW China to Manchuria and Korea. I about 1908 by Ernest Wilson. Subject to canker.

× **charkoviensis** See *P. nigra* 'Charkoviensis'.

**deltoides** MARSH. (*P. monilifera* AIT.) "Cottonwood" "Necklace Poplar". A large, broad-headed, black poplar with rounded or angled twigs and broadly heart-shaped, slender-pointed, bright green leaves. Now almost displaced in cultivation by its hybrid progeny. E North America.

**'Carolin'** (*P. angulata* HORT.) "Carolina Poplar". A large, open-headed male tree, with prominently angled twigs and large heart-shaped leaves. Origin uncertain, probably North America. C about 1789.

**'Cordata'** Similar to 'Carolin' but female. Both have been grown as *P. angulata*.

**'Eugenei'** See *P.* × *canadensis* 'Eugenei'.

× **euramericana** See *P.* × *canadensis*.

**'Gelrica'** See *P.* × *canadensis* 'Gelrica'.

× **generosa** HENRY (*P. deltoides* 'Cordata' × *P. trichocarpa*). We were the first to distribute this remarkably vigorous hybrid, raised by Augustine Henry at Kew in 1912. Young

**POPULUS × generosa**—*continued*

trees sometimes increase in height at the rate of 2m a year. Male and female trees are grown, the males with long crimson-anthered catkins in April. Leaves conspicuously large on young trees, bright soft green above, turning yellow in autumn.

**grandidentata** MICHX. "Large-toothed Aspen". Medium-sized tree with rounded or ovate, deeply and broadly-toothed leaves which are greyish tomentose beneath at first, later glabrous and glaucous. Differing from *P. tremula* in its downy young shoots and from *P. tremuloides* in its large-toothed leaves. E North America. I 1772.

**'Henryana'** See *P. × canadensis* 'Henryana'.

**'Hiltingbury Weeping'** (*P. tremula* 'Pendula' × *P. tremuloides* 'Pendula'). A small tree with long, weeping branches forming a curtain of greyish-green trembling leaves. The result of a deliberate cross made in our Chandler's Ford nursery in 1962.

**jacquemontiana** DODE This species is cultivated in the following form.

**var. glauca** (HAINES) KIMURA (*P. glauca* HAINES) (Schilling 2620) An attractive and vigorous tree with bronze young foliage emerging late in early summer. Leaves up to 17cm long, broadly ovate, heart-shaped at the base, shallowly-toothed at the margin, blue-green above with red veins, glaucous beneath, on a flattened red petiole. I by A.D. Schilling in 1983. E Himalaya.

**koreana** REHD. A handsome balsam poplar of medium size, with conspicuous, large, bright apple-green leaves, white beneath and with red mid-ribs. One of the first trees to come into leaf in the early spring. Korea. Introduced by E.H. Wilson in 1918.

**lasiocarpa** OLIV. A magnificent medium-sized tree with stout, angled, downy twigs. The leaves, often up to 30cm long and 23cm wide, are bright green with conspicuous red veins and leaf stalks. C China. Discovered by Augustine Henry in 1888, introduced by E.H. Wilson in 1900. FCC 1908.

**laurifolia** LEDEB. A slow-growing balsam poplar, making a medium-sized tree of elegant habit. The young shoots are strongly angled. Leaves narrowly ovate or lanceolate, whitish beneath. Siberia. I about 1830.

**'Lloydii'** See *P. × canadensis* 'Lloydii'.

**'Maine'** (*P. × berolinensis* × *P. × candicans*). An interesting American-raised, multiple hybrid of moderate growth.

**'Marilandica'** See *P. × canadensis* 'Marilandica'.

**maximowiczii** HENRY A conspicuous, rapid-growing balsam poplar of medium size, distinguished by its rounded, downy young twigs and its roundish, leathery, deeply-veined leaves with white undersurfaces and a twisted tip. E Asia. I about 1890.

**monilifera** See *P. deltoides*.

**nigra** L. "Black Poplar". A large, heavy-branched tree with characteristic burred trunk and glabrous twigs. Leaves rhomboid to ovate, slender-pointed, bright, shining green. C and S Europe, W Asia. Long cultivated and naturalised in many countries. Often referred to as var. *typica*.

**'Afghanica'** ('Thevestina') A strong-growing, columnar tree, similar to the Lombardy Poplar, but female and with downy young shoots. In the Middle East and hotter climes than the British Isles, it is renowned for its white trunk.

**var. betulifolia** (PURSH) TORR. "Manchester Poplar" "Wilson's Variety". A picturesque, bushy-headed tree characterised by its downy shoots and young leaves. Tolerant of smoke pollution and formerly much planted in the industrial North of England. Native of E and C England.

**'Charkowiensis'** A tree of Russian origin, probably a cross between *P. nigra* and *P. nigra* 'Italica'. A large tree of broadly pyramidal habit.

**'Italica'** ('Pyramidalis') "Lombardy Poplar". A large, narrow, columnar tree with close, erect branches. A male tree and one of the most effective of its habit, particularly suitable for forming a tall screen. Origin before 1750. Introduced to England in 1758.

**'Italica Foemina'** The female form, a broader tree than 'Italica' but of similar outline. The orange twigs are effective in winter.

**'Lombardy Gold'** A striking tree with golden yellow foliage. Discovered in 1974 as a sport on a mature Lombardy Poplar near the village of Normandy in Surrey by John Whitehead. It has already (1990) reached more than 12m at Wisley.

**POPULUS nigra**—*continued*

**'Plantierensis'** A fastigiate tree like the Lombardy Poplar, which it has largely replaced in this country. It differs from the latter in its downy twigs, stronger, lower branching and bushier, broader head. Appears to have the amalgamated characters of var. *betulifolia* and 'Italica'.

**'Pyramidalis'** See 'Italica'.

**'Thevestina'** See 'Afghanica'.

**var. viadri** (RUDIGER) ASCHERS. & GRAEBN. A slender, erect-growing wild form. Introduced to England in 1893.

**'Oxford'** (*P.* × *berolinensis* × *P. maximowiczii*). A vigorous-growing large tree of American origin.

**'Pacheri'** See *P.* × *canadensis* 'Pacheri'.

× **petrowskyana** See *P.* × *berolinensis* 'Petrowskyana'.

**'Regenerata'** See *P.* × *canadensis* 'Regenerata'.

**'Robusta'** See *P.* × *canadensis* 'Robusta'.

**'Rumford'** See *P.* × *berolinensis* 'Rumford'.

**'Serotina'** See *P.* × *canadensis* 'Serotina'.

**'Serotina Aurea'** See *P.* × *canadensis* 'Serotina Aurea'.

**'Serotina Erecta'** See *P.* × *canadensis* 'Serotina de Selys'.

**sieboldii** MIQ. "Japanese Aspen". Medium-sized tree with downy shoots and ovate, minutely-toothed, deep green leaves. Japan. C 1881.

**simonii** CARR. A medium-sized, early-leafing, balsam poplar with slender, angled, glabrous, red-brown twigs and rhomboid leaves, pale beneath. Liable to canker. N China. I 1862.

**'Fastigiata'** A columnar tree, the branches long and upright. Makes an excellent dense hedge or screen. I from China in 1913.

**suaveolens** FISCH. A very ornamental, medium-sized balsam poplar with rounded twigs and ovate-lanceolate, slender-pointed leaves pale beneath. E Siberia. I 1834.

**szechuanica** SCHNEID. A strikingly handsome balsam poplar making a large tree. Leaves large, whitish-glaucescent beneath, with crimson mid-rib, reddish when young. Fast-growing, but needs shelter from late spring frosts. W China. I 1908 by Ernest Wilson.

**var. tibetica** SCHNEID. (*P. violascens* DODE) One of the most ornamental poplars, differing in its larger leaves, which resemble those of *P. lasiocarpa*. It has reached 24m in the Hillier Gardens and Arboretum (1990). W China. I 1904.

**'T.T. 32'** See *P.* 'Balsam Spire'.

**tacamahacca**. See *P. balsamifera*.

**tremula** L. "Aspen". A medium-sized, suckering tree. Leaves prominently-toothed, late in appearing and hanging late in the autumn when they turn a clear butter-yellow. Petioles slender, compressed, causing the leaves to tremble and quiver in the slightest breeze. Catkins long and grey draping the branchlets in later winter or early spring. One of the commonest sources of wood for the match industry. Widely distributed in Europe and Asia extending to N Africa.

**'Erecta'** An uncommon form of narrowly columnar habit. Originated in Sweden. C 1847.

**'Gigas'** A very vigorous and robust, triploid form. Male. C 1935.

**'Pendula'** The "Weeping Aspen"; one of the most effective, small, weeping trees, especially attractive in February with its abundance of long purplish-grey, male catkins.

**tremuloides** MICHX. "American Aspen". A small to medium-sized tree, mainly distinguished from our native species *P. tremula* by the pale yellowish bark of its young trunks and branches, and by its smaller, finely and evenly-toothed leaves. Its catkins are also more slender. One of the most widely distributed of North American trees, being found in the mountains of N Mexico northwards to Alaska. C 1812.

**'Pendula'** "Parasol de St Julien". A small, pendulous, female tree which originated in France in 1865.

**trichocarpa** HOOK. "Black Cottonwood". The fastest and tallest growing of the balsam poplars, reaching a height of over 30m, and up to 60m in its native habitat. Bark of young trees peeling. Buds large and sticky; leaves pale and reticulate beneath, strongly balsam-scented when unfolding. Autumn colour rich yellow. Liable to canker. W North America. I 1892.

**violascens** See *P. szechuanica* var. *tibetica*.

**POPULUS**—*continued*

**wilsonii** SCHNEID. A highly ornamental, medium-sized species, somewhat resembling *P. lasiocarpa*. Leaves large, up to 20cm long, bright sea-green in colour. Branchlets thick, rounded, of a polished violet-green shade. C and W China. I 1907 by Ernest Wilson.

**yunnanensis** DODE A fast-growing, medium-sized balsam poplar similar to *P. szechuanica*. Leaves with white under-surfaces and reddish stalks and mid-ribs. SW China. I before 1905.

**"PORTUGAL LAUREL"** See *Prunus lusitanica*.

**POTENTILLA** L.—**Rosaceae**—A large genus of some 500 species of mainly herbs, natives largely of N temperate regions. The shrubby potentillas are rich in good qualities. They are very hardy, dwarf to medium-sized shrubs, thriving in any soil, and in sun or partial shade. Their flowers, like small, single roses, are displayed over a long season, beginning in May and June and in some forms lasting until November. Though they are shade-tolerant they are mainly best grown in full sun. The cultivars with orange, red or pink flowers tend to fade in the hottest sun and perform better if given a moister soil and a position where they receive light shade when the sun is highest. Many of the cultivars listed are hybrids but have at one time been treated as forms of *P. fruticosa*.

**arbuscula** D. DON (*P. fruticosa* var. *arbuscula* (D. DON) MAXIM.) A dwarf shrub related to *P. fruticosa*, but very distinct with shaggy branches due to the presence of large, brown stipules. Sage-green leaves with 5 leaflets. Large, rich yellow flowers are produced continuously from midsummer to late autumn. Himalaya. AM 1925. AMT 1965.

**'Beesii'** ('Nana Argentea') A delightful dwarf shrub which displays its golden flowers on mounds of silvery foliage. Raised by Bees from Forrest 2437. AMT 1984.

**var. bulleyana** BALF. f. ex FLETCHER A small shrub with silky hairy leaves and bright yellow flowers. Taller growing and more erect than the type. I by Forrest from Yunnan (Forrest 119).

**var. rigida** (D. DON) HAND-MAZZ. (*P. rigida* WALL. ex LEHM.) A small, compact shrub with bristly stems covered with conspicuous papery stipules and leaves with only 3 leaflets; flowers bright yellow. Himalaya. I 1906. We have also grown an attractive form with smaller, silvery leaves and slightly smaller flowers.

**'Beanii'** (Friedrichsenii Group) ('Leucantha') A dwarf shrub with dark foliage and white flowers. C 1910.

**davurica** NESTL. (*P. glabra* LODD.) (*P. glabrata* SCHLECHT.) (*P. fruticosa glabra*) A very variable species, rarely more than 1.5m in height, usually much less. Both stems and leaves may be glabrous or hairy, depending on the form. The flowers are white and freely produced. N China, Siberia. I 1822.

**'Abbotswood'** Dwarf shrub of spreading habit with dark foliage. Flowers white, plentifully and continuously produced. AMT 1965.

**'Abbotswood Silver'** A sport of 'Abbotswood' with the leaflets narrowly margined creamy-white. Quickly reverts.

**'Farrer's White'** A small shrub of somewhat erect habit, with multitudes of white flowers during summer. Raised from seed collected by Farrer in Gansu.

**'Hersii'** A free-flowering, small shrub of erect habit. Leaves sage-green; flowers white. The same clone, or a seedling of it, is offered on the Continent under the name 'Snowflake'.

**'Manchu'** (*P. fruticosa* var. *mandshurica* HORT. not WOLF) A charming, dwarf, low-spreading shrub, bearing a continuous succession of white flowers on mats of greyish foliage. AM 1924.

**'Mount Everest'** A small, robust shrub up to 1.5m, of dense, rounded habit. Flowers white, produced intermittently throughout summer.

**Rhodocalyx group** (*P. fruticosa rhodocalyx*) A small, upright shrub of subtle, gentle quality, the aristocrat of a popular group. The rather small, somewhat cup-shaped flowers with reddish calyces nod on slender stems.

**var. subalbicans** (HAND.-MAZZ.) (*P. fruticosa* var. *subalbicans* HAND.-MAZZ.) A robust shrub up to 1.5m, with stiff, hairy stems, and clusters of comparatively large, white flowers. Gansu, Shanxi.

**POTENTILLA davurica**—*continued*

**var. veitchii** (WILS.) JESSON (*P. fruticosa* var. *veitchii* (WILS.) BEAN) A small, graceful bush, about 1m high, with arching branches bearing pure white flowers. W and C China. I 1900 by Ernest Wilson.

**'Dart's Golddigger'** A splendid, dwarf shrub of Dutch origin. Dense and compact habit, with light grey-green foliage and large butter-yellow flowers. A seedling probably of *P. arbuscula*. C 1970.

**'Daydawn'** A small shrub with flowers of an unusual shade of peach-pink suffused cream. A sport of 'Tangerine'. AGM 1984.

**'Eastleigh Cream'** (*P. parvifolia* 'Gold Drop' × *P.* × *sulphurascens*). A small shrub of dense habit, spreading to form a low mound. Leaves green; flowers cream, 2.5cm across. Raised in our Eastleigh nursery in 1969.

**'Elizabeth'** (Sulphurascens Group) (*P. arbuscula* × *P. davurica* var. *veitchii*) A magnificent hybrid raised in our nurseries about 1950 and named after the daughter of Sir Harold Hillier. A dome-shaped bush 1m × 1.2m and studded from late spring to early autumn with large, rich canary-yellow flowers. This plant was wrongly distributed throughout European nurseries as *P. arbuscula*. AMT 1965. AGM 1984.

× **friedrichsenii** SPAETH (*P. davurica* × *P. fruticosa*) . A vigorous shrub up to 2m, with slightly grey-green foliage and light yellow flowers. Originated as a seedling in Spaeth's Nursery in Berlin, in 1895. The clone in cultivation is sometimes referred to under the name 'Berlin Beauty'. For other clones see 'Beanii' and 'Ochroleuca'. Both the latter and the present plant are excellent as informal hedges.

**fruticosa** L. A dense bush averaging 1-1.5m high, producing yellow flowers from May to September. Leaves small, divided into 5-7 narrow leaflets. This is generally treated as a variable species, being distributed throughout the N hemisphere, including the North of England and the West of Ireland. It is a parent of numerous hybrids.

**var. grandiflora** SCHLECHT. A shrub up to 1.5m, of strong erect growth with sage-green leaves and dense clusters of large, canary-yellow flowers. The clone 'Jackman's Variety' is a seedling of this variety. FCCT 1966.

**'Northman'** A small, erect shrub with sage-green leaves and small, rich yellow flowers.

**var. tenuiloba** SER. Erect-growing shrub up to 1.5m, with narrow leaflets and bright yellow flowers. The clone in cultivation is probably of North American origin.

**glabra** See *P. davurica*.

**'Goldfinger'** A dwarf, compact shrub with pinkish shoots and blue-green leaves with usually 5 leaflets. Large, rich golden yellow flowers profusely borne. Raised in Holland about 1970. AGM 1984.

**'Goldstar'** Habit rather upright, to 80cm. Very large deep yellow flowers up to 5cm across are borne over a long period. C 1976.

**'Hurstbourne'** Small shrub of upright habit with bright yellow flowers.

**'Jackman's Variety'** See under *P. fruticosa* var. *grandiflora*.

**'Katherine Dykes'** (*P.* × *friedrichsenii* × *P. parvifolia*). A shrub up to 2m, producing an abundance of primrose-yellow flowers in summer. Named after the raiser's wife. C 1925. AM 1944. AGM 1984.

**'Lady Daresbury'** A small shrub forming a broad, dome-shaped bush of arching branches; flowers large, yellow, continuously produced, but especially abundant in late spring and autumn. C 1955.

**'Logan'** (Sulphurascens Group) A small shrub up to 1.5m, of bushy habit, producing masses of pale yellow flowers during summer.

**'Longacre'** (Sulphurascens Group) A dense, dwarf, mat-forming shrub. Flowers large, of a bright, almost sulphur-yellow. A seedling raised at Longacre in N Ireland. C 1956. AMT 1965. AGM 1984.

**'Maanelys'** ('Moonlight') A small shrub of Scandinavian origin, producing a continuous succession of soft yellow flowers from May to November. C 1950.

**'Milkmaid'** Small shrub with slender, upright stems and leaves with 3-5 leaflets. Flowers flattened, 2.5-3cm wide, creamy-white, nodding or inclined on slender peduncles. A hybrid of *P. dahurica rhodocalyx*, raised in our nurseries in 1963.

**'Minstead Dwarf'** A dwarf shrub forming a low hummock of green leaves and masses of bright yellow flowers.

**POTENTILLA**—*continued*

**'Ochroleuca'** A small, erect shrub up to 2m, similar to *P. × friedrichsenii*, of which it is a seedling with cream-coloured flowers. Both make an excellent informal hedge. C 1902.

**parvifolia** FISCH. ex LEHM. (*P. fruticosa* var. *parvifolia* (LEHM.) WOLF) A dense, compact shrub of semi-erect habit, seldom exceeding 1m in height. Leaves small, with 7 leaflets, the lower 2 pairs forming a whorl. Flowers golden yellow, comparatively small but abundantly produced during early summer, and more sparingly until October. C Asia, Siberia, Himalaya.

**'Buttercup'** A small shrub of compact habit producing small, deep yellow flowers over a long period.

**'Gold Drop'** A dwarf shrub of compact habit, with small, neat leaves and small, bright golden yellow flowers. Often wrongly grown under the name *P. fruticosa farreri*. C 1953.

**'Klondike'** A first-rate shrub of dwarf habit raised in Holland, similar to 'Gold Drop', but with larger flowers. C 1950. AMT 1965.

**'Pretty Polly'** A low spreading shrub with medium-sized pale pink flowers. A seedling of 'Red Ace'.

**'Primrose Beauty'** A small, spreading, free-flowering shrub with arching branches, grey-green foliage and primrose-yellow flowers with deeper yellow centres. AMT 1965. AGM 1984.

**'Princess'** A compact, dwarf shrub of spreading habit. Flowers a delicate pale pink, yellow centred, sometimes with a few extra petals.

**'Red Ace'** A compact dwarf shrub forming a dense mound with bright green foliage. Leaves with usually 5 narrow leaflets. Flowers bright orange-red, cream on the back of the petals. C 1973. FCC 1975.

**'Royal Flush'** A seedling of 'Red Ace' with deep pink flowers. C 1980.

**'Ruth'** A small shrub of upright habit with nodding, slightly cup-shaped flowers, creamy-yellow at first becoming white, with red-flushed calyces. A hybrid of *P. dahurica rhodocalyx*, raised in our nurseries in 1960 and named after Sir Harold Hillier's daughter.

**salesoviana** STEPHAN An unusual, dwarf shrub with erect, hollow, reddish-brown stems, bearing large, dark green, pinnate leaves, white beneath. Flowers nodding, white, occasionally tinged pink, produced in terminal corymbs in June and July. Siberia, N China, Himalaya. I 1823.

**'Stoker's Variety'** A small shrub up to 1.5m, of upright habit. Small, densely-crowded leaves and abundantly produced rich yellow flowers.

× **sulphurascens** HAND.-MAZZ. (*P. arbuscula × P. davurica*). A rather variable hybrid originally described from Yunnan, which has given rise to several of the best garden potentillas, including 'Elizabeth', 'Longacre' and 'Logan', which see.

**'Sunset'** A small shrub with flowers of an unusual colour varying between deep orange and brick-red. Best grown in partial shade. A sport of 'Tangerine'. AGM 1984.

**'Tangerine'** A dwarf, wide-spreading shrub forming a dense mound. Flowers of a pale coppery-yellow, which is best developed on plants growing in partial shade. Raised at the Slieve Donard Nursery.

**'Tilford Cream'** A dense dwarf bush, broader than tall with rich green foliage and large, creamy-white flowers about 3.5cm across. AGM 1984.

**tridentata** AIT. A prostrate sub-shrub forming low tufts or mats. Leaves trifoliolate, with oblanceolate leaflets, three-toothed at the apex. Flowers white during summer. An excellent plant for paving or scree. E North America. C 1789.

**'Vilmoriniana'** A splendid, erect-branched shrub up to 2m, with very silvery leaves and cream-coloured flowers. The best tall, erect potentilla. AMT 1965. AGM 1984.

**'Walton Park'** A small, very floriferous shrub, forming a low compact bush with large, bright yellow flowers.

**'Whirlygig'** (*P. arbuscula × P. fruticosa* var. *grandiflora*). A strong-growing small shrub, the relatively large leaves with broad, soft green silky hairy leaflets. Flowers bright yellow with curiously twisted and wavy-edged petals. Raised by our Foreman Alf Alford from a cross made in 1969.

**'William Purdom'** (*P. fruticosa purdomii* HORT.) A small shrub of semi-erect growth up to 1.5m, with an abundance of light yellow flowers. FCCT 1966. AGM 1984.

**PRINSEPIA** OLIV.—**Rosaceae**—A small genus of probably only 3 species of uncommon and interesting, usually spiny shrubs, natives of E Asia. All do best in an open position, and succeed in any fertile soil.

**sinensis** (OLIV.) OLIV. ex BEAN A rare, lax-habited shrub up to 2m. Flowers slender-stalked, produced in clusters of 2-5 in the leaf axils of the previous year's wood, buttercup-yellow, 12-20mm across, clustering the arching stems in early spring. Fruits red, produced in August. Manchuria. I 1903.

**uniflora** BATAL. A spreading shrub 1.5-2m high, with spiny grey stems and linear leaves. Flowers white, in axillary clusters of 1-3 on the previous year's wood, in late April or early May. Fruits, purplish-red, like short-stalked Morello cherries, rarely produced except during a hot summer. NW China. Introduced by William Purdom in 1911. AM 1983.

**utilis** ROYLE An attractive, vigorous, small to medium-sized shrub with strongly spiny, arching, green stems. Flowers white, in axillary racemes during late winter and early spring. Himalaya. C 1919.

**"PRIVET"** See *Ligustrum*.

†*****PROSTANTHERA** LABILL.—**Labiatae**—The "Mint Bushes" are a genus of beautiful, small to medium-sized, floriferous, aromatic shrubs, with about 50 species, natives of Australasia. Ideal for the cool conservatory or in a warm sheltered corner in the milder counties. Inclined to become chlorotic on a shallow chalky soil. Established specimens are best pruned back hard immediately after flowering.

**aspalathoides** A. CUNN. ex BENTH. A small, compact shrub with tiny, almost linear, dark green, aromatic leaves and red flowers. Australia.

**'Chelsea Pink'** A small shrub similar to *P. rotundifolia*. Leaves aromatic, grey-green, wedge-shaped at the base. Flowers pale pink with purple anthers. AM 1986.

**cuneata** BENTH. A relatively hardy dwarf shrub of spreading habit with small dark glossy green leaves, toothed at the tip, wedge-shaped at the base. Flowers white flushed lilac, marked with purple inside, borne in May. Survived the hard winters of the 1980s. SE Australia, Tasmania. C 1886, reintroduced by Capt Neil McEachern in 1943.

**lasianthos** LABILL. Medium-sized to large shrub of erect growth. Leaves comparatively large, lanceolate. The purple-tinted white flowers appear in branched, terminal racemes during spring. Tasmania, Australia. I 1808. FCC 1888.

**melissifolia** F. MUELL. A native of SE Australia, this species is represented in cultivation by the following form.

**var. parvifolia** SEALY This pretty shrub has been confused with *P. sieberi*; flowers bright lilac, nearly 2.5cm across, borne abundantly in early summer.

**ovalifolia** R. BR. An elegant, small to medium-sized shrub with small, olive-green leaves and soft lilac-mauve or purple flowers on long, drooping branches in spring. Australia. AM 1952.

**rotundifolia** R. BR. A beautiful small to medium-sized shrub of dense habit, with tiny rounded or ovate leaves. The attractive heliotrope flowers inundate the branches during summer. The massed effect of the flowers is quite staggering. I 1824. AM 1924.

**PRUNUS** L.—**Rosaceae**—A large genus of about 400 species of mainly deciduous trees and shrubs found largely in N temperate regions. Includes many of the most beautiful flowering trees suitable for temperate regions. Under *Prunus* are included the following:- Almond (*P. dulcis*); Apricot (*P. armeniaca*); Bird Cherry (*P. padus*); Common Laurel (*P. laurocerasus*); Peach (*P. persica*) and Portugal Laurel (*P. lusitanica*). For Japanese cherries see end of this section. With the exception of most of the evergreen species, all require an open, preferably sunny position, in any ordinary soil, being particularly happy in soils containing lime or chalk. It must, however, be emphasised that the Cherry Laurel (*P. laurocerasus*) will tend to become chlorotic in poor, shallow chalk soils, and, as an alternative, the Portugal Laurel (*P. lusitanica*) should be planted.

**PRUNUS**—*continued*

**'Accolade'** (*P. sargentii* × *P. subhirtella*). An outstanding cherry; a small tree with spreading branches and semi-double, rich pink flowers 4cm in diameter in pendulous clusters, produced in great profusion in early summer. AM 1952. FCC 1954. AGM 1984.

**americana** MARSH. "American Red Plum". A small tree of graceful habit. Flowers white, 2.5cm across, borne in clusters of 2-5; fruits up to 2.5cm wide, yellow, finally bright red, but not freely produced in the British Isles. United States, S Canada. I 1768.

× **amygdalo-persica** (WEST.) REHD. (*P. dulcis* × *P. persica*). A hybrid between the peach and almond, first recorded about 1623. The following is the most commonly grown form:-

**'Pollardii'** (*P.* × *pollardii* HORT.) This beautiful, small tree differs from the almond in its larger, richer pink flowers. Said to have originated in Australia about 1904. Bears fruit which leaves us in no doubt as to its hybrid origin. Susceptible to peach leaf curl, for which see under *P. dulcis*. FCC 1935.

**amygdalus** See *P. dulcis*.

**armeniaca** L. "Apricot". The wild species. A small, rounded-headed tree with white or pink-tinged, single flowers in March and April, followed by yellow red-tinged fruits. C Asia, China. Widely cultivated and naturalised in S Europe. Clones selected for their fruit are widely cultivated.

**var. ansu** MAXIM. (*P. ansu* (MAXIM.) KOMAR.) A small tree with rounded leaves and pink flowers in April; fruits red. Often confused in gardens with *P. mume* from which it differs in its darker, usually purple-flushed shoots and its larger flowers with strongly reflexed sepals. N China, long cultivated in Japan and Korea. AM 1944.

**'Flore Pleno'** (*P. mume* 'Grandiflora') (*P. mume* 'Rosea Plena') A beautiful form with semi-double flowers, carmine in bud opening to pink, densely clustered on purple-flushed shoots in March or April. AM 1934.

**avium** L. "Gean" "Mazzard" "Wild Cherry". One of the most attractive of our native woodland trees. A medium-sized to large tree with smooth grey bark turning mahogany-red, peeling and deeply fissured with age. The white cup-shaped flowers are borne in clusters and open with the leaves in late April or early May. Fruits small and shiny, reddish-purple, bitter or sweet to the taste. Autumn foliage crimson. From this species are derived most of the sweet cherries. Europe (including British Isles), W Asia.

**'Decumana'** (*P. macrophylla* POIR.) An unusual form with large flowers 2.5cm across, and very large leaves up to 23cm long. Raised in France before 1808.

**'Pendula'** A form with semi-pendulous, rather stiff branches. C 1825.

**'Plena'** ('Multiplex') "Double Gean". One of the loveliest of all flowering trees, its branches wreathed with masses of drooping, double-white flowers. Cultivated since 1700. FCC 1964. AGM 1984.

**besseyi** BAILEY (*P. pumila* var. *besseyi* (BAILEY) WAUGH) "Sand Cherry". A small shrub with greyish-green leaves turning rusty-purple in autumn. Clusters of tiny white flowers are massed along the branches in May. Fruits rounded, black with purplish bloom, rarely produced in the British Isles. C United States. I 1892.

× **blireana** ANDRE (*P. cerasifera* 'Pissardii' × *P. mume* 'Alphandii'). A beautiful large shrub or small tree with leaves of a metallic coppery-purple. Flowers double, over 2.5cm across, slightly fragrant, rose-pink, with the leaves in April. Garden origin 1895. AM 1914. FCC 1923. AGM 1984.

**'Moseri'** Differs in its slightly smaller, pale pink flowers, and paler foliage. C 1894. AM 1912.

†**campanulata** MAXIM. "Formosan Cherry". A delightful, small, round-headed tree. The dark, rose-red flowers are produced in dense clusters during early spring. Only suitable outside in the mildest areas. S China, Taiwan, S Japan. C 1899. AM 1935.

**'Plena'** A form with small, double red flowers.

**canescens** BOIS A shrubby, medium-sized cherry with attractive, dark mahogany, peeling bark and slender, willowy branches. The polished dark brown inner bark is exposed on the older branches. Leaves greyish-green, downy, coarsely-toothed; flowers small, pink-tinted, in early April; fruits red, pleasantly flavoured. China. I 1898.

**canescens** × **serrula** An unusual and not unattractive hybrid. A small tree, retaining the ornamental bark of *P. serrula* and possessing the long, willowy stems of *P. canescens*

**PRUNUS canescens** × **serrula**—*continued*

which, like the leaves, are downy. The flowers also resemble those of the latter, but are slightly larger. Flowering during April.

**capollin** See *P. salicifolia*.

†\***caroliniana** AIT. "Carolina Cherry Laurel". A small, bushy-headed tree in the mildest parts of the country, attaining a large size in the wild. Leaves elliptic, up to 10cm long, dark glossy green, entire or sparsely-toothed. Flowers white, in short axillary racemes in spring, followed by black fruits. SE United States. I 1759.

**cerasifera** EHRH. (*P. myrobalana* (L.) LOISEL.) (*P. korolkowii* VILM.) "Myrobalan" "Cherry Plum". A small tree with greenish young shoots. The myriads of small white flowers crowd the twigs in March, sometimes earlier or later. Mature trees sometimes bear red cherry-plums. An excellent dense hedging shrub. Not known in the wild. C during the 16th century. AM 1977.

**'Atropurpurea'** See 'Pissardii'.

**'Diversifolia'** ('Aspleniifolia') Leaves bronze-purple, varying in shape from ovate to lanceolate, often irregularly toothed or lobed. Flowers white. A sport of 'Pissardii'.

**'Feketiana'** See 'Pendula'.

**'Hessei'** A medium-sized shrubby form with leaves pale green on emerging, becoming bronze-purple and irregularly edged creamy-white to yellowish or pink. Flowers snow-white, crowding the slender purple shoots in late March. C 1906.

**'Lindsayae'** An attractive tree of graceful habit with flat, almond-pink flowers and green leaves. Introduced from Iran by Miss Nancy Lindsay. AM 1948.

**'Nigra'** Leaves and stems blackish-purple; flowers very prolific, pink fading to blush. A very effective, small tree flowering in March and April. C 1916. FCC 1939. AGM 1984. 'Vesuvius' is almost, if not, identical.

**'Pendula'** ('Feketiana') A form with pendulous, interlacing stems, green leaves and white flowers. C 1901.

**'Pissardii'** ('Atropurpurea') "Purple-leaved Plum". A very popular form with dark red young foliage turning to a deep purple. Flowers in great profusion, white, pink in bud, appearing in late March and early April; fruits purple, only occasionally produced. If grown as shrubs, both this and the clone 'Nigra' are excellent hedging plants. Originally discovered as a sport, sometime before 1880 by Mons Pissard, gardener to the Shah of Persia. FCC 1884.

**'Rosea'** Leaves bronze-purple at first, becoming bronze-green, then green in late summer. Flowers small, of a clear salmon-pink, paling with age, crowding the slender purple stems before the leaves emerge, after both 'Nigra' and 'Pissardii'. Distributed by Messrs B. Ruys Ltd, of Holland, who believe the plant to be of hybrid origin (*P. cerasifera* 'Nigra' × *P. spinosa*). Sometimes found in gardens under the name *P. spinosa* 'Rosea'. It is looser and more open in habit than *P. spinosa* with slightly larger flowers less densely crowded on the branchlets, which are sparsely spiny.

**'Trailblazer'** Similar in flower to 'Pissardii'. Leaves larger, becoming bronze-green above.

**'Vesuvius'** See under 'Nigra'.

†**cerasoides** D. DON This species is represented in gardens by the following form.

**var. rubea** INGRAM "Kingdon-Ward's Carmine Cherry". A lovely tree of small to medium size, related to *P. campanulata*. Flowers rose-pink, deeper in bud, but not generally free-flowering in the British Isles. W China, Upper Burma. Introduced by Kingdon-Ward in 1931. AM 1946.

**cerasus** L. "Sour Cherry". Of interest as being one of the parents of the Morello cherries. A small bushy tree with comparatively dark slender stems and producing dense clusters of white flowers in late April or May followed by red or black fruits, acid to the taste. SW Asia. Widely cultivated and naturalised in Europe.

**'James H. Veitch'** See *P.* 'Fugenzo' under Japanese cherries.

**'Rhexii'** (*P. cerasus* f. *ranunculiflora* VOSS) A form with very showy, double white flowers, 2.5-4cm across. Known to have been in cultivation in England since the 16th century.

**'Semperflorens'** "All Saints Cherry". A floriferous, and somewhat pendulous, small tree producing its white flowers intermittently throughout the spring and summer. C 1623.

× **cistena** KOEHNE (*P.* 'Cistena') (*P.* 'Crimson Dwarf') "Purple-leaf Sand Cherry". (*P. pumila* or *P. besseyi* × *P. cerasifera* 'Pissardii'). A beautiful shrub, up to 2m, with red leaves and

**PRUNUS** × **cistena**—*continued*

white flowers in spring; fruits black-purple. An excellent hedging plant. Garden origin in the United States before 1910.

**'Collingwood Ingram'** A small tree resembling 'Kursar' but with deeper coloured flowers. A seedling of 'Kursar' raised at Kalmthout and selected by Jelena de Belder. A fitting tribute to a man to whom we owe the presence of many ornamental cherries in our gardens.

**communis** See *P. dulcis.*

**concinna** KOEHNE A very beautiful, shrubby, small-leaved cherry of medium size, producing its white or pink-tinted flowers profusely before the purplish young leaves, in March or early April. China. Introduced by Wilson in 1907.

**conradinae** KOEHNE This early flowering cherry is a small tree of elegant habit. In a sheltered position its fragrant, white or pinkish flowers, which are produced very freely, give a welcome foretaste of spring, usually during the latter half of February. China. Introduced by E.H. Wilson in 1907. AM 1923.

**'Malifolia'** Carmine buds and pink flowers about 3cm across; slightly later flowering. C 1948.

**'Semiplena'** Flowers longer-lasting with a few extra petals, appearing in late February and March. C 1925. AM 1935.

**cornuta** STEUD. (Subgenus Padus) "Himalayan Bird Cherry". A medium-sized tree differing from *P. padus* in its larger leaves and fruits, the latter being glossy, brown-crimson and carried in drooping, grape-like clusters 10-13cm long from mid-August onwards. Flowers white, carried in long, cylindrical racemes in May. Himalaya. I 1860.

**'Crimson Dwarf'** See *P.* × *cistena.*

**cyclamina** KOEHNE A delightful cherry, forming an elegant, small tree. The bright pink flowers, profusely borne in April, have reflexed sepals. Unfolding leaves bright copper. C China. Introduced by E.H. Wilson in 1907.

× **dasycarpa** EHRH. (*P. armeniaca* × *P. cerasifera*). The "Purple" or "Black Apricot". A small tree with purple twigs and a profusion of white flowers, appearing before the leaves in March. Fruits black, with a purple bloom, apricot-flavoured, rarely produced in the British Isles.

**davidiana** (CARR.) FRANCH. This Chinese peach is one of the earliest trees to bloom, and on that account should be given a sheltered position. A small, erect tree with finely-toothed, long-pointed leaves. The white or rose-coloured flowers open any time between January and March. Like all deciduous trees and shrubs which flower early on the leafless branches, it is very desirable to select a site with a suitable background. China. Introduced by the Abbé David in 1865.

**'Alba'** Flowers white. C 1872. FCC 1892.

**'Rubra'** Flowers pink. C 1867.

× **dawyckensis** SEALY "Dawyck Cherry". A small tree with shining, dark brown bark and downy young shoots and leaves, glaucous beneath. Flowers pale pink in April, followed by amber-red cherries. A tree of uncertain origin, first discovered in the famous gardens at Dawyck, Scotland, and thought to have been introduced by E.H. Wilson in 1907. Rehder suggested that it might be the hybrid *P. canescens* × *P. dielsiana.*

**dielsiana** SCHNEID. (*P. dielsiana* var. *laxa* KOEHNE) A small floriferous tree related to *P. cyclamina*, but later flowering and never so tall. The trunk and primary branches are a dark mahogany-red. Flowers white or pale pink, with conspicuous stamens, borne on long, downy pedicels before the leaves in April or early May; fruits red. C China. Introduced by E.H. Wilson in 1907.

**var. laxa** See *P. dielsiana.*

**divaricata** LEDEB. A small tree closely related to *P. cerasifera* but with smaller, yellow fruits. W to C Asia.

**domestica** L. "Plum". A small, usually spineless tree represented in gardens by forms selected for their fruit. It is of hybrid origin and similar plants occur in the Caucasus. Widely naturalised.

**subsp. insititia** (L.) POIR. (*P. insititia* L.) "Bullace" "Damson". A small tree with occasionally spiny, brownish, pubescent branches and small white flowers in early spring, followed by rounded, purple, red, yellow or green fruits.

**PRUNUS**—*continued*

**dulcis** (MILL.) D.A. WEBB (*P. amygdalus* BATSCH) (*P. communis* (L.) ARCANGELI) "Common Almond". A universal favourite and one of the best spring-flowering trees. A small tree with lanceolate, long-pointed, finely-toothed leaves. Flowers 2.5-5cm across, pink, borne singly or in pairs in March and April. The edible almonds of commerce are mainly introduced from S Europe. Distributed in the wild from N Africa to W Asia, but widely grown and extensively naturalised in the Mediterranean region. Cultivated in England since the 16th century or earlier. Susceptible to peach leaf curl for which we recommend Murphy's Traditional Copper Fungicide.

**'Alba'** Flowers white, single.

**'Erecta'** A broadly columnar form up to 6m or more, with erect branches and pink flowers.

**'Macrocarpa'** Flowers very pale pink or white, up to 5cm across. One of the best of the edible cultivars with large fruits. AM 1931.

**'Praecox'** A form with pale pink flowers opening 2 weeks earlier than normal, very often in late February. FCC 1925.

**'Roseoplena'** "Double Almond". Flowers pale pink, double.

× **dunbarii** REHD. (*P. americana* × *P. maritima*). A large shrub with sharply serrate, acuminate leaves, white flowers and purple fruits. Origin about 1900.

× **effusa** See *P.* × *gondouinii*.

**emarginata** (HOOK.) EATON "Bitter Cherry". In its typical form a shrub with more or less glabrous shoots and leaves, this species is represented in cultivation by the following form. W North America.

**var. mollis** (HOOK.) BREWER & WATSON A small, elegant, deciduous tree with a dense, spreading head and downy shoots. Leaves finely-toothed, downy beneath. Flowers small, creamy-white, produced in dense clusters at the end of the branches in May, followed by small, dark fruits. The bark is bitter to the taste. I 1862.

**fenzliana** FRITSCH A small, wide-spreading, shrubby almond, closely related to *P. dulcis*, but with narrower, sea-green leaves. The flowers, carmine in bud opening soft pink, are conspicuous on the naked branches during March. Caucasus. C 1890.

**fruticosa** PALL. "Ground Cherry". A small, spreading shrub with small, white flowers and dark red fruits. When grown as a standard it forms a neat mop-headed miniature tree. C and E Europe to Siberia. C 1587.

**'Pendula'** A form with slender pendulous branches.

**'Variegata'** Leaves variegated yellowish-white, but not very constant.

**glandulosa** THUNB. "Chinese Bush Cherry". A small, bushy shrub of neat habit with slender, erect shoots covered in April by numerous, small, pink or white flowers. Grows best in a warm , sunny position. C and N China, long cultivated in Japan. C 1835.

**'Alba Plena'** A very beautiful shrub, each shoot pendent with a wealth of comparatively large, double, white flowers in early May. Excellent for forcing. C 1852. AM 1950. AGM 1984.

**'Rosea Plena'** ('Sinensis') (*P. japonica* 'Flore Roseoplena') Flowers double, bright pink. A very popular shrub in Victorian and Edwardian gardens. C 1774. AM 1968. Excellent for forcing.

**'Sinensis'** See 'Rosea Plena'.

× **gondouinii** (POITEAU & TURPIN) REHD. (*P. avium* × *P. cerasus*) (*P.* × *effusa* (HOST) SCHNEID.) "Duke Cherry". A variable medium-sized tree producing white flowers in spring, followed by somewhat acid, red fruits. Several clones are grown for their fruits.

**grayana** MAXIM. (Subgenus Padus) A small, Japanese bird cherry. Leaves coarsely-toothed, flowers white in erect, glabrous racemes 7.5-20cm long, produced in June; fruits small, black. Japan. I 1900.

**'Hally Jolivette'** ([*P. subhirtella* × *P.* × *yedoensis*] × *P. subhirtella*). A small, graceful tree or large shrub raised by Dr Karl Sax at the Arnold Arboretum and named after his wife. Its slender, willowy stems are inundated in early spring with small, semi-double, blush-white flowers which continue over a long period.

**'Hillieri'** A hybrid of *P. sargentii* raised in our nurseries before 1928, the original is now a broad-crowned tree 10m high, and in spring is like a soft pink cloud. In favourable

**PRUNUS 'Hillieri'**—*continued*

seasons the autumn colour is gorgeous. The other parent was possibly *P.* × *yedoensis*. AM 1959.

**'Spire'** See *P.* 'Spire'.

**'Hilling's Weeping'** A small tree with long, slender, almost perpendicularly weeping branches, wreathed with pure white flowers in early April.

†\***ilicifolia** (HOOK. & ARN.) WALP. "Holly-leaved Cherry". A dense, medium-sized to large shrub. Leaves broadly ovate to orbicular, undulate, leathery and edged with spreading spines. Flowers white, in short racemes 5cm long, in June and July, followed by red fruits. California (United States).

**incana** BATSCH "Willow Cherry". A small to medium-sized, erect-branched shrub of loose habit. The slender leaves are white woolly beneath. Flowers pink, contrasting effectively with the grey-green leaves, occasionally followed by red, cherry-like fruits. SE Europe and Asia Minor. I 1815.

**incisa** THUNB. "Fuji Cherry". A lovely Japanese species, generally shrubby, but occasionally a small tree, blooming with the greatest freedom in March. Leaves small, incisely-toothed, beautifully tinted in autumn. Flowers small, white, pink-tinged in bud and appearing pink at a distance; fruits only occasionally produced, small, purple-black. Makes an unusual hedge and long used by the Japanese for Bonsai. C 1910. AM 1927. AGM 1984.

**'February Pink'** An early flowering form with pale pink flowers in February or earlier.

**'Moerheimii'** See *P.* 'Moerheimii'.

**'Omoinoyama'** Profuse double pale pink flowers.

**'Praecox'** A winter-flowering form with white flowers, pale pink in bud. AM 1957. FCC 1973.

**jacquemontii** HOOK. f. "Afghan Cherry". A small to medium-sized shrub of straggling habit, with small leaves. Flowers pink, opening in April. Fruits only occasionally produced, small, red. Happiest in a well drained, sunny position. NW Himalaya, Tibet, Afghanistan. I 1879.

**jamasakura** SIEB. (*P. serrulata* var. *spontanea* (MAXIM.) WILS.) (*P. mutabilis* MIYOSHI) "Hill Cherry". A medium-sized tree of spreading habit with bronze-coloured young foliage. Flowers white or pink in late April and early May. A beautiful cherry, said to be the most adored tree in Japan, one which has inspired her poets and artists and is a prototype of many of the Japanese cherries. It is extremely variable, the best forms having rich, coppery-red young foliage and pure white flowers. Fruit dark purplish-crimson. Japan. I about 1914. AM 1936.

**japonica** THUNB. A small shrub with slender, wiry branches. The small, single white or pale pink flowers appear with the leaves in April; fruits only occasionally produced, dark red. C China east to Korea. Long cultivated in Japan. I 1860.

**var. nakaii** (LEVL.) REHD. A geographical form introduced from Korea in 1918 by Ernest Wilson.

× **juddii** E. ANDERSON (*P. sargentii* × *P.* × *yedoensis*). A small tree with leaves copper-tinted when unfolding, deep crimson in the fall. Flowers pale pink in late April or early May. Originated at the Arnold Arboretum in 1914.

**kansuensis** REHD. Small tree akin to *P. persica*, with long, spray-like branches carrying pink-tinged, white blossoms in January or February. NW China. I 1914. AM 1957.

**kurilensis** See *P. nipponica* var. *kurilensis*.

**'Kursar'** (*P. campanulata* × *P. nipponica* var. *kurilensis*). A very beautiful small tree raised by Capt Collingwood Ingram, who was the leading western authority on Japanese cherries. The flowers, though small, are coloured a rich deep pink and are borne in great profusion with, or just before, the reddish-bronze, young leaves, in March or early April. AM 1952.

**lanata** (SUDW.) MACK. & BUSH. Small tree with a rounded head of branches. Leaves obovate, downy beneath; flowers small, white, occasionally followed by red or yellow fruits. C United States. I 1903.

**lannesiana** (CARR.) WILS. (*P. serrulata* var. *lannesiana* (CARR.) REHD.) (*P. serrulata hortensis* HORT.) Under this name Ernest Wilson described a pink, single-flowered Japanese cherry of garden origin. The wild type with fragrant white flowers he named *P. lannesiana* f.

**PRUNUS lannesiana**—*continued*

*albida* (now *P. speciosa*). Japanese botanists use the name *P. lannesiana* to cover the numerous garden cherries with large single or double flowers many of which are now thought to be forms of either *P. speciosa* or *P. jamasakura* (*P. serrulata* var. *spontanea*).

**f. albida** See *P. speciosa*.

**f. speciosa** See *P. speciosa*.

**latidentata** KOEHNE A small tree or shrub mainly grown in the following form.

**var. pleuroptera** (KOEHNE) INGRAM A small, round-headed tree with a peculiar mottled trunk. Flowers small, white, in drooping clusters with the leaves in April. China. I 1908 by Ernest Wilson.

**\*laurocerasus** L. "Common Laurel" "Cherry Laurel". A vigorous, wide-spreading evergreen shrub attaining 6m or more in height, by as much, or more, across. Leaves large, leathery, dark shining green. Mainly grown for screening purposes or for shelter in game coverts, but attractive in April when bearing its erect axillary and terminal racemes of small, white flowers, followed by cherry-like fruits, red at first, finally black. Not at its best on shallow, chalk soils. E Europe, Asia Minor. Extensively planted and naturalised in the British Isles. I 1576. AGM 1984.

There are few other evergreens more tolerant of shade and drip from overhanging trees than the laurel in its many forms. Several of the more compact, erect-growing cultivars make excellent tub specimens where *Laurus nobilis*, the Bay, is insufficiently hardy.

**'Angustifolia'** A form with ascending branches and narrow leaves similar to those of 'Zabeliana'. C 1802.

**'Camelliifolia'** A large shrub or small tree. Leaves dark green twisted and curled. C 1901.

**'Castlewellan'** See 'Marbled White'.

**'Caucasica'** A vigorous form of upright growth with rather narrow leaves.

**'Herbergii'** Erect-growing form of dense, compact habit, with oblanceolate, polished green leaves. Excellent for hedging. C 1930.

**'Greenmantle'** A medium-sized to large, wide-spreading shrub of open habit with dark glossy green leaves. Found in our nursery in 1965.

**'Latifolia'** ('Macrophylla') A tall, vigorous, large-leaved form. C 1869.

**'Magnoliifolia'** An imposing evergreen with glossy leaves up to 30cm long and 10cm wide. The largest-leaved laurel. C 1869.

**'Marbled White'** ('Castlewellan') A slow-growing dense bush eventually of large size. Leaves green and grey-green, marbled throughout with white. Originally grown as 'Variegata'. C 1811. AM 1986.

**'Mischeana'** A most ornamental clone slowly forming a dense, rather flat-topped mound of dark, lustrous green, oblong leaves. A superb lawn specimen. Attractive also when in flower, the short, erect racemes packed along the stems. C 1898.

**'Otinii'** A large, compact bush with large, very dark green, lustrous leaves. C 1873.

**'Otto Luyken'** A low, compact shrub with erect stems and narrow, shining green leaves. An outstanding clone in both leaf and flower. Raised in 1940. AM 1968. AGM 1984.

**'Reynvaanii'** A small, slow-growing form of compact habit, with stiff branches. C 1913.

**'Rotundifolia'** A bushy form, excellent for hedging. Leaves half as broad as long. C 1865.

**'Rufescens'** For many years we have grown under this name a rather slow-growing, small, rather flat-topped bush with small, neat, oval to obovate leaves.

**'Schipka Holland'** ('Schipkaensis Holland') A selection made in Holland from plants grown as 'Schipkaensis'. A compact, medium-sized, spreading bush differing from 'Schipkaensis' in its smaller, more distinctly toothed leaves. Flowers profusely.

**'Schipkaensis'** An extremely hardy, free-flowering, narrow-leaved form of spreading habit. Found in the wild near the Schipka Pass in Bulgaria. I 1888. AM 1959.

**'Schipkaensis Holland'** See 'Schipka Holland'.

**'Schipkaensis Macrophylla'** A German clone of open habit having ascending branches up to 2m. Leaves oblong-elliptic up to 18cm long. Free-fruiting. C 1930.

**'Serbica'** "Serbian Laurel". More upright than 'Schipkaensis', and with obovate rugose leaves. Originally found in Yugoslavia. C 1877.

**'Variegata'** See under 'Marbled White'.

**PRUNUS laurocerasus**—*continued*

**'Zabeliana'** A low, horizontally branched form, with long, narrow, willow-like leaves; very free-flowering. Makes an excellent ground cover, even under the shade and drip of trees, also useful for breaking the regular outline of a border or bed in the same way as the Pfitzer Juniper. C 1898. AGM 1984.

**litigiosa** SCHNEID. (*P. pilosiucula* var. *barbata* KOEHNE) A splendid small, somewhat conical tree with small white flowers appearing in drooping clusters with the unfolding leaves in April. Worthy of more extensive planting where a fastigiate shape is required. Attractive autumn tints. C China. I 1907 by Ernest Wilson.

**\*lusitanica** L. "Portugal Laurel". An indispensable, large, evergreen shrub or small to medium-sized tree. A beautiful specimen tree when allowed to develop naturally. Leaves ovate, dark green with reddish petioles. Flowers small, white, hawthorn-scented, carried in long slender racemes, in June. Fruits small, red turning to dark purple. Hardier than the Cherry Laurel. Useful as game cover and a splendid hedging plant. Happy even on shallow chalk soils, where it may be used instead of *P. laurocerasus*. Spain, Portugal. I 1648. AGM 1984.

**'Angustifolia'** See 'Myrtifolia'.

**subsp. azorica** (MOUILLEF.) FRANCO A magnificent and very hardy, large evergreen shrub or small tree with larger, thicker leaves of a bright green, reddish when unfolding and with reddish petioles. Azores. I about 1860. FCC 1866. AGM 1984.

**'Myrtifolia'** ('Angustifolia') ('Pyramidalis') Forms a dense cone up to 5m, with polished, deep green leaves, smaller and neater than those of the type. In cold areas may be used as a formal evergreen to replace the conical Bay. C 1892.

**'Variegata'** An attractive form with leaves conspicuously white margined, sometimes pink-flushed in winter. C 1865.

**†\*lyonii** (EASTW.) SARG. (*P. integrifolia* SARG.) "Captain Cherry". A rare evergreen shrub closely related to *P. ilicifolia*, but differing in its flat, mostly entire leaves, longer racemes and nearly black fruits. California. Our stock has toothed, slightly undulate leaves and may be a hybrid with *P. ilicifolia*.

**maackii** RUPR. "Manchurian Cherry". A rare, vigorous, small tree with attractive, shining, golden brown, flaking bark. Flowers small, white, carried in irregular racemes on the previous year's shoots in April; fruits small, black. Manchuria, Korea. I 1878.

**'Amber Beauty'** A Dutch selection with a good amber-coloured bark and a narrow crown.

**macradenia** KOEHNE A small tree or large shrub related to *P. maximowiczii*. Flowers small, white, carried in few-flowered corymbose racemes in May. China. I 1911.

**macrophylla** See *P. avium* 'Decumana'.

**mahaleb** L. "St Lucie Cherry". A very attractive, small to medium-sized tree of spreading or rounded habit, smothered with myriads of small white fragrant blossoms in late April and early May, but not very free-flowering when young. Fruits black. Cherrywood pipes and walking sticks are made from this species. C and S Europe. I 1714.

**'Pendula'** An elegant form with gracefully arching branches. Raised in France in 1847. FCC 1874.

**mandshurica** (MAXIM.) KOEHNE "Manchurian Apricot". An uncommon small tree. Its pale pink flowers, which open in February and March, are of a lively peach-pink colour before expanding. Fruits rounded, yellow. Manchuria, Korea. C 1900. AM 1977.

**maritima** MARSH. "Beach Plum". A small shrub of fairly compact habit, occasionally reaching 2-2.5m. Flowers small, white, produced in May. Fruits rounded, red or purple. Native of the eastern United States where it frequently grows in sandy places near the sea.

**maximowiczii** RUPR. A small, dense-headed tree with small, coarsely-toothed leaves and erect, corymbose racemes of small, creamy-white flowers in May. Fruits red turning black. Manchuria, Ussuri, Korea, Japan. I 1892 by Charles Sargent.

**'Moerheimii'** (*P. incisa* 'Moerheimii') A small, picturesque, weeping tree of wide-spreading, dome-shaped habit. Flowers blush-white, pink in bud, in late March and early April.

**mugus** HAND.-MAZZ. "Tibetan Cherry". Described as growing prostrate in the wild but the plant in general cultivation is a stiff, thick-stemmed, rather compact small bush. The

**PRUNUS mugus**—*continued*

flowers are more curious than beautiful, shell-pink with inflated reddish calyces, usually disposed singly or in pairs. W China. I by George Forrest in 1922.

**mume** SIEB. & ZUCC. "Japanese Apricot". A delightful small tree with green young shoots and single, almond-scented, pink flowers paling with age. Normally in flower during March, occasionally as early as late January or as late as early April. China, Korea, extensively cultivated in Japan. I 1844.

**'Alba'** A vigorous form with usually single, pure white flowers studding the branches in late March or early April.

**'Alboplena'** Flowers semi-double, white, appearing in late winter and early spring.

**'Alphandii'** ('Flore Pleno') A beautiful form with semi-double pink flowers in March, sometimes earlier. C 1902.

**'Beni-shidare'** A striking form with strongly fragrant, double, cup-shaped flowers which are a rich madder-pink, darker in bud and paling slightly with age, appearing in late March or early April. Previously listed as 'Beni-shidon'. AM 1961.

**'Grandiflora'** See *P. armeniaca* var. *ansu* 'Flore Pleno'.

**'Omoi-no-mama'** A charming form with semi-double, cup-shaped, usually white flowers in late March or early April. Occasional petals and sometimes whole flowers are pink. Previously listed as 'O-moi-no-wac'. AM 1991.

**'Pendula'** A small, weeping tree with single or semi-double flowers of a pale pink, in late February or March.

**'Rosea Plena'** See *P. armeniaca* var. *ansu* 'Flore Pleno'.

**munsoniana** WIGHT & HEDR. "Wild Goose Plum". Small tree with lanceolate, shining green leaves and clusters of white flowers in spring, occasionally followed by red fruits. SE United States. C 1911.

**mutabilis** See *P. jamasakura*.

**myrobalana** See *P. cerasifera*.

**nana** See *P. tenella*.

**nigra** AIT. "Canada Plum". A small, narrow-headed tree or large shrub, producing in spring clusters of fragrant white flowers which later turn pink. Red or yellowish plum-like fruits. Canada and E United States. I 1773.

**nipponica** MATSUM. "Japanese Alpine Cherry". A dense shrub or bushy tree 2.5-3m, with chestnut-brown branches. Leaves coarsely-toothed; flowers white or pale pink in May. Fruits small, black. Japan. I 1915.

**var. kurilensis** (MIYABE) WILS. (*P. kurilensis* (MIYABE) MIYABE) Small, bushy shrub of slow growth, with coarsely-toothed leaves rusty-brown when young. Flowers in April, before the leaves, comparatively large, white or pink-tinged; fruits purplish-black. Japan. I 1905.

**'Ruby'** A lovely form of var. *kurilensis*, its erect branches a mass of pale pink blossoms with conspicuous purplish-red calyces in early April. C 1958.

**'Okame'** (*P. campanulata* × *P. incisa*). A small tree, one of the numerous hybrids raised by Capt Collingwood Ingram. This is a very lovely cherry, with masses of carmine-rose flowers opening throughout March. Foliage attractively tinted in autumn. AM 1947. AGM 1984.

**padus** L. (Subgenus Padus) "Bird Cherry". A small to medium-sized native tree widely distributed in the N hemisphere. Flowers small, white, almond-scented, produced in slender, drooping or spreading racemes in May after the leaves; fruits black, bitter to taste. Europe (including British Isles), N Asia to Japan.

**'Albertii'** A very free-flowering form of medium size, strong and erect in growth. C 1902.

**'Colorata'** A remarkable clone with dark purplish shoots, coppery-purple young foliage and pale pink flowers. The leaves in summer are a sombre green with purple-tinged veins and undersurfaces. Found in Sweden in 1953. AM 1974. AGM 1984. 'Purple Queen' is very similar.

**var. commutata** DIPP. (*P. seoulensis* NAKAI) A geographical form from eastern Asia. A medium-sized tree of spreading habit. One of the first heralds of spring, the fresh green leaves appearing before winter has passed. I 1880. AM 1956.

**'Plena'** A form with longer-lasting, larger, double flowers. C 1892.

**'Purple Queen'** See under 'Colorata'.

**PRUNUS padus**—*continued*

**'Watereri'** ('Grandiflora') A medium-sized tree with conspicuous racemes up to 20cm long. C 1914. AM 1969. AGM 1984.

**'Pandora'** (*P. subhirtella* 'Ascendens Rosea' × *P.* × *yedoensis*). A splendid small tree with ascending branches which, in March or early April, are flooded with pale, shell-pink blossoms 2.5cm across. Leaves bronze-red when unfolding, and often colouring richly in autumn. AM 1939.

**pendula** See *P. subhirtella* 'Pendula'.

   **f. ascendens** See *P. subhirtella* var. *ascendens*.

**pensylvanica** L. f. A fast-growing, small to medium-sized tree with bright green, finely-toothed leaves and clusters of white flowers in late April and early May. Fruits small, red. North America. I 1773.

**persica** (L.) BATSCH "Peach". A small bushy tree or large shrub with pale pink flowers, 2.5-4cm wide, in early April. Differing from the almond in its smaller flowers which appear 2 or 3 weeks later, and in its fleshy juicy fruits. Native probably of China, but cultivated since ancient times.

   Susceptible to peach leaf curl, for the treatment of which see under *P. dulcis*.

**'Alba'** Flowers white. C 1829.

**'Alboplena'** Flowers white, double. C 1850. FCC 1899.

**'Alboplena Pendula'** A weeping form with double, white flowers.

**'Atropurpurea'** See 'Foliis Rubris'.

**'Aurora'** Dense clusters of double, rose-pink flowers with frilled petals. AM 1950.

**'Cardinal'** Flowers glowing red, semi-double, rosette-like.

**'Crimson Cascade'** Weeping branches; flowers crimson, double.

**'Foliis Rubris'** ('Atropurpurea') Leaves rich purplish-red when young, becoming bronze-green. Flowers single, fruits reddish-purple. AM 1939.

**'Helen Borchers'** A strong-growing form with large, semi-double, rose-pink flowers. AM 1949.

**'Iceberg'** A very free-flowering form with large, semi-double, pure white flowers. AM 1950.

**'Klara Mayer'** ('Flore Roseoplena') Flowers double, peach-pink. The best double peach for general planting. C 1890.

**'Prince Charming'** A small, upright-growing tree; flowers double, rose-red.

**'Russell's Red'** Flowers double, crimson. AM 1933.

**'Windle Weeping'** A very distinct weeping form with broad leaves and semi-double, cup-shaped flowers of purplish-pink. AM 1949.

**pilosiuscula** KOEHNE Small tree or large shrub producing in April clusters of small, white or pink-tinged flowers with conspicuous protruding anthers, followed by red fruits in June. W China. I 1907 by Ernest Wilson.

**'Pink Shell'** One of the loveliest of cherries in a genus full of floral treasures. A small, elegant tree, the slender, spreading branches drooping beneath a wealth of cup-shaped, delicate, shell-pink blossoms, which blend beautifully with the pale green of the emerging leaves in early April. Possibly a seedling of *P.* × *yedoensis*. AM 1969.

**pleiocerasus** KOEHNE Small tree with small, white flowers in spring. W China. I 1907.

× **pollardii** See *P.* × *amygdalo-persica* 'Pollardii'.

**prostrata** LABILL. "Rock Cherry". A dwarf, spreading shrub usually forming a delightful, low, gnarled hummock reaching 0.7m high by 2m wide in 25 years. Flowers bright pink borne along the wiry stems in April. SE Europe, Mediterranean region, W Asia. I 1802.

**pseudocerasus** LINDL. A small tree, the leafless stems wreathed in clusters of white flowers in early March. N China. I 1819.

   **'Cantabrigiensis'** This interesting, small tree is well worth growing for its early display of fragrant pink blossoms, commencing as early as mid-February. The original plant is growing in the University Botanic Garden, Cambridge. AM 1925.

**pubigera** KOEHNE (Subgenus Padus) A distinct and attractive bird cherry forming a medium-sized tree. Flowers small, creamy-white, in drooping racemes up to 18cm long and 2.5cm wide. W China. AM 1957.

**pumila** L. "Sand Cherry". A spreading shrub to 2m. In May the naked branches are wreathed with multitudes of tiny white flowers. The greyish-green, narrowly obovate leaves become bright red in autumn. Fruits dark red. NE United States. I 1756.

**PRUNUS pumila**—*continued*

**var. besseyi** See *P. besseyi*.

**var. depressa** (PURSH) BEAN A prostrate form less than 15cm tall, good for ground cover. It is studded with white flowers in May. I 1864.

**rufa** HOOK. f. "Himalayan Cherry". A small tree with rusty-hairy young shoots and small clusters of pale pink flowers. Some forms have superb, peeling, reddish-brown or amber bark. Himalaya. I 1897.

**salicifolia** KUNTH (*P. serotina* var. *salicifolia* (KUNTH) KOEHNE) (*P. capollin* ZUCC.) A small tree related to *P. serotina* with lanceolate, long-persisting glabrous and long-pointed leaves and stouter racemes. Remarkably hardy considering its native distribution. Mexico to Peru. I 1820.

**salicina** LINDL. (*P. triflora* ROXB.) "Japanese Plum". A small, bushy tree or large shrub with shining dark twigs. Leaves turning bright red in autumn. The small, white flowers crowd the leafless branches in early April. China. Long cultivated in Japan. I 1870. AM 1926.

**sargentii** REHD. (*P. serrulata* var. *sachalinensis* (F. SCHMIDT) WILS.) Considered by many to be the loveliest of all cherries. A round-headed tree, attaining 15-18m in Japan, but rather less in this country. Bark dark chestnut-brown. Young foliage bronze-red. Flowers single, pink, opening late March or early April. One of the first trees to colour in the autumn, its leaves assuming glorious orange and crimson tints, usually in late September. One of the few cherries that bullfinches appear to ignore. Japan, Sakhalin, Korea. I 1890. AM 1921. FCC 1925. AGM 1984.

**'Rancho'** A narrowly upright form raised in the United States before 1962. Some plants grown under this name are poor forms of *P. sargentii*.

×**schmittii** REHD. (*P. avium* × *P. canescens*). This fast-growing, narrowly conical tree of medium size should have a great future for public planting. The polished brown trunk is a greater attraction than the pale pink flowers in spring. Garden origin in 1923.

†**scoparia** (SPACH) SCHNEID. A remarkable rare, large shrub, with slender, broom-like branches recalling those of *Spartium junceum*, sparsely furnished with small, narrow leaves, reddish-bronze at first becoming bronze-green and finally green. Flowers pale pink, almond-like, in early spring. Iran. C 1934.

**scopulorum** KOEHNE (*P. vilmoriniana* HORT.) A rare tree of upright habit, reaching 11-12m. Flowers tiny, fragrant, white flushed pink in March or April. China.

**serotina** EHRH. (Subgenus Padus) In its native environs a large tree, but of small to medium size in this country. The attractive glossy leaves, recalling those of the Portugal Laurel (*P. lusitanica*) turn clear yellow in the autumn. Flowers white, in racemes up to 15cm long, produced during May to June. E North America, E and S Mexico, Guatemala. I 1629.

**'Aspleniifolia'** An unusual form of graceful habit, with slender leaves strongly-toothed and less than 12mm wide. C 1864.

**var. salicifolia** See *P. salicifolia*.

**serrula** FRANCH. (*P. serrula* var. *tibetica* (BATAL.) KOEHNE) A small, but vigorous tree whose main attraction is the glistening surface of its polished red-brown, mahogany-like new bark. Leaves narrow, willow-like; flowers small, white, produced with the foliage in late April. W China. Introduced by E.H. Wilson in 1908. AM 1944. AGM 1984.

**serrulata** LINDL. (*P. serrulata* 'Alboplena') A small, flat-topped tree with wide-spreading branches, green unfolding leaves and clusters of white, double flowers in late April and early May. An interesting tree of ancient garden origin, introduced from Canton in 1822. It has been suggested by some authorities that this tree may have arisen as a branch sport on the wild Chinese Hill Cherry (*P. serrulata* var. *hupehensis*). It was the first Japanese cherry to be planted in European gardens and is the plant designated by Lindley as the type of the species.

**'Alboplena'** See *P. serrulata*.

**'Autumn Glory'** See *P. verecunda* 'Autumn Glory'.

**f. erecta** See *P.* 'Amanogawa' under Japanese Cherries.

**var. hupehensis** INGRAM (*P. mutabilis stricta* HORT.) "Chinese Hill Cherry". Considered to be the prototype of the cultivated double white cherry, to which Lindley gave the name *P. serrulata*. A medium-sized tree with ascending branches bearing clusters of

**PRUNUS serrulata var. hupehensis**—*continued*

white or blush flowers in April and early May. Young leaves bronze, and autumn foliage attractively tinted. C China. Introduced by E.H. Wilson in 1900.

**var. pubescens** See *P. verecunda*.

**var. sachalinensis** See *P. sargentii*.

**f. sieboldii** See *P. × sieboldii*.

**var. spontanea** See *P. jamasakura*.

**'Shosar'** (*P. campanulata × P. incisa*). A strong-growing, rather fastigiate tree. Flowers single, clear pink. Early. Usually good autumn colour. Raised by Capt Collingwood Ingram.

× **sieboldii** (CARR.) WITTM. (*P. apetala × P. speciosa*). (*P.* 'Takasago') (*P. serrulata* f. *sieboldii* (CARR.) MAK.) (*P. pseudocerasus watereri* HORT.) A small, spreading cherry with downy leaves. Flowers semi-double, pale pink. Mid. Young leaves varying from yellowish-brown to reddish-bronze. I about 1864.

**simonii** CARR. "Apricot Plum". Small tree or large shrub of erect, conical habit, producing white flowers in March and April. Fruits very conspicuous, tomato-shaped, red and yellow, fragrant, edible. N China. I 1863.

**'Snow Goose'** A small tree with ascending branches crowded in spring with pure white, well-formed flowers. A seedling of similar parentage (*P. incisa × P. speciosa*) to 'Umineko', but differing from that cultivar in its broader crown and its larger leaves which appear after the flowers.

**speciosa** (KOIDZ.) INGRAM (*P. lannesiana* f. *albida* (MAK.) WILS.) "Oshima Cherry". A medium-sized tree with ovate-elliptic leaves with aristate teeth and usually terminating in a slender, acuminate apex, bronze-green when unfolding soon turning bright green. In April the fragrant white flowers are carried on long pedicels. This species is regarded as the ancestor of many of the Japanese cherries, for example 'Gioiko', 'Tai Haku' and 'Jo-nioi'. Japan. C 1909.

**spinosa** L. "Blackthorn" "Sloe". A large, dense-habited shrub or small bushy tree with dark, spiny branches, crowded in March or early April with small white flowers. Fruits like small damsons, blue-bloomy at first, later shining black. A familiar native shrub in hedges, its fruits are used in preserves, for winemaking and for flavouring gin, whilst its branches provide the traditional blackthorn sticks and Irish shillalahs. Europe, N Africa, W Asia. Long cultivated.

**'Plena'** An attractive form with double flowers. C 1770. AM 1950.

**'Purpurea'** A neat, compact bush with rich purple leaves and white flowers. One of the elite of purple-leaved shrubs. C 1903.

**'Rosea'** See *P. cerasifera* 'Rosea'.

**'Spire'** (*P. × hillieri* 'Spire') Possibly the best small street tree raised this century. A vase-shaped tree attaining 10m high, and with a width of about 7m with age. Flowers soft pink; leaves with rich autumn tints. It is a sister seedling of *P.* 'Hillieri'.

**subhirtella** MIQ. "Spring Cherry". A small to medium-sized tree. It includes among its forms some of the most delightful of early spring-flowering trees, and in a good year most forms produce attractive autumn tints. Flowers small, pale pink in March and April. Unknown in the wild and probably of hybrid origin. I 1894. AM 1930.

**var. ascendens** WILS. (*P. pendula* f. *ascendens* (MAK.) OHWI) The wild type which as seen in cultivation in this country is a small, semi-erect tree, but is much larger in Japan. Flowers white or pale pink, opening towards the end of March. Japan, China, Korea. C 1916.

**'Ascendens Rosea'** A lovely form with flowers of a clear shell-pink, enhanced by the red-tinged calyces. AM 1960.

**'Autumnalis'** "Autumn Cherry". A small tree up to 7.5m producing its semi-double, white flowers intermittently from November to March. Flowers may be found on this tree on almost any winter's day and a few cut sprays are a welcome indoor decoration. C 1900. AM 1912. FCC 1966. AGM 1984.

**'Autumnalis Rosea'** Similar to 'Autumnalis' but flowers blush. AM 1960. AGM 1984.

**'Flore Pleno'** A rare and splendid form with flattish, many-petalled or double flowers, about 2.5cm across, rich pink in bud, opening white. AM 1935.

**'Fukubana'** This very striking small tree with its profusion of semi-double, rose-madder flowers is certainly the most colourful of the spring cherries. I 1927 from California by Collingwood Ingram.

**PRUNUS subhirtella**—*continued*

**'Pendula'** (*P. pendula* MAXIM.) Raised from Japanese seed, this forms a lovely slender weeping tree of medium size, recalling the most graceful forms of weeping birch. The tiny blush flowers in late March to early April are not conspicuous. I 1862. AM 1930.

**'Pendula Plena Rosea'** A weeping shrub or small tree. Flowers semi-double, rosette-like, rose-madder, similar to those of 'Fukubana', but slightly paler. I 1928 by Collingwood Ingram. AM 1938.

**'Pendula Rosea'** "Weeping Spring Cherry". A small weeping, mushroom-shaped tree. Flowers rich pink in bud passing to pale blush, wreathing the graceful drooping branches in late March and early April. Often grown as *P. subhirtella* 'Pendula'. AGM 1984.

**'Pendula Rubra'** Flowers single, deep rose, carmine in bud, wreathing the long pendulous branches. AM 1983. AGM 1984.

**'Stellata'** A very beautiful form with larger, clear pink, star-shaped flowers produced in crowded clusters along the branches. I about 1955. AM 1949.

**tangutica** (BATAL.) KOEHNE (*P. dehiscens* KOEHNE) A large, bushy shrub with spiny branches. The carmine-pink, almond-like flowers appear from March onwards. W China. I 1910 by Ernest Wilson.

**tenella** BATSCH (*P. nana* (L.) STOKES) (*Amygdalus nana* L.) The "Dwarf Russian Almond" is a charming, small shrub with long glabrous stems. Flowers borne in April, bright pink. SE Europe, W Asia to E Siberia. I 1683. AM 1929.

**'Alba'** Flowers white. C 1845.

**'Fire Hill'** Perhaps the best dwarf almond. An outstanding small shrub, a selection of f. *gessleriana* from the Balkan Alps. The erect stems are wreathed with brilliant, rose-red flowers. AM 1959. AGM 1984.

**georgica** HORT. A tall-growing, geographical form, up to 2m with larger leaves. Flowers pink.

**f. gessleriana** (KIRCHN.) REHD. A small shrub with bright pink flowers darker in bud.

**tomentosa** THUNB. "Downy Cherry". A very variable shrub of medium size and usually erect habit. Young shoots and leaves beneath tomentose. Flowers white or more usually pale pink, produced in late March or early April. Fruits red. N and W China, Korea, Himalaya. C 1870.

**'Leucocarpa'** A form almost completely lacking the red colouration found in the typical form. Flowers white, even in bud, fruits white. C 1930.

**triflora** See *P. salicina*.

**triloba** LINDL. (*P. triloba* f. *simplex* (BUNGE) REHD.) Most frequently grown as the following form, the wild plant differs in its single, pale pink flowers. China. I 1884.

**'Multiplex'** (*P. triloba* f. *multiplex* (BUNGE) REHD.) A medium-sized to large shrub with small, coarsely-toothed, three-lobed leaves. Flowers large, double, rosette-like, clear peach-pink, produced in great profusion at the end of March or early April. Introduced by Robert Fortune from China in 1855. It makes a splendid wall shrub if the old flowering shoots are pruned back immediately after flowering. FCC 1983.

**f. simplex** See *P. triloba*.

**'Umineko'** (*P. incisa* × *P. speciosa*). A narrow-growing, upright tree of considerable merit. Flowers white, single, produced in April with the leaves which tint beautifully in autumn. AM 1928. AGM 1984.

**verecunda** (KOIDZ.) KOEHNE (*P. serrulata* var. *pubescens* (NAKAI) WILS. in part) "Korean Hill Cherry". A medium-sized tree with bronze-green young foliage and white or pink flowers in late April and early May. Often producing rich autumn tints. Intermediate between *P. serrulata* var. *hupehensis* and *P. jamasakura*, differing from both in its hairy petioles and leaf undersurfaces. China, Korea, Japan. I 1907.

**'Autumn Glory'** A form selected by Capt Collingwood Ingram for its consistent, rich, deep crimson and red autumn colours. Flowers pale blush, very prolific. AM 1966.

**vilmoriniana** See *P. scopulorum*.

**virginiana** L. (Subgenus Padus) "Choke Cherry". A small tree or large shrub with glossy green leaves and densely packed racemes of small white flowers in May. Fruits dark red. E North America. I 1724.

**var. demissa** (TORR. & A. GRAY) TORR. "Western Choke Cherry". A small, bushy tree or shrub, mainly of botanical interest. W United States. I 1892.

**PRUNUS virginiana**—*continued*

**'Shubert'** A small tree of conical habit. Young foliage green, quickly changing to deep reddish-purple. C 1950.

**'Wadae'** (*P. pseudocerasus* × *P. subhirtella*). A small twiggy tree or large shrub with bristly-hairy young shoots, the trunk inclined to produce aerial roots. The pale pink flowers, deep rose in bud, are produced in March and are scented of ripe peaches. Garden origin in Japan and named after Mr K. Wada of Yokohama.

×**yedoensis** MATSUM. (*P. speciosa* × *P. subhirtella*). "Yoshino Cherry". A graceful, early flowering, small to medium-sized tree with arching branches. Highly valued for the profusion of its almond-scented, blush-white flowers in late March and early April. Unknown in the wild; introduced from Japan in 1902, possibly earlier. AM 1927. AGM 1984.

**'Ivensii'** Raised in our nurseries from seed of *P.* × *yedoensis* in 1925. A quite remarkable small, vigorous, weeping tree with long, tortuous branches and long, slender, drooping branchlets which, in late March to early April, are transformed into snow-white cascades of delicately fragrant blossom. Named to commemorate our late Manager, Arthur J. Ivens, FLS.

**'Shidare Yoshino'** (*f. perpendens* WILS.) ('Pendula') A small tree with horizontal and arching branches often weeping to the ground. Flowers pale pink in late March and early April. I 1916. AGM 1984.

**'Tsubame'** Branches spreading and slightly weeping, flowers white.

## JAPANESE CHERRIES
### of Garden Origin

The "Sato Zakura" of Japan are a large group of extremely ornamental flowering cherries. Most are of obscure origin, some having been cultivated in Japan for more than 1000 years. Some are hybrids, whilst others are undoubtedly derived from *P. speciosa* and *P. jamasakura (P. serrulata* var. *spontanea)*. No doubt other species have also contributed to their development. Many of the older sorts at least are derived from trees found in the wild, in fact forms of *P. speciosa* identical to some of the Sato Zakura have been found growing wild in Japan.

The majority are small trees of easy cultivation, varying from low and spreading to tall and erect in habit. The leaves of some are bronze in spring, providing a delightful backing to the emerging flowers. The flowers themselves may be single, semi-double or double, and vary in colour from rich pink to white or cream. With few exceptions the leaves turn to shades of yellow or tawny-orange in autumn. Like the edible cherries, they succeed in all types of well drained soils, including chalk soils. During the dormant period the buds are often subject to bird damage, when it is necessary to use a repellant to ensure blossom. Pruning of any kind is rarely necessary, but when unavoidable it is best carried out in late summer so that the cuts heal before winter. Flowering periods are indicated as follows:

Early—late March to early April
Mid—mid to late April
Late—late April to mid May

**'Amanogawa'** (*P. serrulata* f. *erecta* MIYOSHI) A small, columnar tree with erect branches and dense, upright clusters of fragrant, semi-double, shell-pink flowers. Mid to late. Young leaves greenish-bronze. AM 1931.

**'Asagi'** (*P. serrulata* f. *luteoides* MIYOSHI) Similar to 'Ukon', but flowers single or nearly so and paler in colour, opening earlier. Early to mid.

**'Asano'** (*P. serrulata* f. *geraldiniae* INGRAM) A small tree with ascending branches, bearing dense clusters of deep pink, very double flowers. Early. Young leaves greenish-bronze. A beautiful tree, in effect an upright form of 'Cheal's Weeping'. I 1929 by Collingwood Ingram.

**'Benden'** See 'Bendono'.

**'Bendono'** ('Benden') (*P. serrulata* f. *rubida* MIYOSHI) A vigorous tree with ascending branches, similar in size and habit to 'Kanzan'. Flowers single, pale pink. Early. Young leaves reddish-brown or coppery-red. Said to have originated on Mt Nikko.

**'Benifugen'** See 'Daikoku'.

**PRUNUS (Japanese Cherries)**—*continued*

   **'Botan'** (*P. serrulata* f. *moutan* MIYOSHI) A small tree with ascending and spreading branches. Flowers large, nearly 5cm across, single or semi-double, fragrant, lilac-pink in bud opening pale pink or white. Mid. Young leaves bronze-green. Similar to 'Mikuruma-gaeshi' and 'Ojochin' in flower.

   **'Cheal's Weeping'** A small tree with arching or drooping branches, very attractive when wreathed with clear deep pink very double flowers. Early. Young leaves bronze-green, later green and glossy. AM 1915. Often wrongly referred to as 'Kiku-shidare Sakura'.

   **'Choshu-hizakura'** (*P. serrulata splendens* HORT.) A beautiful, small tree with single, deep pink flowers, the calyces attractively tinted purplish-brown. Mid. Young leaves reddish-brown or coppery-red. Previously listed as 'Hisakura', a name which properly applies to 'Ichiyo'.

   **'Daikoku'** A small tree with strong ascending branches. Flowers large up to 5cm across, double, purplish-red in bud opening deep lilac-pink, with a central cluster of small green carpels, carried in loose, drooping clusters. Late. Young leaves yellowish-green. Originally called 'Benifugen', a name which properly applies to 'Fugenzo'. I 1899.

   **'Fudanzakura'** (*P. serrulata* f. *semperflorens* MIYOSHI) A small, round-headed tree opening its single pink-budded, white flowers during spells of mild weather between November and April. Especially useful for cutting for indoor decoration. Young leaves coppery-red or reddish-brown. AM 1930.

   **'Fugenzo'** (*P. cerasus* 'James H. Veitch') (*P. serrulata* f. *fugenzo* MAK.) Resembling 'Kanzan' in some respects, but smaller and with a broader, flat-topped head. Flowers large, double, rose-pink, borne in drooping clusters. Very late. Young leaves coppery-red. A very old cultivar, commonly grown in Japan. I about 1880. FCC 1899.

   **'Fukubana'** See *P. subhirtella* 'Fukubana'.

   **'Gioiko'** (*P. serrulata* f. *tricolor* MIYOSHI) A strong-growing tree with ascending branches; flowers semi-double, creamy-white, streaked green and often tinged with pink, opening a little later than 'Ukon'. Young leaves reddish-brown. I about 1914. AM 1930.

   **'Hata-zakura'** "Flag Cherry". Branches ascending. Flowers fragrant, single, white or pink-flushed. Early. Young leaves green or bronze-tinged. The Japanese name refers to the peculiar tattered edges of the petals.

   **'Hisakura'** See under 'Choshu-hizakura' and 'Kanzan'.

   **'Hokusai'** One of the earliest and most popular introductions. A vigorous, wide-spreading tree, its branches hidden in spring by the large clusters of large, semi-double, pale pink flowers. Mid. Young leaves brownish-bronze. An old cultivar of good constitution, ideally suited to English gardens. I about 1866.

   **'Horinji'** (*P. serrulata* f. *decora* MIYOSHI) A small, upright tree with ascending branches. Flowers semi-double, mauve-pink in bud opening soft pink, contrasting with the purplish-brown calyces, freely borne along the branches. Mid. Young leaves greenish-bronze. I about 1905. AM 1935.

   **'Ichiyo'** (*P. serrulata* f. *unifolia* MIYOSHI) A beautiful tree with ascending branches and double, shell-pink flowers which have a circular, frilled appearance and are borne in long-stalked corymbs. Mid. Young leaves bronze-green. AM 1959.

   **'Imose'** A free-growing tree with double, mauve-pink flowers, abundantly produced in long, loose clusters. Mid. Leaves reddish-copper when young, glossy bright green at maturity, turning yellow in November. Fruits often produced in pairs on the same stalk. I 1927 by Collingwood Ingram.

   **'Itokukuri'** (*P. serrulata* f. *fasciculata* MIYOSHI) A small tree with ascending branches. Flowers semi-double, pale pink or white. Mid. Young leaves greenish-bronze. Cultivated in Japan for more than 400 years.

   **'Jo-nioi'** (*P. serrulata* f. *affinis* MIYOSHI) A strong-growing cherry of spreading habit. The single, white, deliciously-scented blossoms wreathe the branches in spring. The white petals contrast with the purple-brown sepals. Mid. Young leaves pale golden brown. I about 1900.

   **'Kanzan'** ('Sekiyama') (*P. serrulata* f. *purpurascens* MIYOSHI) One of the most popular and commonly planted ornamental cherries. A strong-growing, medium-sized tree with characteristic stiffly ascending branches when young, later spreading. Flowers large and showy, double purplish-pink. Mid. Young leaves coppery-red or reddish-brown. Often

**PRUNUS 'Kanzan'**—*continued*

wrongly grown in cultivation under the name 'Hisakura', for which see under 'Choshu-hizakura', from which it differs in its taller stature and double flowers opening generally a week later. I about 1913. AM 1921. FCC 1937. AGM 1984.

**'Kiku-shidare Sakura'** See under 'Cheal's Weeping'.

**'Kiku-zakura'** (*P. serrulata* f. *chrysanthemoides* MIYOSHI) A small, slow-growing cultivar. Flowers double, each flower being a congested, rounded mass of soft pink petals. Late. Young leaves bronze-green.

**'Kojima'** See 'Mount Fuji'.

**'Kokonoe'** (*P. serrulata* f. *homogena* MIYOSHI) A small tree producing large, semi-double, shell-pink blossoms in great profusion. Early to mid. Young leaves bronze-green.

**'Mikuruma-gaeshi'** (*P. serrulata* f. *diversifolia* MIYOSHI) (*P. serrulata* 'Temari') A distinct tree with long, ascending, rather gaunt, short-spurred branches along which large, mostly single, blush-pink flowers are densely packed. Mid. Young leaves bronze-green. Similar to 'Ojochin' and 'Botan' in flower. AM 1946.

**'Mount Fuji'** This beautiful cherry is one of the most distinct clones. A small vigorous tree with wide-spreading, horizontal or slightly drooping branches, often reaching to the ground. Flowers very large, single or semi-double, fragrant, snow-white, bursting from the soft green young foliage in long, drooping clusters. Mid. The leaves have a distinctive fringed appearance. I about 1905 and long grown as 'Shirotae' which is similar. AGM 1984.

**'Ojochin'** A striking tree easily distinguished by its large leaves and stout growth. Flowers single, 5cm across, pink in bud opening blush, profusely borne in long-stalked clusters of as many as 7 or 8. Mid. Young leaves bronze-brown becoming rather tough and leathery when mature. Similar to 'Botan' and 'Mikuruma-gaeshi' in flower. I before 1905. AM 1924.

**'Okiku'** A small tree of rather stiff habit. Flowers large, double, pale pink, passing to white. Mid. Young leaves bronze-green. AM 1934.

**'Oku Miyako'** See under 'Shogetsu'.

**'Oshokun'** (*P. serrulata* f. *conspicua* MIYOSHI) A small tree of weak growth, but with very lovely, single flowers, carmine-red in bud opening to blush-pink, very freely produced. Mid to late. Young leaves bronze-green.

**'Pink Perfection'** A very striking cultivar raised in this country from 'Shogetsu', presumably pollinated by 'Kanzan'. Habit is intermediate. Flowers bright rosy-pink in bud, opening paler, double, carried in long, drooping clusters. Mid to late. Young leaves bronze. I 1935. AM 1945.

**'Sekiyama'** See 'Kanzan'.

**'Shimidsu'** See 'Shogetsu'.

**'Shirofugen'** (*P. serrulata* f. *alborosea* WILS.) A strong-growing, wide-spreading tree up to 10m. Flowers large, double, dull purplish-pink in bud opening white, then fading to purplish-pink, produced in long-stalked clusters and contrasting superbly with the copper-coloured young leaves. Very late. One of the best clones for general planting, the flowers are late and long-lasting. I about 1900. AM 1951. AGM 1984.

**'Shirotae'** See under 'Mount Fuji'.

**'Shogetsu'** ('Shimidsu') One of the loveliest of Japanese cherries. A small tree with wide-spreading branches forming a broad, flattened crown. The large, fimbriated, double flowers are pink-tinted in bud, opening to pure white, and hang all along the branches in long-stalked clusters. Mid to late. Young leaves green. Wrongly called 'Oku Miyako' in the past. AM 1930. FCC 1989. AGM 1984.

**'Shogun'** A vigorous cherry with deep pink, semi-double flowers, becoming abundant as the tree ages. Mid. Rich autumn colours.

**'Shosar'** See *P.* 'Shosar'.

**'Shujaku'** (*P. serrulata* f. *campanuloides* MIYOSHI) A small tree with double, slightly cup-shaped, pale pink flowers, freely produced. Mid. Young leaves yellowish-bronze. I about 1900.

**'Tai Haku'** "Great White Cherry". A superb, robust tree up to 12m. Flowers very large, single, of a dazzling white, enhanced by the rich coppery-red of the young leaves. Mid. One of the finest cherries for general planting and perhaps the best of the whites. It is

**PRUNUS 'Tai Haku'**—*continued*

one of the many lovely cherries which owes its popularity to Capt Collingwood Ingram, who, when it was lost to cultivation in Japan, found a plant in a Sussex garden in 1923 which had been introduced from Japan in 1900. It was reintroduced to Japan in 1932. AM 1931. FCC 1944. AGM 1984.

**'Taizanfukun'** (*P. serrulata* f. *ambigua* INGRAM) A distinct, erect-growing cherry of twiggy habit, with leathery leaves. Flowers double, pale pink. Mid. Young leaves bronze.

**'Takasago'** See *P. × sieboldii*.

**'Taki-nioi'** (*P. serrulata* f. *cataracta* MIYOSHI) A strong, vigorous, medium-sized tree with spreading branches. The honey-scented, single, white flowers are rather small, but are produced in great abundance and contrast effectively with the reddish-bronze, young leaves. Late.

**'Taoyame'** A floriferous, small tree of slow growth and spreading habit. Flowers fragrant, semi-double, shell-pink becoming pale blush with purplish-brown calyces, effectively backed by the reddish-brown or coppery emerging leaves. Mid. I 1929 by Collingwood Ingram.

**'Ukon'** (*P. serrulata* f. *grandiflora* WAGNER) (*P. serrulata* f. *luteovirens* MIYOSHI) A robust tree of spreading habit. Flowers semi-double, pale yellowish, tinged green, occasionally pink-flushed, freely borne and very effective against the brownish-bronze young leaves. Closely akin to 'Asagi'. Mid. The large, mature leaves turn rusty-red or purplish-brown in autumn. I about 1905. AM 1923. AGM 1984.

**'Umineko'** See *P.* 'Umineko'.

**'Washino-o'** (*P. serrulata* f. *wasinowo* INGRAM) A strong-growing tree with white, slightly fragrant, single flowers. Early. Young leaves soft bronze-green.

**'Yae-murasaki'** (*P. serrulata* f. *purpurea* MIYOSHI) A small, free-flowering tree of slow growth. Flowers semi-double, purplish-pink. Mid. Young leaves coppery-red.

**'Yedo Zakura'** (*P. serrulata* f. *nobilis* MIYOSHI) Small upright tree; flowers semi-double, carmine in bud, almond-pink when expanded. Mid. Young leaves golden coppery. I about 1905.

**'Yokihi'** A small tree with widely ascending or spreading branches and large, semi-double, pale pink flowers in loose clusters, freely produced. Late. Young leaves bronze-green.

**PSEUDOCYDONIA** (SCHNEID.) SCHNEID.—**Rosaceae**—A monotypic genus related to and sometimes included in *Cydonia*.

**sinensis** (THOUIN) SCHNEID. (*Cydonia sinensis* THOUIN) A small, occasionally semi-evergreen tree or large shrub with flaky bark. Shoots hairy when young, bearing obovate to ovate leaves 5-10cm long. Flowers in spring, solitary, pink, followed by large egg-shaped yellow fruits 5-18cm long, which in this country are rarely fully developed. China.

**†\*PSEUDOPANAX** K. KOCH—**Araliaceae**—A small genus of about 6 species of evergreens mainly from New Zealand, with remarkable leaves of variable form, often sword-shaped but varying depending on age of plant. Flowers small, greenish of little or no garden merit. Hardy in mild localities, and succeeding in all types of well drained soil. Some make useful house plants.

**arboreus** (L. f.) W.R. PHILIPSON (*Neopanax arboreum* (L. f.) ALLAN) (*Nothopanax arboreum* (L. f.) SEEM.) The New Zealand "Five Finger" makes a handsome large shrub in cultivation but often a small tree in its native habitat. The large, glossy green leaves are divided into 5-7 coarsely-toothed, stalked leaflets. Flowers in dense rounded clusters, replaced by decorative black fruits. Only suitable for the mildest areas. New Zealand. I 1820.

**crassifolius** (A. CUNN.) K. KOCH "Lancewood". A small, evergreen tree with leaves varying extraordinarily according to the age of the plant. In young unbranched specimens they are rigid and sharply-toothed, up to 0.6m long, 12mm wide, dark green with red mid-rib and purple under-surface. New Zealand. I 1846.

**davidii** (FRANCH.) W.R. PHILIPSON (*Nothopanax davidii* (FRANCH.) HARMS) A relatively hardy medium-sized to large, slow-growing shrub, with variable leaves, simple or divided into 2 or 3 lanceolate leaflets. The flower clusters are followed by black fruits. China.

**PSEUDOPANAX davidii**—*continued*

Introduced by E.H. Wilson in 1907. It does not fit well into this genus but is retained here until its position is clarified.

**ferox** (KIRK) KIRK "Toothed Lancewood". A small, slender-stemmed tree resembling *P. crassifolius* but leaves of juvenile and mature plants always simple. The leaves of young plants are pendent, greyish-green, with strongly hooked teeth. New Zealand.

**laetus** (KIRK) W.R. PHILIPSON (*P. daviesii* HORT.) (*Neopanax laetum* (KIRK) ALLAN) (*Nothopanax laetum* (KIRK) CHEESEM.) A very handsome species, related to but differing from *P. arboreus* in its much larger, drooping, three-lobed, glossy green leaves. New Zealand.

**lessonii** K. KOCH A small tree or large shrub with bright green, compound leaves composed of 3-5, coarsely-toothed or entire, leathery leaflets. New Zealand.

'**Gold Splash**' Leaves conspicuously blotched with yellow. A sport found on a cut stump of *P. lessonii* in New Plymouth, New Zealand about 1969.

'**Purpureus**' Foliage tinged with purple. Possibly a hybrid with *P. discolor*.

'**Trident**' A vigorous large shrub of upright habit. Leaves dark glossy green, varying from simple to three-lobed at the apex. Possibly a hybrid of *P. lessonii* with *P. crassifolius*.

†\***PSEUDOWINTERA** DANDY—**Winteraceae**—A small New Zealand genus of about 3 species related to *Drimys*. Not suitable for shallow chalk soils.

**colorata** (RAOUL) DANDY (*Drimys colorata* RAOUL) "Pepper Tree". A small to medium-sized shrub. Unusual in the colouring of its aromatic, oval, leathery leaves, which are pale yellow-green above, flushed pink, edged and blotched with dark crimson-purple, glaucous beneath. The small greenish-yellow flowers are borne in axillary clusters. Fruits dark red to black, rarely produced in the British Isles. Grows best in sheltered woodland conditions. AM 1975.

†**PSORALEA** L.—**Leguminosae**—A genus of 20 species of herbs and shrubs with usually compound leaves, natives of S Africa. The following species is only suitable for the very mildest areas, but makes an attractive conservatory shrub.

**pinnata** L. Medium-sized to large shrub with very beautiful pinnate leaves. Masses of lovely blue and white pea-flowers cluster the branches in May or June. S Africa. I 1690. AM 1903.

**PTELEA** L.—**Rutaceae**—A small genus of North American aromatic shrubs or small trees of which the "Hop-tree" (*P. trifoliata*) is the best-known. All possess gland-dotted, trifoliolate leaves and monoecious flowers. Suitable for all types of fertile soil.

**baldwinii** TORR. & GR. (*P. angustifolia* BENTH.) Large shrub related to *P. trifoliata*, but differing in its smaller leaves with narrow leaflets and its larger individual flowers. Florida. The cultivated plants under this name belong to var. *crenulata* from California.

**nitens** GREENE A rare species with lustrous leaves, strongly aromatic when crushed. SW United States. C 1912.

**polyadenia** GREENE A rare species akin to *P. trifoliata*. SW United States. I 1916.

**trifoliata** L. "Hop-tree". A low, spreading tree or large shrub. The corymbs of small, yellowish flowers open in June and are probably the most fragrant of any hardy tree, being equal to those of the best scented honeysuckle. They are followed by dense green clusters of persistent, winged, elm-like fruits. E North America, Mexico. I 1704.

'**Aurea**' Leaves soft yellow, contrasting well with purple and dark green-leaved shrubs. FCC 1980.

'**Fastigiata**' A form with erect branches. It has reached 8m in the Hillier Gardens and Arboretum.

**PTEROCARYA** KUNTH—**Juglandaceae**—The "Wing Nuts" are fast-growing, often wide-spreading trees of the walnut family, with handsome, pinnate leaves and monoecious catkin-like inflorescences. About 10 species in Asia, mainly China. The pith of the stems is characteristically chambered. They succeed in all types of fertile soil.

**caucasica** See *P. fraxinifolia*.

**fraxinifolia** (LAM.) SPACH (*P. caucasica* C.A. MEY.) A large, wide-spreading tree, occasionally forming large thickets of suckering stems, and usually with a short trunk and deeply

**PTEROCARYA fraxinifolia**—*continued*

furrowed bark. Leaves 0.3-0.6m long, composed of numerous, oblong, toothed leaflets. Flowers greenish, in pendulous catkins, the females up to 50cm long, draping the branches in summer. Fruits winged. A hardy, fast-growing tree, happiest in a moist, loamy soil, and particularly suitable for planting by lakes or rivers. Caucasus to N Iran. I 1782.

**var. dumosa** SCHNEID. A remarkable medium to large shrub, with smaller leaflets.

×**rehderiana** SCHNEID. (*P. fraxinifolia* × *P. stenoptera*). A large, suckering tree, raised in the Arnold Arboretum in 1879. In general, it is intermediate in character between its parents. The rachis of the leaf is winged but never so pronounced nor toothed as in *P. stenoptera*. It is a first class, hardy tree tolerant of all kinds of soils. The long drooping catkins which later support the fruits are an attractive feature for several months. A tree of 16m in the Hillier Gardens and Arboretum is less than 40 years old (1990).

**rhoifolia** SIEB. & ZUCC. "Japanese Wing Nut". A large, fast-growing tree with leaves about 30cm long, composed of 11-21 finely-toothed leaflets; female catkins 20-30cm long. Japan. I 1888.

**stenoptera** C. DC. (*P. sinensis* REHD.) A large, vigorous tree. Leaves 25-40cm long, the rachis prominently winged. Female catkins 20cm long; wings of fruit narrow and erect. China. I 1860.

**PTEROSTYRAX** SIEB. & ZUCC.—**Styracaceae**—A small genus of 4 species of interesting, large Asiatic shrubs or small trees, conspicuous in their halesia-like leaves and long panicles of small, interesting but not showy flowers. They succeed in all types of good deep soil, even over chalk, but cannot be recommended for poor, shallow, chalk soils.

**corymbosa** SIEB. & ZUCC. A rare, small tree or large spreading shrub with bristle-toothed, ovate leaves and nodding, corymbose panicles of fragrant, white flowers in May and June. Fruits obovoid, five-winged. China, Japan. I 1850.

**hispida** SIEB. & ZUCC. "Epaulette Tree". A large shrub or small tree with oval or obovate leaves. The fragrant, white flowers are borne in June and July in drooping panicles up to 23cm long, followed by spindle-shaped, five-ribbed fruits. Japan, China. I 1875. AM 1964.

†**PUNICA** L.—**Punicaceae**—A small genus of 2 species. The following is the only species in general cultivation.

**granatum** L. "Pomegranate". A large shrub, or small bushy tree, requiring a warm, sunny wall and good drainage in the southern counties. Leaves oblong, deep shining green, coppery when young, yellow in autumn. Flowers funnel-shaped, scarlet or orange-red with crumpled petals, late summer and early autumn. The familiar fruits require a long, hot summer in which to ripen. Naturalised in SE Europe it is spectacular when carrying its brilliant flowers. In the Mediterranean region it is often seen as a dense hedge. SW Asia. Long cultivated in S Europe.

**'Albopleno'** ('Multiplex') Flowers double, creamy-white. Young leaves green. C 1830.

**'Flore Pleno'** ('Rubroplena') A showy form with double, orange-red flowers.

**'Multiplex'** See 'Albopleno'.

**'Nana'** A charming dwarf form, with narrow leaves, plants of 15-23cm producing many orange-scarlet flowers in September and October. Suitable for a selected sunny site on the rock garden. C 1806. AM 1936.

\***PYRACANTHA** ROEM.—**Rosaceae**—The "Firethorns" are related to *Cotoneaster*, but are easily distinguished by their thorny branches and toothed leaves. They are frequently grown as wall shrubs, and will attain a height of 5m or more and, when grown as such, their long growths may be cut back immediately after flowering. They are equally effective, though less tall, grown as specimen shrubs. Their masses of hawthorn-like flowers are borne in early summer, and their red, orange or yellow fruits in autumn and winter. All are hardy, and include some of the best evergreen flowering and fruiting shrubs for north and east walls. They are tolerant of all exposures and pollution and will grow in all kinds of fertile soil. Susceptible to fireblight and canker, though some are more

**PYRACANTHA**—*continued*

resistant than others. In recent years a number of disease-resistant forms have been raised at the US National Arboretum, Washington, DC.

**angustifolia** (FRANCH.) SCHNEID. Medium-sized shrub, occasionally up to 4m high. Very distinct with its narrow, oblong leaves, grey-felted beneath, and conspicuous clusters of orange-yellow fruits which are retained throughout winter. W China. I 1899. FCC 1904.

**atalantioides** (HANCE) STAPF (*P. gibbsii* A.B. JACKS.) A large, robust shrub, occasionally a small tree, with large, oval, dark glossy green leaves. Flowers in May or early June. Fruits scarlet, long-lasting. Excellent on a sunless wall. A splendid species but unfortunately very susceptible to fireblight. China. Introduced by E.H. Wilson in 1907. FCC 1918. In 1967 a deliberate hybrid was made by our propagator Peter Dummer in which the flowers of *Photinia davidiana* were pollinated by pollen of *Pyracantha atalantioides*. It was named × *Pyravaesia* LANCASTER.

**'Aurea'** ('Flava') Fruits rich yellow. AM 1936.

**'Buttercup'** A hybrid of spreading habit with small fruits of a rich yellow.

**coccinea** ROEM. A large shrub with narrowly obovate or oval, finely-toothed leaves. Flowers, in downy corymbs, in June followed by rich red fruits in dense clusters all along the branches. S Europe, SW Asia. I 1629.

**'Lalandei'** Stronger-growing and more erect, with broader leaves and larger, orange-red fruits thickly covering the branches in autumn and winter. Raised in France in 1874 by Mons Lalande. Once the most popular variety but very susceptible to canker.

**crenato-serrata** (HANCE) REHD. (*P. yunnanensis* CHITT.) A large shrub related to *P. atalantioides*. The obovate to oblanceolate leaves, 2.5-8cm long have a broad, rounded apex with shallow, rounded teeth in their upper halves. Flowers in June, followed by innumerable clusters of small, red fruits which often persist until March. C and W China. I 1906.

**crenulata** (D. DON) ROEM. A variable species related to *P. coccinea*, differing in its blunt-tipped leaves, and its smaller flowers and fruits, which are orange-red. Himalaya. I about 1844. AM 1915.

**var. rogersiana** See *P. rogersiana*.

**'Fiery Cascade'** A medium-sized shrub of upright habit with small glossy leaves and profuse, small orange-red fruits, very hardy and disease-resistant.

**gibbsii** See *P. atalantioides*.

**'Golden Charmer'** (*P. coccinea* × *P. rogersiana*). A vigorous shrub with long, arching branches with finely-toothed, bright glossy green leaves. Large, globose, orange-yellow berries are profusely borne and ripen early. C 1960.

**'Golden Dome'** A splendid small shrub making a dense mound of arching branches. A mass of white flowers in June is followed by an equal abundance of small, deep yellow berries. Selected in our nursery before 1973.

**'Harlequin'** An unusual variegated form with pink-flushed leaves margined with cream. Best on a wall.

**koidzumii** (HAYATA) REHD. A rare species akin to *P. crenulata*, with oblanceolate leaves and loose clusters of red fruits. Taiwan.

**'Mohave'** (*P. coccinea* 'Wyatt' × *P. koidzumii*) A dense, medium-sized to large shrub with large, deep green leaves. Masses of bright orange-red, persistent berries ripen early. Very prone to scab. Raised at the US National Arboretum, Washington in 1963. FCC 1984. AGM 1984.

**'Monrovia'** Vigorous, upright habit with dark glossy green pointed leaves. Large orange-red fruits are profusely borne.

**'Navaho'** (a second-generation seedling of the cross *P. angustifolia* × *P.* 'Watereri') A small to medium-sized shrub of dense, spreading habit; leaves narrowly oblong-oblanceolate, to 6 × 1cm, entire apart from a few teeth at the apex. Berries late ripening, small but firm, distinctly flattened, orange becoming orange-red, in very dense clusters. Very resistant to fireblight. Raised at the US National Arboretum, Washington in 1966.

**'Orange Charmer'** A large shrub resembling 'Orange Glow' but fruits deeper orange and more flattened. C 1962.

**'Orange Glow'** A vigorous shrub of dense habit, its branches inundated each autumn with bright, orange-red fruits which last well into winter. Probably *P. coccinea* × *P. crenato-serrata*. AGM 1984.

**PYRACANTHA**—*continued*

**'Red Column'** A dense bushy shrub of upright habit with reddish shoots and ovate to broadly elliptic, sharply-toothed glossy green leaves. Dense clusters of scarlet fruits ripen early.

**'Renault d'Or'** A vigorous shrub with stout reddish-purple shoots and dark glossy green, broad elliptic-oblong leaves reddish when young. Bears dense clusters of clear yellow berries 11mm across.

**rogersiana** (A.B. JACKS.) CHITT. (*P. crenulata* var. *rogersiana* A.B. JACKS.) A large, free-fruiting shrub related to *P. crenulata*, but distinguished by its smaller, oblanceolate leaves and reddish-orange fruits. W China. I 1911. AGM 1937. AM 1953. AGM 1984.

  **'Flava'** Fruits bright yellow. FCC 1919. AGM 1984.

**'Rutgers'** A small, wide-spreading shrub with small, dark glossy green leaves and densely grey-hairy shoots. Profuse orange-red fruits.

**'Shawnee'** A densely-branched, spiny shrub of medium to large size, widely spreading at the base. The masses of white flowers are replaced by an equal abundance of yellow to light orange fruits which begin to colour as early as August. An American cultivar raised at the US National Arboretum as a second-generation seedling of the hybrid *P. crenato-serrata* × *P. koidzumii*. It is claimed by its raisers to be resistant to fireblight and scab. AGM 1984.

**'Soleil d'Or'** A medium-sized upright shrub with reddish stems and dark glossy green, broadly elliptic leaves. Golden yellow berries 1cm across are borne in large clusters. A sport of 'Morettii' raised in France in about 1970.

†**'Sparkler'** A very striking variegated form, the leaves heavily mottled with white, pink-tinged in autumn and winter. Unfortunately tender and best under glass.

**'Teton'** (*P.* 'Orange Glow' × *P. rogersiana* 'Flava'). A large shrub of vigorous, upright habit with reddish shoots and small, bright glossy green, wavy-edged leaves. Berries small, yellow-orange, profusely borne. Very resistant to fireblight. Raised at the US National Arboretum, Washington in 1963.

**'Victory'** A vigorous shrub with arching branches and red often sparsely spiny shoots. Leaves bronze when young, obovate to oblanceolate, sometimes narrowly so, usually truncate to emarginate and mucronate at the apex, rich glossy green, to 6.5 × 1.7cm, entire or sparsely-toothed above the middle. Berries large, distinctly flattened, in large dense clusters, pinkish-red becoming scarlet.

**'Watereri'** (*P. atalantioides* × *P. rogersiana*). A very free-fruiting hybrid of compact growth, smothered annually with clusters of white flowers, followed by bright red fruits. Garden origin. AM 1955. AGM 1969. AGM 1984.

**'Waterer's Orange'** A strong-growing, free-fruiting shrub with orange-yellow fruits. AM 1959.

**yunnanensis** See *P. crenato-serrata*.

× **PYRACOMELES** REHD. (*Pyracantha* × *Osteomeles*)—**Rosaceae**—A remarkable intergeneric hybrid, succeeding in all types of fertile soil. Tolerant of maritime exposure and air pollution.

  **vilmorinii** REHD. (*P. crenato-serrata* × *O. subrotunda*). A small, semi-evergreen shrub with slender, thornless branches. Leaves 2-3cm long, pinnate in the lower half, pinnatisect in the upper half. Flowers 1cm across, white in corymbs in May, followed by small, coral-red fruits. Garden origin in France before 1922.

× **PYRAVAESIA** LANCASTER See under *Pyracantha atalantioides*.

+ **PYROCYDONIA** WINKL. ex DANIEL (+ *Pirocydonia*) (*Pyrus* + *Cydonia*)—**Rosaceae**—Interesting graft hybrids (chimaeras) between pear and quince.

  **danielii** WINKL. ex DANIEL (*Cydonia oblonga* + *Pyrus communis* 'Williams' Bon Chretien'). A remarkable quince-like tree or shrub with ovate, downy leaves and white flowers which are succeeded by large, apple-like fruits which are brown with paler spotting. First recorded in 1902 at the junction of a pear grafted onto a quince in a garden at Rennes in France.

×**PYRONIA** VEITCH (*Cydonia* × *Pyrus*)—**Rosaceae**—A remarkable intergeneric hybrid intermediate between a quince and a pear and succeeding in all types of fertile soil. Tolerant of polluted atmosphere.

**veitchii** GUILL. (*C. oblonga* × *P. communis*). A large shrub or small tree with oval, entire leaves. Flowers white, nearly 5cm across, borne usually 3 together at the tips of branchlets; anthers violet. Fruit ellipsoid, 8cm long, greenish-yellow, spotted red. Raised by John Seden of Messrs Veitch about 1895. This, the original form, should be given the cultivar name 'John Seden' to distinguish it from later forms.

**'Luxemburgiana'** Leaves larger. Flowers about 4cm across, pale rose. Fruits resembling small pears. Probably raised by Veitch.

**PYRUS** L.—**Rosaceae**—The "Pears" are a genus of about 20 species of mainly deciduous trees and shrubs, natives of temperate regions of the Old World. The ornamental pears are small to medium-sized, deep-rooted trees with green to silvery-grey leaves, and white flowers in April. They are quite tolerant both of drought and moisture, and are excellently suited for cold areas. They are also tolerant of smoke pollution and succeed in all types of fertile soil.

**amygdaliformis** VILL. A rare and quaint species from the northern shores of the Mediterranean. A large shrub or small tree with occasionally spiny branches. Leaves narrow, shallowly-toothed or entire, at first silvery, becoming sage-green. Fruits small, globose, yellow-brown. I 1810.

**var. cuneifolia** (GUSS.) BEAN A form with smaller, narrower leaves.

**betulifolia** BUNGE A graceful, slender, small tree of rapid growth. Leaves ovate or rounded, with a slender point, strongly toothed, greyish-green at first, becoming green and glossy above. Fruits small, the size of a large pea, brown. N China. I 1882.

**calleryana** DECNE Medium-sized tree with normally thorny branches and oval or broadly ovate, finely-toothed, glossy green, long-persistent leaves. Fruits small, like large brown peas, on slender stalks. China. I 1908 by Ernest Wilson.

**'Bradford'** A selected, non-thorny seedling, raised at the Plant Introduction Station, Glenn Dale, Maryland (United States) from seed collected in China in 1918. It forms a vigorous, medium-sized, dense-headed tree, flowering profusely in late March or early April, and in suitable conditions the leaves colour attractively in autumn. Highly praised as an ornamental in the United States and commonly planted as a street tree. The original tree was over 15m high and 9m across after forty-four years.

**'Chanticleer'** A selection made in the United States by Edward Scanlon. It is similar to 'Bradford' but much narrower and is proving to be an excellent street tree. AGM 1984. Other more recent selections from North America include 'Autumn Blaze', 'Redspire' and 'Trinity'.

×**canescens** SPACH (*P. nivalis* × *P. salicifolia*). A small tree attractive when in flower. Leaves lanceolate or narrowly oval, finely-toothed, greyish-white, downy when young, eventually becoming green and glossy above. Fruits small, roundish, pale green. A most attractive silvery foliage tree.

**communis** L. The common or garden pear. A medium-sized tree with oval or rounded, glossy green leaves which often give rich autumn tints. The branches in April are smothered with blossom, to be followed by sweet-tasting pears. Long cultivated and said to be a hybrid of multiple parentage. Over a thousand cultivars are known.

**'Beech Hill'** A narrow tree with upright branches. The glossy green leaves often turn to brilliant orange-yellow in autumn.

**cossonii** REHD. (*P. longipes* COSS. & DURIEU) A small tree or large shrub with rounded or ovate, finely-toothed leaves which are glossy green above. Small, rounded, brown fruits. Algeria. I before 1875.

**elaeagnifolia** PALL. A small tree or large shrub with erect, thorny branches and narrow, greyish leaves. Flowers over 2.5cm across, followed by small, rounded or top-shaped fruits. A most attractive grey foliage tree. SE Europe. I 1800.

×**lecontei** REHD. (*P. communis* × *P. pyrifolia*). A small tree with glossy green, finely-toothed leaves and yellow fruits. Rich autumn colour. The cultivars 'Kieffer' and 'Le Conte' originated from this cross. Originated before 1850.

**PYRUS**—*continued*

**longipes** See *P. cossonii.*

× **michauxii** POIR. (*P. amygdaliformis* × *P. nivalis*). A small, round-headed tree with entire, ovate or oval, greyish leaves which later become glossy-green above. Fruits rounded or top-shaped, greenish-yellow, spotted brown.

**nivalis** JACQ. A small tree with stout, ascending branches, most conspicuous in April when the pure white flowers are abundantly produced simultaneously with the white-woolly young leaves. Leaves oval or obovate, entire. Fruits small, rounded, yellowish-green, becoming sweet when over-ripe. A most attractive silvery foliage tree. S Europe. I 1800.

**pashia** D. DON A small, round-headed tree with ovate, finely-toothed leaves sometimes three-lobed on vigorous shoots. Flowers pink-flushed in bud opening white with red anthers. Rounded fruits 2-2.5cm across, brown with paler speckles. Himalaya, W China. I 1825.

**pyraster** (L.) BURGSD. (*P. communis* var. *pyraster* L.) "Wild Pear". A small to medium-sized tree with occasionally thorny branches. Leaves ovate or rounded, crenulate-serrulate, glossy green above. Fruits small, globose or pear-shaped, yellow or brown. The wild counterpart of *P. communis*. Europe, W Asia, doubtfully wild in the British Isles.

**pyrifolia** (BURM. f.) NAKAI (*P. serotina* REHD.) "Sand Pear". A small to medium-sized tree. Leaves ovate-oblong, toothed, glossy green above, 8-12cm long, often giving rich autumn colour. Fruits small, rounded, brown. China. I 1908 by Ernest Wilson.

**var. culta** (MAK.) NAKAI A form with larger leaves and much larger fruits which are hard and gritty. Long cultivated in China and Japan. I 1880.

**salicifolia** PALL. "Willow-leaved Pear". A graceful, small, often weeping tree with silvery, narrow, willow-like leaves eventually becoming greyish-green and shining above. Flowers creamy-white. Fruits small, top-shaped, brown. Caucasus. I 1780.

**'Pendula'** A very elegant and attractive silvery-grey tree with weeping branches. This is the form in general cultivation. AGM 1984.

**syriaca** BOISS. A small, round-headed tree with usually thorny branches. Leaves oblong-lanceolate, finely-toothed, glossy green. Fruits small, globular or top-shaped. SW Asia, Cyprus. I before 1874.

**ussuriensis** MAXIM. A vigorous small to medium-sized tree with ovate or rounded, bristle-toothed leaves, turning bronze-crimson in autumn. The most important of the wild Chinese pears, and one of the earliest in flower. Fruits small, yellow-green. NE Asia. I 1855.


**QUERCUS** L.—**Fagaceae**—The "Oaks" make up a large genus of some 600 species of deciduous and evergreen trees, or occasionally shrubs, widely distributed in the N hemisphere and extending from cold temperate to tropical regions. 2 species are native to the British Isles and are valued for their timber. Many reach noble proportions and live to a great age. Several species possess large or attractively-cut leaves and quite a few give rich autumn tints. Oaks are monoecious, the drooping male catkins appearing with the leaves in spring. They thrive in deep, rich soils and, apart from the North American Red and White Oaks, are mostly lime-tolerant, given a deep soil over chalk, but very few succeed on a shallow chalk soil. One may judge the quality and depth of soil by the rate of growth and ultimate size of our native oaks.

This genus was one in which the late Sir Harold Hillier particularly interested himself. During the 1970s and early 1980s, in his travels to many parts of the world he brought back seed of numerous species. Plants grown from this seed now form part of the National Collection of oaks at the Hillier Gardens and Arboretum.

‡\***acuta** THUNB. (*Q. laevigata* BLUME) A small, slow-growing evergreen tree or large bushy shrub. Leaves leathery, elliptic, slender-pointed, glossy, dark green above. Most attractive when the bright, green, young leaves emerge in late spring and early summer. Japan. I about 1878.

**acutissima** CARRUTH. (Cerris Section) (*Q. serrata* SIEB. & ZUCC.) Medium-sized, free-growing tree with narrowly oblong, chestnut-like, bright, polished green leaves which persist into winter, margined with bristle-tipped teeth. They are downy at first, becoming glabrous above and glabrate beneath, with axillary tufts of hairs. Japan, Korea, China. I 1862 by Richard Oldham.

**QUERCUS acutissima**—*continued*

    **subsp. chenii** (NAKAI) CAMUS A Chinese variety with obovate, glossy green leaves. Late-made, unripened growth is subject to frost damage in cold areas. Not satisfactory on shallow chalk soils.

    **aegilops** See *Q. macrolepis*.

    **\*agrifolia** NEE A small, round-headed, evergreen tree or large shrub occasionally reaching 12m, with smooth, black bark becoming rough and squared with age. Leaves oval or rounded, shortly-stalked, 2.5-5cm long, hard in texture, armed with spine-tipped, marginal teeth; smooth, shiny green above, glabrous except for axillary tufts of hair beneath. Acorns sessile, cone-shaped, 2.5cm long. California, Mexico. Introduced by Hartweg, in 1849.

    **‡alba** L. (Prinus Section) "White Oak". In the British Isles, generally a medium-sized tree with obovate, deeply and irregularly lobed, soft-green leaves, reddish when unfolding, turning purple-crimson in autumn. SE Canada, E United States. I 1724.

    **var. repanda** MICHX. Leaves with broad, shallow lobes.

    **aliena** BLUME (Prinus Section) A small tree with large, obovate to oblong-lanceolate, coarsely-toothed leaves, 15-20cm long, shining dark green above, paler and pubescent beneath. Japan. I 1908.

    **var. acuteserrata** MAXIM. A form with smaller, narrower leaves with gland-tipped teeth. C China, Korea, Taiwan, Japan. I 1905.

    **\*alnifolia** POECH (Suber Section) "Golden Oak of Cyprus". A rare and interesting, slow-growing, medium to large shrub in cultivation. Leaves rounded or broad obovate, hard in texture, hooded at apex, dark glossy green above and yellow-felted beneath. Hardy in sheltered gardens in the Home Counties. Cyprus. I 1815. AM 1989.

    **ambrozyana** See *Q. × hispanica* 'Ambrozyana'.

    **aquatica** See *Q. nigra*.

    **†arizonica** SARG. A large shrub or small tree in cultivation. Leaves long persistent, obovate to oblong-lanceolate, shortly spine-toothed, 5-10cm long. S Central United States, N Mexico.

    **‡bicolor** WILLD. (Prinus Section) A medium-sized tree, with characteristic flaking bark, particularly noticeable on young specimens. Leaves obovate, 13-18cm long, shallowly-lobed, polished green above, thinly whitish or greyish-felted beneath, or sometimes only inconspicuously pubescent. SE Canada, E United States. I 1800.

    **borealis var. maxima** See *Q. rubra*.

‡ × **bushii** SARG. (*Q. marilandica* × *Q. velutina*). Medium-sized tree with leaves intermediate in character between those of the parents, generally obovate and strongly three to seven-lobed, glossy green above, clothed with a pale yellowish pubescence beneath. E United States.

    **canariensis** WILLD. (Robur Section) (*Q. mirbeckii* DURIEU) "Algerian Oak". A handsome, large tree with very dark grey, deeply fissured bark and a dense rounded head of branches; much narrower as a young tree. The large, obovate or oval, shallowly-lobed leaves are dark shining green above, paler or slightly glaucous beneath and remain on the tree until the New Year. An excellent fast-growing tree succeeding equally well on heavy clay or shallow chalky soil, easily recognised in winter by its bold, persistent foliage. N Africa, S Portugal, Spain. I about 1845.

    **canariensis × robur** A fast-growing tree, intermediate in character between the parents, leaves never as large as in *Q. canariensis*. When home-grown seed of *Q. canariensis* is raised, the progeny is almost invariably this hybrid.

    **castaneifolia** C.A. MEY. (Cerris Section) "Chestnut-leaved Oak". A magnificent medium-sized to large tree resembling the Turkey Oak in general appearance. Leaves oblong or narrowly oval, tapered at both ends and margined with coarse, triangular, sharply-pointed teeth, shining dark green above, minutely greyish pubescent beneath. Caucasus, Iran. I 1846.

    **'Green Spire'** A broadly columnar form of compact habit, raised in our nurseries in about 1948. A vigorous, tall tree.

    **castaneifolia × macranthera** (A. & L. 25) This seems to be the parentage of plants grown from seed of *Q. castaneifolia* collected in N Iran by Mrs Ala and Roy Lancaster. A vigorous tree with downy shoots, terminal buds with slender stipules. Leaves obovate,

**QUERCUS castaneifolia** × **macranthera**—*continued*

to 20cm long, 9cm across, dark green above, paler and glossy beneath, with up to 10, broadly triangular, mucronate lobes on each side. It has reached 9m in the Hillier Gardens and Arboretum (1990).

**cerris** L. "Turkey Oak". A large tree and possibly the fastest-growing oak in this country. Excellent in chalky soils and in maritime exposure. Leaves oval or oblong; coarsely-toothed or shallowly-lobed, covered with stellate hairs and slightly rough to the touch. Both the winter buds and the acorn cups are furnished with long, narrow, downy scales. The leaves of sucker shoots and vigorous growths are often variable in size and shape. S Europe, Asia Minor. I 1735. AGM 1984.

**var. ambrozyana** See *Q.* × *hispanica* 'Ambrozyana'.

**'Laciniata'** Leaves pinnatisect, with narrow, spreading, mucronate lobes.

**'Variegata'** Leaves with a conspicuous, creamy-white margin. A most effective variegated tree.

**\*chrysolepis** LIEBM. "Californian Live Oak" "Maul Oak". A variable, small, slow-growing evergreen tree or large shrub. Leaves oval or ovate, spine-toothed, often entire on mature trees, resembling those of *Q. coccifera*, but normally larger and greyish or yellowish downy and minutely gland-dotted beneath, becoming sub-glabrous during the second year. SW United States, Mexico. I 1877 by Charles Sargent.

**var. vacciniifolia** See *Q. vacciniifolia*.

**\*coccifera** L. (Suber Section) "Kermes Oak". A very slow-growing, dense evergreen shrub 2m or more high. The polished, green leaves are very variable and may be small and prickly or flat and nearly smooth. This is the host plant to the Kermes insect, from which is obtained cochineal, a once common scarlet dye. A splendid backcloth for the rock garden. In the south of France it may frequently be seen growing in stony arid ground in company with scrubby *Quercus ilex, Phillyrea angustifolia, Juniperus oxycedrus* and *J. phoenicea*. Mediterranean region, Portugal. Cultivated in England since 17th century.

**subsp. calliprinos** (WEBB) HOLMBOE "Palestine Oak". A form with larger leaves making a medium to large tree in the wild. E Mediterranean region.

**‡coccinea** MUENCHH. "Scarlet Oak". A large tree with attractive, broad, deeply-lobed leaves, each lobe furnished with several bristle-tipped teeth; glossy dark green above during summer, turning in autumn, branch by branch, to a glowing scarlet. Some leaves persist on a few lower branches until Christmas. One of the finest trees for autumn colour, but variable in this respect. SE Canada, E United States. I 1691.

**'Splendens'** A selected form vegetatively propagated. Leaves rich scarlet in autumn. FCC 1893. AGM 1984.

**conferta** See *Q. frainetto*.

**cuspidata** See *Castanopsis cuspidata*.

**densiflora** See *Lithocarpus densiflorus*.

**‡dentata** THUNB. (Prinus Section) (*Q. daimio* K. KOCH) "Daimio Oak". A rare species generally making a small, angular tree or large irregular shrub in the British Isles. Remarkable for its stout shoots and very large, obovate, broadly-lobed leaves which are occasionally over 30cm long and 18cm wide. Japan, Korea, China. I 1830. AM 1901.

**'Pinnatifida'** A rare and striking but very slow-growing form in which the leaves are deeply cut into narrow lobes. C 1879.

**douglasii** HOOK. & ARN. "Blue Oak". A small, Californian tree or large shrub with oblong, occasionally lobed leaves which are sea-green above, paler beneath.

**\*dumosa** NUTT. "Californian Scrub Oak". An evergreen, intricately-branched shrub, with slender stems and tiny, dark green, oblong or rounded, spiny leaves. California, Mexico.

**‡ellipsoidalis** E.J. HILL. A medium-sized to large tree, related to *Q. palustris*, usually with a short trunk and spreading head. The deeply-lobed leaves, on slender petioles, turn deep crimson-purple in autumn, equal to the best forms of *Q. coccinea*. C North America. I 1902.

**faginea** LAM. (*Q. lusitanica* AUCT. not LAM.) "Portuguese Oak". Usually a small, broad-headed tree. Leaves varying from oval to obovate, strongly-toothed and grey-felted beneath. Excellent on all soil types including chalk. Portugal, Spain. I 1824.

**QUERCUS**—*continued*

**frainetto** TEN. (Robur Section) (*Q. conferta* KIT.) (*Q. farnetto* TEN.) (*Q. pannonica* BOOTH ex GORD.) "Hungarian Oak". A magnificent, large, fast-growing tree with fissured bark and wide-spreading, often slightly drooping branches. Leaves obovate, occasionally as much as 20cm long, deeply and regularly-lobed with large oblong lobes. This fine species ought to be more widely planted. For all types of soil including chalk soils, this exotic species, together with *Q. cerris* and *Q. canariensis* is equal to, or even superior in rate of growth to, our 2 native species. SE Europe. I 1838.

**'Hungarian Crown'** We propose this name here for the tree widely grown in Britain and on the Continent as *Q. frainetto*. A splendid, vigorous tree with upright branches making a broadly oval head.

**fruticosa** See *Q. lusitanica*.

**fulhamensis** See *Q.* × *hispanica* 'Fulhamensis'.

**gambelii** NUTT. (Prinus Section) "Shin Oak". A small tree or large shrub with leathery, obovate, deeply-lobed, glossy leaves. SW United States, N Mexico. I 1894.

× **ganderi** C. WOLF (*Q. agrifolia* var. *oxyadenia* × *Q. kelloggii*). A small semi-evergreen tree with leathery, obovate, shallowly and irregularly-lobed leaves with bristle-tipped teeth. California (San Diego Co).

**garryana** HOOK. (Prinus Section) "Oregon Oak". A medium-sized tree in the British Isles with a short, stout trunk and wide-spreading head. Leaves shining green, obovate, deeply cut into oblong lobes. W North America. I 1873.

**glandulifera** BLUME (Prinus Section) (*Q. serrata* THUNB.) A small, slow-growing tree. Leaves variable, oblong-obovate to ovate-lanceolate, up to 18cm long, margined with gland-tipped teeth, bright apple-green above, greyish-white beneath, remaining late in the year. Japan, Korea, China. I 1893 by Charles Sargent.

‡***glauca** THUNB. A rare, small, evergreen tree or more usually a large, bushy shrub with stout, leafy branches. Leaves bronze when young, leathery, elliptic to obovate-oblong with an abrupt point and usually several teeth, glossy green above, glaucous beneath. Japan, Taiwan, China, Himalaya. I 1804.

‡**grisea** LIEBM. "Grey Oak". A variable species in the wild ranging from a shrub to a medium-sized tree. Twigs densely grey-hairy. Leaves leathery, grey-green and softly downy on both sides, oblong, to 5cm long with a few small teeth, persisting well into winter. A specimen in the Hillier Gardens and Arboretum has reached 4m (1990). SW United States, N Mexico.

**grosseserrata** See *Q. mongolica* var. *grosseserrata*.

**haas** See *Q. pedunculiflora*.

‡ × **heterophylla** MICHX. f. (*Q. phellos* × *Q. rubra*). A medium-sized to large tree with oblong or oval leaves varying from entire to strongly-toothed, glabrous except for axillary tufts beneath. Occurring with the parents in the wild. C 1822.

‡***hinckleyi** C.H. MULLER A very rare evergreen shrub, in the wild forming low thickets. Leaves glaucous, very rigid and short-stalked with 2-3 sharp spines on each side, often auricled at the base. Found only near Solitario Peak in SW Texas.

× **hispanica** LAM. (*Q. cerris* × *Q. suber*). A variable hybrid between the Cork Oak and the Turkey Oak but always a magnificent tree and sometimes nearly evergreen, occurring with the parents in the wild in S Europe. The same hybrid has also arisen a number of times in cultivation. All are hardy, semi-evergreen trees of medium to large size, inheriting some of the Turkey Oak's vigour. The bark is thick and fissured, but never as corky as that of the Cork Oak. A very lime-tolerant tree.

**'Ambrozyana'** (*Q. cerris* var. *ambrozyana* (SIMONKAI) ASCHERS. & GRAEBN.) A distinct and attractive semi-evergreen tree differing from the Turkey Oak in its darker leaves which are white beneath and remain on the tree until the following spring. When established, unless in a very exposed position or in an extremely severe winter, this tree remains evergreen. The original tree grows in Mlynany Arboretum, Czechoslovakia, the home of the late Count Ambrozy. When we visited this splendid arboretum under the guidance of the distinguished Director Bencat and his charming interpreter Dr F. Botka we were shown this tree as well as many other exciting plants. C 1909.

**'Crispa'** Originated in 1792 as a seedling of 'Lucombeana', a shorter-stemmed tree with a low, broad crown and dark grey, corky bark with deep, wide fissures. The leaves are

**QUERCUS × hispanica 'Crispa'**—*continued*

variously shaped, but in general are shorter and remain dark green on the tree until spring, except in the hardest winters.

**'Fulhamensis'** (*Q. fulhamensis* ZAB.) "Fulham Oak". A large tree with grey, corky bark and a dense head of drooping branchlets. Leaves grey beneath, coarsely-toothed. Raised at Osborne's nursery at Fulham about 1760. Sometimes incorrectly known as 'Dentata'.

**'Lucombeana'** (*Q. lucombeana* SWEET) "Lucombe Oak". A large, ornamental tree raised by Mr Lucombe in his nursery in Exeter about 1762. The original form is a tall-stemmed tree resembling *Q. cerris*, with pale grey, shallowly-fissured bark and long leaves which mostly fall around the New Year.

× **hybrida** See *Q. × rosacea*.

**hypoleuca** See *Q. hypoleucoides*.

**\*hypoleucoides** CAMUS (*Q. hypoleuca* ENGELM.) A very rare and remarkable small tree with grey tomentose branches. Leaves thick and leathery, narrowly oblong to lanceolate, 5-8cm long, grey, downy beneath. It has attained 9m in the Hillier Gardens and Arboretum. SW United States, N Mexico

**\*ilex** L. "Evergreen Oak" "Holm Oak". A large tree with attractive corrugated bark and a rounded head of branches, the ends of which become pendulous with age. Leaves leathery, dark glossy green above, greyish downy beneath or glabrous, entire or toothed, variable both in shape and size depending on age of tree and growing conditions. Leaves on young bushy specimens in shade are often completely green and glabrous. Thrives in all classes of well drained soil, and is particularly valuable for coastal planting, but is not recommended for the very coldest inland areas. Responds well to clipping and tolerates shade.

Excepting certain conifers, this is probably the most majestic evergreen tree cultivated in the British Isles. A large tree with its lush piles of dark green foliage is a striking sight, particularly in June when the tawny or white woolly young shoots and pendulous, yellow catkins are emerging. There can be few species which exhibit such an extraordinary variation in shape, size and texture of leaf. The Evergreen Oak will make a magnificent rigid hedge resistant to sea winds. Mediterranean region, SW Europe. Cultivated in England since the 16th century. AGM 1984.

**'Bicton'** A form with large, broad leaves. There is a remarkable old specimen at Bicton, S Devon.

**'Fordii'** ('Angustifolia') A distinct small-leaf form of dense, broadly conical habit. Leaves narrow, 2.5-4cm long, and 8-12mm wide. Raised at Exeter before 1843.

‡**ilicifolia** WANGH. "Bear Oak". A spreading shrub or small tree rarely exceeding 5m, with obovate, deeply-lobed leaves that are white-felted beneath, and persist into early winter. Young growths attractively pink-flushed. E United States. I about 1800.

‡**imbricaria** MICHX. "Shingle Oak". A medium-sized tree, occasionally reaching 20m. Leaves oblong or narrowly oval, 10-18cm long, usually entire, shining dark green, displaying rich autumn colours. The English name refers to the use of the wood by early settlers for shingles on roofs. E United States. Introduced by John Fraser in 1786.

**incana** ROXB. See *Q. leucotrichophora*.

**infectoria** OLIVIER A large, semi-evergreen shrub or small tree, closely related to *Q. lusitanica* from which it differs chiefly in its glabrous or nearly glabrous, spine-toothed leaves and branches. SW Asia, Cyprus, Greece. I 1850.

**ithaburensis** DECNE. (*Q. aegilops* var. *pyrami* (KOTSCHY) BOISS.) A small tree of neat habit with rugged bark and deeply cut, often fiddle-shaped leaves. SW Asia.

‡**kelloggii** NEWB. "Californian Black Oak". A medium-sized to large tree with deeply-lobed, bristle-toothed, shining green leaves. California and Oregon. C 1873.

\* × **kewensis** OSBORN (*Q. cerris* × *Q. wislizeni*). A small to medium-sized, vigorous tree, with dense compact head and almost persistent, small dark green, angularly-lobed leaves. Raised at Kew in 1914.

‡**laurifolia** MICHX. "Laurel Oak". Medium-sized, semi-evergreen tree of dense, rounded habit. Leaves glossy green, oblong or oblong-obovate, entire or occasionally shallowly-lobed. Differing from the closely related *Q. nigra* in its narrower, less obovate and usually longer leaves. E United States. I 1786.

**QUERCUS**—*continued*

‡× **leana** NUTT. (*Q. imbricaria* × *Q. velutina*). A medium-sized to large tree with oblong, entire or occasionally lobed leaves 10-18cm long, firm and leathery in texture. Occurring with the parents in the wild. C 1850.

†\***leucotrichophora** CAMUS (*Q. incana* ROXB. not BARTR.) A very striking, small evergreen tree or large shrub for the mildest areas. Leaves narrowly oval, slender-pointed and conspicuously toothed, dark green above, white-felted beneath. It attains a large size in the Himalaya where it is accompanied by *Rhododendron arboreum*. Large, old specimens are said to have attractive flaking bark. I about 1815.

**libani** OLIVIER (Cerris Section) "Lebanon Oak". A small, elegant tree with slender branches and long, persistent, oblong-lanceolate leaves which are glossy green above and margined with triangular, bristle-tipped teeth. Closely related to *Q. trojana*. Syria, Asia Minor. I about 1855.

**lobata** NEE "Valley Oak". A slow-growing, small to medium-sized tree in the British Isles. Leaves elliptic to obovate, with broad, rounded lobes, dark green above, pale downy beneath. California. I 1874.

**lucombeana** See *Q.* × *hispanica* 'Lucombeana'.

‡× **ludoviciana** SARG. (*Q. falcata* var. *pagodifolia* × *Q. phellos*). A most attractive, large, semi-evergreen tree of vigorous habit. Leaves obovate to oblanceolate, usually deeply and irregularly-lobed, shining green above. Rich autumn tints. Occurs with the parents in SE United States. I 1880.

**lusitanica** LAM. (*Q. fruticosa* BROT.) A small to medium-sized semi-evergreen shrub. Leaves leathery, obovate-oblong with mucronate teeth. A scrub oak in Portugal, SW Spain and N Africa. I about 1829. This name has been incorrectly applied to *Q. faginea*.

**macedonica** See *Q. trojana*.

**'Macon'** (*Q. frainetto* × *Q. macranthera*). A vigorous, medium-sized to large tree with stout hairy shoots. Leaves obovate, deeply-lobed, up to 17cm long, tomentose beneath on stout, hairy petioles. Raised by J.R.P. van Hoey-Smith.

**macranthera** FISCH. & MEY. (Robur Section) A splendid, fast-growing tree of medium size, striking on account of its large, broad-obovate, acute, strongly-lobed leaves up to 15cm long. It is easily distinguished from related species by its stout twigs which, like the slender-scaled winter buds and leaf under-surfaces, are clothed with pale grey velvety tomentum. An excellent tree, which may be grown in deep soils over chalk. Often hybridises with *Q. robur* in cultivation. Caucasus, N Iran. I 1873.

‡**macrocarpa** MICHX. (Prinus Section) "Burr Oak" "Mossy-Cup Oak". A remarkable and handsome North American species of medium size. On vigorous young trees the conspicuously-lobed, obovate leaves are sometimes up to 40cm long. Young shoots, buds and under-surfaces of leaves covered by a pale down. Not a tree for the plantsman who wants a perfect specimen with a gun-barrel-like stem. NE and NC North America. I 1811.

**macrolepis** KOTSCHY (Cerris Section) (*Q. aegilops* L.) "Valonia Oak". A small to medium-sized tree with grey tomentose twigs. Leaves somewhat greyish-olive-green, oblong, sharply-lobed, the lobes bristle-tipped and occasionally toothed, grey tomentose beneath. The acorns, ripening the second year, are set in large cups with reflexed, slender scales. S Balkans, SE Italy, W Asia. I 1731.

**var. pyrami** See *Q. ithaburensis*.

‡**marilandica** MUENCHH. "Black Jack Oak". A remarkable, small, slow-growing tree of low, spreading habit. Leaves sometimes almost triangular, broadly obovate, tapered to the base, more or less three-lobed at the broad apex, up to 18cm long and often as much across, glossy green above, tawny-yellow beneath, turning yellow or brown in autumn. E United States. C 1739.

‡**michauxii** NUTT. (Prinus Section) (*Q. prinus* L. in part) "Swamp Chestnut Oak" "Basket Oak". A medium to large round-headed tree with obovate, coarsely-toothed, bright green leaves. Rich yellow autumn colour. E United States. I 1737.

**mirbeckii** See *Q. canariensis*.

‡**mongolica** FISCH. (Prinus Section) "Mongolian Oak". A striking, irregular, small to medium-sized tree with thick glabrous branches. Leaves large, shortly-stalked, obovate to obovate-

**QUERCUS mongolica**—*continued*

oblong, strongly lobed, auricled at the base, borne in dense clusters at the ends of the branches. Japan, Manchuria, Korea, Mongolia, E Siberia. I 1879.

**var. grosseserrata** (BLUME) REHD. & WILS. (*Q. grosseserrata* BLUME) A form with usually narrowly obovate, pointed leaves with rather acute, forward-pointing teeth. Japan.

**montana** See *Q. prinus*.

‡**muhlenbergii** ENGELM. "Chinquapin Oak" "Yellow Chestnut Oak". Medium-sized tree with oblong to oblong-lanceolate, coarsely-toothed leaves, yellowish-green above, pale pubescent beneath, mid-rib and petioles yellow. Rich autumn tints. North America, N Mexico. I 1822.

‡*myrsinifolia BLUME (*Q. bambusifolia* FORT. not HANCE) (*Q. vibrayeana* FRANCH. & SAV.) A small, and very hardy, densely-branched evergreen tree of compact habit. The smooth, somewhat shining leaves are lanceolate with finely tapered points, remotely-toothed, dark green above, paler beneath, purple-red when unfolding. China, Japan. Introduced by Robert Fortune in 1854.

†*myrtifolia WILLD. An evergreen or semi-evergreen shrub or small tree. Leaves up to 5cm long, rigid, glossy bright green above, usually entire or with a few short spines. This interesting species has proved hardy in a sheltered position. SE United States.

‡**nigra** L. (*Q. aquatica* WALT.) "Water Oak". A medium-sized tree, native of the S United States, where it frequents moist areas. Leaves normally obovate, occasionally oblong, variously lobed, particularly on young plants, sometimes entire, glossy, deep rich green on both sides, often persisting into early winter. I 1723.

‡**palustris** MUENCHH. "Pin Oak". A free-growing, large, dense-headed tree resembling *Q. coccinea*, but more elegant with the slender branches drooping gracefully at their extremities. Leaves deeply and sharply-lobed, shining green on both surfaces and with conspicuous tufts of down in the axils below. They are smaller than those of the "Scarlet Oak", but often turn the same rich scarlet in autumn. SE Canada, E United States. I 1800. AGM 1984.

**pedunculata** See *Q. robur*.

**pedunculiflora** (C. KOCH) SCHWARZ (*Q. haas* KOTSCHY) A rare, medium-sized to large tree related to and resembling *Q. robur*, but leaves somewhat glaucous-green above and pubescent beneath. SE Europe.

**petraea** (MATTUSCHKA) LIEBL. (Robur Section) (*Q. sessiliflora* SALISB.) "Sessile Oak" "Durmast Oak". One of our 2 large native species replacing the "Common Oak" (*Q. robur*) in many damper districts or soils, notably in the west. It is distinguished by its often rather larger, long-stalked leaves which are usually pubescent beneath along the midrib, and cuneate, not auricled at the base; also in its sessile fruits. Good for maritime exposure. W, C and SE Europe, Asia Minor.

'Acutifolia' Leaves with pronounced and regular lobes.

'Columna' A densely-branched, columnar tree of medium size. A sport of 'Mespilifolia'.

'Insecata' ('Laciniata') Leaves up to 15cm long, narrow, deeply incised with forward-pointing lobes, occasionally reduced almost to the midrib. This strange form has also been grown as 'Laciniata Crispa'.

'Laciniata' See 'Insecata'.

'Mespilifolia' A form with irregular and crinkled, narrow leaves, 15-20cm long, tapered at both ends and entire or shallowly-lobed.

'Purpurea' ('Rubicunda') Leaves very similar in colour to those of the "Purple Beech".

'Salicifolia' See *Q. robur* 'Holophylla'.

‡**phellos** L. "Willow Oak". A large tree with slender branches and narrow, entire, willow-like leaves which are glossy green above, turning yellow and orange in autumn. The leaves of young trees are often lobed. An attractive species, broad-headed when young. Requires a lime-free soil. E United States. I 1723.

*phillyreoides A. GRAY (Ilex Section) A rare, very hardy, large shrub recalling *Phillyrea latifolia*, generally seen as a dense, rounded bush up to 5m or more, but occasionally a small tree. Leaves oval or obovate, leathery, glossy green on both surfaces, sharply but minutely-toothed, usually bronze-tinted when unfolding. China, Japan. Introduced by Richard Oldham in 1861.

QUERCUS—*continued*

‡**'Pondaim'** A small, rugged tree intermediate between the parents both of which are remarkable plants. Leaves large, obovate and sharply-toothed, dark glossy green above, grey beneath. Raised by J.R.P. van Hoey-Smith about 1960.

‡**pontica** K. KOCH (Robur Section) "Armenian Oak". An unmistakable species, usually shrubby, but occasionally a small tree. Shoots stout; leaves large, oval to obovate, sometimes as much as 25cm long and 12cm wide, strongly ribbed and toothed. The mid-rib and petiole are yellow. Rich yellow autumn colour. Armenia, Caucasus. I 1885.

‡**prinus** L. (*Q. montana* WILLD.) "Chestnut Oak". Medium-sized to large tree with an open, spreading crown. Leaves obovate to oblong-obovate, crenately-dentate, turning rich yellow in autumn. SE Canada, E United States. C 1688.

× **pseudoturneri** See *Q.* × *turneri* 'Pseudoturneri'.

**pubescens** WILLD. (Robur Section) (*Q. lanuginosa* LAM.) A small to medium-sized tree, occasionally shrubby, with densely hairy twigs. Leaves obovate, with wavy margins, deeply-lobed and covered with a thick greyish down. W, C and S Europe.

    **subsp. palensis** (PALASSOU) SCHWARZ A shrubby form with smaller leaves. Pyrenees, N Spain.

**pyrenaica** WILLD. (Robur Section) (*Q. toza* DC.) "Pyrenean Oak". A medium to large-sized tree with a wide-spreading head of pendent branches, tomentose branchlets, and bark of pale grey, deeply fissured into knobbly squares. Leaves variable in size, obovate or broadly oblong, with long, narrow, usually pointed lobes, glossy green above, grey-felted beneath. Its long, drooping, male catkins are attractive in June, turning from grey to gold. SW Europe, N Italy. I 1822.

    **'Pendula'** An elegant form with drooping branches. There are good examples of this tree both at Westonbirt Arboretum and Holland Park, London.

***reticulata** HUMB. & BONPL. (Ilex Section) A rare, evergreen species. A large shrub or small, slow-growing tree of upright habit with densely hairy branches and obovate, spine-toothed, leathery leaves, which are sea-green above, paler, shortly pubescent and strongly reticulate beneath. Hardy given reasonable shelter. S Arizona, New Mexico (United States). I 1839.

**robur** L. (*Q. pedunculata* EHRH.) "Common Oak" "English Oak". This is the better known and more widely distributed of our 2 native species, the other being *Q. petraea*. A large, long-lived tree, developing a broad head of rugged branches when growing in the open. Leaves sessile or almost so, shallowly-lobed and auricled at the base. Fruits one to several on a slender stalk. Almost all the ancient "named" oaks in the British Isles belong to this species rather than *Q. petraea*. Europe, Caucasus, Asia Minor, N Africa. AGM 1984.

    **'Atropurpurea'** A curious, slow-growing form with leaves and shoots a rich vinous-purple, becoming greyish-purple at maturity.

    **'Concordia'** "Golden Oak". A small, rounded tree of very slow growth. Leaves suffused golden yellow throughout spring and summer. Raised in Van Geert's nursery at Ghent in 1843. FCC 1868.

    **'Cristata'** A curious form in which the short, broad, deeply-lobed leaves are folded and curled.

    **'Cucullata'** Leaves long and relatively narrow, the margins variously lobed and inrolled.

    **f. fastigiata** (LAM.) SCHWARZ "Cypress Oak". A large, imposing tree of columnar habit. A splendid specimen tree where space is restricted. AGM 1984.

    **'Fastigiata Purpurea'** Smaller than 'Fastigiata' with young leaves reddish-purple throughout the growing season.

    **'Filicifolia'** (*Q.* × *rosacea* 'Filicifolia') (*Q. robur* 'Pectinata') Leaves pinnately divided into narrow, forwardly pointing segments; petioles long and under-surfaces downy as in *Q. petraea*. Fruits pedunculed. As effective as the better-known "Fern-leaved Beech", though never so large a tree.

    **'Holophylla'** (*Q. petraea* 'Salicifolia') Leaves ovate-oblong to oblong-lanceolate, entire or with an occasional shallow lobe, distinctly stalked. Propagated from the tree in the Trompenburg Arboretum, Rotterdam, whose Director, Mr van Hoey-Smith, is an authority on oaks.

    **'Pectinata'** See 'Filicifolia'.

**QUERCUS robur**—*continued*

**'Pendula'** "Weeping Oak". A small to medium-sized tree with pendulous branches.

**'Strypemonde'** A curious form with relatively narrow, jaggedly-lobed leaves, mottled yellow.

**'Variegata'** Leaves with an irregular, creamy-white margin.

× **rosacea** BECHST. (Robur Section) (*Q. petraea* × *Q. robur*) (*Q.* × *hybrida* BECHST.) A variable hybrid, generally intermediate in character between the parents but sometimes leaning more to one than the other. Occurs with the parents in the wild.

**'Filicifolia'** See *Q. robur* 'Filicifolia'.

‡**rubra** L. (*Q. borealis* var. *maxima* (MARSH.) ASHE) "Red Oak". This large, fast-growing, broad-headed tree thrives in most parts of the British Isles, even in industrial areas, and in some places has reached a height of over 30m. Its large, oval or obovate, lobed leaves turn red and finally red-brown before falling, but on some trees they turn ruby-red or mixed yellow and brown. It differs from the closely related *Q. coccinea* in its stout, more horizontal branches and in its less deeply-lobed, matt leaves. E North America. I 1724. AM 1971. AGM 1984.

**'Aurea'** A small to medium-sized tree, the young leaves of a bright yellow in spring, later turning to yellow-green, finally green. A lovely clone which requires a sheltered position in partial shade otherwise the leaves are inclined to scorch in strong sun. 2 forms are grown under this name. Raised in Holland about 1878. AM 1971.

‡*****rysophylla** WEATHERBY A strong-growing evergreen tree, ultimate height in this country uncertain. Young shoots downy, ridged, buds with linear stipules. Leaves downy on both sides and reddish when young. Mature leaves dark glossy green above and conspicuously bullate, nearly glabrous beneath with small tufts of hair in the vein axils, elliptic, to 25cm long and 8cm wide, auricled at the base, wavy-edged and shallowly-lobed to merely toothed above the middle, the lobes bristle-tipped. This remarkable tree was introduced by Sir Harold Hillier in 1979 from the Horsetail Falls above Monterrey, Mexico. It is proving hardy and has already reached 5m in the Hillier Gardens and Arboretum (1990).

‡*****sadleriana** R. BR. "Deer Oak". A rare and distinct species collected in the Siskiyou Mountains, California. A small, stoutly-branched shrub with conspicuously scaly buds and prominently veined, serrately-toothed leaves. California, SW Oregon.

‡*****salicina** BLUME A rare small tree related to *Q. glauca*. Leaves lanceolate to narrowly so, long-acuminate and sharply-toothed towards the apex, up to 15cm long, green beneath at first becoming glaucous. S Japan, S Korea.

‡ × **schochiana** DIECK (*Q. palustris* × *Q. phellos*). A medium-sized tree of spreading habit, with glossy green, often willow-like leaves, few-toothed or lobed or occasionally entire. A most attractive hybrid, colouring bright yellow in the autumn. Semi-evergreen in sheltered positions. Occurs both in the wild and in cultivation. C 1894.

†*****semecarpifolia** SM. In cultivation a small, rounded tree. Leaves up to 11cm long and 7cm across, leathery, broadly elliptic to oblong, rounded at the apex, heart-shaped or almost auricled at the base, undulate and spiny on the margins on young plants becoming entire, dark glossy green above with a conspicuous midrib. Plants in the Hillier Gardens and Arboretum derive from an old plant in a Hampshire garden and a later introduction by Roy Lancaster. Afghanistan, Himalaya, China.

**serrata** See *Q. acutissima* and *Q. glandulifera*.

**sessiliflora** See *Q. petraea*.

‡**shumardii** BUCKL. (*Q. shumardii* var. *schneckii* (BRITT.) SARG.) A small to medium-sized tree with attractive, deeply-cut leaves turning red or golden brown in the autumn. S and C United States. I 1897.

‡**stellata** WANGEN. "Post Oak". A medium-sized tree with obovate, conspicuously and deeply-lobed leaves which are rough to the touch above and densely clothed beneath with a stellate tomentum. W and C United States. I 1800.

*****suber** L. "Cork Oak". Normally a short-stemmed, wide-spreading tree of medium size, but occasionally reaching 20m. Its bark is thick, rugged and corky and provides the cork of commerce. Leaves oval or oblong, broadly-toothed, leathery, lustrous green above, greenish-grey-felted beneath. Though very frost-resistant, it is not satisfactory in the

**QUERCUS suber**—*continued*

coldest counties. S Europe, N Africa. Extensively cultivated in Spain and Portugal. C 1699.

**trojana** WEBB (Cerris Section) (*Q. macedonica* A. DC.) "Macedonian Oak". A small to medium-sized, densely branched, usually deciduous tree. The rather shiny, obovate-oblong, taper-pointed leaves are margined with large, incurved triangular teeth, and are often retained until the end of the year. Balkans, SE Italy. I about 1890.

×**turneri** WILLD. (*Q. ilex* × *Q. robur*). "Turner's Oak". A distinctive, small to medium-sized, semi-evergreen tree with a compact, rounded head of dark green leaves, which are oblong-obovate to oblanceolate, with 4-6 broad, mucronate teeth on each margin. Good on calcareous soils. Raised in the nursery of a Mr Turner in Essex, during the late 18th century. Cultivated plants belong to 'Pseudoturneri' (*Q. pseudoturneri* WILLD.).

*\*vacciniifolia* KELLOGG (Ilex Section) (*Q. chrysolepis* var. *vacciniifolia* (KELLOGG) ENGELM.) "Huckleberry Oak". A slow-growing, very hardy, small to medium-sized shrub of dense, bushy habit. Leaves 1.5-2.5cm long, pointed, undulate and spine-toothed or entire, greyish-green beneath. SW United States.

**variabilis** BLUME (Cerris Section) A large, elegant tree which develops an attractive, corky bark. Leaves chestnut-like, narrow, oval or oblong, margined with small, bristle-tipped teeth, green above, densely greyish or yellowish-white pubescent beneath and persisting late into the autumn. China, Korea, Taiwan, Japan. I 1861 by Robert Fortune from near Beijing.

‡**velutina** LAM. (*Q. tinctoria* MICHX.) "Black Oak" "Yellow-bark Oak". A large tree with downy buds and young shoots. Leaves large, hard and often 30cm long, deeply and irregularly-lobed, dark green and glossy above, covered by a pale pubescence beneath. The inner bark is a bright yellow, from which is extracted the dye "quercitron". Rich autumn tints. E and C United States. I 1800.

'Rubrifolia' One of the most striking of all oaks with its enormous hooded leaves measuring up to 40cm long and 23cm wide. Colours in autumn warm reddish-brown and yellowish.

‡\***virginiana** MILL. "Live Oak". A small, wide-spreading, evergreen tree with tomentose twigs and elliptic or oblong, leathery leaves which are normally entire, or rarely with a few spiny teeth, glossy dark green above, greyish or whitish, pubescent beneath. SE United States, NE Mexico, W Cuba. I 1739.

**warburgii** A. CAMUS "Cambridge Oak". A rare, large tree of uncertain origin. The large obovate, shallowly-lobed leaves are remarkably like those of *Q. robur*, but are slightly longer-stalked and semi-evergreen, often remaining on the branches until the following March. Our stock is propagated from the original tree growing in the University Botanic Garden, Cambridge. C 1869.

*\*wislizeni* A. DC. A large shrub or small, rounded tree of slow growth. Leaves holly-like, polished, leathery, oblong to ovate, edged with slender spiny teeth. Related to and resembling *Q. agrifolia*, but leaves almost sessile, and glabrous, with acorns maturing the first (not second) autumn. California, Mexico. I 1874.

**var. frutescens** ENGELM. A shrubby variety with smaller, rigidly spiny leaves. California.

"QUICK" See *Crataegus monogyna*.

†*\*QUILLAJA* MOLINA—**Rosaceae**—A small genus of 4 species of tender, evergreen, S American trees or large shrubs, succeeding in all kinds of well drained, fertile soil.

**saponaria** MOLINA "Soap Bark Tree". A small Chilean tree. Leaves oval, toothed, thick, leathery and shining green. Flowers usually solitary in April, rather large, white with purple centre. The bark contains saponin, as well as several minerals used for washing purposes in parts of Chile. Only suitable for the mildest localities. I 1832.

"QUINCE" See *Cydonia oblonga*.

**RAPHIOLEPIS** See *Rhaphiolepis*.

†\*REEVESIA LINDL.—**Sterculiaceae**—A small genus of 3 or 4 species of evergreen, monoecious trees and shrubs, natives of the Himalaya and SE Asia. Only suitable for sheltered woodland gardens in the mildest areas, but excellent conservatory subjects. They require a moist, deep, preferably lime-free loam and sun or semi-shade.

**pubescens** MAST. A rare, small, evergreen tree; leaves ovate, rather leathery with the veins impressed above. Flowers creamy-white, fragrant, borne in terminal corymbs during summer. E Himalaya, SW China. A splendid specimen, like a large bay tree (*Laurus nobilis*) grew for many years at Caerhays Castle, Cornwall and a smaller specimen in a more exposed position at Wakehurst Place, Sussex, but both succumbed to the severe winter of 1962-63. A later planting at Wakehurst survived recent hard winters. I 1910 by Ernest Wilson. AM 1954.

**thyrsoidea** LINDL. A tall, evergreen shrub or small tree with ovate-lanceolate leaves. Flowers fragrant, creamy-white, produced in dense terminal clusters 5-7.5cm across, in July. SE China. I 1826.

‡**REHDERODENDRON** HU—**Styracaceae**—A small genus of 9 or 10 species of deciduous trees, natives of SW China and only known since 1930.

**macrocarpum** HU A small tree with elliptic to oblong-ovate, finely serrate leaves, 7.5-10cm long, usually attractively tinted before falling. Flowers cup-shaped, slightly fragrant, white, tinged pink, with conspicuous, exserted yellow anthers, produced in hanging clusters with the leaves, in May. The pendulous fruits are oblong, 8-10-ribbed, bright red. A magnificent species, in garden merit equal to the best *Styrax*. Requires a moist, lime-free soil. Discovered on Mt Omei, W China by Mr F.T. Wang in 1931, and introduced by Professor Hu in 1934. AM 1947.

**RHAMNUS** L.—**Rhamnaceae**—A large genus of about 125 species of deciduous and evergreen trees and shrubs, widely distributed, mainly in N temperate regions and largely grown for their foliage effect. The flowers, which may be perfect, dioecious or polygamous, are small but numerous in axillary clusters and generally inconspicuous. They will grow in all types of soils in sun or semi-shade.

\***alaternus** L. A useful, large, bushy, fast-growing evergreen shrub. Leaves alternate, small, dark glossy green; flowers yellowish-green in April; fruits red, becoming black. In the mountains of S Spain are found remarkable, small-leaved forms which creep over the rocks. It is splendid for maritime exposure and industrial areas. In warmer, sunnier climes, it rivals the English holly in fruit. Not recommended for the coldest inland areas. Mediterranean region, Portugal. I early in the 17th century.

**'Angustifolia'** A large, compact bush of dense, rounded habit, with narrow conspicuously toothed leaves. A splendid evergreen proving extremely hardy.

**'Argenteovariegata'** Leaves green, marbled grey with an irregular, creamy-white margin. One of the best of all variegated shrubs, but somewhat tender and best given some shelter. AM 1976. AGM 1984.

**alpina** L. "Alpine Buckthorn". A slow-growing, small to medium-sized shrub of compact habit, producing numerous erect stems. Leaves broad elliptic, finely-toothed, glossy green and attractively veined. Fruits black. SW Europe, C Alps, Italy. I 1752.

\***californica** ESCH. (Frangula Section) "Coffee-berry". An interesting, more or less evergreen shrub of medium size with oblong or oval leaves about 5cm, occasionally to 10cm long. Fruits red changing to purple-black. W North America. C 1871.

**subsp. crassifolia** (JEPS.) C.B. WOLF A remarkable variety with larger, thicker leaves which, like the shoots, are conspicuously grey velvety pubescent.

**cathartica** L. "Common Buckthorn". A large, native shrub or small tree, a common hedge or woodland shrub on chalk. Branches spiny, quite attractive in autumn, when laden with masses of shining black fruits. Europe (including British Isles).

**davurica** PALL. "Dahurian Buckthorn". A large shrub or small tree with slender-pointed, oblong leaves and black fruits in autumn. Siberia, Manchuria, N China. I 1817.

**frangula** L. (*Frangula alnus* MILL.) "Alder Buckthorn". A large shrub or small tree with ovate leaves turning yellow in autumn. Fruits red, changing to black and extremely

**RHAMNUS frangula**—*continued*

ornamental when bearing berries of both colours. Its wood makes the best charcoal for gunpowder. Europe (including British Isles).

**'Aspleniifolia'** A curious form in which the leaf blade is reduced to a mere thread 3-5mm wide. Particularly attractive in autumn when the pendulous leaves turn to deep yellow.

**'Columnaris'** "Tallhedge". A compact form of narrowly upright habit. Found in the United States in 1936.

\* × **hybrida** L'HERIT. (*R. alaternus* × *R. alpina*). A medium-sized to large, usually semi-evergreen shrub of spreading habit with dark glossy green, oblong, shallowly-toothed leaves up to 10cm long. C 1788.

**'Billardii'** Leaves smaller, more deeply-toothed.

**imeretina** KIRCHN. The most outstanding of the buckthorns. A medium-sized to large shrub with stout shoots and large, handsome corrugated leaves which are dark green above, downy beneath, usually becoming bronze-purple in autumn. Some leaves may be as much as 30-35cm long and 10-15cm wide. A splendid shrub for a damp, shaded site. W Caucasus. I 1858.

**infectoria** L. "Avignon Berry". A spreading shrub to 2m, with spine-tipped branches and ovate or obovate leaves. The black fruits were once used by dyers. SW Europe.

**japonica** MAXIM. Medium-sized shrub with glossy, pale green obovate leaves, crowded at the ends of the branchlets. The small, faintly-scented, yellowish-green flowers are produced in dense clusters in May. Fruits black. Japan. I 1888.

**parvifolia** BUNGE A spiny, medium-sized shrub with elliptic, dark green polished leaves and black fruits in autumn. It hasn't grown very successfully in our area. NE Asia. I 1910.

**\*procumbens** EDGEW. A prostrate species from the Himalaya, making a low mound of intricate stems, small, shining, bright green leaves, and producing black fruits. Most suitable for the rock garden.

**pumila** TURRA "Dwarf Buckthorn". A dwarf, sometimes prostrate shrub, only a few inches high. Fruits blue-black. Suitable for the rock garden. Mts of S Europe, Alps. C 1752.

**purshiana** DC. (Frangula Section) A small tree or large shrub worthy of inclusion in a representative arboretum. The rather large leaves are prominently veined and downy beneath. Fruits red turning black. The drug "Cascara Sagrada" is obtained from the bark of this tree. W North America. C 1870.

**rupestris** SCOP. (Frangula Section) A small, spreading, sometimes procumbent shrub. Leaves elliptic or rounded. Fruits small, red at first, finally black. W Balkans. C 1800.

**utilis** DECNE. A medium-sized shrub with slender branches and oblong, polished-green leaves. Fruits black. Long cultivated for the dye known as "China Green". C and E China, Japan.

**\*RHAPHIOLEPIS** LINDL. (*Raphiolepis* LINDL.)—**Rosaceae**—A small genus of about 15 species, natives of E Asia. The following are rather slow-growing, evergreen shrubs with firm, leathery leaves. They require a warm, sunny position in a well drained, fertile soil.

† × **delacourii** ANDRE (*R. indica* × *R. umbellata*). A charming shrub usually less than 2m, of rounded habit. Leaves obovate, glossy green, toothed in upper half. Flowers of a lovely rose-pink borne in erect, terminal panicles in spring or summer. Only injured by severe frosts. It makes an attractive wall shrub. Raised by Mons Delacour, near Cannes, France, towards the end of 19th century. AM 1932.

**'Coates' Crimson'** A choice selection with rose-crimson flowers. Named after the Californian raiser. C 1952.

**'Spring Song'** A form with apple blossom-pink flowers borne over a long period.

†**indica** (L.) LINDL. A small shrub with narrow, toothed, leathery leaves 5-7.5cm long. Flowers white, flushed pink, borne in racemes intermittently during spring and summer. Only suitable for the mildest localities or the conservatory. S China. C 1806.

**umbellata** (THUNB.) MAK. (*R. japonica* SIEB. & ZUCC.) A delightful, dense, slow-growing shrub of rounded habit, usually attaining about 1.2m in the open or higher against a wall. Leaves oval, thick and leathery, inconspicuously toothed. Terminal clusters of slightly fragrant, white flowers in June, followed by bronzy-black fruits. Normally hardy, but injured in the severest winters such as 1962-63. Japan, Korea. I about 1862.

**RHAPHITHAMNUS** MIERS—**Verbenaceae**—2 species of evergreen shrubs or small trees, natives of Chile and Argentina.

†*spinosus** (A.L. JUSS.) MOLDENKE (*R. cyanocarpus* (HOOK. & ARN.) MIERS) A medium-sized to large, evergreen, myrtle-like shrub of dense habit. Each pair or cluster of small, sharply-toothed leaves is accompanied by 2 or 3 sharp, needle-like spines. Flowers small, tubular, 1cm long, pale blue, in April, berries deep blue. Requires a warm sunny wall. Introduced by William Lobb in about 1843.

**RHODODENDRON** L. (including *Azalea*)—**Ericaceae**—The rhododendrons are one of the most important and diverse groups of ornamental plants in cultivation. They include many of the most spectacular as well as some of the noblest of flowering trees and shrubs. Late spring and early summer is the height of their flowering season and about nine-tenths flower during the months of April, May and June. The remainder are, nevertheless, an important group, bringing colour to the garden sometimes as early as January or even late December, or as late as August. Many are notable for their handsome foliage and a number of deciduous kinds for their autumn tints. For landscaping, the rhododendrons are unsurpassed. When massed, no other shrub gives such a wealth of colour. The variations in form, colour, texture and size of leaf are so remarkable that even if they never flowered, some species would still be the outstanding evergreens of the temperate world. Those with large leaves are subject to wind damage and should, if possible, be planted in woodland or similar shelter. The dwarf, small-flowered species should be mass planted. They are particularly effective in the open heather garden. The same is true of almost all of the Lapponica Subsection.

Rhododendrons may be grown in a moist yet well drained, fertile soil, so long as no free lime is present. Few rhododendrons will tolerate even a trace of free lime, although applications of Iron Sequestrene to the soil often improve performance in such situations. A sheltered, semi-shaded position is appreciated by all rhododendrons but many, especially the alpine species and that wide range of hybrids popularly known as the Hardy Hybrids, will luxuriate in full exposure to wind and sun. They are also remarkably tolerant of atmospheric pollution. It is better to give an annual mulch up to 8cm deep, preferably in early autumn, to protect and nourish the root system which develops close to the soil surface, rather than loosen the topsoil by annual forking. For this purpose, decaying leaves, bracken, peat or spent hops are excellent. Rhododendrons require no regular pruning, but the removal of the faded trusses immediately after flowering is extremely beneficial. Hardy Hybrids which have become straggly or too large may be hard pruned in April.

**Hardiness**

> H4 Hardy anywhere in the British Isles.
> H3 Hardy in the south and west, also along the seaboard and in sheltered gardens inland.
> H2 Requires protection in the most sheltered gardens.
> H1 Can usually be grown only as a greenhouse plant.
> To facilitate easy reference, rhododendrons have been treated under five main headings, as follows:-
> Rhododendron Species (including Azaleas). See below.
> Rhododendron Hybrids. See page 390.
> Azaleodendrons. See page 416.
> Deciduous Hybrid Azaleas. See page 418.
> Evergreen Hybrid Azaleas. See page 421.

## ‡RHODODENDRON SPECIES
### (including Azaleas)

The genus Rhododendron is one of the largest, containing some 800 species. It is represented mainly in the N hemisphere, reaching its greatest density in the vast expanse of mountain ranges and gorges bordering China, Tibet and Upper Burma. It is thanks to such men as Sir Joseph Hooker, George Forrest, Joseph Rock, Kingdon-Ward and Ernest Wilson that our gardens have such a wide representation of species and forms. Had it not been for the late J.B. Stevenson, many of these would have been lost to

**RHODODENDRON**—*continued*

cultivation during and after the First World War. Gardeners throughout the world owe to him a debt of gratitude for raising and maintaining at Tower Court, Ascot, the most complete set of rhododendron species. After his death this work was bravely continued by his widow (who later became Mrs Harrison) assisted by the Head Gardener, Mr Keir. Fortunately before her death she sold the bulk of her collection to the Commissioner of Crown Lands, so that these plants have been saved for posterity in the Valley Garden made in Windsor Great Park by Sir Eric Savill, that past-master of informal gardening.

The species described below range from tiny, prostrate alpines to trees with enormous leaves. The dwarf species are charming rock-garden shrubs, those belonging to the Subsections Lapponica and Saluenensia of Subgenus Rhododendron associating well with heaths. The massed planting of dwarf and alpine rhododendrons, with all their various colours ranging from white through pink and red to yellow, purple and blue, exhibits a greater colour range than that of the finest heather garden. The large-leaved species require shelter, especially from wind, and will not tolerate very dry conditions for long periods. An ideal site for these is provided by thin oak woodland, with some evergreen shelter.

This account follows the now widely accepted Edinburgh Revision which has so far dealt with subgenus Rhododendron excluding section Vireya (the lepidote species) and subgenus Hymenanthes (the elepidote species excluding Azaleas and their relatives). Subgenus Rhododendron is divided into three sections, Rhododendron into which most species fall, Pogonathum which contains *R. anthopogon* and its relatives and Vireya of which none of the mainly subtropical and tender species are dealt with here. Section Rhododendron is further divided into subsections. Subgenus Hymenanthes contains only one section which is divided into subsections. The subgenus and section/subsection to which each species belongs is indicated in parentheses after the name. The section name for species in Subgenus Rhododendron, section Rhododendron is not given.

Where certain species worthy of horticultural recognition have been relegated to synonymy in the Edinburgh Revision, the RHS Horticultural Revision has been followed in giving these group status.

Except where otherwise stated, the following species and their forms are evergreen.

Awards. Many awards have been given to un-named forms of species, and these are indicated in the text as follows: AM (F) or FCC (F).

We are grateful for the assistance of Mr John Bond with the revision of this section.

**aberconwayi** COWAN (Subgenus Hymenanthes, Subsect. Irrorata) A small to medium-sized shrub with loose trusses of flat, saucer-shaped flowers, white, tinged pink, usually heavily spotted maroon; May and June. Leaves rather rigid and leathery, of medium size. NE Yunnan. I 1937. H3.

**'His Lordship'** Flowers white flashed with crimson. AM 1945.

**adenogynum** DIELS (Subgenus Hymenanthes, Subsect. Taliensia) Small to medium-sized shrub with woolly young shoots; leaves leathery covered with a tawny, suede-like felt beneath. Flowers funnel-shaped, deep rose in bud opening white, shaded rose; April to May. W Yunnan, SW Sichuan, SE Tibet. I by George Forrest in 1910. H3.

**Adenophorum group** (*R. adenophorum* BALF. f. & W.W. SM.) Flowers rose with scattered crimson spots; April. Yunnan. I by George Forrest in 1910. H4.

**adenophorum** See *R. adenogynum* Adenophorum group.

**aechmophyllum** See *R. yunnanense.*

**aemulorum** See *R. mallotum.*

**aeruginosum** See *R. campanulatum* subsp. *aeruginosum.*

**albrechtii** MAXIM. (*Azalea albrechtii* (MAXIM.) KUNTZE) (Subgenus Pentanthera, Sect. Sciadorhodion) A very beautiful, medium-sized, deciduous shrub of open habit. Leaves obovate or oblong-obovate, clustered at the ends of the branches, turning yellow in autumn. Flowers deep rose, 5cm across, appearing before or with the leaves; April and May. Japan. I 1914 by Ernest Wilson. AM 1943. AGM 1984. H4.

**amagianum** (MAK.) MAK. ex NEMOTO (*Azalea amagiana* MAK.) (Subgenus Pentanthera, Sect. Brachycalyx) An outstanding medium-sized to large, deciduous shrub with broad obovate leaves in clusters of threes at the ends of the branches. Flowers funnel-shaped, orange-red, 3-4 in a truss; June and July. AM 1948. Japan. H4.

**RHODODENDRON**—*continued*

**ambiguum** HEMSL. (Subgenus Rhododendron, Subsect. Triflora) An attractive, medium-sized to large shrub, with 5-7.5cm long leaves and clusters of 3-6 funnel-shaped flowers of greenish-yellow, spotted green. April and May. C Sichuan. I 1904 by Ernest Wilson. H4.

**anhweiense** See *R. maculiferum* subsp. *anhweiense*.

**annae** FRANCH. (Subgenus Hymenanthes, Subsect. Irrorata) Medium-sized to large shrub with rather small, narrow leaves; flowers bell-shaped, white to rose-flushed with or without purple spots; June and July. W Yunnan, NE Upper Burma. H3-4.

**anthopogon** D. DON (Subgenus Rhododendron, Sect. Pogonanthum) A dwarf shrub of compact habit with brown, scaly branchlets and leaves up to 3cm long, densely scaly below. Flowers in a tight, terminal cluster, narrowly tubular, varying in colour from cream to deep pink; April. Nepal, Sikkim, Assam, Bhutan, S Tibet. I 1820. AM 1955. H4.

> **subsp. hypenanthum** (BALF. f.) CULLEN (*R. hypenanthum* BALF. f.) Small, tubular, yellow flowers are carried in tight rounded heads; April and May.

> > **'Annapurna'** An attractive form with smaller, dark glossy green leaves and slightly larger flowerheads. AM 1974.

**aperantum** BALF. f. & WARD (Subgenus Hymenanthes, Subsect. Neriiflora) A dwarf, spreading shrub with tomentose shoots and dark green obovate leaves up to 6cm long glaucous beneath. Flowers tubular-campanulate in trusses of 3-6, usually pink or red but varying to white and yellow often flushed pink. Best in a cool, moist, open position. April-May. NE Upper Burma, NW Yunnan. I 1919 by Kingdon-Ward. AM (F) 1931. H4.

**apodectum** See *R. dichroanthum* subsp. *apodectum*.

**arborescens** (PURSH) TORR. (*Azalea arborescens* PURSH) (Subgenus Pentanthera, Sect. Pentanthera) A large, deciduous shrub with obovate or oval, glossy green leaves, pale green or glaucous beneath usually attractively tinted in autumn. Flowers fragrant, funnel-shaped, white, occasionally pink-flushed, style red, long and protruding; June and July. E North America. I 1818. H4.

**arboreum** W.W. SM. (Subgenus Hymenanthes, Subsect. Arborea) A magnificent large shrub or small tree, in its less hardy forms requiring woodland shelter. Leaves up to 20cm long, green above, whitish to brownish-red below, primary veins conspicuously impressed. The bell-shaped, 5cm long flowers are carried in dense, globular heads and vary in colour from white to blood-red; January to April. It usually flowers very early and in cold districts is often ruined by frost. Many of its progeny are, however, hardier. This magnificent species was the first rhododendron introduced from the Himalaya and is the parent of many of our hardy hybrids. Temperate Himalaya, Kashmir to Bhutan, Khasia Hills. I about 1810. H2-4. AGM 1984 (to subsp. *arboreum*).

**'Album'** Flowers white. H4.

**'Blood Red'** Flowers of a striking blood-red. H3.

> **subsp. cinnamomeum** (LINDL.) TAGG Leaves with a thick, cinnamon or rust-coloured tomentum beneath. E Nepal, NE India. I 1820.

> **subsp. delavayi** (FRANCH.) CHAMBERLAIN (*R. delavayi* FRANCH.) Leaves glossy dark green above with a greyish-white tomentum beneath. Flowers usually blood-red, bell-shaped, in a round, compact truss; March to May. E Himalaya to SW China. I about 1884. FCC 1936. H2-3.

> > **var. roseum** LINDL. Flowers rich pink, with darker spots; a lovely form. AM 1973. FCC 1974. H4.

**'Sir Charles Lemon'** See *R.* 'Sir Charles Lemon' under Hybrids.

> **subsp. zeylanicum** (BOOTH) TAGG (*R. zeylanicum* BOOTH) A large shrub or small tree superb in the milder parts of the British Isles. Leaves elliptic-oblong, bullate, very dark green, covered with a dense fawn or tawny indumentum below. Flowers in a dense truss, bell-shaped, red; April and May. One of the most beautiful foliage rhododendrons. Sri Lanka. I in the 1830s. H2-3.

**argenteum** See *R. grande*.

**argyrophyllum** FRANCH. (Subgenus Hymenanthes, Subsect. Argyrophylla) A beautiful large, densely leafy shrub of slow growth, with long leaves, silvery or white-felted beneath.

**RHODODENDRON argyrophyllum**—*continued*

Flowers in a loose head, bell-shaped, white or pink with darker spots. May. Yunnan, Sichuan, Shaanxi. I 1904 by Ernest Wilson. AM (F) 1934. H4.

**'Chinese Silver'** A selection of subsp. *nankingense*. Leaves very silvery beneath, flowers pink, darker on the lobes, 5cm across. AM 1957.

**Cupulare group** (var. *cupulare* REHD.) Flowers smaller, cup-shaped, white spotted with pink.

**subsp. nankingense** (COWAN) CHAMBERLAIN A form with larger leaves and flower trusses. W Sichuan, Guizhou. I 1931.

**'Roseum'** A selection with flowers of a clear rose.

**arizelum** See *R. rex* subsp. *arizelum*.

**atlanticum** (ASHE) REHD. (*Azalea atlantica* ASHE) (Subgenus Pentanthera, Sect. Pentanthera) A charming, small, deciduous, stoloniferous shrub with obovate or oblong-obovate, bright green leaves. Flowers fragrant, funnel-shaped, white or white flushed pink, occasionally with a yellow blotch; May. Mid-eastern United States. I about 1916. H4.

**aucklandii** See *R. griffithianum*.

**augustinii** HEMSL. (Subgenus Rhododendron, Subsect. Triflora) A large, small-leaved shrub. In its best forms this beautiful, blue-flowered, Chinese species is one of the finest of all rhododendrons. It is fairly quick-growing, making an ideal woodland shrub. April and May. The name commemorates Augustine Henry who first found this species. Hubei, E Sichuan. I 1899 by Farges. AM 1926. AGM 1984 (to AM and FCC clones only). H3-4.

**subsp. chasmanthum** (DIELS) CULLEN (*R. chasmanthum* DIELS) A splendid variety with pale lavender to deep lavender-mauve flowers, a little later than the typical form, and borne in rather larger trusses. Yunnan, Sichuan, SE Tibet. AM 1930. FCC 1932. H3.

**'Electra'** A magnificent shrub when bearing clusters of violet-blue flowers marked with greenish-yellow blotches. The flowers are a startling colour, particularly when seen *en masse* on a large bush. Raised by Lionel de Rothschild at Exbury in 1937. It is a hybrid between the typical form and subsp. *chasmanthum*. AM 1940. H3.

**aureum** GEORGI (*R. chrysanthum* PALL.) (Subgenus Hymenanthes, Subsect. Pontica) Prostrate or dwarf shrub up to 30cm. Leaves oblanceolate to obovate 4-7.5cm long. Flowers bell-shaped, pale yellow; May and June. E USSR, Korea, Japan, N China. I 1796. H4.

**auriculatum** HEMSL. (Subgenus Hymenanthes, Subsect. Auriculata) A large shrub, occasion-ally a small tree. Though very distinct and handsome in leaf, this Chinese species is chiefly remarkable for its late flowering, which occurs normally in July and August, but sometimes later. The large, white, funnel-shaped flowers, long-tapered in bud are borne in huge trusses and are richly scented. Hubei, Sichuan, Guizhou. Introduced by E.H. Wilson in 1901. AM 1922. AGM 1984. H4.

**baileyi** BALF. f. (Subgenus Rhododendron, Subsect. Baileya) A small, Tibetan shrub sometimes reaching 2m, the young shoots and small leaves beneath coated with reddish-brown scales. Flowers saucer-shaped, red-purple, usually with darker markings; May. SE Tibet, Bhutan, Sikkim. I 1913. AM 1960. H3-4.

**bakeri** (LEMM. & MCKAY) HUME (Subgenus Pentanthera, Sect. Pentanthera) A deciduous shrub varying in height from dwarf to medium-size. Leaves obovate, glaucous beneath. Flowers in terminal clusters, funnel-shaped, varying in colour from orange to yellow or red; June. SE United States. H4.

**barbatum** G. DON (Subgenus Hymenanthes, Subsect. Barbata) A beautiful, large, spreading shrub or small tree with coloured stems and attractively peeling bark. The branchlets and petioles are clad with conspicuously impressed primary veins. Flowers bell-shaped, of a glowing crimson-scarlet, carried in dense, globular heads; March. N India, S Tibet, Nepal, Bhutan. C 1829. AM 1954. H3-4.

**basilicum** BALF. f. &. W.W. SM. (Subgenus Hymenanthes, Subsect. Falconera) A large shrub or small tree succeeding best in woodland conditions. The large, handsome leaves have winged petioles and are a rich cinnamon beneath. Flowers pale yellow, sometimes crimson-tinged and with a deep crimson basal blotch; April. W Yunnan, NE Upper Burma. I 1912 by George Forrest. AM (F) 1956. H3-4.

**bathyphyllum** BALF. f. & FORR. (Subgenus Hymenanthes, Subsect. Taliensia) Small, densely leafy shrub, the leaves 5-7.5cm long, clothed beneath with a rust-coloured indumentum.

**RHODODENDRON bathyphyllum**—*continued*

Flowers 4-5cm long, bell-shaped, white, spotted crimson; April-May. SE Tibet, NW Yunnan. H4.

**bauhiniiflorum** See *R. triflorum* var. *bauhiniiflorum*.

**beanianum** COWAN (Subgenus Hymenanthes, Subsect. Neriiflora) Medium-sized shrub of open habit, with chestnut-brown or yellowish-brown, woolly tomentum on the undersides of the leaves; flowers in loose trusses, bell-shaped, waxy, usually red, sometimes pink; March to May. NE Upper Burma, NE India. Named after W.J. Bean, one of the greatest-ever authorities on woody plants. AM (F) 1953. H3-4.

**bodinieri** FRANCH. A very hardy, medium-sized shrub with narrow, acuminate leaves. Flowers funnel-shaped, white or pale rose, with purple spots; March and April. Closely related to *R. yunnanense* and probably of hybrid origin. C 1933. H3-4.

**brachyanthum** FRANCH. (Subgenus Rhododendron, Subsect. Glauca) A dwarf or small shrub of neat habit, with aromatic leaves sparsely scaly beneath and bell-shaped, pale yellow flowers; June and July. C Yunnan. Discovered by the Abbé Delavay in 1884, introduced by George Forrest in 1906. AM 1966 (to 'Jaune'). H4.

**subsp. hypolepidotum** (FRANCH.) CULLEN Leaves densely scaly beneath. NE Burma, NW Yunnan, SE Tibet. AM 1951 (to 'Blue Light').

**brachycarpum** D. DON ex G. DON (Subgenus Hymenanthes, Subsect. Pontica) An attractive, hardy species of medium size with leaves covered with a fawn or brownish indumentum beneath. Flowers funnel-shaped, creamy-white, flushed pink; June and July. Japan, Korea. H4.

**subsp. fauriei** (FRANCH.) CHAMBERLAIN (*R. fauriei* FRANCH.) Leaves becoming glabrous beneath, white flowers with a pink flush and green spots.

**brachystylum** See *R. trichocladum*.

**bullatum** See *R. edgeworthii*.

**bureaui** FRANCH. (Subgenus Hymenanthes, Subsect. Taliensia) Medium-sized shrub with attractive, dark, glossy green leaves, covered beneath with a rich red woolly indumentum. Flowers bell-shaped, rose, with crimson markings, 10-15 in a tight truss; April and May. This outstanding species is well worth growing if only for the attractive colours of its young growths which vary between pale fawn and a warm rusty-red. N Yunnan. I by Wilson in 1904. AM 1939 (for flower). AM 1972 (for foliage). AGM 1984. H4.

**caeruleum** See *R. rigidum*.

**caesium** HUTCH. (Subgenus Rhododendron, Subsect. Trichoclada) Small shrub with attractive, shining, pale brown bark and aromatic leaves, green above, bluish-grey and scaly below. Flowers small, 2 or 3 together, funnel-shaped, greenish-yellow, with green flecks within; May. Yunnan. I 1925 by George Forrest. H4.

**calendulaceum** (MICHX.) TORR. (*Azalea calendulacea* MICHX.) (Subgenus Pentanthera, Sect. Pentanthera) A medium-sized to large, deciduous shrub with elliptic or obovate-oblong leaves, turning orange and red in autumn. Flowers funnel-shaped, 5cm across, varying in rich colours from yellow to orange or scarlet, hence the specific epithet (like a marigold); May and June. One of the most vividly coloured of all wild azaleas. E North America. I 1806. H4.

**'Burning Light'** Flowers coral-red with orange throats. AM 1965.

**callimorphum** BALF. f. & W.W. SM. (*R. cyclium* BALF. f. & FORR.) (Subgenus Hymenanthes, Subsect. Campylocarpa) A dainty, medium-sized shrub with small, round leaves, green above, glaucous below. Flowers in loose trusses, bell-shaped, soft pink, deep rose in bud, occasionally with a crimson basal blotch; April to June. W Yunnan. I 1912 by George Forrest. H4.

**var. myiagrum** (BALF. f. & FORR.) CHAMBERLAIN (*R. myiagrum* BALF. f. & FORR.) Flowers white. I 1919 by George Forrest.

**calophytum** FRANCH. (Subgenus Hymenanthes, Subsect. Fortunea) One of the noblest of Chinese species and one of the hardiest of those species with conspicuous large leaves. A large shrub or small tree with thick shoots capped with rosettes of long, narrow, oblanceolate leaves. Large trusses of white or pink, bell-shaped flowers, each with a maroon basal blotch; March and April. Sichuan, Yunnan. First found by the Abbé David, introduced by E.H. Wilson in 1904. AM (F) 1920. FCC (F) 1933. H4.

**RHODODENDRON**—*continued*

**calostrotum** BALF. f. & WARD (Subgenus Rhododendron, Subsect. Saluenensia) A very attractive, dwarf shrub with grey-green foliage and comparitively large, flat or saucer-shaped, bright magenta-crimson flowers; May and June. A fine rock-garden species. NE Upper Burma, W Yunnan. I 1919. AM (F) 1935. H4.

**'Gigha'** ('Red Form') A very splendid selection with flowers of a deep claret-red, contrasting with the grey-green young leaves. The name recalls the lovely garden made by Col Sir James Horlick on the Isle of Gigha off the coast of Argyllshire. FCC 1971. AGM 1984.

**subsp. keleticum** (BALF. f. & FORR.) CULLEN (*R. keleticum* BALF. f. & FORR.) A dwarf shrub forming mats or hummocks of small, densely scaly leaves from which the saucer-shaped, purple-crimson flowers arise, singly or in pairs; May and June. SE Tibet, Yunnan, Upper Burma. I 1919 by George Forrest. AM (F) 1928. H4.

**Radicans group** (*R. radicans* BALF. f. & FORR.) Habit very dwarf, prostrate. The normally solitary, flattish, rose-purple flowers appear in May and June. Suitable for the rock garden. SE Tibet. Introduced by George Forrest in 1921. AM (F) 1926. H4.

**subsp. riparioides** CULLEN Similar to subsp. *riparium* but with larger leaves. NW Yunnan. A plant known as 'Rock's Form' has deep purple flowers.

**subsp. riparium** (WARD) CULLEN (*R. riparium* WARD) Habit upright, leaves not glaucous. NE India, NE Upper Burma, Yunnan, S Tibet. AM 1983.

**Calciphilum group** (*R. calostrotum* var. *calciphilum* (HUTCH. & WARD) DAVIDIAN) A form with very small leaves and rather later pink flowers. Grows on limestone screes in the wild. NE Upper Burma.

**Nitens group** (*R. nitens* HUTCH.) A dwarf, erect shrublet with aromatic leaves and usually deep purple flowers, widely funnel-shaped or saucer-shaped, up to 5cm across; June and July. The last of its series to flower. Upper Burma.

**caloxanthum** See *R. campylocarpum* subsp. *caloxanthum*.

**campanulatum** D. DON (Subgenus Hymenanthes, Subsect. Campanulata) A large shrub, the unfolding leaves covered with a suede-like, fawn or rust-coloured indumentum. Flowers bell-shaped, varying in colour from pale rose to lavender-blue; April and May. A lovely species, said to be one of the commonest rhododendrons in the Himalayan forests. Kashmir to Bhutan. I 1825 by Wallich. H4.

**subsp. aeruginosum** (HOOK. f.) CHAMBERLAIN (*R. aeruginosum* HOOK. f.) A slow-growing compact shrub with the young growths a striking metallic blue-green. Sikkim, Bhutan.

**'Knap Hill'** An attractive selection with lavender-blue flowers. AM 1925.

**campylocarpum** HOOK. f. (Subgenus Hymenanthes, Subsect. Campylocarpa) A small to medium-sized shrub with ovate leaves, glossy green above, glaucous green below. Flowers bell-shaped, of a clear yellow; April and May. The best of its colour for general planting and one of the choicest of all hardy shrubs. In common with its relatives it does not flower when young. E Nepal, Sikkim, Bhutan, Assam, S Tibet. Introduced by Sir Joseph Hooker about 1849. FCC 1892. H3-4.

**subsp. caloxanthum** (BALF. f. & FARR.) CHAMBERLAIN (*R. caloxanthum* BALF. f. & FARR.) (*R. telopeum* BALF. f. & FORR.) Charming, small, free-flowering shrub with small, rounded leaves and clusters of bell-shaped, citron-yellow flowers, tipped orange-scarlet in bud; April and May. One of Reginald Farrer's prettiest introductions. NE Burma, SE Tibet, Yunnan. I 1919 by Reginald Farrer. AM (F) 1934. H3-4.

**Elatum group** Taller and looser in growth. Flowers usually with a crimson basal blotch, orange-vermilion in bud. Collected at a lower elevation than the typical form. H3-4.

**campylogynum** FRANCH. (Subgenus Rhododendron, Subsect. Campylogyna) A delightful, dwarf shrub with small lustrous green leaves glaucous beneath and producing long-stalked, nodding, rose-purple to almost mahogany, bell-shaped, waxy flowers when only a few centimetres high. May and June. Suitable for the rock garden. Yunnan, SE Tibet, NE Burma, NE India. I 1912 by George Forrest. H3-4.

**Charopoeum group** (*R. charopoeum* BALF. f. & FORR.) Leaves and flowers larger.

**Cremastum group** (*R. cremastum* BALF. f. & FORR.) Habit erect, leaves green beneath.

**'Crushed Strawberry'** A selection made in our nurseries in about 1955; flowers pink, a pleasant shade of crushed strawberry.

RHODODENDRON campylogynum—*continued*

**Myrtilloides group** (*R. myrtilloides* BALF. f. & WARD) A charming shrublet, with smaller, delightful, waxy, plum-purple flowers. AM 1925. FCC 1943.

**camtschaticum** PALLAS (*Therorhodion camtschaticum* (PALLAS) SMALL) (Subgenus Therorhodion) A dwarf, spreading, deciduous shrublet, up to 30cm, with curious, comparatively large, saucer-shaped, rose-purple flowers in May. A curious feature is the corolla tube which on the lower side is split almost to the base. Leaves up to 5cm long, giving attractive autumn tints. Requires an open, well drained situation. Alaska, E USSR, Japan. I 1799. AM 1908. H4.

**canadense** (L.) TORR. (*Rhodora canadensis* L.) (Subgenus Pentanthera, Sect. Rhodora) A small, deciduous shrub of erect, twiggy habit. Leaves narrowly oval, sea-green. Flowers appearing before the leaves, saucer-shaped or bell-shaped, rose-purple; April. Thriving in moist situations. NE North America. I 1767. AM 1928 (as *Rhodora canadensis*). H4.

**'Album'** Flowers white.

**canescens** (MICHX.) SWEET (*Azalea canescens* MICHX.) (Subgenus Pentanthera, Sect. Pentanthera) A medium to large, deciduous shrub with oblong or oblanceolate leaves, densely hairy beneath. Flowers funnel-shaped, sweetly-scented, white or pink-flushed with a pink or reddish, gland-covered tube; April and May. SE United States. I 1810. H4.

**cantabile** See *R. russatum*.

**carolinianum** See *R. minus* Carolinianum group.

**catawbiense** MICHX. (Subgenus Hymenanthes, Subsect. Pontica) An extremely hardy, medium-sized to large shrub of dense habit, with oval or oblong, glossy green leaves up to 15cm long. An old plant will develop into a dense thicket of layering stems. Flowers borne in a large truss, bell-shaped, varying in colour from lilac-purple to pink or white; June. A parent of many hardy hybrids. SE United States (Allegheny Mts). I 1809 by John Fraser. H4.

**caucasicum** PALL. (Subgenus Hymenanthes, Subsect. Pontica) A slow-growing, dome-shaped shrub of medium size. Leaves elliptic to oblanceolate, clad with a thin, fawn tomentum beneath. Flowers in a compact truss, widely funnel-shaped, pale sulphur-yellow with pale green markings within; May, occasionally again in late summer. A parent of many of the old hardy hybrids. Now rare in cultivation, the form here described is the plant previously known as 'Cunningham's Sulphur'. Caucasus, NE Turkey. I 1803. H4.

**cephalanthum** FRANCH. (Subgenus Rhododendron, Sect. Pogonanthum) A very beautiful small, slender, aromatic shrub, with small leaves, densely scaly beneath, and dense terminal heads of tubular, white or pinkish, daphne-like flowers; May. Yunnan, Sichuan, SE Tibet, Upper Burma. I 1908. H4.

**Crebreflorum group** (*R. crebreflorum* HUTCH. & WARD) A choice dwarf form from Assam, with pink flowers. A gem for the peat garden. AM 1934.

**cerasinum** TAGG (Subgenus Hymenanthes, Subsect. Thomsonia) A medium-sized to large shrub with elliptic leaves 5-10cm long and drooping trusses of long, bell-shaped flowers varying in colour from white with marginal band of cherry-red to self red or crimson. It was to the former that Kingdon-Ward gave the name "Cherry Brandy"; May. NE Upper Burma, SE Tibet. AM (F) 1938. H4.

**chaetomallum** See *R. haematodes* subsp. *chaetomallum*.

**chamaethomsonii** (TAGG & FORR.) COWAN & DAVIDIAN (*R. repens* var. *chamaethomsonii* TAGG. & FORR.) (Subgenus Hymenanthes, Subsect. Neriiflora) Dwarf, semi-prostrate or spreading shrub producing trusses of 5-6 bell-shaped, crimson or rose-crimson flowers; March to April. NW Yunnan, SE Tibet. H4.

**var. chamaethauma** (TAGG) COWAN & DAVIDIAN (*R. repens* var. *chamaethauma* TAGG) A form with smaller leaves. AM 1932.

**chameunum** See *R. saluenense* subsp. *chameunum*.

**chapmanii** See *R. minus* var. *chapmanii*.

**charianthum** See *R. davidsonianum*.

**charidotes** See *R. saluenense* subsp. *chameunum*.

**charitopes** BALF. f. & FARR. (Subgenus Rhododendron, Subsect. Glauca) A charming shrublet rarely as much as 1.2m, with obovate leaves, glaucous and densely scaly below.

**RHODODENDRON charitopes**—*continued*

Flowers bell-shaped, apple blossom-pink, speckled crimson; April and May. NE Upper Burma, NW Yunnan. I 1924 by George Forrest. H4.

**subsp. tsangpoense** (WARD) CULLEN (*R. tsangpoense* WARD) A variable dwarf to small, aromatic shrub. The leaves are obovate-oblong, 2.5-5cm long, glaucous scaly below, interspersed with pale-green or pink scales which, when viewed through a lens, appear like glistening jewels set in a white satin cloth. Flowers produced very freely, semi-bell-shaped, varying in colour from crushed strawberry to deep-crimson or violet; May and June. S Tibet. AM 1972 to 'Cowtye'. H4.

**chartophyllum** See *R. yunnanense*.

**chasmanthum** See *R. augustinii* subsp. *chasmanthum*.

**chrysanthum** See *R. aureum*.

**chryseum** See *R. rupicola* var. *chryseum*.

**ciliatum** HOOK. f. (Subgenus Rhododendron, Subsect. Maddenia) A beautiful, dome-shaped shrub about 1.2-1.5m, with attractive peeling bark and conspicuously ciliate leaves. Flowers nodding, fragrant, bell-shaped, rose-lilac, borne at an early age; March and April. E Nepal, Sikkim, SE Tibet, Bhutan. I 1850 by Sir Joseph Hooker. AM (F) 1953. H3-4.

**cinnabarinum** HOOK. f. (Subgenus Rhododendron, Subsect. Cinnabarina) This beautiful, medium-sized to large shrub with obovate-elliptic, scaly leaves and tubular flowers of bright cinnabar-red is one of the choicest of the Himalayan species, blooming in May and June. Nepal, Sikkim, Bhutan, SE Tibet. Introduced by Sir Joseph Hooker in 1849. H4.

**'Aestivale'** Flowers later, usually in July.

**'Blandfordiiflorum'** Flowers red outside, yellow within. AM 1945.

**'Caerhays John'** Medium-sized shrub of erect, bushy habit. Flowers funnel-shaped, deep apricot, up to 6cm across; mid. Flowering later than 'Caerhays Lawrence'. A cross between Concatenans and the typical form. H4.

**'Caerhays Lawrence'** Similar in habit to 'Caerhays John', and bearing waxy flowers of a rich orange-yellow. Early to mid. A cross between Concatenans and the typical form. H4.

**'Caerhays Philip'** A beautiful, medium-sized shrub with elliptic leaves and loose trusses of funnel-shaped yellow flowers 6cm across; early. A cross between 'Blandfordiiflorum' and Concatenans. AM 1966. H4.

**'Cinzan'** ('Blandfordiiflorum' × subsp. *xanthocodon*). Flowers rich yellow flushed pink. C 1951.

**Concatenans group** (*R. concatenans* HUTCH.) A distinct and lovely shrub of medium size. Leaves oval to oblong, densely scaly beneath, 4-6cm long, glaucous blue when young; flowers bell-shaped, waxy, apricot-yellow faintly purple-tinged on outside and sometimes conspicuously veined; April and May. SE Tibet. I 1924 by Kingdon-Ward. FCC 1935. AGM 1984. H3.

**Conroy group** (*R.* Conroy) Loose, flat-topped trusses of pendent, narrowly trumpet-shaped, waxen flowers which are light orange with a rose tinge; mid. (1937). A cross between *Concatenans* and *Roylei*. AM 1950. H3.

**'Mount Everest'** A lovely form from the Tower Court collection. Flowers pale apricot, freely produced, less tubular than in the typical form.

**Purpurellum group** (var. *purpurellum* COWAN) A form of subsp. *xanthocodon* with the flowers plum-purple. AM 1951.

**Roylei group** (*R. roylei* HOOK. f.) Leaves glaucous, flowers rose-red to purple-red, shorter than those of the type. A splendid form. Bhutan, SE Tibet. AGM 1984.

**subsp. xanthocodon** (HUTCH.) CULLEN (*R. xanthocodon* HUTCH. ) Clusters of waxy, yellow, bell-shaped to funnel-shaped flowers; May and June. Flowers best when given some form of shelter. NE India, Bhutan, SE Tibet. I 1924 by Kingdon-Ward. AM (F) 1935. H4.

**concatenans** See *R. cinnabarinum* Concatenans group.

**concinnum** HEMSL. (Subgenus Rhododendron, Subsect. Triflora) Medium-sized to large shrub with elliptic or obovate-elliptic, scaly leaves, and clusters of funnel-shaped, purplish flowers; April and May. Sichuan, Hubei. I 1904 by Ernest Wilson. H4.

**RHODODENDRON concinnum**—*continued*

> **Benthamianum group** (var. *benthamianum* (HEMSL.) DAVIDIAN) A form with lavender-purple flowers.

> **Pseudoyanthinum group** (*R. pseudoyanthinum* HUTCH.) A lovely variety with deep ruby-red or purple-red flowers. AM 1951.

**coreanum** See *R. yedoense* var. *poukhanense*.

**coriaceum** FRANCH. (Subgenus Hymenanthes, Subsect. Falconera) A large shrub or small tree with large, narrowly elliptic leaves, silvery at first beneath, later greyish to pale brown. Flowers in large, loose trusses, bell-shaped, white, or rose-flushed, with a crimson basal blotch; April. NW Yunnan, SE Tibet. H3-4.

**coryanum** TAGG & FORREST (Subgenus Hymenanthes, Subsect. Argyrophylla) A large shrub, with long, leathery, cinnamon-backed leaves and lax trusses of bell-shaped, creamy-white, crimson-spotted flowers; April and May. Named after that keen amateur gardener Reginald Cory. NW Yunnan, SE Tibet. H4.

**coryphaeum** See *R. praestans* Coryphaeum group.

**cosmetum** See *R. saluenense* subsp. *chameunum*.

**cowanianum** DAVIDIAN (Subgenus Rhododendron, Subsect. Lepidota) A small, deciduous shrub, the leaves covered with yellow scales beneath. Flowers in clusters of 2-4, bell-shaped, reddish-purple; calyx large; May. C Nepal. H3-4.

**crassum** See *R. maddenii* subsp. *crassum*.

**crebreflorum** See *R. cephalanthum* Crebreflorum group.

**cremastum** See *R. campylogynum* Cremastum group.

**crinigerum** FRANCH. (Subgenus Hymenanthes, Subsect. Glischra) A medium-sized shrub with glandular-hairy shoots and glossy green, rather bullate leaves, covered beneath by a creamy-yellow or buff tomentum. The attractive, bell-shaped flowers are white or blush, with a blood-red basal blotch; April and May. NW Yunnan, SE Tibet, NE Upper Burma. First found by the Abbé Soulié in 1895, introduced by George Forrest in 1914. AM (F) 1935. H4.

**croceum** See *R. wardii*.

**cuneatum** W.W. SM. (*R. ravum* BALF. f. & W.W. SM.) (Subgenus Rhododendron, Subsect. Lapponica) Medium-sized shrub with 2.5cm long, densely scaly leaves and 2.5cm long, widely funnel-shaped flowers in varying shades of rose-lilac; April. Yunnan, Sichuan. I 1913. H4.

**cyanocarpum** (FRANCH.) W.W. SM. (Subgenus Hymenanthes, Subsect. Thomsonia) A large shrub, well distinguished by its rigid, rounded, glaucous leaves and trusses of widely funnel-shaped flowers, varying in colour from white, pink to soft rose; March and April. W Yunnan. AM (F) 1933. H4.

**cyclium** See *R. callimorphum*.

**dasycladum** See *R. selense* subsp. *dasycladum*.

**dauricum** L. (Subgenus Rhododendron, Subsect. Rhodorastra) A charming, early flowering, semi-evergreen shrub of medium size, with elliptic leaves 2-3cm long and one to three-flowered trusses of funnel-shaped, bright rose-purple flowers 2.5-3.5cm across from January to March. Closely related to *R. mucronulatum*, differing in its smaller, blunter, partially evergreen leaves and its smaller flowers. Japan, Korea, N China, Mongolia, E Siberia. C 1780. H4.

> **'Hiltingbury'** An evergreen form of compact habit, leaves bronzing in cold weather. AM 1990.

> **'Midwinter'** A deciduous or semi-evergreen form with flowers of phlox-purple. AM 1963. FCC 1969. AGM 1984.

> **Sempervirens group** A form with persistent leaves. C 1817.

**davidsonianum** REHD. & WILS. (*R. charianthum* HUTCH.) (Subgenus Rhododendron, Subsect. Triflora) A medium to large-sized shrub, with lanceolate leaves. Flowers in both terminal and axillary clusters, funnel-shaped, extremely variable in colour from soft pink to purplish-rose, sometimes spotted. April and May. Sichuan. Introduced by E.H. Wilson in 1904. AM (F) 1935. FCC (F) 1955. AGM 1984 (to pink forms only). H3-4.

> **'Caerhays Pink'** Flowers pink.

**decorum** FRANCH. (Subgenus Hymenanthes, Subsect. Fortunea) This large and beautiful Chinese species should be in every representative collection. Leaves glabrous, oblong-

**RHODODENDRON decorum**—*continued*

obovate, pale beneath, up to 15cm long. Flowers large, funnel-shaped, fragrant, in lax trusses, white or shell-pink, sometimes spotted; May and June. NE Burma, Yunnan, Sichuan, Guizhou. I 1901 by Ernest Wilson. H3-4.

**degronianum** CARR. (*R. pentamerum* (MAXIM.) MATSUM. & NAKAI) (*R. metternichii* f. *pentamerum* MAXIM.) (Subgenus Hymenanthes, Subsect. Pontica) A very hardy, small, dome-shaped bush with dark green leaves up to 15cm long, covered below with a fawn or rufous tomentum. Attractive, bell-shaped, soft pink flowers; May. Japan. I 1870. H4.

**subsp. heptamerum** (MAXIM.) HARA (*R. metternichii* SIEB. & ZUCC.) Flowers seven-lobed, rose-coloured; April and May. Japan. Introduced by Fortune and Siebold in 1860. H4.

**'Wada'** (*R. metternichii* 'Wada') An interesting form of subsp. *heptamerum* with leaves which are deep cinnamon-brown beneath, habit more compact.

**delavayi** See *R. arboreum* subsp. *delavayi*.

**deleiense** See *R. tephropeplum*.

**desquamatum** See *R. rubiginosum* Desquamatum group.

†**diaprepes** BALF. f. & W.W. SM. (Subgenus Hymenanthes, Subsect. Fortunea) A magnificent woodland species. A large shrub or small tree with light green, oblong-elliptic leaves up to 30cm long. Flowers in loose trusses, bell-shaped, fleshy, white with a faint rose flush, slightly fragrant; June and July. A parent of 'Polar Bear'. NE Burma, W Yunnan. I 1913 by George Forrest. AM 1926. H3.

**'Gargantua'** (F. 11958) A triploid form with very large flowers, white flushed green at the base. FCC 1974.

**dichroanthum** DIELS (Subgenus Hymenanthes, Subsect. Neriiflora) A slow-growing, dome-shaped shrub 1.2-2m. Leaves 6-10cm long, oblong-obovate to oblanceolate, with white or grey indumentum beneath. Bearing loose trusses of variably coloured, usually deep orange, bell-shaped flowers in May and June. Calyx large and fleshy, coloured as the corolla. Parent of many hybrids. W Yunnan. First found by Forrest in 1906. AM (F) 1923. H4.

**subsp. apodectum** (BALF. f. & W.W. SM.) COWAN A colourful variety with orange-yellow flowers flushed rose or crimson. W Yunnan, NE Upper Burma. I 1913 by George Forrest.

**subsp. herpesticum** See subsp. *scyphocalyx*.

**subsp. scyphocalyx** (BALF. f. & FORR.) COWAN (*R. scyphocalyx* BALF. f. & FORR.) (*R. dichroanthum* subsp. *herpesticum* (BALF. f. & WARD) COWAN) (*R. herpesticum* BALF. f. & WARD) Flowers in clusters of 3-5, of an unusual coppery-orange, the lobes suffused red, calyx similarly coloured. NE Upper Burma, W Yunnan. I by Forrest in 1919.

**didymum** See *R. sanguineum* subsp. *didymum*.

**dilatatum**. See *R. reticulatum*.

**discolor** See *R. fortunei* subsp. *discolor*.

**dryophyllum** See *R. phaeochrysum*.

**eclecteum** BALF. f. & FORR. (Subgenus Hymenanthes, Subsect. Thomsonia) An early flowering shrub of medium size with distinctive, short-stalked oblong or obovate-oblong leaves. Flowers in loose trusses, bell-shaped, fleshy, varying in colour from white to rose-red; Feb to April. Differing from the closely related *R. stewartianum* in the leaves, which are glabrous beneath. Yunnan, Sichuan, SE Tibet, NE Upper Burma. AM (F) 1949. H3.

**edgarianum** REHD. & WILS. A small shrub 0.6-1m high with small, densely scaly, sage-green leaves and a wealth of attractive, small, blue-purple flowers; May and June. A hybrid of *R. nivale*. Sichuan, Yunnan, SE Tibet. H4.

**edgeworthii** HOOK. f. (*R. bullatum* FRANCH.) (Subgenus Rhododendron, Subsect. Edgeworthia) Medium-sized shrub, its branches coated with a soft fawn or brown, woolly tomentum as are the dark green, bullate leaves beneath. Flowers funnel-shaped, white or pink-tinged, richly scented; April and May. Some forms of this beautiful species may be grown in the open in very mild districts, where it forms a rather straggly shrub. N India, Yunnan, Bhutan, SE Tibet, NE Upper Burma. First found by the Abbé Delavay in 1886, introduced by George Forrest in 1904. AM (F) 1923. FCC (F) 1937. AM (F) 1946. H2-4.

**elaeagnoides** See *R. lepidotum*.

**RHODODENDRON**—*continued*

†**elliottii** WATT (Subgenus Hymenanthes, Subsect. Parishia) Large shrub or small tree requiring woodland conditions, with glossy green leaves and large, bell-shaped, scarlet or crimson flowers; May to July. One of the best red-flowered species and the parent of many good hybrids. Nagaland (NE India). I 1927 by Kingdon-Ward. AM 1934. FCC 1937. H1-2.

**eriocarpum** (HAYATA) NAKAI (*R. indicum* var. *eriocarpum* HAYATA) (*R. simsii* var. *eriocarpum* (HAYATA) WILSON) (Subgenus Tsutsutsi, Sect. Tsutsutsi) A slow-growing, dwarf shrub of dense, compact habit. Flowers pink to lavender, large and frilled, opening in June and July. A variable shrub with several forms. Some authorities regard it as a form of *R. indicum*. S Japan, Taiwan. For some cultivars previously listed here see under Evergreen Hybrid Azaleas.

  '**Album Grandiflorum**' Flowers very large, white with green markings.

  '**Terra Cotta Beauty**' Small flowers of terracotta-pink.

**eriogynum** See *R. facetum*.

**eritimum** See *R. anthosphaerum*.

**erubescens** See *R. oreodoxa* var. *fargesii*.

× **erythrocalyx** BALF. f. & FORR. (*R. selense* × *R. wardii*) A medium-sized shrub with ovate to elliptic leaves. Flowers bell-shaped, white or pink, with or without crimson spots and basal blotch; April and May. SE Tibet, NW Yunnan. H3.

  **Panteumorphum group** (*R. panteumorphum* BALF. f. & W.W. SM.) Medium-sized to large shrub with leaves oblong-elliptic, 5-10cm long, trusses of bell-shaped flowers of a lovely pale yellow; April and May. H4.

**euchaites** See *R. neriiflorum* Euchaites group.

**eximium** See *R. falconeri* subsp. *eximium*.

**exquisitum** See *R. oreotrephes* 'Exquisitum'.

**faberi** HEMSL. (Subgenus Hymenanthes, Subsect. Taliensia) Large shrub or small tree, the young shoots clothed with rust-red, woolly indumentum. Leaves up to 15cm or more long, pale to rusty-brown beneath. Loose trusses of white, bell-shaped flowers; May. Sichuan. H4.

  **subsp. prattii** (FRANCH.) CHAMBERLAIN (*R. prattii* FRANCH.) Medium-sized to large shrub. Its leathery, ovate leaves, 10-15cm long, are coated beneath with a fawn or brown indumentum. Flowers bell-shaped, white, with pink spots, calyx conspicuous and leafy; April and May. One needs patience to wait for this plant to reach flowering age. Sichuan. I 1904 by Ernest Wilson. AM 1967. H4.

**facetum** BALF. f. & WARD (*R. eriogynum* BALF. f. & W.W. SM.) (Subgenus Hymenanthes, Subsect. Parishia) A superb, large shrub of tree-like habit requiring woodland conditions; leaves glaucous below. Flowers bell-shaped, up to 7.5cm long and wide, scarlet or crimson; June and July. The parent of many excellent hybrids. NE Upper Burma, W Yunnan. I 1914 by George Forrest. AM 1924. AM 1938. FCC 1980. H2-3.

**falconeri** HOOK. f. (Subgenus Hymenanthes, Subsect. Falconera) This magnificent, Himalayan rhododendron may be grown in sheltered gardens in most parts of the British Isles, where it makes a large shrub or small tree. Leaves large, broadly obovate with deeply impressed veins. It has huge, dome-shaped trusses of waxy, creamy-yellow, purple-blotched, bell-shaped flowers; April and May. E Nepal, Sikkim, Bhutan. Introduced from Sikkim by Sir Joseph Hooker in 1850. AM 1922. AGM 1984. H3-4.

  **subsp. eximium** (NUTT.) CHAMBERLAIN (*R. eximium* NUTT.) A magnificent, large shrub or small tree, the young growths covered with orange-brown indumentum, as are the large leaves, up to 30cm long and 7.5cm wide. The 5cm long, bell-shaped, fleshy flowers are pink or rose; April to May. NE India. AM 1973. H3-4.

**fargesii** See *R. oreodoxa* var. *fargesii*.

**fastigiatum** FRANCH. (Subgenus Rhododendron, Subsect. Lapponica) A dense, small, dome-shaped bush 0.6-1m high with small, scaly leaves, sea-green when young. Flowers lavender-purple, funnel-shaped; April and May. Yunnan. I 1906 by George Forrest. AM (F) 1914. H4.

**fauriei** See *R. brachycarpum* subsp. *fauriei*.

**ferrugineum** L. (Subgenus Rhododendron, Subsect. Rhododendron) The "Alpen Rose" of Switzerland. A small, flattish dome-shaped or spreading shrub, with leaves reddish-scaly

**RHODODENDRON ferrugineum**—*continued*

beneath. Flowers rose-crimson, tubular, borne in small trusses in June. Pyrenees and Alps of C Europe. C 1740. AM 1990. H4.

**f. album** (D. DON) ZAB. Flowers white. I 1830. AM 1969.

**'Coccineum'** A charming form with crimson flowers.

**fictolacteum** See *R. rex* subsp. *fictolacteum*.

**fimbriatum** See *R. hippophaeoides*.

**fittianum** See *R.* 'Fittianum' under Hybrids.

**flavidum** FRANCH. (*R. primulinum* HEMSL.) (Subgenus Rhododendron, Subsect. Lapponica) A pretty, erect shrub 0.6-1m high, with small, glossy, aromatic leaves, and funnel-shaped, primrose-yellow flowers; March. NW Sichuan. I 1905 by Ernest Wilson. AM 1910 (as *R. primulinum*). H4.

**'Album'** Differs in its laxer habit and larger, white flowers. C 1925.

**fletcherianum** DAVIDIAN (Subgenus Rhododendron, Subsect. Maddenia) Small, bristly shrub, with usually oblong-lanceolate, 5cm long leaves, pale brown-scaly beneath. Flowers widely funnel-shaped, nearly 5cm long, pale yellow, with deeply five-lobed calyx; March and April. Perhaps the hardiest member of the Maddenii Subsection, distinguished by its decurrent leaf base, narrowly winged petioles, and crenulate leaf margin. Collected by Joseph Rock in SE Tibet in 1932, and for long grown under the name *R. valentinianum* to which species it is closely related. Named after Dr Harold Fletcher, Regius Keeper, Royal Botanic Garden, Edinburgh, 1956-70. H4.

**floccigerum** FRANCH. (Subgenus Hymenanthes, Subsect. Neriiflora) A small shrub; leaves oblong-elliptic, glaucous below and covered by a loose tomentum. The trusses of narrowly bell-shaped flowers are usually waxy and scarlet but may vary from rose or crimson, to yellow, margined rose; March and April. Yunnan, SE Tibet. I 1914 by George Forrest. H4.

**floribundum** FRANCH. (Subgenus Hymenanthes, Subsect. Argyrophylla) A pleasing large shrub with dense foliage, the leaves rich green and bullate above, white-felted beneath. Flowers bell-shaped, usually magenta-purple, lavender-purple or rose, with crimson blotch and spots; April. Sichuan. I 1903 by Ernest Wilson. H4.

**forrestii** BALF. f. ex DIELS (Subgenus Hymenanthes, Subsect. Neriiflora) A slow-growing, prostrate shrub, occasionally up to 30cm high, forming mats or low hummocks of dark green, broadly obovate to rounded leaves which are 2.5-3.5cm long and purple beneath. The comparatively large, bell-shaped, bright scarlet flowers are borne singly or in pairs from the tips of short branchlets; April and May. Requires moist soil and partial shade. SE Tibet, NW Yunnan, NE Upper Burma. Discovered by George Forrest in 1905 and introduced by him in 1914. H4.

**Repens group** (*R. repens* BALF. f. & FORR.) A choice creeping variety, differing in its leaves which are pale or glaucous-green below. FCC (F) 1935. A parent of the FCC cultivars 'Ethel', 'Elizabeth' and 'Little Ben'. The cultivars **'Scarlet Pimpernel'** (K.W. 5845) and **'Scarlet Runner'** (K.W. 5846) were both introduced by Kingdon-Ward.

**fortunei** LINDL. (Subgenus Hymenanthes, Subsect. Fortunea) A large shrub or small tree, leaves elliptic, 10-18cm long. Flowers bell-shaped, produced in loose trusses of 6-12, lilac-pink, fragrant in May. Probably the first hardy Chinese species to be introduced. A parent of numerous hybrids. China. Introduced by Robert Fortune in 1855. H4.

**subsp. discolor** (FRANCH.) CHAMBERLAIN (*R. discolor* FRANCH.) A superb, late flowering form making a large shrub. Leaves oblong-elliptic to oblanceolate up to 20cm long. The funnel-shaped, fragrant, pink flowers, with seven-lobed corollas are borne in huge trusses, giving a magnificent display; June and July. A parent of many distinguished hybrids. Sichuan, Hubei. Introduced by E.H. Wilson in 1900. AM 1921. AM (F) 1922. FCC (F) 1922. AGM 1984. H4.

**Houlstonii group** (*R. houlstonii* HEMSL. & WILS.) A choice small tree or large shrub, a form of subsp. *discolor*. Leaves oblong-oblanceolate 7.5-15cm long. Flowers bell-sʼaped, usually soft lilac or pale pink, faintly lined and spotted; May. A parent of the AM hybrid named after our late Manager Arthur J. Ivens. Hubei. Sichuan. I about 1900 by Ernest Wilson. H4.

**'Mrs Charles Butler'** Flowers blush, fading to almost white.

**RHODODENDRON**—*continued*

**fulgens** HOOK.f. (Subgenus Hymenanthes, Subsect. Fulgensia) Medium-sized shrub with broad leaves, dark shining green above, covered with reddish-brown indumentum below. The tight, rounded trusses contain 10-12, bell-shaped flowers of a bright scarlet; Feb to April. The young shoots are adorned with attractive crimson bracts. Bark in some forms attractively peeling. E Nepal, Sikkim, Bhutan, Assam, S Tibet. I 1850 by Sir Joseph Hooker. AM 1933. H4.

**fulvum** BALF. f. & W.W. SM. (*R. fulvoides* BALF. f. & FORR.) (Subgenus Hymenanthes, Subsect. Fulva) A large shrub or small tree, attractive on account of its large, polished dark green leaves which are clothed beneath with a conspicuous, cinnamon indumentum. Flowers bell-shaped, blush to deep rose with or without a crimson blotch; March and April. W Yunnan, NE Upper Burma, SE Tibet. Discovered and introduced by George Forrest in 1912. AM (F) 1933. FCC (F) 1981. H4.

**galactinum** BALF. f. ex TAGG (Subgenus Hymenanthes, Subsect. Falconera) A large shrub or small tree with large, leathery leaves, clothed beneath with buff-grey or pale cinnamon indumentum. Flowers bell-shaped, white to deep rose, with a crimson blotch and spots within; April and May. C Sichuan. Discovered and introduced by E.H. Wilson in 1908. H4.

×**geraldii** (HUTCH.) IVENS (*R. sutchuenense* × *R. praevernum*) A large shrub with splendid foliage. Flowers white, with a deep purplish basal blotch; Feb and March. Occurs in the wild with the parents. AM 1945. H3-4.

**glaucophyllum** HOOK. f. (*R. glaucum* HOOK. f.) (Subgenus Rhododendron, Subsect. Glauca) A small, aromatic shrub with lanceolate leaves, white beneath and bearing attractive, bell-shaped flowers of a pale old-rose to lilac shade; calyx large and leafy; April and May. E Nepal, Sikkim, Bhutan, SE Tibet. I 1850 by Sir Joseph Hooker. H3-4.

**var. luteiflorum** See *R. luteiflorum*.

**var. tubiforme** COWAN & DAVIDIAN Flowers tubular with spreading lobes, pale pink flushed white. I by Ludlow and Sherriff from E Bhutan.

**glischroides** See *R. glischrum* subsp. *glischroides*.

**glischrum** BALF. f. & W.W. SM. (Subgenus Hymenanthes, Subsect. Glischra) Large shrub or small tree. Leaves oblanceolate 10-25cm long. The twigs and petioles covered with gland-tipped bristles. Flowers bell-shaped, varying in colour from white to deep rose, with crimson blotch and spots; April and May. Yunnan, Upper Burma, SE Tibet. I 1914 by George Forrest. H3.

**subsp. glischroides** (TAGG & FORR.) CHAMBERLAIN (*R. glischroides* TAGG & FORR.) Large shrub with bristly young shoots. Leaves oblong-lanceolate 10-15cm long, bristle-clad on the undersurface. Flowers bell-shaped, white or creamy-white, flushed rose, with a crimson basal blotch; March and April. NE Upper Burma. I 1925 by George Forrest. H3-4.

**subsp. rude** (TAGG & FORR.) CHAMBERLAIN (*R. rude* TAGG & FORR.) Medium-sized shrub with bristly twigs and dark green, broad oblong to oblanceolate, 13-20cm long leaves which are hispid above and covered with crisped hairs beneath. Flowers bell-shaped, purplish-crimson, with darker lines; April and May. Yunnan. I 1925 by George Forrest. H4.

**glomerulatum** See *R. yungningense*.

†**grande** WIGHT (*R. argenteum* HOOK. f.) (Subgenus Hymenanthes, Subsect. Grandia) A small tree or large shrub of imposing appearance. The handsome leathery, oblong to oblanceolate leaves are 15-30cm long, dark green and shining above, silvery-white or buff tomentose beneath. Flowers bell-shaped, 5-7.5cm across, ivory-white, with purple basal blotch within, pink in bud, borne in dense rounded trusses; Feb to April. One of the most spectacular species but only suitable for sheltered woodland gardens in the milder counties. There exist some fine examples in Cornwall. E Nepal, Sikkim, Bhutan. Introduced by Sir Joseph Hooker in 1850. FCC (F) 1901. H2-3.

**griersonianum** BALF. f. & FORR. (Subgenus Hymenanthes, Subsect. Griersonia) A splendid, distinct and striking, medium-sized, Chinese rhododendron. Leaves lanceolate, 10-20cm long, matt green above, buff woolly beneath. The brilliant geranium-scarlet, narrowly bell-shaped flowers appear in June and are unlike any others in the genus. It is a prolific parent and its hybrid progeny are now innumerable. Distinct on account of its long,

**RHODODENDRON griersonianum**—*continued*

tapered flower-buds, a character possessed by only one other species, ie *R. auriculatum*. Yunnan, N Burma. Discovered and introduced by George Forrest in 1917. FCC 1924. H3-4.

†**griffithianum** WIGHT (*R. aucklandii* HOOK. f.) (Subgenus Hymenanthes, Subsect. Fortunea) A magnificent, large shrub or small tree, the parent of innumerable award-winning hybrids. Unfortunately, only suitable for the most sheltered gardens in the mildest areas. Bark of branches reddish-brown, attractively peeling. Leaves up to 30cm long. Flowers widely bell-shaped, 7.5cm long, and up to 15cm across, carried in a loose truss of 3-6, white, with faint green speckles, sweetly-scented; May. E Nepal, NE India, Bhutan. Introduced by Sir Joseph Hooker in 1850. FCC 1866. H1-3.

**habrotrichum** BALF. f. & W.W. SM. (Subgenus Hymenanthes, Subsect. Glischra) Medium-sized to large shrub with reddish-bristly young shoots, dark green leaves up to 18cm long, and compact trusses of funnel-shaped flowers of white to deep rose; April and May. W Yunnan, NE Upper Burma. I 1912-13. AM (F) 1933. H3.

**haematodes** FRANCH. (Subgenus Hymenanthes, Subsect. Neriiflora) Generally considered one of the finest of Chinese rhododendrons. A compact, small to medium-sized, slow-growing bush. Leaves oblong-obovate, 4-7.5cm long, dark green, thickly rufous-felted beneath; flowers bell-shaped, brilliant scarlet-crimson; May and June. A parent of several good hybrids. W Yunnan. Introduced by George Forrest about 1911. FCC 1926. H4.

**subsp. chaetomallum** (BALF. f. & FORR.) CHAMBERLAIN (*R. chaetomallum* BALF. f. & FORR.) A very splendid, medium-sized shrub with obovate leaves densely covered beneath with a brown, woolly indumentum. Flowers in loose trusses, blood-red, waxy, bell-shaped; March and April. NE Upper Burma, SE Tibet, NW Yunnan. I 1918 by George Forrest. AM (F) 1959. H4.

**hanceanum** HEMSL. (Subgenus Rhododendron, Subsect. Tephropepla) A dainty, small shrub with bronze-coloured young growths and ovate-lanceolate to obovate leaves which are finely scaly below. Flowers funnel-shaped, 2.5cm long, creamy-white or pale yellow, slightly scented; April. C Sichuan. H4.

**Nanum group** A slow-growing shrub making a neat compact hummock up to 35cm. A choice rock garden shrublet. 'Canton Consul', a selection of this, received an AM in 1957.

**heliolepis** FRANCH. (*R. oporinum* BALF. f. & WARD) (Subgenus Rhododendron, Subsect. Heliolepida) Medium-sized shrub. Leaves elliptic-oblong 6-10cm long, truncate or rounded at the base, intensely aromatic. Flowers in small, loose trusses, funnel-shaped, purple-rose; May and June, sometimes later. Yunnan. I 1912 by George Forrest. AM (F) 1954. H4.

**hemitrichotum** BALF. f. & FORR. (Subgenus Rhododendron, Subsect. Scabrifolia) A small shrub. Leaves oblanceolate about 2.5cm long. Very attractive in April with its numerous small, funnel-shaped flowers, bright red in bud, opening white or pale pink with darker edges. N Yunnan, SW Sichuan. Introduced by Forrest in 1919. H4.

**hemsleyanum** WILS. (Subgenus Hymenanthes, Subsect. Fortunea) A large shrub or occasionally a small tree with auricled leaves up to 20cm long. Flowers trumpet-shaped 8-10cm long, white; May and June. Named after the English botanist William Botting Hemsley (1843-1924) who named and described numerous plants of Chinese origin. Sichuan (Mt Omei). C 1964. H4.

×**hillieri** DAVIDIAN A small shrub sometimes reaching 180cm with bristly hairy shoots and leathery dark green leaves to 6cm long, thinly brown-hairy beneath. Flowers bell-shaped, crimson, to 4cm long in trusses of 3-7. SE Tibet. Discovered by George Forrest in 1922 at 13,000-14,000ft and named after Sir Harold Hillier 'in recognition of his outstanding contributions to the cultivation of rhododendrons'. It is a naturally occurring hybrid, probably involving *R. catacosmum* and *R. temenium*.

**hippophaeoides** BALF. f. & W.W. SM. (*R. fimbriatum* HUTCH.) (Subgenus Rhododendron, Subsect. Lapponica) A small, erect, leafy shrub with small, greyish-green, oblanceolate leaves and usually lavender, lilac or rose-coloured, or occasionally lilac-pink, funnel-shaped flowers; March and April. A fairly tolerant species which will grow even in semi-bog conditions. Yunnan, Sichuan. I 1913 by George Forrest. AM (F) 1927. H4.

**RHODODENDRON hippophaeoides**—*continued*

**'Inshriach'** A choice form raised by Jack Drake in Scotland. Flowers lavender-mauve, darker at margins, in comparatively large, dense clusters.

**hirsutum** L. (Subgenus Rhododendron, Subsect. Rhododendron) Small, twiggy shrub, with bristly shoots and bristle-fringed leaves. Clusters of tubular rose-pink flowers in June. Alps of C Europe. This species has the distinction of being the first rhododendron to be introduced into cultivation. I 1656. H4.

**'Album'** Flowers white.

**hirtipes** TAGG (Subgenus Hymenanthes, Subsect. Selensia) A large shrub or small tree with bristly shoots and broadly obovate leaves up to 12cm long. Flowers bell-shaped, in trusses of 3-5, red in bud opening pink to white, often spotted and streaked with red. SE Tibet. I 1924 by Kingdon-Ward. H3-4.

**hodgsonii** HOOK. f. (Subgenus Hymenanthes, Subsect. Falconera) A large Himalayan shrub or small tree, grown for its very handsome foliage. Leaves up to 30cm long and 13cm wide, dark green above, grey or fawn-tomentose beneath. Flowers bell-shaped, dark magenta, carried in dense trusses; April. E Nepal, NE India, Bhutan, SE Tibet. I 1850 by Sir Joseph Hooker. H4.

†**hookeri** NUTT. (Subgenus Hymenanthes, Subsect. Thomsonia) An unusual species of medium to large size. Leaves pale glaucous-green beneath, the veins studded with small, isolated but conspicuous tufts of hooked hairs, a character possessed by no other known species. Flowers bell-shaped, blood-red or pink, calyx often similarly coloured; March and April. NE India. I 1850. FCC (F) 1933. H3.

**houlstonii** See *R. fortunei* Houlstonii group.

**hunnewellianum** REHD. & WILS. (Subgenus Hymenanthes, Subsect. Argyrophylla) An attractive, large shrub or small tree neat and compact in growth, the long, narrow leaves with conspicuously impressed venation above, loosely grey-felted beneath. Flowers bell-shaped white, tinted pink; March and April. Named in honour of a well-known New England family of great gardeners. C Sichuan. I 1908 by Ernest Wilson. H4.

**hypenanthum** See *R. anthopogon* subsp. *hypenanthum*.

**hyperythrum** HAYATA (Subgenus Hymenanthes, Subsect. Pontica) Small shrub with usually oblong, curiously rigid, polished green leaves, the lower surfaces dotted with reddish specks. Flowers funnel-shaped, pure white or with purple spots; April and May. Taiwan. H3-4.

**impeditum** BALF. f. & W.W. SM. (*R. litangense* BALF. f. & HUTCH.) (Subgenus Rhododendron, Subsect. Lapponica) A dwarf, alpine shrub only a few centimetres high with tiny leaves, forming low, tangled mounds of scaly branches. Flowers funnel-shaped, light purplish-blue; April and May. Frequently confused with *R. fastigiatum*. Most suitable for the rock garden. Yunnan, Sichuan. Introduced by George Forrest in 1911. AM (F) 1944. AGM 1984. H4.

**imperator** See *R. uniflorum* var. *imperator*.

**indicum** (L.) SWEET (*R. macranthum* (BUNGE) D. DON) (*Azalea indica* L.) (*A. macrantha* BUNGE) (Subgenus Tsutsutsi, Sect. Tsutsutsi) A small, dense, semi-evergreen bush rarely reaching medium size. Leaves small, narrow, lanceolate to oblanceolate, often turning crimson or purple in autumn. Flowers single or in pairs, widely funnel-shaped, varying in colour from red to scarlet; June. A variable species with numerous forms. Both this species and *R. simsii* and their forms are often referred to as "Indian Azaleas". S Japan. I about 1877. AMT 1975. H2-3.

**'Balsaminiflorum'** (*R. rosiflorum*) (*Azalea rosiflora*) Charming dwarf form with double, salmon-pink flowers. FCC 1882.

**'Coccineum'** Low, spreading shrub, with large, single, scarlet-red flowers; late.

**'Double Rose'** Flowers double, rose-pink.

**var. eriocarpum** See *R. eriocarpum*.

**'Hakata Shiro'** A low shrub with very large, ivory-white flowers. Earlier flowering and more tender than the type.

**'Kokinshita'** See under Evergreen Azaleas.

**'Misomogiri'** A form with semi-double, salmon-coloured flowers.

**'Salmonea'** Low-growing habit, large, single, salmon-red flowers.

**'Zangetsu'** Flowers pale crimson with white throat.

**RHODODENDRON**—*continued*

**insigne** HEMSL. & WILS. (Subgenus Hymenanthes, Subsect. Argyrophylla) An exceptionally hardy and unmistakable, slow-growing Chinese species eventually attaining a large size. Leaves leathery, oblong-lanceolate, 6-13cm long, rich glossy green above and silvery-white beneath when young, assuming a metallic lustre. Large trusses of bell-shaped flowers, soft pink with dark markings; May and June. C Sichuan. I 1908 by Ernest Wilson. AM 1923. H4.

**intricatum** FRANCH. (Subgenus Rhododendron, Subsect. Lapponica) Small, densely twiggy shrub, 0.6-1m high, with small, olive-green, aromatic leaves. Flowers funnel-shaped, lavender-blue, in small, rounded trusses; April and early May. Suitable for the rock garden. A parent of the AM cultivar 'Bluebird'. N Yunnan, Sichuan. Introduced by E. H. Wilson in 1904. FCC 1907. H4.

**irroratum** FRANCH. (Subgenus Hymenanthes, Subsect. Irrorata) A large shrub or small tree. Leaves oblanceolate or elliptic, 6-13cm long, green on both surfaces. Flowers narrowly bell-shaped, variously coloured, usually white, pink, or creamy-yellow with a more or less broad ray of dark crimson markings or sometimes heavily spotted; March to May. Yunnan, Sichuan. AM (F) 1957. I about 1886 by the Abbé Delavay. H3.

'**Polka Dot**' A very remarkable form, the white flowers being densely marked with purple dots. It received an AM when exhibited by Exbury in 1957.

**japonicum** (A. GRAY) SURINGAR ex WILS. (*R. molle* SIEB. & ZUCC. not G. DON) (*R. sinense* MAXIM) (*Azalea mollis* (SIEB. & ZUCC.) ANDRE not BLUME) (Subgenus Pentanthera, Sect. Pentanthera) A tall, deciduous shrub of medium size with ovate-oblong ciliated leaves 5-10cm long, often giving rich autumn tints. Flowers usually appearing before the leaves, fragrant, funnel-shaped, orange-red or salmon-red, with basal blotch, borne in conspicuous trusses of 6-12; May. This is a dominant parent of many named garden hybrids. Japan. I 1861. H4.

†**johnstoneanum** WATT ex HUTCH. (Subgenus Rhododendron, Subsect. Maddenia) Large shrub with leaves elliptic to obovate, ciliate, 5-10cm long, densely scaly below. The large, fragrant, funnel-shaped flowers are borne in clusters of 3 or 4. They are creamy-white or pale yellow in colour, with red spots and a yellow blotch; May. There are forms with double flowers. Manipur. I 1882. AM (F) 1934. H2-3.

**kaempferi** PLANCH. (*R. obtusum* var. *kaempferi* (PLANCH.) WILS.) (Subgenus Tsutsutsi, Sect. Tsutsutsi) A very beautiful and very hardy deciduous or semi-evergreen shrub of medium size. Leaves 4-7.5cm long and like the young shoots strigose pubescent. Flowers in clusters of 2 to 4, funnel-shaped, varying in colour from biscuit to salmon-red to orange-red, or rose-scarlet; May and June. A parent of many of the Kurume azaleas. Japan. Introduced by Professor Sargent in 1892. AM 1953. AGM 1984. H4.

'**Daimio**' See 'Mikado'.

'**Highlight**' A striking form raised in our nurseries; flowers bright salmon-orange.

'**Mikado**' ('Daimio') Flowers an exquisite shade of apricot-salmon, late June and July. AGM 1984. AM 1988.

**keiskei** MIQ. (Subgenus Rhododendron, Subsect. Triflora) A very attractive, free-flowering, semi-evergreen, dwarf species suitable for the rock garden. Leaves 2.5-7.5cm long, lanceolate. Flowers widely funnel-shaped in trusses of 3-5, lemon-yellow; March to May. Japan. I 1908. AM 1929. H3-4.

'**Yaku Fairy**' A very dwarf or prostrate form collected on Mt Kuromi, Yakushima. AM 1970.

**keleticum** See *R. calostrotum* subsp. *keleticum*.

**keysii** NUTT. (Subgenus Rhododendron, Subsect. Cinnabarina) An interesting, medium-sized to large shrub with oblong-lanceolate, densely scaly leaves; very attractive when bearing its clusters of remarkable tubular, cuphea-like flowers of bright orange-red, tipped yellow and 2cm long; June. SE Tibet, Bhutan, Assam. I 1851. H3-4.

**kiusianum** MAK. (*Azalea kiusiana*) (*R. obtusum* f. *japonicum* (MAXIM.) WILS.) (Subgenus Tsutsutsi, Sect. Tsutsutsi) "Kyushu Azalea". A dwarf, evergreen or semi-evergreen shrub, occasionally up to 1m, of dense, spreading habit. Leaves small, oval. Flowers in clusters of 2-5, funnel-shaped, varying in colour from salmon-red to crimson or purple, but usually lilac-purple; May and June. This is generally regarded as one of the species from

**RHODODENDRON kiusianum**—*continued*

which the Kurume azaleas were developed. It is restricted in the wild to the tops of high mountains on the island of Kyushu (Japan). I 1918 by Ernest Wilson. H3-4. AGM 1984.

**'Hillier's Pink'** A lovely form with flowers of a clear lilac-pink. Raised in our nurseries about 1957.

**kotschyi** See *R. myrtifolium.*

**lacteum** FRANCH. (Subgenus Hymenanthes, Subsect. Taliensia) A beautiful large shrub or rarely a small tree of slow growth. Leaves oblong to oblong-elliptic, covered with a thin, suede-like fawn or brown tomentum below. Flowers bell-shaped, normally clear soft yellow, sometimes with a pink stain or crimson blotch; April and May. Unfortunately of rather weak constitution. W Yunnan. I 1910 by George Forrest. FCC (F) 1926. H4.

**lanatum** HOOK. f. (Subgenus Hymenanthes, Subsect. Lanata) A small to medium-sized, unusual and attractive shrub. Leaves thick, inclined to obovate, 5-10cm long, brown-felted beneath. Flowers bell-shaped, pale yellow with crimson-purple markings; April and May. NE India, Bhutan, S Tibet. Discovered by Sir Joseph Hooker in 1848. I 1850. H4.

**lanigerum** TAGG (*R. silvaticum* COWAN) (Subgenus Hymenanthes, Subsect. Arborea) Large shrub or small tree, the young shoots grey tomentose and the large, oblong-lanceolate leaves 10-23cm long, covered with white, grey or cinnamon-brown tomentum beneath. Flowers in a round, compact truss of 25 or more, bell-shaped, up to 5cm long, rose-purple to dark magenta; March and April. Assam, SE Tibet. I 1928 by Kingdon-Ward. AM 1949. AM 1951 (as *R. silvaticum*). H4.

**'Chapel Wood'** Flowers neyron-rose. AM 1961. FCC 1967.

**'Round Wood'** Flowers crimson. AM 1951.

**'Silvia'** Flowers pale crimson flushed white. AM 1954.

**lapponicum** WAHLENB. (Subgenus Rhododendron, Subsect. Lapponica) A dwarf shrub of dense, compact habit. The tiny leaves are densely scaly. Flowers in clusters of 2 or 3, funnel-shaped, purple; Jan and Feb. A difficult plant to keep in cultivation. Arctic regions of Europe, Asia and America. I 1825. H4.

**ledifolium** See *R.* Mucronatum group under Evergreen Azaleas.

**ledoides** See *R. trichostomum* Ledoides group.

**lepidostylum** BALF. f. & FORR. (Subgenus Rhododendron, Subsect. Trichoclada) A dwarf, deciduous or semi-evergreen shrub occasionally to 1m, of dense, compact habit. The small, bristly, ovate leaves are a conspicuous blue-green above until the winter months. Flowers funnel-shaped, pale yellow, produced singly or in pairs during May and June. A choice shrub for the peat garden or shady rock garden. The most glaucous-leaved of the dwarf rhododendrons. SW Yunnan. I 1924 by George Forrest. AM 1969. H4.

**lepidotum** G. DON (*R. obovatum* HOOK. f.) (*R. elaeagnoides* HOOK. f.) (Subgenus Rhododendron, Subsect. Lepidota) A variable dwarf shrub with conspicuously scaly oblanceolate leaves 2-4cm long. Flowers 1-3 in a small truss, saucer-shaped, scaly on the outside, varying in colour from pink to purple, occasionally yellow or white; June. NW Himalaya to Yunnan. I 1829. H3-4.

**'Reuthe's Purple'** Flowers deep rose-purple, freely borne. AM 1967.

**leucaspis** TAGG (Subgenus Rhododendron, Subsect. Boothia) Dwarf shrub occasionally to 1m, with elliptic to obovate 4-6cm long hairy leaves and scaly stems. The 5cm diameter, lovely saucer-shaped flowers are milky-white, with contrasting chocolate-brown anthers, in clusters of 2 or 3; Feb and March. It should be given a sheltered site. A parent of several fine hybrids. Burma-Tibet frontier. Introduced by Kingdon-Ward in 1925. AM (F) 1929. FCC 1944. H3-4.

**linearifolium** See *R. macrosepalum* 'Linearifolium'.

**var. macrosepalum** See *R. macrosepalum.*

**litangense** See *R. impeditum.*

**litiense** See *R. wardii* Litiense group.

×**lochmium** BALF. f. (Subgenus Rhododendron, Subsect. Triflora) A medium-sized shrub of loose, open habit with leaves densely scaly beneath. Flowers funnel-shaped, white, flushed rosy-purple; May. A natural hybrid probably of *R. davidsonianum* and *R. trichanthum.* H4.

**lopsangianum** See *R. thomsonii* subsp. *lopsangianum.*

**RHODODENDRON**—*continued*

**lowndesii** DAVIDIAN (Subgenus Rhododendron, Subsect. Lepidota) A dwarf, deciduous shrublet of compact habit. Leaves bright green, obovate, bristly, up to 2.5cm long. Flowers solitary or in pairs, widely bell-shaped, 2.5cm across, pale yellow with light reddish spots; June and July. A charming diminutive species for the peat garden or rock garden. Discovered in C Nepal by Col Donald Lowndes in 1950. H3-4.

**ludlowii** COWAN (Subgenus Rhododendron, Subsect. Uniflora) A charming, dwarf shrub for the peat garden. Leaves obovate about 12mm long. Flowers borne singly or in pairs, 2.5cm long and wide, saucer-shaped, yellow, with reddish-brown spots in the centre; calyx large and leafy; April and May. Parent of AM cultivar 'Chikor'. SE Tibet. I 1938 by Ludlow, Sherriff and Taylor. H3-4.

**luteiflorum** (DAVIDIAN) DAVIDIAN (*R. glaucophyllum* var. *luteiflorum* DAVIDIAN) (Subgenus Rhododendron, Subsect. Glauca) A small to medium-sized shrub of compact habit closely related to *R. glaucophyllum* and differing in its yellow flowers. April-May. NE Burma. I 1933 by Kingdon-Ward. H3.

**lutescens** FRANCH. (Subgenus Rhododendron, Subsect. Triflora) A lovely, but variable Chinese species up to 3.6m, requiring shelter on account of its early flowering. Leaves lanceolate, 4-7.5cm long. Its primrose-yellow, funnel-shaped flowers and bronze-red young leaves are especially effective in thin woodland. Feb to April. C Sichuan, Yunnan. Discovered by the Abbé Delavay and introduced by E.H. Wilson in 1904. AGM 1984. H3-4.

**'Bagshot Sands'** Flowers larger, primrose-yellow. Young growth deep bronze-red. AM 1953.

**'Exbury'** Flowers lemon-yellow. FCC 1938. AGM 1984.

**luteum** SWEET (*Azalea pontica* L.) (Subgenus Pentanthera, Sect. Pentanthera) The well-known, common, fragrant, yellow azalea. A medium-sized, deciduous shrub, occasionally reaching 3.5m high and as much or more across. Winter buds and young shoots sticky. Leaves oblong to oblong-lanceolate, 5-10cm long, turning to rich shades of crimson, purple and orange in autumn. Flowers in a rounded truss, funnel-shaped, yellow, viscid on the outside, richly and strongly fragrant; May. Caucasus, E Europe, occasionally naturalised in the British Isles. I 1793. AM 1979. AGM 1984. H4.

**lysolepis** HUTCH. An intricately-branched, small shrub of stiff, erect habit, with small, bright shiny green leaves. Flowers funnel-shaped, rosy-mauve, lavender-blue or purple, in three-flowered trusses; April and May. Probably a natural hybrid of *R. flavidum*. Sichuan. H4.

**macabeanum** WATT ex BALF. f. (Subgenus Hymenanthes, Subsect. Grandia) A magnificent species for woodland conditions. A large, rounded shrub or small tree. The handsome leaves up to 30cm long are dark, shining green and conspicuously veined above, greyish or greyish-white tomentose beneath. The large trusses of bell-shaped, pale-yellow, purple-blotched flowers are borne in March or April. In some forms the flowers are deep canary-yellow. Assam, Manipur. Introduced by Kingdon-Ward about 1928. AM 1937. FCC 1938. AGM 1984. H3-4.

**macranthum** See *R. indicum*.

**macrophyllum** G. DON (*R. californicum* HOOK.) (Subgenus Hymenanthes, Subsect. Pontica) A large shrub with strong, stout stems and leaves like those of *R. ponticum*. Flowers bell-shaped, up to 20 in a compact truss, rose-purple with reddish-brown spots. Opening in May and June. W North America. I 1850 by William Lobb. H4.

**macrosepalum** MAXIM. (*R. linearifolium* var. *macrosepalum* (MAXIM.) MAK.) (Subgenus Tsutsusi, Sect. Tsutsusi) A small semi-evergreen shrub of loose, spreading habit with often densely glandular hairy young shoots. Leaves ovate to ovate-elliptic or lanceolate, densely hairy, some leaves often turn rich crimson in autumn. Flowers fragrant, funnel-shaped, 5cm across, lilac-pink to rose-purple; calyx lobes long and narrow; April and May. Japan. I 1863. H3.

**'Linearifolium'** (*R. linearifolium* SIEB. & ZUCC.) An unusual form with narrower leaves up to 7.5cm long by 6mm wide. The pink flowers are deeply divided into 5 narrow segments. Long cultivated in Japan. C 1808. H3-4.

**maculiferum** FRANCH. (Subgenus Hymenanthes, Subsect. Maculifera) A medium-sized to large shrub or small tree. Leaves 7.5-13cm long, oval to obovate, sea-green beneath.

**RHODODENDRON maculiferum**—*continued*

Flowers in a loose truss, bell-shaped, white or rose-flushed, with a dark black-purple basal blotch; April. Sichuan, Hubei. I 1901 by Ernest Wilson. H3.

**subsp. anhweiense** (WILS.) CHAMBERLAIN (*R. anhweiense* WILS.) Medium-sized shrub with ovate-lanceolate leaves 5-7.5cm long. Rounded heads of bell-shaped, white flowers, usually with a pink flush and reddish-purple spots; April and May. Anhui Province (China). AM 1976. H4.

†**maddenii** HOOK. f. (Subgenus Rhododendron, Subsect. Maddenia) A large shrub or small tree with very fragrant, white or pink flowers. Rather tender in its typical state, the following is more hardy. NE India, Bhutan, SE Tibet. I 1850 by Sir Joseph Hooker. H2-3.

**subsp. crassum** (FRANCH.) CULLEN (*R. crassum* FRANCH.) A medium-sized to large shrub with stout, scaly young shoots. Leaves lanceolate or oblanceolate, 5-12cm long, thick and rigid, glossy dark green above, densely rusty scaly below. Flowers funnel-shaped, 5-8cm long, varying in colour from white to pink, with or without a yellow blotch, sweetly-scented; June and July. In some forms, one of the hardiest members of its group. A beautiful, late flowering shrub, worth growing as a conservatory shrub in cold districts. N Vietnam, Yunnan, SE Tibet, Upper Burma, Manipur. Introduced by George Forrest in 1906. AM (F) 1924. AM 1938. H2-4.

†**magnificum** WARD (Subgenus Hymenanthes, Subsect. Grandia) A magnificent large shrub or small tree for a very sheltered woodland site with leaves 30-45cm long, covered with a white or greyish-white indumentum beneath. Flowers in a dense truss, bell-shaped, 5cm long, rose-purple; Feb and April. Flowers not produced on young plants. Burma-Tibet frontier. I 1931. AM (F) 1950. H2-3.

**makinoi** TAGG (*R. metternichii* var. *angustifolium* (NAKAI) OHWI) (Subgenus Hymenanthes, Subsect. Pontica) A very hardy, medium-sized shrub. The young growths are clothed with a white or tawny woolly indumentum and appear in late summer. Leaves narrow lanceolate, somewhat bullate above, thickly fawn or tawny-woolly tomentose beneath. Flowers bell-shaped, soft pink, sometimes with crimson dots; June. Japan. H3-4.

**mallotum** BALF. f. & WARD (*R. aemulorum* BALF. f.) (Subgenus Hymenanthes, Subsect. Neriiflora) A distinct and beautiful large shrub or small tree, with obovate leaves 7.5-15cm long, covered beneath with red-brown, woolly indumentum. Flowers bell-shaped, dark crimson; March and April. W Yunnan, NE Upper Burma. I 1919 by Reginald Farrer. AM 1933. H4.

**mariesii** HEMSL. & WILS. (Subgenus Tsutsutsi, Sect. Brachycalyx) A medium-sized to large, deciduous shrub. Leaves 3-7.5cm long, prominently reticulate beneath, borne in clusters of 2 or 3 at the ends of the branches. Flowers saucer-shaped or shallowly funnel-shaped, 5cm across, lilac or pale rose, with reddish spots on upper lobes; April. SE and C China, Taiwan. I 1886 by Augustine Henry. H3.

**maximum** L. (Subgenus Hymenanthes, Subsect. Pontica) The "Great Laurel" or "Rose Bay" of the United States. A useful and very hardy, large, evergreen shrub, or small tree, with leaves 10-30cm long. Flowers in compact trusses, funnel-shaped, varying in colour from purple-rose to white, slightly fragrant; July. E North America. I 1736 by Peter Collinson. H4. A plant previously listed as an intergeneric hybrid with *Kalmia latifolia* has the leaves lanceolate-oblong to oblanceolate, 7-10cm long, sometimes twisted, the apex either retuse or mucronate, decurrent at the base into a long slender petiole. A specimen in the Hillier Gardens and Arboretum has not flowered though buds have been produced. It appears to be an abnormal form of *R. maximum*.

**maxwellii** See *R.* 'Maxwellii' under Evergreen Azaleas.

**meddianum** FORR. (Subgenus Hymenanthes, Subsect. Thomsonia) Medium-sized to large shrub with glaucous young shoots and obovate or oval leaves, 5-18cm long. Flowers bell-shaped, fleshy, deep crimson or bright scarlet; April. A parent of the AM cultivars 'Queen of Hearts' and 'Rocket'. W Yunnan, NE Upper Burma. I 1917 by George Forrest. H2-4.

**var. atrokermesinum** TAGG A variety with usually larger, darker flowers and glandular branchlets. NE Upper Burma. AM 1954.

**megeratum** BALF. f. & FORR. (Subgenus Rhododendron, Subsect. Boothia) A charming but fastidious, dwarf species. Leaves glaucous and scaly below; flowers bell-shaped, rich

**RHODODENDRON megeratum**—*continued*
yellow, calyx large; March and April. NW Yunnan, S Tibet, NE India, NE Burma. I 1914 by George Forrest. AM 1935. AM 1970. H3.

**mekongense** FRANCH. (Subgenus Rhododendron, Subsect. Trichoclada) A small semi-evergreen shrub with sea-green leaves. Funnel-shaped yellow or greenish-yellow flowers open in spring or summer. E Nepal, NE Burma, S Tibet, NW Yunnan.

**'Doshong La'** (KW 5829) (Viridescens group) Flowers yellow flushed pink at the tips of the lobes, flecked olive-green inside. Collected by Kingdon-Ward at the Doshong La Pass, Tibet. AM 1972.

**Viridescens group** (*R. viridescens* HUTCH.) A small, evergreen shrub with oblong-elliptic leaves, about 2.5-3.5cm long, glaucous beneath. Flowers funnel-shaped, yellowish-green, spotted green within; June. SE Tibet. I 1924 by Kingdon-Ward.

**var. melinanthum** (BALF. f. & WARD) CULLEN (*R. melinanthum* BALF. f. & WARD) Flowers funnel-shaped, yellow, appearing before the leaves; April and May. The best garden plant of this series. NE Upper Burma, NW Yunnan, SE Tibet.

**melinanthum** See *R. mekongense* var. *melinanthum*.

**metternichii** See *R. degronianum* subsp. *heptamerum*.

**var. angustifolium** See *R. makinoi*.

**'Wada'** See *R. degronianum* 'Wada'.

**micranthum** TURCZ. (Subgenus Rhododendron, Subsect. Micrantha) A very distinct and interesting Chinese species which has racemes of tiny white, bell-shaped flowers resembling those of *Ledum* and entirely different from nearly all other rhododendrons; May to July. A free-growing, small-leaved shrub up to 2m high. China, Korea. I 1901 by Ernest Wilson. H4.

**microgynum** BALF. f. & FORR. (*R. gymnocarpum* BALF. f. ex TAGG) (Subgenus Hymenanthes, Subsect. Neriiflora) Small shrub with leaves 5-7.5cm long, clad with buff tomentum beneath. Flowers bell-shaped, soft rose, spotted crimson; April. NW Yunnan, SE Tibet. AM (F) 1940 (as *R. gymnocarpum*). H4.

**microleucum** See *R. orthocladum* var. *microleucum*.

**minus** MICHX. (Subgenus Rhododendron, Subsect. Caroliniana) A medium-sized to large evergreen shrub most commonly grown in the following forms. SE United States.

**'Album'** (Carolinianum group) Flowers white, with a yellow blotch; leaves also narrower and more pointed. I 1895.

**Carolinianum group** (*R. carolinianum* REHD.) A very attractive, free-flowering shrub attaining 2m. Leaves densely scaly beneath; flowers tubular, soft rose-purple; May and June. N Carolina (United States). I 1812. AM (F) 1968. H4.

**var. chapmanii** (A. GRAY) DUNCAN & PULLEN (*R. chapmanii* A. GRAY) Small shrub of stiff habit, occasionally reaching 2m; leaves scaly below. Flowers in tight clusters, funnel-shaped, pink with greenish spots, and conspicuous chocolate-coloured anthers; April and May. W Florida (United States). I 1936. H4.

**molle** (BLUME) G. DON (*R. sinense* (LODD.) SWEET) (*Azalea mollis* BLUME) (Subgenus Pentanthera, Sect. Pentanthera) A small to medium-sized shrub of upright habit with bristly shoots and oblanceolate leaves softly hairy beneath. Flowers funnel-shaped in large trusses, usually yellow. It is the Chinese equivalent of *R. japonicum*. Best known as a parent of the Mollis and Exbury azaleas. E and C China. I 1823. H4. See also *R. japonicum*.

**mollyanum** See *R. montroseanum*.

**monosematum** See *R. pachytrichum*.

**montroseanum** DAVIDIAN (*R. mollyanum* COWAN & DAVIDIAN) (Subgenus Hymenanthes, Subsect. Grandia) Large shrub or small woodland tree of noble proportions; leaves inclined to oblong, 15-30cm long, silvery-white beneath; flowers in large trusses, bell-shaped, pink with a crimson basal blotch; April and May. Named after the late Duchess of Montrose. S Tibet. I 1925 by Kingdon-Ward. H3-4.

**morii** HAYATA (Subgenus Hymenanthes, Subsect. Maculifera) A medium-sized to large shrub. A rare and beautiful rhododendron from Taiwan. Leaves oblong-lanceolate, 7.5-13cm long, green on both surfaces. The bell-shaped flowers white, with a ray of crimson spots; April and May. Introduced by Wilson in 1918. AM (F) 1956. H4.

**RHODODENDRON**—*continued*

**moupinense** FRANCH. (Subgenus Rhododendron, Subsect. Moupinensia) A delightful, early flowering, small shrub with bristly branchlets. Leaves ovate-elliptic, densely scaly below. Flowers funnel-shaped, white, pink or deep rose, sometimes spotted red, sweetly-scented; Feb and March. C Sichuan. This lovely species was introduced by E.H. Wilson in 1909. It should have some shelter, especially on the east side against early morning frost whilst in flower. It is a parent of the following AM cultivars: 'Bo-Peep', 'Bric-a-Brac', 'Tessa', 'Tessa Roza', 'Seta' and several others. AM (F) 1914. AM (F) 1937. H4.

**mucronatum** See *R.* Mucronatum group under Evergreen Azaleas.

**mucronulatum** TURCZ. (Subgenus Rhododendron, Subsect. Rhodorastra) A slender, medium-sized, normally deciduous shrub. Leaves elliptic-lanceolate up to 5cm long. Flowers 4-5cm long, bright rose-purple, funnel-shaped; Jan to March. Japan, Korea, China, Mongolia, Ussuri. I 1882. AM (F) 1924. AM (F) 1935. AGM 1984. H4.

   **'Winter Brightness'** Flowers rich purplish-rose. FCC 1957.

**myiagrum** See *R. callimorphum* var. *myiagrum*.

**myrtifolium** SCHOTT & KOTSCHY (*R. kotschyi* SIMONKAI) (Subgenus Rhododendron, Subsect. Rhododendron) Dwarf shrub of dense habit, the 1cm long leaves are crenulate and are densely scaly below. Flowers tubular, with spreading lobes, rose-pink, appearing in clusters of 3-8 from May to July. C Europe (Carpathians). I 1846. H3-4.

**myrtilloides** See *R. campylogynum* Myrtilloides group.

**nakaharae** HAYATA (Subgenus Tsutsutsi, Sect. Tsutsutsi) A very attractive and rare dwarf shrub of creeping habit, suitable for the rock garden, with densely adpressed hairy shoots. Leaves small, oblanceolate, persistent. Flowers in small clusters, funnel-shaped, up to 2.5cm long, of an unusual dark brick-red; June and July or even later. Native of mountains in N Taiwan. H4.

   **'Mariko'** Flowers rich orange-red with a deeper flare. AM 1970.

**neriiflorum** FRANCH. (Subgenus Hymenanthes, Subsect. Neriiflora) One of the most desirable species. A medium-sized shrub with narrow leaves, gleaming white beneath, and trusses of fleshy, bell-shaped flowers which vary in colour from deep rose to scarlet or crimson; calyx large, coloured like the corolla; April and May. W Yunnan, SE Tibet, NE Upper Burma. First discovered by the Abbé Delavay and introduced by George Forrest in 1910. H3-4.

   **Euchaites group** (*R. neriiflorum* subsp. *euchaites* (BALF. f. & FORR.) TAGG (*R. euchaites* BALF. f. & FORR.) A lovely form, differing in its taller growth and larger, crimson-scarlet flowers in April. Often considered the finest of its series. AM 1929. I 1913.

   **subsp. phaedropum** (BALF. f. & FARRER) TAGG A form with variably coloured flowers; in the form we grow they are straw-yellow tipped scarlet. SE Tibet, NE Upper Burma, W Yunnan, NE India.

**nigropunctatum** See *R. nivale* subsp. *boreale*.

**niphargum** See *R. uvariifolium*.

**nipponicum** MATSUM. (*Azalea nipponica* (MATSUM.) COPELAND) (Subgenus Pentanthera, Sect. Viscidula) A rare, small, deciduous shrub of stiff, erect habit; older stems with attractive, peeling cinnamon-brown bark. Leaves large up to 15cm long and 7.5cm wide, obovate, turning rich orange or crimson in autumn. Flowers in clusters, appearing with or after the leaves, tubular, white; May and June. Japan. Introduced by E.H. Wilson in 1914. H4.

**nitens** See *R. calostrotum* subsp. *riparium* Nitens group.

**nivale** HOOK. f. (Subgenus Rhododendron, Subsect. Lapponica) A dwarf shrub native of the Himalaya and most commonly grown in the following form.

   **subsp. boreale** PHILIPSON & PHILIPSON (*R. nigropunctatum* FRANCH.) (*R. stictophyllum* BALF. f. & FORR.) (*R. violaceum* REHD. & WILS.) A dwarf, aromatic shrub of dense, twiggy habit, with minute, densely scaly leaves. Flowers solitary or in pairs, small, widely funnel-shaped, pale purple; May and June. NW Yunnan, W Sichuan, SE Tibet. H4.

**niveum** HOOK. f. (Subgenus Hymenanthes, Subsect. Arborea) An attractive, large Himalayan shrub for woodland. Leaves obovate-lanceolate, to 15cm long, young leaves covered with white indumentum, persisting and turning pale brown on the undersurfaces. Flowers

**RHODODENDRON niveum**—*continued*

bell-shaped, smokey-blue to rich purple, in tight globular heads; April and May. Sikkim, Bhutan. I 1849 by Sir Joseph Hooker. AM (F) 1951. H4.

**'Clyne Castle'** A form with larger leaves and rich purple flowers. H4.

**nudiflorum** See *R. periclymenoides*.

†**nuttallii** BOOTH (Subgenus Rhododendron, Subsect. Maddenia) A superb species, but too tender for all but the mildest areas. A medium-sized to large shrub, often epiphytic in nature, of rather straggling habit. Leaves up to 20cm long, bullate and reticulate above, densely scaly beneath, of an enchanting metallic purple when unfolding. The fragrant, funnel-shaped, lily-like flowers are 13cm or more long and appear in loose trusses of 3-9, yellow or white flushed yellow within, tinged pink on the lobes; April and May. An ideal conservatory shrub. NE India, NW Yunnan, SE Tibet. I 1850. FCC 1864. H1-2.

**oblongifolium** (SMALL) MILLAIS (*Azalea oblongifolia* SMALL) (Subgenus Pentanthera, Sect. Pentanthera) A deciduous shrub up to 2m with obovate to oblanceolate leaves pale or glaucous beneath. Flowers appearing after the leaves, funnel-shaped, slightly clove-scented, white or occasionally pale pink; June and July. S Central United States. I 1917. H3.

**obtusum** See *R.* Obtusum group under Evergreen Azaleas.

**occidentale** (TORR. & GRAY) A. GRAY (*Azalea occidentalis* TORR. & GRAY) (Subgenus Pentanthera, Sect. Pentanthera) Medium-sized, deciduous, summer-flowering shrub, with oval or obovate, glossy green leaves, turning yellow, scarlet or crimson in autumn. Flowers normally appearing with the leaves, widely funnel-shaped, fragrant, creamy-white to pale pink with pale yellow or orange-yellow basal stain; June. A parent of many beautiful hybrids. W North America. Introduced by William Lobb about 1851. AM (F) 1944. H4. AGM 1984.

**ochraceum** REHD. & WILS. (Subgenus Hymenanthes, Subsect. Maculifera) A rare, medium-sized shrub with glandular hairy shoots and petioles. Flowers bell-shaped, crimson, in trusses of 8-12; March and April. Sichuan. H3-4.

†**oldhamii** MAXIM. (*Azalea oldhamii* (MAXIM.) MAST.) (Subgenus Tsutsutsi, Sect. Tsutsutsi) "Formosan Azalea". A medium-sized, evergreen shrub with densely glandular hairy young shoots and elliptic, glossy green leaves thickly covered with rust-coloured hairs. Flowers in clusters of 1-3, funnel-shaped, bright brick-red; May. Taiwan. First discovered by Richard Oldham in 1864, introduced by Charles Maries in 1878 and later E.H. Wilson in 1918. H2-3.

**oleifolium** See *R. virgatum* subsp. *oleifolium*.

**oporinum** See *R. heliolepis*.

**orbiculare** DECNE. (Subgenus Hymenanthes, Subsect. Fortunea) An outstanding Chinese species forming a symmetrical, dome-shaped bush up to 3m high. The rounded, heart-shaped leaves held rigidly horizontal are matt green above, glaucous beneath. Flowers bell-shaped, seven-lobed, rose-pink, sometimes with a bluish tinge; March and April. Sichuan, Guanxi. Introduced by E.H. Wilson in 1904. AM 1922. AGM 1984. H4.

**oreodoxa** FRANCH. (*R. haematocheilum* CRAIB) (Subgenus Hymenanthes, Subsect. Fortunea) A very floriferous large shrub, or small tree with oblanceolate-elliptic leaves glaucous beneath. Loose trusses of funnel-shaped pink flowers, deep red in bud; March and April. Sichuan. I about 1904 by Ernest Wilson. AM (F) 1937. H4.

**var. fargesii** (FRANCH.) CHAMBERLAIN Medium-sized to large shrub. Leaves oblong-elliptic, 7.5-12cm long. Flowers funnel-shaped, 5cm long, deep rose-pink on the outside, paler within, up to about 8 in a truss; March and April. Hubei, Sichuan, Yunnan. I 1901 by Ernest Wilson. AM (F) 1926. H4.

**oreotrephes** W.W. SM. (*R. artosquameum* BALF. f. & FORR.) (*R. exquisitum* HUTCH.) (*R. timeteum* BALF. f. & FORR.) (Subgenus Rhododendron, Subsect. Triflora) A free-flowering, large shrub with glaucous young growths and usually oblong-elliptic leaves which are scaly and glaucous beneath. Flowers generally funnel-shaped varying in colour from mauve, mauve-pink or purple to rose, with or without crimson spots; April and May. Semi-deciduous in cold gardens. N Yunnan, SW Sichuan, S Tibet. First introduced by George Forrest in 1910. AM (F) 1932 (as *R. timeteum*). H4.

**'Exquisitum'** (F. 20489) A beautiful form with larger leaves and flowers. AM 1937.

**RHODODENDRON**—*continued*

**orthocladum** BALF. f. & FORR. (Subgenus Rhododendron, Subsect. Lapponica) A small, neat, Chinese shrub with densely scaly branches, and small, greyish, scaly leaves. Flowers small, funnel-shaped, mauve, purplish-blue or lavender-blue, produced with great profusion in April. N Yunnan, SW Sichuan. I 1913 by George Forrest. H4.

**var. microleucum** (HUTCH.) PHILIPSON & PHILIPSON (*R. microleucum* HUTCH.) Flowers white. A dwarf shrub suitable for the rock garden. Yunnan. FCC 1939. H4.

†**ovatum** (LINDL.) MAXIM. (Subgenus Azaleastrum, Sect. Azaleastrum) A medium-sized to large shrub with pale bark and broadly ovate leaves up to 2.5cm long. Flowers solitary, saucer-shaped, white, pink or purple, with purple spots; May and June. E and C China, C Taiwan. Introduced by Robert Fortune in 1844. H3.

†**pachypodum** BALF. f. & W.W. SM. (*R. scottianum* HUTCH.) (Subgenus Rhododendron, Subsect. Maddenia) A beautiful but tender shrub of medium size, with densely scaly branches. Leaves obovate, densely scaly beneath. Flowers widely funnel-shaped, up to 10cm long and across, white, occasionally flushed rose, strongly and sweetly scented; May and June. Only suitable for conservatory treatment. Yunnan, NE Burma. H1.

**pachysanthum** HAYATA (Subgenus Hymenanthes, Subsect. Maculifera) A medium-sized shrub with tomentose young shoots. Leaves oblong, up to 9cm long, silvery or brownish tomentose above when young, densely so beneath. Flowers in large trusses of up to 20, broadly bell-shaped, white to pale pink, sometimes spotted inside. A promising species handsome in foliage and flower. March-April. Taiwan. Introduced in 1972 by John Patrick. AM 1989. H4.

**pachytrichum** FRANCH. (*R. monosematum* HUTCH.) (Subgenus Hymenanthes, Subsect. Maculifera) A slow-growing, medium-sized to large shrub, the young shoots thickly covered with shaggy, brown hairs. Leaves oblong to oblanceolate, 6-13cm long, shining green beneath. Flowers bell-shaped, up to 5cm long, usually soft pink but varying in colour from white to deep pink, with a purple blotch; March and April. W Sichuan, NE Yunnan. I 1903 by Ernest Wilson. H4.

× **pallescens** HUTCH. (*R.* 'Pallescens') (*R. davidsonianum* × *R. racemosum*) A small, slender shrub of thin, open habit with lanceolate leaves, glaucous and scaly below. The funnel-shaped flowers occur in terminal clusters and in the upper leaf axils. They are pale pink in colour, with a white or carmine flush about the margin; mid. A natural hybrid from W China, raised at Exbury from Rock's seed. AM (F) 1933. H4.

**panteumorphum** See *R.* × *erythrocalyx* Panteumorphum group.

**pemakoense** WARD (Subgenus Rhododendron, Subsect. Uniflora) A beautiful, dwarf, suckering, alpine species only a few centimetres high. Small leaves and comparatively large, funnel-shaped, lilac-pink or purple flowers; March and April. A very floriferous species provided the flower-buds escape frost damage. NE India, SE Tibet. I 1924 by Kingdon-Ward. AM (F) 1933. H3-4.

**pentamerum** See *R. degronianum*.

**pentaphyllum** MAXIM. (Subgenus Pentanthera, Sect. Sciadorhodion) A very lovely, medium-sized to large, deciduous shrub. Leaves oval to elliptic-lanceolate, in whorls of 5 at the ends of the branches, turning orange and crimson in autumn. Flowers single or in pairs, appearing before the leaves, saucer-shaped or shallowly bell-shaped, rich clear peach-pink; March and April. Japan. Introduced by E.H. Wilson in 1914. AM (F) 1942. H4.

**periclymenoides** (MICHX.) SHINNERS (*R. nudiflorum* (L.) TORR.) (Subgenus Pentanthera, Sect. Pentanthera) Medium-sized, deciduous shrub with oblong or obovate, bright green leaves. Flowers in clusters; fragrant, funnel-shaped, pale pink with reddish tube; May. A parent of many of the Ghent hybrid azaleas. E North America. Introduced by Peter Collinson in 1734. H4.

**phaeochrysum** BALF. f. & W.W. SM. (*R. dryophyllum* BALF. f. & FORR.) (Subgenus Hymenanthes, Subsect. Taliensia) A variable, medium-sized to large shrub or small tree, with 5-7.5cm long leaves coated on the underside with a suede-like fawn, brown or buff indumentum. Flowers bell-shaped or funnel-shaped, varying in colour from white through pink to rose-purple, sometimes with crimson spots or blotch; April and May. NW Yunnan, W Sichuan, S Tibet. H4.

**planetum** BALF. f. A large shrub with oblong leaves up to 20cm long. Flowers bell-shaped, pink, 8-10 in a truss; March and April. Not known in the wild. Raised at Caerhays from Wilson seed before 1920. H4.

**379**

**RHODODENDRON**—*continued*

**pleistanthum** See *R. yunnanense*.

**pocophorum** BALF. f. ex TAGG (Subgenus Hymenanthes, Subsect. Neriiflora) A medium-sized shrub with oblong-ovate leaves up to 15cm long, covered beneath with brown, woolly indumentum. Flowers bell-shaped, crimson, in a tight head; March and April. NE India, S Tibet, NW Yunnan. H3-4.

**polycladum** FRANCH. (Subgenus Rhododendron, Subsect. Lapponica) A small shrub of upright habit with small scaly leaves and blue to purple flowers. Yunnan. H4. Best known in the following form:

**Scintillans group** (*R. scintillans* BALF. f. & W.W. SM.) Flowers funnel-shaped, lavender-blue, or purple-rose; April and May. I 1913 by George Forrest. AM (F) 1924. FCC (F) 1934. AGM 1984 (to FCC form).

**polylepis** FRANCH. (Subgenus Rhododendron, Subsect. Triflora) A medium-sized to large shrub. Leaves narrowly elliptic-lanceolate, aromatic, densely scaly beneath. Flowers widely funnel-shaped, varying from pale to dark purple, often with yellow spots; April. Sichuan. Introduced by E.H. Wilson in 1904. H4.

**ponticum** L. (Subgenus Hymenanthes, Subsect. Pontica) The commonest and most extensively planted *Rhododendron* in the British Isles, where it has become naturalised, and has inter-bred with garden cultivars to such an extent that the true species has become obscured. Large shrub with mauve to lilac-pink flowers which can look lovely especially in the fading light of evening. Its floral display in May and June is a feature of many districts. Invaluable for shelter belts and forming hedges. It is one of the few shrubs which will grow even under beech trees. Bulgaria, N Turkey, Caucasus, Lebanon, SW Spain, S Portugal. I 1763. H4.

**'Cheiranthifolium'** A curious form with narrow, wavy leaves.

**'Lancifolium'** A relatively low-growing, compact form making a medium-sized shrub with rather short and narrow leaves but not wavy as in 'Cheiranthifolium'.

**'Flore Pleno'** An unusual form with double flowers.

**'Variegatum'** One of the few variegated rhododendrons. Leaves margined creamy-white.

**poukhanense** See *R. yedoense* var. *poukhanense*.

**praestans** BALF. f. & W.W. SM. (Subgenus Hymenanthes, Subsect. Grandia) A large woodland shrub or small tree, bearing immense, leathery, obovate-oblong leaves which are dark green above and covered with a greyish-white or fawn plastered indumentum beneath, borne on large-winged petioles. Flowers in a dense truss, bell-shaped, deep magenta-rose or pink, with a crimson basal blotch; April and May. NW Yunnan, SE Tibet. Originally discovered by George Forrest on the mountains between the Mekong and the Yangtze rivers, in 1914. H3-4.

**Coryphaeum group** (*R. coryphaeum* BALF. f. & FORR.) Flowers creamy-white with basal crimson blotches, produced in April in heads of 20 or more. I 1918 by George Forrest. H3-4.

**praevernum** HUTCH. (Subgenus Hymenanthes, Subsect. Fortunea) An early flowering, medium-sized to large shrub. Leaves elliptic to oblanceolate, 10-18cm long. Flowers up to 6cm long, bell-shaped, white or rose-flushed, with a large, reddish-purple basal blotch. Produced in trusses of 8-15; February to April. SE Sichuan, Hubei. AM 1954. H4.

**prattii** See *R. faberi* subsp. *prattii*.

**primuliflorum** BUR. & FRANCH. (Subgenus Rhododendron, Sect. Pogonanthum) A twiggy, small to medium-sized, aromatic shrub. Leaves small, oblong-elliptic, densely scaly and white beneath. The small, tubular, daphne-like flowers, borne in small, rounded heads are usually white with a yellow tube; April and May. Differing from the very similar *R. cephalanthum* in the deciduous leaf-bud scales. W Yunnan, SW Sichuan, S Tibet. H4.

**primulinum** See *R. flavidum*.

**principis** BUR. & FRANCH. (*R. vellereum* HUTCH.) (Subgenus Hymenanthes, Subsect. Taliensia) A large shrub or small tree to 5m. Leaves silvery-white to fawn tomentose beneath. Flowers in a compact truss, bell-shaped, white or blush with purple or carmine spots; March and April. SE Tibet. H4.

**prinophyllum** See *R. roseum*.

**prostratum** See *R. saluenense* Prostratum group.

**RHODODENDRON**—*continued*

**proteoides** BALF. f. &. W.W. SM. (Subgenus Hymenanthes, Subsect. Taliensia) Small shrub of slow growth. Leaves small, narrowly oblong, with revolute margins and thick, woolly, rufous tomentum below. Flowers in a compact truss, bell-shaped, creamy-yellow or white with crimson spots; April. NW Yunnan, SW Sichuan, SE Tibet. H4.

**protistum** BALF. f. & FORR. (Subgenus Hymenanthes, Subsect. Grandia) A large shrub or small tree with large, dark green broadly obovate leaves up to 45cm long, glabrous or nearly so beneath. Flowers in large trusses of up to 25 or 30, fleshy, with 8 lobes, white to deep pink with a deeper basal blotch; February-March. W Yunnan, NE Upper Burma. I by George Forrest in 1919. H 1-3.

**var. giganteum** (TAGG) CHAMBERLAIN (*R. giganteum* TAGG) Leaves densely brown tomentose beneath at least on mature plants. I by George Forrest in 1919 who discovered it as a tree 25m tall. FCC 1953.

**prunifolium** (SMALL) MILLAIS (*Azalea prunifolia* SMALL) (Subgenus Pentanthera, Sect. Pentanthera) A remarkable late flowering, deciduous, medium-sized to large shrub. Leaves elliptic to obovate, up to 13cm long. Flowers appearing after the leaves, 4 or 5 in a truss, funnel-shaped, 4-5cm across, colour normally brilliant orange-red; July and August. Georgia-Alabama border (United States). Introduced by Professor Sargent in 1918. H3-4.

**pruniflorum** HUTCH. (*R. tsangpoense* var. *pruniflorum* (HUTCH.) COWAN & DAVIDIAN) (Subgenus Rhododendron, Subsect. Glauca) A dwarf shrub allied to *R. brachyanthum*. Leaves obovate, dark green above, glaucous and scaly beneath. Flowers bell-shaped, usually plum-purple. NE India, NE Burma. H4.

**pseudochrysanthum** HAYATA (Subgenus Hymenanthes, Subsect. Maculifera) A slow-growing, medium-sized, dome-shaped shrub of compact habit. Leaves ovate-elliptic 5-7.5cm long, when young covered with a woolly indumentum. Flowers bell-shaped, pale pink or white, with darker lines and spots; April. Taiwan. I 1918 by Ernest Wilson. AM (F) 1956. H4.

**pseudoyanthinum** See *R. concinnum* Pseudoyanthinum group.

**pubescens** BALF. f. & FORR. (Subgenus Rhododendron, Subsect. Scabrifolia) An attractive, small shrub of straggling habit, with bristly stems and densely hairy narrowly lanceolate leaves. Flowers funnel-shaped, pink, produced in clusters of 1-4; April and May. Closely related to *R. scabrifolium*. SW Sichuan, N Yunnan. H4.

**'Fine Bristles'** Flowers white, suffused rose, deep pink in bud. AM 1955.

**pulchrum** See *R.* 'Phoeniceum' under Evergreen Azaleas.

**'Maxwellii'** See *R.* 'Maxwellii' under Evergreen Azaleas.

**'Tebotan'** See *R.* 'Tebotan' under Evergreen Azaleas.

**pumilum** HOOK. f. (Subgenus Rhododendron, Subsect. Uniflora) A dwarf or prostrate shrub of neat habit with small leaves which are narrow, scaly and usually glaucous beneath. The small pink or rose, bell-shaped flowers are borne in clusters of 2 or 3; May and June. E Nepal, Sikkim, Bhutan, NE Burma, S Tibet. I 1924 by Kingdon-Ward. AM (F) 1935. H4.

**puralbum** See *R. wardii* var. *puralbum*.

**purdomii** REHD. & WILS. (Subgenus Hymenanthes, Subsect. Taliensia) A medium-sized shrub with oblong-lanceolate to oblong leaves 6-9cm long. Flowers bell-shaped, white or pink; April and May. Named after William Purdom who collected for the Arnold Arboretum in China during the years 1909-11, and with Reginald Farrer in 1914. Shaanxi (China). H4.

**quinquefolium** BISSET & MOORE (Subgenus Pentanthera, Sect. Sciadorhodion) An exquisitely beautiful azalea, a medium-sized to large, deciduous shrub. Leaves broadly obovate or diamond-shaped, in whorls of 4 or 5 at the ends of the shoots. They are green bordered reddish-brown when young, colouring richly in autumn. Flowers in small clusters, appearing after the leaves, pendulous, saucer-shaped, 4-5cm across, pure white, with green spots; April and May. Japan. I about 1896. AM 1931. H4.

**'Five Arrows'** Flowers white spotted with olive-green. AM 1958. FCC 1967.

**racemosum** FRANCH. (Subgenus Rhododendron, Subsect. Scabrifolia) A variable but invaluable Chinese species, normally a dense, small to medium-sized shrub, a suitable subject for the heather garden. Leaves oblong-elliptic, leathery, glaucous beneath. Flowers funnel-shaped, pale to bright pink, very numerous from axillary buds, forming

**RHODODENDRON racemosum**—*continued*

racemes along the branchlets; March and April. Yunnan, SW Sichuan. Introduced by the Abbé Delavay about 1889. FCC 1892. H4.

**'Forrest's Dwarf'** (F.19404) A dwarf form with red branchlets and bright pink flowers, originally collected by George Forrest in Yunnan in 1921. Admirable shrub for the rock garden.

**'Rock Rose'** (Rock 11265) An extremely floriferous form of compact habit with bright pink flowers. AM 1970.

**'White Lace'** Flowers white. AM 1974.

**radicans** See *R. calostrotum* subsp. *keleticum* Radicans group.

**ravum** See *R. cuneatum*.

**recurvoides** TAGG & WARD (Subgenus Hymenanthes, Subsect. Glischra) Small shrub of dense, compact habit. Leaves narrowly lanceolate, 5-7.5cm long, tawny tomentose beneath, margins recurved; flowers in a compact truss, bell-shaped, white or rose with darker spots; April and May. NE Upper Burma. I 1926 by Kingdon-Ward. AM (F) 1941. H4.

**repens** See *R. forrestii* Repens group.

**reticulatum** D. DON ex G. DON (*Azalea reticulata* K. KOCH) (*R. dilatatum* MIQ.) (*R. rhombicum* MIQ.) (*R. wadanum* MAK.) (Subgenus Tsutsusi, Sect. Brachycalyx) A medium-sized to large, deciduous shrub. Leaves broad obovate, or diamond-shaped, conspicuously reticulate beneath, purplish when young, turning vinous-purple in autumn. Flowers appearing before the leaves, solitary or in pairs, funnel-shaped, bright purple; April and May. Japan. I 1865. AM 1894 (as *R. rhombicum*). H4.

**rex** LEVL. (Subgenus Hymenanthes, Subsect. Falconera) A large shrub or small tree with large, shining dark green leaves covered with grey to pale buff tomentum beneath. Flowers in large trusses, bell-shaped, rose or white, with a crimson basal stain and spots; April and May. S Sichuan, NE Yunnan. FCC (F) 1935. AM (F) 1946. H4.

**subsp. arizelum** (BALF. f. & FORR.) CHAMBERLAIN (*R. arizelum* BALF. f. & FORR.) A large shrub or small tree for moist woodland with magnificent large leaves, covered with a cinnamon indumentum beneath. Compact heads of creamy-yellow bells, sometimes rose-tinted, and with dark crimson blotch. April. W Yunnan, NE Upper Burma. AM (F) 1963. H3-4.

**subsp. fictolacteum** (BALF. f.) CHAMBERLAIN (*R. fictolacteum* BALF. f.) A very handsome, large shrub or small tree, with cinnamon tomentose young shoots and long, dark green leaves, brown tomentose beneath, occasionally as much as 30cm long. Flowers bell-shaped, creamy-white, with a crimson blotch, in large trusses; April and May. One of the hardiest of the large-leaved rhododendrons. W Yunnan, SE Tibet, NE Burma. I about 1885 by the Abbé Delavay. AM (F) 1923. AGM 1984. H4.

**rhombicum** See *R. reticulatum*.

**rigidum** FRANCH. (*R. caeruleum* LEVL. ) (Subgenus Rhododendron, Subsect. Triflora) A beautiful, medium-sized shrub of twiggy habit. Leaves 2.5-6cm long, oblong-elliptic. Flowers funnel-shaped, varying in colour from white to pink; March to May. W Yunnan, SW Sichuan. AM (F) 1939 (as *R. caeruleum*). H4.

**'Album'** A form with white flowers.

**riparium** See *R. calostrotum* subsp. *riparium*.

**ririei** HEMSL. & WILS. (Subgenus Hymenanthes, Subsect. Argyrophylla) A large, early flowering shrub with oblong-elliptic leaves, 10-15cm long, silvery-white or greyish beneath. Flowers bell-shaped, purplish-blue; Feb and March. Sichuan. I 1904 by Ernest Wilson. AM (F) 1931. H4.

**roseum** (LOISEL.) REHD. (*R. prinophyllum* (SMALL) MILLAIS) (*Azalea rosea* LOISEL.) (Subgenus Pentanthera, Sect. Pentanthera) A lovely, medium to large-sized deciduous shrub with oval or obovate leaves. Flowers appearing in clusters with the leaves, clove-scented, funnel-shaped, pale to deep pink; May. E North America. I 1812, perhaps earlier. AM (F) 1955. H4.

**rosiflorum** See *R. indicum* 'Balsaminiflorum'.

**roxieanum** FORREST (Subgenus Hymenanthes, Subsect. Taliensia) A variable, slow-growing, small to medium-sized shrub of compact habit. The narrow leaves, 5-10cm long, are coated below with a fawn or rust-red indumentum. The bell-shaped flowers are creamy-

**RHODODENDRON roxieanum**—*continued*

white usually rose-flushed, appearing 10-15 in a tight truss; April and May. It takes some time to reach flowering age but is well worth growing for its leaves alone. NW Yunnan, SE Tibet, SW Sichuan. I 1913 by George Forrest. H4.

**Oreonastes group** (*R. roxieanum* var. *oreonastes* (BALF. f. & FORR.) HORT. A form with very narrow leaves. AM 1973.

**roylei** See *R. cinnabarinum* Roylei group.

**rubiginosum** FRANCH. (Subgenus Rhododendron, Subsect. Heliolepida) A floriferous, large shrub with ovate to elliptic aromatic leaves, 4-6cm long, covered with rust-coloured scales beneath. Flowers funnel-shaped, pink or rosy-lilac, with brown spots; April and May. SW Sichuan, Yunnan, SE Tibet, NE Burma. Introduced by the Abbé Delavay in 1889. H4.

**'Album'** A lovely form with white flowers.

**Desquamatum group** (*R. desquamatum* BALF. f. & FORR.) A large shrub or small tree, the aromatic leaves oblong-elliptic, dark brown-scaly beneath. Flowers funnel-shaped or almost flat, mauve with darker markings; March and April. Yunnan, Sichuan, Burma, SE Tibet. AM (F) 1938. H4.

**rude** See *R. glischrum* subsp. *rude*.

**rufum** BATAL. (Subgenus Hymenanthes, Subsect. Taliensia) Medium-sized to large shrub, the elliptic-oblong to obovate leaves red-brown beneath. Flowers narrowly bell-shaped, white or pinkish-purple, with crimson spots; April. N Sichuan, Gansu. AM 1980. H4.

**rupicola** W.W. SM. (Subgenus Rhododendron, Subsect. Lapponica) A dwarf shrub of spreading habit with oblong-obovate leaves up to 2.5cm long, dark glossy green above and densely scaly on both sides, revolute at the margins. Flowers saucer-shaped, 3cm across, in small, dense clusters, deep purple in bud opening to mauve. April-May. SE Tibet, N Burma, Yunnan, SW Sichuan. I 1910 by George Forrest. H4.

**var. chryseum** (BALF. f. & WARD) PHILIPSON & PHILIPSON (*R. chryseum* BALF. f. & WARD) Flowers bright yellow. Calyx not scaly. NE Burma, NW Yunnan, SE Tibet. I 1918 by George Forrest.

**russatum** BALF. f. & FORR. (*R. cantabile* BALF. f.) (Subgenus Rhododendron, Subsect. Lapponica) A first-rate garden plant, making compact growth up to 1 or 1.2m high. Leaves oblong-lanceolate, densely scaly below and about 2.5cm long. Flowers funnel-shaped, deep blue-purple or violet with a white throat; April and May. NW Yunnan, Sichuan. I 1917 by George Forrest. AM (F) 1927. FCC (F) 1933. AGM 1984. H4.

**saluenense** FRANCH. (Subgenus Rhododendron, Subsect. Saluenensia) Small, densely matted shrub of variable habit. The small, ovate-elliptic, aromatic leaves are hidden by clusters of funnel-shaped, rose-purple or purplish-crimson flowers; April and May. SE Tibet, NW Yunnan, NE Burma. I 1914 by George Forrest. AM (F) 1945. H4.

**subsp. chameunum** (BALF. f. & FORR.) CULLEN (*R. chameunum* BALF. f. & FORR.) (*R. charidotes* BALF. f. & FARRER) (*R. cosmetum* BALF. f. & FORR.) Dwarf shrub with erect stems and bristle-clad branchlets. The small leaves are brown-scaly beneath. Flowers saucer-shaped, with wavy margin, rose-purple, with crimson spots, borne in loose clusters of up to 6; April and May. N Yunnan, NE Burma, SE Tibet, SW Sichuan. H4.

**Prostratum group** (*R. prostratum* W.W. SM.) A form of subsp. *chameunum* of prostrate habit with very small leaves. Introduced by George Forrest in 1910. H4.

**sanguineum** FRANCH. (Subgenus Hymenanthes, Subsect. Neriiflora) A very variable, dwarf or small shrub, with 4-6cm long, obovate or narrow oblong leaves, greyish-white beneath. Flowers bell-shaped, bright crimson, in trusses of 3-6, not produced on young plants; May. NW Yunnan, SE Tibet. I 1917 by George Forrest. H4.

**var. didymoides** TAGG & FORR. (subsp. *roseotinctum* BALF. f. & FORR.) COWAN A medium-sized shrub with rose or yellowish-red flowers.

**subsp. didymum** (BALF. f. & FORR.) COWAN (*R. didymum* BALF. f. & FORR.) Flowers of an unusual black-crimson. A parent of several good hybrids. SE Tibet.

**var. haemaleum** (BALF. f. & FORR.) CHAMBERLAIN Flowers dark blackish-red.

**subsp. roseotinctum** See var. *didymoides*.

**sargentianum** REHD. & WILS. (Subgenus Rhododendron, Sect. Pogonanthum) Dwarf, twiggy shrub of dense, compact habit. Leaves small, aromatic when bruised. Flowers small, tubular, lemon-yellow or white; April and May. A gem for a cool spot on the rock

**RHODODENDRON sargentianum**—*continued*

garden but not an easy plant to grow. C Sichuan. I 1903-4 by Ernest Wilson. AM (F) 1923. H4.

**'Whitebait'** Flowers pale primrose-yellow. AM 1966.

**scabrifolium** FRANCH. (Subgenus Rhododendron, Subsect. Scabrifolia) A small to medium-sized, straggly shrub with oblanceolate leaves, 4-5cm long, roughly hairy above, tomentose and reticulate beneath. Flowers funnel-shaped, varying in colour from white to deep rose; March and April. N Yunnan. I 1885. H3.

**var. spiciferum** (FRANCH.) CULLEN (*R. spiciferum* FRANCH.) A small, moderately hardy shrub from Yunnan with wiry, bristly stems and bristly, narrowly oblanceolate leaves. Flowers borne in profusion, funnel-shaped, rose or pink; April and May. C and S Yunnan. I 1921 by Kingdon-Ward. H3.

†**scabrum** G. DON (Subgenus Tsutsutsi, Sect. Tsutsutsi) A small to medium-sized shrub of bushy habit. Leaves elliptic to oblanceolate, 6-10cm long. Flowers with a large, green calyx, funnel-shaped, rose-red to brilliant scarlet; April and May. Islands of Japan. I about 1909. AM 1911. H2.

**'Red Emperor'** A striking form with large, scarlet flowers, usually a little later than those of the typical form.

**schlippenbachii** MAXIM. (*Azalea schlippenbachii* (MAXIM.) KUNTZE) (Subgenus Pentanthera, Sect. Sciadorhodion) This exquisitely beautiful azalea, though winter hardy, is subject to injury by late spring frosts. A medium-sized to large, deciduous shrub of rounded habit. The large, broadly obovate leaves are produced in whorls of five at the ends of the branches. They are suffused purplish-red when young, turning to yellow, orange and crimson in autumn. Flowers appearing before or with the leaves, saucer-shaped, 7.5cm across, pale pink to rose-pink, occasionally white; April and May. Korea, Manchuria. First discovered by Baron Schlippenbach in 1854, introduced by James Veitch in 1893. AM (F) 1896. FCC (F) 1944. AGM 1984. H4.

**scintillans** See *R. polycladum* Scintillans group.

**scottianum** See *R. pachypodum*.

**scyphocalyx** See *R. dichroanthum* subsp. *scyphocalyx*.

**searsiae** REHD. & WILS. (Subgenus Rhododendron, Subsect. Triflora) An attractive, medium-sized shrub with leaves densely scaly and glaucous beneath. Flowers freely produced, widely funnel-shaped, white, rose or purplish-mauve, with pale green spots; April and May. SW Sichuan. Introduced by E.H. Wilson in 1908. H4.

**selense** FRANCH. (Subgenus Hymenanthes, Subsect. Selensia) Medium-sized shrub with oblong to obovate, dark green leaves and bell-shaped, pink or rose flowers, occasionally with a crimson basal blotch, in April and May. SE Tibet, NW Yunnan. I 1917 by George Forrest. H4.

**subsp. dasycladum** (BALF. f. & W.W. SM.) CHAMBERLAIN (*R. dasycladum* BALF. f. & W.W. SM.) Medium-sized shrub with glandular hairy, young shoots and leaves varying from 3-8cm long. The small, funnel-shaped flowers may be white or rose, with or without a dark basal stain; April and May. W Yunnan, SW Sichuan. H4.

**semibarbatum** MAXIM. (Subgenus Mumeazalea) Medium-sized to large, deciduous shrub, often giving rich orange-yellow and crimson autumn colour. Leaves elliptic, 2.5-5cm long. Flowers small, solitary, funnel-shaped, white or yellowish-white, flushed pink, spotted red; June. A very unusual species. Japan. H4.

**serotinum** HUTCH. A large, late flowering shrub related to *R. decorum* of which it is probably a hybrid. Leaves up to 15cm long. Flowers bell-shaped, sweetly-scented, 5cm long, white flushed pink on the outside, spotted pink within and with a yellow basal stain. With its flowers opening in August and September it is one of the last rhododendrons to flower. I by the Abbé Delavay before 1889. AM (F) 1925. H4.

**serpyllifolium** (A. GRAY) MIQ. (*Azalea serpyllifolia* A. GRAY) (Subgenus Tsutsutsi, Sect. Tsutsutsi) A remarkable, small, deciduous shrub, in fact a true mini azalea, of dense habit with slender, interlacing stems and very tiny leaves. Flowers appearing after the leaves, solitary or in pairs, small and funnel-shaped, rose-pink; April and May. Japan. I by Charles Maries about 1879. H4.

**serrulatum** (SMALL) MILLAIS (Subgenus Pentanthera, Sect. Pentanthera) A small to medium-sized deciduous shrub closely related to the common *R. viscosum* and differing in its

**RHODODENDRON serrulatum**—*continued*

more finely-toothed leaves and longer corolla tube. Flowers white or pink-flushed; late. SE United States. H3-4.

**setosum** D. DON (Subgenus Rhododendron, Subsect. Lapponica) A small shrub with densely bristly branches and bristly, scaly, aromatic leaves. Flowers funnel-shaped, reddish-purple; May. Nepal, Sikkim, W Bengal, SE Tibet. I 1825. H4.

**sherriffii** COWAN (Subgenus Hymenanthes, Subsect. Fulgensia) A medium-sized shrub with elliptic to oblong-elliptic leaves, 7.5cm long, covered with a thick dark brown indumentum beneath. Flowers bell-shaped, deep rich carmine, with crimson, bloomy calyx. March and April. S Tibet. I 1926 by Ludlow and Sherriff. AM 1966. H4.

**shweliense** BALF. f. & FORR. (Subgenus Rhododendron, Subsect. Glauca) Dwarf, aromatic shrub, with densely scaly twigs and leaves oblong-obovate, 2.5-5cm long. Flowers bell-shaped, pink with yellow flush and purple spots, scaly on the outside; May. SW Yunnan. I 1924 by George Forrest. H4.

**sidereum** BALF. f. (Subgenus Hymenanthes, Subsect. Grandia) A large shrub or small tree closely related to *R. grande* with bold leaves up to 25cm long, silvery-grey to fawn beneath. Flowers bell-shaped, creamy-white to clear yellow with a crimson basal blotch. April. NE Upper Burma, W Yunnan. I 1919. H2-3.

**'Glen Rosa'** Flowers primrose-yellow blotched deep crimson. AM 1964.

**siderophyllum** FRANCH. (Subgenus Rhododendron, Subsect. Triflora) A medium-sized to large shrub of upright habit. Leaves oblanceolate, glossy green and slightly scaly above, densely scaly beneath, up to 6cm long. Flowers in small clusters in May, greenish in bud opening very pale pink with a large patch of reddish spots on the upper lobe, open funnel-shaped, 4cm across. Yunnan, Guizhou. AM 1945. H4.

**silvaticum** See *R. lanigerum.*

†**simsii** PLANCH. (*Azalea indica* SIMS not L.) (Subgenus Tsutsutsi, Sect. Tsutsutsi) A tender evergreen or semi-evergreen shrub up to 2m, of dense, spreading habit. Leaves up to 5cm long, broadly oval. Flowers funnel-shaped, 5-6cm across, in clusters of 2-6, rose-red to dark red, with darker spots; May. A parent of the greenhouse "Indica" hybrid azaleas. China, Taiwan. I early in the 19th century. FCC (F) 1933. H2.

**var. eriocarpum** See *R. eriocarpum.*

**'Queen Elizabeth'** A beautiful form reminiscent of the greenhouse azaleas, but hardier. Flowers large, 7.5-9cm across, double, white, edged rose-opal.

**'Queen Elizabeth White'** Flowers double, pure white.

†**sinogrande** BALF. f. & W. W. SM. (Subgenus Hymenanthes, Subsect. Grandia) A large shrub or small tree for woodland. Magnificent as a foliage plant, the shining dark green leaves being sometimes as much as 0.8m long and 30cm wide, the lower surface with a silvery-grey or fawn indumentum. Flowers in huge trusses, creamy-white with a crimson blotch; April. W Yunnan, NE Upper Burma, SE Tibet. Discovered and introduced by George Forrest in 1913. AM (F) 1922. FCC (F) 1926. H3-4.

**smirnowii** TRAUTV. (Subgenus Hymenanthes, Subsect. Pontica) A very hardy, compact, slow-growing shrub of medium to large size, with oblong-obovate leaves, 10-15cm long, grey or pale brown-felted beneath. Flowers bell-shaped, rose-purple or rose-pink; May and June. NE Turkey, Georgia (USSR). I 1886. H4.

**smithii** NUTT. & HOOK. (Subgenus Hymenanthes, Subsect. Barbata) Large shrub or small tree with attractive plum-coloured bark and bristly-hairy shoots. Leaves oblong-lanceolate, 10-15cm long, loosely tomentose below. Flowers bell-shaped, scarlet-crimson, in compact trusses; March. NE India, Bhutan, SE Tibet. I 1850. H3.

**souliei** FRANCH. (Subgenus Hymenanthes, Subsect. Campylocarpa) A beautiful, hardy, medium-sized shrub with almost round leaves, 5-7.5cm long, and saucer-shaped, white or soft pink flowers; May to June. Said to do best in the eastern counties. Sichuan. I 1903 by Ernest Wilson. FCC (F) 1909. H4.

**sperabile** BALF. f. & FARRER (Subgenus Hymenanthes, Subsect. Neriiflora) A small shrub, occasionally reaching 2m. Leaves elliptic-lanceolate, 6-10cm long, with a thick, tawny or cinnamon tomentum beneath. Flowers bell-shaped, fleshy scarlet or deep crimson; April and May. NW Yunnan, NE Upper Burma. Discovered and introduced by Reginald Farrer in 1919. AM (F) 1925. H3-4.

**sphaeranthum** See *R. trichostomum.*

**RHODODENDRON**—*continued*

**sphaeroblastum** BALF. f. & FORR. (Subgenus Hymenanthes, Subsect. Taliensia) A medium-sized shrub with glabrous shoots and ovate-lanceolate leaves up to 15cm long, densely brown tomentose beneath. Trusses up to twenty-flowered. Corolla bell-shaped, white or pink with crimson spots. April-May. N Yunnan, SW Sichuan. H4.

**spiciferum** See *R. scabrifolium* var. *spiciferum*.

**spinuliferum** FRANCH. (Subgenus Rhododendron, Subsect. Scabrifolia) A quite remarkable, medium-sized shrub, one of the many discovered by the Abbé Delavay. Leaves oblanceolate and bullate, 5-7.5cm long, and like the stems softly pubescent; flowers in erect clusters, produced in the axils of the upper leaves, tubular, 2.5cm long, red, with protruding stamens; April. C and S Yunnan. I 1907. H3.

**stewartianum** DIELS (Subgenus Hymenanthes, Subsect. Thomsonia) An early flowering, medium-sized to large shrub with loose trusses of bell-shaped flowers, varying in colour from white to yellow, rose or crimson; Feb to April. Differing from the very similar *R. eclecteum* in its leaves, the undersurfaces of which are minutely hairy and covered by a thin, creamy-yellow, farinose indumentum. SE Tibet, NW Yunnan, NE Upper Burma. I 1919 by Farrer and Cox. AM 1934. H4.

**stictophyllum** See *R. nivale* subsp. *boreale*.

**strigillosum** FRANCH. (Subgenus Hymenanthes, Subsect. Maculifera) A large, Chinese shrub with bristly young shoots. Leaves oblong-lanceolate, 10-18cm long, bristly-hairy. Magnificent when bearing its trusses of brilliant crimson, bell-shaped flowers in February and March. A sheltered woodland site is necessary. Sichuan, NE Yunnan. Introduced by E.H. Wilson in 1904. AM (F) 1923. H3-4.

**suberosum** See *R. yunnanense*.

**succothii** DAVIDIAN (Subgenus Hymenanthes, Subsect. Barbata) A large shrub with glabrous shoots and very shortly-stalked oblong, glabrous leaves to 13cm long, heart-shaped at the base. Flowers bell-shaped, crimson, in dense trusses of up to 15. March to April. Bhutan, NE India. I 1937 by Ludlow and Sherriff. H4.

**sutchuenense** FRANCH. (Subgenus Hymenanthes, Subsect. Fortunea) An outstanding, large, Chinese shrub with stout shoots and drooping, oblong-oblanceolate leaves, up to 30cm long. In favourable seasons its floral display is magnificent, the flowers, 7cm long, bell-shaped, varying from palest pink to rosy-lilac, with purple spots; Feb and March. China. Introduced by E.H. Wilson in 1900. H4.

'Geraldii' See *R. × geraldii*.

'**Seventh Heaven**' (Wils. 1232) Flowers white suffused pale lilac, spotted red in the throat. Raised at Borde Hill in Sussex. AM 1978.

**taliense** FRANCH. (Subgenus Hymenanthera, Subsect. Taliensia) A medium-sized shrub with tomentose shoots and dark green, broadly ovate leaves to 10cm long, densely brown-felted beneath. Flowers bell-shaped, creamy-white to yellow flushed pink with red spots, borne in trusses of up to 20. April to May. W Yunnan. I by George Forrest about 1910. H4.

**tapetiforme** BALF. f. & WARD (Subgenus Rhododendron, Subsect. Lapponica) A dwarf, scaly-branched shrub with terminal clusters of 2 or 3 pale mauve-pink or purple, funnel-shaped flowers; April. NE Burma, NW Yunnan, SE Tibet. H4.

**tatsienense** FRANCH. (Subgenus Rhododendron, Subsect. Triflora) A medium-sized to large shrub related to *R. davidsonianum* with reddish young growths and elliptic dark green leaves scaly on both sides. Flowers broadly funnel-shaped, pink to pale purple, borne in clusters of up to 6. April-May. N Yunnan, SW Sichuan. I by George Forrest. H3-4.

**tebotan** See *R.* 'Tebotan' under Evergreen Azaleas.

**telmateium** BALF. f. &. W.W. SM. (Subgenus Rhododendron, Subsect. Lapponica) A small, erect shrub with small, oblanceolate, scaly leaves and branches. Flowers solitary or in clusters of 2 or 3, small, funnel-shaped, deep rose-purple, with white throat; April and May. Suitable for the rock garden. Introduced by George Forrest in 1914. Yunnan, SW Sichuan. H4.

**telopeum** See *R. campylocarpum* subsp. *caloxanthum*.

**tephropeplum** BALF. f. & FARRER (*R. deleiense* HUTCH. & WARD) (Subgenus Rhododendron, Subsect. Tephropepla) A dwarf or small shrub occasionally to 1.5m, narrow, oblong-lanceolate leaves, 3.5-10cm long, glaucous and dark scaly beneath. Flowers in profusion,

**RHODODENDRON tephropeplum**—*continued*

bell-shaped, varying in colour from pink to carmine-rose; April and May. Young leaves an attractive plum-purple beneath. NE Burma, NW Yunnan, SE Tibet, Assam. I 1921 by George Forrest. AM (F) 1929. AM 1935 (as *R. deleiense*). H3-4.

**thomsonii** HOOK. f. (Subgenus Hymenanthes, Subsect. Thomsonia) A well-known and desirable Himalayan species. A large shrub or small tree with attractive, smooth, plum coloured or cinnamon bark and rounded or oval leaves, 3.5-8cm long, which are glaucous when young. Flowers in loose trusses, bell-shaped, deep blood-red, calyx large, cup-shaped; April to May. Even after flowering the fruiting clusters are most attractive, with apple-green calyces and glaucous capsules. Because of its often consistent and prodigious flowering this magnificent species appreciates an annual feed and mulch. E Nepal, N India, Bhutan. Introduced by Sir Joseph Hooker in 1850. A parent of many fine hybrids. AGM 1984. AM 1973. H3.

**subsp. lopsangianum** (COWAN) CHAMBERLAIN (*R. lopsangianum* COWAN) A small shrub up to 2m. Leaves 3-6cm long, glaucous beneath. Flowers narrowly bell-shaped, fleshy, deep crimson; April. Named after the late Dalai Lama of Tibet. SE Tibet. H3-4.

**tosaense** MAK. (Subgenus Tsutsutsi, Sect. Tsutsutsi) A densely-branched, semi-evergreen shrub, occasionally reaching 2m. Leaves narrow, pubescent, turning crimson-purple in autumn. Flowers in clusters of 1-6, funnel-shaped, 2.5-3cm across, lilac-purple; April to May. Japan. I 1914 by Ernest Wilson. H3-4.

**'Barbara'** A lovely selection with flowers of a clear pink. Raised in our nurseries in 1958.

**traillianum** FORR. & W.W. SM. (Subgenus Hymenanthes, Subsect. Taliensia) A large shrub or small tree related to *R. phaeochrysum*. Leaves obovate to elliptic, to 13cm long, dark green and glabrous above, brown-felted beneath. Flowers funnel-campanulate, white or flushed with pink and spotted red, in trusses of up to 15. April to May. W Yunnan, SW Sichuan. H4. Named after G.W. Traill, George Forrest's father-in-law.

**trichanthum** REHD. (*R. villosum* HEMSL. & WILS.) (Subgenus Rhododendron, Subsect. Triflora) Large shrub, the branches densely beset with bristles. Leaves ovate-elliptic, 5-10cm long, pubescent. Flowers widely funnel-shaped, usually dark violet-purple, sometimes paler, 3-5 in a truss; May and June. NW Sichuan. I 1904 by Ernest Wilson. H4.

**trichocladum** FRANCH. (*R. brachystylum* BALF. f. & FORR.) (Subgenus Rhododendron, Subsect. Trichoclada) Small, deciduous shrub with hairy twigs. Leaves ovate-oblong, 2.5-3.5cm long. Flowers funnel-shaped, greenish-yellow, spotted dark green; April and May. NE Upper Burma, Yunnan. I 1910 by George Forrest. H4.

**trichostomum** FRANCH. (*R. sphaeranthum* BALF. f. & W.W. SM.) (Subgenus Rhododendron, Sect. Pogonanthum) A small, twiggy, aromatic shrub, with slender shoots bearing small, narrow leaves about 2.5cm long and tight terminal heads of tubular, white, pink or rose, daphne-like flowers; May and June. N Yunnan, Sichuan. I 1908 by Ernest Wilson. AM 1925 (as *R. sphaeranthum*). H3-4.

**Ledoides group** (*R. ledoides* BALF. f. & W.W. SM.) Corolla without scales. AM 1925. FCC 1976.

**Radinum group** (var. *radinum* (BALF. f. & W.W. SM.) COWAN & DAVIDIAN) Flowers more scaly, of equal garden merit. AM 1972.

**triflorum** HOOK. f. (Subgenus Rhododendron, Subsect. Triflora) A slender shrub of medium to large size, with attractive peeling bark. Leaves ovate-lanceolate, 5-7.5cm long. Flowers funnel-shaped, lemon-yellow with a ray of green spots borne in trusses of 3; May and June. E Nepal, N India, Bhutan, S Tibet, NE Burma. I 1850 by Sir Joseph Hooker. H4.

**var. bauhiniiflorum** (*R. bauhiniiflorum* WATT ex HUTCH.) Flowers flat, saucer-shaped, lemon-yellow. Manipur. I 1928 by Kingdon-Ward. H3-4.

**Mahogani group** (var. *mahogani* HUTCH.) Flowers with a mahogany-coloured blotch or suffused mahogany. Discovered and introduced by Kingdon-Ward, from SE Tibet.

**tsangpoense** See *R. charitopes* subsp. *tsangpoense*.

**var. pruniflorum** See *R. pruniflorum*.

**tsariense** COWAN (Subgenus Hymenanthes, Subsect. Lanata) A small shrub with yellow-tomentose young shoots and obovate to elliptic-obovate leaves, covered with a dense woolly indumentum beneath. Flowers in a loose truss, bell-shaped, varying in colour from pale blush to cream or white, spotted red within; April and May. SE Tibet, NE India, Bhutan. I 1936 by Ludlow and Sherriff. H4.

**RHODODENDRON**—*continued*

**tsusiophyllum** See *Tsusiophyllum tanakae.*

**ungernii** TRAUTV. (Subgenus Hymenanthes, Subsect. Pontica) Large shrub notable for its hardiness and late flowering, producing its trusses of funnel-shaped, pinky-white flowers in July. Handsome, oblong-oblanceolate leathery leaves, 12-20cm long, greyish-white to fawn, tomentose beneath. NE Turkey, Georgia (USSR). I 1886. AM 1973. H4.

**uniflorum** WARD (Subgenus Rhododendron, Subsect. Uniflora) A small shrub closely related to *R. pemakoense* with oblong-elliptic, mucronate leaves up to 2.5cm long, densely scaly on both sides. Flowers funnel-shaped, pale to rose-purple, spotted red, borne singly or in pairs. April-May. SE Tibet. I by Kingdon-Ward in 1924. H4.

**var. imperator** (HUTCH. & WARD) CULLEN (*R. imperator* HUTCH. & WARD) A dwarf shrub, often creeping, with small, narrow leaves and normally solitary, funnel-shaped flowers of pink or rose-purple, 2.5cm across appearing even on very young plants; May. Best in an open sunny position and very suitable for the rock garden. NE Burma. Introduced by Kingdon-Ward in 1926. AM (F) 1934. H3-4.

**uvariifolium** DIELS (*R. niphargum* BALF. f. & WARD) (Subgenus Hymenanthes, Subsect. Fulva) A large shrub or small tree, the young growths in spring of a beautiful silvery appearance. Leaves up to 25cm long, oblanceolate to obovate, dark shining green above, white or grey tomentose beneath. Flowers bell-shaped, white or pale rose, with or without crimson spots, produced in March or April. NW Yunnan, SW Sichuan, SE Tibet. I 1913 by George Forrest. H4.

**'Reginald Childs'** Flowers white, flushed and spotted red. AM 1976.

**valentinianum** FORR. ex HUTCH. (Subgenus Rhododendron, Subsect. Maddenia) A small shrub with densely scaly and bristly young shoots. Leaves about 3cm long, oval or obovate, densely scaly beneath, clustered at the ends of the branches; flowers narrowly bell-shaped, 3.5cm long, pubescent and scaly on the outside, bright buttercup-yellow; April. NE Burma, NW Yunnan. Introduced by George Forrest in 1917 and later by Joseph Rock. Remarkably hardy for the Maddenia Subsection. AM 1933. H3-4.

**vaseyi** A. GRAY (*Azalea vaseyi* (A. GRAY) REHD.) (Subgenus Pentanthera, Sect. Rhodora) A beautiful, medium-sized to large deciduous shrub with narrowly oval leaves up to 13cm long, often turning fiery red in autumn. Flowers appearing before the leaves, widely funnel-shaped, 3.5-5cm across, pale pink, rose-pink or white, with orange-red spots; April and May. North Carolina (United States). I about 1880. AGM 1984. H4.

**†veitchianum** HOOK. (Subgenus Rhododendron, Subsect. Maddenia) A tender, small to medium-sized shrub with densely scaly leaves up to 13cm long. Flowers comparatively large, widely funnel-shaped, fragrant, deeply five-cleft, with crinkled petals, white, with a faint green tinge; May to July. Only suitable for the conservatory. Burma, Laos, Thailand. I 1850 by Thomas Lobb. H1.

**vellereum** See *R. principis.*

**venator** TAGG (Subgenus Hymenanthes, Subsect. Venatora) A medium-sized shrub of bushy habit with glandular hairy young shoots. Leaves oblong-lanceolate, 10cm long. Scarlet, bell-shaped flowers in trusses of 4 or 6; May and June. SE Tibet. I 1924 by Kingdon-Ward. AM (F) 1933. H3.

**villosum** See *R. trichanthum.*

**violaceum** See *R. nivale* subsp. *boreale.*

**†virgatum** HOOK. f. (Subgenus Rhododendron, Subsect. Virgata) A small to medium-sized, leggy shrub with ovate leaves, 3.5-6cm long, scaly below. Flowers inclined to be tubular, varying from purple through pink to white, usually lilac-purple; April and May. E Nepal, N India, Bhutan, S Tibet. Introduced by Sir Joseph Hooker in 1850. AM (F) 1928. H2-3.

**subsp. oleifolium** (FRANCH.) CULLEN (*R. oleifolium* FRANCH.) Differs in its smaller, pink flowers. Yunnan, SE Tibet. I 1906. H3.

**viridescens** See *R. mekongense* Viridescens group.

**viscosum** (L.) TORR. (*Azalea viscosa* L.) (Subgenus Pentanthera, Sect. Pentanthera) "Swamp Honeysuckle". A medium-sized, deciduous, summer-flowering shrub of bushy habit. Leaves up to 3.5cm long, dark green above, glaucous green beneath. Flowers appearing after the leaves, narrowly funnel-shaped, 2.5-3.5cm across, viscid on the outside, delight-

**RHODODENDRON viscosum**—*continued*

fully and spicily fragrant, white, sometimes with a pink stain; June and July. E North America. I 1734. AM (F) 1921. AGM 1984. H4.

**wallichii** HOOK. f. (Subgenus Hymenanthes, Subsect. Campanulata) Medium-sized to large shrub with elliptic-obovate leaves, 5-10cm long, dark green and glabrous above, paler and dotted with tiny, powdery tufts of reddish-brown hair below. Flowers bell-shaped, lilac with rose spots, 6-10 in a truss; April. E Nepal, Sikkim, Bhutan, Assam, S Tibet. I 1850. Closely related to *R. campanulatum*. H4.

**wardii** W.W. SM. (*R. croceum* BALF. f. & W.W. SM.) (Subgenus Hymenanthes, Subsect. Campy-locarpa) A compact, medium-sized to large Chinese shrub, with oblong-elliptic or rounded leaves, 5-10cm long. Flowers in loose trusses, saucer-shaped, clear yellow, sometimes with a crimson basal blotch; May. NW Yunnan, SW Sichuan, SE Tibet. A beautiful species discovered and introduced in 1913 by Kingdon-Ward after whom it is named. A parent of several superb hybrids. AM (F) 1926. AM (F) 1931. H4.

**Litiense group** (*R. litiense* BALF. f. & FORR.) A very beautiful shrub. Flowers widely bell-shaped or saucer-shaped, clear soft yellow without markings; May. Leaves oblong, waxy glaucous beneath. Yunnan. AM 1 931. FCC 1953. H3.

**var. puralbum** (BALF. f. & W.W. SM.) CHAMBERLAIN (*R. puralbum* BALF. f. & W.W. SM.) Flowers white. Leaves oblong-elliptic, 5-7.5cm long, dark green. Yunnan. I 1913 by George Forrest. H3.

**wasonii** HEMSL. & WILS. (Subgenus Hymenanthes, Subsect. Taliensia) A small to medium-sized shrub of compact growth with stout, greyish-white young shoots. Leaves 5-10cm long, usually oval, glossy green above, white beneath becoming reddish-brown. Flowers bell-shaped, varying in colour from white to pink, rose or rarely yellow, with crimson spots; May. C Sichuan. Introduced by E.H. Wilson in 1904. H4.

**weyrichii** MAXIM. (Subgenus Pentanthera, Sect. Brachycalyx) A very splendid, medium-sized to large, deciduous shrub with broad ovate or rounded leaves in clusters of 2 or 3 at the ends of the branches. Flowers opening before the leaves, widely funnel-shaped, variable in colour, usually bright brick-red, with a purple blotch; April and May. Japan and the island of Chejudo (Quelpaert), S Korea. I 1914 by Ernest Wilson. H4.

**wightii** HOOK. f. (Subgenus Hymenanthes, Subsection Taliensia) A large, usually rather lax shrub, the oblong-elliptic leaves up to 20cm long, covered with a fawn or rust-coloured suede-like tomentum below. Flowers in a loose, one-sided truss, bell-shaped, cream or pale yellow, spotted crimson, rarely white; May. C and E Nepal, N India, Bhutan, S Tibet. AM (F) 1913. I 1850 by Sir Joseph Hooker. H3-4.

**williamsianum** REHD. & WILS. (Subgenus Hymenanthes, Subsect. Williamsia) A charming, Chinese shrub with attractive, bronze young growths, small, round, heart-shaped leaves and delightful, bell-shaped, shell-pink flowers; April. It is generally of dwarf, spreading habit, but may reach a height of 1-1.5m. C Sichuan. Discovered and introduced by E. H. Wilson in 1908. A parent of several good hybrids including 'Arthur J. Ivens'. AM 1938. AGM 1984 . H3.

†**wilsoniae** HEMSL. & WILS. (Subgenus Azaleastrum, Sect. Choniastrum) A medium-sized evergreen shrub with narrowly oval, glossy leaves up to 12cm long. Flowers deeply five-lobed, funnel-shaped, flesh-pink and slightly fragrant. April-May. W Hubei. I by Ernest Wilson in 1900 and named after his wife. AM 1971. H2-3.

**wiltonii** FRANCH. (Subgenus Hymenanthes, Subsect. Taliensia) A medium-sized to large shrub with distinct dark green, deeply veined, oblong-obovate leaves, 7.5-13cm long, white turning to cinnamon-felted beneath. The bell-shaped flowers are usually pale pink with red markings; April and May. C Sichuan. I 1904 by Ernest Wilson. AM (F) 1957. H4.

**wongii** HEMSL. & WILS. A rare, small shrub with densely scaly twigs and terminal clusters of pale yellow, funnel-shaped flowers; May and June. Probably the same as *R. ambiguum* but differing in its smaller stature, smaller, obtuse leaves and flowers without scales. Sichuan. H4.

**xanthocodon** See *R. cinnabarinum* subsp. *xanthocodon*.

**yakushimanum** NAKAI (*R. metternichii* var. *yakushimanum* (NAKAI) OHWI) (Subgenus Hymenanthes, Subsect. Pontica) A remarkable species, forming a compact, dome-shaped bush up to 1.3m high and more in width. Young growths silvery. Leaves leathery,

**RHODODENDRON yakushimanum**—*continued*

recurved at the margins, dark glossy green above, densely brown tomentose beneath. Flowers in a compact truss, bell-shaped, rose in bud, opening to apple blossom-pink and finally white; May. Only found on the windswept, rain-drenched, mountain peaks of Yakushima Island, Japan. I 1934. Now the parent of many new hybrids. H4.

**'Koichiro Wada'** This selection of the original introduction is the best form of the species. The original plant grows at Wisley. FCC 1947. AGM 1984.

**yanthinum** See *R. concinnum*.

**yedoense** MAXIM. (*R.* 'Yodogawa') (Subgenus Anthodendron, Sect. Tsutsutsi) A small, usually deciduous shrub of dense, spreading habit. Leaves narrow, 5-9cm long, often colouring prettily in autumn. Flowers funnel-shaped, double, rosy-purple; May. Long cultivated in Japan and Korea. C 1886. H4.

**var. poukhanense** (LEVL.) NAKAI (*R. poukhanense* LEVL.) (*R. coreanum* REHD.) "Korean Azalea". A small, usually deciduous shrub of dense, spreading habit. Leaves narrow, up to 8cm long, dark green, turning to orange and crimson in autumn. Flowers in clusters of two or more, appearing before or with the leaves, 5cm wide, fragrant, funnel-shaped, lilac-rose to pale lilac-purple; May. Korea, Japan. I 1905. AM 1961. H4.

**yungningense** BALF. f. (*R. glomerulatum* HUTCH.) (Subgenus Rhododendron, Subsect. Lapponica) A small shrub 0.6-1m high resembling *R. russatum*. Leaves ovate-elliptic 1-2cm long, densely scaly. The clusters of light purple-mauve, funnel-shaped flowers are encircled by semi-persistent bud-scales; March to May. N Yunnan, SW Sichuan. H4.

**yunnanense** FRANCH. (*R. aechmophyllum* BALF. f. & FORR.) (*R. chartophyllum* FRANCH.) (*R. suberosum* BALF. f. & FORR.) (Subgenus Rhododendron, Subsect. Triflora) A very hardy and exceedingly floriferous Chinese shrub up to 4m. Leaves lanceolate or oblanceolate, semi-deciduous in cold or exposed gardens. Flowers funnel-shaped, usually pink, with darker spots; May. Sichuan, Yunnan, Guizhou, NE Burma. Introduced by the Abbé Delavay in about 1889. AM 1903. AGM 1984 (to good forms only). H4.

**Hormophorum group** (*R. hormophorum* BALF. f. & FORR.) A small to medium-sized, floriferous shrub, the leaves lanceolate, 2.5-7.5cm long, covered with pale yellow scales below; flowers funnel-shaped, rose-lilac or lavender, usually with a ray of brown markings; May. AM (F) 1943. H4.

**'Praecox'** An early flowering form.

**zaleucum** BALF. f. & W.W. SM. (Subgenus Rhododendron, Subsect. Triflora) A large shrub with lanceolate to obovate leaves, white beneath. Flowers in terminal and axillary trusses, widely funnel-shaped, varying in colour from white to purple, usually lilac-mauve, with or without crimson spots; April. N Burma, Yunnan. Introduced by Forrest in 1912. AM (F) 1932. H3-4.

**zeylanicum** See *R. arboreum* subsp. *zeylanicum*.

## ‡*RHODODENDRON HYBRIDS

The earliest hybrids began to appear about 1825, when *R. arboreum* flowered for the first time in this country. From this date up to the beginning of the present century, a large number of hybrids were raised, derived mainly from *R. catawbiense* and *R. maximum* (United States); *R. arboreum* (Himalaya); *R. caucasicum* (Caucasus); *R. ponticum* (Turkey); and to a lesser extent *R. fortunei* (China) and *R. griffithianum* (Himalaya). Most of the hybrids produced from these species have several things in common, namely hardiness, ample foliage, firm and full flower trusses, and an ability to withstand exposure, and hence they are often referred to as the "Hardy Hybrids" (HH). As a group they are indispensable for planting in cold or exposed districts and are unsurpassed for landscape effect, whilst many are ideal as informal hedges or screens. More recently *R. yakushimanum* has played an important part in the development of many new hybrids suitable for smaller gardens.

With the exploration of China and the E Himalaya during the first thirty years of the present century, a vast wealth of new and exciting species flooded British gardens. From this glorious palette has been raised a whole range of colourful and ornamental hybrids which continue to flow unabated. They show a much greater variation in foliage, flower and habit than the older hybrids and though most are hardy, few will tolerate the extreme conditions often weathered by the "Hardy Hybrids".

**RHODODENDRON**—*continued*

Among the many raisers of hybrid rhododendrons mention must be made of the following, whose names will always remain in association with this great genus, namely the late Lord Aberconway of Bodnant, N Wales; Sir Edmund Loder of Leonardslee, Sussex; the late Edward Magor of Lamellan, Cornwall; Lionel de Rothschild, creator of the Exbury Gardens, Hampshire; Mr and Mrs J.B. Stevenson of Tower Court, Ascot, Berks; and J.C. Williams of Caerhays, Cornwall. In more recent years many fine hybrids have been raised in the Savill Gardens, Windsor, and in the RHS Gardens, Wisley.

The following hybrids, all of which are evergreen, vary from prostrate alpines to small trees, and unless otherwise stated may be taken as averaging 1.8-3m in height. The date of introduction of a hybrid (when known) is given in parentheses at the end of each description. A number of the descriptions represent original work done by our late Manager Arthur J. Ivens.

Dates in parentheses indicate the approximate year of introduction into commerce.

We are grateful for the assistance of Alan Hardy with the revision of this section.

Flowering seasons are indicated as follows:

**Early**—April

**Mid**—May to mid June

**Late**—Mid June onwards

**'A. Gilbert'** (*R. campylogynum* × *R. fortunei* subsp. *discolor*). An exceedingly free-flowering hybrid, similar to 'Lady Bessborough', but more compact. Leaves oblong-obovate, to 11cm long. Flowers fragrant, in loose trusses, apricot yellow in bud, opening to pale cream with 2 small crimson flashes, 6cm across. Mid. (1925). AM 1925. H3.

**'Adder'** (*R. diphrocalyx* × *R. thomsonii*). Beautiful blood-red, bell-shaped flowers with large petaloid calyces. Early. (1933). H3.

**'Aladdin'** (*R. auriculatum* × *R. griersonianum*). A very beautiful shrub with large, widely expanded, brilliant salmon-cerise flowers in loose trusses. Late. (1930). AM 1935. H3.

**Albatross group** (*R. fortunei* subsp. *discolor* × *R.* Loderi group). One of the glories of Exbury. A large, robust shrub or a small tree with terminal clusters of large leaves and magnificent, lax trusses of richly fragrant, trumpet-shaped flowers 13cm across. Mid. (1930). AM 1934. AMT 1953. H3.

**'Townhill Pink'** (*R. fortunei* subsp. *discolor* × *R.* Loderi group 'King George'). Flowers in enormous trusses, deep pink in bud, opening shell-pink. Mid. Both this and the white form were raised by Frederick Rose from seed given to him by Lionel de Rothschild. (1945). AM 1945.

**'Townhill White'** A lovely form differing only in its comparatively shorter, broader leaves and white flowers, which are pale yellowish-green within. Mid.

**'Albert Schweitzer'** A large shrub of upright habit with large conical trusses of rose-bengal flowers with a deeper blotch. Parentage unknown. Mid. (1960). H4.

**'Alice'** (HH) A hybrid of *R. griffithianum*, large, vigorous and upright in habit. Flowers funnel-shaped, rose-pink with lighter centre, borne in tall, conical trusses. Mid. (1910). AM 1910. H4.

**'Alison Johnstone'** (*R. cinnabarinum* Concatenans group × *R. yunnanense*). A dainty hybrid with oval leaves and trusses of slender-tubed flowers, greenish in bud opening to pale yellow flushed orange or pink. Mid. (1945). AM 1945. AGM 1984. H4.

**'Alpine Glow'** See *R.* Avalanche group 'Alpine Glow'.

**'Amor'** (*R. griersonianum* × *R. thayerianum*). A dense, bushy shrub with narrow dark green leaves thickly brown-felted beneath, up to 13cm long. Flowers 8-10 in a truss, scarlet in bud opening white, stained pink. Late. (1927). AM 1951. H3.

**'Angelo'** (*R. fortunei* subsp. *discolor* × *R. griffithianum*). A group of magnificent hybrids raised first at Caerhays and later by Lionel de Rothschild at Exbury. 'Exbury Angelo' makes a large shrub or small tree with handsome foliage. Huge, shapely trusses of large, fragrant, trumpet-shaped, white flowers, 14cm across, with green markings within. Mid. (1933). AM 1935. FCC 1948. H3. See also 'Solent Queen'.

**'Anna Baldsiefen'** (*R.* 'Pioneer' selfed). A dwarf shrub of compact upright habit with light green leaves, bronze-red in winter, to 2.5cm long. Flowers profusely borne, vivid phlox-pink, funnel-shaped, 3cm across with deeper coloured, wavy margins. Early. (1964). H4.

**RHODODENDRON**—*continued*

    **'Anna Rose Whitney'** (*R.* 'Countess of Derby' × *R. griersonianum*). A vigorous, medium-sized spreading shrub with dark green leaves to 11cm long. Flowers in dense, rounded trusses, widely funnel-shaped, 10cm across, deep rose-pink spotted with brown on the upper lobes. Mid. (1954). AMT 1987. H4.

    **'Antonio'** (*R. fortunei* subsp. *discolor* × *R.* 'Gill's Triumph'). A splendid, large hybrid, notable for the rich scent of its beautiful, funnel-shaped, pink flowers which are blotched and spotted crimson within; rich pink in bud. Mid. (1933). AM 1939. H3.

    **'April Chimes'** (*R. hippophaeoides* × *R. mollicomum*) (*R.* 'Hippomum'). A charming, small shrub of upright habit, similar in leaf to *R. hippophaeoides*. Flowers appearing in the axils of the upper leaves and in terminal umbels, the whole forming a compact ball of funnel-shaped, rosy-mauve flowers, normally at their best during late April. A floriferous hybrid of neat habit, excellent as a cut bloom for indoor decoration. Raised as a chance seedling in our nurseries from seed of *R. hippophaeoides* in 1938. H3-4.

    **'Arborfield'** (*R.* 'Crest' × *R.* Loderi group 'Julie'). Mimosa-yellow with slight pink flush and deeper base with a crimson tinge, bell-shaped on long pedicels, 11.5cm across. AM 1963.

    **'Arctic Tern'** (*R. trichostomum* hybrid). A vigorous, compact, free-flowering shrub of upright habit with glossy green leaves to 3.5cm long. Flowers 1cm long, white tinged with green, in compact, globular trusses. It has been suggested that a *Ledum* sp. is involved in the parentage. Mid. (1982). AMT 1984 (as × *Ledudendron* 'Arctic Tern'). AMT 1989 (as *Rhododendron* 'Arctic Tern'). H4.

    **'Argosy'** (*R. auriculatum* × *R. fortunei* subsp. *discolor*). A vigorous, large shrub or small tree with handsome, large leaves and very fragrant, trumpet-shaped, white flowers with a ray of dull crimson at base of throat. Late. (1933). H3-4.

    **'Ariel'** (*R. fortunei* subsp. *discolor* × *R.* 'Memoir'). A large shrub with freely-produced pale pink flowers. Mid. (1933). H3.

    **'Arthur Bedford'** A charming hybrid of unknown parentage, possibly *R. ponticum* × mauve seedling making a large, very floriferous shrub. Compact, conical trusses of pale mauve flowers spotted with dark rose-madder within. Named after a Head Gardener at Exbury. Mid. (1936). AM 1936. FCCT 1958. H4.

    **'Arthur J. Ivens'** (*R. fortunei* Houlstonii group × *R. williamsianum*). A medium, dome-shaped bush, resembling *R. williamsianum* in leaf shape and the attractive coppery-red tints of its young foliage. Flowers shallowly bell-shaped, 7.5cm across, deep pink in bud, opening delicate rose-pink with 2 small crimson flashes. Early. Raised by and named after our late Manager. (1938). AM 1944. H4.

    **'Arthur Osborn'** (*R. griersonianum* × *R. sanguineum* subsp. *didymum*). A small, late flowering shrub with small, narrowly oblong leaves, pale cinnamon beneath. Flowers drooping, funnel-shaped, ruby-red with orange-scarlet tube. Late. Sometimes continuing until early autumn. A useful, low-growing shrub, flowering when quite small. (1929). AM 1933. H3.

    **'Arthur Stevens'** (*R.* 'Coronation Day' × *R. souliei*). A lovely hybrid of rounded habit. Young shoots, petioles and buds bright yellow. The loose trusses of bell-shaped flowers are pale pink fading to white, with a deep rose-red basal stain. A seedling raised in our nurseries and named in memory of our late Foreman. Mid. (1960). AM 1976. H3.

    **'Ascot Brilliant'** A hybrid of *R. thomsonii* with an unknown garden hybrid. Lax trusses of funnel-shaped, rose-red flowers, darker at margins. Early to mid. Requires woodland treatment for the best results. (1861). H4.

    **Augfast group** (*R. augustinii* × *R. fastigiatum*). A small, dense, rounded shrub with small scattered leaves and scaly young shoots. Flowers small, funnel-shaped, in terminal clusters. Forms of our own raising vary in colour from dark lavender-blue to heliotrope. Early. (1921). AGM 1984. H4.

    **'Aurora'** (*R.* Loderi group × *R. thomsonii*). A large, fast-growing shrub or small tree of rather open habit. The fragrant, trumpet-shaped, rose-coloured flowers are borne in flat trusses 20cm. across. Early to mid. (1922). AM 1922. H3.

    **Avalanche group** (*R. calophytum* × *R.* Loderi group). A large shrub with bold foliage and large trusses of enormous, fragrant, widely funnel-shaped, snow-white flowers which are pink-flushed in bud and possess a red basal stain within. The conspicuous red pedicels

**RHODODENDRON Avalanche group**—*continued*

and bracts contrast superbly with the white of the flowers. Early. (1933). AM 1934. FCC 1938. H3.

**'Alpine Glow'** A handsome, large shrub with long, rich green leaves and flowers in large trusses, widely funnel-shaped, 10cm across, delicate pink with a deep crimson blotch at the base, sweetly-scented. Mid. (1933). AM 1938. H3.

**'Azor'** (*R. fortunei* subsp. *discolor* × *R. griersonianum*). A large shrub bearing trusses of large, trumpet-shaped flowers of soft salmon-pink; late. (1927). AM 1933. H3-4.

**'Bad Eilsen'** (*R.* 'Essex Scarlet' × *R. forrestii* Repens group). Dwarf shrub of spreading habit, free-flowering. Flowers funnel-shaped, red, with waved and crinkled margins; mid. H4.

**'Baden Baden'** (*R.* 'Essex Scarlet' × *R. forrestii* Repens group). Dwarf, compact, spreading shrub with small, dark glossy green, rather twisted leaves. Deep waxy-red flowers are profusely borne. Mid. H4.

**'Bagshot Ruby'** A vigorous hybrid of *R. thomsonii*, raised by John Waterer, Sons & Crisp, producing dense rounded trusses of widely funnel-shaped, ruby-red flowers; mid. (1916). AM 1916. H4.

**'Bambi'** (*R.* 'Fabia Tangerine' × *R. yakushimanum*). A small shrub of compact habit with dark green, deeply veined leaves, felted pale brown when young. Flowers red in bud opening pale pink flushed yellow. (About 1964). H3.

**Barclayi group** (*R.* 'Glory of Penjerrick' × *R. thomsonii*). A beautiful hybrid raised by Robert Barclay Fox at Penjerrick, Cornwall in 1913. Unfortunately, it is somewhat tender and is only seen at its best in Cornwall and similarly favourable areas. H2.

**'Helen Fox'** Flowers deep scarlet; early.

**'Robert Fox'** Flowers of a glowing deep crimson; early. AM 1921.

**'Bashful'** (*R.* 'Doncaster' × *R. yakushimanum*). A medium-sized shrub of wide-spreading habit with narrow red-tinged leaves silvery when young. Flowers light pink with a rust-red blotch fading to white. (1971). AMT 1989. H4.

**'Beatrice Keir'** (*R. lacteum* × *R.* 'Damaris Logan'). A large shrub with handsome foliage and large trusses of funnel-shaped lemon-yellow flowers. Early. AM 1974. H3.

**'Beau Brummell'** (*R. facetum* × *R.* 'Essex Scarlet'). Scarlet, funnel-shaped flowers, with conspicuous black anthers, as many as thirty in a neat globular truss. Late. (1934). AM 1938.

**'Beauty of Littleworth'** (HH) One of the first *R. griffithianum* hybrids. A very striking, large shrub with immense conical trusses of white, crimson-spotted flowers. Mid. Still one of the best hardy hybrids. Raised by Miss Clara Mangles at Littleworth, Surrey, about 1900. FCC 1904. FCCT 1953. AGM 1984. H4.

**'Beefeater'** (*R. elliottii* × *R.* 'Fusilier'). A superb Wisley hybrid with well-filled, flat-topped trusses of geranium-lake flowers. Mid. AM and Cory Cup 1958. FCC 1959. H3.

**'Belle Heller'** (*R.* 'Catawbiense Album' × white *R. catawbiense* seedling). A compact small shrub with dark geen leaves bearing large, dense, conical trusses of white flowers marked with a gold flash. Mid. (1958). H4.

**'Ben Mosely'** A compact small shrub bearing light purplish-pink, funnel-shaped, frilly margined flowers with a deep red flair in dense rounded trusses. Mid. (1981). H4.

**'Betty Wormald'** (*R.* 'George Hardy' × red garden hybrid). (HH) A magnificent hybrid with immense trusses of large, widely funnel-shaped, wavy-edged flowers which are rich crimson in bud opening to deep rose-pink, lighter in the centre and with a broad pattern of blackish-crimson markings within. Mid. (Before 1922). AMT 1935. FCCT 1964. AGM 1984. H4.

**'Bibiani'** (*R. arboreum* × *R.* 'Moser's Maroon'). A large shrub with good foliage, producing compact trusses of rich crimson, funnel-shaped flowers with a few maroon spots. Mid. (1934). AM 1934. H4.

**'Billy Budd'** (*R. elliottii* × *R.* 'May Day'). A Wisley hybrid. Flowers Turkey-red in a loose flat-topped truss. Early. (1954). AM 1957. H3.

**'Binfield'** (*R.* 'China A' × *R.* 'Crest'). A large shrub with the flowers primrose-yellow stained red in the throat, open bell-shaped in large, rounded trusses. Mid. AM 1964. H4.

**'Biskra'** (*R. ambiguum* × *R. cinnabarinum* Roylei group). A large, slender, floriferous shrub carrying rather flat trusses of pendent, narrowly funnel-shaped, vermilion flowers. Early. (1934). AM 1940. H3.

**RHODODENDRON**—*continued*

**'Blewberry'** (*R. roxieanum* × *R. maculiferum* subsp. *anhweiense*). A small shrub of compact habit, leaves resembling those of *R. roxieanum*, narrow and pointed, to 9cm long with down-curved margins and a loose, pale brown indumentum beneath. Flowers widely bell-shaped, 4cm across, white with reddish-purple spots. It is named after a village in Oxfordshire. Mid. (1968). AM 1968. FCCT 1983. H4.

**'Bluebird'** (*B. augustinii* × *R. intricatum*). A neat, dwarf, small-leaved shrub suitable for the rock garden or the front row of borders. Flowers of a lovely violet-blue borne in small, compact trusses. Early. Raised by the late Lord Aberconway at Bodnant in 1930. AM 1943. H4.

**'Blue Chip'** (*R.* 'Blue Diamond' × *R. russatum*). A dwarf shrub with dark green leaves to 5.5cm long scaly beneath. Flowers violet-purple, widely funnel-shaped and deeply five-lobed. Early to mid. AM 1978. H4.

**'Blue Diamond'** (*R. augustinii* × *R.* 'Intrifast'). A slow-growing, compact bush, up to 1m high or more, with terminal clusters of rich lavender-blue saucer-shaped flowers in tight clusters; early to mid. Raised by Mr J.J. Crosfield at Embley Park, Hampshire. (1935). AM 1935. FCC 1939. AGM 1984. H4.

**'Blue Peter'** (HH) A vigorous, very free-flowering hybrid of upright habit. Flowers in compact, conical trusses, funnel-shaped, frilled at the margin, cobalt violet, paling to white at throat, with a ray of maroon spots. Mid. (1930). AMT 1933. FCCT 1958. H4.

**'Blue Star'** (*R. impeditum* × *R.* 'Saint Tudy'). Mauve-blue, 3cm across. (1961). H4.

**'Blue Tit'** (*R. augustinii* × *R. impeditum*). A Caerhays hybrid very similar to Augfast, forming dense bushes up to 1m high, and as much in width. The small, widely funnel-shaped flowers are borne in clusters at the tips of branchlets. They are a lovely lavender-blue in colour, which intensifies with age, as in 'Blue Diamond'. Early. A first class shrub for the rock garden or heather garden. (1933). AGM 1984. H4.

**'Boddaertianum'** ('Bodartianum'). (HH) A large, fast-growing hybrid, developing into a small tree. Leaves long and narrow, dark green above, slightly bronzed beneath. Flowers in a compact, rounded truss, widely funnel-shaped, lavender-pink in bud, opening very pale pink or nearly white, with a wide ray of crimson-purple markings, 6cm across. Early. Said to be *R. arboreum* × *R. campanulatum*, but in our opinion white forms of both *R. arboreum* and *R. ponticum* are the parents. (1863). H4.

**'Bodnant Yellow'** (Lady Chamberlain group). A beautiful rhododendron with flowers of orange-buff, flushed red on the outside. Mid. FCC 1944. H3.

**'Bonito'** (*R. fortunei* subsp. *discolor* × *R.* 'Luscombei'). Flowers pink in bud opening to white, with a basal chocolate-coloured blotch within. Mid. (1934). AM 1934. H4.

**'Bo-peep'** (*R. lutescens* × *R. moupinense*). A small Exbury hybrid of slender, loose habit. Flowers widely funnel-shaped primrose-yellow with two broad bands of pale orange spots and streaks, 4cm across, borne in clusters of 1 or 2 in March. Very floriferous and a splendid sight when in full flower. (1934). AM 1937. H3.

**'Bow Bells'** (*R.* 'Corona' × *R. williamsianum*). A charming shrub of bushy, compact habit, with bright coppery young growths. Flowers widely bell-shaped, 8cm across, long-stalked and nodding, deep cerise in bud, opening to soft pink within, shaded rich pink outside, borne in loose trusses. Early to mid. (1934). AM 1935. AGM 1984. H4.

**'Bray'** (*R. griffithianum* hybrid × *R.* 'Hawk'). A Windsor hybrid in which the flowers deep pink in bud open mimosa-yellow, shaded pale pink on the outside. Mid. AM 1960. H3.

**'Bric-a-brac'** (*R. leucaspis* × *R. moupinense*). A small, neat, floriferous shrub, bearing pure white, wide-open flowers, 6cm across, with bright chocolate-coloured anthers. Although hardy, it is best given a sheltered position to protect its flowers which appear in March or earlier in a mild season. Raised by Lionel de Rothschild, at Exbury. (1934). AM 1945. H3.

**'Britannia'** (*R.* 'Queen Wilhelmina' × *R.* 'Stanley Davies'). (HH) A superb shrub of slow growth, forming a compact, rounded bush generally broader than high. Flowers gloxinia-shaped, of a glowing crimson-scarlet, carried in compact trusses backed by bold, handsome foliage. Mid. One of the most popular of all hardy hybrids and an excellent wind resister. Raised by C.B. van Nes & Sons of Boskoop, Holland. (1921). AM 1921. FCCT 1937. AGM 1984. H4.

## RHODODENDRON—*continued*

**'Brocade'** A dome-shaped shrub, strongly resembling 'Arthur J. Ivens' in habit and foliage. Flowers in loose trusses, bell-shaped, 7cm across, with frilly margins, vivid carmine in bud, opening to peach-pink. Early to mid. This pretty shrub was raised at Exbury and is stated to be a cross between 'Vervaeniana' and *R. williamsianum*. The latter parent is obvious, but there seems little evidence of the other. H4.

**'Brookside'** (*R.* 'Goshawk' × *R. griersonianum*). A Windsor hybrid of flamboyant appearance. The tubular campsis-like flowers are ochre-yellow, shaded paler yellow and flame, blood-red in bud. Mid. AM 1962. H3-4.

**'Bruce Brechtbill'** A sport of 'Unique' which it closely resembles but the flowers pale pink with a yellow throat. Early to mid. (1970). H4.

**'Butterfly'** (*R. campylocarpum* × *R.* 'Mrs Milner'). A very pretty hybrid bearing rounded trusses of widely funnel-shaped, primrose-yellow flowers with a broad ray of crimson speckles. Early to mid. (1940). AMT 1940. H4.

**'Buttermint'** (*R.* 'Unique' × [*R.* Fabia group × *R. dichroanthum* subsp. *apodectum*]). A compact dwarf shrub with dark glossy green leaves bronze when young. Bright yellow bell-shaped flowers edged with deep pink open from orange-red buds. Mid. (1979). H4.

**'Buttersteep'** (*R.* 'Crest' × *R.* 'Jalisco'). Barium-yellow with a small red blotch, open funnel-shaped and seven-lobed in loose trusses. Mid. AM 1971. H4.

**'C.I.S.'** (*R.* 'Fabia' × *R.* 'Loder's White'). A vigorous, free-flowering medium-sized shrub of upright habit with dark green leaves to 12.5cm long. Flowers in compact, globular trusses, widely funnel-shaped with wavy margins, 6cm across; red in bud opening orange-yellow, flushed and veined with red, speckled orange-brown in the throat. The initials stand for Claude I. Sersanous, once President of the American Rhododendron Society. Mid. (1952). AMT 1975. H4.

**'Cadis'** (*R.* 'Caroline' × *R. fortunei* subsp. *discolor*). A vigorous medium-sized shrub with handsome dark green leaves red-tinged when young. Flowers large, funnel-shaped with wavy edges, lilac-pink fading to nearly white on red stalks, borne in large, rounded trusses. Mid. (1958). H4.

**'Caerhays John'** See *R. cinnabarinum* 'Caerhays John'.

**'Caerhays Lawrence'** See *R. cinnabarinum* 'Caerhays Lawrence'.

**'Caerhays Philip'** See *R. cinnabarinum* 'Caerhays Philip'.

**Calfort group** (*R. calophytum* × *R. fortunei*). A vigorous large shrub with dark glossy green leaves raised by Collingwood Ingram. Flowers white to pale pink blotched with red in very large trusses. Several cultivars have been named. Mid. H4. AM 1932.

    **'Bounty'** Flowers off-white with red-purple blotch. AM 1967.

**'Carex White'** (*R. oreodoxa* var. *fargesii* × *R. irroratum*). A tall, pyramidal, very free-flowering hybrid from Exbury. Flowers in a lax truss, bell-shaped, fragrant, pink-flushed in bud, opening white, freely spotted maroon within, opening in March or April. (1932). H4.

**Carita group** (*R. campylocarpum* × *R.* 'Naomi'). A beautiful Exbury hybrid bearing well-filled trusses of large, bell-shaped flowers of the palest shade of lemon, with a small basal blotch of cerise within. Early. (1935). AM 1945. H3-4.

    **'Charm'** Deep pink in bud, opening to cream, flushed and overlaid deep peach-pink.

    **'Cream'** Pink in bud opening pale cream.

    **'Golden Dream'** Flowers deep cream, flushed and shaded pink, becoming ivory-white at maturity.

    **'Inchmery'** Pink with biscuit-yellow centre, red in bud, usually with 6 lobes.

    **'Pink'** Flowers soft lilac-pink.

**'Carmen'** (*R. forrestii* Repens group × *R. sanguineum* subsp. *didymum*). A dwarf or prostrate shrub carrying waxy, bell-shaped flowers of a glistening dark crimson. Mid. (1935). AMT 1989. H4.

**'Caroline Allbrook'** (*R.* 'Purple Splendour' × *R. yakushimanum*). A vigorous small shrub of compact, spreading habit with dark green leaves to 11cm long. Flowers widely funnel-shaped with very wavy margins, lavender-pink with a paler centre fading with age, borne in compact, globular trusses to 12.5cm across. Mid. (1975). AMT 1977. H4.

**'Cary Ann'** (*R.* 'Corona' × *R.* 'Vulcan'). A compact small shrub with dark green leaves and dense, rounded trusses of coral-pink flowers. Mid. (1962). H4.

RHODODENDRON—*continued*

**'Charlotte de Rothschild'** (Sir Frederick Moore group). Similar to 'Sir Frederick Moore' but flowers clear pink spotted chocolate. AM 1958.

**'Cheer'** (*R. catawbiense* hybrid × *R.* 'Cunningham's White'). A dense medium-sized shrub with glossy green leaves. Flowers shell-pink blotched with red, freely borne in conical trusses. (1958). H4.

**'Chelsea Seventy'** A sister seedling of 'Vintage Rosé' which it resembles. Flowers salmon-pink flushed rose-pink from purple buds. (1972).

**'Chevalier Felix de Sauvage'** (*R. caucasicum* × hardy hybrid). (HH) A very old hybrid and still among the best. A medium-sized to large shrub of dense habit with trusses of deep rose-pink, dark-blotched flowers 6cm across, wavy at the margin. Mid. (1870). H4.

**'Chikor'** (*R. rupicola* var. *chryseum* × *R. ludlowii*). A choice dwarf shrub with small leaves and clusters of yellow flowers. Mid. Raised by E.H.M. and P.A. Cox at Glendoick, Perthshire. AM 1962. FCCT 1968. H4.

**'China'** (*R. fortunei* × *R. wightii*). A strong-growing plant with particularly handsome foliage and large, loose trusses of creamy-white flowers with a basal blotch of rose-carmine. Mid. (1936). AM 1940. AMT 1948. FCCT 1982. H4.

**'China A'** Similar to China but flowers pale yellow and smaller. (1946).

**'Chink'** (*R. keiskei* × *R. trichocladum*). An early flowering, dwarf shrub raised at Windsor Great Park, bearing lax trusses of drooping, bell-shaped flowers of an unusual Chartreuse-green, with occasional darker spotting on the lower lobe, opening in March. (1961). AM 1961. H4.

**'Chionoides'** An extremely hardy hybrid of *R. ponticum* making a medium-sized compact shrub with narrowly elliptic, acute leaves to 10cm long. Flowers funnel-shaped, 4cm across, in rounded heads, pink-tinged in bud, opening pure white apart from a conspicuous patch of yellow spots on the upper lobe. Late. Raised by Waterer's before 1865. H4.

**'Christmas Cheer'** (HH) An old *R. caucasicum* hybrid of rather dense, compact habit. Flowers pink in bud, fading to white. Normally flowering in March, occasionally February, the name referring to the one-time practice of forcing this plant for Christmas decoration although very occasionally in mild weather it is in flower by Christmas. AM 1990. H4.

**Cilpinense group** (*R. ciliatum* × *R. moupinense*). A beautiful, free-flowering, Bodnant hybrid forming a neat rounded bush up to 1m high with glossy green bristle-margined leaves. Flowers in loose trusses, shallowly bell-shaped, 6cm across, sparkling white, flushed pink, deeper in bud, opening in March. (1927). AM 1927. FCC 1968. AGM 1984. H4.

**Cinnkeys group** (*R. cinnabarinum* × *R. keysii*). A choice hybrid of upright habit with oval, glossy green leaves. Flowers tubular, 3.5cm long, bright orange-red, shading to pale apricot on the lobes, produced in dense, drooping clusters. Mid. (1926). AM 1935. H4.

**Colonel Rogers group** (*R. falconeri* × *R. niveum*). A large shrub of open habit with large, deeply veined leaves thinly tomentose beneath. Flowers pale lilac-pink in large trusses, often fading to nearly white. Mid. (1917). H3-4.

**'Concessum'** (HH) Compact trusses of widely funnel-shaped, bright pink flowers with paler centres. Mid to late. (Before 1867). H4.

**Conroy** See *R. cinnabarinum* Conroy group.

**'Cool Haven'** (*R.* 'Chaste' × *R. wardii* Litiense group). A lovely hybrid named by us and raised at Embley Park, Hants in 1945. A compact, leafy shrub with dark green, ovate leaves up to 10 × 5cm. Flowers in a well-filled, rounded truss, widely funnel-shaped, pale Dresden-yellow, flushed pink on the outside, with a broad ray of crimson spots; faintly fragrant. Mid. H3.

**'Coral Reef'** (*R.* 'Fabia' × *R.* 'Goldsworth Orange'). A lovely hybrid, raised at Wisley. Flowers in a lax, open truss, narrowly bell-shaped, 8cm across, with large lobes, salmon-pink tinged apricot in the throat and pink at the margin. Mid. AM 1954. H4.

**'Cornish Cross'** (*R. griffithianum* × *R. thomsonii*). A large shrub of rather open habit, producing lax trusses of narrowly bell-shaped, waxy flowers which are mottled rose-pink, shaded darker on the outside. Early to mid. A lovely hybrid raised at Penjerrick in Cornwall. (Before 1930). H3.

**'Cornubia'** (*R. arboreum* 'Blood Red' × *R.* 'Shilsonii'). A rather sparsely-leaved, large shrub or small tree. The blood-red, bell-shaped flowers are produced in compact, rounded trusses during March and April. A magnificent Penjerrick hybrid only suitable for sheltered gardens. (Before 1911). AM 1912. H3.

**'Corona'** (HH) Forms a very charming, slow-growing compact mound. Flowers funnel-shaped, 5cm across, rich coral-pink, in rather elongated trusses. Mid. (Before 1911). AM 1911. H4.

**'Corry Koster'** (HH) A strong-growing hybrid of uncertain origin. Perfectly formed, conical trusses of frilly-edged, widely funnel-shaped flowers, which are rich pink in bud opening pink, paling to white at the margin and with a ray of brownish-crimson spots. Mid. (1909). H4.

**'Cosmopolitan'** (*R.* 'Cunningham's White' × *R.* 'Vesuvius'). A medium-sized shrub of dense, spreading habit with dark glossy green leaves. Flowers pale pink flared with deep red, in rounded trusses. Mid. (1957). H3.

**'Countess of Athlone'** (*R.* 'Catawbiense Grandiflorum' × *R.* 'Geoffrey Millais'). (HH) An attractive hybrid of compact growth, well furnished with glossy, olive-green leaves. Flowers widely funnel-shaped, wavy-edged, purple in bud, opening mauve with greenish-yellow markings at base; carried in conical trusses. Mid. (1923). H4.

**'Countess of Derby'** (*R.* 'Cynthia' × *R.* 'Pink Pearl'). (HH) A large shrub bearing perfectly formed, conical trusses of large, widely funnel-shaped flowers which are a striking pink in bud, opening pink, paling slightly on the lobes and marked with reddish-brown spots and streaks within. Mid. (1913). AM 1930. H4.

†**'Countess of Haddington'** (*R. ciliatum* × *R. dalhousiae*). A beautiful but tender hybrid of rather straggling habit. Leaves usually 5 in a terminal cluster, glaucous-green and gland-dotted beneath. Flowers richly fragrant, borne in umbels of 2-4, trumpet-shaped, white, flushed pale rose. Early. A charming conservatory shrub. (1862). FCC 1862. H1.

**'Cowslip'** (*R. wardii* × *R. williamsianum*). A small shrub of neat, rounded habit. Flowers bell-shaped, 5-6cm across, cream or pale primrose with a pale pink flush when young, carried in loose trusses. Mid. (1937). AM 1937. H4.

**'Creeping Jenny'** See 'Jenny'.

**'Crest'** See *R.* Hawk group 'Crest'.

**'Curlew'** (*R. fletcherianum* 'Yellow Bunting' × *R. ludlowii*). A most attractive dwarf, spreading shrub with small, dark green, obovate leaves and widely funnel-shaped flowers 5cm across, pale yellow marked with greenish-brown, profusely borne. Best in a cool position. Raised by Peter Cox. Mid. FCC 1969. AMT 1981. AGM 1984. FCCT 1986. H4.

**'Cutie'** A hybrid of *R. calostrotum* making a small, compact shrub the leaves to 2.5cm long with a slight tan indumentum. Small lilac-pink flowers are profusely borne. Mid. (1959). H4.

**'Cynthia'** (*R. catawbiense* × *R. griffithianum*). (HH) One of the best rhododendrons for general planting, thriving in a great variety of situations. A large, vigorous, dome-shaped bush bearing magnificent conical trusses of widely funnel-shaped, rose-crimson flowers, each with a narrow ray of blackish-crimson markings within. Mid. Raised by Messrs Standish and Noble of Bagshot before 1870. AGM 1984. H4.

**'Dairy Maid'** A hybrid of *R. campylocarpum*. A dense, slow-growing shrub bearing compact trusses of pale creamy-yellow flowers streaked and spotted with red inside. Mid. (1930). AMT 1934. H4.

**Damaris group** (*R. campylocarpum* × *R.* 'Dr Stocker'). A broadly dome-shaped bush with oval leaves. Flowers in a lax truss, widely bell-shaped, glossy pale canary-yellow, shading to ivory at the margin. Early to mid. (1926). H3.

> **'Logan'** A lovely form with Dresden-yellow flowers admirably set-off by the rich green, glossy foliage. Early to mid. (1948). AM 1948.

**'Damozel'** A wide-spreading hybrid of *R. griersonianum*. Dome-shaped trusses of funnel-shaped, ruby-red flowers up to 8cm across, with darker spots within. Mid. (1936). AM 1948. H3-4.

**'David'** (*R.* 'Hugh Koster' × *R. neriiflorum*). Compact, rounded trusses of funnel-shaped, frilly-margined, deep blood-red flowers, slightly spotted within. Mid. (1939). FCC 1939. AMT 1957. H4.

**'Daydream'** (*R. griersonianum* × *R.* 'Lady Bessborough'). A beautiful Exbury hybrid of open, spreading habit with large, loose trusses of broadly funnel-shaped flowers which are rich

**RHODODENDRON 'Daydream'**—*continued*

crimson in bud, opening to pink, flushed crimson and fading to creamy-white, flushed pale pink on tube. Mid. (1936). AM 1940. H3.

**'Diana Colville'** A vigorous and free-flowering large shrub of compact habit with dark matt green leaves to 5cm long. Flowers 5cm across, widely funnel-shaped with wavy edges, pale lilac-purple spotted with red and with a yellow throat are borne in dome-shaped trusses 10cm across. A seedling of *R. yunnanense* raised by Lt-Col N.R. Colville in 1949. Mid. AMT 1968. FCCT 1972.

**'Diana Pearson'** (*R.* 'Glamour' × *R. yakushimanum*). A vigorous and compact, small shrub of spreading habit bearing dense, globular trusses to 14cm across of funnel-shaped very pale pink flowers spotted inside with red. Mid. AMT 1980. H4.

**'Doc'** (*R.* 'Corona' × *R. yakushimanum*). A small, compact, free-flowering shrub with dull green leaves to 8cm long. Flowers in globular trusses, funnel-shaped, 4cm across with wavy margins, rose-pink with deeper edges and spots, fading to creamy-white. Mid. (1972). H4.

**'Doncaster'** (HH) A very popular, distinct and easily recognised hybrid of *R. arboreum*. A small shrub, broadly dome-shaped in habit, with somewhat glossy, very dark green, leathery leaves, held very stiffly on the shoots. Flowers in a dense truss, funnel-shaped, brilliant crimson-scarlet, with a ray of black markings within. Mid. Raised by Anthony Waterer at Knap Hill. H4.

**'Dopey'** ([*R. facetum* hybrid × *R.* Fabia group] × [*R. yakushimanum* × *R.* Fabia group 'Tangerine']). A small to medium-sized shrub of compact habit. Flowers bell-shaped, wavy-edged, bright orange-red, paler towards the margin, spotted with orange-brown, freely borne in globular trusses. Mid. (1971). AMT 1977. FCCT 1979. H4.

**'Dora Amateis'** (*R. minus* Carolinianum group × *R. ciliatum*). A vigorous, compact, mound-forming shrub with ovate-lanceolate, dark dull green leaves to 7cm long, scaly on both sides. Flowers freely produced in open clusters, funnel-shaped, pale pink in bud opening white, faintly spotted with yellow, 5cm across. Early. (1955). AMT 1976. FCCT 1981. AGM 1984. H4.

**'Dormouse'** (*R.* 'Dawn's Delight' × *R. williamsianum*). A small to medium-sized, compact, dome-shaped bush with loose clusters of delicate pink, bell-shaped flowers set amid kidney-shaped leaves, which are copper-coloured when young. Mid. (1936). H4.

**'Dr Stocker'** (*R. caucasicum* × *R. griffithianum*). (HH) A dome-shaped bush, broader than high, bearing loose trusses of large, widely bell-shaped flowers, which are milk-white tinged cream and delicately marked brown-crimson. Early to mid. (1900). AM 1900. H3.

**'Dusky Maid'** (*R. fortunei* subsp. *discolor* × *R.* 'Moser's Maroon'). A tall, erect bush of robust habit. Tight rounded trusses of very attractive dark, dusky-red flowers. Mid to late. (1936). H4.

**'Dusty Miller'** (*R. yakushimanum* hybrid). A compact and rather slow-growing dwarf shrub, the leaves with a persistent silvery-white indumentum. Flowers pale pink flushed red, fading to cream. Mid. (1975). H4.

**'Earl of Athlone'** (*R.* 'Queen Wilhelmina' × *R.* 'Stanley Davies'). A splendid hybrid from the same pod as 'Britannia', but less hardy. Compact trusses of glowing, deep blood-red, bell-shaped flowers. Early to mid. FCCT 1933. H3.

**'Earl of Donoughmore'** A hybrid of *R. griersonianum*, produced by M. Koster and Sons in 1953. Flowers bright red, with an orange glow. Mid. H4.

**'Egret'** (*R. racemosum* 'White Lace' × *R. campylogynum*, white form). A compact and free-flowering dwarf shrub of neat habit with dark glossy green leaves to 2.5cm long. Flowers 2cm across, widely funnel-shaped, white tinged green, in open trusses 7cm across. Mid. (1982). AM 1982. AMT 1987. H4.

**'Eider'** (*R. minus* Carolinianum group 'Album' × *R. leucaspis*). A vigorous and compact, free-flowering shrub of spreading habit, the leaves to 6cm long. Flowers 5cm across, widely funnel-shaped, white, in compact globular trusses to 7cm across. Early to mid. (1979). H4.

**'El Camino'** (*R.* 'Anna' × *R.* 'Marinus Koster'). A vigorous large shrub with dark green leaves and very large, wavy-edged, glowing red flowers with darker spots. Mid. H4.

**RHODODENDRON**—*continued*

**'Eleanore'** (*R. augustinii* × *R. rubiginosum* Desquamatum group). A large, pretty shrub with pale mauve flowers nearly 7.5cm across. Early to mid. Suitable for woodland planting. (1937). AM 1943. H3.

**'Electra'** See *R. augustinii* 'Electra' under species.

**'Elisabeth Hobbie'** (*R.* 'Essex Scarlet' × *R. forrestii* Repens group). A dwarf shrub; loose umbels of 6-10 translucent, scarlet-red, bell-shaped flowers. Early. (1945). AMT 1986. H4.

**'Elizabeth'** (*R. forrestii* Repens group × *R. griersonianum*). A dwarf or small, spreading shrub raised at Bodnant. Flowers trumpet-shaped, 7.5cm across, rich dark red, carried in clusters of five or six in April. (1939). AM 1939. FCC 1943. AGM 1984. H4.

**'Elizabeth Lockhart'** A small, mound-forming shrub with oval to oblong leaves which are deep bronze purple. Loose clusters of bell-shaped, deep red flowers are borne in spring. A sport of 'Humming Bird'. (1965). H4.

**'Emasculum'** (*R. ciliatum* × *R. dauricum*). A medium-sized shrub of upright habit with elliptic leaves up to 3cm long, slightly glossy above and scaly on both sides. Flowers borne in pairs or singly, mauve-pink in bud opening very pale lilac-pink, broadly funnel-shaped, 4cm across. The stamens are present but are much reduced in size, not reaching above the ovary and bearing sterile anthers. Early. AM 1976. H4.

**'Emerald Isle'** (*R.* 'Idealist' × *R.* 'Naomi'). An unusual hybrid with bell-shaped flowers of Chartreuse-green. May. (1956). AM 1956. H4.

**'Ethel'** (*R.* 'F.C. Puddle' × *R. forrestii* Repens group). A dwarf Bodnant hybrid of low spreading habit. Large trumpet-shaped flowers of crimson-scarlet. Early. (1940). FCC 1940. H3.

**'Everestianum'** A very old hybrid of *R. catawbiense* making a medium-sized, dense bush. Flowers widely funnel-shaped with frilly lobes, pale lilac with a broad band of brown or reddish spots. Mid. (Before 1853). H4.

**Exburiense group** (*R. kyawii* × *R. sanguineum* var. *didymum*). A medium-sized spreading shrub with dark green leaves and bell-shaped dark waxy-red flowers. Late. (1937). H4.

**'Exbury Angelo'** See under 'Angelo'.

**'Exbury Isabella'** (*R. auriculatum* × *R. griffithianum*). A large shrub or small tree with large trusses of enormous, fragrant, trumpet-shaped white flowers. Late. (1948). H3.

**Fabia group** (*R. dichroanthum* × *R. griersonianum*). A very beautiful, widely-dome-shaped bush bearing loose, flat trusses of funnel-shaped flowers which are scarlet, shaded orange in the tube and freely speckled with pale brown markings. Mid. Raised at Bodnant. (1934). AM 1934. AGM 1984. FCC 1989. H4.

**'Tangerine'** Flowers vermilion in colour, shaded geranium-red around the mouth and poppy-red in the throat. As in Fabia, the calyx is large and petaloid with incised margin. Mid. AM 1940.

**'Waterer'** Salmon-pink, with a tint of orange. Late. Compact habit. A splendid selection.

**'Faggetter's Favourite'** A hybrid of *R. fortunei* raised by W.C. Slocock of Woking. A tall grower, with fine foliage and producing large trusses of sweetly-scented, shell-pink flowers with white shading. Mid. (1933). AM 1933. AMT 1955. H4.

**'Fastuosum Flore Pleno'** (*R. catawbiense* × *R. ponticum*). (HH) A very hardy hybrid, forming a large, dome-shaped bush. Flowers in a lax truss, funnel-shaped with wavy margins, rich mauve with a ray of brown-crimson markings within, filaments unevenly petaloid. Mid. Raised at Ghent, Belgium sometime before 1846. AGM 1984. H4.

**'Fire Bird'** (*R. griersonianum* × *R.* 'Norman Shaw'). A tall, vigorous shrub, producing large trusses of glowing salmon-red flowers with a deeper orange-red eye. The bright green young leaves are strikingly set against long crimson bracts. Mid. (1938). H3-4.

**'Fireball'** (*R.* 'Ascot Brilliant' × *R. barbatum*). An early flowering shrub requiring woodland conditions. Flowers bell-shaped, with frilly margins, glowing carmine-scarlet, carried in rounded trusses in March. Raised by Richard Gill and Sons of Penryn, Cornwall, before 1925. AM 1925. H3-4.

**'Fireman Jeff'** (*R.* 'Jean Marie de Montague × *R.* 'Grosclaude'). A small shrub with dark green leaves and dense trusses of deep blood-red flowers. Mid. (1977). H4.

**'Fittianum'** (*R. fittianum* BALF. f.) A small to medium-sized shrub. Sometimes considered to be a form of *R. dauricum*, but the 2.5cm wide, mauve-pink flowers not opening until

**RHODODENDRON 'Fittianum'**—*continued*

mid-April. A natural hybrid of *R. racemosum* raised in 1913 at Werrington Park from Forrest 10278 and named after the then Head Gardener. H4.

**'Fittra'** (*R.* 'Fittianum' × *R. racemosum*). A very free-flowering, dwarf, compact shrub, raised in our nurseries. The vivid, deep rose-pink flowers are borne in dense trusses of up to 30 blooms, often completely covering the plant. Early to mid. (1938). AM 1949. H4.

**Flava group** (*R. wardii* × *R. yakushimanum*). A compact small shrub with dark glossy green leaves. Flowers bell-shaped, pale yellow blotched with red in dense, dome-shaped trusses. This hybrid has been raised many times and several cultivars have been named. Mid. H4.

**Fortune group** (*R. falconeri* × *R. sinogrande*). A splendid hybrid raised at Exbury and like its parents needing a sheltered woodland situation. A large, stoutly branched shrub, the dark glossy green, deeply veined leaves with a brown indumentum beneath. Flowers pale yellow blotched with deep red in huge trusses. Early to mid. FCC 1938. H3.

†**'Fragrantissimum'** (*R. edgeworthii* × *R. formosum*). A beautiful hybrid of medium size with attractive, dark green, corrugated leaves, paler beneath. Flowers appearing in terminal umbels of 4, extremely fragrant, widely funnel-shaped up to 7.5cm long, white, flushed rose without and greenish within at base; stamens with brown anthers. Early. Requires conservatory treatment except in the mildest areas. FCC 1868. H1.

**'Francis Hanger'** (*R. dichroanthum* × *R.* 'Isabella'). Flowers with frilly margins, chrome-yellow, edged with a delicate tinge of pale rose. Mid. (1942). AM 1950. Raised at Exbury and named after the late Curator of the RHS Gardens, Wisley. AM 1950.

**'Frank Baum'** (*R.* 'Jasper' × *R.* 'Mars'). A small shrub with red-stalked leaves and coral-watermelon-coloured flowers in dense, rounded trusses. Late. (1968). H4.

**'Fred Rose'** (*R.* 'Gladys Swaythling' × *R. lacteum*). A medium-sized shrub with dark matt green leaves to 12.5cm long. Flowers 6cm diameter, widely bell-shaped and wavy margined, lemon-yellow spotted red in the throat, borne in compact, dome-shaped trusses 12.5cm across. Mid. (1962). H4.

**Fulgarb group** (*R. arboreum* 'Blood Red' × *R. fulgens*). A large shrub or tree bearing small compact trusses of rich crimson flowers in February. AM 1937. H3.

**'Furnivall's Daughter'** Similar to 'Mrs Furnivall' but stronger-growing, with larger leaves and flowers, which are widely funnel-shaped, light rose-pink with a bold splash of dark markings. Mid to late. AMT 1958. FCCT 1961. AGM 1984. H4.

**'Fusilier'** (*R. elliottii* × *R. griersonianum*). A magnificent Exbury hybrid, a dense bush furnished with long, narrow leaves brown tomentose beneath and bearing large trusses of brilliant red, funnel-shaped flowers darker spotted on all lobes, 8cm across. Mid. (1938). AM 1938. FCC 1942. H3.

**'Gartendirektor Glocker'** (*R.* 'Doncaster' × *R. williamsianum*). A compact small shrub of domed habit with rounded deep blue-green leaves bronze when young. Deep rose-red, funnel-shaped flowers are borne in loose trusses. Mid. (1952). H4.

**'General Eisenhower'** A hybrid of *R. griffithianum*, bearing large trusses of widely funnel-shaped deep carmine flowers with frilly lobes darker spotted within. Mid. (1946). H4.

**'General Sir John du Cane'** (*R. fortunei* subsp. *discolor* × *R. thomsonii*). A very fine hybrid producing large, lax trusses of fragrant, widely funnel-shaped flowers which are rose-madder, fading to pink, with a dark crimson basal flash within. Mid. (1933). H4.

**'George Hardy'** A tall, fast-growing shrub, a hybrid of *R. griffithianum*. Leaves dark glossy green, to 15cm long. Flowers in large conical trusses, bright rose in bud opening to glistening, waxy-white with crimson markings, broadly bell-shaped, fragrant, to 10cm across. Mid. H4.

**'Geraldii'** See *R.* × *geraldii* under species.

**'Ginny Gee'** (*R. keiskei* 'Yaku Fairy' × *R. racemosum*). An excellent dwarf shrub of compact, spreading habit with profusely borne, widely funnel-shaped, pale pink flowers deeper in bud and fading to nearly white edged pink. Early to mid. (1979). H4.

**'Golden Bee'** (*R. keiskei* 'Yaku Fairy' × *R. mekongense* var. *melinanthum*). A dwarf, semi-evergreen shrub of compact habit bearing small funnel-shaped bright yellow flowers in open trusses. Early to mid. (1982). H4.

**RHODODENDRON**—*continued*

**'Golden Horn'** (*R. dichroanthum* × *R. elliottii*). A brilliantly coloured, small, Exbury hybrid. Flowers drooping, bell-shaped, salmon-orange, freely speckled with brownish markings within; calyx large, double, same colour as corolla. Mid. (1939). AM 1945. H3-4.

**'Golden Horn Persimmon'** See *R.* 'Persimmon'.

**'Golden Orfe'** (Comely group) (*R. cinnabarinum* Concatenans group × *R.* Lady Chamberlain group). A Tower Court hybrid resembling *R. cinnabarinum*. Flowers 5cm long, orange-yellow. AM 1964.

**'Golden Oriole'** (*R. moupinense* × *R. sulfureum*). A small shrub of upright habit with attractive red young shoots. Leaves ovate or obovate, to 5cm long, glaucous beneath with long bristles on the margins. Flowers usually in twos or threes, funnel-shaped, primrose-yellow with two patches of orange spots inside. The newly opened flowers contrast effectively with the bright pink bud scales densely clustered at their bases. Early. AM 1947. H4.

**'Golden Oriole Talavera'** Similar to 'Golden Oriole' but flowers clear pale yellow. FCC 1963.

**'Golden Star'** (*R. fortunei* × *R. wardii*). A vigorous, medium-sized to large shrub with handsome, dark glossy green leaves. Flowers pale yellow flushed with pink in bud, freely borne. Mid. (1966). H4.

**'Golden Torch'** (*R.* 'Bambi' × [*R.* 'Grosclaude' × *R. griersonianum*]). A small, compact shrub with leaves to 6cm long. Flowers bell-shaped, 5cm across, salmon-pink in bud opening pale yellow, borne in compact trusses. The parentage is doubtful. Mid. (1972). AMT 1984. H3.

**'Goldfort'** (*R. fortunei* × *R.* 'Goldsworth Yellow'). Flowers pink in bud, opening creamy-yellow, tinted with apricot-pink. Mid. (1937). H4.

**'Goldkrone'** ([*R. wardii* × *R.* 'Alice Street'] × *R.* 'Hachmann's Marina'). A small shrub making a compact mound. Large trusses of golden yellow funnel-shaped flowers are profusely borne over a long period. One of the best small yellows. Mid. (1983). H4.

**'Goldstrike'** (*R. oreotrephes* × *R.* Royal Flush group). A medium-sized shrub of upright habit with dark green leaves. Flowers yellow, nodding, borne in open terminal clusters. Mid. (1962). H4.

**'Goldsworth Orange'** (*R. dichroanthum* × *R. fortunei* subsp. *discolor*). A low, spreading bush bearing large trusses of pale orange flowers, tinged with apricot-pink. Late. (1938). AMT 1959. H4.

**'Goldsworth Pink'** A hardy shrub raised from *R. griffithianum* crossed with an unnamed garden hybrid. Lax, conical trusses of widely funnel-shaped flowers which are deep rose in bud, opening to mottled rose-pink and fading to white. Mid. (1933). AMT 1958. FCCT 1987. H4.

**'Goldsworth Yellow'** (*R. campylocarpum* × *R. caucasicum*). A leafy, dome-shaped bush, broader than high and very hardy. Flowers in a well-filled, rounded truss, funnel-shaped, apricot-pink in bud, opening primrose-yellow, with a large ray of warm brown markings. Usually flowering at "bluebell time". Mid. Raised by W.C. Slocock at Goldsworth Nurseries, Woking. (1925). AM 1925. H4.

**'Gomer Waterer'** (HH) A very beautiful, medium-sized bush of dense habit, a hybrid of *R. catawbiense*. Leaves dark green, large and leathery, oval or oblong-obovate, with deflexed margins, to 13cm long. The buds in the leaf axils are reddish and rather conspicious. Flowers fragrant, in a large, dense, rounded truss, funnel-shaped, but deeply divided, white, flushed pale mauve towards the edges, with a mustard-coloured basal blotch, 8cm across. Mid to late. (Before 1900). AM 1906. AGM 1984. H4.

**'Goosander'** (*R. ludlowii* × *R. lutescens*). A vigorous and compact, free-flowering dwarf shrub with dark green leaves to 3cm long bronze when young. Flowers 4cm across, open funnel-shaped, pale yellow flushed green and spotted red, in compact, dome-shaped trusses up to 6cm across. Early to mid. AMT 1981. H3.

**'Grace Seabrook'** (*R.* 'Jean Marie de Montague' × *R. strigillosum*). A vigorous and tough, medium-sized shrub with dark green, pointed leaves. Flowers deep red, paler at the margins, in compact, broadly conical trusses. Early to mid. (1965). H4.

**RHODODENDRON**—*continued*

**'Grayswood Pink'** (*R. venator* × *R. williamsianum*). A small, dense bush with obovate-oblong, dark glossy green leaves to 7.5cm long. Flowers narrowly bell-shaped, rose-pink, darker spotted within. Mid. (1949). H4.

**'Grenadier'** (*R. elliottii* × *R.* 'Moser's Maroon'). An Exbury hybrid, a tall shrub of compact growth, bearing magnificent trusses of deep blood-red flowers. Mid to late. (1939). FCC 1943. H3.

**'Gristede'** A compact dwarf shrub resembling 'Blue Diamond' with glossy green leaves and clusters of funnel-shaped, violet-blue flowers. A hybrid of *R. impeditum*. Early to mid. (1977). H4.

**'Grosclaude'** (*R. facetum* × *R. haematodes*). An Exbury hybrid of neat, compact habit, producing lax trusses of bell-shaped, waxen, blood-red flowers darker spotted within, with wavy margins. Calyx petaloid. Mid. (1941). AM 1945. H3-4.

**'Grumpy'** (*R. yakushimanum* × unknown hybrid). Small shrub of compact, spreading habit. Leaves dark dull green to 8cm long. Flowers in rounded trusses, freely borne, funnel-shaped, 5cm across, cream tinged pale pink at margins, spotted with orange-yellow. AMT 1979.

**'Gwillt-King'** (*R. griersonianum* × *R. arboreum* subsp. *zeylanicum*). A vigorous and attractive shrub for woodland planting. Flowers bell-shaped, rich Turkey-red. Mid. (1938). AM 1952. H2-3.

**'Hachmann's Polaris'** (*R. yakushimanum* 'Koichiro Wada' × *R.* 'Omega'). A small shrub making a compact mound with hairy leaves. Flowers light rhodamine-pink edged with fuchsia-purple, carmine-red in bud. Mid. (1963). H4.

**'Halcyone'** (*R.* 'Lady Bessborough' × *R. souliei*). A lovely hybrid bearing rather lax, flat-topped trusses of delicate pink, wide-open flowers with a basal flash of crimson spots. Mid. (1940). H4.

**'Halfdan Lem'** (*R.* 'Jean Marie de Montague' × red Loderi). A vigorous medium-sized shrub with dark green somewhat twisted leaves. Bright red flowers are borne in large trusses. Mid. (1974). H4.

**'Hallelujah'** (*R.* 'Kimberley' × *R.* 'Jean Marie de Montague'). A small shrub with thick, dark green leaves bent downwards from the middle. Rose-red flowers are borne in large, dense trusses. Mid. (1976). H4.

**'Hampshire Belle'** A very distinct small shrub of compact upright habit with linear-oblong to lanceolate leaves up to 8 × 1cm. Flowers in dense, hemispherical trusses of about 18; corolla funnel-shaped, 5cm across, pink in bud opening lilac-pink fading to white in the centre, heavily blotched with red. Mid. H4. A seedling found in about 1970 in the Hillier Gardens and Arboretum by Head Gardener E.W. (Bill) George and probably a hybrid of *R. ponticum*.

**'Harvest Moon'** (*R. campylocarpum* hybrid × *R.* 'Mrs Lindsay Smith'). A lovely hybrid with bell-shaped, creamy-white flowers marked with a broad ray of carmine spots within. Mid. AMT 1948. H4.

**Hawk group** (*R.* 'Lady Bessborough' × *R. wardii*). A magnificent Exbury hybrid with oblong, glossy green leaves to 14cm long on long, slender, purplish petioles. Bears loose, flat-topped trusses of large, sulphur-yellow, funnel-shaped flowers marked with red at the base, apricot in bud. Mid. (1940). AM 1949. H3. See also 'Crest'.

**'Crest'** A magnificent, Exbury hybrid with reddish-purple shoots and dark glossy green leaves up to 10cm long, bearing large trusses of bell-shaped, primrose-yellow flowers, orange in bud, which have a slight darkening in the throat. The individual flowers are 10cm across. Mid. (1953). FCC 1953. H3.

**'Jervis Bay'** A superb rounded shrub with dark green, ovate leaves to 11cm long. Flowers widely funnel-shaped in firm, rounded trusses, golden yellow tinged orange in bud, primrose-yellow when open with a large maroon blotch at the base and maroon marks inside. Mid. AM 1951. H3.

**'Hélène Schiffner'** A small, dense, rounded bush of German origin, bearing rounded trusses of widely funnel-shaped flowers which are mauve in bud, opening to pure white, occasionally with an inconspicuous ray of greenish markings within. A hybrid of *R. arboreum*. Mid. FCC 1893. H4.

**RHODODENDRON**— *continued*

**'Honey Bee'** (*R. hanceanum* × *R. ludlowii*). A slow-growing dwarf shrub of compact habit with bronze young growths and pale yellow flowers. Mid. H4.

**'Hoppy'** (*R.* 'Doncaster' × *R. yakushimanum*) selfed. A vigorous, compact, free-flowering small shrub with dark green leaves to 8cm long. Flowers 5cm across, funnel-shaped, pale lilac fading to white spotted with yellow, in compact globular trusses up to 18cm across. Mid. (1972). AMT 1977. H4.

**'Hotei'** (*R.* 'Goldsworth Orange' × [*R. souliei* × *R. wardii*]). A compact medium-sized shrub with narrow, dark green leaves to 12cm long. Deep yellow, widely bell-shaped flowers. The parent of many new hybrids. Mid. (1964). AM 1974. H3.

**'Hugh Koster'** (*R.* 'Doncaster' hybrid × *R.* 'George Hardy'). (HH) A sturdy, leafy bush with stiff, erect branches. Flowers in a well-formed truss, funnel-shaped, glowing crimson-scarlet, with black markings within. Mid. A fine, hardy hybrid resembling 'Doncaster', but foliage slightly wavy at the margins and flowers lighter in colour. (1915). AMT 1933. H4.

**'Humming Bird'** (*R. haematodes* × *R. williamsianum*). A small, compact dome-shaped bush of distinctive appearance. Flowers half nodding, widely bell-shaped, carmine, shaded glowing scarlet inside the tube. Early. (1933). H3.

**'Hydon Dawn'** (*R.* 'Springbok' × *R. yakushimanum*). A compact dwarf shrub with dark, slightly glossy green leaves to 10cm long with a cream indumentum when young. Flowers 5cm across, funnel-shaped with wavy margins, light pink with paler margins and reddish brown spots, borne in compact globular trusses 12.5cm across. Mid. (1969). AMT 1986. FCCT 1987. H4.

**'Hydon Hunter'** (*R.* 'Springbok' × *R. yakushimanum*). A vigorous and compact small shrub of upright habit with dark, slightly glossy green leaves to 10cm long. Flowers funnel-shaped, 5.5cm across in compact dome-shaped trusses 12cm across, white flushed pale pink and spotted with yellow. Mid. (1972). AM 1976. FCCT 1979. H4.

**'Idealist'** (*R.* 'Naomi' × *R. wardii*). A very floriferous large shrub or small tree, striking when in flower. Leaves broadly elliptic, bright green above, to 9cm long on purple petioles. Flowers in large, compact, clustered trusses which appear to weigh down the branches. Corolla widely funnel-shaped, to 8cm across with 5-7 lobes, coral-pink in bud, opening to pale creamy-yellow with lines of reddish markings at the base. Early to mid. (1941). AM 1945. H3.

**'Ilam Violet'** (*R. augustinii* 'Electra' × *R. russatum*). A very free-flowering small shrub of upright habit with dark green leaves to 4cm long reddish when young. Flowers 4cm across, widely funnel-shaped with wavy margins, deep violet blue, in globular trusses 6.5cm across. Early to mid. (1947). AMT 1983. H4.

**Impeanum group** (*R. hanceanum* × *R. fastigiatum*). A dwarf, spreading shrub with small crowded leaves. Smothered with small clusters of saucer-shaped flowers of a striking cobalt-violet. Mid. An excellent shrub for the rock garden or heather garden. Cross made at Kew in 1915. FCC 1934. H4.

**'Impi'** (*R.* 'Moser's Maroon' × *R. sanguineum* subsp. *didymum*). A medium-sized shrub of upright growth. Leaves broadly elliptic, bullate above, to 8cm long. Flowers funnel-shaped, 5cm across, in small trusses, nearly black in bud opening to a very deep, vinous-crimson, faintly black-spotted within. Brilliant when viewed by transmitted light. Late. AM 1945. H4.

**Intrifast group** (*R. fastigiatum* × *R. intricatum*). A dwarf shrub of dense habit producing innumerable clusters of small, violet-blue flowers. Mid. H4.

**'Isabel Pearce'** (*R.* 'Anna' × *R.* 'Lem's Goal'). A stiffly-branched large shrub of upright habit with long, narrow leaves. Flowers rose-red fading to pink with deeper margins conspicuosly blotched and spotted, in large trusses. Mid. (1975). H3.

**'Isabella'** (*R. auriculatum* × *R. griffithianum*). A beautiful Leonardslee hybrid. A large shrub or small tree with oblong-lanceolate leaves to 20cm long on long, yellowish-green petioles. Bears large trusses of enormous, fragrant, trumpet-shaped, frilly-edged, white flowers, 11cm across with a patch of rose-red markings near the base. Late. (1934). H3.

**'Jacksonii'** (*R. caucasicum* × *R.* 'Nobleanum'). (HH) A broadly dome-shaped, slow-growing, medium-sized bush. Flowers in a well-formed truss, widely funnel-shaped, 6cm across, bright rose-pink, with maroon markings and paler spotting within; normally opening in

**RHODODENDRON 'Jacksonii'**—*continued*

April, occasionally in March. One of the earliest raised hybrids, tolerant of industrial pollution and thriving where many other rhododendrons would fail. (1835). H4.

**Jalisco group** (*R.* 'Dido' × *R.* 'Lady Bessborough'). A most attractive hybrid raised at Exbury. Flowers straw-coloured, tinted orange-rose at the tips. Late. (1942). H3-4.

**'Eclipse'** Flowers primrose-yellow, streaked crimson on the outside and blotched and spotted crimson at the base within. Calyx yellow edged with red. AM 1948.

**'Elect'** Flowers primrose-yellow, with paler lobes, the margins slightly frilled, marked with brownish-red spots within. Calyx yellow. AM 1948. FCCT 1987.

**'Emblem'** Flowers very pale yellow or nearly white, with a dark maroon basal blotch within. Calyx white veined red. (1948).

**'Goshawk'** Mimosa-yellow spotted with crimson. FCC 1954.

**'Janet'** Flowers apricot-yellow. (1948).

**'Jubilant'** Red in bud opening buttercup-yellow, deeper in the throat. AM 1966.

**'James Barto'** (*R. orbiculare* × *R. williamsianum*). A compact small shrub with elliptic leaves to 7.5cm long. Flowers pink, funnel-shaped and slightly fragrant. Early to mid. (1953). H4.

**'James Burchett'** (*R. catawbiense* hybrid × *R. fortunei* subsp. *discolor*). A vigorous large shrub of dense habit with dark green leaves. Flowers white tinged mauve with a bronze-green flare, in compact trusses. Late. AMT 1960. H4.

**'Jenny'** ('Creeping Jenny') (Elizabeth group). A prostrate shrub raised at Bodnant, carrying large, deep red, bell-shaped flowers. Mid. H4.

**'Jervis Bay'** See *R.* Hawk group 'Jervis Bay'.

**'John Barr Stevenson'** (*R. lacteum* × *R.* Damaris group 'Logan'). A splendid Tower Court hybrid bearing lemon-yellow, red-blotched, broadly bell-shaped flowers in large trusses. Early to mid. AM 1971. H4.

**'John Walter'** (HH) A semi-erect branched shrub of compact habit. Flowers in dense, globular trusses, cherry-red fading to lilac-red with dark spotting, funnel-shaped, wavy at the margin. Late. (1860). H4.

**'July Fragrance'** (*R. diaprepes* × *R.* 'Isabella'). A strong-growing bush, young leaves flushed bronze. Flowers in a large, loose truss, trumpet-shaped, white with a crimson basal stain within, deliciously fragrant. Late. Raised in our nurseries. (1967). H3.

**'Jutland'** (*R.* 'Bellerophon' × *R. elliottii*). Flowers in a large, dome-shaped truss, widely bell-shaped, geranium lake, flecked darker red. Late. (1942). AM 1947. H3.

**'Karkov'** (*R. griersonianum* × *R.* 'Red Admiral'). A vigorous-growing, Exbury hybrid bearing large, globular trusses of widely funnel-shaped, frilly-edged flowers which are carmine-rose, faintly and evenly spotted. Early to mid. (1943). AM 1947. H3.

**'Kate Waterer'** (HH) A medium-sized to large, dense shrub with oblong-ovate leaves to 12cm long. Flowers funnel-shaped, to 6cm across, rose-crimson passing to clear rose, the upper lobe with a ray of greenish-yellow spots on a white background. Mid. (Before 1876). H4.

**'Kilimanjaro'** (*R.* 'Dusky Maid' × *R. elliottii*). A superb Exbury hybrid, with compact, globular trusses of funnel-shaped, currant-red, wavy-edged flowers, spotted chocolate within. Mid to late. (1943). FCC 1947. H3.

**'Kluis Sensation'** (*R.* 'Britannia' × un-named seedling). A hardy shrub with flowers of a bright scarlet, with darker spots on upper lobes. Mid. (1948). H4.

**'Kluis Triumph'** A splendid *R. griffithianum* hybrid with outstanding deep red flowers. Mid. AMT 1969. FCCT 1971. H4.

**'Lady Alice Fitzwilliam'** (*R. ciliatum* × *R. edgeworthii*). A beautiful but tender medium-sized shrub with dark green, deeply veined leaves. Flowers 10cm across, funnel-shaped, white flushed pink with yellow markings in the throat, very fragrant. Mid. FCC 1881. H2.

**Lady Bessborough group** (*R. campylocarpum* Elatum group × *R. fortunei* subsp. *discolor*). A tall, erect-branched hybrid bearing trusses of funnel-shaped, wavy-edged flowers which are apricot in bud, opening to creamy-white, with a flash of maroon on a deeper cream ground within. Mid. Raised at Exbury. FCC 1933. H4.

**'Roberte'** A beautiful form with loose trusses of daintily fringed flowers of a bright salmon-pink colour, tinged with apricot and spotted with crimson in the throat. Mid. FCC 1936.

**RHODODENDRON**—*continued*

**Lady Chamberlain group** (*R. cinnabarinum* Roylei group × *R.* Royal Flush group, orange form). Undoubtedly one of the loveliest rhododendrons grown in gardens. It forms a stiffly-branched shrub with neat, sea-green leaves, and bears with the utmost freedom clusters of drooping, waxy, long, narrowly bell-shaped flowers. The typical colour is mandarin-red, shading to orange-buff on the lobes. Mid. It was raised by Lionel de Rothschild at Exbury. (1930). FCC 1931. H3. It is a variable hybrid.

**'Chelsea'** Flowers orange-pink.

**'Exbury'** Flowers yellow, overlaid salmon-orange. FCC 1931. AGM 1984.

**'Gleam'** Flowers orange-yellow, with crimson-tipped lobes.

**'Ivy'** Flowers orange.

**'Salmon Trout'** Flowers salmon-pink.

**'Seville'** Flowers bright orange inside, reddish outside.

**'Lady Clementine Mitford'** (HH) A large shrub, a hybrid of *R. maximum*, with large, glossy green leaves. Flowers in a firm truss, widely funnel-shaped, peach-pink, shading to white in centre, with a V-shaped pattern of pink, olive-green and brown markings within. Mid to late. (1870). AMT 1971. AGM 1984. H4.

**'Lady Eleanor Cathcart'** (*R. arboreum* × *R. maximum*). (HH) A magnificent large, dome-shaped bush or small tree with handsome and very distinctive foliage. Flowers in a rounded truss, widely funnel-shaped, bright clear rose with slightly darker veins and a conspicuous maroon basal blotch within. Mid to late. Said to have originated at Sandleford Park, near Oxford, before 1844. H4.

**'Lady Grey Egerton'** A hybrid of *R. catawbiense*. Flowers in a loose truss, pale lilac, nearly white in the centre with a broad patch of yellow spots, funnel-shaped, 6cm across. Mid to late. (Before 1888). H4.

**'Lady Longman'** An excellent hardy hybrid with large vivid rose flowers with a chocolate eye. Mid to late. H4.

**Lady Roseberry group** (*R. cinnabarinum* Roylei group × *R.* Royal Flush group, pink form). Similar to 'Lady Chamberlain', except in colour, pink shades predominating. Typical colour is deep pink graduating to a lighter shade at the margins. Mid. Raised by Lionel de Rothschild at Exbury. (1930). AM 1930. FCC 1932. H3.

**'Dalmeny'** Flowers soft pink.

**'Pink Beauty'** A lovely pink form. (1955).

**'Pink Delight'** A beautiful shrub with flowers of a glistening pink, paler within. AGM 1984.

**'Lamplighter'** (*R.* 'Britannia' × *R.* 'Mme F.R. Chauvin'). A vigorous large shrub of open habit with narrow, pointed dark green leaves. Bright red flowers are borne in large trusses. Mid. (1955). H3.

**'Lava Flow'** (*R. griersonianum* × KW 13225). A late flowering hybrid of dwarf bushy habit, the dark green leaves with a buff coloured indumentum beneath. Flowers trumpet-shaped, 7cm across, deep scarlet with darker spots. The Kingdon-Ward introduction used as one parent is similar to *R. sanguineum* subsp. *didymum*. Late. (1955). H3.

**'Lavender Girl'** (*R. fortunei* × *R.* 'Lady Grey Egerton'). A vigorous, free-flowering hybrid of compact habit producing dome-shaped trusses of fragrant, funnel-shaped flowers which are lilac-mauve in bud opening pale lavender, darker at margins with pinkish-yellow throat. Mid. (1950). AMT 1950. FCCT 1967. H4.

**'Lee's Dark Purple'** (HH) A compact rounded bush resembling *R. catawbiense* in habit and foliage. Flowers in a dense rounded truss, widely funnel-shaped, royal purple, with a ray of greenish-brown or ochre markings within. Mid. H4.

**'Lem's Cameo'** (*R.* 'Anna' × *R.* 'Dido'). A medium-sized upright shrub with dark matt green leaves to 16cm long bronze when young. Flowers funnel-shaped, to 9cm across, red in bud opening cream and apricot flushed with red and spotted pink, borne in rounded trusses. Mid. (1962). H4.

**'Lem's Monarch'** (*R.* 'Anna' × *R.* 'Marinus Koster'). A vigorous large shrub of spreading habit with thick-textured, pointed leaves. Flowers pale pink fading to white, edged with pink, in very large, conical trusses. Mid. (1971). H4.

**'Letty Edwards'** (*R. campylocarpum* Elatum group × *R. fortunei*). (Gladys group). Free-flowering shrub of compact habit. Flowers funnel-shaped, pale sulphur-yellow with a deeper flush, pale pink in bud. Mid. AMT 1946. FCCT 1948. H4.

**RHODODENDRON**— *continued*

**'Lionel's Triumph'** (*R. lacteum* × *R.* 'Naomi'). An outstanding Exbury hybrid with long leaves and large trusses of bell-shaped flowers of Dresden-yellow, spotted and blotched crimson at the base within; individual flowers are 10cm across. Early to mid. AM 1954. FCC 1974. H3.

**'Little Ben'** (*R. forrestii* Repens group × *R. neriiflorum*). A dwarf, spreading shrub producing an abundance of waxy, bell-shaped flowers 4cm long, of a brilliant scarlet, in March or April. (1937). FCC 1937. H4.

**Lodauric group** (*R. auriculatum* × *R.* Loderi group). Magnificent in leaf and flower. A large shrub or small tree, bearing nodding trusses of rich-scented, trumpet-shaped, pure white flowers 13cm across, with 2 streaks of brownish-crimson at base within. Late. (1939). H3.

**'Lodauric Iceberg'** Similar to Lodauric but with more flowers in the truss. AM 1958.

**Loderi group** (*R. fortunei* × *R. griffithianum*). Generally considered to be the finest hybrid rhododendron. A strong-growing, large, rounded bush or small tree bearing enormous trusses of very large, lily-like, trumpet-shaped, richly scented flowers 13-15cm across, varying in colour from white to cream and soft pink. Early to mid. Raised by Sir Edmund Loder at Leonardslee in 1901. H3. From the original and subsequent crosses a great number of slightly different clones have been raised. AGM 1984.

**'Julie'** Cream, suffused sulphur. The nearest to a yellow Loderi. AM 1944.

**'King George'** Perhaps the "best of the bunch". Flowers soft pink in bud, opening to pure white, with a basal flash of pale green markings within. AM 1968. FCC 1970. AGM 1984.

**'Patience'** Flowers carmine-rose in bud, opening to white with a faint flash of crimson and green at the base within.

**'Pink Diamond'** Flowers similar to those of 'King George', but slightly smaller and a delicate pink in colour, with a basal flash of crimson, passing to green flushed brown. FCC 1914. AGM 1984.

**'Venus'** Deep pink in bud, opening to rhodamine-pink, passing to pale pink with a very faint greenish flash at the base within. AGM 1984.

**'White Diamond'** Pure white, pink-flushed in bud. FCC 1914.

**'Loder's White'** (*R.* 'Album Elegans' × *R. griffithianum*). (HH) A large, dome-shaped shrub, clothed to the ground with handsome foliage. Flowers in a magnificent, conical truss, widely funnel-shaped, mauve-pink in bud, opening to pure white, edged with pink and marked with a few scattered crimson spots. Mid. Raised by J.H. Mangles before 1884. AM 1911. AGM 1984. H4.

**'Logan Damaris'** See *R.* Damaris group 'Logan'.

**'Lori Eichelser'** (*R. forrestii* Repens group × *R.* 'Bowbells'). A free-flowering dwarf shrub of compact, spreading habit with glossy green, rounded leaves. Flowers cherry-red in loose trusses. Mid. (1966). H4.

**'Lord Roberts'** (HH) An old hybrid of erect growth. Flowers in a dense, rounded truss, funnel-shaped, dark crimson with an extensive V-shaped pattern of black markings. Mid to late. AGM 1984. H4.

**'Lucy Lou'** (*R. leucaspis* × [*R. ciliatum* × *R. leucaspis*]). A free-flowering dwarf shrub of compact habit with attractive dark green, hairy leaves and pure white flowers. Early. (1956). H3.

**'Luscombei'** (*R. fortunei* × *R. thomsonii*). A large shrub forming a broadly dome-shaped bush. Flowers in a loose truss, trumpet-shaped, deep rose, with a well-defined ray of crimson markings within. Early to mid. (1875). H3.

**'Madame de Bruin'** (*R.* 'Doncaster' × *R.* 'Prometheus'). (HH) A vigorous, leafy hybrid with dark green leaves marked by the conspicuous pale green midrib. Conical trusses of cerise-red flowers. (1904). H4.

**'Madame Masson'** (*R. catawbiense* × *R. ponticum*). (HH) An old hybrid, bearing trusses of white flowers, deeply cut into 5 lobes, with a yellow basal blotch within. Mid. (1849). H4.

**'Manderley'** (*R.* 'Fabia' × *R.* 'Scandinavia'). A compact small shrub with dark matt green leaves to 9cm long reddish when young. Flowers funnel-shaped, 9cm across, cardinal-red with darker spots. Mid. (1965). AMT 1983. H4.

RHODODENDRON— *continued*

**'Marchioness of Lansdowne'** An old hybrid of *R. maximum* raised by Waterer's before 1879. A medium-sized to large shrub, the dense trusses of pale magenta-pink, funnel-shaped flowers 7cm across with a very dark flare borne over a long period. Late. H4.

**'Mariloo'** (*R.* 'Dr Stocker' × *R. lacteum*). A handsome, woodland rhododendron with bold foliage and bearing large trusses of lemon-yellow flowers, flushed green. Early to mid. Named after Mrs Lionel de Rothschild, one of the greatest experts on rhododendron hybrids, a subject she loved and shared with her most distinguished husband. (1941). H3.

**'Marinus Koster'** A magnificent, hardy, free-flowering shrub, a hybrid of *R. griffithianum*. Flowers 10cm across, in large trusses, deep pink in bud, opening to white shading to pink at the margins, with a large purple blotch within. Mid. (1937). AMT 1937. FCCT 1948. H4.

**'Marion Street'** (*R.* 'Stanley Davies' × *R. yakushimanum*). A vigorous small shrub of dense, spreading habit with dark green leaves to 10cm long brown-felted beneath. Flowers widely funnel-shaped, up to 7cm across, white edged and flushed pale pink, fading to white. Mid. (1965). AM 1978. AMT 1989. H4.

**'Markeeta's Prize'** (*R.* Loderi group 'Venus' × *R.* 'Anna'). A medium-sized to large shrub of upright habit with dark green foliage. Scarlet flowers with darker spots are freely borne in large, flat-topped trusses. Mid. (1967). H4.

**'Mary Fleming'** (*R.* Keisrac group × *R. keiskei*). A very hardy dwarf shrub of compact habit, the foliage bronzing in cold weather. Flowers buff-yellow flushed with pink at the margins in small clusters. Early to mid. (1967). H4.

**'Matador'** (*R. griersonianum* × *R. strigillosum*). A Bodnant hybrid making a large shrub of spreading habit with leaves densely rusty hairy beneath. Flowers 5cm across, in a large, loose truss, funnel-shaped, brilliant, dark orange-red. Early to mid. (1945). AM 1945. FCC 1946. H3.

**'May Day'** (*R. griersonianum* × *R. haematodes*). A magnificent, comparatively low, wide-spreading shrub bearing loose trusses of slightly-drooping, funnel-shaped flowers which are a brilliant signal-red or orange-red; calyces large and similarly coloured. Mid. (1932). AGM 1984. H3.

**'Merganser'** (*R. campylogynum*, white form × *R. luteiflorum*). A vigorous, free-flowering dwarf shrub of compact, upright habit with dark green leaves to 3.5cm long. Flowers 3cm across, funnel-shaped, pale primrose-yellow, in compact conical trusses 6cm across. Early to mid. (1967). H4.

**'Michael Waterer'** (HH) A slow-growing, free-flowering *R. ponticum* hybrid of compact habit. Flowers in a well-formed truss, funnel-shaped, crimson-scarlet, fading to rose-crimson. Mid to late. (Before 1894). H4.

**'Michael's Pride'** (*R. burmanicum* × *R. dalhousiae*). Tubular, lily-like, creamy-yellow, waxy and fragrant flowers open from lime-green buds. Bronze young foliage. (1964). H1.

**'Midsummer Snow'** (*R. diaprepes* × *R.* 'Isabella'). A handsome hybrid, raised in our nurseries. Buds and young shoots bright yellow-green. Flowers in a large, loose truss, large, trumpet-shaped, pure white, richly fragrant. Late. (1967). H3.

**'Moerheim'** A dwarf shrub of compact habit with glossy green leaves turning maroon in winter. Clusters of small, aster-violet flowers are freely produced. Probably a hybrid of *R. impeditum*. Mid. (1966). H4.

**'Moerheim's Pink'** (*R.* 'Genoveva' × *R. williamsianum*). A very attractive small, dome-shaped bush of dense habit with broadly ovate leaves to 8cm long. Flowers funnel-shaped, deep pink in bud opening pale lilac spotted rose inside with slightly frilled lobes. Raised by Dietrich Hobbie. Mid. AMT 1972. H4.

**'Mohamet'** (*R. dichroanthum* × *R. facetum*). An Exbury hybrid producing brilliant, rich orange-coloured flowers, with frilly margins and large, coloured, petaloid calyces. Mid. AM 1945. H3.

**'Moonshine Crescent'** Similar to 'Moonshine Supreme' but with clear yellow flowers. AMT 1960.

**'Moonshine Supreme'** (*R.* 'Adriaan Koster' × *R. wardii* Litiense group). A Wisley hybrid with compact, dome-shaped trusses of saucer-shaped, primrose-yellow flowers, with a darker staining on upper segment and indistinct spotting. Early to mid. (1953). AM 1953. H4.

**RHODODENDRON**—*continued*

**'Moonstone'** (*R. campylocarpum* × *R. williamsianum*). A small, dome-shaped bush, bearing attractive, bell-shaped flowers which are rose-crimson in bud opening cream or pale primrose. Early to mid. (1933). H3.

**'Morning Red'** ['Morgenrot'] (*R.* 'Spitfire' × *R. yakushimanum* 'Koichiro Wada'). A small shrub of compact, rounded habit with dark green leaves. Flowers in large trusses, deep red in bud opening rose-red. Mid. (1983). H4.

**'Moser's Maroon'** A vigorous, tall-growing hybrid of French origin, with copper-red young growths. Flowers maroon-red, with darker markings within. Mid to late. Used by the late Lionel de Rothschild as a parent for many of his hybrids. AM 1932. H4.

**'Mother of Pearl'** A lovely hybrid, a sport of 'Pink Pearl', raised in the Bagshot nursery of Messrs Waterer, Sons & Crisp, before 1914. Flowers rich pink in bud, opening to a delicate blush and fading to white, with a few external pink streaks. Mid. AM 1930. H4.

**'Mount Everest'** (*R. campanulatum* × *R. griffithianum*). A large shrub of vigorous growth and very free-flowering. Conical trusses of narrow, bell-shaped flowers of pure white, with reddish-brown speckling in throat; large yellow stigma. Early. (1930). AMT 1953. FCCT 1958. H4.

**'Mrs A.M. Williams'** (HH) A superb *R. griffithianum* hybrid. A large shrub of dense habit with dark green leaves up to 15cm long and well-filled, rounded trusses of bright crimson-scarlet, funnel-shaped flowers with wavy margins and a broad ray of blackish spots. Mid. (1896). AM 1926. AMT 1933. FCCT 1954. H4.

**'Mrs A.T. de la Mare'** (*R.* 'Halopeanum' × *R. fortunei* 'Mrs Charles Butler'). (HH) A free-flowering, hardy hybrid of vigorous, upright, compact habit. Flowers in a compact, dome-shaped truss, funnel-shaped, with frilly margins, white, with greenish-yellow spotting in throat, pink-tinged in bud. Mid. AMT 1958. AGM 1984. H4.

**'Mrs Charles Butler'** See *R. fortunei* 'Mrs Charles Butler' under species.

**'Mrs Charles E. Pearson'** (*R.* 'Catawbiense Grandiflorum' × *R.* 'Coombe Royal'). (HH) A robust hybrid with stout, erect branches. Flowers in a large, conical truss, widely funnel-shaped, 10cm across, mauve-pink in bud, opening pale pinky-mauve passing to nearly white, with a ray of Burnt Sienna within. Mid. (1909). AMT 1933. FCCT 1955. H4.

**'Mrs Davies Evans'** (HH) A vigorous, free-flowering hybrid of upright, compact habit. Flowers in a compact globular truss, funnel-shaped, with frilly margins imperial-purple, with a white basal blotch and yellow spots within. Mid. (Before 1915). AMT 1958. H4.

**'Mrs E.C. Stirling'** (HH) A widely dome-shaped bush, a hybrid of *R. griffithianum*, bearing handsome, conical trusses of flattened, crinkly-edged, mauve-pink flowers, with a paler centre, rich rose in bud. Mid. AM 1906. H4.

**'Mrs Edwin Hillier'** (*R. griffithianum* hybrid × *R.* 'Monsieur Thiers'). A medium-sized shrub of lax habit with dark matt green leaves to 19cm long. Flowers vivid pink in rounded trusses, funnel-shaped, 7cm across. Mid. (1933). H4.

**'Mrs Furnivall'** (*R. caucasicum* hybrid × *R. griffithianum* hybrid). (HH) A magnificent dense-growing bush, producing compact trusses of widely funnel-shaped, light rose-pink flowers, with a conspicuous blotch of Sienna and crimson markings within. Mid to late. One of the finest hardy hybrids ever produced. (1920). AMT 1933. FCCT 1948. AGM 1984. H4.

**'Mrs G.W. Leak'** (*R.* 'Chevalier Felix de Sauvage' × *R.* 'Coombe Royal'). (HH) A splendid hybrid of Dutch origin making a large, dense shrub with dark green leaves to 15cm long. Flowers in a rather lax, conical truss, widely funnel-shaped, 8cm across, mottled light rosy-pink, darkening in tube and with a conspicuous splash of blackish-brown and crimson markings within, nectaries blood-red. Mid. (1916). FCCT 1934. AGM 1984. H4.

**'Mrs J.C. Williams'** A tall, rounded bush with narrowly elliptic to oblanceolate leaves to 22cm long. Bears compact, rounded trusses of white flowers with a ray of crimson markings within, pink in bud. Mid to late. AMT 1960. H4.

**'Mrs Lionel de Rothschild'** A compact, erect-branched shrub with large, firm trusses of fleshy, widely funnel-shaped flowers, white, edged with apple blossom-pink and marked with a conspicuous ray of dark crimson. Mid. AM 1931. H4.

**'Mrs P.D. Williams'** A free-flowering hybrid. Flowers in a compact flattened truss, ivory-white with a large brown blotch on the upper lobes. Mid to late. AMT 1936. H4.

**RHODODENDRON**—*continued*

**'Mrs R.S. Holford'** (HH) A Knap Hill hybrid of vigorous growth, apt to become leggy with age. Flowers in a large truss, widely funnel-shaped, salmon-rose with a small pattern of crimson spots within. Mid to late. (1866). H4.

**'Mrs T.H. Lowinsky'** A vigorous, tall hardy hybrid with broad elliptic-obovate leaves to 9cm long. Flowers open funnel-shaped, 7-8cm across, lilac, whitish towards the centre, heavily spotted orange brown. The parentage includes *R. ponticum*, *R. maximum*, and *R. catawbiense*. Not to be confused with 'Mrs Tom Lowinsky', a tender hybrid of *R. griffithianum*. Raised at Knap Hill before 1917. AM 1919. H4.

**'Mrs W.C. Slocock'** A dense-growing bush, a hybrid of *R. campylocarpum*. Flowers apricot-pink, shading to buff. Mid. (1929). AM 1929. H4.

**Naomi group** (*R.* 'Aurora' × *R. fortunei*). A wonderful Exbury hybrid. A large shrub or small tree producing large, shapely trusses of fragrant, widely-expanded flowers which are a lovely soft lilac-mauve shading to greenish-yellow in the tube, with a ray of faint brown markings. Early to mid. (1926). AM 1933. H3-4.

**'Astarte'** Flowers pink shaded yellow, with a yellow throat.

**'Early Dawn'** Pale soft pink, deeper outside, yellowish towards the base, slightly rose spotted inside, 6cm across.

**'Exbury'** Lilac, tinged yellow.

**'Glow'** Bright pink, deepening in throat.

**'Hope'** Pink, tinged mauve.

**'Nautilus'** Large frilled flowers of deep rose, flushed pale orange-yellow on the tube, becoming paler with age. AM 1938.

**'Nereid'** Lavender and yellow.

**'Pink Beauty'** Satiny-pink.

**'Stella Maris'** Buff, shaded lilac-pink, slightly larger and fuller in the truss than other forms and longer in leaf. FCC 1939.

**'New Comet'** (*R.* 'Idealist' × *R.* 'Naomi'). An attractive hybrid producing large, heavy, globular trusses of shallowly funnel-shaped, mimosa-yellow flowers flushed pale pink, mauve-pink in bud, 9cm across, slightly scented. Early to mid. AM 1957. H3.

**Nobleanum group** (*R. arboreum* × *R. caucasicum*). (HH) A large, slow-growing shrub or small tree with dull, dark green leaves covered beneath with a thin, plastered, buff indumentum. Flowers in a compact truss, widely funnel-shaped, brilliant rose-scarlet in bud, opening to rich rose, flushed white within and with a few crimson spots; nectaries dark crimson. One of the earliest rhododendron hybrids, first raised by Anthony Waterer at Knap Hill about 1832. It is also one of the first to flower, opening from January to March, or earlier in sheltered gardens. AGM 1984. H4.

**'Album'** (*R. arboreum* 'Album' × *R. caucasicum*). (HH) A dense bush of compact habit. Flowers in a compact truss, pink in bud, opening to white or blush, with purplish spots inside and reddish-purple nectaries, faintly marked with a small ray of yellowish-green. Jan. to March. Raised by Messrs Cunningham & Fraser of Edinburgh.

**'Coccineum'** (HH) A large conical bush bearing trusses of bell-shaped flowers of a deep rose, marked with a few dark crimson spots at the base within. January to March.

**'Venustum'** (*R. arboreum venustum*). (HH) A very old hybrid, a densely leafy bush of broadly dome-shaped habit, up to 2m high and 3m across. Flowers in a compact truss, funnel-shaped, glistening pink, shading to white in the centre, with a small pattern of dark crimson markings at base within; nectaries crimson. Flowering in late winter, but occasionally opens in December in a mild season. Raised by William Smith at Norbiton Common, near Kingston, Surrey in 1829. AM 1973. AGM 1984.

**'Nova Zembla'** (*R.* 'Parson's Grandiflorum' × red-flowered hybrid). An excellent and very hardy medium-sized shrub of rather upright habit with dark green, deeply veined leaves. Deep red flowers with a conspicuous dark blotch are borne in compact trusses. Mid. (1902). H4.

**'Odee Wright'** (*R.* 'Idealist' × *R.* 'Mrs Betty Robinson'). A small to medium-sized compact shrub with dark glossy green leaves. Flowers widely funnel-shaped with frilled lobes, pale yellow tinged with pink and spotted red. Mid. (1964). H4.

**'Old Copper'** (*R.* Fabia group × *R.* 'Vulcan'). A medium-sized to large shrub of compact, upright habit. The large, bell-shaped flowers in loose trusses are an unusual coppery colour, opening from red buds. Mid to late. (1958). H4.

**RHODODENDRON**—*continued*

**'Old Port'** (HH) A vigorous, leafy, dome-shaped bush with very glossy foliage, a hybrid of *R. catawbiense*. Flowers up to 6.5cm across, in a dense truss, widely funnel-shaped, with frilled lobes, of a rich plum colour, with a well-defined pattern of blackish-crimson markings. Mid to late. Raised at Knap Hill in 1865. H4.

**'Olive'** (*R. dauricum* × *R. moupinense*). An attractive, floriferous, small to medium-sized shrub of upright habit. Leaves ovate-elliptic, to 4cm long, bright fresh green above. Flowers in twos or threes, funnel-shaped, mauve-pink with deeper spots, up to 4cm across. Very early. (1936). AM 1942. H4.

**'Olympic Lady'** (*R.* Loderi group 'King George' × *R. williamsianum*). A small shrub of compact habit with dark green leaves 5cm long. Flowers bell-shaped, 6cm across, pink in bud opening white, in lax conical trusses to 11cm wide. Mid. (1960). AMT 1977. H4.

**Oreocinn group** (*R. cinnabarinum* × *R. oreotrephes*). A delightful Lamellen hybrid of slender, twiggy habit, with sea-green leaves and pastel flowers of a soft apricot. Mid. We were fortunate to obtain the original plant for our collection. (1926). H4.

**'Oudijk's Sensation'** A small shrub forming a dense mound, the young foliage attractively bronze-tinged. Flowers in open, flat-topped trusses, bell-shaped, of a striking bright pink with a few deeper spots on the upper lobe, 7cm across. Mid. H4.

**'P.J. Mezitt'** (*R. minus* Carolinianum group × *R. dauricum*). A small, free-flowering shrub with broad elliptic leaves to 5cm long, blackish-green above, purple-tinged in cold weather, with a bronzy lustre beneath, densely scaly on both sides. Flowers in small dense clusters, saucer-shaped, up to 4cm across, lilac with 2 patches of indistinct pink spots. Early. AM 1972. It is a selection of the P.J.M. hybrids raised in Massachusetts in 1943 and popular for their extreme hardiness in North America where several selections have been made. H4.

**'Pallescens'** See *R.* × *pallescens* under species.

**'Patty Bee'** (*R. fletcherianum* × *R. keiskei* 'Yaku Fairy'). A compact and vigorous dwarf shrub, the dark green leaves to 4.5cm long bronzing in winter. Flowers pale yellow, funnel-shaped with wavy margins, 4.5cm across borne in compact trusses. Early. (1977). AMT 1989.

**'Peace'** (*R. cinnabarinum* Concatenans group × *R. rigidum*). A very attractive Bodnant hybrid making a densely branched medium-sized shrub with broadly elliptic leaves to 6cm long, densely brown scaly beneath. Flowers funnel-shaped, borne in loose trusses, yellowish in bud opening white marked with yellow inside, 6cm across. Has flowered at Christmas here in mild weather. Mid. AMT 1946. H4.

**'Penheale Blue'** (*R. concinnum* Pseudoyanthinum group × *R. russatum*). A small, compact, rounded shrub with dark glossy green leaves to 2.5cm long. Flowers freely borne in small, dense clusters, widely funnel-shaped, 3.5cm across, deep violet-blue flushed red. One of the best of the deep blues. Early. (1975). AMT 1974. FCCT 1981. H4.

**Penjerrick group** (*R. campylocarpum* Elatum group × *R. griffithianum*). One of the choicest of all hybrid rhododendrons. Loose trusses of bell-shaped, fragrant, creamy-yellow, or pale pink flowers, with crimson nectaries. Early. Both colour forms are available. AM 1923. H3. One of the many fine hybrids raised by Mr Smith, Head Gardener at Penjerrick.

**'Percy Wiseman'** (*R.* Fabia group 'Tangerine' × *R. yakushimanum*) selfed. A small compact shrub with dark glossy green leaves to 7.5cm long. Flowers funnel-shaped, 5cm across, cream flushed with pink, fading to creamy white, in globular trusses. Mid. (1971). AMT 1982.

**'Persimmon'** (Golden Horn group). A colourful hybrid of medium size, more compact in habit than 'Golden Horn'. Flowers orange-red, with a large calyx of similar colour. Mid. (1939). H3-4.

**'Peter Koster'** (*R.* 'Doncaster' hybrid × *R.* 'George Hardy'). (HH) A handsome shrub of sturdy, bushy habit. Flowers in a firm truss, trumpet-shaped, rosy-crimson, paling towards the margins, darker in bud. Mid to late. (1909). AMT 1946. H4.

**'Pink Cherub'** (*R.* 'Doncaster' × *R. yakushimanum*). A vigorous small shrub of compact habit with dark green leaves to 9cm long. Flowers very freely borne in large, compact, rounded trusses, corolla funnel-shaped, wavy-margined, pink in bud opening to nearly white flushed pale pink, throat with greenish spots. AMT 1968. FCCT 1988. H4.

**RHODODENDRON**—*continued*

**'Pink Drift'** (*R. calostrotum* × *R. polycladum* Scintillans group). A dwarf shrub of neat, compact habit with small, aromatic leaves and clusters of soft lavender-rose flowers. Mid. (1955). Suitable for the rock garden. AGM 1984. H4.

**'Pink Pearl'** (*R.* 'Broughtonii' × *R.* 'George Hardy'). (HH) One of the most popular of all rhododendrons. A strong-growing shrub, ultimately tall, and bare at the base. Flowers in a magnificent, large, conical truss, widely funnel-shaped, rose-coloured in bud, opening to deep lilac-pink, fading to white at the margins, with a well-defined ray of crimson-brown markings. Mid. Raised by J. Waterer & Sons at Bagshot. AM 1897. FCC 1900. AGM 1984. H4.

**'Pink Pebble'** (*R. callimorphum* × *R. williamsianum*). A free-flowering dense small shrub bearing loose trusses of widely bell-shaped rose-pink flowers from red buds. Mid. (1954). H4.

**'Polar Bear'** (*R. auriculatum* × *R. diaprepes*). A superb, late flowering hybrid forming a large shrub or small tree with handsome, large leaves. Flowers in large trusses, trumpet-shaped, richly fragrant, like pure white lilies, with a light green flash within. Late. Raised by J.B. Stevenson at Tower Court, Ascot in 1926. This lovely rhododendron is most suitable for woodland conditions. Unfortunately, flowers are not produced on young specimens. FCC 1946. AGM 1984. H3.

**Praecox group** (*R. ciliatum* × *R. dauricum*). An extremely popular, small, early flowering hybrid of compact growth. Leaves sometimes partially deciduous, aromatic when crushed. Flowers produced in twos and threes at the tips of the shoots. They are widely funnel-shaped in appearance, purplish-crimson in bud, opening to glistening rosy-purple, slightly darker on the outside. February to March. Raised by Isaac Davies of Ormskirk, Lancashire, about 1855. (1860). AGM 1984. FCC 1978. H4.

**'Princess Alice'** (*R. ciliatum* × *R. edgeworthii*). A small shrub of open habit with dark green leaves to 10cm long. Flowers white flushed pink from pink buds, very fragrant, 7.5cm across, borne in clusters of 3. Raised by Veitch and named after one of Queen Victoria's daughters. Tender but worth trying on a wall except in very cold areas. Mid. FCC 1862. H2.

**'Princess Anne'** (*R. hanceanum* × *R. keiskei*). A very attractive dwarf shrub of dense habit with light matt green, elliptic, pointed leaves to 6cm long. Flowers greenish in bud opening pale yellow with faint greenish spots, funnel-shaped, 3cm across. Early to mid. Sometimes grown as 'Golden Fleece'. AMT 1978. FCCT 1983. H4.

**'Professor Hugo de Vries'** (*R.* 'Doncaster' × *R.* 'Pink Pearl'). Similar in habit to 'Countess of Derby'. Flowers in a large, conical truss, widely funnel-shaped, rich rose in bud, opening to lilac-rose, with a ray of reddish-brown markings on a light ground. Mid. AM 1975. H4.

**Prostigiatum group** (*R. fastigiatum* × *R. prostratum*). A dwarf shrub of dense habit resembling *R. impeditum*, producing clusters of violet-purple flowers. Early. (1924). AM 1924. H4.

**'Ptarmigan'** (*R. leucaspis* × *R. orthocladum* var. *microleucum*). A floriferous, low, spreading shrub of compact habit with scaly leaves 1-2cm long. Flowers usually in threes, saucer-shaped, 3cm across, pure white. Early. FCC 1965. H4.

**'Purple Splendour'** (HH) A sturdy, leafy bush with erect branches, a hybrid of *R. ponticum*. Flowers in a well-formed truss, widely funnel-shaped, rich royal purplish-blue, with a well-defined ray of black, embossed markings on a purplish-brown ground. Mid to late. A fine hybrid, looking well against 'Goldsworth Yellow', which flowers about the same time. (Before 1900). AM 1931. AGM 1984. H4.

**'Queen Elizabeth II'** (*R.* 'Crest' × *R.* 'Idealist'). A medium-sized shrub with lanceolate to narrowly elliptic leaves up to 14cm long. The seven-lobed, pale Chartreuse-green flowers are widely funnel-shaped and 11cm across, borne in trusses of up to 12. Mid. AM 1967. AGM 1984. H3.

**'Queen of Hearts'** (*R. meddianum* × *R.* 'Moser's Maroon'). One of the last hybrids raised by Lionel de Rothschild. A striking shrub, producing dome-shaped trusses of widely funnel-shaped flowers of a deep, glowing crimson, speckled black within, enlivened by the white filaments. Early to mid. AM 1949. H3.

**411**

**RHODODENDRON**—*continued*

**Racil group** (*R. ciliatum* × *R. racemosum*). A small, free-flowering shrub, with obovate leaves to 6cm long and clusters of funnel-shaped flowers 2.5cm across, pink in bud opening lilac-pink, darker on the margins. Early. (1937). H4.

**'Ramapo'** (*R. fastigiatum* × *R. minus* Carolinianum group). A dwarf, very hardy shrub of compact habit with attractive blue-grey young foliage. The clusters of small, violet-purple flowers are freely borne. Best in sun. Early to mid. (1940). H4.

**'Razorbill'** (*R. spinuliferum* hybrid) A very ornamental small shrub of compact habit with dark green leaves to 5cm long, scaly beneath. Flowers tubular, 2cm long, deep pink in bud opening rose-pink outside, paler inside, held upright in dense trusses. Early to mid. (1976). AM 1978. AMT 1981. FCCT 1983. H4.

**'Red Carpet'** (*R. 'Amerika'* × *R. forrestii* Repens group). A dwarf shrub of compact, spreading habit with leaves to 6.5cm long. Bright red bell-shaped flowers 5.5cm across with wavy margins are borne in lax trusses. Mid. (1967). AMT 1983. H4.

**'Red Riding Hood'** (*R. 'Atrosanguineum'* × *R. griffithianum*). A tall-growing shrub bearing large, conical trusses of brilliant deep red flowers. Mid. (1933). H4.

**'Remo'** (*R. lutescens* × *R. valentinianum*). A Tower Court hybrid of compact habit making an attractive small bush with scaly leaves to 7cm long. Flowers 3.5cm across, in loose trusses, bright yellow with darker spots inside. Early. (1943). H3.

**'Repose'** (*R. fortunei* subsp. *discolor* × *R. lacteum*). A beautiful hybrid raised at Exbury. The deeply bell-shaped flowers are whitish-cream, with a faint greenish suffusion and greenish-crimson speckling in the throat. Mid. (1956). AM 1956. H4.

**'Review Order'** (*R. neriiflorum* Euchaites group × *R. 'May Day'*). A dense, medium-sized shrub of spreading habit. Leaves densely tomentose beneath; flowers in a lax truss, bell-shaped, blood-red, faintly brown-spotted within. Mid. (1954). AM 1954. H3.

**Riplet group** (*R. forrestii* Repens group × *R. 'Letty Edwards'*). A small shrub bearing rounded trusses of bell-shaped, neyron-rose flowers, white in the throat with crimson spots. Early to mid. AM 1961. H4.

**'Romany Chai'** (*R. griersonianum* × *R. 'Moser's Maroon'*). A lovely hybrid raised at Exbury, the name meaning "Gypsy Children". Large compact trusses of rich terracotta, with a dark maroon basal blotch. Mid to late. (1912). AM 1932, when it was also awarded the Cory Cup. H3-4.

**'Romany Chal'** (*R. facetum* × *R. 'Moser's Maroon'*). Another Exbury hybrid, the name meaning "Gypsy Girl". A tall bush, bearing lax trusses of bell-shaped, cardinal-red flowers, with a ray of black markings within. Mid to late. Magnificent in a woodland setting. AM 1932. FCC 1937. H3.

**'Roseum Elegans'** (HH) A very old hybrid of *R. ponticum* making a large shrub. Rosy-lilac, funnel-shaped flowers 6cm across with a small pattern of brown markings are borne in rounded trusses. Mid to late. (1851). H4.

**'Roza Stevenson'** ('Roza Harrison') (*R. Loderi* group 'Sir Edmund' × *R. wardii*). A superb hybrid raised by, and named in memory of, one who was a great lover of rhododendrons (see note under Rhododendron Species). Flowers saucer-shaped, 10-12cm across, deep lemon-yellow, darker in bud, borne in attractive trusses. FCC 1968. H3.

**'Rubicon'** (*R. 'Kilimanjaro'* × *R. 'Noyo Chief'*). A medium-sized shrub with handsome, dark glossy green, deeply veined leaves. Bright red flowers spotted with black are produced in dense, rounded trusses. Mid. (1979). H3.

**'Ruby Hart'** ([*R. 'Carmen'* × *R. 'Elizabeth'*] × *R. elliottii*). A promising small shrub, the glossy green leaves to 7cm long with a thin brown indumentum beneath. Bell-shaped, waxy, very deep red flowers to 4.5cm long are borne in open trusses. Mid. (1976). AM 1988. H3-4.

**Russautinii group** (*R. augustinii* × *R. russatum*). A first class compact shrub of upright habit, combining the best features of its distinguished parents. Leaves obovate, dull bluish-green, aromatic, to 4cm long. Flowers in clusters of 5-6, deep lavender-blue, reddish on the ribs, with brownish spots on the upper lobes. In very mild weather can be in flower at Christmas. Early to mid. (1936). H4.

**'Saffron Queen'** (*R. burmanicum* × *R. xanthostephanum*). A beautiful hybrid with narrowly elliptic leaves, glossy green above, with scattered brown scales beneath. Flowers tubular, sulphur-yellow, with darker spotting on the upper lobes. Mid. (1948). AM 1948. H3.

RHODODENDRON—*continued*

**'Saint Breward'** (*R. augustinii* × *R. impeditum*). A beautiful, small, compact, rounded shrub bearing tight, globular trusses of shallowly bell-shaped flowers of a soft lavender, darker at the margins, anthers pale blue. Early to mid. FCC 1962. H4.

**'Saint Merryn'** (*R. impeditum* × *R.* 'Saint Tudy'). A free-flowering, compact dwarf shrub of spreading habit with dark glossy green leaves 1cm long. Flowers broadly funnel-shaped with wavy margins, 3cm across, deep violet-blue, darker at the margins, in trusses 5cm across. Mid. (1971). AM 1970. FCC 1973. AMT 1983. FCCT 1986. H4.

**'Saint Tudy'** (*R. augustinii* × *R. impeditum*). A small shrub of dense, bushy habit, bearing dense trusses of shallowly bell-shaped, lobelia-blue flowers. Early to mid. Raised by Maj Gen Harrison at Tremeer, St Tudy, Cornwall. AM 1960. FCCT 1973. AGM 1984. H4.

**'Sapphire'** (*R.* 'Blue Tit' × *R. impeditum*). A dwarf, small-leaved shrub of open habit, resembling *R. impeditum*. Flowers of a pale, lavender-blue. Early. AMT 1967. AGM 1984. H4.

**'Sappho'** (HH) A very free-growing bush of rounded or dome-shaped habit with dark glossy green leaves to 18cm long. Flowers in handsome, conical trusses, widely funnel-shaped, mauve in bud, opening to pure white, with a conspicuous blotch of rich purple overlaid black. Mid. Raised by Anthony Waterer at Knap Hill, before 1867. AMT 1974. H4.

**'Sarita Loder'** (*R. griersonianum* × *R.* Loderi group). An outstanding hybrid producing loose trusses of large, bright pink flowers, deep crimson in bud. Mid. (1934). AM 1934. H3.

**Sarled group** (*R. sargentianum* × *R. trichostomum* Ledoides group). A dwarf shrub suitable for the rock garden with tiny leaves and rounded trusses of small flowers pink in bud, opening creamy-white. Mid. AM 1974. H4.

**'Scarlet Wonder'** A very hardy, dwarf shrub forming a compact mound of dense foliage. Flowers trumpet-shaped, frilly-margined, ruby-red, borne in loose trusses at the ends of the shoots. Mid. This very useful shrub was raised by Mr Dietrich Hobbie of Germany. AGM 1984. AMT 1989. H4.

**'Seta'** (*R. moupinense* × *R. spinuliferum*). An exceedingly pretty, medium-sized Bodnant hybrid of erect habit producing umbels of unspotted narrowly bell-shaped flowers 4cm long which are white at base, shading to vivid pink in the lobes. One of the first hybrids to flower, in March or April. (1933). AM 1933. FCC 1960. AGM 1984. H3-4.

**'Seven Stars'** (*R.* Loderi group 'Sir Joseph Hooker' × *R. yakushimanum*). A large, vigorous, free-flowering hybrid raised at Windsor Great Park. Flowers bell-shaped, with wavy margins, white, flushed pink, reddish in bud. Mid. AM 1967. FCCT 1974. AGM 1984. H3-4.

**'Shamrock'** (*R. keiskei*, dwarf form × *R. hanceanum* Nanum group). A dwarf shrub of compact, spreading habit with glossy green leaves. Pale yellow flowers open from yellow-green buds. Early to mid. (1978). H4.

**'Shilsonii'** (*R. barbatum* × *R. thomsonii*). A strong-growing, rounded, symmetrical bush or small tree with attractive metallic-coloured stems; intermediate in habit and foliage between the parents. Flowers in a loose truss, bell-shaped, blood-red, with darker veins and inconspicuous dark brown markings; calyx large, cup-shaped, pale green, flushed crimson. Early. Raised by Richard Gill before 1900. AM 1900. H3-4.

**'Silver Cloud'** ['Silberwolke']. (*R.* 'Album Novum' × *R. yakushimanum* 'Koichiro Wada'). A dwarf shrub of dense, rounded habit with dark green leaves. Flowers pale purple, darker outside, spotted with yellow-green and with frilled margins. Raised in 1963. H4.

**'Sir Charles Lemon'** (*R. arboreum* 'Sir Charles Lemon') A magnificent large shrub or small tree with handsome leaves rusty-brown beneath. Flowers white in dense trusses. Probably *R. arboreum* × *R. campanulatum*. C 1868. H3.

**'Sir Frederick Moore'** (*R. fortunei* subsp. *discolor* × *R.* 'St Keverne'). A tall, hardy hybrid, with long leaves and bearing large, compact, rounded trusses of large, widely funnel-shaped, wavy-edged flowers which are clear pink, heavily spotted crimson at base within. Mid. (1935). AM 1937. FCCT 1972. H3-4.

**'Snow Lady'** (*R. ciliatum* × *R. leucaspis*). A compact small shrub of spreading habit with bristly hairy leaves to 7.5cm long. Fragrant white flowers are borne in lax trusses. Mid. (1955). H3.

**'Snow Queen'** (*R.* 'Halopeanum' × *R.* Loderi group). A lovely, free-flowering Leonardslee hybrid. A large, compact bush, bearing dome-shaped trusses of large, funnel-shaped

**RHODODENDRON 'Snow Queen'**—*continued*

flowers which are dark pink in bud, opening to pure white, with a small red basal blotch within. Mid. (1926). AM 1934. AMT 1946. FCCT 1970. H3-4.

**'Solent Queen'** (Angelo group) A large Exbury hybrid producing magnificent trusses of large, widely funnel-shaped, fragrant flowers each about 13cm across; white flushed pink at margins and with a central ray of green. Mid. AM 1939. H3.

**'Songbird'** (*R.* 'Blue Tit' × *R. russatum*). A charming, small shrub producing clusters of violet, bell-shaped flowers. Early. Raised by Col Sir James Horlick, at Gigha, Argyllshire, Scotland. (1954). AM 1957. H4.

**'Souvenir de Dr S. Endtz'** (*R.* 'John Walter' × *R.* 'Pink Pearl'). A compact bush showing the influence of the former parent in its habit and that of the latter parent in its foliage and flowers. Flowers in a dome-shaped truss, widely funnel-shaped, rich rose in bud, opening to rich, mottled pink, paler in the centre and marked with a ray of crimson, nectaries crimson. Mid. Raised by L.J. Endtz & Co. of Boskoop before 1924. AM 1924. AGM 1984. FCCT 1970. H4.

**Spinulosum group** (*R. racemosum* × *R. spinuliferum*). An erect shrub, bearing compact trusses of narrowly bell-shaped, deep pink flowers, with protruding anthers. Mid. Raised at Kew. (1926). AM (F) 1944. H4.

**'Spring Magic'** (*R.* 'Essex Scarlet' × *R. forrestii* Repens group). A compact, spreading small shrub with dark green leaves. Flowers deep currant-red with darker spots. Mid. AMT 1969. H4.

**'Streatley'** (*R. aberconwayi* × *R. yakushimanum*). A small shrub, flowers white flushed rose-pink spotted red from magenta buds. Mid. AM 1965. H4.

**'Surrey Heath'** ([*R. facetum* × *R.* Fabia group] × [*R. yakushimanum* × *R.* 'Britannia']). Small bushy shrub of spreading habit with narrow leaves white tomentose above when young. Flowers funnel-shaped, 4.5cm across in globular trusses, pale rose-pink, deeper at the margins with brownish spots inside. Mid. (1975). AMT 1982. H4.

**'Susan'** (*R. campanulatum* × *R. fortunei*). A tall, bushy hybrid bearing large trusses of bluish-mauve flowers, darker at margins and spotted purple within. Early to mid. AM 1930. AMT 1948. FCC 1954. AGM 1984. H4.

**'Sweet Sue'** ([*R. facetum* × *R.* 'Fabia'] × [*R. yakushimanum* × *R.* 'Fabia Tangerine']). A vigorous small shrub of upright habit with leaves to 11cm long. Flowers bell-shaped, 7cm across with wavy margins, orange-red spotted red and margined pale pink, in compact dome-shaped trusses 14cm across. Mid to late. (1972). H4.

**'Tally Ho'** (*R. facetum* × *R. griersonianum*). A broadly dome-shaped bush bearing compact, rounded trusses of brilliant scarlet, funnel-shaped flowers. Mid to late. A superb woodland plant raised by J.J. Crosfield at Embley Park. (1933). FCC 1933. H3.

**'Taurus'** (*R.* 'Jean Marie de Montague' × *R. strigillosum*). A stoutly-branched large shrub of upright growth with handsome dark green, prominently veined leaves. Vivid red, widely funnel-shaped flowers with frilled margins are borne in large rounded trusses. Early to mid. (1972). H4.

**'Teal'** (*R. brachyanthum* var. *hypolepidotum* × *R. fletcherianum*). A compact dwarf shrub of rather upright habit with pale green leaves to 5.5cm long, developing peeling bark with age. Flowers primrose-yellow, broadly bell-shaped, to 3.5cm across. Mid. AM 1977. H4.

**'Temple Belle'** (*R. orbiculare* × *R. williamsianum*). A charming shrub of neat, rounded habit, much resembling the former parent. The rounded leaves are attractively glaucous beneath. Flowers in a loose cluster, bell-shaped, of a uniform Persian-rose without markings. Early to mid. (1916). AGM 1984. H3.

**'Tessa'** (*R. moupinense* × *R.* Praecox group). A small bush up to 1m. Flowers in loose flattened umbels, soft, slightly purplish-pink, with a ray of crimson spots, opening in March or early April. (1935). AM 1935. AGM 1984. H4.

**'Tessa Roza'** A selection from 'Tessa' which it resembles but with deeper pink flowers. Early. AM 1953. H4.

**'The Hon Jean Marie de Montague'** A vigorous, medium-sized shrub of compact, spreading habit with dark green leaves to 15cm long. Flowers widely funnel-campanulate with wavy margins, 8cm across, deep scarlet-crimson with darker spots in the throat, borne

**RHODODENDRON 'The Hon Jean Marie de Montague'**—*continued*

in compact, dome-shaped trusses to 15cm wide. A hybrid of *R. griffithianum*. Mid. (1921). AMT 1989. H4.

**'The Master'** (*R.* 'China' × *R.* 'Letty Edwards'). Huge globular trusses of large, funnel-shaped, pink flowers with a dark red basal blotch within. Mid. AMT 1966. H3-4.

**'Thomwilliams'** (*R. thomsonii* × *R. williamsianum*). A compact, medium-sized shrub with broadly ovate or nearly orbicular leaves, deeply cordate at the base, to 7.5cm long. Flowers widely bell-shaped, 7.5cm across, in open trusses, deep crimson in bud opening deep reddish-pink, unspotted. Early. (1927). AM 1935. H4.

**'Thor'** (*R. haematodes* × *R.* 'Felis'). A compact small shrub of rounded habit, the dark green leaves covered beneath with a thick indumentum. Flowers bright scarlet with a showy, petaloid calyx, in open trusses. Mid. (1962). H3.

**'Tidbit'** (*R. dichroanthum* × *R. wardii*). A small shrub of dense, spreading habit with dark glossy green leaves to 7cm long. The bell-shaped flowers 3cm across with wavy margins are straw-yellow, red in the throat and are borne in compact, domed trusses. Mid. (1957). H4.

**'Titian Beauty'** ([*R. facetum* × *R.* Fabia group 'Tangerine'] × [*R.* Fabia group 'Tangerine' × *R. yakushimanum*]). A small shrub of compact, rather upright habit, the dark green leaves with a thin brown indumentum beneath. Flowers waxy-red. Mid. (1971). H4.

**'Too Bee'** (*R. campylogynum* 'Patricia' × *R. keiskei* 'Yaku Fairy'). A most attractive compact dwarf shrub of spreading habit with dark green leaves to 4cm long, slightly scaly beneath. Flowers tubular to bell-shaped, 3cm long, deep pink outside, pale pink to white inside, borne in clusters of 3-4. Early to mid. (1983). AM 1988. H4.

**'Tortoiseshell Champagne'** (*R.* 'Goldsworth Orange' × *R. griersonianum*). Rich yellow funnel-shaped flowers fading to pale yellow tinged pink at the margins of the lobes. Mid to late. AMT 1967. H3-4.

**'Tortoiseshell Orange'** (*R.* 'Goldsworth Orange' × *R. griersonianum*). A Goldsworth hybrid bearing large, deep orange flowers. Mid to late. (1945). H3-4.

**'Tortoiseshell Wonder'** (*R.* 'Goldsworth Orange' × *R. griersonianum*). Salmon-pink. AM 1947.

**'Tottenham'** A dwarf shrub, an old hybrid of *R. ferrugineum* with dark green leaves and clusters of small, pale pink flowers. Mid to late. H4.

**'Treasure'** (*R. forrestii* Repens group × *R. williamsianum*). Dwarf, mound-forming shrub with gnarled branches and neat oval or rounded leaves, bronze when young. Flowers bell-shaped, deep rose, 5cm across. Early to mid. H3-4.

**'Trewithen Orange'** (*R. cinnabarinum* Concatenans group × *R.* 'Full House'). A remarkable hybrid, bearing loose, pendent trusses of deep orange-brown flowers with a faint rosy blush. Early to mid. Raised at Trewithen, near St Austell, Cornwall. FCC 1950. H3-4.

**'Trude Webster'** (*R.* 'Countess of Derby' selfed). A strong-growing medium-sized to large shrub, the winner of several awards in North America. Flowers clear pink, white on the lobes, with darker spots, borne in very large, rounded trusses. Mid to late. (1961). H4.

**'Unique'** A leafy, dense-habited bush, a hybrid of *R. campylocarpum*. Flowers in a dense, dome-shaped truss, funnel-shaped, creamy-white with a faint blush and marked by scattered, faint, crimson spots within. Early to mid. AMT 1934. FCCT 1935. H4.

**Vanessa group** (*R. griersonianum* × *R.* 'Soulbut'). A spreading, rather shapely bush bearing loose trusses of soft pink flowers 9cm across, spotted carmine at the base within. Mid to late. Raised at Bodnant, this was the first hybrid of *R. griersonianum* to be exhibited at the RHS. Cross made in 1924. FCC 1929. H3-4.

　　**'Pastel'** A lovely clone with flowers of a soft rose-pink, flushed biscuit with a deep crimson eye, 10cm across. Mid to late. (1946). AM 1946. FCCT and Cory Cup 1971. AGM 1984.

**'Venetian Chimes'** ([*R. facetum* × *R.* 'Fabia'] × [*R.* 'Britannia' × *R. yakushimanum*]). A vigorous small shrub of compact, spreading habit. Flowers bell-shaped, 5cm across, in compact globular trusses to 13cm across, brick-red flushed scarlet towards the base and spotted with blackish-red. Mid to late. (1971). H4.

**'Vintage Rosé'** (*R. yakushimanum* × [*R.* 'Jalisco Eclipse' × *R.* 'Fusilier']). A small vigorous shrub, the dark matt green leaves to 10cm long, with a thick indumentum beneath.

**RHODODENDRON 'Vintage Rosé'**—*continued*

Flowers funnel-shaped, wavy margined, 6cm across, rose-pink, deeper in the centre, in large conical trusses 13cm across. Mid to late. (1974). H4.

**'Virginia Richards'** ([*R. wardii* × *R.* 'F.C. Puddle'] × *R.* 'Mrs Betty Robertson'). A small shrub of vigorous upright habit. Leaves to 9cm long. Flowers in large globular trusses of up to 16cm across, funnel-shaped, wavy margined, pale orange in the centre flushed rose-pink at the margins, deeper at the base with red spots inside. Mid. (1962). AMT 1985. H4.

**'Vulcan'** (*R. griersonianum* × *R.* 'Mars'). A medium-sized shrub of compact habit. Funnel-shaped, wavy margined, bright red flowers 6cm across are borne in dome-shaped trusses. Mid. (1938). AMT 1957. H4.

**'W.F.H.'** (*R. haematodes* × *R.* 'Tally Ho'). A small, spreading shrub bearing clusters of brilliant scarlet, funnel-shaped flowers. Mid. Named after Mr W.F. Hamilton, one-time Head Gardener at Pylewell Park near Lymington, Hampshire. (1941). H3.

**'Wigeon'** (*R. calostrotum* 'Gigha' × *R. minus* Carolinianum group). A compact, free-flowering dwarf shrub with dark green leaves to 4.5cm long. Flowers open funnel-shaped with wavy margins, 4cm across, deep lavender-pink with darker spots, in dome-shaped trusses 7cm across. Mid. (1982). AMT 1987. H4.

**'Wilgen's Ruby'** (*R.* 'Britannia' × *R.* 'John Walter'). A popular and very hardy medium-sized compact shrub. Bears handsome large rounded trusses of deep red funnel-shaped flowers with darker spots. Mid to late. (1951). H4.

**'Willbrit'** (*R.* 'Britannia' × *R. williamsianum*). A small shrub of compact, rounded habit with dark green leaves to 8cm long reddish when young. Deep pink, bell-shaped flowers, paler at the margin are borne in open trusses. Mid to late. (1960). H4.

**'Windlesham Scarlet'** (*R.* 'Britannia' × *R.* 'Doncaster'). A vigorous medium-sized shrub of compact habit. Dome-shaped trusses bear widely bell-shaped, deep crimson, frilly margined flowers speckled with black inside. Mid to late. (1950). AMT 1968. FCCT 1971. H4.

**'Windsor Lad'** A hybrid of *R. ponticum* making a medium-sized shrub. Widely funnel-shaped flowers 6-7cm across open lilac-purple with a prominent green patch from deep purple buds. Mid to late. (1958). H4.

**'Winsome'** (*R. griersonianum* × *R.* 'Humming Bird'). A lovely Bodnant hybrid making a small bush with deep coppery young growths. Leaves dark green above, with a thin rusty tomentum beneath, to 9cm long. Flowers funnel-shaped, 6cm across, in loose, pendent clusters, corolla scarlet in bud opening deep rose-pink, reddish towards the base, contrasting effectively with the young leaves. Mid. (1939). AM 1950. H3-4.

**'Wishmoor'** (*R. wardii* Litiense group × *R. yakushimanum*). A compact small shrub with glossy green leaves. Seven-lobed, bell-shaped flowers 8cm across open pale primrose-yellow, deeper in the throat from orange-red buds. Mid. AM 1972. FCC 1987. H4.

**'Woodcock'** (*R.* 'Elizabeth' × *R. hyperythrum*). A very distinct, small, rounded shrub of compact habit raised at Wisley. Leaves rich green, to 10cm long, deeply veined and with recurved margins. Flowers in flat-topped trusses of about 10. Corolla funnel-shaped, clear pale pink with a few red spots contrasting effectively with the deep strawberry-pink buds. (1972). AMT 1986. H4.

**'Wren'** (*R. ludlowii* × *R. keiskei* 'Yaku Fairy'). A prostrate, mound-forming dwarf shrub with deep glossy green leaves scaly beneath and reddish young growths. Flowers clear yellow. Early to mid. AM 1970. H4.

**'Yaku Princess'** (*R.* 'King Tut' × *R. yakushimanum* 'Koichiro Wada'). A small, very hardy shrub of dense rounded habit, the leaves with a pale brown indumentum beneath. Flowers apple blossom-pink with greenish spots, in dense rounded trusses. Mid to late. (1977). H4.

**'Yellow Hammer'** (*R. flavidum* × *R. sulfureum*). A charming, rather slender hybrid raised at Caerhays. Flowers in pairs from terminal and axillary buds, tubular or narrowly bell-shaped, bright yellow. Early. (Before 1931). AGM 1984. H3-4.

## ‡AZALEODENDRONS

A group of attractive hybrids between deciduous azaleas and evergreen species of other series. Very hardy, mostly semi-evergreen shrubs of small to medium size, flowering in May or June. H4.

**RHODODENDRON (AZALEODENDRONS)**—*continued*

*\*'Azaleoides'* (*R. nudiflorum* × *R. ponticum*). A dense-habited, slow-growing shrub with slender branches. Leaves oblanceolate, dull, dark green above, pale green or faintly glaucous beneath; flowers in rounded trusses, funnel-shaped, deliciously scented, purplish-lilac in bud, opening white, edged purplish-lilac and faintly spotted within; June. The first recorded rhododendron hybrid, which occurred as an accidental cross in the nursery of a Mr Thompson, at Mile End, London, about 1820.

**'Broughtonii Aureum'** ([*R. maximum* × *R. ponticum*] × *R. molle*) ('Norbitonense Broughtonianum'). A small shrub of rounded habit. Leaves elliptic to oblanceolate, persistent, 7.5-10cm long, dark green above, paler beneath, often bronze-flushed in winter. Flowers in a compact truss, widely funnel-shaped, deep creamy-yellow, with light brown markings, flushed pink in bud; June. Raised in the village of Broughton, Peeblesshire, Scotland, about 1830. FCC 1935.

**'Dot'** Small to medium-sized shrub. Leaves green, oblanceolate to elliptic-obovate, 6-10cm long. Large clusters of rose-crimson flowers. AM 1945.

**'Galloper Light'** A most pleasing, leafy bush raised at Exbury, bearing loose trusses of funnel-shaped flowers which are cream in the tube shading to soft salmon-pink in the lobes, with a chrome-yellow blotch (general effect creamy-pink). Late; May to early June. AM 1927.

**'Gemmiferum'** A small shrub of loose, open habit. Leaves elliptic to obovate, 3-5cm long, leathery, dark green above, paler beneath. Flowers in a compact, rounded truss, funnel-shaped, dark crimson in bud, opening to rose, heavily flushed crimson; late May to early June. Brought into cultivation by T. Methven & Son, of Edinburgh, in 1868. Of similar origin to 'Azaleoides'.

**'Glory of Littleworth'** A superb, small, azalea-like, semi-evergreen shrub of stiff, erect habit. Leaves oblong to oblong-lanceolate, 7.5-11cm long, often curled and undulate. Flowers funnel-shaped, cream at first becoming milk-white with conspicuous coppery blotch, fragrant. May. Raised by H.J. Mangles. AM 1911.

**'Govenianum'** An erect, densely-branched bush up to 2m or more in height. Leaves crowded at the tips of the shoots, elliptic to oblanceolate, leathery, 5-6cm long, smooth, dark green and reticulate above, pale green beneath. Buds red in winter. Flowers funnel-shaped, fragrant, delicate lilac-purple, slightly paler on lobes, stained crimson on the ridges outside and faintly green-spotted within; June. Brought into cultivation by T. Methven & Son, of Edinburgh, about 1868. Said to be a hybrid rhododendron (*R. catawbiense* × *R. ponticum*) crossed with an unknown azalea.

**'Jill Dolding'** A small, stiffly upright, semi-evergreen shrub with oblanceolate leaves to 9 × 3cm, turning deep purple above in winter. Flowers funnel-shaped, rose-purple shading to lilac with orange and rose-red spots on the upper lobe, borne in a rather open truss in May. Occurred as a chance seedling in our nurseries and is probably *R. ponticum* hybrid × *R.* (deciduous azalea) 'Marconi'.

**'Martine'** (*R. racemosum* ×? *R.* 'Hinomayo'). A small, densely-branched shrub of Dutch origin. Leaves elliptic to elliptic-oblong, 1-2cm long, bright glossy green. Flowers funnel-shaped, shell-pink, abundantly produced. Mid.

**'Nellie'** (*R. occidentale* × *R.* 'The Monitor'). A small, azalea-like shrub, resembling the former parent in habit, but much broader in outline. Leaves narrowly elliptic to oblanceolate, dull green above, paler beneath. Flowers in a rounded truss, fragrant, funnel-shaped, pure white with a conspicuous deep yellow blotch; May.

**'Norbitonense Aureum'** See 'Smithii Aureum'.

**'Norbitonense Broughtonianum'** See 'Broughtonii Aureum'.

*\*'Odoratum'* (*R. nudiflorum* × *R. ponticum*). A small, dense, bushy shrub. Leaves obovate to obovate-elliptic, 5-6cm long, green above, glaucous at first beneath. Flowers blush or pale lilac, fragrant. I before 1875.

**'Smithii Aureum'** ([*R. maximum* × *R. ponticum*] × *R. molle*) ('Norbitonense Aureum'). A small shrub resembling 'Broughtonii Aureum', but differs in the leaves which are oblanceolate, 7-9cm long, glaucous beneath, and the paler yellow flowers; late May to early June. The leaves assume a distinctive purplish or plum-colour in winter. Raised by W. Smith, at Norbiton, Surrey, about 1930.

## RHODODENDRON (AZALEODENDRONS)—*continued*

**'Torlonianum'** An azalea-like shrub to 2m high. Leaves elliptic, 5-10cm long, dark shining green. Flowers in a neat rounded truss, funnel-shaped, lilac-rose, darker at the margins, with a conspicuous orange blotch; late May to early June.

## DECIDUOUS HYBRID AZALEAS

The first deciduous hybrid azaleas began to appear in the early part of the 19th century and today number in hundreds. Their average height varies from 1.5-2.5m, but many clones may reach greater heights in moist, woodland gardens. Flowers are normally trumpet-shaped and single, though a number have double flowers. Colours range from the delicate pastel shades of the Occidentale Hybrids to the riotous reds, flames and golds of the Mollis Azaleas and Knap Hill Hybrids. The flowers of such groups as the Ghent Azaleas and the Occidentale Hybrids are deliciously fragrant, particularly in the evening. Many exhibit rich autumn colours.

**Ghent Hybrids** (Gh)—A popular group of azaleas first raised in Ghent, Belgium in the early 19th century and later in England, between 1830 and 1850. More recently cultivars of this group have been produced in the United States. Among the species involved are *RR. atlanticum, calendulaceum, luteum, periclymenoides, roseum, speciosum* and *arborescens*. They are distinguished by their usually fragrant, long-tubed, honeysuckle-like flowers. In growth they are taller and more twiggy than the Mollis Azaleas, and their flowering season is later, commencing about the end of May. Average height when growing in an open position 1.8-2.5m. H4.

**Knap Hill Hybrids** (Kn)—A large and colourful group of hardy azaleas probably derived from *R. calendulaceum × molle*, Ghent Hybrids × *R. molle* as well as *RR. occidentale* and *arborescens*. Originally developed in the Knap Hill Nursery by Anthony Waterer, and more extensively by the late Lionel de Rothschild at Exbury, Hants (the latter are often referred to as the Exbury Azaleas and are marked Kn-Ex). Further development by the late Edgar Stead at Christchurch, New Zealand gave the Ilam Hybrids. New cultivars from several sources continue to appear, swelling the ranks of an already formidable assemblage. Members of the group are characterised by their trumpet-shaped, usually scentless flowers in a wide range of colours, opening in May. Average height when growing in an open position 1.8-2.5m. H4.

**Mollis Azaleas** (M)—This attractive group originated as selections of *R. japonicum*, made by L. van Houtte in 1873, and later on by other Belgian nurserymen. At a later date this species was crossed with *R. molle* to produce a range of seedlings, with flowers of more intense and diverse colouring. Their large, scentless flowers are borne in handsome trusses usually in early May, before the leaves. Average height when growing in an open position 1.2-1.8m. H4.

**Occidentale Hybrids** (O)—A group of hybrids derived mainly from *R. molle × R. occidentale*. All have delicate, pastel-coloured, fragrant flowers, opening in late May, usually a fortnight later than the Mollis Azaleas. Average height when growing in an open position 1.8-2.5m. H4.

**Rustica Hybrids** (R) (Rustica Flore Pleno Hybrids)—A group of double-flowered hybrid azaleas produced by crossing double-flowered forms of Ghent azaleas with *R. japonicum*. They are compact in habit, with attractive, sweetly-scented flowers, opening in late May and early June. Average height when growing in an open position 1.2-1.5m. H4.

**'Aida'** (R) Deep peach-pink with a deeper flush, double. (1888).

**'Annabella'** (Kn) Orange and yellow in bud, opening to golden yellow, overlaid and flushed orange-rose. (1947).

**'Babeuff'** (M) Bright salmon shaded orange. (1918).

**'Ballerina'** (Kn-Ex) White, with orange flush, suffused flesh-pink in bud; large flowers with frilled edges.

**'Balzac'** (Kn-Ex) Nasturtium-red with orange flash; fragrant. AM 1934.

**'Basilisk'** (Kn-Ex) Rich creamy-yellow in bud, opening to cream with bright orange flare. AM 1934.

## RHODODENDRON (DECIDUOUS HYBRID AZALEAS)—*continued*

**'Beaulieu'** (Kn-Ex) Deep salmon-pink in bud, opening soft salmon-pink, with deep orange flush; young foliage bronze-red.

**'Berryrose'** (Kn-Ex) Rose-pink with a yellow flash; young foliage coppery. AM 1934.

**'Bouquet de Flore'** (Gh) Vivid red blotched with yellow. C 1869.

**'Brazil'** (Kn-Ex) Bright tangerine-red, darkening with age; frilly margins. (1934).

**'Buzzard'** (Kn) Pale straw-yellow, edged and tinted pink, with deep yellow flare. (1947).

**'Cecile'** (Kn-Ex) Dark salmon-pink in bud, opening to salmon-pink with yellow flare; large. (1947). AGM 1984.

**'Christopher Wren'** (M) ('Goldball') Orange-yellow flushed flame, with dark orange spotting; flushed red in bud.

**'Coccineum Speciosum'** (Gh) Brilliant orange-red. Still one of the best of the old azaleas. (Before 1846). AGM 1984.

**'Comte de Gomer'** (M) Rose-pink with orange flare. (1872). FCC 1879.

**'Comte de Papadopoli'** (M) Bright pink, illuminated orange. (1873).

**'Corneille'** (Gh) Cream, flushed deep pink on outside, pink in bud; double. Especially good autumn leaf colour. AMT 1958. AGM 1984.

**'Coronation Lady'** Yellowish-pink with orange-yellow blotch.

**'Corringe'** (Kn-Ex) Flame.

**'Daviesii'** (Gh) White with yellow flare, fragrant; a hybrid between *R. molle* and *R. viscosum*. (About 1840). AGM 1984. AM 1989.

**'Devon'** (Kn) Orange-red. AMT 1952.

**'Diorama'** ([*R. viscosum* × *R.* 'Koster's Brilliant Red'] × *R.* 'Fireglow'). Deep red, fragrant.

**'Directeur Moerlands'** (M) ('Golden Sunlight') Golden yellow, deepening in throat, with orange flare; buds Chinese-white.

**'Dracula'** (Kn) An unusual colour; blackish-red in bud opening to a smouldering nasturtium-red, overlaid crimson; margins frilled. Young leaves bronze-tinted. The buds appear almost black from a distance. Raised in our nurseries. (1970).

**'Dr M. Oosthoek'** (M) Deep orange-red. (1920). AM 1920. AMT 1940.

**'Embley Crimson'** (Kn) Crimson; compact habit. A seedling from Embley Park, Hampshire.

**'Exbury White'** (Kn-Ex) White blotched orange-yellow, large.

**'Exquisitum'** (O) Flesh-pink, flushed deep pink on outside, orange flare and frilly margins. Fragrant. (1901). AMT 1950. FCCT 1968.

**'Fanny'** (Gh) ('Pucella') Deep rose-magenta, with darker tube and orange flare, becoming rose with age.

**'Fawley'** (Kn-Ex) Flushed pink in bud, opening white flushed pink at margins with orange flare. (1947).

**'Fireball'** (Kn-Ex) Deep orange-red. Young foliage deep copper-red. (1951).

**'Firefly'** (Kn-Ex) Rose-red with faint orange flare. (1947).

**'Floradora'** (M) Orange-red, deeply spotted. (1910). AM 1910.

**'Freya'** (R) Pale pink tinted orange-salmon; double. (1888). AM 1897. AMT 1953.

**'Frills'** (Kn-Ex) Orange-red, semi-double with frilly margins. (1951).

**'Frome'** (Kn) Saffron-yellow, overlaid fiery red in throat, margins waved and frilled. (1958). AMT 1958.

**'Gallipoli'** (Kn-Ex) Rose-red buds, opening pale tangerine, flushed pink with a warm yellow flare; very large. (1947).

**'George Reynolds'** (Kn) Deep butter-yellow with chrome-yellow and green spotting, pink flushed in bud. A tall clone with large flowers. AM 1936.

**'Gibraltar'** (Kn-Ex) Large, flame-orange flowers with warm yellow flash and crinkly petals; deep crimson-orange in bud. (1947). AGM 1984.

**'Ginger'** (Kn-Ex) Orange-carmine in bud, opening to brilliant orange with warm golden upper petal. (1947).

**'Gloria Mundi'** (Gh) Bright orange with yellow flare, frilled at the margins. (1846).

**'Glowing Embers'** (Kn-Ex) Vivid reddish-orange with orange blotch.

**'Gog'** (Kn) Orange-red with yellow flash, flushed dark red on outside. (1926).

**'Gold Dust'** (Kn-Ex) Pale yellow with gold flare. (1951).

**'Goldball'** See 'Christopher Wren'.

**RHODODENDRON (DECIDUOUS HYBRID AZALEAS)**—*continued*

'**Golden Eagle**' (Kn) Reddish-orange with orange-yellow veins, blotched vivid orange. A hybrid of *R. calendulaceum*.

'**Golden Horn**' (Kn-Ex) Flowers straw-yellow with deep yellow flash tinged rose on the outside, and in bud, fading to ivory. Leaves bronze-tinted, greyish, hoary. (1947).

'**Golden Oriole**' (Kn) Deep golden-yellow, with orange flare; young leaves bronze-tinted. (1939). AM 1947.

'**Golden Sunset**' (Kn) Vivid yellow. AM 1956.

'**Harvest Moon**' (Kn) Straw-yellow with chrome-yellow flare; slightly scented. (1938). AMT 1953.

'**Homebush**' (Kn) Rose-madder, with paler shading, semi-double, in tight rounded heads. A most attractive azalea. (1926). AMT 1950. AGM 1984.

'**Hortulanus H. Witte**' (M) Bright orange-yellow, red-tinged in bud. (1892).

'**Hotspur**' (Kn-Ex) Dazzling flame-red with darker markings on upper petals. AM 1934.

'**Hotspur Red**' (Kn-Ex) Rich reddish-orange with orange blotch.

'**Hugh Wormald**' (Kn-Ex) Deep golden yellow, with a darker flare.

'**Ignea Nova**' (Gh) Deep yellowish-orange with orange blotch. C 1876.

'**Il Tasso**' (R) Rose-red, tinted salmon; double. (1892).

'**Irene Koster**' (O) Rose-pink with small yellow blotch; late.

'**Kathleen**' (Kn-Ex) Salmon-pink with orange blotch, darker in bud. (1947).

'**Klondyke**' (Kn-Ex) A wonderful glowing orange-gold, large flowers, tinted red on back and flushed red in bud; young foliage coppery-red. One of the most striking of its group. (1947).

'**Koningin Emma**' (M) ('Queen Emma') Deep orange, with salmon glow.

'**Koster's Brilliant Red**' (M) Glowing orange-red. Perhaps the best of its colour. Very close to typical *R. japonicum*. (1918).

'**Lapwing**' (Kn) Pale yellow tinged orange and pink, upper lobe deeper with a greenish blotch. C 1935. AMT 1953.

'**Lemonara**' (M) Apricot-yellow, tinged red on outside. (1920).

'**Magnificum**' (O) Creamy-white, flushed pink, with orange flare; rose-flushed in bud. Fragrant. (1910).

'**Marion Merriman**' (Kn) Chrome-yellow with large orange flash, petals with crimpled margins. AM 1925. AMT 1950.

'**Mrs Peter Koster**' (M) Deep red, with orange glow. AMT 1953.

'**Multatuli**' (M) Deep glowing orange-red. (1918).

'**Nancy Buchanan**' (Kn-Ex) Pale straw-yellow, flushed pink with orange flare. (1947).

'**Nancy Waterer**' (Gh) Brilliant golden yellow; large. (Before 1876). AGM 1984.

'**Narcissiflorum**' (Gh) Pale yellow, darker in centre and on outside; double; sweetly-scented; vigorous, compact habit. (Before 1871). AMT 1954. AGM 1984.

'**Norma**' (R) Rose-red with salmon glow; double. (1888). AM 1891. AMT 1959. AGM 1969.

'**Orange Truffles**' (Kn) Apricot, illuminated chrome-yellow within, flushed nasturtium-red on the outside, double, with frilly margins, borne in a tight, compact, rounded truss. Young foliage coppery-red. Raised in our nurseries in 1966.

'**Oxydol**' (Kn-Ex) White with yellow blotch. C 1947.

'**Pallas**' (Gh) Orange-red, with orange-yellow flare. (Before 1875).

'**Peregrine**' (Kn) Rich orange-red, darker in bud. (1949).

'**Persil**' (Kn) White, with orange-yellow flare. AGM 1984.

'**Pink Ruffles**' Pink with orange blotch.

'**Pucella**' See 'Fanny'.

'**Queen Emma**' See 'Koningin Emma'.

'**Raphael de Smet**' (Gh) White, flushed rose, double; excellent autumn colour. (Before 1889). AM 1893.

'**Rosta**' (*R. viscosum* × *R*. 'Koster's Brilliant Red'). Deep pink with darker veins, fragrant. H4.

'**Royal Command**' (Kn-Ex) Vivid reddish-orange.

'**Royal Lodge**' (Kn-Ex) Deep vermilion-red, becoming crimson-red with age, long protruding stamens. (1947).

'**Sang de Gentbrugge**' (Gh) Bright signal-red. (1873).

**RHODODENDRON (DECIDUOUS HYBRID AZALEAS)**—*continued*

**'Satan'** (Kn) Geranium-red, darker in bud. (1926).

**'Scarlet Pimpernel'** (Kn-Ex) Flowers dark red in bud opening to red, with a faint orange flare; young foliage coppery-tinted. (1947).

**'Silver Slipper'** (Kn-Ex) White flushed pink, with orange flare; young foliage copper-tinted. (1948). AMT 1962. FCCT 1963. AGM 1984.

**'Soir de Paris'** Purplish-pink with orange blotch, fragrant. C 1965.

**'Spek's Orange'** (M) Orange, deeper in bud. Late flowering for its group. AMT 1948. FCCT 1953. AGM 1984.

**'Strawberry Ice'** (Kn-Ex) Flesh-pink, mottled deeper pink at margins with a gold flare, deep pink in bud. (1947). AMT 1963. AGM 1984.

**'Sugared Almond'** (Kn-Ex) Pale pink. C 1951.

**'Summer Fragrance'** (O) (*R. luteum* × *R. occidentale*). Pale yellow with vivid yellow blotch, fragrant, flowering in June. A compact small shrub with good autumn colour.

**'Sun Chariot'** (Kn-Ex) Vivid yellow with orange-yellow blotch. AMT 1963. FCCT 1967.

**'Sunbeam'** (M) A hybrid of 'Altaclerense' with larger flowers which are bright yellow, with an orange blotch. (1895). AMT 1952.

**'Tangiers'** (Kn-Ex) Tangerine, flushed pink; large with frilly margins.

**'Tay'** (Kn) Chinese-yellow, with orange blotch and crinkled margins. (1959). AMT 1959.

**'Toucan'** (Kn) Pale straw-yellow, with conspicuous saffron-yellow flare, fading with age; pink-tinged margins. (1941).

**'Trent'** (Kn) Chrome-yellow, tinged salmon at margins, with golden yellow flare; buds pink-tinged. (1958). AMT 1958.

**'Tunis'** (Kn) Deep crimson with orange flare, darker in bud. (1926).

**'Unique'** (Gh) Vivid orange-red in bud, opening to yellowish-orange, in a dense, ball-like truss. (Before 1875). AMT 1952.

**'Westminster'** (O) Clear rich almond-pink, with faint orange flash. Fragrant.

**'White Swan '** (Kn-Ex) White with yellow flare.

**'Whitethroat'** (Kn) Pure white, double, with frilly margins; compact habit. (1941). AMT 1962.

**'Wryneck'** (Kn) Straw-yellow, darker at margins, deeper yellow flash, darker and pink-tinged in bud.

**'Wye'** (Kn) Apricot-yellow darker in throat, with orange flare and crinkled margins; pink-flushed in bud.

### ‡*EVERGREEN HYBRID AZALEAS

The hardy evergreen and semi-evergreen species of the Azalea series have given rise to a prodigious number of hybrids, many of which have arisen in Europe and the United States. The majority, however, have been received from Japan, from where E.H. Wilson introduced the beautiful "Kurume" azaleas. In woodland glades, a close planting of dwarf, evergreen Kurume azaleas creates a spectacular effect, like a colourful patchwork quilt.

Evergreen azaleas will thrive in full sun if their roots are kept moist, but some shelter from cold winds is desirable and partial shade should be provided if possible, as in some clones the flowers are liable to bleach. The flowering season is April and May (the majority in May) when their blossom is often produced with such freedom that the foliage is completely hidden. Individual flowers are normally single but certain clones possess "hose-in-hose" flowers (one flower within another). Unless otherwise stated, their average height is 0.6-1.2m. The date of introduction of a hybrid where known is given in parentheses at the end of each description.

The main groups are as follows:

**Exbury Hybrids** (E)—Hybrids between various species raised by Lionel de Rothschild at Exbury, about 1933. The flowers of this group are normally large, being 6-7.5cm across. Previously listed as Oldhamii Hybrids.

**Gable Hybrids** (G)—A large group of hybrids developed by Joseph B. Gable at Stewartstown, Pennsylvania, United States, and introduced about 1927. Many are the

**RHODODENDRON (EVERGREEN HYBRID AZALEAS)**—*continued*

result of *R. kaempferi* × *R. poukhanense* but several other species and named hybrids have been used. Flowers medium-sized—4-6cm across.

**Glenn Dale Hybrids** (GD)—A large and varied group of hybrids in which innumerable species and hybrids have been used. They have been developed since 1935 by B.Y. Morrison of the United States Department of Agriculture at Glenn Dale, Maryland. Flowers vary from medium to very large—5-10cm across.

**Indian or Indica Azaleas** (I)—A large group of mainly tender hybrids developed in Belgium and England and to a lesser extent in France and Germany during the 19th century. Several species are involved in their parentage including *R. indicum*, *R. mucronatum* and *R. simsii*. The numerous greenhouse azaleas forced for Christmas and offered by florists belong here. The flowers of this group are large—6-7cm across.

**Kaempferi Hybrids** (Kf)—A large group of hybrids which originated in Holland about 1920. They were produced by crossing *R. kaempferi* with *R.* 'Malvaticum'. At a later date several new clones were raised using *R.* 'Maxwellii'. The flowers of this group are usually of medium size—4-5cm across.

**Kurume Azaleas** (K)—The Kurume azaleas originated in Kurume, Japan, during the last century. That great plant collector, E.H. Wilson, was responsible for their introduction into the West when, in 1920, he introduced his famous "Wilson's Fifty". Since the original introduction, numerous other clones have been raised, particularly in the United States. The main species responsible for the original Kurumes are *RR. kaempferi, kiusianum* and 'Obtusum'. The flowers of this group are characteristically small, being 2.5-3.5cm across.

**Oldhamii Hybrids** See Exbury Hybrids.

**Sander Hybrids** (Sr)—Hybrids between Indian azaleas and Kurume azaleas. Developed originally in 1890 by Charles Sander of Brookline, Massachusetts. The flowers of this group are medium to large.

**Satsuki Hybrids** (S)—Introduced by the Chugai Nursery, Kobe, Japan to America during 1938-39. They are mainly the result of *R. indicum* × *R. simsii*, but various Belgian hybrids have also played a part. They are notorious for their tendency to sport and produce flowers of various colours. The flowers of this group are medium to large.

**Vuyk Hybrids** (V)—A group of hybrids which originated in the Vuyk van Nes Nursery, Boskoop, Holland, in 1921. The flowers of this group are normally large, being 5-7.5cm across.

**Wada Hybrids** (W)—Hybrids of mixed parentage, raised by K. Wada, of Yokohama, Japan, before 1940. The flowers of this group are medium to large.

**'Addy Wery'** (K) (*R.* 'Malvaticum' × *R.* 'Flame'). Deep vermilion-red. (1940). AMT 1950. AGM 1984. H4.

**'Adonis'** (K) White, hose-in-hose, with frilly margins.

**'Advance'** (GD) Rosy-red, 5cm across. H4.

**'Aladdin'** (K) (*R. kaempferi* hybrid × *R.* Kurume Hybrid). Intense geranium-red fading to salmon.

**'Alexander'** (*R. nakaharae* × *R.* 'Kin no sai'). Deep reddish-orange with purplish-red blotch. Dwarf, spreading habit.

**'Alice'** (Kf) (*R.* 'Malvaticum' × *R. kaempferi*). Salmon-red with dark flash. (1922). H4.

**'Appleblossom'** See 'Ho o'.

**'Atalanta'** (Kf) (*R.* 'Malvaticum' × *R. kaempferi*). Soft lilac. H4.

**'Azuma Kagami'** (K) Phlox-pink with darker shading, hose-in-hose. Up to 1.8m, best in semi-shade. (Wilson 16). AMT 1950. H3.

**'Beethoven'** (V) Orchid-purple, with deeper blotch; petals fringed. (1941). H4.

**'Bengal Beauty'** (*R. kaempferi* 'Daimio' × *R. simsii*). Purplish-pink with wavy margins. C 1964.

**'Bengal Fire'** (E) (*R. kaempferi* × *R. oldhamii*). Fiery orange, ultimately 1.8m high. (1934). H4.

**'Beni Giri'** (K) Bright crimson. (1910). H4.

**'Betty'** (Kf) (*R.* 'Malvaticum' × *R. kaempferi*). Salmon-pink with deeper centre. (1922). AMT 1940. FCCT 1972. H4.

**'Bijou de Ledeberg'** (I) Rose-red. Leaves dark green margined with white. (1865). H3.

## RHODODENDRON (EVERGREEN HYBRID AZALEAS)—*continued*

**'Blaauw's Pink'** (K) Salmon-pink with paler shading, early. (1953). AGM 1984. H4.

**'Blue Danube'** (Kf) Bluish-violet. A most distinctive and striking colour. AMT 1970. FCCT 1975. AGM 1984.

**'Buccaneer'** (GD) (*R.* 'Hinode Giri' × *R.* 'Late Salmon'). Vivid reddish-orange. Vigorous.

**'Bungo Nishiki'** (W) Orange-scarlet, semi-double; late. H4.

**'Chanticleer'** (GD) Amaranth-purple, brilliant in effect, very floriferous. Bushy, dense habit. H4.

**'Chippewa'** Purplish-red with darker blotch.

**'Christina'** (Kf) (*R.* 'Florida' × *R.* 'Louise Gable'). Red, hose-in-hose or double, large.

**'Commodore'** (GD) Vivid red blotched purple, 7cm across. H4.

**'Christmas Cheer'** See 'Ima Shojo'.

**'Connie'** (Kf) Reddish-orange.

**'Double Beauty'** (*R.* double seedling × *R.* 'Vuyk's Scarlet'). Purplish-red, hose-in-hose; low, compact habit. C 1966.

**'Eddy'** (E) (*R.* 'Apollo' × *R. kaempferi*). Deep salmon-red; ultimately 1.5m high. (1933). AM 1944. H3.

**'Favorite'** (*R.* 'Hinodegiri' × *R. kaempferi*). Deep rosy-pink. (1920). H4.

**'Fedora'** (Kf) (*R.* 'Malvaticum' × *R. kaempferi*). Pale pink with darker flash. (1922). AM 1931. FCCT 1960. H4.

**'Firefly'** See 'Hexe'.

**'Florida'** (V) (*R.* unknown seedling × *R.* 'Vuyk's Scarlet'). Deep red, hose-in-hose with some petaloid stamens. C 1962.

**'Gaiety'** (GD) (*R. indicum* × *R.* 'Hazel Dawson' ). Purplish-pink with darker blotch, large.

**'General Wavell'** (S) Deep yellowish-pink flushed yellow at the base with red spots, large. H3.

**'Greenway'** (K) Pink. C 1975.

**'Gumpo'** (S) Large, wavy-petalled white flowers, occasionally flecked red. AM 1934.

**'Hana Asobi'** (K) Bright rose-carmine, with white anthers. (Wilson 50). H4.

**'Hardy Gardenia'** Dwarf, spreading habit. Flowers 6cm across, double, white. H4.

**'Helen Close'** (GD) White blotched with pale yellow, to 7.5cm across. H4.

**'Hexe'** (I) ('Firefly') Glowing crimson; hose-in-hose. (1885). AM 1907. H4. Used in some Continental nurseries as an understock.

**'Hino Crimson'** (K) Crimson-scarlet. AGM 1984. H4.

**'Hinode Giri'** (K) Bright crimson. A popular clone. (Wilson 42). AMT 1965. AGM 1984. H4.

**'Hinode no Taka'** (K) Crimson, with red anthers. (Wilson 48). H4.

**'Hinomayo'** (K ) Clear pink, a most lovely clone up to 1.5m in height. Obtained by C.B. van Nes & Sons from the Emperor's Garden in Tokyo, Japan, about 1910. AM 1921. FCCT 1945. AGM 1984. H4.

**'Ho o'** (K) ('Appleblossom') Pale pink with white throat. (Wilson 9). AMT 1950. H4.

**'Ima Shojo'** (K) ('Christmas Cheer') Bright red; hose-in-hose. (Wilson 36). AMT 1959. H4.

**'Iroha Yama'** (K) White, margined pale lavender, with faint chestnut-brown eye. (Wilson 8). AMT 1952. H4.

**'Ivette'** (Kf) Brilliant rose-pink, low, compact habit.

**'Jeanette'** (Kf) Phlox-pink, with darker blotch. (1920). AMT 1948. H4.

**'Jitsugesuse'** (S) Flowers pale mauve.

**'Johanna'** (*R.* 'Florida' × *R.* unnamed seedling). Deep red. FCCT 1988.

**'John Cairns'** (Kf) Dark orange-red. AMT 1940. AGM 1984. H4.

**'Kermisina'** Vivid purplish-red; low, compact habit. A hybrid of *R. kiusianum*.

**'Killarney'** (GD) Broad, spreading habit. Flowers white blotched with greenish-yellow, to 7.5cm across.

**'Kirin'** (K) Deep rose, shaded silvery-rose, hose-in-hose. (Wilson 22). AM 1927. AMT 1952. H4.

**'Kiritsubo'** (K) Rosy-mauve. (Wilson 24). AMT 1974. H4.

**'Koningin Wilhelmina'** (V) ('Queen Wilhelmina'). Vermilion-red; dwarf; best in semi-shade. H4.

**RHODODENDRON (EVERGREEN HYBRID AZALEAS)**—*continued*

**'Kumo no Ito'** (K) ('Suga no Ito') Lavender-pink with white throat. (Wilson 31). AMT 1952. H4.

**'Kure no Yuki'** (K) ('Snowflake') White, hose-in-hose. Dwarf habit. (Wilson 2). AMT 1952. AGM 1984. H4.

**'Lemur'** (*R. nakaharae* 'Mariko' × *R.* 'Vuyk's Scarlet'). Deep pink; dwarf, prostrate habit with red winter buds. Raised by Peter Cox.

**'Leo'** (E) (*R.* 'Malvaticum' × *R. kaempferi*). Bright orange; late; dwarf and spreading in habit. (1933). H4.

**'Louise Dowdle'** (GD) Brilliant Tyrian-pink with Tyrian-rose blotch; large. AMT 1974. FCCT 1976. H4.

**'Louise Gable'** (*R. indicum* × [*R. yedoense* var. *poukhanense* × *R. kaempferi*]). Deep pink with darker blotch. Low, compact, spreading habit.

**'Madame van Hecke'** Small, rosy-pink. H4.

**'Martha Hitchcock'** (GD) White margined reddish-purple, 7.5cm across. Spreading habit. H4.

**'Mary Helen'** ([*R.* 'Mucronatum' × *R.* 'Vittata Fortunei'] × *R.* 'Kagetsu'). White with yellow spotting and wavy margins.

**'Maxwellii'** (*R. pulchrum* 'Maxwellii') Similar to 'Phoeniceum' but with larger flowers of a bright rose-red with a darker blotch. AMT 1960.

**'Merlin'** (GD) A semi-evergreen hybrid of *R. poukhanense*. Large mauve flowers 7.5cm across. H4.

**'Mimi'** (Kf) Pale purplish-pink with darker blotch. C 1962.

**'Mother's Day'** Rose-red. A cross between a Kurume hybrid and an Indian azalea. AMT 1959. AGM 1984. FCCT 1970. H4.

**Mucronatum group** (*R. mucronatum* (BLUME) G. DON) (*R. ledifolium* (HOOK.) G. DON) A very lovely small, evergreen or semi-evergreen shrub of wide-spreading, dome-shaped habit. Flowers fragrant, funnel-shaped, pure white in May. Long cultivated in Japan but unknown in the wild and probably of hybrid origin. I 1819. AMT 1958. AGM 1984. H4.

**'Bulstrode'** A floriferous shrub; large white flowers with a faint yellowish-green stain.

**'Lilacinum'** Flowers soft lilac-mauve.

**'Noordtianum'** A form with slightly larger white flowers green at the throat, occasionally red striped.

**'Naomi'** (Kf) (*R.* 'Malvaticum' × *R. kaempferi*). Salmon-pink, very late; ultimately to 1.8m high. Raised at Exbury. (1933). H4.

**'Niagara'** (GD) ([*R.* 'Lilacinum' × *R.* 'Willy'] × [*R.* 'Mrs Carmichael' × *R.* 'Willy']). White with frilly margin and yellow-green blotch.

**Obtusum group** (*R. obtusum* (LINDL.) PLANCH.) (*Azalea obtusa* LINDL.) "Kirishima Azalea". A dwarf, densely-branched, evergreen or semi-evergreen, wide-spreading shrub seldom reaching 1m. Branches densely hairy, clothed with small, oval, glossy green leaves and flowering with prodigious freedom in spring. Flowers in clusters of 1-3, 2.5cm across, funnel-shaped; bright red, scarlet or crimson; May. Said by some authorities to be wild on a few high mountains on the island of Kyushu (Japan), but now generally regarded as being of hybrid origin. Long cultivated, both in Japan and China, and a parent of many of the Kurume azaleas. Introduced from China by Robert Fortune in 1844. AM 1898. H4.

**'Amoenum'** (*Azalea amoena* LINDL.) The hardiest form. A rather taller, wide-spreading shrub. Flowers hose-in-hose, brilliant magenta or rose-purple. Introduced from Japanese gardens in 1845. AM 1907. AMT 1965. AGM 1984.

**'Amoenum Coccineum'** A branch sport of 'Amoenum' with carmine-rose, hose-in-hose flowers. Tends to revert.

**'Amoenum Splendens'** A low, wide-spreading shrub with single, pale mauve flowers.

**'Kokinshita'** A dwarf shrub with rose-salmon flowers in June and July.

**'Macrostemon'** Low spreading bush with single, salmon-orange flowers 4cm wide.

**'Orange Beauty'** (Kf) (*R.* 'Hinode Giri' × *R. kaempferi*). Salmon-orange. (1920). AMT 1945. FCC 1958. AGM 1984. H4.

**RHODODENDRON (EVERGREEN HYBRID AZALEAS)**—*continued*

**'Palestrina'** (V) White, with faint ray of green; very distinct and attractive. (1926). AM 1944. FCC 1967. AGM 1984. H4.

**'Phoeniceum'** (*R. pulchrum* SWEET) A small to medium-sized shrub, with densely hairy twigs and elliptic to obovate leaves. Flowers in clusters of 1-4, funnel-shaped, 5-6cm across, rose-purple, with dark spots; May. Unknown in the wild and possibly of hybrid origin, perhaps *R. scabrum* × *R.* Mucronatum group. Long cultivated in Japan and China. I early in the 19th century. H3.

**'Pink Gumpo'** (S) Large flowers, peach-pink with deeper flecks.

**'Prinses Juliana'** (V) Light orange-red. H4.

**'Purple Splendor'** (*R. yedoense* var. *poukhanense* × *R.* 'Hexe'). Vivid reddish-purple.

**'Purple Triumph'** (V) Deep purple. (1951). AMT 1960. H4.

**'Queen Wilhelmina'** See 'Koningin Wilhelmina'.

**'Rasho Mon'** (K) Scarlet. (Wilson 37). H4.

**'Rose Greeley'** White with yellow-green blotch, hose-in-hose, fragrant. Low, compact, spreading habit.

**'Rosebud'** (K) Rose-pink, hose-in-hose; late. Low spreading habit. AMT 1972. AGM 1984. H4.

**'Royal Pink'** (Kf) Rich purplish-pink. C 1969.

**'Sakata Red'** (Kurume hybrid × *R. kaempferi*). Fiery red. AMT 1952. H4.

**'Satsuki'** (I) Pink, with dark blotch. H4.

**'Shin Seikai'** (K) White, hose-in-hose; dwarf habit. (Wilson 3). AM 1921. AMT 1952. H4.

**'Silver Moon'** (GD) White, with pale green blotch, frilled. Broad spreading habit. H4.

**'Silvester'** (K) (*R.* 'Aladdin' × *R.* 'Amoenum'). Purplish-red with paler margins, early. C 1964.

**'Sir William Lawrence'** (E) (*R.* 'Hinode Giri' × *R. kaempferi*). Pale pink.

**'Snowflake'** See 'Kure no Yuki'.

**'Squirrel'** (*R.* 'Galathea' × *R. nakaharae*). Deep reddish-orange. A dwarf, compact shrub.

**'Stewartsonianum'** (G) Vivid red. Foliage reddish in winter.

**'Suga no Ito'** See 'Kumo no Ito'.

**'Surprise'** (K) Light orange-red. (1939). H4.

**'Takasago'** (K) Cherry blossom-pink, hose-in-hose. (Wilson 11). H4.

**'Tebotan'** (*R. pulchrum* 'Tebotan') Flowers double, soft purple, with tiny, undeveloped, green leaves in centre.

**'Ukamuse'** (K) Pale salmon-rose with darker flash, hose-in-hose. (Wilson 47). AMT 1952. H4.

**'Vida Brown'** (K) Clear rose-pink, hose-in-hose. AMT 1960. H4.

**'Violetta'** (GD) (*R.* 'Malvaticum' × *R. indicum*). Light purplish-pink blotched purplish-red to 5cm, early.

**'Vuyk's Rosyred'** (V) Deep satiny-rose with darker flash. (1954). AMT 1962. H4.

**'Vuyk's Scarlet'** (V) Bright red with wavy petals. (1954). AMT 1959. FCCT 1966. AGM 1984. H4.

**'Willy'** (Kf) Soft pink. H4.

**'Wombat'** A prostrate shrub good for ground cover with profusely borne pink flowers. A hybrid of *R. nakaharae*.

**RHODODENDRON maximum × Kalmia latifolia** See under *Rhododendron maximum*.

‡†\***RHODOLEIA** CHAMP. ex HOOK.—**Hamamelidaceae**—A small genus of trees native to SE Asia. A warm, sheltered position in woodland conditions is preferred, but only suitable for the mildest areas.

**championii** HOOK. A beautiful shrub or occasionally a small tree with the general habit of a rhododendron and large, thick, shining green leaves, glaucous beneath, crowding the tips of the stems. The drooping flower-clusters consist of numerous silky-hairy, multi-coloured bracts through which emerge the bright, rose-madder petals and black anthers. These are borne in the axils of the leaves in spring. Only suitable for the very mildest gardens, but a superb conservatory shrub. S China. First introduced in 1852 and more recently by Kingdon-Ward.

‡***RHODOTHAMNUS** REICHENB.—**Ericaceae**—2 species of dwarf shrubs related to *Phyllodoce* and requiring a cool, moist pocket on the rock garden.

**chamaecistus** (L.) REICHENB. A charming, dwarf, evergreen shrublet rarely above 25cm high. The pale rose, saucer-shaped flowers resemble those of *Rhododendron calostrotum*, and are produced during April and May. In common with others of the family it is not suited to chalky soil in cultivation, though it grows on hard limestone formations in the wild. E European Alps. I 1786. AM 1925.

**RHODOTYPOS** SIEB. & ZUCC.—**Rosaceae**—A monotypic genus most closely related to *Kerria*, differing, among other things, in its opposite leaves and white flowers. All types of soil, in sun or half shade.

**scandens** (THUNB.) MAK. (*R. kerrioides* SIEB. & ZUCC.) A free-flowering shrub with erect branches to 1.2m. The paper-white flowers, 4-5cm across, appear from May to July like white dog roses and are followed by conspicuous, shining black fruits. China, Korea, Japan. I 1866.

**RHUS** L.—**Anacardiaceae**—The "Sumachs" are a genus of easily cultivated shrubs and trees, thriving in any fertile soil and mainly grown for their often striking foliage and rich autumn colours. There are about 200 species, a few of them climbers, widely distributed in temperate regions, with some in the tropics. They are dioecious or monoecious and the individual flowers are small and rarely of merit, but in several species are succeeded by fruits which are colourful in the mass. The sap of some species is a severe irritant to the skin of those so allergic. The genus includes the "Poison Ivy" of North America (*Rhus toxicodendron*). Both *R. glabra* and *R. typhina* make handsome foliage plants when pruned to the ground each or every other year in February.

**aromatica** AIT. (*R. canadensis* MARSH.) "Fragrant Sumach". A small, spreading, downy shrub with coarsely-toothed, trifoliolate leaves, aromatic when bruised, giving attractive orange and purple-red tints in autumn. The yellowish flowers, though small, are produced in conspicuous clusters in April. E United States. I 1759.

**chinensis** MILL. (*R. javanica* AUCT.) (*R. osbeckii* (DC.) CARR.) A small, dioecious, broad-headed tree or large irregular shrub here attaining about 6m. The pinnate, coarsely-toothed leaves colour richly in autumn, and have a peculiarly winged rachis. Flowers yellowish-white, produced in large, terminal panicles in late summer. Late made, unripened growths are often cut back by winter frosts. Manchuria, Japan, China, Korea to Malaysia. I 1737.

**copallina** L. "Dwarf Sumach". A small to medium-sized, downy shrub. The lustrous leaves are pinnate, the usually entire leaflets being attached to a strongly winged rachis. The dense, erect clusters of small, greenish-yellow flowers are of little beauty, but the autumn colour of the foliage is rich red or purple and combines well with red fruit clusters. E North America. I 1688. AM 1973.

**coriaria** L. "Tanner's Sumach". A small to medium-sized shrub or small tree. Leaves pinnate, with 7-21 ovate to oblong, coarsely-toothed leaflets, the rachis winged or partially so. The greenish-white, female flowers are followed by brownish-purple, hispid fruits. This species is extremely rare in cultivation in Britain. The "Sumach" of commerce is obtained from the leaves, and tannin from both leaves and shoots is used in the preparation of morocco leather. It requires a warm, sunny position in a well drained soil. SE Europe.

**cotinoides** See *Cotinus obovatus*.

**cotinus** See *Cotinus coggygria*.

**glabra** L. "Smooth Sumach". A wide-spreading, medium-sized shrub with glabrous, glaucous stems and attractive glabrous, pinnate leaves which are glaucous beneath and usually turn an intense red or orange-yellow in autumn. The erect, scarlet, hairy, plume-like fruit-clusters of the female plant are also conspicuous in autumn. E North America. C 1620.

**'Laciniata'** A splendid foliage plant, the fern-like leaves with deeply incised leaflets, turning to orange, yellow and red in autumn. Inclined to revert. FCC 1867. AGM 1984.

**RHUS**—*continued*

**potaninii** MAXIM. (*R. henryi* DIELS) A small, round-headed tree which, planted at the beginning of the century, reached 6m on chalk soil in our Winchester nursery. Leaves pinnate, colouring richly in autumn. The greenish-white flowers and red fruits have not yet appeared on our tree. C and W China. Discovered by Augustine Henry in 1888 and introduced by E.H. Wilson in 1902. AM 1932.

×**pulvinata** GREENE (*R. glabra* × *R. typhina*) (*R.* × *hybrida* REHD.) A medium-sized to large shrub with downy stems, intermediate between the parents. Leaves turning to rich scarlet, orange and flame in autumn. Occurs with the parents in the wild. I 1923.

†**succedanea** L. "Wax Tree". A small tree with large, pinnate leaves which are a lustrous, dark green above, paler beneath, colouring richly in autumn. Succeeds only in the mildest areas. The fruits of the female tree yield a wax which was once used for making candles in Japan. Taiwan, China, Japan, Malaysia, India. I 1862.

**sylvestris** SIEB. & ZUCC. A small to medium-sized shrubby tree, with pinnate leaves, giving conspicuous autumn colour. Fruits brownish-yellow. Taiwan, China, Korea, Japan. I 1881.

**trichocarpa** MIQ. A splendid large shrub or small tree with large, pinnate, downy leaves coppery-pink when young, turning deep orange in autumn. Fruits yellow, bristly, borne in drooping clusters on female plants in autumn. Japan, Korea, China. I 1894. AM 1979.

**trilobata** TORR. & A. GRAY A small shrub occasionally to 2m, closely related to *R. aromatica*, but more erect in growth and leaves with smaller leaflets and an unpleasant scent. W North America. I 1877.

**typhina** L. "Stag's-horn Sumach". A wide-spreading, sparsely-branched, small tree or an irregular large shrub, developing a gaunt, flat-topped appearance, particularly noticeable in winter. The thick, pithy branches are covered, when young, with a dense coat of reddish-brown hairs. The large, pinnate leaves turn to rich orange, yellow, red or purple in autumn. Large, erect, green clusters of male flowers and smaller, female clusters are borne on separate plants. The dense conical clusters of crimson, hairy fruits are most decorative at the end of the year. Sometimes forming small thickets of suckering stems. E North America. C 1629.

**'Dissecta'** ('Laciniata') A striking, female form with deeply incised leaflets, creating a fern-like effect; orange and yellow autumn colours. AM 1910. AGM 1984.

**'Laciniata'** See 'Dissecta'.

**verniciflua** STOKES "Varnish Tree". Medium-sized tree with large, handsome, pinnate leaves; flowers in large, drooping panicles, followed on female trees by yellowish fruits. This is the source of the famous varnish or lacquer of Japan where it is cultivated in the warmer areas. The sap has been known to cause a severe rash when applied to the skin. Japan, China, Himalaya. C before 1862. FCC 1862.

**RIBES** L.—**Grossulariaceae**—About 150 species natives of temperate regions of the N hemisphere and S America. The flowering currants and ornamental gooseberries are a group of evergreen and deciduous, mainly spring-flowering shrubs of easy cultivation in all types of soil. Some are very showy in flower. The majority are extremely hardy. Leaves mostly three or five-lobed, rarely of special merit. Straggly or untidy specimens may be hard-pruned immediately after flowering.

**alpinum** L. A small to medium-sized, semi-erect shrub of neat, densely-twiggy habit suitable for hedging. Flowers greenish-yellow, small, usually dioecious; berries red. Extremely shade-tolerant. N and C Europe (including British Isles).

**'Aureum'** A small shrub usually wider than high with leaves yellow when young. FCC 1881.

**'Pumilum'** A very dense, compact, rounded bush slowly reaching up to 1m, wider than high, with small, neat leaves. C 1827.

**ambiguum** MAXIM. A small, sparsely-branched shrub with shortly lobed or toothed, orbicular leaves. Flowers greenish, solitary or in pairs in spring. Fruits rounded, green and glandular, hispid. In the wild it is found as an epiphyte on tree trunks and branches in mountain forests, but it is growing quite happily, though slowly, in an open border in our garden. Japan. I 1915.

**RIBES**—*continued*

**americanum** MILL. "American Blackcurrant". A small shrub up to 1.8m, resembling the common blackcurrant in habit, leaf and smell, but differing in its longer, funnel-shaped, rather insipid yellowish flowers. The foliage turns to gorgeous crimson and yellow shades in autumn. E North America. I 1729.

**'Variegatum'** Leaves mottled pale green and cream.

**aureum** See under *R. odoratum.*

**bracteosum** HOOK. "Stink Currant". A medium-sized shrub of upright habit with large, five to seven-lobed, aromatic leaves up to 20cm across on petioles to 20cm. Flowers pinkish-green in bracteate racemes to 25cm, pendulous in fruit. Berries blue-black conspicuously bloomed with white. W North America. I 1895.

× **culverwellii** MACFARL. (*R. uva-crispa* × *R. nigrum*). A small, thornless shrub of spreading habit with leaves and flowers resembling those of the gooseberry. Fruits like small, rounded gooseberries, green becoming dark red. Scarlet-purple autumn colour. First raised by Mr Culverwell of Yorkshire, about 1880.

**emodense** REHD. Small shrub with leaves glandular beneath; flowers greenish, with purplish tinge, berries red or black. Himalaya, C China. I 1908.

**var. verruculosum** REHD. Differs in its smaller leaves, which are dotted on the petiole and on the veins beneath with small wart-like glands. Berries red. N China. I 1921.

**fasciculatum** SIEB. & ZUCC. A small to medium-sized, dioecious shrub with coarsely-toothed leaves. Flowers fascicled, creamy-yellow and fragrant but not showy; female plants bear scarlet berries which persist well into winter. Japan, Korea, China. C 1884.

**var. chinense** MAXIM. A taller, more vigorous variety with larger, longer persistent leaves of a distinctive bright green. N China to Korea. C 1867. AM 1976.

*****gayanum** (SPACH) STEUD. A small suckering, evergreen shrub with soft green velvety leaves. The bell-shaped, pale yellow flowers are honey-scented and densely packed into erect, cylindrical racemes, in early June. Chile. C 1858.

**glutinosum** See *R. sanguineum* var. *glutinosum.*

× **gordonianum** LEM. (*R. odoratum* × *R. sanguineum*). An extremely hardy, vigorous and rather pleasing shrub, intermediate in habit between its parents. Flowers in drooping racemes, bronze-red on the outside, yellow within. Garden origin 1837. AM 1989.

*****henryi** FRANCH. A rare and very worthy, almost prostrate, evergreen, dioecious shrub with glandular-bristly young shoots and large, obovate to orbicular, pale green leaves. Flowers in drooping racemes, greenish-yellow, produced with the new growths in February and March. It is related to *R. laurifolium*, differing in its dwarfer habit, hairy shoots and broader, thinner-textured leaves. Native of C China; introduced inadvertently by E.H. Wilson in 1908, with seed of *Sinowilsonia henryi.*

**lacustre** (PERS.) POIR. "Swamp Currant". A subtly attractive, small shrub with slender, erect stems, which are closely beset with rich brown bristles. Flowers disc-like, small, but numerous, in long drooping racemes; petals pale yellow or white, spotted with red or pink, opening from late May to June or July. Growing in wet situations in its native environs. North America. I 1812.

*****laurifolium** JANCZ. An excellent, dwarf, evergreen, dioecious shrub with large, leathery, narrow-elliptic, glabrous leaves and drooping racemes of dioecious, greenish-white flowers in February and March. Berries red then blackish. An interesting early flowering shrub for the rock garden. The male form is sometimes referred to as *R. vicarii.* W China. Discovered and introduced by E.H. Wilson in 1908. AM 1912.

**menziesii** PURSH. A small shrub with erect, bristly and spiny stems to 2m. The small, fuchsia-like flowers appear in pairs in the axils of the leaves in May, petals white, calyx reddish-purple, a delightful contrast; berries reddish, bristly. W North America. I 1830.

**odoratum** WENDL. (*R. aureum* HORT. not PURSH.) "Buffalo Currant". A small to medium-sized shrub of loose, erect habit. Leaves glabrous, shining green, colouring richly in autumn. Lax racemes of golden yellow flowers in April, deliciously clove-scented. Berries black. Long cultivated in gardens as *R. aureum*, which is a rarer, less ornamental species with smaller flowers. C United States. I 1812.

**roezlii** REG. A small, spiny, loosely-branched shrub with pubescent young shoots. Flowers 1-3 in the leaf axils, petals rosy-white, calyx purplish, pubescent. Berries globular, purple, densely beset with slender bristles. California and S Oregon (United States). C 1899.

**RIBES**—*continued*

**sanguineum** PURSH. The popular "Flowering Currant", extensively planted throughout Britain. A medium-sized shrub with a characteristic pungent smell. Flowers deep rose-pink, petals white, produced during April in racemes which are drooping at first, later ascending. Berries black, bloomy. Useful for cutting for the home and easily forced, but tending to pale in colour. W North America. First discovered by Archibald Menzies in 1793 and introduced in 1817.

**'Albescens'** Flowers whitish, tinged pink.

**'Album'** Flowers white.

**'Atrorubens'** ('Atrosanguineum') Flowers deep blood-crimson. C 1837.

**'Brocklebankii'** A small, slower-growing shrub with attractive golden yellow leaves and pink flowers. Tends to burn in full sun. AM 1914.

**'Carneum Grandiflorum'** Flowers of a deep flesh-pink.

**var. glutinosum** (BENTH.) LOUD. (*R. glutinosum* BENTH.) A Californian variety, differing little from the type, but in cultivation flowering two to three weeks earlier. I 1832. AM 1988.

    **'Albidum'** Flowers white, tinged pink, similar in effect to *R. sanguineum* 'Albescens', but earlier. C 1840.

**'King Edward VII'** Flowers of an intense crimson. Rather lower-growing than the typical form. AM 1904.

**'Lombartsii'** Flowers larger than those of the type, rose-pink with white centre.

**'Plenum'** Flowers double.

**'Pulborough Scarlet'** A selected form with deep red flowers the same colour as *Spiraea japonica* 'Anthony Waterer'. AM 1959. AGM 1984.

**'Splendens'** Flowers rosy-crimson, in larger, longer racemes. C 1900.

**'Tydeman's White'** The best white-flowered form. Both the racemes and individual flowers are larger than those of 'Album'.

**speciosum** PURSH. An attractive medium-sized, semi-evergreen shrub with reddish-bristly stems and fruits and shining green leaves. The beautiful, slender, fuchsia-like, rich red flowers are borne in pendulous clusters during April and May. In cold areas it is best grown against a sunny wall. California. I 1828. AGM 1984.

†\***viburnifolium** A. GRAY A medium-sized, evergreen shrub with long scandent stems. Leaves shining green, emitting a pleasant turpentine-like odour when crushed. Flowers small, terracotta-red, in short, erect racemes in April; berries red. Requires a warm wall in all but the mildest areas. It is not very hardy with us. California. I 1897.

**vilmorinii** JANCZ. A medium-sized, densely-branched, dioecious shrub closely related to and resembling *R. alpinum*. The greenish or brown-tinted flowers are followed by black berries. W China. I 1902.

‡\***RICHEA** R. BR.—**Epacridaceae**—A small genus of some 10 species of very distinct and subtly attractive evergreen shrubs, natives mainly of Tasmania with one species in SE Australia. The following require a moist preferably acid soil.

†**dracophylla** R. BR. An erect, small to medium-sized shrub, with long thick, spreading, lanceolate leaves crowded at the ends of the bare stems almost suggesting Liliaceae. Flowers in terminal, crowded panicles, white, the branches subtended by brown, rigidly pointed bracts. Tasmania.

**scoparia** HOOK. f. An unusual, hardy, small, spreading shrub, resembling a dwarf, shrubby "Monkey Puzzle". The stems are clothed with stiff, sharply-pointed leaves. Flowers pink, produced in erect, terminal, spike-like panicles, 5-10cm long, in May. Tasmania. AM 1942.

**ROBINIA** L.—**Leguminosae**—A small genus of about 8 species of fast-growing trees and shrubs, confined in the wild to the United States and N Mexico. They are characterised by their attractive, pinnate leaves, often spiny stems and pendulous racemes of pea-flowers. All are hardy and suitable for any ordinary soil, being especially useful in dry, sunny situations. All species are tolerant of atmospheric pollution. As suckering trees and shrubs they are useful for fixing sand banks and shifting soil. To avoid damage to the brittle branches we recommend that small trees are hard-pruned after flowering.

**ROBINIA**—*continued*

× **ambigua** POIR. (*R. pseudoacacia* × *R. viscosa*). A small tree with slightly viscid young shoots and racemes of pale pink flowers in June. Garden origin before 1812.

'**Bella-rosea**' An elegant form with slightly stickier shoots and rather large, pink flowers. Raised about 1860.

'**Decaisneana**' (*R. pseudoacacia* 'Decaisneana') A vigorous form of medium size, producing large racemes of pale pink flowers. FCC 1865.

**boyntonii** ASHE Medium-sized shrub generally with smooth, spineless branches and loose racemes of pink flowers in May and June, pods glandular-bristly. E United States. I 1914.

**elliottii** ASHE (*R. hispida* 'Rosea') A small to medium-sized shrub. Flowers large, rose-lilac, appearing in May and June; pods bristly. Branches rather brittle. SE United States. I about 1901.

**fertilis** ASHE A small to medium-sized, suckering shrub with bristly stems and rosy-pink flowers in June; pods densely bristly. Closely related to *R. hispida*, differing in its smaller flowers and pubescent leaflets. Branches rather brittle. SE United States. C 1900.

'**Monument**' A more compact form up to 3m.

**hartwigii** KOEHNE A large shrub, the downy shoots are liberally sprinkled with glandular hairs. Flowers varying in colour from pale lilac to soft rose, borne 20-30 together in dense racemes during June and July, pods glandular-bristly. SE United States. C 1904.

× **hillieri** See *R.* × *slavinii* 'Hillieri'.

**hispida** L. "Rose Acacia". A medium-sized, suckering shrub of irregular habit with long, glandular-bristly branches. Short racemes of large, deep rose flowers, 2.5-4cm long, in May and June; pods, when produced, glandular-bristly. An excellent small tree when grafted onto stems of *R. pseudoacacia*, but rather brittle and requires a sheltered position. It may also be grown effectively against a sunny wall. SE United States. I 1743. AM 1934.

'**Macrophylla**' A less bristly form with larger leaflets and larger flowers, resembling a pink wisteria.

× **holdtii** BEISSN. (*R. luxurians* × *R. pseudoacacia*). Resembling the latter parent in habit and vigour and bearing long, loose racemes of pale pink flowers in June or July, often continuing almost to autumn, followed by attractive red, bristly seed pods. Garden origin about 1890.

'**Britzensis**' A form with nearly white flowers. Raised in 1893.

**kelseyi** COWELL ex HUTCHINS. A graceful shrub or small tree with slender branches and elegant foliage, producing its slightly fragrant, lilac-pink flowers in June; pods glandular-bristly. Branches somewhat brittle. S Allegheny Mts (United States). I 1901. AM 1910. FCC 1917.

**luxurians** (DIECK) SCHNEID. A vigorous large shrub or small tree with spiny stipules, producing short racemes of pale rose flowers in June, frequently again in August; pods bristly. SE United States, N Mexico. I 1887.

× **margaretta** ASHE (*R. hispida* × *R. pseudoacacia*). A large suckering shrub or small tree occurring in the wild with the parents. Generally resembles *R. pseudoacacia* but with the leaflets downy beneath and with pink flowers.

'**Pink Cascade**' ('Casque Rouge') A vigorous form with profusely borne, large, purplish-pink flowers. Raised in the United States about 1934.

**pseudoacacia** L. "Common Acacia" "False Acacia" "Black Locust". A large, suckering tree, often of picturesque "oriental" appearance. Bark rugged and deeply furrowed, twigs with spiny stipules. Flowers slightly fragrant, white, with a yellow stain at the base of the standard, produced in long racemes in June; pods smooth. A commonly planted tree thriving in any well drained soil and tolerant of industrial pollution. Its flowers are especially attractive to bees. Native of the E United States, introduced to France in 1601 and now widely naturalised both in that country and elsewhere in Europe especially in the vicinity of railways.

'**Aurea**' Leaves soft yellow in early summer, becoming green later. C 1864. FCC 1873. Now superseded by 'Frisia'.

'**Bessoniana**' A small to medium-sized, compact, round-headed tree, usually spineless. Perhaps the best clone for street planting. C 1871.

**ROBINIA pseudoacacia**—*continued*

**'Coluteoides'** A small tree of dense habit. Flowers and racemes smaller but abundantly produced.

**'Decaisneana'** See *R.* ×*ambigua* 'Decaisneana'.

**'Erecta'** See 'Monophylla Fastigiata'.

**'Fastigiata'** See 'Pyramidalis'.

**'Frisia'** An outstanding, small to medium-sized tree with leaves which are a rich golden yellow from spring to autumn, creating a brilliant splash of colour. It associates particularly well with large, purple-leaved shrubs such as *Cotinus coggygria* 'Royal Purple'. Also good if stooled each spring as a shrub. Raised at the nursery of W. Jansen in Holland, in 1935. AM 1964. AGM 1984.

**var. inermis** DC. Shoots without thorns. For the "Mop-head Acacia" grown under this name see 'Umbraculifera'.

**'Microphylla'** ('Angustifolia') A small to medium-sized, slow-growing tree with dainty, small, fern-like leaves with small leaflets; flowers rarely produced while young.

**'Monophylla'** See 'Unifoliola'.

**'Monophylla Fastigiata'** ('Erecta') A medium-sized tree of narrow, upright habit, leaves with 1-3 leaflets.

**'Pyramidalis'** ('Fastigiata') A slender, columnar tree of medium size, with spineless, closely erect branches. C 1843.

**'Rehderi'** A large bush or small bushy tree with rather erect, spineless branches. Raised in 1859.

**'Rozynskyana'** An elegant and beautiful, large shrub or small spreading tree, the branches drooping at their tips and bearing large, drooping leaves. C 1903.

**'Semperflorens'** Flowers produced intermittently throughout summer. C 1874.

**'Tortuosa'** A picturesque, slow-growing, small to medium-sized tree with somewhat contorted branches.

**'Umbraculifera'** A small tree with a compact, rounded head of spineless branches. A commonly planted street tree, but requires protection from strong winds. Flowers are rarely produced. Usually grown as 'Inermis'. C 1811.

**'Unifoliola'** ('Monophylla') A curious form with leaves reduced to a single large leaflet or accompanied by 1 or 2 normal-sized leaflets. Raised about 1855.

×**slavinii** REHD. This hybrid was first raised in the United States in 1914. The following form was raised in our nurseries in about 1930.

**'Hillieri'** (*R.* ×*hillieri* HORT.) (*R. kelseyi* × *R. pseudoacacia*). An elegant, small tree with delicate foliage, developing a rounded head of branches. Flowers slightly fragrant, lilac-pink in June. An excellent tree for the small garden. AM 1962.

**viscosa** VENT. "Clammy Locust". A small tree, occasionally to 12m, with characteristic viscid young shoots and leaf-stalks. Flowers in short racemes towards the end of June, pale rose, stained yellow on the standard. SE United States. I 1791.

**"ROCK ROSE"** See *Helianthemum* and *Cistus*.

**ROMNEYA** HARV.—**Papaveraceae**—The "Tree Poppies" or "Matilija Poppies" include 2 species of sub-shrubby, Californian perennials with glaucous stems and deeply cut leaves, producing large, white, poppy-like flowers with a central mass of golden yellow stamens. Sometimes difficult to establish, but once settled they spread quickly by underground stems (rhizomes). Best in a warm, sunny position.

**coulteri** HARV. Small to medium-sized perennial bearing large, solitary, fragrant flowers, 10-15cm across, from July to October. Flower buds smooth, slightly conical and somewhat beaked. I 1875. FCC 1888. AGM 1984.

×**hybrida** HORT. See *R.* 'White Cloud'.

**trichocalyx** EASTW. Closely resembling *R. coulteri*, but stems more slender, peduncles leafy, buds bristly and rounded, not beaked. Some plants grown as *R. coulteri* belong here.

**'White Cloud'** (*R.* ×*hybrida* 'White Cloud') (*R. coulteri* × *R. trichocalyx*). A strong-growing, large-flowered hybrid of American origin.

**ROSA** L.—**Rosaceae**—The wild "Rose" species possess a beauty and charm rarely to be found in the vast assemblage of today's popular garden hybrids. Indeed their often graceful elegance, plus their floral and fruiting qualities, are a refreshing change from the comparatively vivid blowsiness of many Hybrid Tea and Floribunda roses. Not that the species are without colour. Their flowers vary from the most delicate pastels, to reds and scarlets of exceptional brilliance, and colourful fruits bring a welcome bonus which sometimes lasts well into winter, brightening the doleful days which follow Christmas. Their leaves are normally pinnate and deciduous and their stems armed with prickles. There are about 100 species mainly in N temperate regions.

They are of the easiest cultivation, thriving in most soils except those which are wet and acid. Most flower better when planted in full sun and the more ornamental species react favourably to an annual or bi-annual manuring.

The species and hybrids here described range in habit from trailing, or low, suckering shrubs (excellent as ground cover) to large shrubs and tall climbers. The more vigorous shrubs are best planted as isolated specimens in lawns or borders, whilst the climbing species are useful for training over fences, pergolas, against walls and into trees.

Pruning. Once established the species require very little pruning, except to remove dead wood or to thin out dense and overcrowded specimens which threaten to destroy their support. This may be carried out immediately after flowering unless fruits are expected, in which case prune in February.

We record our appreciation of the work done in popularising these roses by Graham Thomas, author of several books on the subject, which we have freely consulted.

**acicularis** LINDL. A small, vigorous shrub rarely above 1.3m high, with densely bristly stems and leaves with 5-9 sea-green leaflets. Flowers 5-6cm across, bright rose-pink; fruits 2.5cm long, pear-shaped, bright rose. North America, N Europe, NE Asia, Japan. I 1805.

**'Agnes'** (*R. foetida* 'Persiana' × *R. rugosa*). An erect shrub of Canadian origin, with arching branches and densely arranged, bright green leaves. The amber-tinted, double, butter-yellow flowers are deliciously and intriguingly scented. C 1922. AM 1951.

× **alba** L. The "White Rose of York". A medium-sized shrub with strong, prickly stems. Leaves with 5-7 broad, greyish-green leaflets. Flowers 7.5cm across, white, usually semi-double, richly scented; fruits oblong, red. The origin of this famous rose is still a source of argument. Its hybrid origin is generally agreed and probably involves *R. gallica*, *R. arvensis* and a relative of *R. canina*. It is known to have been in cultivation since before 1600 and research by the late Dr C.C. Hurst confirms the opinions of those who claim that it was grown by the Greeks and Romans. During the Wars of the Roses it was traditionally adopted as an emblem by the Yorkists. It is the type of a group of old hybrids and in one or more of its forms is cultivated in SE Europe for Attar of Roses.

**'Albert Edwards'** (*R. hugonis* × *R. pimpinellifolia* 'Grandiflora'). A medium-sized shrub, the arching branches wreathed in May with fragrant lemon-yellow flowers 5-6cm across. A choice hybrid raised in our Sarum Road nursery, Winchester in about 1938 and named after our then Rose-Foreman.

**alpina** See *R. pendulina*.

**'Andersonii'** A medium-sized, strong-growing shrub with arching, prickly stems and leaves with usually 5 long-pointed leaflets, downy beneath. Flowers 5-7.5cm across, rich, clear, rose-pink, scented, freely produced and showy over a long period. Fruits urn-shaped, scarlet, similar to those of the "Dog Rose" (*R. canina*). A hybrid of unknown origin possibly *R. canina* × *R. gallica*. C 1912.

**anemoniflora** FORT. ex LINDL. (*R. triphylla* REHD. & WILS. not ROXB. ex LINDL.) A rambling or climbing shrub, the leaves with 3-5 leaflets. Flowers 2.5-4cm across, double and anemone-like, blush-white. Introduced from a garden in Shanghai by Robert Fortune in 1844. It is not known in the wild and is most probably a hybrid of the group *R. banksiae*, *R. laevigata*, *R. multiflora*. It is subject to frost damage and is best grown against a sunny wall.

**'Anemonoides'** (*R. laevigata* 'Anemonoides') A lovely rose, a hybrid of *R. laevigata* with a Tea Rose, producing over several weeks single, 10cm wide, silver-pink flowers shaded

**ROSA 'Anemonoides'**—*continued*

rose, like a pink 'Mermaid'. Garden origin about 1895. AM 1900. Less vigorous than *R. laevigata*, but requiring similar conditions.

**"Apothecary's Rose"** See *R. gallica* var. *officinalis*.

**arkansana** PORTER "Arkansas Rose". A small, densely-prickly shrub usually less than 1m high. Leaves with 5-11 leaflets. Flowers 3-4cm across, pink, followed by small, globular red fruits. C United States. C 1917.

**'Arthur Hillier'** (*R. macrophylla* × *R. moyesii*). A vigorous, large shrub with semi-erect branches. The multitudes of large, rose-crimson flowers in June and July are followed in autumn by conspicuous, bright red, flask-shaped fruits. Occurred in our Sarum Road nursery, Winchester, in about 1938. AM 1977.

**arvensis** HUDS. "Field Rose". A trailing or climbing species forming dense mounds or drapes of slender stems. Leaves with 5-7 shining green leaflets persisting late into winter. Flowers 4-5cm across, white, with little or no fragrance, appearing in July; fruits rounded or oval, dark red. A common native species of woodlands and hedgerows. Europe.

**'Splendens'** "Myrrh-scented Rose". A charming form, or possibly a hybrid, with long-persisting leaves. The small, double, soft pink flowers are scented of myrrh.

**"Austrian Briar"** See *R. foetida*.

**"Austrian Copper"** See *R. foetida* 'Bicolor'.

**"Austrian Yellow"** See *R. foetida*.

**banksiae** R. BR. "Banksian Rose" "Lady Banks' Rose". A tall-growing, vigorous, semi-evergreen climber reaching 7.5m or above in a suitable position. The slender shoots are thornless or nearly so and the leaves are composed of 3-5 leaflets. This beautiful and well-known rose and its several forms do not flower when young. They thrive best on a warm wall in full sun which is needed to ripen growths. Plants grown in cold areas or in shady positions elsewhere are liable to frost damage which reduces, if not prevents, flowering. Named (from 'Alba Plena') after Lady Banks, wife of Sir Joseph Banks, one of the greatest-ever Directors of the Royal Botanic Garden, Kew.

**'Alba Plena'** Flowers 3cm across, double and rosette-like, white and delicately fragrant of violets, borne in densely-packed umbels during May and June. Introduced to Kew from a garden in Canton, China, by William Kerr in 1807.

**'Lutea'** "Yellow Banksian". Flowers double yellow, rosette-like. A few sensitive noses are reputed to detect in this beautiful rose a delicate fragrance. It was introduced from China via the Calcutta Botanic Garden by J.D. Parks some time before 1824. AM 1960.

**'Lutescens'** Flowers single, yellow, sweetly fragrant. I before 1870.

**'Normalis'** Flowers single, creamy-white, sweetly fragrant. The wild form, said to have been introduced to Megginch Castle, Strathtay, Scotland, by Robert Drummond in 1796. It remained in obscurity until 1909 when E.H. Woodall, who had four years previously obtained cuttings, flowered it in his garden in Nice. Ernest Wilson has described his finding of this plant in C and W China, where it is abundant in glens and ravines, forming tangled masses on low trees and scrub.

**"Banksian Rose"** See *R. banksiae*.

**banksiopsis** BAK. A vigorous, medium-sized shrub with leaves composed of 7-9 leaflets. Flowers 2.5cm across, rose-red, borne in corymbs and followed by flask-shaped, orange-red fruits. W China. I 1907 by Ernest Wilson.

**bella** REHD. & WILS. An attractive, small to medium-sized shrub with slender-spined stems and leaves with 7-9, small, glaucescent leaflets. The bright, cherry-red flowers 3-4cm across are slightly fragrant and appear singly or in clusters along the branches in June. Fruits small, orange-scarlet. N China. I 1910.

**biebersteinii** LINDL. (*R. horrida* FISCH.) (*R. ferox* BIEB.) A dwarf, dense shrub with rigid, prickly stems. Leaves small, composed of 5-7 rounded, coarsely-toothed leaflets. The white flowers 2.5-4cm across are followed by globose, red fruits. The curious nature of this species reminds one of a small gooseberry bush. SE Europe, W Asia. I 1796.

**blanda** AIT. "Smooth Rose" "Meadow Rose". A small shrub with nearly thornless stems and leaves with 5-7, pale green leaflets. Flowers 6-7.5cm across, rose-pink. Fruits small, globular or pear-shaped, red. North America. I 1773.

**ROSA**—*continued*

**'Blanc Double de Coubert'** (*R. rugosa* 'Blanc Double de Coubert') A hybrid of *R. rugosa* with more open, taller growth. Flowers semi-double, white, blush-tinted in bud. Garden origin in 1892. AM 1895. AGM 1984.

†**\*bracteata** WENDL. "Macartney Rose". A medium-sized to large evergreen shrub with rambling stems which are thick and stout and clothed with prickles and dense brownish down. Leaves deep green, composed of 5-11 closely set shining leaflets. Flowers 7.5-10cm across, lemon-scented, white, with attractive golden anthers; each head surrounded by conspicuous leaf-like bracts. Fruits globose, orange-red. A most ornamental species, requiring a warm, sunny, sheltered wall. SE China, Taiwan. I 1795 by Lord Macartney.

**brunonii** LINDL. (*R. moschata* HORT. not HERRM.) "Himalayan Musk Rose". A rampant climbing species reaching 9-12m on a building or tree. Leaves limp, composed of 5-7, narrow, sea-green leaflets. (Plants found in E Nepal, 1972, possess glossy, dark green leaflets.) The richly fragrant, white flowers, 2.5-5cm across are carried in tight, downy-stalked corymbs; June and July. This vigorous species thrives best in full sun and a warm climate. Often wrongly grown in cultivation as *R. moschata*. Himalaya. I 1822.

**'Betty Sherriff'** A very vigorous form. Flowers reddish-pink in bud opening white flushed pink towards the tips of the petals. Probably introduced from Bhutan by Ludlow and Sherriff in 1949. AM 1985.

**'La Mortola'** (*R. moschata* 'La Mortola') A superb hardier selection raised at the celebrated Hanbury garden, La Mortola in Italy. Its leaves are larger and more greyish-downy and the larger pure white flowers are borne in more ample clusters. Richly fragrant. It requires a sheltered position and full sun to ripen growth.

**"Burgundian Rose"** See *R.* 'Parvifolia'.

**"Burnet Rose"** See *R. pimpinellifolia*.

**"Burr Rose"** See *R. roxburghii*.

**"Cabbage Rose"** See *R. centifolia*.

**"Cabbage Rose, Crested"** See *R. centifolia* 'Cristata'.

**californica** CHAM. & SCHLECHT. A medium-sized shrub with stout-prickled stems and leaves composed of 5-7 leaflets. Flowers 3cm across, pink, borne in corymbs. Fruits globose, usually with a prominent neck, red. W United States. C 1878.

**'Plena'** A most attractive, free-flowering form bearing corymbs of semi-double, rich dark pink flowers fading to rose and purple. AM 1958. AGM 1984.

**'Canary Bird'** A beautiful shrub of medium size with arching stems and fresh green, small, fern-like leaves. The bright canary-yellow flowers wreathe the branches during late May and early June. The parents of this hybrid are almost certainly *R. hugonis* × *R. xanthina*.

**canina** L. "Dog Rose". A familiar native rose of hedgebanks and downs. A medium-sized to large shrub with strong prickly stems and leaves with 5-7 leaflets. Flowers 4-5cm across, white or pink, scented, followed by bright red, egg-shaped fruits. Perhaps the most variable of all roses, countless varieties and subspecies having received names. Europe, W Asia.

**'Cantabrigiensis'** (*R. hugonis* × *R. sericea*). A medium-sized shrub with densely bristly, arching stems and fragrant, fern-like leaves composed of 7-11 leaflets. Flowers 5cm across, soft yellow, passing to cream. A lovely hybrid raised in the University of Cambridge Botanic Garden. AM and Cory Cup 1931. AGM 1984.

**carolina** L. A small, suckering shrub forming dense thickets of erect stems. Leaves composed of 5-7 leaflets. The fragrant, rose-pink flowers 5-6cm across, are produced in clusters from June to August. Fruits orange-shaped, red and glandular hairy. E North America. C 1732.

**centifolia** L. "Cabbage Rose" "Provence Rose". A small shrub with erect prickly stems and fragrant leaves with 5-7, broadly oval leaflets. Flowers large, double, rose-pink and richly fragrant. *R. centifolia* or a form of it is also known as the "Rose des Peintres" in recognition of its association with the old Dutch painters. The cabbage rose had long been regarded as the most ancient of roses until the late Dr C.C. Hurst proved otherwise. It appeared in its present familiar form in the 18th century. Dr Hurst further proved that it was born of complex hybrid origin in which the following species played a part, *R. canina*, *R. gallica*, *R. moschata* and *R. phoenicea*. There are many forms of *R. centifolia* and it is a parent of numerous hybrids.

**ROSA centifolia**—*continued*

**'Cristata'** "Crested Cabbage Rose" "Crested Moss". A charming form in which the sepals are beautifully crested to such an extent that the flower buds are completely enveloped. Flowers large, rosy-pink. Said to have been found in the crevice of a wall at Fribourg, Switzerland, in 1820.

**'Muscosa'** (*R. muscosa* AIT.) "Moss Rose". Differs in the dense, moss-like, glandular-bristly covering of the stems, branches, petioles, flower-stalks and calyx tubes. This unusual and characteristic clothing is sticky to the touch and gives off a resinous or balsam-like odour when bruised. The clear pink, globular, double flowers later open flat and are richly scented. C 1720.

**'Parvifolia'** See *R.* 'Parvifolia'.

**'Cherokee Rose'** See *R. laevigata*.

**'China Rose'** See *R. chinensis*.

**chinensis** JACQ. (*R. indica* AIT. f. not L.) "China Rose". A small to medium-sized shrub with stout branches and leaves with 3-5 shining green leaflets. Flowers 5cm across, crimson or pink, occasionally white, appearing continuously from June to September. Fruits scarlet, obovoid. This rose more than any other holds claim to being the ancestor of most of our modern garden hybrids. It was first introduced in the late 1700s and early 1800s in several garden forms and not until about 1900 was the wild form discovered in C China by Dr Augustine Henry.

**'Minima'** "Miss Lawrence's Rose". A miniature shrub up to 15cm high, bearing small leaves and small, single, pink flowers, 2-3cm across.

**'Mutabilis'** See *R.* × *odorata* 'Mutabilis'.

**'Old Blush'** The "Monthly Rose" is an old favourite of compact habit and small to medium size. Flowers scented of sweet peas, pink with darker veins, deepening with age. They are produced over a very long period and after a mild autumn may even be present at Christmas.

**'Viridiflora'** The so-called "Green Rose". A curious small shrub with double flowers consisting of numerous crowded, greenish, petal-like scales. Said to have been in cultivation as early as 1743.

**cinnamomea** See *R. majalis*.

**'Complicata'** A lovely, medium-sized shrub which will, if allowed, clamber into small trees, or cover fences and hedges. The multitudes of very large, clear, deep peach-pink, white-eyed flowers are delicately fragrant. A flowering shrub of unsurpassed beauty, a hybrid of *R. gallica*. AM 1951. FCC 1958. AGM 1984.

**'Coryana'** A strong-growing, medium-sized shrub resembling *R. roxburghii*, of which it is a seedling, the other parent being possibly *R. macrophylla*. Flowers 5-6cm across, deep pink appearing in June. Raised at the University Botanic Garden, Cambridge in 1926 and named after Mr Reginald Cory.

**corymbifera** BORKH. (*R. dumetorum* THUILL.) A medium-sized shrub with stout-prickled stems and leaves with 5-9, hairy leaflets. Flowers 4-5cm across, white or pale pink; fruits ovoid, orange-red. Closely related to *R. canina*, but differing mainly in its rather more sea-green, hairy leaves. Europe, W Asia, N Africa. C 1838.

**corymbulosa** ROLFE A small shrub with erect or somewhat climbing, almost spineless stems and leaves with 3-5 downy leaflets, which often turn reddish-purple beneath in autumn. Flowers 4-5cm across, rose-pink with a whitish eye. Fruits globose, coral-red. C and W China. I 1908.

**damascena** MILL. "Damask Rose". A small shrub with densely thorny stems and greyish-green leaves with 5-7 leaflets. Flowers large, usually in corymbs, fragrant, varying in colour from white to red, followed by obovoid, red, bristle-clad fruits. An ancient rose probably of garden origin in Asia Minor, introduced to Europe in the 16th century. Its petals are used in the perfume industry, particularly those of 'Trigintipetala', which are used more than any other in the production of Attar of Roses in Bulgaria. It is represented in cultivation by numerous named forms and hybrids.

That distinguished geneticist and rosarian, the late Dr C.C. Hurst, regarded the damask rose as being of hybrid origin. He further regarded it as constituting two distinct

**ROSA damascena**—*continued*

groups, i.e. *R. damascena* MILL., the "Summer Damask" (*R. gallica* × *R. phoenicea*) and *R.* × *bifera* (POIR.) PERS. (*R. damascena* var. *semperflorens*), the "Autumn Damask" (*R. gallica* × *R. moschata*).

'**Trigintipetala**' A form with rather small, loosely double flowers of a soft pink, richly scented.

'**Versicolor**' "York and Lancaster Rose". An unusual form with loosely-double flowers which are white, irregularly but lightly flaked pink or blotched rose. Often confused with *R. gallica* 'Versicolor'. Cultivated prior to 1629.

"**Damask Rose**" See *R. damascena*.

**davidii** CREP. A strong-growing, medium-sized shrub of erect, open habit. Leaves composed of 7-9, conspicuously veined leaflets. Flowers 4-5cm across, bright rose-pink, carried in large, many-flowered corymbs. The ovoid, scarlet, pendulous fruits have a distinctly long neck. Originally discovered in W Sichuan, China, by the great French missionary and naturalist Armand David, it was later introduced by E.H. Wilson in 1903. AM 1929.

'**Acicularis**' (*R. persetosa* ROLFE) (*R. davidii* var. *persetosa* (ROLFE) BOULENGER) An attractive, medium-sized shrub with densely-bristly stems and leaves with 5-9 leaflets. Flowers pink, 2-3cm across, borne in corymbs, followed by red fruits. I 1895.

var. **elongata** REHD. & WILS. A variety with rather longer leaflets, fewer flowers and larger fruits. W China. I 1908.

'**Glaucescens**' (*R. macrophylla* 'Glaucescens') (Forrest 14958) In this form the flowers are rose-purple and the leaves conspicuously glaucous on both surfaces. The leaflets are more narrowly elliptic than those of 'Rubricaulis'. The stems are also glaucous. A form of var. *elongata*. I 1917.

var. **persetosa** See 'Acicularis'.

'**Rubricaulis**' (*R. macrophylla* 'Rubricaulis') (Forrest 15309) A very distinct form which is conspicuous by its red stems overlaid with a plum-like bloom. The peduncles, petioles, bracts and primary veins are also usually red. The flowers have more lilac-blue in them than those of the type and the plant is noticeably glaucous. It is unfortunate that this distinct form is less hardy than the type. A form of var. *elongata*. I 1917.

"**Dog Rose**" See *R. canina*.

**dumetorum** See *R. corymbifera*.

'**Dupontii**' (*R. moschata* var. *nivea* (DUPONT) LINDL.) A strong-growing, medium-sized shrub of loose habit, sometimes needing a little support, with leaves composed of 3-7 leaflets, downy beneath. Flowers large, fragrant, 7.5cm across, blush, passing to creamy-white, borne in corymbose clusters in July. A magnificent rose of hybrid origin possibly *R. gallica* crossed with *R. moschata* or one of its old hybrids. C 1817. AM 1954.

'**Earldomensis**' (*R. hugonis* × *R. sericea* f. *pteracantha*). A quite distinct and pleasing, medium-sized, rather wide-spreading shrub with conspicuously flattened reddish thorns, small fern-like leaves and canary-yellow flowers in early June.

**ecae** AITCH. A small shrub of dainty appearance and comparatively compact, with very prickly, slender, arching, dark chestnut-brown branches. The small leaves 2-2.5cm long are composed of 5-9 oval leaflets. The small, buttercup-yellow flowers 2.5cm across are borne all along the branches during late May and June. Fruits small, globular, red. Afghanistan. Introduced by Dr Aitchison in 1880 and named after his wife, using her initials E.C.A. AM 1933.

'**Helen Knight**' See *R.* 'Helen Knight'.

**eglanteria** L. (*R. rubiginosa* L.) "Sweet Briar" "Eglantine". A strong-growing, medium-sized shrub with stout, erect, densely prickly and glandular stems. The deliciously aromatic leaves are composed of 5-7 rounded leaflets and the clear pink, fragrant, beautifully formed flowers, 3-4cm across, stud the arching branches during summer. Fruits bright red, oval, lasting well into winter. A lovely native species famed for its fragrance both of flower and foliage. It makes a pleasant if vigorous hedge. Europe. It is a parent of innumerable hybrids and has given rise to several hundred forms, few of which are now in cultivation. AM 1975.

"**Eglantine**" See *R. eglanteria*.

**elegantula** ROLFE (*R. farreri* STAPF ex STEARN) A charming species up to 2m high, with spreading branches and dainty fern-like leaves composed of 7-9 leaflets. The pale pink or white flowers, 2-2.5cm across, in June are followed by bright coral-red ovoid fruits

**ROSA elegantula**—*continued*

which are effectively set against the purple and crimson autumn foliage. Introduced from S Gansu (China) in 1915 by Reginald Farrer, one of the greatest and most descriptive of horticultural writers.

**'Persetosa'** "Threepenny-bit Rose". The form in general cultivation, originally selected from a batch of Farrer's seedlings by that great gardener and plantsman, E.A. Bowles. It differs in its smaller leaves and smaller flowers which are coral-red in bud opening soft pink.

**ernestii** See *R. rubus*.

**fargesii** See *R. moyesii* 'Fargesii'.

**farreri** See *R. elegantula*.

**var. persetosa** See *R. elegantula* 'Persetosa'.

**fedtschenkoana** REGEL An erect-growing, medium-sized shrub with sea-green leaves composed of 5-7 leaflets. The white flowers, 5cm across, are produced continuously throughout summer. These are replaced by orange-red, bristly, pear-shaped fruits. An interesting and ornamental species with distinctive foliage. Turkestan.

**filipes** REHD. & WILS. A strong-growing, rambling or climbing species forming large curtains over suitable support. Leaves with 5-7 leaflets. The fragrant, white flowers, 2.5cm across, are borne in large panicles in late June and July. Fruits globose, red. W China. Introduced by E.H. Wilson in 1908.

**'Kiftsgate'** An extremely vigorous clone with light green foliage, which is richly copper-tinted when young. Its panicles may contain as many as a hundred or more sweetly-scented flowers, and it is almost as spectacular when bearing its numerous small, red fruits. It should be grown wherever space allows. C 1938.

**foetida** HERRM. (*R. lutea* MILL.) "Austrian Yellow" "Austrian Briar". A small shrub with erect, slender, prickly chestnut-brown stems and bright green leaves composed of 5-9 leaflets. Flowers rich yellow, 5-6cm across. Plant in full sun and in a well drained site. Cultivated since the 16th century this species and its forms has figured in the ancestry of many of our modern garden roses. Though naturalised in S and C Europe (including Austria), it is a native of SW Asia.

**'Bicolor'** "Austrian Copper". A remarkably beautiful plant requiring plenty of sun and a good, rich, well-drained soil. The flowers are brilliant coppery-red, with brilliant yellow reverse. Very rarely completely yellow flowers are produced on the same bush. Cultivated since at least 1590.

**'Persiana'** "Persian Yellow Rose". A beautiful form with golden yellow, double flowers. First introduced to the West in 1837, it has since been used as a parent for innumerable garden hybrids.

**foliolosa** TORR. & A. GRAY A low-growing, suckering shrub rarely exceeding 1m in height. Leaves with 7-9 narrow, glossy green leaflets. Flowers fragrant, bright pink, 4-5cm across, appearing usually in late July and continuing often into September. Fruits orange-shaped, red. Often good autumn colour. SE United States. C 1888.

**forrestiana** BOULENGER A strong-growing, medium-sized shrub with arching stems up to 2m. Leaves with 5-7 oval or rounded leaflets. The rose-crimson, strongly fragrant flowers, 3-4cm across, are borne in clusters surrounded by leafy bracts. These are followed by equally attractive pillar-box-red, bottle-shaped fruits, which appear like highly coloured nuts encircled by the persistent green bracts. W China. I 1918 by George Forrest.

**"Fortune's Double Yellow"** See *R.* ×*odorata* 'Fortune's Double Yellow'.

×**fortuneana** LINDL. A tall-growing climber, reputedly a hybrid between *R. banksiae* and *R. laevigata*. It resembles the former in general appearance, but differs in its larger leaflets and bristly pedicels. The flowers, too, are larger, 6-7.5cm across, double and white. This rose seldom flowers with sufficient freedom to be conspicuous. It requires a south-facing, sunny wall. Introduced from Chinese gardens by Robert Fortune in 1850.

**'Fru Dagmar Hastrup'** A hybrid of *R. rugosa* making a compact shrub up to 1.8m with lush dark green foliage and flowers of a pale rose-pink, with cream coloured stamens. Large crops of rich crimson fruits. Makes an excellent hedge. Garden origin 1914. AM 1958. AGM 1984.

**gallica** L. (*R. rubra* LAM.) "French Rose". A small, suckering shrub with erect, slender stems densely covered with prickles and bristles, and leaves composed of 3-7 leaflets. Flowers

**ROSA gallica**—*continued*

deep pink, 5-7cm across, followed by rounded or top-shaped, brick-red fruits. A native of C and S Europe, but cultivated in one form or another from time immemorial. It is a parent of countless hybrids and is the probable ancestor of the modern garden rose in Europe.

**var. officinalis** THORY The "Apothecary's Rose", also known as the "Red Rose of Lancaster". A small shrub producing richly fragrant, semi-double, rosy-crimson flowers, with prominent yellow anthers. An old rose known in cultivation since at least 1310. Its petals retain their fragrance even when dried and powdered and gave rise to a once important industry in preserves and confections. The centre of this industry was the town of Provins in France where the apothecaries were instrumental in its development. Sometimes referred to as the "Old Red Damask".

**'Versicolor'** ('Rosa Mundi') An old and well-loved rose which arose as a branch sport of the "Apothecary's Rose". Flowers semi-double, usually rose-red, striped white, and carrying a few entirely red blossoms. Some seasons all the flowers may be of a self red. AM 1961. AGM 1984. Sometimes confused with *R. damascena* 'Versicolor', the "York and Lancaster Rose".

**gigantea** COLLETT (*R. odorata* var. *gigantea* (CREP.) REHD.) A vigorous, tall-growing, semi-evergreen climber. Leaves with 5-7 leaflets. Flowers white, 5-7.5cm across, fragrant followed by globose, bright red fruits. SW China, Burma. I 1889.

**'Cooperi'** See *R. laevigata* 'Cooperi'.

**giraldii** CREP. A strong-growing, medium-sized shrub with leaves composed of 7-9 leaflets. Flowers pink, 1.5-2.5cm across, followed by globular or ovoid, red fruits. N and C China. C 1897.

**glauca** POURR. (*R. rubrifolia* VILL.) A most useful and ornamental species, forming a medium-sized shrub with reddish-violet, almost thornless stems. The great attraction of this rose is its foliage, which is a glaucous purple in a sunny position and greyish-green, with a mauve tinge, when in shade. Flowers clear pink, 2.5-5cm across, followed by ovoid, red fruits. Invaluable for coloured foliage schemes. Mts of C and S Europe. C before 1830. AM 1949. AGM 1984.

**'Golden Chersonese'** (*R.* 'Canary Bird' × *R. ecae*). A beautiful shrub of medium size, with slender arching stems and delightful, small, frond-like leaves. The deep buttercup-yellow flowers are sweetly-scented, wreathing the branches during late May. Raised in 1963 by the distinguished rosarian E.F. Allen who kindly permitted us to be the first distributors under Licence Grant No. 269 (Plant Breeders Rights). It was awarded an AM at the Chelsea Show of 1966.

**"Green Rose"** See *R. chinensis* 'Viridiflora'.

× **hardii** CELS (*R. clinophylla* × *R. persica*) (× *Hulthemosa hardii* (CELS) ROWLEY) One of the most remarkable and beautiful of all roses. A small to medium-sized shrub with slender stems and leaves composed of 1-7 oblanceolate leaflets. Flowers 5cm across, yellow, with a red blotch at the base of each petal. Requires a warm, sunny position and perfect drainage; ideal for a sunny, south-facing wall, or sprawling over rock in a scree garden. A difficult plant to establish. Garden origin, Paris in 1836.

**'Harisonii'** (*R. lutea* var. *hoggii* D. DON) "Harison's Yellow" "Hogg's Double Yellow". A small, free-flowering shrub occasionally reaching 2m. A hybrid of *R. pimpinellifolia*, probably with *R. foetida*. It bears brilliant yellow, semi-double flowers which possess a similar odour to those of *R. foetida*. These are followed by small blackish fruits. Raised by George Harison of New York in 1830. AM 1949.

**'Headleyensis'** A vigorous but graceful, medium-sized shrub, thought to be the hybrid (*R. hugonis* × *R. pimpinellifolia* 'Grandiflora'). Leaves neat and fern-like. The primrose-yellow, fragrant flowers are carried along the arching branches in May. Garden origin about 1922. Raised by that distinguished botanist and amateur gardener Sir Oscar Warburg.

**'Helen Knight'** (*R. ecae* × *R. pimpinellifolia* 'Grandiflora') Similar to *R. ecae* but reaching a larger size with larger flowers. Raised at Wisley in 1966.

**helenae** REHD. & WILS. A vigorous rambling or climbing species reaching 6m or more in a tree. Leaves with 7-9 leaflets. The creamy-white, fragrant flowers 2-4cm across are borne in dense corymbs in June and are followed in autumn by large, drooping bunches of

**ROSA helenae**—*continued*

narrowly ovoid, orange-red fruits. W and C China. Introduced by Ernest Wilson in 1907 and named after his wife, Helen.

**hemisphaerica** HERRM. (*R. sulphurea* AIT.) (*R. glaucophylla* EHRH.) The "Sulphur Rose" is a rare, medium-sized shrub of rather loose growth requiring a little support. The leaves are composed of 5-9 sea-green leaflets. Flowers double, sulphur-yellow and sweetly-scented, 5cm across. This beautiful rose does best when given a warm, sheltered wall and even then it only flowers well during a warm summer. W Asia. C before 1625.

**hemsleyana** TACKHOLM A vigorous, medium-sized shrub related to *R. setipoda*, with leaves composed of 7-9 leaflets. Flowers rose-pink, 4-5cm across, in several-flowered corymbs, followed by hispid, bottle-shaped, red fruits. C China. I 1904.

×**hibernica** SM. (*R. corymbifera* × *R. pimpinellifolia*). A vigorous, medium-sized shrub producing delightful, clear, bright shell-pink flowers 5cm across, followed by globose, red fruits. First found near Belfast in 1802.

**'Highdownensis'** A medium-sized shrub resembling in general appearance *R. moyesii*, of which it is a seedling. The dainty leaves are somewhat glaucous beneath. Flowers 6cm across, light velvety crimson, with a ring of pale buff anthers, freely borne on the stout, semi-erect branches. Fruits flagon-shaped, orange-scarlet. Raised by that great amateur gardener the late Sir Frederick Stern at Highdown, nr Goring, Sussex, before 1925. AM 1928. AGM 1984.

**'Hillieri'** (*R.* ×*pruhoniciana* 'Hillieri') A very beautiful rose, a seedling of *R. moyesii* raised in our nurseries in about 1924. It resembles *R. willmottiae* in its elegant habit, whilst its flowers recall those of *R. moyesii*, but of a darker shade of crimson. It is perhaps the darkest coloured of all single roses.

**hispida** See *R. pimpinellifolia* 'Hispida'.

**horrida** See *R. biebersteinii*.

**hugonis** HEMSL. (*R. xanthina* CREP. not LINDL.) A very graceful shrub up to 2m. The long, arching branches are clothed with neat, fern-like leaves composed of 5-11 fresh green leaflets, often becoming bronze-hued in autumn. By mid-May the branches are wreathed with hundreds of soft yellow flowers, 5cm across. These are followed by small, rounded, dark red fruits. Deservedly the most popular single yellow rose. It may be used to make a most delightful, informal hedge. C China. I 1899. AM 1917. AGM 1925.

**'Flore Pleno'** Flowers double. Not so graceful a plant as the single form.

**indica** See *R. chinensis*.

**jundzillii** BESSER (*R. marginata* AUCT. not WALLR.) A vigorous, erect shrub of medium size with few prickled stems and leaves composed of 5-11 glandular-toothed leaflets. Flowers 5-7.5cm across, pink changing to white, followed by dark scarlet fruits. W Asia. C 1870. AM 1964.

**"Lady Banks' Rose"** See *R. banksiae*.

**'Lady Penzance'** (*R.* ×*penzanceana* REHD.) (*R. foetida* 'Bicolor' × *R. eglanteria*). A medium-sized shrub with arching branches, fragrant leaves and single flowers which are copper-tinted, with bright yellow centres. AM 1891.

**laevigata** MICHX. (*R. sinica* AIT. not L.) "Cherokee Rose". A strong-growing, semi-evergreen rambler or climber with beautiful, dark glossy green leaves composed of 3 coarsely-toothed, glabrous leaflets. Flowers white, fragrant, 7.5-10cm across, borne singly on bristly stalks during late May and June. Fruits large and bristly. An attractive species with impressive foliage. Requires a warm, sheltered wall. A native of China, but long naturalised in the S United States where the common name arose. AM 1954.

**'Anemonoides'** See *R.* 'Anemonoides'.

**'Cooperi'** (*R. gigantea* 'Cooperi') "Cooper's Burmese Rose". A beautiful rose reaching 12m in a suitable position. Flowers large, slightly fragrant, pure white, occasionally with a pink stain and with golden anthers. Best grown against a south-facing wall. I 1921.

**latibracteata** BOULENGER A medium-sized shrub which has been confused with *R. multibracteata* from which it differs in its larger, cherry-pink flowers, 4cm across, carried in many-flowered corymbs. The conspicuous leafy flower bracts are three times the size of those of *R. multibracteata*. The leaves, sepals and thorns are also distinctly larger. W China. I 1936.

**ROSA**—*continued*

**longicuspis** BERTOL. (*R. lucens* ROLFE) A remarkable, semi-evergreen rambler or climber of rampant growth. Leaves 12-28cm long, composed of 5-9 slender-pointed, glabrous, dark glossy green leaflets. The white, banana-scented flowers, 5cm across, are borne in large terminal panicles. Fruits ovoid, scarlet or orange-red. A distinguished species with bold foliage and polished, dark reddish-brown shoots and copper-tinted young growths. E Nepal, NE India and W China. C 1915. AM 1964. AGM 1984. Often confused with the closely related and similar *R. sinowilsonii*.

**lucida** See *R. virginiana*.

**lutea** See *R. foetida*.

**'Lutea Maxima'** (*R. pimpinellifolia* 'Lutea') One of the best single yellow roses. A small shrub with few scattered thorns and bright green foliage, amongst which the buttercup-yellow flowers, 5cm across, nestle. Probably a hybrid between *R. pimpinellifolia* and *R. foetida*.

**lutescens** See *R. pimpinellifolia* 'Hispida'.

**"Macartney Rose"** See *R. bracteata*.

**'Macrantha'** A small, variable, wide-spreading shrub with prickly, arching branches neatly set with conspicuously-veined leaves composed of 5-7 leaflets. Flowers large, 7-10cm across, pink in bud opening clear almond-pink, changing to almost white, deliciously fragrant and with conspicuous stamens. Fruits rounded, red. A magnificent rose of mound-like habit with loose, often procumbent stems, ideal for clothing banks, covering stumps, etc. A hybrid of uncertain origin. C 1888.

**macrophylla** LINDL. A vigorous, distinctive, medium-sized to large shrub with large leaves composed of 5-11 leaflets. Flowers 5-7.5cm across, bright cerise-pink, carried singly or in clusters of 2-3. Fruits pear-shaped, glandular-bristly, bright red. Himalaya. I 1818. AM 1897.

**'Glaucescens'** See *R. davidii* 'Glaucescens'.

**'Master Hugh'** A superb form collected in the wild by Stainton, Sykes and Williams under the number 7822. The deep pink flowers are followed by large orange-red, changing to bright red, fruits, possibly the largest fruited rose in cultivation. When exhibited by that distinguished amateur gardener, Mr Maurice Mason, it was given an Award of Merit in 1966.

**'Rubricaulis'** See *R. davidii* 'Rubricaulis'.

**majalis** HERRM. (*R. cinnamomea* L.) "Cinnamon Rose". A strong-growing, medium-sized shrub with leaves composed of 5-7, coarsely-toothed leaflets, glaucous beneath. Flowers 5cm across, deep lilac-pink but variable, spicily fragrant. Fruits small, red. Europe, N and W Asia. C before 1600.

**marginata** See *R. jundzillii*.

**'Mariae-graebneriae'** A beautiful, low, spreading shrub reputedly a hybrid between *R. virginiana* and possibly *R. palustris*. Leaves with shining, coarsely-toothed leaflets often colouring well in autumn. Flowers bright rose-pink, 5cm across, carried often in many-flowered corymbs from June to August. Fruits orange-shaped, red. C 1880.

**'Max Graf'** (*R. rugosa* × *R. wichuraiana*). A superb rose with long, trailing stems, excellent as a ground cover for sunny banks. The fragrant, rose-pink, golden-centred flowers, 5cm across, are borne over a long period. C 1919. AM 1964.

**'Mermaid'** A beautiful, free-growing evergreen rose of rambling habit, with long stems and glossy green, ample foliage. Flowers 13-15cm across, sulphur-yellow with deep amber stamens, coloured even after the petals have fallen. Seen at its best in warmer, southern areas of the British Isles. A hybrid of *R. bracteata* and like that species best grown on a warm sheltered wall. Raised by Messrs W. Paul of Waltham Cross. AM 1917. AGM 1984.

**microphylla** See *R. roxburghii*.

× **micrugosa** HENKEL (*R. roxburghii* × *R. rugosa*). Medium-sized shrub of dense bushy habit resembling *R. rugosa* in its foliage. Flowers pale pink followed by bristly, rounded, orange-red fruits. Garden origin before 1905.

**mollis** SM. An erect-stemmed, native shrub up to 2m. Leaves composed of 5-7 downy leaflets. Flowers rose-red, 4-5cm across, in short clusters, followed by rounded, scarlet, bristle-clad fruits. Europe (including British Isles), Caucasus.

**"Monthly Rose"** See *R. chinensis* 'Old Blush'.

ROSA—*continued*

'**Morletii**' (*R. pendulina* 'Morletii') A medium-sized shrub with long arching branches. Flowers double, magenta, opening flat and revealing petaloid stamens. Young foliage tinted in spring.

**moschata** HERRM. "Musk Rose". A strong-growing rather lax shrub up to 3.5m. Leaves composed of 5-7 dark green, polished leaflets. The sweetly musk-scented, creamy-white flowers 5cm across, are carried in large branching heads during late summer and autumn. A rare species in cultivation, other roses often bearing its name (see *R. brunonii*). It is a parent of many old garden hybrids and in particular that group known as Hybrid Musks. It is notable for its richly fragrant flowers in autumn. Origin uncertain, perhaps W Asia.

**moschata** HORT. See *R. brunonii*.

'**La Mortola**' See *R. brunonii* 'La Mortola'.

"**Moss Rose**" See *R. centifolia* 'Muscosa'.

**moyesii** HEMSL. & WILS. A medium-sized to large, erect-branched shrub of rather loose, open habit with few-prickled stems and leaves with 7-13 leaflets. Flowers rich blood-crimson 6-7.5cm across, either 1 or 2 terminating each short spur in June and July. They are followed by equally beautiful large, flagon-shaped, bright crimson fruits. One of the most beautiful species in cultivation and a parent of several lovely hybrids. W China. Introduced by A.E. Pratt in 1894 and again by E.H. Wilson in 1903. AM 1908. FCC 1916. AGM 1984.

'**Fargesii**' Flowers of a glowing, vivid colour, perhaps best described as shining carmine. AM 1922.

'**Geranium**' Slightly more compact in habit and with flowers of a brilliant geranium-red. The fruits too are slightly larger and smoother. Raised at Wisley in 1938. AM 1950.

**multibracteata** HEMSL. & WILS. A very graceful shrub of medium size with stout, prickly stems and attractive, fragrant, fern-like leaves composed of 7-9 leaflets. The bright rose-lilac flowers, 2.5-4cm across, are produced intermittently over a long period. The small, rounded, red fruits are covered with glandular bristles. W China. I 1908 by Ernest Wilson. AM 1936.

**multiflora** THUNB. (*R. polyantha* SIEB. & ZUCC.) A vigorous, large shrub or rambler with long stems, which will clamber 6m into trees if suitably placed. Leaves composed of 7-9 leaflets. Flowers fragrant, white, 2-3cm across, abundantly borne in large, conical heads followed by small, pea-like, bright fruits which last into winter. A dense-growing species suitable for hedging and covering ugly banks. An ancestor of the Hybrid Polyantha roses. Japan, Korea. I 1804.

'**Carnea**' Flowers double, pink. A sport of var. *cathayensis* REHD. & WILS. from China. I from China in 1804.

'**Grevillei**' ('Platyphylla') The "Seven Sisters Rose". Flowers double, cerise-purple at first changing to mauve-pink and fading to white. An old favourite, vigorous and free-flowering. Introduced from Japan by Sir Charles Greville about 1816.

'**Platyphylla**' See 'Grevillei'.

"**Musk Rose**" See *R. moschata*.

"**Musk Rose, Himalayan**" See *R. brunonii*.

**mutabilis** See *R.* × *odorata* 'Mutabilis'.

"**Myrrh-scented Rose**" See *R. arvensis* 'Splendens'.

**nitida** WILLD. A charming dwarf shrub of suckering habit producing numerous, slender, reddish stems which are densely clothed with fine prickles and bristles. Leaves with 7-9 slender, shining green leaflets which turn crimson and purple in autumn. Flowers rose-red, 5cm across, followed by slightly bristly scarlet fruits. An excellent carpeting shrub with rich autumn colour. E North America. I 1807.

**nutkana** PRESL. A strong-growing, medium-sized shrub, the leaves with 5-9 leaflets. Flowers bright pink, 5cm across, followed by globose red fruits which persist into winter. W North America. Introduced about 1876.

× **odorata** (ANDR.) SWEET (*R. chinensis* × *R. gigantea*). "Tea Rose". A group of old and variable hybrids raised in Chinese gardens. They are best grown against a sunny, sheltered wall where they will reach several metres high.

**ROSA** × **odorata**—*continued*

**'Fortune's Double Yellow'** ('Pseudindica') Also known as "Beauty of Glazenwood" and "Gold of Ophir". An old rose up to 3m with semi-double flowers which are salmon-yellow or coppery-yellow, flushed coppery-scarlet, richly scented. As it flowers on the second-year wood it should not be pruned like an ordinary climber. Discovered by Robert Fortune in a mandarin's garden at Ningpo in China and introduced by him in 1845.

**var. gigantea** See *R. gigantea*.

**'Mutabilis'** (*R. chinensis* 'Mutabilis') (*R.* 'Tipo Ideale') A vigorous small to medium-sized, few-spined shrub of slender habit, with deep purplish young shoots and coppery young foliage. The slender-pointed, vivid-orange buds open to buff, shaded carmine flowers, changing to rose and finally crimson, borne over a very long period. They are richly tea-scented and expand to 7.5-10cm. An unusual and very versatile rose. AM 1957.

**'Pseudindica'** See 'Fortune's Double Yellow'.

**omeiensis** See *R. sericea* var. *omeiensis*.

**oxyodon** See *R. pendulina* var. *oxyodon*.

**'Parvifolia'** (*R. centifolia* 'Parvifolia') (*R. burgundiaca* ROESS.) "Burgundian Rose". A slow-growing, small, almost thornless rose of erect habit, its stems densely leafy. The small, flat, pompon flowers are deep rose, suffused claret. Cultivated at least since 1764.

**'Paulii'** (*R. arvensis* × *R. rugosa*). A low-growing, mound-forming shrub with extremely thorny, procumbent stems reaching 3-4m in length. Leaves and flowers like those of *R. rugosa*, the latter white and slightly clove-scented. A vigorous shrub excellent as ground cover in sun, or for growing beneath taller shrubs. Garden origin before 1903.

**pendulina** L. (*R. alpina* L.) A small, semi-erect shrub with smooth or few-thorned green or purplish stems and leaves with 5-11 leaflets. Flowers magenta-pink, 4-5cm across, followed by red, flask-shaped fruits. Mts of C and S Europe.

**'Morletii'** See *R.* 'Morletii'.

**var. oxyodon** (BOISS.) REHD. (*R. oxyodon* BOISS.) (*R. haematodes* CREP.) Flowers deep pink; fruits dark red, conspicuous during late summer. Caucasus. C 1896.

× **penzanceana** See *R.* 'Lady Penzance'.

**persetosa** See *R. davidii* 'Acicularis'.

**persica** MICHX. ex JUSS. (*R. berberifolia* PALL.) (*Hulthemia persica* (MICHX. ) BORNM.) A rare species of dwarf habit with slender, suckering shoots and simple, greyish-green, downy leaves. The solitary flowers, 2.5cm across, are brilliant yellow, each petal with a scarlet blotch at its base. The small, globose green fruits are clothed with minute prickles. A difficult plant to establish. It requires perfect drainage and a dry, sunny position. Iran, Afghanistan, C Asia. C 1790.

**pimpinellifolia** L. (*R. spinosissima* L.) "Scotch Rose" "Burnet Rose". A small, native, suckering shrub producing dense, low thickets of slender, erect stems thickly beset with bristles and tiny prickles. Leaves composed of 5-9 deep green and glabrous leaflets. The small, white or pale pink flowers, 4-5cm across, are borne in profusion during May and June, followed by rounded, shining black or maroon-black fruits. A common native shrub of coastal sand dunes. Europe, N Asia. This species has given rise to many forms and hybrids.

**var. altaica** See 'Grandiflora'.

**'Canary'** A small, compact shrub intermediate in habit between 'Grandiflora' and *R.* 'Lutea Maxima', with comparatively large, single, yellow flowers, intermediate in shade of colour.

**'Glory of Edzell'** A very beautiful, early flowering shrub reaching 2m in height. The clear pink, lemon-centred flowers garland the slender branches in May. Possibly of hybrid origin.

**'Grandiflora'** (var. *altaica* REHD. not (WILLD.) THORY (*R. altaica* HORT. not WILLD.) A stronger-growing variety up to 2m high and more across. The large, creamy-white flowers, 5-6cm across, crowd the branches and are replaced by shining maroon-black fruits. An excellent free-flowering rose which, because of its dense, suckering habit makes a useful hedge. I from Siberia about 1820.

**'Hispida'** (*R. lutescens* PURSH) An unusual variety with densely bristly stems up to 1.5m. Flowers creamy-yellow 5-6cm across. Siberia. Introduced before 1781.

**ROSA pimpinellifolia**—*continued*

    **'Lutea'** See *R.* 'Lutea Maxima'.

    **'William III'** A dwarf, suckering shrub of dense, bushy habit with short branches and greyish-green leaves. Flowers semi-double, magenta-crimson changing to rich plum colour, paler on the reverse. Fruits black.

    **'Williams' Double Yellow'** See *R.* 'William's Double Yellow'.

  **pisocarpa** GRAY. A dense-growing, medium-sized shrub with leaves composed of 5-7 coarsely-toothed leaflets. Flowers fragrant, lilac-pink, 2.5-3cm across, borne in corymbose clusters from June to August. Fruits rounded to ellipsoid, red. W North America. I about 1882.

× **polliniana** SPRENGEL (*R. arvensis* × *R. gallica*). A rambling shrub forming a low mound up to 1m high and 3m across, clambering into trees and shrubs if allowed. Flowers slightly fragrant, 6-7.5cm across, rose-pink in bud, opening blush, with yellow anthers. C 1820.

  **polyantha** See *R. multiflora*.

  **'Polyantha Grandiflora'** A climbing or rambling rose reaching 6m on a suitable support. Leaves glossy, deep green. Flowers strongly fragrant, creamy-white, with orange-yellow stamens, followed by oval, orange-red fruits lasting well into winter. A fine free-flowering rose of uncertain origin. Probably a hybrid of *R. multiflora*. FCC 1888.

  **pomifera** See *R. villosa*.

  **"Prairie Rose"** See *R. setigera*.

  **prattii** HEMSL. An exceedingly attractive shrub of medium size with dainty foliage and clusters of deep rose flowers, 2.5-3cm across, in July. The crimson, bottle-shaped fruits are very ornamental. W China. I 1903 by Ernest Wilson.

  **primula** BOULENGER A beautiful, medium-sized shrub with arching stems and leaves composed of 7-13 dark glossy leaflets which emit a strong incense-like odour when crushed. Flowers fragrant, 4cm across, primrose-yellow passing to white, opening in mid-May. Fruits globose, red. Turkestan to N China. I 1910. AM 1962.

  **"Provence Rose"** See *R. centifolia*.

× **pruhoniciana 'Hillieri'** See *R.* 'Hillieri'.

  **"Ramanas Rose"** See *R. rugosa*.

  **"Red Rose of Lancaster"** See *R. gallica* var. *officinalis*.

× **reversa** WALDST. & KIT. (*R. pendulina* × *R. pimpinellifolia*) A small, suckering shrub resembling the Burnet Rose in general appearance. The small, semi-double, carmine flowers, white at base, are followed by scarlet fruits. Occurs in the wild with the parents. C 1820.

  **'Rosa Mundi'** See *R. gallica* 'Versicolor'.

  **'Rose d'Amour'** (*R. virginiana* 'Plena') "St Mark's Rose". A medium-sized shrub with almost thornless stems up to 2m and leaves with 5-7 leaflets. Flowers double, fragrant, deep pink, with paler outer petals, continuing over several weeks from mid to late summer. A vigorous, free-flowering rose, a hybrid between *R. virginiana* and another species, possibly *R. carolina*. Garden origin before 1820. FCC 1980.

  **"Rose des Peintres"** See under *R. centifolia*.

  **'Roseraie de l'Hay'** A hybrid of *R. rugosa*. The long, pointed buds are dark purplish-red opening to a rich crimson-purple with cream stamens, expanding 10-12cm across, double, very fragrant. A superb rose of vigorous growth and an excellent hedge. Garden origin in 1901. AGM 1984.

  **roxburghii** TRATT. (*R. microphylla* ROXB. ex LINDL.) "Burr Rose" "Chestnut Rose". A very distinct, viciously-armed shrub of medium to large size. Leaves composed of 9-15 neatly-paired leaflets. Flowers fragrant, 6-7.5cm across, shell-pink, with prickly receptacles, calyces and pedicels, followed by orange-yellow, tomato-shaped fruits covered with stiff prickles. The twisted, spreading, grey to cinnamon-coloured stems with their flaky bark give a gnarled effect to this interesting rose. Introduced from China in 1908 by Ernest Wilson.

  **'Plena'** The double-flowered form from which the species was named. I before 1814.

  **rubiginosa** See *R. eglanteria*.

  **rubra** See *R. gallica*.

  **rubrifolia** See *R. glauca*.

  **rubus** LEV. & VANIOT (*R. ernestii* STAPF ex BEAN) A strong-growing, vigorous rambler with good foliage. The long stems possess large prickles and the leaves are composed of

**ROSA rubus**—*continued*

usually 5 leaflets. Flowers fragrant, 3cm across, pinkish in bud, opening creamy-white with orange anthers, borne in dense corymbs and replaced by dark scarlet, oval fruits. Related to *R. helenae*, but even more vigorous, reaching 9m in a suitable position. C and W China. I 1907 by Ernest Wilson.

**rugosa** THUNB. "Ramanas Rose". A strong-growing, perpetual-flowering shrub with stout, densely prickly and bristly stems, 1.5-2m high. Leaves up to 18cm long, composed of 5-9 oblong, conspicuously veined, rugose leaflets, downy beneath. Flowers fragrant, 8-9cm across, purplish-rose, followed by bright red, tomato-shaped fruits, 2.5cm across. A well-known rose, parent of innumerable hybrids. Its vigorous, suckering habit enables it to form dense thickets and it is an excellent hedge plant. In Japan it grows on sandy sea-shores and is occasionally found naturalised in similar situations in the British Isles. NE Asia. I 1796. AM 1896.

**'Alba'** Flowers white, blush-tinted in bud. Very vigorous. Exceptional in fruit.

**'Blanc Double de Coubert'** See *R.* 'Blanc Double de Coubert'.

**'Fru Dagmar Hastrup'** See *R.* 'Fru Dagmar Hastrup'.

**'Roseraie de l'Hay'** See *R.* 'Roseraie de l'Hay'.

**'Rubra'** Flowers wine-crimson, fragrant. Fruits large and conspicuous. AM 1955.

**'Scabrosa'** See *R.* 'Scabrosa'.

**"Sacramento Rose"** See *R. stellata* var. *mirifica*.

**'Scabrosa'** A vigorous hybrid of *R. rugosa* with excellent foliage. The enormous violaceous-crimson flowers are up to 14cm across. Fruits large, like small tomatoes, with persistent sepals. AM 1964. AGM 1984.

**"Scotch Rose"** See *R. pimpinellifolia*.

**serafinii** VIV. A dwarf shrub, occasionally up to 1m with densely prickly stems and leaves composed of 5-7 rounded glandular and aromatic leaflets. The small, bright pink flowers are followed by small, bright red, rounded fruits. Mediterranean region, SE Europe. C 1914.

**sericea** LINDL. An extremely variable species, forming a dense shrub of medium size with usually conspicuously bristly and thorny stems and leaves with generally 7-15 leaflets. The white to yellow, usually four-petalled flowers, 2.5-5cm across, rather resemble a Maltese Cross and are borne all along the branches in May and early June. They are followed by bright, parti-coloured crimson and yellow, edible, pear-shaped fruits which fall during summer. Himalaya to W and C China. I 1822. The following forms were previously listed under *R. omeiensis*.

**'Atrosanguinea'** Fruits deep crimson.

**'Chrysocarpa'** Fruits yellow.

**'Lutea'** An attractive form with yellow flowers and translucent crimson thorns.

**var. omeiensis** (ROLFE) ROWLEY (*R. omeiensis* ROLFE) "Mount Omei Rose". Pedicel fleshy in fruit, leaflets more than 11.

**var. polyphylla** ROWLEY A form with more numerous leaflets and smoother, less spiny stems.

**f. pteracantha** FRANCH. A distinct variety, its stems furnished with flat, broad-based, translucent crimson thorns which are particularly pleasing when illuminated by the rays of a winter sun. They are especially conspicuous on young and vigorous, basal shoots and may be encouraged by an annual or bi-annual pruning. Himalaya, W China. I 1890. FCC 1905. AM 1976.

**setigera** MICHX. "Prairie Rose". A small, wide-spreading shrub with long trailing stems and trifoliolate leaves, the leaflets deep green, coarsely-toothed and 5-7.5cm long. Flowers 5cm across, rose-pink, fading to blush, fragrant, appearing in July and August. Fruits small, globose, red. Useful as a ground cover or for training over bushes and low walls. E United States. I 1800.

**setipoda** HEMSL. & WILS. A free-growing, medium-sized shrub with stout, erect, few-thorned stems. Leaves composed of 7-9 leaflets which are glandular beneath and possess a delightful sweet-briar-like fragrance when crushed. The clear pink, beautifully-formed flowers 5-6cm across are borne on contrasting purplish pedicels all along the branches and are followed by large flagon-shaped, crimson, glandular-bristly fruits. W China. I 1901 by Ernest Wilson.

**ROSA**—*continued*

**"Seven Sisters Rose"** See *R. multiflora* 'Grevillei'.

**'Silver Moon'** A vigorous, rambling rose up to 9m, with glossy, dark green leaves and large creamy-white, richly scented flowers which are butter-yellow in bud. Usually regarded as *R. laevigata* × *R. wichuraiana*, but the "Magnolia Rose" (*R.* 'Devoniensis') may have also played a part.

**sinica** See *R. laevigata*.

**sinowilsonii** HEMSL. & WILS. A magnificent climbing species, related to *R. longicuspis*. Its shining, reddish-brown stems are clothed with attractive leaves composed of usually 7, long-pointed, corrugated leaflets which are deep glossy green above, purple-flushed beneath. The white flowers, 5cm across, are borne in panicles during summer. Superb foliage plant requiring a warm sunny wall in a sheltered garden. Introduced by E.H. Wilson from W China in 1904. The name refers to the collector's nickname "Chinese Wilson".

**soulieana** CREP. A large shrub with long, scandent, pale spiny stems, forming great mounds. Leaves grey-green, with 7-9 leaflets. Flowers 2.5-4cm across, creamy-yellow in bud, opening white, borne on well-established, mature plants in large corymbs followed by small, ovoid, orange-red fruits. A strong-growing species requiring plenty of space in which to develop. It looks well covering an old decrepit tree. W China. I 1896.

**spinosissima** See *R. pimpinellifolia*.

× **spinulifolia** DEMATRA A hybrid between *R. pendulina* and probably *R. tomentosa*. A small shrub of stiff habit with leaves which are glaucous at first becoming green. Flowers fragrant, 4-5cm across, bright cherry-pink, followed by bright red, bottle-shaped fruits. Occurs in the wild with the parents.

**stellata** WOOT. A dwarf shrub with wiry, greyish-green stems forming dense, low thickets. Leaves trifoliolate, with wedge-shaped, coarsely-toothed leaflets. Flowers 5-6cm across, deep pink, with yellow anthers. Fruits small, dull red. Mts of SW United States. I 1902.

**var. mirifica** (GREENE) COCKERELL "Sacramento Rose". A rare shrub, slightly more robust than the typical form. It also differs in its hairless stems clothed with ivory-coloured prickles and its generally glabrous leaves with 3-5, or occasionally 7, leaflets. Flowers rose-purple, paling with age, followed by red, top-shaped fruits. It requires a warm sunny position in a well drained soil. New Mexico. I 1916. AM 1924.

**stylosa** DESV. A medium-sized, native shrub with long, arching stems and leaves with 5-7 leaflets. Flowers 3-5cm across, pale pink to white followed by ovoid, red fruits. Europe.

**"Sweet Briar"** See *R. eglanteria*.

**sweginzowii** KOEHNE A strong-growing shrub 3-4m high with strongly thorny stems and leaves with 7-11 leaflets, in general appearance very like *R. moyesii*. The bright rose-pink flowers, 4cm across, are carried often in clusters on glandular, bristly stalks and are followed by flagon-shaped, bright red, hispid fruits. The latter are about equal in size and colour to those of *R. moyesii*, but ripen earlier. NW China. I 1903 by Ernest Wilson. AM 1922.

**"Tea Rose"** See *R.* × *odorata*.

**"Threepenny Bit Rose"** See *R. elegantula* 'Persetosa'.

**triphylla** See *R. anemoniflora*.

**villosa** L. (*R. pomifera* HERRM) "Apple Rose". A vigorous, medium-sized shrub with leaves composed of 5-7 bluish-green, downy leaflets, fragrant when crushed. Flowers 5cm across, carmine in bud, opening clear pink followed in early autumn by large, apple-shaped, bristle-clad, crimson fruits. C and S Europe, W Asia. I 1771. AM 1955.

**'Duplex'** See *R.* 'Wolley-Dod'.

**virginiana** MILL. (*R. lucida* EHRH.) A small, suckering shrub forming thickets of slender, erect stems. Leaves composed of 7-9 glossy green leaflets which turn first to purple then to orange-red, crimson and yellow in autumn. Flowers 5-6cm across, bright pink, deeper in bud, appearing continuously from June to July into August. Fruits small, orange-shaped, bright glistening red. A most attractive species, excellent in sandy soils, particularly by the sea. E North America. I before 1807. AM 1953. AGM 1984.

**'Plena'** See *R.* 'Rose d'Amour'.

**wardii** MULLIGAN The typical form of this rare Tibetan species is thought not to be in cultivation and is represented by the following form:

**ROSA wardii**—*continued*

**'Culta'** A lax-growing shrub up to 2m with arching branches and leaves similar to those of *R. moyesii*. Flowers also similar to those of the latter, but petals creamy-white, with a mahogany-red disc surrounded by yellow stamens. SE Tibet. I 1924 by Kingdon-Ward.

**webbiana** ROYLE A graceful and slender shrub up to 2m, with arching branches and leaves composed of 7-9 small, rounded leaflets. The clear, almond-pink flowers, 4-5cm across, are carried along the stems creating a charming effect in June. They are followed in late summer by bottle-shaped, shining sealing-wax-red fruits. W Himalaya. I 1879. AM 1955. AGM 1969.

**'Wedding Day'** A vigorous climbing or rambling shrub with red-thorned, green stems reaching 10m in a suitable tree. Leaves rich green and glossy. Flowers richly scented, in large trusses, deep yellow in bud, opening creamy-white with vivid orange-yellow stamens, fading to pink. Raised before 1950 by the late Sir Frederick Stern at Highdown, Sussex, by selfing a hybrid from the cross *R. sinowilsonii* × *R. moyesii*. AM 1950.

**"White Rose of York"** See *R. × alba*.

**wichuraiana** CREP. A vigorous, semi-evergreen species with trailing stems up to 6m long. Leaves small, dark shining green, composed of 7-9 leaflets. Flowers 4-5cm across, white, richly scented, borne in small, conical clusters during late summer, followed by tiny, globose, red fruits. An excellent ground cover, the stems rooting as they grow. Also suitable for clothing tree-stumps and unsightly objects. A parent of numerous hybrids including 'Alberic Barbier', 'Albertine' and 'Dorothy Perkins'. E Asia. Introduced from Japan in 1891. AGM 1973. AM 1985.

**'Grandiflora'** A splendid form with larger flowers.

**'William's Double Yellow'** (*R. pimpinellifolia* 'William's Double Yellow') Rather taller in habit than *R. pimpinellifolia*, bearing fragrant double yellow flowers with a central cluster of green carpels. Probably *R. pimpinellifolia* × *R. foetida*.

**willmottiae** HEMSL. An elegant shrub of medium size, with gracefully arching branches and small, sea-green, fern-like leaves composed of 7-9 leaflets, pleasantly fragrant when crushed. Flowers 3-4cm across, lilac-pink, with cream-coloured anthers. Fruits pear-shaped, orange-red. One of the loveliest species, when in flower. Introduced from the Tibetan border region of W China by E.H. Wilson in 1904, and named after that great gardener and rosarian, Miss Ellen Willmott. AM 1958.

**'Wisley'** Flowers of a deeper shade of lilac-pink.

**'Wintonensis'** (*R. moyesii* × *R. setipoda*). A beautiful hybrid raised in our nurseries in 1928. In general appearance it shows a leaning towards *R. setipoda*, which is apparent in the sweet-briar-like fragrance of the foliage. Flowers rich rose-pink, several in a cluster, with long leafy sepals and very glandular-hairy receptacles.

**'Wolley-Dod'** (*R. villosa* 'Duplex') "Wolley-Dod's Rose". An attractive medium-sized shrub resembling *R. villosa*. Flowers semi-double, clear pink, fruits dark red. Raised in the garden of the Rev Wolley-Dod. AM 1954.

**woodsii** LINDL. A very variable shrub up to 2m, the leaves with 5-7 leaflets. Flowers 3-4cm across, lilac-pink, followed by red, globose fruits. C and W North America. I 1815.

**var. fendleri** RYDB. The most beautiful form of this species and a truly first class garden shrub. It forms a densely leafy bush to about 1.5m high and carries bright lilac-pink flowers, followed by conspicuous sealing-wax-red fruits which persist long into winter. W North America. C 1888.

**xanthina** LINDL. (*R. xanthina* 'Flore Pleno') A beautiful, medium-sized shrub with gracefully arching branches and small, dainty, fern-like leaves composed of 7–13 rounded leaflets. Flowers semi-double, 4cm across, golden yellow. A garden form, said to have been cultivated in N China and Korea for over 100 years. Reintroduced to the Arnold Arboretum in 1907 by that indefatigable collector, Fredrick N. Meyer. AM 1945.

**f. spontanea** REHD. The wild form, reaching 3m in time, the branches clothed with pale sea-green foliage and bedecked in May and early June with single, comparatively large yellow flowers, followed by dark red fruits. A parent of 'Canary Bird'. N China, Korea. I 1907. AM 1945. AGM 1969.

**"York and Lancaster Rose"** See *R. damascena* 'Versicolor'.

**"ROSE OF SHARON"** See *Hypericum calycinum*.

**"ROSEMARY"** See *Rosmarinus officinalis*.

**\*ROSMARINUS** L.—**Labiatae**—A genus of 2 species of evergreen, aromatic shrubs, with romantic associations, long cultivated in W European gardens, thriving in all types of well drained soil in full sun.

    **lavandulaceus** See under *R. officinalis* 'Prostratus'.

    **officinalis** L. "Common Rosemary". A dense shrub up to 2m, and as much through, the stems thickly clothed with linear, green or greyish-green leaves, white beneath. Flowers blue, produced in numerous axillary clusters along the branches of the previous year in May or earlier. Makes an attractive, informal hedge which may be lightly pruned if necessary, immediately after flowering. S Europe, Asia Minor. Cultivated in Britain for over four hundred years. AGM 1984.

        **'Albus'** Flowers white.

        †**'Benenden Blue'** A smaller-growing, distinct form with very narrow, dark green leaves and bright blue flowers. A selected clone of var. *angustifolius*. AM 1933.

        **'Fastigiatus'** See 'Miss Jessopp's Upright'.

        **'Majorca'** A lovely clone, with flowers of bluebird blue, with a dark spot on the lower petals. AM 1961.

        **'Miss Jessopp's Upright'** ('Fastigiatus') A strong-growing form of erect habit. 'Pyramidalis' is very similar. AGM 1984.

        †**'Prostratus'** (*R. lavandulaceus* HORT.) A low-growing form making large, dense, prostrate mats, studded with clusters of blue flowers in May and June. Ideal for draping sunny wall-tops, but somewhat tender.

        **'Pyramidalis'** See under 'Miss Jessopp's Upright'.

        **'Roseus'** A small shrub with lilac-pink flowers.

        **'Severn Sea'** A dwarf shrub with arching branches and brilliant blue flowers. Raised by that dedicated gardener Norman Hadden, at West Porlock, Somerset. AGM 1984. AM 1989.

        **'Sissinghurst Blue'** A form of upright habit with profuse rich blue flowers. A chance seedling raised at Sissinghurst Castle. About 1958. AM 1983.

        †**'Tuscan Blue'** A small shrub with broader leaves and brighter coloured, deep blue flowers. Often flowers in winter.

**"ROWAN"** See *Sorbus aucuparia*.

**RUBUS** L.—**Rosaceae**—A large genus of more than 250 species widely distributed as well as numerous apomicts in Europe and North America. The ornamental brambles are a varied throng, many species thriving in the poorest of soils and other adverse conditions. Several species have attractive flowers and foliage, whilst others have striking white stems in winter, and all have prickles unless otherwise stated. Those grown for their ornamental stems should have the old flowering stems cut down to ground level each year, immediately after flowering. See also under CLIMBERS.

    **amabilis** FOCKE A small shrub of graceful habit, usually less than 1.2m. Leaves pinnate, with 7-9, deeply-toothed leaflets, borne along the slender, fairly erect stems. Flowers solitary, 4-5cm across, white, in June and July. Fruits large, red, edible but sparingly produced. W China. I 1908 by Ernest Wilson.

    **\*australis** FORST. An evergreen, dioecious climber with long, wiry, prickle-clad stems. Leaves with 3-5 leaflets, variable in shape and size. Flowers small, white, in long panicles, only produced on adult plants. Juvenile plants creep along the ground, forming dense hummocks. Requires a well drained, sheltered position. New Zealand.

    **'Benenden'** (*R.* Tridel 'Benenden') (*R. deliciosus* × *R. trilobus*). A beautiful hybrid, raised by Capt Collingwood Ingram, in 1950. A vigorous shrub producing erect, peeling, thornless shoots up to 3m high. Leaves three to five-lobed. Flowers 5cm across, glistening white, with a central boss of golden yellow stamens, produced singly all along the arching branches in May. AM 1958. FCC 1963.

    **biflorus** BUCH.-HAM. ex SM. A vigorous, medium-sized shrub, the semi-erect, prickly stems are green, but covered with a vivid white, waxy bloom. Leaves composed of 5,

**RUBUS biflorus**—*continued*

occasionally 3, leaflets, white-felted beneath. The small white flowers are produced in small terminal clusters and are followed by edible yellow fruits. Himalaya. I 1818.

**caesius** L. "Dewberry". A native species of little ornamental merit, with long, slender, creeping stems, forming extensive carpets. Leaves usually trifoliolate. Flowers small, white, followed by bloomy-black fruits. Europe to N Asia.

**\*calycinoides** KOIDZ. (*R. fockeanus* HORT.) A creeping alpine evergreen, forming dense mats of short-jointed, rooting stems. The small, three to five-lobed, mallow-like leaves are glossy green and bullate above, grey-felted beneath. The white flowers are borne singly or in short clusters in summer, but are usually concealed beneath the leaves. A most useful ground cover for the rock garden, scree or peat wall, even in shade. Taiwan. The Chinese *R. fockeanus* is very similar.

**cissoides var. pauperatus** See *R. squarrosus*.

**cockburnianus** HEMSL. (*R. giraldianus* FOCKE) A strong-growing species of medium size, the purple arching stems overlaid with a vivid white bloom. The attractively pinnate, fern-like leaves are composed of 7-9 leaflets, white or grey beneath. Flowers small, rose-purple, of little merit, borne in dense terminal panicles and followed by bloomy-black fruits. N and C China. I 1907 by Ernest Wilson. AGM 1984.

**deliciosus** TORR. A medium-sized, thornless shrub, the arching branches with peeling bark. Leaves three to five-lobed. Flowers like white dog roses, 5cm across, borne in May and June. Fruits purplish but seldom maturing. A delightful flowering shrub and for this purpose, one of the best in the genus. Native of the Rocky Mountains, Colorado (United States). I 1870. FCC 1881.

**fockeanus** HORT. See *R. calycinoides*.

× **fraseri** REHD. (*R. odoratus* × *R. parviflorus*). A vigorous, medium-sized, suckering shrub with palmate leaves and comparatively large, fragrant, rose-coloured flowers from June to August. Particularly useful for covering shady areas beneath trees. Garden origin in 1918.

**fruticosus** L. "Bramble" "Blackberry". A common and familiar scrambling native which may be found growing in just about every type of soil and situation. It is immensely variable and in the British Isles alone several hundred species or microspecies are recognised. Only a few are of any ornamental merit, for which see *R. laciniatus* and *R. ulmifolius* 'Bellidiflorus'.

**var. laciniatus** See *R. laciniatus*.

**giraldianus** See *R. cockburnianus*.

**illecebrosus** FOCKE "Strawberry-Raspberry". A dwarf sub-shrub with a creeping, woody rootstock. Stems erect, bearing pinnate leaves and solitary or terminal clusters of white flowers 2.5-4cm across, in July. Fruits large, red, sweet, but rather insipid. Japan. C 1895.

**laciniatus** WILLD. (*R. fruticosus* var. *laciniatus* WESTON). "Fern-leaved" or "Cut-leaved Bramble". This bramble is not known in a wild state and yet it breeds true from seed. It is a vigorous species with long scrambling, prickly stems. The leaves are composed of usually 5 pinnately-lobed leaflets, the lobes incisely toothed, creating an attractive fern-like effect. The rather insignificant flowers are replaced by prolific, sweet, black fruits. Origin before 1770. There is also a similar form with thornless stems.

**leucodermis** TORR. & GR. A species of medium size with both erect and spreading, glaucous blue stems. Leaves with 3-5 coarsely-toothed leaflets, white-felted beneath. Flowers small, white, borne in terminal clusters in June; fruits purplish-black, edible. W North America. Introduced by David Douglas about 1829.

†**lineatus** REINW. In our area a semi-evergreen shrub with rambling, silky-hairy stems, usually less than 1.2m. Leaves unique and beautiful, with 5 leaflets, dark green above, covered with a shining, silvery, silky down beneath, conspicuously veined. Prickles few or absent. Flowers white in small axillary clusters. Fruits small, red or yellow. Requires a warm sheltered position. E Himalaya, W China, Malaya. I 1905 by George Forrest.

**linkianus** SER. (*R. thyrsoideus* 'Plenus') A robust, medium-sized shrub with long, scrambling stems. Leaves with 5 leaflets. Flowers double, white, in large, erect, conical panicles in July and August. A conspicuous shrub for the wild garden, also useful in semi-shade. C before 1770.

**RUBUS**—*continued*

**mesogaeus** FOCKE A strong-growing shrub producing erect, velvety stems up to 3m high. Leaves trifoliolate, with large, coarsely-toothed leaflets, grey-tomentose beneath. Flowers small, pinkish-white in June. Fruits black. C and W China. I 1907.

**microphyllus 'Variegatus'** A small, suckering shrub producing dense mounds of slender, prickly, glaucescent stems. Leaves 4-7.5cm long, prettily three-lobed, green, mottled cream and pink. The typical form is a native of Japan.

**\*nepalensis** (HOOK. f.) KUNTZE (*R. nutans* WALL. ex EDGEW.) A dwarf evergreen creeping shrub with densely soft-bristly stems and short-stalked, trifoliolate leaves. The attractive, nodding white flowers 2.5-4cm across, are borne on erect, leafy shoots in June, followed by purple edible fruits. A charming carpeting shrub for a shady border or bank. Himalaya. I 1850, reintroduced in 1971 (BL & M 152). A hybrid between this species and *R. tricolor* was raised in 1976 by our propagator Peter Dummer; on this plant the leaves varied from broadly ovate to three-lobed or trifoliolate.

×**nobilis** REG. (*R. idaeus*×*R. odoratus*). A small, thornless shrub with erect, peeling stems and large, downy, trifoliolate leaves. Flowers purple-red, in terminal clusters in June and July. A vigorous hybrid with the same potential as *R. odoratus*. C 1855.

**nutans** See *R. nepalensis*.

**odoratus** L. A vigorous, suckering shrub with erect, peeling thornless stems up to 2.5m high. Young shoots densely glandular hairy. Leaves large and velvety, palmate. Flowers in branched clusters, 4-5cm across, fragrant, purplish-rose, opening from June to September. Fruits flat and broad, red, edible. An excellent shrub for the wild garden or semi-shade beneath trees. E North America. I 1770.

    **'Albus'** A form with white flowers.

**parviflorus** NUTT. (*R. nutkanus* MOCINO ex SER.) "Thimbleberry". A strong-growing shrub with erect, peeling thornless stems, 1.8-2.5m high. Leaves large, palmate, softly downy. Flowers white, 4-5cm across, in terminal clusters in May and June. Fruits large and flattened, red. W North America. I 1827 by David Douglas.

†**\*parvus** BUCH. A low-growing shrub with long, creeping or semi-climbing stems. Leaves narrow and prickly-toothed, dark or bronze-green above, paler beneath. Flowers unisexual, solitary or in small panicles, white, in May and June. Fruits red. Related to *R. australis*, forming attractive ground cover in sheltered places. New Zealand. C 1916.

**peltatus** MAXIM. A remarkable, vigorous small shrub of spreading and suckering habit. Shoots zig-zag, conspicuously glaucous bloomed in winter. Leaves shallowly five-lobed and coarsely-toothed, about 25cm across with large, glaucous stipules. Flowers white, to 6cm across, pendulous on short pedicels, borne singly at the tips of short shoots in May. Japan.

**phoenicolasius** MAXIM. "Wineberry". A conspicuous shrub with reddish, glandular-bristly stems 2.5-3m high. Leaves large, trifoliolate, the leaflets coarsely-toothed, white-felted beneath. Flowers in July, in terminal glandular bristly clusters, small, pale pink. Fruits bright orange-red, sweet and edible. Japan, China, Korea. I about 1876. FCC 1894.

**spectabilis** PURSH. "Salmonberry". A vigorous, suckering shrub, producing erect, finely-prickly stems, 1.2-1.8m high. Leaves trifoliolate. Flowers solitary or in small clusters, 2.5-4cm across, bright magenta-rose, fragrant, in April. Fruits large, ovoid, orange-yellow, edible. Excellent in the wild garden or as ground cover beneath trees. A rather striking double-flowered form is also in cultivation. W North America. Introduced by David Douglas in 1827.

†**squarrosus** FRITSCH (*R. cissoides* var. *pauperatus* KIRK) A curious species, forming a dense, tangled mass of dark, slender stems, bearing numerous, scattered, tiny, ivory-white prickles. Leaves variably shaped, sparse, usually thread-like. Flowers in racemes or panicles, small, yellowish. Fruits seldom seen in this country, orange-red. Normally found in cultivation as a congested mound or scrambling over neighbouring shrubs, but in its native habitat it develops into a tall climber. New Zealand.

**thibetanus** FRANCH. (*R. veitchii* ROLFE) An attractive species with semi-erect, purplish-brown stems covered with a blue-white bloom, 1.8-2m high. Leaves pinnate, fern-like, with 7-13, coarsely-toothed leaflets, which are greyish silky hairy above, white or grey-felted beneath. Flowers small, purple; fruits black or red. W China. I 1904 by Ernest Wilson. AM 1915.

**RUBUS thibetanus**—*continued*
   **'Silver Fern'** A dainty form with small, silvery-grey leaves.
   **\*tricolor** FOCKE (*R. polytrichus* FRANCH.) An attractive evergreen ground cover with long trailing, densely bristly stems. Leaves cordate, 7.5-10cm long, dark glossy green above, white-felted beneath. Flowers white 2.5cm across, produced singly in the leaf axils in July, sometimes followed by large, bright red, edible fruits. An excellent ground cover in shady places, forming extensive carpets even under beech trees. W China. First discovered by the Abbé Delavay; introduced by E.H. Wilson in 1908. AGM 1984.
   **Tridel** See *R.* 'Benenden'.
   **trilobus** SER. A lovely medium-sized shrub with strong, spreading, thornless stems. Leaves resembling those of *R. deliciosus*, but larger and cordate-ovate. Flowers 5cm across, pure white, with yellow stamens, borne intermittently along the arching stems from May to July. Mexico. I 1938. AM 1947.
   **ulmifolius** SCHOTT. A vigorous shrub with long, scrambling, rambling, plum-coloured stems and leaves with 3-5 leaflets which are white-felted beneath. A common native bramble of which the following is the only form in general cultivation:
   **'Bellidiflorus'** Large panicles of showy, double pink flowers in July and August. Too vigorous for all but the wild garden.

**"RUE"** See *Ruta graveolens*.

**\*RUSCUS** L.—**Ruscaceae**—A small genus of about 6 species of evergreen sub-shrubs distributed from Madeira to Iran and spreading by underground stems. The apparent leaves are really flattened stems (cladodes), which carry out the functions of the true leaves, these being reduced to tiny, papery scales. The flowers are minute and are borne, during spring, on the surface of the cladodes, male and female on separate plants. Useful plants for dry shady places in all types of soil, the females bearing attractive fruits.
   **aculeatus** L. "Butcher's Broom". A small, erect, native shrub forming thick clumps of green, thick but flexible stems 0.5-1m high. Cladodes small, spine-tipped, densely borne on the branches in the upper parts of the stems. Berries resembling bright, sealing-wax-red cherries, sometimes abundantly produced when plants of both sexes are present. Tolerant of dense shade, where few other plants will grow. S Europe (including S England).
   **hypoglossum** L. A dwarf shrub forming broad clumps of green "leafy" stems. The comparatively large, leaf-like cladodes carry a tiny, green flower on their upper surface and on female plants large, red, cherry-like fruits. Excellent ground cover in shade. S Europe. C since 16th century.
   × **microglossus** BERTOLONI (*R. hypoglossum* × *R. hypophyllum*). An interesting hybrid forming extensive suckering patches of erect or ascending stems up to 60cm high. Cladodes elliptic to obovate, petioled and slender-pointed, smaller and more elegantly posed than those of *R. hypoglossum*. The flower bracts are also much smaller and scale-like. N Italy and adjacent parts of France and Yugoslavia. The plants in general cultivation are female and probably belong to a single clone.
   **racemosus** See *Danae racemosa*.

**RUTA** L.—**Rutaceae**—A small genus of about 7 species of aromatic shrubs and perennial herbs natives of Europe and SW Asia. They thrive in a sunny, well drained position in almost any soil.
   **\*graveolens** L. "Rue". A small, evergreen shrub up to 1m with glaucous, much divided, fern-like leaves and terminal corymbs of small, mustard-yellow flowers from June to August. A popular herb, long cultivated for its medicinal properties. The foliage can sometimes cause a skin rash. S Europe. Cultivated in England since about 1652, perhaps earlier.
   **'Jackman's Blue'** A striking form with vivid, glaucous-blue foliage and compact, bushy habit. AGM 1984.
   **'Variegata'** Leaves variegated creamy-white.

**"ST JOHN'S WORT"** See *Hypericum*.

**SALIX** L.—**Salicaceae**—The "Willows" are a numerous and diverse genus of 300 or more species, varying from tiny, creeping alpines from high northern altitudes, to large, noble lowland trees scattered throughout the temperate regions of the world, mainly in the N hemisphere. All may be grown in ordinary loamy soils and many flourish in damp situations. Only a few are happy on chalky uplands, but almost all except the alpine species are at home in water meadows, chalky or otherwise. Few waterside trees are as beautiful as the weeping willows, despite the attentions of various diseases. Several willows, including *S. alba* 'Britzensis', *S. alba* var. *vitellina*, *S. daphnoides* and *S. irrorata* have attractive young stems in winter and to encourage the production of these it is necessary to hard prune each or alternate years in March. The willows with coloured stems, if planted with silver birches, white-stemmed brambles, red and yellow-stemmed dogwoods, the snake-barked maples and the mahogany-barked *Prunus serrula*, create an effective winter garden. A number of creeping species and their hybrids are excellent as ground cover, hiding large bare or unsightly areas with their dense, leafy stems.

Willows are normally dioecious, male and female catkins being borne on separate plants. They generally appear in late winter or early spring, before or with the young leaves. The catkins of *S. bockii* are unusual in appearing in autumn. In the majority of species the male catkins are the more showy.

Large shrubs and trees should be sited away from drains which can be invaded by the root systems.

**acutifolia** WILLD. (*S. daphnoides* var. *acutifolia* (WILLD.) DOELL) (*S. pruinosa* BESS.) A very graceful, large shrub, occasionally a small tree, with lanceolate, long-pointed leaves and slender, damson-coloured shoots overlaid with a white bloom. Catkins appearing before the leaves. Closely related to *S. daphnoides* from which it differs in its more slender, darker twigs, smaller, narrower catkins and narrower, longer tapered and more numerously veined leaves. Russia. C 1890. AGM 1984.

**'Blue Streak'** A male clone of Dutch origin, with polished, blackish-purple stems covered with a vivid blue-white bloom.

**'Pendulifolia'** A beautiful, male form with conspicuously drooping leaves.

**adenophylla** See *S. cordata*.

**aegyptiaca** L. (*S. medemii* BOISS.) (*S. muscina* HORT.) "Musk Willow". A large shrub or occasionally a small tree, with densely grey-pubescent twigs. Leaves lanceolate, grey pubescent beneath. Its large conspicuous bright yellow male catkins occur in February and March, making this a very beautiful early spring flowering tree. SW to C Asia. C 1820. AM 1925 (as *S. medemii*). AM 1957 (as *S. aegyptiaca*).

**alba** L. "White Willow". A familiar native species of water meadows and riversides. A large, elegant tree of conical habit, with slender branches, drooping at the tips. The lanceolate, silky-hairy leaves occur in great, billowy masses, creating a characteristic silvery appearance from a distance. The slender catkins appear with the young leaves in spring. A vigorous, fast-growing tree, much planted in moist, sandy areas by the sea. Europe, W Asia.

**f. argentea** See var. *sericea*.

**'Aurea'** A less vigorous tree with yellowish-green branches and pale yellow leaves.

**'Britzensis'** ('Chermesina') "Scarlet Willow". A remarkable form, most conspicuous in winter when the branches are brilliant orange-scarlet, especially if pruned severely every second year. The clone 'Chrysostela' is similar, if not identical. AM 1976. AGM 1984.

**var. caerulea** (SM.) SM. (*S.* 'Caerulea') (*S.* × *caerulea* SM.) "Cricket-bat Willow". A large tree of conical habit, with spreading branches and lanceolate leaves which are sea-green above and somewhat glaucous beneath. The best willow for cricket bats and long planted for this purpose in E England. The original tree is said to have been found in Norfolk about 1700. The female form is most commonly grown.

**'Chermesina'** See 'Britzensis'.

**'Chrysostela'** See under 'Britzensis'.

**'Liempde'** A vigorous male form with upright branches making a narrowly conical tree. Selected in Holland where it is commonly planted. C 1968.

**SALIX alba**—*continued*

**var. sericea** GAUDIN (f. *argentea* WIMM.) ('Sericea') ('Regalis') A smaller, less vigorous, rounder-headed tree with leaves of an intense silvery hue, striking when seen from a distance. AGM 1984.

**'Tristis'** See *S.* × *sepulcralis* 'Chrysocoma'.

**var. vitellina** (L.) STOKES (*S. vitellina* L.) "Golden Willow". A smaller tree than the type. The brilliant yolk-of-egg-yellow shoots are made more conspicuous by severe pruning every second year. AMT 1967. AGM 1984.

**'Vitellina Pendula'** See *S.* × *sepulcralis* 'Chrysocoma'.

**amygdalina** See *S. triandra*.

**apoda** TRAUTV. A dwarf species with prostrate stems closely hugging the ground and glossy green leaves paler beneath. The erect, silvery-furry, male catkins appear all along the branches in early spring, before the leaves, and gradually elongate until 2.5-3cm long, when they are decked in bright yellow anthers. A superb plant for the rock garden or scree. Both *S. retusa* and *S. uva-ursi* are occasionally wrongly grown under his name. Caucasus, Turkey. C before 1939. AM 1948.

**arbuscula** L. (*S. formosa* WILLD.) A dwarf, creeping shrub forming close mats of green leaves, glaucous beneath. Catkins long and slender, produced with the young leaves in spring. Scandinavia, N Russia, Scotland.

**'Erecta'** See *S. waldsteiniana*.

**arbutifolia** PALL. (*S. eucalyptoides* MEYER ex SCHNEID.) (*Chosenia arbutifolia* (PALL.) SKVORTS.) (*Chosenia bracteosa* (TURCZ.) NAKAI) Said to attain large tree size in its native habitats. Long willowy stems covered by a conspicuous white bloom. Leaves lanceolate, bright green and bloomy at first. A rare tree or large shrub of elegant habit. It is distinct among the willows in its pendulous, not erect, male catkins, its glandless flowers and other botanical characters. N Asia. I 1906.

**atrocinerea** See *S. cinerea* subsp. *oleifolia*.

**aurita** L. "Eared Willow". A small to medium-sized, native shrub with small, wrinkled, dull green leaves, grey woolly beneath. Catkins produced before the leaves in early April. A common willow of bogs and streamsides on acid soils. N and C Europe (including Britain).

**babylonica** L. "Weeping Willow". An attractive tree of medium size with a wide-spreading head of long, pendulous, glabrous, brown branches. Leaves long and narrow, green above, bluish-grey beneath; catkins slender, appearing with the young leaves in spring. A native of China, but long cultivated in E Europe, N Africa and W Asia. Said to have been first introduced to W Europe during the late 17th century and into England about 1730. Most of the trees cultivated in this country are said to be female. At one time widely cultivated as a waterside tree, it has now largely been superseded by *S.* × *sepulcralis* 'Chrysocoma' and other similar hybrids.

**'Crispa'** ('Annularis') A curious form in which the leaves are spirally curled.

**var. pekinensis** HENRY (*S. matsudana* KOIDZ.) "Pekin Willow". A medium-sized, graceful tree of conical habit, with slender stems and long, narrow, slender-pointed leaves which are green above and glaucous beneath. Catkins appearing with the leaves in spring. Only the female form is in general cultivation. N China, Manchuria, Korea. I 1905.

**'Pendula'** A very graceful tree and one of the best weeping willows, showing resistance to scab and canker.

**'Tortuosa'** "Dragon's Claw Willow". A curious form with branches and twigs much twisted and contorted. AGM 1984.

**'Ramulis Aureis'** See *S.* × *sepulcralis* 'Chrysocoma'.

× **balfourii** LINTON (*S. caprea* × *S. lanata*). A splendid, strong-growing, medium-sized to large bush, intermediate in character between the parents. Young leaves grey woolly becoming green and downy later in the year. Catkins appearing before the leaves in early April, yellowish and silky-hairy, with tiny red bracts. A remarkable and useful shrub, especially for damp sites. Said to have originated in Scotland. Ours is a male clone.

**'Basfordiana'** See *S.* × *rubens* 'Basfordiana'.

**bicolor** See *S. schraderiana*.

× **blanda** See *S.* × *pendulina* 'Blanda'.

**SALIX**—*continued*

**bockii** SEEMEN An attractive small to medium-sized shrub, usually seen as a neat, spreading bush, 1-1.2m high. The numerous, slender, reddish twigs are greyish downy when young and in spring are thickly peppered with the bright green emerging leaf-clusters. The numerous, small, greyish catkins appear along the current year's growth in late summer and autumn, the only willow in general cultivation to flower at this time of the year. W China. Introduced by E.H. Wilson in 1908.

×**boydii** LINTON (*S. lapponum* × *S. reticulata*). A dwarf, erect, slow-growing shrub of gnarled appearance, with rounded, grey downy leaves becoming green above. A female clone, with rarely produced small, dark grey catkins. An ideal shrub for a trough or for a pocket on the rock garden or scree. Found in the 1870s, only on a single occasion in the mountains of Angus in Scotland. AM 1958.

**'Caerulea'** See *S. alba* var. *caerulea.*

×**calliantha** KERN. (*S. daphnoides* × *S. purpurea*). A small tree or large shrub with non-bloomy stems and lanceolate to oblanceolate, serrated leaves, glossy dark green above, sea-green beneath. Ours is a female clone. C 1872.

**caprea** L. "Goat Willow" or "Great Sallow". A common and familiar native species, particularly noticeable in early spring when the large, yellow, male catkins are gathered as "Palm" by children. The female form known as "Pussy Willow" has silver catkins. A large shrub or small tree with stout twigs and oval or obovate leaves, grey tomentose beneath. Europe, W Asia.

**'Kilmarnock'** ('Pendula' in part) "Kilmarnock Willow". A small, umbrella-like, male tree with stiffly pendulous branches; rarely reaching 3m. Attractive silvery catkins studded with golden anthers in late winter. C 1853. AM 1977. AGM 1984.

**'Pendula'** See 'Kilmarnock' and 'Weeping Sally'.

**'Weeping Sally'** ('Pendula' in part) Similar to 'Kilmarnock' but female. More vigorous but less effective in flower. C 1880.

**caspica** PALL. A large shrub or small tree with long, whip-like, pale grey stems and linear-lanceolate leaves. A rare species from SE Russia, W and C Asia.

×**chrysocoma** See *S.* × *sepulcralis* 'Chrysocoma'.

**cinerea** L. "Grey Sallow". A large shrub or occasionally a small tree. It has stout pubescent twigs and obovate leaves which are grey tomentose beneath. Catkins appearing before the leaves in early spring. Europe (including British Isles), W Asia, Tunisia.

**subsp. oleifolia** MACREIGHT (subsp. *atrocinerea* (BROT.) SILVA & SOBRINHO) (*S. atrocinerea* BROT.) "Common Sallow". Similar in general habit, but branches more erect and leaves more leathery, glaucous beneath and with rust-coloured hairs. Perhaps its only claim to cultivation is its toughness and usefulness for planting in derelict areas, such as slag heaps, where it will help in the task of reclamation and reafforestation. Both this species and *S. caprea* are familiar hedgerow shrubs throughout the British Isles. Europe, S Russia.

**'Tricolor'** ('Variegata') Leaves splashed and mottled yellow and creamy-white. Perhaps the only form of this species which can claim garden merit.

**cordata** MICHX. (*S. adenophylla* HOOK.) "Furry Willow". A loosely branched, large shrub or small tree, with densely grey downy twigs, clothed with ovate, finely-toothed, silky-hairy leaves up to 5cm long. Catkins before the leaves in early spring. NE North America. C 1900.

×**cottetii** LAGGER ex KERN (*S.* × *gillotii* HORT.) (*S. myrsinifolia* × *S. retusa*). A vigorous, low-growing shrub with long trailing stems forming carpets several metres across. Leaves dark, shining green above, paler beneath; catkins before the leaves in early spring. Our plant is a male clone. Too vigorous for the small rock garden, but an excellent ground cover. European Alps. C 1905.

**dahurica** See *S. miyabeana.*

**daphnoides** VILL. "Violet Willow". A fast-growing, small tree with long, purple-violet shoots which are attractively overlaid with a white bloom. Catkins before the leaves in spring. Extremely effective in winter especially when hard pruned each or every other year in late March. Female trees are narrower and more columnar in habit than the male. N Europe, C Asia, Himalaya. C 1829. AM 1957.

**var. acutifolia** See *S. acutifolia.*

**SALIX daphnoides**—*continued*

**'Aglaia'** A male clone with large, handsome, silvery then bright yellow catkins in early spring. Stems not bloomed, red in winter.

× **dasyclados** WIMM. A large shrub or small tree with downy stems and ovate to oblong-lanceolate, sharply-pointed leaves, glaucescent and downy beneath. A willow of obscure origin, possibly the hybrid *S. caprea* × *S. cinerea* × *S. viminalis*.

**'Grandis'** A particularly vigorous form.

**'Decipiens'** See *S. fragilis* var. *decipiens*.

**discolor** MUHL. A strong-growing, large shrub, occasionally a small tree with stout, downy shoots, glabrous in the third year. Leaves grey tomentose beneath. Catkins appearing before the leaves in March or early April. E North America. I 1811.

× **doniana** SM. (*S. purpurea* × *S. repens*). A small to medium-sized shrub with oblong or lanceous leaves, glaucous beneath. Catkins before the leaves in spring, the males with red anthers, ripening to yellow. Occurs with the parents in the wild. C 1829.

× **ehrhartiana** SM. (*S. alba* × *S. pentandra*). A large shrub or small to medium-sized tree with polished, olive-brown twigs and oblong-lanceolate, shining green leaves. Catkins appearing with or after the leaves. Europe (including British Isles). C 1894.

**elaeagnos** SCOP. (*S. incana* SCHRANK) (*S. rosmarinifolia* HORT. not L.) "Hoary Willow". A beautiful, medium-sized to large shrub of dense, bushy habit. Leaves linear, like elongated leaves of rosemary, greyish hoary at first becoming green above and white beneath, thickly clothing the slender, reddish-brown, wand-like stems. Catkins slender, appearing with the young leaves in spring. One of the prettiest willows for waterside planting. C and S Europe, Asia Minor. I about 1820. AGM 1984. AM 1989 (for foliage).

**'Elegantissima'** See *S.* × *pendulina* 'Elegantissima'.

× **erdingeri** KERN. (*S. caprea* × *S. daphnoides*). An attractive large shrub or small tree, its greenish stems covered with bluish-white bloom. Leaves obovate to oblong, glossy green above, appearing after the catkins in spring. Ours is a female clone. Europe. C 1872.

**eriocephala** MICHX. (*S. missouriensis* BEBB) Small to medium-sized tree with slender, spreading, reddish-brown branches, pubescent when young and narrowly lanceolate leaves, hairy at first, later almost glabrous. Catkins before the leaves. E and C North America. I 1898.

× **erythroflexuosa** See *S.* × *sepulcralis* 'Erythroflexuosa'.

**eucalyptoides** See *S. arbutifolia*.

**exigua** NUTT. "Coyote Willow". A beautiful, large, erect shrub or a small tree with long, slender, greyish-brown branches clothed with linear, silvery-silky, minutely-toothed leaves. Catkins slender, appearing with the leaves. W North America, N Mexico. I 1921. AGM 1984.

**fargesii** BURK. A medium-sized to large shrub of rather open habit, with stout, glabrous shoots which are a polished, reddish-brown in their second year. Winter buds reddish, large and conspicuous. Leaves elliptic to oblong-elliptic, up to 18cm long and deep glossy green with impressed venation. Catkins appearing with or after the leaves, slender and ascending, the females 10-15cm long. C China. I 1911 by Ernest Wilson. Closely related to *S. moupinensis*. AGM 1984.

× **finnmarchica** WILLD. (*S. myrtilloides* × *S. repens*). A dwarf shrub, forming a low wide-spreading patch, with slender, ascending shoots and small leaves. The small catkins crowd the stems before the leaves in early spring. Ours is a female clone. Excellent for the rock garden, or as ground cover. Found in the wild with the parents in N and C Europe.

**foetida** SCHLEICHER ex LAM. A dwarf shrub with trailing stems and dark green, sharply-toothed leaves. Catkins produced with the leaves in spring. Mts of Europe (W and C Alps, C Pyrenees).

**formosa** See *S. arbuscula*.

**fragilis** L. "Crack Willow". A large, native tree with wide-spreading branches, as familiar as the White Willow, the two often growing together by rivers and streams. Bark rugged and channelled, twigs brittle at their joints. Leaves lanceolate, glabrous, sharply-toothed, glossy dark green above, green or sometimes bluish-green beneath. Catkins slender, appearing with the leaves in spring. Europe, N Asia.

**'Basfordiana'** See *S.* × *rubens* 'Basfordiana'.

**SALIX fragilis**—*continued*

**var. decipiens** (HOFFM.) KOCH (*S.* 'Decipiens') "White Welsh Willow". A small tree or large bush with polished yellowish-grey branches which are orange or rich red on the exposed side when young. The lanceolate, toothed leaves are shining green above. Usually male.

**'Ginme'** See *S.* × *tsugaluensis* 'Ginme'.

**glaucosericea** B. FLOD. An attractive grey, dwarf shrub suitable for the rock garden. Leaves narrowly elliptic to elliptic-lanceolate, densely grey hairy at first, less so by autumn. European Alps, Pyrenees.

**gracilistyla** MIQ. A very splendid, vigorous, medium-sized shrub with stout, densely grey pubescent young shoots. Leaves silky grey downy at first, gradually becoming green and smooth, remaining late in the autumn. Catkins appearing before the leaves in early spring, the young males are grey and silky, through which the reddish, unopened anthers can be seen; later they are bright yellow. One of the most effective catkin-bearing shrubs. Japan, Korea, Manchuria, China. I 1895. AM 1925. AGM 1984.

**'Melanostachys'** (*S. gracilistyla* var. *melanostachys* (MAK.) SCHNEID.) (*S.* 'Melanostachys') (*S. melanostachys* MAK.) (*S.* 'Kureneko') (*S.* 'Kurome') (*S.* 'Kuroyanagi'). An attractive and unusual form. Quite outstanding in the remarkable colour combination of its catkins appearing before the leaves, very dark, with blackish scales and brick-red anthers, opening to yellow. The stout twigs are thickly clustered with oblanceolate leaves, glaucous beneath at first and sharply serrate. A male clone, known only in cultivation. Differs from the typical form in its glabrous twigs, non-silky catkins, longer, darker coloured bracts, shorter glands, etc. AM 1976. AGM 1984.

**× grahamii** BORR. ex BAK. (*S. aurita* × *S. herbacea* × *S. repens*). A dwarf, procumbent shrub forming large patches of slender stems and broad elliptic to oblong-elliptic, shining green leaves, 2.5-4cm in length. Catkins erect, appearing with or after the leaves. Ours is a female clone. Occurring wild with the parents in Sutherland, Scotland, originally found about 1830 by Prof Robert Graham.

**'Moorei'** (*S.* × *moorei* F.B. WHITE) A dwarf shrub for the rock garden or scree, forming a low, wide-spreading mound of slender stems. Leaves small, shining green; catkins before the leaves in spring. An excellent ground cover, not too vigorous. A female form found by David Moore in Co Donegal in 1886.

**hastata** L. A small shrub with obovate to elliptic leaves, which are sea-green beneath. Catkins produced before or with the leaves in spring. C and S Europe to NE Asia and Kashmir. I 1780.

**'Wehrhahnii'** (*S. wehrhahnii* BONST.) A slow-growing, small to medium-sized shrub of spreading habit. In spring the stout twigs become alive with pretty, silvery-grey, male catkins which later turn yellow. Found in Switzerland about 1930. AM 1964. AGM 1984.

**helvetica** VILL. A small, bushy shrub, the young stems, leaves and catkins clothed in a soft, greyish pubescence. The small, oblanceolate leaves are grey-green above, white beneath. Catkins appearing with the young leaves in spring. An attractive foliage shrub for the rock garden. European Alps. C 1872. AGM 1984.

**herbacea** L. "Dwarf Willow". A tiny, alpine species and one of the smallest British shrubs, forming mats of creeping, often underground stems. Leaves rounded, up to 2cm long, glossy green and prominently reticulate, borne in pairs or in threes at the tips of each shoot. Catkins up to 2cm long, appearing with the leaves in spring. Suitable for a moist position in the peat garden or rock garden. Arctic and mountainous regions of Europe and North America.

**'Hippophaifolia'** See *S.* × *mollissima* var. *hippophaifolia*.

**hookeriana** BARR. A medium-sized to large shrub or small tree with glossy, reddish-brown branches, tomentose when young. Leaves oblong, acute, glossy green above, densely felted beneath. Catkins with the leaves. W North America. C 1891.

**humilis** MARSH. "Prairie Willow". A vigorous, medium-sized shrub. Leaves obovate or oblong-lanceolate, dark green above, glaucous and tomentose beneath. Catkins appearing before the leaves, the males with brick-red, later yellow anthers, the females with brick-red stigmas. E North America. I 1876.

**incana** See *S. elaeagnos*.

**SALIX**—*continued*

**integra** THUNB. (*S. purpurea* var. *multinervis* (FRANCH. & SAV.) KOIDZ.) (*S.* 'Axukime') A large shrub or small tree of elegant habit. Branches long and slightly drooping, leaves generally in pairs, oblong, bright green, almost sessile. The slender catkins grace the polished stems in early April, before the leaves. A graceful fast-growing species, ideally suitable for waterside planting. Japan, Korea.

**'Hakuro Nishiki'** ('Albomaculata') Leaves conspicuously blotched with white. I from Japan in 1979 by the Dutch botanist Harry van de Laar.

**irrorata** ANDERSS. A vigorous, medium-sized shrub, the long shoots green when young, then purple and covered with a striking white bloom, particularly noticeable in winter. Leaves lanceolate or oblong-lanceolate, glossy green above, glaucous beneath. Catkins appearing before the leaves, the males with brick-red anthers turning to yellow. An attractive species for contrasting with the red and yellow-stemmed clones. SW United States. I 1898. AMT 1967.

**japonica** THUNB. A large shrub with long, slender, pale stems of elegant disposition. Leaves slenderly-pointed, serrulate, bright green above, glaucous beneath. Catkins slender, appearing with the leaves. Japan. C 1874.

**kinuyanagi** KIMURA (*S.* 'Kishu') A strong-growing, large shrub or small tree with long, stout, greyish-brown-felted shoots and long, narrow leaves, silky-hairy beneath. Catkins bright yellow, closely arrayed along the stems in March. Only the male form is known. Native of Korea and introduced to Japan where it is widely cultivated. It is related to our native osier (*S. viminalis*), which it closely resembles.

**'Kishu'** See *S. kinuyanagi*.

**koriyanagi** KIMURA (*S. purpurea* var. *japonica* NAKAI) A large, erect-growing shrub or small tree with slender, whip-like stems. The sub-opposite, bright green leaves are suffused an attractive orange-red on emerging. Catkins slender, in rows along the stems, the males with orange anthers. Korea; widely cultivated in Japan for basket-making and furniture. AM 1990.

**'Kureneko'** See *S. gracilistyla* 'Melanostachys'.

**'Kurome'** See *S. gracilistyla* 'Melanostachys'.

**'Kuroyanagi'** See *S. gracilistyla* 'Melanostachys'.

**lanata** L. "Woolly Willow". An attractive, slow-growing shrub usually 0.6-1.2m high, or occasionally more, with ovate to rounded, silvery-grey downy leaves and stout, erect, yellowish-grey woolly catkins in spring. The female catkins elongate considerably in fruit, sometimes measuring 10cm long. A rare native alpine species suitable for the rock garden. N Europe (including Scotland). AGM 1984.

**'Stuartii'** See *S.* 'Stuartii'.

**lapponum** L. "Lapland Willow". A small, densely-branched shrub with grey, downy leaves, 2.5-5cm long. The silky, grey catkins are produced before the leaves in spring. Mts of Europe (including British Isles), Siberia. C 1789.

**lasiandra** BENTH. "Pacific Willow". A large, strong-growing tree with the general appearance of *S. fragilis*. Leaves lanceolate, sharply glandular-toothed, glaucous at first beneath. Catkins with the leaves in spring. W North America. C 1883.

**lasiolepis** BENTH. A large shrub or small tree with linear, toothed leaves dull green above, glaucous beneath. An elegant species, with attractive, grey, female catkins before the leaves in early spring. W United States, N Mexico.

**livida** See *S. starkeana*.

**lucida** MUHL. "Shining Willow". A large shrub or a small to medium-sized tree with glossy young shoots and lanceolate, slender-pointed, glossy green leaves. Catkins produced with the leaves in spring. NE North America. C 1830.

**mackenzieana** (HOOK.) BARR. A small tree of upright habit, with long, slender, pale yellow-green stems and lanceolate leaves. W North America.

**magnifica** HEMSL. A large shrub or small tree of sparse habit, bearing large, oval or obovate, magnolia-like leaves up to 20cm long and 13cm wide. Catkins produced with the leaves in spring, the females often 15-25cm in length. A most impressive and unusual species, native of W China, introduced by Ernest Wilson in 1909 who, when he first found it, thought he had discovered a new magnolia. AM 1913.

**SALIX**—*continued*

**'Mark Postill'** (*S. hastata* 'Wehrhahnii' × *S. lanata*). A dwarf shrub of spreading habit with purplish-brown winter shoots. Leaves pale green when young becoming sparsely white hairy then dark green. Stout green catkins, silvery as they emerge are produced over a long period with and after the leaves. Raised by our propagator Alan Postill in 1967 and named after his son.

**matsudana** See *S. babylonica* var. *pekinensis*.

**medemii** See *S. aegyptiaca*.

**medwedewii** DODE A small shrub, related to *S. triandra* of which it is possibly only a form. Leaves long and narrow, vividly glaucous beneath. Catkins produced with the leaves in spring. Asia Minor. C 1910.

**'Melanostachys'** See *S. gracilistyla* 'Melanostachys'.

× **meyeriana** ROSTK. ex WILLD. (*S. fragilis* × *S. pentandra*). A vigorous, medium-sized to large tree with oval, glossy green leaves, glaucescent beneath. Catkins appearing with the leaves in spring. Europe (including British Isles). C 1829.

**missouriensis** See *S. eriocephala*.

**miyabeana** SEEM. (*S. dahurica* TURCZ. ex KAKSCHEWITZ) A large shrub or small tree with long, slender, polished brown stems which, in spring and summer, are heavily clothed with narrow, pale green leaves. Catkins before the leaves. NE Asia. I 1897.

× **mollissima** HOFFM. ex ELWERT (*S. triandra* × *S. viminalis*) (*S. trevirani* SPRENG.) A variable hybrid forming a large shrub or small tree, the catkins appearing with the young leaves in spring. Occurs with the parents in the wild, though the typical form has not been found in Britain.

**var. hippophaifolia** (THUILL.) WIMM. A large shrub or small tree with olive-brown twigs and long, narrow leaves. Catkins similar to those of *S. triandra*, but with reddish anthers. Ours is a male form. England.

× **moorei** See *S.* × *grahamii* 'Moorei'.

**moupinensis** FRANCH. A very beautiful, medium-sized shrub of great quality, related to and generally resembling *S. fargesii*, with which it has long been confused in gardens. It differs from that species mainly in its slightly smaller, normally glabrous leaves. Both species are extremely ornamental at all times of the year. China. Introduced by Armand David in 1869 and by E.H. Wilson in 1910.

**muscina** HORT. See *S. aegyptiaca*.

**myrsinifolia** SALISB. (*S. nigricans* SM.) A medium-sized to large, native shrub with downy twigs and downy, variably shaped leaves, dark green above, generally glaucous beneath. Catkins appearing before the leaves. N and C Europe.

**myrsinites** L. "Whortle Willow". A prostrate, native species forming dense carpets of shortly ascending stems clothed with shining, bright green leaves and bearing large, attractive catkins in April. An ideal species for the rock garden. N Europe, N Asia.

**nigricans** See *S. myrsinifolia*.

**nitida** See *S. repens* var. *argentea*.

× **pendulina** WENDEROTH (*S. babylonica* × *S. fragilis*). A small to medium-sized, normally female, weeping tree similar to *S. babylonica* but of better constitution. Originated in Germany in the early 19th century.

**'Blanda'** (*S.* × *blanda* ANDERSS.) A small to medium-sized tree with a wide-spreading head of weeping branches. Leaves lanceolate, glabrous, bluish-green beneath. Catkins produced with the leaves. C 1830.

**'Elegantissima'** (*S.* × *elegantissima* C. KOCH) "Thurlow Weeping Willow". Similar to 'Blanda' in habit but more strongly weeping. Both trees are sometimes found in cultivation under the name *S. babylonica*.

**pentandra** L. "Bay Willow". A beautiful small to medium-sized tree, or occasionally a large shrub, with glossy twigs and attractive, bay-like lustrous green leaves, pleasantly aromatic when unfolding or when crushed. Catkins produced with the leaves in late spring, the males bright yellow. Found wild in N parts of the British Isles, planted elsewhere. Used as a substitute for bay in Norway. Europe, N Asia.

**phylicifolia** L. "Tea-leaf Willow". A medium-sized, native shrub with dark, glabrous twigs and leaves which are shining green above and glaucous beneath. Catkins appearing before the leaves. N Europe.

**SALIX**—*continued*

×**pontederiana** See *S.* × *sordida*.

**pruinosa** See *S. acutifolia*.

**purpurea** L. "Purple Osier". A graceful, medium-sized to large shrub with long, arching, often purplish shoots. Leaves narrowly oblong, dull green above, paler or glaucous beneath, often in opposite pairs. Catkins slender, produced all along the shoots in spring before the leaves. The wood of the young shoots is a bright yellow beneath the bark, a character which is normally present in its hybrids. Europe (including British Isles), C Asia.

**'Eugenei'** See *S.* × *rubra* 'Eugenei'.

**'Gracilis'** See 'Nana'.

**var. japonica** See *S. koriyanagi*.

**'Nana'** ('Gracilis') A dwarf, compact, slender-branched cultivar. A useful low hedge for a damp site.

**'Pendula'** An attractive form with long, pendulous branches; trained as a standard it forms a charming, small, weeping tree. AGM 1984.

**pyrifolia** ANDERSS. (*S. balsamifera* BARRATT ex BEBB) "Balsam Willow". A large shrub or occasionally a small tree, with shining reddish-brown twigs and red winter buds. Leaves ovate-lanceolate, glaucous and reticulate beneath. Catkins appearing with the leaves in spring. Canada, NE United States. I 1880.

**rehderiana** SCHNEID. A large shrub or small tree with lanceolate, bright green leaves, grey silky beneath. W China. I 1908 by Ernest Wilson.

**repens** L. "Creeping Willow". Normally a small, creeping shrub, but in some forms occasionally 1.8-2.5m high, forming large patches or dense clumps of slender, erect stems clothed with small, greyish-green leaves, silvery-white beneath. Catkins small, crowding the naked stems in spring. A common native species of heaths, bogs and commons, particularly on acid soils. Europe, N Asia. AM 1988 (for flower).

**var. argentea** (SM.) WIMM. & GRAB. (var. *nitida* WENDEROTH) (*S. arenaria* L.) An attractive, semi-prostrate variety with silvery-silky leaves. Abundant in moist, sandy areas by the sea. Grown as a standard it makes an effective miniature weeping tree. Atlantic coasts of Europe. AGM 1984.

**var. subopposita** See *S. subopposita*.

**'Voorthuizen'** A charming little plant of Dutch origin, the slender prostrate stems bearing small, silky leaves and tiny female catkins. Suitable for the small rock garden or scree.

**reticulata** L. A dwarf, native shrub with prostrate stems, forming dense mats. Leaves small, orbicular or ovate, entire, dark green and attractively net-veined above, glaucous beneath. Catkins erect, appearing after the leaves. A dainty, pretty little willow suitable for a moist ledge on the rock garden. Artic and mountain areas of North America, Europe and N Asia. C 1789. AM 1981 (to a male plant).

**retusa** L. A prostrate species forming extensive carpets of creeping stems and small, notched, polished green leaves. Catkins erect, 12-20mm long, appearing with the leaves. Mts of Europe. I 1763.

**rosmarinifolia** See *S. elaeagnos*.

×**rubens** SCHRANK (*S. alba* × *S. fragilis*). (*S.* × *viridis*) A common and variable native hybrid generally intermediate in character between the parents, with some clones leaning more to one than the other. A large, fast-growing tree with lanceolate leaves, green or glaucous beneath. Occurring in the wild either with or without the parents.

**'Basfordiana'** (*S.* 'Basfordiana') (*S. fragilis* 'Basfordiana') A medium-sized to large tree with long narrow leaves and conspicuous, orange-red twigs in winter. A male clone with long, slender, yellow catkins appearing with the leaves in spring. Said to have been found originally in the Ardennes, about 1863, by Mr Scaling, a nurseryman of Basford, Nottinghamshire.

**'Sanguinea'** A female clone similar to 'Basfordiana' but with smaller leaves and redder shoots.

×**rubra** HUDS. (*S. purpurea* × *S. viminalis*). A large shrub or small tree with glossy, yellow-brown shoots and narrow, dark glossy green leaves. Catkins borne before the leaves. Commonly found with the parents. Europe.

**SALIX** × **rubra**—*continued*

**'Eugenei'** (*S. purpurea* 'Eugenei') An erect-branched, small tree of slender conical habit producing an abundance of subtly attractive, grey-pink male catkins.

**sachalinensis** See *S. udensis*.

**'Sekka'** See *S. udensis* 'Sekka'.

× **salamonii** See *S.* × *sepulcralis* 'Salamonii'.

**schraderiana** WILLD. (*S. bicolor* WILLD.) A medium-sized shrub, closely related to *S. phylicifolia*. Shoots stout, with yellowish bud in winter. Leaves glossy green above, glaucous beneath. Catkins with reddish anthers, opening to yellow. Mts of Europe, but not the Alps.

× **sepulcralis** SIMONK. (*S.* × *salamonii* CARR. ex HENRY) (*S. alba* × *S. babylonica*). Hybrids between these two species have arisen fairly frequently. For the plant previously grown under this name see 'Salamonii'.

**'Chrysocoma'** (*S.* × *chrysocoma* DODE) (*S. alba* var. *vitellina* × *S. babylonica*) (*S. alba* 'Vitellina Pendula') (*S. alba* 'Tristis') (*S. babylonica* 'Ramulis Aureis') Possibly the most beautiful weeping tree hardy in our climate. A medium-sized, wide-spreading tree producing vigorous, arching branches which terminate in slender, golden yellow, weeping branchlets, ultimately of great length. Leaves lanceolate; catkins appearing with the leaves in April, both male and female flowers in the same catkin, or occasionally catkins all male or all female. Frequently seen planted in small gardens for which it is not suitable. C 1888. AGM 1984. Unfortunately subject to scab and canker, which may be controlled on young trees by spraying with a suitable fungicide.

**'Erythroflexuosa'** (*S.* × *erythroflexuosa* RAG.) (*S.* × *sepulcralis* 'Chrysocoma' × *S. babylonica* 'Tortuosa'). A curious, ornamental, small tree discovered in Argentina. The vigorous, orange-yellow, pendulous shoots are twisted and contorted, as are the narrow leaves.

**'Salamonii'** A medium-sized tree of weeping habit with long, slender, pendulous stems and linear-lanceolate, glossy-green leaves, glaucous beneath at first. Catkins appearing with the leaves in spring. A vigorous tree resembling *S. babylonica*, but less pendulous. Garden origin before 1864.

× **seringeana** GAUD. (*S. caprea* × *S. elaeagnos*) (*S. salviifolia* LINK.) A large shrub or small tree of erect habit, with grey tomentose stems and lanceolate or narrowly oblong, softly grey downy leaves, pale beneath. A most ornamental, grey-leaved hybrid. C 1872.

**'Setsuka'** See *S. udensis* 'Sekka'.

× **smithiana** WILLD. (*S. cinerea* × *S. viminalis*). A strong-growing, variable, large native shrub or small tree, with long, stout branches, tomentose when young. Leaves lanceolate, silky-hairy beneath. Catkins produced before the leaves in spring. Ours is a female form. Found in the wild only in the British Isles. The most commonly used stem for top-working.

× **sordida** (*S.* × *pontederiana* WILLD.) (*S. cinerea* × *S. purpurea*). A medium-sized to large shrub with branches hairy at first. Leaves obovate-lanceolate, silky-hairy and glaucous beneath. Catkins produced in March, before the leaves. Ours is a male form with yellow anthers prettily red-tinted when young. Europe. C 1820.

**'Spaethii'** A small tree with stout, densely hairy shoots, long leaves and female catkins. Of Continental origin.

**starkeana** WILLD. (*S. livida* VAHL) Small to medium-sized shrub with broad elliptic leaves, glossy green above, glaucous green beneath. Catkins appearing before the leaves. N and C Europe, N Asia. C 1872.

**'Stipularis'** A vigorous, small tree or large shrub with tomentose shoots and lanceolate leaves, glaucous and downy beneath. Conspicuous on account of its large foliaceous stipules.

**'Stuartii'** (*S. lanata* 'Stuartii') A dwarf, gnarled shrublet, conspicuous in winter with its yellow shoots and orange buds. Its leaves are smaller, but its catkins larger than those of *S. lanata*. Probably *S. lanata* × *S. lapponum*.

**subopposita** MIQ. (*S. repens* var. *subopposita* (MIQ.) SEEM.) A rare and very distinct dwarf shrub with slender, erect and spreading stems and small leaves which are opposite or nearly so. Catkins before the leaves in early spring, the male with brick-red anthers turning to yellow. This unusual little willow has the stance of a *Hebe*. Japan, Korea.

**SALIX**—*continued*

× **tetrapla** WALKER ex SM. (*S. myrsinifolia* × *S. phylicifolia*). Small to medium-sized native shrub of stiff habit with stout, glossy, yellowish-green twigs and oblong-elliptic leaves, glossy green above, glaucous beneath. Occasionally found with the parents in the wild. C 1829.

**trevirani** See *S.* × *mollissima*.

**triandra** L. (*S. amygdalina* L.) "Almond-leaved Willow". A large shrub or small tree with flaky bark and lanceolate, glossy green, serrated leaves, glaucous beneath. Catkins produced with the leaves in spring, the males fragrant and almost mimosa-like. Europe to E Asia. Long cultivated in Europe for basket-making.

    **var. hoffmanniana** BAB. An uncommon variety with smaller, oblong-lanceolate leaves, green beneath.

× **tsugaluensis** KOIDZ. (*S. integra* × *S. vulpina*). This hybrid occurs in the wild in Japan. The following is considered to belong here.

    **'Ginme'** A medium-sized to large shrub of vigorous, spreading habit. Leaves oblong, bright green, paler beneath and orange-tinged when young. Catkins silvery, slender and recurved appearing all along the naked stems in spring. A female clone of Japanese origin.

**udensis** TRAUTV. & MEY. (*S. sachalinensis* F. SCHMIDT) A large shrub or small tree of spreading habit, with young shoots of a polished chestnut-brown. Leaves lanceolate, slender-pointed, shining green above, pale or glaucous beneath. Catkins appearing before the leaves, the males large and conspicuous. NE Asia. I 1905. A vigorous, ornamental willow usually seen in the following clone.

    **'Sekka'** ('Setsuka') A male clone of Japanese origin, noted for its occasional curiously flattened and recurved stems, which may be encouraged by hard pruning. Useful when cut for "Japanese" floral arrangements.

**uva-ursi** PURSH. "Bearberry Willow". A prostrate shrub forming dense carpets of creeping stems clothed with small, glossy green leaves. Catkins appearing with the young leaves in spring. A superb plant for the rock garden or scree. Has been confused with *S. apoda* and *S. retusa*. Canada, NE United States. I 1880.

**viminalis** L. "Common Osier". A large, vigorous shrub or a small tree with long, straight shoots thickly grey tomentose when young. Leaves long and narrow, tapering to a fine point, dull green above, covered with silvery silky hairs beneath. Catkins appearing before the leaves. A very common native species of rivers, streamsides, lakes and marshes. Long cultivated for basket-making. Europe to NE Asia and Himalaya.

× **viridis** See *S.* × *rubens*.

**vitellina** See *S. alba* var. *vitellina*.

**waldsteiniana** WILLD. (*S. arbuscula* 'Erecta') A medium-sized upright-branched shrub closely related to *S. arbuscula*. Leaves glossy green, longer than in *S. arbuscula*, entire or slightly-toothed. Catkins about 2.5cm long, borne with the leaves on leafy peduncles to 1.5cm long. SE Europe.

**wehrhahnii** See *S. hastata* 'Wehrhahnii'.

**wilhelmsiana** BIEB. A large, elegant shrub with slender, wand-like stems and narrow, obscurely-toothed leaves which, like the stems, are silky-hairy at first, later shining green. Catkins appearing with the leaves in spring. SE Russia to SC Asia. C 1887.

× **wimmeriana** GREN. & GODR. (*S. caprea* × *S. purpurea*). A medium-sized shrub with slender branches and oblong to lanceolate leaves, glaucescent beneath. Catkins borne all along the stems before the leaves in early April. The male catkins are very pretty when both brick-red emerging anthers and yellow ripened anthers are apparent at the same time. Ours is a male form. Occurs with the parents in the wild. C 1872.

**yezoalpina** KOIDZ. A prostrate shrub with long, trailing stems bearing attractive, long-stalked, rounded or obovate glossy green leaves with reticulate venation. Catkins appearing with the leaves in spring. A rare alpine species, suitable for the rock garden or scree. Now considered to be a variety of the Japanese *S. nakamurana*. Japan.

**"SALLOW"** See *Salix caprea* and *S. cinerea*.

**SALVIA** L.—**Labiatae**—A large genus of some 900 species of often aromatic, flowering plants containing mainly herbs and numerous sub-shrubs, of which all but *S. officinalis* are

**SALVIA**—*continued*

tender in varying degrees. Widely distributed. They require a warm, dry, well drained position in full sun. The more tender species make excellent cool-house subjects. The two-lipped flowers are normally borne in whorls along the stems during late summer or early autumn.

**ambigens** See *S. guaranitica*.

†**aurea** L. A small species with round, hoary leaves and rusty-yellow flowers. S. Africa. I 1731.

**bethellii** See *S. involucrata* 'Bethellii'.

**caerulea** See *S. guaranitica*.

†**elegans** VAHL (*S. rutilans* CARR.) "Pineapple-scented Sage". A small species up to 1m, suitable for a sunny south wall, with softly downy, heart-shaped leaves, scented of pineapple and loose leafy panicles of magenta-crimson flowers throughout summer. Mexico. C before 1873.

†**fulgens** CAV. "Mexican Red Sage". A small species up to 1m with heart-shaped leaves and long racemes of showy, densely hairy, scarlet flowers, 5cm long, in late summer. Mexico. I 1829. AM 1937.

†**gesneriiflora** LINDL. & PAXT. An attractive, small species related to *S. fulgens*, but with even larger, showier flowers of an intense scarlet. Mexico. I 1840. AM 1950.

**grahamii** See *S. microphylla*.

†**greggii** A. GRAY A small, slender species up to 1.2m, suitable for a sunny south wall. Similar in some respects to *S. microphylla*, but leaves smaller and narrower and flowers rose-scarlet. Texas, Mexico. C 1885. AM 1914.

**guaranitica** ST HIL. ex BENTH. (*S. ambigens* BRIQ.) (*S. caerulea* BENTH.) A small shrub with erect stems up to 1.5m. Softly downy, heart-shaped leaves and long racemes of deep, azure-blue flowers about 5cm long, during summer and autumn. S America. I 1925. AM 1926.

'**Black and Blue**' Flowers deep blue, calyx black. Previously grown as *S. caerulea*. AM 1989.

'**Blue Enigma**' Shorter, with smaller, paler flowers, calyx green. Previously grown as *S. ambigens*.

†**interrupta** SCHOUSB. A small, glandular, hairy sub-shrub up to 1m. Leaves varying from entire, with two basal lobes, to pinnate, with 2 pairs of leaflets. Flowers violet-purple, with a white throat, produced in loose terminal panicles from late spring to midsummer. Morocco. I 1867.

†**involucrata** CAV. Small species with ovate, long-pointed leaves and spike-like racemes of rose-magenta flowers which are sticky to the touch. Late summer to autumn. Mexico. I 1824.

'**Bethellii**' (*S. bethellii* HORT.) A robust form with large, heart-shaped leaves and stout racemes of magenta-crimson flowers from midsummer onwards. Garden origin. FCC 1880.

**lavandulifolia** VAHL A dwarf species with narrow, grey, downy leaves and spike-like racemes of blue-violet flowers in early summer. Spain.

†**mexicana** L. This species is most frequently grown in the following form.

**var. minor** BENTH. A vigorous, small to medium-sized sub-shrub with large, ovate leaves and terminal spike-like racemes of showy, violet-blue flowers, in late winter. Differing from the typical variety in its small calyces. Only suitable for the cool greenhouse. Mexico. I 1720.

†**microphylla** H.B.K. (*S. grahamii* BENTH.) A variable, small shrub up to 1.2m. Bright red fading to bluish-red flowers, 2.5cm long, from June into late autumn. Mexico. I 1829.

**var. neurepia** (FERN.) EPLING (*S. neurepia* FERN.) Differs in its larger, paler green leaves 3-5cm long, and showier, rosy-red flowers in late summer and autumn. Mexico.

**neurepia** See *S. microphylla* var. *neurepia*.

**officinalis** L. "Common Sage". A well-known, dwarf, semi-evergreen species long cultivated as a herb. Leaves grey-green and strongly aromatic. Flowers bluish-purple, during summer. S Europe. Cultivated in England since 1597, possibly before.

'**Aurea**' See under 'Icterina'.

'**Alba**' Flowers white.

**SALVIA officinalis**—*continued*

**'Icterina'** Leaves variegated green and gold. Low, spreading habit. Sometimes grown as 'Aurea'. AGM 1984.

**'Kew Gold'** Leaves golden yellow. A sport of 'Icterina' raised at Kew. Sometimes reverts.

**'Purpurascens'** "Purple-leaf Sage". Stems and young foliage suffused purple. Particularly effective in coloured foliage groups for blending or contrasts. AGM 1984.

**'Tricolor'** A distinct, compact form with leaves grey-green, splashed creamy-white, suffused purple and pink. Rather tender but well worth planting each year.

**rutilans** See *S. elegans.*

**SAMBUCUS** L.—**Caprifoliaceae**—The "Elders" are a genus of about 20 species of shrubs, small trees and perennial herbs widely distributed in temperate and subtropical regions. The cultivated species are hardy and tolerant of almost all soils and situations. Few are eye-catching in flower, but many have ornamental foliage and fruits. All species possess pinnate leaves and serrated leaflets. To encourage the production of large flowerheads or lush foliage the lateral branches may be cut back to within a few centimetres of the previous year's growth in March. Ideal subjects for the wild garden.

**callicarpa** GREENE A small to medium-sized shrub, the leaves with 5-7 leaflets. Flowers whitish, in a round head, 7-10cm across, in June to July, followed by small, scarlet fruits. W North America. I about 1900.

**canadensis** L. "American Elderberry". A stout, strong-growing shrub of medium to large size, the leaves with 5-11, usually 7, large leaflets. Flowers white in convex heads, 13-20cm across, appearing in July, followed by purple-black fruits. SE Canada, E United States. I 1761. AM 1905. AM 1948.

**'Aurea'** An unusual form with yellow foliage and red fruits.

**'Maxima'** A handsome form with leaves 30-45cm long and enormous flowerheads 30cm or more across. The rosy-purple flower-stalks, which remain after the flowers have fallen, are an added attraction. A bold shrub which should be pruned each spring to encourage the production of new shoots. A bold subject for the wild garden. AM 1951.

**'Rubra'** An unusual form with red fruits.

**var. submollis** REHD. A variety with leaflets softly greyish pubescent beneath.

**ebulus** L. "Dane's Elder". An unusual herbaceous species, throwing up annually stout, grooved stems 1-1.2m high, in time forming dense colonies. Leaves with 9-13 leaflets. Flowers white, tinged pink in flattened heads, 7.5-10cm across, during late summer. Fruits black. Europe, N Africa, naturalised in the British Isles.

**nigra** L. "Common Elder". A familiar, native, large shrub or small tree, with a rugged, fissured bark and leaves with 5-7 leaflets. The flattened heads of cream-coloured, sweetly fragrant flowers in June are followed by heavy bunches of shining black fruits. Both flowers and fruits are used in country-winemaking. A useful plant for extremely chalky sites. Europe, N Africa, W Asia. Long cultivated.

**'Albovariegata'** See 'Marginata'.

**'Aurea'** "Golden Elder". Leaves golden yellow, deepening with age. One of the hardiest and most satisfactory of golden foliaged shrubs. C 1883. AGM 1984.

**'Aureomarginata'** Leaflets with an irregular, bright yellow margin.

**'Fructuluteo'** An unusual form with yellow fruits.

**'Guincho Purple'** ('Purpurea') ('Foliis Pupureis') Leaves green when young becoming deep blackish-purple, red in autumn. Flowers contrasting well with the foliage, pink in bud opening white flushed pink on the backs of the lobes, stalks stained with purple. AM 1977.

**'Heterophylla'** See 'Linearis'.

**f. laciniata** (L.) ZAB. "Fern-leaved Elder". An attractive form with finely divided fern-like leaves. AM 1988 (for flower and foliage).

**'Linearis'** ('Heterophylla') A curious shrub with leaflets of variable form, often reduced to thread-like segments.

**'Marginata'** ('Albovariegata') ('Argenteomarginata') Leaflets with an irregular, creamy-white margin. AM 1892.

**'Plena'** A form with double flowers.

**f. porphyrifolia** E.C. NELSON This name covers all forms with purple leaves.

**SAMBUCUS nigra**—*continued*

    **'Pulverulenta'** A slow-growing but very effective form in which the leaves are striped and mottled white.

    **'Purpurea'** See 'Guincho Purple'.

    **'Pyramidalis'** A form of stiff, erect habit, wider above than below; leaves densely clustered on the stems.

  **pubens** MICHX. A large shrub related to *S. racemosa*. Leaves with 5-7 leaflets, like the stems pubescent when young. Flowers cream-coloured, borne in rounded or conical heads during May. Fruits red. North America. I 1812.

  **racemosa** L. "Red-berried Elder". A medium-sized to large shrub, the leaves with 5-7 coarsely-toothed leaflets. Flowers yellowish-white in conical heads, crowding the branches in April followed in summer by dense clusters of bright, scarlet fruits. Europe, W Asia. Planted as game cover in parts of N England and Scotland. Cultivated in England since the 16th century. AM 1936.

    **'Plumosa Aurea'** ('Serratifolia Aurea') A colourful shrub with beautiful, deeply cut, golden foliage. One of the elite of golden foliaged shrubs; slower-growing and best in light shade. Rich yellow flowers. AM 1895. AM 1956. AGM 1984.

    **'Sutherland Gold'** An excellent plant similar to 'Plumosa Aurea' but slightly coarser in texture and less liable to scorching in sun. Raised in Canada.

    **'Tenuifolia'** A small, slow-growing shrub forming a low mound of arching branches and finely divided, fern-like leaves. As beautiful as a cut-leaved Japanese maple and a good substitute on chalky soils. A good plant for the rock garden. AM 1917.

**\*SANTOLINA** L.—**Compositae**—The "Lavender Cottons" are low-growing, mound-forming, evergreen sub-shrubs with dense grey, green or silvery, finely divided foliage, and dainty, button-like flowerheads on tall stalks, in July. They require a sunny position and well drained soil. About 5 species, natives of the Mediterranean region.

  **chamaecyparissus** L. (*S. incana* L.) A charming dwarf species, valued for its woolly, silver-hued, thread-like foliage. Flowerheads bright lemon-yellow. S France, Pyrenees. Cultivated in England since the 16th century. AGM 1984.

    **var. corsica** See 'Nana'.

    **'Nana'** (var. *corsica* HORT. not FIORI) A dwarfer, denser, more compact variety, ideal for the rock garden. AGM 1984.

  **incana** See *S. chamaecyparissus*.

  **neapolitana** See *S. pinnata* subsp. *neapolitana*.

  **pinnata** VIV. A dwarf sub-shrub related to *S. chamaecyparissus*. Differing in its longer, finely divided green leaves and flowerheads of an off-white. NW Italy. Mainly grown in the following forms.

    **subsp. neapolitana** (JORD. & FOURR.) GUINEA (*S. neapolitana* JORD. & FOURR.) A dwarf sub-shrub similar to *S. chamaecyparissus*, but rather looser in growth and with longer, more "feathery" leaves. Flowers bright lemon-yellow. NW and C Italy. AGM 1984.

    **'Edward Bowles'** A charming form originally given to us by E.A. Bowles, after whom we named it. It is similar to 'Sulphurea', but the foliage is more grey-green and the flowerheads of a paler primrose, almost creamy-white.

    **'Sulphurea'** Foliage grey-green; flowerheads pale primrose-yellow.

  **rosmarinifolia** L. (*S. virens* MILL.) (*S. viridis* WILLD.) An attractive, dwarf species with thread-like leaves of a vivid green colour. Flowerheads bright lemon-yellow. SW Europe. C 1727.

    **subsp. canescens** (LAG.) NYMAN Foliage grey-green. S Spain.

    **'Primrose Gem'** A lovely form with flowerheads of a pale primrose-yellow. Originated as a seedling in our nursery before 1960.

  **virens** See *S. rosmarinifolia*.

  **viridis** See *S. rosmarinifolia*.

**SAPINDUS** L.—**Sapindaceae**—A small genus of about 13 species of mainly tropical trees and shrubs of which the following are relatively hardy. They require a well drained soil in sun or semi-shade.

**SAPINDUS**—*continued*

**drummondii** HOOK. & ARN. "Soapberry". An interesting small tree with pinnate, robinia-like leaves. The tiny, cream-coloured flowers are borne in dense, conical panicles in June. Central S United States, N Mexico. C 1900.

†**\*mukorossi** GAERTN. A large shrub or small tree with late persisting, pinnate leaves, consisting of 8-12 leathery, reticulately-veined leaflets. Flowers yellowish-green, in terminal panicles. Japan, Taiwan, China to India. C 1877.

**SAPIUM** P. BROWNE—**Euphorbiaceae**—A large genus of 100 or more species of trees and shrubs almost all of which are found in the tropics.

**japonicum** (SIEB. & ZUCC.) PAX. & HOFFM. A rare, small tree or shrub here proving hardy, with greyish, glabrous branches and smooth, dark green, elliptic or obovate-elliptic, entire leaves, turning glowing crimson in autumn. Flowers unisexual, inconspicuous, appearing in June in slender, axillary, catkin-like, greenish-yellow racemes. Capsules like large capers, three-lobed, green, finally brown, pendulous. Japan, China, Korea.

†**sebiferum** (L.) ROXB. "Chinese Tallow Tree". A small tree with broadly ovate or rounded, abruptly-pointed leaves and slender racemes of greenish-yellow flowers. The waxy coating of the seeds is used in the manufacture of candles in China. The leaves often turn a brilliant red in autumn. Only suitable for the mildest gardens of the British Isles. China, Taiwan. C 1850.

†**\*SARCANDRA** GARDNER—**Chloranthaceae**—A small genus of about 15 species of mainly tropical shrubs natives of E and SE Asia.

**glabra** (THUNB.) NAKAI (*Chloranthus brachystachys* BLUME) Small evergreen shrub with oblong leaves and spikes of bright orange fruits. A conservatory plant in most areas. S India to SE Asia.

**\*SARCOCOCCA** LINDL.—**Buxaceae**—The "Christmas Boxes" make up a genus of about 14 species natives of E and SE Asia. Attractive, shade-bearing, dwarf or small shrubs, with evergreen, glossy foliage suitable for cutting. The small, white, fragrant, male flowers open during late winter, the tiny female flowers occurring in the same cluster. Succeed in any fertile soil, being especially happy in chalk soils. They slowly attain 1.2-1.5m high unless otherwise indicated.

**confusa** SEALY A useful hardy shrub of dense spreading habit. Leaves elliptic, taper-pointed; flowers with cream-coloured anthers, very fragrant; fruits shining black. Similar in general appearance to *S. ruscifolia* var. *chinensis*, but the stigmas vary from 2 to 3 and the berries are black. Origin uncertain, probably China. C 1916. AGM 1984. AM 1989.

**hookeriana** BAILL. A rare, erect-growing species, with shortly pubescent, green stems, lanceolate leaves and white flowers, the female flowers with 3 stigmas. Berries black. Not quite so hardy as the var. *digyna*. Himalaya. AM 1936. AM 1983 (to Schilling 1260).

**var. digyna** FRANCH. More slender and with narrower leaves. Female flowers with only 2 stigmas. Berries black. W China. I 1908 by Ernest Wilson. AM 1970. AGM 1984.

**'Purple Stem'** An attractive form with the young stems, petioles and midribs flushed purple.

**var. humilis** REHD. & WILS . (*S. humilis* (REHD. & WILS.) STAPF) A dwarf, densely-branched shrub, suckering to form extensive clumps and patches seldom exceeding 60cm high. Leaves elliptic, shining deep green. Male flowers with pink anthers; berries black. W China. I 1907 by Ernest Wilson.

**humilis** See *S. hookeriana* var. *humilis*.

**orientalis** C.Y. WU A strong-growing upright small shrub with stout green shoots. Leaves ovate-lanceolate, to 9cm long, three-veined and cuneate at the base, slenderly taper-pointed at the apex. Flowers fragrant, males with pink-tinged anthers and sepals, females with 2-3 stigmas. Fruits black. Jiangxi, E China. I 1980 by Roy Lancaster.

**ruscifolia** STAFF A small, slow-growing shrub. Leaves broad ovate, thick, shining dark green. Berries dark red. Uncommon in cultivation. C China. I 1901 by Ernest Wilson. AM 1908.

**SARCOCOCCA ruscifolia**—*continued*

var. **chinensis** (FRANCH.) REHD. & WILS. A more vigorous shrub, commoner in cultivation, differing in its comparatively longer, narrower leaves. It is very similar in general appearance to *S. confusa*, having the same long, slender-pointed leaves and attaining the same dimensions, but the berries are dark red and the female flowers have 3 stigmas. C and W China.

†**saligna** (D. DON) MUELL.-ARG. (*S. pruniformis* LINDL. in part) A small shrub with erect, glabrous, green stems. Leaves tapering, lance-shaped, up to 13cm long; flowers greenish-white, with little if any scent. Berries purple. W Himalaya. C 1908.

**SAROTHAMNUS scoparius** See *Cytisus scoparius*.

‡**SASSAFRAS** TREW—**Lauraceae**—A small genus of 3 species of deciduous trees requiring a lime-free loam and a slightly sheltered position such as in woodland.

**albidum** (NUTT.) NEES (*S. officinale* var. *albidum* (NUTT.) BLAKE) An attractive and very distinct, aromatic, medium-sized, suckering tree of broadly conical habit with flexuous twigs and branches, particularly noticeable in winter. Leaves variable in shape from ovate to obovate, entire or with 1 or 2 conspicuous lobes, some leaves resembling those of the fig in outline, dark green above, rather glaucous or pale green beneath, colouring attractively in autumn. Flowers greenish-yellow, inconspicuous, appearing in short racemes in May. E United States. I 1633.

var. **molle** (RAF.) FERN. Leaves and young shoots downy.

‡†*SCHIMA REINW. ex BLUME—**Theaceae**—A small genus of uncommon evergreen shrubs and trees requiring a lime-free soil in a sheltered position such as woodland. Now usually regarded as containing one variable species.

**argentea** PRITZ. A medium-sized to large shrub of erect, bushy habit. Leaves elliptic to elliptic-oblong, tapering to both ends, polished dark green above, usually glaucous beneath. Flowers creamy-white, like small camellias, about 4cm across, produced on the young wood in late summer. This distinct and attractive member of the camellia family has been growing successfully here in woodland conditions for nearly forty years and has reached 5m in the Hillier Gardens and Arboretum. Native of W China, Assam and Taiwan, where it is said to attain large tree size. AM 1955.

**khasiana** DYER A large shrub to medium-sized tree bearing lustrous, dark green, elliptic, serrated leaves, 15-18cm long. Flowers white, 5cm across, with a central mass of yellow stamens, produced on the young wood during September and October. There are splendid examples in Cornwall, but it is not hardy in our area. Assam, Burma, China. AM 1953.

**noronhae** REINW. ex BLUME A small to medium-sized shrub in cultivation, with oblanceolate or narrow elliptic, acuminate leaves covered above when mature with a bluish bloom. Flowers 4-5cm across, cream-coloured, with a central boss of golden stamens produced in the axils of the terminal leaves during late summer and autumn. Only for the mildest areas, but a suitable conservatory shrub. Tropical Asia. I 1849.

**wallichii** CHOISY A small tree in cultivation with elliptic-oblong leaves, pubescent and reticulate beneath. Flowers white, fragrant, 4-5cm across, produced on the young wood in late summer. Not hardy in our area. Sikkim, Nepal, E Indies.

†*SCHEFFLERA FORST. & FORST. f.—**Araliaceae**—A large genus of some 200 species of trees and shrubs confined to warm and tropical regions of the world and containing several popular houseplants.

**impressa** (C.B. CLARKE) HARMS A large, stoutly-branched spreading shrub or small tree. Leaves palmately compound with 7-9 oblanceolate leaflets up to 20cm long on petioles to 50cm. This remarkable plant lived for many years in front of Jermyns House in the Hillier Gardens and Arboretum but was badly damaged in the 1978-79 winter and eventually died in 1981. Yunnan, China.

**SCHINUS** L.—**Anacardiaceae**—A small genus of 27 species of usually dioecious shrubs and trees with simple or compound leaves. Natives of Mexico and S America.

**SCHINUS**—*continued*

**dependens** See *S. polygamus*.

†\***molle** L. "Pepper Tree". A small, evergreen tree with gracefully drooping branches and attractive, pinnate leaves. The small, yellowish-white flowers are borne in short panicles in spring, followed, on female trees, by rosy-red, pea-shaped fruits. Commonly planted as a street tree in S Europe and best grown as a conservatory tree in the British Isles. S America.

\***polygamus** (CAV.) CABRERA (*S. dependens* ORT.) A medium-sized to large, evergreen shrub, the shoots often spine-tipped. Leaves small, obovate, 1-2cm long. The tiny yellowish flowers crowd the branches in May; fruits purplish, the size of peppercorns. Chile. I 1790.

**"SEA BUCKTHORN"** See *Hippophae rhamnoides*.

**SECURINEGA** COMM. ex JUSS—**Euphorbiaceae**—A small genus of botanical interest related to *Andrachne* with about 25 species in temperate and subtropical regions.

**suffruticosa** (PALL.) REHD. (*S. ramiflora* (AIT.) MUELL.-ARG.) A small, densely-branched shrub with slender, arching stems and oval leaves, 2.5-5cm long. Flowers small, greenish-yellow, produced during late summer and early autumn. NE Asia to C China, Taiwan. I 1783.

**SEDUM** L.—**Crassulaceae**—A large genus of more than 300 species of mainly herbs, well represented in our herbaceous borders and rock gardens. Natives of N temperate regions and mountains in the tropics. The following is one of the few hardy shrubby species.

**populifolium** L. A dwarf sub-shrub of erect habit with reddish-brown bark, peeling on old stems. Leaves with slender stalks, ovate, coarsely-toothed, cordate at base, pale green and fleshy. Flowers sweetly hawthorn-scented, white or pink-tinged, with purple anthers, borne in small, dense, flattened heads in July and August. Siberia. I 1780.

**SENECIO** L.—**Compositae**—A very large genus of 1500 or more species of annual and perennial herbs, shrubs and climbers, widely distributed throughout the world. The shrubby members are mostly evergreen and bear heads or panicles of white or yellow daisy flowers during summer. All are sun-lovers and make excellent seaside shrubs. With rare exception, the woody species will not withstand low Continental temperatures but are excellent wind resisters. Unless otherwise stated, the following are natives of New Zealand.

The New Zealand shrubby members of this genus are included in *Brachyglottis* by some authorities.

\***bidwillii** HOOK. f. A striking, dwarf, alpine shrub of compact rigid habit, occasionally very slowly reaching 0.75m. Leaves elliptic to obovate, up to 2.5cm, long, remarkably thick, shining above and covered beneath, like the stems, in a soft white or buff tomentum. Flowers not conspicuous. N Island with a variety in S Island.

†\***compactus** T. KIRK A small, compact shrub attaining 0.9-1m, like *S.* 'Sunshine' but less spreading. Leaves oval, 2.5-5cm long, wavy-edged, white-felted beneath, as are the young shoots and flower stalks. Flowerheads bright yellow in few-flowered racemes. Subject to injury in severe winters. See also *S.* Dunedin Hybrids. N Island where it is restricted to one locality.

\***Dunedin Hybrids** This name covers the various hybrids and backcrosses which have occurred between *S. compactus*, *S. greyi* and *S. laxifolius* and are now more commonly grown than any of the parents. The most frequently seen form, previously grown as *S. greyi* and *S. laxifolius*, has been named 'Sunshine'.

\***elaeagnifolius** HOOK. f. A rigid, densely-branched shrub of medium size with oval, leathery leaves, 7.5-15cm long, glossy above, thickly buff-felted beneath, as are the young shoots and flower stalks. Flowerheads in terminal panicles, of little ornament. An excellent coastal shrub. N Island .

**var. buchananii** (ARMSTR.) T. KIRK Smaller in all its parts.

**SENECIO**—*continued*

†\***greyi** HOOK. f. A small, spreading shrub with grey hairy shoots. Leaves white tomentose on both sides when young, becoming glossy green above. Flowerheads bright yellow. Very rare in cultivation, the plant previously grown under this name is *S.* 'Sunshine', see also under Dunedin Hybrids. N Island.

†\***hectoris** BUCH. A medium-sized to large, semi-evergreen shrub of erect, rather open habit. Leaves oblanceolate, 13-25cm long, often pinnately lobed at base and conspicuously-toothed, white tomentose beneath. Flowerheads white, 4-6cm across, in large terminal corymbs. H.G. Hillier was first introduced to this unusual Daisy Bush by that great gardener the late Sir Herbert Maxwell, who was growing it in sheltering woodland. Unlike its allies this handsome, large-leaved species cannot be expected to grow in an exposed, windy position. S Island. I 1910.

†\***heritieri** DC. A small, loose-growing shrub with broadly ovate, toothed or shallowly lobed leaves, 10-15cm long. Both the young stems and the leaf undersurfaces are covered by a dense, white tomentum. Flowerheads white and crimson with purple centres, violet-scented, recalling the popular cineraria, borne in large panicles from May to July. Only suitable for the mildest areas or conservatory. Canary Isles (Tenerife). I 1774.

†\***huntii** MUELL. "Rautini". A medium-sized shrub of compact, rounded habit, with glandular downy young shoots and narrowly obovate leaves up to 11cm long. Flowerheads yellow, in terminal panicles. Chatham Islands. I 1909.

†\***kirkii** HOOK. f. (*S. glastifolius* HOOK. f.) "Kohurangi". A glabrous shrub of medium size, with brittle stems. Leaves fleshy, varying in shape from narrow-obovate to elliptic-oblong, few-toothed or dentate. Flowerheads white, in large, flat terminal corymbs. Only for the mildest areas or conservatory. N Island.

\***laxifolius** BUCH. A small shrub related to *S. greyi*, but with smaller, thinner, pointed leaves. Flowerheads yellow, in loose terminal panicles. The true species is rare in cultivation. See also *S.* Dunedin Hybrids. S Island.

†\*"**Leonard Cockayne**' (*S. greyi* × *S. reinoldii*). A wide-spreading medium-sized shrub with white-backed, wavy margined grey-green leaves up to 15cm long. The yellow flowerheads are borne in large panicles in summer. Excellent in coastal areas.

**leucostachys** See *S. viravira*.

\***monroi** HOOK. f. A small shrub of dense habit often forming a broad dome, easily recognised by its oblong or oval, conspicuously undulate leaves which are covered beneath, like the young shoots and flower stalks, with a dense white felt. Flowerheads yellow, in dense terminal corymbs. As attractive and useful in gardens as *S.* 'Sunshine'. S Island. AGM 1984.

†\***perdicioides** HOOK. f. "Raukumara". A small to medium-sized shrub, with dull green, glabrous leaves which are finely-toothed and 2.5-5cm long. Flowerheads yellow in terminal corymbs. Only for the mildest areas. N Island.

\***reinoldii** ENDL. (*S. rotundifolius* HOOK. f.) "Muttonbird Scrub". A medium-sized shrub of dense, rounded habit with thick, leathery, rounded leaves, 5-13cm long, glabrous and shining green above, felted beneath. Flowerheads yellowish in terminal panicles, not conspicuous. One of the best shrubs for windswept gardens by the sea. It will take the full blast of the Atlantic Ocean. S Island, Stewart Island etc.

**rotundifolius** See *S. reinoldii*.

\*'**Sunshine**' (*S. greyi* HORT.) A popular and attractive grey shrub forming a dense, broad mound up to 1m high and twice as much across. Leaves silvery-grey when young becoming green above. Flowerheads yellow, in large open corymbs. A hybrid between the true *S. greyi* and another species, possibly *S. compactus*. AGM 1984.

†\***viravira** HIERONYMUS (*S. leucostachys* HORT. not BAKER) (*S. argentinus* BAKER) A striking and beautiful, lax, silvery-white shrub of medium size with finely divided pinnate leaves. Its almost scandent branches and tender nature demand a sunny wall. Flowers whitish in summer, not very ornamental. Patagonia. I 1893. AM 1973.

†**SENNA** (K. BAUHIN) MILL. (*Cassia* L. in part)—**Leguminosae**—A large genus of about 240 species of trees, shrubs and herbs with a wide tropical and subtropical distribution. Leaves evenly pinnate. The pods of several species produce the Senna of medicine. The following species require a warm, sheltered, sunny site or conservatory.

**SENNA**—*continued*

**corymbosa** (LAM.) IRWIN & BARNABY (*Cassia corymbosa* LAM.) Less robust than *S. ×floribunda*, with more slender growths. A medium-sized shrub, the leaves with 2 or 3 pairs of narrow, acuminate leaflets, flowers also smaller and paler yellow, in late summer and autumn. Uruguay, Argentina, widely naturalised in warm countries. I 1796. AM 1933.

**× floribunda** (CAV.) IRWIN & BARNABY (*S. multiglandulosa × S. septemtrionalis*). A very handsome and vigorous wall shrub, the pinnate leaves with 4-5 pairs of leaflets. Flowers large, rich deep yellow, in terminal clusters during late summer and autumn. This plant is often grown as *Cassia corymbosa* or *C. obtusa*. The true *Cassia obtusa*, a native of Chile and now correctly known as *Senna candolleana*, is rarely cultivated. C 1800.

**septemtrionalis** (VIV.) IRWIN & BARNABY This species has also been grown as both *Cassia corymbosa* and *C. obtusa*. It makes a large shrub or small tree, the leaves with 3-4 pairs of ovate, taper-pointed leaflets. The bright yellow flowers open from summer to winter. Mexico, C and northern S America, widely naturalised and a weed in many tropical areas.

**SHEPHERDIA** NUTT.—**Elaeagnaceae**—A small genus of 3 species of dioecious shrubs related to *Elaeagnus* and *Hippophae*, differing from both in the opposite leaves. Shrubs for full exposure, excellent in coastal areas.

**argentea** (PURSH) NUTT. "Buffalo Berry". A slow-growing, occasionally spiny shrub of medium size with oblong, silvery, scaly leaves. The tiny yellow flowers appear in small, dense clusters during March or earlier and are followed, on female plants, by scarlet, edible berries. C North America. I 1818.

**canadensis** (L.) NUTT. A dense, bushy shrub of medium size, with brownish, scaly shoots and elliptic to ovate leaves, which are silvery hairy and speckled with brown scales below. The inconspicuous flowers in spring are followed, on female plants, by yellowish-red berries. North America. I 1759.

**SIBIRAEA** MAXIM.—**Rosaceae**—A genus of 2 species closely related to and sometimes included in *Spiraea*, but differing in the entire leaves and various small botanical characters. The following species is best in a well drained sunny position.

**laevigata** (L.) MAXIM. (*S. altaiensis* (LAXM.) SCHNEID.) (*Spiraea laevigata* L.) An erect shrub occasionally up to 1.8m. The stout, glabrous branches are clad with narrowly obovate, sea-green leaves, 7.5-10cm long. The panicles of whitish flowers are produced from the tips of the shoots in late spring and early summer, but they are of little ornament. Mts of C Asia. I 1774.

**var. croatica** (DEGEN) SCHNEID. In cultivation smaller in its parts. Yugoslavia.

**SINOCALYCANTHUS** CHENG & CHANG—**Calycanthaceae**—A monotypic genus closely related to *Calycanthus* and originally included in it.

**chinensis** (CHENG & CHANG) CHENG & CHANG A medium-sized deciduous shrub reaching about 3m. Leaves opposite, broadly elliptic to obovate, abruptly acuminate, up to 15cm long, glossy green turning yellow in autumn. Flowers 7cm across, nodding, borne singly at the ends of the shoots in June, with numerous tepals in 2 whorls of about 10 each; outer tepals white, sometimes flushed pink, inner tepals smaller, pale yellow, white at the base with maroon markings. This remarkable plant first flowered in this country in the garden of Roy Lancaster in 1989 and in the Hillier Gardens and Arboretum the following year. Zhejiang (E China). I 1983.

**‡SINOJACKIA** HU—**Styracaceae**—A small genus of 2 species of deciduous, Chinese small trees or large shrubs, requiring a moist, lime-free soil.

**rehderiana** HU A very rare, small, styrax-like, loosely-branched, small tree or large shrub, with thin, elliptic, alternate leaves. Flowers white, the corolla divided to the base into 4-6 lobes, appearing singly or in short, axillary racemes in May and June. Alfred Rehder, after whom this species is named, was a giant among botanists. It is to him we all owe a tremendous debt for his *Manual of Cultivated Trees and Shrubs*, one of his many

**SINOJACKIA rehderiana**—*continued*

works, but like so many botanists he was not "good company" in the garden. E China. I 1930.

**xylocarpa** HU A small tree differing from *S. rehderiana* in its broader leaves, longer-stalked flowers and curious ovoid fruits. E China. I 1934.

‡**SINOWILSONIA** HEMSL.—**Hamamelidaceae**—A rare monotypic genus related to the witch hazels and mainly of botanical interest. Introduced from China by E.H. Wilson ("Chinese Wilson"), in whose honour it is named. In a walk round the nurseries with Ernest Wilson it seemed impossible to find a tree, shrub or herbaceous plant with which he was not familiar. A first class botanist, perhaps the greatest of the plant hunters, and like W.J. Bean, a tremendous companion in the garden.

**henryi** HEMSL. A large shrub or occasionally a small, spreading tree. The large, bristle-toothed leaves, 7.5-15cm long, recall those of a lime and are covered beneath with stellate pubescence. Flowers in May monoecious, small and greenish, the males in slender, pendulous catkins, the females in pendulous racemes lengthening to 15cm in fruit. C and W China. I 1908.

***SKIMMIA** THUNB.—**Rutaceae**—A small genus of 4 species of slow-growing, aromatic, evergreen shrubs or trees, natives of the Himalaya and E Asia. *S. japonica* subsp. *japonica*, *S. × confusa* and *S. anquetilia* bear male and female flowers on separate plants and both sexes are required for the production of the brightly coloured fruits which persist through the winter. All are tolerant of shade and are excellent shrubs for industrial areas and seaside gardens. Plants once thought to be hybrids between *S. japonica* and *S. reevesiana* are considered to belong to *S. japonica* subsp. *japonica*.

**anquetilia** N.P. TAYLOR & AIRY SHAW A small shrub of open habit with oblanceolate taper-pointed leaves, 7.5-15cm long, clustered at the ends of the shoots in the manner of *Daphne laureola*. When crushed they emit a strong pungent smell. The small terminal clusters of greenish-yellow flowers with upright petals are borne in spring. These are followed on female plants by bright red fruits. Himalaya. I 1841. AM 1977.

×**confusa** N.P. TAYLOR (*S. anquetilia* × *S. japonica*). (*S. melanocarpa* HORT.) A small, mound-forming shrub thriving in sun or shade with oblanceolate, pointed, aromatic leaves. The large, conical clusters of very fragrant, creamy-white flowers make it the best of the genus for flower. Previously distributed as *S. laureola* male. The male form is commonest in cultivation.

**'Chelsea Physic'** A male form similar to 'Kew Green' but lower-growing with smaller leaves and inflorescences. Found in the Chelsea Physic Garden.

**'Isabella'** A female form reaching 3m. Berries bright red.

**'Kew Green'** A splendid form selected at Kew with broad leaves and very large flower clusters. Male.

**fortunei** See *S. japonica* subsp. *reevesiana*.

**japonica** THUNB. A variable, small, dome-shaped shrub of dense habit, with leathery, obovate to elliptic leaves. The terminal panicles of white, often fragrant flowers in April and May are followed, on female plants, by clusters of globular, bright red fruits. A most adaptable shrub in all its forms, equally at home on chalk or acid soils. Japan. C 1838. FCC 1863.

**'Fisheri'** See 'Veitchii'.

**'Foremanii'** See under 'Veitchii'.

**'Fragrans'** A free-flowering male clone of broad, dome-shaped habit with dense panicles of white flowers scented of lily-of-the-valley. AGM 1969.

**'Fructo-albo'** A rather weak, low-growing, female clone of compact habit. Leaves small, fruits white.

**var. intermedia** KOMATSU (var. *repens* (NAKAI) OHWI) A very slow, low-growing, often creeping form from the mountains of Japan, Sakhalin and Kuriles.

**'Nymans'** An extremely free-fruiting form with oblanceolate leaves and comparatively large fruits.

**var. repens** See var. *intermedia*.

**SKIMMIA japonica**—*continued*

> **subsp. reevesiana** (FORT.) N.P. TAYLOR & AIRY SHAW (*S. reevesiana* (FORT.) FORT.) (*S. fortunei* MAST.) A dwarf shrub, rarely reaching 0.9m, forming a low, compact mound. Leaves narrowly elliptic, often with a pale margin. Flowers hermaphrodite, white, produced in short, terminal panicles in May, followed by obovoid, matt crimson-red fruits which last through the winter and are usually present when the flowers appear again in spring. It is not satisfactory on chalky soils. S China, SE Asia. I 1849. AM 1982. AGM 1984.
>
>> **'Chilan Choice'** A form recently introduced from Taiwan with spherical fruits and the leaves pink-crimson on the backs.
>>
>> **'Robert Fortune'** This name has been given to the commonly grown clone deriving from the original introduction and described above.
>
> **'Rogersii'** A dense, compact, dwarf, female clone of slow growth with somewhat curved or twisted leaves and large, red fruits. AGM 1969.
>
> **'Rogersii Nana'** A free-flowering male clone resembling 'Rogersii' but more dwarf and compact, slower-growing and with smaller leaves.
>
> **'Rubella'** (*S. rubella* CARR.) A male clone with large, open panicles of red buds throughout the winter which open in the early spring into white, yellow-anthered flowers. AM 1962. AGM 1984.
>
> **'Ruby King'** Narrow, taper-pointed, dark green leaves and large conical panicles of flowers from deep red buds. Male.
>
> **'Veitchii'** ('Fisheri') A vigorous female clone with distinctly broad-obovate leaves and large bunches of brilliant red fruits. FCC 1888. Usually grown as 'Foremanii'.
>
> **laureola** (DC.) SIEB. & ZUCC. ex WALPERS The true plant of this name has been introduced but is rare in cultivation. It is a small creeping shrub with very dark green leaves, fragrant, hermaphrodite or unisexual flowers and black fruits. E Himalaya, W China. For the plant previously distributed as *S. laureola* male, see *S. × confusa*; for the plant distributed as *S. laureola* female, see *S. anquetilia*.
>
> **melanocarpa** See *S. × confusa*.
>
> **reevesiana** See *S. japonica* subsp. *reevesiana*.
>
> **rubella** See *S. japonica* 'Rubella'.

**"SLOE"** See *Prunus spinosa*.

**"SMOKE TREE"** See *Cotinus coggygria*.

**"SNOWBALL"** See *Viburnum opulus* 'Roseum'.

**"SNOWBALL, JAPANESE"** See *Viburnum plicatum*.

**"SNOWBERRY"** See *Symphoricarpos albus*.

**"SNOWDROP TREE"** See *Halesia carolina*.

**"SNOWY MESPILUS"** See *Amelanchier*.

**SOLANUM** L.—**Solanaceae**—A very large genus of about 1500 species of mainly herbaceous plants widely distributed throughout the world and containing several species of economic importance such as the potato (*Solanum tuberosum*). The following semi-woody species are only suitable for the mildest localities. See also under CLIMBERS.

> **crispum** See under CLIMBERS.
>
> **jasminoides** See under CLIMBERS.
>
> **†laciniatum** AIT. f. "Kangaroo Apple". A beautiful sub-shrub with purple stems up to 1.8m high. Leaves lanceolate, usually deeply cut. Flowers comparatively large and very attractive, violet, with a yellow staminal beak, borne in loose, axillary racemes during summer, followed by small, egg-shaped fruits which change from green to yellow. A

**SOLANUM laciniatum**—*continued*

vigorous species for the very mildest areas or conservatory. Generally confused in cultivation with *S. aviculare* which differs in its lilac or white flowers, with pointed (not notched) lobes. Australia, New Zealand. I 1772.

†**valdiviense** DUNAL A vigorous, more or less climbing shrub for a sunny, sheltered wall. The arching shoots lengthen to 2.5 or 3m, bearing entire, pointed leaves. Flowers usually pale mauve or lavender, with a central beak of yellow anthers, borne in axillary racemes during May. Valdivia (Chile). Introduced by Harold Comber in 1927. AM 1931.

**SOPHORA** L.—**Leguminosae**—A genus of about 80 species of deciduous and evergreen, sun-loving trees, shrubs and herbs. The following are much valued for their elegant, pinnate leaves and floral display. Succeeding in all well drained, fertile soils.

**davidii** (FRANCH.) SKEELS (*S. viciifolia* HANCE) A medium-sized to large shrub with greydowny, later spiny branches and leaves with 7-10 pairs of leaflets, silky hairy beneath. The small bluish-white pea-flowers are borne in short terminal racemes in June. China. I 1897. AM 1933.

**japonica** L. "Japanese Pagoda Tree". A medium-sized to large tree, normally of rounded habit. Leaves up to 30cm long, composed of 9-15 leaflets. The creamy-white pea-flowers are produced in large, terminal panicles during late summer and autumn but, unfortunately, not on young trees. It flowers prodigiously in the hot dry summers of SE Europe. Native of China, widely planted in Japan. I 1753.

'**Pendula**' A picturesque, small, weeping tree with stiffly drooping branches. An admirable lawn specimen, also suitable for forming a natural arbour.

**var. pubescens** (TAUSCH) BOSSE Leaflets softly pubescent beneath, up to 8cm long. Flowers tinged lilac.

'**Regent**' A vigorous form selected in North America with dark glossy green leaves and flowering at a relatively early age.

'**Variegata**' Leaflets mottled creamy-white.

'**Violacea**' A late flowering form with wing and keel-petals flushed with rose-violet.

†*****macrocarpa** SM. (*Edwardsia chilensis* MIERS ex LINDL.) An attractive evergreen shrub of medium size, flowering at an early age. Leaves up to 13cm long with 13-25 leaflets. Flowers comparatively large, rich yellow, borne in short axillary racemes in May. Chile. I 1822. AM 1938.

†*****microphylla** AIT. (*S. tetraptera* var. *microphylla* (AIT.) HOOK. f.) A large shrub or occasionally a small tree, closely related to and resembling *S. tetraptera*, but with smaller, more numerous leaflets and slightly smaller flowers. Juvenile plants are dense and wiry in habit. New Zealand, Chile. I 1772. AM 1951.

'**Sun King**' An extremely hardy form of bushy habit with large, bright yellow flowers profusely borne over a long period during late winter and spring. A selection of Chilean origin which has survived several cold winters in an exposed position in the Hillier Gardens and Arboretum.

†*****prostrata** BUCH. (*S. tetraptera* var. *prostrata* (BUCH.) KIRK) A small shrub, occasionally prostrate, usually forming a broad, rounded hummock of tangled, interlacing, wiry stems. Leaves with 6-8 pairs of tiny leaflets. The small, brownish-yellow to orange pea-flowers are produced singly or in clusters of 2 or 3 during May. New Zealand.

†*****tetraptera** J. MILL. The New Zealand "Kowhai" is best grown against a south-west-facing, sunny wall in the British Isles. It forms a large shrub or small tree with spreading or drooping branches covered, when young, by a fulvous tomentum. Leaves with 20-40 ovate to elliptic-oblong leaflets. Flowers pea-shaped, but rather tubular, yellow, 4-5cm long, produced in drooping clusters in May. The curious seed pods are beaded in appearance and possess 4 broad wings. I 1772. AM 1943.

'**Grandiflora**' A form with large leaflets and slightly larger flowers. AM 1977.

**viciifolia** See *S. davidii*.

**SORBARIA** (DC.) A. BRAUN—**Rosaceae**—Handsome, vigorous shrubs with elegant, pinnate leaves which serve to distinguish them from *Spiraea*, with which they are commonly associated. All bear white or creamy-white flowers in terminal panicles during summer

**SORBARIA**—*continued*

and early autumn. Even in winter their brownish or reddish stems and seed heads possess a sombre attraction. They thrive in most soils, flowering best in full sun. The old flowering stems may be hard pruned in late February or March, to encourage the production of strong, vigorous shoots with extra large leaves and flower panicles. They look very well in association with water.

**aitchisonii** (HEMSL.) REHD. A very elegant shrub of medium size closely related to *S. tomentosa*, the branches long and spreading, reddish when young. Leaves glabrous, with 11-23 sharply-toothed and tapered leaflets. Flowers in large, conical panicles in July and August. Afghanistan, Kashmir. I 1895. AM 1905. AGM 1984.

**arborea** SCHNEID. A large, robust shrub with strong, spreading stems and large leaves composed of 13-17 slender-pointed leaflets which are downy beneath. Flowers produced in large, conical panicles at the end of the current year's growths in July and August. An excellent large specimen shrub for lawn or border. C and W China. Introduced by Ernest Wilson in 1908. AM 1963.

**assurgens** VILM. & BOIS ex REHD. A vigorous shrub of medium size closely related to *S. arborea* with large leaves composed of 13-17 sharply, double-toothed leaflets, glabrous or slightly downy on the veins beneath. Flowers borne in dense, erect, terminal panicles in July. China. I 1896.

**sorbifolia** (L.) A. BRAUN A small to medium-sized, suckering shrub with erect stems and leaves composed of 13-25 sharply-toothed, glabrous leaflets. Flowers produced in narrow, stiffly erect panicles, in July and August. N Asia. I 1759.

**tomentosa** (LINDL.) REHD. (*S. lindleyana* (WALL.) MAXIM.) A large, strong-growing shrub of spreading habit. Leaves large, composed of 11-23 deeply-toothed leaflets, hairy beneath. Flowers in large, terminal, downy panicles, from July to September. Himalaya. C 1840.

× **SORBARONIA** SCHNEID. (*Sorbus* × *Aronia*)—**Rosaceae**—Hardy, slow-growing shrubs or small, spreading trees of a certain quality, intermediate in character between *Sorbus* and *Aronia*. Though of no outstanding ornamental merit, they are interesting on account of their unusual origin and add autumn tints to the garden. Any ordinary soil, in sun or semi-shade.

**alpina** (WILLD.) SCHNEID. (*S. aria* × *A. arbutifolia*). A large shrub or small tree with oval or obovate, finely-toothed leaves, which are usually attractively tinted with soft orange in autumn. Flowers white, borne in terminal clusters during May; fruits 1.5cm long, rounded, dark reddish-purple, speckled brown. Garden origin before 1809.

**dippelii** (ZAB.) SCHNEID. (*S. aria* × *A. melanocarpa*). Similar to × *S. alpina* in general appearance, but leaves narrower in outline and permanently grey-felted beneath. Fruits dark reddish-purple with an orange pulp. Garden origin before 1870.

**fallax** (SCHNEID.) SCHNEID. (*S. aucuparia* × *A. melanocarpa*). A medium-sized shrub or small tree with wide-spreading branches. Leaves elliptic, obtuse or acute, deeply divided below into 2 or 3 pairs of serrulate lobes or leaflets, turning to orange and red in autumn. Flowers white; fruits purplish. Garden origin before 1878.

**hybrida** (MOENCH.) SCHNEID. (*S. aucuparia* × *A. arbutifolia*). A wide-spreading shrub or small tree. Leaves variable in form, ovate to elliptic, broader and larger than those of × *S. fallax*, rounded at the apex, deeply divided into 2 or 3 pairs of broad, overlapping leaflets, which give autumn colours of red and orange. Flowers white, hawthorn-like in spring; fruits purplish-black. Garden origin before 1785.

**sorbifolia** (POIR.) SCHNEID. (*S. americana* × *A. melanocarpa*). A medium-sized to large shrub or small tree similar to × *S. fallax* in general appearance, but with leaves shortly acuminate and young growths less downy. Fruits blackish. Garden origin before 1893.

× **SORBOCOTONEASTER** POJARK. (*Sorbus* × *Cotoneaster*)—**Rosaceae**—A rare, intergeneric hybrid of slow growth, originally found with the parents in pine forests in Yakutskland, E Siberia. Two forms are said to occur, one tends towards the *Sorbus* parent and the other to the *Cotoneaster* parent.

**pozdnjakovii** POJARK. (*S. sibirica* × *C. melanocarpus*). A medium-sized shrub of somewhat erect habit. Leaves ovate, deeply cut into 1-3 pairs of oval lobes or leaflets, dark green

× **SORBOCOTONEASTER pozdnjakovii**—*continued*

above, densely hairy beneath. Flowers white, up to 10 in a corymb. Fruits red. We are indebted for this interesting plant to Dr D.K. Ogrin of the Faculty of Agriculture, Ljubljana, Jugoslavia who was instrumental in having scions sent to us from Siberia in 1958.

× **SORBOPYRUS** SCHNEID. (*Sorbus* × *Pyrus*)—**Rosaceae**—A rare intergeneric hybrid usually forming a small to medium-sized tree. Any ordinary soil in an open position.

**auricularis** (KROOP) SCHNEID. (*S. aria* × *P. communis*) "Bollwyller Pear". A remarkable small to medium-sized tree of rounded habit, with oval or ovate, coarsely-toothed leaves which are grey-felted beneath. Flowers white, produced in corymbs in May. Fruits pear-shaped, 2.5-3cm long, green then reddish, edible. Garden origin before 1619. AM 1982.

**'Malifolia'** ( × *S. malifolia* (SPACH) SCHNEID.) Probably a seedling of × *S. auricularis*, differing in its broader, often rounded leaves, heart-shaped at base, its larger flowers in late April and May and its larger pear-shaped fruits 5cm long which are yellow when ripe. Garden origin in Paris, before 1834. Previously listed as 'Bulbiformis'.

**SORBUS** L.—**Rosaceae**—A large and horticulturally important genus ranging from dwarf shrubs to large trees, with 100 or more species in N temperate regions, the majority of which are quite hardy. Quite attractive in flower, they are mainly grown for their ornamental foliage, which, in many species, colours richly in autumn, and for their colourful, berry-like fruits. On average the forms with white or yellow fruits retain their attractions longer into the winter than those with red or orange fruits. Unless otherwise stated, the flowers are white and appear in May and early June. Easily grown in any well drained, fertile soil. Some of the species and clones of the Aucuparia Section are not long-lived on shallow chalk soils. Like many of their relatives in this family they are susceptible to fireblight.

The majority of *Sorbus* may conveniently be referred to the first two of three groups:

**Aria Section** Leaves simple, toothed or lobed. Excellent on chalky soil.

**Aucuparia Section** Leaves pinnate with numerous leaflets.

**Micromeles Section** A smaller group differing from the Aria Section in the fruits having deciduous calyces. Sometimes regarded as a distinct genus.

**alnifolia** (SIEB. & ZUCC.) K. KOCH (Micromeles Section) A small to medium-sized tree with a dense head of purplish-brown branches. Leaves ovate to obovate, strongly veined, double-toothed, recalling those of the hornbeam. Fruits small, oval, of a bright red. Rich scarlet and orange tints in autumn. Japan, Korea, China. I 1892. AM 1924.

**'Skyline'** A columnar form of upright habit, the leaves turning yellow in autumn. A seedling selected by our Foreman Alf Alford in our Eastleigh nursery in 1962.

**var. submollis** REHD. Leaves broader, softly pubescent beneath, particularly when young. Japan, Korea, Manchuria, China and Ussuri.

**alnifolia × aria** A small to medium-sized tree with glabrous reddish-brown shoots. Leaves elliptic to oblong-elliptic, doubly serrate, dark green and glabrous above, paler and thinly tomentose beneath, grey downy when young.

**americana** MARSH. (Aucuparia Section) A small tree of vigorous growth, with ascending branches and long-pointed, red sticky buds. Leaves with 13-17 sharply-toothed, long-acuminate leaflets. Fruits small, bright red, borne in large, densely packed bunches. Rich autumn tints. E North America. I 1782. AM 1950.

**'Nana'** See *S. aucuparia* 'Fastigiata'.

**anglica** HEDL. (Aria Section) A medium-sized, native shrub or small bushy tree related to the whitebeam (*S. aria*). Leaves inclined to obovate, shallowly lobed and toothed, glossy green above, grey tomentose beneath, turning golden brown in autumn; flowers white, with pink anthers, followed in autumn by globose, crimson fruits. Found only in western parts of the British Isles (except Scotland) and Killarney.

**'Apricot Lady'** (Aucuparia Section) A small tree, a seedling of *S. aucuparia* originating in our nurseries. Fruits apricot-yellow, large, in bold corymbs, contrasting with the neatly-cut, bright green foliage which colours richly in autumn. AM 1973.

**aria** (L.) CRANTZ "Whitebeam". A small to medium-sized, native tree with a compact, usually rounded head of branches. Leaves oval or obovate, greyish-white at first, later bright

**SORBUS aria**—*continued*

green above, vivid white tomentose beneath, turning to gold and russet in autumn when the bunches of deep crimson fruits are shown to advantage. A familiar tree, particularly on chalk formations in the south of England, where it usually accompanies the yew. One of the best trees for windswept or maritime districts and industrial areas. Europe.

**'Aurea'** Leaves tinted soft yellow-green.

**'Chrysophylla'** Leaves yellowish throughout summer, particularly effective in late spring, becoming a rich butter-yellow in autumn.

**'Cyclophylla'** A form with broad oval or orbicular leaves.

**'Decaisneana'** See 'Majestica'.

**'Lutescens'** Upper surface of leaves covered by a dense creamy-white tomentum, becoming grey-green by late summer. An outstanding tree in spring. AM 1952. AGM 1984.

**'Magnifica'** A form of upright habit with large, glossy green leaves and large clusters of red fruits. C 1916.

**'Majestica'** ('Decaisneana') A handsome form with larger, elliptic leaves, 10-15cm long, and slightly larger fruits. AGM 1984.

**'Pendula'** A delightful, small, weeping tree, usually less than 3m high, with slender branches and smaller, narrower leaves. Tends to revert.

**'Quercoides'** A slow-growing shrub or small tree of dense, compact, twiggy and congested growth. Leaves oblong, sharply and evenly lobed, the margins curving upwards.

**'Salicifolia'** An attractive form, graceful in habit, with lax branches and leaves relatively narrow and long.

**arranensis** HEDL. (Aria Section) A large shrub or small tree of upright habit. Leaves ovate to elliptic, deeply lobed, green above, grey tomentose beneath. Fruits red, longer than broad. A rare, native species only found wild in two glens on the Isle of Arran.

**aucuparia** L. "Mountain Ash" "Rowan". A familiar, native tree of small to medium size, with greyish downy winter buds. Leaves pinnate, with 11-19 sharply-toothed leaflets. Fruits bright red, carried in large, dense bunches during autumn, but soon devoured by hungry birds. An easily grown species, quite the equal to its Chinese counterparts, but not long-lived on very shallow, chalk soils. Very tolerant of extreme acidity. A parent of numerous hybrids. Europe. AM 1962. AGM 1984.

**'Aspleniifolia'** ('Laciniata') An elegant tree with deeply cut and toothed leaflets, giving the leaves a fern-like effect.

**'Beissneri'** An interesting tree with a dense head of erect branches. Young shoots and sometimes the leaf petioles of a dark coral-red. Leaves yellow-green, particularly when young, the leaflets varying in form from deeply incised to pinnately lobed, many having an attractive, fern-like appearance. The trunk and stems are a warm copper or russet colour. C 1899. AGM 1984.

**'Cardinal Royal'** A form of upright habit with profuse bright red fruits.

**'Dirkenii'** Leaves yellow when young, becoming yellowish-green. Raised about 1880.

**'Edulis'** ('Moravica') ('Dulcis') A strong-growing, extremely hardy tree, differing in its larger leaves with longer, broader leaflets, toothed mainly near the apex, and its larger fruits which are sweet and edible and carried in heavier bunches. Originated about 1800.

**'Fastigiata'** (*S. scopulina* HORT. not GREENE) (*S. americana* 'Nana') (*S. decora* 'Nana') A remarkable, slow-growing, columnar shrub or small tree up to 5.5m, with stout, closely erect stems. Leaves large, with 11-15 dark green leaflets. Fruits sealing-wax-red, large, borne in large, densely-packed bunches. A distinct plant with a confusing history. AM 1924 (as *S. americana* 'Nana').

**'Fructu Luteo'** ('Xanthocarpa') ('Fifeana') Fruits amber-yellow. AM 1895. AGM 1984.

**'Moravica'** See 'Edulis'.

**'Pendula'** A small, ungainly, wide-spreading tree with weeping branches.

**'Rossica Major'** Similar to 'Edulis', but leaflets with stronger and more regular teeth. Previously grown as 'Rossica'.

**'Sheerwater Seedling'** A vigorous, upright small tree with a compact, ovoid head of ascending branches, and large clusters of orange-red fruits. Excellent as a street tree. AGM 1984.

**'Xanthocarpa'** See 'Fructu Luteo'.

**SORBUS**—*continued*

**'Autumn Glow'** (*S. commixta* 'Embley' × *S. vilmorinii*). A small tree of upright habit, the pinnate leaves turning to purple and orange-red in autumn. Fruits pinkish-white then yellow flushed red. Raised in our Eastleigh nursery by our Foreman Alf Alford in 1967.

**bakonyensis** (JAV.) KARPATI (Aria Section) A small tree related to *S. latifolia*. Leaves broadly elliptic-ovate, coarsely double-toothed above the middle, glossy green above, densely grey tomentose beneath. Fruits large, scarlet, speckled with lenticels. Hungary.

**bristoliensis** WILMOTT (Aria Section) A small, native tree with a compact, often rounded head of branches. Leaves oval or rhomboidal, shortly lobed, with a wedge-shaped base, green above, grey downy beneath. Fruits orange-red, carried in dense clusters. Only found wild in the Avon Gorge, near Bristol.

**caloneura** (STAPF) REHD. (Micromeles Section) A large shrub or small tree with erect stems. Leaves oval to oblong, double-toothed and boldly marked by 9-16 pairs of parallel veins. Fruits small, brown, globular with a flattened apex. C China. I 1904 by Ernest Wilson.

**cascadensis** G.N. JONES A medium-sized to large shrub of upright habit with stout shoots. Leaves with usually 9-11 broadly oblong leaflets which are glossy green above. Large bright orange fruits ripen early. Plants previously listed as *S. sitchensis* belong here. W. North America.

**cashmiriana** HEDL. (Aucuparia Section) A beautiful, small tree of open habit. Leaves composed of 17-19 strongly serrated leaflets. Flowers soft pink in May. Fruits gleaming white, 12mm across. A distinct species with its loose, drooping clusters of fruits like white marbles, remaining long after the leaves have fallen. Kashmir. C 1934. AM 1952. FCC 1971. AGM 1984.

**chamaemespilus** (L.) CRANTZ (Aria Section) A small, slow-growing shrub of dense, compact habit up to 1.8m. Twigs stout, bearing elliptic, sharply-toothed leaves which are glossy dark green above, paler beneath, turning rich yellow, orange and russett in autumn. Flowers pink, densely packed in terminal corymbs. Fruits 12mm long, red. A distinct species of neat appearance. Mts of C and S Europe. I 1683.

**'Chinese Lace'** (Aucuparia Section) A small tree of upright habit, leaves with deeply cut and divided leaflets giving a charming, lace-like effect and turning red-purple in autumn. Fruits dark red. Possibly *S. aucuparia* 'Aspleniifolia' × *S. esserteauana*.

**commixta** KOEHNE (Aucuparia Section) (*S. discolor* HORT.) (*S. randaiensis* HORT) A small, variable tree of columnar habit when young, broadening somewhat in maturity. Winter buds long-pointed and sticky. Leaves glabrous, with 11-15 slender-pointed, serrated leaflets, bright, glossy green above, coppery when young, colouring richly in autumn. Fruits small and globular, red or orange-red, borne in large, erect bunches. One of the best species for autumn colour. Japan, Sakhalin, Korea. C 1880. AM 1979.

**'Embley'** (*S.* 'Embley') A superb small tree, with its leaves consistently glowing red in autumn, colouring generally later and remaining on the branches longer. Large, heavy bunches of glistening orange-red fruits. AM 1971. AGM 1984.

**'Jermyns'** (*S.* 'Jermyns') A splendid form giving good autumn tints. Fruits in large bunches, deep amber turning to orange-red. Originated in our nursery from a batch of seed received as *S. sargentiana*.

**var. rufoferruginea** SHIRAI ex SCHNEID. (*S. rufoferruginea* (SCHNEID.) SCHNEID.) Differs in its slightly villous buds and the presence of soft brown hairs on the inflorescence and along the leaf midrib beneath. Japan. I 1915. AM 1958 (as *S. matsumurana*).

**'Serotina'** (*S. serotina* KOEHNE) Leaves composed of 15-17 sharply-toothed leaflets, colouring richly in late autumn. Fruits small, bright orange-red.

× **confusa** See *S.* × *vagensis*.

**conradinae** KOEHNE See *S. esserteauana*.

**conradinae** HORT. See *S. pohuashanensis*.

**cuspidata** See *S. vestita*.

**danubialis** (JAV.) KARPATI A small tree related to *S. umbellata*. Leaves broadly elliptic to obovate to 8 × 6cm, broadly cuneate at the base, coarsely double-toothed above the middle, glossy green above, grey tomentose beneath. Fruits scarlet with few lenticels, about 12mm across. SE Europe.

**decora** HORT. (Aucuparia Section) An attractive, medium-sized shrub of loose, open growth. Leaves with 13-17 sea-green, obtuse leaflets. Fruits borne in dense clusters, coloured a

**SORBUS decora**—*continued*

conspicuous orange when young, later turning to red. The plant grown under this name is possibly of hybrid origin. The true species is a close relative of *S. americana*.

**'Nana'** See *S. aucuparia* 'Fastigiata'.

**decurrens** See *S.* × *thuringiaca* 'Decurrens'.

**discolor** HEDL. (Aucuparia Section) A small tree with an open head of ascending branches. Leaves glabrous with 11-15 toothed leaflets, colouring richly in autumn. Flowers opening generally earlier than the others of the group, in some years by 2-3 weeks. Fruit creamy-yellow, tinged pink, ovoid to obovoid, carried on red stalks in rather loose clusters. N China. Introduced about 1883. It is doubtful whether the true species is in cultivation. The plant here described is probably of hybrid origin.

**discolor** HORT. See *S. commixta*.

**domestica** L. "Service Tree". A medium-sized tree, with open, spreading branches, rough scaly bark and sticky, shining winter buds. Leaves pinnate, turning orange-red or yellow in autumn, composed of 13-21 leaflets. Fruits pear-shaped or apple-shaped, 2.5-3cm long, green, tinged red on the sunny side, edible when bletted. S and E Europe. Long cultivated.

**var. pomifera** HAYNE (var. *maliformis* (HAYNE) LODD.) Fruits apple-shaped, pedicel 1.5cm, leaves with 6-7 pairs of leaflets. AM 1983.

**var. pyrifera** HAYNE (var. *pyriformis* (HAYNE) LODD.) Fruits pear-shaped, pedicel 2.5cm, leaves with 8-9 pairs of leaflets.

**'Eastern Promise'** (*S. commixta* 'Embley' × *S. vilmorinii*). A small oval-headed tree of upright habit, the pinnate leaves with 15-19 leaflets which are dark green above on a red tinged-rachis, turning to purple then fiery orange in autumn. Fruits deep rose-pink in dense, hanging clusters which weigh down the branches. Raised in our nurseries in 1967.

**'Edwin Hillier'** A slow-growing shrub or small tree. The mother plant was raised in our nursery from seed received as *S. poteriifolia*, and has the appearance of having a member of the Aria Section as the pollinator. Winter buds rounded and ferruginous. Leaves ovate to elliptic or lanceolate, the lower half divided into 1-3 pairs of serrated leaflets or lobes, the upper half strongly lobed and toothed, dark green above, densely grey or brownish-grey tomentose beneath. Flowers pink in terminal corymbs. Fruits oval, rose-red.

**'Embley'** See *S. commixta* 'Embley'.

**epidendron** HAND.-MAZZ (Micromeles Section) A very rare shrub or small tree inclined to the equally rare *S. rhamnoides*, with slightly glaucous shoots. Leaves obovate to narrowly elliptic, long-pointed, serrulate dark green above, rusty pubescent beneath. Fruits globose, brownish-green in colour. W China. Introduced by George Forrest in 1925.

**esserteauana** KOEHNE (Aucuparia Section) (*S. conradinae* KOEHNE not HORT.) A small tree of open habit, occasionally up to 11m. Stipules large and leafy. Leaves composed of usually 11-13, sharply-toothed leaflets, dark matt green above, grey downy beneath. The small scarlet fruits colour later than most other species and are borne in dense broad clusters. The foliage gives rich autumn tints. W China. I 1907. AM 1954.

**'Flava'** Fruits of a rich, lemon-yellow borne in crowded flattened corymbs. A superb clone. AM 1954.

**'Ethel's Gold'** (Aucuparia Section) A small tree with bright green, sharply serrated leaflets and bunches of golden amber fruits. A seedling of hybrid origin which originated in our nurseries before 1959. Probably a seedling of *S. commixta*, which it resembles in leaf. The attractively coloured fruits persist into the New Year if the birds allow. Named after Sir Harold Hillier's mother. AM 1989.

**fennica** See *S. hybrida*.

**folgneri** (SCHNEID.) REHD. (Micromeles Section) A graceful, small tree of variable habit, usually with spreading or arching branches. Leaves variable, oval to narrowly so, double-toothed, dark green above, white or grey tomentose beneath, often assuming rich autumnal colours. Fruits variable in size, ovoid or obovoid, dark red or purplish-red, in drooping clusters. C China. I 1901. AM 1915.

**'Lemon Drop'** A graceful tree with slender, arching and drooping branches. Fruits bright yellow, set amid deep green leaves which are white beneath. Originated in our nurseries before 1950.

**SORBUS**—*continued*

**forrestii** MCALLISTER & GILLHAM (Forr. 19583) A very graceful small tree of open habit related to *S. hupehensis*. Leaves blue-green with usually 13-15 oblong leaflets toothed above the middle. Fruits small, white, tinged with pink on the calyx. An excellent small garden tree. Yunnan, China. I by George Forrest in 1921 but not named until 1980.

**'Golden Wonder'** (Aucuparia Section) A small tree of upright habit with stout shoots and grey hairy buds. Leaves with 13-15 deep blue-green leaflets, sharply-toothed nearly to the base and turning yellow and red in autumn. Golden yellow fruits are borne in large clusters.

**gracilis** (SIEB. & ZUCC.) K. KOCH (Aucuparia Section) A small tree or shrub of medium size. Leaves with 7-11 matt-green leaflets, toothed at the apex, stipules persistent, large and leafy. Flowers in few-flowered corymbs, fruits elongated pear-shape, oblong or obovoid, 15mm long, orange-red. Japan. C 1934.

**graeca** (SPACH) KOTSCHY (Aria Section) (*S. umbellata* var. *cretica* (LINDL.) SCHNEID.) A medium-sized shrub or small tree of dense, compact habit. Leaves obovate or rounded, double-toothed, green above, greenish-white tomentose beneath. Fruits crimson. SE and EC Europe. C 1830.

†**harrowiana** (BALF. f. & W.W. SM.) REHD. (Aucuparia Section) Related to *S. insignis*, this is perhaps the most remarkable and distinct of the pinnate-leaved species. A large shrub or small tree of compact habit, with stout ascending branches. Leaves 20-30cm long and as much across, pinnate with 2-4 pairs of sessile leaflets and a long-stalked terminal leaflet; leaflets 15-18cm long by 4-4.5cm across, the lateral ones conspicuously uneven at base, glossy dark green above, pale glaucous-green and slightly reticulate beneath. Flowers small, dull white, borne in large flattened corymbs, followed by equally small pink or pearly white fruits. Discovered by George Forrest in Yunnan in 1912, and later reintroduced by Kingdon-Ward. Plants of the latter introduction survived with little injury the severe winters of 1962-63 and the 1980s, whilst those of Forrest's introduction have been killed by severe winters except in the mildest localities. AM 1971.

**hedlundii** SCHNEID. (Aria Section) A strikingly handsome, medium-sized tree related to *S. vestita* with large leaves which are silvery-white tomentose beneath, with rust-coloured midrib and veins. E Himalaya.

× **hostii** (JACQ.) K. KOCH (*S. chamaemespilus* × *S. mougeotii*). A small tree or large shrub of compact habit. Leaves oval or obovate, sharply-toothed, green above, grey pubescent beneath. Flowers pale pink, followed by bright red fruits which ripen early. Occurring with the parents in the wild. C 1820. AM 1974.

**hupehensis** SCHNEID. (Aucuparia Section) A small, but strong-growing tree developing a bold, compact head of ascending, purple-brown branches. Leaves large, with a distinctive bluish-green cast, easily recognisable from a distance. Leaflets 11-17, sharply-toothed in the upper half. Stipules large and leafy. Fruits white or sometimes pink-tinged. Borne in loose, drooping bunches and lasting late into winter. The leaves turn a glorious red in autumn. W China. Introduced by E.H. Wilson in 1910. AM 1955. AGM 1984.

**var. obtusa** SCHNEID. Under this name is grown a most attractive form with pink fruits. Leaves with usually 11 leaflets, toothed only near the obtuse apex. Various selections have been named including 'Rosea' and 'Rufus', both with pink fruits. FCC 1977.

**hybrida** L. (Aria Section) (*S. fennica* (KALM) FRIES) A small to medium-sized, compact tree. Leaves broad ovate, one to one and a half times as long as broad, divided at the base into one or two pairs of long leaflets, the upper half variously toothed and lobed, green above, grey tomentose beneath. Fruits red, globose, almost 12mm across, in large clusters. Probably originated as a hybrid between *S. aucuparia* and *S. rupicola*. Wild in Scandinavia.

**'Fastigiata'** See *S.* × *thuringiaca* 'Fastigiata'.

**'Gibbsii'** (*S. pinnatifida* 'Gibbsii') A selected clone of more compact habit and with larger fruits. AM 1925 (as *Pyrus firma*). AM 1953.

**var. meinichii** See *S. meinichii*.

× **hybrida** HORT. See *S.* × *thuringiaca*.

**insignis** (HOOK. f.) HEDL. (K.W. 7746) (Aucuparia Section) A magnificent, small tree for a reasonably sheltered site, with stout, stiffly ascending, purplish-brown branches. Leaves pinnate, up to 25cm long, composed of 11-15 oblong-lanceolate, shallowly-toothed

**SORBUS insignis**—*continued*

leaflets which are dark polished green and reticulate above, glaucous beneath. They are retained long on the tree and turn red in early winter. Petioles with a large, conspicuous clasping base. Fruits small, oval, pink, borne in large heads. They seem to hold little attraction for the birds and persist almost to Easter. In winter the large buds are conspicuous. Related to *S. harrowiana*, but hardier, this tree has grown in the Hillier Gardens and Arboretum for many years where it has reached 5.5m. Introduced by Kingdon-Ward from the Naga Hills (Assam) in 1928. Also found in E Nepal.

**intermedia** (EHRH.) PERS. (Aria Section) "Swedish Whitebeam". A small to medium-sized tree with a dense, usually rounded head of branches. Leaves ovate to broad elliptic, lobed in the lower half, coarsely-toothed above, dark green and glossy above, grey tomentose beneath. Fruits 12mm across, orange-red, in bunches. NW Europe.

'**Brouwers**' A selected form with ascending branches making an oval crown. An excellent street tree.

**japonica** (DECNE.) HEDL. (Micromeles Section) A rare tree of medium size, the young branches, inflorescence and leaves beneath covered with a dense, white pubescence. Leaves ovate-orbicular to broadly ovate, shallowly-lobed and toothed. Fruits obovoid, red, with brown speckles. Attractive autumn tints. Japan.

**var. calocarpa** REHD. An attractive form with leaves whiter beneath and fruits larger, orange-yellow, without speckles. Rich yellow autumn tints. C Japan. I 1915.

'**Jermyns**' See *S. commixta* 'Jermyns'.

'**John Mitchell**' See *S. thibetica* 'John Mitchell'.

'**Joseph Rock**' (Rock 23657) (Aucuparia Section) An outstanding, small tree up to 9m or more high, with an erect, compact head of branches. Leaves composed of 15-19, narrowly-oblong, sharply-toothed leaflets, turning to shades of red, orange, copper and purple in autumn. The rich autumn tints provide an ideal setting for the clusters of globular fruits, which are creamy-yellow at first deepening to amber-yellow at maturity, remaining on the branches well after leaf fall. The origin of this tree remains a mystery. It is probably a form of a variable Chinese species. Unfortunately very susceptible to fireblight. AM 1950. FCC 1962. AGM 1984.

**keissleri** (SCHNEID.) REHD. (Micromeles Section) A very rare and quite distinct small tree up to 12m or a large shrub, with stiffly ascending branches. Leaves obovate, leathery, glossy green. Flowers greenish-white, sweetly-scented, borne in dense, terminal clusters and followed by small, crab-apple-like fruits which are green, with a bloomy, red cheek. C and W China. I 1907 by Ernest Wilson.

× **kewensis** HENSEN (Aucuparia Section) (*S. pohuashanensis* HORT. not HEDL.) A first class, hardy, free-fruiting rowan, a hybrid between our native species (*S. aucuparia*), and the best of the Chinese species (*S. pohuashanensis*). The orange-red fruits are borne in large, heavy bunches, and severely test the strength of the branches, providing in autumn a feast both for the eyes and the birds. It is commonly grown in gardens under the name *S. pohuashanensis* from which it differs mainly in that the leafy stipules below the inflorescence are normally shed before the fruits develop. Raised originally at Kew Gardens. AM 1947. FCC 1973 (as *S. pohuashanensis*). AGM 1984.

**koehneana** SCHNEID. (Aucuparia Section) A medium-sized shrub or small, elegant tree. Leaves with 17-33, narrow, toothed leaflets. The small, porcelain-white fruits are borne in slender, drooping clusters. C China. I 1910 by Ernest Wilson.

**lanata** See *S. vestita*.

**latifolia** (LAM.) PERS. (Aria Section) "Service Tree of Fontainbleau". A small to medium-sized tree with downy young shoots and shaggy, peeling bark. Leaves ovate or broad elliptic, sharply lobed, glossy green above, grey-felted beneath. Fruits globular, russet-yellow with large, brownish speckles. An apomictic species derived from a hybrid between *S. torminalis* and a species of the Aria Section. EC Portugal to SW Germany. AM 1973. FCC 1987.

'**Leonard Messel**' (*S. aucuparia* × *S. harrowiana*). A splendid but unfortunately rather neglected small tree with upright branches making a dense, oval crown. Winter buds conical, red with brown hairs at the apex. Leaves large with usually 9-11 leaflets on a pink rachis, turning red and purple in autumn. Leaflets oblong, to 11 × 2.8cm, sharply-toothed above the middle, blue-green above, glaucous beneath. Distinctive bright pink

**SORBUS 'Leonard Messel'**—*continued*

fruits are borne in broad, hanging clusters. Raised in 1949 by Col L.C.R. Messel. It has reached 9m in the Hillier Gardens and Arboretum. AM 1973. FCC 1987.

**megalocarpa** REHD. A remarkable large shrub of loose spreading habit. Twigs brown-purple, stout, bearing large, oval to obovate, deep glossy green, coarsely-toothed leaves, which sometimes turn to crimson in autumn. The large flower-buds open before the leaves in early spring, producing a conspicuous corymb of cream flowers which have too pungent a smell for indoor decoration. These are followed by hard, brown fruits the size and colour of small partridge eggs. The large, red, sticky bud scales and red young leaves in spring are very striking. W China. Introduced by E.H. Wilson in 1903.

**var. cuneata** REHD. More vigorous, making a small tree with arching branches. Leaves matt green, short-stalked, and finely-toothed, with white tufts of hair in the vein axils beneath. I by Ernest Wilson in 1910.

**meinichii** (HARTM.) HEDL. (*S. hybrida* var. *meinichii* (HARTM.) REHD.) A small, erect tree with a compact head of fastigiate branches. Leaves with 4-6 pairs of distinct leaflets and a deeply-toothed or lobed terminal portion, green above, grey tomentose beneath. Fruits rounded, red. Now accepted by many authorities as a species, it is said to have originated as a hybrid between *S. aucuparia* and *S. rupicola*, though it resembles more the former. Wild in S and W Norway.

**meliosmifolia** REHD. (Micromeles Section) A small tree or large bushy shrub with stiffly ascending, purplish-brown branches. Leaves up to 18cm long, bright green, with 18-24 pairs of parallel veins. One of the first trees to flower once winter has passed. Fruits 12mm long, brownish-red. A rare species sometimes confused in cultivation with *S. caloneura*, from which it differs in its larger, shorter-stalked, more numerously-veined leaves. W China. I 1910 by Ernest Wilson.

**minima** (LEY) HEDL. (Aria Section) A slender-branched, native shrub of medium size. Leaves elliptic or oblong-elliptic, 5-7.5cm long, shallowly-lobed, green above, grey tomentose beneath. Fruits small, scarlet, with a few speckles. Only found in the wild on limestone crags near Crickhowell, Brecon, Wales.

**'Mitchellii'** See *S. thibetica* 'John Mitchell'.

**mougeotii** SOY-WILLEM. & GODRON (Aria Section) Generally a large shrub or small tree, with ovate or obovate, shallowly lobed leaves, green above, whitish-grey tomentose beneath. Fruits slightly longer than wide, red, with a few speckles. European Alps (mainly in the west), Pyrenees. C 1880. AM 1984.

**pallescens** REHD. (Aria Section) A beautiful, small tree of upright growth. Leaves narrowly elliptic to elliptic-lanceolate, acuminate, sharply double-toothed, green above, silvery-white tomentose beneath, with conspicuous veins. Older trees have shreddy bark and elliptic to oblong leaves. Fruits pear-shaped or rounded, up to 12mm long, green with a red cheek, borne in loose clusters. W China. I 1908.

**'Pearly King'** (Aucuparia Section) A small, slender-branched tree with pinnate, fern-like leaves composed of 13-17 narrow, sharply-toothed leaflets. Fruits 15mm across, rose at first, changing to white with a pink flush, borne in large, loosely pendulous bunches. A hybrid of *S. vilmorinii*, which originated in our nurseries.

**'Pink Pearl'** A small tree of upright habit, the attractive pinnate leaves with sharply-toothed leaflets. Fruits white, heavily flushed and spotted pink, borne in heavy clusters. A seedling raised in our Eastleigh nursery in 1958 by our Foreman Alf Alford.

**pinnatifida** See *S.* × *thuringiaca*.

**'Gibbsii'** See *S. hybrida* 'Gibbsii'.

**pohuashanensis** (HANCE) HEDL. not HORT. (Aucuparia Section) (*S. conradinae* HORT. not KOEHNE) (*S. sargentiana warleyensis* HORT.) A splendid tree, possibly the best Chinese rowan, attaining up to 11m with a dense head of spreading and ascending branches. Leaves with usually 11-15, sharply-toothed leaflets which are green above, grey pubescent beneath. Stipules large and leafy, persistent, especially below the inflorescence even when fruiting. Fruits red, borne in conspicuous bunches, causing the branches to bow under their concentrated weight. One of the most reliable and spectacular of *Sorbus* in fruit. Easily grown and very hardy. A parent of several hybrids, the true plant is rare in cultivation, its place most often being taken by the hybrid *S.* × *kewensis*. N China. I 1883. AM 1946.

**SORBUS**—*continued*

**pohuashanensis** HORT. See *S.* × *kewensis*.

**poteriifolia** HAND.-MAZZ. (*S. pygmaea* HORT.) (Aucuparia Section) The smallest known *Sorbus*. A very rare, tiny shrublet, difficult to cultivate. Leaves composed of 9-15 sharply-toothed leaflets. Flowers pale rose to crimson in terminal clusters, followed by globular, white fruits. Related to *S. reducta* it is best given a moist, peaty soil. N Burma, NW Yunnan. I from Burma in 1926 by Kingdon-Ward and again in 1953. Until recently the only plants in cultivation grew in the Hillier Gardens and Arboretum.

**poteriifolia** HORT. See *S.* sp. McLaren D. 84.

**prattii** KOEHNE (Aucuparia Section) (*S. prattii* f. *subarachnoidea* (KOEHNE) REHD.) An elegant large shrub or occasionally a small tree, with slender branches and leaves composed of 21-29 coarsely-toothed leaflets. Fruits small, globose, pearly-white, borne in small, drooping clusters all along the branches. W China. I by E.H. Wilson in 1910. AM 1971.

    **f. subarachnoidea** See *S. prattii*.

**pygmaea** HORT. See *S. poteriifolia* HAND.-MAZZ.

**randaiensis** (HAYATA) KOIDZ. (Aucuparia Section) A small tree closely related to *S. commixta* and differing in the narrower leaflets. Plants previously grown under this name are *S. commixta*. The true species has now been introduced to cultivation. Taiwan.

**'Red Marbles'** (Aucuparia Section) A small tree with stout twigs which originated in our Eastleigh nurseries in 1961. Leaves with purple stalks and 13-15 large, broadly and boldly-toothed leaflets. Fruits red with pale spots, 12-17mm across, borne in loose, heavy bunches. A magnificent fruiting tree, believed to be *S. aucuparia* 'Edulis' × *S. pohuashanensis*.

**reducta** DIELS (Aucuparia Section) An unusual small, suckering shrub forming thickets of slender, erect stems, 60cm to 1m high. Leaves with red petioles, composed of 13-15 sharply serrate, dark, shining green leaflets, turning to bronze and reddish-purple in autumn. Fruits small, globular, white flushed rose. A charming species when associated with heathers, dwarf conifers and other dwarf shrubs. Some plants under this name are similar in leaf and fruit but grow on a single stem and do not sucker. N Burma, W China. Introduced by Kingdon-Ward in 1943. AM 1974.

**rhamnoides** REHD. The true species of this name, a native of the E Himalaya, belongs to the Micromeles Section and is not in cultivation. The plant grown under this name is of uncertain identity. A small tree of loose habit. Leaves elliptic, 13-15cm long, serrate, slender-stalked, green above, thinly grey downy beneath at first. Fruits green becoming yellowish-brown flushed red with persistent calyx, remaining on the tree until late winter.

**'Rose Queen'** (Aucuparia Section) (*S. commixta* 'Embley' × *S.* sp. McLaren D. 84). An attractive, small tree raised in our Eastleigh nurseries in 1963. Leaves composed of 13-17 sharply serrate leaflets. Fruits of a bright rose-red, produced in large, loose bunches.

**rufoferruginea** See *S. commixta* var. *rufoferruginea*.

**rupicola** (SYME) HEDL. (Aria Section) (*S. salicifolia* (MYRIN) HEDL.) A medium-sized, native shrub of rather stiff habit. Leaves obovate or oblanceolate, tapering to the base, coarsely-toothed, green above, white tomentose beneath. Fruits broader than long, carmine, with scattered brown speckles. British Isles, Scandinavia.

**sargentiana** KOEHNE (Aucuparia Section) A magnificent species, slowly developing into a rigidly-branched tree up to 9m and as much through. Winter buds large and sticky, like those of a horse chestnut, but crimson. Leaves large and attractive, up to 30cm long, composed of 7-11 slender-pointed leaflets, each 7.5-13cm long. Leaf-stalks red, stipules large, leafy and persistent. Fruits small, scarlet, late in ripening, produced in large, rounded heads up to 15cm across. Rich red autumn colour. W China. Discovered by E.H. Wilson in 1903, and introduced by him in 1908. AM 1954. FCC 1956. AGM 1984.

**'Savill Orange'** A small tree bearing dense clusters of large, orange-red berries. A seedling of *S. aucuparia* 'Xanthocarpa' which originated in the Valley Gardens, Windsor Great Park about 1970. AM 1979.

**scalaris** KOEHNE (Aucuparia Section) A small tree of distinct appearance with wide-spreading branches and neat, attractive, frond-like leaves. They are composed of 21-33 narrow leaflets, which are dark glossy green above, grey downy beneath, turning to rich

**SORBUS scalaris**—*continued*

red and purple late in autumn. Fruits small, red, densely packed in flattened heads. W China. Discovered and introduced by E.H. Wilson in 1904. AM 1934. AGM 1984.

**scopulina** HORT. See *S. aucuparia* 'Fastigiata'.

**serotina** See *S. commixta* 'Serotina'.

**'Signalman'** A small tree of columnar habit raised in our Eastleigh nursery in 1968 as the result of crossing *S. domestica* with *S. scopulina*. Leaves similar to those of the former parent, but slightly smaller and more densely arranged. Fruits large, bright orange, borne in dense clusters. Should prove to be an excellent tree for the small garden and for street planting.

**sitchensis** ROEM. (Aucuparia Section) This species is rare in cultivation. Plants previously listed under this name are *S. cascadensis*.

**sp. Ghose** (Aucuparia Section) A superb, small tree of upright habit showing some affinity to *S. insignis* but hardier. Probably a new species and worthy of extensive planting. Leaves large, composed of 15-19, sharply serrate leaflets which are dark, dull green above, glaucescent beneath and rusty pubescent, at least along the midrib. Fruits small, rose-red, produced in large, densely packed bunches which remain on the branches until late in the season. Introduced by us from the Himalaya.

**sp. Lowndes** See *S. ursina*.

**sp. McLaren D. 84** (*S. poteriifolia* HORT.) (Aucuparia Section) A beautiful, slow-growing, small tree with erect, purplish-brown branches. Leaves composed of 15-19 sharply serrate, dark green, downy leaflets. Fruits globular, of a delightful deep rose-pink, carried in large, loose bunches. China. AM 1951.

**sp. Yu 8423** See under *S. thibetica*.

×**splendida** HEDL. (Aucuparia Section) (*S. americana* × *S. aucuparia*). A small, robust tree intermediate in character between its parents. Buds sticky but rusty pubescent at tips. Fruits orange-red, in large, dense bunches. Garden origin before 1850.

**subcuneata** WILMOTT A small British endemic tree with glossy brown, white hairy shoots. Leaves glossy green above, thinly grey tomentose beneath, sharply-toothed or lobed to about one quarter of the way to the midrib, truncate or shallowly cuneate at the base. Fruits bright red. Somerset, N Devon.

**'Sunshine'** A small tree of erect habit when young. Leaves dark glossy green with 7-8 pairs of sharply-toothed leaflets. Fruits golden yellow, borne in large, dense clusters and colouring before 'Joseph Rock' of which it is a seedling. Raised in our nurseries in 1968.

**'Theophrasta'** A small, round-headed tree with broadly ovate, double-toothed leaves grey tomentose beneath. Fruits relatively large, brownish and conspicuously lenticelled at first becoming dull orange. Origin unknown.

**thibetica** (CARDOT) HAND.-MAZZ. This species is mainly represented in gardens by 'John Mitchell' described below. For the Kingdon-Ward introduction previously distributed under this name (KW 21175) see *S. wardii*.

**'John Mitchell'** (*S.* 'Mitchellii') (*S.* 'John Mitchell') A handsome, medium-sized to large tree, eventually developing a broad, rounded head. The mature leaves are large, about 15cm long by as much across and remarkably rounded, green above, white tomentose beneath. The original tree from which our stock was raised is growing in the Westonbirt Arboretum, Glos. AGM 1984.

**Yu 8423** A distinct, slow-growing form making an erect, small tree of narrow, columnar habit. Leaves oval to obovate, 10-13cm long, toothed, green above, grey tomentose beneath. Winter buds green and viscid. Fruits pear-shaped, orange flushed red. China.

×**thuringiaca** (ILSE) FRITSCH (*S. aria* × *S. aucuparia*) (*S. pinnatifida* HORT.) (*S.* × *hybrida* HORT.) A small tree with a dense head of ascending branches. Leaves narrowly oval to oblong, lobed and toothed, divided at the base into 1-3 pairs of leaflets, dull green above, grey tomentose beneath. Fruits scarlet with a few brown speckles. Occurs rarely with the parents in the wild. Frequently confused with *S. hybrida* in cultivation, it differs in its stricter, more compact habit, and in its slightly larger, more elongated leaves with smaller, oval leaflets. AM 1924 (as *S. pinnatifida*).

**'Decurrens'** Leaves pinnate except for the terminal three leaflets which are often joined. C 1834.

**SÒRBUS × thuringiaca**—*continued*

**'Fastigiata'** (*S. hybrida* 'Fastigiata') A most distinctive, small tree with an ovoid head of closely packed, ascending branches. Leaves and fruits as in type. A first class tree possessing most of the qualities sought by those interested in public planting.

**'Neuillyensis'** Leaves with several of the upper pairs of leaflets joined. C 1893.

**tianschanica** RUPR. A slow-growing shrub or low rounded tree up to 4m high. Leaves pinnate with 9-15 sharply-toothed, glossy green leaflets, colouring in autumn. Flowers and fruits are rarely carried on trees in the British Isles, though they are said to be conspicuous on specimens growing in more suitable climes. Flowers 20mm across followed by globular red fruits. Turkestan. I 1895.

**torminalis** (L.) CRANTZ (Aria Section) "Chequer Tree" "Wild Service Tree". An attractive, medium-sized, native tree with ascending branches, spreading with age, scaly bark and brown twigs, woolly pubescent when young. Leaves maple-like, ovate, sharply and conspicuously lobed, glossy dark green above, pubescent beneath at first, turning bronzy-yellow in autumn; fruits longer than broad, russety-brown. Europe including England, Asia Minor, N Africa.

**'Tundra'** A small upright tree, the fern-like dark green leaves with about 10 pairs of sharply-toothed leaflets, turning reddish-purple in autumn. Fruits pale Chartreuse-green at first becoming creamy-white providing an effective contrast as the leaves colour. A seedling of 'Joseph Rock' raised in our nursery in 1968.

**umbellata var. cretica** See *S. graeca.*

**ursina** SCHAUER (*S.* sp. Lowndes) (Aucuparia Section) An attractive, small, erect-growing tree with stout, ascending, greyish branches. Buds red, ferruginous hairy at the tips. Leaves composed of 15-21 sharply-toothed, elliptic-oblong, conspicuously reticulated leaflets. Fruits white or pink-tinged, borne in dense bunches. A very distinct and beautiful species, introduced by Col Donald Lowndes from the Himalaya in 1950. AM 1973.

**× vagensis** WILMOTT (Aria Section) (*S. aria × S. torminalis*) (*S. × confusa* GREMLI ex ROUY-CAMUS) A small to medium-sized tree of compact habit. Leaves ovate to elliptic, sharply lobed, not as deeply as in *S. torminalis,* glossy green above, thinly grey tomentose beneath. Fruits obovoid; greenish-brown, with numerous brown speckles. Occurs with the parents in the wild, in England only in the Wye Valley.

**vestita** (G. DON) LODD. (Aria Section) (*S. cuspidata* (SPACH) HEDL.) (*S. lanata* HORT. not (D. DON) SCHAUER) "Himalayan Whitebeam". A medium-sized tree of erect habit when young, later spreading. Leaves broad-elliptic, decurrent onto the petiole, 15-25cm long, green above, silvery-white or buff tomentose beneath. Fruits green, speckled and flushed warm brown, 15-20mm across, resembling small crab apples or miniature pears, borne in loose bunches. A magnificent species with bold foliage, quite one of the handsomest of all hardy trees. Himalaya. I 1820.

**'Sessilifolia'** Large elliptic leaves tapering towards base and apex, sea-green above, grey-white tomentose beneath, sessile or very shortly-stalked.

**vilmorinii** SCHNEID. (Aucuparia Section) A beautiful, small tree or medium-sized shrub of elegant, spreading habit. Leaves often in clusters, fern-like, composed of 11-31 small leaflets, each 12-20mm long, turning to red and purple in autumn. The loose, drooping clusters of fruits are rose-red at first, gradually passing through pink to white flushed rose. A charming species suitable for the smaller garden. W China. Introduced by the Abbé Delavay in 1889. AM 1916. AGM 1984.

**wardii** MERR. (K.W. 21127) (Aria Section) A specimen of this rare species in the Hillier Gardens and Arboretum is growing strongly and is over 9m high. Its branches are rather stiff and erect giving the tree a distinct columnar habit. Leaves elliptic to obovate, green and ribbed above, thinly hairy beneath; young leaves grey downy. Fruits in loose corymbs, globular, 12mm in diameter, amber, speckled greyish-brown. Tibet, Bhutan. A splendid silvery whitebeam for sites where space is limited. Introduced by Kingdon-Ward. Previously listed as *S. thibetica.*

**'White Wax'** A small tree with a conical head of branches and blackish buds covered with grey down. Leaves fern-like with up to 23 oblong, sharply-toothed leaflets. Fruits pure white, 1cm across, in drooping clusters.

**'Wilfrid Fox'** (Aria Section) (*S. aria × S. cuspidata*). Named in memory of a generous friend and great gardener who did much to beautify the roadside plantings of England and was the creator of the famous Winkworth Arboretum in Surrey. This handsome hybrid tree

**SORBUS 'Wilfrid Fox'**—*continued*

has been growing in our nurseries for more than fifty years. It forms a round-headed tree 12m in height. A broadly columnar tree when young, with densely packed, ascending branches. Leaves elliptic, 15-20cm long, with a slender petiole, 2.5-4cm long, shallowly lobed and doubly serrate, dark glossy green above, greyish-white tomentose beneath. Fruits marble-like, green at first turning to deep amber speckled grey.

**'Winter Cheer'** (Aucuparia Section) (*S. esserteauana* 'Flava' × *S. pohuashanensis*). A seedling raised in our Eastleigh nursery in 1959. A small to medium-sized, open-branched tree. The large, flat bunches of fruits are a warm, chrome-yellow at first, ripening to orange-red. They begin to colour in September and last well into winter. AM 1971.

**zahlbruckneri** HORT. See *S. alnifolia*.

**"SOUTHERNWOOD"** See *Artemisia abrotanum*.

†**SPARMANNIA** L. f.—**Tiliaceae**—A small genus of 3 species of tender shrubs and trees natives of tropical and S Africa.

**africana** L. f. "African Hemp" "House Lime". A large, stellately-hairy, apple-green shrub of vigorous habit. Leaves large, often 30cm or more across, palmately-lobed. Flowers white, 4cm wide, with sensitive, yellow stamens, borne in conspicuous cymose umbels during spring. An excellent conservatory shrub. This marvellous plant not only tolerates but appears to thrive on the cigarette and cigar-ends and tea and coffee dregs of the second class Continental cafés. S Africa. I 1790. AM 1955.

**SPARTIUM** L.—**Leguminosae**—A monotypic genus closely related to *Cytisus* and *Genista*, differing in its one-lipped, spathe-like calyx. Thrives in a well drained, sunny position. An excellent seaside shrub. Specimens drawn up in sheltered gardens are apt to become tall and leggy. These may be hard pruned in March, taking care not to cut into the old hard wood.

**junceum** L. "Spanish Broom". A strong-growing shrub of loose habit, with erect green, rush-like stems up to 3m. Leaves small and inconspicuous. The comparatively large, fragrant, yellow, pea-flowers, 2.5cm long, are borne in loose, terminal racemes throughout summer and early autumn. A wonderful shrub when kept low and bushy by the sea wind's blast. Mediterranean region, SW Europe. Introduced to England about 1548. AM 1968. FCC 1977. AGM 1984.

**SPARTOCYTISUS nubigenus** See *Cytisus supranubius*.

†*****SPHACELE** BENTH.—**Labiatae**—A small genus of 25 species of sage-like shrubs and sub-shrubs, natives of Mexico and S America. Only suitable for the mildest areas of the British Isles.

**chamaedryoides** BRIQUET (*S. campanulata*) A small shrub with wrinkled leaves and loose racemes of pale blue, tubular flowers during summer. It makes a lovely conservatory shrub. Chile. I 1875.

**SPHAERALCEA** ST.-HIL.—**Malvaceae**—A genus of about 60 species of herbs, shrubs and sub-shrubs, natives mainly of North and South America with a few species in S Africa. The following requires a warm, sunny site and a well drained soil.

†**fendleri** A. GRAY A dwarf sub-shrub with downy shoots and three-lobed leaves. The 2.5cm wide, mallow-like flowers are pale reddish-orange in colour and are borne in axillary clusters during summer and autumn. A pretty little shrublet, suitable for a sunny border. N Mexico.

**"SPICE BUSH"** See *Lindera benzoin*.

**"SPINDLE"** See *Euonymus*.

**SPIRAEA** L.—**Rosaceae**—A varied and useful genus of hardy flowering shrubs, many of which are graceful in habit and pleasing in foliage. About 70 species in N temperate regions. They are easily grown in any ordinary soil and a sunny position though a few become chlorotic in very shallow chalk soils. Those of the *japonica-douglasii* type which flower on the current year's shoots may be pruned to the ground in March, whilst those of the *henryi-nipponica-veitchii* type which flower on shoots of the previous year may require thinning out and the old flowering shoots cut to within a few centimetres of the old wood, immediately after flowering. Untidy specimens of *S.* 'Arguta' and *S. thunbergii* may be hard pruned immediately after flowering. *S. douglasii, S. salicifolia, S. tomentosa* and other thicket-forming species should only be planted where space permits.

**aitchisonii** See *Sorbaria aitchisonii.*

**albiflora** See *S. japonica* 'Albiflora'.

**arborea** See *Sorbaria arborea.*

**arcuata** HOOK. f. A medium-sized shrub related to *S. gemmata*, with pubescent, angular stems and entire leaves. Flowers white, carried in small umbels all along the arching branches in May. Himalaya. C 1908.

**'Arguta'** (*S.* × *multiflora* × *S. thunbergii*). "Bridal Wreath" "Foam of May". A dense-growing, medium-sized shrub with graceful, slender branches. Leaves oblanceolate, to narrowly oval, entire or few-toothed, usually glabrous. Flowers pure white, produced in small clusters all along the branches in April and May. One of the most effective and free-flowering of the early spireas. C before 1884. AGM 1984.

**assurgens** See *Sorbaria assurgens.*

**baldshuanica** B. FEDTSCHENKO A dwarf shrub of rounded, compact habit, with slender, glabrous, twiggy branches. Leaves small, obovate, sea-green, toothed at the apex. Flowers white, in small, terminal corymbs in summer. SE Russia.

**bella** SIMS A small shrub occasionally 1.5m high, with angular branches, downy when young. Leaves broadly ovate, toothed at apex, glaucous beneath. Very attractive when carrying its bright rose-pink flowers in terminal corymbs in June. Not happy in really shallow chalk soils. Himalaya. I 1818.

**betulifolia** PALL. A dwarf shrub occasionally up to 1m high, forming mounds of reddish-brown, glabrous branches and broadly ovate to rounded leaves, 2-4cm long. Flowers white, borne in dense corymbs, 2.5-6.5cm across, in June. Suitable for the rock garden. NE Asia, Japan. I about 1812.

× **billiardii** HERINCQ (*S. douglasii* × *S. salicifolia*). Medium-sized, suckering shrub with erect, hairy stems. Leaves oblong to oblong-lanceolate, sharply-toothed, greyish pubescent beneath. Flowers bright rose, borne in narrow, densely crowded panicles throughout summer. Not happy on shallow chalky soils. C before 1854.

'Triumphans' (*S. menziesii* 'Triumphans') A beautiful shrub with dense, conical panicles of purplish-rose flowers during summer. Not happy on shallow, chalky soils.

× **brachybotrys** LANGE (*S. canescens* × *S. douglasii*). A strong-growing, medium-sized shrub with gracefully arching branches. Leaves oblong or ovate, toothed at apex, grey downy beneath. Flowers pale rose, borne in dense, terminal panicles during summer. Not recommended for very shallow, chalky soils. C before 1867.

**bracteata** See *S. nipponica.*

**bullata** See *S. japonica* 'Bullata'.

× **bumalda** See *S. japonica* 'Bumalda'.

'Anthony Waterer' See *S. japonica* 'Anthony Waterer'.

'Coccinea' See *S. japonica* 'Coccinea'.

'Froebelii' See *S. japonica* 'Froebelii'.

'Goldflame' See *S. japonica* 'Goldflame'.

**calcicola** W.W. SM. A small, graceful shrub with angular, glabrous stems. Leaves very small, fan-shaped, prettily three-lobed and toothed, borne on slender petioles. Flowers white, tinted rose without, produced in numerous small umbels along the arching stems in June. China. I 1915.

**canescens** D. DON A graceful, medium-sized shrub with long, angular, downy branches. Leaves oval or obovate, 1-2.5cm long, toothed at apex, grey downy beneath. Flowers in corymbs, white, wreathing the arching stems in June and July. Himalaya. I 1837.

'Myrtifolia' Leaves oblong, dark green above, glaucescent beneath.

**SPIRAEA**—*continued*

**cantoniensis** LOUR. (*S. reevesiana* LINDL.) A wide-spreading, graceful shrub up to 1.8m high, with slender, arching, glabrous branches. Leaves rhomboidal, deeply-toothed or three-lobed, glaucous beneath. Flowers white, borne in rounded clusters along the branches in June. China, long cultivated in Japan. I 1824.

'**Flore Pleno**' ('Lanceata') An attractive form with lanceolate leaves and double flowers.

**chamaedryfolia** L. A suckering shrub, producing erect, angular, glabrous shoots up to 1.8m high. Leaves ovate to ovate-lanceolate, coarsely-toothed, glaucescent beneath. Flowers white, borne in corymbs along the stems, in May. Widely distributed in the wild from C and E Europe to Siberia. C 1789.

**var. ulmifolia** (SCOP.) MAXIM. A more robust form with taller stems and ovate, double-toothed leaves. Flowers in large, fluffy heads, in late May or June.

×**cinerea** ZAB. (*S. cana* × *S. hypericifolia*). A small, densely-branched shrub with downy arching stems and narrow, entire leaves, grey downy when young. The small, white flowers are abundantly produced in dense clusters all along the branches in late April and early May; resembling *S.* 'Arguta' in general effect.

'**Grefsheim**' A fine-flowering clone of Norwegian origin. AGM 1984.

**crispifolia** See *S. japonica* 'Bullata'.

**decumbens** KOCH A dwarf, compact, alpine shrub with procumbent glabrous stems and ascending branches, up to 20cm high. Leaves narrow, elliptic, toothed at apex. Flowers white in small, terminal corymbs, from June to September. A choice little shrub for the rock garden or scree. SE European Alps.

**subsp. tomentosa** (POECH) DOSTAL (*S. hacquetii* FENZL & K. KOCH) (*S. lancifolia* HOFFMANNS) Stems greyish-pubescent, leaves grey tomentose beneath. I 1885.

**densiflora** NUTT. A small shrub with dark red branches and oval or oblong, sharply-toothed leaves. Flowers rose-pink, borne in dense corymbs in June. W United States. C 1861.

**var. splendens** (BAUMANN) ABRAMS (*S. splendens* BAUMANN) Differs from the typical form in its downy shoots. C 1875.

**discolor** See *Holodiscus discolor*.

‡**douglasii** HOOK. A rampant, suckering shrub, forming in time dense thickets of erect, reddish shoots 1.5-1.8m high. Leaves narrowly oblong, coarsely-toothed, grey-felted beneath. Flowers purplish-rose, produced in dense, terminal panicles in June and July. Not recommended for shallow chalk soils. W North America. Discovered and introduced by David Douglas in 1827. Naturalised in parts of N and C Europe.

**var. menziesii** (HOOK.) PRESL (*S. menziesii* HOOK.) A small to medium-sized, vigorous shrub of suckering habit, with erect, brown stems and lanceolate to oval, coarsely-toothed leaves. Flowers bright purplish-rose, borne in dense, terminal, pyramidal panicles, in July and August. W North America. I 1838.

**fritschiana** SCHNEID. A small, mound-forming shrub with glabrous, yellowish or orange-brown young shoots. Leaves ovate, glabrous, blue-green on both sides. Flowers white tinged pink in broad, dense terminal corymbs in June. Introduced to our nurseries from Korea in 1976 by Carl Miller and Sir Harold Hillier. E China, Korea.

**gemmata** ZAB. An elegant shrub of medium size, with glabrous, angular stems and characteristic long, slender leaf-buds. Leaves narrowly oblong, entire or three-toothed at apex, glabrous. Flowers white, borne in small corymbs along the arching branches in May. Mongolia. C 1886.

**hacquetii** See *S. decumbens* subsp. *tomentosa*.

**henryi** HEMSL. A strong-growing, medium-sized to large shrub of arching habit, with reddish-brown, sparsely hairy stems. Leaves 4-8cm long, narrowly oblong or oblanceolate, coarsely-toothed at apex. Flowers white, produced in rounded corymbs all along the arching branches, in June. C China. Discovered by Augustine Henry, introduced by Ernest Wilson in 1900. AM 1934.

**hypericifolia** L. A dense, bushy shrub producing graceful, arching branches up to 1.5-1.8m high. Leaves obovate, entire or three-toothed at apex. Flowers white, produced in small clusters along the branches during May. The form in general cultivation is subsp. *obovata* (WALDST. & KIT) H. HUBER. SE Europe. Naturalised in parts of North America. C 1640.

**SPIRAEA**— *continued*

**japonica** L.f. (*S. callosa* THUNB.). A small, erect shrub with lanceolate to ovate, coarsely-toothed leaves. Flowers pink, borne in large, flattened heads, from midsummer onwards. A variable species, very popular in gardens. Japan, Korea, China to the Himalayas. Naturalised in parts of C Europe. C 1870.

**'Alba'** See 'Albiflora'.

**'Albiflora'** ('Alba') (*S. albiflora* (MIQ.) ZAB.) A dwarf, "front-row" shrub of compact habit. Flowers white, borne in dense, terminal corymbs. I before 1868.

**'Alpina'** See 'Nana'.

**'Anthony Waterer'** (*S.* × *bumalda* 'Anthony Waterer') Flowers bright crimson. An excellent, dwarf shrub for the front of borders or for mass effect. The foliage is occasionally variegated cream and pink. FCC 1893. AGM 1984.

**'Atrosanguinea'** Young growths red; flowers crimson. A selection of var. *fortunei*.

**'Bullata'** (*S. crispifolia* HORT.) (*S. bullata* MAXIM.) A dwarf, slow-growing shrub of compact habit. Leaves small, broadly ovate, bullate above. Flowers rose-crimson, in terminal, flat-topped clusters in summer. A splendid companion for 'Nana'. Garden origin in Japan. C before 1881. FCC 1884.

**'Bumalda'** (*S.* × *bumalda* BURVEN.) A dwarf shrub with glabrous stems and sharply-toothed, ovate-lanceolate leaves. Flowers deep pink, carried in broad, flattened, terminal panicles on the current year's shoots, continuously throughout summer. The leaves are often variegated with pink and cream. C before 1890.

**'Coccinea'** (*S.* × *bumalda* 'Coccinea') Flowers of a rich crimson.

**'Crispa'** Leaves dark glossy green, reddish-purple when young, deeply and sharply-toothed. Often grown as var. *fortunei*.

**'Fastigiata'** A vigorous, small shrub of stiff, erect habit. Flowers white in exceptionally wide flat heads.

**var. fortunei** REHD. The common Chinese form, differing from the type chiefly in its much larger, glabrous, incisely-toothed leaves. E and C China. I about 1850.

**'Froebelii'** (*S.* × *bumalda* 'Froebelii') Flowers bright crimson in July.

**'Gold Mound'** A dwarf shrub of compact habit with yellow foliage. Bears small heads of pale pink flowers.

**'Golden Dome'** A compact, dome-shaped dwarf shrub, the foliage golden yellow in spring and early summer.

**'Goldflame'** (*S.* × *bumalda* 'Goldflame') A very popular dwarf shrub. Young leaves in spring emerging reddish-orange becoming bright yellow and eventually green. Flowers deep rose red. AGM 1984.

**'Little Princess'** A dwarf, compact form forming a low mound with rose-crimson flowers.

**'Macrophylla'** Not the best form in flower, but perhaps the best Spiraea for autumn leaf colour. Leaves large and bullate, reddish-purple when young. A selection of var. *fortunei*.

**'Nana'** ('Alpina') ('Nyewoods') A superb dwarf shrub forming a dense, compact mound, 45-60cm high and rather more across with proportionately smaller leaves and flower-heads. Spectacular when closely studded with tiny heads of rose-pink flowers. Worthy of a position in every garden and window-box, and should be mass-planted where space permits. AGM 1984.

**'Ruberrima'** A dense, rounded shrub with rose-red flowers. A selection of var. *fortunei*.

**'Shirobana'** An unusual dwarf form producing a mixture of deep pink and white flowers on the same and different heads.

**laevigata** See *Sibiraea laevigata*.

**lancifolia** See *S. decumbens* subsp. *tomentosa*.

**latifolia** (AIT.) BORKH. (*S. salicifolia* var. *latifolia* AIT.) A rampant, suckering shrub producing erect, angular, reddish stems, 1.5-1.8m high. Leaves variable in shape, coarsely-toothed. Flowers white or pale pink, produced in broad, conical, glabrous panicles at the ends of the current year's growth during summer. Not suitable for shallow chalk soils. North America. C 1789.

**lindleyana** See *Sorbaria tomentosa*.

**'Margaritae'** (*S.* × *margaritae* ZAB.) (*S. japonica* × *S.* 'Superba'). A small shrub with erect, downy, reddish shoots and narrowly oval or oblong, coarsely-toothed leaves. Flowers

**SPIRAEA 'Margaritae'**—*continued*
bright rose-pink, borne in large, flattened heads from July onwards. Foliage brightly tinted in autumn. C before 1890.

**media** F. SCHMIDT (*S. confusa* REG. & KOERNICKE) A small shrub of compact habit, with erect, rounded, glabrous stems and ovate to oblong leaves, toothed at the apex or entire. Flowers white, borne in long racemes in late April and May. Widely distributed from E Europe to Siberia and Japan. I 1789.

**f. glabrescens** (SIMONKAI) ZAB. Differing only in its glabrous or sparsely hairy nature.

**menziesii** See *S. douglasii* var. *menziesii*.

**'Triumphans'** See *S.* × *billiardii* 'Triumphans'.

**micrantha** HOOK. f. A small to medium-sized shrub related to *S. amoena*. Leaves ovate-lanceolate, 7.5-15cm long, acuminate and toothed. Flowers pale pink, borne in loose, leafy corymbs in June. E Himalaya. I 1924.

**mollifolia** REHD. A pretty, grey-leaved shrub with strongly angled, purplish shoots 1.2-1.8m high. Leaves oval or obovate, silky-hairy. Flowers creamy-white, borne in small corymbs along the arching branches in June and July. W China. I 1909.

**nipponica** MAXIM. (*S. bracteata* ZAB.) Among the best June-flowering shrubs. A strong-growing, glabrous, medium-sized shrub of dense, bushy habit. Stems long and arching. Leaves oval or broadly obovate or rounded, toothed at apex. Flowers white, borne in clusters which crowd the upper sides of the branches in June. Each tiny flower is subtended by a small green bract. A bush in full flower is a lovely sight. Japan. Introduced by Siebold about 1885.

**'Rotundifolia'** One of the best June-flowering shrubs, and excellent on chalky soils. A strong-growing form with broader, almost orbicular leaves and slightly larger flowers than the type. This is the form most frequently seen in the older British gardens. I 1830. AM 1955.

**'Snowmound'** (*S. nipponica* var. *tosaensis* HORT. not (YATABE) MAK.) A small shrub of dense, mound-like habit. Leaves oblong to oblanceolate, entire or crenate at apex. Flowers smaller than those of the type, but just as freely produced, smothering the branches in June. Japan. AM 1982. AGM 1984.

**var. tosaensis** See 'Snowmound'.

× **nobleana** See *S.* × *sanssouciana* 'Nobleana'.

× **oxyodon** ZAB. (*S. chamaedryfolia* × *S. media*). A small, suckering shrub developing large patches of erect stems. Leaves small, obovate, toothed at apex, thickly crowding the branches. Flowers white, borne in small umbels along the stems during summer. C before 1884.

**pectinata** See *Luetkia pectinata*.

**prunifolia** SIEB. & ZUCC. (*S. prunifolia* f. *simpliciflora* NAK.) The single-flowered form of this species is a plant of little horticultural merit. It was not discovered until after the double-flowered form had been introduced. China.

**'Plena'** A dense shrub with arching branches up to 1.8m high. Leaves ovate, finely-toothed, turning orange or red in autumn. Flowers white, double, borne in tight, button-like, stalkless clusters along the branches in April and May. Introduced from Japan about 1845 by Siebold. AM 1980.

**reevesiana** See *S. cantoniensis*.

**salicifolia** L. "Bridewort". A vigorous, suckering shrub producing, in time, dense thickets of erect stems. Leaves lanceolate to elliptic, sharply-toothed, green and glabrous on both surfaces. Flowers pink, borne in dense, cylindrical downy panicles in June and July. A good plant for stabilising poor soils subject to erosion but not satisfactory on shallow chalk soils. C and EC Europe, NE Asia, Japan. Naturalised in many parts of Europe, including the British Isles. C 1586.

**var. latifolia** See *S. latifolia*.

× **sanssouciana** K. KOCH (*S. douglasii* × *S. japonica*) This hybrid is grown mainly in the following form.

**'Nobleana'** (*S.* × *nobleana* HOOK.) A small shrub with erect, brown, grey-felted stems and oblong to narrowly oval, coarsely-toothed leaves, grey downy beneath. Flowers bright rose, borne in broad, flattened heads in July. Not recommended for shallow chalk soils. Garden origin before 1857.

**SPIRAEA**—*continued*

**sargentiana** REHD. A graceful, medium-sized shrub with arching shoots and 2.5cm long, narrowly oval to narrowly obovate leaves, toothed near the apex. Flowers creamy-white, carried in dense corymbs all along the branches in June. W China. I 1908 by Ernest Wilson. AM 1913.

× **semperflorens** ZAB. (*S. japonica* × *S. salicifolia*). This hybrid is represented in gardens by the following form in which the *S. japonica* parent was 'Albiflora'.

**'Syringiflora'** (*S.* × *syringiflora* LEMOINE) A small shrub of spreading habit with lanceolate leaves and terminal corymbose panicles of rose-pink flowers. Garden origin before 1885.

**'Snowmound'** See *S. nipponica* 'Snowmound'.

**sorbifolia** See *Sorbaria sorbifolia*.

**splendens** See *S. densiflora* var. *splendens*.

× **syringiflora** See *S.* × *semperflorens* 'Syringiflora'.

**thunbergii** SIEB. A popular small to medium-sized, spreading shrub of dense, twiggy habit, with slender, angular, downy stems and narrow, glabrous, sharply-toothed leaves, 2.5-3cm long. Flowers white, borne in numerous clusters along the branches during March and April. Generally the earliest of the spiraeas in bloom, the pure white flowers often smothering the wiry stems. Native of China, but widely cultivated and naturalised in Japan, from which country it was first introduced about 1863.

**tomentosa** L. "Steeplebush". A small, vigorous, suckering shrub, eventually forming a dense thicket of erect, brownish stems which are clothed with brownish felt when young. Leaves ovate, coarsely-toothed, yellowish-grey-felted beneath. Flowers purplish-rose, produced in dense, terminal panicles during late summer. E United States. I 1736.

**trichocarpa** NAKAI A vigorous, graceful shrub with glabrous, angular shoots up to 1.8m high. Leaves apple-green, oblong or oblanceolate, entire or toothed at apex. Flowers white, borne in rounded corymbs along the arching branches in June. Korea. Introduced by Ernest Wilson in 1917. AM 1942.

**trilobata** L. A small shrub of dense, compact habit. Leaves up to 2.5cm long, rounded in outline and coarsely-toothed, occasionally shallowly three to five-lobed. Flowers white, borne in crowded umbels on the previous year's shoots in June. N Asia. I 1801.

× **vanhouttei** (BRIOT) ZAB. (*S. cantoniensis* × *S. trilobata*). A vigorous shrub with gracefully arching branches up to 1.8m high. Leaves obovate to rhomboidal, coarsely-toothed, sometimes three to five-lobed. Flowers white, borne in dense umbels along the branches in June. Excellent for early forcing. Garden origin before 1866. AM 1984.

**veitchii** HEMSL. A strong-growing shrub up to 3m high, with long, arching, reddish branches. Leaves oval to oblong, 2.5-5cm long, entire. Flowers white, borne in dense corymbs all along the branches in June and July. A superb species well worth a place in the garden, where space permits. C and W China. I 1900 by Ernest Wilson. AM 1909.

× **watsoniana** ZAB. (*S. densiflora* var. *splendens* × *S. douglasii*). An attractive shrub with erect, downy shoots to 1.5-1.8m high. Leaves elliptic to oblong, toothed toward the apex, grey downy beneath. Flowers rose, borne in dense, terminal panicles in June and July. Has occurred both in cultivation and with the parents in the wild (Oregon).

**wilsonii** DUTHIE A medium-sized shrub with long, arching shoots. Leaves oval to obovate, 2.5-5cm long, entire or toothed near apex. Flowers white, borne in dense corymbs which crowd the branches in June. Closely related to *S. veitchii*, but never as large and with glabrous corymbs and leaves downy above. C and W China. I 1900.

**yunnanensis** FRANCH. An elegant shrub up to 1.8m high, with orbicular-ovate to obovate leaves which are doubly-toothed or shallowly lobed, white or grey tomentose beneath. Flowers white, borne in small, densely pubescent umbels in May or June. W China. C 1923.

**STACHYURUS** SIEB. & ZUCC.—**Stachyuraceae**—The sole representative of its family, embracing 5 or 6 species, natives of E Asia, only 2 of which are hardy throughout the British Isles. The stiffly pendulous inflorescences are formed in the leaf axils before the leaves fall in autumn, but the flowers do not open until the early spring. The individual flowers are normally hermaphrodite, but there are in cultivation clones possessing unisexual flowers. *Stachyurus* will grow in all fertile soils and in sun or semi-shade.

**chinensis** FRANCH. A medium-sized to large shrub of spreading habit, with purplish branchlets. Leaves ovate-oblong to elliptic-oblong or oblong-lanceolate, narrowing into a long taper point, dull green and slightly bullate above, shining pale green beneath. Racemes drooping, 10-13cm long, composed of 30-35 soft yellow, cup-shaped flowers, at Winchester generally opening two weeks later than *S. praecox*. A rare species of considerable merit. Introduced from China by E.H. Wilson in 1908. AM 1925.

**'Magpie'** Leaves grey-green above with an irregular, creamy-white margin, splashed pale green and tinged rose. Tends to produce shoots of all-white foliage. Originated in our nurseries about 1945.

†**himalaicus** HOOK. f. & THOMS. ex BENTH. A strong-growing shrub producing long, yellowish-brown shoots up to 3m high or more. Leaves oblong-lanceolate, slightly bullate above, 13-23cm long, with a long taper point and reddish petiole and midrib. Racemes 4-5cm long, flowers cup-shaped, wine-purple to rose-pink, opening in early April. A rare and unusual species of extremely vigorous habit, worthy of a wall in all but the mildest areas. E Himalaya, N Burma, W and C China.

**japonicus** See *S. praecox*.

**lancifolius** See *S. praecox* var. *matsuzakii*.

**praecox** SIEB. & ZUCC. (*S. japonicus* STEUD.) A medium-sized to large shrub with reddish-brown branchlets. Leaves ovate-oblong to elliptic or broad-elliptic, shortly taper-pointed, larger and broader than those of *S. chinensis*. Racemes stiffly drooping, 4-7cm long, composed of 15-24 cup-shaped, pale yellow flowers, opening in March or earlier in mild weather. Differing from *S. chinensis* in its stouter growths, larger leaves and usually shorter racemes. Japan. I 1864. AM 1925. AGM 1984. FCC 1976.

**'Gracilis'** A form with female flowers, otherwise differing little from the typical form.

†**var. matsuzakii** (NAKAI) MAK. (*S. lancifolius* KOIDZ.) Differs in its stouter, pale green, glaucescent stems and its long-stalked, larger and longer leaves. Flowers yellow, opening in early April. A tender shrub usually cut back to ground level each year by frost and, therefore, only suitable for the mildest areas. Coastal areas of Japan.

**STAPHYLEA** L.—**Staphyleaceae**—The "Bladder Nuts" are a small genus of 11 species of mainly hardy flowering shrubs, natives of temperate regions of the N hemisphere, whose seeds are enclosed in curious, inflated, two or three-celled bladder-like capsules. Easily grown in any fertile soil, in sun or semi-shade.

**bumalda** DC. A spreading shrub with glabrous, greyish-brown branches, usually less than 1.8m high. Leaves trifoliolate. Flowers white, borne in short racemose panicles in May and June. Foliage usually giving attractive red tints in autumn. Japan, Korea, China, Manchuria. I 1812.

**colchica** STEV. A strong-growing shrub with erect branches, 2.5-3.6m high. Leaves composed of three to five ovate-oblong leaflets, which are shining green beneath. Flowers white, carried in conspicuous erect panicles up to 13cm long, in May. Capsules up to 10cm long. S Caucasus. I 1850. FCC 1879.

**'Coulombieri'** See *S. × coulombieri*.

**'Hessei'** (*S. × elegans* 'Hessei') An attractive form with red-purple-flushed flowers. AM 1927.

**var. kochiana** MEDWED. A minor form distinguished by its hairy filaments.

× **coulombieri** ANDRE (*S. × elegans* ZAB.) (*S. colchica × S. pinnata*). A vigorous large shrub intermediate between the parents. Leaves with 3-5 leaflets. Panicles compact, more or less erect. Fruits smaller than in *S. colchica*. C 1872. AM 1927.

× **elegans** See *S. × coulombieri*.

**'Hessei'** See *S. colchica* 'Hessei'.

**holocarpa** HEMSL. A beautiful, large shrub or small, spreading tree. Leaves trifoliolate, with oblong-lanceolate leaflets. Flowers white, rose in bud, produced in short, dense, drooping panicles in April and May. First discovered by Augustine Henry in C China; introduced by Ernest Wilson in 1908. AM 1924.

**'Rosea'** A lovely spring flowering shrub or small tree, its spreading branches strung with drooping clusters of soft pink flowers. Young leaves bronze. C 1908. AM 1953.

**STAPHYLEA**—*continued*

**pinnata** L. A large shrub of vigorous, erect habit. Leaves pinnate, composed of usually 5, sometimes 7 or 3 leaflets, pale dull green beneath. Flowers white, borne in long, narrow, drooping panicles in May and June. C Europe. First recorded as being cultivated in 1596.

**trifolia** L. A large shrub with glabrous shoots and trifoliolate leaves. Leaflets broadly ovate, acuminate, finely-toothed, more or less glabrous above, downy beneath. Flowers creamy-white in short, drooping panicles in May, followed by three-celled fruits. E United States. C 1640.

**STEPHANANDRA** SIEB. & ZUCC.—**Rosaceae**—A small genus of 4 species of shrubs allied to *Spiraea* and natives of E Asia. Though of subtle beauty in flower, their graceful habit and attractive foliage qualifies them for a place in the garden. They are happy in most soils, in sun or semi-shade. The leaves often give rich tints in autumn. Untidy specimens may be hard pruned in March.

**incisa** (THUNB.) ZAB. (*S. flexuosa* SIEB. & ZUCC.) A small to medium-sized shrub of dense habit, with slender, warm brown, zig-zag stems. Leaves 2.5-7.5cm long, ovate, incisely-toothed and lobed. Flowers greenish-white in crowded panicles in June. Japan, Korea. I 1872.

'**Crispa**' A dwarf shrub with small, crinkled leaves forming dense, low mounds. Excellent as ground cover especially in full exposure. AGM 1984.

**tanakae** (FRANCH. & SAV.) FRANCH. & SAV. A medium-sized shrub producing long, arching, rich brown stems. Leaves broadly ovate or triangular, 7.5-13cm long, three to five-lobed and incisely-toothed. An elegant shrub with stouter growths and larger leaves than *S. incisa*, the flowers also are a little larger though not showy. Japan. I 1893. AGM 1984.

**STERCULIA platanifolia** See *Firmiana simplex.*

**STEWARTIA** See *Stuartia.*

**STRANVAESIA** See *Photinia.*

× **STRANVINIA** See *Photinia.*

"**STRAWBERRY TREE**" See *Arbutus unedo.*

**STUARTIA** L.—**Theaceae**—(*Stewartia*) A small but valuable genus of ornamental shrubs and trees allied to *Camellia*, requiring a semi-shaded position and a moist, loamy, lime-free soil, revelling in woodland conditions. All have white or cream flowers which, although soon falling, are produced in continuous succession over several weeks in July and August. Rich autumn colour is another attribute, whilst the beautiful trunks and flaking bark of the older trees is no less attractive. They resent disturbance and, once planted, are best left alone. Like *Eucryphia*, *Oxydendrum* and *Cornus nuttallii*, they enjoy having their roots shaded from the hot sun.

**gemmata** See *S. sinensis.*

**koreana** See *S. pseudocamellia* var. *koreana.*

**malacodendron** L. A large shrub or occasionally a small tree, with ovate to obovate leaves, hairy beneath. Flowers solitary in the leaf axils, 6-8.5cm across, white, with purple stamens and bluish anthers. A beautiful shrub, the purple-eyed flowers studding the branches in July and August. SE United States. C 1742. FCC 1934.

**monadelpha** SIEB. & ZUCC. A large shrub or small tree with ovate to ovate-lanceolate, acuminate leaves which yield attractive autumn tints. Flowers solitary in the leaf axils, 2.5-4cm across, white with spreading petals, the stamens with violet anthers. Japan, Cheju Do, Korea (Quelpart Island). C 1903.

**ovata** (CAV.) WEATHERBY (*S. pentagyna* L'HERIT.) A large bushy shrub with ovate to elliptic, acuminate leaves. Flowers solitary in the leaf axils, 6-7.5cm across, cup-shaped, with conspicuous orange anthers. SE United States. Introduced before 1785.

**STUARTIA**—*continued*

**pseudocamellia** MAXIM. (*S. grandiflora* CARR.) Small to medium-sized tree with attractive flaking bark and glabrous shoots. Leaves ovate to obovate, shortly acuminate. Flowers white, solitary in the leaf axils, 5-6cm across, cup-shaped, anthers bright yellow. The leaves turn to yellow and red in autumn. A free-growing tree of open habit, one of the best for general planting. Japan. C before 1878. FCC 1888. AGM 1984.

**var. koreana** (REHD.) SEALY (*S. koreana* REHD.) A splendid form giving exceptionally bright autumn colour. Flowers similar but opening wider, the petals spreading. Korea. Introduced by E.H. Wilson in 1917. AGM 1984.

†\***pteropetiolata** CHENG (*Hartia sinensis* DUNN) A very interesting large, semi-evergreen woodland shrub. Leaves dark glossy green, glandular serrate. Stems softly bristly. Flowers white, 3-4cm across, resembling those of *Camellia sinensis*. Only suitable for the mildest localities. Yunnan. I 1912 by George Forrest.

**serrata** MAXIM. A small tree with attractive, warm brown stems and ovate-elliptic or elliptic, acuminate leaves which are rather leathery in texture. Flowers solitary in the leaf axils, 5-6cm across, cup-shaped, white, stained red on the outside at base, anthers yellow, opening in June, earlier than other species. Rich autumn tints. Japan. C before 1915. AM 1932.

**sinensis** REHD. & WILS. (*S. gemmata* CHIEN & CHENG) A large shrub or small tree with attractive, flaking bark. Leaves elliptic to elliptic-oblong, acuminate. Flowers solitary in the leaf axils, 4-5cm across, cup-shaped, fragrant. Rich crimson autumn colour. C China. I 1901 by Ernest Wilson.

**STYRAX** L.—**Styracaceae**—A genus of some 120 species of trees and shrubs widely distributed in temperate and tropical regions of the N hemisphere. The cultivated species are very distinguished and beautiful trees and shrubs, thriving in a moist, loamy, lime-free soil, in sun or semi-shade. The name "Snowbell" has been given to them in America, an allusion to their pure white, pendulous flowers which appear in late spring and summer.

**americana** LAM. A medium-sized shrub with ascending branches and narrowly oval or obovate, minutely-toothed leaves. The slender-stalked, narrow-petalled, bell-shaped flowers hang from the branchlets in June and July. Not one of the easiest species to grow. SE United States. I 1765.

**calvescens** PERKINS A rare, small tree or large shrub with minutely and stellately-hairy shoots. Leaves elliptic, acuminate, serrate, lustrous green on both surfaces, rather thin in texture. Flowers borne in short racemes in June or July. China.

†**dasyantha** PERKINS A large shrub or small tree. Leaves obovate to broad-elliptic, minutely-toothed in the upper half. Flowers pendulous, borne in slender, terminal racemes in July. Not the hardiest species and best grown against a wall except in the mildest areas. C China. First discovered by Augustine Henry. Introduced by Ernest Wilson in 1900.

**var. cinerascens** REHD. Leaves grey or white downy beneath. We previously distributed this plant as *S. philadelphoides* or *S. serrulata*.

**hemsleyana** DIELS An attractive, small, openly-branched tree. Leaves broad, elliptic or almost orbicular, oblique at base, 10-13cm long. Flowers white, with a central cone of yellow anthers, borne in long, lax racemes in June. A lovely species similar in some respects to *S. obassia*, but differing in its less downy leaves and exposed chocolate-brown leaf buds. C and W China. Introduced by E.H. Wilson in 1900. AM 1930. FCC 1942. AGM 1984.

**japonica** SIEB. & ZUCC. A very beautiful large shrub or small tree, with wide-spreading, fan-like branches, often drooping at the slender tips. Leaves ovate to narrowly oblong, acuminate. Flowers bell-shaped, white, with yellow, staminal beak, coating the undersides of the branches in June. The commonest species in cultivation and deservedly the most popular, combining daintiness and elegance with a hardy constitution. Best planted where one can admire the flowers from beneath. Japan, Korea. Introduced by Richard Oldham in 1862. FCC 1885. AGM 1984.

**'Benibana'** See under 'Pink Chimes'.

**'Fargesii'** This is more tree-like, with slightly larger leaves. I 1924. AM 1945. FCC 1971.

**'Pink Chimes'** A very floriferous form with pale pink flowers deeper at the base. Branches pendulous on young plants. Raised in Japan before 1976. In Japan the name Benibana,

**STYRAX japonica 'Pink Chimes'**—*continued*
which means pink-flowered, is applied to forms with pink flowers which are raised from seed.

**obassia** SIEB. & ZUCC. A beautiful, large shrub or small, round-headed tree with handsome, large, broadly ovate to orbicular leaves, 10-20cm long and clothed beneath with a soft, velvety tomentum. The petioles are enlarged at the base enclosing the leaf buds. Bark of second-year shoots chestnut and exfoliating. Flowers fragrant, bell-shaped, 2.5cm long, carried in long, lax, terminal racemes in June. Japan. Introduced by Charles Maries in 1879. FCC 1888.

**officinalis** L. A medium-sized to large shrub bearing ovate leaves 7-9cm long. The short, drooping clusters of comparatively large, fragrant flowers are borne at the tips of the shoots in June. It requires a warm sheltered position. The gum-like sap of this species is used as incense and the seeds for rosaries. Mediterranean region. AM 1984.

**serrulata** See under *S. dasyantha* var. *cinerascens*.

**shiraiana** MAK. A large shrub or small tree with stellately hairy young shoots. Leaves obovate to orbicular, coarsely-toothed or lobed in upper half, downy beneath. Petioles swollen at base, enclosing the leaf buds. Flowers funnel-shaped, borne in short, densely hairy racemes in June. Japan. I 1915.

**veitchiorum** HEMSL. & WILS. A very rare large spreading shrub or a small tree with greyish, hairy young shoots. Leaves downy, lanceolate, taper-pointed, 7.5-13cm long. Flowers pendulous, borne in slender panicles up to 20cm long in June. China. I 1900.

**wilsonii** REHD. A beautiful medium-sized shrub of dense, twiggy habit. Leaves tiny, ovate, 1-2.5cm long, toothed or occasionally three-lobed at apex, glaucous and downy beneath. Flowers pendulous, solitary or in clusters, opening in June. A pretty shrub flowering when quite young, but requiring a sheltered position. W China. I 1908. AM 1913.

**SUAEDA** FORSSK. ex SCOP.—**Chenopodiaceae**—About 110 species of herbs and sub-shrubs widely distributed in both hemispheres, the majority of no horticultural merit.

**fruticosa** See *S. vera*.

**\*vera** FORSSK. ex J. GMEL. (*S. fruticosa* AUCT. not FORSSK.) A small, native, maritime sub-shrub of dense habit. Leaves narrow, blue-green and fleshy, semi-evergreen. Flowers inconspicuous. The whole plant sometimes turns a bronze-purple in autumn. It grows best in a sandy soil in full sun and is most suitable for seaside gardens. Sea coasts of S and W Europe, N Africa to India (including the British Isles).

**"SUMACH, STAG'S HORN"** See *Rhus typhina*.

**"SUMACH, VENETIAN"** See *Cotinus coggygria*.

**"SUN ROSE"** See *Helianthemum* and *Cistus*.

**†SUTHERLANDIA** R. BR.—**Leguminosae**—A small genus of 5 species of S African shrubs of which one species is occasionally seen in the British Isles.

**frutescens** R. BR. A medium-sized to large shrub with downy shoots and pinnate leaves composed of 13-21 narrow leaflets. The large, conspicuous, terracotta, pea-flowers are carried in axillary racemes in June. Seed pods inflated as in *Colutea*. Suitable for a warm, sunny wall in the mildest areas. S Africa. C 1683.

**"SWAMP BAY"** or **"SWEET BAY"** See *Magnolia virginiana*.

**"SWEET BRIAR"** See *Rosa eglanteria*.

**"SWEET CHESTNUT"** See *Castanea sativa*.

**"SWEET FERN"** See *Comptonia peregrina*.

**"SWEET GALE"** See *Myrica gale*.

**"SWEET GUM"** See *Liquidambar styraciflua*.

**"SWEET PEPPER BUSH"** See *Clethra alnifolia*.

**"SYCAMORE"** See *Acer pseudoplatanus*.

× **SYCOPARROTIA** ENDRESS & ANLIKER (*Parrotia* × *Sycopsis*)—**Hamamelidaceae**—An interesting intergeneric hybrid between 2 outstanding plants. Unfortunately the following has not proved to be an improvement on either of its parents.

**semidecidua** ENDRESS & ANLIKER (*P. persica* × *S. sinensis*). A medium-sized to large, semi-evergreen, open, spreading shrub with the habit of *Parrotia* and the foliage resembling *Sycopsis*. Leaves ovate, elliptic or obovate, acuminate, toothed above the middle, glossy green but lighter and thinner than *S. sinensis*. Some leaves turn yellow in autumn while others remain until winter. Flowers resembling *Sycopsis* with dense clusters of yellow anthers tinged orange-red in late winter. Raised in Switzerland in about 1950.

**\*SYCOPSIS** OLIV.—**Hamamelidaceae**—A small genus of 7 species of evergreen shrubs and trees, natives of the Himalaya, China and SE Asia. The following requires the same conditions as *Hamamelis*. Only one species is in general cultivation.

**sinensis** OLIV. A medium-sized to large, evergreen, monoecious shrub or small tree of dense, upright habit. Leaves elliptic-lanceolate, acuminate, somewhat bullate, leathery and glabrous. Flowers without petals, consisting of small clusters of yellow, red-anthered stamens, enclosed by chocolate-brown, tomentose scales, opening in February and March. C China. Introduced by E.H. Wilson in 1901. AM 1926.

**tutcheri** See under *Distylium racemosum*.

**SYMPHORICARPOS** DUHAMEL—**Caprifoliaceae**—A small genus of about 17 species of deciduous shrubs, natives of North America and Mexico with one species in China. Their flowers are bell-shaped, but small and relatively insignificant. They are mainly grown for their often abundant display of white or rose-coloured berries, which appear in autumn and generally last well into winter, being untouched by birds. Several forms are excellent for hedging and all grow well in shade even among the roots and drip of overhanging trees. They are quite hardy and will grow in all types of soils. Untidy specimens may be hard pruned in March.

**albus** (L.) BLAKE (*S. racemosus* MICHX.) "Snowberry". A small shrub with slender, erect, downy shoots, forming dense clumps. Leaves oval to ovate-oblong, downy beneath, lobed on sucker shoots. Berries globose or ovoid, 12mm across, white. E North America. I 1879.

**var. laevigatus** (FERN.) BLAKE (*S. rivularis* SUKSD.) "Snowberry". A strong-growing shrub forming dense thickets of erect, glabrous stems up to 1.8m high. Leaves elliptic to elliptic-oblong, 4-7.5cm long, commonly lobed on vigorous, suckering shoots. Berries in great profusion, like large glistening white marbles. The common snowberry of English plantations. Ideal for game cover and for poor soils or dark, shaded corners. W North America. I 1817. FCC 1913.

× **chenaultii** REHD. (*S. microphyllus* × *S. orbiculatus*). A dense-growing shrub, 0.6-1m high, resembling *S. microphyllus* in general habit. Berries purplish-red on exposed side, pinkish-white elsewhere, carried in clusters or spikes. Garden origin in 1910.

**'Hancock'** An outstanding form of dwarf, wide-spreading habit. An excellent ground cover, particularly beneath trees. Raised about 1940. AGM 1984.

× **doorenbosii** See *S.* Doorenbos Hybrids.

**Doorenbos Hybrids** A very useful group of attractive hybrids raised by Mr Doorenbos of The Hague, one of the greatest Dutch horticulturists of this century and involving *S. albus* var. *laevigatus*, *S.* × *chenaultii* and *S. orbiculatus*.

**'Erect'** A vigorous, but compact shrub of erect habit producing trusses of rose-lilac berries. Excellent as a small hedge.

**SYMPHORICARPOS Doorenbos Hybrids**—*continued*

**'Magic Berry'** A small shrub of compact, spreading habit, bearing large quantities of rose-pink berries.

**'Mother of Pearl'** The first named clone, probably *S. albus* var. *laevigatus* × *S. × chenaultii*. A small, dense shrub, the branches weighed down by heavy crops of white, rose-flushed, marble-like berries. AM 1971. AGM 1984.

**'White Hedge'** A small shrub of strong, upright, compact growth, freely producing small, white berries in erect clusters. An excellent, small, hedging shrub. AGM 1984.

**occidentalis** HOOK. "Wolfberry". A small shrub of dense, erect habit with rounded leaves and clusters of globular, white berries. North America. C 1880. AM 1910.

**orbiculatus** MOENCH. (*S. vulgaris* MICHX.) "Indian Currant" "Coral Berry". A dense, bushy shrub up to 2m high, with thin, downy, densely leafy stems. Leaves oval or ovate, glaucescent beneath. Berries purplish-rose, rounded to ovoid, very small but borne in dense clusters along the stems. E United States. I 1730.

**'Foliis Variegatis'** ('Variegatus') Leaves smaller, irregularly margined yellow. A graceful plant and one of the most pleasing variegated shrubs of medium size but inclined to revert if planted in shade. A form is also in cultivation with white-margined leaves.

**'Variegatus'** See 'Foliis Variegatis'.

**rivularis** See *S. albus* var. *laevigatus*.

**vulgaris** See *S. orbiculatus*.

**SYMPLOCOS** JACQ.—**Symplocaceae**—A large genus of some 250 species of evergreen and deciduous trees and shrubs widely distributed in tropical and subtropical regions excluding Africa. Only one is generally hardy in the British Isles.

‡**paniculata** (THUNB.) MIQ. (*S. crataegoides* BUCH.-HAM. ex D. DON) A deciduous shrub or occasionally a small tree of dense, twiggy habit. Leaves variable in shape, 1.5-4.5cm long. Flowers small, white, fragrant, borne in panicles in May and June, followed by brilliant ultramarine blue fruits in autumn which persist into winter. It is usually necessary to plant two or more specimens in order to achieve successful fertilization; fruits are most abundant after a long, hot summer. Himalaya, China, Taiwan, Japan. I 1871. AM 1938 (flower). AM 1947 (fruit). FCC 1954.

**SYRINGA** L.—**Oleaceae**—The "Lilacs" are a genus of hardy, deciduous, flowering shrubs and small trees, containing some of the most elegant and colourful of May and June-flowering, woody plants. The flowers of many species and hybrids are accompanied by a delicious fragrance, which has become an inseparable part of their magic. The numerous, large-flowered garden lilacs, hybrids and cultivars of *S. vulgaris*, need no introduction and their continued popularity is ensured. The species are perhaps less well known, and their good qualities deserve much wider recognition. The lilacs are happy in most well drained soils, especially so in those of a chalky nature, and revel in full sun. Unless otherwise stated, it may be assumed that they are strong-growing shrubs of large size, often tree-like, and that they flower in May and June. For "Mock Orange", often wrongly referred to as "Syringa", see *Philadelphus*. Pruning consists of removing the old flowering wood immediately after flowering. Summer pinching of extra strong shoots is often desirable.

**affinis** See *S. oblata* var. *alba*.

**afghanica** HORT. See *S. protolaciniata*.

**amurensis** See *S. reticulata* var. *mandshurica*.

**var. japonica** See *S. reticulata*.

×**chinensis** WILLD. (*S. × laciniata* × *S. vulgaris*) "Rouen Lilac". A medium-sized shrub of dense, bushy habit with ovate leaves and large, drooping panicles of fragrant, soft lavender flowers in May. Raised in the Botanic Garden at Rouen about 1777.

**'Alba'** Flowers very pale lilac, nearly white. C 1885.

**'Metensis'** Flowers a charming shade of pale lilac-pink. C 1871.

**'Saugeana'** ('Rubra') Flowers lilac-red. Raised about 1809.

+**correlata** BRAUN (*S. × chinensis* + *S. vulgaris*). This interesting lilac is a periclinal chimaera, composed of an outer layer of *S. vulgaris* (white flowered form), and an inner core of

494

**SYRINGA** +**correlata**—*continued*

> *S.* × *chinensis*. Its erect panicles of flowers are normally very pale lilac, nearly white, but occasional shoots of typical *S.* × *chinensis* are produced.

× **diversifolia** REHD. (*S. oblata* var. *giraldii* × *S. pinnatifolia*). A medium-sized to tall shrub with both entire, ovate-oblong leaves and pinnatifid, three to five-lobed leaves. Raised at the Arnold Arboretum in 1929.

> **'William H. Judd'** Flowers white, scented; early May.

**emodi** WALL. ex ROYLE "Himalayan Lilac". A distinct large shrub of robust habit. Leaves ovate to obovate, 10-20cm long, pale or whitish beneath. Flowers pale lilac in bud fading to white, not very pleasantly scented, borne in erect panicles in June. A noteworthy species claiming a position in every well-stocked shrub garden. Himalaya. I 1838.

> **'Aurea'** Leaves suffused soft yellow. Best when grown in semi-shade.

> **'Aureo-variegata'** Leaves yellow, with green centre.

**'Ethel M. Webster'** A medium to large-size shrub of compact habit. Flowers flesh-pink, borne in broad, loose panicles in May and June. Possibly a *S.* × *henryi* hybrid. C 1948.

**formosissima** See *S. wolfii*.

× **henryi** SCHNEID. (*S. josikaea* × *S. villosa*). A tall variable hybrid raised by Mons Louis Henry at the Jardin des Plantes, Paris, in 1896.

> **'Alba'** A graceful shrub, more lax in habit than 'Lutèce'. Flowers white.

> **'Floréal'** See *S.* × *nanceiana* 'Floréal'.

> **'Lutèce'** A large, erect shrub with leaves resembling the *villosa* parent. Flowers violet, paling as they age, fragrant, borne in large panicles in June.

> **'Prairial'** See *S.* 'Prairial'.

× **hyacinthiflora** (LEMOINE) REHD. (*S. oblata* × *S. vulgaris*). An attractive, but variable hybrid first raised by Lemoine in 1876. More recently several clones have been raised by W.B. Clarke of San José, California, using *S. oblata* var. *giraldii*. The flowers appear quite early, usually in late April or early May.

> **'Alice Eastwood'** Claret-purple in bud, opening cyclamen-purple; double. C 1942 (Clarke).

> **'Blue Hyacinth'** Mauve to pale blue; single. C 1942 (Clarke).

> **'Buffon'** Soft pink, petals slightly reflexed, faintly scented; single, late April to early May. C 1921 (Lemoine). AM 1961.

> **'Clarke's Giant'** Rosy-mauve in bud, opening lilac-blue, large florets and large panicles up to 30cm long; single. C 1948 (Clarke). AM 1958.

> **'Esther Staley'** Buds red, opening pink, very floriferous; single. C 1948 (Clarke). AM 1961. AGM 1984.

> **'Lamartine'** Flowers blue-lilac, in large panicles; single. Young growths flushed bronze. C 1911 (Lemoine). AM 1927.

> **'Plena'** Victor Lemoine's original hybrid (*S. vulgaris* 'Azurea Plena' × *S. oblata*). Flowers in dense, erect panicles, double, bright purple in bud, opening to a delicate shade of violet. Leaves bronze-tinged when unfolding.

> **'Purple Heart'** Deep purple; large florets. C 1949 (Clarke).

**japonica** See *S. reticulata*.

× **josiflexa** PRESTON ex J.S. PRINGLE (*S. josikaea* × *S. reflexa*). A very beautiful race of hybrids raised in Ottawa by Miss Isabella Preston. Medium-sized to large shrubs, with fine, deep green leaves and bearing loose, plume-like panicles of fragrant, rose-pink flowers in May or June.

> **'Bellicent'** An outstanding clone, the best of this excellent hybrid, with enormous panicles of clear rose-pink flowers. FCC 1946. AGM 1984.

**josikaea** JACQ. f. ex REICHENB. "Hungarian Lilac". A large shrub related to *S. villosa*. Leaves ovate to obovate, 5-13cm long, glossy dark green above, paler beneath. Flowers fragrant, deep violet-mauve, borne in erect panicles in June. C and E Europe. I 1830.

**julianae** SCHNEID. A graceful shrub, 1.8-2.5m in height by as much through. Leaves oval, privet-like, grey downy beneath. Flowers in slender, upright panicles, fragrant, pale lilac in May and early June. A choice shrub of free-flowering habit. Ideal for the small garden. W China. Introduced by E.H. Wilson in 1900. AM 1924.

**'Kim'** See *S.* × *prestoniae* 'Kim'.

**komarowii** SCHNEID. (*S. sargentiana* SCHNEID.) A vigorous, tall-growing shrub related to *S. reflexa* with large, deep green, oval or ovate-lanceolate leaves up to 18cm long. Flowers

**SYRINGA komarowii**—*continued*

deep rose-pink borne in nodding, cylindrical panicles during May and early June. China. I 1908 by Ernest Wilson.

×**laciniata** MILL. (*S. protolaciniata* × *S. vulgaris*). A graceful small shrub with prettily dissected, three to nine-lobed leaves and small panicles of lilac flowers in May. Probably originated in cultivation in SW Asia. Introduced from Turkey in the 17th century. AM 1965. Not to be confused with the wild *S. protolaciniata*, a species which is rare in cultivation.

**meyeri** SCHNEID. A dense, compact, rather slow-growing, small-leaved shrub, to about 1.8m high. Leaves oval or obovate, about 4-5cm long. Flowers violet-purple, in short, dense panicles in May, even on young plants. Sometimes a second crop of flowers appears in September. China, where it is known only in cultivation. I 1908.

**'Palibin'** (*S. palibiniana* HORT.) (*S. patula* HORT.) (*S. velutina* HORT.) A slow-growing, eventually medium-sized shrub of dense habit. Flowers pale lilac-pink in numerous, elegant panicles even on young plants. A lovely form suitable for the small garden. AM 1984. AGM 1984.

**microphylla** DIELS A very pretty, small-leaved shrub up to 2m high. Leaves ovate, usually pointed at apex, 1-5cm long. Flowers rosy-lilac, darker externally, fragrant, borne in small panicles in June and again in September. N and W China. Introduced by William Purdom in 1910. AM 1937.

**'Superba'** A selected form of free-flowering habit. Flowers rosy-pink in May and intermittently until October. AM 1957. AGM 1984.

×**nanceiana** MCKELVEY (*S.* × *henryi* × *S. sweginzowii*). A variable hybrid raised by Lemoine in 1925 and mainly grown in the following form.

**'Floréal'** (*S.* × *henryi* 'Floréal') A graceful shrub of lax habit, with panicles of fragrant, lavender-mauve flowers in May.

**oblata** LINDL. A large shrub or small tree related to *S. vulgaris*, with broadly heart-shaped or reniform leaves up to 10cm wide and 7.5cm long. Flowers lilac-blue, produced in broad panicles in late April or early May. The unfolding leaves are bronze-tinted. Liable to damage by late spring frost. N China. Introduced by Robert Fortune from a garden in Shanghai, in 1856.

**var. alba** HORT. ex REHD. (*S. affinis* L. HENRY) A form with smaller leaves and white flowers.

**var. dilatata** (NAKAI) REHD. A variety of medium height. Leaves ovate-acuminate, bronze when unfolding, richly tinted in autumn. Flowers violet-purple, in loose panicles. Korea. I 1917 by Ernest Wilson.

**var. giraldii** (LEMOINE) REHD. Differs in its taller, more open habit and the larger, looser panicles of darker (purplish-violet) flowers in late April. N China. I 1895.

**'Nana'** A dwarf form with bluish flowers.

**palibiniana** HORT. See *S. meyeri* 'Palibin'.

**patula** HORT. See *S. meyeri* 'Palibin'.

**pekinensis** RUPR. (*Ligustrina pekinensis* (RUPR.) DIECK) A small tree with ovate to ovate-lanceolate, long-tapered leaves. Flowers creamy-white, densely crowded in large panicles in June. N China. Discovered by the Abbé David. Introduced by Dr Bretschneider in 1881.

**'Pendula'** A graceful form with drooping branches.

×**persica** L. "Persian Lilac". A charming, slender-branched shrub of rounded, bushy habit, 1.8-2.5m high and as much across. Leaves lanceolate, entire, 2.5-6cm long. Flowers lilac, fragrant, borne in small panicles in May. Said to have been cultivated in England in 1640. It is possibly a backcross between *S.* × *laciniata* and *S. vulgaris*. AGM 1984.

**'Alba'** Flowers white.

**'Laciniata'** See *S.* × *laciniata*.

**pinetorum** W.W. SM. A medium-sized shrub with ovate to ovate-lanceolate leaves and panicles of pale lavender-rose flowers with yellow anthers, in June. SW China.

**pinnatifolia** HEMSL. An unusual species reaching a height of about 2.5m. Leaves 4-8cm long, pinnate with 7-11 separate leaflets. Flowers white or lavender-tinted, produced in small, nodding panicles in May. So unlike a lilac as to create an amusing "legpull" or conundrum for the uninitiated. W China. Introduced by E.H. Wilson in 1904.

**SYRINGA**—*continued*

**potaninii** SCHNEID. An elegant, medium-sized shrub with oval, slender-pointed leaves, downy above, grey-felted beneath. Flowers white to pale rose-purple, with yellow anthers, fragrant, borne in loose panicles in June. W China. I 1905. AM 1924.

**'Prairial'** (*S.* × *henryi* × *S. tomentella*) (*S.* × *henryi* 'Prairial') An elegant shrub producing large panicles of soft lavender flowers in May. Raised by Lemoine about 1933.

× **prestoniae** MCKELVEY (*S. reflexa* × *S. villosa*). An extremely hardy race of late flowering hybrid lilacs, first raised by Miss Isabella Preston at the Central Experimental Farm, Division of Horticulture, Ottawa, Canada, in 1920. Usually referred to as "Canadian Hybrids", they are vigorous, medium-sized to large shrubs, producing large, erect or drooping panicles of flower in late May and June, on shoots of the current year. Red-purple is the dominant colour.

**'Audrey'** Flowers deep pink in June. C 1927. AM 1939.

**'Elinor'** Flowers dark purplish-red in bud, opening to pale lavender, borne in rather erect panicles in May and June. C 1928. AM 1951. AGM 1984.

**'Hiawatha'** Flowers rich reddish-purple in bud, opening pale pink. C 1934.

**'Isabella'** Flowers mallow-purple, borne in rather erect panicles in May and June. C 1927. AM 1941.

**'Juliet'** Flowers lilac-pink.

**'Kim'** (*S.* 'Kim') An elegant, medium-sized shrub with dark green, oblong-lanceolate leaves and large, freely-branching panicles of mallow-purple flowers in late May and early June. C 1934. AM 1958.

**'Royalty'** Flowers violet-purple.

**'Virgilia'** Flowers deep lilac-magenta in bud, opening pale lilac. Compact habit.

**'W.T. Macoun'** Lilac-pink, in large panicles.

**protolaciniata** P.S. GREEN & M.-C. CHANG (*S. laciniata* HORT. not MILL.) A beautiful, small shrub with dark, slender stems and small, dainty, pinnately-cut leaves. Flowers lilac in slender panicles in May. W China. The form in cultivation was probably introduced from a garden in Afghanistan and has been named 'Kabul'.

**reflexa** SCHNEID. A distinct, large shrub of considerable quality, bearing large, oval leaves up to 20cm long and rough to the touch. Flowers rich purplish-pink outside, whitish within, densely packed in long, narrow, drooping panicles, 15-20cm long in late May and June. One of the best of the species and very free-flowering. C China. Discovered and introduced by E.H. Wilson in 1904. AM 1914.

**reticulata** (BLUME) HARA (*S. amurensis* var. *japonica* (MAXIM.) FR. & SAV.) (*S. japonica* DECNE.) A robust, large shrub readily trained to a stout, short tree with an attractive trunk. Leaves broad rotund-ovate, reticulate and pubescent beneath. Flowers creamy-white, fragrant, borne in large, dense panicles in late June. Japan. I 1878. FCC 1887.

**var. mandshurica** (MAXIM.) HARA (*S. amurensis* RUPR.) "Amur Lilac". An elegant shrub with ovate, taper-pointed leaves and large, loose panicles of white flowers in June. The older bark peels, revealing the dark, chestnut-brown, new bark marked with horizontal lenticels. Subject to injury by late spring frost after growth has commenced. Manchuria to Korea. I 1855.

× **swegiflexa** HESSE ex J.S. PRINGLE (*S. reflexa* × *S. sweginzowii*). A beautiful, strong-growing, variable hybrid of open habit with large, dense, cylindrical panicles of usually pink flowers, red in bud. Raised by Messrs Hesse of Weener, NW Germany, about 1934. AM 1977.

**'Fountain'** A medium-sized shrub of compact habit. Flowers pale pink, fragrant, in long, drooping panicles in May and June.

**sweginzowii** KOEHNE & LINGELSH. A vigorous, medium-sized shrub of elegant habit. Leaves ovate, acute or acuminate, 5-7.5cm long. Flowers flesh-pink, sweetly fragrant, borne in long, loose panicles in May and June. W China. Introduced by G.N. Potanin in 1894. AM 1915.

**'Superba'** A selected form with somewhat larger panicles. AM 1918.

**tigerstedtii** H. SM. A medium-sized shrub related to *S. yunnanensis*. Flowers fragrant, pale or whitish-lilac, produced in erect panicles in June. W China. I 1934 by the Swedish plant collector Harry Smith.

**SYRINGA**—*continued*

**tomentella** BUR. & FRANCH. (*S. wilsonii* SCHNEID.) A strong-growing, wide-spreading species up to 3.6-4.5m high. Leaves ovate to elliptic, 5-13cm long, dark green and corrugated above, grey-downy beneath. Flowers sweetly-scented, deep lilac-pink, white inside, paling with age, produced in broad, terminal panicles in late May and June. W China. I 1904. AM 1928.

**velutina** See *S. meyeri* 'Palibin'.

**villosa** VAHL (*S. bretschneideri* LEMOINE) A medium-sized to large, erect-branched shrub of compact habit. Leaves oval to oblong, 5-15cm long, dull dark green above, glaucous beneath. Flowers lilac-rose, carried in stiff, compact, erect panicles in late May and early June. N China. I 1882. AM 1931.

**vulgaris** L. "Common Lilac". A large, vigorous shrub or small tree of suckering habit. Leaves ovate or heart-shaped. Flowers richly scented, lilac, borne in dense, erect, pyramidal panicles in May. Mountains of E Europe. A common garden escape readily naturalised. Introduced in the 16th century. Plants raised from seed are variable in flower colour.

The vast range of garden lilacs have originated from this species. There is probably no other shrub or tree which has given rise to so many cultivars. More than 500 selections have been named, their differences being confined almost entirely to the colour of their single or double flowers. For a representative selection of the better cultivars see CULTIVARS of SYRINGA VULGARIS.

'**Alba**' Flowers white; leaves and winter-buds pale green. Long cultivated.

'**Aurea**' Leaves yellow when young, later yellowish-green.

**wilsonii** See *S. tomentella*.

**wolfii** SCHNEID. (*S. formosissima* NAKAI) An extremely hardy species related to *S. villosa*. A medium-sized to large shrub, with pale ash-grey branches and elliptic-lanceolate, taper-pointed leaves, 8-12cm long. Flowers fragrant, pale violet-purple, borne in long, wide, loose panicles in June. Korea, Manchuria. I 1904.

**yunnanensis** FRANCH. "Yunnan Lilac". A beautiful, medium-sized to large shrub, occasionally up to 4m, of loose, open habit. Leaves elliptic to oblong-lanceolate, glaucous beneath. Flowers fragrant, pink in bud, opening lilac-pink, paling with age, carried in slender panicles in June. Discovered by the Abbé Delavay in 1887, introduced by George Forrest in 1907. AM 1928.

'**Alba**' Flowers white. A distinct plant, possibly of hybrid origin.

'**Rosea**' A superior form selected in our nurseries. Flowers rose-pink, in long, slender panicles. In foliage too, it is distinct and attractive.

## CULTIVARS of SYRINGA VULGARIS

Medium to large-sized shrubs or occasionally small trees of strong erect habit. Flowers produced in dense, erect, conical panicles in May or early June, varying in colour from white through creamy-yellow to red, blue or purple, single or double. All are sweetly scented. The garden lilacs will always be associated with the names of Victor Lemoine and his son Emile, who raised so many lovely cultivars at their nursery at Nancy, France, towards the end of the 19th century and in the early part of the present century. The lover of the lilac also owes a great deal to Alice Harding for her great work and magnificent book on this genus. As with other plants which have become the victims of the specialist, far too many sorts have been selected and named. It requires a highly cultivated imagination to detect the differences in shade of colour, as they vary from hour to hour which makes naming very difficult.

After transplanting it takes 2-3 years before full flower and truss size are achieved.

### SINGLE

'**Ambassadeur**' Azure-lilac with a white eye; large, broad panicles. C 1930 (Lemoine).

'**Blue Hyacinth**' See *S.* × *hyacinthiflora* 'Blue Hyacinth'.

'**Buffon**' See *S.* × *hyacinthiflora* 'Buffon'.

'**Capitaine Baltet**' Light carmine-pink, blue tinged in bud; large panicles. C 1919 (Lemoine).

'**Charles X**' Purplish-red, long, conical panicles. A very popular lilac. C before 1830 and named after the King of France.

## SYRINGA vulgaris—*continued*

**'Clarke's Giant'** See *S. × hyacinthiflora* 'Clarke's Giant'.

**'Congo'** Rich lilac-red in large, compact panicles, paling with age. C 1896 (Lemoine).

**'Esther Staley'** See *S. × hyacinthiflora* 'Esther Staley'.

**'Etna'** Deep claret-purple, fading to lilac-pink; late. C 1927 (Lemoine).

**'Firmament'** Clear lilac-blue; early. C 1932 (Lemoine). AGM 1984.

**'Glory of Horstenstein'** Rich lilac-red, changing to dark lilac. C 1921 (Wilke).

**'Hugo Koster'** Purple-crimson. C 1913 (Koster). AM 1913.

**'Jan van Tol'** Pure white, in long, drooping panicles. C about 1916 (van Tol). AM 1924.

**'Lamartine'** See *S. × hyacinthiflora* 'Lamartine'.

**'Lavaliensis'** ('Lavanensis'). Pale pink. C 1865 (Leroy).

**'Madame Charles Souchet'** Soft lilac-blue, large florets and broad panicles; early. C 1924 (Lemoine).

**'Madame Florent Stepman'** Creamy-yellow in bud, opening white. C 1908 (Stepman).

**'Madame Francisque Morel'** Mauve-pink, large florets, enormous panicles. Erect habit. C 1892 (Morel).

**'Marceau'** Claret-purple, broad panicles. C 1913 (Lemoine).

**'Maréchal Foch'** Bright carmine-rose, large flowers in broad, open panicles. C 1924 (Lemoine). AM 1935.

**'Marie Legraye'** White, creamy-yellow in bud, inflorescences rather small. Popular and much used for forcing. C 1879 (Legraye). FCC 1880.

**'Massena'** Deep reddish-purple, large florets, broad panicles; late. C 1923 (Lemoine). AM 1928. AGM 1930.

**'Maud Notcutt'** Pure white, large panicles up to 30cm long. C 1956 (Notcutt). AM 1957.

**'Mont Blanc'** Greenish-white in bud, opening white, long, well-filled panicles. C 1915 (Lemoine).

**'Pasteur'** Claret-red, long, narrow panicles. C 1903 (Lemoine). AM 1924.

**'President Lincoln'** Purple in bud, opening light bluish-violet; early. C about 1916 (Dunbar).

**'Primrose'** Pale primrose-yellow, small, dense panicles. Originated as a sport in Holland. C 1949 (Maarse). AM 1950.

**'Prodige'** Deep purple, large florets. C 1928 (Lemoine).

**'Purple Heart'** See *S. × hyacinthiflora* 'Purple Heart'.

**'Réaumur'** Deep carmine-violet, broad panicles; late. C 1904 (Lemoine). AM 1916.

**'Sensation'** Purplish-red florets edged white, large panicles. A sport of 'Hugo de Vries'. Inclined to revert and lose its marginal variegation. C 1938 (Maarse).

**'Souvenir de Louis Späth'** ['Andenken an Ludwig Späth']. Wine-red. Perhaps the most popular lilac, one of the most consistent and reliable. C 1883 (Spaeth). FCC 1894. AGM 1984.

**'Vestale'** Pure white, broad, densely-packed panicles. A magnificent lilac. C 1910 (Lemoine). AGM 1984.

### DOUBLE

**'Alice Eastwood'** See *S. × hyacinthiflora* 'Alice Eastwood'.

**'Ami Schott'** Deep cobalt-blue, with paler reverse. C 1933 (Lemoine).

**'Belle de Nancy'** Purple-red in bud, opening lilac-pink, large panicles. C 1891 (Lemoine).

**'Charles Joly'** Dark purplish-red, late. A reliable and popular lilac. C 1896 (Lemoine). AGM 1984.

**'Condorcet'** Lavender, long, massive panicles. C 1888 (Lemoine).

**'Edith Cavell'** Creamy-yellow in bud, opening pure white, large florets. C 1918 (Lemoine).

**'Ellen Willmott'** Cream in bud opening pure white, long, open panicles. C 1903 (Lemoine). AM 1917.

**'General Pershing'** Purplish-violet, long panicles. C 1924 (Lemoine).

**'Katherine Havemeyer'** Purple-lavender, fading to pale lilac-pink, broad, compact panicles. Quite first class. C 1922 (Lemoine). AM 1933. AGM 1984.

**'Madame Abel Chatenay'** Pale greenish-yellow in bud, opening milk-white, broad panicles; late. C 1892 (Lemoine). FCC 1900.

**'Madame Antoine Buchner'** Rose-pink to rosy-mauve, loose, narrow panicles; late. C 1900 (Lemoine). AM 1982. AGM 1984.

**SYRINGA vulgaris**—*continued*

**'Madame Casimir Perier'** Cream in bud, opening white. C 1894 (Lemoine).

**'Madame Lemoine'** Creamy-yellow in bud, opening pure white. An old and popular lilac. C 1890 (Lemoine). AM 1891. FCC 1894. AGM 1984.

**'Michel Buchner'** Pale rosy-lilac, large, dense panicles. C 1885 (Lemoine). AM 1891.

**'Monique Lemoine'** Pure white, large panicles; late. C 1939 (Lemoine). AM 1958.

**'Mrs Edward Harding'** Claret-red, shaded pink, very free-flowering; late. A superb and popular lilac. C 1922 (Lemoine). AGM 1984.

**'Paul Thirion'** Carmine in bud, opening claret-rose, finally lilac-pink; late. C 1915 (Lemoine).

**'Président Grévy'** Lilac-blue, massive panicles. C 1886 (Lemoine). AM 1892.

**'Président Poincare'** Claret-mauve, large florets. C 1913 (Lemoine).

**'Princesse Clementine'** Creamy-yellow in bud, opening white, very floriferous. C about 1908 (Mathieu).

**'Souvenir d'Alice Harding'** Alabaster-white, tall panicles; late May to early June. C 1938 (Lemoine).

**TALAUMA coco** See *Magnolia coco.*

**"TAMARISK"** See *Tamarix.*

**TAMARIX** L.—**Tamaricaceae**—About 50 species of shrubs or small trees, natives of Europe, Asia and N Africa. The "Tamarisks" are excellent wind-resisters and are most commonly planted near the sea, but will thrive inland in full sun, and any soil, except shallow chalk soils. All have graceful, slender branches and plume-like foliage. The tiny pink flowers are borne in slender racemes towards the ends of the branches, the whole creating large, plumose inflorescences which contribute a colourful splash to any landscape. As plants are apt to become straggly in habit, pruning is usually necessary in order to maintain a balance. Those species which flower on growths of the current year should be pruned in late February or March, whilst those which flower on the previous year's wood should be pruned immediately after flowering.

**anglica** See *T. gallica.*

**caspica** HORT. See *T. tetrandra.*

**chinensis** LOUR. (*T. japonica* HORT. ex DIPP.) (*T. juniperina* BUNGE) (*T. plumosa* HORT. ex CARR.) A large shrub or small tree of dense habit. Branches extremely slender, clothed with distinctive pale green foliage. Flowers bright pink, opening in May on shoots of the previous year. E and C Asia. C 1877.

**gallica** L. (*T. anglica* WEBB) A large, spreading, glabrous shrub or small tree, with dark purple-brown branches and sea-green foliage. Flowers during summer, pink, crowded into lax, cylindrical racemes on shoots of the current year. SW Europe. Naturalised along many stretches of the English coast.

**germanica** See *Myricaria germanica.*

**japonica** See *T. chinensis.*

**juniperina** See *T. chinensis.*

**odessana** See *T. ramosissima.*

**parviflora** DC. (*T. tetrandra* var. *purpurea* (DC.) BOISS.) A large shrub or small tree with long, brown or purple branches, clothed with bright green foliage. Flowers deep pink, borne in May on shoots of the previous year. SE Europe, W Asia. Long cultivated and naturalised in C and S Europe. C 1853.

**pentandra** See *T. ramosissima* and *T. ramosissima* 'Rosea'.

**plumosa** See *T. chinensis.*

**ramosissima** LEDEB. (*T. odessana* STEV. ex BUNGE) (*T. pentandra* PALL. in part) A large, glabrous shrub or small tree with reddish-brown branches. Flowers pink in slender racemes during summer, on shoots of the current year. W and C Asia. I about 1885. AM 1903. AGM 1984.

**'Rosea'** Flowers rose-pink borne on shoots of the current year in late summer and early autumn. One of the finest late flowering shrubs, the whole bush becoming a feathery

**TAMARIX ramosissima 'Rosea'**—*continued*

mass of rose-pink, intermingled with the delightful foliage. C 1883. AM 1933. Previously listed as *T. pentandra*.

**'Rubra'** A splendid selection with darker-coloured flowers. AGM 1984.

**tetrandra** PALL. (*T. caspica* HORT.) A large shrub of loose, open growth, with long dark coloured branches and green foliage. Flowers in May or early June, light pink, borne in slender racemes on the branches of the previous year, the whole forming long, large panicles. SE Europe, W Asia. I 1821. AGM 1984.

**var. purpurea** See *T. parviflora*.

‡\***TELOPEA** R. BR.—**Proteaceae**—A small Australasian genus of 3 or 4 species thriving under conditions congenial to Embothriums but welcoming more sun. The "Australian Waratah" (*T. speciosissima* (SM.) R. BR.) requires a warmer clime.

**truncata** R. BR. "Tasmanian Waratah". A remarkably hardy, medium-sized to large shrub or occasionally a small tree with stout, downy shoots and rather thick, oblanceolate, evergreen leaves. Flowers rich crimson, borne in dense terminal heads in June. Hardy when planted among other evergreens in moist, but well drained soil. Thrives in conditions suitable to *Rhododendron*. Introduced by Harold Comber from Tasmania in 1930. A specimen in the Hillier Gardens and Arboretum has reached 4.5m tall and 2.5m across. AM 1934. FCC 1938.

**f. lutea** A.M. GRAY An unusual form with pale yellow flowers. Occurs rarely in the wild and mostly gives red flowered plants when grown from seed due to open pollination. A clone of this, named 'Essie Huxley' in Tasmania, first flowered in the Hillier Gardens and Arboretum in May 1989; it should only be propagated vegetatively. We received cuttings from the original plant in Miss Huxley's garden in Tasmania in 1975.

‡\***TERNSTROEMIA** MUTIS ex L. f.—**Theaceae**—A genus of about 85 species of evergreen trees and shrubs mainly native to tropical regions. They differ from the closely related *Eurya* in their entire leaves and hermaphrodite flowers and from *Cleyera* in various small floral characters.

**gymnanthera** (WIGHT & ARN.) SPRAGUE (*T. japonica* THUNB. in part) A medium-sized shrub with stout branches. The thick, leathery, obovate leaves are blunt tipped and generally clustered towards the ends of the shoots. Flowers white, borne in the leaf axils in July. Only suitable for mild areas, requiring a sheltered position in semi-shade. E and SE Asia.

**'Variegata'** A beautiful form. The dark green leaves are marbled grey and possess a creamy-white margin which turns to rose in autumn.

**TETRACENTRON** OLIVER—**Tetracentraceae**—A rare, monotypic genus of disputable allegiance, included under both *Magnoliaceae* and *Trochodendraceae* in the past. It bears a superficial resemblance to *Cercidiphyllum*, but its leaves are alternate and its hermaphrodite flowers are borne in catkins. It thrives in woodland conditions, but makes an elegant lawn specimen. It is lime-tolerant and has grown for many years on the site of our West Hill nursery in Winchester but grows with greater freedom in an acid or neutral soil.

**sinense** OLIVER A large shrub or small to medium-sized tree of wide-spreading habit. Leaves ovate or heart-shaped, with a long slender point, red-tinted when young. Flowers minute, yellowish, borne in dense, pendulous catkin-like spikes, 10-15cm long, which drape the leafy branches in summer. A graceful tree from C and W China and the Himalaya where it was seen by C.R. Lancaster in E Nepal in 1971. First discovered by Augustine Henry. Introduced by E.H. Wilson in 1901.

**TETRADIUM** LOUR.—**Rutaceae**—9 species of trees with pinnate leaves (with not more than 3 leaflets in *Euodia*), natives of the Himalaya, E and SE Asia. Related and similar in general appearance to *Phellodendron* but differing in the exposed winter buds and the

**TETRADIUM**—*continued*

fruits consisting of dehiscent pods. Flowers unisexual (bisexual in *Euodia*). The hardy species in cultivation are deciduous trees succeeding in all types of soil.

**daniellii** (BENN.) HARTLEY (*Euodia daniellii* (BENN.) HEMSL.) (*Euodia hupehensis* DODE) (*Euodia velutina* REHD. & WILS.) A variable, fast-growing small to medium-sized tree with large, pinnate leaves and corymbs of small, white, pungently scented flowers with yellow anthers in late summer and early autumn, succeeded by red to purplish or black fruits. China, Korea. I 1905. AM 1949. FCC 1976 (both as *Euodia hupehensis*).

**TEUCRIUM** L.—**Labiatae**—A genus of about 100 species of herbs, shrubs and sub-shrubs widely distributed in warm temperate regions of the world particularly in the Mediterranean region. The shrubby members are useful flowering and foliage plants, requiring a sunny, well drained position. All have square stems and two-lipped flowers.

**\*chamaedrys** L. "Wall Germander". A dwarf, bushy, aromatic sub-shrub with creeping rootstock and erect, hairy stems, densely clothed with small, prettily-toothed leaves. Flowers rose-pink with darker veins, produced in axillary whorls from July to September. Suitable for walls. C and S Europe. C in England about 1750.

†**\*fruticans** L. "Shrubby Germander". A small, evergreen shrub, the stems and the undersides of the ovate leaves covered with a close white tomentum. Flowers pale blue, in terminal racemes, throughout the summer. It requires a sunny, well drained position with the shelter of a wall. S Europe, N Africa. I 1714. AM 1982 (for foliage). AGM 1984.

**'Azureum'** A slightly more tender form with darker blue flowers contrasting better with the foliage. AM 1936.

**\*polium** L. A dwarf, evergreen shrub with procumbent stems forming low hummocks a few centimetres high. Leaves narrow and grey-felted. Flowers white or yellow in terminal heads during summer. Suitable for the rock garden. Mediterranean region. C 1562.

**\*subspinosum** POURR. ex WILLD. A dwarf, grey spiny shrublet of unusual appearance. Flowers mauve-pink, produced in late summer. A worthy plant for the rock garden or scree. Balearic Islands (Mallorca).

**THEA sinensis** See *Camellia sinensis*.

**"THORN"** See *Crataegus*.

**"THORN, CHRIST'S"** See *Paliurus spina-christi*.

**"THORN, GLASTONBURY"** See *Crataegus monogyna* 'Biflora'.

†**TIBOUCHINA** AUBLET—**Melastomataceae**—A large genus of some 350 species of mainly trees and shrubs, natives of Tropical America. None are hardy though several are suitable for walls or pillars in the conservatory.

**\*urvilleana** (DC.) COGNIAUX (*T. semidecandra* HORT.) "Glory Bush". A large shrub with four-angled stems and velvety hairy, prominently veined leaves. The large, vivid royal purple flowers are produced continuously throughout summer and autumn. Old plants tend to become straggly and should be pruned in early spring. S Brazil. I 1864. FCC 1868 (as *T. semidecandra*).

**TILIA** L.—**Tiliaceae**—The "Limes" or "Lindens" make up a genus of about 45 species of deciduous trees widely distributed in N temperate regions. They are all very amenable to cultivation, many growing into stately trees. Because of their tolerance of hard pruning they have been widely used in the past for roadside planting and "pleaching". They will grow in all types of fertile soils and situations. Sticky honey-dew produced by aphids is a problem with *T.* × *europaea* and *T. platyphyllos* and their forms. Unless otherwise stated the small, fragrant, creamy-yellow flowers of the Common Lime are common to all the species and are borne in numerous clusters in July; in *T. tomentosa* and its forms they are toxic to bees. They hybridise readily when grown from seed.

**alba** See *T. tomentosa*.

**TILIA**—*continued*

**americana** L. "American Lime" "Basswood". A medium-sized tree with glabrous shoots and enormous broad leaves up to 30cm long. They are coarsely-toothed, green on both sides, and glabrous, except for minute axillary tufts beneath. It is conspicuous on account of the large leaves but like the American Beech it does not luxuriate in the British Isles. The bark of old trees is rough, almost corky in appearance. E and C North America. I 1752.

**'Dentata'** Leaves coarsely-toothed, a striking plant particularly when young.

**'Fastigiata'** A narrow, conical form with ascending branches. Raised in New York about 1927.

**'Pendula'** See *T. tomentosa* 'Petiolaris'.

**'Redmond'** A selected form said to be of dense conical habit. Garden origin, Nebraska, about 1926. Originally introduced as a form of *T. × euchlora*.

**amurensis** RUPR. A small to medium-sized tree related to *T. cordata*, with broadly ovate, coarsely-toothed leaves. It is unlikely to prove an outstanding tree in the British Isles. Manchuria, Korea. C 1909.

**argentea** See *T. tomentosa*.

**begoniifolia** STEV. (A. & L. 16) A vigorous tree related to *T. platyphyllos*. Shoots glabrous, turning red in winter. Leaves large, broadly ovate, to 15cm long, coarsely-toothed at the margin, obliquely cordate at the base, dark green above, paler and glabrous beneath except for tufts of down in the leaf axils, turning bright yellow in autumn. N Iran and adjacent USSR. I 1972 by Mrs Ala and Roy Lancaster from N Iran. It has reached 9m in the Hillier Gardens and Arboretum (1990).

**caroliniana** MILL. A medium-sized tree with tomentose, reddish-brown or yellowish twigs. Leaves broad ovate and coarsely-toothed, dark yellowish-green above, stellate tomentose beneath. SE United States.

**subsp. floridana** (SMALL) E. MURR. Mature leaves nearly glabrous. C 1915.

**caucasica** RUPR. (*T. dasystyla* REHD. in part not STEV.) A medium-sized tree with greenish twigs, pubescent at first, and orbicular-ovate, sharply and conpicuously bristle-toothed leaves, dark glossy green above, paler with yellow axillary tufts beneath. SE Europe, Caucasus to N Iran. C 1880.

**chinensis** MAXIM. A distinct small to medium-sized tree with glabrous, glossy shoots and ovate to broadly-ovate, sharply-toothed, slender-pointed leaves, thinly pubescent beneath. Bark of older trees flaking. W and C China. I 1925.

**cordata** MILL. (*T. parvifolia* EHRH.) "Small-leaved Lime". A medium-sized to large, native tree of rounded habit. Leaves heart-shaped, 5-7.5cm long, rather leathery, glossy dark green above, pale green, with reddish-brown axillary tufts beneath. The characteristic spreading inflorescences appear in late July, generally after those of the Common Lime and Large-leaved Lime; flowers ivory-coloured and sweetly-scented. Europe (including the British Isles).

**'Greenspire'** A fast-growing American selection of upright habit making a narrowly oval crown. C 1961.

**'Rancho'** A small to medium-sized tree of dense, conical habit with small, glossy green leaves. C 1961.

**'Swedish Upright'** A most attractive, columnar form with spreading branches. Introduced by Alfred Rehder from Sweden to the Arnold Arboretum in 1906. Suitable for planting in broad thoroughfares and city squares.

**dasystyla** STEV. This species, a native of the Crimea, may not be in cultivation. Plants grown under this name are usually *T. caucasica* or *T. × euchlora*.

**× euchlora** K. KOCH (*T. × dasystyla* HORT.) (*T. cordata* ×? *T. dasystyla*). A medium-sized tree with generally glabrous green twigs. Leaves orbicular-ovate, intermediate in size between those of the parents, shining dark green above, paler almost glaucous, with brown axillary tufts beneath. An elegant tree when young with glossy leaves and arching branches, becoming dense and twiggy with pendulous lower branches in maturity. It is a "clean" lime, being free from aphids, but its flowers tend to have a narcotic effect on bees. Possibly a form of *T. caucasica*. C 1860. FCC 1890. AGM 1984.

**× europaea** L. (*T. cordata* × *T. platyphyllos*) (*T. × vulgaris* HAYNE) (*T. × intermedia* DC.) "Common Lime". A familiar avenue tree and at least in the past the most commonly

**TILIA** × **europaea**—*continued*

planted lime. A large, vigorous tree with glabrous, greenish zig-zag shoots. Leaves broadly ovate or rounded, obliquely heart-shaped at base, sharply-toothed, glabrous except for axillary tufts beneath. A long-lived tree, easily recognised by its densely suckering habit. Occasionally found with its parents in the wild. The honey-dew produced by aphids on this tree is a problem in late summer.

**'Pallida'** "Kaiser Linden". Branches ascending forming a broadly conical crown, reddish in winter. Leaves yellowish-green beneath. This is the lime of Unter den Linden in Berlin.

**'Wratislaviensis'** Leaves golden yellow when young becoming green with age. A splendid tree whose young growths give the effect of a yellow halo. A sport of 'Pallida'.

**floridana** See *T. caroliniana* subsp. *floridana*.

**grandifolia** See *T. platyphyllos*.

**'Harold Hillier'** (*T. insularis* × *T. mongolica*). A handsome and vigorous, medium-sized tree of narrowly conical habit with glabrous shoots. Leaves variable in size, up to 15cm long, usually less, maple-like and 3-lobed, edged with bristle-tipped teeth, dark green above, grey-green and glabrous beneath except for pale brown tufts of hair in the vein axils. Autumn colour a lovely butter-yellow. A clean lime with good potential as a street tree. Raised in 1973 by Nigel Muir who kindly suggested we name it after the late Sir Harold Hillier.

**henryana** SZYSZ. A very rare, medium-sized tree with broadly ovate leaves up to 13cm long, oblique at the base and edged with conspicuous, bristle-like teeth. They are softly downy on both surfaces with axillary tufts beneath and are often conspicuously carmine-tinged when young. Flowers in autumn. Very slow-growing in cultivation. C China. Discovered by Augustine Henry in 1888. Introduced by Ernest Wilson in 1901.

**heterophylla** VENT. (*T. heterophylla* var. *michauxii* (NUTT.) SARG.) A medium-sized tree with glabrous branches and large, broadly ovate, coarsely-toothed leaves which are dark green above and covered beneath by a close silvery tomentum. E United States. C 1755.

**var. michauxii** See *T. heterophylla*.

**insularis** NAKAI A small to medium-sized tree in cultivation with heart-shaped coarsely-toothed, green leaves, tufted in the vein axils beneath. Fragrant flowers are profusely borne in summer. Cheju Do (Quelpart), S Korea. I 1919 by Ernest Wilson.

**japonica** (MIQ.) SIMONK. A distinct and attractive, medium-sized, small-leaved tree related to, and resembling our native *T. cordata*, but leaves slightly larger and abruptly acuminate. Japan, E China. I 1875.

**kiusiana** MAK. & SHIRAS. A remarkable unlime-like, slow-growing shrub, rarely a small tree, with slender stems and small ovate leaves about 4-6cm long, oblique at base, serrately-toothed, thinly downy on both surfaces and with axillary tufts beneath. One of the most distinct of all limes. S Japan. I 1930.

**mandshurica** RUPR. & MAXIM. A striking small to medium-sized tree with downy young shoots and large, heart-shaped, coarsely-toothed leaves, which are equal in size to those of *T. americana*, but greyish beneath, both surfaces stellately downy. Subject to injury by late spring frosts. NE Asia. I about 1860.

**maximowicziana** SHIRAS. A medium-sized to large tree with downy, yellowish shoots and broadly ovate to rounded leaves, 10-18cm long, edged with broad, mucronate teeth. They are stellately hairy above, greyish tomentose beneath, with conspicuous axillary tufts. Flowers appearing in June. N Japan. C 1880. AM 1976.

**miqueliana** MAXIM. A very distinct, slow-growing tree of small to medium size, with grey-felted shoots. Leaves ovate, tapering to an acuminate apex, coarsely-toothed or slightly lobed, grey-felted beneath, long persisting. Flowers appearing in August, conspicuous and fragrant. Jiangsu, E China. Long cultivated in Japan, particularly around temples. I before 1900.

× **moltkei** SPAETH ex SCHNEID. (*T.* × *spectabilis* DIPP.) (*T. americana* × *T. tomentosa* 'Petiolaris'). A strong-growing tree of medium to large size, with arching, slightly pendulous branches. Leaves broad ovate or rounded 15-20cm long, greyish downy beneath. Flowers fragrant, in large clusters, July. Raised by Messrs Späth in Berlin.

**mongolica** MAXIM. "Mongolian Lime". A small tree of compact rounded habit and dense twiggy growth, with glabrous, reddish shoots. Leaves 4-7.5cm long on red stalks,

**TILIA mongolica**—*continued*

coarsely-toothed or three to five-lobed, particularly on young trees, glossy green and glabrous except for axillary tufts beneath, turning bright yellow in autumn. An attractive species with prettily lobed, ivy-like leaves. E Russia, Mongolia, N China. I 1880.

**monticola** SARG. Medium-sized tree with reddish young twigs. Leaves ovate, acuminate, deep lustrous green above, pale beneath. Closely related to and, by some authorities, united with *T. heterophylla*. SE United States. C 1888.

**neglecta** SPACH. A large tree with red, glabrous shoots and broadly ovate, green leaves, stellately hairy beneath. Closely related to *T. americana*. E and C North America. C 1830.

**oliveri** SZYSZ. An elegant, medium-sized to large tree with glabrous shoots inclined to be pendulous. Leaves broadly ovate or rounded, finely-toothed, dark green above, silvery-white tomentose beneath. Closely related to *T. tomentosa* and like it free from aphids, differing in its glabrous young shoots. C China. Discovered by Augustine Henry in 1888. Introduced by E.H. Wilson in 1900.

**'Orbicularis'** See *T. tomentosa* 'Orbicularis'.

**parvifolia** See *T. cordata*.

**petiolaris** See *T. tomentosa* 'Petiolaris'.

**'Chelsea Sentinel'** See *T. tomentosa* 'Chelsea Sentinel'.

**platyphyllos** SCOP. (*T. grandifolia* EHRH.) "Broad-leaved Lime". A large, vigorous tree of rounded habit with downy shoots. Leaves roundish-ovate, sharply-toothed, shortly pubescent above, densely so beneath, especially on veins and midrib. Flowers appearing in late June or early July. A commonly planted tree, especially in parks. Suckers are produced, though not as prolifically as in *T. × europaea*, but it still has the same aphid problems. C and S Europe to N France and SW Sweden. Possibly native in the Wye Valley and S Yorkshire. FCC 1892.

**'Aspleniifolia'** An elegant, small to medium-sized tree with leaves deeply and variously divided into narrow segments. Perhaps a sport of the variable 'Laciniata'.

**'Aurea'** ('Aurantiaca') (*T. grandifolia* 'Aurantia') Young shoots yellow, becoming olive-green. Most conspicuous in winter.

**'Corallina'** See 'Rubra'.

**'Fastigiata'** ('Pyramidalis') An erect-branched form of broadly conical habit.

**'Laciniata'** A small to medium-sized tree of dense, conical habit. Leaves deeply and irregularly cut into rounded and tail-like lobes.

**'Örebro'** A large tree of upright habit forming a broad, conical crown. Found in Sweden in 1935.

**'Pendula'** Branches spreading, branchlets pendulous.

**'Prince's Street'** A vigorous form of upright habit, the young shoots bright red in winter.

**'Rubra'** ('Corallina') "Red-twigged Lime". Young shoots bright brownish-red, particularly effective in winter. The best cultivar for street planting owing to its uniformly, semi-erect habit of branching. Excellent in industrial areas.

**spectabilis** DIPP. See *T. × moltkei*.

**tomentosa** MOENCH. (*T. argentea* DC.) (*T. alba* AIT. in part) "Silver Lime". A handsome, but variable, large tree of stately habit. Branches erect, often pendulous at their tips, shoots white-felted. Leaves shortly-stalked, ovate-orbicular, sharply-toothed, dark green above, silvery-white tomentose beneath. They are particularly effective when disturbed by a breeze. Free from aphid problems but flowers toxic to bees. SE and EC Europe. I 1767. AGM 1984.

**'Brabant'** A Dutch selection of upright habit developing a dense, broadly conical crown. C 1970.

**'Chelsea Sentinel'** Resembles 'Petiolaris' in its long-stalked leaves and attractively weeping branches but has a distinctly columnar habit. The original tree grew in the grounds of the Royal Hospital, Chelsea until it was destroyed in the hurricane of October 1987. Fortunately we had already propagated it and were happy to present a replacement that H.M. the Queen planted to commemorate the 75th Chelsea Flower Show.

**'Orbicularis'** (*T. × orbicularis* (CARR.) JOUIN) A vigorous, medium-sized tree of conical habit, with somewhat pendulous branches. Leaves large, orbicular, glossy green above,

**TILIA tomentosa 'Orbicularis'**—*continued*

grey tomentose beneath; flowers fragrant. Raised by Messrs Simon-Louis, near Metz, NE France, about 1870.

**'Petiolaris'** (*T. petiolaris* DC.) (*T. americana* 'Pendula') "Weeping Silver Lime". One of the most beautiful of all large, weeping trees. A large, round-headed tree with graceful, downward-sweeping branches. Leaves long-stalked, broadly ovate to rounded, sharply-toothed, dark green above, white-felted beneath, especially attractive when ruffled by a breeze. Flowers richly scented, but narcotic to bees. A tree of uncertain origin. C 1840. AGM 1984.

× **vulgaris** See *T.* × *europaea*.

**TOONA** (ENDL.) M. ROEMER—**Meliaceae**—A small genus of 6 species of trees natives of China, SE Asia and N Australia. The genus *Cedrela* is restricted to tropical America with 8 species.

**sinensis** (A. JUSS.) M. ROEMER (*Cedrela sinensis* A. JUSS.) (*Ailanthus flavescens* CARR.) A medium-sized fast-growing tree with handsome, large pinnate leaves often bronze when young, in which the terminal leaflet is sometimes absent, and fragrant white flowers in panicles often 30cm long. Lovely yellow tints in autumn. N and W China. I 1862.

**'Flamingo'** (*Cedrela sinensis* 'Flamingo') Young foliage brilliant pink turning to cream then green. Raised in Australia before 1930.

**\*TRACHYCARPUS** H. WENDL.—**Palmae**—A small genus of 4 species of usually dioecious palms with very large, fan-shaped leaves, natives of the Himalaya and E Asia. The following species is hardy in the British Isles but it deserves a sheltered position to protect its leaves from being shattered by strong winds.

**fortunei** (HOOK.) H. WENDL. (*T. excelsus* H. WENDL.) (*Chamaerops excelsus* MART. not THUNB.) "Chusan Palm" "Chinese Windmill Palm". A remarkable species of small to medium size, developing a tall, single trunk, thickly clothed with the fibrous remains of the old leaf bases. Leaves large, fan-shaped, 1-1.5m across, borne on long, stout petioles in a cluster from the summit of the trunk, persisting many years. Flowers yellow, small, numerously borne in large, terminal, decurved panicles in early summer, sometimes both sexes on the same tree; fruits marble-like, bluish-black. C China. First introduced by Philip von Siebold in 1830 and later by Robert Fortune in 1849. AM 1970.

**"TREE DAISY"** See *Olearia*.

**"TREE OF HEAVEN"** See *Ailanthus altissima*.

**"TREE LUPIN"** See *Lupinus arboreus*.

**"TREE POPPY"** See *Romneya*.

**TRIPETALEIA** See *Elliottia*.

‡**\*TROCHOCARPA** R. BR.—**Epacridaceae**—A small genus of about 12 species of evergreen shrubs and small trees distributed from Tasmania to Borneo.

**thymifolia** (R. BR.) SPRENG. A dwarf or prostrate, heath-like shrub with downy shoots and tiny, densely arranged, narrowly ovate dark green leaves, three-veined beneath. Small deep pink flowers white within are borne in short, pendulous spikes in early spring and often again in autumn, followed by fleshy, bluish fruits. Tasmania. C 1940.

‡**\*TROCHODENDRON** SIEB. & ZUCC.—**Trochodendraceae**—A monotypic genus growing in most fertile soils except shallow chalky soils, in sun or shade. During the severe winter of 1962/63 when most evergreens looked bedraggled, this species was unharmed and quite outstanding.

**aralioides** SIEB. & ZUCC. A large, glabrous, evergreen shrub or small tree of slow growth and spreading habit, the bark aromatic. The long-stalked, obovate, leathery leaves are

**TROCHODENDRON aralloides**—*continued*
bright apple-green or yellowish-green in colour and prettily scalloped at the margins. Flowers green, borne in erect, terminal racemes during spring and early summer. A striking and unusual shrub desired by flower arrangers. Japan, Taiwan, S Korea. C 1894. AM 1976.

‡**TSUSIOPHYLLUM** MAXIM.—**Ericaceae**—A monotypic genus sometimes united with *Rhododendron*, from which it differs in its three-celled ovary and dehiscent anthers. Requires a moist, lime-free soil.

**tanakae** MAXIM. (*Rhododendron tsusiophyllum* SUGIM.) A dwarf or small semi-evergreen shrub of dense, twiggy habit, with myriads of tiny leaves, glaucous beneath. The tiny, bell-shaped, white flowers appear in one to three-flowered clusters during June and July. A delightful little species. Japan. I 1915 by Ernest Wilson. AM 1965.

**"TULIP TREE"** See *Liriodendron tulipifera*.

**"TUPELO"** See *Nyssa sylvatica*.

**TWEEDIA coerulea** See *Oxypetalum caeruleum*.

**ULEX** L.—**Leguminosae**—About 20 species of spiny shrubs native of W Europe and N Africa. Variously known as "Furze", "Gorse" or "Whin". The 3 native species are usually found on poor, dry, heath or downland, and are valuable for covering dry banks, and for windswept, maritime sites.

If our native gorses were rare exotics, they would be sought by connoisseur and garden designer alike. It would be impossible to imagine in any landscape a richer mass of chrome-yellow, intermixed with the occasional splash of deep lemon-yellow, than one sees covering the downs around Slieve Donard in N Ireland in April. This dazzling feast of colour is provided by *U. europaeus*. In August and September along the Welsh mountainsides, as one approaches C Wales from Herefordshire, the countryside is enriched by lower-growing masses of *U. gallii*.

Many of us have roved those lovely downs which rise from Salcombe harbour in S Devon and which, in late summer, become a patchwork quilt of golden gorse and purple heather. In parts of the New Forest we meet *U. minor*, our third native species, which also flowers in the autumn with the heather.

Gorse should be pot grown, otherwise it is difficult to establish. It is not recommended for shallow, chalk soils. Strong-growing plants are apt to become leggy and bare at the base. They may be cut to the ground after flowering. Gorse is one of those shrubs which, like heather, grows best in poor, dry, acid soil.

**europaeus** L. "Common Gorse". A densely-branched, green, viciously spiny, native shrub, 1.2-1.8m high, much more in sheltered or shaded sites. The chrome-yellow, pea-flowers crowd the branches from March to May and intermittently throughout the year. W Europe extending eastwards to Italy. Extensively naturalised in C Europe.

**'Flore Pleno'** ('Plenus') A superb shrub when in April and May its lower-growing compact hummocks are smothered in long-lasting, semi-double flowers. C 1828. AM 1967. AGM 1984.

**'Strictus'** ('Hibernicus') ('Fastigiatus') A slow-growing, unusual form with erect, slender, shortly and softly spiny shoots forming a dense, compact bush. It resembles more a form of *U. gallii* than *U. europaeus* and, though it rarely flowers, makes an excellent low hedge.

**gallii** PLANCH. A dwarf shrub, often prostrate in maritime areas, usually more robust and stronger-spined than *U. minor*, but much less so than *U. europaeus*. Flowers smaller than those of the Common Gorse, deep golden yellow, opening in the autumn from August to October. W Europe (including the British Isles).

**minor** ROTH (*U. nanus* T.F. FORSTER ex SYMONS) A dwarf, often prostrate shrub with slender, softly spiny shoots. Flowers half the size of those of the Common Gorse, golden yellow,

**ULEX minor**—*continued*

opening during autumn and particularly spectacular in September. A low-growing species which must be given "starvation diet" to prevent it becoming tall and lanky. SW Europe northwards to the British Isles, but not Ireland.

**ULMUS** L.—**Ulmaceae**—The "Elms" are a genus which included, until recently, some of the noblest, deciduous, hardy trees in this country. They all thrive in almost any type of soil and in exposed positions, the Wych Elm being one of the few trees which may be planted near the sea in full exposure to Atlantic gales. The golden and variegated forms are colourful trees in the landscape, while the weeping forms are picturesque and useful for the shade they give. In most species the leaves turn glowing yellow in the autumn sunshine. The flowers of the elm are small and reddish in colour and hermaphrodite; unless otherwise stated, they are borne on the naked twigs in early spring. The fruits (samaras) which follow are greenish, winged and disc-like.

The English Elm (*U. minor* var. *vulgaris*) was an inseparable part of the English landscape. Unfortunately its presence in certain areas has, in recent years, been drastically reduced due to the depredations of the Dutch Elm Disease. The name does not connect it with the Dutch Elm or imply that it originated in Holland, but refers to the fact that early work on the disease was carried out there. This disease is caused by a fungus (*Ceratocystis ulmi*), spores of which are transmitted from diseased trees to healthy trees through the agency of various elm-bark beetles (*Scolytus scolytus* and *S. multistriatus*). Death is caused by the blockage of vessels which transport water from the roots. It was first reported in 1918 and reached epidemic proportions in the 1930s. After this it died down but returned in the early 1970s in a very aggressive form. Most of the forms mentioned here as being resistant were only resistant to earlier introductions of the disease. At present most disease-resistance is shown by Asiatic species such as *U. japonica*. An account of the disease and its occurrence in the British Isles is available from the Forestry Commission (Bulletin No 33).

In dealing with this serious disease landowners and gardeners are asked to co-operate by checking the condition of all elms (whatever the species) growing on their property. Badly infected trees should be completely removed, but where isolated branches are infected these should be dealt with in the same manner and burnt. To prevent the disease from spreading, it is necessary to remove all possible breeding sites for the elm-bark beetles, and to this end all dead or dying trees and branches should be destroyed. Elm logs or stumps left in the open should have their bark removed.

**alata** MICHX. "Winged Elm". A small to medium-sized tree developing a rounded head. Branches glabrous or nearly so, with 2 opposite corky wings. Leaves narrowly obovate or ovate-oblong, glabrous above. Fruits hairy. SE United States. I 1820.

**americana** L. "White Elm". A large, vigorous, attractive tree with ash-grey bark and a wide-spreading head of graceful branches. The ovate to obovate, slenderly-pointed leaves, 10-15cm long, are double-toothed along the margins and unequal at the base. Fruits ciliate. E and C North America. I 1752.

**angustifolia** See *U. minor*.

    **var. cornubiensis** See *U. minor* var. *cornubiensis*.

**belgica** See *U.* × *hollandica* 'Belgica'.

**campestris** L. A confused name which has been applied to several species, in Britain mainly to *U. procera*.

    **'Major'** See *U.* × *hollandica* 'Major'.

    **var. stricta** See *U. minor* var. *cornubiensis*.

    **var. sarniensis** See *U. minor* 'Sarniensis'.

**carpinifolia** See *U. minor*.

    **var. cornubiensis** See *U. minor* var. *cornubiensis*.

    **'Dampieri'** See *U.* × *hollandica* 'Dampieri'.

    **'Italica'** See *U.* × *hollandica* 'Australis'.

    **f. sarniensis** See *U. minor* 'Sarniensis'.

    **'Variegata'** See *U. minor* 'Variegata'.

**chinensis** See *U. parvifolia*.

**crassifolia** NUTT. A slow-growing, small, round-headed tree in cultivation, with downy young shoots and occasionally opposite or subopposite winter buds. Leaves ovate to

**ULMUS crassifolia**—*continued*
  oblong, blunt-tipped, leathery, 2.5-5cm long, rough to the touch above, downy beneath.
  Flowers produced in axillary clusters in late summer and early autumn. Fruits downy. S
  United States, NE Mexico. I 1876.

**davidiana** PLANCH. A medium-sized tree related to *U. minor* with downy shoots and broad,
  obovate or ovate leaves, pubescent beneath. Fruits hairy in the centre. NE Asia. I 1895.
    **var. japonica** See *U. japonica*.

**effusa** See *U. laevis*.

**elegantissima** See *U. minor*.

  **'Jacqueline Hillier'** See *U. minor* 'Jacqueline Hillier'.

**exoniensis** See *U. glabra* 'Exoniensis'.

**foliacea** See *U. minor*.

**fulva** See *U. rubra*.

**glabra** HUDS. (*U. montana* STOKES) "Wych Elm" "Scotch Elm". A large native tree, usually
  developing a dome-shaped crown with spreading branches, arching or pendulous at their
  extremities. Leaves shortly stalked, large and rough to the touch above, coarsely-toothed,
  markedly unequal at base, abruptly acuminate. Fruits downy at apex, effective in early
  spring when they crowd the branches. It is said to be the only native elm which
  reproduces itself freely and regularly from seed. An excellent tree for planting in exposed
  situations either inland or along the coast. Many forms have been named. Europe, N
  and W Asia. Probably the only elm native to Britain, the others having been introduced
  by man.

  **'Camperdownii'** (*U. pendula* 'Camperdownii') "Camperdown Elm". A small, neat and
  compact tree with pendulous branches, forming a globose or dome-shaped head in
  marked contrast to the more spreading, stiffer-looking crown of the equally common
  **'Horizontalis'**. Suitable as an isolated specimen on a lawn. C 1850.

  **'Crispa'** ('Aspleniifolia') ('Urticifolia') An unusual form of slow growth and generally
  loose habit, with narrow leaves which are curiously infolded, with jaggedly-toothed
  margins.

  **'Exoniensis'** ('Fastigiata') (*U. scabra* 'Pyramidalis') (*U. exoniensis* HORT.) An erect tree
  of medium to large size, narrowly columnar when young, broadening with age. Leaves
  broad, jaggedly-toothed, occurring in clusters on the ascending branches. Found near
  Exeter, about 1826.

  **'Fastigiata'** See 'Exoniensis'.

  **'Horizontalis'** ('Pendula') "Weeping Wych Elm". A small tree occasionally reaching 9m,
  developing a wide head of spreading branches with long pendulous branchlets. Suitable
  as an isolated specimen for the large garden or park.

  **'Lutescens'** (*U. americana* 'Aurea') Leaves soft cream-yellow in spring, becoming yellowish-
  green. A very beautiful free-growing tree.

  **'Pendula'** See 'Horizontalis'.

  **'Vegeta'** See *U.* × *hollandica* 'Vegeta'.

× **hollandica** MILL. (*U. glabra* × *U. minor*). An extremely variable, natural hybrid wide-spread
  in W Europe. According to Dr R. Melville this hybrid, in its numerous forms, constitutes
  almost the entire elm population of Germany, Holland, Belgium and France, as well as
  being quite abundant in East Anglia and the Midlands. R.H. Richens has more recently
  expressed the view that it is less common but occurs where the parents grow together.
    The cultivars described below under this name are of similar parentage, but of
  independent origin. The majority are very vigorous and, unless otherwise stated, attain
  a large size.

  **'Australis'** (*U. procera* 'Australis') (*U. carpinifolia* 'Italica') An interesting tree with
  conspicuously and numerously veined leaves which are rather leathery in texture. It is
  said to occur in the wild in SE France, Switzerland and Italy.

  **'Bea Schwarz'** A Dutch selection raised for its resistance to Dutch Elm Disease. First
  introduced in 1948.

  **'Belgica'** (*U. belgica* WEST.) "Belgian Elm". A natural hybrid strongly resembling *U.
  glabra*. A vigorous tree forming a broad crown with almost glabrous twigs and obovate-
  elliptic leaves with a long, serrated point. This was the clone usually grown as

**ULMUS** × **hollandica 'Belgica'**—*continued*

    *U.* × *hollandica* in Belgium and Holland where it was commonly planted in parks and along roads. C 1694.

**'Christine Buisman'** An attractive disease-resistant clone of Dutch origin. Introduced in 1937.

**'Commelin'** A disease-resistant clone of Dutch origin differing from the type in its narrower habit and smaller leaves.

**'Dampieri'** A narrow, conical tree, with broadly-ovate, double-toothed leaves, densely crowded on short branchlets.

**'Dampieri Aurea'** ('Wredei') ('Wredei Aurea') A narrowly conical tree in which the crowded broad leaves are suffused golden yellow. A sport of 'Dampieri'. FCC 1893.

**'Hillieri'** A graceful, compact, slow-growing, miniature, weeping tree to shrub, usually less than 1.2m high, which originated as a chance seedling in our Pitt Corner nursery, Winchester in 1918. The slender branchlets carry small leaves which, under favourable conditions, turn crimson and yellow in autumn.

**'Major'** (*U. major* SMITH) "Dutch Elm". A large, suckering tree with a short trunk and wide-spreading branches. Young shoots glabrous or almost so. Leaves broad elliptic with a long serrated point and markedly unequal at base. Branchlets often prominently ridged. This is the *U.* × *hollandica* of England, where it was commonly planted.

**'Pendula'** See 'Smithii'.

**'Serpentina'** A remarkable small tree with curved and twisted, zig-zag pendulous branches, forming a dense conical or globose crown.

**'Smithii'** ('Pendula') "Downton Elm". An elegant small to medium-sized tree with ascending branches and long, pendulous branchlets. Leaves dark green, smooth and shining above.

**'Vegeta'** (*U. vegeta* (LOUD.) LEY) (*U. glabra* 'Vegeta') "Huntingdon Elm" "Chichester Elm". A magnificent large tree with a short trunk and long, ascending branches. Young shoots sparsely hairy. Leaves large, elliptic, very unequal at base, long-pointed; smooth, shining dark green above, jaggedly-toothed and conspicuously veined. One of the most vigorous elms, raised from seed of trees growing in Hinchingbrook Park, Cambs about 1750.

**'Wredei'** See 'Dampieri Aurea'.

**japonica** (REHD.) SARG. (*U. davidiana* var. *japonica* (REHD.) NAKAI) "Japanese Elm". A graceful tree with downy twigs and elliptic or obovate leaves, rough to the touch above. Fruits glabrous. Japan.

**laciniata** (TRAUTV.) MAYR (*U. montana* var. *laciniata* TRAUTV.) A small tree closely related to *U. glabra* with large, thin, obovate leaves which are usually three to nine-lobed at the apex, rough to the touch above and sharply double-toothed. Fruits glabrous. NE Asia. I 1905.

**laevis** PALL. (*U. effusa* WILLD.) (*U. pedunculata* FOUG.) "European White Elm". A large tree with a wide-spreading head and rounded to ovate or obovate, double-toothed leaves, softly downy below, markedly unequal at base. Fruits ciliate. CE and SE Europe to W Asia.

**macrocarpa** HANCE "Large-fruited Elm". A small, bushy tree with corky winged branches and roughly hairy leaves. Distinguished from other elms by the large, winged fruits up to 3cm long, which are bristly, like the leaves. N China. I 1908.

**major** See *U.* × *hollandica* 'Major'.

**minor** MILL. (*U. angustifolia* (WEST.) WEST.) (*U. carpinifolia* GLEDITSCH) (*U. elegantissima* HORWOOD) (*U. nitens* MOENCH) (*U. foliacea* GILIB.) "Field Elm" "Smooth-leaved Elm". A large tree of graceful, open habit, with slender, often pendulous shoots. Leaves narrowly oval to oblanceolate, markedly unequal at base, double-toothed and rather leathery in texture, glabrous, shining dark green above, hairy in the vein axils beneath. Fruits glabrous. An attractive but variable species, usually developing a conical head, or spreading and round-topped when exposed to gales near the coast, where it is invaluable as a wind-break. Europe, N Africa, SW Asia. It was possibly introduced to England during the Bronze Age.

**'Argenteo-variegata'** Leaves green, splashed and striped silvery-grey and white. A large tree is particularly conspicuous. A form of var. *vulgaris*. Long cultivated.

**ULMUS minor**—*continued*

**var. cornubiensis** (WEST.) RICHENS (*U. stricta* (AIT.) LINDL.) (*U. angustifolia* var. *cornubiensis* (WEST.) MELV.) (*U. carpinifolia* var. *cornubiensis* (WEST.) REHD.) "Cornish Elm". A familiar elm easily recognised by its dense, conical head of ascending branches, eventually attaining a large size and then more open and looser in growth. Leaves small, obovate or ovate; fruits glabrous. Occurs wild in Devon and Cornwall in England, and in Brittany in France, from where it was probably introduced to Cornwall in Anglo-Saxon times. An excellent maritime tree.

**'Dicksonii'** (*U. sarniensis* 'Dicksonii') (*U. sarniensis* 'Aurea') (*U.* 'Wheatleyi Aurea') "Dickson's Golden Elm". A very slow-growing tree with leaves of a beautiful bright golden yellow.

**'Jacqueline Hillier'** (*U. elegantissima* 'Jacqueline Hillier') A small to medium-sized, suckering shrub of dense habit. The slender, brown pubescent twigs are neatly clothed with small, double-toothed, scabrid leaves 2.5-3.5cm long. An unusual elm which was found in a garden in Birmingham several years ago. Its neat, dense habit lends itself to planting as a low hedge or for bonsai.

**var. lockii** (DRUCE) RICHENS (*U. plotii* DRUCE) "Lock's Elm". A large, erect tree with short, horizontal or ascending branches and long, pendulous branchlets. Leaves small, smooth above. Differs from the "Cornish Elm" in its looser habit and arching leader, particularly noticeable when young. A native of C and N England, most common in Lincolnshire. It is of uncertain origin and may be a sport of var. *minor* of which the original Plot's Elm was a form.

**'Louis van Houtte'** ('Van Houttei') A handsome tree with golden yellow foliage throughout the summer.

**'Sarniensis'** (*U. minor* var. *sarniensis* (LOUD.) DRUCE) (*U. sarniensis* (LOUD.) BANCROFT) (*U. carpinifolia* f. *sarniensis* (LOUD.) REHD.) (*U. wheatleyi* (BEAN) DRUCE) "Guernsey Elm" "Wheatley Elm". A large tree of conical habit with strictly ascending branches, developing a narrower, denser crown than the Cornish Elm. Leaves small, ovate to obovate, broader than those of the Cornish Elm. Fruits glabrous. One of the finest of all trees for roadside planting, especially near the coast. Occurs in Guernsey and the other Channel Islands. Commonly planted elsewhere. Probably a selection from N France. R.H. Richens, in his book *Elm*, has pointed out that we were instrumental in the early distribution of this tree.

**'Silvery Gem'** (*U. procera* 'Silvery Gem') Leaves with irregular but conspicuous creamy-white margin.

**'Purpurea'** (*U. sarniensis* 'Purpurea') A medium-sized tree with spreading branches. The leaves and shoots are suffused dull purple when young. Strong, vigorous shoots on young plants bear large, roughly hairy leaves.

**'Variegata'** (*U. carpinifolia* 'Variegata') Leaves densely mottled white, giving a silvery-grey effect.

**'Viminalis'** (*U. viminalis* LODD. ex BEAN) (*U. procera* 'Viminalis') (*U. antarctica* KIRCHN.) An extremely graceful, medium-sized tree recalling *Zelkova × verschaffeltii*, of slow growth, with arching and drooping branches. Leaves small, oblanceolate to narrowly oval, tapered at base, the margins deeply toothed. Long cultivated.

**'Viminalis Aurea'** (*U. viminalis* 'Aurea') (*U. campestris* 'Rosseelsii') (*U. campestris* 'Aurea') A picturesque form with leaves suffused golden yellow when young, becoming yellowish-green as the summer advances. C about 1865.

**'Viminalis Marginata'** (*U. viminalis* 'Marginata') (*U. viminalis* 'Argentea') Leaves mottled greyish-white, especially near the margins.

**var. vulgaris** (AIT.) RICHENS (*U. procera* SALISB.) (*U. campestris* L. in part) "English Elm". A large, stately tree inseparably associated with the English landscape. Shoots downy; leaves appearing earlier than those of the Wych Elm, oval or rounded, acute, rough to the touch above, sharply double-toothed. Fruits glabrous, but rarely produced. There are few more pleasing sights than a tall mature tree in autumn when the clear, butter-yellow of its fading leaves is intensified by the rays of the setting sun and a background mist. SW Europe. Probably introduced to England from NW Spain. It does not produce seed in this country but spreads extensively by suckers.

**montana** See *U. glabra*.

**ULMUS**—*continued*

**nitens** See *U. minor*.

   **var. wheatleyi** See *U. minor* 'Sarniensis'.

**parvifolia** JACQ. (*U. chinensis* PERS.) (*U. sieboldii*) "Chinese Elm". A medium-sized tree with young shoots densely pubescent. Leaves small, 2.5-8cm long, leathery and glossy green. Flowers produced in early autumn. One of the most splendid elms having the poise of a graceful *Nothofagus*, and with small, rich green leaves which persist halfway through the winter. We have never seen this tree affected by disease. N and C China, Korea, Taiwan, Japan. I 1794.

   **'Frosty'** A charming, slow-growing, shrubby form, the tiny, neatly-arranged leaves bearing white teeth.

   **'Pinnato-ramosa'** (*U. pumila* var. *arborea* HORT. not *U. pumila* var. *arborescens* LITV.) A small tree, recognisable by the pinnate arrangement of its small, bright green leaves. C 1894.

**plotii** See *U. minor* var. *lockii*.

**procera** See *U. minor* var. *vulgaris*.

   **'Viminalis'** See *U. minor* 'Viminalis'.

**pumila** L. "Dwarf Elm" "Siberian Elm". A variable species varying from a large shrub to a medium-sized tree, the latter being the form in general cultivation. Leaves ovate to ovate-lanceolate, 2.5-3.5cm long, thin in texture, simply toothed. Fruits glabrous. N Asia. I 1770.

   **var. arborea** See under *U.* 'Pinnato-ramosa'.

**racemosa** See *U. thomasii*.

**rubra** MUHL. (*U. fulva* MICHX.) (*U. elliptica* KOEHNE) "Slippery Elm" "Red Elm". A striking, medium-sized tree with a spreading head of branches. Twigs densely pubescent. Leaves large, oval or obovate, velvety-hairy beneath, rough to the touch above. Fruits reddish-brown. Its large velvety leaves make this one of the most distinct elms. C and E North America. C 1830.

**'Sapporo Autumn Gold'** (*U. japonica* × *U. pumila*). A fast-growing, medium-sized tree of spreading habit with glossy green leaves, red-tinged when young turning yellow-green in autumn. Selected at the University of Wisconsin from plants grown from seed of *U. pumila* sent from Japan where it had crossed with *U. japonica*. Proving resistant to the aggressive strain of Dutch Elm Disease.

**sarniensis** See *U. minor* 'Sarniensis'.

**serotina** SARG. A large tree forming a spreading head of drooping branches. Leaves oblong to obovate, slender-pointed, markedly unequal at base, bright glossy green above. Flowers produced during early autumn; fruits ciliate with silvery-white hairs. SE United States. C 1903.

**sieboldii** See *U. parvifolia*.

**stricta** See *U. minor* var. *cornubiensis*.

**thomasii** SARG. (*U. racemosa* THOMAS) "Rock Elm". A slow-growing, small to medium-sized tree of conical habit when young. Winter buds large and, like the young shoots, downy. Leaves oval to obovate, unequal at base and abruptly pointed, glabrous and glossy green above, downy beneath. Flowers in short racemes; fruits downy all over. E North America. I 1875.

**vegeta** See *U.* × *hollandica* 'Vegeta'.

   **'Commelin'** See *U.* × *hollandica* 'Commelin'.

**villosa** BRANDIS ex GAMBLE A large, noble tree of vigorous growth and wide-spreading habit with smooth, silvery-grey bark, becoming fissured and greyish-brown. Leaves of a fresh pale green and softly downy. W Himalaya. AM 1974.

**viminalis** See *U. minor* 'Viminalis'.

   **'Aurea'** See *U. minor* 'Viminalis Aurea'.

   **'Marginata'** See *U. minor* 'Viminalis Marginata'.

**wallichiana** PLANCH. A rare, medium-sized to large tree with downy, red-tinged young shoots and obovate, coarsely-toothed leaves ending in a slender point. Himalaya.

**wheatleyi** See *U. minor* 'Sarniensis'.

   **'Wredei Aurea'** See *U.* × *hollandica* 'Dampieri Aurea'.

**\*UMBELLULARIA** (NEES) NUTT.—**Lauraceae**—A monotypic evergreen genus resembling the Bay in general appearance and requiring a warm, sunny position in a well drained soil.

**californica** (HOOK. & ARN.) NUTT. "Californian Laurel" "Californian Bay". A strongly aromatic, large shrub or small to medium-sized tree of dense leafy habit. Leaves oblong to oblong-lanceolate, entire, bright green or yellowish-green in colour. Flowers small, yellowish-green, borne in small umbels during April, occasionally followed by oval, green fruits, 2.5cm long, turning dark purple when ripe. In exposed positions the young shoots are subject to injury by late spring frosts. The pungent aroma emitted by the leaves when crushed can cause a headache when inhaled. The "old school" of gardeners indulged in extravagant stories of the prostrate Dowager overcome by the powerful aroma. California and Oregon. Introduced by David Douglas in 1829.

**"UMBRELLA TREE"** See *Magnolia tripetala*.

**‡VACCINIUM** L.—**Ericaceae**—A large genus of some 450 species of evergreen and deciduous shrubs widely distributed over the N hemisphere, also occurring in SE Africa and on mountains in S America. They require much the same conditions as heathers, but are more tolerant of shade and moisture. In fact some species demand these conditions. While autumn colour of leaf and berry is their most notable attribute, their flowers and modest beauty at other seasons qualify them for inclusion in any representative collection of shrubs. Excellent subjects for extremely acid soils.

**angustifolium** AIT. (*V. pensylvanicum* var. *angustifolium* (AIT.) A. GRAY) "Low-bush Blueberry". A dwarf shrub of compact habit with thin, wiry twigs and bristle-toothed, lanceolate leaves, richly tinted in autumn, sometimes earlier. Flowers cylindrical or bell-shaped, white or red-tinted, produced in dense clusters in April and May. Berries blue-black, bloomy, sweet and edible. Grown commercially for its fruits in North America. NE North America.

**var. laevifolium** HOUSE (*V. pensilvanicum* LAM. not MILL.) A variable, taller-growing form with larger, lanceolate to narrowly oval or oblong leaves. I 1772. FCC 1890.

**arboreum** MARSH. "Farkleberry". A medium-sized to large, deciduous or semi-evergreen shrub, sometimes a tree of up to 10m in some of its native haunts. Leaves ovate to obovate, up to 5cm long, leathery, glabrous and dark glossy green above, giving rich autumn tints. Flowers white, bell-shaped, in small racemes during summer, followed by black inedible berries. S and E United States. I 1765.

**arctostaphylos** L. "Caucasian Whortleberry". A splendid, slow-growing shrub of medium size and loose, wide-spreading habit with reddish young shoots. Leaves large, up to 10 or even 13cm long, narrowly elliptic to obovate, reticulately veined and finely-toothed, turning purplish-red in autumn and often remaining until Christmas. The waxy, white or crimson-tinted, bell-shaped flowers are carried in conspicuous racemes in summer and again during autumn, followed by rounded, shining black berries. Caucasus. I 1800. AM 1970. AGM 1984.

**atrococcum** (A. GRAY) HELLER A small to medium-sized shrub with oval, entire leaves, densely pubescent beneath. Flowers urceolate, greenish-white, tinged red, carried in dense racemes during May, often before the leaves. Berries black and shining. It is closely related to *V. corymbosum* and, like that species, gives rich autumn colours. E North America. I before 1898.

**\*bracteatum** THUNB. A charming evergreen shrub up to 2m in height with narrowly oval, glabrous leaves, copper-red when young. The cylindrical or ovoid, fragrant, white flowers are borne in numerous leafy racemes during late summer and autumn, sometimes earlier. Berries red. Easily recognised when in flower by the presence of small, leaf-like bracts on the main flower-stalk. Japan, Korea, China, Taiwan. I 1829.

**caespitosum** MICHX. "Dwarf Bilberry". A dwarf, spreading shrub with green or reddish shoots and small, finely-toothed leaves. Flowers pinkish-white, borne singly in April-May followed by blue-black, bloomy berries. North America. I 1823.

**corymbosum** L. "Swampy Blueberry" "High-bush Blueberry". A colourful small to medium-sized shrub forming a dense thicket of erect branching stems. Leaves ovate to ovate-

**VACCINIUM corymbosum**—*continued*

lanceolate, up to 8.5cm long, bright green and reticulate, turning to vivid scarlet and bronze in autumn. The clusters of pale pink or white, urn-shaped flowers are borne in May. Berries comparatively large, black with a blue bloom, sweet and edible, like small, black grapes. Extensively cultivated in the United States for commerical fruit production. Several cultivars selected for fruit quality are also available. E North America. I 1765. AGM 1984.

**\*crassifolium** ANDR. "Creeping Blueberry". A dwarf evergreen shrub of creeping habit, with slender, reddish stems up to 15cm high. Leaves oval, shining green and leathery, densely crowding the twigs. The small, bell-shaped, rose-red flowers are borne in terminal racemes in May and June. Berries black. SE United States. I 1787.

**cylindraceum** SM. (*V. longiflorum* WIKSTR.) A superb, semi-evergreen species. An erect, medium-sized to large shrub with bright green, finely-toothed and reticulate leaves, often green until well into the New Year. Flowers cylindrical, 12mm long, densely packed in short racemes along the previous year's branchlets during late summer and autumn, red in bud, opening to pale yellow-green, tinged red, recalling *Agapetes serpens*. They are followed by cylindrical blue-black, bloomy berries. AM 1990 (for fruit). Azores.

**\*delavayi** FRANCH. A neat, compact, evergreen shrub slowly reaching 1.8m, densely set with small, box-like, leathery leaves which are usually notched at the apex. The tiny, pink-tinged whitish flowers are borne in small racemes terminating the shoots in late spring or early summer. Berries purplish-blue, rounded. In its native state it grows on cliffs and rocks and as an epiphyte on trees. Discovered by the Abbé Delavay in Yunnan. I by George Forrest before 1923. AM 1950.

**deliciosum** PIPER A dwarf, tufted, glabrous shrub, with oval or obovate leaves. The solitary, pinkish, globular flowers in May are replaced by sweet, edible, black, bloomy berries. NW United States. I 1920.

**\*floribundum** H.B.K. (*V. mortinia* BENTH.) A beautiful, small, evergreen shrub with attractive red young growths and small, ovate, dark green leaves, purplish-red when young, densely crowding the spray-like branches. Flowers cylindrical, rose-pink, carried in dense racemes in June. Berries red, edible. Although its native haunts are close to the equator, it is remarkably hardy in the southern counties. Ecuador. I about 1840. AM 1935 (as *V. mortinia*).

**†\*gaultheriifolium** (GRIFF.) HOOK. f. ex C.B. CL. A small to medium-sized, evergreen shrub of loose habit with bloomy young shoots. Leaves elliptic, 7.5-13cm long, acuminate, glossy green and attractively veined above, paler and covered by a blue-white bloom beneath, entire or minutely-toothed. Flowers white in corymbs in late summer. Related to *V. glauco-album*, but more graceful in habit, and with larger, slender-pointed leaves. E Himalaya, W China.

**\*glauco-album** HOOK. f. ex C.B. CL. An attractive evergreen shrub, suckering and forming patches 1.2-1.8m in height. Leaves comparatively large, oval or ovate, grey-green above, vividly blue-white beneath. Flowers cylindrical, pale pink, borne amongst conspicuous rosy, silvery-white bracts in racemes during May and June. Berries black, blue bloomy, often lasting well into winter. Liable to damage by frost in cold areas of the British Isles. E Himalaya, S Tibet. C 1900. AM 1931.

**hirsutum** BUCKL. "Hairy Huckleberry". A small, suckering shrub producing dense thickets of slender, hairy stems with ovate or elliptic, entire leaves. Flowers cylindrical, white tinged pink, produced in short racemes during May. Berries blue-black, rounded, covered with tiny, glandular hairs, sweet and edible. Often colouring well in autumn. SE United States. I 1887.

**\*macrocarpon** AIT. (*Oxycoccus macrocarpus* (AIT.) PURSH) "American Cranberry". A prostrate shrublet with slender, creeping, wiry stems and small, delicate, oval or oblong leaves, glaucous beneath. Flowers small, drooping, pink, the petals curving back to reveal a beak of yellow anthers, carried in short racemes during summer. Berries red, globular, 12-20mm across, edible but acid in flavour. Selected clones of this species are the commercially grown Cranberry of the United States. It requires a moist, peaty or boggy soil in which to thrive. E North America. I 1760.

**membranaceum** DOUGL. ex TORR. A small, erect-growing shrub with glabrous, angular branches and ovate to oblong, bright green leaves. Flowers urn-shaped, greenish-white

**VACCINIUM membranaceum**—*continued*

or pink-tinged, produced singly in the leaf axils in June, followed by purplish-black, edible berries. Closely related to our native Bilberry which it much resembles. C and E North America. I 1828.

**mortinia** See *V. floribundum*.

**\*moupinense** FRANCH. A neat-growing, dwarf, evergreen shrub of dense habit. Leaves narrowly obovate or ovate, 12mm long, leathery and usually entire, densely crowding the branches. Flowers urn-shaped, mahogany-red, borne on similarly coloured stalks in dense racemes during May and June. Berries purplish-black, rounded. Resembling *V. delavayi* in many ways, differing in its leaves which are rounded, not notched at the apex, and in its glabrous inflorescence. W China. I 1909 by Ernest Wilson.

**\*myrsinites** LAM. "Evergreen Blueberry". A dwarf, spreading, evergreen shrub of compact habit with small, neat, oval, finely-toothed leaves. Flowers white or pink-tinged, rose in bud, borne in terminal and axillary clusters during April and May. Berries blue-black. SE United States. C 1813.

**myrtillus** L. "Bilberry" "Whortleberry" "Whinberry" "Blaeberry". A familiar native species of heaths and moors, forming a dense, suckering patch of slender, bright green, angular stems. Leaves ovate, finely-toothed. Flowers globular, greenish-pink, produced singly or in pairs in the leaf axils from late April to June, followed by bloomy black edible berries. Europe to Caucasus and N Asia.

**†\*nummularia** HOOK. f. & THOMS. ex C.B. CL. This is probably the most attractive dwarf species in cultivation. A compact, evergreen shrub with bristly-hairy, arching shoots neatly clothed with a double row of small, leathery, dark glossy-green, orbicular-ovate leaves. The small, cylindrical rose-red flowers are borne in small, dense clusters at the ends of the shoots in May and June, followed by globular, black, edible berries. Although hardy only in mild localities, this choice little shrub makes an ideal alpine house plant. It is an excellent shrub for a not too dry, sheltered, shady bank. Himalaya. I about 1850. AM 1932.

**\*ovatum** PURSH "Box Blueberry". An attractive evergreen shrub of medium size and dense, compact habit. The 1-4cm long ovate to oblong, leathery leaves are bright coppery-red when young, becoming polished dark green, thickly crowding the downy branches. Flowers bell-shaped, white or pink, appearing in short racemes during May and June. Berries red at first, ripening to black. A useful evergreen for cutting. W North America. Introduced by David Douglas in 1826.

**\*oxycoccos** L. (*Oxycoccus palustris* PERS.) "Cranberry". A prostrate, native, evergreen shrublet of moorland and mountain bogs, producing far-reaching wiry stems bearing tiny, silver-backed leaves. The tiny, nodding flowers with pink, recurved petals and a yellow staminal beak are borne on short, erect, thread-like stems and recall those of a *Dodecatheon* (Shooting Star), but are much smaller. They appear during May and June and are followed by edible, red, rounded fruits which possess an agreeable acid taste. Requires a moist, peaty soil in which to thrive. Widely distributed in the cooler regions of the N hemisphere, from North America eastwards to Japan. C 1789.

**padifolium** SM. (*V. maderense* LINK) "Madeiran Whortleberry". A strong-growing, medium-sized shrub of rather stiff, erect growth. Leaves ovate, 2.5-6cm long, reticulately veined. Flowers bell-shaped, greenish, with a pale brown "eye" of stamens, appearing in clusters in June. Berries globular, purplish-blue. The leaves often remain green until the New Year. Remarkably hardy in view of its origin. Mts of Madeira. I 1777.

**pallidum** AIT. A small shrub with arching branches and oval, wavy-edged leaves which are slender-pointed, glaucous beneath. The pale pink, cylindrical flowers in June are followed by round, purplish-black bloomy berries, which are sweet and edible. Rich autumn colours. E United States. C 1878.

**parvifolium** SM. "Red Bilberry". A variable, small to medium-sized shrub, usually of erect habit, with sharply angled stems densely furnished with variably shaped, entire leaves. Flowers globular, pinkish, borne singly in the leaf axils in May and June, followed by conspicuous red berries, edible but acid. W North America to Alaska. I 1881.

**pensilvanicum** See *V. angustifolium* var. *laevifolium*.

**praestans** LAMB. A creeping shrub forming dense patches of shortly ascending shoots 3-10cm high. Leaves obovate to broadly ovate, 2.5-6cm long. Flowers bell-shaped, white

**VACCINIUM praestans**—*continued*

to reddish, borne singly or in clusters of 2 or 3 in June. The comparatively large, edible berries which follow are globular, 12mm across, bright glossy red, fragrant and sweet to the taste. A choice little species for a moist, cool place. Its leaves colour richly in autumn. NE Asia, Japan. Introduced by Ernest Wilson in 1914.

**\*retusum** (GRIFF.) HOOK. f. ex C.B. CL. A dwarf evergreen shrub slowly reaching 0.6-1m, with stiff, downy shoots and small, bright green, oval, leathery leaves which are retuse and mucronate at the apex. The small, urn-shaped, pink flowers are carried in short, terminal racemes in May. Rare and shy-flowering. E Himalaya. I about 1882.

**smallii** A. GRAY A small, erect-branched shrub with elliptic to broadly ovate leaves. Flowers bell-shaped, greenish-white to pinkish, borne 1-3 together in clusters in May and June. Berries purple-black, globular. Japan. I 1915.

**uliginosum** L. "Bog Whortleberry". An uncommon native species, a dwarf shrub of bushy habit with small, obovate or oval blue-green leaves. Flowers pale pink, single or in clusters in the leaf axils, in May and June. Berries globular, black and bloomy, sweet to the taste, but said to produce headache and giddiness if eaten in quantity. Cool moorland and mountainous regions of the N hemisphere including N England and Scotland.

**†\*urceolatum** HEMSL. An evergreen shrub producing strong, downy shoots, 1.2 or occasionally to 1.8m in height. Leaves thick and leathery, ovate-elliptic to oblong-elliptic, slenderly-pointed. Flowers urn-shaped, red-tinged, borne in axillary clusters in June. Berries globular, black. W China. I 1910.

**virgatum** AIT. "Rabbiteye Blueberry". An attractive small to medium-sized graceful shrub of elegant habit. The long, slender branches arch at their extremities and bear narrow ovate to lanceolate leaves, which turn to rich shades of red in autumn. Flowers white or pink-tinged, borne in axillary clusters in May and June. Berries black. E North America. I 1770.

**\*vitis-idaea** L. "Cowberry". A dwarf, creeping, evergreen shrub native of moors and woods in the north and west of the British Isles. Leaves small, box-like, glossy dark green above, paler and gland-dotted beneath. Flowers bell-shaped, white, tinged pink, borne in short, terminal racemes from June to August, followed by globular, red, edible berries, acid to the taste. An excellent ground-cover plant in shade. Northern regions of North America, Europe and Asia, and mountains of C and S Europe.

**'Koralle'** An attractive, free-fruiting form bearing relatively large, bright red berries. C 1969. AM 1976.

**subsp. minus** (LODD.) HULTEN ('Nana') An interesting miniature form with leaves half the size of the typical form. N United States, Canada. C 1825.

**'Variegata'** A form with creamy-white margined leaves, not very constant.

**†VALLA** MUTIS ex L. f.—**Elaeocarpaceae**—A monotypic genus.

**stipularis** L. f. An unusual large shrub or small tree. Leaves glabrous, somewhat fleshy and very variable, ovate and entire to three-lobed and ivy-like, deeply cordate at the base, grey and reticulate beneath, with small, kidney-shaped stipules. The deep pink flowers, with five, three-lobed petals and numerous stamens are usually borne in early summer. Best against a wall in most areas. Andes from Colombia to Bolivia. C 1928. AM 1978.

**VELLA** L. (*Pseudocytisus* KUNTZE)—**Cruciferae**—A small genus of 4 species of deciduous and evergreen shrubs, natives of the W Mediterranean region; some of the few shrubby members of the cabbage family.

**\*pseudocytisus** L. (*Pseudocytisus integrifolius* (SALISB.) REHD.) A small, evergreen shrub suitable for maritime exposure, with spiny bristly stems and small, obovate, bristly leaves. Long, erect, terminal racemes of small, yellow, four-petalled flowers in late May to early June. Requires a hot, dry, well drained position to succeed. Spain. C 1759.

**†VERBENA** L.—**Verbenaceae**—A large genus of some 250 species of mostly annual and perennial herbs, widely distributed but largely in S America. The following woody species is fairly hardy in most areas of the British Isles, enjoying a warm, sunny position in a well drained soil.

**VERBENA**—*continued*

**\*tridens** LAG. This very unusual shrub looks like an ungainly tree heath with its stiffly erect, rigid stems thickly crowded with tiny, downy, often spiny leaves. It attains a height of 1-1.5m. Flowers white to rosy-lilac, strongly vanilla-scented, produced in terminal spikes in July. In its native land it is often collected and used as fuel. Patagonia. Introduced by Clarence Elliott in 1928. AM 1934.

**VERONICA** The shubby members of this genus may be found under *Hebe* and *Parahebe*.

**†\*VESTIA** WILLD.—**Solanaceae**—A monotypic genus related to *Cestrum*, requiring the same conditions.

**foetida** (RUIZ & PAVON) HOFFMANNS. (*V. lycioides* WILLD.) A small, evergreen shrub of erect habit, foetid when bruised. Leaves oblong to obovate, 2.5-5cm long. Flowers nodding, tubular, pale yellow, profusely borne in the axils of the upper leaves from April to July, followed by small, yellow fruits. Only suitable for the milder areas of the British Isles, where it requires a warm, sunny position in a well drained soil. It has succeeded with us for several years planted against a south-east wall. Chile. I 1815.

**VIBURNUM** L.—**Caprifoliaceae**—A large genus of about 150 species of evergreen and deciduous shrubs and small trees, widely distributed mainly in N temperate regions, extending south to Malaysia and S America. Most have white flowers, some very fragrant, in flat heads or round corymbs, often followed by brightly coloured fruits. Several of the evergreen species are most effective in leaf whilst many of the deciduous species give rich autumn colour. Those species grown for their fruits often give the most satisfactory results when planted 2 or more together to assist cross-pollination.

**acerifolium** L. "Dockmackie". A small shrub up to 2m high, bearing three-lobed, maple-like leaves which are coarsely-toothed, and covered with black dots beneath. Flowers white, borne in terminal corymbs in June, but not particularly attractive. Fruits ovoid, red at first turning purplish-black later. The foliage turns a rich dark crimson in autumn. E North America. I 1736.

**alnifolium** See *V. lantanoides*.

**'Anne Russell'** See *V.* × *burkwoodii* 'Anne Russell'.

**\*atrocyaneum** C.B. CLARKE An attractive evergreen shrub of medium to large size and dense, bushy habit. Leaves ovate, acute, glandular-toothed, dark green above, copper-tinted when young. Fruits small, steely-blue, effective in winter. Sometimes grown under the name *V. wardii*. I 1931 by Kingdon-Ward. Himalaya.

**betulifolium** BATAL. A large, erect-growing shrub with ovate to rhomboid, coarsely-toothed leaves and corymbs of white flowers in June. A magnificent sight in autumn when the long swaying branches are heavy with innumerable bunches of red-currant-like fruits which persist into the winter. Unfortunately, they are none too freely borne on young plants. One of the finest fruiting shrubs but to ensure fruiting, plant several in a group from different sources. W and C China. Introduced by E.H. Wilson in 1901. AM 1936. FCC 1957.

**bitchiuense** MAK. A medium-sized shrub of slender, open habit similar to *V. carlesii* to which it is closely related but rather taller and more lax. Leaves ovate-elliptic, dark metallic green. The sweetly-scented, flesh-pink flowers are produced in clusters during late April and May. Japan. I 1911. AGM 1948.

× **bodnantense** STEARN (*V. farreri* × *V. grandiflorum*). A medium-sized to large shrub of strong, upright habit with densely-packed clusters of sweetly-scented, rose-tinted flowers, which are freely produced over several weeks from October onwards. Its flowers are remarkably frost-resistant and provide a cheering sight on a cold winter's day. A splendid hybrid, first raised at the Royal Botanic Garden, Edinburgh in 1933 and later at Bodnant in 1935.

**'Charles Lamont'** Similar in vigour and habit to 'Dawn' but flowers of a purer pink resembling *V. farreri*. One of the original seedlings raised at Edinburgh.

**'Dawn'** The first-named clone, a vigorous, hardy shrub with leaves approaching those of *V. grandiflorum* and ample clusters of richly fragrant flowers during late autumn and winter. Anthers pink. AM 1947. AGM 1984.

**VIBURNUM** × **bodnantense**—*continued*

'**Deben**' A lovely clone producing clusters of sweetly-scented flowers which are pink in bud, opening white during mild spells from October to April. Anthers cream. AM 1962. FCC 1965. AGM 1984.

**bracteatum** REHD. A rare shrub of medium size related to *V. dentatum*, with rounded leaves and cymose clusters of white flowers in May and June, followed by bluish-black fruits. The name refers to the conspicuous bractlets which accompany the flowers. SE United States (Georgia). C 1904.

**buddlejifolium** C.H. WRIGHT A medium-sized, nearly evergreen shrub of distinctive appearance. Leaves oblong-lanceolate, up to 20cm long, pale green and softly pubescent above, thickly grey-felted beneath. Flowers white, borne in clusters 7.5cm across, in June. Fruits red at first, finally black. C China. I 1900 by Ernest Wilson.

**burejaeticum** REG. & HERD. A large shrub with downy young shoots and ovate or elliptic leaves, pubescent beneath. Flowers white produced in downy, cymose clusters during May. Fruits bluish-black. A rare species akin to *V. lantana*. Manchuria, N China. C 1900.

\* × **burkwoodii** BURKW. & SKIPW. ex ANON (*V. carlesii* × *V. utile*). A medium-sized, evergreen shrub, taller-growing than *V. carlesii*, from which it inherits its clusters of fragrant, pink-budded, white flowers, produced from January to May. Its ovate leaves are dark shining green above and brownish-grey-felted beneath. Raised by Messrs Burkwood and Skipwith in 1924. AM 1929. AGM 1984.

'**Anne Russell**' A lovely hybrid with clusters of fragrant flowers. The result of a backcross with *V. carlesii*. Raised about 1951. AM and Cory Cup 1957. AGM 1984.

'**Chenaultii**' A medium-sized, semi-evergreen shrub, similar in general appearance to *V.* × *burkwoodii* and with the same qualities.

'**Fulbrook**' A medium-sized shrub producing clusters of comparatively large, sweetly-scented flowers which are pink in bud opening white. Like 'Anne Russell' the result of a backcross with *V. carlesii*. AM 1957. AGM 1984.

'**Mohawk**' A backcross with *V. carlesii* raised at the U.S. National Arboretum, Washington and selected in 1959. Flowers bright red in bud opening white, red on the outside, strongly fragrant. Leaves glossy green, orange-red in autumn.

'**Park Farm Hybrid**' A strong-growing shrub of more spreading habit than typical *V.* × *burkwoodii*, and with fragrant, slightly larger flowers produced in April and May. AM 1949.

\***calvum** REHD. (*V. schneiderianum* HAND.-MAZZ.) A medium-sized to large, evergreen shrub, akin to *V. tinus*, with ovate or elliptic, wavy-edged, sage-green leaves. The corymbs of small white flowers appear in June and July, to be followed by glossy, bluish-black fruits. W China. C 1933.

**canbyi** See *V. dentatum*.

× **carlcephalum** BURKW. & SKIPW. ex A.V. PIKE (*V. carlesii* × *V. macrocephalum*). A splendid medium-sized shrub of compact habit, producing rounded corymbs, 10-13cm across, of comparatively large, very fragrant, pink-budded, white flowers in May. The leaves often colour richly in autumn. Raised about 1932. AM 1946. AGM 1984.

'**Cayuga**' A backcross with *V. carlesii* raised at the U.S. National Arboretum, Washington and selected in 1960. It is more compact than the typical form with smaller but more profuse heads of fragrant white flowers pink in bud.

**carlesii** HEMSL. One of the most popular of all shrubs. A medium-sized shrub of rounded habit, with ovate, downy leaves which are dull green above, greyish beneath, often colouring in autumn. The rounded clusters of pure white flowers are pink in bud and emit a strong, sweet daphne-like fragrance during April and May. Fruits jet black. Korea. I 1902. AM 1908. FCC 1909.

'**Aurora**' An outstanding selection made by the Slieve Donard Nursery, with red flower buds opening to pink and deliciously fragrant. AGM 1984.

'**Charis**' Another Donard selection, extremely vigorous in growth, bearing flowers which are red in bud, passing to pink and finally white, and richly scented.

'**Diana**' A strong-growing clone of compact habit with flower-buds opening red, passing to pink, strongly fragrant. Young foliage with a distinct purple tinge.

**VIBURNUM**—*continued*

‡**cassinoides** L. "Withe-rod". A medium-sized shrub of rounded habit with scurfy young shoots. The ovate-elliptic, leathery, dull dark green leaves are bronze-coloured when unfolding and in autumn change to crimson and scarlet. The small, creamy-white flowers in June are replaced by rounded, red fruits changing to metallic blue, finally black. E North America. Not satisfactory on thin soils over chalk. I 1761.

'**Nanum**' ('Bullatum') A remarkable, slow-growing shrub, having large, peculiarly-formed, wavy leaves which colour richly in autumn.

'**Chenaultii**' See *V.* × *burkwoodii* 'Chenaultii'.

'**Chesapeake**' (*V.* × *carlcephalum* 'Cayuga' × *V. utile*). A small shrub forming a dense mound broader than tall with dark glossy green, long-persistent leaves. Flowers pink in bud opening white, followed by red fruits turning black.

*****cinnamomifolium** REHD. A large, handsome, evergreen shrub with large, dark glossy, leathery leaves, similar to those of *V. davidii*, but thinner and entire, or almost so. Flowers small, dull white, carried in cymose clusters, 10-15cm across, in June followed in autumn by small, shining, egg-shaped, blue-black fruits. An imposing species when well grown, it requires a more sheltered position than *V. davidii* and is equally happy in semi-shade. China. Introduced by Ernest Wilson in 1904.

‡**corylifolium** HOOK. f. & THOMS. A medium-sized shrub with reddish-brown, hairy shoots and broad, ovate or rounded, hairy leaves which colour attractively in autumn. Flowers white, carried in flattened heads during May and June. Fruits bright red, long-lasting. E Himalaya, C and W China. I 1907.

**cotinifolium** D. DON A medium-sized to large shrub with densely hairy young shoots and leaf undersurfaces. Leaves broadly ovate to rounded, up to 13cm long, sometimes turning crimson in autumn and hanging for several weeks. Flowers white, flushed pink, borne in terminal cymes in May; fruits ovoid, red then black. Related to our native *V. lantana*. Afghanistan, Himalaya. I 1830.

*****cylindricum** BUCH.-HAM. ex D. DON (*V. coriaceum* BLUME) A large, evergreen shrub or occasionally a small tree, with glabrous, warty shoots and comparatively large, narrowly oval or oblong, to broadly ovate, dull green leaves, paler beneath, older leaves tending to hang. The upper surface is covered by a thin, waxy film which cracks and turns grey when bent or rubbed. The characteristic tubular, white flowers have protruding, lilac stamens and are carried in conspicuous flattened heads from July to September. Fruits egg-shaped, black. Subject to injury in severe winters. Himalaya, W China. I 1881.

**dasyanthum** REHD. A medium-sized shrub of upright habit with ovate, slender-pointed leaves, glabrous except for hairs on the veins and in the vein axils beneath. Flowers white, borne in branched corymbs in June and July, followed by showy bunches of bright red, egg-shaped fruits. Closely related to *V. hupehense*. C China. I 1907 by Ernest Wilson. AM 1916.

*****davidii** FRANCH. A small, evergreen shrub of compact habit, generally forming a low, wide-spreading mound and creating good ground cover. The large, narrowly oval, leathery leaves are conspicuously three-nerved and are a glossy dark green above, paler beneath. Flowers small, dull white, borne in terminal cymes in June. The bright turquoise-blue, egg-shaped fruits are never too plentiful but are particularly striking during winter, combining effectively with the lustrous green foliage. Several plants should be planted together to effect cross-pollination. Some plants seem dominantly male and others female whilst others are possibly mules, it is all in the luck of the draw. A popular, widely planted species introduced from W China by Ernest Wilson in 1904. AM 1912. AM 1971 (to female plant). AGM 1984.

**dentatum** L. (*V. canbyi* SARG.) (*V. pubescens* var. *canbyi* (REHD.) BLAKE) "Southern Arrow Wood". A medium-sized to large shrub, bearing broad ovate to rounded, coarsely-toothed leaves which are hairy beneath at least on the veins. Flowers white, borne in slender-stalked cymes during May and June. Fruits egg-shaped, blue-black. The strong, straight basal shoots are said to have been used for making arrows by the native Indians. E North America. I 1736.

var. **lucidum** AIT. (*V. recognitum* FERN.) "Arrow Wood". Leaves glossy green and glabrous, except for occasional axillary tufts beneath. Has been confused with the typical form.

**VIBURNUM dentatum**—*continued*

> **var. pubescens** AIT. (*V. pubescens* (AIT.) PURSH) Leaves thicker and more hairy beneath. I 1731.

**dilatatum** THUNB. An excellent shrub of medium size, with downy young shoots and ovate to obovate or rounded, coarsely-toothed leaves, hairy on both surfaces. Flowers pure white, pungently scented, produced in numerous trusses in late May and June. Fruits vivid red, borne in heavy bunches and often lasting well into winter. Does particularly well in the eastern counties. Japan. I before 1875. AM 1968.

> **'Catskill'** A seedling selected at the U.S. National Arboretum in 1958. Dense, mound-like habit to 1.5m tall and twice as much across. Leaves smaller, colouring well in autumn.

> **f. xanthocarpum** REHD. A form with yellow fruits. AM 1936.

**edule** (MICHX.) RAF. (*V. pauciflorum* (RAF.) TORR. & A. GRAY) "Mooseberry". A small, straggling shrub with broad, oval or rounded leaves, weakly three-lobed at apex. Flowers white, produced in small clusters during May. Fruits red. Requires a moist, shaded position. North America. I 1880.

**erosum** THUNB. A medium-sized, compact shrub with sharply-toothed, rounded, almost sessile leaves. Flowers white, produced in cymes during May, followed in autumn by red fruits. Not as a rule free-fruiting. Japan. I 1844 by Robert Fortune.

†**erubescens** WALL. A medium-sized shrub or occasionally a small tree with ovate to obovate, acuminate leaves. Flowers fragrant, white, tinted pink, borne in loose, pendulous clusters in July. One of the few viburnums with paniculate flower-clusters. Fruits red then black. A lovely shrub, but too tender for cold or exposed gardens. Himalaya.

> **var. gracilipes** REHD. A perfectly hardy form with elliptic, usually glabrous leaves and longer panicles of fragrant flowers. Free-fruiting. C China. I 1910 by Ernest Wilson. FCC 1988.

**'Eskimo'** (*V.* × *carlcephalum* 'Cayuga' × *V. utile*). A small, semi-evergreen shrub of dense habit with leathery, dark glossy green leaves. Compact, snowball-like inflorescences, 7.5cm across, of white flowers open from creamy buds tinged with pink.

**farreri** STEARN (*V. fragrans* BUNGE not LOISEL.) A medium-sized to large shrub with the primary branches stiff and erect but as the shrub ages it forms a broad rounded outline. Leaves oval or obovate, strongly-toothed and with conspicuous, parallel veins, bronze when young. Flowers produced in both terminal and lateral clusters, pink in bud, opening white, sweetly-scented. Fruits red, only occasionally produced in cultivation. One of the most popular of all shrubs and a favourite for the winter garden. Its flowers appear in November and continue through winter. N China. First introduced by William Purdom in 1910, later by Reginald Farrer. AM 1921 (as *V. fragrans*). AGM 1984.

> **'Candidissimum'** ('Album') A distinct form with green unfolding leaves and pure white flowers. AM 1926.

> **'Farrer's Pink'** Deep pink in bud opening white flushed pink. Flowering profusely in late autumn and early winter.

> **'Nanum'** ('Compactum') A dwarf form of dense mound-like habit; not free-flowering. AM 1937.

**foetens** DECNE. A beautiful, fragrant, winter-flowering shrub of medium size. It is closely related to *V. grandiflorum*, differing in its looser, more spreading habit, large, smoother leaves and its white flowers which are occasionally pale pink in bud, opening from January to March. Fruits are said to be red turning to black. It is not one of the easiest plants to make happy. It seems to appreciate a good deep moist loam in half shade and grows well on chalk on the site of our West Hill nursery in Winchester. W Himalaya. C 1937.

**foetidum** WALL. (*V. foetidum* var. *ceanothoides* (C.H. WRIGHT) HAND.-MAZZ.) (*V. ceanothoides* C.H. WRIGHT) A medium-sized to large semi-evergreen shrub with oval to oblong leaves which may be entire or coarsely-toothed and are often three-lobed at the apex. Flowers white, with purple anthers, borne in rounded clusters in July. Fruits scarlet-crimson. Large specimens in full fruit are extremely effective in autumn. Himalaya, W China. I 1901 by Ernest Wilson. AM 1934.

> **var. ceanothoides** See *V. foetidum*.

**fragrans** See *V. farreri*.

**VIBURNUM**—*continued*

**'Fulbrook'** See *V.* × *burkwoodii* 'Fulbrook'.

‡**furcatum** BLUME A large shrub closely related to and resembling *V. lantanoides*, but of more upright habit. Leaves broadly ovate or rounded, up to 15cm long, conspicuously veined and colouring richly over a long period during late summer and autumn. Flowers in May, in flattened terminal corymbs, surrounded by several sterile ray-florets, resembling a lacecap hydrangea. Fruits red, becoming black at maturity. A beautiful species of elegant charm, an excellent woodland plant. Japan, Taiwan. I 1892. AM 1944.

\* × **globosum** COOMBES (*V. calvum* × *V. davidii*). A small to medium-sized, evergreen shrub of dense, rounded habit. Leaves leathery, narrowly-elliptic to lanceolate, 8-12cm long, shallowly and distantly toothed, sometimes twisted or undulate, dark green and reticulate above, borne on slender, reddish petioles. The small white flowers are produced in flat-topped clusters in late spring and often at other times of the year. Fruits ovoid, bluish-black. An interesting hybrid which occurred in our West Hill nursery, Winchester in 1964. It was raised from seed collected from *V. davidii* which grew close to a specimen of *V. calvum*. The habit is intermediate between those of the parents, but much more dense and compact than either.

**'Jermyns Globe'** The best clone, of dense, rounded habit, selected from the original seedlings.

**grandiflorum** WALL. ex DC. (*V. nervosum* AUCT. not D. DON) A medium-sized shrub of stiff, upright habit and related to *V. farreri*. Leaves elliptic to ovate, of firm texture with parallel veins. Flowers fragrant, carmine-red in bud, opening deep pink, fading to blush, produced in dense clusters during February and March. It differs from *V. farreri* in its more hairy, multi-veined leaves and slightly larger individual flowers. Himalaya. I 1914. AM 1937.

**'Snow White'** (Lowndes 1409) Flowers deep pink in bud, nearly white inside when open, flushed pink on the backs of the lobes. I from Nepal by Col Donald Lowndes in 1950. AM 1970. FCC 1974.

\***harryanum** REHD. A medium-sized shrub of dense, bushy growth. A distinct species on account of its small, neat, orbicular leaves which are dark green above and 1-2cm long. On strong shoots they appear in whorls of 3. The small white flowers appear in late spring; fruits ovoid, shining black. Introduced by Ernest Wilson from China in 1904, and named after Sir Harry Veitch who did more than any other nurseryman to introduce new plants to western gardens.

\***henryi** HEMSL. A medium-sized, evergreen shrub of open, erect habit with rather stiff branches and narrowly elliptic, glossy green, leathery leaves recalling those of *Ilex fargesii*. Flowers white, fragrant, carried in pyramidal panicles in June followed by colourful, bright red, then black, ellipsoid fruits. C China (Hubei). First discovered by Augustine Henry in 1887. Introduced by E.H. Wilson in 1901. FCC 1910.

**hessei** See *V. wrightii* 'Hessei'.

× **hillieri** STEARN (*V. erubescens* × *V. henryi*). A semi-evergreen shrub of medium size with spreading and ascending branches and narrowly oval leaves which are copper-tinted when unfolding and suffused bronze-red in winter. Flowers creamy-white, profusely borne in panicles in June. Fruits red, finally black. An attractive hybrid which originated in our nurseries in 1950. Wilson also reports having seen this hybrid in W Hubei (China).

**'Winton'** The original selected clone which received the Award of Merit in 1956.

**hupehense** REHD. A very tough shrub of medium size with broadly ovate, coarsely-toothed leaves. Flowers white in clusters during May and June. The egg-shaped, orange-yellow, finally red fruits are conspicuous in autumn. The leaves colour early in autumn. C China. I 1908 by Ernest Wilson. AM 1952.

**ichangense** REHD. A small to medium-sized, slender-branched shrub with ovate to ovate-lanceolate, slender-pointed leaves. Flowers white, fragrant, borne in clusters during May. Fruits bright red. C and W China. I 1901 by Ernest Wilson.

\***japonicum** (THUNB.) SPRENG. (*V. macrophyllum* BLUME) A handsome, medium-sized, evergreen shrub with firm, leathery, often bullate leaves up to 15cm long and 10cm wide. They may be entire or undulately-toothed in the upper half and are glossy dark green above, paler and minutely punctate beneath; petioles stout, grooved above. Flowers white,

**VIBURNUM japonicum**—*continued*

fragrant, borne in dense, rounded trusses in June, but not on young plants; fruits red. Japan. I about 1879 by Charles Maries.

**'Jermyns Globe'** See *V.* × *globosum* 'Jermyns Globe'.

× **juddii** REHD. (*V. bitchiuense* × *V. carlesii*). A delightful small to medium-sized shrub of bushy habit, freely producing its terminal clusters of sweetly-scented, pink-tinted flowers during April and May. A plant of better constitution than *V. carlesii* and less susceptible to aphis attack. Raised in 1920 by William Judd, one-time propagator at the Arnold Arboretum. AGM 1984.

**kansuense** BATAL. A medium-sized, loose-growing shrub with deeply lobed, maple-like leaves. The pink-flushed, white flowers in June and July are followed by red fruits. Succeeds best in half shade. Not very lime-tolerant. W China. I 1908 by Ernest Wilson.

**lantana** L. "Wayfaring Tree". A large, native shrub, a familiar hedgerow plant, particularly on the chalk downs of the South. Leaves broadly ovate, covered beneath as are the young shoots with a dense, stellate tomentum, sometimes turning a dark crimson in autumn. Flowers creamy-white in May and June, followed by oblong fruits which slowly mature from red to black. C and S Europe, N Asia Minor, N Africa.

**var. discolor** HUTER (*V. maculatum* PANTOCZEK) An interesting, geographical form from the Balkans with smaller, neater leaves which are white or pale grey tomentose beneath.

**'Mohican'** A form of dense habit with dark green foliage and orange-red fruits. Selected in 1956 at the U.S. National Arboretum, Washington.

**'Variegatum'** ('Auratum') Young growths yellowish; not very exciting.

‡**lantanoides** MICHX. (*V. alnifolium* MARSH.) "Hobble Bush". A distinct and attractive shrub of medium size, with comparatively large, strongly-veined leaves. In shape they are broadly ovate or orbicular, 10-20cm long, downy above at first, more densely so beneath, turning a deep claret in autumn. The first inflorescences appear in May and June and recall those of a lacecap hydrangea, having a marginal row of conspicuous white, sterile florets. Fruits red, turning to blackish-purple. Thrives in woodland conditions. A low suckering shrub as seen in the forests of New England but reaching 2-2.5m in cultivation in this country. E North America. I 1820. AM 1952.

**lentago** L. "Sheep-berry". A strong-growing, large shrub or small tree of erect habit, with ovate to obovate leaves, dark shining green above, giving rich autumn tints. Flowers creamy-white, produced in terminal cymes during May and June. Fruits blue-black and bloomy, like small Merryweather damsons. E North America. I 1761.

**lobophyllum** GRAEBN. A medium-sized shrub allied to *V. betulifolium* and *V. dilatatum*. Leaves variable in shape, usually ovate or rounded with an abrupt point and coarsely-toothed. Flowers white followed by bright red fruits. W China. Introduced by Ernest Wilson in 1901. AM 1947.

**macrocephalum** FORT. (*V. macrocephalum* f. *keteleeri* (CARR.) REHD.) A semi-evergreen, medium-sized shrub of rounded habit. Leaves ovate to elliptic, 5-10cm long. Flowers white, in lacecap-like heads margined with large, sterile florets. China.

**'Sterile'** Flowers sterile, gathered together in large, globular heads, 7.5-15cm across, like the sterile forms of *Hydrangea macrophylla*, giving a spectacular display in May. Best grown against a warm, sunny wall in cold districts. A garden form, introduced from China in 1844 by Robert Fortune. AM 1927.

**molle** MICHX. A medium-sized shrub with broadly ovate to rounded, coarsely-toothed leaves. Flowers white in flattened heads in June. Fruits blue-black. The bark of older stems is flaky. N United States. I 1923.

**nervosum** See *V. grandiflorum*.

‡**nudum** L. A medium-sized shrub of upright growth, related to *V. cassinoides*, but differing in its dark glossy green leaves, colouring attractively in autumn. Flowers yellowish-white, borne in long-stalked cymes in June. Fruits oval, blue-black. E United States. I 1752.

†\***odoratissimum** KER.-GAWL. A large, evergreen shrub of noble aspect, bearing striking glossy green, oval to obovate, leathery leaves. They vary in size from 10-20cm long and are shallowly serrate in the upper half. Older leaves often colour richly during winter and early spring. The fragrant, white flowers are carried in large, conical panicles during late summer; fruits red turning black. A magnificent species for gardens in mild areas. India, Burma, S China, Taiwan, Japan. I about 1818.

**VIBURNUM**—*continued*

**'Oneida'** (*V. dilatatum* × *V. lobophyllum*). An erect, medium-sized shrub with dark green leaves of variable shape and size. The creamy-white, pungently scented flowers are abundantly produced in May and intermittently throughout summer and are followed by glossy, dark red fruits which persist well into winter. A hybrid of American origin.

**opulus** L. "Guelder Rose" "Water Elder". A large, vigorous shrub of spreading habit with three to five-lobed, maple-like leaves which colour richly in autumn. The flattened corymbs in June or July are edged with showy white ray-florets, the effect being similar to that of a lacecap hydrangea. These are followed in autumn by glistening red, translucent fruits which persist long into winter. A familiar native of hedgerows and woods, particularly rampant in wet or boggy situations. Europe, N and W Asia, N Africa (Algeria).

**'Aureum'** A striking form of compact habit with bright yellow leaves. Tends to burn in full sun.

**'Compactum'** A small shrub of dense, compact habit which flowers and fruits freely. AM 1962. AGM 1984.

**'Fructuluteo'** Fruits lemon-yellow, with a strong pink tinge, maturing to chrome-yellow with a faint hint of pink.

**'Nanum'** A curious, dwarf form of dense, tufted habit; seldom, if ever, flowering but often colouring in autumn.

**'Notcutt's Variety'** A selected form with larger flowers and fruits. AM 1930. AGM 1984.

**'Roseum'** ('Sterile') "Snowball". One of the most attractive and popular hardy, flowering shrubs. The flowers are all sterile and gathered into conspicuous, globular, creamy-white heads. AGM 1984.

**'Sterile'** See 'Roseum'.

**'Xanthocarpum'** Fruits differing from those of 'Fructuluteo' in being clear golden yellow at all stages, becoming a little darker and almost translucent when ripe. AM 1932. FCC 1966. AGM 1984.

**'Park Farm Hybrid'** See *V.* × *burkwoodii* 'Park Farm Hybrid'.

**parvifolium** HAYATA A rare, small shrub with small, ovate to obovate, toothed leaves up to 2.5cm in length. Flowers white, followed by globular, red fruits. Taiwan.

**pauciflorum** See *V. edule.*

**phlebotrichum** SIEB. & ZUCC. A medium-sized shrub of slender habit, with strong, erect shoots and narrow, ovate-oblong, acuminate, bronze-green leaves which, in the adult state, have spiny teeth and are prettily net-veined. Flowers white or pink-tinged in small nodding trusses. Fruits crimson-red. Rich autumn tints. Japan. C 1890.

**plicatum** THUNB. (*V. plicatum* f. *tomentosum* (THUNB.) REHD.) (*V. tomentosum* THUNB. not LAM.) A wide-spreading, medium-sized to large shrub of architectural value, with a distinctive mode of branching. The branches are produced in layers creating, in time, an attractive and characteristic tiered effect. The bright green pleated, ovate to oval leaves are followed in May and early June by 7.5-10cm wide umbels of small, fertile, creamy-white flowers surrounded by conspicuous, white ray-florets. The inflorescences sit in double rows along the upper sides of the branches giving the appearance, from a distance, of icing on a cake. Fruits red, finally black. The leaves are often attractively tinted in autumn. China, Japan, Taiwan. I about 1865.

**'Grandiflorum'** Similar to 'Sterile', with larger heads of sterile, white florets flushed pink at the margins. AM 1961. AGM 1984.

**'Lanarth'** A very fine form resembling 'Mariesii', but stronger in growth and less horizontal in habit of branching. AM 1930.

**'Mariesii'** A superb shrub with a tabulate arrangement of branching. Its abundance of flower gives the effect of a snow-laden bush. The ray florets are also relatively large and the leaves colour well in autumn. AGM 1984.

**'Nanum Semperflorens'** ('Watanabe') A slow-growing form of dense habit with white flowers produced over a long period during summer and autumn. It was found as a seedling in the wild in Japan by Kenji Watanabe about 1956. Dwarf plants reaching 50cm and found in the wild at the foot of Mt Fuji in Japan have been described as f. *watanabei* ( HONDA) HARA.

**VIBURNUM plicatum**—*continued*

**'Pink Beauty'** A charming selection in which the ray-florets change to a delightful pink as they age. Free-fruiting.

**'Rowallane'** Similar to 'Lanarth', but a little less vigorous. The marginal ray-florets are larger and it has the added attraction of usually producing a conspicuous show of fruits which very seldom occur on 'Mariesii'. Good autumn colour. AM 1942. FCC 1956.

**'Shasta'** A profusely flowering, wide-spreading form, similar to 'Lanarth' but with larger ray-florets. Fruits bright red, turning black. Raised at the U.S. National Arboretum in 1970. AM 1988.

**'Sterile'** "Japanese Snowball". This popular shrub of medium size and dense, spreading habit is in the front rank of hardy, ornamental shrubs. The conspicuous, white sterile florets are gathered into globular heads 5-7.5cm across. They are produced in late May and early June, in a double row along the length of each arching branch, persisting for several weeks. This is a garden form, long cultivated in both China and Japan. It was introduced from the former by Robert Fortune in 1844 several years before the wild form. FCC 1893. Previously listed as *V. plicatum* of which it is a selected form.

**'Summer Snowflake'** A medium-sized shrub with tiered branches and lacecap-like flowerheads in May and through summer. Leaves red to purple in autumn.

**f. tomentosum** See *V. plicatum*.

**'Watanabe'** See 'Nanum Semperflorens'.

*****'Pragense'** (*V. rhytidophyllum* × *V. utile*). An attractive, spreading, evergreen shrub of medium to large size. The elliptic, corrugated leaves, 5-10cm long, are lustrous dark green above and white-felted beneath. Flowers creamy-white, buds pink, produced in terminal branched cymes during May. This hybrid was raised in Prague and is extremely hardy.

***propinquum** HEMSL. A small to medium-sized evergreen shrub of dense, compact habit. Leaves three-nerved, ovate to elliptic, polished dark green above, paler beneath. Flowers greenish-white, borne in umbellate cymes during summer, followed by blue-black, egg-shaped fruits. C and W China, Taiwan. I 1901 by Ernest Wilson.

**'Lanceolatum'** A form with narrower leaves.

**prunifolium** L. "Black Haw". A large, erect shrub, or small tree, with shining, bright green, ovate to obovate leaves which colour richly in autumn, and clusters of white flowers in April and May. Fruits comparatively large, bloomy, blue-black, sweet and edible. E North America. I 1731.

**pubescens** See *V. dentatum* var. *pubescens*.

**var. canbyi** See *V. dentatum*.

**rafinesquianum** SCHULT. "Downy Arrow-Wood". A medium-sized to large shrub with ovate to elliptic, coarsely-toothed, polished leaves. Flowers white, borne in cymes during May and June. Fruits blue-black. The leaves often colour richly in autumn. NE United States, E Canada. C 1883.

* × **rhytidocarpum** LEM. (*V. buddlejifolium* × *V. rhytidophyllum*). A large, more or less evergreen shrub, intermediate in habit and leaf between its parents. C 1936.

× **rhytidophylloides** SURING. (*V. lantana* × *V. rhytidophyllum*). A very vigorous, large shrub with elliptic-ovate to oblong-ovate, rugose leaves and stout cymes of yellowish-white flowers. In general effect intermediate between the parents. A splendid shrub for screen planting.

**'Alleghany'** Leaves leathery and dark green, fruits brilliant red ripening to black. Selected at the U.S. National Arboretum, Washington in 1958 from a batch of seedlings obtained from a plant raised by crossing *V. rhytidophyllum* with *V. lantana* 'Mohican'.

**'Holland'** The name given to the original clone, raised about 1925 and described above.

***rhytidophyllum** HEMSL. A large, fast-growing, handsome, evergreen shrub, with large, elliptic to oblong, attractively-corrugated leaves which are dark glossy green above, densely grey tomentose beneath. The small, creamy-white flowers are produced in stout, tomentose cymes during May. Fruits oval, red, finally black. It is necessary to plant 2 or more in close proximity, as single specimens do not fruit freely. A magnificent foliage shrub and a splendid chalk plant, creating the effect of a large-leaved *Rhododendron*. C and W China. Introduced by Ernest Wilson in 1900. FCC 1907. AGM 1984.

**VIBURNUM rhytidophyllum**—*continued*

**'Roseum'** A form with rose-pink-tinted flowers. The plant we grow originated in our nurseries.

**'Variegatum'** Leaves conspicuously blotched with pale yellow when young turning to creamy-white. Of curiosity value only. C 1935.

**rigidum** See *V. tinus* subsp. *rigidum*.

**rufidulum** RAF. "Southern Black Haw". A large shrub of rigid habit with rusty-tomentose young shoots. Leaves elliptic-obovate, leathery, polished green, often colouring in autumn. Flowers white; fruits blue-black. SE United States. I 1883.

**rugosum** See *V. tinus* subsp. *rigidum*.

**sargentii** KOEHNE A large, vigorous shrub related to and resembling *V. opulus*, but the maple-like leaves are larger, the bark corky and the flowers have purple anthers (not yellow). The fruits also are a little larger, of a bright, translucent red, lasting well into winter. Rich autumn tints. NE Asia. I 1892. AM 1967.

**f. flavum** REHD. ('Fructuluteo') An unusual form with translucent yellow fruits. The flowers have yellow anthers.

**'Onondaga'** A splendid form with deep maroon young leaves turning reddish-purple in autumn. Fertile flowers deep red in bud, surrounded by a ring of white, sterile flowers, the inflorescence contrasting effectively with the young foliage. A seedling raised at the U.S. National Arboretum, Washington and selected in 1959. Although originally described as globose, it has retained a strong upright habit here.

**scabrellum** CHAPM. Medium-sized shrub related to *V. dentatum* with scabrous shoots and ovate to ovate-oblong leaves. The white flowers in June are followed by blue-black, rounded fruits. E United States. C 1830.

**schensianum** MAXIM. A medium-sized to large shrub with downy young shoots and ovate to elliptic leaves which are downy beneath. Flowers creamy-white, borne in flattened cymes in May or June followed by red, finally black egg-shaped fruits. It belongs to the same group as *V. lantana*. NW China. I about 1910.

**schneiderianum** See *V. calvum*.

**setigerum** HANCE (*V. theiferum* REHD.) A distinct and attractive shrub of medium size and open, lax growth. From time of unfolding until early winter, the ovate-lanceolate to oblong, slender-pointed leaves are constantly changing colour from metallic-blue-red through shades of green to orange-yellow in autumn. Its corymbs of white flowers in early summer are followed by conspicuous clusters of comparatively large, orange-yellow, finally brilliant red, somewhat flattened, oval fruits. C and W China. Introduced by E.H. Wilson in 1901. AM 1925.

**sieboldii** MIQ. A vigorous shrub of medium to large size. The unfolding foetid leaves in spring, and the falling leaves in autumn, are attractively bronze-tinted and only emit an objectionable smell if crushed. They have a conspicuous impressed venation and throughout the summer are soft yellow-green. Flowers creamy-white in May and June. The oval, comparatively large fruits are pink, changing to red then blue-black. Japan. C 1880.

**'Seneca'** A form raised and selected at the U.S. National Arboretum, Washington for its large, drooping clusters of long-persistent red fruits.

†*****suspensum** LINDL. (*V. sandankwa* HASSK.) A medium-sized, evergreen shrub bearing leathery, ovate or rotund, glossy green leaves, 7.5-13cm long. The flat panicles of fragrant, rose-tinted flowers are produced in early spring. Fruits, when produced, globular, red. An attractive species for mild localities where it is best grown against a warm, sheltered wall. Ryukyus, Taiwan. Long cultivated in S Japan from which country it was introduced about 1850.

**theiferum** See *V. setigerum*.

*****tinus** L. "Laurustinus". One of the most popular evergreens. A medium-sized to large shrub of dense, bushy habit with luxurious masses of dark glossy green, oval leaves. The flattened cymes of white, pink-budded flowers appear continuously from late autumn to early spring. Fruits ovoid, metallic-blue, finally black. An excellent winter-flowering shrub for all but the coldest areas. Makes an attractive, informal hedge and is also tolerant of shade and succeeds well in maritime exposure. Mediterranean region, SE Europe. Cultivated in Britain since the late 16th century.

**VIBURNUM tinus**—*continued*

**'Eve Price'** A selected form of dense, compact habit with smaller leaves than the type and with very attractive, carmine buds and pink-tinged flowers. AM 1961. AGM 1984.

**'French White'** A strong-growing form with large heads of white flowers.

**'Gwenllian'** A compact form with small leaves. Flowers rich, deep pink in bud opening to white flushed with pink on the backs of the lobes. Raised at Kew. AGM 1984.

**f. hirtum** HORT. (*V. hirtulum*) A distinct form with larger, thicker, densely ciliate leaves. Both shoots, petioles and leaf bases are clothed with bristly hairs. Less hardy than the type, but an excellent shrub for mild maritime areas. AM 1939.

**'Lucidum'** A vigorous form with comparatively large, glossy green leaves. The flowerheads too are larger than those of the type, opening white in March and April. AM 1972.

**'Pink Prelude'** Flowers opening white then turning through pale to deep pink. C 1966.

**'Purpureum'** A form with very dark green leaves, purple-tinged when young.

**'Pyramidale'** ('Strictum') A selected form of more erect habit.

**†subsp. rigidum** (VENT.) P. SILVA (*V. rigidum* VENT.) (*V. rugosum* PERS.) Differs in its more open habit and larger leaves 7.5-15cm long, hairy on both surfaces. Flowers white, borne in flattened corymbs from February to April. A tender form for a specially favoured position. Canary Isles. I 1778.

**'Variegatum'** Leaves conspicuously variegated creamy-yellow. Not recommended for cold districts.

**tomentosum** See *V. plicatum*.

**'Sterile'** See *V. plicatum* 'Sterile'.

**trilobum** MARSH. (*V. americanum* AUCT. not MILL.) A large shrub, related to and closely resembling *V. opulus*, from which it differs in the usually long terminal lobe of the leaf, the petiole of which is only shallowly grooved and bears small glands. The petioles of *V. opulus* are broadly grooved and bear large, disc-like glands. The red fruits colour in July and persist throughout winter. Rich autumn tints. N North America. I 1812.

**'Compactum'** A small form of dense, compact growth.

**\*utile** HEMSL. A graceful, evergreen shrub of medium size and elegant, rather sparingly-branched habit. The long, slender stems bear narrowly ovate or oblong, glossy dark green leaves which are white tomentose beneath. The white, sweetly-scented flowers are produced in dense, rounded clusters in May. Fruits bluish-black. C China. Introduced by E.H. Wilson in 1901. AM 1926.

**veitchii** C.H. WRIGHT A shrub of medium to large size, related to *V. lantana*. Leaves ovate, wrinkled above. Flowers white, borne in flattened heads during May and June. Fruits bright red at first, passing through purple to black. C China. I 1901 by Ernest Wilson.

**wilsonii** REHD. A medium-sized shrub related to *V. hupehense*, with oval leaves. Flowers white, appearing in corymbs in June, followed by bright red, downy, egg-shaped fruits. W China. I 1908 by Ernest Wilson.

**wrightii** MIQ. A medium-sized shrub with broadly ovate to obovate, abruptly pointed leaves. Flowers white, borne in corymbs in May, followed in autumn by glistening red fruits. The metallic green leaves often colour richly in autumn. Closely related to *V. dilatatum*, from which it differs in its almost glabrous nature. Japan, Sakhalin, Korea, China. I 1892.

**'Hessei'** A dwarf form with broad, ovate, attractively veined leaves. The flowers are followed by conspicuous sealing-wax-red fruits which appear each autumn with remarkable consistency. An excellent shrub for the border front.

**VILLARESIA mucronata** See *Citronella mucronata*.

**\*VINCA** L.—**Apocynaceae**—The "Periwinkles" are a genus of 7 species of herbs and shrubs natives of Europe, N Africa and W and C Asia. The following are vigorous, evergreen, trailing shrubs forming extensive carpets and ideal as ground cover in both shade or full sun. Growing in all fertile soils.

**difformis** POURR. (*V. acutiflora* BERTOL.) (*V. media* HOFFMANS. & LINK) An uncommon species usually herbaceous in cold areas. Leaves ovate, 4-7.5cm long. Flowers solitary in the leaf axils, pale lilac-blue, with rhomboid lobes, resembling a five-bladed propeller,

**VINCA difformis**—*continued*

produced during autumn and early winter. In general appearance, it resembles the hardier *V. major*, but is quite glabrous in all its parts. W Mediterranean region.

**major** L. "Greater Periwinkle". A rampant species with shortly ascending shoots which later lengthen and trail along the ground, rooting only at their tips. Leaves ovate, 2.5-7.5cm long, dark glossy green and ciliate. Flowers bright blue, 4cm across, borne in the leaf axils, produced continuously from late April to June. An excellent shrub for covering unsightly banks or waste ground. C and S Europe, N Africa. Long cultivated and naturalised in the British Isles.

**'Elegantissima'** See 'Variegata'.

**subsp. hirsuta** (BOISS.) STEARN A more pubescent form. N Turkey, Georgia. See also 'Oxyloba'.

**'Maculata'** Leaves with a central splash of greenish-yellow, more conspicuous on young leaves in an open position.

**'Oxyloba'** (var. *hirsuta* HORT. not BOISS.) A form with narrower, somewhat pubescent leaves and violet-blue flowers with narrower, pointed lobes.

**'Reticulata'** Leaves conspicuously veined with yellow when young, later green.

**'Variegata'** ('Elegantissima') Leaves blotched and margined creamy-white; a conspicuous plant, as vigorous as the green-leaved form. AM 1977. AMT 1982. AGM 1984.

**minor** L. "Lesser Periwinkle". A familiar cottage-garden plant with long, trailing stems rooting at intervals. Leaves oval or elliptic-lanceolate, 2.5-5cm long. The bright blue flowers, 2.5cm across, are borne singly in the leaf axils of short, erect, flowering shoots. They appear continuously from April to June and intermittently until autumn. There are numerous named selections. Europe, W Asia. Doubtfully a British native, though frequently found in woods, copses and hedgebanks.

**'Alba'** Flowers white.

**'Argenteo-variegata'** Leaves variegated creamy-white; flowers blue. Previously listed as 'Variegata'.

**'Atropurpurea'** Flowers deep plum-purple. AMT 1983.

**'Aureovariegata'** Leaves blotched yellow; flowers blue.

**'Azurea Flore Pleno'** Flowers sky-blue, double. AMT 1983.

**'Bowles' Variety'** Flowers pale blue, small. AGM 1984. See also 'La Grave'.

**'Gertrude Jekyll'** A selected form with glistening white flowers. AMT 1983. AGM 1984.

**'La Grave'** Flowers azure-blue, larger than those of the type. Has been confused with 'Bowles' Variety'. AMT 1983.

**'Multiplex'** Flowers plum-purple, double.

**'Variegata'** See 'Argenteo-variegata'.

**VITEX** L.—**Verbenaceae**—A large genus of some 250 species of mainly evergreen trees and shrubs widely distrubuted mostly in the tropics and subtropics. The species grown in temperate climes are deciduous shrubs which succeed better in a continental rather than an insular climate. In the British Isles *Vitex* need good drainage and full sun to ripen growth and produce flower, hence they make excellent subjects for a sunny wall. Pruning consists of the removal of the old flowering shoots in late February or March.

**agnus-castus** L. "Chaste Tree". An attractive, spreading, aromatic shrub of medium size. The compound leaves composed of 5-7, short-stalked, ovate-lanceolate leaflets are borne in pairs along the elegant, grey downy shoots. Flowers violet, fragrant, produced in slender racemes at the ends of the current year's shoots in September and October. Mediterranean region to C Asia. Said to have been cultivated in the British Isles since 1570. AM 1934.

**f. alba** (WEST.) REHD. Flowers white. AM 1959.

**f. latifolia** (MILL.) REHD. (*V. macrophylla* HORT.) A more vigorous and hardy form with broader leaflets. AM 1964.

**macrophylla** See *V. agnus-castus* f. *latifolia*.

†**negundo** L. A graceful shrub of medium to large size, with long four-angled stems. Leaves compound, with 3-5, stalked, ovate-lanceolate leaflets. The attractive lavender flowers are borne in loose panicles during late summer or early autumn. India, China, Taiwan. I about 1697.

**var. heterophylla** (FRANCH.) REHD. Leaflets finely cut.

**"WALNUT"** See *Juglans.*

**"WATER ELM"** See *Planera aquatica.*

**"WATTLE"** See *Acacia.*

**"WAX MYRTLE"** See *Myrica cerifera.*

**"WAYFARING TREE"** See *Viburnum lantana.*

**WEIGELA** THUNB.—**Caprifoliaceae**—A small genus of about 10 species of hardy, flowering shrubs, natives of temperate E Asia and differing from the closely related *Diervilla* in the almost regular corolla (two-lipped in *Diervilla*) which is larger and varies in colour from white to pink and red. Very decorative and easily grown shrubs, growing to an average height of 2m and excellent for town gardens, particularly in industrial areas. The tubular, foxglove-like flowers appear in May and June all along the shoots of the previous year. Occasionally a small second crop is produced in late summer or early autumn. Thin out and cut back old flowering shoots to within a few centimetres of the old wood immediately after flowering.

**coraeensis** THUNB. (*W. grandiflora* (SIEB. & ZUCC.) K. KOCH) An elegant shrub of medium size with glabrous shoots and oval to obovate, abruptly pointed leaves. Flowers bell-shaped, white or pale rose at first, deepening to carmine. June. Japan. C 1850.

**'Alba'** Flowers cream changing to pale rose.

**decora** (NAKAI) NAKAI (*W. nikoensis* NAKAI) A medium-sized shrub related to *W. japonica*. Leaves obovate-elliptic, abruptly acuminate, slightly glossy above. Flowers white, becoming reddish with age, opening in May and June. Japan. C 1933.

**florida** (BUNGE) A. DC. (*W. rosea* LINDL.) A medium-sized shrub with ovate-oblong to obovate, acuminate leaves. Flowers funnel-shaped, reddish or rose-pink on the outside, paler within, opening during May and June. Perhaps the commonest and most popular species in cultivation. A parent of many attractive hybrids. Japan, Korea, N China, Manchuria. Introduced by Robert Fortune in 1845.

**'Foliis Purpureis'** A slower-growing, dwarfer form of compact habit with attractive purple-flushed leaves and pink flowers. AGM 1984.

**'Variegata'** A form of more compact habit, the leaves edged creamy-white; flowers pink. One of the best variegated shrubs for general planting. Of hybrid origin. AM 1968. AGM 1984. AM 1988.

**var. venusta** (REHD.) NAKAI A free-flowering form, the flowers being a little larger and of a brighter rose-pink. Korea. I 1905.

**'Versicolor'** Flowers creamy-white changing to red. 'Dart's Colourdream' is very similar.

**hortensis** (SIEB. & ZUCC.) K. KOCH A small to medium-sized shrub with ovate-elliptic to obovate, acuminate leaves which are densely white pubescent beneath. Flowers reddish in May and June. The typical form is rare in cultivation and is less hardy than most other species. Japan. C 1870.

**'Nivea'** ('Albiflora') A lovely form with comparatively large white flowers. FCC 1891.

**japonica** THUNB. Medium-sized shrub with ovate or oval, taper-pointed leaves. The flowers in May are pale rose or nearly white at first, later changing to carmine. Japan. I 1892.

**var. sinica** (REHD.) BAILEY The Chinese form. A taller-growing variety with pale pink flowers deepening with age. C China. I 1908 by Ernest Wilson.

**maximowiczii** (S. MOORE) REHD. A small shrub of spreading habit, with ovate-oblong to obovate, abruptly pointed, rather narrow leaves. The greenish-yellow, or pale yellow flowers open in April and May. Japan. I 1915.

**middendorffiana** (TRAUTV. & MEY.) K. KOCH A small shrub of no mean quality, with exfoliating bark and broader ovate leaves than those of *W. maximowiczii*. They are also more abruptly pointed. Flowers bell-shaped, sulphur-yellow, with dark orange markings on the lower lobes, produced during April and May. An ornamental species of compact growth, best grown in a sheltered and partially shaded position. Japan, N China, Manchuria. I 1850. AM 1931.

**WEIGELA**—*continued*

**nikoensis** See *W. decora.*

**praecox** (LEMOINE) BAILEY A vigorous, medium-sized shrub with ovate to ovate-oblong leaves. The comparatively large, honey-scented flowers are rose-pink with yellow markings in the throat. They commence to open in early May. Japan, Korea, Manchuria. C 1894.

**'Variegata'** An attractive form with leaves variegated creamy-white. Of hybrid origin.

**rosea** See *W. florida.*

## CULTIVARS AND HYBRIDS OF WEIGELA

A colourful selection of hardy hybrids of medium size, flowering on the old wood during May and June and often a second time in early autumn. Pruning consists of the shortening or removal of the flowering stems immediately after flowering.

**'Abel Carrière'** Free-flowering cultivar with large, bright rose-carmine flowers, flecked gold in the throat; buds purple-carmine. C 1876. AGM 1984.

**'Avalanche'** A vigorous cultivar with numerous panicles of white flowers.

**'Ballet'** A hybrid between 'Boskoop Glory' and 'Newport Red'. Flowers dark pinkish-red.

**'Bristol Ruby'** Vigorous, erect-growing cultivar, free-flowering with flowers of a sparkling ruby-red. A hybrid between *W. florida* and *W.* 'Eva Rathke'. AM 1954. AGM 1984.

**'Buisson Fleuri'** Early flowering cultivar with large, fragrant flowers, rose, spotted yellow in throat.

**'Conquête'** An old favourite with very large flowers, almost 5cm long, of a deep rose-pink. C 1907.

**'Espérance'** An early flowering cultivar with large flowers of pale rose-salmon, white within. C 1906.

**'Eva Rathke'** An old favourite and still one of the best reds. A slow-growing cultivar of compact growth. Flowers bright red-crimson, with straw-coloured anthers, opening over a long season. FCC 1893.

**'Eva Supreme'** Growth vigorous; flowers bright red. A cross between 'Eva Rathke' and 'Newport Red'.

**'Evita'** A dwarf shrub of low, spreading habit. Bright red flowers are borne over a long period.

**'Féerie'** Flowers large and numerous, rose-pink, in erect trusses.

**'Fiesta'** A hybrid between 'Eva Rathke' and 'Newport Red'. Growth lax. Flowers of a shining uniform red, produced in great abundance.

**'Fleur de Mai'** Flowers salmon-rose inside, marbled purple-rose outside, purple in bud. Usually the first to bloom.

**'Gracieux'** Erect-growing, free-flowering cultivar with large flowers of salmon-rose, with sulphur-yellow throat. Said to be a selection of *W. praecox.*

**'Gustave Malet'** Very floriferous, with long-tubed, deep red flowers. Said to be a selection of *W. florida.*

**'Heroine'** An erect-growing cultivar with large flowers of a pale rose.

**'Idéal'** Flowers carmine-rose inside, bright carmine outside, in large clusters, early and free-flowering.

**'Lavallei'** Crimson, with protruding white stigma.

**'Le Printemps'** Large, peach-pink flowers, very floriferous.

**'Looymansii Aurea'** Very pleasing in spring and early summer, when the pink flowers enhance the effect of the light golden foliage. Best in partial shade. Found as a seedling in 1873.

**'Majestueux'** An erect, early flowering cultivar producing masses of large, erect flowers, madder-pink flushed carmine in the throat.

**'Mont Blanc'** Vigorous cultivar with large, white, fragrant flowers. Perhaps the best of the whites. C 1898. AGM 1984.

**'Newport Red'** ('Vanicek') A superb cultivar, more upright than 'Eva Rathke', with larger flowers of a lighter red.

**WEIGELA**—*continued*
**'Perle'** Vigorous cultivar with large flowers in rounded corymbs, pale cream with rose edges, the mouth clear yellow.
**'Rubidor'** Flowers carmine-red. Leaves yellow or green with a broad yellow margin. Tends to burn in full sun.
**'Styriaca'** Vigorous cultivar with carmine-red flowers produced in great abundance. C 1908.

†\***WEINMANNIA** L.—**Cunoniaceae**—A large genus of nearly 200 species of mainly tropical, evergreen trees and shrubs, widely distributed. The following species require a loamy soil and are only suitable for sheltered gardens in the mildest areas of the British Isles.
**racemosa** L. "Kamahi". A small, graceful tree or large shrub remarkable on account of the variability of its leaves which, on adult trees, are simple, ovate to oval and coarsely-toothed, and on juvenile specimens vary from simple to three-lobed, or trifoliolate with coarsely-toothed leaflets. Flowers white, produced in slender racemes during summer. New Zealand.
**trichosperma** CAV. A slender, small to medium-sized tree or large shrub, with pinnate leaves composed of 9-19 small, neat, oval or obovate, toothed leaflets. The rachis in between each leaflet bears a pair of small, triangular wings. The white flowers, produced in dense racemes during May and June, are succeeded by small, coppery-red capsules. Chile. AM 1927.

†\***WESTRINGIA** SM.—**Labiatae**—A small genus of about 25 species of tender, evergreen shrubs native of Australia.
**rosmariniformis** SM. "Victoria Rosemary". A small to medium-sized shrub bearing whorls of narrow, rosemary-like leaves which, like the shoots, are silvery hoary beneath. Flowers white, borne in axillary clusters in July. An interesting shrub for a wall in a warm, sunny, well drained position in mild areas. E Australia. I 1791.

**"WHINBERRY"** See *Vaccinium myrtillus*.

**"WHITEBEAM"** See *Sorbus aria*.

**"WHITEBEAM, SWEDISH"** See *Sorbus intermedia*.

**"WHORTLEBERRY"** See *Vaccinium myrtillus*.

**"WINEBERRY"** See *Rubus phoenicolasius*.

**"WILD IRISHMAN"** See *Discaria toumatou*.

**"WILLOW"** See *Salix*.

**"WING NUT"** See *Pterocarya*.

**"WINTER JASMINE"** See *Jasminum nudiflorum*.

**"WITCH HAZEL"** See *Hamamelis*.

**"WYCH ELM"** See *Ulmus glabra*.

**XANTHOCERAS** BUNGE—**Sapindaceae**—A monotypic genus related to *Koelreuteria*, but very different in general appearance. The erect flower panicles recall those of the horse chestnut.
**sorbifolium** BUNGE A beautiful, large shrub or small tree of upright growth. Leaves pinnate, composed of 9-17 sessile, lanceolate, sharply-toothed leaflets. The 2.5cm wide flowers, which are white with a carmine eye, are borne in erect panicles on the shoots of the

**XANTHOCERAS sorbifolium**—*continued*

previous year in May. Fruit a top-shaped, three-valved, walnut-like capsule containing numerous small chestnut-like seeds. It may be grown in all types of fertile soil, its thick, fleshy, yellow roots take kindly to a chalk formation. N China. I 1866. FCC 1876.

**XANTHORHIZA** MARSH. (*Zanthorhiza* L'HERIT.)—**Ranunculaceae**—A monotypic genus related to the buttercups but very different in general appearance from other members of the family.

**simplicissima** MARSH. (*Z. apiifolia* L'HERIT.) "Yellow Root". A small, suckering shrub forming in time a thicket of erect stems up to 1m. The very attractive, pinnate leaves are composed of 3-5 sessile, deeply-toothed leaflets which turn the colour of burnished bronze, often with a purple cast, in autumn. The tiny, delicate, deep purple flowers are produced in loose, drooping panicles with the emerging leaves during March and April. The roots and inner bark are coloured a bright yellow and are bitter to the taste. Thrives in a moist or clay soil but is not at home on shallow chalk. E United States. I 1776. AM 1975 (for foliage effect).

**XANTHOXYLUM** See *Zanthoxylum*.

†\***XYLOSMA** FORST. f.—**Flacourtiaceae**—Evergreen trees and shrubs, normally with spiny branches and dioecious flowers. About 85 species, found mainly in the tropics and subtropics.

**japonica** (THUNB.) A. GRAY (*X. racemosa* (SIEB. & ZUCC.) MIQ.) A large shrub or small bushy tree sparsely armed with axillary spines when young. Leaves ovate to oblong-ovate, leathery and dark glossy green. Flowers dioecious, small, yellow, fragrant, produced in short, axillary racemes in late summer. Berries blackish-purple. Japan. Ryukyus, Taiwan, China.

**var. pubescens** REHD. & WILS. Shoots hairy. Most cultivated plants belong here. I by Ernest Wilson.

**"YELLOW ROOT"** See *Xanthorhiza simplicissima*.

**"YELLOW WOOD"** See *Cladrastis lutea*.

\***YUCCA** L.—**Agavaceae**—These remarkable evergreens, with rosettes or clumps of narrow, usually rigid leaves, and tall racemes or panicles of drooping, bell-shaped, lily-like flowers are of great architectural value and help to create a subtropical effect in the garden. There are about 40 species native of C America, Mexico and S United States. Several species are hardy in the British Isles where they prefer a hot, dry, well drained position in full sun.

**angustifolia** See *Y. glauca*.

†**arizonica** MCKELVEY A stemless species bearing narrow, rigidly recurved leaves which are channelled above and clothed with white threads along the margins. Flowers creamy-white, in attractive panicles in late summer. Arizona.

†**brevifolia** ENGELM. "Joshua Tree". A small tree-like species with an erect trunk ending in several stout branches. Leaves green, narrow and recurved, channelled above, margined with fine teeth. Flowers cream to greenish-white, borne in a dense panicle during late summer. SW United States.

**var. jaegeriana** MCKELVEY Differs in its shorter stature, smaller leaves and panicles. SW United States.

**filamentosa** L. A stemless species producing dense clumps of spreading or erect, lanceolate, slightly glaucous leaves. The leaf margins are clothed with numerous, curly, white threads. The creamy-white flowers, each 5-7.5cm long, are borne in erect, glabrous, conical panicles 1-2m tall, in July and August, even on young plants. SE United States. C 1675. AGM 1984.

**'Bright Edge'** Leaves with a narrow golden yellow margin.

**'Variegata'** Leaves margined with creamy-white. AGM 1984.

**YUCCA**—*continued*

**flaccida** HAWORTH A stemless species forming tufts of long, lanceolate, green or glaucous leaves. The terminal portion of each leaf bends down and the margins are furnished with curly, white threads. Flowers creamy-white, 5-6.5cm long, borne in erect, downy panicles, 0.6-1.2m tall in July and August. As in the related *Y. filamentosa*, this species spreads by short basal sidegrowths. SE United States. I 1816.

'**Golden Sword**' Leaves with a broad central band of creamy-yellow.

'**Ivory**' Large panicles of creamy-white, green stained flowers. AM 1966. FCC 1968. AGM 1984.

**glauca** NUTT. (*Y. angustifolia* PURSH) A low-growing, short-stemmed species producing a rounded head of linear, greyish leaves which are margined white and edged with a few threads. The greenish-white flowers, 5-7.5cm long, are carried in an erect raceme, 1-1.5m tall in July and August. The species is hardy in our area but young plants do not flower. South C United States. I 1696.

**gloriosa** L. "Adam's Needle". A small, tree-like species with a stout stem, 1.2 to 2.5m tall, and few or no branches. Leaves straight and stiff, almost dangerously spine-tipped, glaucous green, 0.3-0.6m long, by 7.5-10cm wide, gathered into a dense, terminal head. Flowers creamy-white, sometimes tinged red on the outside, borne in an erect, crowded, conical panicle, 1-2m high or more, from July to September. SE United States. I about 1550. AM 1975.

'**Variegata**' Leaves margined and striped creamy-yellow, fading to creamy-white on older leaves. FCC 1883. AGM 1984.

× **karlsruhensis** GRAEBN. (*Y. filamentosa* × *Y. glauca*). A hardy stemless plant with long, linear, greyish leaves and panicles of creamy-white flowers during late summer. It resembles *Y. glauca* in general appearance, but the leaves possess numerous marginal threads.

**parviflora var. engelmannii** See *Hesperaloe parviflora* var. *engelmannii*.

**recurvifolia** SALISB. A medium-sized species, usually with a short stem and several branches. The long, tapered leaves, 0.6-1m long, are glaucous at first becoming green with age. All but the upper, central leaves are characteristically recurved. Flowers creamy-white, borne in dense, erect panicles, 0.6-1m high during late summer. Perhaps the best species for town gardens. Similar to *Y. gloriosa*, but differing in the recurved leaves. SE United States. I 1794. AGM 1984.

'**Variegata**' Leaves with a pale green central band.

†**whipplei** TORR. (*Hesperoyucca whipplei* (TORR.) TREL.) A stemless species developing a dense, globular clump of long, narrow, rigid, spine-tipped leaves which are finely-toothed and glaucous. The large, fragrant flowers are greenish-white, edged with purple. They are produced in a densely-packed panicle at the end of an erect, 1.8-3.6m scape, in May and June. Though able to withstand frost, this magnificent species can only be recommended for sunny places in the mildest counties and requires a very well drained position. California. I 1854. AM 1945.

"**YULAN**" See *Magnolia denudata*.

**ZANTHOXYLUM** L. (*Xanthoxylum* MILL.)—**Rutaceae**—A large and rather neglected genus of some 200 species of mainly deciduous trees and shrubs widely distributed particularly in warm regions of the world. Branches normally spiny, leaves aromatic when crushed. The flowers are small but the diversity of the usually compound leaves is always attractive and in some species they are as beautiful as the fronds of a fern, and in others, as spectacular as those of the Tree of Heaven. The fruits too, which may be jet-black or bright red, have a subtle quality. Easily grown in any ordinary soil, sun or shade.

**ailanthoides** SIEB. & ZUCC. A very vigorous, sparsely-branched large shrub or small tree with thorny branches and stout, glaucous young shoots. Leaves pinnate, 0.3-0.6m long, composed of 11-23 ovate to ovate-lanceolate, acuminate leaflets. The greenish-yellow flowers are produced in flattened heads, 13cm or more across, during early autumn. An extremely attractive foliage tree of subtropical appearance. It has reached 7.5m tall with a spread of 12m in the Hillier Gardens and Arboretum (1990). Japan, Korea, China, Ryukyus, Taiwan.

**ZANTHOXYLUM**—*continued*

**alatum var. planispinum** See *Z. planispinum.*

**americanum** MILL. "Toothache Tree" "Prickly Ash". A large, rather gaunt shrub or short-stemmed tree with short stout spines and pinnate leaves composed of 5-11 ovate or oval leaflets. The small, yellowish-green flowers are produced in short axillary clusters in spring, followed by conspicuous, capitate clusters of jet-black fruits. The twigs and fruits are said to have been chewed by the North American Indians to alleviate toothache, the acrid juice having a numbing effect. E North America. I about 1740.

**bungei** See *Z. simulans.*

**piperitum** (L.) DC. "Japan Pepper". A medium-sized shrub of neat, compact habit with pairs of flattened spines. The attractive pinnate leaves are composed of 11-19 sessile, broadly lanceolate or ovate leaflets. The small, greenish-yellow flowers are produced on the old wood in May or June and are followed by small, reddish fruits. The black seeds are crushed and used as a pepper in Japan. Leaves turn a rich yellow in autumn. Japan, Korea, Manchuria, China. C 1877.

**planispinum** SIEB. & ZUCC. (*Z. alatum* var. *planispinum* (SIEB. & ZUCC.) REHD. & WILS.) A large, spreading shrub with a pair of prominently flattened spines at the base of each leaf. Leaves with 3 or 5 ovate or lanceolate, sessile leaflets and a conspicuously winged petiole. The small, yellow flowers in spring are followed by small, red, warty fruits. Japan, Ryukyus, Taiwan, China, Korea. C 1880.

**schinifolium** SIEB. & ZUCC. A graceful, medium-sized shrub, the branches bearing single thorns and fern-like leaves, which are pinnate and composed of 11-21, lanceolate leaflets. The small, flat clusters of green-petalled flowers, in late summer, are followed by red fruits. A pretty shrub, resembling *Z. piperitum*, but with solitary spines and flowers on the current year's shoots in August. Japan, Korea, E China. C 1877.

**simulans** HANCE (*Z. bungei* PLANCH.) A medium-sized to large shrub or small tree of spreading habit with spiny branches. Leaves pinnate, composed of 7–11, broadly ovate, shining green leaflets. The greenish-yellow flowers, in early summer, are followed by small, reddish fruits. China. I 1869.

†**ZAUSCHNERIA** C. PRESL—**Onagraceae**—A small genus of 4 species of dwarf sub-shrubs, or perennials, requiring a warm, sunny, well drained position. They make excellent subjects for the rock garden.

**californica** PRESL. "Californian Fuchsia". A bushy sub-shrub with several erect, green or grey downy, more or less glandular stems densely clothed with narrow, downy, grey-green leaves. The tubular fuchsia-like flowers are red with a scarlet tube and are borne in long, loose spikes during late summer and autumn. California. I 1847.

    **'Dublin'** Flowers borne over a very long period from August to October. Selected at Glasnevin Botanic Garden. AM 1983. AGM 1984.

    **subsp. latifolia** (HOOK.) KECK (*Z. canescens* EASTW.) More herbaceous in nature, with broader leaves. SW United States. AM 1928.

    **subsp. mexicana** (PRESL) RAVEN Similar to the typical form and equally floriferous but with broader, green leaves.

**cana** GREENE (*Z. microphylla* (A. GRAY) MOXLEY) A grey, dwarf sub-shrub with linear leaves crowding the stems and loose spikes of red, scarlet-tubed flowers during late summer and autumn. California. AM 1928 (as *Z. microphylla*).

**canescens** See *Z. californica* subsp. *latifolia.*

**microphylla** See *Z. cana.*

**ZELKOVA** SPACH—**Ulmaceae**—A small genus of 5 species of smooth-barked trees or rarely shrubs, natives of Asia with one species in Crete. They are allied to the elms, differing in their simple (not double) toothed leaves and unwinged fruits. The small, greenish flowers (male and bisexual on the same tree) and the fruits which follow are of little ornament. They thrive in deep, moist, loamy soils and are fairly tolerant of shade. The Zelkovas are trees of considerable quality, their garden value may be paralleled with the deciduous *Nothofagus.*

**abelicea** (LAM.) BOISS. (*Z. cretica* SPACH) A large, wide-spreading shrub with slender twigs and small, ovate to oblong, coarsely-toothed leaves up to 2.5cm long. The small, whitish

**ZELKOVA abelicea**—*continued*

flowers are scented. A rare species in cultivation and the wild. Mts of Crete. I about 1924.

**acuminata** See *Z. serrata*.

**carpinifolia** (PALL.) K. KOCH (*Z. crenata* (MICHX. f.) SPACH) (*Planera richardii* MICHX.) A long-lived, slow-growing tree eventually attaining a large size. The bark is smooth and grey like a beech, but flakes with age. As seen in the British Isles the trunk is generally comparatively short, soon giving way to numerous, erect, crowded branches which form a characteristic dense, conical head. On old trees the trunk is often buttressed. The hairy shoots bear 4-7.5cm long, ovate to elliptic, coarsely-toothed leaves which are rough to the touch above. Caucasus, N Iran. I 1760.

**crenata** See *Z. carpinifolia*.

**cretica** See *Z. abelicea*.

**serrata** (THUNB.) MAK. (*Z. acuminata* (LINDL.) PLANCH.) (*Z. keaki* (SIEB.) MAXIM.) (*Planera acuminata* LINDL.) "Keaki". A medium-sized, occasionally large tree of graceful, wide-spreading habit, forming a rounded crown, with smooth, grey, later flaky bark. The attractive, ovate to ovate-lanceolate, acuminate leaves are 5-12cm long and edged with slender-pointed, coarse teeth. In autumn they turn to bronze or red. Japan, Korea, Taiwan, China. I 1861. This was the largest tree (supplied by us) planted on the Thames embankment site for the Festival of Britain in 1951. It weighed over 2 tons and had a branch spread exceeding 10m, and throughout its journey from the ancient capital of Winchester to the "new" capital London it was honoured by a police escort.

**sinica** SCHNEID. A medium-sized tree with smooth, grey bark flaking with age. Twigs slender and short-pubescent. Leaves small and neat, ovate to ovate-lanceolate, coarsely-toothed, 2.5-6cm long, harsh to the touch. The young growths are pink-tinted in spring. C and E China. Introduced by E.H. Wilson in 1908.

× **verschaffeltii** (DIPP.) NICHOLS. (*Z. carpinifolia* × *Z. serrata*). Normally a splendid large shrub or small, bushy-headed tree of graceful habit, with slender shoots and oval to ovate, conspicuously toothed leaves rough to the touch above, and in shape recalling those of *Ulmus* × *viminalis*. In the Westonbirt Arboretum is a large tree with a grey and rich brown, mottled bark and deeply lobed leaves. Origin unknown. C 1886. FCC 1886 (as *Ulmus pitteursii pendula*).

× **ZENOBIA** D. DON—**Ericaceae**—A monotypic genus requiring a lime-free soil and preferably semi-shade. One of the most beautiful and most neglected of early summer-flowering shrubs. One suspects that this glorious little shrub flowers during the "London Season"? how else can it have been so unnoticed.

**pulverulenta** (BARTR. ex WILLD.) POLLARD A beautiful, small, deciduous or semi-evergreen shrub of loose habit with bloomy young shoots. The oblong-ovate, shallowly-toothed leaves are covered by a conspicuous, glaucous bloom which tends to fade above as the leaves age. The white, bell-shaped flowers, resembling those of a large lily-of-the-valley, are aniseed-scented and appear in pendulous, axillary clusters in June and July. E United States. I 1801. AM 1932. FCC 1934.

**f. nitida** (MICHX.) FERN. (var. *nuda* (VENT.) REHD.) A form with green leaves. This variety is said to occur with the typical form in the wild. Some authorities regard it as a distinct species, but seed-grown plants in cultivation contain forms which appear intermediate between the two. AM 1965.

**var. nuda** See f. *nitida*.

# CLIMBERS

Only true climbers are listed here. For other wall plants see TREES AND SHRUBS.

Climbers may roughly be divided into three main categories, based on their mode of growth, namely:

Group 1 consists of those climbers which, due to the presence of aerial roots (as in ivy), or adhesive tendril tips (as in Virginia Creeper), are self-clinging and have the ability to scale a wall or tree-trunk without added support.

Group 2 consists of climbers with twining stems (as in Honeysuckle), curling tendrils (as in vine), or curling petioles (as in Clematis), which require support other than that of a flat surface up which to grow.

Group 3 consists of climbers with hooked thorns (as in Climbing Roses), or with long scandent stems (as in *Berberidopsis*), which require the support of a wall or tree over or into which to scramble.

All climbers require careful attention on a support until established. Even the self-clingers of group 1 usually require the support of a little string or wire until their adhesive organs establish permanent contact with the wall or tree surface.

In the absence of trees or suitable walls the climbers of groups 2 and 3 may be trained up specially constructed wooden supports, or over hedges.

Many climbers, particularly those in groups 1 and 3, may be used as ground cover when, particularly on unsightly banks, a rapid and often ornamental effect may be obtained.

Several climbers are dioecious, the females often bearing attractive fruits. Where fruits are required plants of both sexes are best planted together over or against the same support.

**ACTINIDIA** LINDL.—**Actinidiaceae**—About 30 species of climbers, natives of E Asia. Vigorous, generally hardy twining climbers with simple leaves, unisexual, bisexual or polygamous flowers and sometimes edible, juicy berries. They are excellent for covering old walls or tall stumps and will grow in most fertile soils in sun or semi-shade. Those grown for their fruits are best planted in pairs.

**arguta** (SIEB. & ZUCC.) MIQ. A strong-growing species climbing to the tops of lofty trees in its native land. Leaves broadly ovate, 7.5-13cm long, bristly-toothed. Flowers white, with purple anthers, slightly fragrant, 1-2cm across, opening in June and July. Fruits oblong, greenish-yellow, 2.5cm long, edible but insipid. Japan, Korea, Manchuria. C 1874.

**var. cordifolia** DUNN A form with heart-shaped leaves.

**chinensis** PLANCH. "Chinese Gooseberry" "Kiwi Fruit". A vigorous species reaching a height of 9m with densely reddish hairy shoots and large, heart-shaped leaves, 15-23cm long and up to 20cm wide. Flowers creamy-white, turning to buff-yellow, 4cm across, fragrant, produced in axillary clusters in late summer. Fruits edible, green then brown, 4-5cm long, resembling a large, elongated gooseberry and with a similar flavour. To obtain fruit it is necessary to plant both sexes; only one male is needed for several females in reasonable proximity. Selected clones are cultivated for their fruits, notably in New Zealand. Native of China. I 1900 by Ernest Wilson. AM 1907.

**'Aureovariegata'** Leaves splashed and marked with cream and yellow. Tends to revert.

†**coriacea** DUNN A vigorous, almost evergreen species with leathery, slender-pointed leaves to 13cm long. Flowers 12mm across, fragrant, an attractive rose-pink in May and June. Fruits brown, spotted white, egg-shaped to 2.5cm long. Requires a warm, sunny sheltered position. On a west-facing wall at Winchester it survived, in spite of injury, the severe winter of 1962/63. W China. I 1908 by Ernest Wilson.

**giraldii** DIELS A strong-growing species related to *A. arguta* with ovate or elliptic leaves and white flowers during summer. C China. C 1933.

**kolomikta** (MAXIM. & RUPR.) MAXIM. A striking, slender, dioecious climber reaching 4.5-6m. Remarkable on account of the tri-coloured variegation of many of its leaves, the terminal half being creamy-white, flushed pink. The variegation is not apparent on very young

**ACTINIDIA kolomikta**—*continued*

plants. Flowers white, slightly fragrant, 12mm across, opening in June; fruits ovoid, 2.5cm long, yellowish and sweet. The form in general cultivation appears to be a male plant. Japan, N China, Manchuria. I about 1855. AM 1931. AGM 1984.

**melanandra** FRANCH. A vigorous species, reaching a great height in a tree. Leaves oblong or narrowly oval, 7.5-10cm long, glaucous beneath. Flowers unisexual, white, with purple anthers, opening in June and July. Fruits egg-shaped, 2.5-3cm long, reddish-brown, covered by a plum-like bloom. C China. I 1910 by Ernest Wilson.

**polygama** (SIEB. & ZUCC.) MAXIM. "Silver Vine". A slender-branched species up to 4.5-6m in a tree. Leaves broadly ovate to elliptic, 7.5-13cm long, bronze tinted when unfolding, becoming blotched with silvery-white. The fragrant white flowers, 2cm across, are produced in June. Fruits ovoid, beaked, 2.5-4cm long, yellow and edible. C Japan.

**purpurea** REHD. Strong-growing species, reaching 6-7.5m in a tree. Leaves oval to ovate-oblong, 7.5-13cm long. Flowers white, 1-2cm across, opening in June. Fruit ovoid or oblong, 2.5cm long, purple in colour, edible and sweet. W China. I 1908 by Ernest Wilson.

**AKEBIA** DECNE.—**Lardizabalaceae**—A genus of 5 species of vigorous, hardy, semi-evergreen, monoecious, twining plants with attractive foliage and flowers. Succeeding in most soils, in sun or shade. They are excellent for training over hedges, low trees, bushes or old stumps. A mild spring (for the flowers) and a long hot summer are usually required before the conspicuous and unusual fruits are produced.

**lobata** See *A. trifoliata*.

×**pentaphylla** (MAK.) MAK. (*A. quinata* × *A. trifoliata*). A strong-growing, rare hybrid, the leaves with usually 5 oval leaflets. Flowers similar to those of *A. trifoliata*. Japan.

**quinata** (HOUTTUYN) DECNE. A semi-evergreen climber up to 9 or 12m in a tree. Leaves composed of normally 5 oblong or obovate, notched leaflets. Flowers fragrant, red-purple, male and female in the same racemes in April. Fruits 5-10cm long, sausage-shaped, turning dark purple, containing numerous black seeds embedded in a white pulp. Japan, Korea, China. Introduced by Robert Fortune in 1845. AM 1956.

**trifoliata** (THUNB.) KOIDZ. (*A. lobata* DECNE.) An elegant climber up to 9m in a tree. Leaves trifoliolate, with broadly ovate, shallowly-lobed or undulate leaflets. Flowers dark-purple, male and female produced in a drooping raceme in April. Fruits sausage-shaped, often in groups of 3, 7.5 -13cm long, pale violet, containing black seeds in a white pulp. Japan, China. I 1895.

**AMPELOPSIS** MICHX.—**Vitaceae**—A small genus of about 20 species of ornamental vines climbing by means of curling tendrils; natives mainly of North America and E Asia. At one time they were included under *Vitis*, but differ in having free (not united) petals and usually compound leaves. They are excellent subjects for covering walls, fences, hedges, etc, and with initial support will clamber into trees. Valuable for their attractive foliage and for their fruits which, however, require a long, hot summer and a mild autumn in which to develop. The inconspicuous flowers appear in late summer or early autumn. They will grow in any ordinary soil and in sun or semi-shade, but for those species with attractive fruits a warm, sunny, sheltered position is recommended. See also *Parthenocissus* and *Vitis*.

**aconitifolia** BUNGE (*Vitis aconitifolia* (BUNGE) HANCE) A vigorous, luxurious climber. Leaves variable in shape, composed of 3 or 5 sessile, lanceolate or rhomboid, coarsely-toothed or lobed leaflets. The whole leaf is 10-13cm across and a deep glossy green above. Fruits small, orange or yellow. N China. C 1868.

**bodinieri** (LEVL. & VANT.) REHD. (*Vitis micans* (REHD.) BEAN) A slender climber up to 6m with smooth, often purplish stems. Leaves simple, triangular-ovate or rounded, 7.5-13cm long, coarsely-toothed and occasionally three-lobed, dark shining green above, somewhat glaucous beneath. The small rounded fruits are dark blue. C China. I 1900 by Ernest Wilson.

**brevipedunculata** (MAXIM.) TRAUTV. (*Cissus brevipedunculata* MAXIM.) A vigorous, luxuriant climber with three-lobed or occasionally five-lobed, cordate leaves 5-15cm across,

**AMPELOPSIS brevipedunculata**—*continued*

resembling those of the hop. After a hot summer the masses of small fruits vary between verdigris and deep blue but in the mass are porcelain-blue and are exceedingly attractive. NE Asia. C 1870.

**'Citrulloides'** Leaves more deeply five-lobed. An attractive foliage plant. Fruits similar to those of the typical form. C 1875.

**'Elegans'** ('Variegata') ('Tricolor') An attractive form with leaves densely mottled white and tinged pink. Relatively weak-growing and therefore useful for planting where space is restricted. An excellent patio plant. Introduced by P. von Siebold before 1847.

**'Tricolor'** See 'Elegans'.

**'Variegata'** See 'Elegans'.

**chaffanjonii** (LEVL.) REHD. (*Ampelopsis watsoniana* WILS.) A large-leaved climber suitable for walls and wooden supports. Leaves pinnate, 15-30cm long, composed of 5 or 7 oval or oblong, deep glossy green leaflets which are purple-tinted beneath, and often colour richly in autumn. Fruits red, later black. C China. I 1900 by Ernest Wilson. AM 1907.

**megalophylla** DIELS & GILG (*Vitis megalophylla* VEITCH) A strong but rather slow-growing aristocratic climber of considerable quality, reaching 9m or more in a suitable tree. Leaves bi-pinnate, 30-60cm long, with ovate to ovate-oblong leaflets usually glaucous beneath, coarsely-toothed and 5-15cm in length. The loose bunches of top-shaped fruits are purple at first, finally black. W China. I 1894. AM 1903.

**orientalis** (LAM.) PLANCH. (*Cissus orientalis* LAM.) A bushy shrub of loose growth or occasionally climbing. Leaves variable, pinnate, bi-pinnate or bi-ternate, with ovate to obovate, coarsely-toothed leaflets. After a hot summer the bunches of redcurrant-like fruits are most attractive. Asia Minor, Syria. I 1818.

**sempervirens** HORT. See *Cissus striata*.

**veitchii** See *Parthenocissus tricuspidata* 'Veitchii'.

†\***ARAUJIA** BROT.—**Asclepiadaceae**—A small genus of 2 or 3 species of mainly tropical twining climbers requiring full sun. Natives of S America.

**sericifera** BROT. "Cruel Plant". A vigorous evergreen climber with pale green, ovate-oblong leaves. The slightly fragrant, creamy-white, salver-shaped flowers are borne in short racemes close to the leaf axils during late summer. These are followed after a long, hot summer by large grooved yellowish-green pods 10-13cm long, containing numerous silky-tufted seeds. Only suitable for the mildest areas of the British Isles. The common name refers to the peculiar fact that in its native habitats, night-flying moths visiting the flowers are held trapped by their long proposces until daytime when they are usually able to release themselves. S Brazil. I 1830. AM 1975.

AHₙSTOLOCHIA L.—**Aristolochiaceae**—A large genus of about 300 species of shrubs, climbers and herbaceous plants, with cordate leaves and peculiarly-shaped flowers; widely distributed especially in warm regions. The species here described are excellent, twining plants for covering unsightly walls, fences or stumps and equally effective in trees and on wooden supports such as arbours, archways, etc, and will grow in most fertile soils, in sun or shade.

**altissima** See *A. sempervirens*.

**durior** See *A. macrophylla*.

**chrysops** (STAPF) HEMSL. A rare species up to 6m with hairy shoots and hairy, auricled, ovate leaves 5-13cm long. Flowers shaped like a small, tubby, greyish saxophone, 4cm long, with a flared purplish-brown mouth and a mustard-yellow throat, appearing singly on long, slender, pendulous stalks during late May and June. W China. I 1904.

**macrophylla** LAM. (*A. sipho* L'HERIT.) (*A. durior* HILL.) "Dutchman's Pipe". A vigorous species reaching 9m in a suitable tree. Leaves heart-shaped or kidney-shaped up to 30cm long. Flowers tubular, bent in the lower half, like a siphon, 2.5-4cm long, yellowish-green, the flared mouth brownish-purple, produced in June in axillary pairs. E United States. Introduced by John Bartram in 1763.

†\***sempervirens** L. (*A. altissima* DESF.) An evergreen species with long, lax stems up to 3m, trailing along the ground unless trained. Leaves glossy green, heart-shaped and slender-

**ARISTOLOCHIA sempervirens**—*continued*

pointed to 10cm long. The solitary, yellowish-brown to dull purple flowers are funnel-shaped and curved. They are produced singly in the leaf axils during late spring or early summer. May be cut to ground level during winter, but invariably appears the following spring, particularly if given winter protection. E Mediterranean region, N Africa. I 1727.

**sipho** See *A. macrophylla*.

**tomentosa** SIMS. A vigorous species related to and somewhat resembling *A. macrophylla*, but downy in almost all its parts. Its leaves are also smaller and its flowers possess a distinctly three-lobed, yellowish, flared mouth. SE United States. I 1799.

†\***ASTERANTHERA** KLOTZSCH & HANST.—**Gesneriaceae**—A monotypic genus related to *Mitraria* and climbing by means of aerial roots. It requires a cool, leafy soil, preferably neutral or acid, and is happiest in a sheltered woodland or against a north wall in the milder areas of the British Isles.

**ovata** (CAV.) HANST. A beautiful evergreen trailing creeper which will climb up the trunks of trees or the surface of a wall where conditions are suitable, otherwise it makes a charming ground cover. Leaves opposite, rounded or ovate, 1-4cm long. The tubular, two-lipped flowers are 5cm long and appear in June. They are red, the lower lip having blood-red veins, accentuated by a white throat. In the forests of the Chilean Andes it adheres closely to the trunks of trees and attains a height of 3-6m. Introduced from Chile by Harold Comber in 1926. AM 1939.

†\***BERBERIDOPSIS** HOOK. f.—**Flacourtiaceae**—A monotypic genus requiring an open or sandy loam and a sheltered position in shade, succeeding best in an acid or neutral soil. Correctly sited it is moderately hardy. A shaded site and a moist soil are essential.

**corallina** HOOK. f. "Coral Plant". A beautiful evergreen, scandent shrub attaining a length of 4.5-6m on a shaded wall. Leaves heart-shaped or ovate, thick and leathery, the margins set with spiny teeth, dark green above, glaucous beneath. Flowers deep crimson, 12mm across, borne singly on slender stalks or in pendent racemes during late summer. Chile. Introduced by Richard Pearce in 1862. AM 1901.

**BERCHEMIA** NECKER ex DC.—**Rhamnaceae**—A small genus of about 12 species of twining climbers natives of E Asia, E Africa and North America. They have rather insignificant white or greenish flowers and small fruits which, however, are rarely freely produced in British gardens. Their elegant foliage makes them unusual climbers for walls, hedges, or bushy-headed trees. Easy to grow in most fertile soils in sun or semi-shade.

**giraldiana** SCHNEID. A graceful species attaining 4.5-6m, with reddish-brown shoots and ovate-oblong, parallel veined leaves 2.5-6cm long, which are dark sea-green above, glaucous beneath. Fruits sausage-shaped, 8mm long, red at first, then black. C and W China. C 1911.

**lineata** DC. An elegant climber with neat, elliptic parallel veined leaves 6mm to 4cm long. The tiny fruits ripen to blue-black. China, Taiwan, Himalaya.

**racemosa** SIEB. & ZUCC. A strong-growing, scandent shrub up to 4.5m with pretty ovate, parallel veined leaves 4-7.5cm long, pale or glaucescent beneath. Fruits small, oblong, changing from green to red, then black. A spreading species ideal for growing over hedges, low trees and bushes. The leaves turn clear yellow in autumn. Japan. I 1880.

**'Variegata'** Leaves, particularly when young, conspicuously variegated creamy-white.

\***BIGNONIA** L.—**Bignoniaceae**—As now understood a monotypic genus which at one time included *Campsis* and *Tecoma*.

**capreolata** L. (*Doxantha capreolata* (L.) MIERS) A vigorous evergreen or semi-evergreen climbing by means of twining leaf tendrils. Leaves composed of two oblong to ovate-lanceolate leaflets, 5-13cm long. The tubular flowers 4-5cm long are orange-red, paler within, carried in axillary clusters in June. A rampant climber for a sunny sheltered wall or tree. Hardy in the southern counties. SE United States. C 1653. AM 1958.

†***BILLARDIERA** SM.—**Pittosporaceae**—A small genus of about 8 species of low-growing Australasian twining plants. The following is suitable for a warm, sunny position in the milder areas of the British Isles. It makes an unusual conservatory subject.

**longiflora** LABILL. A slender climber up to 2m. Leaves lanceolate, 2.5-4cm long. The solitary, bell-shaped flowers hang on slender stalks from the leaf axils during summer and autumn. They are greenish-yellow in colour, 2cm long and are replaced by brilliant deep blue, oblong fruits 2-2.5cm in length. A charming plant against a wall or clambering over a large boulder on the rock garden or scrambling through a low bush. Tasmania. I 1810. AM 1924.

**'Fructualbo'** ('Alba') Fruits white.

**"BLUEBELL CREEPER"** See *Sollya heterophylla*.

**CAMPSIS** LOUR.—**Bignoniaceae**—A genus of only 2 species of attractive, deciduous, scandent shrubs related to *Bignonia*, and equally brilliant in flower. Both require a position in full sun to ripen growth and produce flowers. They are excellent when trained over walls or the roofs of outhouses or tree stumps. Specimens which have become too large and tangled may be pruned in late February or March.

**chinensis** See *C. grandiflora*.

**grandiflora** (THUNB.) K. SCHUM. (*C. chinensis* (LAM.) VOSS) This beautiful oriental climber will attain a height of 6m or more in a suitable position. Leaves pinnate, composed of 7 or 9 ovate, coarsely-toothed, glabrous leaflets. Flowers trumpet-shaped, 5-9cm long, deep orange and red, carried in drooping panicles from the tips of the current year's growths during late summer and early autumn. China. I 1800. AM 1949.

**'Thunbergii'** A form with shorter-tubed, red trumpets and reflexed lobes. I by Siebold in 1856.

**radicans** (L.) SEEM. "Trumpet Vine". A tall, strong-growing species which normally climbs by aerial roots, but is best given a little support until established. Leaves pinnate, composed of 9 or 11, coarsely-toothed leaflets which are downy beneath, at least on the veins. Flowers trumpet-shaped, 5-8cm long, brilliant orange and scarlet, produced in terminal clusters on the current year's growths in August and September. SE United States. C 1640.

**'Flava'** ('Yellow Trumpet') This attractive form with rich yellow flowers received an AM when exhibited by us in 1969.

× **tagliabuana** (VIS.) REHD. (*C. grandiflora* × *C. radicans*). A variable hybrid intermediate in habit between the parents. Leaflets varying from 7-11, slightly downy on the veins beneath.

**'Madame Galen'** A vigorous climber with panicles of salmon-red flowers during late summer. Requires support up which to clamber. C 1889. AM 1959.

**CELASTRUS** L.—**Celastraceae**—A genus of some 30 species, widely distributed. Vigorous twining and scandent climbers with tiny insignificant flowers, followed in autumn by attractive, long-persistent capsules containing brightly coloured seeds. The flowers are often unisexual; therefore, when grown for fruit the species are best planted in pairs. Sometimes male and female clones are available. All species are tall-growing, rampant climbers and are best accommodated in an old tree or tall bush. They are also excellent for covering large stumps, hedges, unsightly walls, etc in full sun or shade.

**articulatus** See *C. orbiculatus*.

**hypoleucus** (OLIVER) LOES. (*C. hypoglaucus* HEMSL.) A large climber, the young shoots covered with a purplish bloom. Leaves oblong or obovate, up to 15cm long, strikingly glaucous beneath. The yellow-lined green capsules split to reveal the red seeds. A handsome species well distinguished by its terminal inflorescences and the glaucous undersurfaces of its leaves. C China. Introduced by E.H. Wilson about 1900.

**orbiculatus** THUNB. (*C. articulatus* THUNB.) A strong-growing climber reaching a height of 12m or more in a tree. The twining, young shoots are armed with a pair of short spines at each bud. Leaves varying from obovate to orbicular, 5-13cm long, turning clear yellow

**CELASTRUS orbiculatus**—*continued*

in autumn. Also in autumn the brownish capsules split open to reveal a yellow lining containing colourful red seeds. A beautiful climber in autumn, when the scarlet and gold-spangled fruits glisten against a backcloth of yellow. The most consistent species for fruiting. NE Asia. I 1860. AM 1914. FCC 1958 (to a hermaphrodite form). AGM 1984 (to hermaphrodite forms).

**rosthornianus** LOES. A vigorous scandent shrub reaching 5-6m in a tree. Leaves ovate to ovate-lanceolate, 4-8cm long, glossy green above. Capsules orange-yellow, containing scarlet seeds, long-persistent. W China. I 1910 by Ernest Wilson.

**rugosus** REHD. & WILS. A vigorous climber up to 6m with warty shoots and ovate or elliptic, strongly-toothed and wrinkled leaves up to 15cm long. Capsules orange-yellow, containing bright red seeds. W China. I 1908 by Ernest Wilson.

**scandens** L. Vigorous climber up to 7m with ovate to ovate-oblong, sharply-pointed leaves. Female plants produce orange-lined capsules containing scarlet-coated seeds. Not very free-fruiting in the British Isles. North America. Introduced by Peter Collinson in 1736.

†**CISSUS** L.—**Vitaceae**—A large genus of some 350 species of shrubs and herbaceous plants, widely distributed, mainly in tropical regions, the majority climbing by means of twining tendrils. Only the following species may be grown out-of-doors in the British Isles and then only in the mildest areas.

\***antarctica** VENT. "Kangaroo Vine". A strong-growing, vine-like climber with ovate-oblong, cordate leaves, rather leathery in texture, glossy green and 8-10cm long. An excellent climber or trailer for the conservatory and a popular house plant, succeeding in sun or shade. E Australia. I 1790.

\***striata** RUIZ & PAVON (*Vitis striata* (RUIZ & PAVON) MIQ.) (*Ampelopsis sempervirens* HORT.) A luxuriant evergreen climber for a sunny wall. Leaves 5-7.5cm across, composed of 5 obovate or oblanceolate, dark glossy green leaflets which are coarsely-toothed towards the apex. Fruits like reddish-purple currants. Chile and S Brazil. I about 1878.

**CLEMATIS** L.—**Ranunculaceae**—The species of this most popular genus are, on the whole, much more easy to establish than the large-flowered hybrids, though, like the latter, they thrive best in full sun, with their roots in cool, moist, well drained soil. The climbing species support themselves by means of their petioles which twine round any slender support available. The stronger-growing species are ideal when grown in trees or over large bushy shrubs and most others are very effective on walls, fences or wooden support. As well as flowers, some species have attractive silken seed-heads. The flower of a clematis is composed of 4-8 sepals which are usually large and colourful and sometimes referred to as tepals. The true petals are absent or in a few species (Atragene Section) reduced to small petaloid staminodes. *C. orientalis*, *C. tangutica* and their allies belong to Sect. Meclatis.

The only pruning needed is the removal of dead or useless wood, and the shortening of shoots which have extended beyond their allotted space, but, if necessary, the later summer-flowering species may be pruned hard every spring. See also under "Large-Flowered Garden Clematis".

**aethusifolia** TURCZ. A slender-stemmed climber reaching about 2m with deeply and finely divided leaves. Flowers borne in late summer, bell-shaped, 2cm long, with recurved lobes, pale primrose-yellow and fragrant, nodding on slender stems. N China. I about 1875.

**afoliata** BUCHAN. (*C. aphylla* KUNTZE) A curious species with slender leafless stems up to 3m long, clambering into bushes or, when no support is available, forming dense mounds. Worth growing for its unusual form, and for the fragrance of its small, unisexual, greenish-white flowers which are borne in May. Requires a warm, sunny, sheltered position. New Zealand. AM 1915.

**akebioides** (MAXIM.) HORT. ex VEITCH (Sect. Meclatis) A relative of *C. tibetana* growing to about 4m. Leaves pinnate, with up to 7, glaucous and rather fleshy, crenately toothed leaflets. Flowers bell-shaped, yellow or tinged with green to purple outside, borne on long stalks in late summer and early autumn. W China.

**CLEMATIS**—*continued*

**alpina** (L.) MILL. (Sect. Atragene) A lovely species with slender stems up to 2.5m long. Leaves with 9 ovate-lanceolate, coarsely-toothed leaflets. Flowers solitary, 2.5-4cm long, blue or violet-blue with a central tuft of white staminodes. They are borne on long, slender stalks during April and May, followed by silky seed-heads. Superb when grown over a low wall or scrambling over a large rock or small bush. N Europe, Mts of C Europe, N Asia. I 1792. AM 1894.

**'Frances Rivis'** ('Blue Giant') A vigorous, free-flowering clone with larger flowers, up to 5cm long, with a contrasting sheaf of white stamens and staminodes in the centre. Raised by Sir Cedric Morris before 1961. AM 1965 (as 'Blue Giant'). AGM 1984.

**'Helsingborg'** Flowers deep blue.

**'Pamela Jackman'** Large rich blue flowers. Outer staminodes tinged blue, the inner white. C 1960.

**'Ruby'** Flowers rose-red, with creamy-white staminodes. Raised by Ernest Markham in 1935.

**var. sibirica** (L.) SCHNEID. (var. *alba* DAVIS) Flowers creamy-white. NE Europe, Norway, Siberia. I 1753.

**'White Moth'** See *C. macropetala* 'White Moth'.

**'Willy'** Flowers mauve-pink with a deep pink blotch at the base of each sepal. C 1971.

**aphylla** See *C. afoliata*.

**\*armandii** FRANCH. A strong-growing, evergreen climber with stems 4.5-6m long. Leaves composed of 3, long, leathery, glossy dark green leaflets. The creamy-white flowers, 5-6.5cm across are carried in axillary clusters during April or early May. A beautiful species; subject to injury in severe winters and best planted on a warm, sunny wall. Seed-raised plants often produce smaller, inferior flowers. C and W China. Introduced by Ernest Wilson in 1900. FCC 1914.

**'Apple Blossom'** The true plant is a superb form with broad sepals of white shaded pink, especially on the reverse. Leaves bronze-green when young. A poor form that is easy to propagate has recently been distributed under this name. AM 1926. FCC 1936.

**'Snowdrift'** Flowers pure white. AGM 1984.

× **aromatica** LEN. & KOCH (*C. flammula* × *C. integrifolia*). A small sub-shrub, dying back to near ground level each winter. Leaves pinnate, with 3-7 short-stalked leaflets. Flowers fragrant, dark bluish-violet produced in terminal cymes from July to September.

**\*australis** KIRK A slender-stemmed, usually dioecious, scrambling species, the dark glossy green trifoliolate leaves with deeply cut leaflets. Flowers creamy to greenish-yellow, with 5-8 sepals, very fragrant, females about 3.5cm across, males slightly smaller, profusely borne either singly or in small panicles, April-May. New Zealand (S Island).

**'Bill Mackenzie'** (*C. tangutica* × *C. tibetana* subsp. *vernayi*). A vigorous, floriferous climber, the bright green leaves with sharply-toothed leaflets. Flowers long-stalked, up to 6cm across, with 4 wide-spreading, rather thick sepals, bright yellow with purple filaments. AM 1976.

**'Blue Bird'** (*C. alpina* × *C. macropetala*). A vigorous hybrid between 2 popular species which it resembles. Flowers 7.5cm across, purple-blue, semi-double. C 1965.

**†brachiata** THUNB. A tender species only suitable for the mildest areas or the conservatory. Flowers greenish-white, deliciously fragrant. S Africa. AM 1975.

**campaniflora** BROT. A vigorous climber up to 6m with pinnate leaves, the leaflets in groups of 3. Its small, bowl-shaped, blue-tinted flowers, borne profusely from July to September, are most effective in the mass. Portugal, S Spain. I 1810.

**chrysocoma** FRANCH. A beautiful species resembling the well-known *C. montana*, but less rampant. Leaves trifoliolate, covered, as are the shoots and flower-stalks, with a thick yellowish down. The soft pink flowers are 4-6cm across, generally smaller than those of *C. montana* and carried on usually longer and stouter peduncles. They are profusely borne from early May to June and successively on the young growths in late summer. W China. I about 1890. AM 1936. AGM 1984.

**var. sericea** SCHNEID. (*C. spooneri* REHD. & WILS.) An attractive variety with white flowers produced singly or in pairs on the older growths in late spring. W China. I 1909.

**\*cirrhosa** L. (*C. balearica* PERS.) An evergreen species up to 3m with leaves varying from simple to compound, with 3-6 leaflets. Flowers 4-6.5cm across, yellowish-white, opening during winter and followed by silky seed-heads. S Europe, Asia Minor. I 1596.

**CLEMATIS cirrhosa**—*continued*

**var. balearica** (RICH.) WILLK. & LANGE (*C. balearica* RICH.) "Fern-leaved Clematis". An elegant evergreen climber with slender stems, 3.5-4.5m long. Leaves prettily divided into several segments, becoming bronze-tinged in winter. Flowers pale yellow, spotted reddish-purple within, 4-5cm across, produced throughout winter. Balearic Isles. I before 1783. AM 1974.

**'Freckles'** Flowers very heavily spotted and streaked with red. AM 1989.

**'Wisley Cream'** Large, creamy-white, unspotted flowers.

**colensoi** See *C. hookeriana*.

**connata** DC. A vigorous species allied to *C. rehderiana* and distinguished by the flattened bases of the petioles which surround the stem. Flowers nodding, bell-shaped, pale yellow and slightly fragrant, borne in panicles in early autumn. Himalaya, W China. C 1885.

**crispa** L. A slender stemmed, semi-woody climber to about 2.5m with angled stems and pinnate leaves with up to 5 entire leaflets. Flowers borne during summer, bell-shaped, the reflexed lobes with crisped margins, pale to deep blue, solitary at the ends of the shoots. SE United States. I 1726.

× **durandii** KUNTZE (*C. integrifolia* × *C.* × *jackmanii*). A lovely hybrid up to 3m. Leaves simple, entire, 7.5-15cm long. The dark blue, four-sepalled flowers sometimes exceed 10cm in diameter and have a central cluster of yellow stamens. They appear from June to September. Garden origin in France about 1870. AGM 1984.

× **eriostemon** DECNE. (*C. integrifolia* × *C. viticella*). The original hybrid was raised in France before 1852.

**'Hendersonii'** A beautiful clematis, semi-herbaceous in habit, each year throwing up slender stems of 2-2.5m. Leaves simple or pinnate. Flowers deep bluish-purple, widely bell-shaped, slightly fragrant, 5-6.5cm across, nodding, borne singly on slender peduncles from July to September. Raised by Messrs Henderson of St John's Wood in about 1830. It is best given some support. AM 1965.

**fargesii** See *C. potaninii*.

**var. souliei** See *C. potaninii* var. *souliei*.

†\***finetiana** LEVL. & VAN. (*C. pavoliniana*) An evergreen climber up to 5m, related to *C. armandii*, but differing in its smaller flowers. Leaves composed of 3 dark green, leathery leaflets. Flowers white, fragrant, 2.5-4cm wide, borne in axillary clusters in June. Best grown on a warm, sheltered wall except in milder areas. C to W China. Introduced by E.H. Wilson in 1908.

**flammula** L. A strong-growing climber, 4-5m high, forming a dense tangle of glabrous stems clothed with bright green bi-pinnate leaves. From August to October, the loose panicles of small, white, sweetly-scented flowers are abundantly scattered over the whole plant, followed by silky seed-heads. An ideal climber for clothing tall, unsightly walls or hedges. S Europe. Cultivated in England since the late 16th century. AM 1984. AGM 1984.

**florida** THUNB. An elegant species with wiry stems, 3-5m long, and glossy green, compound leaves. Flowers 6-10cm across, solitary on long, downy stalks, sepals creamy-white, with a greenish stripe on the reverse, stamens dark purple, opening in June and July. A native of China and Japan and a parent of many garden hybrids. I 1776.

**'Alba Plena'** ('Plena') In this striking form each flower is fully double, a dense mass of greenish-white sepals, long-lasting and borne over a long period.

**'Sieboldii'** ('Bicolor') A beautiful and striking form recalling a passion flower. Flowers white, 8cm across, with a conspicuous central boss of violet-purple petaloid stamens. Introduced from Japan before 1836. AM 1914.

**forrestii** See *C. napaulensis*.

\***forsteri** GMEL. A usually dioecious, scrambling species related to *C. indivisa* but differing in its paler green, thinner leaves which are bright apple-green. Flowers verbena-scented, star-like, the males up to 4cm across with 5-8 white to creamy-yellow sepals, females smaller. New Zealand.

**glauca** See *C. intricata*.

**grata** WALL. The typical form from the Himalaya is rare in cultivation. It is mainly represented by the Chinese variety:-

**var. grandidentata** REHD. & WILS. A strong-growing climber reaching 9m in a suitable position. Leaves 15 cm long, composed of 3-5, coarsely-toothed leaflets. Flowers white,

**CLEMATIS grata var. grandidentata**—*continued*

2.5cm wide, borne in small axillary and terminal panicles during May and June. It is a hardy species related to *C. vitalba* and was introduced from W China by E.H. Wilson in 1904.

**\*hookeriana** ALLAN (*C. colensoi* HOOK. f. 1864 not 1852) An unusual species of subtle charm, up to 3m, bearing fern-like, compound leaves with glossy green leaflets. The delightfully fragrant, star-shaped flowers, 4cm across, have yellowish-green, silky sepals and are borne in profusion during May and June. Succeeds best against a sunny wall. New Zealand. Introduced by Collingwood Ingram in 1935. AM 1961.

**indivisa** WILLD. (*C. paniculata* GMEL.) A usually dioecious New Zealand species, the trifoliolate leaves with dark glossy green, entire or shallowly lobed or toothed leaflets. Flowers often fragrant, the males larger than those of the female and up to 10cm across, sepals 6-8, white, stamens yellow, with pink anthers. I 1840.

**'Lobata'** A juvenile form with coarsely-toothed or lobed leaflets and slightly larger flowers.

**intricata** BUNGE (*C. glauca* HORT. not WILLD.) (Sect. Meclatis) A slender climber up to 6m, with pinnate or bi-pinnate, glaucous leaves. The slender-stalked, bell-shaped flowers are 5cm across when fully open and deep orange-yellow. They are produced during August and September and are followed by silky seed-heads. S Mongolia, N China.

× **jackmanii** MOORE (*C. lanuginosa* × *C. viticella*). A superb large-flowered hybrid, raised in the nursery of Messrs Jackman of Woking in 1858. A spectacular climber, 3-4m high, with pinnate leaves. Flowers 10-13cm across, consisting of normally 4 conspicuous, rich, violet-purple sepals. They are borne in great profusion singly or in threes from July to October, on the current year's growth. Many clones have been named for which see "Large-Flowered Garden Clematis". FCC 1863.

× **jouiniana** SCHNEID. (*C. heracleifolia* var. *davidiana* × *C. vitalba*). A vigorous, somewhat shrubby climber up to 3.5m high. Leaves composed of 3-5 coarsely-toothed leaflets. Effective in autumn with its profusion of small, white, lilac-tinted flowers. An excellent plant for covering low walls, mounds or tree stumps. Garden origin before 1900.

**'Cote d'Azur'** A charming form with azure-blue flowers.

**'Mrs Robert Brydon'** Closer to *C. heracleifolia*, reaching 2m. Flowers very pale blue with white stamens.

**'Praecox'** A vigorous, early flowering form with slightly larger, pale blue flowers.

**lasiandra** MAXIM. An uncommon species, bearing leaves with 3-9, ovate-lanceolate, coarsely-toothed leaflets 5-10cm long. The purple, bell-shaped flowers 12mm long, are borne in short axillary cymes during autumn. White-flowered forms occasionally appear. Japan, China. I 1900.

**macropetala** LEDEB. (Sect. Atragene) A charming, slender-stemmed climber up to 2.5m, with prettily divided leaves. Flowers 6.5-7.5cm across, violet-blue, with conspicuous paler petaloid staminodes, giving the effect of doubling, produced from May or June onwards. Seed-heads silky, becoming fluffy and grey with age. A beautiful species for a low wall or fence. N China, Siberia. Introduced by William Purdom in 1910. AM 1923. AGM 1984.

**'Blue Bird'** See *C.* 'Blue Bird'.

**'Lagoon'** ('Blue Lagoon') Similar to 'Maidwell Hall' but with slightly deeper blue flowers. C 1959.

**'Maidwell Hall'** Flowers deep lavender-blue. C 1956.

**'Markham's Pink'** ('Markhamii') A lovely form with flowers the shade of crushed strawberries. AM 1935. AGM 1984.

**'White Moth'** (*C. alpina* 'White Moth') Flowers pure white. C 1955.

**'White Swan'** See *C.* 'White Swan'.

**maximowicziana** See *C. terniflora*.

**†\*meyeniana** WALP. A strong-growing evergreen species up to 6m or more, resembling *C. armandii* in leaf. Flowers white, 2.5cm across, borne in large, loose panicles during spring. A rare species for a warm, sheltered wall in the milder areas. S Japan, Ryukyus, Taiwan, S China, Philippines. C 1821. AM 1920.

**CLEMATIS**—*continued*

**montana** DC. A popular species of vigorous, often rampant growth and strong constitution; stems 6-9m long with trifoliolate, almost glabrous leaves. Flowers white, 5-6.5cm across, borne on long stalks in great profusion during May. A lovely climber for any aspect, excellent for growing in trees, over walls, outhouses and arbours, particularly those with a northern aspect. Himalaya. Introduced by Lady Amherst in 1831.

**'Alexander'** A lovely form with creamy-white, sweetly-scented flowers. Introduced from N India by Col R.D. Alexander.

**'Elizabeth'** A lovely clone with large, slightly fragrant, soft pink flowers in May and June. AGM 1984.

**'Freda'** Deep cherry-pink, the sepals with darker edges; young foliage bronze. A seedling of 'Pink Perfection' raised by and named after Mrs Freda Deacon.

**f. grandiflora** REHD. A strong-growing, Chinese variety, occasionally up to 12m, producing an abundance of white flowers in May and June. Excellent on a north-facing wall. AGM 1984.

**'Marjorie'** Semi-double, creamy-pink with salmon-pink centre. A seedling of var. *wilsonii*.

**'Picton's Variety'** Deep rosy-mauve with up to 6 tepals.

**'Pink Perfection'** Fragrant flowers similar to but slightly deeper coloured than 'Elizabeth'.

**var. rubens** WILS. A beautiful variety with bronze-purple shoots and leaves and rose-pink flowers during May and June. W and C China. Introduced by E.H. Wilson in 1900. AM 1905. AGM 1984.

**'Tetrarose'** An excellent tetraploid form of Dutch origin, with bronze foliage and lilac-rose flowers up to 7.5cm across, during May and June. AGM 1984.

**var. wilsonii** SPRAGUE A Chinese variety producing masses of fragrant, rather small, white flowers in late June.

†**napaulensis** DC. (*C. forrestii* W.W. SM.) A semi-evergreen climber reaching 6-9m, with leaves composed of 3-5 glabrous leaflets. Flowers cup-shaped, 1-2.5cm long, creamy-yellow, with conspicuous purple stamens. They are produced in axillary clusters on the young growths during winter. Only suitable for the milder areas. N India, SW China. Collected by G. Forrest in 1912. AM 1957.

**nutans** HORT. See *C. rehderiana*.

**orientalis** L. (Sect. Meclatis) Graceful climber to 5m with downy shoots. Leaves pinnate with up to 3 pairs of widely spaced glaucous grey leaflets, toothed or lobed. Flowers small, nodding, with 4 strongly reflexed pale yellow tepals slightly streaked with red towards the base and contrasting with the deep purplish-red filaments of the clustered stamens. Flowers late September to October, best after a hot summer. SE Europe to W China. The true species is rare in cultivation. For the plant commonly grown under this name see *C. tibetana* subsp. *vernayi*.

**paniculata** GMEL. See *C. indivisa*.

**paniculata** THUNB. See *C. terniflora*.

**patens** MORR. & DECNE. A slender species up to 3m, closely related to and resembling *C. florida*. The form we grow has flowers 10-15cm across with creamy-white sepals, appearing during late summer and early autumn. Several of the large-flowered garden hybrids are derived from this species. Japan, China. I 1836.

**pavoliniana** See *C. finetiana*.

†**phlebantha** L.H.J. WILLIAMS A recently named species discovered and introduced by O. Polunin, W. Sykes and L.H.J. Williams from W Nepal in 1952 (under the number P.S. & W. 3436). Described as a trailing shrub in the wild. The greatest attraction of this lovely climber is its glistening silvery-silky pinnate leaves and stems. The flowers are 2.5-4.5cm across, with 5-7 creamy-white, prettily veined sepals. They are borne singly in the leaf axils of the young growths during summer. It is sad that this beautiful plant is not proving more hardy. Planted against a south-east wall here it has survived for many years but is cut back most winters. It is certainly worthy of a selected site in full sun against a south-facing wall or on a well drained sunny bank. An excellent conservatory climber. I 1952. AM 1968.

**pitcheri** TORR. & A. GRAY A relative of *C. texensis* reaching about 3-4m, the leaves with up to 9 entire or lobed, reticulate leaflets. Flowers pitcher-shaped, purplish-blue, deeper

**CLEMATIS pitcheri**—*continued*

inside, with recurved sepals, solitary on long stalks. Named after its discoverer, Zina Pitcher. C United States. I 1878.

**potaninii** MAXIM. (*C. fargesii* FRANCH.) A strong-growing climber up to 6m, with comparatively large, compound leaves. Flowers white, 4-5cm across, produced in the leaf axils continuously from June to September. W China. It is represented in cultivation by the following variety:-

**var. souliei** (*C. fargesii* var. *souliei* FINET & GAGNEP.) This is the form in general cultivation, differing little from the typical form. W China. I 1911.

**rehderiana** CRAIB (*C. nutans* HORT. not ROYLE) (*C. veitchiana* CRAIB) A charming species, reaching 7.5m in a tree. Leaves pinnate or bipinnate with 7-9, coarsely-toothed leaflets. The nodding, bell-shaped flowers up to 2cm long are soft primrose-yellow and deliciously scented of cowslips. They are carried in erect panicles 15-23cm long during late summer and autumn. W China. I 1898. AM 1936. AGM 1984.

**'Rosy O'Grady'** A hybrid between *C. alpina* and *C. macropetala* with large rose-pink, semi-double flowers. C 1967.

**serratifolia** REHD. (Sect. Meclatis) A slender species up to 3m, related to *C. tangutica*, with prettily divided green leaves. Flowers 2.5cm long, yellow, with purple stamens, borne very profusely in August and September, followed by attractive silky seed-heads. Korea, NE China, E USSR. I about 1918.

**songarica** BUNGE A low, rambling shrub of greyish-green hue, with narrow, simple leaves up to 10cm long. Flowers 2.5cm across, creamy-white, produced during summer and autumn, followed by feathery seed-heads. Siberia to Turkestan. I before 1880.

**spooneri** See *C. chrysocoma* var. *sericea*.

**tangutica** (MAXIM.) KORSH. (Sect. Meclatis) A dense-growing climber up to 4.5m, closely related to *C. orientalis*. A delightful, easily grown species with prettily divided sea-green leaves and rich yellow, lantern-like flowers, 4-5cm long. They are nodding at first, produced on long, downy stalks during autumn, the later ones intermingled with masses of silky seed-heads. Perhaps the best yellow-flowered species, excellent for low walls, fences, trellises, large boulders and banks. Mongolia to NW China. C 1890. AGM 1984.

**subsp. obtusiuscula** (REHD. & WILS.) GREY-WILSON A free-flowering, strong-growing variety differing in having fewer teeth on the leaves and the flowers opening more widely with blunt sepals. W Sichuan, China. I by Ernest Wilson in 1908. AM 1913.

**terniflora** DC. (*C. maximowicziana* FRANCH. & SAV.) (*C. paniculata* THUNB. not GMEL.) A vigorous species up to 10m often forming a dense tangle of growth. Leaves with 3-5 long-stalked leaflets. The hawthorn-scented, white flowers, 2.5-4cm wide, are borne in panicles on the current year's growth in autumn. In the British Isles this species only flowers in profusion after a hot summer. Korea, China, Japan. I about 1864.

**texensis** BUCKL. (*C. coccinea* ENGELM.) A distinct species with pinnate leaves, composed of 4-8, stalked, glaucous leaflets. The red, pitcher-shaped, nodding flowers 2.5cm long, are produced on penduncles 13-15cm long during the summer and autumn. In the British Isles this attractive climber is usually semi-herbaceous in habit and requires some form of protection in winter. It is a parent of several hybrids. Texas (United States). I 1868.

**tibetana** O. KUNTZE (Sect. Meclatis) The typical form of this species, a native of N India, is not in cultivation. It is represented by the following form.

**subsp. vernayi** (FISCH.) GREY-WILSON (*C. orientalis* HORT.) A vigorous and graceful climber with finely divided glaucous leaves. Flowers nodding, yellow to greenish-yellow or purple-flushed, with purple stamens, bell-shaped at first, the sepals later spreading; borne singly or up to 3 together. Remarkable in its thick, spongy sepals which have given it the name of "Orange Peel Clematis". Nepal, Tibet. I from SE Tibet in 1947 by Ludlow and Sherriff (L. & S. 13342). AM 1950. AGM 1984 (to L. & S. 13342).

×**triternata** DC. (*C. flammula* × *C. viticella*) (*C. × violacea*) A vigorous climber up to 5m with leaves pinnate or bi-pinnate. Flowers up to 3cm wide, pale violet, borne in terminal panicles during late summer. Origin before 1840.

**'Rubromarginata'** The fragrant flowers are white, margined reddish-violet, and when borne in masses during late summer give the effect of dark, billowing clouds.

†***uncinata** BENTH. An evergreen climber up to 4.5m, with compound leaves, the leaflets up to 10cm long, glaucous beneath. Flowers about 2.5cm across, white, fragrant, borne in

**CLEMATIS uncinata**—*continued*

large panicles in June and July. A beautiful species requiring a warm, sheltered wall. W China. First discovered by Augustine Henry in 1884. Introduced by Ernest Wilson in 1901. AM 1922.

× **vedrariensis** VILM. (*C. chrysocoma* × *C. montana* var. *rubens*). A strong-growing climber up to 6m. Leaves trifoliolate with coarsely-toothed, dull purplish-green leaflets. Flowers 5-6.5cm wide, with 4-6, broad, delicate rose sepals, surrounding the bunched yellow stamens. Flowering from late May onwards. Raised by Mons Vilmorin prior to 1914. AM 1936.

**veitchiana** See *C. rehderiana*.

× **violacea** See *C.* × *triternata*.

**vitalba** L. "Travellers Joy" "Old Man's Beard". A rampant, familiar native climber of hedgerows and roadsides, especially in chalk areas, often clambering high into trees, its rope-like stems forming long columns or dense curtains. Leaves variable in size, pinnate. The small, greenish-white, faintly scented flowers in late summer and early autumn are followed by glistening silky seed-heads which become fluffy and grey with age, remaining throughout winter. Too vigorous for all but the wild garden. S, W and C Europe (including British Isles), N Africa, Caucasus.

**viticella** L. A slender climber up to 3.5m with pinnate leaves. The violet, reddish-purple or blue flowers 4cm across are profusely borne on slender stalks during summer and early autumn. S Europe. Cultivated in England since the 16th century. Small-flowered hybrids of this species are included here.

**'Abundance'** Delicately veined flowers of soft purple. AGM 1984.

**'Alba Luxurians'** Flowers white, tinted mauve. AGM 1984.

**'Kermesina'** Flowers crimson. AGM 1984.

**'Little Nell'** White with pale pink margins, 5cm across, very profuse. C 1900.

**'Minuet'** Flowers erect, larger than those of the type, creamy-white, with a broad band of purple terminating each sepal.

**'Purpurea Plena Elegans'** Flowers double, up to 6cm across, with numerous sepals, lilac-purple, paler in the centre. FCC 1987.

**'Royal Velours'** Flowers deep velvety-purple. AM 1948. AGM 1984.

**'White Swan'** (*C. macropetala* 'White Swan') (*C. alpina* var. *sibirica* × *C. macropetala*) A hybrid raised in Canada and selected in 1961. The pure white, double flowers are up to 12cm across.

## LARGE-FLOWERED GARDEN CLEMATIS

The large-flowered clematis, a selection of which are described below, share with the rose a special place in the garden. They are among the most colourful of flowering plants and, when well placed, their effect is charming and often spectacular. Like the species from which they are derived they are fairly adaptable, but being less easily established, require and fully deserve more care in the selection of the site and preparation of the soil.

They are best planted where their "heads" are in the sun and their roots are shaded. They succeed best in a good loamy soil in which well rotted manure plus lime in some form have been mixed. Good drainage is essential. They may be trained to wires on a wall or grown over pergolas, trellises, or tripods or into shrubs or small trees. They may also be encouraged to grow with wall shrubs or climbing roses, their flowers often combining effectively. When considering training a clematis over or into a tree or bush, care should be taken to plant it, where practicable, well away from the roots of the intended host.

Clematis are gross feeders and respond to an annual mulch of well rotted manure or compost, plus an ample supply of water.

Generally speaking, clematis flower most abundantly in full sun, but many are almost as prolific in a shady or north-facing position. The paler and more delicately coloured cultivars, such as 'Nelly Moser', tend to bleach when exposed to a hot sun.

The large-flowered clematis are sometimes subject to a puzzling disease known as "Clematis Wilt", for which at present there seems to be no known cure. Young plants

**CLEMATIS**—*continued*

are mainly affected, the sudden collapse of a single shoot or of the whole plant whilst in full growth being the usual symptom.

**Pruning.** For pruning purposes the large-flowered clematis can be divided into 2 groups.

(*a*) Applies to the FLORIDA, LANUGINOSA and PATENS groups which flower on the previous year's wood. These normally flower in May and June and the only pruning required is to trim back the old flowering growths immediately after flowering. Old, dense-habited plants may also be hard pruned in February, but the first crop of flowers will thus be lost.

(*b*) Applies to the JACKMANII, TEXENSIS and VITICELLA groups which flower on the current year's shoots. These normally flower in late summer and autumn and may be hard pruned to within 30cm of the ground in February or March. Old unpruned plants tend to become bare at the base.

The letters in parentheses following the names indicate the groups to which the cultivars belong, viz:—(F)—FLORIDA, (J)—JACKMANII, (L)—LANUGINOSA, (P)—PATENS, (T)—TEXENSIS and (V)—VITICELLA.

**'Asao'** Large, with 6-7 broad rose-carmine sepals.

**'Ascotiensis'** (V) Azure-blue to 13cm across with pointed sepals, very floriferous; July to September. C 1871.

**'Barbara Dibley'** (P) Pansy-violet, with deep carmine stripe along each sepal, to 20cm across or more; May and June and again in September.

**'Barbara Jackman'** (P) Deep violet striped magenta to 15cm with cream stamens. May-June. C 1952. AGM 1984.

**'Beauty of Worcester'** (L) Blue-violet, to 15cm, with contrasting creamy-white stamens; occasionally produces double flowers; May to August. C 1900. AGM 1984.

**'Bee's Jubilee'** (P) Blush-pink banded carmine, to 18cm. C 1958. AGM 1984.

**'Belle of Woking'** (F) Pale mauve, double, 10cm, May and June.

**'Blue Gem'** (L) Sky-blue, large, to 15cm; June to October.

**'Capitaine Thuilleaux'** ('Souvenir de Capitaine Thuilleaux') (P) Creamy-pink with deeper bar, to 16cm across.

**'Carnaby'** (L) Deep raspberry-pink with deeper bar. Good in shade. Compact and free-flowering. C 1983.

**'Comtesse de Bouchaud'** (J) Beautiful soft rose-pink, with yellow stamens, to 15cm across, vigorous and free-flowering; June to August. C 1903. AM 1936. AGM 1984.

**'Corona'** (P) Purple suffused pink with orange highlights, 18cm across, dark red anthers. May-June and August. C 1972.

**'Countess of Lovelace'** (P) Double and single, bluish-lilac with cream anthers, 15cm across. May-July. C 1876.

**'Daniel Deronda'** (P) Large violet-blue, paler at centre, up to 20cm across with creamy stamens; flowers often double; June to September.

**'Dawn'** Pale pink shading white towards the base, 15cm across with conspicuous red anthers. Best in shade. May-June. C 1969.

**'Dr Ruppel'** (P) Deep pink with carmine bar and yellow stamens. Up to 20cm across. C 1975.

**'Duchess of Albany'** (T) Flowers tubular, nodding, bright pink, shading to lilac-pink at margins; July to September. AM 1897.

**'Duchess of Edinburgh'** (F) Large double, rosette-like, white with green shading, scented, to 10cm across; May and June. C 1875.

**'Duchess of Sutherland'** (V) Petunia-red with a darker bar on each tapered sepal, to 15cm across, often double; July and August.

**'Edith'** (L) Similar to 'Mrs Cholmondley' of which it is a seedling but flowers white with red anthers.

**'Elsa Späth'** (P) Large, lavender-blue to 20cm with red stamens. May-June and September. AGM 1984.

**'Ernest Markham'** (V) Glowing petunia-red, with a velvety sheen, to 15cm across, sepals rounded; June to September. C 1938. AGM 1973.

**CLEMATIS**—*continued*

**'Etoile Rose'** (T) ([*C. scottii* × *C. texensis*] × *C. viticella*). Semi-herbaceous. Flowers nodding, bell-shaped, 5cm long, deep cherry-purple with a silvery-pink margin. Summer. AM 1959. AGM 1984.

**'Etoile Violette'** (V) Vigorous and free-flowering, deep purple, to 10cm across with 4-6 sepals. July-September. C 1885. AGM 1984.

**'Fair Rosamond'** Fragrant, to 15cm across, pale blush-pink with carmine bar fading to white, purple anthers. May-June. C 1871. FCC 1873.

**'Fairy Queen'** (L) Pale flesh-pink, with bright central bars, 18cm across; May and June. FCC 1875.

**'General Sikorski'** (L) Mid blue, reddish at the base of the sepals, to 15cm across. Raised in Poland. June-July.

**'Gipsy Queen'** (J) Rich velvety violet-purple to 12cm across with broad, rounded sepals; vigorous and free-flowering; July to September. C 1871.

**'Gravetye Beauty'** (T) Flowers bell-shaped at first, the sepals later spreading, cherry-red; July to September. AM 1935.

**'H.F. Young'** (P) A good blue, up to 20cm across with broad, overlapping sepals and white stamens. May-June and September. C 1962. AGM 1984.

**'Hagley Hybrid'** (J) Shell-pink with contrasting chocolate-brown anthers, to 15cm across, free-flowering; June to September. C 1956. AGM 1984.

**'Henryi'** (L) Large, creamy-white, to 18cm across with pointed sepals and dark stamens; vigorous and free-flowering; May and June and again in August and September. Raised by and named after Isaac Anderson-Henry. C 1858. AGM 1973.

**'Huldine'** (V) Pearly-white, the pointed sepals with a mauve bar on the reverse; vigorous and free-flowering; requires full sun; July to October. AM 1934. AGM 1984.

**'Jackmanii'** See *C.* × *jackmanii* under species.

**'Jackmanii Alba'** (J) White veined with blue, to 13cm across, early flowers double, later single. Very vigorous. C 1878. FCC 1883.

**'Jackmanii Superba'** (J) Large, rich violet-purple with broad sepals; vigorous and free-flowering; July to September. C 1878. AGM 1984.

**'John Huxtable'** (J) An excellent late flowering white. A seedling of 'Comtesse de Bouchaud' which it resembles in all but flower colour. July-August.

**'John Warren'** (L) Pinkish-lilac with deeper bar and margins and red stamens, fading after opening, to 25cm across.

**'Kathleen Wheeler'** (P) Deep mauve-blue, the prominent stamens with lilac filaments, large, 18cm across. May to June with smaller flowers in autumn. C 1967.

**'King George V'** (L) Flesh-pink, each sepal with a dark central bar, 15cm across; July and August.

**'Lady Betty Balfour'** (V) Deep velvety purple, 12cm across with golden stamens; very vigorous, best in full sun; August to October. C 1910. AM 1912.

**'Lady Londesborough'** (P) Pale mauve at first, becoming silvery-grey, to 15cm across with dark stamens and broad, overlapping sepals; free-flowering; May and June. FCC 1869.

**'Lady Northcliffe'** (L) ('Beauty of Worcester' × 'Otto Froebel'). Rich violet-blue with broad, wavy sepals and cream stamens, to 15cm across. June-September and later. AM 1906.

**'Lasurstern'** (P) Deep lavender-blue, to 18cm across with conspicuous white stamens and broad, tapering, wavy-margined sepals; May and June and again in early autumn. AGM 1984.

**'Lincoln Star'** (P) Brilliant raspberry-pink 15cm across with dark red stamens. May-June. Flowers in September paler with deep pink bar. C 1954.

**'Lord Nevill'** (P) Vigorous with bronze young foliage. Flowers deep purplish-blue, to 18cm across with darker veins. June and September. C 1878.

**'Mme Baron Veillard'** (J) Vigorous, to 4m with pale lilac-pink flowers 13cm across, sepals 6. July to September. C 1885.

**'Mme Edouard André'** (J) Rich crimson, 12cm across with yellow stamens and pointed sepals; very free-flowering; June to August. C 1893.

**'Mme Grangé'** (J) Velvety deep purplish-red, to 12cm across. July-September. C 1873. FCC 1877.

**CLEMATIS**—*continued*

**'Mme Julia Correvon'** (V) A hybrid of *C. viticella* and 'Ville de Lyon'. Flowers rose-red, up to 13cm across with cream stamens, very freely borne. July-September. C 1900. AGM 1984.

**'Mme Le Coultre'** See 'Marie Boisselot'.

**'Marcel Moser'** (P) Mauve, to 20cm across, each tapered sepal with a deep carmine central bar; May and June. AM 1897.

**'Margot Koster'** (V) A hybrid of *C. viticella*. Flowers deep rose-pink, to 10cm across with up to 6 reflexed sepals. July-September.

**'Marie Boisselot'** ('Mme Le Coultre') (P) Large, to 20cm across, pure white, with cream stamens and broad, rounded, overlapping sepals; vigorous and free-flowering. May to October. C 1900. AGM 1984.

**'Miss Bateman'** (P) Large, white, 15cm across, banded pale green when first open. May-June. C 1869.

**'Mrs Cholmondely'** (J) Large, pale blue, 20cm across with long-pointed sepals; vigorous and free-flowering; May to August. FCC 1873. AGM 1984.

**'Mrs George Jackman'** (P) White, to 18cm across, with broad, overlapping sepals. Similar to 'Marie Boisselot' but the sepals with a cream bar and the darker anthers are more prominent. May-June and September. C 1873.

**'Mrs Hope'** Pale blue with deeper bar and purple anthers, to 18cm across with overlapping sepals.

**'Mrs N. Thompson'** (P) Violet, 12cm across with scarlet bar. May-June and September. C 1961.

**'Mrs Spencer Castle'** (V) Large, pale heliotrope, sometimes double; May and June and again in early autumn.

**'Nelly Moser'** (L) One of the most popular. Large, pale mauve-pink, to 20cm across, each sepal with a carmine central bar; very free-flowering, but best on a north wall or in a shady position to prevent bleaching. May and June and again in August and September. C 1897. AGM 1984.

**'Niobe'** (J) The best red. Deep red, to 15cm across with yellow anthers. C 1975. AGM 1984.

**'Perle d'Azur'** (J) Light blue, with broad sepals; vigorous and free-flowering; June to August. C 1885. AGM 1984.

**'Proteus'** (F) Deep mauve-pink, to 15cm across, double with numerous sepals; later flowers single. June and September. FCC 1876.

**'Richard Pennell'** (P) Lavender flushed white, to 20cm across with wavy-margined sepals, red filaments and cream anthers. Raised from a cross between 'Vyvyan Pennell' and 'Daniel Deronda'. May-June and September. C 1974.

**'Rouge Cardinal'** (J) Crimson velvet, to 15cm across with brown anthers. June-August. C 1968.

**'Sealand Gem'** (L) Pale mauve-pink with carmine bar, to 15cm across. Tends to fade in sun. May-June and September. C 1950.

**'Sensation'** (L) Bright satiny mauve; May and June. FCC 1867.

**'Souvenir de Capitaine Thuilleaux'** See 'Capitaine Thuilleaux'.

**'Star of India'** (J) Red-purple becoming violet-purple with a redder central bar, up to 16cm across with broad sepals. June-September. FCC 1867.

**'Sylvia Denny'** Pure white, semi-double and rosette-like. From the cross 'Duchess of Edinburgh' × 'Marie Boisselot'.

**'The President'** (P) A popular clematis. Deep purple-blue with silvery reverse, to 18cm across; free-flowering; June to September. FCC 1876. AGM 1984.

**'Venosa Violacea'** (V) A very distinct hybrid of *C. viticella* possibly with *C. florida*. Flowers up to 10cm across, the 5 or 6 sepals with a white centre, veined and edged with purple, anthers blackish-purple. June-September. C 1910. AGM 1984.

**'Victoria'** (J) Rose-purple with 3 darker ribs on each sepal, to 15cm across with white stamens. Vigorous and free-flowering. June-September. FCC 1870.

**'Ville de Lyon'** (V) Bright carmine-red, deeper at margins, with golden stamens; July to October. AM 1901. AGM 1984.

**'Voluceau'** (V) Large, to 14cm across, petunia-red with yellow stamens. C 1970.

**CLEMATIS**—*continued*

**'Vyvyan Pennell'** (P) Described by its raisers as the best double clematis yet raised. Deep violet-blue, suffused purple and carmine in centre, to 15cm across. Fully double and produced from May to July. Single lavender-blue flowers are also produced in autumn. A cross between 'Daniel Deronda' and 'Beauty of Worcester'. C 1959. AGM 1984.

**'W.E. Gladstone'** (L) Very large, to 25cm across, silky lavender, with purple anthers; vigorous and free-flowering. June to September. FCC 1881.

**'Wada's Primrose'** (P) Pale creamy-yellow, best in shade. C 1979.

**'William Kennet'** (L) Lavender-blue with dark stamens and sepals with crimpled margins; June to August.

**'Yellow Queen'** Large, pale creamy-yellow with yellow stamens. June-August.

**CLEMATOCLETHRA** MAXIM.—**Actinidiaceae**—About 25 species of twining climbers natives of China. They are related to *Actinidia*, but differ in the solid pith and the flowers having 10 stamens and a single style (numerous in *Actinidia*). Useful subjects for a wall or tree in sun or semi-shade.

**integrifolia** MAXIM. A climber up to 7.5m, with ovate-oblong leaves, 4-7cm long, bristle-toothed, glaucous beneath. Flowers solitary or in clusters, small, white and fragrant, produced in June. NW China. I 1908 by Ernest Wilson.

**lasioclada** MAXIM. Attains up to 6m, with downy shoots. Leaves ovate, 5-10cm long, bristle-toothed. Flowers white, borne in axillary cymes in July. W China. I 1908 by Ernest Wilson.

**strigillosa** FRANCH. A rare and distinct species with compara-tively broad leaves. China.

**"CLIMBING HYDRANGEA"** See *Hydrangea petiolaris*.

**COCCULUS** DC.—**Menispermaceae**—A small genus of twining climbers suitable for growing into trees and hedges or on trellis-work in sun or semi-shade. About 11 species, widely distributed mainly in the tropics.

**orbiculatus** (L.) DC. (*C. trilobus* (THUNB.) DC.) A variable species up to 4.5m, with long persistent leaves entire or three-lobed, orbicular to ovate acuminate. Flowers small and inconspicuous, borne in axillary clusters in August. Fruits rounded, black, with a blue bloom. Japan, China. I before 1870.

**trilobus** See *C. orbiculatus*.

**DECUMARIA** L.—**Hydrangeaceae**—A genus of 2 perfectly hardy species of shrubs climbing by means of aerial roots. They are related to *Hydrangea*, but differ in that all their flowers are fertile. Like the climbing hydrangeas and schizophragmas they succeed in sun or shade on a wall or tree trunk.

**barbara** L. A semi-evergreen climber up to 9m. Leaves ovate 7.5-13cm long. The small, white flowers are carried in small corymbs in June and July. Native of SE United States where it climbs the trunks of trees. I 1785.

**\*sinensis** OLIV. A rare evergreen species up to 5m with obovate or oblanceolate leaves 2.5-9cm long. The small, green and white flowers are profusely carried in corymbs in May and are deliciously honey-scented. C China. I 1908 by Ernest Wilson. AM 1974.

**†DREGEA** E. MEYER (*Wattakaka* (DECNE.) HASSK.)—**Asclepiadaceae**—A genus of 3 species from warm regions of the Old World. The following species may be grown outside on a warm, sheltered wall, or in a conservatory.

**sinensis** HEMSL. (*Wattakaka sinensis* (HEMSL.) STAPF) A moderately hardy species with slender stems up to 3m long requiring some support. Leaves ovate, grey-felted beneath. The deliciously scented flowers, which bear a close resemblance to those of a *Hoya*, are white, with a central zone of red spots. They are borne in long-stalked, downy umbels during summer. China. I 1907 by Ernest Wilson. AM 1954.

**ECCREMOCARPUS** RUIZ & PAVON—**Bignoniaceae**—A small genus of about 5 species of evergreen or nearly evergreen climbers climbing by means of coiling leaf tendrils; natives

**ECCREMOCARPUS**—*continued*

of Chile and Peru. The following species is hardy in a sheltered corner in southern gardens, but in colder areas may be treated either as a conservatory subject or as a half-hardy annual.

**scaber** RUIZ & PAVON A vigorous, fast-growing climber, quickly covering a support with its angular stems 3-4.5m long. Leaves bi-pinnate ending in a slender tendril. The scarlet to orange or yellow, tubular flowers, 2.5cm long, are borne in racemes which are continuously produced throughout summer and autumn. Fruit a capsule, packed with small, winged seeds. Chile. I 1824. AGM 1984.

**†\*ELYTROPUS** MUELL. ARG.—**Apocynaceae**—A rare, monotypic genus.

**chilensis** MUELL. ARG. A strong-growing, twining, evergreen climber 3-4.5m high, with slender, bristly stems. Leaves opposite, elliptic to elliptic-oblong, acuminate, bristly hairy and conspicuously fringed. The small, white, lilac-flushed flowers are produced singly, or in pairs, in the axils of the leaves in spring. Fruits when produced are green, ripening to yellow. A rare climber suitable for a small tree or trellis or against a sheltered wall in milder areas of the British Isles, perhaps preferring semi-shade to full sun. Chile, Argentina.

**\*ERCILLA** A. JUSS.—**Phytolaccaceae**—A genus of 2 species of evergreen climbers supporting themselves by means of aerial roots; natives of Chile. May be grown on a wall in sun or shade, or as a ground cover.

**volubilis** JUSS. (*E. spicata* (HOOK. & ARN.) MOQUIN) (*Bridgesia spicata* HOOK. & ARN.) A self-clinging evergreen climber with rounded leathery leaves and dense sessile spikes of small, purplish-white flowers during spring. Chile. Introduced by Thomas Bridges in 1840, and more recently by Harold Comber. AM 1975.

**FALLOPIA** ADANS.—**Polygonaceae**—A genus of 9 species of perennial herbs and woody climbers, natives of N temperate regions. The species here described are hardy, twining climbers of vigorous, rampant growth, ideal for covering and concealing unsightly objects. They also look effective when trained into trees and are among the best plants for clothing old stumps, bare banks, etc.

**aubertii** (L. HENRY) HOLUB (*Polygonum aubertii* L. HENRY) (*Bilderdykia aubertii* (L. HENRY) DUMORT.) A rampant climber, with densely twining stems up to 12m long. Closely resembling and often mistaken in gardens for *F. baldschuanica* but differing in its white or greenish-white flowers which only become pinkish in fruit, and are borne on short, lateral branchlets. The branches of the inflorescence are minutely scabrid. W China, Tibet. Occasionally naturalised in Europe (including British Isles). I 1899.

**baldschuanica** (REG.) HOLUB (*Polygonum baldschuanicum* REG.) (*Bilderdykia baldschuanica* (REG.) WEBB) "Russian Vine". A rampant climber with stems up to 12m long. Leaves ovate or heart-shaped, pale green. Flowers pink-tinged. Though individually small, they are borne in conspicuous, crowded panicles on terminal and short lateral branches throughout summer and autumn. Less common in cultivation than *F. aubertii*, with which it is often confused. The almost smooth branches of the inflorescence contrast with the scabrid branches of *F. aubertii*. When in flower, covering a 12m high tree, it creates a remarkable picture. SE Russia (Tadzhikistan). C 1883. AM 1899.

**†\*GELSEMIUM** JUSS.—**Loganiaceae**—A genus of 2 or 3 species of tender evergreen, twining shrubs producing attractive flowers; natives of North America and SE Asia. The following species requires a sunny, sheltered wall.

**sempervirens** (L.) J. ST. HILL. "Yellow Jessamine". A species with stems up to 6m long bearing oblong or ovate-lanceolate, glossy green leaves 3.5-5cm long and fragrant, yellow, funnel-shaped flowers 2.5cm long during late spring or early summer. S United States.

**"GRANADILLA"** See *Passiflora edulis*.

**\*HEDERA** L.—**Araliaceae**—The "Ivies" make up a small genus of about 12 species of evergreen climbers attaching themselves to walls or tree trunks by means of aerial roots or covering the ground with a dense carpet; native from Europe and N Africa to Japan. There are no other self-clinging evergreens comparable with the ivies, thriving as they do in almost any soil, or situation, climbing without artificial aid to great heights or clothing bare ground beneath trees or shrubs where not even grass would grow. When large specimens on walls are becoming too dense, they may be pruned severely. The ivies are excellent for industrial sites and for withstanding atmospheric pollution. The leaves of the climbing (sterile) shoots are often markedly different from those of the flowering (fertile) shoots, this is particularly noticeable in the "Common Ivy"—*H. helix*. The flowers of the ivy are small and inconspicuous, borne in greenish umbels and replaced by usually black berry-like fruits.

**algeriensis** HIBB. A strong-growing species with large, dark green leaves up to 15cm or even 20cm across. Those of the climbing shoots are kidney-shaped, sometimes obscurely three-lobed, those of the flowering shoots rounded with a cordate base. They are a bright green during summer, often turning a deep bronze with green veins in winter, particularly if growing in a dry situation. Usually grown as *H. canariensis*. N Africa. C 1833.

**'Gloire de Marengo'** (*H. canariensis* 'Gloire de Marengo') (*H. canariensis* 'Variegata') An attractive and colourful form with large leaves, deep green in the centre, merging into silvery-grey and margined white. Admirably suitable for patio gardens and low walls, etc. Less hardy than green-leaved forms. It is a popular house plant. FCC 1880. AMT 1979. AGM 1984.

**'Margino-maculata'** (*H. canariensis* 'Margino-maculata') Leaves deep green and pale green mottled creamy-white, often producing shoots bearing leaves similar to 'Gloire de Marengo' but with a mottled margin. Often grown as a house plant; outside the leaves become heavily mottled with creamy-white. A sport of 'Gloire de Marengo'. C 1942.

**amurensis** See *H. colchica*.

**azorica** CARR. (*H. canariensis* 'Azorica') A distinct and hardy species with broad leaves of a light matt green, those of the climbing shoots with 5-7 blunt lobes. Azores.

**†canariensis** WILLD. (*H. helix* var. *canariensis* (WILLD.) DC.) "Canary Island Ivy". The true species of this name is a vigorous ivy with stout, reddish shoots. Leaves often large, deep bronze when young becoming mid to dark green and matt or only slightly glossy above. In shape they are rounded and almost entire to shallowly lobed or angled, deeply heart-shaped at the base. The most tender species, it can be killed by frost in hard winters even in the south of England. Canary Islands. For the plant usually grown under this name see *H. algeriensis*.

**'Azorica'** See *H. azorica*.

**'Gloire de Marengo'** See *H. algeriensis* 'Gloire de Marengo'.

**'Margino-maculata'** See *H. algeriensis* 'Margino-maculata'.

**'Variegata'** See *H. algeriensis* 'Gloire de Marengo'.

**chrysocarpa** See *H. helix* subsp. *poetarum*.

**colchica** (K. KOCH) K. KOCH (*H. amurensis* HIBB.) (*H. roegneriana* HIBB.) "Persian Ivy". A handsome, strong-growing species with leaves the largest in the genus, ovate or elliptic and 15-20cm long or more on the climbing shoots, smaller and oblong-ovate on the flowering shoots; all leaves are dark green, thick and leathery. Caucasus. C 1850. AGM 1984.

**'Arborescens'** A shrubby form developing into a small, densely leafy mound with large, oblong-ovate leaves. Raised from a cutting of the flowering growth, free-fruiting.

**'Dentata'** A spectacular climber with leaves even larger and somewhat more irregular in outline, slightly softer green and with occasional teeth. AMT 1979.

**'Dentata Variegata'** A most ornamental ivy with large, broad, ovate to elliptic often elongated leaves which are bright green shading to grey and conspicuously margined creamy-yellow when young, creamy-white when mature. Hardier than *H. algeriensis* 'Gloire de Marengo', and just as effective in patio gardens, on walls, etc. AM 1907. FCCT 1979. AGM 1984.

**'Sulphur Heart'** ('Gold Leaf') ('Paddy's Pride') An impressive variegated ivy. The large, broadly ovate leaves are boldly marked by an irregular central splash of yellow, merging

**HEDERA colchica 'Sulphur Heart'**—*continued*

into pale green and finally deep green. Occasionally almost an entire leaf is yellow. On old leaves the yellow splash becomes pale yellow-green. AMT 1979. AGM 1984.

**helix** L. "Common Ivy". One of the most adaptable and variable of all plants. It makes an excellent ground cover and is particularly useful where little else will grow. Several forms are commonly grown as house plants and in window boxes. Leaves of climbing shoots variable, three to five-lobed, those of the flowering shoots ovate to rhomboidal, entire. Europe, Asia Minor to N Iran.

**'Adam'** Leaves rather small, shallowly three-lobed, green and grey-green in the centre, margined creamy-white. C 1968. AGM 1984.

**'Arborescens'** A shrubby form developing into a broad, densely leafy mound. Originated as a cutting from flowering shoots.

**'Atropurpurea'** Leaves entire, or with 2 short lateral lobes. Dark purplish-green, darker in winter, often with bright green veins. C 1884. AMT 1979.

**'Aureovariegata'** See 'Chrysophylla'.

**'Bird's Foot'** See 'Caenwoodiana'.

**'Buttercup'** The best golden form of the Common Ivy. Leaves of a rich yellow, becoming yellowish-green or pale green with age. Slow-growing. C 1925. AGM 1984.

**'Caenwoodiana'** ('Bird's Foot') ('Pedata') A charming form with small leaves regularly divided into narrow lobes, of which the middle lobe is longest. C 1863.

**'Cavendishii'** A pretty form with small, angular green leaves mottled grey and broadly margined creamy-white. C 1867.

**'Chicago'** A form with small, dark green leaves frequently stained or blotched bronze-purple. C 1962.

**'Chicago Variegated'** See 'Harald'.

**'Chrysophylla'** ('Aureovariegata') Leaves irregularly suffused soft yellow, but liable to revert.

**'Congesta'** An upright, non-climbing form similar to 'Erecta' but differing in its more congested habit and smaller leaves. C 1887.

**'Conglomerata'** A dense, slow-growing form with rigid stems forming a low hummock. Leaves with or without lobes, obtuse at the apex and with a distinct wavy margin. Excellent for rock garden or woodland garden. FCC 1872. AMT 1979.

**'Cristata'** See 'Parsley Crested'.

**'Deltoidea'** See *H. hibernica* 'Deltoidea'.

**'Digitata'** See *H. hibernica* 'Digitata'.

**'Erecta'** ('Conglomerata Erecta') A slow-growing form with stiffly erect shoots. Leaves three-lobed, arrow-shaped with acute apex. An excellent plant for growing by a boulder on the rock garden or against a low tree stump. C 1898. It has been confused with 'Congesta' q.v.

**'Eva'** Leaves green and grey-green with a broad, creamy-white margin. A popular house plant. A sport of 'Harald'. C 1966.

**'Feastii'** See 'Königer's Auslere'.

**'Glacier'** Leaves silvery-grey with a narrow white margin. C 1950. AMT 1979. AGM 1984.

**'Glymii'** ('Tortuosa') Leaves ovate, somewhat curled or twisted, especially during cold weather. Often turning reddish-purple in winter. C 1867.

**'Goldchild'** Leaves when young bright green and pale green in the centre with a broad, golden yellow margin becoming blue-green and grey-green margined creamy-yellow. A very attractive ivy but best as a house plant. AM 1971.

**'Goldheart'** A most striking form of neat growth, the leaves with a large, conspicuous central splash of yellow. C about 1950. AM 1970. Wrongly called 'Jubilee' in recent years. AGM 1984.

**'Gracilis'** A slender form with prettily lobed leaves. C 1864.

**'Green Feather'** ('Meagheri') An unusual cultivar with small, pointed, deeply cut leaves. C 1939.

**'Green Ripple'** An attractive form with small, jaggedly lobed leaves, the central lobe long and tapering. A sport found in 1939. AMT 1979.

**HEDERA helix**—*continued*

**'Harald'** ('Chicago Variegated') Leaves shallowly five-lobed, green and grey-green in the centre margined with creamy-white. C 1958.

**'Hibernica'** See *H. hibernica*.

**'Ivalace'** A compact ivy with bright green, shallowly five-lobed leaves, stiffly curled at the margins. Very good for ground cover. C 1955. FCCT 1979. AGM 1984.

**'Kolibri'** A striking ivy, the leaves dark green broadly and conspicuously blotched and streaked with creamy-white. Best grown under cover. A sport of 'Ingrid' raised in Germany in the 1970s.

**'Königer's Auslese'** ('Feastii') A neat-growing form with five-lobed leaves, the central lobe large and triangular. Frequently grown as 'Sagittifolia'.

**'Little Diamond'** A dwarf, bushy plant of dense growth. Leaves diamond-shaped, entire or three-lobed, green mottled grey with a creamy-white margin. C 1970. AMT 1979. AGM 1984.

**'Luzii'** An attractive form popular as a house plant. Leaves shallowly five-lobed, green mottled with pale green, often developing a pale green margin when grown out-of-doors. Previously listed as 'Marmorata Minor'. C 1951.

**'Manda's Crested'** ('Curly Locks') An attractive ivy suitable for ground cover. Leaves with 5 pointed lobes which point upwards while the sinuses point down giving a wavy-edged effect, bronzing in winter. C 1940. FCCT 1979.

**'Marginata'** ('Argentea Elegans') Leaves triangular-ovate, broadly margined white, often tinged pink in winter.

**'Marginata Elegantissima'** See 'Tricolor'.

**'Marmorata Minor'** See 'Minor Marmorata' and 'Luzii'.

**'Meagheri'** See 'Green Feather'.

**'Minor Marmorata'** ('Marmorata Minor') An unusual form with small leaves mottled and marbled with cream and grey, occasionally pink-tinged during winter. C 1868. See also 'Luzii'.

**'Palmata'** A rather slow-growing form with palmately-lobed leaves. C 1846.

**'Parsley Crested'** ('Cristata') A distinct and unusual form with pale green, often rounded leaves which are attractively twisted and crimpled at the margin. C 1956. AMT 1979.

**'Pedata'** See 'Caenwoodiana'.

**'Persian Carpet'** A vigorous form good for ground cover or a wall with green shoots and light green, shallowly lobed leaves. Found in a public park in Tehran by John Whitehead in 1978.

**subsp. poetarum** NYMAN (*H. chrysocarpa* WALSH) "Poets' Ivy" "Italian Ivy". An attractive ivy distinguished by its bright green, shallowly-lobed leaves and the yellow fruits of the adult growth. In winter, the older leaves often turn a bright copper colour with green veins. Greece and Turkey (naturalised in Italy and France), N Africa, SW Asia. 'Emerald Gem' is a named clone.

**var. rhombea** See *H. rhombea*.

**'Sagittifolia'** Leaves bluntly three-lobed, arrow-shaped. C 1872. For the plant commonly grown under this name see 'Königer's Auslese'.

**'Sagittifolia Variegata'** Similar to 'Königer's Auslese' but leaves grey-green margined creamy-white. C 1965. AGM 1984.

**'Shamrock'** "Clover-Leaf Ivy". A very distinct form with small, bright green leaves which are entire to deeply three-lobed at the base, bronzing in winter. C 1954.

**'Sicilia'** Similar to 'Parsley Crested' with crisped leaf margins but edged with creamy-white.

**'Silver Queen'** See 'Tricolor'.

**'Tortuosa'** See 'Glymii'.

**'Tricolor'** ('Marginata Elegantissima') ('Marginata Rubra') ('Silver Queen') A pretty form with small leaves of greyish-green, margined white and edged rose-red in winter.

**hibernica** BEAN (*H. helix* 'Hibernica') "Irish Ivy". The common ivy of W England and the only species native to Ireland. It is closely related to *H. helix* but often produces larger leaves and is further distinguished by the rays of the scale hairs lying parallel with the leaf surface (upright in *H. helix*). The commonly grown form or forms of this species

**HEDERA hibernica**—*continued*

have large, dark green, usually 5-lobed leaves 7.5 to 15cm across. A vigorous ivy particularly useful as ground cover. AMT 1979. AGM 1984.

**'Deltoidea'** (*H. helix* 'Deltoidea') A distinct form of neat, close growth. The leaves possess 2 basal lobes which are rounded and overlapping. Becoming bronze-tinged in winter. C 1872.

**'Digitata'** (*H. helix* 'Digitata') Leaves broad, divided into 5 finger-like lobes. Originally found in Ireland. C 1826.

**maderensis** K. KOCH This ornamental and vigorous species is proving very hardy. Most closely resembling *H. hibernica* and with potential as a ground-cover plant. Leaves broad, slightly glossy, bronzing in cold weather, attractively held above the ground on long, pink stalks. Madeira.

**nepalensis** K. KOCH (*H. cinerea* (HIBB.) BEAN) (*H. himalaica* TOBLER) "Himalayan Ivy". A strong-growing species with greyish-green, ovate to ovate-lanceolate, taper-pointed leaves, 5-13cm long, occasionally with 2 basal lobes and several blunt teeth. Fruits usually yellow or rarely red. Himalaya. C 1880.

**var. sinensis** (TOBLER) REHD. Leaves unlobed or nearly so. W China.

**pastuchowii** VORONOV A vigorous species with leaves from entire to shallowly lobed or toothed. It was introduced to our nurseries in 1972 by Mrs Ala and Roy Lancaster from N Iran. These plants have dark blackish-green, heart-shaped and unlobed leaves with pale green veins, the midrib red beneath. The ivy native to Cyprus is a close relative of this. Caucasus, N Iran.

**rhombea** (MIQ.) BEAN (*H. helix* var. *rhombea* MIQ.) "Japanese Ivy". The Japanese equivalent of our native ivy, differing from the common species in its ovate or triangular-ovate leaves with sometimes 2 shallow lobes. Japan.

**'Variegata'** Leaves with a narrow creamy-white margin. C 1867.

**\*HOLBOELLIA** WALL.—**Lardizabalaceae**—A small genus of some 5 species, related to *Stauntonia*, of luxuriant, evergreen, monoecious, twining plants with compound leaves; natives of the Himalaya and China. They will grow in any fertile soil in sun or shade, but require sun for flower and fruit. Differs from *Stauntonia* in the free stamens.

**coriacea** DIELS A vigorous, hardy species up to 6m or more. Leaves composed of 3, stalked, glossy green leaflets, 7.5-15cm long. Flowers appearing in April and May, the purplish male flowers in terminal clusters, the greenish-white, purplish-tinged, female flowers in axillary clusters. Fruit a purplish, fleshy pod 4-7.5cm long, filled with rows of black seeds. A useful climber for growing on walls, drainpipes or into trees. C China. Introduced by Ernest Wilson in 1907.

**latifolia** WALL. (*Stauntonia latifolia* (WALL.) WALL.) An attractive, but slightly tender species with leaves consisting of 3–7, stalked leaflets, 7.5-18cm long. The fragrant flowers are borne in short racemes during March, the male flowers greenish-white, the female flowers purplish. Fruit an edible, purple, sausage-shaped, fleshy pod 5-7.5cm long. Hand-pollination is usually required to ensure fruiting. May be distinguished from *H. coriacea* by the more pronounced reticulate venation. Himalaya. I 1840.

**"HONEYSUCKLE"** See *Lonicera*.

**"HONEYSUCKLE, CAPE"** See *Tecomaria capensis*.

**"HOP"** See *Humulus*.

**HUMULUS** L.—**Cannabidaceae**—A small genus of 3 species of monoecious, perennial climbers natives of Europe and Asia. Though herbaceous the following species and its attractive golden-leaved form are vigorous plants and useful for giving summer clothing to unsightly objects, hedges, etc.

**lupulus** L. "Hop". A familiar, native climber with long, twining stems 3-6m long. Commonly seen scrambling in hedges and thickets. Leaves 7.5-15cm long, deeply three to five-lobed and coarsely-toothed. The female flowers are borne in drooping, yellowish-green, cone-

**HUMULUS lupulus**—*continued*

like clusters during late summer, enlarging in fruit. The fruit clusters are a valuable constituent of the best beers, for which purpose this plant is extensively cultivated in certain districts. S Europe, W Asia.

**'Aureus'** An attractive form with soft yellow leaves. Best grown in full sun. It is most effective when trained on a pergola or a wooden tripod.

**HYDRANGEA** L.—**Hydrangeaceae**—The species here described are climbing shrubs, attaching themselves to trees or walls by means of aerial roots. They are splendid in such positions and are equally happy in sun or semi-shade in all types of soils. Excellent for industrial sites and withstanding atmospheric pollution.

**altissima** See *H. anomala*.

**anomala** D. DON (*H. altissima* WALL.) A vigorous climber reaching a height of 12m or above in a suitable tree. Mature bark brown and peeling. Leaves ovate or elliptic, coarsely-toothed. Flowers arranged in slightly domed corymbs, 15-20cm across, in June, small, yellowish-white with several conspicuous, white, sterile florets along the margin. Himalaya to W China. I 1839.

**integerrima** See *H. serratifolia*.

**petiolaris** SIEB. & ZUCC. (*H. scandens* MAXIM. not (L. f.) SER.) (*H. anomala* subsp. *petiolaris* (SIEB. & ZUCC.) MCCLINTOCK) "Climbing Hydrangea". A strong-growing, self-clinging species reaching 18-25m in suitable trees and excellent on a north-facing or otherwise shady wall; in addition it is very picturesque when grown as a shrub. Leaves broadly ovate, abruptly pointed and finely-toothed. Flowers in corymbs 15-25cm across in June, dull, greenish-white, with several large, conspicuous, white, sterile florets along the margin. Vigorous enough when once established, it may require initial support until its aerial roots become active. Japan, Kuriles, Sakhalin, S Korea. I 1865. AGM 1984.

**\*serratifolia** (HOOK. & ARN.) PHIL. f. (*H. integerrima* (HOOK. & ARN.) ENGLER) An evergreen species with stout, elliptic to obovate, leathery leaves which are entire and usually marked with curious, tiny pits in the vein axils beneath. Flowers small, creamy-white, borne in crowded, columnar panicles, 7.5-15cm long, in late summer. Best grown against a wall in sun or shade, though in its native forests it is known to reach 15m or more in suitable trees. Chile. Introduced by Harold Comber in 1925/27. AM 1952.

**"IVY"** See *Hedera*.

**"IVY, BOSTON"** See *Parthenocissus tricuspidata*.

**"JASMINE"** See *Jasminum*.

**"JASMINE, CHILEAN"** See *Mandevilla laxa*.

**JASMINUM** L.—**Oleaceae**—The climbing "Jasmines" or "Jessamines" are easily grown in most fertile soils, preferring a sunny position. They are excellent for training up walls or pergolas and several are useful for covering unsightly banks. The hardy species are excellent for withstanding industrial sites. See also TREES AND SHRUBS.

†**\*angulare** VAHL (*J. capense* THUNB.) A choice but tender species with rather thickish, dark green, trifoliolate leaves. The sweetly-scented, white flowers, 5cm long, are borne in large panicles during late summer. Only suitable for the mildest localities, but a beautiful conservatory subject. S Africa. AM 1956.

†**\*azoricum** L. (*J. trifoliatum* MOENCH) A beautiful, twining species with trifoliolate leaves and clusters of white, sweetly-scented flowers, purple-flushed in bud, opening in summer and winter. Only suitable for the mildest localities. An excellent conservatory plant. Madeira, where it is very rare. I late 17th century. AM 1934.

**beesianum** FORR. & DIELS A vigorous, scandent shrub developing a dense tangle of slender stems, 2.5-3.5m long. Leaves tapering to a long point, dark, dull green. Flowers fragrant, rather small, of an unusual deep velvet red, appearing in May and June; followed by

**JASMINUM beesianum**—*continued*

shining black berries which often last well into winter. SW China. I 1907 from Yunnan by George Forrest.

**†dispermum** WALL. A delightful climber with twining stems and leaves varying from trifoliolate to pinnate on the same plant. The fragrant, white, pink-flushed flowers are borne in axillary and terminal cymes during summer. Only suitable for the mildest localities, but admirable as a conservatory plant. Himalaya, W China. C 1849. AM 1937.

**diversifolium** See *J. subhumile*.

**†\*floridum** BUNGE An evergreen species of scandent growth, with angular shoots and alternate, usually trifoliolate leaves. Flowers yellow, appearing in terminal clusters during late summer and early autumn. Requires a warm, sunny wall. W China. I 1850.

**humile** See TREES AND SHRUBS.

**†\*mesnyi** HANCE (*J. primulinum* HEMSL.) "Primrose Jasmine". A singularly beautiful, evergreen species with four-angled shoots and opposite trifoliolate leaves, 2.5-7.5cm long. Flowers bright yellow, 4cm long, semi-double and produced in succession from March to May. A strong-growing species with scandent stems up to 4.5m long. Best grown against a warm sheltered sunny wall in favoured localities or in a conservatory. Introduced from SW China by E.H. Wilson in 1900. FCC 1903.

**nudiflorum** See TREES AND SHRUBS.

**officinale** L. "Common White Jasmine" "Poets' Jasmine". A strong-growing, scandent or twining climber, reaching 6-9m in a suitable tree. Leaves pinnate, composed of 5-9 leaflets. Flowers white, deliciously fragrant, borne in terminal clusters from June to September. An old favourite cottage-garden plant, said to have been introduced into Britain as long ago as 1548. It requires a sheltered corner in cold northern districts. Caucasus, N Iran and Afghanistan, through the Himalaya to China. AGM 1984.

**f. affine** (LINDL.) REHD. ('Grandiflorum') A superior form with slightly larger flowers which are usually tinged pink on the outside. Not to be confused with *J. grandiflorum* L., a tender species for the greenhouse.

**'Argenteovariegatum'** A very striking form, the leaves grey-green margined with creamy-white. C 1770.

**'Aureum'** ('Aureovariegatum') Leaves variegated and suffused yellow; a very effective plant. C 1914.

**'Grandiflorum'** See f. *affine*.

**†\*polyanthum** FRANCH. A beautiful, vigorous, twining species up to 7.5m, related to *J. officinale*, but tender. Leaves pinnate, composed of 5-7 leaflets. The intensely fragrant, white flowers, flushed rose on the outside, are borne in numerous panicles from May until late summer, earlier under glass. Requires a warm wall or trellis in mild localities, but makes an excellent conservatory subject elsewhere providing it is kept under control by rigorous pruning. China. I 1891. AM 1941. FCC 1949.

**primulinum** See *J. mesnyi*.

**× stephanense** LEMOINE (*J. beesianum × J. officinale*). A vigorous climber up to 7.5m, with slender green, angular shoots. Leaves simple or pinnate, with 3-5 leaflets. Flowers fragrant, pale pink, borne in terminal clusters in June and July. The leaves of young or vigorous shoots are often flushed creamy-yellow. Interesting on account of it being the only known hybrid jasmine. It is a beautiful plant where space permits its full development, such as when covering an outhouse. It was raised at Saint-Etienne in France just prior to 1920 and occurs with the parents in the wild in Yunnan (China), where it was found by Delavay in 1887. AM 1937. AGM 1984.

**†suavissimum** LINDL. A tall-growing conservatory species with slender twining stems and linear leaves 2.5-6cm long. The white, sweetly fragrant flowers are borne in loose panicles during late summer. They will perfume the whole conservatory. Australia.

**†subhumile** W.W. SM. (*J. diversifolium* KOBUSKI) (*J. heterophyllum* ROXB.) A scandent shrub with purplish young shoots and alternate dark glossy green, leathery, privet-like leaves, which are simple or occasionally with 1 or 2 small, slender subsidiary leaflets. Flowers small, yellow, star-like, in slender glabrous cymes during late spring. The form we grow is the variety *glabricymosum*, differing little from typical form. E Himalaya, W China. I 1820.

†\*KADSURA JUSS.—**Schisandraceae**—A small genus of evergreen, monoecious, twining plants related to *Schisandra*. About 20 species natives of E and SE Asia.

**japonica** (L.) DUNAL A slender climber up to 3.6m, with dark green, oval or lanceolate leaves, 5-10cm long, glossy green, often turning red in autumn. Flowers solitary, cream-coloured, 2cm across, appearing during summer and early autumn. Fruits scarlet, in clusters. Requires a warm, sheltered wall; best in mild localities. Japan, China, Taiwan. I 1860.

'**Variegata**' Leaves with a broad margin of creamy-yellow.

†\*LAPAGERIA RUIZ & PAVON—**Philesiaceae**—A monotypic genus requiring a cool, moist, lime-free soil in shade or semi-shade. Succeeding best on a sheltered wall. It is an excellent conservatory plant, but detests long exposure to strong sunlight.

**rosea** RUIZ & PAVON "Chilean Bellflower". One of the most beautiful of all flowering climbers, the national flower of Chile. An evergreen with strong, wiry, twining stems reaching 3-4.5m on a suitable wall. Leaves ovate-lanceolate to cordate, leathery. The rose-crimson, fleshy, bell-shaped flowers, 7.5cm long by 5cm wide, are borne singly or in pendulous clusters from the axils of the upper leaves during most of summer and autumn. A lovely plant for a shaded sheltered wall in the milder counties. Chile, Argentina. I 1847. FCC 1974.

var. **albiflora** HOOK. Flowers white.

'**Flesh Pink**' Flowers flesh-pink.

'**Nash Court**' Flowers soft pink marbled with deeper pink. FCC 1884.

†\*LARDIZABALA RUIZ & PAVON—**Lardizabalaceae**—A genus of 2 species of evergreen twining plants with compound leaves and unisexual flowers; natives of Chile. Suitable for a sheltered wall in sun or semi-shade, but only in mild localities.

**biternata** RUIZ & PAVON A fairly vigorous climber with leaves composed of 3-9 dark green, glossy, oblong leaves. Flowers chocolate-purple and white, the males in pendulous racemes, the females solitary, appearing during winter. Fruits sweet, sausage-shaped, edible, dark purple, 5-7.5cm long. Chile. I 1844.

LONICERA L.—**Caprifoliaceae**—The climbing "Honeysuckles" include some of the loveliest and most popular of all twining plants. All are worth cultivating, though none surpasses the fragrance of our common native hedgerow species *L. periclymenum*. They are probably seen at their best when scrambling over other bushes, or tree stumps, trellises or pergolas, but are very adaptable to other purposes and some are even occasionally grown as small standards. Although some flower best with their "heads" in full sun, many honeysuckles luxuriate in half-shade or even complete shade and in such positions are less susceptible to aphis. They are happy in almost all soils. The funnel-shaped or trumpet-shaped flowers are pollinated by hawk-moths and bumble-bees, etc.

\***acuminata** WALL. A vigorous, even rampant, evergreen or semi-evergreen species related to *L. japonica*; excellent as a rapid ground cover. *L. japonica* has been grown under this name. Himalaya.

\***alseuosmoides** GRAEBN. An evergreen species with glabrous shoots and narrowly oblong, ciliate leaves. Flowers small, funnel-shaped, 12mm long, yellow outside, purple within, carried in short, broad panicles on the young growths from July to October. Berries black, blue bloomy. W China. I by Wilson about 1904.

× **americana** (MILL.) K. KOCH (*L. caprifolium* × *L. etrusca*) (*L. grata* AIT.) (*L. italica* TAUSCH) A magnificent, extremely free-flowering, vigorous climber reaching a height of 9m under suitable conditions. Leaves broad elliptic to obovate. Flowers 4-5cm long, fragrant, white, soon passing to pale and finally deep yellow, heavily tinged purple outside, appearing in whorls at the ends of the shoots and providing one of the most spectacular floral displays of late June and July. C before 1730. AM 1937. AGM 1984.

× **brownii** (REG.) CARR. (*L. hirsuta* × *L. sempervirens*) "Scarlet Trumpet Honeysuckle". A deciduous or semi-evergreen climber of moderate vigour. Leaves up to 8.5cm long, downy and glaucous beneath, the upper leaves perfoliate. Flowers 2.5-4cm long, orange-

**LONICERA** × **brownii**—*continued*

scarlet, borne in whorls at the ends of the branches in late spring, and again in late summer. Garden origin, before 1850.

**'Dropmore Scarlet'** A tall-growing climber, producing clusters of bright scarlet, tubular flowers, from July to October. This is now the commonest form of this hybrid in cultivation but is very susceptible to attack by aphids. AGM 1984.

**'Fuchsioides'** This clone of equal beauty is scarcely distinguishable from the typical form. AGM 1984.

**'Plantierensis'** Flowers coral-red, with orange lobes.

**caprifolium** L. (*L.* 'Early Cream') "Perfoliate Honeysuckle". A fairly vigorous climber up to 6m, with obovate or oval, glaucous leaves, the upper pairs of which are perfoliate. Flowers 4-5cm long, fragrant, creamy-white, very occasionally tinged pink on the outside, borne in whorls at the ends of the shoots in June and July. Berries orange-red. A popular species commonly planted in cottage gardens. The perfoliate upper leaves easily distinguish it from *L. periclymenum*. C and S Europe, Caucasus, Asia Minor. Long cultivated and occasionally naturalised in the British Isles. AGM 1984.

**'Pauciflora'** Flowers rose-tinged on the outside. AGM 1984.

**ciliosa** (PURSH) POIR. "Western Trumpet Honeysuckle". An American honeysuckle related to *L. sempervirens*, but differing in its ciliate leaves, the upper pairs of which are perfoliate. Flowers 2.5-4cm long, yellow, tinged purple on the outside, borne in whorls at the ends of the shoots in June. W North America. I 1825. AM 1919.

**dioica** L. A bushy twining shrub with ovate or elliptic glabrous leaves to 7cm long, glaucous beneath. Flowers deep yellow tinged red, fragrant, borne in dense groups of terminal whorls above a pair of perfoliate leaves in June. Corolla, two-lipped, about 2.5cm long and across. Berries red. E North America. I 1776.

**'Dropmore Scarlet'** See *L.* × *brownii* 'Dropmore Scarlet'.

**etrusca** SANTI A very vigorous deciduous or semi-evergreen climber with purplish young shoots and oval or obovate, glaucous, usually downy leaves which become perfoliate at the ends of the shoots. Flowers 4cm long, fragrant, opening cream, often flushed red, deepening to yellow, borne in whorls at the ends of the shoots in June and July, but not on young plants. A superb species revelling in sun and seen at its best in the drier counties. Mediterranean region. I about 1750.

**'Donald Waterer'** Young shoots red, flowers red outside white inside, becoming orange-yellow. Found in the French Pyrenees about 1973 by Donald Waterer. AM 1985.

**'Michael Rosse'** Flowers pale yellow at first deepening with age. Derived from a plant in the National Trust garden at Nymans, West Sussex. AM 1982.

**flexuosa** See *L. japonica* var. *repens*.

*****giraldii** REHD. An evergreen species forming a dense tangle of slender, hairy stems. Leaves narrowly oblong, heart-shaped at base, 4-9cm long and densely velvety hairy. Flowers 2cm long, purplish-red, with yellow stamens, yellowish pubescent on the outside, produced in terminal clusters in June and July. Berries purplish-black. Useful for growing over a low wall or parapet. NW China. I 1899.

*****glabrata** WALL. A very vigorous evergreen climber with densely hairy shoots and dark glossy green, lanceolate leaves cordate at the base and hairy on both sides. Flowers two-lipped, slightly fragrant, opening yellow tinged red becoming white tinged deep pink, borne in terminal clusters and in pairs from the axils of young leaves in early summer and again in autumn. Berries black. Himalaya. I by Harry van de Laar from E Nepal in 1973 (VdL 4120).

**glaucescens** RYDB. A bushy shrub with twining stems and obovate to narrow elliptic leaves, green above, glaucous and pubescent beneath. Flowers 2cm long, orange-yellow, borne in terminal whorls in June and July followed by dense clusters of orange-red fruits. North America. C 1890.

**grata** See *L.* × *americana*.

× **heckrottii** REHD. (*L.* × *americana* × *L. sempervirens*). A shrubby plant with scandent branches. Leaves oblong or elliptic, glaucous beneath, the upper ones perfoliate. Flowers 4-5cm long, fragrant, yellow, heavily flushed purple, abundantly borne in whorls at the ends of the shoots from July to August or September. Origin uncertain, before 1895.

**LONICERA** × **heckrottii**—*continued*

**'Gold Flame'** According to the Dutch botanist Harry van de Laar this is a distinct clone. It differs from the plant described above in being less evergreen and more of a climber, with deeper green leaves turning blue-green in autumn; it also has shorter racemes and brighter flowers. The name 'American Beauty' has been proposed for the form described above.

**\*henryi** HEMSL. (*L. henryi* var. *subcoriacea* REHD.) A vigorous evergreen or semi-evergreen species with downy shoots and oblong, slender-pointed, ciliate leaves, 4-10cm long, dark green above, paler and glossy beneath. Flowers yellow, stained red, 2cm long, borne in terminal clusters in June and July, followed by black berries. W China. I 1908 by Ernest Wilson. A handsome plant introduced by Keith Rushforth is close to this species but has bristly shoots. The leaves are very large and glossy, deep bronze when young. Flowers opening white with a pink tube becoming deep yellow, followed by blue-black berries.

**var. subcoriacea** See *L. henryi*.

**†\*hildebrandiana** COLL. & HEMSL. "Giant Honeysuckle". This magnificent species is a giant in every respect. A strong-growing, evergreen climber, in its native forests reaching into lofty trees. Leaves broadly oval, 7.5-15cm long. Flowers 9-15cm long, fragrant, creamy-white at first, changing to rich yellow occasionally flushed orange-yellow, produced in the terminal leaf axils from June to August; berries 2.5-3cm long. This wonderful species is only suitable for the very mildest localities of the British Isles, but makes a spectacular, if rampant, climber for the conservatory. It is the largest in size, leaf, flower and fruit of all the honeysuckles. Shy-flowering when young. Burma, Thailand, SW China. First discovered in the Shan Hills (Burma) by Sir Henry Collet in 1888. FCC 1901.

**\*implexa** SOL. An evergreen or semi-evergreen climber with glabrous shoots and ovate to oblong leaves, glaucous beneath, the upper ones perfoliate. Flowers 4-5cm long, yellow, flushed pink on the outside, borne in whorls at the ends of the shoots from June to August. Our propagator was shaken when he first received this species as cuttings by air from Mr H.G. Hillier in 1934, who was then on honeymoon. S Europe. I 1772.

**italica** See *L.* × *americana*.

**\*japonica** THUNB. A rampant evergreen or semi-evergreen species reaching 6-9m on a suitable support. Leaves ovate to oblong, often lobed on young or vigorous shoots. Flowers fragrant, 2.5-4cm long, white, changing to yellow with age, produced continuously from June onwards. An excellent climber or creeper for covering and concealing unsightly objects. As a ground cover it must be kept under control; it is a serious weed in parts of North America. Japan, Korea, Manchuria, China. I 1806.

**'Aureoreticulata'** A delightful form of var. *repens*, the neat, bright green leaves with a conspicuous golden reticulation. I by Robert Fortune before 1862. AGM 1984.

**'Halliana'** Flowers white, changing to yellow, very fragrant. Considered by some authorities to be the typical form. AGM 1984.

**'Hall's Prolific'** Selected in Holland from plants grown as 'Halliana', this flowers profusely even when young.

**var. repens** REHD. (*L. flexuosa* THUNB.) A distinct variety, the leaves and shoots flushed purple; flowers flushed purple on the outside, very fragrant. Japan, China. Introduced early in the 19th century.

**periclymenum** L. "Woodbine". The common honeysuckle of our hedgerows and woods. A vigorous species climbing, scrambling or trailing in habit. Leaves ovate to oblong, glaucous beneath. Flowers 4-5cm long, strongly and sweetly fragrant, creamy-white within, darkening with age, purplish or yellowish outside, appearing in terminal clusters from June to September. Berries red. A pretty climber, long connected with old cottage-gardens. Europe, N and C Morocco.

**'Belgica'** "Early Dutch Honeysuckle". Flowers reddish-purple on the outside fading to yellowish, produced during May and June and again in late summer. Cultivated since the 17th century. AGM 1984.

**'Graham Thomas'** Flowers white in bud and when first open, becoming yellow, borne over a long period. Found in Warwickshire about 1960.

**'Munster'** Flowers deep pink in bud opening white streaked pink on the tube and the backs of the lobes, fading to cream.

**LONICERA periclymenum**—*continued*

'**Serotina**' ('Late Red') "Late Dutch Honeysuckle". Flowers rich reddish-purple outside, appearing from July to October. AGM 1984. AM 1988.

**prolifera** (KIRCHN.) REHD. A vigorous twining shrub with glaucous bloomed shoots. Leaves glaucous green above, glaucous beneath. Upper leaves perfoliate, intensely glaucous, forming a conspicuous rounded disk. Flowers creamy-yellow, pink-tinged with exserted yellow anthers, borne in several terminal whorls in May, not fragrant. Fruits red. Has been confused with *L. glaucescens*. North America.

*****sempervirens** L. "Trumpet Honeysuckle". A high-climbing, usually semi-evergreen species, with elliptic to obovate, rich-green leaves, glaucous and slightly downy beneath, the upper ones perfoliate. Flowers 4-5cm long, rich orange-scarlet outside, yellow within, borne in axillary whorls towards the ends of the shoots during summer. A striking and very hardy species which does not seem to be troubled by aphids like *L. × brownii* 'Dropmore Scarlet'. E United States. I 1656. AM 1964.

**f. sulphurea** (JACQUES) REHD. Flowers yellow.

*****similis** HEMSL. This species is represented in cultivation by the following variety.

**var. delavayi** (FRANCH.) REHD. (*L. delavayi* FRANCH.) A slender half-evergreen climber with ovate-lanceolate leaves which are white and downy beneath. Flowers fragrant, 3-4cm long, white changing to pale yellow, produced in the axils of the terminal leaves during late summer and early autumn. W China. I 1901.

†*****splendida** BOISS. A rather fastidious evergreen, or sometimes semi-evergreen, species with oval or oblong, very glaucous leaves, the upper ones perfoliate. Flowers 4-5cm long, fragrant, reddish-purple outside, yellowish-white within, borne in dense terminal clusters during summer. A beautiful climber, succeeding best in the milder areas of the British Isles. Spain. Introduced about 1880.

× **tellmanniana** SPAETH (*L. sempervirens × L. tragophylla*). A superb hybrid with oval or ovate leaves, the upper ones perfoliate. Flowers 5cm long, rich coppery-yellow, flushed red in bud, borne in large terminal clusters in June and July. Succeeds best in semi-shade or even in full shade. Raised at the Royal Hungarian Horticultural School, Budapest, sometime prior to 1927. AM 1931. AGM 1984.

**tragophylla** HEMSL. A climber of great ornamental merit. Leaves 7.5-10cm long, oblong to oval, glaucous and downy beneath. Flowers 6-9cm long, bright golden yellow, produced in June and July, in large terminal clusters. Berries red. An extremely showy species, requiring almost complete shade. Best grown into a tree. W China. Discovered by Augustine Henry. Introduced by Ernest Wilson in 1900. AM 1913. AGM 1984.

†**MANDEVILLA** LINDL.—**Apocynaceae**—More than 100 species of mainly twining climbers of the periwinkle family, with characteristic milky sap; natives of tropical America. The following species requires a warm, sheltered wall and a well drained soil in the milder counties. It makes an attractive conservatory plant.

**laxa** (RUIZ & PAVON) WOODSON (*M. suaveolens* LINDL.) "Chilean Jasmine". An elegant, sun-loving climber with slender stems 3-4.5m long, or more. Leaves heart-shaped, slender-pointed, bearing tufts of white down in the vein axils beneath. The fragrant, white, periwinkle-like flowers, 5cm across, are borne in corymbs from the leaf axils during summer. Well worth growing for its sweetly scented flowers. Bolivia, N Argentina. Introduced in 1837 by H.J. Mandeville. AM 1957.

**suaveolens** See *M. laxa*.

**MENISPERMUM** L.—**Menispermaceae**—A genus of 2 species of semi-woody, twining, dioecious plants suitable for growing into small trees or over walls, sheds, etc, best in full sun. In cold districts they may be cut to the ground each winter, but will invariably produce new shoots again in spring. They are distinctive in leaf, but to obtain fruit, plants of both sexes are required.

**canadense** L. "Moonseed". A climber spreading by suckers and making a dense tangle of slender shoots up to 4.5m long. The conspicuous, long-stalked leaves, 10-18cm across, are ovate to heart-shaped, with 5-7 angular lobes. The inconspicuous, greenish-yellow flowers are borne in slender axillary racemes in summer and on female plants are

**MENISPERMUM canadense**—*continued*

followed by blackcurrant-like fruits, each containing a single, crescent-shaped seed (hence the common name). E North America. C 1646.

**"MOONSEED"** See *Menispermum canadense*.

**MUEHLENBECKIA** MEISSNER—**Polygonaceae**—A small genus of about 15 species of dioecious, creeping or climbing plants natives of Australasia and S America. They are of little beauty in flower, but amusing and interesting botanically. *M. complexa* is useful for covering and concealing unsightly objects in mild areas.

**axillaris** (HOOK. f.) WALP. A hardy, slow-growing, prostrate species forming dense carpets of intertwining thread-like stems clothed with small ovate to orbicular leaves 2-5mm long. Fruits white, bearing a shiny black nutlet. Useful as ground cover on rock gardens and screes. New Zealand, Australia, Tasmania.

†**complexa** (CUNN.) MEISSN. A twining species with slender, dark, interlacing stems occasionally up to 6m or more, forming dense tangled curtains or carpets. Leaves variable in shape and size from 3-20mm long and from roundish or oblong to fiddle-shaped. The minute, greenish flowers in autumn are followed on female plants by small, white, fleshy fruits, enclosing a single, black shining nutlet. New Zealand. I 1842.

**var. trilobata** (COL.) CHEESEMAN (*M. varians* MEISSN.) (*M. trilobata* COL.) A curious and amusing form in which the larger leaves are distinctly fiddle-shaped. In habit it is just as vigorous and as twining as the typical variety and makes excellent cover for old stumps, walls and banks in mild areas.

**varians** See *M. complexa* var. *trilobata*.

*****MUTISIA** L. f.—**Compositae**—The "Climbing Gazanias" are a genus of about 60 species of erect or climbing evergreens, the climbing species attaching themselves to a support by means of leaf tendrils; natives of S America, particularly Chile. They may be grown on a wall, but are perhaps best planted near an old or unwanted shrub or small bushy tree, so that their stems may be encouraged to grow into the support provided. They require a warm, sunny position in a rich but well drained soil. The colourful gazania-like flowerheads are produced singly on long stalks.

†**clematis** L. f. A strong-growing species for the conservatory. Leaves pinnate, composed of 6-10 oblong-ovate leaflets which are white woolly beneath. Flowerheads pendulous, cylindrical at base, 5-6cm across, with brilliant orange petals, produced in summer and early autumn. Andes of Colombia and Ecuador. I 1859. AM 1926.

**decurrens** CAV. A rare species up to 3m, with narrowly oblong, sessile leaves 7.5-13cm long. Flowerheads 10-13cm across, with brilliant orange or vermilion petals, borne continuously during summer. A superb but difficult species to establish. It succeeds in a warm, sheltered position such as a partially shaded west wall and in a rich friable sandy loam. Chile. Introduced by Richard Pearce in 1859. FCC 1861.

**ilicifolia** CAV. A vigorous, hardy species, with stems 3-4.5m long. Leaves sessile, ovate-oblong, the margins strongly-toothed, dark green above, pale woolly beneath. Flowerheads 5-7.5cm across, yellow, with lilac-pink petals, borne in summer and early autumn. Chile. I 1832.

**oligodon** POEPP. & ENDL. A very beautiful, suckering species usually easy to establish growing through a sparsely branched shrub, forming a low thicket of straggling stems rarely reaching 1.5m. Leaves oblong, sessile, coarsely-toothed, auriculate at base. Flowerheads 5-7.5cm across, with salmon-pink petals, appearing continuously throughout summer and intermittently into autumn. A lovely species more compact in habit than *M. ilicifolia* and with shorter stems. In a sunny site supported by a low trellis or a low to small-sized shrub, it is a most attractive plant except that in winter it can look almost dead, with only an occasional green shoot. Chile. Introduced by Harold Comber in 1927. AM 1928.

†**OXYPETALUM** R. BR.—**Asclepiadaceae**—About 100 species of erect or climbing herbs and sub-shrubs, natives of C and S America. The following species may be grown outside

**OXYPETALUM**—*continued*

only in the very mildest localities. It makes an exceptionally attractive conservatory climber.

**caeruleum** (D. DON) DECNE. (*Tweedia caerulea* D. DON) A beautiful sub-shrub with twining stems and oblong or heart-shaped, sage-green leaves. The remarkable flowers are powder-blue at first and slightly tinged green, turning to purplish and finally lilac. They are freely borne in erect, few-flowered cymes during summer. Temperate SE South America. I 1832. AM 1936.

**PAEDERIA** L.—**Rubiaceae**—A small genus of some 20 species of twining plants emitting a foetid smell when bruised; natives of temperate and tropical Asia and S America. The following requires a sunny sheltered position in any fertile soil.

**scandens** (LOUR.) MERR. (*P. chinensis* HANCE) A strong-growing climber up to 5m, with ovate, slender-pointed, dark green leaves, often rather downy beneath. Flowers tubular, white, with a purple throat, carried in slender terminal panicles throughout summer, followed by small, orange fruits. China, Taiwan, Japan, Korea. I 1907.

†\***PANDOREA** (ENDL.) SPACH—**Bignoniaceae**—A small genus of about 6 species of evergreen, twining plants, natives of SE Asia and Australia. The following requires a warm, sheltered position in very mild localities, but is best grown in a conservatory.

**jasminoides** SCHUM. (*Bignonia jasminoides* HORT.) (*Tecoma jasminoides* LINDL.) The "Bower Plant" of Australia, a beautiful climber with pinnate leaves composed of 5-9 slender-pointed leaflets. The attractive funnel-shaped flowers, 4-5cm long, are white, stained crimson and are borne in panicles during summer. E Australia.

**PARTHENOCISSUS** PLANCHON—**Vitaceae**—A small genus of about 10 species of high-climbing vines, related to *Vitis* and attaching themselves to supports by means of leaf tendrils which either twine or adhere by adhesive pads; natives of the United States, Mexico, E Asia and the Himalaya. The self-clinging species are excellent on walls or tree trunks whilst those with twining tendrils may be trained over hedges, large coarse shrubs or small bushy trees. The leaves are often richly coloured in autumn. The attractive, small fruits are only produced following a hot, dry summer. See also *Ampelopsis* and *Vitis*.

**henryana** (HEMSL.) DIELS & GILG (*Vitis henryana* HEMSL.) A beautiful, self-clinging species. Leaves digitate, composed of 3-5 obovate or narrowly oval leaflets, dark green or bronze, with a silvery-white veinal variegation, particularly when growing in half-shade, turning red in autumn. Fruits dark blue. Best grown on a wall. C China. First discovered by Augustine Henry about 1885. Introduced by Ernest Wilson in 1900. AM 1906. AGM 1984.

**himalayana** (ROYLE) PLANCHON (*Vitis himalayana* BRANDIS) A strong-growing, more or less self-clinging climber, differing mainly from the Virginia Creeper in its larger leaflets. These turn rich crimson in autumn. Fruits deep blue. Himalaya. C 1894.

**var. rubrifolia** (LEVL. & VANIOT) GAGNEP. An attractive variety, leaflets smaller, purple when young. W China. I 1907.

**inserta** (KERNER) FRITSCH (*Vitis vitacea* (KNERR) BEAN) A vigorous vine with twining tendrils climbing into small trees or scrambling over hedges. Leaves with 5, stalked, ovate to obovate leaflets, shining green beneath, colouring richly in autumn. Fruits blue-black. Ideal for covering unsightly objects, differing most markedly from the closely related Virginia Creeper in its non-adhesive tendrils and bright green leaves. E United States. C before 1800.

**quinquefolia** (L.) PLANCHON (*Vitis quinquefolia* (L.) LAM.) (*Vitis hederacea* EHRH.) "Virginia Creeper". A tall-growing, more or less self-clinging vine excellent for high walls, trees, towers, etc. Leaves composed of usually 5 oval to obovate, stalked leaflets which are dull green and glaucescent beneath, turning brilliant orange and scarlet in autumn. Fruits blue-black. Reaching to the tops of lofty trees in its native habitats. The plant still commonly and incorrectly referred to as Virginia Creeper is *P. tricuspidata*, the Boston Ivy. E United States. I 1629. AGM 1984.

**sinensis** See *Vitis piasezkii*.

**PARTHENOCISSUS**—*continued*

**thomsonii** (M.A. LAWS. ) PLANCHON (*Vitis thomsonii* M.A. LAWS.) A beautiful vine of slender habit. Leaves composed of 5 oval or obovate, glossy green leaflets. The young growths in spring are purple, whilst in autumn the foliage turns to rich crimson and scarlet. Fruits black. Himalaya, China. I 1900 by Ernest Wilson. FCC 1903 (as *Vitis thomsonii*).

**tricuspidata** (SIEB. & ZUCC.) PLANCHON (*Vitis inconstans* MIQ.) "Boston Ivy". A vigorous, self-clinging vine, almost as ubiquitous as the common ivy. Leaves extremely variable, broadly ovate and toothed, or trifoliolate on young plants, ovate and conspicuously three-lobed on old plants. Turning rich crimson and scarlet in autumn. Fruits dark blue and bloomy. A commonly planted vine, densely covering walls in urban districts and a familiar sight in many of our older cities and towns. Japan, Korea, China, Taiwan. Introduced from Japan by J.G. Veitch in 1862. FCC 1868. AGM 1984.

**'Lowii'** A selection with small, curiously crisped, palmate, three to seven-lobed leaves and rich autumn colour. AM 1907.

**'Veitchii'** (*Ampelopsis veitchii* HORT.) (*Vitis inconstans* 'Purpurea') A selected form with slightly smaller, ovate or trifoliolate leaves, purple when young.

†**PASSIFLORA** L.—**Passifloraceae**—The "Passion Flowers" make up a large genus of some 350 species of mainly climbers, attaching themselves to a support by means of twining tendrils; natives mainly of tropical S America. The majority are too tender for planting outside in the British Isles, but the remaining few contain some of the most beautiful and exotic of flowering creepers. They are best planted on a sunny, sheltered, south-facing wall. The beautiful and fascinating flowers, usually borne singly on long stalks, are composed of a tubular calyx with 5 lobes or sepals. These are often the same size, shape and colour as the 5 petals and collectively are referred to as tepals. Inside the tepals are situated rings of "filaments" which are usually thread-like and coloured, collectively referred to as the "corona". The 5 stamens are carried on a long central column and are topped by the ovary and 3 nail-like stigmas. The fruits vary in size and shape and contain numerous seeds in an edible, jelly-like pulp. Out-of-doors they are normally only produced after a long, hot summer.

The delightful story connected with the origin of the name "Passion Flower" is worth recounting. According to Dr Masters it was used originally by the Spanish priests in S America, because of the resemblance their piety led them to detect between the various parts of the flower and the instruments of Christ's Passion. The 3 stigmas representing the 3 nails; the 5 anthers representing the 5 wounds; the corona representing the crown of thorns or the halo of glory; the 10 tepals representing the apostles—Peter and Judas being absent; the lobed leaves and the whip-like tendrils representing the hands and scourges of His persecutors.

× **allardii** LYNCH (*P. caerulea* 'Constance Elliott' × *P. quadrangularis*). A choice hybrid raised at the University Botanic Garden, Cambridge. A strong-growing climber with large, three-lobed leaves. Flowers 9-11.5cm across, tepals white, shaded pink, corona white and deep cobalt-blue, appearing throughout summer and autumn. May be grown outside in the milder counties.

**antioquiensis** KARST. (*Tacsonia vanvolxemii* LEM.) A beautiful climber with slender, downy stems and leaves of 2 kinds—lanceolate, unlobed leaves, and deeply three-lobed leaves, the lobes long and slender-pointed, downy beneath. Flowers pendulous, 10-13cm across, tube 2.5-4cm long, rich rose-red, with a small violet corona, borne singly on long peduncles during late summer and autumn. May be grown outside only in the most favoured localities, otherwise a plant for the conservatory. Colombia. I 1858.

**caerulea** L. "Blue Passion Flower". A vigorous, usually rampant species often forming a dense blanket of tangled stems, evergreen in mild localities. Leaves palmately five to seven-lobed. Flowers slightly fragrant, 7.5-10cm across, tepals white or occasionally pink-tinged; the conspicuous corona has the outer filaments blue at the tips, white in the middle and purple at the base. They appear continuously throughout summer and autumn, often until the first frosts. Fruits ovoid, orange-red, 2.5-4cm long. Hardy on a warm, sunny wall in the south and surviving often many winters in the Home Counties. S Brazil, Argentina. I 1609. AGM 1984.

**PASSIFLORA caerulea**—*continued*

**'Constance Elliott'** A superb clone with ivory-white flowers. FCC 1884.

× **caerulea-racemosa** SABINE A vigorous climber with deeply five-lobed leaves. Flowers, borne singly, the tepals deeply flushed violet, corona deep violet-purple, column apple-green, stigmas purple and green. A free-flowering hybrid, rampant when established. Only suitable for the mildest localities.

**edulis** SIMS. "Purple Granadilla". A tender, vigorous climber with angular stems and ovate, deeply three-lobed leaves. Flowers 6cm across, tepals white, green without, corona with curly, white filaments, banded with purple, produced throughout summer. Fruits ovoid, 5cm long, yellow or dull purple, pulp edible. Commonly cultivated in warmer countries for its fruit which is sometimes produced in the mildest gardens of the British Isles. Brazil. I 1810.

**'Exoniensis'** (*P. antioquiensis* × *P. mollissima*) (*Tacsonia* 'Exoniensis') A beautiful hybrid with downy stems and deeply three-lobed, downy leaves. Flowers pendulous, 10-13cm across, the tube 6cm long, tepals rose-pink, corona small, whitish, appearing during summer. Only for the conservatory. Raised by Messrs Veitch of Exeter about 1870.

**mollissima** (H.B.K.) L.H. BAILEY A vigorous climber with downy shoots and deeply three-lobed, toothed leaves densely hairy beneath. Flowers pendulous, to 7.5cm across with a long tube 7-8cm long; petals and sepals pink, corona a purple, warty ridge. Fruits yellow, edible. S America. C 1843.

**quadrangularis** L. "Granadilla". A vigorous climber with 4-angled, winged stems and unlobed leaves up to 20cm long. Flowers fragrant, 8cm across, greenish outside, white, pink, red or violet within, the corona banded with reddish-purple, blue and white. Fruit edible, yellow, 20-30cm long. Origin unknown but widely grown in tropical America for its fruit.

**racemosa** BROT. (*P. princeps* LODD.) "Red Passion Flower". A climber with ovate, usually three-lobed leaves. Flowers vivid scarlet, with purple, white-tipped outer filaments, borne in drooping, terminal racemes during summer. A magnificent species requiring conservatory treatment. Brazil. I 1815.

**umbilicata** (GRISEB.) HARMS (*Tacsonia umbilicata* GRISEB.) A fast-growing species with small, violet flowers and round, yellow fruits. Proving one of the hardiest, thriving in the open in the SW counties. Bolivia, Paraguay, N Argentina. I 1954.

**"PASSION FLOWER"** See *Passiflora*.

**PERIPLOCA** L.—**Asclepiadaceae**—A small genus of about 10 species of deciduous and evergreen shrubs and twining climbers, exuding a poisonous, milky juice when cut. Suitable for growing on pergolas, fences, etc, requiring a sunny position in any type of fertile soil.

**graeca** L. "Silk Vine". A vigorous climber, reaching 9-12m, on a suitable support. Leaves ovate or lanceolate, long persistent. Flowers 2.5cm across, greenish outside, brownish-purple within, possessing a heavy odour, borne in cymes during July and August. Seedpods in pairs, 12cm long, packed with small silky-tufted seeds. SE Europe, W Asia. C 1597.

†**laevigata** AIT. A tender, strong-growing, semi-evergreen climber, differing from *P. graeca* in its lanceolate, sessile leaves, subsessile cymes and smaller, greenish-yellow flowers. Canary Islands. I 1770.

*\*PILEOSTEGIA* HOOK. f. & THOMS.—**Hydrangeaceae**—A small genus of 3 species of evergreen shrubs climbing by means of aerial roots; natives of E Asia. The following species, the only one in general cultivation, requires a wall or tree trunk in sun or shade and will grow in all types of fertile soil.

**viburnoides** HOOK. f. & THOMS. A rather slow-growing, evergreen, self-clinging species reaching 6m on a suitable surface. Leaves entire, leathery, narrow-oblong to ovate-lanceolate, 7.5-15cm long, strongly veined and minutely pitted beneath. Flowers in crowded terminal panicles, creamy-white, appearing during late summer and autumn. One of the best climbers for any aspect including shady or north-facing walls. Khasia

**PILEOSTEGIA viburnoides**—*continued*
Hills (India), S China, Ryukyus. The first meeting Mr H.G. Hillier had with this plant was in 1922 in Orleans when the leading French nurseryman of that time, Mons Chenault, proudly pointed to a plant covering the front of his house. Introduced by Ernest Wilson in 1908. AM 1914.

**POLYGONUM aubertii** See *Fallopia aubertii*.
**baldschuanicum** See *Fallopia baldschuanica*.

**†PUERARIA** DC.—**Leguminosae**—A small genus of about 20 species of herbaceous and woody, twining climbers with trifoliolate leaves and often attractive pea-flowers. Natives of E and SE Asia.
**lobata** (WILLD.) OHWI (*P. thunbergiana* (SIEB. & ZUCC.) BENTH.) "Kudzu Vine". A vigorous species up to 6m, woody at base, stems climbing or trailing. Leaves trifoliolate, the middle leaflets 15-18cm long. Flowers fragrant, violet-purple, borne in long racemes in July and August. The long stems are often cut back during winter, but spring again from the base. Useful for growing over large, unwanted shrubs or old hedges, in full sun. Japan, Korea, China. I 1885.

**"PURPLE BELLS"** See *Rhodochiton atrosanguineum*.

**†RHODOCHITON** ZUCC. ex OTTO & DIETR.—**Scrophulariaceae**—A monotypic genus requiring conservatory treatment, though it makes an unusual summer creeper.
**atrosanguineum** (ZUCC.) ROTHM. (*R. volubile* ZUCC.) "Purple Bells". A slender plant with stems up to 3m long, climbing by means of its twining petioles and peduncles. Leaves cordate, few-toothed. The curious flowers, consisting of a broadly bell-shaped, almost black-purple calyx and a long tubular, purplish red corolla are borne in endless succession during summer. Mexico. AM 1985.

**RUBUS** L.—**Rosaceae**—The climbing members of this large genus are fairly vigorous shrubs with long, prickly, scandent stems. They may be trained up wooden supports or into small trees or hedges. Of little beauty in flower or fruit, they are mainly grown for their ornamental foliage. Thriving in all types of well drained soil. See also TREES AND SHRUBS.
**bambusarum** See *R. henryi* var. *bambusarum*.
**\*flagelliflorus** FOCKE An evergreen species with long, white-felted, minutely-prickly stems. Leaves broad ovate to ovate-lanceolate, 10-18cm long, shallowly lobed and toothed, felted beneath. The small, white flowers are borne in axillary clusters in June, followed by black, edible fruits. Mainly grown for its striking ornamental foliage. China. I 1901 by Ernest Wilson.
**\*henryi** HEMSL. & KTZE. An evergreen species with long, scandent stems, reaching a height of 6m on a suitable support. Leaves deeply three-lobed, 10-15cm long, glossy dark green above, white-felted beneath. Flowers pink, borne in slender racemes during summer, followed by black fruits. Both the species and the following variety are grown for their habit and attractive foliage. C and W China. First discovered by Augustine Henry. Introduced by Ernest Wilson in 1900.
**var. bambusarum** (FOCKE) REHD. (*R. bambusarum* FOCKE) An elegant variety with the leaves composed of 3 distinct lanceolate leaflets. C China. I 1900. FCC 1907.
**hupehensis** See *R. swinhoei*.
**lambertianus** SER. A semi-evergreen species with scandent, four-angled, prickly stems which are viscid when young. Leaves ovate, 7.5-13cm long, shallowly three to five-lobed and toothed, glossy on both surfaces. Flowers small, white, borne in terminal panicles during summer, followed by red fruits. C China. I 1907 by Ernest Wilson.
**\*parkeri** HANCE An evergreen species with slender, scandent, biennial stems, densely clothed with greyish hairs. Leaves oblong-lanceolate, with wavy, finely-toothed margins, densely covered with a reddish-brown down beneath. Flowers small, white, produced in panicles during summer, followed by black fruits. C China. I 1907 by Ernest Wilson.

**RUBUS**—*continued*

**swinhoei** HANCE (*R. hupehensis* OLIVER) A vigorous scandent shrub with erect branches which can reach 3m or more in one season. Shoots purplish and loosely floccose when young, later glabrous and reddish-green with a few small spines. Leaves glossy green above, grey-felted beneath at first, oblong-lanceolate, to 18cm long. Flowers in terminal racemes, white, the filaments spreading and turning red, forming a conspicuous corona around the small, blackberry-like, insipid fruits. Hubei, China. I 1907 by Ernest Wilson.

**"RUSSIAN VINE"** See *Fallopia baldschuanica*.

**SCHISANDRA** MICHX.—**Schisandraceae**—Some 25 species of deciduous and evergreen, monoecious or dioecious, twining shrubs of considerable charm and quality; natives of E and SE Asia with 1 species in North America. Flowers borne in clusters in the leaf axils, followed on female plants by long, pendulous spikes of attractive berries. They are suitable for growing on walls or fences or over shrubs and into trees.

**chinensis** (TURCZ.) BAILL. A high-climbing species reaching 9m on a suitable support. Leaves obovate to oval, 5-10cm long. Flowers fragrant, 1-2cm across, usually white or palest pink, produced on slender, drooping stalks during late spring. Berries scarlet. Usually dioecious. China, Japan. I 1860.

**grandiflora** (WALL.) HOOK. f. A rare species with obovate, somewhat leathery leaves and conspicuous venation, 7.5-10cm long. Flowers 2.5-3cm across, white or pale pink, borne on drooping stalks during May and June. Berries scarlet. Temperate Himalaya.

**var. cathayensis** SCHNEID. A variety with smaller leaves and clear rose-pink flowers. W China. I 1907.

**var. rubriflora** See *S. rubriflora*.

**propinqua** (WALL.) BAILL. The typical form of this species is a native of the Himalaya. It is mainly grown as the following form.

**var. chinensis** OLIV. This Chinese variety is hardier and is notable for bearing its short-stalked, yellowish terracotta flowers during late summer and autumn. Leaves oblong to lanceolate, persistent, 5-10cm long. Berries scarlet. C and W China. I 1907.

**rubriflora** REHD. & WILS. (*S. grandiflora* var. *rubriflora* (REHD. & WILS.) SCHNEID.) Closely related to *S. grandiflora* but flowers deep crimson, borne on pendulous stalks during late spring. Berries scarlet. W China, N India, N Burma. I 1908. AM 1925 (for fruit).

**sphenanthera** REHD. & WILS. A strong-growing climber with noticeably warty shoots. Leaves obovate, 5-10cm long, green beneath. Flowers a distinct shade of orange-red or terra-cotta, borne on slender stalks during May and June. Berries scarlet. W China. I 1907 by Ernest Wilson.

**SCHIZOPHRAGMA** SIEB. & ZUCC.—**Hydrangeaceae**—A small genus of 4 species of ornamental climbers supporting themselves by means of aerial roots. The small, creamy-white flowers are densely borne in large, flattened cymes, each cyme attended by several conspicuous, cream-coloured, marginal bracts (really enlarged sepals of sterile flowers). Their requirements are similar to those of *Hydrangea petiolaris* and they are suitable for north-facing or otherwise shady walls, though flowering best on a sunny wall. They are most effective when allowed to climb a large tree or old stump. Although eventually tall, they are slow starters and need cultural encouragement in their early years.

**hydrangeoides** SIEB. & ZUCC. A superb climber, reaching 12m. Leaves broadly rotund-ovate and coarsely-toothed (by which it is distinguished from *S. integrifolium*). Flowerheads 20-25cm across, appearing in July, bracts 2.5-4cm long. Native of Japan where it is found in woods and forests in the mountains often accompanied by *Hydrangea petiolaris*. C 1880. FCC 1885.

**'Roseum'** A lovely form with rose-flushed bracts. AM 1939.

**integrifolium** (FRANCH.) OLIV. A climber reaching 12m or more under suitable conditions. Leaves broad ovate to elliptic-oblong, slender-pointed, entire or thinly set with small, narrow teeth. Flowerheads often as much as 30cm across, the bracts 6-9cm long, borne freely in July. A magnificent species, larger in all its parts than *S. hydrangeoides*. Native of C China where it is said to grow on rocky cliffs. Introduced by E.H. Wilson in 1901. AM 1936. FCC 1963. AGM 1984.

**SENECIO** L.—**Compositae**—Probably the largest genus of flowering plants in the world. Only a few are climbers and of these the following is the only hardy species likely to be met with in cultivation.

†**scandens** G. DON A fairly vigorous, half-evergreen, semi-woody climber with long scandent stems 4.5-6m long. Leaves narrowly triangular or ovate, coarsely-toothed, sometimes lobed at the base. The small, bright yellow, groundsel-like flowerheads are produced in large panicles during autumn. Best planted where it may scramble over bushes and hedges or into small, densely-branched trees. It requires a sunny, sheltered site and though in cold areas it is frequently cut to ground level in winter, it will normally spring up again from the base. Given mild weather, a well established specimen is one of the most conspicuous flowering plants in the garden during October and November. Japan, Taiwan, China, Philippines, India, E Nepal. I 1895.

**SINOFRANCHETIA** HEMSL.—**Lardizabalaceae**—A monotypic genus related to *Holboellia* but deciduous and dioecious. It requires a sunny or semi-shady position in any ordinary soil.

**chinensis** (FRANCH.) HEMSL. A vigorous, hardy, twining climber reaching a height of 9m in a suitable tree or on a high wall. Leaves trifoliolate, glaucous beneath. Flowers white, inconspicuous, borne in drooping racemes during May. These are followed, on female plants, by conspicuous, large, elongated bunches of lavender-purple, rounded fruits. C and W China. I 1907 by Ernest Wilson. AM 1948.

**SINOMENIUM** DIELS—**Menispermaceae**—A monotypic genus related to *Cocculus*. Suitable for growing into a tree or against a large wall in sun or semi-shade; any ordinary soil.

**acutum** (THUNB.) REHD. & WILS. A hardy, twining climber up to 12m. Leaves variable in shape, ovate and entire to kidney-shaped, often shallowly lobed or with 3-5 lanceolate lobes, shining deep green. Flowers small, yellowish, borne in long, slender, pyramidal panicles in June, followed, on female plants, by small globular, bloomy black fruits. E Asia. I 1901 by Ernest Wilson.

**var. cinereum** (DIELS) REHD. & WILS. The form occasionally seen in cultivation, with leaves greyish pubescent beneath. I 1907 by Ernest Wilson.

**SMILAX** L.—**Smilacaceae**—A large genus of 200 or more species of evergreen and deciduous, mainly climbing plants. Their often prickly stems are tough and wiry, bearing stipular tendrils by which they are able to support themselves, scrambling over bushes, hedges or similar support. They are normally grown for their rich, often glossy green foliage and are excellent for covering stumps, low walls, etc. Sun or shade in any ordinary soil. They are normally dioecious, with flowers of little beauty.

†*****aspera** L. An evergreen climber with prickly, angular zig-zag stems and ovate-lanceolate to heart-shaped, glossy green, leathery leaves which are often attractively blotched with grey. The racemes of small, fragrant, pale green flowers are produced in late summer and early autumn, often followed by small, red fruits. An established plant forms a dense tangle of thorny stems. It requires a warm sunny position and is not suitable for cold areas. S Europe, N Africa, Canary Isles. C 1648. AM 1903.

**biflora** SIEB. ex MIQ. This remarkable species is not a climber but makes a dwarf, congested bush about 10cm tall, spreading by suckers. Stems zig-zag, somewhat spiny. Leaves glossy green above, glaucous beneath, three-nerved, broadly ovate, mucronate, about 1cm long. Flowers in few-flowered umbels, followed by red fruits. S Japan.

**china** L. "China Root". A deciduous shrub with rounded, prickly scrambling stems. Leaves variable in shape, usually roundish-ovate with a heart-shaped base, often turning red in autumn. Flowers greenish-yellow in May. Fruits bright red. The large, fleshy root is said to be eaten by the Chinese. It also contains a drug known as China Root, once valued as a cure for gout. China, Japan, Korea. I 1759.

**discotis** WARB. A deciduous species with generally prickly stems up to 3-4.5m long. Leaves ovate, heart-shaped at base, glaucous beneath. Fruits blue-black. W China. I 1908.

*****excelsa** L. (A. & L. 15) A vigorous evergreen or semi-evergreen climber with four-angled stems and glossy green, heart-shaped leaves, purple-tinged in winter. Fruits bright red,

**SMILAX excelsa**—*continued*

in axillary umbels in autumn. SE Europe, W Asia. Our stock was introduced by Mrs Ala and Roy Lancaster from the Caspian Forests of N Iran in 1972.

**hispida** MUHL. "Hag Brier". A vigorous, deciduous climber with slightly angled,´ densely bristly-spiny stems. Leaves broadly ovate, heart-shaped at the base, acuminate at the apex, five to seven-nerved, minutely toothed at the margin. Fruits blue-black. E North America.

**\*pumila** WALT. An unusual species of low, trailing habit with slender, rounded, spineless stems. Leaves glossy above and red-tinged in winter with a dense, white tomentum beneath, five-veined with conspicuous secondary veins, ovate, cordate at the base, to 13cm long. Flowers yellowish, fruits red. SE United States.

**SOLANUM** L.—**Solanaceae**—The climbing members of this large genus make spectacular wall climbers for sheltered gardens. They require full sun and a south or west aspect and are not fastidious as to soil.

**crispum** RUIZ & PAVON A vigorous, semi-evergreen shrub with scrambling, downy, normally herbaceous stems 4.5-6m long. Leaves ovate to ovate-lanceolate, variable in size, minutely downy. Flowers very slightly fragrant, 2.5-3cm across, resembling those of a potato, but rich purple-blue, with a bright yellow staminal beak, borne in loose corymbs very freely from July to September. Fruits small, yellowish-white. A pleasing species suitable for training on a wall and equally effective when allowed to scramble over small fences, sheds and similar structures. It is hardier than *S. jasminoides* and luxuriates in a chalky soil. Chile. I about 1830. AM 1989.

**'Glasnevin'** ('Autumnale') A selected form with a longer flowering season. AM 1955. AGM 1984.

**†jasminoides** PAXT. A slender, fast-growing, semi-evergreen climber with twining stems in mild areas reaching 6-9m long. Leaves ovate-acuminate, glossy green and thin in texture. Flowers 2cm across, pale slate-blue, with a yellow staminal beak, profusely borne in loose clusters from midsummer until checked by autumn frosts. This species needs the protection of a south or west-facing sunny wall. Brazil. I 1838.

**'Album'** Flowers white, with a yellow staminal beak.

**†\*SOLLYA** LINDL.—**Pittosporaceae**—A genus of 3 species of extremely beautiful evergreen, twining plants only suitable for the mildest localities or for the conservatory; natives of SW Australia. They require a sunny, sheltered position and a well drained soil. The following are delightful when grown against a low wall or allowed to scramble over low shrubs.

**drummondii** See *S. parviflora*.

**heterophylla** LINDL. (*S. fusiformis* PAYER) "Bluebell Creeper". A beautiful plant with slender stems up to 2m or more. Leaves variable, usually ovate to lanceolate, 2.5-5cm long. The nodding clusters of delicate bell-shaped, sky-blue flowers are freely borne during summer and autumn. I 1830.

**parviflora** TURCZ. (*S. drummondii* MORR.) A delightful species, differing from *S. heterophylla* in its even more slender shoots, smaller, linear leaves and its smaller darker blue flowers produced usually singly or in pairs during summer and autumn. I 1838. AM 1922.

**\*STAUNTONIA** DC.—**Lardizabalaceae**—A small genus of about 6 species of evergreen, twining shrubs closely related to *Holboellia*, but monoecious and with united stamens (free in *Holboellia*). The following requires a warm, sheltered wall in full sun or semi-shade.

**hexaphylla** (THUNB.) DECNE. A strong-growing climber up to 10m or more. Leaves large, composed of 3-7, stalked, leathery, dark green leaflets. Flowers 2cm across, fragrant, male and female in separate racemes, white, tinged violet, appearing in spring. The egg-shaped, pulpy, purple-tinged fruits, 2.5-5cm long, are edible, but are only produced after a warm, dry summer. Japan, Korea, Ryukyus, Taiwan. I 1874. AM 1960.

**latifolia** See *Holboellia latifolia*.

**TACSONIA** See *Passiflora*.

†\*TECOMARIA (ENDL.) SPACH—**Bignoniaceae**—A monotypic genus related to *Campsis* and only suitable for mild localities. The following requires a warm, sunny wall in a sheltered position.

**capensis** (THUNB.) SPACH "Cape Honeysuckle". A vigorous, self-clinging, twining or scandent shrub with glabrous stems up to 4.5m long. Leaves pinnate, composed of 5-9 toothed leaflets. The brilliant scarlet, trumpet-shaped flowers, 5cm long, are borne in terminal racemes during late summer. In colder districts it makes an excellent conservatory climber. E and S Africa. I 1823.

†\*TRACHELOSPERMUM LEMAIRE—**Apocynaceae**—A genus of about 20 species, natives of E and SE Asia with 1 in the SE United States. Given a sunny, sheltered wall, these beautiful, self-clinging, evergreen, twining shrubs may be successfully grown in all but the coldest localities. Their attractive, sweetly-scented, jasmine-like flowers are borne in July and August. The stems and leaves exude a milky juice when cut.

**asiaticum** (SIEB. & ZUCC.) NAKAI (*T. divaricatum* KANITZ) (*T. crocostemon* STAPF) (*T. majus* NAKAI not HORT.) A very beautiful species, when grown on a wall presenting a dense leafy cover up to 6m high or more and as much across. Leaves oval, 2.5-5cm long, dark glossy green. Flowers 2cm across, creamy-white with buff-yellow centre, changing to yellow, fragrant. Hardier than *T. jasminoides* and neater and more compact in growth. It also differs from that species in its smaller leaves and flowers, the latter with exserted stamens and longer-pointed in bud. Japan, Korea.

**divaricatum** See *T. asiaticum*.

**japonicum** See *T. jasminoides* 'Japonicum'.

**jasminoides** (LINDL.) LEM. (*Rhyncospermum jasminoides* LINDL.) A lovely, rather slow-growing climber up to 7m high or more and as much across. Leaves narrowly oval, 5-7.5cm long, dark polished green. Flowers 2.5cm across, very fragrant, white, becoming cream with age. It requires a warm, sheltered wall. In cold areas it is a very worthy candidate for the conservatory. C and S China, Taiwan. Introduced by Robert Fortune from Shanghai in 1844. AM 1934. AGM 1984.

**'Japonicum'** (*T. japonicum* HORT.) (*T. majus* HORT. not NAKAI) A vigorous selection, a form of var. *pubescens* MAK. which is taller-growing with larger leaves than the typical form. When established it will clothe a wall as effectively as ivy. Leaves downy beneath, often colouring richly in winter.

**'Variegatum'** Leaves margined and splashed creamy-white, often with a crimson suffusion in winter. A very pretty plant.

**'Wilsonii'** An unusual form introduced from China by Ernest Wilson under his number W.776. Leaves varying from ovate to almost linear-lanceolate, with an attractive veining, often turning crimson in winter.

**majus** See *T. asiaticum* and *T. jasminoides* 'Japonicum'.

TRIPTERYGIUM HOOK. f.—**Celastraceae**—A small genus of 2 interesting species of deciduous, scandent shrubs, requiring a moist loamy soil. They are best planted where they may clamber into a suitable tree or large bush or over a pergola or outhouse. They flower best in full sun, but grow freely in shade.

**forrestii** See *T. wilfordii*.

**regelii** SPRAGUE & TAK. A large, scandent shrub with long, reddish-brown conspicuously warty branches, reaching a height of 6m in a suitable tree. Leaves ovate or elliptic, slender-pointed, up to 15cm long, dark green above, paler beneath. Flowers small, greenish-white, borne in large, brown pubescent panicles in late summer, followed by pale green, three-winged fruits. Japan, Korea, Manchuria. I 1905.

**wilfordii** HOOK. f. (*T. forrestii* LOES.) A large, scandent shrub with long, angular, downy stems, up to 6m long. Leaves ovate or elliptic, 5-15cm long, green above, glaucous beneath. Flowers small, greenish-white, borne in large, rusty tomentose panicles in early autumn. Fruits three-winged, purplish-red. Proving hardy here. S China, Taiwan, Japan, Burma. Introduced from Yunnan by George Forrest in 1913. AM 1952.

**TWEEDIA caerulea** See *Oxypetalum caeruleum*.

**"VINE, ORNAMENTAL"** See *Ampelopsis, Parthenocissus* and *Vitis.*

**"VINE, RUSSIAN"** See *Fallopia baldschuanica.*

**"VINE, SILK"** See *Periploca graeca.*

**"VINE, TRUMPET"** See *Campsis radicans.*

**"VIRGINIA CREEPER"** See *Parthenocissus quinquefolia.*

**VITIS** L.—**Vitaceae**—The ornamental vines are a genus of 60 or so species of woody climbers, supporting themselves by twining tendrils; widely distributed throughout N temperate regions, particularly North America. They are variable in leaf and several species give rich autumn colour. The majority are of vigorous habit and are most effective when allowed to clamber into a large tree or cover an old hedge or stump. They may also be trained to cover walls, pergolas, bridges and fences. The small, greenish flowers are carried in panicles or racemes during summer and though of little beauty are followed after a hot, dry season by bunches of small grapes. See also *Ampelopsis* and *Parthenocissus.*

**aconitifolia** See *Ampelopsis aconitifolia.*

**amurensis** RUPR. A strong-growing species with reddish young shoots. Leaves broadly ovate, 10-25cm across, three to five-lobed, sometimes deeply so. Fruits small, black. Autumn colours of rich crimson and purple. Manchuria, Amur region. I about 1854.

**betulifolia** DIELS & GILG. A high-climbing vine with ovate to oblong-ovate leaves, 5-10cm long, toothed and occasionally slightly three-lobed, covered with white or tawny floss when young. Rich autumn tints. Fruits small, blue-black. C and W China. I 1907. AM 1917.

**'Brant'** (*V. vinifera* 'Brant') One of the most popular of hardy fruiting vines. A vigorous grower, reaching 9m high or above on a suitable support. It produces numerous cylindrical bunches of sweet, aromatic grapes which are dark purple-black and bloomy when ripe. In addition the attractive, deeply three to five-lobed leaves turn to shades of dark red and purple, with greenish or yellow veins. Often wrongly regarded as a form of the common Grape Vine (*Vitis vinifera*), it is in fact a seedling of multiple parentage, *V.* 'Clinton' (*V. labrusca* × *V. riparia*) crossed with *V. vinifera* 'Black St Peters'. It was raised at Paris, Ontario (Canada) in the early 1860s by Charles Arnold. AM 1970. AGM 1984.

**coignetiae** PULLIAT ex PLANCH. Perhaps the most spectacular of all vines. A strong-growing species climbing to the tops of lofty trees. The broadly ovate or rounded leaves often measure 30cm across. They possess a heart-shaped base and 3-5 obscure lobes, clothed with rust-coloured tomentum beneath. Fruits 12mm across, black with purple bloom. The large, handsome leaves turn to crimson and scarlet in autumn, giving a magnificent display. Best colours are obtained in poor soils or when root run is restricted, such as against a wall. Japan, Korea, Sakhalin. C 1875. AGM 1984.

**davidii** (CARR.) FOEX (*V. armata* DIELS & GILG) (*Spinovitis davidii* CARR.) A vigorous climber, its shoots covered with gland-tipped, hooked spines. Leaves heart-shaped, coarsely toothed, 10-25cm long, shining dark green above, glaucous and glandular-bristly beneath, turning a rich crimson in autumn. Fruits black, edible. A luxuriant vine easily recognised by its spiny shoots. China. C 1885. AM 1903.

**var. cyanocarpa** (GAGNEP.) SARG. A variety with less prickly shoots, rather larger leaves and bluish, bloomy fruits. Rich autumn colour. AM 1906.

**flexuosa** THUNB. An elegant species with slender stems. Leaves roundish-ovate, 5-9cm across, rather thin in texture, glossy green above. Fruits black. Japan, Korea, China.

**major** See *V. pulchra.*

**var. parvifolia** (ROXB.) GAGNEP. A pretty variety with smaller leaves which are a pleasing shade of bronze-green above, with a metallic sheen, purple beneath when young. Himalaya to C China. I 1900 by Ernest Wilson. AM 1903.

**VITIS**—*continued*

**henryana** See *Parthenocissus henryana*.

**himalayana** See *Parthenocissus himalayana*.

**inconstans** See *Parthenocissus tricuspidata*.

    **'Purpurea'** See *Parthenocissus tricuspidata* 'Veitchii'.

**labrusca** L. "Fox Grape". A vigorous, luxuriant vine with woolly young shoots. Leaves broadly ovate or rounded, 7.5-18cm wide, varying from shallowly-toothed to three-lobed, normally rather thick in texture, dark green above, white then rusty pubescent beneath. Fruits black-purple; edible and musky-flavoured. A parent of most of the cultivated American grapes. E United States. I 1656.

**megalophylla** See *Ampelopsis megalophylla*.

**micans** See *Ampelopsis bodinieri*.

**odoratissima** See *V. riparia*.

**orientalis** See *Ampelopsis orientalis*.

**piasezkii** MAXIM. (*Parthenocissus sinensis* (DIELS & GILG.) SCHNEID.) A vigorous, but slender species with remarkably variable leaves, 7.5-15cm long. They vary from three-lobed to compound, with 3-5 oval or obovate leaflets. All are dark green above, brown tomentose beneath. Fruits black-purple. Rich spring and autumn tints. C China. I 1900. AM 1903.

**pulchra** REHD. (*V. flexuosa major* HORT.) A climber with reddish shoots and roundish-ovate, coarsely-toothed leaves, 7.5-15cm across. Young leaves reddish, autumn foliage brilliant scarlet. A handsome, vigorous, hardy vine, possibly a hybrid between *V. coignetiae* and *V. amurensis*. C about 1880.

**quinquefolia** See *Parthenocissus quinquefolia*.

**riparia** MICHX. (*V. odoratissima* DONN) (*V. vulpina* HORT.) "Riverbank Grape". A vigorous, high-climbing species with ovate to broadly ovate, coarsely-toothed and usually three-lobed leaves, 7.5-20cm across. Fruits purple-black, with an intense blue bloom. A useful species worth growing for its attractive bright green foliage and delightfully mignonette-scented male flowers. E North America. C 1656.

**striata** See *Cissus striata*.

**thomsonii** See *Parthenocissus thomsonii*.

**vinifera** L. "Grape Vine". The grape vine has been cultivated for so long that its native country is now a matter of conjecture. Most authorities regard it as having originated in Asia Minor and the Caucasus region. Many vines grown for their fruits are hybrids between this and other species. The following clones are particularly useful for their ornamental foliage as well as fruits.

    **'Apiifolia'** ('Laciniosa') "Parsley Vine". An attractive form with deeply divided leaves recalling *Ampelopsis aconitifolia*.

    **'Brant'** See *V*. 'Brant'.

    **'Fragola'** An unusual form with small fruits with a distinct musky flavour, which to some palates is of strawberries, and to others, of gooseberries!

    **'Incana'** "Dusty Miller Grape". Leaves grey-green, covered with a white, cobwebby down, three-lobed or unlobed. Fruits black. A most effective form when grown with purple-leaved shrubs.

    **'Laciniosa'** See 'Apiifolia'.

    **'Purpurea'** "Teinturier Grape". Leaves at first claret-red, later deep vinous purple, particularly effective when grown with grey or silver foliage shrubs. An attractive combination may be achieved by training a specimen into a weeping willow-leaved pear (*Pyrus salicifolia* 'Pendula'). AM 1958. AGM 1984.

**vitacea** See *Parthenocissus inserta*.

**vulpina** See *V. riparia*.

**WATTAKAKA sinensis** See *Dregea sinensis*.

**WISTERIA** NUTT. (*Wistaria*)—**Leguminosae**—A small genus of about 6 species of deciduous twiners; natives of E Asia and North America. There are perhaps no more beautiful climbers, when draped with their multitude of long racemes of white, pink, blue or mauve pea-flowers. May and June is the normal flowering season, but later blooms are

**WISTERIA**—*continued*

often produced. The attractive leaves are pinnate. Planting in full sun is advised, and if the soil is chalky, some good loam should be added. They are excellent subjects for walls and pergolas or for growing into old trees. They may even be trained into small standards by careful cultivation. Large, vigorous specimens on walls, etc, may require an annual hard pruning in late winter to keep them within bounds. A second pruning consists of shortening the leafy shoots in August.

**chinensis** See *W. sinensis*.

**floribunda** (WILLD.) DC. "Japanese Wisteria". A lovely climber up to 4m or more. Leaves composed of 13-19 ovate, dark green leaflets. Flowers fragrant, violet-blue or bluish-purple, carried in slender racemes, 13-25cm long with the leaves and opening successively from the base onwards. Seed pods velvety. The stems twine in a clockwise direction. Japan. Introduced by Philipp von Siebold in 1830. AM 1894.

**'Alba'** (*W. multijuga* 'Alba') Flowers white, tinted lilac on keel, in racemes 45-60cm long. AM 1931. AGM 1984.

**'Issai'** Flowers lilac-blue, borne in short trusses 18-25cm long, even on young shoots. Possibly a hybrid between *W. floribunda* and *W. sinensis*, the trusses resembling the latter whilst the stems twine in a clockwise direction like the former.

**f. macrobotrys** (NEUBERT) REHD. & WILS. A group of forms with racemes 0.3-1m or more long. They were originally selected in Japan and grown there for many years where racemes up to 1.8m long have been recorded. The most commonly grown form is 'Multijuga'. In this form the flowers are fragrant, lilac, tinged blue-purple. Best grown on a wooden bridge, pergola or high arch to allow for the drop of the long racemes. Introduced from Japan to Belgium by Siebold, and thence to England in 1874. AGM 1984.

**'Rosea'** (*W. multijuga* 'Rosea') Flowers pale rose, tipped purple, in long racemes.

**'Violacea'** Flowers violet-blue.

**'Violacea Plena'** Flowers violet-blue; double.

× **formosa** REHD. (*W. floribunda* 'Alba' × *W. sinensis*). An attractive hybrid of American origin; shoots silky downy, flowers pale violet-pink, opening almost simultaneously on racemes 25cm long. Raised in the garden of the late Professor Sargent of the Arnold Arboretum in 1905.

**frutescens** (L.) POIR. A rare species in cultivation with long climbing stems and leaves composed of 5-17 ovate leaflets. Flowers fragrant, pale lilac-purple, with a yellow spot, crowded into racemes 10-15cm long which are borne on the current year's shoots during summer. Seed pods glabrous. Less vigorous in cultivation than the Asiatic species. SE United States. I 1724.

**multijuga** See under *W. floribunda* f. *macrobotrys*.

**'Alba'** See *W. floribunda* 'Alba'.

**'Rosea'** See *W. floribunda* 'Rosea'.

**sinensis** (SIMS) SWEET (*W. chinensis* DC.) "Chinese Wisteria". Perhaps the most popular of all wisterias and one of the noblest of all climbers, reaching 18-30m in a suitable tree. Leaves with 9-13, mostly 11 elliptic to elliptic-oblong leaflets. The fragrant, mauve or deep lilac flowers, 2.5cm long, are carried in racemes 20-30cm long before the leaves, the flowers opening simultaneously. Seed pods velvety. A large specimen in full flower against an old house wall is one of the wonders of May. The stems twine in an anti-clockwise direction. China. First introduced in 1816 from a garden in Canton. AGM 1984.

**'Alba'** Flowers white. FCC 1892. AGM 1984.

**'Black Dragon'** Flowers double, dark purple.

**'Plena'** Flowers double, rosette-shaped, lilac.

**venusta** REHD. & WILS. A strong-growing climber up to 9m or more. Leaves with 9-13 oval to ovate, downy leaflets. Flowers, the largest in the genus, white, slightly fragrant, borne in racemes 10-15cm long. Seed pods velvety. C 1912. Introduced from Japan where it is only known in cultivation. AM 1945. FCC 1948.

**f. violacea** REHD. The wild form, with violet-coloured flowers. Japan.

# CONIFERS

There are few hardy evergreen trees apart from the conifers. Their beauty, wide range of shape, form and colour, plus their adaptability and valuable timber qualities render them indispensable for forest, shelter and ornamental planting. As a general principle it may be stated that, climatic conditions being suitable, they will grow in most soils except very shallow chalky land, pure sand, barren peat or water-logged ground; but there are species adaptable even to these extreme conditions and reference is made to them in the text. Some are excellent for maritime exposures and others, in particular those which respond well to clipping such as *Thuja* and *Taxus*, lend themselves to hedgemaking.

Species, including several from extremely cold Arctic conditions, which start into growth very early and are, therefore, subject to injury by spring frosts, are unsuitable for low-lying land and similar "frost pockets". On other sites the risk of injury may be reduced by planting them on the west side of shelter trees, where they are screened from the early morning sun.

The term 'Conifer', as used in gardens, has a different meaning to its use botanically. In horticulture, the conifers are generally regarded as including all the Gymnosperms with the exception of *Ephedra* (a course which is followed here). Botanically, the conifers (Class Pinopsida) also exclude *Ginkgo*, *Taxus* and *Torreya*.

The conifers are mainly distributed in the temperate and subtropical regions of the world (a small proportion occur at high elevations in the tropics). Only 3 species, namely *Juniperus communis* ("Juniper"), *Pinus sylvestris* ("Scots Pine") and *Taxus baccata* ("Yew") are native to the British Isles, though many foreign species are commonly planted and sometimes naturalised.

The leaves of conifers are, with few notable exceptions, evergreen. They vary from the long, bundled needles of the Pines (*Pinus*) to the shorter, often sharp-pointed leaves of the Firs (*Abies*), Spruces (*Picea*) and Junipers (*Juniperus*). Very different in appearance are the small, scale-like leaves of the Cypresses (*Cupressus*), False Cypresses (*Chamaecyparis*) and Arborvitae (*Thuja*). Of the deciduous conifers the following genera are here described: *Larix*, *Pseudolarix*, *Metasequoia*, *Taxodium*, *Ginkgo* and *Glyptostrobus*.

The flowers of conifers are small and primitive and are borne in usually short, catkin-like structures known as strobili. The male and female are borne on separate strobili on the same or on different plants. Pollination is by wind.

The fruits of conifers vary from a woody cone, as in pine and larch, to a fleshy, berry-like fruit as in juniper and yew.

A great deal of work on the growth and heights of conifers in the British Isles has been carried out by Alan Mitchell, late of the Forestry Commission and the author of several books on trees in this country.

**Dwarf Conifers** Recent years have witnessed a tremendous upsurge in the development and interest in miniature to semi-dwarf conifers. Few species are truly dwarf, they include the creeping or low-growing junipers, particularly *Juniperus horizontalis* and its cultivars, *Podocarpus nivalis* and *Dacrydium laxifolium*. Used in a broad sense the term includes all those cultivars which have originated both in the wild and in cultivation as seedling variants, or as sports or mutations; quite a few have come into being as propagations from Witches' Brooms, whilst some prostrate cultivars are the result of vegetative reproduction of horizontally-growing side branches.

With the reduction in size of the modern garden there is not room for the large-growing timber-producing species, but a miniature forest is a thing of beauty and infinite interest for every day of the year. Dwarf conifers have reproduced, in miniature, evergreen trees displaying the full range of colour and contour which exist in the great pinetums and natural forests of the temperate world.

Dwarf conifers associate well with heathers and many are suitable as specimens on the small lawn or the rock garden. The miniature "bun" forms make excellent subjects for the alpine-house or for growing in troughs, etc.

**\*ABIES** MILLER—**Pinaceae**—The "Silver Firs" are a genus of more than 50 species of evergreen trees, widely distributed in the N hemisphere, reaching as far south as C America and Taiwan. Many of them reach a great size, particularly in the wild. They differ from *Picea* in the disc-like leaf-scars and their erect cones which break up whilst still on the tree. The majority of species are conical in outline, at least when young, the branches borne in more or less regular whorls, flattened in a horizontal manner. The leaves are linear and usually flattened, bearing several greyish or white lines of stomata on their lower surface and, in some species, on the upper surface too. Male and female strobili are borne on the same tree during spring. The cones are borne on the upper sides of the branchlets and, in many species, are an attractive blue-purple or violet when young.

The firs require a deep, moist soil for best development. Most dislike industrial atmosphere and shallow chalk soils, the chief exceptions being *A. cephalonica*, *A. pinsapo*, and their hybrid *A. × vilmorinii*.

**alba** MILLER (*A. pectinata* DC.) "European Silver Fir". The common species of C Europe, being particularly predominant in the mountains of France, Switzerland and Germany. A large, or very large tree, with a smooth, grey bark when young. Leaves 2-3cm long, in 2 usually horizontal ranks, dark shining green above, marked with 2 glaucous bands beneath. Cones cylindrical, 10-16cm long, greenish-brown when young, with exserted reflexed bracts. Subject to injury from late spring frosts and one of the least satisfactory species for the southern counties of the British Isles. Europe. I about 1603.

**'Pendula'** An unusual tree of medium size with long, weeping branches, often hanging down the trunk. Originated as a seedling in France about 1835.

**'Pyramidalis'** ('Pyramidalis Compacta') A medium-sized tree of conical habit, narrower and fastigiate when young, the crowded, ascending branches bearing short, dark shining green leaves. C 1851.

**‡amabilis** (DOUGLAS) FORBES "Red Silver Fir". A beautiful large tree with silvery-white bark when young and small, very resinous winter buds. Leaves 2.5-3cm long, dark shining green above, white beneath, smelling of oranges when crushed, crowded on the upper sides of the branchlets, pectinate below. Cones 8-15cm long, purplish when young, bracts hidden. A rare tree in the British Isles and unsuitable for chalky or dry soils. W North America. I 1830.

**'Spreading Star'** ('Procumbens') A low-growing cultivar up to 1m high with wide-spreading, horizontally arranged branches. Raised in Holland. C 1960.

**arizonica** See *A. lasiocarpa* var. *arizonica*.

**‡balsamea** (L.) MILLER "Balsam Fir" "Balm of Gilead". A medium-sized tree common in North America and extending into the Arctic regions, but not well adapted for our climate. One of the species from which Canada Balsam is obtained. Winter buds very resinous. Leaves 1.5-3cm long, strongly balsam-scented, glossy dark green above except for a patch of glaucous stomata at tip, and with 2 narrow greyish bands beneath, spreading upwards on the upper sides of the branchlets, parted beneath. Cones 6-10cm long, violet-purple when young. I 1696.

**'Hudsonia'** A dwarf shrub. Habit dense and compact with a flattish top. Leaves short and densely arranged on the branchlets. A specimen in our nursery attained 0.75m × 1.2m in about thirty years. More lime-tolerant than the typical form. I before 1810. AGM 1984.

**borisii-regis** MATTF. A strong-growing, large tree. Leaves 2.5-3cm long, dark glossy green above, marked with 2 glaucous bands beneath, crowded on the upper surfaces of the branchlets, pectinate below. Cones cylindrical, 10-15cm long, bracts exserted and reflexed. A variable species more or less intermediate between *A. alba* and *A. cephalonica*, from which it is perhaps derived as a hybrid. Balkan Peninsula. AM 1974.

**bornmuelleriana** MATTF. A large tree resembling *A. nordmanniana* in habit, with branches down to the ground. Leaves densely arranged on the upper sides of the branchlets, up to 2-3cm long, green above, often with stomata at tip, marked with 2 white bands of stomata beneath. Cones 12-15cm long, bracts exserted and reflexed. Sometimes regarded as a natural hybrid between *A. cephalonica* and *A. nordmanniana*. N Turkey.

**ABIES**—*continued*

**brachyphylla** See *A. homolepis*.

**bracteata** (D. DON) NUTT. (*A. venusta* (DOUGL.) K. KOCH) "Santa Lucia Fir". One of the most outstanding and beautiful of the firs, forming a large tree. Distinct on account of its pale brown, spindle-shaped winter buds up to 2.5cm long, and its 3.5-5cm long, rigid, spine-tipped dark green leaves which occur on the branchlets in 2 ranks. Cones 7-10cm long, bracts long exserted, spine-tipped, giving the cones a remarkable whiskery appearance. Succeeds on deep soil over chalk. Mts of S California. Introduced by William Lobb in 1852. FCC 1915.

**cephalonica** LOUD. "Greek Fir". A large, handsome tree reaching 30m in the wild. Leaves rigid, sharp-pointed, shining green, 1.5-2.5cm long, white beneath, spreading more or less all round the branchlets but not so noticeably so as *A. pinsapo*. Cones 12-16cm long, with exserted, reflexed bracts. One of the best species for chalky soils and for freedom from disease, but breaks into growth early and therefore should not be planted in frost pockets. Mts of S Greece. I 1824.

**'Meyer's Dwarf'** ('Nana') A dwarf cultivar with horizontally spreading branches, rigid branchlets and shorter leaves. C 1963.

**chengii** RUSHFORTH A medium-sized tree related to *A. forrestii* and described in 1984 from a specimen at Westonbirt. Leaves dark glossy green, up to 6cm long, notched at the apex and with 2 pale green bands of stomata beneath, adpressed beneath the shoots, parted above. Cones pale violet when young, to 9cm long, the tips of the bracts slightly exserted. Probably introduced from Yunnan in 1931 by George Forrest. It has reached 15m in the Hillier Gardens and Arboretum (1990).

**chensiensis** VAN TIEGH. A medium-sized tree with conspicuous rough grey bark. Leaves 1.5-3.5cm long, thick and rigid, shining dark green above, marked with 2 grey or bluish stomatic bands beneath, arranged in V-shaped formation. Cones 8-10 cm long, greenish when young, bracts hidden. Very rare in cultivation. C China. Introduced by Ernest Wilson in 1907.

**cilicica** CARR. "Cilician Fir". Medium to large-size tree. Bark greyish, deeply fissured on old trees. Leaves 2-3.5cm long, light green above, marked with 2 narrow, greyish stomatic bands beneath, arranged on the branchlets in a V-shaped formation. Cones cylindrical, 16-25cm long, bracts hidden. S Turkey, NW Syria, Lebanon. I 1855.

**concolor** (GORD.) LINDL. "Colorado White Fir". A very beautiful large tree with smooth, grey bark, grooved and scaly on old trees. Leaves up to 5.5cm long, thick, almost round in section, of an attractive blue-green or grey-green colour, arranged mainly in 2 ranks, but also standing above the shoot. Cones 8-14cm long, pale green when young sometimes purplish bloomy, bracts hidden. SW United States. I 1873. AGM 1984.

**'Candicans'** A striking cultivar with vivid grey or silvery-white leaves. Raised in France before 1929.

**'Compacta'** ('Glauca Compacta') A dwarf shrub of compact but irregular habit, leaves of an attractive greyish-blue colour. A wonderful plant, the most outstanding dwarf Silver Fir, suitable for the large rock garden or as an isolated lawn specimen. A specimen in the Hillier Gardens and Arboretum has exceeded 2m tall and across. C 1891. AGM 1984.

**var. lowiana** (GORD.) LEMM. (*A. lowiana* (GORD.) A. MURR.) "Pacific White Fir". A large tree, the side-branches very even in length and short in comparison with the height of the tree and diameter of the trunk. It has greyish-green young shoots and smaller winter buds with the leaves pectinate above or arranged in V-shaped formation. SW United States. Introduced by William Lobb in 1851.

**'Violacea'** Leaves glaucous-blue. C 1875.

**'Wattezii'** A small to medium-sized tree, leaves creamy-yellow when young, becoming silvery-white later. Raised in Holland before 1900.

**delavayi** FRANCH. A medium-sized, handsome tree of somewhat variable nature. The densely set leaves, 2-3cm long, are revolute, bright shining green above and gleaming silvery-white beneath. Cones barrel-shaped, 6-10cm long, dark bluish-violet with very slightly exserted bracts. W Yunnan, China, N Burma, N India. I 1918. AM 1980 (to K.W. 21008).

**ABIES delavayi**—*continued*

**var. fabri** See *A. fabri.*

**var. faxoniana** See *A. fabri* subsp. *minensis* and *A. fargesii.*

**var. forrestii** See *A. forrestii.*

**var. georgei** See *A. georgei* and *A. forrestii* var. *smithii.*

**'Major Neishe'** ('Nana') A dwarf, slow-growing form. Winter buds orange-brown. Leaves more or less radially arranged, 1-1.5cm long, the margins recurved.

**'Nana'** See 'Major Neishe'.

**ernestii** See *A. recurvata* var. *ernestii.*

**fabri** (MASTERS) CRAIB (*A. delavayi* var. *fabri* (MASTERS) HUNT) A medium-sized tree with brown scaly bark. Leaves 2-3cm long, dark green above, gleaming white beneath, with recurved margins, often rather loosely and irregularly arranged. Cones 6-8cm long, bluish-black, bracts exserted and reflexed. W Sichuan, China. I 1901.

**subsp. minensis** (BORDERES-REY & GAUSS.) RUSHF. A more vigorous form with longer, flatter leaves. Plants grown as *A. delavayi* var. *faxoniana* belong here.

**fargesii** FRANCH. (*A. faxoniana* REHD. & WILS.) (*A. delavayi* var. *faxoniana* (REHD. & WILS.) A.B. JACKS.) (*A. sutchuenensis* (FRANCH.) REHD. & WILS.) A strong-growing, medium-sized tree with glossy purple young shoots. Leaves loosely two-ranked, 3-5cm long, notched, dark green above, marked with 2 glaucous bands beneath. Cones 6-10cm long, purplish-brown when young. Bracts shortly exserted and reflexed. A splendid species and one of the best of the Asiatic Silver Firs in cultivation. N China. First discovered by Père Farges and introduced by Ernest Wilson in 1901.

**faxoniana** See *A. fabri* subsp. *minensis* and *A. fargesii.*

‡**firma** SIEB. & ZUCC. "Japanese Fir" "Momi Fir". A large tree which can reach 40m or more in the wild. The comparatively broad, stiff, leathery leaves, 1.5-4cm long, are yellowish-green above, with 2 greyish-green, stomatic bands beneath. They are conspicuously notched on the lateral branches, densely crowded, with a V-shaped parting, on the upper sides of the shoots, loosely pectinate below. Cones 8-15cm long, yellowish-green when young. Bracts slightly exserted. Japan. I 1861. FCC 1863.

**forrestii** ROGERS (*A. delavayi* var. *forrestii* (ROGERS) A.B. JACKS.) A very distinct and beautiful, small to medium-sized tree. Leaves variable in length and arrangement, but usually 2-4cm long and almost radial, dark green above, conspicuously silvery-white beneath. Cones barrel-shaped, 8-15cm long, sloe-black with exserted bracts. NW Yunnan, China, SE Tibet. Introduced by George Forrest about 1910. AM 1930.

**var. smithii** VIGUIE & GAUSS. This form differs in its stout, densely hairy shoots. Plants previously grown as *A. delavayi* var. *georgei* belong here.

**fraseri** (PURSH) POIR. Medium-sized tree with a slender, conical crown. Leaves short, 1-2cm long, crowded on the upper sides of the twigs, pectinate below, dark shining green above, with a few short lines of stomata near the tip, marked with 2 white stomatic bands beneath. Cones 3-5cm long, purple when young. Bracts long-exserted and reflexed. One of the least satisfactory of the North American Silver Firs in cultivation and very prone to disease. SE United States, rare in the wild. Introduced by John Fraser in 1811.

**gamblei** HICKEL (*A. pindrow* var. *brevifolia* DALLIM. & JACKS.) A very distinct tree with pale brown or reddish-brown shoots and leaves 2-3.5cm long. Cones up to 12cm long, violet blue when young. N India. C 1860.

**georgei** ORR (*A. delavayi* var. *georgei* (ORR) MELVILLE) This species is probably not in cultivation. For plants previously grown under this name see *A. forrestii* var. *smithii.*

**grandis** (DOUGL.) LINDL. "Giant Fir". This remarkably fast-growing tree quickly attains a large size. Leaves varying from 2-6cm long, dark shining green above, marked with 2 glaucous-grey bands beneath, spreading horizontally on either side of the shoot. Cones 7.5-10cm long, bright green when young. Grows best in areas with a heavy rainfall and prefers a moist but well drained soil. A good shade-bearing species and moderately lime-tolerant; the leaves are delightfully fragrant when crushed. W North America. Introduced by David Douglas in 1830.

**'Aurea'** Leaves yellowish. C 1890.

**ABIES**—*continued*

**holophylla** MAXIM. "Manchurian Fir". A large tree, rare in cultivation. Leaves 2.5-4cm long, bright green above, with 2 greyish-green stomatic bands beneath, densely arranged on the upper sides of the shoots, pectinate below. Cones 10-13cm long, green when young. Closely related to *A. homolepis*. Manchuria, Korea. I 1908.

**homolepis** SIEB. & ZUCC. (*A. brachyphylla* MAXIM.) "Nikko Fir". A splendid, large tree, very tolerant of atmospheric pollution. Leaves 1.5-3cm long, green above, with 2 chalk-white, stomatic bands beneath, crowded on the upper sides of the branchlets, pectinate below. Cones 7.5-10cm long, purple when young. Japan. I 1861.

**kawakamii** (HAYATA) ITO A very rare, small to medium-sized tree with very pale or whitish corky bark. Leaves 1.5-3cm long, bloomy at first above, later green, marked with 2 pale bands beneath, crowded and curved on the upper sides of the branchlets, loosely spreading below. Cones 5-7.5cm long, purple when young. Mountains of Taiwan. I before 1930.

**koreana** WILS. A small, slow-growing tree of neat habit. Leaves 1-2cm long, dark green above, gleaming white beneath, radially arranged on strong shoots, loosely arranged on others. An interesting species, producing its violet-purple, cylindrical cones, 5-7.5cm long, even on specimens half a metre high. A tall-growing but very poor form is in cultivation. S Korea. I 1905. AGM 1984.

**'Compact Dwarf'** A small, compact form, spreading horizontally, without a leader. Non-coning. C 1964.

**'Horstmann's Silberlocke'** See 'Silberlocke'.

**'Piccolo'** A slow-growing dwarf form differing from 'Compact Dwarf' in its much shorter leaves, mainly pointing forwards and upwards on the shoots and not radially arranged. Raised in Holland before 1979.

**'Silberlocke'** ('Horstmann's Silberlocke') A slow-growing form, the leaves twisted upwards revealing their white undersides. Raised in Germany before 1983.

**lasiocarpa** (HOOK.) NUTT. "Subalpine Fir". A medium-sized tree distinct on account of its pale greyish-green leaves, 1.5-3.5cm long, densely but irregularly arranged on the branchlets in 2 ranks. Cones 5-10cm long, purple when young. Moderately lime-tolerant. W North America.

**var. arizonica** (MERRIAM) LEMM. (*A. arizonica* MERRIAM) "Cork Fir". A medium-sized tree with greyish or buff-coloured, shortly pubescent branchlets and thick, soft, corky bark. Leaves 2.5-3.5cm long, silvery-grey. Cones smaller. SW United States. I 1903.

**'Compacta'** (*A. arizonica* 'Compacta') A slow-growing shrub of compact, conical habit, leaves of a conspicuous blue-grey. C 1927.

**lowiana** See *A. concolor* var. *lowiana*.

‡**magnifica** A. MURR. "Californian Red Fir". A beautiful large tree of slender, cone-shaped habit, attaining 60m in its native habitats. Bark of young trees whitish. Leaves long and curved, 2-4cm long, grey-green or blue-green on both surfaces, densely clothing the upper sides of the branchlets, pectinate below. Cones 15-22cm long, purple when young. Not suitable for chalk soils. Oregon, California. I 1851.

**'Glauca'** Leaves of a deep glaucous-green. C 1891.

**'Prostrata'** ('Nana') A dwarf form with wide-spreading branches.

‡**mariesii** MAST. "Maries' Fir". Medium-sized to large tree with persistently reddish-brown, downy young shoots. Winter buds very resinous. Leaves 1.5-2.5cm long, shining dark green above, with 2 conspicuous white bands of stomata below, crowded on the upper sides of the branchlets, pectinate below. Cones 7.5-10cm long, violet-purple when young. Japan. Introduced by Charles Maries about 1879.

**marocana** TRABUT "Moroccan Fir". A medium-sized tree closely related to *A. pinsapo*. Young shoots yellowish-grey and glabrous. Winter buds resinous. Leaves 1-1.5cm long, green above, with white stomatic bands beneath, arranged in 2 horizontal ranks. Cones cylindrical, 12-15cm long, pale brown. Rare in cultivation. Morocco. I about 1905.

**nebrodensis** (LOJAC.) MATTEI A small to medium-sized tree, related to *A. alba*, but differing in its smaller size and the broader, flatter crown of mature specimens. The leaves are

**ABIES nebrodensis**—*continued*

also stiffer and slightly shorter and densely arranged on the upper sides of the branchlets. Cones to 15cm long, with exserted bracts. A very rare species at one time almost extinct in the wild and restricted to a few trees in the mountains of N Sicily. A specimen in the Hillier Gardens and Arboretum has reached 12m. Coning material from this tree received the Award of Merit in 1990.

**nobilis** See *A. procera*.

**nordmanniana** (STEVEN) SPACH "Caucasian Fir". A noble species of great ornamental value. A large to very large tree reaching 50-60m in its native habitats, with tiered branches sweeping downwards. Winter buds reddish-brown. Leaves 2-3cm long, shining green above, marked with 2 white stomatic bands beneath, densely arranged on the branchlets, pointing forwards and overlapping above, pectinate below. Cones 15-20cm long, greenish when young, scales long-exserted and reflexed. A very satisfactory, generally disease-resistant species. W Caucasus. I 1840.

**'Aureospica'** Growth irregular. Leaves tipped golden yellow. C 1891.

**'Golden Spreader'** ('Aurea Nana') A dwarf, slow-growing cultivar with wide-spreading branches. Leaves 1-2.5cm long, light yellow above, pale yellowish-white beneath. C 1960.

**'Pendula'** A wide-spreading, semi-prostrate form, the branchlets with pendulous tips. C 1870.

**numidica** CARR. "Algerian Fir". A large tree of conical habit. Leaves radially arranged, but all curving upwards, 1-2cm long, dark green above, with a greyish stomatic patch near the apex, marked with 2 white bands beneath. Cones 12-18cm long, brown. Only native in a small mountainous area of E Algeria. I 1861. AM 1976. AM 1987 (both for foliage and cones).

**'Pendula'** A slow-growing form with pendulous branchlets.

†**oaxacana** MARTINEZ A rare, medium-sized tree with conspicuous glabrous, orange-brown young shoots. Leaves 2-4cm long, dark green above, marked with 2 glaucous, stomatic bands beneath. Cones 8-11cm long, bracts exserted. Resembles both *A. religiosa* and *A. vejari*, at least when young. Mexico.

**pectinata** See *A. alba*.

**pindrow** ROYLE "West Himalayan Fir". A rare and beautiful large tree of slender, conical habit. Leaves normally 3-6cm long, bright shining green above, with 2 greyish-white, stomatic bands beneath, loosely arranged but concealing the branchlets above, pectinate below. W Himalaya, where it forms mixed forests with *Cedrus deodara* and *Picea smithiana* and ranges into *A. spectabilis*. Introduced by Dr Royle about 1837.

**var. brevifolia** See *A. gamblei*.

**var. intermedia** See *A. spectabilis* var. *intermedia*.

**pinsapo** BOISS. "Spanish Fir". A medium-sized to large tree, easily recognised by its short, rigid, dark green leaves up to 1.5cm long which radiate from all sides of the branchlets. Cones 10-15cm long, purplish-brown when young. One of the best species for chalk soils and one of the only 2 species with radially-spreading leaves, the other being *A. cephalonica* although *A. numidica* and some forms of *A. forrestii* approach this condition. Mts of S Spain near Ronda, where it is planted in the streets. Pinsapo is the Spanish name of the tree. I 1839.

**'Aurea'** Leaves suffused golden yellow. Usually a medium to large shrub or small tree of rather poor constitution. C 1868.

**'Glauca'** A large tree selected for its striking blue-grey leaves. C 1867.

‡**procera** REHD. (*A. nobilis* LINDL.) "Noble Fir". A most beautiful, large to very large tree. Leaves 2.5-3.5cm long, bluish-green above, with 2 narrow, glaucous bands beneath, crowded on the upper sides of the branchlets, pectinate and decurved below. The magnificent cylindrical cones are 16-25cm long, green when young, with long-exserted, reflexed bracts. W United States. Introduced by David Douglas in 1830. AM 1973. FCC 1979. AGM 1984.

**'Glauca'** A selection with blue-grey leaves. C 1863.

**'Glauca Prostrata'** ('Prostrata') A low bush with spreading or prostrate branches and glaucous leaves. Originated in our Shroner Wood Nursery in about 1895.

**recurvata** MAST. "Min Fir". A medium-sized tree closely resembling *A. chensiensis* but with shorter leaves. Leaves 1.5-2.5cm long, thick and rigid, those on the upper sides of the

**ABIES recurvata**—*continued*

terminal branchlets strongly recurved, dark shining green or sometimes slightly glaucous above, paler beneath. Cones 5-10cm long, violet-purple when young. NW Sichuan, China. I 1910.

**var. ernestii** (REHD.) KUAN (*A. ernestii* REHD.) Differs in its longer, notched leaves. Some plants grown as *A. chensiensis* belong here.

**religiosa** (H.B.K.) SCHLECH T. "Sacred Fir". A rare tree of small to medium size with down-sweeping stems. Leaves 1.5-3.5cm long, peculiarly tapered and curved, dark green above, marked with 2 greyish stomatic bands beneath, densely arranged and forward-pointing on the upper sides of the branchlets, pectinate below. Cones 10-15cm long, bluish when young, bracts exserted and reflexed. In Mexico the branches are used to decorate mission buildings during religious festivals. Reasonably lime-tolerant, it grew in our nursery for more than 50 years and a specimen in the Hillier Gardens and Arboretum has reached 14m (1990). C Mexico. I 1838.

**sachalinensis** (SCHMIDT) MAST. "Sachalin Fir". A medium-sized tree with leaves very densely arranged, 1.5-3.5cm long, light green above, marked with 2 greyish bands beneath. Cones 7-8cm long, olive-green when young, bracts exserted and reflexed. Less susceptible to spring frosts. Differs from the closely related *A. sibirica* in its furrowed shoots not densely white pubescent. N Japan, Sakhalin, Kurile Isles. I 1878.

**var. mayriana** MIYABE & KUDO A Japanese variety differing mainly in its shorter leaves, 1.5-2.5cm long, and slightly larger cones.

**spectabilis** (D. DON) SPACH (*A. webbiana* LINDL.) "Himalayan Fir". A magnificent large tree closely resembling forms of *A. delavayi*. Young shoots reddish-brown, stout and rough, downy in the grooves. Winter buds large and globular, very resinous. The densely two-ranked leaves, 1.5-5cm or occasionally 6cm long, are shining dark green above and gleaming silvery-white beneath. Cones cylindrical, 14-18cm long, violet-purple when young, bracts hidden or slightly exserted. Unfortunately, this striking species is susceptible to spring frosts. Nepal, Sikkim, Bhutan. I 1822. AM 1974.

**var. intermedia** HENRY (*A. pindrow* var. *intermedia* HENRY) A very distinct variety with leaves 4.5-6cm long, dark green above, gleaming silvery-white beneath, loosely two-ranked. A striking fir of uncertain origin. C 1870. AM 1944.

**squamata** MAST. "Flaky Fir". A very rare, small to medium-sized tree with conspicuous shaggy, peeling, purplish-brown bark. Leaves 1-2.5cm long, greyish-green above with 2 greyish bands beneath, sharply-pointed, densely arranged on the upper sides of the branchlets. Cones 5-6cm long, violet, the bracts with exserted, reflexed tips. It has reached 19m on the site of our Chandler's Ford nursery (1990). Introduced by E.H. Wilson from W China, in 1910.

**sutchuenensis** See *A. fargesii*.

× **vasconcellosiana** FRANCO (*A. pindrow* × *A. pinsapo*). A very rare, medium-sized tree which occurred in a park in Portugal in 1945. Resembling *A. pindrow* in general habit. Leaves 1-3cm long, slightly curved, glossy dark green above, prominently marked with 2 greyish stomatic bands beneath. Cones 12-15cm long, dark purple when young.

‡**veitchii** LINDL. A beautiful, large, fast-growing tree. The densely-arranged, upcurved leaves, 1-2.5cm long, are glossy dark green above and silver-white beneath. Cones 5-7cm long, bluish-purple when young, tips of bracts exserted. This handsome species thrives better in the vicinity of large towns than most others. C Japan. First discovered by John Gould Veitch on Mt Fuji in 1860; introduced by Charles Maries in 1879. AM 1974.

**vejari** MARTINEZ A small to medium-sized tree of relatively recent introduction. Leaves up to 3.5cm long, dark green above, marked with 2 grey stomatic bands beneath. Cones 5-8cm long, purple when young, bracts with exserted tips. Young specimens resemble *A. religiosa*. Mexico. I 1964.

**venusta** See *A. bracteata*.

× **vilmorinii** MAST. (*A. cephalonica* × *A. pinsapo*). A medium-sized to large tree; leaves 2-3cm long, marked with 2 grey bands beneath, radially-arranged but more densely so on the upper sides of the branchlets. Cones 14-20cm long, bracts exserted and reflexed at tips. An intentional cross raised in 1867 by Maurice L. de Vilmorin, whose arboretum at Des Barres was and still is one of the largest and richest in Europe. It was to M. Vilmorin that the plant-collecting French missionaries such as David, Delavay and Farges sent

**ABIES** × **vilmorinii**—*continued*

from China seed of so many new and exciting woody plants. This same hybrid frequently occurs where the 2 parent species are growing in close proximity.

**webbiana** See *A. spectabilis*.

†***AGATHIS*** SALISB.—**Araucariaceae**—A genus of 13 species of large, usually monoecious, evergreen trees with massive trunks, related to *Araucaria*, natives of SE Asia to Queensland and New Zealand. The following is the hardiest species but is only suitable for the mildest localities. The thick, scaly, resinous bark emits a thick, milky liquid when wounded.

**australis** SALISB. "Kauri Pine". An exotic-looking tree with thick spreading branches. Leaves variable, on young trees they are narrowly lanceolate, 2.5-8cm long, spreading, leathery and lime-green in colour, on old trees they are shorter, oblong and sessile. Young plants are bronze or purple-flushed. Cones 6-8cm across, subglobose. These were produced on a tree which grew for many years on chalk soil in our West Hill nursery in a cold house. Outside it grew for several years at the Ventnor Botanic Garden. It attains small tree size in the British Isles, but in New Zealand giants of 45m high with trunks 6-7m in diameter are recorded. Native of New Zealand (N Island) where it is of economic importance for its timber and resin. I 1823.

***ARAUCARIA*** JUSS.—**Araucariaceae**—A genus of about 18 species of evergreen trees found in Oceania, Queensland and S America. Young trees remarkable for their symmetrical habit, with branches usually borne in whorls down to ground level. The long-persistent, spirally-arranged leaves are usually leathery and overlapping, but vary in size and shape often on different parts of the same tree. Male and female strobili normally borne on different trees, occasionally on different branches of the same tree. The globular or ovoid cones break up while still on the tree. Apart from the following, the only hardy species, the "Norfolk Island Pine" (*A. heterophylla* (SALISB.) FRANCO) is a commonly grown conservatory plant.

**araucana** (MOL.) K. KOCH (*A. imbricata* PAVON) "Chile Pine" "Monkey Puzzle". A medium-sized to large tree of unique appearance with long spidery branches and densely overlapping, rigid, spine-tipped, dark green leaves. Cones globular, 11-18cm long, taking 3 years to mature. One of the few S American trees hardy in the British Isles and an excellent wind resister. It grows best in a moist, loamy soil. In industrial areas it loses its lower branches and becomes ragged in appearance. Extensively planted in Victorian times. Chile, Argentina. First introduced by Archibald Menzies in 1795 and later by William Lobb in 1844. AM 1980.

***ATHROTAXIS*** D. DON—**Taxodiaceae**—The "Tasmanian Cedars", with their small cones and usually short, thick, imbricated leaves, are unique in appearance and slow-growing. Male and female strobili borne on the same tree. Cones small, ripening the first year. Leaves of the main branchlets are larger than those of the subsidiary branchlets. All 3 species are native to Tasmania and require a warm, sheltered position. *A. cupressoides* and *A. laxifolia* have grown successfully here without injury for more than fifty years, but *A. selaginoides* is less hardy and can be injured or killed in a very severe winter.

**cupressoides** D. DON A small, erect tree with very small, closely-imbricated, dark green, scale-like leaves, obtuse at the tips and pressed close to the stems. Cones 8-12mm across. I 1848.

**laxifolia** HOOK. A small to medium-sized tree differing from *A. cupressoides* in its laxer habit and larger, usually pointed leaves which are slightly spreading. Cones 16-18mm across, often profusely borne and then very ornamental. I 1857.

†**selaginoides** D. DON A small to medium-sized tree larger in all its parts than the other 2 species. Closer to *A. laxifolia*, but leaves larger—up to 12mm long, more spreading, showing the conspicuous glaucous bands above, and with a long-pointed apex. Cones up to 18mm long and broad. I about 1857. AM 1931.

***AUSTROCEDRUS*** FLORIN & BOUTELJE—**Cupressaceae**—A monotypic genus closely related to and sometimes united with *Libocedrus*. Leaves scale-like, borne in unequal opposite

**AUSTROCEDRUS**—*continued*

pairs, marked with glaucous stomatic bands, forming flattened sprays. Male and female strobili borne on the same tree. Cones small, solitary.

**chilensis** (D. DON) FLORIN & BOUTELJE (*Libocedrus chilensis* (D. DON) ENDL.) "Chilean Cedar". A remarkably beautiful and distinct species, here slow-growing, but hardy and making a small, columnar tree. The branchlets are flattened and beautifully moss-like or fern-like in their ultimate divisions. Leaves in V-shaped pairs, of a pleasant shade of sea-green. This tree grew successfully in our nursery for more than forty years. Chile, Argentina. I 1847.

'**Viridis**' Leaves bright green, lacking the glaucous, stomatic bands.

†\***CALLITRIS** VENT.—**Cupressaceae**—With about 14 species, the "Cypress Pines" of Australia and New Caledonia are evergreen trees and shrubs thriving in dry, arid conditions. Their branchlets are long and thread-like, densely clothed with small, narrow or scale-like leaves arranged in whorls of 3. Male and female strobili borne on the same tree. The globular, ovoid or conical cones, with 6-8 scales, are often borne in clusters and persist for several years. All species are tender and should be grown in the conservatory or in sheltered woodland in mild localities.

**oblonga** A. & L.C. RICH. "Tasmanian Cypress Pine". An erect bush of medium size. The densely-arranged, spray-like branchlets bear short, adpressed, scale-like leaves. Cones up to 2.5cm long, woody, with clawed scales; produced singly or in clusters. Tasmania. AM 1931.

**rhomboidea** R. BR. ex A. & L.C. RICH. (*C. cupressiformis* D. DON ex LOUD.) (*C. tasmanica* (BENTH.) R.T. BAK. & H.G. SM.) "Oyster Bay Pine". A rare species in cultivation attaining small tree size. Branchlets finely divided, clothed with bright green or glaucous scale-like leaves. Cones ovoid, 8-13mm across, purplish-brown. E Tasmania, Australia (Queensland, New South Wales, Victoria).

**tasmanica** See *C. rhomboidea*.

\***CALOCEDRUS** KURZ—**Cupressaceae**—A small genus of 3 species of evergreen trees allied to *Thuja* and, by some authorities, united with *Libocedrus*; natives of SE Asia and North America. The branchlets are arranged in broad, flattened sprays. Leaves scale-like, flattened, densely borne in opposite pairs. Male and female strobili borne on different branches of the same tree. Cones woody, ripening the first year.

**decurrens** (TORR.) FLORIN (*Libocedrus decurrens* TORR.) "Incense Cedar". A large tree with a conical head of spreading branches in the wild state. Most cultivated trees belong to the form 'Columnaris' ('Fastigiata'). The characteristic columnar habit renders it unmistakable among cultivated trees and ideal as a single specimen or for grouping for skyline or formal effect. The dark green leaves are crowded into dense, fan-like sprays. Cones ovoid, pendulous, up to 2.5cm long. W North America. I 1853. AGM 1984.

'**Aureovariegata**' A cultivar in which sprays of golden leaves occur irregularly about the branches. An attractive, slow-growing, medium-sized tree. C 1894.

'**Berrima Gold**' A slow-growing form with orange bark and pale yellow-green foliage tipped with orange in winter. Ultimate height uncertain. Introduced in 1976 by Sir Harold Hillier from an Australian nursery.

'**Fastigiata**' See 'Columnaris' under *C. decurrens*.

'**Intricata**' A remarkable dwarf form making a dense, rigid column with thick, flat and twisted recurving branchlets. 1.2m high by 0.6m wide after 20 years and 2.5m high by 1.2m wide after 40 years in the Hillier Gardens and Arboretum. Previously listed as 'Nana'. Seed raised by James Noble of San Francisco in 1938.

'**Nana**' See 'Intricata'.

†**formosana** (FLORIN) FLORIN (*Libocedrus formosana* FLORIN) A distinct species. A small tree of open habit showing kinship with *C. macrolepis*, but differing in its more slender branchlets and bright green leaves, yellowish-green beneath. Only suitable for the mildest localities. Plants have survived several winters here, growing among shelter trees. Taiwan.

†**macrolepis** KURZ (*Libocedrus macrolepis* (KURZ) BENTH. & HOOK.) A beautiful, small, open-branched tree with broad, elegant, fan-like sprays of flattened branchlets. The large,

**CALOCEDRUS macrolepis**—*continued*

flattened leaves are sea-green above and glaucous beneath. Only suitable for the mildest localities. SW China, E Burma. Introduced by Ernest Wilson in 1900. FCC 1902 (as *Libocedrus macrolepis*).

**\*CEDRUS** TREW—**Pinaceae**—The "Cedars" are a small genus of 4 species of evergreen trees, renowned for their grandeur and longevity. Young trees are conical in outline, developing often a massive trunk and large horizontal branches as they age. They are among the most popular of all trees for specimen planting, but owing to their eventual size are only suitable for parks, open areas and large gardens.

The narrow, needle-like leaves are sparsely arranged in spirals on the terminal shoots and borne in rosettes on the numerous, spur-like side growths. Male and female strobili are borne usually on the same tree, the bright yellow males peppering the flattened branchlets in autumn. Cones barrel-shaped, erect, maturing in 2 years and breaking up while still on the tree. *C. atlantica, C. brevifolia* and *C. libani* are very closely related and differ only in small details.

**atlantica** MANETTI "Atlas Cedar". A large or very large tree of rapid growth when young. Leaves 2-3.5cm long, green or grey-green, thickly covering the long branches which, though somewhat ascending at first, eventually assume the horizontal arrangement generally associated with *C. libani*. Cones 5-7cm long. The "Atlas Cedar" is said to differ from the "Cedar of Lebanon" in a number of characters such as hairier shoots, larger leaf rosettes, etc, but these minor differences are not consistent, varying from tree to tree. It is perhaps best considered as a geographical subspecies of *C. libani*. Atlas Mts in Algeria and Morocco (N Africa). I about 1840.

**'Aurea'** A medium-sized tree; leaves shorter than in the type, distinctly golden yellow. Not always a satisfactory grower. C 1900.

**'Fastigiata'** A large, densely-branched tree of erect habit, the branches sharply ascending, branchlets short and erect. Leaves bluish-green. C 1890.

**Glauca group** (f. *glauca* BEISSN.) "Blue Cedar". Perhaps the most spectacular of all "blue" conifers and a very popular tree for specimen planting. Leaves silvery-blue, extremely effective. It occurs both in the wild and in cultivation. FCC 1972. AGM 1984.

**'Glauca Pendula'** A superb small tree with weeping branches and glaucous leaves. Most effective when well positioned. C 1900.

**'Pendula'** A small, weeping tree with green or greyish-green leaves. C 1875.

**brevifolia** HENRY. "Cyprian Cedar". A rare species of slow growth, but eventually making a tree of medium size. The arrangement of the branches is similar to that of *C. libani*, but the usually green leaves are much smaller—1-1.25cm long, or up to 2cm on young trees. Mts of Cyprus. I 1879.

**deodara** G. DON. The "Deodar" is a most beautiful, large tree of somewhat pendent habit. The leaves are glaucous when young, soon deep green. It is readily distinguished from all other species by its drooping leader and by its longer leaves which occasionally measure 5cm long. Cones 7-10cm long. W Himalaya. I 1831. AGM 1984.

**'Albospica'** Tips of young shoots creamy-white. An elegant tree, particularly effective in late spring. C 1867.

**'Aurea'** "Golden Deodar". A tree with leaves golden yellow in spring, becoming greenish-yellow later in the year. C 1866.

**'Aurea Pendula'** Branches weeping; leaves yellow during late spring and summer, yellow-green during winter.

**'Golden Horizon'** A Dutch-raised selection of spreading habit with golden yellow foliage. C 1975.

**'Karl Fuchs'** An extremely hardy form with good blue foliage. C 1979. Raised in Germany from seed collected by Karl Fuchs in Paktia province, Afghanistan.

**'Pendula'** ('Prostrata') A form with pendulous branches spreading over the ground, eventually growing too large for the rock garden. C 1866. Attractive as a wide-spreading low bush if controlled by pruning, but if permitted to develop unchecked it tends to produce a leader and lose its dwarf habit.

**'Pygmy'** ('Pygmaea') An extremely slow-growing, dwarf form increasing at about 1.5cm per year. It is of American origin, making a tiny hummock of blue-grey foliage and is best suited to the alpine-house. C 1943.

**CEDRUS deodara**—*continued*

**'Robusta'** A wide-spreading tree of medium height with irregular drooping branches and long, stout, dark blue-green leaves up to 8cm long. C 1850.

**'Verticillata Glauca'** A dense-growing, small bushy tree with horizontal branches and almost whorled (verticillate) branchlets. Leaves dark glaucous-green. C 1867.

**libani** A. RICH. "Cedar of Lebanon". A large, wide-spreading tree, slower-growing than *C. atlantica* and, like that species, conical when young, gradually assuming the familiar, picturesque, flat-topped and tiered arrangement of a mature tree. Leaves green or greyish-green, 2-3.5cm long. Cones 8-10cm long. This interesting tree has innumerable scriptural and historical associations. It is a native of Asia Minor and Syria and is thought to have been first introduced into England sometime before 1650, possibly 1645. AGM 1984.

**'Aurea Prostrata'** See 'Golden Dwarf'.

**'Comte de Dijon'** A slow-growing, conical form of dense, compact growth, eventually making a medium-sized bush. C 1867.

**'Golden Dwarf'** ('Aurea Prostrata') A slow-growing, horizontal, dwarf bush with yellow leaves. Stems sometimes prostrate. C 1960.

**'Nana'** A very slow-growing, dense, conical bush of medium size, similar to 'Comte de Dijon', but with slightly broader, shorter leaves, 1-2.5cm long. C 1838.

**'Sargentii'** ('Pendula Sargentii') A slow-growing, small bush with a short trunk and dense, weeping branches; leaves blue-green. A superb plant, ideal for the rock garden. C 1919.

**var. stenocoma** (SCHWARZ) DAVIS A conical or broadly columnar tree, intermediate in leaf and cone between *C. atlantica* and *C. libani*. A geographical form native to SW Anatolia, Turkey. I about 1938.

**\*CEPHALOTAXUS** SIEB. & ZUCC. ex ENDL.—**Cephalotaxaceae**—A small genus of 4 species of shrubs or shrubby trees, best described as large-leaved yews; natives of the Himalaya and E Asia. Like the yews they grow well in shade and in the drip of other trees, even conifers, and thrive on calcareous soils. The plants are normally dioecious, the females producing large, olive-like fruits ripening the second year. They differ from *Taxus* both in their fruits and in their longer leaves which have 2 broad, silvery bands beneath. From the closely related *Torreya* they are distinguished by their non-spine-tipped leaves.

**drupacea** See *C. harringtonia* var. *drupacea*.

**fortunei** HOOK. "Chinese Plum Yew". A handsome, large shrub or small bushy tree wider than high, with dark glossy green, lanceolate leaves, 6-9cm long, arranged spirally on the erect shoots and in 2 opposite rows along the spreading branchlets. Fruits ellipsoid or ovoid, 2-3cm long, olive-brown. An excellent shade-bearing evergreen. C and SW China. Introduced by Robert Fortune in 1849. AM 1975.

**'Grandis'** An attractive female form with long leaves. C 1928.

**'Prostrata'** See 'Prostrate Spreader'.

**'Prostrate Spreader'** ('Prostrata') A low-growing shrub with wide-spreading branches and large, deep green leaves. A superb ground-cover plant, eventually covering several yards. It originated in our nurseries before the First World War as a side cutting. The original plant reached 0.8m high by 4.5m across.

**harringtonia** (FORBES) K. KOCH (*C. pedunculata* SIEB. & ZUCC.) (*C. drupacea* var. *pedunculata* (SIEB. & ZUCC.) MIQUEL) A large shrub or small bushy tree of dense growth. Leaves 3.5-6.5cm long, densely arranged along the spreading branchlets in 2 irregular ranks, usually shorter and stiffer than those of *C. fortunei*, also rather paler green. Fruits ovoid to obovoid, 2-2.5cm long, olive-green, borne on drooping peduncles 6-10mm long. Origin unknown, probably China, but cultivated in Japan for many years. I 1829.

**var. drupacea** (SIEB. & ZUCC.) KOIDZ. (*C. drupacea* SIEB. & ZUCC.) "Cow's Tail Pine" "Japanese Plum Yew". In cultivation a medium-sized shrub rarely above 3m, of dense, compact habit. This is the wild form native to Japan and C China. It differs from var. *harringtonia* in its smaller size (in cultivation) and in its smaller leaves 2-5cm long, which are ascending, creating a V-shaped trough on the upper sides of the branchlets. Large plants develop into beautiful large mounds with elegant, drooping branchlets. Fruits obovoid, 2-3cm long, olive-green. I 1829.

**CEPHALOTAXUS harringtonia**—*continued*

**'Fastigiata'** An erect-branched shrub of medium to large size, resembling the Irish Yew in habit. Leaves almost black-green, spreading all round the shoots. Probably derived as a sport from *C. harringtonia*. Garden origin in Japan. I 1861.

**'Gnome'** A dwarf form with shortly ascending stems, and radially-arranged leaves, forming a flat-topped dome. A sport from 'Fastigiata', raised in our Crook Hill nursery in 1970.

**'Prostrata'** (*C. drupacea* 'Prostrata') A dwarf form with low spreading branches. Similar to var. *drupacea* except in habit. Originated in our West Hill nursery as a sport from 'Fastigiata' before 1920.

**pedunculata** See *C. harringtonia*.

**\*CHAMAECYPARIS** SPACH—**Cupressaceae**—The "False Cypresses" are a small genus of about 7 species of evergreen trees, natives of North America, Japan and Taiwan. They differ from *Cupressus* in their flattened frond-like branchlets and smaller cones. Young trees are conical in outline, broadening as they mature. Leaves opposite, densely arranged, awl-shaped on seedling plants, soon becoming small and scale-like. Male and female strobili borne on the same tree, the males minute but usually an attractive yellow or red. Cones small, globose, composed of 6-12 shield-like scales, usually maturing during the first year. They thrive best in a moist, well drained soil, being slower-growing on a dry, chalk soil. Unlike *Cupressus* they do not resent disturbance and may be moved even as small specimen trees.

Though the species are few in number they have given rise in cultivation to an astonishing number of cultivars covering a wide range of shapes and sizes, with foliage varying in form and colour. A few are really dwarf, others are merely slow-growing, whilst many are as vigorous as the typical form. Forms with juvenile foliage (awl-shaped leaves) were formerly separated under the name *Retinispora*.

**formosensis** MATSUM. "Taiwan Cypress" "Taiwan Cedar". In its native land a giant of up to 60m; in the British Isles a medium-sized tree of loose conical or bushy habit. Young trees are most attractive in their bright green foliage which becomes darker and bronzed in autumn. Leaves sharp-pointed making the sprays rough to the touch, sometimes whitish beneath, smelling of seaweed when bruised. Slow-growing in our climate; established trees are proving hardy. Taiwan. I 1910.

**henryae** LI An interesting, medium-sized tree, closely related to *C. thyoides*, from which it differs in its smoother bark, less flattened branchlets and the much lighter yellowish-green foliage especially pronounced on young specimens. The leaves also differ in being slightly larger and more adpressed. Juvenile leaves are green, not glaucous beneath. The male strobili are pale not dark in colour and the cones are slightly larger and green, or only slightly glaucous. Large specimens are said to resemble more *C. nootkatensis* than *C. thyoides*. Named after that indefatigable traveller and collector of American plants the late Mrs J. Norman Henry, who first collected it and from whom we received this plant in 1968. Coastal plains of Florida, Alabama and Mississippi.

**lawsoniana** (MURR.) PARL. "Lawson Cypress". A large conical tree with drooping branches and broad fan-like sprays of foliage, arranged in horizontal though drooping planes. Leaves pointed, green or glaucous green, marked with indistinct white streaks beneath. Male strobili usually pinkish or red in spring. Native of SW Oregon and NW California where trees of 60m have been recorded. It was first introduced in 1854 when seeds were sent to Lawson's nursery of Edinburgh.

It is a most useful and ornamental tree and makes an excellent hedge or screen even in exposed positions and shade. Its numerous cultivars vary from dwarf shrubs suitable for the rock garden to stately, columnar trees in many shades of green, grey, blue and yellow, also variegated.

**'Albospica'** A slow-growing, small conical tree. Foliage green, speckled white, with tips of scattered shoots creamy-white. C 1884. FCC 1869.

**'Alumii'** A medium-sized tree of columnar habit; branches dense, compact and ascending; foliage blue-grey, soft, in large, flattened sprays. A popular and commonly planted cultivar. C 1891.

**CHAMAECYPARIS lawsoniana**—*continued*

**'Alumigold'** A sport of 'Alumii' of more compact habit with the young foliage tipped with golden yellow.

**'Argenteovariegata'** A strong-growing, broadly columnar tree of medium size with green foliage interspersed with creamy-white patches. C 1862.

**'Aurea Densa'** A small, slow-growing, conical bush of compact habit, eventually up to 2m. Foliage golden yellow in short, flattened, densely packed sprays, stiff to the touch. One of the best golden conifers for the rock garden. Raised by Messrs Rogers Ltd, of Red Lodge Nurseries, Southampton, who produced many excellent dwarf conifers during the early part of the present century. C 1938.

**'Aureovariegata'** A small to medium-sized tree. Foliage in flattened sprays, green with scattered patches of creamy-yellow. C 1868.

**'Backhouse Silver'** See 'Pygmaea Argentea'.

**'Bleu Nantais'** A slow-growing small shrub of conical habit with striking silvery-blue foliage. Raised in France and probably a sport of 'Ellwoodii'.

**'Blom'** A dense columnar bush of medium size with ascending branches and vertically flattened sprays of glaucous foliage. A sport of 'Alumii', raised in Holland about 1930.

**'Blue Surprise'** A slow-growing form of Dutch origin making a narrowly conical bush with striking silvery-blue juvenile foliage.

**'Bowleri'** A dense, globular, small bush; branches very slender, spreading, drooping at the tips; foliage dark green. C 1883.

**'Caudata'** A small, curious, rather flat-topped shrub. The crowded branches bear apical tufts of green stems and occasional long, tail-like stems. Raised in Holland before 1934.

**'Chilworth Silver'** A slow-growing, broadly columnar bush, with densely packed, silvery-blue juvenile foliage. A sport which originated on a plant of 'Ellwoodii ' at Chilworth near Southampton before 1968.

**'Columnaris'** ('Columnaris Glauca') A small, narrow, conical tree with densely packed, ascending branches and flattened sprays which are glaucous beneath and at the tips. One of the best narrow-growing conifers for the small garden. Raised by Jan Spek of Boskoop about 1940. AGM 1984.

**'Darleyensis'** A medium-sized tree of conical habit; branches open, loosely held; leaves with a pale yellow or cream overlay, borne in large, flattened sprays. C 1880.

**'Depkenii'** Medium-sized tree of slender, conical habit; branches slender; foliage yellowish-white, becoming green in winter. Raised in Germany in 1901.

**'Dow's Gem'** A large bush of dense, rounded habit with bluish-green foliage in drooping sprays. Similar to 'Knowefieldensis' but larger. Seed-raised in California.

**'Duncanii'** A small bush of compact habit forming a wide-based, flat-topped dome; branches narrow, thread-like; leaves glaucous green. A specimen in the Hillier Gardens and Arboretum has reached 2.5m tall and more across after 30 years. Raised in New Zealand before 1953.

**'Elegantissima'** A beautiful, small tree of broadly conical habit, with pale yellow shoots and broad, flattened, drooping sprays of silvery-grey or greyish-cream foliage. Raised in our nurseries before 1920.

**'Ellwoodii'** A slow-growing, columnar bush of medium to large size. The short, feathery sprays of grey-green foliage are densely arranged and become steel-blue in winter. A deservedly popular and commonly planted conifer, excellent as a specimen for the lawn or large rock garden. A juvenile form raised in Swanmore Park, Bishops Waltham before 1929 and named after the Head Gardener. AM 1934. AGM 1984.

**'Ellwood's Gold'** A neat, compact, columnar form of slow growth. The tips of the sprays are yellow-tinged giving the whole bush a warm glow. A sport of 'Ellwoodii'. C 1968. AGM 1984.

**'Ellwood's Pillar'** A narrow and compact form of 'Ellwoodii' with feathery, blue-grey foliage.

**'Ellwood's White'** ('Ellwoodii Variegata') A sport of 'Ellwoodii', with creamy-white or pale yellow patches of foliage. Slow-growing. C 1965.

**'Erecta'** ('Erecta Viridis') A medium-sized to large tree of dense, compact growth, columnar when young, broadening in maturity. Foliage bright, rich green, arranged in large, flattened, vertical sprays. It normally forms numerous long, erect branches which

**CHAMAECYPARIS lawsoniana 'Erecta'**—*continued*

require tying-in to prevent damage by heavy snow. An old but still very popular cultivar. FCC 1870.

**'Erecta Alba'** A medium-sized to large, conical tree with stout, shortly spreading branches, foliage grey-green; tips of young growths white. FCC 1882.

**'Erecta Aurea'** A slow-growing, eventually medium-sized or large bush of dense, compact habit with erect sprays of golden foliage which tends to scorch in full sun. Raised in Holland in 1874.

**'Erecta Filiformis'** ('Masonii') Medium-sized tree of dense, conical habit; branches ascending with long, spreading and drooping thread-like tips, foliage bright, rich green. C 1896.

**'Erecta Witzeliana'** See 'Witzeliana'.

**'Erecta Viridis'** See 'Erecta'.

**'Filifera'** A large shrub or small tree of loose habit, with slender, green, drooping, filiform branchlets. Less strong-growing than 'Filiformis' and without the long projecting terminals. C 1887. AM 1896.

**'Filiformis'** A medium-sized to large tree of broadly conical habit; branches whip-like, drooping, with thread-like sprays of green foliage and long, slender, projecting terminals. The branches of mature trees form enormous hanging curtains. C 1877.

**'Filiformis Compacta'** ('Globosa Filiformis') Dwarf bush of globular habit; branchlets thread-like, drooping, with dark green foliage. C 1891.

**'Fletcheri'** A well-known and commonly planted cultivar, forming a dense, compact column up to 5m or more. Normally seen as a broad, columnar bush with several main stems. The semi-juvenile foliage is similar to that of 'Ellwoodii', but more greyish-green in colour, becoming bronzed in winter. Because of its slow growth it is often planted on the rock garden where it soon becomes too large. Named after Fletcher Bros who introduced it. A specimen in the Bedgebury Pinetum was 11m high in 1971. FCC 1913. AGM 1984.

**'Fletcheri Somerset'** See 'Somerset'.

**'Fletcher's White'** ('Fletcheri Variegata') A large, columnar bush with greyish-green, close foliage, boldly variegated with white or creamy-white. C 1965.

**'Forsteckensis'** A small, slow-growing bush of dense, globular habit; branchlets short, in congested fern-like sprays; foliage greyish-blue-green. A specimen in our nursery reached $0.9 \times 1.2$m after 30 years. Recalling 'Lycopodioides' but branchlets not so cord-like and twisted. Raised at Forsteck, near Kiel, Germany before 1891.

**'Fraseri'** Medium-sized tree of narrowly conical or columnar habit; branches erect; foliage grey-green, in flattened, vertically arranged sprays. Similar to 'Alumii' and, like that cultivar, commonly planted. It differs, however, in its greener foliage and neater base. C 1891.

**'Gimbornii'** A dwarf, dense, globular bush of slow growth; foliage bluish-green, tipped mauve. Suitable for the rock garden. Named after van Gimborn on whose estate in Holland it arose before 1938.

**'Glauca'** A dense, broadly columnar tree with glaucous foliage. Similar forms commonly turn up in seedbeds and occur in the wild. A selected form is known as 'Blue Jacket'.

**'Gnome'** A dwarf, very slow-growing, rounded bush suitable for the rock garden. Foliage in flattened sprays and densely branched tufts. Raised at Warnham Court, Surrey.

**'Golden King'** A medium-sized, conical tree with rather sparse spreading branches and large, flattened sprays of golden yellow foliage, becoming bronzed in winter. A seedling of 'Triomf van Boskoop', raised in Holland before 1931.

**'Golden Wonder'** A medium-sized, broadly conical tree with bright yellow foliage. Raised as a seedling in Holland about 1955.

**'Gracilis Nova'** Medium-sized tree of conical habit, branches slender, foliage bluish-green, in whorled sprays. C 1891.

**'Gracilis Pendula'** Small tree with slender, thread-like, pendulous branches, foliage dark green, with a bluish bloom. C 1881.

**'Grayswood Feather'** A small tree of slender columnar habit with upright sprays of dark green foliage.

**'Grayswood Gold'** Similar to 'Grayswood Feather' but with golden yellow foliage.

**CHAMAECYPARIS lawsoniana**—*continued*

**'Grayswood Pillar'** A medium-sized tree of narrow columnar habit, with tightly packed, ascending branches and grey foliage. It occurred as a sport of 'Blue Jacket' and the original tree reached about 9 × 0.5m after 16 years. AM 1969.

**'Green Globe'** A very dense, dwarf bush of rounded habit becoming more irregular with age. Foliage deep bright green in short, tightly congested sprays. Raised in New Zealand before 1973.

**'Green Hedger'** An erect, medium-sized to large tree of dense conical habit with branches from the base; foliage rich green. Excellent for hedges and screens. A seedling raised by Jackman's before 1949. AGM 1984.

**'Green Pillar'** Conical tree of upright habit, the ascending branches clothed in bright green foliage, tinted gold in early spring. C 1940.

**'Headfort'** A medium-sized tree of graceful habit with spreading branches and large, loosely-borne, flattened sprays of blue-green foliage, silvery-white beneath. Named after the late Lord Headfort, one of the most enthusiastic growers of this century, who planted a very complete pinetum at Kells, County Meath and staged an outstanding exhibit at Westminster at the Conifer Conference of 1930.

**'Hillieri'** Medium-sized tree of dense, conical habit; foliage in large, floppy, feathery sprays, bright golden yellow. Selected by Edwin Hillier before 1920.

**'Hollandia'** A medium-sized to large tree of conical habit; branches thick, spreading, bearing flattened sprays of dark green foliage. Raised in Holland before 1895.

**'Intertexta'** A superb large tree of open, ascending habit. Branches loosely borne, with widely spaced, drooping branchlets and large, thick, flattened, fan-like sprays of dark glaucous green foliage. A most attractive conifer of distinct growth resembling a columnar form of *Cedrus deodara* from a distance. Raised at Lawson's nursery, Edinburgh about 1869.

**'Kilmacurragh'** A medium-sized to large tree of dense, narrow, columnar habit. The short, ascending branches bear irregular sprays of dark green foliage. A superb tree similar to the "Italian Cypress" in effect and perfectly hardy, and due to the angle of branching remarkably resistant to snow damage. Raised at Kilmacurragh, Co Wicklow before 1951. AGM 1984.

**'Knowefieldensis'** A dwarf, dense, flat-topped, dome-shaped bush; foliage deep sea-green, in short, overlapping, plumose sprays. C 1911.

**'Kooy'** ('Glauca Kooy') Medium-sized, conical tree with spreading branches and fine sprays of glaucous blue foliage. Raised in Holland about 1925.

**'Krameri'** A semi-dwarf, globular, rather flat-topped bush with densely and irregularly arranged branches, cord-like terminal growths and dark green foliage. C 1909.

**'Krameri Variegata'** A sport of 'Krameri', with silver or cream variegated growths.

**'Lane'** ('Lanei') A columnar tree of medium size; thin, feathery sprays of golden yellow foliage. One of the best golden cypresses. Named after Lane's Nurseries, Berkhampstead who introduced it. C 1938. AGM 1984.

**'Little Spire'** A slow-growing small tree of narrowly conical habit with the distinctive foliage of 'Wisselii'. Raised from a cross between 'Wisselii' and 'Fletcheri'.

**'Lutea'** A medium-sized tree of broad columnar habit, with a narrow, drooping spire-like top; foliage golden yellow in large, flattened, feathery sprays. An old and well-tried cultivar. FCC 1872.

**'Lutea Nana'** A small, slow-growing bush of narrowly conical habit, eventually attaining 2m in height. Foliage golden yellow, densely arranged in short, flattened sprays. Raised in the Rogers nursery, Eastleigh. C 1930.

**'Luteocompacta'** A small to medium-sized tree of dense, conical habit; foliage golden yellow in loosely held sprays. C 1938.

**'Lycopodioides'** A slow-growing, broadly conical, medium-sized to large bush, eventually a small, fat tree. The curious grey-green branchlets are cylindrical in form and become twisted and tangled like whipcord. Seed-raised in Holland about 1890.

**'Minima'** A small, slow-growing, globular bush, eventually about 2m high with numerous ascending stems and densely packed, often vertically arranged, neat sprays of green foliage. Suitable for the rock garden. C 1863.

**CHAMAECYPARIS lawsoniana**—*continued*

**'Minima Aurea'** A dense-growing, dwarf, conical bush with often vertically held sprays of golden yellow foliage, soft to the touch. One of the best golden conifers for the rock garden. Specimens in our nursery attained 1.1 × 0.8m in 30 years. Raised in the Rogers nursery. C 1929. AGM 1984.

**'Minima Glauca'** A dense, globular, small bush of slow growth. Foliage sea-green, borne in short, densely packed, often vertically arranged sprays. A specimen in our nursery attained 1 × 1.2m in 25 years. C 1863. AGM 1984.

**'Naberi'** Medium-sized tree of conical outline; foliage green with sulphur-yellow tips, paling to creamy-blue in winter. A very distinct shade of colour. Raised by Naber & Co of Gouda, Holland. C 1929.

**'Nana'** A small, dense, semi-globular bush, slowly growing to 2m and developing a thick central trunk in later years; foliage dark glaucous green, in short, generally horizontal sprays. A specimen in our nursery attained 2 × 1.5m in about 35 years. It differs from the rather similar 'Minima' in its generally pointed top, thick and obvious central trunk (on old plants) and rather horizontally held branchlets. Raised in France in 1861.

**'Nana Argentea'** A remarkably attractive, dwarf, slow-growing bush. The inner previous year's foliage is cream, whilst the current season's growth is silver-grey, with an occasional cream fleck. C 1884.

**'Nidiformis'** A slow-growing form of dense habit, ultimately a small tree. Foliage green, borne in large horizontally flattened sprays, drooping gracefully at the tips. A specimen here reached 6m high by 3.5m wide. Not to be confused with 'Nidifera' which is a form of *C. nootkatensis*. C 1901.

**'Parsons'** A beautiful, dense, compact, dome-shaped bush, eventually of medium size; foliage green in large, flattened, arching and drooping, overlapping, fern-like sprays. One of the most graceful of the smaller Lawson cultivars.

**'Patula'** A graceful, conical tree of medium size; foliage greyish dark green in narrow, outward-curving sprays. C 1903.

**'Pembury Blue'** A medium-sized, conical tree with sprays of silvery-blue foliage. A very striking cultivar. Perhaps the best blue Lawson Cypress. AGM 1984.

**'Pena Park'** An attractive, slow-growing, wide-spreading bush with glaucous green foliage. The original plant in Portugal was stated to measure 2.5m high × nearly 35m in circumference after approx 80 years.

**'Pendula'** A medium-sized, rather open tree of conical shape; branches pendulous; foliage dark green. C 1870. FCC 1870.

**'Pottenii'** A medium-sized, columnar tree of dense, slow growth; foliage sea-green partly juvenile, in soft crowded, feathery sprays. Very decorative. AM 1916.

**'Pygmaea Argentea'** ('Backhouse Silver') A dwarf, slow-growing bush of rounded habit; foliage dark bluish-green with silvery-white tips. Suitable for the rock garden. Perhaps the best dwarf, white variegated conifer. Raised by James Backhouse and Son of York before 1891. AM 1900. AGM 1984.

**'Pyramidalis Alba'** A small to medium-sized tree of narrow columnar habit; branches erect, foliage dark green, with creamy-white tips. C 1887.

**'Robusta Glauca'** A large tree of broadly columnar habit; branches stout, rigid and spreading; foliage in short, thick, greyish-blue sprays. C 1891.

**'Rogersii'** ('Nana Rogersii') A small, slow-growing bush of dense, globular habit, old specimens are broadly conical, foliage grey-blue, in thin, loose sprays. Eventually attains a height of about 2m. Raised in the Rogers nursery. C 1930.

**'Shawii'** Dwarf, globular bush of slow growth, foliage light glaucous green, in loose sprays. Suitable for a large rock garden. C 1891.

**'Silver Queen'** Medium-sized to large conical tree with elegantly spreading branches; foliage greyish-green, creamy-white when young, in large, flattened sprays. Not one of the best variegations; 'Elegantissima' is much better. C 1883.

**'Smithii'** ('Smithii Aurea') ('Lutea Smith') Medium-sized conical tree of slow growth; branches spreading, foliage golden yellow, in large drooping horizontal sprays. C 1898.

**'Somerset'** ('Fletcheri Somerset') A densely columnar, small tree or large bush, a sport of 'Fletcheri'. The blue-grey, feathery foliage is yellowish-tinged during summer, becoming bronze-tinged in winter.

**CHAMAECYPARIS lawsoniana**—*continued*

**'Stardust'** An outstanding, columnar or narrowly conical tree raised in Holland with yellow foliage suffused bronze at the tips.

**'Stewartii'** A medium-sized to large tree of elegant, conical habit; branches slightly erect bearing large, flattened sprays of golden yellow foliage, changing to yellowish-green in winter. A very hardy, popular cultivar and one of the best golden Lawsons for general planting. Raised by Stewart and Son of Bournemouth. C 1890.

**'Summer Snow'** A small shrub of bushy habit with conspicuous white young growth.

**'Tabuliformis'** A small to medium-sized shrub of dense spreading habit with overlapping, flattened sprays of green foliage.

**'Tamariscifolia'** Slow-growing, eventually medium-sized to large bush with several ascending and spreading main stems, flat-topped and spreading when young, eventually umbrella-shaped; foliage sea-green in horizontally arranged flattened fan-like sprays. One of many fine conifers raised by James Smith and Son at their Darley Dale nursery, near Matlock in Derbyshire. There are several large attractive specimens in the Bedgebury Pinetum including one at 5.5m high and 4.5m across. C 1923.

**'Tharandtensis Caesia'** Dwarf to medium-sized bush of globular habit when young, broadly conical and sometimes flat-topped when older; branches short; foliage glaucous, in dense, curly, moss-like sprays. C 1890.

**'Triomf van Boskoop'** ('Triomphe de Boskoop') At one time a very popular cultivar, growing into a large tree of open, conical habit; foliage glaucous blue, in large, lax sprays. Needs trimming to obtain density. Raised in Holland about 1890.

**'Van Pelt'** A narrowly conical small tree with deep blue-grey later blue-green foliage. An improvement on 'Columnaris'.

**'Versicolor'** A medium-sized tree, broadly conical in outline, with spreading branches and flattened sprays of green foliage, mottled creamy-white and yellow. Raised in Holland about 1882.

**'Westermannii'** Medium-sized tree of broadly conical habit, branches loose and spreading; foliage in large sprays, light yellow when young becoming yellowish-green. Raised in Holland about 1880.

**'White Spot'** Foliage grey-green, the young growth flecked with creamy-white.

**'Winston Churchill'** A dense, broadly columnar tree of small to medium size; foliage rich golden yellow all the year round. One of the best golden Lawsons. Raised in Sussex before 1945.

**'Wisselii'** A most distinct and attractive, fast-growing tree of medium to large size. Slender and conical with widely spaced, ascending branches. The stout, upright branchlets bear crowded, short, fern-like sprays of bluish-green foliage. The rather numerous red male strobili are very attractive in the spring. Named after the raiser, F. van der Wissel of Epe, Holland. C 1888. AM 1899.

**'Witzeliana'** ('Erecta Witzeliana') A small narrow, columnar tree with long, ascending branches and vivid green, crowded sprays. An effective cultivar, like a slender green flame. Probably a sport of 'Erecta'. C 1931.

**'Yellow Transparent'** Young foliage yellowish, transparent in summer with the sun behind it, bronzing in winter. A slow-growing sport of 'Fletcheri' raised at Boskoop in Holland in about 1955.

**'Youngii'** A beautiful, medium-sized to large, conical tree, with loosely spreading branches and long, frond-like firm sprays of shining dark green foliage. One of the best of the green forms. Raised by and named after Maurice Young of Milford. C 1874.

**nootkatensis** (D. DON) SPACH "Nootka Cypress". A large tree of conical habit, often broadly so. Branchlets drooping, with long, flattened sprays of green foliage which is rough to the touch due to the sharp-pointed, scale-like leaves. A handsome specimen tree differing from *C. lawsoniana* in its coarser, stronger smelling, duller green foliage and the yellow male strobili in May. W North America. First discovered by Archibald Menzies in 1793. I about 1853. AM 1978.

**'Aureovariegata'** A medium-sized tree with conspicuous deep yellow variegated foliage. Raised by Maurice Young of Milford before 1872. FCC 1872.

**'Compacta'** A medium-sized to large bush of dense, globular habit; foliage light green, in crowded sprays. C 1873.

**CHAMAECYPARIS nootkatensis**—*continued*

**'Glauca'** A medium to large, conical tree with dark sea-green foliage. C 1858.

**'Lutea'** ('Aurea') Medium-sized, conical tree; foliage yellow when young, becoming yellowish-green. C 1891.

**'Pendula'** A superb specimen tree of medium to large size. Branchlets hanging vertically in long, graceful streamers. There are 2 forms of this tree in cultivation. C 1884. AGM 1984. AM 1988.

**'Variegata'** ('Argenteovariegata') A medium-sized tree, foliage with splashes of creamy-white. C 1873.

**obtusa** (SIEB. & ZUCC.) ENDL. "Hinoki Cypress". A large tree of broad, conical habit. Branches spreading horizontally, foliage deep shining green, in thick, horizontally flattened sprays. Differing from other species in its unequal pairs of usually blunt-tipped leaves, with white, X-shaped markings below and in its larger cones. One of the most important timber trees in Japan and held to be sacred by followers of the Shinto faith. The garden cultivars of this species, including many of Japanese origin, are almost as numerous as those of *C. lawsoniana* and include several excellent dwarf or slow-growing forms. I by P.F. von Siebold and J.G. Veitch in 1861.

**'Albospica'** Small tree of compact habit; young shoots creamy-white changing to pale green. C 1863.

**'Aurea'** A conical tree with flattened sprays of golden-yellow foliage. Introduced by Robert Fortune in 1860. See also 'Crippsii'.

**'Bassett'** ('Nana Bassett') A very dwarf bush similar to 'Juniperoides', but taller-growing and foliage a darker green. A rock garden plant.

**'Caespitosa'** ('Nana Caespitosa') A slow-growing, miniature bush of dense bun-shaped habit, a gem for the alpine garden or trough; foliage light green, in short, crowded, shell-like sprays. One of the smallest conifers, raised by Messrs Rogers and Son of the Red Lodge Nursery, Southampton, sometime before 1920, from seed of 'Nana Gracilis'.

**'Chabo-yadori'** A dwarf or small bush of dome-shaped or conical habit. Both juvenile and adult foliage are present in irregular fan-like sprays. A most attractive cultivar imported from Japan.

**'Compacta'** Medium-sized to large bush of dense, compact, conical habit; foliage deep green. C 1875.

**'Compact Fernspray'** ('Filicoides Compacta') A miniature, rather stunted form of 'Filicoides'.

**'Coralliformis'** Small to medium-sized bush, with densely arranged, twisted, cord-like branchlets; foliage dark green, branchlets brown. A specimen in the Hillier Gardens and Arboretum has reached 2.5m × 2.5m. C 1903.

**'Crippsii'** A small, slow-growing, loosely conical tree, with spreading branches and broad, frond-like sprays of rich golden yellow foliage. One of the loveliest and most elegant of small golden conifers. Raised by Thomas Cripps and Sons of Tunbridge Wells before 1899. FCC 1899. AGM 1984.

**'Densa'** See 'Nana Densa'.

**'Fernspray Gold'** A small to medium-sized shrub similar to 'Filicoides' but with golden yellow foliage in fern-like sprays. Originally grown in New Zealand as 'Tetragona Aurea'.

**'Filicoides'** "Fern-spray Cypress". A bush or small tree of open, irregular, often gaunt habit, branches long and straggly, clothed with dense pendulous clusters of fern-spray, green foliage. A specimen in our nursery reached 2.4m high by as much through in 25 years. I by Siebold to Germany from Japan about 1860.

**'Filicoides Compacta'** See 'Compact Fernspray'.

**'Flabelliformis'** ('Nana Flabelliformis') A miniature bush of globular shape, with small, fan-shaped branchlets of slightly bloomy, light green foliage. Very similar to 'Juniperoides'. Suitable for the alpine-house or trough. Raised by Rogers before 1939.

**var. formosana** (HAYATA) REHD. A rare, small to medium-sized tree in cultivation, smaller in all its parts than the typical form. Distinct in its *Thuja*-like foliage, green beneath. One of the most important timber trees in Taiwan where it reaches a large size. I 1910.

**'Graciosa'** A large shrub of compact, conical habit with bright green foliage. A sport of 'Nana Gracilis' raised in Holland about 1935.

**CHAMAECYPARIS obtusa**—*continued*

**'Hage'** Dwarf, slow-growing bush of dense, compact, conical habit; foliage bright green in crowded, twisted sprays. A seedling of 'Nana Gracilis' raised by the Hage nursery in Holland before 1928.

**'Intermedia'** ('Nana Intermedia') A miniature, slow-growing bush of slightly loose, conical habit, with short, loose sprays of green foliage. Regarded as intermediate between 'Caespitosa' and 'Juniperoides'. Suitable for the alpine-house or trough. Raised by Rogers about 1930.

**'Juniperoides'** ('Nana Juniperoides') A miniature bush of very slow growth; globular habit, with loose branches and small cupped sprays of foliage. Suitable for alpine-house or trough. Raised by Rogers before 1923. AM 1980.

**'Juniperoides Compacta'** Similar to 'Juniperoides' in general appearance, but slightly more compact and dense as an old plant. Raised by Rogers before 1939.

**'Kosteri'** ('Nana Kosteri') A dwarf bush, intermediate in growth between 'Nana' and 'Pygmaea'. Conical in habit with flattened and mossy sprays of bright green foliage, bronzing in winter. Suitable for the rock garden. C 1915.

**'Lycopodioides'** A medium-sized bush of informal habit often gaunt with age; branches sparse, heavy with masses of dark bluish-green, mossy foliage becoming particularly congested towards the ends of the branches. A specimen in our nursery attained 1.8m × 2.4m in about 30 years. Introduced from Japan in 1861 by Siebold.

**'Lycopodioides Aurea'** A slower-growing form of 'Lycopodioides' with soft, yellow-green foliage. Introduced from Japan in about 1890.

**'Magnifica'** Small, broadly conical tree with broad, fan-shaped, heavy sprays of deep green leaves. C 1874.

**'Mariesii'** ('Nana Variegata') Small, slow-growing bush of cone-shaped habit and open growth. Foliage in loose sprays, creamy-white or pale yellow during summer, yellowish-green during winter. In the Hillier Gardens and Arboretum it has reached 1.8m tall and 1.4m across. C 1891.

**'Minima'** ('Nana Minima') Miniature bush, forming a moss-like, flat pin-cushion; foliage green, in tightly packed, erect, quadrangular sprays. Perhaps the smallest conifer of its kind. Suitable for the alpine-house or trough. Raised by Messrs Rogers and Son before 1923.

**'Nana'** A miniature, flat-topped dome, comprising tiers of densely packed, cup-shaped fans of black-green foliage. One of the best dwarf conifers for the rock garden. A specimen in our nursery attained 0.75m high by 1m wide at base in 40 years. Introduced from Japan by Philip von Siebold in about 1861. The stronger-growing plant found under this name in many collections throughout Europe is 'Nana Gracilis'. AGM 1984.

**'Nana Aurea'** A looser, slightly taller-growing plant than 'Nana' with golden yellow foliage. Perhaps the best dwarf golden conifer. Ideal for the rock garden. Introduced from Japan by Veitch. C 1867. AGM 1984.

**'Nana Densa'** ('Densa') A slow-growing, miniature bush of dense, dome-shaped habit; foliage in densely crowded and congested cockscombs. Suitable for the rock garden or trough. A specimen in our nursery attained 0.6m high by a little greater width after 35 years. C 1923.

**'Nana Gracilis'** A conical bush or eventually a small tree of dense, compact habit; foliage dark green, in short, neat, shell-like sprays. Perhaps the most commonly planted dwarf conifer, eventually attaining several metres in height. C 1874. AGM 1984. It was from seeds of this cultivar that Messrs Rogers & Son of Southampton, England, raised a whole selection of dwarf and miniature bun-shaped conifers which included 'Caespitosa', 'Juniperoides', 'Minima' and 'Intermedia'.

**'Nana Pyramidalis'** Dwarf bush of dense, conical habit; foliage dark green in short, shell-like sprays. Suitable for the rock garden. A seedling of 'Nana Gracilis' raised in Holland about 1905.

**'Nana Rigida'** See 'Rigid Dwarf'.

**'Pygmaea'** A small, wide-spreading bush with loose sprays of bronze-green foliage, tinged reddish-bronze in winter, arranged in flattened tiers. Introduced from Japan by Robert Fortune in 1861.

**CHAMAECYPARIS obtusa**—*continued*

**'Pygmaea Aurescens'** Resembling 'Pygmaea' in growth, but foliage permanently yellow-bronze, richer in winter. A sport of 'Pygmaea' which occurred in Holland before 1939.

**'Pygmaea Densa'** A smaller, more compact form of 'Pygmaea'.

**'Repens'** ('Nana Repens') Dwarf bush with prostrate branches and loose sprays of bright green foliage, yellow-tinged in winter. A sport of 'Nana Gracilis'. A most attractive cultivar of spreading habit. C 1929.

**'Rigid Dwarf'** ('Nana Rigida') A small, slow-growing bush of stiff, rigid, almost columnar habit; foliage almost black-green, with conspicuous white markings beneath, in shell-like sprays. Most effective amongst the bun-shaped clones.

**'Sanderi'** See *Thuja orientalis* 'Sanderi'.

**'Spiralis'** ('Contorta') ('Nana Spiralis') A dwarf, ascending bush with attractively twisted branchlets, resembling 'Nana' as a young plant. A specimen in our nursery attained 0.75 × 0.45m in about 30 years. Raised by Rogers before 1930.

**'Suiryuhiba'** Medium-sized shrub of loose habit with long cord-like branchlets which are often curiously twisted and contorted.

**'Tempelhof'** A dense, conical bush of small to medium size. Foliage deep green, in broad, dense, shell-like sprays. Found in the Tempelhof nurseries in Holland before 1965.

**'Tetragona Aurea'** An unusual large shrub or small tree of angular appearance. Branches sparse, usually wide-spreading, thickly covered with golden yellow, moss-like sprays of foliage. A very distinct and attractive cultivar which associates well with heathers. Introduced from Japan in about 1870. The green form 'Tetragona', which is said to have been introduced at the same time, now appears lost to cultivation. In our opinion both may have arisen as sports of 'Filicoides', the Fern-spray Cypress. FCC 1876.

**'Tonia'** A dwarf sport of 'Nana Gracilis' making a dense small bush of irregular habit, the shoots occasionally white-tipped. Raised in Holland about 1928.

**'Tsatsumi'** A dwarf, globular bush of loose habit, with slender, thread-like branchlets and drooping sprays of foliage.

**pisifera** (SIEB. & ZUCC.) ENDL. "Sawara Cypress". A large tree of broadly conical habit, with spreading branches and horizontally flattened sprays of dark green foliage. The sharply-pointed, scale-like leaves, with white markings below, plus its small cones 6mm across, distinguish it from other species. It has given rise to numerous cultivars, many of which have juvenile foliage. Japan. Introduced by Robert Fortune in 1861. FCC 1861.

**'Argenteovariegata'** ('Albovariegata') A medium-sized tree with foliage speckled silvery-white. Introduced from Japan by Robert Fortune in 1861.

**'Aurea'** Young foliage yellow, passing to soft green during summer. Introduced from Japan by Robert Fortune in 1861. FCC 1862.

**'Aurea Nana'** Dwarf, slow-growing form of flattened, globular habit. One of the most consistent rich yellow, dwarf conifers; suitable for the rock garden. C 1891. FCC 1861.

**'Aureovariegata'** A slow-growing, small tree or large bush with golden variegated foliage. C 1874.

**'Boulevard'** ('Cyanoviridis') An outstanding, medium-sized bush of dense, conical habit. The steel-blue foliage is soft to the touch, becoming attractively purple-tinged in winter. A juvenile form which originated as a sport of 'Squarrosa' in the Boulevard nurseries, United States about 1934. It has now become one of the most popular of all conifers.

**'Cyanoviridis'** See 'Boulevard'.

**'Filifera'** A small to medium-sized tree or large shrub of broadly conical habit, usually broader than high. Branches spreading, with long, drooping, whip-like branchlets and string-like sprays of green foliage. Introduced from Japan by Robert Fortune in 1861.

**'Filifera Aurea'** Smaller and slower-growing than 'Filifera', making a medium-sized to large bush with attractive golden yellow foliage. Can burn in full sun. See also 'Sungold'. C 1889. AGM 1984.

**'Filifera Aureovariegata'** A small to medium-sized bush. The whip-like branches, and branchlets are splashed with sections of yellow foliage. C 1891.

**'Filifera Nana'** A dense, rounded, flat-topped, dwarf bush with long, string-like branchlets. Suitable for the rock garden. C 1897.

**'Filifera Nana Aurea'** See 'Golden Mop'.

**CHAMAECYPARIS pisifera**—*continued*

**'Gold Spangle'** Small, densely conical tree with both loose and congested sprays of golden yellow foliage. A sport of 'Filifera Aurea'. Reverting shoots should be removed. C 1900.

**'Golden Mop'** ('Filifera Nana Aurea') ('Filifera Aurea Nana') Small, dense-growing, bright golden form of 'Filifera Nana'.

**'Nana'** A dwarf, slow-growing bush forming a flat-topped dome with crowded flattened sprays of dark green foliage. Old specimens will form a top tier, resembling a cottage loaf. A very consistent cultivar. A specimen in our nursery attained $0.6 \times 1.4$m after about 30 years. C 1891.

**'Nana Aureovariegata'** Similar in habit to 'Nana', but foliage possessing a golden tinge. Excellent for the rock garden. C 1874.

**'Nana Variegata'** Similar to 'Nana', but foliage flecked with a creamy-white variegation. C 1867.

**'Parslorii'** ('Nana Parslorii') A dense, dwarf shrub of flattened, bun-shaped habit, with foliage in short crowded sprays. Suitable for the rock garden.

**'Plumosa'** A small to medium-sized conical tree or large, compact bush with densely packed branchlets and plumose sprays of bright green, juvenile foliage, soft to the touch. Introduced from Japan by Veitch in 1861. FCC 1866.

**'Plumosa Albopicta'** Foliage speckled with white, otherwise similar to 'Plumosa'. C 1881.

**'Plumosa Aurea'** Young growths bright yellow deepening with age to soft yellow-green, stained bronze-yellow. I by Fortune from Japan in 1861.

**'Plumosa Aurea Compacta'** Dwarf, dense, conical bush of slow growth; foliage soft yellow, more especially in spring. C 1891.

**'Plumosa Aurescens'** A small conical tree with plumose branchlets, the tips of which are light yellow in summer, changing to bluish-green in autumn. C 1909.

**'Plumosa Compressa'** A dwarf, slow-growing, rather flat-topped bush, usually forming a tight, rounded bun with both 'Plumosa' and 'Squarrosa' foliage which, on young plants, is crisped and moss-like. A sport of 'Squarrosa' raised in Holland before 1929. AM 1925.

**'Plumosa Compressa Aurea'** Similar to 'Plumosa Compressa', but foliage gold-tinged in summer.

**'Plumosa Flavescens'** A small conical bush with foliage similar to 'Plumosa' but pale sulphur-yellow when young. Introduced by Siebold from Japan in about 1866.

**'Plumosa Rogersii'** A small upright bush with golden yellow foliage which in its long needles is closer to 'Squarrosa'. A sport of 'Plumosa Aurea' raised by Rogers about 1930.

**'Pygmaea'** ('Plumosa Pygmaea') Small, slow-growing bush of compact, conical habit with densely crowded juvenile foliage.

**'Snow'** ('Squarrosa Snow') A dwarf, bun-shaped bush with mossy, blue-grey foliage tipped creamy-white, green in winter. Tends to burn in full sun or cold wind. It has reached 60cm tall by 1m across in the Hillier Gardens and Arboretum.

**'Squarrosa'** A small to medium-sized tree of broadly conical outline with spreading branches and dense, billowy sprays of glaucous juvenile foliage, soft to the touch. A commonly planted cultivar. Introduced from Japan by Veitch in 1861. FCC 1862.

**'Squarrosa Aurea Nana'** A dwarf, slow-growing form of dense, compact habit with yellow foliage paling in winter.

**'Squarrosa Dumosa'** Foliage similar to 'Squarrosa' but a compact, dwarf, rounded bush, grey-green bronzing in winter. It was found in Berlin Botanic Garden before 1891.

**'Squarrosa Intermedia'** ('Squarrosa Minima') ('Squarrosa Argentea Pygmaea') ('Dwarf Blue') A dense, dwarf, globular bush with densely-packed and congested, greyish-blue, juvenile foliage through which occasional longer shoots protrude. An unsatisfactory plant unless one is prepared to trim annually. C 1923.

**'Squarrosa Boulevard'** See 'Boulevard'.

**'Squarrosa Sulphurea'** Similar to 'Squarrosa' in habit; foliage sulphur-yellow, especially in spring. C before 1894. AM 1894.

**'Sungold'** Similar to 'Filifera Aurea' but not as bright yellow and withstands full sun.

## CHAMAECYPARIS—*continued*

‡**thyoides** (L.) B.S.P. "White Cypress". A small to medium-sized tree in the British Isles, of conical habit. Branchlets bearing erect, fan-shaped sprays of aromatic, glaucous green foliage. Cones small and bloomy. Unsuitable for shallow chalk soils. E United States. Introduced by Peter Collinson in 1736.

**'Andelyensis'** ('Leptoclada') A medium-sized, slow-growing bush of dense, narrowly columnar habit, with short sprays of dark bluish-green adult and juvenile foliage. Attractive in late winter when peppered with its tiny red male strobili. A specimen in the Bedgebury Pinetum was 6m high in 1971. Raised at Les Andelys, France about 1850. FCC 1863.

**'Andelyensis Nana'** ('Leptoclada Nana') A small shrub of slow growth with mostly juvenile foliage, forming a dense, rather flat-topped bush. A specimen in our nursery attained 1.1 × 0.9m after about 30 years. C 1939.

**'Aurea'** A slow-growing form, the foliage bright yellow in summer, bronzing in winter. C 1872.

**'Conica'** A slow-growing dwarf bush of dense, conical habit with both sea-green adult and some juvenile foliage which turns bronze-purple in winter. Differs from 'Andelyensis' in its much slower growth and from 'Andelyensis Nana' in its conical habit. C 1949.

**'Ericoides'** An attractive, small, compact, conical form with sea-green juvenile foliage, soft to the touch, becoming bronze or plum-purple in winter. C 1840.

**'Glauca'** ('Kewensis') Foliage glaucous-blue. C 1897.

**'Purple Heather'** A slow-growing dwarf bush of bun-shaped habit. The grey-green juvenile foliage turns to deep plum-purple in winter. 'Heatherbun', 'Red Star' and 'Rubicon' all appear to be the same or very similar.

**'Variegata'** Foliage speckled with yellow. C 1831.

## *CRYPTOMERIA D. DON—Taxodiaceae*—A monotypic genus. Male and female strobili borne on the same tree, the males orange or reddish in March. Cones solitary, globular, maturing the first year.

**fortunei** See *C. japonica* var. *sinensis*.

**japonica** D.DON "Japanese Cedar". A large, fast-growing tree of broadly columnar habit with reddish shredding bark and spreading or decurved branches. Leaves awl-shaped, densely crowded on long slender branchlets. It resembles in some ways the "Wellingtonia" (*Sequoiadendron giganteum*), but its leaves are longer and its bark has not the spongy thickness of the American tree. Easily cultivated and thriving best in moist soils. Many cultivars are in cultivation. Japan (var. *japonica*), China (var. *sinensis*). I 1842. AGM 1984.

**'Araucarioides'** See under 'Viminalis'.

**'Bandai-sugi'** A small, slow-growing compact bush becoming more irregular in old age. Foliage in congested, moss-like clusters with intermittent normal growth, turning bronze in very cold weather. C 1939.

**'Compressa'** A dwarf bush of very slow growth similar to 'Vilmoriniana', forming a compact, rather flat-topped globe. Foliage densely crowded, turning reddish-purple in winter. Suitable for the rock garden or scree. 'Birodo-sugi' appears identical. I from Japan to Holland in 1942.

**'Cristata'** A conical bush eventually making a small to medium-sized tree. Many of the branches are flattened (fasciated) into great cockscomb-like growths. C 1901.

**'Elegans'** A beautiful form of tall bushy habit, eventually making a small tree. The soft, feathery juvenile foliage is retained throughout life and becomes an attractive red-bronze during autumn and winter. Introduced by Thomas Lobb from Japan in 1854. FCC 1862.

**'Elegans Aurea'** Similar to 'Elegans' but slower-growing with yellow-green foliage, bronzing in very cold weather. C 1935.

**'Elegans Compacta'** A slower-growing, smaller shrub than 'Elegans', with even softer, more plumose foliage, forming a medium-sized billowy bush. Leaves turn rich purple in winter. A sport of 'Elegans'. C 1881. AGM 1984.

**CRYPTOMERIA japonica**—*continued*

**'Elegans Nana'** A very dense, slow-growing small shrub with juvenile foliage, bronze in winter. Differs from 'Elegans Compacta' in its tighter habit and straight, not curved leaves which are fairly stiff to the touch. C 1923.

**'Globosa'** A small, dense, dome-shaped bush of neat and compact habit. Foliage adult, rust-red in winter. Ideal for the large rock garden attaining about $0.6 \times 0.8$m in 15 years. C 1923.

**'Globosa Nana'** A dwarf, dense, flat-topped bush of slow growth. Branchlets and foliage agreeing with 'Lobbii'. Numerous, somewhat arching branchlets fan out to make a perfect low dome, previously listed as 'Lobbii Nana'.

**'Jindai-Sugi'** A small, dense, slow-growing bush developing an irregular but rather flattened top. Foliage of a cheerful bright green, densely crowded. A specimen in our nursery attained $1.2 \times 1.2$m in 25 years. I from Japan before 1932.

**'Knaptonensis'** See under 'Nana Albospica'.

**'Lobbii'** A very desirable medium-sized to large conical tree, differing from the type in its longer branchlets more clustered at the ends of the shorter branches. Leaves deep rich green and more adpressed to the shoots. Introduced by Thomas Lobb in about 1850.

**'Lobbii Nana'** See under 'Globosa Nana'.

**'Lycopodioides'** See under 'Viminalis'.

**'Midare-sugi'** A small bush of loose growth resembling 'Elegans' in foliage, except for scattered bunches of congested growths at the base of shoots.

**'Monstrosa'** A medium-sized bush up to 3m. Growth irregular, shoots long at first, then becoming dense and crowded, forming large, congested clusters over the whole bush. C 1909.

**'Nana'** A small, slow-growing, compact bush with slender branchlets ending in recurved tips. C 1850.

**'Nana Albospica'** ('Albovariegata') ('Argenteovariegata') A dwarf, slow-growing, flat-topped bush; foliage green, young growths creamy-white. The creamy tips are often browned by sun or frost and a sheltered position is desirable. 'Knaptonensis' is very similar in general appearance, being perhaps a little more compact and slower-growing.

**'Pygmaea'** A slow-growing, eventually compact, small bush of dense, irregular habit. Branchlets short and drooping, borne in congested clusters at the shoot tips. Has been confused with 'Nana' but differs in its much more compact growth and the fact that the outer foliage turns rich bronze-red in winter. C 1850.

**'Pyramidata'** A conical bush or small tree of rather open growth with small, densely-packed leaves concealing the slender branchlets. C 1891.

**'Sekkan-sugi'** A small tree with the young foliage pale creamy-yellow.

**'Selaginoides'** See under 'Viminalis'.

**var. sinensis** SIEB. & ZUCC. (*C. fortunei* HOOIBR. ex OTTO & DIETR.) The Chinese form differs from the Japanese tree in its looser habit, slender, more drooping branches and fewer-scaled cones. Some cultivars described here may belong to this variety. I by Capt Sir Edward Hume in 1842.

**'Spiralis'** "Grannies Ringlets". There is a large tree of this cultivar in the gardens at Nymans in Sussex and at Fota in SW Ireland, but as grown in general cultivation, it forms a small, slow-growing bush of dense, spreading habit. The leaves are spirally twisted around the stems. The whole bush is a pleasant, bright green in colour. Introduced from Japan in 1860.

**'Spiraliter Falcata'** ('Spiralis Elongata') Similar in effect to 'Spiralis', but with longer, thinner, almost whipcord-like branchlets with pendulous tips. A medium-sized bush of loose growth. C 1876.

**'Vilmoriniana'** An exceedingly slow-growing, dwarf bush with very small, crowded branchlets and leaves, forming a dense, rigid globe. Turning reddish-purple in winter. One of the most popular dwarf conifers for the rock garden, very similar to 'Compressa', but leaves a little shorter and more congested on the branchlets. A specimen in our nursery attained $0.6\text{m} \times 1$m in about 30 years. Raised in France by M de Vilmorin in 1890 from Japanese seed. AGM 1984.

**'Viminalis'** A large, irregular bush with long, slender, whip-like branches bearing terminal whorls of elongated branchlets. A specimen in our nursery attained $4.6 \times 4.6$m in about

**CRYPTOMERIA japonica 'Viminalis'**—*continued*

40 years. 'Araucarioides', 'Athrotaxoides', 'Lycopodioides' and 'Selaginoides' are very similar, some appearing identical.

**\*CUNNINGHAMIA** R. BR. ex L.C. RICH.—**Taxodiaceae**—A small genus comprising probably 2 species of very distinct trees recalling *Araucaria*. They are fairly hardy, but thrive best in a sheltered position. Male and female strobili are borne on the same tree. The whorled branches are densely clothed with spirally arranged leaves which are twisted at the base so as to appear in 2 ranks.

†**konishii** HAYATA A small tree mainly differing from *C. lanceolata* in its smaller leaves and cones. Young plants of both species are very similar. As may be expected this tree is less hardy than the Chinese Fir and is not suitable for the colder areas of the British Isles. Taiwan. I 1910. AM 1980.

**lanceolata** (W.J. LAMB.) HOOK. (*C. sinensis* L.C. RICH.) "Chinese Fir". A small to medium-sized, exotic-looking, hardy tree. Leaves lanceolate, 3-7cm long, irregularly arranged, emerald-green above, marked with 2 white bands of stomata beneath, becoming dark and bronzy by autumn. Cones usually in clusters, ovoid or rounded, 3-4cm across. It would be unwise to plant this tree in a windswept site. C and S China. First introduced by William Kerr in 1804. AM 1977.

**'Glauca'** Leaves with a conspicuous glaucous bloom. A particularly hardy form with very lush foliage.

**\* × CUPRESSOCYPARIS** DALLIM. (*Cupressus × Chamaecyparis*)—**Cupressaceae**—Interesting intergeneric hybrids, all of which have arisen in cultivation. They are extremely fast-growing trees with many uses, and are rapidly becoming one of the most popular conifers. Their requirements are similar to those of *Chamaecyparis*.

**leylandii** (DALLIM. & JACKS.) DALLIM. (*Cupressus macrocarpa × Chamaecyparis nootkatensis*) "Leyland Cypress". A large noble tree of dense columnar habit, extremely vigorous in growth. Foliage borne in flattened or irregular, slightly drooping sprays, similar to those of *C. nootkatensis*, but less strong-smelling when bruised. In general appearance it resembles more the *Chamaecyparis* parent; the cones are intermediate. It is the fastest-growing conifer in the British Isles, indeed the fastest-growing evergreen, apart from some *Eucalyptus* species. Even on a relatively poor site plants from cuttings have reached a height of 15m in 16 years. Such is its vigour and adaptability that it is unsurpassed for tall screens but is generally too vigorous to be used for hedging in the small garden. When trimmed it is important that only the young growth is cut into. It is tolerant of a wide range of conditions including coastal areas and chalk soils.

'Rostrevor' is now believed to be the earliest form of the hybrid. It derives from a tree that used to grow at Rostrevor, Co Down and probably originated about 1870. The cross later occurred at Leighton Hall, Powys, Wales in 1888 (6 seedlings) and again in 1911 (2 seedlings), also in a garden at Ferndown, Dorset in 1940 (2 seedlings). AM 1941. AGM 1984.

**'Castlewellan Gold'** ('Galway Gold') Young foliage golden yellow on small plants tending to become bronzy-green with age. Slower-growing and more suitable for hedging than the green forms. A seedling raised at Castlewellan, Co Down in 1962. The female parent was *Cupressus macrocarpa* 'Lutea' while the male parent was *Chamaecyparis nootkatensis* 'Lutea'. AGM 1984.

**'Galway Gold'** See 'Castlewellan Gold'.

**'Gold Rider'** Raised from a sport found in Holland this has foliage of a much better yellow than other forms such as 'Castlewellan Gold'. It stands full sun and does not burn.

**'Green Spire'** (Clone 1) A dense, narrow column of bright green foliage, arranged in irregular sprays. Eventually very similar to 'Haggerston Grey'. Raised at Leighton Hall in 1888.

**'Haggerston Grey'** (Clone 2) Perhaps the commonest clone in cultivation, more open in growth than 'Leighton Green'; foliage green or with a slight pale grey cast, arranged in dense, irregular sprays. Raised at Leighton Hall in 1888.

× **CUPRESSOCYPARIS leylandii**—*continued*

**'Harlequin'** A sport of 'Haggerston Grey' which occurred at Weston Park, found by the late Lord Bradford in 1975. Foliage flecked with creamy-white.

**'Hyde Hall'** The first dwarf Leyland and the best form for small gardens. A conical shrub of upright habit with bright green foliage.

**'Leighton Green'** (Clone 11) One of the clones most commonly propagated. It forms a tall column of green foliage arranged in more or less flattened fern-like sprays. Cones often present. Raised at Leighton Hall in 1911.

**'Naylor's Blue'** (Clone 10) A narrow columnar tree with greyish-green foliage most noticeably glaucous during winter, arranged in more or less irregular sprays. Raised at Leighton Hall in 1911.

**'Robinson's Gold'** Similar to 'Castlewellan Gold' but of a better colour. The foliage resembles 'Leighton Green'. A seedling raised at Belvoir Castle, Co Down in about 1962 and named after the Head Gardener who found it.

**'Rostrevor'** A form similar to 'Leighton Green' but more vigorous. It originated in Ireland about 1870 and was probably the first Leyland Cypress.

**'Silver Dust'** Foliage conspicuously blotched with creamy-white. Originated at the U.S. National Arboretum, Washington, DC in 1960 as a sport of a plant of 'Leighton Green' which had been supplied by us. I to England in 1966.

**'Stapehill'** A dense columnar tree with more or less flattened sprays of green foliage.

**notabilis** MITCHELL (*Chamaecyparis nootkatensis* × *Cupressus glabra*). An attractive medium-sized tree raised at the Forestry Commission's Research Station at Alice Holt Lodge, Surrey. The original seed was collected in 1956 from a specimen of *Cupressus glabra* growing at Leighton Hall, Powys. In 1970 the original 2 seedlings were reported as being 9m and 7.5m tall respectively, and growing fast. Trees have since reached 12m and are described by A.F. Mitchell as having sinuous, upswept branches draped with flattened sprays of dark grey-green foliage. AM 1986.

**ovensii** MITCHELL (*Chamaecyparis nootkatensis* × *Cupressus lusitanica*). An interesting hybrid raised by Mr H. Ovens in his nursery at Talybont, Dyfed, from seed collected in 1961 from a specimen of *Cupressus lusitanica* growing in Silkwood, Westonbirt Arboretum, Gloucestershire. This hybrid exhibits a strong influence of the "Nootka" parent and produces large flattened sprays of drooping dark, glaucous green foliage. It promises to reach a medium size and has exceeded 10m in cultivation.

**\*CUPRESSUS** L.—**Cupressaceae**—The "Cypresses" are a genus of about 20 or so species of evergreen trees of mostly conical or columnar habit. Male and female strobili borne on the same tree, the males often quite effective in the mass. Cones globular, composed of 6-12 shield-like scales, maturing during their second year, becoming woody and remaining on the branches often for several years. They do not take kindly to clipping. The species of *Cupressus* differ from those of *Chamaecyparis* in their irregular, rounded or quadrangular branchlet systems and larger cones, and on the whole they are less hardy. They do not transplant easily from the open ground, hence young trees are pot-grown. They are tolerant of a wide range of soil conditions (excepting wet soils) and several species will grow even in shallow chalk soils.

**abramsiana** C.B. WOLF "Santa Cruz Cypress". A fast-growing, symmetrical tree of dense, columnar habit. Branches ascending bearing both ascending and spreading, finely divided branchlets clothed with green foliage. Similar in general effect to a narrow-growing "Monterey Cypress". Cones irregularly globose, 2-2.5cm long, scales with a slight boss. A specimen in our nursery, grown from seed received in 1950, was 18.5m in 1971. Santa Cruz Mts (California). C 1935.

**arizonica** GREENE not HORT. (*C. arizonica* var. *bonita* LEMM. not HORT.) A small to medium-sized tree of dense conical or broadly columnar habit with grey and brown, stringy and slightly ridged bark. Foliage green. Cones 1-2.5cm across, globose, the scales with prominent bosses. Arizona, New Mexico, N Mexico. A rare and graceful species in cultivation, most trees grown under this name are the related *C. glabra*.

**var. bonita** See *C. arizonica* and *C. glabra*.

**bakeri** JEPS. "Modoc Cypress". A small to medium-sized tree of loose conical habit, with reddish-grey, flaking bark. Branches spreading, branchlets drooping, much divided into

**CUPRESSUS bakeri**—*continued*

greyish-green, thread-like sections, liberally speckled with resin. Cones globular 1.25cm across, scales with prominent bosses. N California. C 1930.

**subsp. matthewsii** C.B. WOLF "Siskiyou Cypress". In the wild a taller tree with longer branches. Small specimens passed the severe winter of 1962-63 without injury and have proven hardy ever since. California, Oregon. I 1917.

†**cashmeriana** (ROYLE) CARR. (*C. pendula* GRIFF.) "Kashmir Cypress". One of the most graceful and beautiful of all conifers. A small to medium-sized tree of conical habit. The branches are ascending and are draped with long, pendulous branchlets. Foliage a conspicuous blue-grey, in flattened sprays. We have here grown this plant out-of-doors for 20 years, but it is only seen at its best in the mildest parts of the British Isles. It makes an excellent specimen for the large conservatory. It has variously been regarded as a juvenile form of both *C. funebris* and *C. torulosa*. Origin unknown, probably the Himalaya. I 1862. FCC 1971.

**corneyana** KNIGHT & PERRY ex CARR. (*C. torulosa* var. *corneyana* (KNIGHT & PERRY ex CARR.) CARR.) The identity of the plant originally described under this name is not certain but most plants in cultivation have proved to be *C. lusitanica*. The name is currently applied to a cypress native to Bhutan where it is endemic and from where it has recently been introduced (1975). It is related to *C. torulosa* and reaches 40m in the wild. Foliage green, in flattened, drooping sprays, cones glaucous when young, to 2.5cm across.

**duclouxiana** HICKEL A graceful, small to medium-sized species forming a conical tree with reddish-brown bark. Branchlets finely divided into greyish-green, thread-like segments. Cones globular and smooth, 2-2.5cm across, like miniature footballs. SW China.

**dupreziana** CAMUS An extremely rare relative of *C. sempervirens*, of which it is sometimes regarded as a geographical form, differing from that species in a few minor points, including its flattened branchlets and smaller, longer cones. Only found in the Tassile Mountains in the Sahara, where it is now almost extinct, only 14 or so ancient trees surviving in a remote valley there. It has grown outside in the Hillier Gardens and Arboretum for many years where it has reached 5.5m (1990).

**forbesii** JEPS. A rare and little-known species related to *C. guadalupensis* and proving hardy here. A small, slender tree with attractive brown and red flaking bark, resembling a *Stuartia* in this respect. Branches spreading, with loose and irregular branchlet systems and green foliage. Cones irregularly globose, 2-2.5cm across. California. C 1927.

**funebris** ENDL. "Mourning Cypress" "Chinese Weeping Cypress". An elegant, small to medium-sized tree, erect in growth when young, becoming more open and pendulous with age. Branches spreading, eventually drooping, branchlets pendulous; adult foliage sage-green in flattened sprays. Until it forms its adult leaves it makes a very attractive pot-plant with soft glaucous-green juvenile foliage. In this form, before the last world war, it was often used as the central table piece in cafes and restaurants in London and other large cities and was dispensed by growers as *Juniperus bermudiana*. A native of C China where it reaches a large size and is commonly found near temples and monasteries. I 1849.

**gigantea** CHENG & L.K. FU (L. & S. 13345) A large tree in the wild, a species related to *C. duclouxiana* and only described in 1975. In cultivation it has made a medium-sized tree of narrowly columnar habit with grey-green foliage. Cones not yet produced in this country. It has reached 8.5m in the Hillier Gardens and Arboretum (1990). Previously listed as *Juniperus indica*. SE Tibet. I by Ludlow and Sherriff.

**glabra** SUDW. (*C. arizonica* HORT. not GREENE) (*C. arizonica* var. *bonita* HORT. not LEMM.) "Smooth Arizona Cypress". A small to medium-sized tree of dense, conical habit with ascending branches and an attractive, peeling, red bark, blistering and purple with age. Foliage greyish-green or grey, resin-speckled. Cones globular, 2-3cm long, with prominent bosses. A common tree in cultivation, usually under the name *C. arizonica*, a somewhat similar but rarer species which differs mainly in its usually green foliage and less attractive bark. C Arizona (United States). I 1907.

**'Aurea'** A broadly conical form. Leaves suffused yellow during summer, paling towards winter. Originated in Australia.

**CUPRESSUS glabra**—*continued*

**'Compacta'** ('Nana') (*C. arizonica* 'Compacta') A beautiful, dwarf, globular bush with attractive grey-green adult foliage and red-brown branchlets. Suitable for the rock garden or scree. C 1913.

**'Hodgins'** A strong-growing tree with ascending and spreading branches covered with silvery-grey foliage which is conspicuously resin-speckled, strong-smelling when bruised and rough to the touch.

**'Pyramidalis'** (*C. arizonica* 'Pyramidalis') (*C. arizonica* 'Conica') A dense, compact, conical tree of medium size, with blue-grey foliage. The small, yellow male strobili pepper the branchlets during late winter. Cones freely produced. One of the best formal blue conifers in cultivation. C 1928. AGM 1984.

**'Variegata'** A slow-growing, conical tree with blue-green foliage interspersed with creamy-white growths. Requires a sheltered position.

**goveniana** GORD. "Gowen Cypress" "Californian Cypress". A small to medium-sized tree of conical or broadly columnar habit with loosely arranged ascending branches and long, drooping, irregularly-divided branchlets; foliage dark green, fragrant when crushed. Cones globular, 2cm long, the scales with prominent bosses. Restricted in the wild to Monterey (California) where it occurs with *C. macrocarpa*. I 1846.

**var. pygmaea** LEMMON (*C. pygmaea* (LEMMON) SARG.) Foliage dark green. Cones 1.5cm across, the scales with inconspicuous bosses. Sometimes grows on infertile soils in the wild where it remains very dwarf. We are indebted to Mr Brian Mulligan of the University of Washington Arboretum, Seattle, for this rare variety. California.

**guadalupensis** S. WATS. "Tecate Cypress". A very beautiful, fast-growing tree of medium-size, with attractive, peeling, cherry-red bark. Branches ascending, with finely divided crowded branchlets and greyish-green foliage. Cones globular, 3-4.5cm across, the scales with conspicuous bosses. Proving hardy in the Home Counties. Guadalupe Island (Baja California). I 1880. AM 1978 (for foliage and fruit).

**lusitanica** MILL. "Mexican Cypress" "Cedar of Goa". A medium-sized to large, graceful tree with rich brown, peeling bark. Branches spreading, with pendulous branchlets and greyish-green foliage. Cones glaucous, globular, 12mm across, the scales with slender, pointed bosses. Though surprisingly hardy, it cannot be recommended for cold districts. Mexico, Guatemala, Honduras. C 1682.

**var. benthamii** (ENDL.) CARR. A very distinct tree of narrowly conical habit, in which the bright, shining green branchlet systems are decidedly flattened, giving an attractive fern-like appearance. Not recommended for cold areas. NE Mexico. I about 1838.

**'Flagellifera'** A rare form. A small to medium-sized tree with long, pendulous, cord-like, green branchlets. Cones up to 2cm across. C 1927.

**'Glauca'** Foliage an attractive bluish-green. Found in Portugal before 1910.

**'Glauca Pendula'** A beautiful form selected by Edwin Hillier, with a spreading crown and graceful, drooping, glaucous blue branchlets. Makes a small, wide-spreading tree. C 1925. AM 1944.

**lusitanica × macrocarpa** A strong-growing tree of graceful habit with spreading branches, drooping branchlets and green foliage. Hardier than *C. lusitanica* and eventually attaining a large size. We received this plant in 1966 from the E African Agriculture and Forestry Organisation in Kenya.

**macnabiana** MURR. "McNab's Cypress". A small tree or large shrub with comparatively wide-spreading branches, conspicuous, red-tinged branchlets and pale glaucous green foliage. Cones 2-2.5cm across, the scales with conical curved bosses. A rare tree in cultivation and one of the hardiest cypresses, even on shallow chalk soils. N California. I 1854 by William Lobb.

**macrocarpa** GORD. (*C. lambertiana* GORD.) "Monterey Cypress". A popular, very fast-growing tree of medium to large size, conical or broadly columnar in habit when young, becoming broad-crowned with age when it resembles almost a Lebanon Cedar in outline. Foliage bright green, in densely packed sprays. Cones 2.5-3.5cm across, the scales with a short boss. A valuable shelter tree in coastal districts. Young plants are subject to damage in cold areas. The yellow-foliaged forms colour best in an open position, becoming green when in shade. California. I about 1838.

**CUPRESSUS macrocarpa**—*continued*

**'Conybearii'** A small, wide-spreading tree of loosely conical habit, bearing drooping branches and long filiform yellow or yellowish-green branchlets. An unusual form of Australian origin, recalling *Chamaecyparis pisifera* 'Filifera' in habit.

**'Crippsii'** ('Sulphurea') A form with stiffly spreading, horizontal branches and short, stiff branchlets which are cream-yellow at the tips when young. C 1874.

**'Donard Gold'** A conical or broadly columnar tree of medium size. Foliage rich, deep golden yellow. An improvement on 'Lutea'. Raised in the Slieve Donard Nursery in 1935.

**'Globe'** ('Globosa') A dwarf, globular bush of dense, compact habit, with scale-like leaves. If reversions occur they should be removed.

**'Goldcrest'** A medium-sized tree of narrowly columnar form and dense, compact habit. Feathery juvenile foliage of a rich yellow. Raised by Messrs Treseder of Truro about 1948. One of the best of its colour. AGM 1984.

**'Golden Cone'** A dense, conical tree with golden yellow foliage.

**'Golden Pillar'** A small tree of narrow habit with golden yellow foliage. A seedling raised in Holland before 1955.

**'Gold Spread'** ('Horizontalis Aurea') A very distinct and ornamental form of compact, wide-spreading habit reaching about 1m tall with bright golden yellow foliage. Excellent ground cover except in the coldest areas and the brightest conifer for this purpose. Probably raised in Australia.

**'Horizontalis Aurea'** See 'Gold Spread'.

**'Lutea'** A tall, broadly columnar tree of medium size and compact growth. Foliage soft yellow, becoming green. C before 1893. FCC 1893.

**'Minima'** ('Minimax') A dwarf, slow-growing, low bush of mainly juvenile foliage. If reversions occur they should be cut away. Raised by Mr R. Menzies at the Golden Gate Park, San Francisco, and sent to the late Alfred Nisbet of Brooker's Farm, Gosport, Hants, who, until his death, had gathered together one of the best collections of dwarf conifers in the British Isles.

**'Pendula'** A broad tree of medium size. The wide-spreading branches droop at their extremities. The original tree at Glencormac, Bray, Co Wicklow was 15m tall in 1971.

**'Pygmaea'** A very slow-growing dwarf form differing from 'Woking' in having mainly adult foliage at least on older plants. Raised in 1929 by the late Mr Marcham of Carshalton Nursery, Surrey.

**'Variegata'** ('Lebretoni') Foliage with irregular creamy-white variegation. C 1866. FCC 1867.

**'Woking'** The best miniature of the species. The tiny scale-like leaves are in 4 ranks, very closely set, concealing the stem and recalling *Pilgerodendron*. This remarkable dwarf originated in Jackman's nursery near Woking before 1962.

**pygmaea** See *C. goveniana* var. *pygmaea*.

**sargentii** JEPS. "Sargent Cypress". A small to medium-sized tree, with dark-coloured bark and soft green foliage. Cones 2-2.5cm long, scales with inconspicuous bosses. This tree is succeeding here where it has been growing for more than 30 years. California. C 1908.

**sempervirens** L. "Italian Cypress" or "Mediterranean Cypress". The cypress of the ancients. A medium-sized tree of narrow columnar habit, with strictly ascending branches and dark green foliage. Cones 2-3cm across, the scales with small bosses. A familiar tree in the Mediterranean region where it is widely distributed and cultivated. Young plants are subject to injury in cold areas. The form described here, sometimes known as 'Fastigiata' or 'Stricta', is unknown in the wild state. Mediterranean region, W Asia.

**'Gracilis'** A narrowly columnar form of dense, compact growth raised in New Zealand.

**'Green Pencil'** A very slender and hardy form with bright green foliage selected in our nurseries. The original plant in the Hillier Gardens and Arboretum stood at 10.5m tall with a spread of only 80cm in 1990. It was originally distributed as 'Green Spire'.

**var. horizontalis** GORD. The wild form, differing from the above in its more spreading branches, forming a conical crown. E Mediterranean region.

**'Swane's Golden'** A compact, columnar form with golden-tinged foliage. One of the best tree-sized golden conifers for the small garden. Raised in Australia.

**stephensonii** C.B. WOLF "Cuyamaca Cypress". A rare, small tree related to *C. glabra*. Smooth cherry-like bark and grey-green foliage. Cones globose, scales with inconspicuous bosses. This tree has been growing successfully here for more than 30 years. California.

**CUPRESSUS**—*continued*

**torulosa** D. DON A graceful, usually small to medium-sized tree, but occasionally attaining large proportions. It is conical in habit, with horizontal branches and flattened sprays of whip-like branchlets and dark green foliage. Cones 1-2cm across, dark brown with a violet bloom, the scales with small bosses. Himalaya. I 1824.

**var. corneyana** See *C. corneyana*.

**'Majestica'** A distinct, slow-growing form with thickened branches and rather congested moss-like foliage. C 1855.

**"CYPRESS"** See *Cupressus, Chamaecyparis* and × *Cupressocyparis*.

**\*DACRYDIUM** SOL.—**Podocarpaceae**—A small genus of about 25 species of evergreen trees and shrubs allied to *Podocarpus*; natives of SE Asia to Australasia. The leaves are scale-like on adult trees and awl-shaped on juveniles. Male and female strobili are normally borne on different trees. Fruits consist of an ovoid nut-like seed seated in a cup-like aril. The only species which here survives our severest winters outside is *D. laxifolium*.

**†biforme** PILGER (*D. colensoi* KIRK not HOOK.) A rare species recently received by us from Messrs Duncan & Davies of New Plymouth, New Zealand, who describe it as a slow-growing, alpine conifer up to 6m. The leaves of juvenile plants are likened to those of a yew, spreading in 2 opposite ranks. Leaves of adult plants are smaller and scale-like. New Zealand.

**†colensoi** HOOK. "Westland Pine". A small, conical tree of rather loose habit, branchlets long and slender. The wood is highly prized in New Zealand where it is a native.

**†cupressinum** SOL. "Rimu" or "Red Pine". A small, graceful, conical tree with arching branches and pendulous string-like branchlets. Considered by the botanist Cheeseman to be "as beautiful and attractive as any tree in New Zealand". Slow-growing in the British Isles even in a sheltered position. It makes a charming specimen for the conservatory. New Zealand.

**†franklinii** HOOK. f. The "Huon Pine" of Tasmania. In the milder parts of this country forms a large, graceful shrub or small conical tree. The slender, drooping branches are clothed with bright green, scale-like leaves. Subject to injury in severe winters. The wood is highly prized for furniture and cabinet work in Tasmania.

**†intermedium** KIRK A small tree or large bush with spreading branches. Widely distributed in New Zealand where its wood is used for railway sleepers, boat-building and telegraph poles.

**laxifolium** HOOK. f. "Mountain Rimu" "Pygmy Pine". A prostrate or scrambling conifer forming mats of slender, wiry stems and tiny scale-like leaves which turn plum-purple in winter. Perhaps the smallest conifer in the world, coning at 8cm high. When it was first discovered it was mistaken for a moss; it is found in mountain districts of New Zealand.

**'Blue Gem'** A form with blue foliage, selected in the wild near Homers Tunnel, New Zealand.

**\*DISELMA** HOOK. f.—**Cupressaceae**—A monotypic, Tasmanian genus related to *Fitzroya*. Male and female strobili are borne on separate plants. The cones are small and composed of 2 pairs of scales.

**archeri** HOOK. f. A beautiful, medium-sized to large bush of lax habit. Leaves scale-like, adpressed to and concealing the slender branchlets. This species was lost to cultivation until reintroduced by Lord Talbot de Malahide to whom we are indebted.

**"FIR"** See *Abies*.

**\*FITZROYA** HOOK. f. ex LINDL.—**Cupressaceae**—A monotypic genus, closely allied to *Diselma*. Male and female strobili borne on the same or on separate plants.

**cupressoides** (MOL.) JOHNSTON (*F. patagonica* HOOK. f. ex LINDL.) The only species is a beautiful large tree of cypress-like habit and in cultivation forms a surprisingly hardy, graceful, large shrub or small, dense tree with scale-like leaves borne in threes, banded white, carried on drooping branchlets. Cones small, consisting of 9 scales. Chile,

**FITZROYA cupressoides**—*continued*

Argentina. Introduced by William Lobb in 1849 and later by Richard Pearce. There is a splendid tree of this species at Killerton near Exeter. This magnificent collection was planted by the late Sir Francis Acland, and is now maintained by the National Trust.

**\*FOKIENIA** HENRY & THOMAS—**Cupressaceae**—A genus of 1, possibly 2 species, related to both *Cupressus* and *Calocedrus*. Resembling *Calocedrus macrolepis* in foliage. Male and female strobili are borne on the same plant. The cones, up to 2.5cm long, are similar to those of a *Chamaecyparis*, ripening the second year. The following species is best given a sheltered position in woodland.

**hodginsii** HENRY & THOMAS A small to medium-sized shrub of very slow growth. The very distinct and characteristic spine-tipped, paired, scale-like leaves are bright, glossy green above, marked with conspicuous silvery-white bands of stomata beneath. They are borne in large, flattened sprays somewhat resembling those of a *Thujopsis*, but more delicate and graceful. Probably the best specimen in cultivation is at Borde Hill, planted by that great amateur gardener the late Col Stephenson Clarke. This rare and remarkable conifer is a native of SE China and was first discovered in the province of Fujian (previously Fokien or Fukien) by Captain Hodgins in 1908, and was introduced the following year by Sir Lewis Clinton-Baker. AM 1911.

**GINKGO** L.—**Ginkgoaceae**—A remarkable and distinct, monotypic genus of great ornamental, botanical and geographical interest. *G. biloba* is the sole living survivor of an ancient family whose ancestors occurred in many parts of the world (including the British Isles) about 160 million years ago. Male and female strobili occur on separate plants. The yellow, plum-shaped fruits are produced in pairs or threes at the end of a slender stalk, ripening and falling in autumn, when, if crushed, they emit a strong offensive odour. It is regarded as a sacred tree in the East and is commonly planted in the vicinity of Buddhist temples. Long considered to be extinct in a wild state, it is known to have survived in Zhejiang and Guizhou Provinces, China.

**biloba** L. (*Salisburia adiantifolia* SM.) "Maidenhair Tree". A medium-sized to large, deciduous tree of conical habit when young. Easily recognised by its peculiar fan-shaped, undivided leaves which turn a beautiful clear yellow before falling in autumn. Perfectly hardy and suitable for most soils. It is tolerant of industrial areas and is magnificent either as a single specimen or as an avenue tree. It was first introduced in about 1727 and to England in about 1758. AGM 1984.

**'Fastigiata'** A columnar form with semi-erect branches. C 1906.

**'Pendula'** A remarkable selection with spreading or weeping branches. C 1855.

**'Tremonia'** A very narrowly columnar form raised as a seedling in Dortmund Botanic Garden in 1930. We are indebted for this form to the late Dr G. Krüssmann, once Director of the celebrated gardens at Dortmund. Dr Krüssmann was a very rare example of a botanist who was also a horticulturist.

**'Variegata'** Leaves streaked with creamy-white. Slow-growing and very prone to reversion. C 1855.

**†GLYPTOSTROBUS** ENDL.—**Taxodiaceae**—A monotypic genus related to *Taxodium*. Male and female strobili are borne on the same plant. Cones pear-shaped, 2cm long, borne on long stalks. Not recommended for cold localities.

**lineatus** See *G. pensilis*.

**pensilis** (STAUNTON) K. KOCH (*G. lineatus* AUCT. not (POIR.) DRUCE) (*G. sinensis* HENRY ex LODER) An extremely rare, deciduous conifer, attaining a large bush or small tree. The soft sea-green, narrow leaves turn a rich brown in autumn. This remarkable species has grown slowly in the Hillier Gardens and Arboretum without protection for many years. It is a native of the province of Canton, S China, where it is often found on the banks of streams and in similarly moist situations.

**"HEMLOCK"** See *Tsuga*.

# CONIFERS

**\*JUNIPERUS** L.—**Cupressaceae**—The"Junipers" are a genus of about 60 species of trees and shrubs, ranging from prostrate or creeping alpines to dense, bushy shrubs and tall, conical or columnar trees. They are widely distributed almost throughout the N hemisphere from Mexico to China and from the Arctic Circle to the mountains of tropical E Africa.

The leaves of juvenile plants are awl-shaped and usually pointed, those of adult plants are normally scale-like and crowded, although in some species they retain their juvenile form. The awl-shaped leaves bear white or glaucous stomatal bands above (ie on the inner surface) but because of the often horizontal disposition of the branches the bands appear to be on the lower surface. Male and female strobili are borne on the same or on separate plants. The fruits are usually rounded or ovoid, becoming fleshy and berry-like.

The junipers are a very versatile genus, containing plants for most soils and situations. They are amongst the most suitable conifers for calcareous soils. They range in colour from green to yellow, grey and steel-blue. The prostrate forms are excellent as ground cover in sun and several of the small, columnar forms are effective in the heather garden.

†**ashei** BUCHH. A large, slow-growing, dioecious shrub or occasionally a small tree of conical habit. Foliage awl-shaped and sage-green on young plants, scale-like and dark green on mature plants. Fruits rounded, 6-8mm across, deep blue and covered with a glaucous bloom, sweet and aromatic to the taste. A rare species for a sheltered site in the milder counties. It occurs with *J. virginiana* in the wild. S United States, Mexico. I 1926.

**'Blue Cloud'** (*J. × media* 'Pfitzeriana' × *J. virginiana* 'Glauca'). A wide-spreading medium-sized shrub similar in habit to 'Pfitzeriana', but lower-growing and less vigorous, with slender, almost thread-like branchlets and glaucous blue foliage. C 1955.

†**californica** CARR. "Californian Juniper". A large bush or small tree; foliage yellowish-green, scale-like. Fruits reddish-brown, bloomy. Only for mild areas. California, Oregon. Introduced by William Lobb in 1853.

**canadensis** See *J. communis* subsp. *depressa*.

†**cedrus** WEBB & BERTH. "Canary Island Juniper". An erect-growing, dioecious, small tree of graceful habit, with slender, drooping, whitish branchlets densely clothed with sharply-pointed awl-shaped leaves which are arranged in whorls of 3. Fruits 10-12mm across, reddish-brown, bloomy. A tender species closely related to *J. oxycedrus*. Native of the Canary Isles where it is now very rare. Large trees are still to be found on the island of Palma growing in inaccessible parts of the volcanic crater. It has been grown outside in the Home Counties for many years.

**chinensis** L. (*J. sheppardii* (VEITCH) VAN MELLE) "Chinese Juniper". An extremely variable, dioecious species distributed in the wild over a wide area. In cultivation it is typically a tall, conical or columnar, grey or greyish tree of medium size and dense, compact habit, with both awl-shaped juvenile and scale-like adult foliage on the same plant. Fruits rounded or top-shaped, 5-7mm across, glaucous, ripening in the second year. See also *J. × media*. China, Japan. Originally introduced before 1767. Introduced into England by William Kerr in 1804.

**'Albovariegata'** See 'Variegata'.

**'Ames'** Medium-sized to large bush of rather spreading growth; leaves awl-shaped, bluish-green at first later green. Selected in the United States in 1935.

**'Armstrongii'** See *J. × media* 'Armstrongii'.

**'Aurea'** "Young's Golden Juniper". A tall, slender, slow-growing conical or columnar tree with golden foliage, inclined to burn in full sun. A male clone exhibiting both juvenile and adult foliage. Raised as a sport at Milford, Surrey about 1855. FCC 1871.

**'Blue Alps'** A vigorous large shrub with striking steel-blue foliage. Found in a garden in Austria in 1968.

**'Columnaris'** Similar in habit to and of the same origin as 'Columnaris Glauca'. It differs in its slightly coarser, green foliage.

**'Columnaris Glauca'** Small tree of dense, columnar habit, slightly broader at base and tapering gradually to summit. Leaves awl-shaped, sharply-pointed and glaucous. Sometimes wrongly referred to under the name 'Pyramidalis Glauca'. A seedling selected

**JUNIPERUS chinensis 'Columnaris Glauca'**—*continued*

at the U.S. Dept of Agriculture from seed collected by Frank N. Meyer in Hubei, China in 1905.

**'Echiniformis'** A dwarf, tight ball of prickly leaves. Originally thought to be a form of *J. communis*. Not one of the easiest plants to grow. C 1850. AM 1961.

**'Excelsa Stricta'** See 'Pyramidalis'.

**'Expansa'** See *J. davurica* 'Expansa'.

**'Fairview'** Small to medium-sized tree of narrow habit; leaves bright green, mostly juvenile. Raised from seed in the United States in about 1930.

**'Globosa Cinerea'** See *J.* × *media* 'Globosa Cinerea'.

**'Iowa'** Medium-sized shrub of spreading habit; leaves green, slightly bluish, both scale-like and awl-like present on the same plant. Female. C 1935.

**'Japonica Oblonga'** See 'Oblonga'.

**'Japonica Variegata'** ('Kaizuka Variegata') A compact, medium-sized bushy shrub of conical habit. Foliage mainly adult, flecked with creamy-yellow and silvery-white. C 1867.

**'Kaizuka'** (*J. sheppardii* var. *torulosa* BAILEY) A large, erect-growing shrub, eventually a small tree, with long, spreading branches clothed with characteristic dense clusters of scale-like, bright green foliage. A very distinct form, particularly effective in the heather garden or as an isolated lawn specimen. Introduced from Japan in about 1920.

**'Kaizuka Variegata'** See 'Japonica Variegata'.

**'Keteleeri'** (*J. virginiana* 'Keteleeri') Small, conical tree of dense habit; crowded masses of vivid green, scale-like leaves and an abundance of small, light green fruits. C 1910.

**'Maney'** Medium-sized shrub with ascending branches; leaves bluish bloomy, awl-shaped. C 1935.

**'Monarch'** An upright, conical bush of open habit with ascending or spreading, arm-like branches bearing a mixture of adult and juvenile foliage. Raised from seed of Japanese origin. C 1935.

**'Mountbatten'** Medium-sized bush or small tree of columnar habit; leaves greyish-green, awl-shaped. Raised by the Sheridan Nurseries, Ontario, Canada. C 1948.

**'Obelisk'** Medium-sized shrub of erect, columnar habit; foliage bluish-green, awl-shaped, densely packed. Raised from Japanese seed in Holland in 1930.

**'Oblonga'** ('Japonica Oblonga') A small shrub of irregular, rounded habit with densely crowded branches, those in the lower part of the bush bearing prickly, dark green, awl-shaped leaves, those in the upper part projecting and clothed with scale-like leaves. A sport of 'Japonica' raised in the United States. C 1932.

**'Olympia'** Medium-sized shrub or small tree of columnar habit; leaves glaucous both scale-like and awl-shaped. Raised in Holland before 1956.

**'Parsonsii'** See *J. davurica* 'Expansa'.

**'Pfitzeriana'** See *J.* × *media* 'Pfitzeriana'.

**'Plumosa'** See *J.* × *media* 'Plumosa'.

**var. procumbens** See *J. procumbens*.

**'Pyramidalis'** A dense, slow-growing, columnar bush with almost entirely juvenile, prickly, glaucous leaves. I from Japan to Holland by Siebold in 1843. FCC 1868 (as *J. excelsa stricta*).

**'San Jose'** Dwarf shrub with prostrate branches; leaves grey-green, mostly juvenile. Selected in California in 1935.

**var. sargentii** See *J. sargentii*.

**'Sheppardii'** (*J. sheppardii* (VEITCH) VAN MELLE) (*J. chinensis fortunei* HORT) (*J. fortunei* C. DE VOS) A large, usually multistemmed shrub with orange-brown, peeling bark and loose, bushy growth. Branches ascending and gracefully spreading at the tips. The branches of older plants become rather congested, with characteristic projecting filiform shoots. Leaves green, mainly adult with occasional small sprays of juvenile leaves. SE China. According to Van Melle, probably first introduced by Robert Fortune in about 1850. There may be more than one form in cultivation. Ours is a male clone and in late winter and early spring is rendered easily recognisable by its multitudes of male strobili.

**'Spartan'** A narrowly conical, erect-branched large shrub or small tree of dense habit with rich green foliage. C 1961.

**JUNIPERUS chinensis**—*continued*

'**Stricta**' A large shrub of compact, conical habit with erect branches. Foliage juvenile, soft to the touch and glaucous. C 1949.

**var. torulosa** See 'Kaizuka'.

'**Variegata**' ('Albovariegata') Usually a large conical bush of dense, compact habit. Leaves mostly juvenile, glaucous, with scattered sprays of white variegation. Introduced from Japan about 1860.

**communis** L. "Common Juniper". A variable species, usually found as a medium-sized to large shrub. Its silver-backed leaves are awl-shaped, prickly to the touch and arranged in whorls of 3. Fruits rounded, 5-6mm across, black, covered by a glaucous bloom, ripening during the second or third year and are sometimes used to flavour gin. This species has probably a wider distribution than any other tree or shrub, occurring from North America eastwards through Europe and Asia to Korea and Japan. It is one of our 3 native conifers, being particularly plentiful on the chalk downs of the south of England. It is one of the most accommodating of conifers, its prostrate forms especially being useful as ground cover in sun, whilst the slender columns of the Irish Juniper are a conspicuous feature of many gardens. AM 1890.

**subsp. alpina** (SUTER) CELAK (subsp. *nana* SYME) (var. *jackii* REHD.) (var. *montana* AIT.) (var. *saxatilis* PALL.) (*J. nana* WILLD.) (*J. sibirica* BURGSD.) A slow-growing, prostrate form, its densely packed stems hugging the ground and forming mats or carpets of dark green leaves. In the wild it is found on rocks, mountains and moors and in the north of Scotland may be seen draping sea-cliffs in the teeth of cold, briny winds. W North America, Greenland, British Isles and through Europe, the Himalaya to Japan.

'**Compressa**' A gem for the rock garden or scree. A dwarf, compact, slow-growing column. Resembling a miniature Irish Juniper. Several specimens planted with variously coloured prostrate junipers creates a charming miniature landscape. C 1855. AGM 1984.

'**Cracovia**' A conical or broadly columnar geographical form of Polish origin with ascending branches and branchlets with drooping tips. C 1855.

**subsp. depressa** (PURSH) FRANCO (*J. canadensis* LODD. ex BURGSD.) "Canadian Juniper". A dwarf, wide-spreading variety to about 0.6m, forming large patches of densely packed, slightly ascending stems clothed with comparatively broad, yellowish or brownish-green, silver-backed leaves which are bronze-coloured above during winter. A wild variety from the mountains of North America and one of the best of all dwarf carpeting conifers, excellent as ground cover in sun.

'**Depressa Aurea**' Leaves and young shoots golden yellow during early summer. Growth as in subsp. *depressa*. C 1887. AGM 1984.

'**Dumosa**' A dwarf spreading shrub forming large patches. Leaves green, silvery-white beneath, turning coppery bronze or brown in winter. A form of subsp. *depressa* which originated in Holland. A splendid ground cover for an open situation. A specimen in our arboretum attained 0.6 × 1.5m in 15 years. Raised in Holland about 1934.

'**Effusa**' A wide-spreading, semi-prostrate form. The leaves green above, silvery-white beneath, point forward and lie along the branches, which they more or less conceal. An excellent dwarf carpeting conifer, its leaves usually remaining green in winter contrasting effectively with the bronze of subsp. *depressa* and 'Dumosa'. Raised in Holland about 1944.

'**Gold Cone**' ('Suecica Aurea') Similar to f. *suecica* in habit but slower-growing and with golden yellow foliage.

'**Green Carpet**' Dense, low-growing and wide-spreading with bright green foliage. Found in Norway before 1975.

'**Hibernica**' ('Stricta') (*J. hibernica* HORT.) "Irish Juniper". A dense-growing, compact form of slender, columnar habit attaining 3m or occasionally 5m in height. Leaves densely arranged. A very popular conifer, excellent for use in formal landscapes and gardens. To some extent the counterpart of the Italian Cypress of the warmer S European gardens though never so tall. C 1838. AGM 1984.

'**Hornibrookii**' ('Prostrata') A dwarf, creeping ground cover taking on the shape of the object over which it creeps. Leaves comparatively small, loosely spreading, sharply-

**JUNIPERUS communis 'Hornibrookii'**—*continued*

pointed, silvery-white beneath. A seedling collected in Co Galway, Ireland, by that great authority on dwarf conifers, Murray Hornibrook. C 1923. AGM 1984.

**var. jackii** See subsp. *alpina*.

**var. montana** See subsp. *alpina*.

**subsp. nana** See subsp. *alpina*.

**'Oblonga Pendula'** An elegant, erect shrub of compact habit up to 3-5m, with slightly ascending branches drooping at the tips, branchlets pendulous. Leaves sharply-pointed, bronze during winter. Recalling *J. oxycedrus*, but with rounded shoots. C 1838.

**'Prostrata'** See 'Hornibrookii'.

**'Repanda'** A dwarf, carpet-forming shrub with densely-packed, semi-prostrate stems and forward-pointing, loosely arranged leaves which sometimes become slightly bronze-tinged in winter. Although of different origin this cultivar is for garden purposes identical with 'Effusa'. Both make excellent ground cover in full sun. Discovered in Ireland by the late Maurice Prichard. C 1934. AGM 1984.

**var. saxatilis** See subsp. *alpina*.

**'Sentinel'** A very narrowly columnar form with densely packed erect branches. The deep bluish-green leaves contrast well with the reddish-purple shoots. Reaches 4m tall and 50cm wide in 30 years. Raised in Canada before 1961.

**'Stricta'** See 'Hibernica'.

**f. suecica** (MILL.) BEISSN. (*J. suecica* MILL.) "Swedish Juniper". A medium-sized shrub similar to 'Hibernica' in habit, but the ascending branches are open and drooping at the tips. Occurs wild in Scandinavia. C 1768.

**'Vase'** ('Vase Shaped') Dwarf shrub up to 0.7m with low, obtusely spreading branches and leaves turning bronze in winter. C 1936.

**conferta** PARL. (*J. litoralis* MAXIM.) "Shore Juniper". A prostrate species with shortly ascending branches, forming large patches of bright green, prickly leaves which possess a white stomatal band on the upper surface. Fruits globose, 8-12mm across, purplish-black and bloomy. An invaluable ground-cover species, its dense prickly carpets of apple-green foliage contrasting effectively with the prostrate dark green forms of *J. communis* and the blue and grey forms of *J. horizontalis*. A native of Japan and Sakhalin where it is found on sandy seashores. Introduced by Ernest Wilson in 1915.

**'Blue Pacific'** Leaves broader and less prickly, darker green and not bronzing in winter.

**davurica** PALL. Regarded by the botanist Van Melle as an extremely variable hybrid with a distribution through N Asia. It is represented in cultivation by the following cultivars:

**'Expansa'** (*J. chinensis* 'Parsonsii') (*J. chinensis* 'Expansa') A dwarf shrub with rigid, wide-spreading, almost horizontal, thick branches, eventually developing into a low mound up to 1m high in the centre and 3m or more across. The scale-like, sage-green leaves are arranged in attractive dense, spray-like heavy clusters along the branches. Introduced from Japan by the Parsons Nursery of New York State in 1862.

**'Expansa Aureospicata'** Smaller and slower-growing, with predominantly juvenile leaves. Greyish-green, with scattered yellow splashes. C 1940.

**'Expansa Variegata'** (*J. chinensis* 'Parsonsii Variegata') Similar in habit and foliage, but with scattered, creamy-white sprays. C 1933.

**'Parsonsii Variegata'** See 'Expansa Variegata'.

**deppeana** STEUD. (*J. deppeana* var. *pachyphlaea* (TORR.) MARTINEZ) (*J. pachyphlaea* TORR.) "Chequer-barked" or "Alligator Juniper". A small, dioecious tree of conical habit, with reddish-brown bark deeply furrowed into square plates. Leaves glaucous; fruits globular, 10-12mm across, reddish-brown and bloomy. Particularly conspicuous as a young plant when it is the most vividly silver-blue of all junipers. Not an easy subject to cultivate, coming as it does from the dry mountain slopes of the SW United States and Mexico. I 1904.

**var. pachyphlaea** See *J. deppeana*.

**distans** FLORIN A rare, large shrub or small tree of loosely columnar habit with drooping branchlets. Leaves mainly juvenile, awl-shaped, grey-green; fruits ovoid, 8-12mm long, reddish-brown. SW China. I 1926.

**drupacea** LABILL. "Syrian Juniper". A striking and distinctive dioecious species of narrow columnar habit, at least in cultivation. A small tree, branches short and densely crowded

**JUNIPERUS drupacea**—*continued*

with sharply-pointed, awl-shaped leaves which are fresh green, broadly banded white on the inner surface. Fruits ovoid or globose, 2-2.5cm across, bluish-black and bloomy, ripening during the first season when they are edible. So far fruits have not been reported in the British Isles. A remarkable species easily recognised in gardens by its habit, together with its comparatively broad, prickly leaves. SW Asia, Greece. I in about 1854.

**excelsa** BIEB. "Greek Juniper". Small tree or large shrub of conical or loosely columnar habit, with long sprays of thread-like branchlets densely clothed with tiny grey-green leaves spreading at tips. Fruits ripening the second year, globose, 9-12mm across, deep purplish-brown and bloomy. SE Europe, SW Asia. I 1806.

**'Stricta'** A columnar form with mainly juvenile foliage. Unfortunately this name has been erroneously used in gardens for *J. chinensis* 'Pyramidalis'.

**flaccida** SCHLECT. "Mexican Juniper". A small tree with attractive scaly bark, slender branches and pendulous branchlets; leaves scale-like, grey-green, bright grass-green on mature trees. Fruits ripening the second year, globose, 10-15mm across, reddish-brown, bloomy. This species has grown in the Hillier Gardens and Arboretum for more than 30 years. Mexico, Texas. I 1838.

**†formosana** HAYATA "Prickly Cypress". A beautiful, small, dioecious tree of loose elegant habit with drooping branchlets. Leaves awl-shaped, in whorls of 3, sharp-pointed, glaucous above. Fruits sub-globose, 6-12mm across, olive-green, with 3 conspicuous white grooves at the apex, ripening to dark brown the second year. A graceful but tender species similar in aspect to *J. oxycedrus*. S China, Taiwan. I about 1844.

**'Grey Owl'** ( *J. virginiana* 'Grey Owl') A splendid medium-sized, vigorous shrub with widely-spreading branches; foliage soft silvery-grey. It is thought to be a hybrid between *J. virginiana* 'Glauca' and *J.* ×*media* 'Pfitzeriana', possessing a habit similar to the latter but in other respects appears typical *J. virginiana*. Originated in 1938. AM 1968. AGM 1984.

**hibernica** See *J. communis* 'Hibernica'.

**'Holger'** (*J.* ×*media* 'Pfitzeriana Aurea' × *J. squamata* 'Meyeri'). (*J. squamata* 'Holger') A small, spreading shrub with glaucous blue foliage, creamy-yellow when young. Raised in 1946 by Holger Jensen in Sweden. See also *J.* 'Hunnetorp'.

**horizontalis** MOENCH. "Creeping Juniper". A dwarf or prostrate shrub with long, sometimes procumbent branches, forming in time carpets several metres across. Leaves on cultivated plants mostly juvenile crowding the branchlets, glaucous green, grey-green or blue, varying in intensity and often plum-purple in winter. Fruits rarely produced in cultivation. One of the best species for use as ground cover, contrasting effectively with the green prostrate forms of *J. communis*. It is a native of North America where it inhabits sea-cliffs, gravelly slopes, even swamps. C 1830. AGM 1984.

**'Alpina'** A form with prostrate branches and ascending branchlets up to 0.6m high. Leaves greyish-blue, purple-tinged during autumn and winter. C 1836.

**'Andorra Compact'** Similar to but an improvement on 'Plumosa', of denser habit with bronze-purple winter foliage. C 1955.

**'Banff'** A low-growing form, the short arching shoots clothed with bright blue-grey foliage. Found in the Banff National Park near Calgary, Alberta, Canada before 1975.

**'Bar Harbor'** A prostrate form with branches closely hugging the ground and spreading in all directions. The shortly ascending branchlets are clothed with glaucous, grey-green, scale-like leaves. C 1930. AGM 1984.

**'Blue Chip'** A prostrate form with foliage bright blue throughout the year. Raised in Denmark about 1940.

**'Blue Rug'** See 'Wiltonii'.

**'Coast of Maine'** Low-growing form making flattened mounds. Leaves awl-shaped, grey-green, purple-tinted in winter.

**'Douglasii'** "Waukegan Juniper". A low-growing, procumbent form up to 0.5m high with long, spreading branches and sprays of both adult and juvenile leaves. The whole plant is a bright, glaucous, grey-green in summer, purple-tinged in autumn and winter. C 1916.

**'Emerald Spreader'** Very low-growing forming dense mats of bright green foliage. C 1973.

**JUNIPERUS horizontalis**—*continued*

**'Glauca'** Prostrate, branches long with slender whipcord tips hugging the ground. Leaves steel-blue in slender sprays. C 1939.

**'Hughes'** A vigorous form with ascending branches and grey-green foliage. Raised in the United States.

**'Montana'** A prostrate form with long branches, slender and filiform at their tips. Branchlets shortly-ascending, plumose and densely packed, bearing scale-like leaves of an intense glaucous blue. In our opinion, one of the best forms.

**'Plumosa'** A dense, procumbent form of compact habit with ascending, plumose branchlets up to 0.6m high. Leaves awl-shaped, grey-green, becoming purple-tinged in winter. C 1919. AGM 1984.

**'Prince of Wales'** A low-growing form of dense habit forming mats up to 15cm tall. Foliage bright green tinged blue, flushed with purple in winter. Found in Alberta in 1931.

**'Prostrata'** A prostrate form with shortly-ascending branchlets clothed with awl-shaped and scale-like, glaucous leaves, bronze-tinged in winter. C 1938.

**'Wiltonii'** ('Blue Rug') One of the best forms, its branches long and prostrate, forming flattened, glaucous blue carpets. C 1914. AGM 1984.

**'Youngstown'** Similar to 'Andorra Compact' but usually greener in winter.

**'Hunnetorp'** A sister seedling of 'Holger' under which name it has been distributed. It differs in its permanently glaucous blue foliage.

**indica** BERTOL. A rare species in cultivation, varying in the wild from a small, spreading shrub to a small, conical tree. Foliage dense and crowded, varying from deep to grey-green. From high altitudes in the Himalaya. For the plant previously listed here see *Cupressus gigantea*.

**japonica** HORT. See *J. × media* 'Plumosa'.

**macrocarpa** See *J. oxycedrus* subsp. *macrocarpa*.

**× media** VAN MELLE (*J. chinensis × J. sabina*). A variable hybrid which, according to the author, occurs in the wild in NE Asia. Van Melle was of the opinion that 4 commonly cultivated junipers previously regarded as forms of *J. chinensis* belonged to this hybrid group and existed in a wild state. Whilst agreeing with his concept of their hybrid origin, we prefer here to treat them as cultivars originally selected from wild material rather than varieties having a distinct geographical distribution. We also regard *J. chinensis* in its broader concept as a parent rather than Van Melle's *J. sphaerica*. Many authorities disagree with Van Melle's conclusions, whilst others prefer to remain neutral until such time that the whole of the *J. chinensis* complex has been thoroughly studied and unravelled.

**'Armstrongii'** (*J. chinensis* 'Armstrongii') In habit resembling a dense and compact Pfitzer Juniper. Leaves mainly scale-like, greyish. The juvenile leaves are mostly confined to the centre of the bush. A sport of 'Pfitzeriana' introduced in 1932 by the Armstrong Nurseries of California.

**'Blaauw'** A strong-growing shrub up to 1.5m with strongly ascending main branches and shorter outer branches, all densely clothed with feathery sprays of mainly scale-like, greyish-blue leaves. It is often confused in gardens with 'Globosa Cinerea' which it resembles as a young plant, but it is stronger and much more irregular in habit when older. C 1924.

**'Blue and Gold'** A small spreading shrub reaching about 1.5m. Foliage blue-grey flecked creamy-yellow. C 1972.

**'Blue Cloud'** See *J.* 'Blue Cloud'.

**'Globosa Cinerea'** (*J. chinensis* 'Globosa Cinerea') A strong-growing, small to medium-sized shrub with ascending branches, clothed with blue-grey, mostly adult leaves. C 1923. It is very similar to 'Blaauw'.

**'Gold Coast'** A flat-topped, low-growing and wide-spreading form with golden foliage.

**'Hetzii'** A medium-sized to large, wide-spreading shrub similar to 'Pfitzeriana', but stems more ascending. The glaucous, mainly adult foliage is also softer to the touch. C 1920.

**'Kosteri'** (*J. virginiana* 'Kosteri') A small shrub with prostrate and ascending plumose branches clothed with grey-green, scale-like and awl-shaped leaves, sometimes purple-tinged in winter. C 1884.

**JUNIPERUS** × **media**—*continued*

'**Mint Julep**' A spreading, flat-topped bush with arching shoots resembling 'Pfitzeriana' but with bright green foliage. C 1960.

'**Mordigan Gold**' Similar to 'Pfitzeriana Aurea' of which it is a sport, but more compact. Bright golden summer foliage.

'**Old Gold**' A sport of 'Pfitzeriana Aurea', from which it differs in its more compact habit, and bronze-gold foliage which does not fade in winter. C 1958. AGM 1984.

'**Pfitzeriana**' (*J. chinensis* 'Pfitzeriana') "Pfitzer Juniper". One of the most popular and commonly planted of all conifers. An eventually medium-sized, wide-spreading shrub with stout, ascending arm-like branches, drooping at the tips. Leaves mainly green and scale-like, but with scattered sprays of juvenile leaves with glaucous upper surfaces, particularly in the centre of the bush. An excellent conifer either as a lawn specimen or when used to break the regular outline of a border or bed. It is often used effectively to cover unsightly structures of low stature such as manhole covers and inspection pits. C 1896. AGM 1984.

Its true origin has given rise to much wrangling amongst botanists and horticulturists. It was first mentioned by the great German nursery firm of Spaeth who named it after W. Pfitzer, a nurseryman at Stuttgart. Van Melle suggested that it was a wild form from the Ho Lan Shan Mountains, Inner Mongolia, and may possibly have been introduced by the French missionary Armand David in about 1866.

'**Pfitzeriana Aurea**' "Golden Pfitzer". Terminal shoots and foliage suffused golden yellow in summer, becoming yellowish-green in winter. A sport of 'Pfitzeriana' which originated in the United States in 1923.

'**Pfitzeriana Compacta**' A sport of 'Pfitzeriana', more dense and compact in habit, with a preponderance of juvenile awl-shaped leaves. C 1930. AGM 1984.

'**Pfitzeriana Glauca**' A sport of 'Pfitzeriana' raised in the United States. It is a little denser in habit with mainly awl-shaped, grey-glaucous leaves. It may be described as a glaucous 'Pfitzeriana Compacta'. C 1940.

'**Plumosa**' (*J. chinensis* 'Plumosa') (*J. japonica* HORT.) A low-growing male shrub with wide-spreading branches bearing crowded plume-like sprays of densely set, green, scale-like leaves. Occasionally a few sprays of juvenile awl-shaped leaves are present in the centre of the bush. Originally introduced from Japan as *J. japonica*, under which name it was commonly grown in cultivation. *J. japonica* of Carrière is *J. chinensis* 'Japonica'. C before 1920.

'**Plumosa Albovariegata**' (*J. japonica* 'Albovariegata') Dwarf spreading shrub of slow growth; foliage scale-like, deep-green speckled white. C 1867.

'**Plumosa Aurea**' (*J. japonica* 'Aurea') A most attractive and ornamental form of 'Plumosa', with ascending branches arching at the tips, densely clothed with plumose sprays of yellow, scale-like leaves which ripen to bronze-gold in winter. C 1885.

'**Plumosa Aureovariegata**' (*J. japonica* 'Aureovariegata') Similar in habit to 'Plumosa Aurea', but lower and slower-growing, its green foliage irregularly variegated deep yellow. C 1873.

'**Reptans**' (*J. virginiana* 'Reptans') A low-growing shrub with rigid, slightly ascending branches. Leaves both scale-like and awl-shaped, grey-green. The foliage is rough to the touch. C 1896.

'**Sulphur Spray**' A sport of 'Hetzii' which it resembles in habit but slower-growing to about 2m tall and across. Foliage a striking pale sulphur-yellow. C 1962.

†**monosperma** (ENGELM.) SARG. "Cherrystone Juniper". A large, densely-branched shrub or small tree, with fibrous reddish-brown bark and greyish-green, scale-like foliage. SE United States, N Mexico. I about 1900.

**morrisonicola** HAYATA "Mount Morrison Juniper". A medium-sized to large shrub of usually dense, erect habit with bluish-green, awl-shaped leaves crowding the short branchlets. Fruits single-seeded, 6mm long, black when ripe. A rare species restricted in the wild to Mount Morrison, Taiwan, where it forms impenetrable scrubby thickets on rocky slopes, reaching small tree size in more sheltered ravines. Botanically it is close to *J. squamata*.

**JUNIPERUS**—*continued*

**nana** See *J. communis* subsp. *alpina*.

†**osteosperma** (TORR.) LITTLE (*J. utahensis* (ENGELM.) LEMM.) "Utah Juniper". Small, monoecious, conical tree with brown fibrous bark, and green, scale-like leaves. Fruits rounded, 6-16mm long, reddish-brown and bloomy. SW United States. I 1900.

**oxycedrus** L. "Prickly Juniper". A large dioecious shrub or small tree of open, drooping habit. Leaves in threes, awl-shaped, ending in a sharp point, green above marked with 2 white stomatic bands beneath. Fruits ovoid or globose, 9-13mm long, shining reddish-brown when ripe in the second year. The fragrant wood produces an "Oil of Cade" which is used medicinally, particularly in the treatment of certain skin diseases. Mediterranean region, W Asia. C 1739.

**subsp. macrocarpa** (SIBTH. & SM.) BALL (*J. macrocarpa* SIBTH. & SM.) A large shrub or small tree, occasionally prostrate in the wild. It differs in its larger fruits.

**pachyphlaea** See *J. deppeana* var. *pachyphlaea*.

**phoenicea** L. "Phoenicean Juniper". A large shrub or small tree of dense, rounded or broadly conical habit. Leaves green, awl-shaped on juvenile plants. Fruits rounded, 6-14mm across, ripening the second year. It has been growing successfully here for several years without protection. Mediterranean region. I 1683.

**var. turbinata** PARL. Differing in its egg-shaped or top-shaped fruits. Occurs on hills and by the sea in Spain, Italy, Sicily, Dalmatia and Algeria.

†**pinchotii** SUDWITH "Red Berry Juniper". A rare, large shrub with wide-spreading branches; leaves dark yellowish-green, awl-shaped on juvenile plants, scale-like on adult plants. SW United States.

†**procera** HOCHST. ex ENDL. "East African Juniper". A tall tree in E Africa where it occurs at high elevations in the mountains. In cultivation it is usually seen as a large shrub or small tree with green, scale-like leaves, awl-shaped on juvenile plants. Fruits rounded, 5mm across, glaucous. Only suitable for the mildest localities.

**procumbens** SIEB. ex MIQ. (*J. chinensis* var. *procumbens* (SIEB. ex MIQ.) ENDL.) "Creeping Juniper". A dwarf, procumbent species with long stiff branches, forming carpets up to 30cm high (in the centre) and several metres across. The tightly packed branchlets are crowded with awl-shaped, glaucous green, sharply-pointed leaves. An excellent ground cover for an open, sunny position on a well drained soil. A native of Japan where it is said to inhabit seashores. I 1843. AGM 1984.

**'Bonin Isles'** Similar to 'Nana' but more vigorous.

**'Nana'** A more compact plant with shorter branches. Introduced from Japan in about 1900. AGM 1984.

**recurva** BUCH.-HAM. ex D. DON "Drooping Juniper". A large shrub or small tree of broadly conical habit, with stringy, shaggy bark and drooping branchlets. Leaves awl-shaped, in threes, green or greyish-green, usually with white stomatal bands above, occasionally green. Fruits ovoid, 7-10mm long, glossy olive-brown, ripening to black, containing a single seed. It is an extremely variable species and in the wild appears to intergrade with *J. squamata*. Some forms in cultivation seem intermediate in character between the 2 species though they always retain their characteristic drooping habit. The wood of *J. recurva*, particularly that of the variety *coxii*, is burned for incense in Buddhist temples in the E Himalaya. E Himalaya, from Nepal to Yunnan and Upper Burma. I about 1822.

**'Castlewellan'** A small tree of loose open habit, the branches lax, like fishing rods, the branchlets drooping in long, slender sprays of soft, thread-like foliage.

**var. coxii** (A.B. JACKS.) MELVILLE An elegant, small tree with gracefully drooping branchlets which are longer and more pendulous. Leaves are also more loosely arranged, sage-green in colour. Introduced from Upper Burma in 1920 by E.H.M. Cox and Reginald Farrer.

**'Embley Park'** See *J. squamata* 'Embley Park'.

**'Nana'** A dwarf form of spreading habit, the branches strongly decurving; foliage greyish-green.

**var. viridis** See *J. squamata* 'Embley Park'.

**rigida** SIEB. & ZUCC. An elegant, large, dioecious shrub or small tree, bearing spreading branches and gracefully drooping branchlets. Leaves rigid, awl-shaped and sharply-pointed, marked with glaucous bands above, bronze-green during winter. Fruits globose,

**JUNIPERUS rigida**—*continued*

6-8mm across, black and bloomy, ripening the second year. A lovely species, native of Japan, Korea and N China. Introduced by J.G. Veitch in 1861.

**sabina** L. "Savin". A common and extremely variable, usually dioecious species of spreading or procumbent habit. In its typical form it is a low, spreading shrub, with branches extending 2-3m and slender, ascending, plumose branchlets. Its pungent, disagreeable smell will usually separate this species from forms of *J. virginiana*. Leaves green or grey-green, mostly scale-like, but scattered sprays of paired, awl-shaped leaves occur even on old plants. Fruits ovoid or globose, 5-7mm across, bluish-black and bloomy. Widely distributed in the wild, from the mountains of S and C Europe to Caucasus. It is said to have been cultivated since ancient times and has been known in England since 1548.

**'Arcadia'** A dense, dwarf shrub with short branchlets clothed with predominantly scale-like, greyish-green leaves. Similar in effect to var. *tamariscifolia*. Here attained 30-45cm by 1m after 10 years. C before 1949.

**'Blue Danube'** A low-growing shrub with spreading branches and crowded branchlets. Leaves mostly scale-like, grey-blue. C 1956.

**'Cupressifolia'** A low-growing form throwing out long, more or less horizontal branches seldom exceeding 0.6m above ground, clothed with mostly adult, dark green leaves. Female. C 1789.

**'Erecta'** A strong-growing, medium-sized, female shrub with ascending branches clothed with predominantly scale-like, green leaves. This is the form usually distributed as *J. sabina*. It is also sometimes wrongly grown as 'Cupressifolia' which is lower-growing. C 1891.

**'Fastigiata'** A large shrub of dense, columnar habit with tightly packed, ascending branches; leaves dark green, mainly scale-like. A most unusual form. C 1891.

**'Hicksii'** A strong-growing shrub with spreading or ascending, later procumbent branches and semi-erect, plumose branchlets crowded with greyish-blue, awl-shaped leaves. A most splendid and vigorous semi-prostrate shrub, to all practical intents and purposes a blue Pfitzer. It soon reaches 1.2m and sends out its 3-4m long, plumose steely grey-blue branches. C 1940.

**'Mas'** A male clone, similar in habit to 'Cupressifolia'. Leaves mainly awl-shaped, dark green. C 1940.

**'New Blue'** See 'Tam no Blight'.

**'Skandia'** ('Scandens') An excellent, low, creeping shrub with dark green, mainly awl-shaped leaves. A plant here attained 20cm by 2m after 10 years. C 1953.

**'Tam no Blight'** ('New Blue') A form of var. *tamariscifolia* resistant to the blight which often affects the commonly grown form of that plant. C 1970.

**var. tamariscifolia** AIT. A low-growing, compact variety with horizontally-packed branches, forming in time a wide-spreading, flat-topped bush. Leaves mostly awl-shaped, bright green. An extremely popular juniper of architectural value, equally suitable for clothing dry banks, wall tops or the edges of lawns. Mts of S Europe. In the Spanish Pyrenees large carpets several metres across are occasionally met with. Long cultivated. AGM 1984.

**'Tripartita'** (*J. virginiana* 'Tripartita') (*lusitanica* HORT.) A strong-growing, medium-sized shrub, with strongly-ascending, nearly erect branches densely clothed with both green, scale-like leaves and glaucous, awl-shaped leaves. It is a juniper of rather heavy, ponderous habit which has now been superseded by the many forms of the Pfitzer Juniper. C 1867.

**'Variegata'** A small shrub with low, slightly ascending branches and dark green, adult foliage flecked with white. C 1855.

**'Von Ehren'** A strong-growing shrub eventually reaching up to 2.5m high, with wide, horizontally spreading, slender branches forming a unique plateau 5m or more across. Branchlets ending in slender sprays; leaves awl-shaped green. C 1912.

**sanderi** See *Thuja orientalis* 'Sanderi'.

**sargentii** (HENRY) TAK. (*J. chinensis* var. *sargentii* HENRY) A prostrate shrub slowly forming dense carpets 2m across. Leaves mostly scale-like, green and bloomy. Fruits blue. A pleasing ground cover in an open position. Native of Japan, S Kuriles and Sakhalin

**JUNIPERUS sargentii**—*continued*

where it inhabits rocky mountain cliffs and seashores. Introduced by Prof Sargent in 1892.

**'Glauca'** A slower-growing form with glaucous grey-green foliage. A good small rug for the scree.

**scopulorum** SARG. "Rocky Mountain Juniper". A small cypress-like tree of conical habit, often with several main stems. Bark red-brown and shredding. Branches stout and spreading, with slender branchlets and tightly adpressed scale-like leaves, varying in colour from light green to bluish-green and glaucous. Fruits rounded, 6mm across, dark blue and bloomy. A native of the Rocky Mountains from British Columbia to Arizona, Texas and N Mexico. It has given rise to many forms. I 1839.

**'Blue Heaven'** A small conical tree with striking blue foliage.

**'Erecta Glauca'** An erect, loosely columnar form with ascending branches and both scale-like and awl-shaped, silvery-glaucous leaves becoming purple-tinged in winter.

**'Glauca Pendula'** Dwarf to medium-sized shrub of loose, open habit, branches ascending, branchlets drooping; foliage awl-shaped, greyish-green. With us forming a plant of rather weak constitution.

**'Hillborn's Silver Globe'** Small, dense shrub of irregular, rounded habit with silvery-blue, mainly awl-shaped leaves.

**'Hill's Silver'** A compact, narrowly columnar form with silvery, grey-blue foliage. C 1922.

**'Moonglow'** A small tree of compact, conical habit with blue-grey foliage.

**'Pathfinder'** A small, narrow, conical tree with flat sprays of bluish-grey foliage. C 1937.

**'Repens'** A dwarf, carpeting shrub with prostrate branches clothed with bluish-green, awl-shaped leaves. C 1939.

**'Skyrocket'** (*J. virginiana* 'Skyrocket') A spectacular form of extremely narrow columnar habit. Our tallest specimen measured 5m high by 30cm in diameter in 1970. In the Hillier Gardens and Arboretum it reached 7.5m tall in 26 years. Foliage blue-grey. One of the narrowest of all conifers and as such an excellent plant for breaking up low or horizontal planting schemes. Particularly effective in the heather garden. It was found in the wild as a seedling. C 1949. AGM 1984.

**'Springbank'** Small tree of erect, columnar habit; branches ascending and spreading branchlets slender; foliage silvery grey-green.

**'Table Top'** A compact, small to medium-sized shrub of spreading habit with silvery-blue foliage. C 1956.

**'Tolleson's Weeping'** A small tree of open, spreading habit with arching branches from which hang long, thread-like shoots clothed in silvery-grey foliage.

**'Wichita Blue'** A small tree of compact, broadly upright habit with bright silvery-blue foliage.

**sheppardii** See *J. chinensis* 'Sheppardii'.

    **var. torulosa** See *J. chinensis* 'Kaizuka'.

**sibirica** See *J. communis* subsp. *alpina*.

**silicicola** (SMALL) BAILEY A medium-sized tree closely related to *J. virginiana* from which it differs in its more slender shoots and smaller cones. SE United States (coastal regions).

**sp. Yu 7881** See *J. squamata* 'Chinese Silver'.

**squamata** BUCH.-HAM. ex LAMB. An extremely variable species ranging in habit from a prostrate shrub to a small bushy tree. Approaching some forms of *J. recurva* in character. All forms have characteristic nodding tips to the shoots and short, awl-shaped leaves which are channelled and white or pale green above. Fruits ellipsoid, 6-8mm across, reddish-brown becoming purplish-black, containing a single seed. The old leaves tend to persist, turning brown. It is widely distributed in the wild throughout Asia, from Afghanistan eastwards to China. I 1824.

**'Blue Carpet'** A low-growing form with spreading branches and blue-grey foliage. AGM 1984.

**'Blue Spider'** A dwarf shrub, a sport of 'Meyeri', highest in the centre, the spreading branches with silvery-blue foliage. C 1980.

**'Blue Star'** A low-growing bush of dense habit making a compact, dwarf bun with comparatively large, silvery-blue awl-shaped leaves. A very desirable cultivar. AGM 1984.

**JUNIPERUS squamata**—*continued*

**'Chinese Silver'** (Yu 7881) A beautiful, medium-sized to large, multi-stemmed shrub of dense habit with recurved terminal shoots. Leaves awl-shaped of an intense silvery blue-green.

**'Embley Park'** (*J. recurva* 'Embley Park') (*J. recurva* var. *viridis* HORT.) A very distinct, small, spreading shrub with reddish-brown, ascending branches clothed with rich grass-green, awl-shaped leaves. Raised at Exbury and Embley Park, Hampshire, from seed collected by George Forrest in China.

**var. fargesii** REHD. & WILS. An erect-growing variety slowly attaining small tree size. Bark greyish-brown peeling in long strips. Branches ascending, branchlets drooping, densely packed, clothed with awl-shaped, apple-green leaves. It is said to be the arborescent form of the species, occurring in woodlands throughout the China-Tibet borderland, closely approaching forms of *J. recurva*. I 1908.

**'Holger'** See *J.* 'Holger'.

**'Loderi'** A small, slow-growing shrub of dense, compact, usually conical habit, eventually reaching 3m. The branchlets nod at their tips and are densely set with short, awl-shaped leaves which are marked with 2 white bands above. As a young plant it is an ideal subject for the rock garden. Raised by Sir Edmund Loder at Leonardslee, Sussex, in 1925. It has been confused in gardens with 'Wilsonii'.

**'Meyeri'** A popular and easily recognised juniper of semi-erect habit, with stout, ascending, angular branches and densely packed, glaucous blue, awl-shaped leaves. Although usually seen as a small to medium-sized shrub it will eventually reach a large size. Introduced from a Chinese garden by Frank N. Meyer in 1914. AM 1931.

**'Pygmaea'** A low-growing plant which forms a dwarf, dense, spreading little bush with shortly ascending branches.

**'Wilsonii'** Similar in foliage to 'Loderi' but making a rounded bush to about 2m tall and as much across. This is one of several seedlings raised from seed, collected by E.H. Wilson in W China in 1909.

**suecica** See *J. communis* f. *suecica*.

**thurifera** L. "Spanish Juniper". A large, dioecious shrub or small tree of tight, columnar habit. In the wild developing a rounded or spreading head and stems with a large girth. Adult leaves scale-like, greyish-green borne on slender, thread-like branchlets. Fruits globose, 7-11mm across, blue, ripening to black, bloomy. A rare species in cultivation and unsuitable for the coldest areas. Mts of S, C and E Spain, French Alps, NW Africa (Atlas Mts). C 1752.

**virginiana** L. "Pencil Cedar". One of the hardiest and most accommodating of conifers, forming a medium-sized to large tree of broadly conical habit. Branchlets slender; clothed with small, sharp-pointed, scale-like leaves and scattered patches of awl-shaped, glaucous, juvenile leaves. Fruits rounded or ovoid, 5mm across, brownish-purple and bloomy, ripening the first year. A variable species which can be confused with *J. chinensis* but the latter has broader juvenile leaves. There are numerous cultivars. E and C North America. C 1664.

**'Burkii'** An excellent columnar form of dense, compact habit, with ascending branches and both scale-like and awl-shaped, steel-blue leaves which are bronze-purple in winter. C 1932.

**'Canaertii'** Small, conical tree of rather dense habit. Foliage bright green, very attractive when peppered with small, cobalt-blue to purple-bloomed, violet fruits. C 1868.

**'Chamberlaynii'** ('Pendula Nana') A female clone of dense habit. A dwarf, spreading or prostrate shrub with drooping branchlets and glaucous, mainly awl-shaped leaves. C 1850.

**'Cupressifolia'** A dense, conical or columnar form with densely packed, slender, fastigiate branches clothed with dark green, scale-like foliage. C 1932.

**'Elegans'** A small tree of graceful habit. Branches ascending, drooping at the tips, branchlets spreading or arching. Leaves scale-like, bright green. FCC 1875.

**'Glauca'** A dense, columnar form with spreading branches clothed with silvery-grey, mainly scale-like leaves. A most attractive small to medium-sized tree. C 1855.

**'Globosa'** Dwarf shrub of dense, rounded habit. The densely packed branches are clothed with mainly scale-like, bright green leaves. C before 1904.

# CONIFERS

**JUNIPERUS virginiana**—*continued*

**'Grey Owl'** See *J.* 'Grey Owl'.

**'Hillii'** ('Pyramidiformis Hillii') A slow-growing, columnar form of dense, compact habit up to 4m. Leaves awl-shaped, glaucous or bluish-green, turning to purplish-bronze in winter. C 1914.

**'Keteleeri'** See *J. chinensis* 'Keteleeri'.

**'Kosteri'** See *J.* × *media* 'Kosteri'.

**'Manhattan Blue'** A small, conical, male tree of compact habit, foliage bluish-green. C 1963.

**'Nana Compacta'** Dwarf shrub, similar to 'Globosa', but less regular in shape and bearing mainly juvenile leaves of a greyish-green, becoming purple-tinged in winter. C 1887.

**'Pendula'** An elegant, small tree with spreading or arching branches and drooping branchlets. Leaves mainly awl-shaped, green. C 1850.

**'Pseudocupressus'** Slender, columnar form of compact habit. Leaves awl-shaped, light green, bluish-green when young. C 1932.

**'Reptans'** See *J.* × *media* 'Reptans'.

**'Pyramidiformis Hillii'** See 'Hillii'.

**'Schottii'** Small tree of dense, narrowly conical habit; foliage scale-like, light green. C 1855.

**'Skyrocket'** See *J. scopulorum* 'Skyrocket'.

**'Tripartita'** See *J. sabina* 'Tripartita'.

**wallichiana** PARL. (*J. pseudosabina* HOOK. f. not FISCH. & MEY.) A dioecious, large shrub or small tree of densely, narrowly conical habit when young. Branches ascending, densely packed, bearing dense bunches of scale-like, green leaves and scattered sprays of juvenile leaves, the latter more apparent on young plants. Fruits ripening the second year, ovoid 6mm long, black when mature. Himalaya. Introduced by Sir Joseph Hooker in 1849. Sometimes found in cultivation under the name *J. pseudosabina* which is an irregular shrub with smaller, often rounded fruits.

**\*KETELEERIA** CARR.—**Pinaceae**—A genus of 2 species of evergreen trees related to *Abies* and resembling them in general appearance. Young trees are rather conical in habit, gradually becoming flat-topped with age. The oblong-lanceolate or linear leaves are arranged in 2 ranks on the lateral shoots, leaving a circular scar (as in *Abies*) when they fall. Leaves of juvenile plants are usually spine-tipped. Male and female strobili are borne on the same tree, the males in clusters. The erect cones ripen during the second year, falling intact.

**davidiana** (BERTR.) BEISSN. A small to medium-sized tree, old specimens developing buttress-like roots. Leaves sharply-pointed and 4-6cm long on young trees, blunter and 2-4cm long on adult trees. Cones cylindrical, 12-20cm long, reddish when young, maturing pale brown. Perhaps the hardiest species, although the young shoots are subject to damage by late spring frosts. C and W China, Taiwan. Discovered by Père David in 1869; introduced by Augustine Henry in 1888.

**†fortunei** (MURR.) CARR. A small tree in cultivation, resembling *K. davidiana*, but with shorter leaves and larger seeds. It requires a sheltered position and is subject to damage by late spring frosts. SE China. First introduced by Robert Fortune in 1844.

**LARIX** MILL.—**Pinaceae**—The "Larches" make up a small genus of mostly fast-growing, deciduous, monoecious trees combining utility and beauty. The branches are borne in irregular whorls ending in long, slender, flexible branchlets which, on older trees, tend to droop or hang in a graceful manner. Leaves linear, borne in dense rosettes on short spurs on the older wood, bunched on short side shoots and spirally-arranged on the young growing shoots. They are generally of a bright green or occasionally blue-green during spring and summer, turning to butter-yellow or old gold in autumn. In early spring the attractive red, pink, yellow or green female strobili and the more numerous but small yellow male strobili stud the, as yet, leafless branchlets. The small, erect, rounded or oblong cones which follow, shed their seed usually in the autumn of the

**LARIX**—*continued*

first year, but remain intact for an indefinite period and as such are commonly made use of for Christmas decoration in the home.

Several of the larches are extremely valuable for their timber which is strong, heavy and durable. They are adaptable to most soils, though wet sites and dry shallow chalk soils are best avoided. There is no more refreshing tint of spring than the pale green of their awakening buds, or a more mellow shade than the autumn colour of their foliage.

**americana** See *L. laricina*.

**dahurica** See *L. gmelini*.

**decidua** MILL. (*L. europaea* DC.) "European Larch" "Common Larch". A large tree with a slender, cone-shaped crown when young. Branches and branchlets drooping on old specimens. Shoots yellowish or grey, glabrous. Rosette leaves 1.5-3.5cm long, light green. Cones ovoid, 2-4cm long, bracts hidden. One of the most important afforestation trees. Native of the European Alps and Carpathians. Commonly planted elsewhere. Long cultivated; perhaps first introduced into the British Isles in about 1620.

**'Corley'** A slow-growing, small, leaderless bush of rounded habit. Propagated from a Witches Broom found by Mr R.F. Corley.

**'Fastigiata'** A narrow, conical form with short, ascending branches. C 1868.

**'Pendula'** A tall tree of irregular habit; branches arching downwards, branchlets pendulous. C 1836.

**'Repens'** A form in which the lower branches elongate and spread out along the ground. C 1825.

× **eurolepis** HENRY (*L. decidua* × *L. kaempferi*) "Hybrid Larch" "Dunkeld Larch". A vigorous large tree of great commerical value. It differs from *L. decidua* in its faintly glaucous shoots and its slightly broader, somewhat glaucous leaves. From *L. kaempferi* it differs in its less glaucous, brown or pale orange shoots and shorter, less glaucous leaves. This important hybrid forest tree is less suspectible to disease than the Common Larch. It originated at Dunkeld, Perthshire, in about 1904.

**europaea** See *L. decidua*

**gmelini** (RUPRECHT) KUZENEVA (*L. dahurica* TURCZ. ex TRAUTV.) "Dahurian Larch". A variable species of medium size in cultivation, with usually glabrous, yellowish shoots which may be reddish during winter. Leaves 2-3cm long, bright green. Cones 1.5-3cm long. Not one of the best species for the British Isles, being liable to damage by spring frosts. NE Asia. I 1827.

**var. japonica** (REG.) PILG. "Kurile Larch". A medium-sized tree differing in its denser branching system, shorter leaves and smaller cones. Shoots reddish-brown and downy. Slow-growing and liable to injury by late spring frosts. Sakhalin, Kurile Isles. I 1888.

**var. olgensis** (HENRY) OSTENFELD & LARSEN Similar growth to var. *japonica*, but shoots even more densely reddish-hairy and both leaves and cones smaller. Like its relatives this larch is conditioned to much longer and severer winters than are experienced in the British Isles and is too easily tempted into premature growth by warm periods and then damaged by subsequent inclement conditions. E Siberia. I about 1911.

**var. principis-rupprechtii** (MAYR) PILG. A more vigorous form with reddish-brown, glabrous shoots, much longer bright green leaves, up to 10cm long on vigorous shoots, and larger cones. Korea, Manchuria, NE China. I 1903.

†**griffithiana** (LINDL. & GORD.) CARR. (*L. griffithii* HOOK. f. & THOMS.) "Himalayan Larch". A beautiful tree of medium size with long, drooping branchlets and downy shoots which turn reddish-brown the second year. Leaves 2.5-3.5cm long, bright green. Cones large, cylindrical, 7-10cm long, with exserted, reflexed bracts. A graceful species for the milder districts easily distinguished by its weeping branchlets and large cones. E Nepal, Sikkim, Bhutan, SE Tibet. Introduced by Sir Joseph Hooker in 1848. AM 1974.

**kaempferi** (LAMB.) CARR. (*L. leptolepis* (SIEB. & ZUCC.) GORDON) "Japanese Larch". A vigorous tree of large size, with reddish shoots. Leaves 2-3.5cm long, sea-green, broader than those of *L. decidua*. Cones ovoid, 2-3cm long with scales turned outward and downward at tips. A commonly planted larch used extensively for afforestation, withstanding exposure well. The reddish twigs appear to create a purple haze above a plantation on a sunny afternoon in late winter. Japan. Introduced by John Gould Veitch in 1861.

**LARIX kaempferi**—*continued*

**'Blue Haze'** A selected clone with leaves of an attractive glaucous blue.

**'Diana'** A gracefully-branched upright tree with fresh green foliage. Selected in Germany before 1982.

**'Hobbit'** A compact, slow-growing dwarf form found as a Witches Broom by our salesman Stan Dolding in 1960.

**'Pendula'** A beautiful, tall, elegant tree with long weeping branches. C 1896. 'Dervaes' is very similar.

**'Wolterdingen'** A dense, dwarf, bun-shaped bush of slow growth with blue-grey foliage. Found in a park in Wolterdingen, Germany in 1970.

**laricina** (DU ROI) K. KOCH (*L. americana* MICHX.) "Tamarack". A small to medium-sized tree, vigorous when young. Shoots glabrous and glaucous at first, later reddish-brown. Leaves 2-3cm long, bright green. Cones cylindric-ovoid, 1-1.5cm long. Though of great value in North America it is less successful in the British Isles and has been little planted. It is interesting on account of its small, neat cones. E North America. I about 1760, possibly before (see note under *L. × pendula*).

**leptolepis** See *L. kaempferi*.

**lyallii** PARL. A small to medium-sized tree in its native habitat, often forming a gnarled, windswept, small tree or shrub. It is easily recognised by its densely felted young shoots and its four-angled, greyish-green leaves, 2.5-3.5cm long. Cones oblong-ovoid, 3.5-5cm long with conspicuous, long-pointed, exserted bracts. Regarded by some authorities as an alpine form of *L. occidentalis*. One of the least adaptable species for the British Isles and appears to require a colder climate. W North America. I about 1904.

**occidentalis** NUTT. "Western Larch". A large tree, attaining 60m in its native habitat. Young shoots pale straw, hairy in the grooves, pale orange-brown and glabrous the second year. Leaves 2.5-4cm long, greyish-green. Cones ovoid, 2.5-3.5cm long, with long-pointed, exserted bracts. North America. Originally discovered by David Douglas. C 1880.

**× pendula** SALISB. "Weeping Larch". A large tree with long branches, pendulous branchlets and shoots which are glabrous and pinkish when young, becoming purple in summer.

The origin of this attractive larch has long been obscure. It was first recorded in cultivation in Peter Collinson's garden at Peckham where it had been planted in 1739. It was at that time claimed to be growing wild in America, but no one since then has found any evidence of its existence there. Most authorities favour the explanation of its origin as a hybrid between *L. decidua* and *L. laricina*. Mr Desmond Clarke has pointed out that the tree originally described by the botanist Solander was not the Peckham tree but a tree growing in Collinson's garden at Mill Hill which some authorities assumed was the same tree which Collinson had simply transplanted from one garden to another. From this it seems highly probable that Collinson's original tree at Peckham was in fact *L. laricina* and that the later, Mill Hill tree (*L. × pendula*) was a seedling, the result of a cross with *L. decidua*.

**potaninii** BATAL. (*L. thibetica* FRANCH.) "Chinese Larch". A beautiful, medium-sized tree with comparatively long, blue-green leaves and graceful, drooping branchlets and orange-brown or purplish, usually glabrous shoots. Leaves four-angled, 2-3cm long. Cones oblong-ovoid, 2.5-5cm long, with long-pointed exserted bracts; the common larch of W Sichuan and said to be the most valuable coniferous timber tree in W China. Unfortunately, it is not a tree of robust constitution in the British Isles. Introduced by E.H. Wilson in 1904.

**russica** See *L. sibirica*.

**sibirica** LEDEB. (*L. russica* (ENDL.) TRAUTV.) "Siberian Larch". A medium-sized tree of conical habit when young. Shoots yellow, hairy or glabrous. Leaves 2-4cm long, sharply-pointed. Cones conical, 3-4cm long. Like several of its relatives this species requires a colder, more even climate than can be expected in the British Isles. The young shoots are very subject to damage by spring frost. NE Russia, W Siberia. I 1806.

**thibetica** See *L. potaninii*.

**"LEYLAND CYPRESS"** See × *Cupressocyparis leylandii*.

**\*LIBOCEDRUS** ENDL.—**Cupressaceae**—A small genus of 5 species allied to *Thuja*. Evergreen trees and shrubs from the S hemisphere. The branches are regularly divided into flattened fern-like sprays of scale-like leaves. Male and female strobili occur on the same plant. Cones short-stalked, ripening the first year. The following species are only suitable for the mildest areas of the British Isles.

**bidwillii** HOOK. f. "Pahautea". A rare species differing from *L. plumosa* in its smaller leaves and cones and the four-sided character of the branchlets. This fastigiate tree is hardier than *L. plumosa* and has here survived outside uninjured for many years. New Zealand.

**chilensis** See *Austrocedrus chilensis*.

**decurrens** See *Calocedrus decurrens*.

**doniana** See *L. plumosa*.

**formosana** See *Calocedrus formosana*.

**macrolepis** See *Calocedrus macrolepis*.

**plumosa** (D. DON) DRUCE (*L. doniana* (HOOK.) ENDL.) "Kawaka". A small tree often shrubby in cultivation with peculiar flattened, fern-like branchlets clothed with bright green, scale-like leaves. Cones ovoid, 1-2cm long. New Zealand.

**tetragona** See *Pilgerodendron uviferum*.

**"MAIDENHAIR TREE"** See *Ginkgo biloba*.

**METASEQUOIA** MIKI ex HU & CHENG—**Taxodiaceae**—The first specimen of this monotypic genus was found by Mr T. Kan in a village in C China in 1941. Not until 1944 were further trees discovered and specimens collected, and in the following year the sensational news was released that a living relic of a fossil genus had been discovered. Not unlike *Taxodium* in general appearance it differs in several botanical characters, including its leaves and ultimate branchlets, both of which are oppositely arranged.

**glyptostroboides** HU & CHENG "Dawn Redwood". A strong-growing, vigorous, deciduous tree of conical habit when young, with shaggy, cinnamon-brown bark. Leaves linear, flattened, borne in 2 opposite ranks on short, deciduous branchlets, the whole resembling a pinnate feathery leaf. They are bright larch-green during summer, becoming tawny pink and old gold in autumn. Male and female strobili borne on the same tree, the males in large racemes or panicles. Cones pendulous, on long stalks, globose or cylindrical, 15-20mm across, dark brown and mature the first year.

The ease with which it is propagated and its rapid growth, plus its ornamental qualities, have combined to make this perhaps the most popular coniferous species in the shortest possible time. It thrives best in moist but well drained conditions. On chalk soils it is slower-growing. It has proved quite hardy and is equally successful in industrial areas. After only 40 years in cultivation some plants in North America are more than 30m. Trees growing in the British Isles from seeds received from the Arnold Arboretum in 1948 have already exceeded 25m in height. Mature trees in its native habitat were reported to be 28-35m in height with rounded crowns. Native of SE China (NE Sichuan and W Hubei). First seen in 1941, and introduced in 1947. AM 1969. AGM 1984.

**'Emerald Feathers'** A fine tree of regular, conical habit with lush green foliage.

**'National'** A more narrowly conical form, selected by the National Arboretum, Washington in 1958.

**\*MICROBIOTA** KOMAROV—**Cupressaceae**—A monotypic genus related to *Juniperus*, differing in its fruits which possess hardened, almost woody scales, breaking up when mature. Male and female strobili are borne on separate plants.

**decussata** KOMAROV A densely branched, prostrate, evergreen shrub with wide-spreading branches bearing small, opposite, almost scale-like leaves, although awl-shaped leaves are present on some branches. Fruits very small, berry-like, 3mm long. It is confined in the wild to the Valley of the Suchan, to the east of Vladivostock, E Siberia where it was discovered in 1921. AM 1973.

**\*MICROCACHRYS** HOOK. f.—**Podocarpaceae**—A monotypic genus related to *Podocarpus*, with slender stems and scale-like leaves. Male and female strobili are borne on the same plant.

**MICROCACHRYS**—*continued*

**tetragona** HOOK. f. A splendid and hardy, dwarf bush with snake-like, four-angled, arching branches clad with minute, scale-like leaves arranged in 4 ranks. Both male and female strobili are conspicuous when present. Fruits egg-shaped, bright red, fleshy and translucent. A rare conifer, restricted in the wild to the summits of 2 mountains in Tasmania. I 1857. AM 1971. FCC 1977.

†\***MICROSTROBOS** GARDEN & JOHNSON—**Podocarpaceae**—2 species of very rare evergreen shrubs related to *Microcachrys*. The adult leaves are scale-like and spirally-arranged along the slender stems. Male and female strobili are borne on the same plant. Cones about 2mm long, containing several pale brown or greyish seeds. Both species are found in moist conditions in the wild.

**fitzgeraldii** (F. MUELL.) GARDEN & JOHNSON (*Pherosphaera fitzgeraldii* (F. MUELL.) F. MUELL. ex HOOK. f.) A small, semi-prostrate, densely-branched shrub with slender stems, clothed with tiny, olive-green, scale-like leaves. Differs from *M. niphophilus* in its looser growth and longer, less congested leaves. Usually only found at the foot of waterfalls in the Blue Mountains of New South Wales, Australia. It has grown successfully in the Hillier Gardens and Arboretum for many years.

**niphophilus** GARDEN & JOHNSON (*Pherosphaera hookeriana* HOOK. f.) A slender-branched, small to medium-sized shrub with short, stiff branches, densely clothed with tiny green, overlapping, scale-like leaves. Resembles *Dacrydium franklinii* in general appearance. Only found in high alpine regions in Tasmania, normally frequenting the margins of lakes, streams and waterfalls. Rare, even in the wild.

**"MONKEY PUZZLE"** See *Araucaria araucana.*

\***PHYLLOCLADUS** RICH. ex MIRBEL—**Phyllocladaceae**—A small genus of 4 species of evergreen trees and shrubs of unusual appearance, suggesting a primitive origin. The branches are normally arranged in whorls and bear peculiar and attractive leaf-like, flattened branchlets (cladodes), which perform the functions of the true leaves, these being scale-like and found mainly on seedlings. Male and female strobili are found on the same or on separate plants, the males produced in clusters at the tips of the shoots, the females borne on the margins of the cladodes. Fruits consisting of one to severai seeds, each in a cup-like, fleshy receptacle. Suitable only for the mildest districts, except *P. alpinus*, which has grown here successfully for more than 30 years and was uninjured by the severe winter of 1962-63, when we lost all other species of the genus.

**alpinus** HOOK. f. "Alpine Celery-topped Pine". A small to medium-sized shrub, often dwarf and stunted, usually with a single main stem. As seen here of erect, narrowly conical habit bearing numerous, small, green, diamond-shaped cladodes up to 3.5cm long. The clusters of reddish male strobili are small, but attractive. This species is perfectly hardy here and is a splendid miniature tree for the rock garden. New Zealand.

**'Silver Blades'** A small to medium-sized shrub of slow growth. Small, neat, diamond-shaped cladodes of silvery-blue. The best colour is retained on plants under glass.

†**aspleniifolius** (LABILL.) HOOK. f. (*P. rhomboidalis* L.C. & A. RICH.) "Celery-topped Pine". A small tree with glaucous, fan-shaped cladodes up to 2.5-5cm long, usually toothed or lobed. Suitable only for the conservatory or sheltered corners in the mildest areas. Tasmania.

†**glaucus** CARR. "Toa toa". An attractive, small tree bearing cladodes of 2 kinds. Those of the main stem are solitary and fan-shaped with coarsely-toothed margins. On the branchlets they are arranged in whorls and resemble pinnate leaves 10-25cm long, with 9-17 coarsely-toothed, fan-shaped or diamond-shaped "leaflets". Male and female strobili are borne on separate plants. New Zealand (N Island).

**rhomboidalis** See *P. aspleniifolius.*

†**trichomanoides** D. DON "Tanekaha". A large shrub or small tree with fan-shaped or ovate, entire or lobed, green cladodes which are pinnately arranged in attractive "fronds". The young emerging cladodes are a reddish-brown in colour. New Zealand.

**\*PICEA** A. DIETR.—**Pinaceae**—The "Spruces" form a genus of about 35 species found throung-out N temperate regions, particularly in E Asia. Evergreen trees, usually of conical habit, with branches borne in whorls. The shoots and branchlets are rough to the touch due to numerous, tiny, peg-like projections left by the fallen leaves. The leaves are short and needle-like, flattened or quadrangular and arranged spirally or in 2 ranks. Male and female strobili are produced on the same tree, the male axillary and the often colourful females, terminal. Cones pendulous varying from ovoid to cylindrical, ripening in the autumn of the first year, remaining intact and falling usually late in the second year.

The spruces are an extremely ornamental group of trees, containing a wide range of shapes and sizes with foliage varying in shades of green and grey. They thrive in a variety of soils, but cannot be recommended for really poor, shallow, chalky or dry soils, nor as single isolated specimens or narrow shelter-belts in very exposed places. They differ from the superficially similar *Abies* in their plug-like leaf scars and pendulous cones which fall intact. There are numerous dwarf forms, particularly of the Norway Spruce, *P. abies.*

**abies** (L.) KARSTEN (*P. excelsa* LINK) "Common Spruce" "Norway Spruce". The commonest spruce in general cultivation and the species popularly known as the "Christmas Tree". A large tree with orange or reddish-brown, usually glabrous shoots. Leaves 1-2.5cm long, shining dark green, densely clothing the upper sides of the branchlets, pectinate below. Cones cylindrical, 10-15cm long. This species is extensively used for afforestation and the white or cream-coloured wood for a wide variety of articles. The young shoots and leaves are the basis of "Spruce Beer". Widely distributed in the wild over N and C Europe, often in large forests. Introduced to the British Isles about 1500.

Under cultivation it has given rise to numerous forms, differing mainly in size and habit. Most of the dwarf forms are extremely slow-growing and suitable for the large rock garden.

**'Acrocona'** A large, spreading bush or small tree with semi-pendulous branches which, even at an early age, usually terminate in a precocious cone. C 1890.

**'Argenteospica'** Young foliage tipped with creamy-white. Raised in Germany by Hesse before 1891.

**'Aurea'** Unfolding leaves bright yellow, changing as they age to soft yellow-green. C 1838. FCC 1862.

**'Capitata'** Dense, small, globular bush with clustered terminal branches. Terminal buds large, more or less concealed by the erect leaves. A specimen in our collection attained $1.2 \times 1.2$m after 35 years. C 1889.

**'Cincinnata'** A small tree with weeping branches. C 1897.

**'Clanbrassiliana'** A dense, small, flat-topped bush, wider than high. In the dormant season it is conspicuous by its innumerable brown winter buds and small crowded leaves on branchlets which are noticeably variable in vigour. A specimen in our collection attained $1.2 \times 2.4$m after 40 years. One of the oldest cultivars, originally discovered in N Ireland about 1790.

**'Cranstonii'** A curious, small, irregular tree of loose, open habit with long, lax branches often without branchlets. C 1855.

**'Cupressina'** A medium-sized tree of columnar habit, with ascending branches. An attractive form of dense growth. C 1855.

**'Doone Valley'** A remarkable, extremely slow-growing bush forming a minute bun of tightly congested growth. Almost unrecognisable as a spruce. Suitable for the scree or the alpine trough garden. Named after "Doone Valley", the one-time garden of Mr W. Archer.

**'Echiniformis'** An exceedingly slow-growing, little hummock of dense, congested growth. It may be confused with 'Gregoryana', but is slower-growing, never so large and its leaves are more rigid and prickly. A specimen in our collection attained $23 \times 53$cm after 20 years. Most suitable for the rock garden. C 1875.

**'Effusa'** A dense, compact, dwarf bush of irregular dome-shaped habit. Suitable for the rock garden.

**'Fastigiata'** See 'Pyramidata'.

**PICEA abies**—*continued*

**'Finedonensis'** ('Argentea') Small tree with spreading branches and silver foliage. Tends to scorch in strong sun. Originally found as a seedling at Finedon Hall, Northamptonshire. C 1862.

**'Gregoryana'** A dense, compact, dwarf bush developing into a somewhat billowy, rounded, flat-topped dome. Its radially-arranged sea-green leaves are conspicuous. A specimen in our collection attained $0.5 \times 1.2$m after 30 years. One of the most popular dwarf forms. C 1862. AGM 1984.

**'Humilis'** A dwarf, slow-growing bush of dense, compact, conical habit with crowded and congested branchlets. Suitable for the rock garden. Differs from the very similar 'Pygmaea' in its pale or yellowish-brown winter buds. C 1891.

**'Inversa'** ('Pendula') An unusual form usually seen as a large shrub with depressed branches. It is taller, less rigid and softer to the touch than 'Reflexa'. A magnificent specimen exceeding a hundred years old is growing in the celebrated garden of Mr and Mrs de Belder, at Kalmthout, Belgium. C 1855.

**'Little Gem'** A dwarf, slow-growing bun of globular habit with tiny, densely crowded leaves. Originated as a sport of 'Nidiformis' in the nurseries of F.J. Grootendorst of Boskoop.

**'Maxwellii'** A squat, dwarf, rounded, slow-growing dome with coarse, rigid, spine-pointed, sea-green leaves. C about 1860.

**'Nana'** A slow-growing, dwarf bush of conical habit with densely crowded branches and sharply-pointed, small leaves. C 1855.

**'Nidiformis'** A very popular and commonly planted form of German origin, making a dwarf, dense, flat-topped bush of spreading habit, the branches forming a series of tight, horizontal layers. A specimen in our collection attained $0.6 \times 1.8$m after 30 years. C 1907. AGM 1984.

**'Ohlendorffii'** Small, conical bush of dense habit; leaves yellowish-green, rather small, recalling those of *P. orientalis*. Freer-growing than most it will reach $1.8 \times 1.2$m after 30 years. C about 1845.

**'Pachyphylla'** Dwarf, slow-growing bush with few short, stout branches and exceptionally thick, forwardly-directed, rigid leaves. An excellent specimen of this distinct cultivar is growing at Glasnevin Botanic Garden, Ireland. C 1923.

**'Pendula'** See 'Inversa'.

**'Pendula Major'** A strong-growing, conical tree with mainly spreading branches, some decurving and pendulous bearing branchlets which are also decurving or pendulous. C 1868.

**'Phylicoides'** A slow-growing, medium-sized to large shrub of irregular growth, conspicuous by its short, thick, distantly-spaced leaves. A specimen in our collection attained $1.8 \times 1.5$m after 30 years. C 1855.

**'Procumbens'** A dwarf, flat-topped, wide-spreading bush with densely layered branches, the branchlets ascending at the tips. A specimen in our collection attained $0.6 \times 3$m after 30 years. C 1850.

**'Pseudoprostrata'** ('Prostrata') Dwarf, broad-spreading shrub with flattened top. Denser growing than 'Procumbens'. A specimen in our collection attained $0.6 \times 1.5$m after 25 years. C 1923.

**'Pumila'** A dwarf, slow-growing, flat-topped bush of spreading, compact but irregular habit. Branches and branchlets densely packed and congested. A specimen in our collection attained $0.6 \times 1.5$m after 30 years. C 1874.

**'Pumila Nigra'** Dwarf bush, similar to 'Pumila', but leaves shining dark green. 'Pumila Glauca' is almost if not identical.

**'Pygmaea'** A dwarf, extremely slow-growing form of globular or broadly dome-shaped habit, with tightly congested branchlets forming a neat, compact but irregular outline. It is one of the slowest-growing of all *P. abies* cultivars, attaining $45 \times 30$cm in about 30 years. It is also one of the oldest, having been known since about 1800.

**'Pyramidata'** ('Fastigiata') ('Pyramidalis') A strong-growing, narrowly conical tree with strongly ascending branches. Excellent where space is limited. C 1853.

**'Reflexa'** A dense, rigid, more or less prostrate or creeping bush of irregular habit with normal-sized branchlets and leaves. Unless it is trained to a single upright stem it forms

**PICEA abies 'Reflexa'**—*continued*

a low dome with long prostrate branches extending carpet-like for several metres. A specimen in our collection, 25 years old, measured 0.5m high at the raised centre and 4m across. An excellent ground cover. C 1890.

**'Remontii'** A dense, slow-growing, conical bush, similar to *P. glauca* var. *albertiana* 'Conica' in shape, eventually attaining 2-2.5m. C 1874.

**'Repens'** A slow-growing, dwarf, flat-topped bush with branches in layers. A low, wide-spreading clone suitable for the large rock garden. It appears very similar to 'Pseudo-prostrata'. C 1898.

**'Rubra Spicata'** Under this name is grown a form in which the young growths are red.

**'Tabuliformis'** A small, slow-growing bush with tabulated growth and flattened top. A specimen in our collection attained 1.75 × 3.5m after 30 years. C 1865.

**'Virgata'** A medium-sized tree of curious habit, with long, whorled, sparsely produced branches. They are undivided and snake-like in appearance or with a few pendulous branchlets. The leaves are radially arranged. C 1853. AM 1978.

**'Waugh'** Medium-sized, sparsely-branched bush with thick shoots and thick, widely-spaced leaves.

**'Will's Zwerg'** An attractive, slow-growing form of dense, conical habit, eventually a medium-sized bush.

**alba** See *P. glauca*.

**asperata** MAST. A medium-sized tree similar to and resembling *P. abies* in general appearance, with pale yellowish-brown young shoots. Leaves 1-2cm long, four-angled, dull greyish-green sometimes bluish-green, rigid and sharply-pointed. Cones cylindrical, to 13cm long. This very hardy, lime-tolerant species is the Chinese counterpart of the European *P. abies*. W China. I 1910 by Ernest Wilson. AM 1981.

    **var. notabilis** REHD. & WILS. A variety with slightly longer, glaucous green leaves and rhombic-ovate cone scales.

    **var. retroflexa** (MAST.) BOOM (*P. retroflexa* MAST.) Differing but little from the type, the leaves green and pectinate below.

**bicolor** (MAXIM.) MAYR A medium-sized to large tree of broad conical shape, with long branches upcurved at tips and with yellowish-brown to reddish-brown, glabrous or hairy young shoots. Leaves 1-2cm long, green or bluish-green above, somewhat glaucous beneath, densely crowded on the upper surfaces of the branchlets. Cones to 12cm long, reddish-purple when young. Japan. Introduced by J.G. Veitch in 1861.

    **var. acicularis** SHIR. & KOYAMA An uncommon variety differing in its more densely arranged leaves. Japan. I 1868.

    **var. reflexa** SHIR. & KOYAMA An obscure variety from Japan in which the cone scales are elongated and reflexed. It is the most ornamental form, with more conspicuous stomatic lines.

**brachytyla** (FRANCH.) PRITZ. (*P. sargentiana* REHD. & WILS.) (*P. ascendens* PATSCHKE) A beautiful, medium-sized to large tree, conical when young but developing a rounded head in maturity. The long, spreading branches are gracefully ascending, then arching at the tips. Young shoots shining pale brown, bearing attractive chestnut-brown buds in winter. Leaves to 20mm long, vividly white beneath, crowded on the upper surface of the branchlets. Cones oblong-cylindric, 6-9cm long, greenish or purple-tinged when young. A most ornamental species with its slenderly upcurved branches and drooping branchlets. W and C China. I 1901 by Ernest Wilson.

    **var. complanata** (MAST.) CHENG ex REHD. Differs in its slightly longer, sharply-pointed leaves, up to 2.5cm and its brown or purplish-brown young cones.

**breweriana** S. WATS. "Brewer's Weeping Spruce". Perhaps the most beautiful of all spruces and one of the most popular of all ornamental conifers. A small to medium-sized, broadly conical tree, with spreading or decurved branches from which hang slender, tail-like branchlets, 1.8-2.5m long. Leaves to 3cm long, shining dark blue-green above, marked with 2 white bands beneath. Cones up to 10cm long, green at first, turning purple later. FCC 1974.

There are few more breathtaking sights than a fine specimen of this spruce with its curtained branches, rising like a majestic green fountain. It is sometimes confused with *P. smithiana*, particularly when young, but differs from this species in its smaller,

**PICEA breweriana**—*continued*

flattened, dark blue-green leaves, smaller, dome-shaped buds and hairy shoots. It is a rare tree in the wild state, being confined to a few isolated localities in the Siskiyou Mountains of NW California and SW Oregon. I 1897. AM 1958. AGM 1984.

‡**engelmannii** (PARRY) ENGELM. "Engelmann Spruce". A small to medium-sized tree with pale yellowish-brown young shoots. Leaves four-angled, 1.5-2.5cm long, sharply-pointed, greyish-green, emitting a pungent odour when bruised, crowded on the upper surfaces of the branchlets. Cones to 7.5cm long. W North America. I 1862.

**f. glauca** BEISSN. Leaves glaucous, a very attractive form.

**excelsa** See *P. abies*.

**glauca** (MOENCH) VOSS (*P. alba* LINK) "White Spruce". A large tree of dense, conical habit, with decurved branches, ascending at the tips. Leaves four-angled, to 20mm long, glaucous green, emitting a foetid odour when bruised, densely arranged and standing above the upper surfaces of the branchlets. Cones to 6cm long. A very hardy species, useful for planting in cold, exposed positions. Canada. NE United States. I 1700.

**var. albertiana** (BROWN) SARG. "Alberta White Spruce". An uncommon variety, differing in its less upright habit, slightly longer leaves which are less glaucous beneath and its smaller cones. C North America. Introduced by H.J. Elwes in 1906. AM 1920.

'**Alberta Globe**' Raised in Holland this is a form of very dense habit making a compact, rounded bun. C 1968.

'**Conica**' A slow-growing, perfectly cone-shaped bush of dense, compact habit with leaves of a bright grass-green. A deservedly popular cultivar, in 30 years making a pointed cone of symmetrical shape, 2m high × 1.2m at base. Originally found in the Canadian Rockies, near Alberta in 1904 by Dr J.G. Jack and Prof Alfred Rehder. AM 1933. AGM 1984.

'**Lilliput**' A very slow-growing form, similar in habit to 'Conica' but more dwarf.

'**Caerulea**' An attractive form with densely-arranged, silvery, grey-blue leaves. C 1866.

**var. densata** BAILEY A slow-growing, eventually large shrub or small tree of dense, compact habit. Dakota. C 1920.

'**Echiniformis**' Dwarf, slow-growing, globular bush of dense habit; leaves glaucous grey-green, forward-pointing, concealing both branchlets and buds. A first class miniature conifer for the rock garden. C 1855.

'**Nana**' A dwarf or small, slow-growing bush of dense, globular habit, with radially-arranged greyish-blue leaves. A specimen in our collection attained 1.4 × 1.8m after 30 years. C 1828.

**glehnii** (F. SCHMIDT) MAST. "Sakhalin Spruce". A small to medium-sized, slender, conical tree with reddish or chocolate-brown, flaking bark. Young shoots conspicuously reddish-orange. Leaves bluish-green above, glaucous beneath, 1.5cm long, densely arranged on the upper surfaces of the branchlets. Cones to 8cm long, violet when young. Similar in effect to *P. abies*, but less vigorous and with shorter leaves. S Sakhalin, E and N Hokkaido (Japan). I 1877.

× **hurstii** DE HURST (*P. engelmannii* × *P. pungens*). A vigorous, medium-sized tree, more or less intermediate in character between the parents. Young shoots pale orange, usually glabrous. Buds slightly resinous. Leaves four-sided, 10-12mm long, greyish-green, spreading all round the branchlets or loosely parted below.

**jezoensis** (SIEB. & ZUCC.) CARR. "Yezo Spruce". A medium-sized to large tree with deflexed branches and shining pale brown to yellowish-brown young shoots. Leaves flattened, 1-2cm long, glossy dark green above, silvery-white beneath, densely crowded and overlapping on the upper surfaces of the branchlets. Cones to 7.5cm long, reddish when young. The young growths are subject to injury by late spring frosts. NE Asia, Japan. Introduced by J.G. Veitch in 1861.

**var. hondoensis** (MAYR) REHD. "Hondo Spruce". A variety with shorter leaves, dull green above. In cultivation less susceptible to damage by spring frosts. Mts of Hondo (Japan). I 1861. AM 1974.

**koyamae** SHIRAS. A small to medium-sized tree of narrowly conical habit, with reddish-orange young shoots. Leaves to 12mm long, green or slightly glaucous, densely packed on the upper surfaces of the branchlets. Cones to 10cm long, pale green when young. A rare tree both in the wild and in cultivation. Distinguished from all other Japanese

**PICEA koyamae**—*continued*

species by its resinous buds. Found in the wild only on Mount Yatsuga in C Japan. Discovered by Mitsua Koyama in 1911. Introduced by E.H. Wilson in 1914.

**likiangensis** PRITZ. A most ornamental, vigorous and accommodating tree of medium size, showing considerable variation within the species. Upper branches with ascending terminals. Young shoots pale brown or reddish. Leaves flattened, 1-2cm long, green or bluish-green above, glaucous beneath, loosely packed on the upper surfaces of the branchlets. Cones to 10cm long, reddish-pink when young, freely produced. In April and May when loaded with its male flowers and brilliant red young cones it is spectacularly beautiful. W China. C 1910. AM 1961. FCC 1974.

**var. balfouriana** (REHD. & WILS.) E.H. HILLIER A variety with densely hairy branchlets, dark green or glaucous, obtuse leaves and violet-purple young cones.

**var. purpurea** See *P. purpurea*.

× **lutzii** LITTLE (*P. glauca* × *P. sitchensis*). A medium-sized tree intermediate in character between the parents. Young shoots yellowish and glabrous. Leaves greyish-green. Cones to 6cm long. Found in the wild with the parents in S Alaska in 1950. It has also been artificially raised in cultivation in Europe.

**mariana** (MILL.) B.S. & P. (*P. nigra* (AIT.) LINK) "Black Spruce". A medium-sized, rather narrowly conical tree with brown, densely hairy young shoots. Leaves to 12mm long, dark bluish-green, densely crowding the upper surfaces of the branchlets. Cones to 3.5cm long, produced in large quantities, dark purple when young. NW North America. C 1700.

**'Aurea'** Leaves yellow when young, becoming glaucous green later. Tends to lose its colour when growing in shade. C 1891.

**'Doumetii'** Eventually a large bush of dense, rather irregular but somewhat globular habit. C 1850.

**'Nana'** A slow-growing, dwarf, mound-forming bush of dense habit, with grey-green leaves. A good dwarf conifer, suitable for the rock garden. C 1884. AGM 1984.

× **mariorika** BOOM (*P. mariana* × *P. omorika*). A medium-sized tree intermediate in character between the parents, with some forms closer to one parent than the other. Resembles *P. omorika* in general appearance, but usually broader in habit with narrower, more sharply-pointed leaves, and smaller cones 3.5-4.5cm long. Raised in the nurseries of G.D. Boehlje at Westerstede, Germany in 1925.

**maximowiczii** REG. ex MAST. A small to medium-sized, densely-branched tree of conical habit with yellowish-brown or reddish, glabrous young shoots and white resinous buds in winter. Leaves four-sided, 10-15mm long, dark shining green, densely arranged above, pectinate below. Cones to 6cm long, pale green when young. It resembles an intermediate between *P. abies* and *P. orientalis*. Mts of Japan. First discovered on Mt Fujiyama in 1861. Introduced in 1865.

**morinda** See *P. smithiana*.

**morrisonicola** HAYATA "Mount Morrison Spruce". A rare and graceful, small to medium-sized tree with white or pale brown, glabrous shoots. Leaves four-sided, 1-2cm long, green, very slender, sharply-pointed, crowded forward on the upper surfaces of the shoots. Cones to 8cm long. Taiwan.

**nigra** See *P. mariana*.

**obovata** LEDEB. "Siberian Spruce". A medium-sized to large tree often a large bush, closely related to *P. abies*, but differing in its usually shorter duller leaves and smaller cones, 6-8cm long. Rare in cultivation. N Europe, N Asia. I 1852.

**omorika** (PANCIC) PURKYNE "Serbian Spruce". One of the most beautiful and adaptable spruces in cultivation, quickly forming a tall, graceful, slender tree. A medium-sized to large tree with relatively short, drooping branches which curve upwards at the tips. Young shoots pale brown. Leaves flattened, 1-2cm long, dark green above, glaucous beneath, densely arranged on the upper surfaces of the branchlets, loosely parted below. The leaves of young plants are narrower, sharply-pointed and more spreading on the shoots than those of the adult. Cones ovoid-conic, 4-6cm long, bluish-black when young. It is one of the best spruces for industrial areas and chalk soils and would make an excellent evergreen street tree. A superb species, native of Yugoslavia where it inhabits

**PICEA omorika**—*continued*

limestone rocks on both sides of the River Drina. It was discovered in 1875 and introduced to England in 1889. AGM 1984.

**'Expansa'** A low, wide-spreading bush with shortly ascending branches up to 0.8m. Tends to revert. C 1940.

**'Nana'** A medium-sized, densely conical bush of compact habit. The conspicuous stomatal bands add considerably to its attraction. A specimen in our collection attained 1.2 × 1.2m after 15 years. C 1930.

**'Pendula'** A very beautiful, slender tree with drooping, slightly twisted branches displaying the glaucous upper surfaces of the leaves. C 1920.

**orientalis** (L.) LINK "Oriental Spruce". A large, densely-branched tree of broadly conical habit, with branches to ground level. Young shoots pale brown. Leaves to 8mm long, with blunt tips, dark shining green, densely pressed on the upper surfaces of the branchlets. Cones to 9cm long, purple when young. One of the best and most adaptable species in cultivation, easily recognised by its dense, conical habit and small, closely-pressed leaves. Asia Minor, Caucasus. I about 1839. AGM 1984.

**'Aurea'** ('Aureospicata') Young shoots creamy-yellow, becoming golden yellow later, finally green. A spectacular tree in spring. C 1873. FCC 1893.

**'Gracilis'** ('Nana Gracilis') A slow-growing, rounded bush of dense habit, eventually developing into a small, conical tree up to 5 or 6m. A specimen in our collection attained 2.4 × 1.8m after 22 years. C 1923.

**'Pendula'** See 'Weeping Dwarf'.

**'Skylands'** A beautiful, slow-growing small tree similar to 'Aurea' but the foliage golden yellow throughout the year.

**'Weeping Dwarf'** ('Pendula') A compact, slow-growing form with weeping branches.

**polita** (SIEB. & ZUCC.) CARR. "Tiger-tail Spruce". A medium-sized to large tree of dense, broadly conical habit, with nearly horizontal branches. Young shoots stout, shining yellowish-brown, often white. Leaves to 2cm long, green, sickle-shaped and spine-pointed, stiffly spreading all round the branchlets. Cones to 10cm long, yellowish-green when young. A distinct species, easily recognised by its stout, prickly leaves which are more difficult to handle than any other species. Japan. Introduced by J.G. Veitch in 1861. FCC 1873.

**pungens** ENGELM. "Colorado Spruce". A medium-sized to large tree of conical habit, with stout orange-brown young shoots, which are glaucous at first. Leaves rigid, to 3cm long, sharply-pointed, green to grey, spreading all round the branchlets, but denser on the upper surfaces. Cones to 10cm long, green when young. The typical form is uncommon in cultivation due to the popularity of its glaucous-leaved forms of which there are a considerable number. SW United States. I about 1862. FCC 1877.

**'Compacta'** A medium-sized, flat-topped bush of dense, compact habit, with horizontally spreading branches and grey-green leaves. C 1874.

**Glauca group** (f. *glauca* (REG.) BEISSN.) "Blue Spruce". A medium-sized to large tree with glaucous leaves. A variable form occurring both in the wild and in cultivation. The leaves tend to lose their intensity as they age, those at the base of the branches being greyish-green or green. In cultivation the most glaucous forms are usually small to medium-sized trees. FCC 1890.

**'Globosa'** ('Glauca Globosa') (Glauca group) Dwarf, flat-topped, globular bush of dense habit; leaves glaucous blue. C 1937.

**'Hoopsii'** (Glauca group) An excellent small to medium-sized tree of densely conical habit, with vividly glaucous blue leaves. C 1958. AGM 1984.

**'Hoto'** (Glauca group) A Dutch selection. Not the best for colour but strong-growing with a dense, conical habit. Foliage blue-grey. C.1972.

**'Koster'** (Glauca group) The most popular form of Blue Spruce. A small to medium-sized, conical tree with leaves of an intense silver-blue. C 1885. AGM 1984.

**'Moerheimii'** (Glauca group) A small to medium-sized tree of dense, conical habit with intensely glaucous blue leaves. One of the most satisfactory of the group. C 1912.

**'Montgomery'** (Glauca group) A dwarf, slow-growing bush of compact habit. The sharply-pointed leaves are greyish-blue. C 1934.

**PICEA pungens**—*continued*

**'Oldenburg'** A German selection of dense, broadly conical habit with striking blue-grey foliage. C. 1976.

**'Pendula'** (Glauca group) A slow-growing small tree with down-swept branches and glaucous blue leaves. FCC 1898.

**'Procumbens'** ('Glauca Procumbens') (Glauca group) Dwarf shrub with low, spreading branches in all directions; branchlets pendulous. Leaves glaucous blue. If terminal reversions occur they should be removed. C 1910.

**'Spekii'** (Glauca group) Small to medium-sized, conical tree with glaucous blue leaves. Introduced by the Jan Spek nurseries of Boskoop in about 1925.

**'Thomsen'** (Glauca group) A beautiful, conical tree of small to medium-size bearing leaves of a striking silvery-blue. C 1928.

**purpurea** MAST. (*P. likiangensis* var. *purpurea* (MAST.) DALLIM. & JACKS.) Previously regarded as a variety of *P. likiangensis* but developing a narrower more pointed upper crown, the upper branches with erect terminals. Leaves also darker green, smaller and more closely pressed on the upper surfaces of the branchlets. Cones smaller, violet-purple. W China. I 1910.

**retroflexa** See *P. asperata* var. *retroflexa*.

‡**rubens** SARG. (*P. rubra* LINK not A. DIET.) "Red Spruce". A medium-sized to large tree with reddish-brown, scaly bark. Young shoots light reddish-brown. Leaves to 1.5cm long, twisted, densely set on the upper surfaces of the branchlets. Cones to 5cm long, green or purple when young. At its best in moist conditions and unsuitable for chalk soils. NE North America. I before 1755.

**rubra** See *P. rubens*.

**schrenkiana** FISCH. & MEY. "Schrenk's Spruce". A medium-sized tree with greyish young shoots and resinous buds. Leaves to 3cm long, sage-green, rigid and sharply-pointed, arranged all around the branchlets, but more densely above than below. Cones to 9cm long. It resembles *P. smithiana* in its leaves which, however, are slightly shorter, more glaucous and less radially arranged. C Asia. I 1877.

**sitchensis** (BONG.) CARR. "Sitka Spruce". A fast-growing, large to very large, broadly conical tree primarily of economic importance. Leaves 18mm long, rigid, and sharply-pointed, green above marked with 2 glaucous bands beneath, spreading all round the branchlets, or sometimes loosely parted below. Cones to 10cm long, yellowish-brown when young. A remarkable, prickly-leaved spruce, thriving particularly well in damp sites.

It is one of the most important afforestation trees and is the most commonly planted conifer for this purpose in the British Isles, particularly in the north and in Wales. W North America, from California to Alaska. Originally discovered by Archibald Menzies in 1792, and introduced by David Douglas in 1831.

**'Papoose'** Although commonly cultivated the Sitka Spruce has given rise to surprisingly few cultivars. This form makes a very slow-growing dwarf with blue-grey foliage. C 1982.

**smithiana** (WALL.) BOISS. (*P. morinda* LINK) "West Himalayan Spruce". A large and extremely beautiful tree with branches upcurved at tips and long, pendulous branchlets. Leaves to 4cm long, dark green, needle-like and flexible, spreading all round the branchlets. Cones to 17cm long, green when young, becoming purplish. An attractive and ornamental tree recognisable at all ages by its drooping branches, long leaves and glabrous shoots. Young plants are occasionally subject to injury by late spring frosts, but established trees are quite hardy and develop into a specimen second only in elegance to *P. breweriana*. W Himalaya. I 1818. AM 1975.

**spinulosa** (GRIFF.) HENRY A medium-sized to large tree, reaching 60m and above in its native environs. Branches spreading, branchlets pendulous. Leaves to 3.5cm long, green below, glaucous above, spreading all round the branchlets. Cones to 10cm long, green or reddish-grey when young. A rare and remarkable semi-weeping tree but perhaps a little gaunt and sparsely branched when compared with *P. breweriana* or *P. smithiana*. E Himalaya. I about 1878.

**wilsonii** MAST. (*P. watsoniana* MAST.) A small tree remarkable on account of its conspicuous marble-white, glabrous, young shoots, attractive buds and narrow leaves. Leaves to 2cm

**PICEA wilsonii**—*continued*

long, dark green, densely clothing the upper surfaces of the branchlets. Cones to 5cm long. C and W China. Introduced by Ernest Wilson in 1901.

**\*PILGERODENDRON** FLORIN—**Cupressaceae**—A monotypic genus differing from the closely related *Libocedrus* in its uniformly four-ranked leaves. Male and female strobili are borne on the same plant.

**uviferum** (PILG.) FLORIN (*Libocedrus uviferum* PILG.) "Alerce". A rare, small, slow-growing tree of stiff, upright habit when young. The small, green, scale-like leaves are borne in 4 ranks, giving the shoots a quadrangular appearance. Cones ovoid, 8-13mm long, with 4, woody, brown scales. This remarkable tree, a native of Chile, has proven hardy here. I 1849.

**\*PINUS** L.—**Pinaceae**—The "Pines" make up a genus of more than 100 species of evergreen trees widely distributed in the temperate regions of the N hemisphere, south to C America and Indonesia. Young trees are normally conical in habit, broadening and becoming bushy or flat-topped with age. The leaves are long and needle-like, borne in bundles of from 2-5. Male and female strobili are borne on the same tree and are often attractive in late spring and early summer. Cones varying in shape from rounded and conical to banana-shaped, ripening at the end of the second year. In most species the cones release their seed on ripening, but in a few species the cones remain intact until they fall. Under natural conditions certain species such as *P. radiata* retain their cones intact on the tree for many years until forced to open by forest fires.

The pines serve a great variety of purposes, many being highly ornamental as well as useful. Some species will succeed in the poorest soils whether alkaline or acid but as a rule the five-needled species are not long satisfactory on shallow chalk soils, whilst others are invaluable as wind-breaks, especially in coastal districts. All species dislike shade and very few will tolerate smoke-polluted air. Numerous dwarf or slow-growing forms have appeared in cultivation, many of which are suitable for the rock garden where they combine effectively with dwarf spruces, firs and junipers.

**albicaulis** ENGELM. A small tree related to *P. flexilis* from which it differs in its dense, short leaves and its cones which do not open when ripe. Young shoots reddish-brown, sparsely downy or glabrous. Leaves in fives to 6.5cm long, green or greyish-green. Cones to 7.5cm long, falling intact. Seeds edible. A rare species in cultivation. W North America. Introduced by John Jeffrey in 1852.

**'Nana'** See 'Noble's Dwarf'.

**'Noble's Dwarf'** ('Nana') A dwarf shrubby form of compact habit. Our plant was propagated from material received from the late Mr Nisbet of Gosport who in turn received his plant from the late Mr Noble of California.

**aristata** ENGELM. "Bristlecone Pine". A small tree or large shrub, with stout, reddish-brown, hairy young shoots. Leaves in fives, to 4cm long, flecked with white resin, tightly bunched and closely pressed to the branchlets. Cones to 9cm long, the scales with slender-spined, bristle-like bosses. Native of the SW United States (Colorado, Arizona, New Mexico), where trees aged up to 2,000 years have been recorded. I 1863. See also *P. longaeva*.

**arizonica** ENGELM. (*P. ponderosa* var. *arizonica* (ENGELM.) SHAW) "Arizona Pine". A large tree closely related to *P. ponderosa* with deeply fissured, almost black bark, glaucous young shoots and long, slender leaves in bundles of five or occasionally in threes or fours. SW United States, N Mexico.

**armandii** FRANCH. "Armand's Pine". An attractive tree of medium size. Leaves in fives, 10-15cm long, glaucous. Cones usually borne in clusters of 2 or 3, barrel-shaped, to 19cm long, becoming pendulous. A very ornamental species with its drooping, glaucous leaves and decorative cones. It grows well in the British Isles. SE Tibet, W China, with a variety in Taiwan. I 1895.

**attenuata** LEMM. (*P. tuberculata* GORD.) "Knobcone Pine". A small to medium-sized tree with an open, upswept crown of long branches. Leaves in threes, 10-18cm long, greyish-green. Cones to 13cm long, the scales armed with sharp prickles, appearing singly or in whorls of 2-4. They remain intact for many years and in the wild are usually opened as a result of forest fires. Closely related to *P. radiata*. SW United States. I about 1847.

**PINUS**—*continued*

**ayacahuite** EHRENB. "Mexican White Pine". A large tree with a spreading head of branches and stout, pale brown or greyish young shoots. Leaves in fives, slender and spreading, to 20cm long, glaucous-green. Cones to 20cm long, sometimes longer. They are pendulous and borne singly or in clusters of 2 or 3 towards the ends of the branches, even on quite young trees. An attractive species with its long greyish leaves and resin-smeared cones. Mexico and C America. I 1840. AM 1960. FCC 1961.

**var. veitchii** (ROEZL) SHAW Some plants grown under the above name belong here. It differs in its larger seeds and cones with larger, thicker scales. C Mexico.

‡**banksiana** LAMB. "Jack Pine". A very hardy tree of medium size, occasionally gnarled and shrubby. Leaves in pairs, to 4cm long, curved or twisted. Cones usually in pairs, to 5cm long. It is adaptable to most soils except shallow chalk soils and is particularly good in moist soils. Easily recognised on account of its crooked branches and uneven cones. It occurs further north than any other American pine. N United States, Canada. C 1783.

**brutia** TENORE (*P. halepensis* var. *brutia* (TENORE) HENRY) A medium-sized tree in cultivation differing from *P. halepensis* mainly in its green young shoots, leaves to 16cm long and almost sessile, spreading or forward-pointing cones. E Mediterranean.

**bungeana** ZUCC. "Lace-bark Pine". A small to medium-sized tree or a large shrub, typically branching from near the base. On trees in cultivation the smooth, grey-green bark flakes away creating a beautiful patchwork of white, yellow, purple, brown and green. Leaves in threes 5-10cm long, rigid. Cones to 7cm long. One of the most ornamental of all pines. Closely allied to *P. gerardiana*. China. First discovered by Dr Bunge in a temple garden near Peking in 1831. Introduced by Robert Fortune in 1846.

†**canariensis** C. SMITH "Canary Island Pine". A very beautiful tree reaching a large size in its native habitats, but smaller and only suitable for the mildest localities in the British Isles. A graceful pine with spreading branches and drooping branchlets. Leaves in threes, 20-30cm long, conspicuously glaucous on very young plants, bright green later. Cones to 23cm long, solitary or in clusters, deflexed. Small plants in pots are excellent for conservatory decoration. Canary Isles.

†**caribaea** MORELET "Caribbean Pine". In the British Isles a small tree suitable only for the most sheltered positions in the mildest areas. Leaves in threes, occasionally in fours or fives, 15-23cm long, crowded at the ends of the branchlets. Cones to 10cm long. Bahamas to C America.

**cembra** L. "Arolla Pine". A small to medium-sized tree of characteristic, dense, conical or columnar habit in cultivation. Leaves in fives, 5-8cm long, densely crowded and of a dark blue-green with blue-white inner surfaces. Cones deep blue, to 8cm long, never opening, the seeds being liberated due to the scales rotting or by the attentions of squirrels or birds. An ornamental tree of almost formal aspect which has distinct landscape possibilities. Mountains of C Europe and N Asia. C 1746. AGM 1984.

**'Aureovariegata'** A pleasing form with yellow-tinged leaves. C 1865.

**'Jermyns'** An exceedingly slow-growing, compact bush of dwarf, conical habit, raised in our nurseries.

**'Stricta'** ('Columnaris') A columnar form with closely ascending branches. C 1855.

**cembroides** ZUCC. "Mexican Nut Pine". A small, short-stemmed tree or large bush with a dense, rounded head of branches. Leaves normally in threes, but varying from 2-5 on some trees, sickle-shaped, to 5cm long. Cones to 6cm long, containing large, edible seeds. S Arizona to Mexico.

**var. edulis** See *P. edulis*.

**var. monophylla** See *P. monophylla*.

†**chihuahuana** ENGELM. (*P. leiophylla* var. *chihuahuana* (ENGELM.) SHAW) A small to medium-sized, tender tree, closely related to *P. leiophylla*, and resembling it in most characters. Leaves in threes or fours, occasionally in pairs or fives, 7-10cm long. S Arizona and New Mexico.

‡**contorta** LOUD. "Beach Pine". A medium-sized to large tree, occasionally a large bush, with short branches. Leaves in pairs, to 5cm long, twisted and yellowish-green. Cones to 5cm long, occurring in pairs or clusters, the scales bearing a slender recurved spine. Not adaptable to chalky soils, but a suitable species for light stony or sandy land. It is a

**PINUS contorta**—*continued*

vigorous species, used for fixing sand-dunes in maritime areas. W North America. Introduced by David Douglas in 1831.

**subsp. latifolia** (ENGELM.) CRITCHFIELD "Lodgepole Pine". A medium-sized tree, less vigorous than the type and with slightly broader leaves 6-8.5cm long and larger cones. The common name derives from its use by the North American Indians as the central pole of their huts. Mountains of W North America. Introduced by John Jeffrey in about 1853.

**'Spaan's Dwarf'** ('Minima') A slow-growing dwarf form producing numerous upright and spreading shoots densely clothed with short, dark green leaves.

**coulteri** D. DON "Big-Cone Pine". A remarkable and striking tree of medium to large size with very stout shoots. Leaves in threes, to 30cm long, stiff and curved, pale bluish-grey-green. Cones very large and long-persistent, to 35cm long. The largest cones may weigh up to 2kg. S California, N Mexico. Discovered by Dr Coulter in 1832 and introduced by David Douglas in the same year. It was given an AM by the RHS when shown by us in 1961.

**culminicola** ANDRESEN & BEAMAN A small, slow-growing shrub of spreading habit. Leaves in fives, densely clustered, grey-green and up to 5cm long. This remarkable species was introduced to our nursery by Sir Harold Hillier from the high sierra near Saltillo, Mexico in 1979. There he found several thousand bushy plants on average 1-1.2m tall. It is proving perfectly hardy in cultivation. N Mexico.

‡**densiflora** SIEB. & ZUCC. "Japanese Red Pine". A medium-sized to large tree. Leaves in pairs, to 12cm long, twisted. Cones shortly-stalked, solitary or in clusters of 2 or 3, to 5cm long. It is the Japanese counterpart of our native Scots Pine and has similar reddish young bark. Japan. I 1852.

**'Oculus-draconis'** "Dragon-eye Pine". A curious form whose branches, when viewed from above, show alternate yellow and green rings, hence the name. C 1890.

**'Pendula'** A dwarf shrub with prostrate branches. C 1890.

**'Umbraculifera'** A miniature tree of extremely slow growth, with a dense umbrella-like head of branches, bearing tiny cones. Our largest specimen attained 2m × 2.4m in 30 years. C 1890.

‡**echinata** MILL. "Short-leaf Pine". A small to medium-sized tree with green, violet-flushed young shoots. Leaves usually in pairs, sometimes in threes or fours, to 13cm long, twisted, dark grey-green. Cones usually clustered, to 6cm long, normally remaining on the branches after the seeds have been shed. Best suited to well drained soils. E and SE United States. I 1739.

**edulis** ENGELM. (*P. cembroides* var. *edulis* (ENGELM.) VOSS) "Two-leaved Nut Pine". A small to medium-sized, compact tree in the wild related to *P. cembroides*. Leaves normally in pairs, occasionally in threes or single. Cones rounded, with large, edible seeds. SW United States. I 1848.

‡†**elliottii** ENGELM. "Slash Pine". A small tree in cultivation only suitable for the mildest areas of the British Isles. Young shoots orange-brown at first. Leaves in pairs or threes, to 25cm long, occasionally longer. Cones to 14cm long, the scales armed with a stout prickle. SE United States.

**excelsa** See *P. wallichiana*.

**flexilis** JAMES "Limber Pine". A medium-sized tree of conical outline. Leaves in fives, 3.5-7.5cm long, crowded towards the ends of the branches, entire, or almost so. Cones to 15cm long, spreading. Rocky Mts of W North America. I 1861.

**gerardiana** WALL. "Gerard's Pine". A rare, small tree in cultivation, its main attraction being the beautiful patchwork bark which is greyish-pink, flaking to reveal green, yellow and brown new bark. Leaves in threes, 5-10cm long. Cones to 20cm long. An extremely ornamental tree, allied to *P. bungeana* from which it mainly differs in its longer leaves and larger cones. NW Himalaya, Afghanistan. First discovered by Captain Gerard of the Bengal Native Infantry. Introduced by Lord Auckland in 1839.

**greggii** ENGELM. A medium-sized tree thriving best in a sheltered position. Leaves in threes, bright green, 7.5-15cm long. Cones ovoid-conic, shining creamy-brown, 8-15cm long, borne in reflexed clusters. A beautiful pine rendered conspicuous at all times of the year

**PINUS greggii**—*continued*

by the bright grass-green of the younger leaves. It has grown here for many years without winter damage. NE Mexico.

**griffithii** See *P. wallichiana*.

**halepensis** MILL. "Aleppo Pine". A medium-sized tree with glaucous, glabrous young shoots. Leaves in pairs, very distant, sparse, slightly twisted, 5-10cm long, bright fresh green. Cones deflexed, to 10cm long. Naturally found in warm, dry regions this species is suitable for maritime areas in the south. It will also grow on dry, shallow chalk soils. Mediterranean region, W Asia. C 1683.

**var. brutia** See *P. brutia*.

**hartwegii** LINDL. (*P. montezumae* var. *hartwegii* (LINDL.) ENGELM.) A large tree related to *P. montezumae*. Leaves green to grey-green in clusters of 3-5, to 15cm long. Cones very dark, to 16cm. It grows at higher altitudes than *P. montezumae* and is hardy. Mexico, C America.

× **holfordiana** A.B. JACKS. (*P. ayacahuite* var. *veitchii* × *P. wallichiana*). A large, fast-growing tree with wide-spreading branches. In leaf and cone characters it is close to *P. wallichiana* and resembles that species in general appearance. A most ornamental hybrid with its long, silvery-green leaves and long, banana-shaped, resin-flecked cones. Originated in the Westonbirt Arboretum about 1906. AM 1977.

× **hunnewellii** A.G. JOHNSON (*P. parviflora* × *P. strobus*). A vigorous, medium-sized tree of loose, open habit, similar in some respects to *P. strobus*, but with larger cones and hairy young shoots. Leaves 7.5-8.5cm long, grey-green. Originated in the Hunnewell Aboretum, Wellesley, Massachusetts in 1949.

**insignis** See *P. radiata*.

**jeffreyi** BALF. (*P. ponderosa* var. *jeffreyi* (BALF.) VASEY) A large, imposing tree with a conical or spire-like crown. Young shoots stout, glaucous. Leaves in threes, to 22cm long, dull bluish-green or pale grey, crowded towards the ends of the branchlets. Cones terminal and spreading, conical-ovoid, 13-20cm long, the scales with a slender recurved spine. Differs from *P. ponderosa* mainly in its black or purple-grey bark and its stouter, longer, bluish-green leaves which are invariably in threes. SW United States. I 1852, possibly earlier.

†**kesiya** ROYLE ex GORD. (*P. khasia* ROYLE) A small tree in cultivation, with pale brown young shoots. Leaves in threes, very slender, green or greyish-green, to 23cm long. Cones to 7.5cm long. A rare species only suitable for the mildest areas. SE Asia, Philippines.

**koraiensis** SIEB. & ZUCC. "Korean Pine". A medium-sized tree of loose, conical habit. Young shoots green, covered by a dense, reddish-brown pubescence. Leaves usually in fives, to 12cm long, stiff and rough to the touch, blue-green. Cones short-stalked, to 14cm long. Closely related to *P. cembra* from which it differs in its openly branched habit and its usually longer, more glaucous leaves which are toothed to the apex and possess 3 as against 2 resin canals. E Asia. Introduced by J.G. Veitch in 1861.

**'Compacta Glauca'** (*P. cembra* 'Compacta Glauca') A strong-growing, compact form with short, stout branches and attractive, densely-packed, conspicuously glaucous leaves. C 1949.

**'Winton'** A large, bushy form wider than high, with glaucous leaves. It possesses characters intermediate between the above species and *P. cembra*. The leaves are not toothed to the apex and the resin canals vary from 2 to 3. A specimen in our collection attained 2m × 4.5m in 30 years.

**lambertiana** DOUGL. "Sugar Pine". The largest of all pines, attaining a height of 75m or more in its native habitats. In the British Isles it is a medium-sized tree. Leaves in fives, to 14cm long, sharply-pointed and conspicuously twisted. Cones pendulous, to 50cm long (the longest in the genus). A sweet exudation from the heartwood has in the past been used as a substitute for sugar. Oregon and California. Introduced by David Douglas in 1827 and later by William Lobb in 1851.

‡‡**leiophylla** SCHL. & CHAM. "Smooth-leaved Pine". A small tree in the mildest areas of the British Isles. Young shoots glaucous. Leaves in fives, 7.5-10cm long, slender and greyish-green. Cones stalked, solitary or in clusters, ovoid, 4-6cm long. Mexico.

**PINUS**—*continued*

**leucodermis** ANT. (*P. heldreichii* var. *leucodermis* (ANT.) MARKG. & FITSCH.) "Bosnian Pine". A very distinct medium-sized tree with smooth greenish-grey bark, possessing a dense, ovoid habit. Young shoots glaucous. Leaves in pairs, to 9cm long, rigid and erect, dark almost black-green. Cones to 7.5cm long, bright blue the first year. Particularly suitable for dry soils and shallow soils over chalk. Italy, Balkan Peninsula. I 1864.

**'Compact Gem'** A very slow-growing, eventually medium-sized bush, of compact, rounded habit with dark green leaves. C 1964.

**'Pygmy'** See under 'Schmidtii'.

**'Satellit'** A narrowly conical form with the leaves densely clustered and pressed against the shoots on the young growths, later spreading. A seedling of Dutch origin.

**'Schmidtii'** A slow-growing, dwarf or small form developing into a dense, compact mound. Discovered in the wild by the late Mr Schmidt of Czechoslovakia. C 1952. Previously listed as 'Pygmy'.

**longaeva** BAILEY This species, only described in 1970, is closely related to *P. aristata* but it differs in its leaves which lack the white specks of resin present in that species. Specimens in the White Mountains of California have been proved to be up to 5,000 years old, the oldest living plants. California, Nevada and Utah. Both these species are known as "Bristlecone Pines".

**longifolia** See *P. palustris* and *P. roxburghii*.

‡†**luchuensis** MAYR. "Luchu Pine". A rare, small to medium-sized tree with characteristic smooth, greyish bark. Leaves in pairs, 15-20cm long. Cones ovoid-conic, 5cm long. Luchu Isles (Japan).

**maritima** POIR. See *P. pinaster*.

†**massoniana** LAMB. A small to medium-sized tree with reddish young bark and glabrous young shoots; winter buds conic-cylindric, resinous. Leaves in pairs, 14-20cm long, very slender. Cones ovoid, 3.5-6cm long. SE China, N Taiwan. I 1829.

†**michoacana** MARTINEZ. A small to medium-sized tree in the mildest areas of the British Isles, closely related to *P. montezumae*. Leaves in fives, 25-43cm long, spreading and drooping. Cones oblong-ovoid, 25-30cm long. Mexico.

**monophylla** TORR. & FREM. (*P. cembroides* var. *monophylla* (TORR. & FREM.) VOSS) "One-leaved Nut Pine". An unusual large shrub or small tree related to *P. cembroides*. Leaves borne singly or occasionally in pairs, stiff, glaucous green, up to 5cm long. Cones up to 8cm, with large, edible seeds. Hardy but best in a hot, dry position. SW United States to Mexico. I 1848.

**montana** See *P. mugo*.

**montezumae** LAMB. "Montezuma Pine". A magnificent, medium-sized to large tree with rough and deeply fissured bark and a large domed crown. Young shoots glabrous, stout, orange-brown; winter buds ovoid, pointed. Leaves usually in fives but varying from 3-8 on some trees, 18-25cm long, bluish-grey, spreading or drooping. Cones varying from ovoid-conic to cylindrical, 7.5-25cm long. A bold and imposing tree, hardy given reasonable shelter. Mts of Mexico. I 1839.

**var. hartwegii** See *P. hartwegii*.

†**var. lindleyi** LOUD. (*P. lindleyana* GORD.) A beautiful but more tender variety with slender, drooping, apple-green leaves, 15-25cm long, and pale brown cones.

**var. rudis** See *P. rudis*.

‡**monticola** D. DON "Western White Pine". A medium-sized to large tree of narrowly conical habit. Leaves in fives, to 10cm long, dark blue-green with white inner surface. Cones solitary or in clusters, to 25cm long, pendulous after the first year. W North America. I 1831.

**mugo** TURRA (*P. mughus* SCOP.) (*P. montana* MILL.) "Mountain Pine". A very hardy, large shrub or small tree of dense, bushy habit. Leaves in pairs, 3-4cm long, rigid and curved, dark green. Cones solitary or in clusters, to 6cm long. A variable species in the wild, all forms succeeding in almost all soils. Very lime-tolerant. Several of the smaller forms are excellent in association with heathers, whilst the dwarf, slow-growing cultivars are suitable for the rock garden or scree. Mts of C Europe.

**'Gnom'** A small, compact selection forming a dense, dark green, globular mound. C 1937.

**PINUS mugo**—*continued*

**'Humpy'** Very dwarf and slow-growing with very short needles. Raised in Holland and selected in 1970.

**'Mops'** Dwarf, globular bush of dense, slow growth. C 1951. AGM 1984.

**'Ophir'** A compact, bun-shaped dwarf with golden yellow winter foliage.

**var. pumilio** (HAENKE) ZEN. A dwarf form often prostrate, but occasionally reaching 2m. Alps of C Europe.

**var. rostrata** See *P. uncinata*.

**'Trompenburg'** A dwarf, spreading form making a dense, hemispherical mound about twice as broad as tall. Found as a seedling in the Trompenburg Arboretum.

**'Winter Gold'** A dwarf, spreading bush of open habit. Foliage golden yellow during winter.

‡**muricata** D. DON "Bishop Pine". A very picturesque, medium-sized to large tree forming a dense, rather flat head of branches. Leaves in pairs, to 15cm long, stiff and curved or twisted, dark bluish-grey or yellowish-grey-green. Cones solitary or in clusters, to 9cm long, often remaining unopened on the branches for many years. In the wild the cones have been known to remain intact for 30 or 40 years, the seeds eventually being liberated by forest fires. This species is suitable for exposed areas. California. I 1848.

**nigra** ARNOLD (*P. nigra* var. *austriaca* (HOESS) ASCHERS. & GRAEBN.) "Austrian Pine". A commonly planted and familiar large tree with rough, greyish-brown or dark brown bark and a dense head of large branches. Leaves in pairs, dark green, 8-12cm long, stiff and stout, densely crowded on the branchlets. Cones solitary or in clusters, to 8cm long. All forms of *P. nigra* are excellent for maritime areas and are tolerant of most soils. It thrives better than any other in chalky soils and in bleak exposures and makes an excellent wind-break. Europe, from Austria to C Italy, Greece and Yugoslavia. I by Messrs Lawson of Edinburgh in 1835. AGM 1984.

**var. calabrica** See subsp. *laricio*.

**var. caramanica** See subsp. *pallasiana*.

**var. cebennensis** See subsp. *salzmannii*.

**'Hornibrookiana'** A dwarf form of very slow growth. Originated from a Witches Broom on an Austrian Pine in Seneca Park, Rochester (United States) before 1932.

**subsp. laricio** (POIR.) MAIRE (*P. nigra* var. *calabrica* (LOUD.) SCHNEID.) (*P. nigra* var. *maritima* (AIT.) MELV.) "Corsican Pine". A large tree with a straight main stem to summit of crown, more open and with fewer, shorter, more level branches than the Austrian Pine. It also differs in the more slender and flexible, grey-green leaves which occur less densely and more spreading on the branchlets. The Corsican Pine is extensively used for forestry purposes and is happy in almost any soil or situation. The wood is used throughout the Mediterranean region, especially for general construction purposes. S Italy and Corsica. Introduced by Philip Miller in 1759.

**var. maritima** See subsp. *laricio*.

**subsp. pallasiana** (LAMB.) HOLMB. (*P. nigra* var. *caramanica* (LOUD.) REHD.) "Crimean Pine". A large tree of broad, conical habit, with usually many long, stout, erect branches; leaves to 18cm long. Cones to 10cm long. Rarer in cultivation than the Austrian Pine from which it mainly differs in its more compact, conical habit, longer, thicker leaves and usually larger cones. Balkan Peninsula, S Carpathians, Crimea, W Asia. I 1798.

**'Pygmaea'** See *P. sylvestris* 'Moseri'.

**subsp. salzmannii** (DUNAL) FRANCO (*P. nigra* var. *cebennensis* (GREN. & GODR.) REHD.) "Pyrenees Pine". A medium-sized tree with drooping branches forming a widely-spreading, low-domed crown. Leaves 10-15cm long, greyish-green, very slender and soft to the touch. Cones 4-6cm long. Cevennes, Pyrenees and C and E Spain. I 1834.

†**oaxacana** (MARTINEZ) MIROV (*P. pseudostrobus* var. *oaxacana*) A tender species related to *P. pseudostrobus* and sometimes regarded as a variety of it. Leaves 20-30cm long, cones 13-14cm long. Mexico.

†**oocarpa** SCHEIDE ex SCHLECHT. A rare and beautiful, small to medium-sized tree allied to *P. patula*. Young shoots glaucous. Leaves variable in number, in threes, fours or fives, to 30cm long, sea-green. Cones long-stalked, to 9cm long. A tender species only suitable for the very mildest areas. C America.

**PINUS**—*continued*

‡**palustris** MILL. (*P. longifolia* SALISB.) "Southern Pitch Pine". A low, erect-growing, small to medium-sized tree requiring a warm, moist soil. Young shoots stout, orange-brown. Leaves in threes, to 25cm long, up to 45cm long on young, vigorous plants, flexible, densely crowded on the branchlets. Cones cylindrical, to 25cm long, the scales with a reflexed spine. E United States. I 1730.

**parviflora** SIEB. & ZUCC. "Japanese White Pine". A small to medium-sized tree, conical when young, flat-topped in maturity. Leaves in fives, 5-7.5cm long, slightly curved, deep blue-green with blue-white inner surfaces. Cones solitary or in clusters, erect or spreading, 5-8cm long. This picturesque Japanese tree or large shrub is the pine of the "Willow Tree" pattern and is commonly cultivated in that country, particularly for bonsai purposes. Introduced by John Gould Veitch in 1861. AM 1977.

'**Adcock's Dwarf**' A slow-growing eventually medium-sized bush of rather compact, upright habit. Leaves 1.5-2.5cm long, greyish-green, produced in congested bunches at the tips of the shoots. A seedling raised in our Jermyns Lane Nursery in 1961, it has reached 2.5m tall and 1.3m across at the Hillier Gardens and Arboretum (1990). Named after our propagator, Graham Adcock.

'**Brevifolia**' A small tree with tight bunches of short, stiff, blue-green leaves. C 1900.

'**Tempelhof**' A vigorous form with glaucous blue foliage.

‡†**patula** SCHL. & CHAM. An extremely beautiful, small to medium-sized tree of graceful habit, with reddish bark, long spreading branches and pendulous, glaucous green, glabrous young shoots. Leaves bright green, usually in threes, occasionally in fours or fives, to 30cm long. Cones in clusters, curved, to 10cm long. An elegant species with gracefully drooping foliage. This lovely tree has grown uninjured in our nurseries for more than 30 years, but is not recommended for the coldest northern areas. Mexico.

‡**peuce** GRISEB. "Macedonian Pine". An attractive, medium-sized to large tree, recalling *P. cembra* in its narrowly conical habit. Young shoots shining green and glabrous. Leaves in fives, to 10cm long, deep blue-green with white inner surfaces, densely packed on the branchlets. Cones to 15cm long. Balkan Peninsula. I 1864.

**pinaster** AIT. (*P. maritima* POIR) "Maritime Pine" "Bournemouth Pine". Usually a sparsely-branched, medium-sized tree but occasionally a large tree with a bare stem and thick, reddish-brown or dark purple bark in small squares. Leaves in pairs, to 25cm long, rigid and curved, dull grey. Cones to 18cm long, rich shining brown, often remaining intact on the branches for several years.

An excellent species for sandy soils and seaside districts, particularly in the warmer parts of the British Isles. It is commonly planted along the South Coast, especially in the Bournemouth area. It is an important source of resin and the chief centre of the industry is in W France, from whence large quantities of turpentine and resin are distributed. W Mediterranean region. Cultivated since the 16th century.

**pinea** L. "Umbrella Pine" "Stone Pine". A very distinct tree of small to medium size developing a characteristic dense, flat-topped or umbrella-shaped head. Leaves in pairs, to 15cm long, stiff and slightly twisted, sharply-pointed. Cones stalked, to 15cm long, shining nut-brown. Seeds large and edible. A picturesque pine particularly suitable for sandy soils and maritime areas. Mediterranean region.

**ponderosa** LAWSON. 'Western Yellow Pine'. A large tree of striking appearance with usually a tall, clear trunk, scaly cinnamon bark and stout, spreading or drooping branches. Young shoots stout, orange-brown or greenish, glabrous. Leaves in threes, to 25cm long, stiff and curved, spreading and crowded at the ends of the branchlets. Cones to 16cm long, the scales armed with a small spine. A variable species with several named varieties. W North America. Introduced by David Douglas in 1826. AM 1980.

**var. arizonica** See *P. arizonica*.

**var. jeffreyi** See *P. jeffreyi*.

**subsp. scopulorum** (S. WATS.) WEBER A form with usually drooping branches, shorter leaves 7.5-15cm long, and smaller cones, to 7.5cm long. Dakota, Nebraska and E Wyoming.

‡†**pseudostrobus** LINDL. A tender tree of small to medium size, only suitable for the mildest areas of the British Isles. Young shoots glaucous. Leaves usually in fives, apple-green, to

**PINUS pseudostrobus**—*continued*

25cm long, pendulous. Cones to 14cm long. It is closely allied to *P. montezumae*, differing in its glaucous shoots and smooth bark. Mexico, C America. I 1839.

**var. oaxacana** See *P. oaxacana*.

‡**pumila** (PALL.) REG. (*P. cembra* var. *pumila* PALL.) "Dwarf Siberian Pine". Variable in habit, usually a dwarf shrub of spreading growth, occasionally a dense, medium-sized or large bush. Leaves in fives, to 7 or occasionally 10cm long, blue-white on the inner surfaces, densely bundled and crowding the branchlets. Cones 5cm long. Closely related to *P. cembra* and often difficult to distinguish from dwarf forms of that species. *P. pumila* and its forms are excellent conifers for the heather garden and the large rock garden. Widely distributed in E Asia, usually growing in cold, exposed places high in the mountains. I about 1807.

**'Compacta'** A small shrub up to 2m of dense, erect, bushy habit; the branches crowded with large bunches of glaucous leaves. Very effective on a large rock garden or border edge.

‡**pungens** MICHX. f. "Hickory Pine". A small to medium-sized tree, often of bushy habit, with thick, reddish-brown bark. Leaves in pairs or occasionally in threes, to 7.5cm long, rigid and twisted, sharply-pointed, densely crowded on the branchlets. Cones to 9cm long, often remaining intact on the tree for several years. E North America. I 1804.

‡**radiata** D. DON (*P. insignis* DOUGL. ex LOUD.) "Monterey Pine". A large tree with deeply fissured, dark brown bark and a dense head of branches. Leaves in threes, to 15cm long, bright green, densely crowded on the branchlets. Cones to 15cm long, borne in whorls along the branches, often remaining intact for many years. An attractive, rapid-growing tree for mild inland and coastal areas. Excellent for withstanding sea winds. Monterey Peninsula (California). Introduced by David Douglas in 1833. AGM 1984.

‡**resinosa** AIT. "Red Pine". Small to medium-sized tree of rather heavy appearance, with a broad, conical head of branches. Leaves in pairs, 12-18cm long, slender and flexible. Cones to 6cm long. An important timber tree in North America. E Canada, NE United States. C 1736.

‡**rigida** MILL. "Northern Pitch Pine". A medium-sized tree with strongly ridged young shoots. Leaves in threes, to 10cm long, thick, stiff and spreading. Cones usually in clusters, to 9cm long. A peculiarity of this species is the tendency to produce tufts of leaves on the trunk. E North America. C 1759.

†**roxburghii** SARG. (*P. longifolia* ROXB. ex LAMB.) " Long-leaved Indian Pine". A small tree in cultivation closely related to *P. canariensis*. Young shoots clothed with scale-like leaves. Leaves in threes, to 35cm long, light green. Cones to 20cm long, borne on short, stout stalks. A rare species, only suitable for the milder areas of the British Isles. Himalaya. I 1807.

**rudis** ENDL. (*P. montezumae* var. *rudis* (ENDL.) SHAW) A medium-sized tree related to *P. montezumae* with dark, fissured bark. Leaves generally 5 or 6 in a cluster, 10-15cm long, grey-green and spreading from the shoot. Cones up to 13cm long, bluish-black when young becoming dark brown. It is hardier than *P. montezumae*. Mts of Mexico.

**sabiniana** DOUGL. "Digger Pine". A remarkable pine, related to *P. coulteri*. A medium-sized tree usually of gaunt open habit, with straggly branches. Leaves in threes, to 30cm long, spreading or drooping, glaucous green, sparsely arranged on the branchlets. Cones to 25cm long. The edible seeds were once an important article of food for the American Indians. California. Introduced by David Douglas in 1832.

‡ × **schwerinii** FITSCH. (*P. strobus* × *P. wallichiana*). A large tree resembling *P. wallichiana* in general appearance. Leaves in fives, to 13cm long, loose and pendulous, glaucous green. Cones slightly curved, to 15cm long. It differs from *P. wallichiana* mainly in its densely hairy shoots and shorter leaves. An attractive hybrid which originated on the estate of Dr Graf von Schwerin, near Berlin, in 1905.

‡**strobus** L. "Weymouth Pine" "White Pine". A large tree of conical habit when young, later developing a rounded head. Leaves in fives, to 15cm long, somewhat glaucous green. Cones to 20cm long, pendent on slender stalks liberally flecked with resin. Once the most commonly planted of the five-needled pines, due to its ornamental habit and fast growth. It owes its English name to Lord Weymouth, who made extensive plantings of

**PINUS strobus**—*continued*

this species at Longleat, Wiltshire, in the early 1700s. E North America. Cultivated since the mid 16th century.

**'Compacta'** A dwarf, slow-growing bush of dense habit.

**'Contorta'** ('Tortuosa') A curious form, developing twisted branches and densely set, conspicuously twisted leaves. C 1932.

**'Densa'** A dwarf bush of dense habit. Similar to 'Nana'.

**'Fastigiata'** An erect-branched form of conical or broadly columnar habit. C 1884.

**'Nana'** A small form developing into a dense bush. There are several slight variations of this form, some of which are more vigorous and larger-growing.

**'Nivea'** An attractive form in which the glaucous leaves are tipped milky-white, giving the whole tree an unusual silver-white colour.

**'Pendula'** A form with long, drooping branches.

**'Prostrata'** A remarkable prostrate form, the branches lying flat on the ground or shortly ascending and forming a low mound. Originally found by Alfred Rehder in the Arnold Arboretum. C 1893.

**sylvestris** L. "Scots Pine". Our only native pine. A familiar tree usually seen as a large, tall-stemmed and, occasionally, a low, picturesque, spreading tree. It is easily recognised by its characteristic and attractive, reddish young bark. Leaves in pairs, 3-10cm long, twisted, grey-green or blue-green. Cones to 7.5cm long, on short stalks.

A common tree which combines beauty with utility. In the British Isles, truly wild stands of this species may only be found in parts of N Scotland, but it was once found naturally throughout England and Wales. Due to extensive planting in the past it has become naturalised in many areas, particularly on heaths and moors. There are numerous geographical variants of which our native form is var. *scotica*. Many garden forms have arisen, several of which are suitable for the rock garden. The Scots Pine may be grown in all types of soil but does not reach its maximum proportions or maximum age either in damp acid soils or shallow dry chalk soils. AGM 1984.

**'Argentea'** See 'Edwin Hillier'.

**'Aurea'** A slow-growing, small tree with leaves of a striking golden yellow in winter. AM 1964. AGM 1984.

**'Beuvronensis'** This miniature Scots Pine forms a small, compact, dome-shaped shrublet. A superb subject for the rock garden. C 1891. AM 1968. AGM 1984.

**'Compressa'** A dwarf bush of conical habit, with short, crowded, glaucous leaves. C 1867.

**'Doone Valley'** A dwarf form of compact, somewhat conical habit. Leaves glaucous. Named after "Doone Valley", the one-time garden of Mr W. Archer.

**'Edwin Hillier'** A beautiful form selected by Edwin Hillier with silvery-blue-green leaves and reddish stems. Previously listed as 'Argentea', it has no connection with f. *argentea* STEVEN described from the Caucasus.

**'Fastigiata'** A remarkable Scots Pine, the shape of a Lombardy Poplar. C 1856.

**var. lapponica** FRIES A geographical variety, usually developing a narrow head of branches. Lapland, C and N Scandinavia, N Finland.

**'Moseri'** A very slow-growing, miniature tree of dense, globular or ovoid shape, the leaves turning yellow or yellow-green in winter. Previously listed as *P. nigra* 'Pygmaea'. C 1900.

**'Nana'** Dwarf, bushy form of slow growth; differing from the very similar 'Beuvronensis' in its non-resinous winter buds. C 1855.

**'Pumila'** See 'Watereri'.

**'Pygmaea'** A rare, slow-growing, dwarf form of dense, rounded habit. C 1891.

**var. rigensis** ASCH. & GRAEBN. A geographical form with a slender trunk and a conical head of branches. Baltic Coast.

**'Viridis Compacta'** Dwarf bush of conical habit, superficially resembling a dwarf form of *P. nigra*, with its long, vivid, grass-green leaves. C 1923.

**'Watereri'** ('Pumila') A slow-growing, medium-sized bush or rarely a small tree, conical in habit at first, later becoming rounded. It is suitable for the heather garden, but eventually becomes too large for the normal rock garden. Found on Horsell Common,

**PINUS sylvestris 'Watereri'**—*continued*

Surrey, by Mr Anthony Waterer in about 1865. The original plant in the Knap Hill Nursery is about 8m high.

**'Windsor'** Dwarf, bun-shaped form of slow growth. Leaves very small, greyish-green. Originated as a Witches Broom.

**tabuliformis** CARR. (*P. sinensis* MAYR. not LAMB.) "Chinese Pine". An uncommon species, usually a small to medium-sized flat-headed tree in cultivation. Leaves in pairs or threes, 10-15cm long, densely crowding the branchlets. Cones to 6.5cm long. N China. C 1862.

**var. yunnanensis** See *P. yunnanensis*.

**taeda** L. "Loblolly Pine". A small to medium-sized tree with glabrous and glaucous young shoots. Leaves in threes, to 25cm long, slender and flexible and slightly twisted. Cones to 10cm long. Suitable for southern and drier parts of the British Isles. S and E United States. A distinct and effective tree which should be in every pinetum. I 1741.

**†taiwanensis** HAYATA A rare tree of small to medium size; leaves in pairs. Only suitable for the conservatory or sheltered sites in mild areas. Taiwan.

**thunbergii** PARL. "Black Pine". A distinct and splendid large tree with stout, twisted branches. Leaves in pairs, 7-18cm long, rigid and twisted. Cones to 6cm long, borne singly or in large clusters. The Black Pine is one of the most important timber trees in Japan, where it often occurs by the seashore. In the British Isles it is useful as a wind-break in maritime areas and for growing in poor, sandy soils. Japan, Korea. I 1852.

**'Globosa'** ('Compacta') A dense-growing large bush.

**'Oculus-draconis'** An unusual form in which the leaves are marked with two yellowish bands.

**†torreyana** PARRY ex CARR. A small tree or a gnarled bush, sometimes prostrate in the wild. Leaves in fives, 20-30cm long, borne in dense bunches at the ends of the branchlets. Cones to 13cm long, stalked. Seeds sweet and edible. Only suitable for the milder, drier areas of the British Isles. S California. I 1853.

**tuberculata** See *P. attenuata*.

**uncinata** MIRBEL (*P. mugo* var. *rostrata* (ANT.) HOOPES) "Mountain Pine". A medium-sized tree, closely related to *P. mugo*, differing in both its habit and its larger cones, 5-7cm long. A splendid dense, bushy, broadly conical tree for creating shelter against the coldest winds. Succeeding in all types of soil including shallow chalk soils. Pyrenees to E Alps.

**‡virginiana** MILL. "Scrub Pine". Small to medium-sized tree with purplish, bloomy young shoots. Leaves in pairs, to 6cm long, stiff and twisted. Cones to 7cm long, the scales ending in a short, recurved prickle. It dislikes shallow, chalk soils. E United States. I 1739.

**wallichiana** A.B. JACKS. (*P. griffithii* MCCLELLAND not PARL.) (*P. excelsa* WALL. ex D. DON not LAMB.) "Bhutan Pine". An elegant, large, broad-headed tree, retaining its lowest branches when isolated. Leaves in fives, to 20cm long, blue-green, slender and drooping with age. Cones stalked, solitary or in bunches, banana-shaped, 15-25cm long. A most attractive species with its graceful foliage and ornamental, resin-smeared, pendulous cones. Moderately lime-tolerant but not recommended for shallow chalk soils. Temperate Himalaya. I about 1823. AM 1979. AGM 1984.

**'Nana'** See under 'Umbraculifera'.

**'Umbraculifera'** A small, dome-shaped, glaucous bush of slow growth and dense habit. Previously listed as 'Nana'.

**'Zebrina'** Leaves with a creamy-yellow band below the apex. C 1889.

**‡washoensis** MASON & STOCKWELL A rare, medium-sized tree allied to *P. jeffreyi* from which it differs mainly in its smaller leaves, 10-15cm long, and smaller cones, 5-7.5cm long. Nevada and California.

**yunnanensis** FRANCH. (*P. tabuliformis* var. *yunnanensis* (FRANCH.) SHAW) A medium-sized tree related to *P. tabuliformis* and differing in its stout, glabrous, shining pink shoots, its longer, more slender and drooping leaves, 20-30cm long, borne usually in threes, and in the larger, darker brown cones up to 9cm long. A very distinct, rather sparsely-branched tree creating the effect of *P. montezumae*. W China. I 1909 by Ernest Wilson.

**\*PODOCARPUS** L'HERIT. ex PERS.—**Podocarpaceae**—A genus of some 90 or so species of evergreen trees and shrubs mainly confined in the wild to the S hemisphere in warm temperate and tropical countries. Leaves are variable in shape, usually spirally arranged. Fruits consist of a fleshy, coloured, usually red, receptacle in which the seed is inserted. Several species are suitable for the milder areas of the British Isles and a few may be classed as hardy. They succeed in most types of soil whether acid or alkaline. It has recently been proposed that *Podocarpus* be divided into several genera.

**acutifolius** KIRK "Needle-leaved Totara". A small to medium-sized, moderately hardy shrub usually of dense, prickly habit. Leaves linear, 1-2.5cm long, sharply-pointed, bronze-green. Although it reaches small tree size in its native habitat it remains dense and slow-growing in cultivation and, as such, is an interesting plant for a prominent position on the large rock garden. This plant has grown successfully on the scree at the Hillier Gardens and Arboretum for many years. New Zealand (S Island).

**alpinus** HOOK. f. A remarkably hardy, dwarf species, forming a low, densely-branched mound or a creeping carpet extending 1-2m or more across, sometimes a small bush of upright or pendulous habit. Leaves yew-like, narrow, blue or grey-green, crowding the stems. Suitable for the rock garden or as ground cover. In its native habitat it is often found on stony mountain sides and helps to prevent erosion. SE Australia, Tasmania.

**andinus** ENDL. (*Prumnopitys elegans* PHIL.) (*Prumnopitys andina* (POEP. & ENDL.) DE LAUB.) "Plum-fruited Yew" "Chilean Yew". A small to medium-sized tree or large shrub somewhat resembling a yew in habit. Leaves linear, 1-2.5cm long, bright green above, twisted to reveal the glaucous green undersurface. Fruits like small damsons, glaucous black, borne on slender scaly stalks. This species grows excellently on good soils over chalk. It is a native of the Andes of S Chile and was introduced by Robert Pearce for Messrs Veitch in 1860. FCC 1864.

**chilinus** See *P. salignus*.

**cunninghamii** See *P. hallii*.

**†dacrydioides** A. RICH. (*Dacrycarpus dacrydioides* (A. RICH.) DE LAUB.) "Kahikatea" "White Pine". An extremely beautiful small tree in the mildest areas of the British Isles, but reaching 45m and above in its native habitat. The long, slender, gracefully drooping branchlets are clothed with small, narrow, bronze-green, two-ranked leaves, which on young trees are scale-like, spirally-arranged on older trees. An elegant species which makes an attractive conservatory specimen. New Zealand.

**†elatus** R. BR. A small to medium-sized tree of elegant habit, its branches clothed with narrowly oblong, bright green leaves varying from 5-15cm long, or longer on young vigorous specimens. Only possible in the mildest areas, but suitable for the conservatory. SE Australia.

**†falcatus** (THUNB.) R. BR. ex MIRB. (*Nageia falcata* (THUNB.) O. KUNTZE) A small to medium-sized tree; leaves long and narrow, variable in length and arrangement, up to 13cm long on young plants. Suitable only for the mildest areas or for the conservatory. S Africa.

**†ferrugineus** D. DON (*Prumnopitys ferruginea* (D. DON) DE LAUB.) "Miro". A graceful small tree. Leaves rather yew-like in shape but a softer yellow-green, arranged in irregular ranks along the slender branches which are pendulous at their extremities. This rare and attractive species is doing well in the beautiful garden made by Mrs Vera Mackie at Helen's Bay, N Ireland. Native of New Zealand where it is an important timber tree.

**†gracilior** PILGER An attractive and elegant, small to medium-sized tree with willow-like leaves, up to 10cm long on young plants. An important timber tree in its native land. Only suitable for the mildest gardens in the British Isles or the conservatory. E Africa.

**†hallii** KIRK (*P. totara* var. *hallii* (KIRK) PILGER) (*P. cunninghamii* COL.) A small tree or large, bushy shrub, related and similar to *P. totara*, but differing in its longer leaves, 2.5-5cm on young plants, and its thin, papery, peeling bark. There is a good specimen growing very well at Castlewellan in that splendid pinetum planted by Mr Gerald Annesley in N Ireland. New Zealand.

**'Aureus'** See *P. totara* 'Aureus'.

**‡macrophyllus** (THUNB.) D. DON "Kusamaki". One of the hardiest species, forming a shrub or small tree of very distinct appearance. Leaves 10-13cm long, up to 18cm on vigorous plants, 12mm wide, bright green above, glaucous beneath, arranged in dense spirals on

**PODOCARPUS macrophyllus**—*continued*
the stems. Not suitable for chalky soils. It has withstood 28 degrees of frost here. Native of China and of Japan where it is occasionally grown as an unusual and effective hedge.
**'Angustifolius'** A form with narrower leaves. C 1864.
**'Argenteus'** A slow-growing form, its narrower leaves with an irregular white border. C 1861. FCC 1865.
†**nagi** (THUNB.) MAKINO (*Nageia nagi* (THUNB.) O. KUNTZE) A small, slow-growing tree or large, bushy shrub. Leaves opposite or nearly so, ovate or broadly lanceolate, 4-5cm long, leathery, dark green above, paler below. Not hardy enough to survive long in the Home Counties. Japan, China, Taiwan.
**nivalis** HOOK. f. "Alpine Totara". One of the hardiest species succeeding throughout the British Isles and doing well in chalky soils. Normally seen as a low, spreading mound of shortly erect and prostrate stems, densely branched and crowded with small, narrow, leathery, olive-green leaves, 6-20mm long. An excellent ground cover. A large plant growing in shade in the Bedgebury Pinetum, Kent, formed a carpet 2-3m across. Native of New Zealand where it is found on mountain slopes.
**'Bronze'** ('Aureus') Leaves bronze-tinged, more noticeable in the young growths.
**nubigenus** LINDL. A distinct, slow-growing, beautiful shrub rarely reaching the size of a small tree. The usually spirally-arranged, sharply-pointed, narrow leaves are 3.5-4.5cm long, deep green above and glaucous beneath. Here injured only in the coldest winters. Mts of Chile, Patagonia, Valdivia and Chiloe.
†**salignus** D. DON (*P. chilinus* RICH.) A most attractive and elegant, small tree or large shrub, with drooping branches and long, narrow, bright grey-green leaves, 5-15cm long. A well-grown specimen creates an almost tropical effect with its lush piles of glossy evergreen, willow-like foliage. Hardy in the South-West when given the shelter of other evergreens. Chile.
†**spicatus** MIRBEL (*Prumnopitys spicata* (MIRB.) MAST.) The "Matai" or "Black Pine" of New Zealand. An interesting small tree in the mildest areas of the British Isles. Young trees possess numerous, slender, drooping branches and branchlets, towards the tips of which occur the small, narrow, bronze-tinted leaves.
†**totara** D. DON A tall tree in New Zealand, but usually a slow-growing large shrub in this country. Leaves yellowish-green, scattered or two-ranked, up to 2cm long on adult plants, 2.5cm long on young plants, leathery, stiff and sharply-pointed. Correctly sited among sheltering evergreens this unusual shrub is more or less hardy in the Home Counties.
**'Aureus'** (*P. hallii* 'Aureus') Leaves yellow-green.
**var. hallii** See *P. hallii.*

**PRUMNOPITYS elegans** See *Podocarpus andinus.*

‡**PSEUDOLARIX** GORDON—**Pinaceae**—A monotypic genus differing from *Larix* in several small botanical characters. The linear leaves, which are borne in dense clusters on short spurs on the older wood, are spirally-arranged on the young shoots. Male and female strobili are borne on the same tree. It requires a lime-free soil.
**amabilis** (NELSON) REHD. (*P. fortunei* MAYR) (*P. kaempferi* AUCT. not (LINDL.) GORD.) "Golden Larch". A beautiful and very hardy, slow-growing, deciduous, medium-sized tree of broadly conical habit. The long, larch-like, light green leaves, 3-6cm long, turn a clear golden yellow in autumn. Cones ripening the first year. On a large tree they stud the long, slender branches, resembling small, pale green artichokes, bloomy when young, reddish-brown when ripe. S China. I by Robert Fortune in 1852. AM 1976.

‡**PSEUDOTSUGA** CARR.—**Pinaceae**—A small genus of 4 or more species of evergreen trees of broadly conical habit, with whorled branches and spindle-shaped buds recalling those of the Common Beech, natives of E Asia, W North America and Mexico. The leaves are linear, soft to the touch and marked with 2 glaucous, stomatic bands beneath. Male and female strobili are borne on the same tree. Cones pendulous, ripening in one season. The members of this genus may be distinguished from *Abies* by the pendulous

**PSEUDOTSUGA**—*continued*

cones which fall intact, and from *Picea* by the three-lobed cone-bracts. The majority of species dislike chalky soils, thriving best in moist, but well drained soils. *P. menziesii* is of great economic importance.

**douglasii** See *P. menziesii*.

**glauca** See *P. menziesii* var. *glauca*.

**japonica** (SHIRASAWA) BEISSN. The "Japanese Douglas Fir" is rare in cultivation and makes a small, bushy tree. Leaves to 2.5cm long, notched, pale green, arranged on the branchlets in 2 ranks. Cones to 5cm long. Distinguished from other species by its glabrous shoots, smaller cones and shorter leaves. SE Japan. I 1898. AM 1984.

**macrocarpa** (TORR.) MAYR "Large-coned Douglas Fir". A rare, medium-sized tree with the young shoots reddish-brown. Leaves to 3cm long, arranged on the branchlets in 2 ranks. Cones 10-18cm long, the largest in the genus. Native of S California. There is a specimen 16m tall in the Hillier Gardens and Arboretum (1990). Introduced by H. Clinton-Baker in 1910.

**menziesii** (MIRB.) FRANCO (*P. taxifolia* (LAMB.) SUDW.) (*P. douglasii* (LINDL.) CARR.) "Oregon Douglas Fir". A fast-growing, large tree. The lower branches of large specimens are down-swept and the bark thick, corky and deeply furrowed. Leaves to 3cm long, arranged on the branchlets in 2, usually horizontal ranks, fragrant when crushed. Cones to 10cm long, with conspicuous exserted bracts. This well-known conifer is an important timber tree both here and in North America. It is one of the stateliest conifers, being particularly effective when planted in groups, as in the New Forest and at Knightshayes Court in Devon. It is unsatisfactory on chalk soils. It is a native of W North America, reaching its finest proportions in Washington and British Columbia where specimens of 90m and above are recorded. It was originally discovered by Archibald Menzies in about 1792 and introduced by David Douglas in 1827. AM 1984.

**'Brevifolia'** A small, shrubby form, occasionally a miniature tree up to 2m, with leaves only 6-15mm long, densely spreading all round the shoots. It differs from the similar 'Fretsii' in its narrower leaves, and is less lime-tolerant. FCC 1886.

**var. caesia** (SCHWERIN) FRANCO "Fraser River Douglas Fir" or "Grey Douglas Fir". Differs in its slower growth and grey-green leaves which are arranged in 2 ranks, with a V-shaped parting above. Because of its extreme hardiness it has been used for afforestation purposes in Finland and similar Arctic climates. It is found wild in British Columbia.

**'Densa'** Dwarf, slow-growing, shrubby form of dense habit, with spreading branches and green leaves to 2cm long. C 1933.

**'Elegans'** See under 'Glauca Pendula'.

**'Fletcheri'** (*P. glauca* 'Fletcheri') A slow-growing, shrubby form developing into an irregular, flat-topped, globular bush, eventually reaching 1.5-2m in height. Leaves blue-green, 2-2.5cm long, loosely arranged. Originated as a seedling of var. *glauca* in 1906. AM 1912.

**'Fretsii'** An unusual, slow-growing form. The short, broad, obtuse leaves, 10-12mm long, resemble those of a *Tsuga*, but the arrangement is radial. Specimens in our nurseries at 30 years made irregular bushes about 1.2m high by 1.8m across. More lime-tolerant than 'Brevifolia'. The colour of the leaves suggests kinship with var. *caesia*. C 1905.

**var. glauca** (MAYR) FRANCO (*P. glauca* (MAYR) MAYR) "Blue Douglas Fir". A medium-sized tree of narrow conical habit. Leaves shorter, glaucous above, smelling of turpentine when crushed. Cones 6-7.5cm long, the bracts reflexed. Hardier but slower and more lime-tolerant. Native of the Rocky Mountains, from Montana to N Mexico.

**'Glauca Pendula'** A small, weeping tree of graceful habit. Branchlets ascending, clothed with bluish-green leaves, 3-5cm long. C 1891. FCC 1895. We have received plants under the name 'Elegans' which appear identical with this clone.

**'Holmstrup'** A small to medium-sized shrub or miniature tree of rather compact, upright habit, with green leaves to 1.5cm long, densely and radially arranged on the branchlets.

**'Nana'** (*P. glauca* 'Nana') Small to medium-sized bush, conical when young. Leaves 2-2.5cm long, glaucous-green, almost radial. Originated as a seedling of var. *glauca*, in 1915.

**'Pendula'** An unusual form with weeping branches, a clone of var. *caesia*. C 1868.

**639**

**PSEUDOTSUGA**—*continued*

**sinensis** DODE A small tree in cultivation, with reddish-brown, young shoots. Leaves to 3.5cm long, notched at apex, arranged in 2 ranks. Cones to 5cm long. This rare, slow-growing species is susceptible to damage by spring frost. SW China. I 1912.

**taxifolia** See *P. menziesii*.

**"REDWOOD"** See *Sequoia sempervirens*.

**RETINISPORA** ZUCC. (*Retinospora* SIEB. & ZUCC.) An obsolete generic name which was at one time used to cover those forms of *Chamaecyparis* with permanently juvenile (awl-shaped) foliage.

**\*SAXEGOTHAEA** LINDL.—**Podocarpaceae**—A monotypic genus resembling *Podocarpus andinus* in general appearance. The branchlets are arranged in whorls of 3 or 4. Male and female strobili borne on the same plant. The genus is named in honour of Prince Albert, consort of Queen Victoria, after the Prussian province from which he came. It forms a connecting link between Podocarpaceae and Araucariaceae, resembling a *Podocarpus* in foliage and an *Araucaria* in the female strobili. It occurs in dense forests in Chile and Patagonia.

**conspicua** LINDL. "Prince Albert's Yew". An unusual large shrub or small tree of loose habit, with laxly spreading branches and drooping branchlets. Leaves linear, 1.5-2cm long, dark green above, marked with 2 glaucous bands beneath, rather twisted and arranged on the lateral branches in 2 ranks. Fruits 12-20mm across, soft and prickly. An attractive conifer and botanically very interesting. Introduced by William Lobb in 1847.

**‡\*SCIADOPITYS** SIEB. & ZUCC.—**Taxodiaceae**—A monotypic genus of unique appearance. Thriving in a lime-free soil, it should be planted in every representative collection of conifers. It does well in partial shade.

**verticillata** SIEB. & ZUCC. "Umbrella Pine". A slow-growing, very hardy, monoecious tree of medium size. Dense and conical when young usually with a single trunk, sometimes with several main stems. Bark peeling to reveal the reddish-brown new bark. Branches horizontal, bearing lush clusters of rich, glossy green foliage. The apparent single linear leaves, up to 13cm long, are, in fact, fused pairs and are arranged in characteristic dense whorls like the spokes of an umbrella, hence the English name. The attractive cones, 6-10cm long, are green at first, ripening to brown the second year. Native of Japan where it is restricted in the wild to 2 small areas in C Honshu. First introduced as a single plant by Thomas Lobb in 1853, later more successfully by both Robert Fortune and J. G. Veitch in 1861. AM 1979.

**\*SEQUOIA** ENDL.—**Taxodiaceae**—A well-known monotypic genus named after Sequoiah (1770-1843), a Cherokee half-breed of Georgia, who invented the Cherokee alphabet. An interesting character is that the butt of a felled tree will produce a sheaf of suckers, which is unusual in a conifer. Given 60cm depth of soil, it will succeed in chalk areas.

**gigantea** See *Sequoiadendron giganteum*.

**sempervirens** (D. DON) ENDL. (*Taxodium sempervirens* D. DON) "Californian Redwood". A very large, evergreen, monoecious tree, reaching over 100m tall in its native forests, possessing a thick, fibrous, reddish-brown outer bark which is soft and spongy. Branches slightly drooping, yew-like, bearing two-ranked, linear-oblong leaves, 1-2cm long, dark green above, marked with 2 white stomatic bands beneath. Leaves on leading shoots and fertile shoots smaller and spirally arranged. Cones pendulous, ovoid to globose, 2-3cm long, ripening the first season.

This majestic tree is a native of California and Oregon where it is found on the seaward side of the coastal mountain range. It was first discovered by Archibald Menzies in 1794 and first introduced into Europe (St Petersburg) in 1840. Three years later Hartweg sent seed to England. The Redwood has the distinction of being the world's tallest living tree, the record at present being held by the "Harry Cole" tree in the

**SEQUOIA sempervirens**—*continued*

Humbolt State Redwood Park which, in 1988, measured 113m (371ft). The tallest tree ever recorded was a specimen of *Eucalyptus regnans* in Victoria, SE Australia estimated to have been more than 150m in 1872. The tallest Redwood in the British Isles is found at Bodnant and measured 47m (153ft) in 1984. It is also a long-lived tree, the average age being 500-700 years. Several trees have reached 2,000 years and the oldest known specimen, felled in 1934, was dated at 2,200 years.

**'Adpressa'** ('Albospica') The tips of the young shoots are creamy-coloured, and the short leaves regularly disposed in one plane. It is often grown as a dwarf shrub but unless frequently cut back will eventually make a large tree. C 1867. FCC 1890.

**'Cantab'** A remarkable form with the distinctive foliage of 'Prostrata' but making a strong-growing tree. Occasionally originates when 'Prostrata' produces vigorous, upright shoots. A specimen in the Hillier Gardens and Arboretum has reached 12.5m (1990).

**'Prostrata'** A most remarkable dwarf form with spreading branches thickly clothed with comparatively broad, glaucous green, two-ranked leaves. Originated as a branch sport on a tree at the University Botanic Garden, Cambridge. See also 'Cantab'. C 1951. AM 1951.

**wellingtonia** See *Sequoiadendron giganteum*.

**\*SEQUOIADENDRON** BUCHHOLZ—**Taxodiaceae**—A monotypic genus, once included under *Sequoia*, differing in its naked winter buds, awl-shaped leaves and larger cones, ripening during the second year. It is quite hardy and reasonably lime-tolerant but will not succeed on thin chalky soils.

**giganteum** (LINDL.) BUCHHOLZ (*Sequoia gigantea* (LINDL.) DECNE.) (*Sequoia wellingtonia* SEEM.) "Wellingtonia" "Mammoth Tree". The "Big Tree" of California attains a very large size. The deeply furrowed, reddish-brown outer bark is similar to that of *Sequoia sempervirens* in texture. As a young tree it develops a densely-branched, conical habit. On older trees the branches are more widely spaced and conspicuously down-swept. Sometimes the lower part of the trunk is clear of branches for several metres, revealing the ornamental bark. Leaves awl-shaped, 6-12mm long, bright green, spirally arranged, persisting for up to 4 years. Cones ovoid, 5-7.5cm long, green at first maturing to reddish-brown the second year. It is a familiar tree of parks and estates and resembles no other hardy cultivated conifer, except perhaps *Cryptomeria japonica* which has similar leaves and similarly coloured bark. I 1853. AGM 1984.

It is a native of California where it grows on the western slopes of the Sierra Nevada. Although never as tall as the "Redwood", in its native state it attains a greater girth and the "General Sherman" tree, with a height of 84m (275ft), a girth of 25m (82ft) at 1.4m, and a total trunk volume of 1400m³ (50,000 cubic feet), is generally acknowledged to be the world's largest living thing. It is estimated to weigh 2,500 tonnes and be up to 3,000 years old. Specimens of 30m and above are not uncommon in the British Isles, among the tallest was one at Endsleigh, Devon which, in 1970, measured 49m (165ft), with a girth (at 1.5m or 5ft) of 6.71m (22ft). The Wellingtonia is regarded as one of the oldest living things in the world (see also *Pinus longaeva*). The oldest authenticated age of a felled tree is about 3,200 years, whilst several standing trees appear to be about 1,500-2,000 years old.

**'Glaucum'** A form of narrowly conical habit with glaucous leaves. It has reached 13.5m in the Hillier Gardens and Arboretum. C 1860.

**'Pendulum'** A tree of unique appearance often assuming the most fantastic shapes, but usually forming a narrow column with long branches hanging almost parallel with the trunk. C 1863. FCC 1882.

**'Pygmaeum'** Small to medium-sized bush of dense, conical habit. If reversions occur they should be removed. C 1891.

**'Variegatum'** Leaves flecked with a white variegation. Not a beauty. C 1890.

**"SPRUCE"** See *Picea*.

**\*TAIWANIA** HAYATA—**Taxodiaceae**—A genus of only 2 species of remarkable conifers both rare in cultivation, related to and somewhat resembling *Cryptomeria* in general appearance. Male and female strobili are borne on the same tree.

†**cryptomerioides** HAYATA A rare tree of conical habit, attaining heights of 50m or more in its native habitats. In cultivation it forms a small, sparsely-branched tree with slender, drooping, whip-like branchlets, densely clothed with glaucous green, linear, sickle-shaped, sharply-pointed leaves which become shorter and more scale-like on adult trees. Cones cylindrical, 12mm long. This unusual conifer requires a moist but well drained soil and a sheltered site to succeed. Western slopes of Mount Morrison, Taiwan. I 1920 by Ernest Wilson. AM 1931.

**flousiana** GAUSSEN "Coffin Tree". An attractive species closely resembling *T. cryptomerioides*, but with greener, slightly longer, less rigid leaves, softer to the touch. It has proved a hardier tree. A specimen in our Chandler's Ford nursery grew slowly for many years uninjured by severe winters. It is a native of SW and C China and also N Burma, where it was discovered by Kingdon-Ward. Its wood is used in China for making coffins and it is this species rather than *J. recurva* var. *coxii* which is in danger of extinction through over-felling.

‡**TAXODIUM** RICH.—**Taxodiaceae**—A genus of 3 species of deciduous trees. Leaves linear and flattened or awl-shaped, arranged alternately in 2 opposite ranks on short, deciduous branchlets, the whole resembling a pinnate leaf. On persistent branchlets they are radially arranged. Male and female strobili are borne on the same tree, the males in long, drooping, terminal panicles. Cones shortly-stalked, with thick woody, shield-like scales, ripening during the first year. These beautiful North and Central American trees, with their attractive frond-like foliage, can be successfully grown in all soils other than chalky soils. They are remarkable on account of their adaptability for growing in water-logged conditions, but it is essential that they be "mound planted" in such sites.

**ascendens** BRONGN. A small to medium-sized tree of narrowly conical or columnar habit, with spreading branches and erect branchlets. Leaves awl-shaped, 5-10mm long, incurved and adpressed, bright green. In cultivation in the British Isles it tends to be slower-growing than *T. distichum*, but it is worth growing for its habit and rich brown autumn foliage. Native of swampy places in the SE United States.

'**Nutans**' A beautiful columnar tree with shortly spreading or ascending branches. The thin, crowded branchlets are erect at first, later nodding, clothed with adpressed, awl-shaped leaves up to 5mm long. C 1789.

**distichum** (L.) RICH. "Deciduous Cypress" "Swamp Cypress". A strikingly beautiful tree and the most suitable conifer for wet soils. A large tree with fibrous, reddish-brown bark and strongly buttressed trunk. Leaves linear and flattened, 1-1.5cm long, grass-green, pectinate on short, deciduous shoots, spirally arranged on the persistent branchlets, turning bronze-yellow in autumn. When grown by water, large specimens produce peculiar "knee-like" growths from the roots, which project above ground. Native of wet places, rivers and swamps in the S United States, and the dominant tree in the famous Everglades region of Florida. In America it is known as the "Bald Cypress". I by John Tradescant about 1640. AM 1973. AGM 1984.

'**Hursley Park**' A dwarf, dense bush which originated from a Witches Broom on a tree at Hursley Park, Hampshire, in 1966.

'**Pendens**' A form with drooping branchlets and branch tips. C 1855.

†**mucronatum** TENORE "Mexican Cypress". A small to medium-sized tree, closely resembling *T. distichum*, but leaves semi-persistent in warm areas. It is too tender for all but the mildest areas of the British Isles. A famous specimen near Oaxaca, Mexico has the largest girth of any tree. In 1982 it had a circumference of 36m (118ft) at 1.5m and was 41m (135ft) tall. Mexico.

**sempervirens** See *Sequoia sempervirens*.

**\*TAXUS** L.—**Taxaceae**—The "Yews" are a small genus of about 7 species of evergreen trees and shrubs widely distributed in N temperate regions, south to C America and Indonesia.

**TAXUS**—*continued*

They bear linear, two-ranked or radial leaves which are marked by 2 yellowish-green or greyish-green bands beneath. Male and female strobili borne during spring, usually on separate plants. Fruits with a fleshy, often brightly coloured cup (aril) containing a single poisonous seed. The yews are of great garden value, tolerant of most soils and situations, including dry chalk soils and heavy shade. They are very useful for hedges and the columnar forms for formal planting.

**baccata** L. "Common Yew" "English Yew". One of our 3 native conifers, usually found in the wild on chalk formations. A small to medium-sized tree or large shrub with dark, almost black-green leaves, to 3cm long. Fruits with a red aril. A well-known tree, a common and familiar resident of churchyards where specimens of great age may occasionally be found. The low prostrate forms make wonderful ground-cover plants, even in dense shade. The yew has given rise to numerous forms varying in habit and colour. Given good drainage the yew will grow on almost pure chalk or in very acid soils. Europe, W Asia, Algeria. AGM 1984.

**'Adpressa'** A large shrub or small tree, a female clone of dense, spreading habit, with ascending branches and short crowded branchlets clothed with small, dark green leaves, 5-10mm long. C 1828.

**'Adpressa Aurea'** See under 'Adpressa Variegata'.

**'Adpressa Erecta'** ('Adpressa Stricta') A taller female form with more ascending branches, forming a broad shrub with dark green leaves up to 1.5cm long. C 1886. FCC 1886.

**'Adpressa Variegata'** A male form of 'Adpressa'. The unfolding leaves are old gold, passing to yellow, a colour which is confined to the margin as the leaves age. This is the form usually grown wrongly under the name 'Adpressa Aurea'. C 1866. FCC 1889.

**'Amersfoort'** A curious, small to medium-sized shrub of open habit. The stiffly ascending branches are clothed with numerous, small, radially-arranged, oblong-ovate leaves, 5-7mm long. A botanical conundrum quite un-yew-like in appearance, and recalling *Olearia nummulariifolia*. The mother plant, of French origin, is growing at the Psychiatric Hospital of Amersfoort, Holland.

**'Argentea'** See 'Variegata'.

**'Argentea Minor'** See 'Dwarf White'.

**Aurea group** (*T. baccata* f. *aurea* PILGER) "Golden Yew". A large shrub of compact habit, with golden yellow leaves turning green by the second year. This name is used to cover all golden or gold margined forms, the most popular of which is 'Elegantissima'. C 1855.

**'Cavendishii'** A low-growing, female form less than 1m high, with wide-spreading branches drooping at the tips. In time forming a semi-prostrate mound several metres across. An excellent ground cover, even for heavy shade. C 1932.

**'Cheshuntensis'** An erect-growing, female clone, in habit intermediate between the Common and Irish Yews. It was raised as a seedling of the latter in Messrs Paul's Nursery at Cheshunt about 1857.

**'Decora'** A dwarf, slow-growing shrub forming a low, flat-topped hummock with arching branches and dark, polished green, upward-curving leaves which are 3cm long and 3-4mm broad.

**'Dovastoniana'** "Westfelton Yew". A very distinct, wide-spreading, small, elegant tree with tiers of long, horizontal branches and long, weeping branchlets. Leaves blackish-green. It is normally female. The original tree, planted in 1777, is at Westfelton, Shropshire. Plants which have lost their leader when young form wide-spreading, shallowly vase-shaped bushes several metres across. AGM 1984.

**'Dovastonii Aurea'** ('Dovastonii Aurea Pendula') Similar to 'Dovastoniana' in habit, but leaves margined bright yellow. A splendid male form raised in France. C 1891. AGM 1984.

**'Dwarf White'** ('Argentea Minor') A delightful small, slow-growing, female shrub with drooping branchlets. The leaves have a narrow, white margin.

**'Elegantissima'** The most popular of the golden yews. A dense-growing, large bush with ascending branches and yellow young leaves, which later pass to straw-yellow when the colour is confined to the margin. Female. C 1852.

**TAXUS baccata**—*continued*

    **'Erecta'** Fulham Yew. An erect-branched, broadly columnar, open-topped, female bush, eventually of large size. Raised from seed of the "Irish Yew". C 1838.

    **'Ericoides'** A medium-sized to large, slow-growing bush of erect habit; leaves narrow and spreading. C 1855.

    **'Fastigiata'** "Irish Yew". A female clone of erect habit, forming a dense, compact, broad column of closely-packed branches. As a young specimen it is narrowly columnar. Leaves black-green, radially arranged. A very popular yew and a familiar resident of church-yards. Originally found as 2 plants on the moors in County Fermanagh in 1780. There is also a male form of slightly broader habit. FCC 1863. AGM 1984.

    **'Fastigiata Aureomarginata'** "Golden Irish Yew". A male form, similar in appearance to 'Fastigiata', but leaves with yellow margin. C 1880.

    **'Fructoluteo'** See 'Lutea'.

    **'Glauca'** ('Nigra') "Blue John". A male form of loose yet upright habit with leaves a characteristic dark bluish-green almost black-green above, paler below. One of the most easily recognised forms particularly in early spring when the male strobili crowd the sombre foliage. C 1855.

    **'Lutea'** ('Fructoluteo') ('Xanthocarpa') "Yellow-berried Yew". An unusual and attractive form, the fruits with yellow arils are often abundant and then quite spectacular. C about 1817. AM 1929.

    **'Nana'** A dwarf, slow-growing bush of compact habit. C 1855.

    **'Nigra'** See 'Glauca'.

    **'Nutans'** A small, flat-topped bush. Leaves irregular in shape, often small and scale-like. A specimen in our collection attained 1m × 0.8m after thirty years. C 1910.

    **'Pygmaea'** An extremely slow-growing, dwarf shrub of dense conical or ovoid habit, bearing small, polished, black-green, radially arranged leaves. C 1910.

    **'Repandans'** A low-growing, often semi-prostrate, female bush, with long spreading branches, drooping at the tips. A splendid ground-cover plant doing well in sun or dense shade. C 1887.

    **'Repens Aurea'** A low, spreading, female bush with leaves margined with yellow when young, turning to cream later. Recalls a low form of 'Dovastonii Aurea'. Like all golden-foliaged plants it loses its colour when in deep shade.

    **'Semperaurea'** A slow-growing, male bush of medium size with ascending branches and short, crowded branchlets well clothed with foliage. The unfolding leaves are old gold, passing with age to rusty-yellow, a colour which they retain throughout the year. C 1908. AM 1977. AGM 1984.

    **'Standishii'** ('Fastigiata Standishii') A slow-growing, female form of 'Fastigiata Aurea'. It is of dense, columnar habit with erect, tightly packed branches and radially arranged, golden yellow leaves. The best of its colour and habit, but slow in growth. C 1908. AGM 1984.

    **'Summergold'** A low shrub with broadly spreading branches. Foliage yellow in summer becoming green margined yellow. Does not burn in full sun.

    **'Variegata'** ('Argentea') A female form with obtusely ascending branches, in habit simulating the Pfitzer Juniper. The unfolding leaves are creamy-yellow, maturing to a slender marginal band of greyish-white. C 1770.

    **'Washingtonii'** A vigorous, female form with ascending branches forming a broad, medium-sized bush. Young leaves rich yellow, ageing to yellowish-green, becoming bronzed during winter. C 1874.

    **'Xanthocarpa'** See 'Lutea'.

    **canadensis** MARSH. "Canadian Yew". A small, erect-growing, monoecious shrub up to 1.8m high, with crowded branches and irregularly-arranged, often two-ranked leaves, 1-2cm long. Fruits with a red aril. In the wild the main shoots are loose, often becoming semi-prostrate and taking root, in time forming extensive carpets. Canada, NE United States. I 1800.

    **celebica** (WARBURG) LI "Chinese Yew". A splendid large shrub or small tree of loose, spreading habit easily confused with *Torreya grandis*. Leaves two-ranked, 1-3cm long, of a characteristic yellowish-green or pale green colour. Fruits with a red aril. SE Asia.

**TAXUS**—*continued*

**cuspidata** SIEB. & ZUCC. "Japanese Yew." In its native habitats a small to medium-sized tree, but usually shrubby in cultivation. Leaves 1-2.5cm long, dark green above, yellowish-green beneath, ascending from the branchlets. Fruits with a red aril. In colder climes it proves hardier than our native yew. Japan. Introduced by Robert Fortune in 1855.

**'Aurescens'** A low-growing, compact form with deep yellow young leaves changing to green the second year. C 1920.

**'Densa'** A dwarf, compact, female shrub forming a mound of crowded, erect stems. C 1917.

**'Minima'** An extremely slow-growing, dwarf bush of irregular habit. C 1932.

**var. nana** REHD. A dense, small, male bush with ascending branches, nodding at the tips. Leaves radially arranged. Old specimens in cultivation have attained 1.2-1.5m high by 3m or more across. C 1861.

**floridana** CHAPMAN "Florida Yew". Medium-sized to large shrub with crowded, ascending branches and dark green, sickle-shaped leaves, 2-2.5cm long. Fruits with a red aril. Rare in cultivation. Florida.

× **hunnewelliana** REHD. (*T. canadensis* × *T. cuspidata*). A vigorous, large, very wide-spreading shrub with obtusely-ascending branches and an open centre. It resembles one of the wide-spreading forms of *T.* × *media* from which it differs in its longer, narrower, deep green leaves. A specimen in our collection planted in 1954 reached 3m high and 6m across in 15 years. Raised in the Hunnewell Pinetum, Wellesley, Massachusetts. C 1900.

× **media** REHD. (*T. baccata* × *T. cuspidata*). A vigorous, medium-sized to large shrub of spreading habit, more or less intermediate between the parents. Leaves usually two-ranked. Raised by T.D. Hatfield at the Hunnewell Pinetum, Wellesley, Massachusetts about 1900. There are several named clones in cultivation. Some of the wide-spreading clones develop a peculiar twisting character in the branches, shoots and older leaves.

**'Brownii'** A broadly columnar male form with semi-erect branches. Excellent as a hedge. C 1950.

**'Hatfieldii'** A dense, compact, male form with sharply ascending branches. An excellent subject for hedging. C 1923.

**'Hicksii'** A broadly columnar, female bush. It makes an excellent hedge. C 1900.

**'Nidiformis'** A dense, broad, open-centred, male bush with obtusely ascending branches. C 1953.

**'Sargentii'** An erect-growing, female form of dense habit, excellent for hedging.

**'Thayerae'** A broad, vigorous, male shrub with widely-ascending branches and open centre. In habit somewhat like *T.* × *hunnewelliana* but with shorter, broader leaves and probably not so tall. C 1930.

†*TETRACLINIS MASTERS—**Cupressaceae**—A monotypic genus related to *Callitris*, only suitable for the conservatory or outside in the mildest localities. Male and female strobili borne on the same plant.

**articulata** (VAHL) MAST. A rare evergreen species attaining tree size in its native environs, but generally shrubby in the British Isles. Branches dense and ascending, terminating in flat, jointed, spray-like branchlets clothed with scale-like leaves which are decurrent at the base and arranged in fours. Cones solitary, rounded, 8-12mm across, composed of 4, thick, woody, glaucous scales. Both the wood and resin are of commercial importance. Native to Algeria, Morocco, Mogador, Malta and SE Spain, in which countries it grows in dry places and withstands considerable periods of drought.

*THUJA L. (*Thuya* L.)—**Cupressaceae**—Popularly known as "Arbor-vitae", these comprise a small genus of 6 species of hardy, evergreen trees and shrubs widely disributed in N temperate regions. They differ from the superficially similar *Chamaecyparis* in the usually pleasantly aromatic foliage and cones with overlapping scales. Most form trees of attractive conical habit with small, scale-like, overlapping leaves arranged in 4 ranks and borne in often large, flattened, fan-like sprays. Male and female strobili are borne on the same tree in early spring, the males reddish. Cones small, oblong or subglobose,

**THUJA**—*continued*

and composed of 3-10 pairs of woody, overlapping scales which are attached at their base, maturing the first year. The Thujas will thrive in almost any soil, providing it is well drained.

2 species (*T. occidentalis* and *T. plicata*) are invaluable for hedges and screens, whilst a good number of cultivars are dwarf or slow-growing and thus suitable for the rock garden. There are several excellent coloured forms though the range is less than in *Chamaecyparis*.

**japonica** See *T. standishii.*

**koraiensis** NAKAI "Korean Arbor-vitae". A striking species, usually densely shrubby in habit, but occasionally a small tree with decurved branches and dark brown, peeling bark. Foliage borne in large, flattened, frond-like sprays, green or sea-green above, conspicuously white beneath, pungently aromatic when crushed. Korea. Introduced by Ernest Wilson in 1917.

**lobbii** See *T. plicata.*

**occidentalis** L. "American Arbor-vitae". An extremely hardy, medium-sized columnar tree with reddish-brown, peeling bark. Branches spreading, upcurved at the tips. Leaves with conspicuous resin glands, dark green above, pale green beneath, borne in numerous, flattened sprays, usually bronze during winter. The foliage possesses a pleasant fruity odour when crushed. An important timber tree in the United States. E North America. I about 1534. Innumerable forms have arisen in cultivation.

**'Aurea'** ('Mastersii Aurea') A broadly conical, medium-sized to large bush with golden yellow leaves. C 1857.

**'Aureospicata'** An erect-growing form with young shoots becoming yellow, intensified in winter to a rich burnished old gold.

**'Beaufort'** An open, slender-branched, large shrub or small tree with leaves variegated white. C 1963.

**'Bodmeri'** Medium-sized bush of open, conical habit. Branches thick and stout; foliage dark green, in large, monstrous sprays. C 1877.

**'Buchananii'** Small tree of narrow, conical habit, with ascending branches and long branchlets with sparse foliage. C 1887.

**'Caespitosa'** A dwarf, slow-growing bush forming a rounded hummock, wider than high. Foliage irregular and congested. Excellent for the rock garden. C 1923.

**'Cristata'** A slow-growing, dwarf bush with short, flattened, crest-like branchlets, recalling those of the Fern-Spray Cypress. C 1867.

**'Danica'** A dwarf bush of dense, compact, globular habit. Foliage vertically held in erect, flattened sprays.

**'Ellwangeriana Pygmaea Aurea'** See under 'Rheingold'.

**'Ericoides'** A small, dense, rounded or cone-shaped bush with soft, loose branchlets and dull green, juvenile foliage which becomes donkey-brown in winter. Very liable to damage by snow. C 1867.

**'Europe Gold'** A Dutch selection of narrowly conical habit making a large shrub or small tree with golden yellow foliage.

**'Fastigiata'** ('Columnaris') ('Pyramidalis') ('Stricta') A narrowly conical or columnar form of dense, compact growth. An excellent small, formal tree. C 1865.

**'Filiformis'** A slow-growing, fairly compact bush with drooping "whipcord" branchlets. In 30 years reaching 2m × 1.2m. C 1901.

**'Globosa'** A compact, globular bush, slowly reaching about 1.3m high by 2m wide. C 1875. The clones 'Globularis' and 'Tom Thumb' are almost, if not wholly, identical.

**'Golden Globe'** A small shrub of dense, rounded habit with year-round golden yellow foliage. C 1965.

**'Hetz Midget'** An extremely slow-growing, dwarf bush of globular habit. Perhaps the smallest form of all. C 1928.

**'Holmstrup'** ('Holmstrupii') ('Holmstrupensis') A slow-growing, medium-sized to large, narrowly conical bush of dense, compact habit with rich green foliage throughout the year in vertically arranged sprays. C 1951.

**'Holmstrup Yellow'** A sport of 'Holmstrup' with golden yellow foliage. Raised in Denmark before 1951.

**THUJA occidentalis**—*continued*

'**Hoveyi**' A slow-growing bush of globular or ovoid habit, eventually reaching a height of 3m. The yellowish-green foliage is arranged in vertically held sprays. C 1868.

'**Indomitable**' A large shrub or small tree with spreading branches and dark green foliage, rich reddish-bronze in winter. C 1960.

'**Little Gem**' Dwarf, globular bush of dense, slightly flat-topped habit; foliage deep green, in crowded crimpled sprays. The clone 'Recurva Nana' is very similar. C 1891.

'**Lutea Nana**' A small conical bush of dense habit with deep golden yellow winter foliage, yellow-green in summer. C 1891.

'**Malonyana**' A striking small to medium-sized tree of narrow, columnar habit, leaves a uniform rich green, borne in short, dense, crowded sprays. This architectural tree forms a perfect avenue in the late Count Ambroze's garden, Mlynany Arboretum, Czechoslovakia.

'**Mastersii**' ('Plicata') A small, conical tree with large, flat sprays of foliage, arranged in a vertical plane and tipped old gold in the spring. C 1847.

'**Ohlendorffii**' ('Spaethii') One of the most distinct and curious of dwarf or semi-dwarf conifers, carrying dense clusters of soft juvenile foliage, and long, erect, slender, whipcord-like branches, clothed with adult foliage. C 1887.

'**Pendula**' "Weeping American Arbor-vitae". Small tree with openly ascending branches and pendulous branchlets. C 1857.

'**Pygmaea**' ('Plicata Pygmaea') ('Mastersii Pygmaea') A dwarf bush of dense but irregular growth, with crowded sprays of sea-green foliage.

'**Recurva Nana**' A low-growing, flat-topped dome, the branchlets noticeably recurved at the tips. 'Little Gem' is very similar.

'**Rheingold**' A slow-growing bush of ovoid or conical habit eventually making a large shrub. Foliage mainly adult, of a rich deep old gold, shaded amber. A very popular plant, perhaps the richest piece of radiant old gold in the garden in the dead of the winter. It is an excellent companion to heathers and heaths and contrasts most effectively with darker conifers. C before 1902. AM 1902 (as *T. occidentalis* 'Ellwangeriana Pygmaea Aurea'). AGM 1984.

The name 'Rheingold' is sometimes retained for small plants raised from cuttings of juvenile shoots. In the course of time these revert to the plant here described and appear inseparable from the cultivar 'Ellwangeriana Aurea'.

'**Smaragd**' ('Emerald') A narrowly conical small tree with bright green foliage.

'**Spiralis**' A narrowly columnar small tree of densely-branched habit with short, pinnately-arranged sprays of dark green foliage. A splendid formal tree. C 1923.

'**Sunkist**' A dense, small shrub of broadly conical, round-topped habit with golden yellow foliage in summer.

'**Tiny Tim**' A very slow-growing dwarf bush of rounded habit. Raised in Canada.

'**Vervaeneana**' A large bush or small tree of dense, conical habit, with crowded sprays of light green and yellow foliage, becoming bronzed in winter. C 1862.

'**Wansdyke Silver**' An attractive, small, slow-growing bush of conical habit, the foliage conspicuously variegated with creamy-white. C 1966.

'**Wareana**' ('Robusta') A compact, slow-growing, small bush of conical habit with short, thickened sprays of green foliage. Raised in the nursery of Messrs Weare at Coventry in about 1827.

'**Wareana Lutescens**' ('Lutescens') Similar to 'Wareana', but more compact and with pale yellow foliage. C 1884.

'**Wintergreen**' ('Lombarts' Wintergreen') Small to medium-sized tree of columnar habit, with foliage green throughout the year.

'**Woodwardii**' A dense, ovoid bush, taller than broad, eventually reaching 1m in height, with typical *T. occidentalis* foliage remaining green in winter.

**orientalis** L. (*Biota orientalis* (L.) ENDL.) "Chinese Arbor-vitae". A large shrub or small tree of dense, conical or columnar habit when young. Branches erect, the leaves borne in frond-like, vertical sprays. This species is distinct in its formal habit, its foliage less aromatic than others and its cone scales which have conspicuous recurved hooks. There are several forms suitable for the rock garden. N and W China. I about 1690.

**THUJA orientalis**—*continued*

'**Athrotaxoides**' An extremely slow-growing, small shrub with noticeably thick branches and branchlets, lacking the spray-like foliage typical of the species. Originated in the Jardin des Plantes, Paris, in 1867.

'**Aurea Nana**' A dwarf, globular bush of dense habit, with crowded, vertically-arranged sprays of light, yellow-green foliage. C 1804. AGM 1984.

'**Compacta**' See 'Sieboldii'.

'**Conspicua**' A medium-sized to large bush of dense, compact, conical habit. The golden foliage is retained longer than in most other forms of similar colour. C 1804.

'**Decussata**' See 'Juniperoides'.

'**Elegantissima**' A medium-sized to large bush of dense columnar habit. Foliage golden yellow, tinged old gold, becoming green in winter. C 1858. AGM 1984.

'**Filiformis Erecta**' An unusual form of ovoid habit forming a large bush or small tree, with erect, whip-like stems, clothed with yellowish-green leaves, bronzed in winter. C 1868.

'**Hillieri**' A small to medium-sized bush of dense, compact, ovoid habit. Leaves soft yellow-green, becoming green in winter. Raised in our nurseries prior to 1924.

'**Juniperoides**' ('Decussata') A dwarf, rounded bush with soft, juvenile foliage which is greyish-green in summer turning a rich, purplish-grey in winter. It is a most attractive form requiring shelter from cold winds. C 1850. AM 1973.

'**Meldensis**' A dwarf bush of dense, globular habit. The semi-juvenile foliage is sea-green in summer turning a delightful plum-purple in winter. Raised in 1852.

'**Minima Glauca**' A beautiful, dwarf bush of dense, globular habit. Foliage semi-juvenile, sea-green in summer, turning a warm yellow-brown in winter. C 1891.

'**Rosedalis**' ('Rosedalis Compacta') A dense, ovoid bush with soft juvenile foliage which, in early spring, is a bright canary-yellow, changing by midsummer to sea-green, and in winter glaucous plum-purple. In 15 years it will attain 80cm in height. Its soft-to-the-touch foliage and its spring colour distinguish it from 'Meldensis'. C 1923.

'**Sanderi**' (*Chamaecyparis obtusa* 'Sanderi') A dwarf, slow-growing, juvenile form with short, thick leaves. The whole bush is delightfully sea-green in summer, becoming plum-coloured in winter. It is somewhat wind-tender and requires a sheltered, well drained position or a pot in the alpine-house. It was originally introduced from Japan in 1894 and for many years was considered to be a juniper. Recently H.J. Welch and the late L.J. Gough, using gas chromatography to analyse leaf extracts, have shown that it most likely belongs here. AM 1899.

'**Semperaurea**' A dense, rounded bush of medium size with foliage yellow throughout summer, becoming bronzed later. C 1870. FCC 1870.

'**Sieboldii**' ('Nana') ('Compacta') A small, rounded bush of dense, compact habit. Foliage golden yellow at first, turning to mid-green later, borne in delicate lace-like, vertical sprays. C 1859.

**plicata** D. DON (*T. lobbii* HORT. ex GORD.) (*T. gigantea* NUTT.) "Western Red Cedar". A large, fast-growing, ornamental tree with shredding bark and spreading branches. Leaves of a bright glossy green above, faintly glaucous beneath, carried in large, drooping sprays and with a pleasant, fruity odour when crushed. An important timber tree in North America. It makes a splendid hedge or screen, withstanding clipping well; it is also tolerant of shade and shallow chalk soils. W North America. Introduced by William Lobb in 1853. The most commonly grown clone is sometimes listed under the name 'Atrovirens' (AGM 1984).

'**Aureovariegata**' See 'Zebrina'.

'**Aurea**' An outstanding form with foliage of a rich, old gold. FCC 1897.

'**Collyer's Gold**' A slow-growing form similar to 'Stoneham Gold' but with foliage of a brighter yellow.

'**Cuprea**' A dense, very slow-growing, conical bush, the growths tipped in various shades of deep cream to old gold. A splendid plant for the rock garden. Raised by Messrs Rogers and Sons of Southampton about 1930.

'**Fastigiata**' ('Stricta') A tall-growing, narrowly columnar form with densely arranged, slender, ascending branches. Excellent as a single specimen tree or for hedging when only the minimum of clipping is necessary. C 1867. AGM 1984.

**THUJA plicata**—*continued*

**'Gracilis'** A large bush of conical habit with finely-divided sprays of green foliage. C 1923.

**'Gracilis Aurea'** Medium-sized, slow-growing bush with slender branchlets and yellow-tipped foliage. A sport of 'Gracilis'. C 1949.

**'Hillieri'** ('Nana') A slow-growing, dense, compact, rounded bush of medium size. The green foliage is arranged in curious moss-like clusters on branchlets which are thick and stiff, with irregular crowded growths. Our original plant, which occurred in our Shroner Wood nursery about 1880, had attained 2.4 × 2.1m when it was sold about 1925. A specimen about 35 years old in the Hillier Gardens and Arboretum was 3m tall and 4m across in 1990.

**'Irish Gold'** Similar to 'Zebrina' but the foliage more strongly flecked with deeper yellow.

**'Rogersii'** ('Aurea Rogersii') A slow-growing, dwarf, compact bush of conical habit, with densely crowded gold and bronze-coloured foliage. It will attain about 1.2 × 1m in 30 years. Raised by Messrs Rogers of Southampton about 1928.

**'Semperaurescens'** An extremely vigorous, large tree worthy of inclusion in any pinetum or as a tall screen where colour variation is desired. Young shoots and leaves tinged golden yellow, becoming bronze-yellow by winter. C 1923.

**'Stoneham Gold'** A slow-growing, eventually large bush of dense, narrowly conical habit. Foliage bright gold, tipped coppery-bronze. A superb plant for the large rock garden. C 1948.

**'Zebrina'** ('Aureovariegata') A conical tree, the sprays of green foliage banded with creamy-yellow. A strong-growing, large tree, certainly one of the best variegated conifers, the variegations being so crowded as to give a yellow effect to the whole tree. C 1868. FCC 1869. AGM 1984.

**standishii** (GORD.) CARR. (*T. japonica* MAXIM.) "Japanese Arbor-vitae". A small to medium-sized tree of conical habit with loosely spreading or upcurved branches and drooping branchlets. Leaves yellowish-green above, slightly glaucous beneath, carried in large, gracefully drooping sprays. An attractive species, easily recognised by its characteristic yellowish-green appearance and loose habit. The foliage when crushed smells of Lemon Verbena. C Japan. Introduced by Robert Fortune to the Standish Nurseries, Bagshot in 1860.

**\*THUJOPSIS** SIEB. & ZUCC. ex ENDL.—**Cupressaceae**—A monotypic genus related to *Thuja*, differing in its broader, flatter branchlets and larger leaves. It thrives in all types of well drained soil including shallow chalk soils. Male and female strobili are borne on the same tree.

**dolabrata** (L. f.) SIEB. & ZUCC. (*Thuja dolabrata* L. f.) "Hiba". A distinct and attractive, small to medium-sized tree or large shrub of dense, broadly conical habit. Branchlets flattened, bearing sprays of large, four-ranked, scale-like leaves, shining dark green above, marked with conspicuous silver-white bands beneath. Cones to 20mm long. Japan. I 1853. FCC 1864.

**'Aurea'** Leaves suffused golden yellow. A splendid yellow conifer which deserves to be much more frequently planted. C 1866.

**var. hondae** MAKINO The northern form of the species, attaining 30m in its native habitat. It tends to be more compact in habit, with smaller, blunter leaves.

**'Nana'** (var. *laetevirens* (LINDL.) MAST.) A dwarf, compact, spreading, flat-topped bush, smaller in all its parts. I 1861.

**'Variegata'** A strong-growing clone with scattered patches of creamy-white foliage. Not very stable. I 1859.

**THUYA** See *Thuja*.

**\*TORREYA** ARN.—**Taxaceae**—A small genus of about 7 species of evergreen trees and shrubs allied to *Cephalotaxus*; natives of E Asia and North America. Leaves linear, rigid and spine-tipped, marked with 2 glaucous bands beneath, spirally arranged on leading shoots, twisted to appear in 2 ranks on the lateral shoots. Male and female strobili

**TORREYA**—*continued*

borne on the same or different trees. Fruits plum-like, fleshy, containing a single seed. They are excellent trees for chalk soils and are good shade-bearers.

**californica** TORR. (*T. myristica* HOOK.) "Californian Nutmeg". A small to medium-sized, broadly conical tree, well furnished to ground level, like a majestic yew. Leaves rigid, 3-7.5cm long, shining dark green above, spine-tipped. Fruits ovoid or obovoid, 3-4cm long, green, streaked with purple when ripe. Native of California. Discovered and introduced by William Lobb in 1851.

'**Spreadeagle**' A low-growing form with long, spreading branches. Originated in our Crook Hill nursery in 1965.

**grandis** FORTUNE A rare small tree or large shrub in cultivation. Leaves spine-tipped, to 2.5cm long, yellowish-green above. Fruits to 3cm long, brownish when ripe. A species similar to *T. nucifera*, differing in its paler green, slightly smaller leaves which lack the familiar aromatic scent of the Japanese species and may be confused with those of the Chinese Yew (*Taxus celebica*). China. Introduced by Robert Fortune in 1855.

**nucifera** (L.) SIEB. & ZUCC. "Kaya Nut". Although a large tree in its native habitat, in the British Isles it is usually seen as a large shrub or occasionally a small slender, thinly-foliaged tree. Leaves smaller than those of *T. californica*, to 3cm long, sickle-shaped and spine-tipped and rather more consistently in a flat plane, pungent when crushed. Fruits to 2.5cm long, green, clouded purple when ripe. I 1764.

**taxifolia** ARN. "Stinking Cedar". A small tree, rare in cultivation. It most resembles *T. californica* but has smaller leaves, 2-4cm long. Fruits to 4cm long. NW Florida. I 1840.

**\*TSUGA** CARR.—**Pinaceae**—A small genus of about 10 species of extremely elegant, evergreen trees of broadly conical habit with spreading branches and gently drooping or arching branchlets; natives of E Asia and North America. The leaves are short and linear, arranged on the branchlets so as to appear two-ranked, except in *T. mertensiana*. Male and female strobili are borne on the same tree. The cones are small and pendulous, ripening during the first year, but remaining until the second year. They are good shade-bearers and thrive best in a moist, but well drained, loamy soil. *T. canadensis* may be grown in moderately deep soils over chalk.

**albertiana** See *T. heterophylla*.

**brunoniana** See *T. dumosa*.

**canadensis** (L.) CARR. "Eastern Hemlock". A large tree often with several main stems from near the base. The best species for limey soil. Leaves to 15mm long, marked with 2 whitish bands beneath. Cones ovoid, slender-stalked, 1.5-2.5cm long. It has given rise to innumerable cultivars, a selection of which are here listed, many of them suitable for the rock garden and stone troughs. It differs from the closely related *T. heterophylla* in its usually forked trunk and its leaves which are more tapered to the apex and not so noticeably banded beneath. Another characteristic is the line of the leaves lying under-sides uppermost, along the uppersides of the branchlets. E North America. I 1736.

'**Albospica**' A slower-growing, more compact form in which the growing tips of the shoots are creamy-white. Particularly effective during spring and summer. C 1884.

'**Armistice**' A slow-growing, dwarf form developing into a flat-topped mound. C 1965.

'**Aurea**' A slow-growing, dwarf form of compact, conical habit. Leaves rather broad and crowded, golden yellow when unfolding, becoming yellowish-green later. C 1866.

'**Bennett**' ('Bennett's Minima') A slow-growing, dwarf shrub of spreading habit and dense, crowded growth. C 1920.

'**Cinnamomea**' Dwarf, slow-growing bush of dense, congested, globular habit. Young stems densely covered with a cinnamon pubescence. C 1929.

'**Cole**' ('Cole's Prostrate') A remarkable prostrate plant with long branches flattened along the ground, in time forming extensive carpets. Similar in habit to 'Prostrata'.

'**Compacta**' Dwarf bush with short, crowded branchlets. C 1868.

'**Curly**' A curious small shrub in which the young leaves are crowded and curled around the shoots.

'**Dwarf Whitetip**' A small, broadly conical bush, the young shoots creamy-white, changing to green in late summer. C 1939.

**TSUGA canadensis**—*continued*

**'Fantana'** A small bush as broad as high, with wide-spreading branches. C 1913.

**'Fremdii'** A small, slow-growing, eventually broadly conical, small tree of compact, bushy habit, with crowded branchlets and leaves. C 1887.

**'Globosa'** Dwarf, globose bush with pendulous tips to the branchlets. C 1891.

**'Greenwood Lake'** Slow-growing, medium-sized to large bush with crowded branchlets and no definite leader. C 1939.

**'Horsford'** ('Horsford's Dwarf') A dwarf, slow-growing, globular bush with congested branchlets and small, crowded leaves.

**'Hussii'** Medium-sized to large bush of slow growth. Habit dense and irregular with no definite leader. C 1900.

**'Jeddeloh'** A reliably dwarf bush of compact habit with the branches arching from a depressed centre. Selected in W Germany. C 1965.

**'Jervis'** See 'Nearing'.

**'Lutea'** A slow-growing tree, the golden foliage most conspicuous in winter.

**'Macrophylla'** Large, bushy shrub or small, densely-branched tree with relatively large leaves. Inclined to revert to typical growth. C 1891.

**'Many Cones'** A slow-growing bush of open habit with gracefully arching branches, free-coning.

**'Microphylla'** ('Parvifolia') A distinct and interesting large bush or small tree with tiny heath-like leaves. C 1864.

**'Minima'** A slow-growing, wide-spreading, small bush with arching and drooping branches. C 1891.

**'Minuta'** An extremely slow-growing, miniature bun of tightly congested growth, with small, crowded leaves. I 1927.

**'Nana'** A small, slow-growing bush of graceful, spreading habit. Suitable for large rock gardens. C 1855.

**'Nana Gracilis'** Dwarf, mound-forming bush of graceful habit with slender, arching stems.

**'Nearing'** ('Jervis') An extremely slow-growing, dwarf bush of compact but irregular habit, with crowded, congested growths. A gem for the rock garden.

**'Pendula'** A most attractive form developing into a low mound of overlapping, drooping branches. A superb plant for a prominent position on a large rock garden or isolated on a lawn. In 40 years it reached about $2 \times 3.7$m here. I before 1876. AGM 1984.

**'Prostrata'** A rather slow-growing, prostrate form with stems which press themselves to the ground and lie in all directions, eventually forming large mats. C 1933.

**'Pygmaea'** A dwarf, irregular globe, with short, congested growths.

**'Rugg's Washington Dwarf'** A dwarf, globular or mound-forming bush with dense, congested growth.

**'Stranger'** Small, slow-growing tree of compact habit; leaves rather broad and thick. C 1939.

**'Taxifolia'** Dwarf to medium-sized, irregular bush of compact habit, the leaves crowded at the ends of each year's growth, longer than in the type. C 1938.

**'Warner's Globe'** ('Warner Globosa') A globular bush with relatively short, broad leaves.

‡**caroliniana** ENGELM. "Carolina Hemlock". Although a handsome, large, conical tree in its native habitats, it is rarely more than a compact, small tree or large shrub in this country. Young shoots grey, yellow-brown or red-brown and shining, with short pubescence scattered along the grooves. Leaves 1-1.2cm long, soft yellowish-green, marked with 2 white bands beneath. Cones ovoid or oblong, 2-3.5cm long. SE United States. I 1881.

**'La Bar Weeping'** A very compact dwarf form of spreading habit making a dense mound of arching shoots.

**chinensis** (FRANCH.) PRITZ. Usually a small tree in cultivation. Leaves to 2.5cm long, comparatively broad, marked with 2 inconspicuous, greyish-green bands beneath. Cones to 2.5cm long. A distinct hardy species not subject to damage by spring frost and to a considerable degree lime-tolerant. It most resembles *T. heterophylla*. C and W China. I 1902 by Ernest Wilson.

**TSUGA**—*continued*

‡**diversifolia** (MAXIM.) MAST. "Northern Japanese Hemlock". In cultivation a small horizontally-branched tree. Leaves glistening deep green, 5-15mm long, notched at the apex, marked with 2 chalk-white bands beneath, oblong, very regular. Cones ovoid, 2cm long. An attractive species easily distinguished by its combination of hairy shoots and leaves with entire margins. Japan. Introduced by J.G. Veitch in 1861.

†**dumosa** (D. DON) EICHL. (*T. brunoniana* CARR.) "Himalayan Hemlock". A distinct tender species only likely to be confused with *T. yunnanensis*, scarcely more than shrubby in most districts, but has attained about 21m in Cornwall. Branches gracefully drooping. Leaves to 3cm long, marked with 2 vivid, silvery-white bands beneath. Cones to 2.5cm long. A beautiful species when growing well, but very subject to injury by spring frosts. It is moderately lime-tolerant. Native of the Himalaya where it attains heights of over 30m in sheltered valleys. First introduced by Captain Webb in 1838. AM 1931.

†**formosana** HAYATA "Taiwan Hemlock". A rare species in cultivation allied to *T. sieboldii*, differing in its shorter leaves and smaller cones. It had appeared hardy here for more than 20 years until being badly mauled by the severe winter of 1962-63. Taiwan. I about 1934.

**forrestii** DOWNIE The tree received under this name from Borde Hill is quite different from *T. chinensis*, a species to which it is referred by some botanists. In its longer, narrower leaves, white beneath, it approaches *T. dumosa*, but is decidedly hardier. It has reached 5.5m in the Hillier Gardens and Arboretum. I by George Forrest.

‡**heterophylla** (RAF.) SARG. (*T. albertiana* (A. MURR.) SENECL.) "Western Hemlock". A large, fast-growing tree with gracefully spreading branches. Leaves to 20mm long, marked with 2 bright white bands beneath. Cones to 2.5cm long. A beautiful conifer, particularly when grown as a single specimen, developing into an elegant tree with a spire-like crown. It is an important timber tree in North America and is extensively planted in the British Isles. It is not suitable for chalk soils but is tolerant of shade. It makes a better specimen tree than the allied *T. canadensis*, but has given rise to few cultivars. W North America. First discovered by David Douglas in 1826, it was introduced by John Jeffrey in 1851. AGM 1984.

'**Conica**' A medium-sized bush of dense, conical or ovoid habit, the branches ascending, drooping at the tips. Raised in the arboretum of van Gimborn, Doorne, Netherlands, about 1930.

'**Greenmantle**' A graceful, tall, narrow tree with pendulous branches, which originated at Windsor Great Park.

'**Laursen's Column**' A striking tree of loosely columnar habit, recalling *Podocarpus andinus* in general appearance. Leaves irregularly, almost radially arranged on the ascending branches. A seedling found by Mr Asger Laursen in 1968. It has reached 6.5m in the Hillier Gardens and Arboretum (1990).

× **jeffreyi** (HENRY) HENRY (*T. heterophylla* × *T. mertensiana*). A comparatively slow-growing, eventually medium-sized to large tree, first raised at Edinburgh in 1851. W North America.

**mertensiana** (BONG.) CARR. (*T. pattoniana* (A. MURR.) ENGELM.) A beautiful species, a large tree of spire-like habit. Young shoots brownish-grey and densely pubescent. Leaves radially arranged, 1-2.5cm long, pointing forwards, greyish-green or blue-grey on both surfaces. Cones sessile, oblong-cylindrical, 5-8cm long. A distinct species easily recognised by its radially arranged leaves and comparatively large cones. W North America. Introduced by Jeffrey in 1851.

'**Glauca**' A beautiful, slow-growing form with glaucous leaves. C 1850.

**pattoniana** See *T. mertensiana*.

**sieboldii** CARR. "Japanese Hemlock". In the British Isles usually a small to medium-sized, dense tree or large bush, but reaching greater proportions in the wild. Leaves to 2.5cm long, glossy green above, marked with white bands beneath. Cones ovoid, 2.5-3cm long. S Japan. Introduced by Philip von Siebold in about 1850.

†**yunnanensis** (FRANCH.) MAST. A rare and rather tender, small tree with reddish-grey, densely pubescent young shoots. Leaves serrated, 1-2cm long, marked with 2 broad, vividly chalk-white bands beneath. Cones ovoid, 1-2cm long. Subject to injury by spring frosts. Yunnan and W Sichuan (China). I 1906. AM 1931.

**"WELLINGTONIA"** See *Sequoiadendron giganteum*.

†\***WIDDRINGTONIA** ENDL.—**Cupressaceae**—A genus of 3 species of evergreen, cypress-like trees from C and S Africa. Male and female strobili normally borne on the same tree. Leaves are spirally arranged and linear on young plants, scale-like on adult trees. The erect, woody cones remain for some time after shedding their seed. All are tender and require conservatory treatment except in the mildest areas. They are excellent conifers for hot, dry climes.

**cedarbergensis** MARSH (*W. juniperoides* ENDL.) "Clanwilliam Cedar". A small tree with elegant sprays of linear, glaucous green juvenile leaves, 1-2cm long, soft to the touch. Adult leaves scale-like closely pressed to the shoot. S Africa (Cedarberg Mts, SW Cape Province).

**cupressoides** See *W. nodiflora*.

**juniperoides** See *W. cedarbergensis*.

**nodiflora** (L.) POWRIE (*W. cupressoides* (L.) ENDL.) (*W. whytei* RENDLE) "Sapree Wood". A tree of conical habit when young, reaching 42m with a spreading crown in Malawi, smaller and sometimes shrubby in S Africa. Juvenile leaves linear, up to 2.5cm long, sea-green and soft to the touch. Adult leaves scale-like and closely pressed. S and E Africa.

**schwarzii** MAST. "Willowmore Cedar". A small tree, but reaching 27m in its native habitat. Leaves scale-like, glaucous, in closely pressed pairs. An attractive tree. Young plants growing under glass differ strikingly from the other species here described, in their conspicuously glaucous and scale-like leaves. S Africa (Willowmore district, Cape Province).

**whytei** See *W. nodiflora*.


**"YEW"** See *Taxus*.

# BAMBOOS
## (Gramineae)

Members of the Grass family, some of the most beautiful and elegant of all evergreens are included under this heading.

The majority of the species described below are perfectly hardy, but they are not suitable for windswept sites and it is a mistake to imagine that, because they are moisture-lovers, they will grow in permanently wet land. Many are excellent for growing in shade and all succeed in good soils over chalk.

When skilfully placed they are amongst the most ornamental features of any planting scheme, but it is as waterside plants that they show to their best advantage.

Though the transplanting period need not be restricted, early autumn and late spring are usually the most satisfactory times.

The flowering of bamboos is still not completely understood. Most species will live a great many years before flowering, whilst some flower over a period of years. Contrary to what is often said, death does not always follow flowering.

In their native habitats many of the following species reach great heights, but the ultimate heights quoted below are approximate under average conditions of soil and aspect in the British Isles. The leaves of most species are long and narrow, rich green above, pale green or greyish-green beneath.

It is important to avoid using near bamboos any selective weed killer designed to destroy Couch Grass or other grasses.

**ARUNDINARIA** MICHX. A genus of about 50 species of bamboos of tufted growth or with creeping underground stems. Many species form extensive patches or thickets and should only be planted where space permits. Differing from *Phyllostachys* and *Sasa* in the usually more numerous branches to each cluster and also from *Phyllostachys* in the rounded (terete) internodes, those of the latter being flattened or broadly grooved on alternate sides.

†**amabilis** MCCLURE A little-known species suitable for sheltered gardens in the mildest parts of the British Isles, where it will reach a height of 2.5-4.5m. Leaves variable in size from 10-35cm long by 1-4cm wide. China.

**anceps** See *Sinarundinaria anceps*.

**angustifolia** See *A. chino* f. *angustifolia*.

**auricoma** MITF. (*Arundinaria viridi-striata* (ANDRE) MAK.) (*Pleioblastus viridi-striatus* (ANDRE) MAK.) A very hardy species with erect, purplish-green canes 1-2m high, forming small patches. Leaves variable in size, 7.5-20cm long, 1-4cm wide, dark green, striped rich yellow, often more yellow than green. The best of the variegated bamboos, quite small when grown in shade and an excellent tub plant. Old canes may be cut to ground level in autumn to encourage the production of new canes with brightly coloured young foliage. It has flowered at the tips of the canes in several localities over a considerable period (since 1898) without any ill effect. Japan. I about 1870. AM 1972.

**chino** (FRANCH. & SAV.) MAK. (*Pleioblastus chino* (FRANCH. & SAV.) MAK.) (*Arundinaria simonii* var. *chino* (FRANCH. & SAV.) MAK.) An erect-growing bamboo with a creeping root-stock and dark green, purple-flushed canes, 3-4m high. Leaves 10-25cm long by 2-2.5cm wide, borne in stiff, plume-like clusters. Has flowered several times in cultivation without any ill effect. Japan. I 1876.

**f. angustifolia** (MITF.) CHAO & RENV. (*Arundinaria angustifolia* (MITF.) DE LEHAIE) (*Bambusa angustifolia* MITF.) (*Bambusa vilmorinii* HORT.) A narrow-leaved form reaching 2m tall. I about 1895.

**chrysantha** MITF. (*Pleioblastus chrysanthus* (MITF.) MCCLINTOCK) (*Sasa chrysantha* (MITF.) CAMUS) A fast-growing species forming dense thickets. Canes 1-2m high, deep olive green. Leaves 7.5-18cm long by 1.5-2.5cm wide, bright green, striped yellow, not very constant. A vigorous bamboo, useful as a ground cover. Japan. I 1892.

**disticha** See *A. pygmaea* var. *disticha*.

**falconeri** See *Thamnocalamus falconeri*.

## ARUNDINARIA—*continued*

**fastuosa** See *Semiarundinaria fastuosa*.

**fortunei** (VAN HOUTTE) NAKAI (*Arundinaria variegata* (MIQ.) MAK.) (*Pleioblastus variegatus* (MIQ.) MAK.) A low, tufted species forming dense thickets of erect, zig-zag, pale green canes 0.8-1.2m high. Leaves 5-20cm long by 1-2.5cm wide, dark green, with white stripes, fading to pale green. The best of the white variegated bamboos and suitable for the rock garden or tub culture. Japan. C 1863.

**'Gauntlettii'** See *A. humilis* 'Gauntlettii'.

**gigantea** (WALT.) CHAPM. (*A. macrosperma* MICHX.) "Cane Reed". A strong-growing bamboo, forming dense thickets under suitable conditions, but rarely invasive. Canes 4.5-6m or above in sheltered gardens, but usually 2.5-3m and dull greenish-yellow in colour. Leaves variable in size, 10-30cm long by 2-4cm wide, glabrous or nearly so above, sheaths deciduous. Native of the SE United States where it frequently forms dense thickets known as "cane brakes" on the swampy margins of rivers. It requires a sheltered position and is not suitable for cold areas.

**subsp. tecta** (WALT.) MCCLURE (*A. tecta* (WALT.) MUHL.) Canes up to 2m high bearing coarsely textured leaves up to 25cm long by 2cm wide, hairy on both sides, sheaths persistent.

**graminea** (BEAN) MAK. (*Pleioblastus gramineus* (BEAN) NAK.) A fast-growing species forming dense clumps or patches. Canes up to 3m tall, pale green, maturing to dull yellowish-green. Leaves very narrow in proportion to their length, 10-25cm long by 8-12mm wide. An excellent screening plant and one of the few hardy bamboos that prefers shade. It has flowered in several localities in recent years and good seed is usually produced. Ryukyu Islands (Japan). I 1877.

**hindsii** HORT. not MUNRO (*Pleioblastus hindsii* HORT. not (MUNRO) NAK.) A strong-growing species forming dense thickets of erect, olive-green canes, 2.5-3.5m high. Leaves variable in size, 15-23cm long by 1.5-2.5cm wide, of a rich sea-green, thickly clustered towards the summits of the canes. A useful bamboo which is equally happy in sun or dense shade and makes an excellent hedge or screen. Origin probably Japan. I 1875.

**hookeriana** See *Sinarundinaria hookeriana*.

**humilis** MITF. (*Pleioblastus humilis* (MITF.) NAK.) A rampant species forming low patches or thickets. Canes slender, dark green, 0.6-1.8m high, but usually under 1.2m. Leaves 5-20cm long by 1-2cm wide, slightly downy beneath. An excellent ground cover beneath trees or for covering unsightly banks or waste places. A few canes have flowered at their tips in several localities in recent years without any apparent ill effect. Japan. I about 1892.

**'Gauntlettii'** (*A.* 'Gauntlettii') (*Sasa gauntlettii*) A small clump-forming bamboo with bright green, later dull purple canes up to 0.8m high. Leaves 7.5-18cm long by 1-2cm wide. Very compact and tending not to spread. An uncommon bamboo of obscure, possibly Japanese origin. It was named by Messrs Gauntlett of Chiddingfold, Surrey.

**intermedia** See *Sinarundinaria intermedia*.

**japonica** See *Pseudosasa japonica*.

**jaunsarensis** See *Sinarundinaria anceps*.

**macrosperma** See *A. gigantea*.

**maling** See *Sinarundinaria maling*.

**marmorea** See *Chimonobambusa marmorea*.

**murielae** See *Thamnocalamus spathaceus*.

**nitida** See *Sinarundinaria nitida*.

**nobilis** See *Thamnocalamus falconeri*.

**pumila** MITF. (*Pleioblastus pumilus* (MITF.) NAK.) A very hardy, dwarf bamboo forming dense carpets of slender, dull purple canes 0.3-0.8m in height, with conspicuously hairy nodes. Leaves 5-18cm long by 1-2cm wide. A far-creeping species, useful as a ground cover. Japan. I late 19th century.

**pygmaea** (MIQ.) MITF. (*Pleioblastus pygmaeus* (MIQ.) NAK.) A dwarf species with far-reaching rhizomes forming carpets of slender stems up to 25cm long, taller in shade. Leaves up to 13cm long by 2cm wide. An excellent ground-cover plant. Japan.

**var. disticha** (MITF.) CHAO & RENV. (*Arundinaria disticha* (MITF.) PFITZER) A more vigorous form to 1m with larger, distinctly two-ranked leaves. I about 1870 from Japan where it is known only in cultivation.

**ARUNDINARIA**—*continued*

**quadrangularis** See *Chimonobambusa quadrangularis*.

**racemosa** HORT. See *Sinarundinaria maling*.

**ragamowskii** See *Indocalamus tessellatus*.

**simonii** (CARR.) RIV. (*Pleioblastus simonii* (CARR.) NAK.) A vigorous bamboo of erect habit, forming dense clumps or patches of tall, olive-green canes up to 4.5m high or more. The first-year canes are liberally dusted with a white bloom. Young shoots in spring edible. Leaves 7.5-30cm long by 1-3cm wide. The leaf under-surface is green down one side, greyish-green down the other. A hardy species with luxuriant foliage, useful as a hedge or screen. It has flowered in several localities in recent years and produced good seed. China. I 1862.

    **var. chino** See *Arundinaria chino*.

    **'Variegata'** (*Bambusa albostriata* HORT.) Some of the smaller leaves striped creamy-white, not consistent.

**spathiflora** See *Thamnocalamus spathiflorus*.

**tecta** See *A. gigantea* subsp. *tecta*.

**tessellata** See *Thamnocalamus tessellatus*.

**vagans** See *Sasa ramosa*.

**variegata** See *A. fortunei*.

**veitchii** See *Sasa veitchii*.

**viridi-striata** See *A. auricoma*.

**BAMBUSA albostriata** See *Arundinaria simonii* 'Variegata'.

**angustifolia** See *Arundinaria chino* f. *angustifolia*.

**metake** See *Pseudosasa japonica*.

**vilmorinii** See *Arundinaria chino* f. *angustifolia*.

**CHIMONOBAMBUSA** MAK. A genus of about 12 species, native to E and SE Asia.

**marmorea** (MITF.) MAK. (*Arundinaria marmorea* (MITF.) MAK.) A normally low-growing bamboo forming clumps or patches of 1-2m canes which are green at first maturing to deep purple when grown in a sunny position. The new shoots are an attractive pale green, mottled brown and silvery-white, tipped and striped pink. Leaves 5-15cm long by 1-1.5cm wide. A few canes have flowered on old clumps in recent years. Japan. I 1889.

**quadrangularis** (FENZI) MAK. (*Arundinaria quadrangularis* (FENZI) MAK.) (*Tetragonocalamus quadrangularis* (FENZI) MAK.) "Square-stemmed Bamboo". A rare species with a creeping root-stock. The bluntly four-angled canes reach 2.5-3m in height and in colour are dark green, occasionally splashed purple. The young shoots in spring are edible. Leaves 7.5-23cm long by 2.5-3cm wide. An attractive and unusual bamboo, only succeeding in a sheltered position. Not suitable for cold areas. China. Long cultivated and naturalised in Japan.

**CHUSQUEA** KUNTH A genus of about 95 species of graceful, mainly S American bamboos, distinct in their numerous, densely clustered branches, and their solid stems. Because of this latter characteristic Chusqueas are useful for cutting, as their leaves do not flag as easily as do those of the hollow-stemmed bamboos.

**breviglumis** HORT. See *C. couleou* var. *tenuis*.

**couleou** E. DESV. A hardy species, forming broad dense clumps. The deep olive-green canes, 2.5-3.5m high or occasionally up to 9m, produce dense clusters of slender, short, leafy branches along their entire length, giving them a characteristic bottlebrush effect. The first-year canes possess conspicuous white sheaths at each node. Young shoots in spring, edible. Leaves 2.5-7.5cm long by 6-10mm wide, slender-pointed. Chile. I 1890 and again by Harold Comber in 1926. AM 1974.

    **var. tenuis** MCCLINTOCK (*C. breviglumis* HORT. not PHIL.) A very distinct and ornamental form with numerous, spreading olive-green canes to 1.2m. This rare bamboo was introduced from Chile by Harold Comber.

**INDOCALAMUS** NAKAI A genus of about 15 species, natives of China, only the following generally grown.

**INDOCALAMUS**—*continued*

**tessellatus** (MUNRO) KENG (*Arundinaria ragamowskii* (NICHOLSON) PFITZER) (*Sasa tessellata* (MUNRO) MAK. & SHIB.) Not to be confused with the rare S African *Thamnocalamus tessellatus* q.v. This remarkable species forms dense thickets of slender, bright green canes up to 2m tall. The shining green leaves up to 60cm long by 5-10cm wide are the largest of all hardy bamboos and such is their collective weight that the canes bend down, giving the clump an almost dwarf habit. China. I 1845.

**PHYLLOSTACHYS** SIEB. & ZUCC. Tall, graceful bamboos usually less invasive than many of the Arundinarias from which they differ most markedly in the usually zig-zag stems, the internodes of which are flattened or shallowly grooved on alternate sides. Branches normally in pairs at each node. Some 60 species, natives of China.

**aurea** A. & C. RIV. A very graceful species, forming large clumps 2.5-3.5m high. Canes bright green at first, maturing to pale creamy-yellow, dull yellow in full sun. Leaves 7.5-18cm long by 1-2cm wide. A hardy bamboo characterised by the peculiar crowding of the nodes at the base of each cane and the curious swelling beneath each node. Young shoots in spring, edible. The canes are used in the Far East for walking sticks, umbrella handles, etc and in America for fishing rods. It has flowered on several occasions. China. Long cultivated in Japan. I before 1870.

**bambusoides** SIEB. & ZUCC. (*P. quiloi* (CARR.) RIV.) A very hardy and highly ornamental bamboo forming large clumps. Canes 3-4.5m high, deep shining green at first becoming deep yellow-green and finally brown at maturity. Leaves 5-19cm long by 1.5-3cm wide. In warmer countries canes are known to grow as much as 23m high and almost 15cm in diameter. In China, Japan and the United States it is cultivated on a commercial scale and its canes put to a wide range of uses. Young shoots in spring, edible. China. I 1866.

**'Allgold'** See *P. sulphurea*.

**'Sulphurea'** See *P. sulphurea*.

**boryana** See *P. nigra* 'Boryana'.

**edulis** (CARR.) DE LEHAIE (*P. heterocycla* var. *pubescens* (DE LEHAIE) OHWI) (*P. mitis* HORT. not A. & C. RIV.) (*P. pubescens* DE LEHAIE) A strong-growing bamboo with bright green, later dull yellow canes up to 4.5m high. Young shoots edible and much prized for this purpose in warmer climes. Leaves 7.5-10cm long by 2cm wide. Best grown in a sheltered position. China.

**'Heterocycla'** (*P. heterocycla* (CARR.) MITF.) (*P. pubescens* 'Heterocycla') (*P. pubescens* 'Kikkochiku') "Tortoise-shell Bamboo". An unusual form of vigorous growth differing in the curious appearance of the cane bases caused by the alternate swelling of the internodes. China. I 1893.

**flexuosa** A. & C. RIV. A graceful bamboo, 2.5-3m high, throwing up slender, somewhat wavy canes which are bright green at first, becoming darker at maturity. In time large thickets are formed. Young shoots in spring, edible. Leaves 5-13cm long by 1-2cm wide. Extensively cultivated in France for use as fishing rods. Excellent as a screening plant. Strong shoots are noticeably zig-zag at base. N China. I 1864.

**henonis** See *P. nigra* var. *henonis*.

**heterocycla** See *P. edulis* 'Heterocycla'.

**var. pubescens** See *P. edulis*.

**mitis** HORT. See *P. edulis*.

**nidularia** MUNRO A rare Chinese species with tall canes up to 6m in sheltered positions.

**nigra** (LODD.) MUNRO "Black Bamboo". A beautiful clump-forming bamboo of gracefully arching habit. Canes normally 2.5-3.5m, green the first year becoming mottled dark brown or black and finally an even jet black. In colder gardens the canes often remain a mottled brownish-green. Young shoots in spring, edible. Leaves 5-13cm long by 6-12mm wide. This distinct and attractive species enjoys a sunny position. China. I 1827. AM 1975.

**'Boryana'** ('Bory') (*P. boryana* MITF.) An elegant bamboo producing luxuriant masses of arching, leafy stems. Canes 2.5-4m high, green at first, changing to yellow and splashed purple. Young shoots in spring, edible. Leaves 5-9cm long by 6-12mm wide. A magnificent specimen plant in isolation. Originated in Japan.

**PHYLLOSTACHYS nigra**—*continued*

    **var. henonis** (MITF.) RENDLE ('Henon') (*P. henonis* MITF.) A handsome bamboo throwing up tall, graceful canes, 2.5-4m high, swathed in dark green clouds of shining leaves. Canes bright green at first maturing to brownish-yellow. Young shoots in spring, edible. Leaves 7.5-11cm long by 1-2cm wide. One of the best for planting as a specimen in a lawn or similarly prominent position. The common wild form of the species. C about 1890.

    **'Punctata'** Canes 2.5-3.5m high, green, mottled black, never wholly black as in *P. nigra*. Young shoots in spring, edible. Leaves 5-10cm long by 6-12mm wide. Originated in China.

  **quiloi** See *P. bambusoides*.

  **ruscifolia** See *Shibataea kumasaca*.

  **sulphurea** (CARR.) A. & C. RIV. (*P. bambusoides* 'Allgold') (*P. bambusoides* 'Sulphurea') A very attractive bamboo related to *P. bambusoides*, differing in its generally smaller leaves and its rich yellow canes, which are sometimes striped with green along the internodal grooves. E China. I 1865.

  **viridi-glaucescens** (CARR.) A. & C. RIV. A graceful, extremely hardy clump-forming species. Canes 4-6m high, green at first changing to dull yellowish-green. Leaves 7.5-15cm long, 1-2cm wide, brilliant green above, glaucous beneath. Forms a thicket in ideal conditions, but otherwise an attractive specimen plant in isolation. E China. I 1846.

  **vivax** MCCLURE An erect-growing species of compact, clump-forming habit. The tall green, thin-walled canes will attain 8m in mild areas and bear heavy drooping foliage. It resembles *P. bambusoides*, but is faster-growing. E China. I 1908 (to North America).


**PLEIOBLASTUS chino** See *Arundinaria chino*.

  **chrysanthus** See *Arundinaria chrysantha*.

  **gramineus** See *Arundinaria graminea*.

  **hindsii** See *Arundinaria hindsii*.

  **humilis** See *Arundinaria humilis*.

  **pumilus** See *Arundinaria pumila*.

  **pygmaeus** See *Arundinaria pygmaea*.

  **simonii** See *Arundinaria simonii*.

  **variegatus** See *Arundinaria fortunei*.

  **viridi-striatus** See *Arundinaria auricoma*.


**PSEUDOSASA** NAKAI A genus of 4 species of bamboos from E Asia, only the following is in cultivation here.

  **japonica** (STEUD) NAKAI (*Arundinaria japonica* STEUD.) (*Bambusa metake* MIQ.) This extremely adaptable and very hardy species is the bamboo most commonly cultivated in the British Isles. It forms dense thickets of olive-green canes, 3-4.5m, occasionally up to 6m high, arching at the summit and bearing lush masses of dark glossy green leaves 18-30cm long by 2-5cm wide. The greyish under-surface of the leaf has a characteristic greenish marginal strip. Branches borne singly from each of the upper nodes. Isolated plants and odd canes have flowered sporadically in cultivation. Japan, S Korea. I 1850.


**SASA** MAK. & SHIB. A genus of about 50 species of small, thicket-forming bamboos with a typically low habit, usually solitary branches arising from each node and relatively broad oblong or ovate-oblong leaves. Natives of Japan, Korea and China.

  **albo-marginata** See *S. veitchii*.

  **palmata** (BURB.) E.G. CAMUS (*Bambusa palmata* BURB.) A rampant, large-leaved bamboo forming extensive thickets of bright green canes 2-2.5m high. Leaves up to 35cm long by 9cm wide, the margins often withering during a hard winter. It has been flowering profusely for several years now. Although too invasive for the small garden it provides an excellent shelter plant where space permits. Japan. I 1889. FCC 1896.

    **f. nebulosa** (MAK.) SUZUKI The commonly grown form distinguished by its purple blotched stems.

  **ramosa** (MAK.) MAK. & SHIB. (*Sasaella ramosa* (MAK.) MAK.) (*Arundinaria vagans* GAMBLE) (*Pleioblastus viridi-striatus* var. *vagans* (GAMBLE) NAKAI) A dwarf, creeping species,

**SASA ramosa**—*continued*

quickly forming extensive carpets of bright green foliage. Canes 0.4-1.1m high, bright green at first, becoming deep olive-green, bearing solitary branches from each node. Leaves 5-15cm long by 1-2cm wide, downy on both surfaces. Too rampant for most gardens, but an excellent ground cover where little else will grow, even in dense shade. Japan. I 1892. It flowered at Kew in 1981, the first time outside Japan.

**tessellata** See *Indocalamus tessellatus.*

**veitchii** (CARR.) REHD. (*S. albo-marginata* (MIQ.) MAK.) (*Arundinaria veitchii* (CARR.) N.E. BROWN) A small, dense-growing species forming large thickets of deep purplish-green, later dull purple canes 0.6-1.2m high. Leaves 10-25cm long by 2.5-6cm wide, withering and becoming pale straw-coloured or whitish along the margins in autumn, providing an attractive and characteristic variegated effect, which lasts throughout winter. Japan. I 1880. AM 1898.

**SASAELLA ramosa** See *Sasa ramosa.*

**SEMIARUNDINARIA** NAKAI About 20 species of bamboos native to E Asia.

**fastuosa** (MITF.) NAKAI (*Arundinaria fastuosa* MITF.) An extremely hardy, vigorous bamboo of stiff, erect habit, forming tall, dense clumps of deep glossy green canes, 4.5-7.5m high which are useful as stakes. Leaves 10-25cm long by 1.5-2.5cm wide. A handsome species of distinct habit which has been flowering sporadically in cultivation for several years. The young shoots in spring are edible. An excellent screen or tall hedge. Japan. I 1892. AM 1953.

**SHIBATAEA** NAKAI A genus of 5 species, natives of Japan and China. Low-growing bamboos with a creeping root-stock. Stems flattened on one side between the nodes. Branches short and leafy, borne in clusters of 3-5 at each node.

**kumasaca** (STEUD.) NAKAI (*Phyllostachys ruscifolia* (MUNRO) SATOW) A very distinct bamboo of dwarf, compact habit. Canes 0.5-0.8m high characteristically zig-zag and almost triangular in outline, pale green at first, maturing to dull brownish. Leaves broadly lanceolate to ovate-oblong, 5-10cm long by 2-3cm wide. It has flowered in recent years with no apparent ill effect. A charming species forming dense leafy clumps, particularly happy in a moist soil. Japan. I 1861. FCC 1896.

**SINARUNDINARIA** NAKAI A genus of some 50 species, natives of Asia, C America and Africa.

**anceps** (MITF.) CHAO & RENV. (*Arundinaria anceps* MITF.) (*A. jaunsarensis* GAMBLE) A beautiful but rampant species, ideal for screens and hedges and the mature canes for use in the garden. The straight, erect, deep glossy green canes reach a height of 3-3.5m or more in mild localities. The arching tips bear masses of glossy green leaves, 10-15cm long by 12mm wide. Has flowered in various parts of the British Isles. NW Himalaya. I 1865.

**'Pitt White'** A vigorous form which, in the garden of Dr Mutch at Pitt White, Lyme Regis, Dorset reached a height of 9m, the canes bearing great plumes of small, narrow leaves, 7.5cm long by 1.25cm wide. It was originally misidentified as *Arundinaria niitakayamensis*, a dwarf species native to Taiwan and the Philippines which is not in cultivation.

†**hookeriana** (MUNRO) CHAO & RENV. (*Arundinaria hookeriana* MUNRO) An attractive but tender bamboo suited for the conservatory, or outside only in the mildest localities. Canes up to 3.5-5.5m in height, golden yellow when mature, with deep striations. Leaves 7.5-30cm long by 1.25-3.75cm wide, glaucous when young. Assam, Nepal to Bhutan. Plants flowered, seeded then died at Kew in 1899.

†**intermedia** (MUNRO) CHAO & RENV. (*Arundinaria intermedia* MUNRO) A vigorous but tender species with erect, green canes, 2.5-3.5m high, forming a dense clump. Leaves 7.5-20cm long by 1.5-2.5cm wide. Only suitable for the mildest localities, but an attractive tub plant for the conservatory. E Himalaya. Flowered and died at Kew in 1899.

**maling** (GAMBLE) CHAO & RENV. (*Arundinaria maling* GAMBLE) (*A. racemosa* HORT. not MUNRO) A rare bamboo with a creeping root-stock. Canes brownish-green at first,

**SINARUNDINARIA maling**—*continued*

maturing to dull brown, 2.5-3.5m high or more. Leaves 5-15cm long by 12mm wide. Similar to *Thamnocalamus spathiflorus* in general appearance, but habit more robust and foliage of a darker green. The internodes are extremely rough to the touch. Nepal, Sikkim.

**murielae** See *Thamnocalamus spathaceus.*

**nitida** (MITF.) NAKAI (*Arundinaria nitida* MITF.) This beautiful clump-forming species is often confused with *Thamnocalamus spathaceus*, but differs most noticeably in its purple-flushed canes and narrower leaves. It is one of the most elegant and ornamental of all bamboos, with canes 3-3.8m high, or more, arching at the summit under the weight of foliage. Leaves 5-8cm long by 6-12mm wide, thin and delicate. It thrives best in a little shade and makes an excellent specimen plant. It may also be grown most effectively in a large tub. China. C 1889. FCC 1898. AGM 1930.

**TETRAGONOCALAMUS quadrangularis** See *Chimonobambusa quadrangularis.*

**THAMNOCALAMUS** MUNRO 6 species, natives of China, the Himalaya and Africa.

**falconeri** MUNRO (*Arundinaria falconeri* (MUNRO) RIVIERE) (*A. nobilis* HORT.) A strong-growing, but tender species forming dense clumps up to 6m or more in sheltered gardens, but normally 1.8-3m. Canes olive-green, maturing to dull yellow in a sunny position, thin and pliable. Leaves 5-10cm long by 12mm wide, delicate and paper-thin. Flowered during 1875-77, 1903-07 and again profusely during 1966 and 1967 producing large, gracefully branched panicles of chocolate-red spikelets. All clumps subsequently died, but seed was produced from which fresh stocks were grown. This beautiful species has grown for many years in a sheltered position in the Hillier Gardens and Arboretum. Originally distributed wrongly as *Arundinaria pantlingii*. NE Himalaya. Introduced by Col Madden in 1847.

**spathaceus** (FRANCH.) SODERSTROM (*Arundinaria murielae* GAMBLE) (*Sinarundinaria murielae* (GAMBLE) NAKAI) An elegant species forming graceful arching clumps 2.5-3.5m high or more. Canes bright green at first, maturing to a dull yellow-green. Leaves 6-10cm long by 1-2cm wide, of a bright pea-green. This beautiful bamboo, which is undoubtedly one of the best species in cultivation, was introduced from China in 1913 by Ernest Wilson, after whose daughter Muriel it was subsequently named. Excellent as an isolated specimen plant or in a large tub. AGM 1973.

**spathiflorus** (TRIN.) MUNRO (*Arundinaria spathiflora* TRIN.) A beautiful clump-forming species of neat, erect habit. Canes densely packed, up to 4.5m high, but more usually 2.5-3m, bright green ripening to a pinkish-purple shade on the exposed side, white bloomy during their first season. Leaves 7.5-15cm long by 6-12mm wide. A lovely bamboo, thriving best in a little shade and shelter. NW Himalaya. I 1882.

**tessellatus** (NEES) SODERSTROM & ELLIS (*Arundinaria tessellata* (NEES) MUNRO) A rare species not to be confused with *Indocalamus tessellatus*, forming clumps or patches. Canes 2.5-3.5m high, pale green at first, darkening and maturing to a deep purple. Cane sheaths conspicuous, white the first year, cream later. Leaves 5-14cm long by 1cm wide. The only bamboo native to S Africa, where it occurs in the mountains from Table Mountain northwards. The canes are said to have been used by the Zulus in the construction of shields, etc.

# Botanical Names

The study of plant names is a fascinating subject and one which never goes unrewarded. Learning about names can be fun, and knowledge of their derivation and meaning makes them and the plants they apply to easier to remember.

To the uninitiated, however, botanical names can be a confusing barrier to a better understanding of plants. Why can't plants be known only by English names? Botanical names are written in Latin and are accepted the world over. Vernacular or common names are often easier to remember and pronounce but they can be a source of much confusion and misunderstanding. For example, the names "Bilberry", "Whortleberry", "Blaeberry", "Huckleberry" and "Whinberry" are all English names used in different parts of the British Isles for the same plant—*Vaccinium myrtillus*. Mention "Huckleberry" to an American gardener and he would probably think of a *Gaylussacia*. Mention any of the above to a Russian, Chinese, French or any other non-English-speaking horticulturist and he would shake his head, but mention the botanical name and there is a reasonable chance that he would understand. Another example is the "Swamp Honeysuckle" of the United States. An English gardener would probably imagine this to be a species of *Lonicera* and be surprised to learn that it is in fact the American name for *Rhododendron viscosum*. Thus it will be seen that botanical names are worth learning and using. They need not be tiresome and boring; on the contrary, botanical names usually tell us something about a plant.

**Generic Names** These are always nouns. Their origins and meanings are occasionally obscure, but the majority are derived from older names in Greek, Latin, Arabic and other languages.

Some generic names are based on characters in Greek mythology, eg

> **DAPHNE** named after the river god's daughter
>
> **ANDROMEDA** named after the daughter of Cepheus and Cassiope
>
> **PHYLLODOCE** name of a sea nymph

whilst others commemorate people, such as botanists, patrons, etc, eg

> **BUDDLEJA** named after Rev Adam Buddle
>
> **DEUTZIA** named after J. Deutz
>
> **ESCALLONIA** named after Signor Escallon
>
> **FUCHSIA** named after Leonard Fuchs
>
> **LONICERA** named after Adam Lonicer

**Specific Epithets** The term epithet is used here rather than name because, unlike generic names, these will not stand on their own. Those used to describe species are varied and fall into four main categories (see also under Nomenclature and Classification, page 19) namely:

A   Epithets which indicate the origin of a plant, eg continent, country, region, etc.

B   Epithets that describe the habitat of a plant (where it grows in the wild), eg, in woods, on mountains, by rivers, etc.

C   Epithets that describe a plant or a particular feature, such as size, habit, leaf shape, colour of flower, etc.

D   Epithets which commemorate people, eg botanists, plant collectors, patrons, famous horticulturists, etc.

The following lists are merely a selection of the most commonly used specific epithets and their meanings.

### Epithets which are Geographical

| | | |
|---|---|---|
| **atlantica(um)(us)** | (*Cedrus atlantica*) | —of the Atlas Mountains (North Africa) |
| **australe(is)** | (*Cordyline australis*) | —southern |
| **boreale(is)** | (*Linnaea borealis*) | —northern |
| **californica(um)(us)** | (*Fremontodendron californicum*) | —of California |

## Epithets which are Geographical *continued*

| | | |
|---|---|---|
| capense(is) | (*Phygelius capensis*) | —of the Cape (South Africa) |
| europaea(um)(us) | (*Euonymus europaeus*) | —of Europe |
| himalaica(um)(us) | (*Stachyurus himalaicus*) | —of the Himalaya |
| hispanica(um)(us) | (*Genista hispanica*) | —of Spain |
| japonica(um)(us) | (*Camellia japonica*) | —of Japan |
| lusitanica(um)(us) | (*Prunus lusitanica*) | —of Portugal |
| nipponica(um)(us) | (*Spiraea nipponica*) | —of Japan |
| occidentale(is) | (*Thuja occidentalis*) | —western |
| orientale(is) | (*Thuja orientalis*) | —eastern |
| sinense(is) | (*Wisteria sinensis*) | —of China |

### Epithets describing Habitat

| | | |
|---|---|---|
| alpina(um)(us) | (*Daphne alpina*) | —alpine, of the Alps or growing in alpine regions |
| arvense(is) | (*Rosa arvensis*) | —of fields or cultivated land |
| aquatica(um)(us) | (*Nyssa aquatica*) | —of water, or growing by water |
| campestre(is) | (*Acer campestre*) | —of plains or flat areas |
| littorale(is) | (*Griselinia littoralis*) | —of sea shores |
| maritima(um)(us) | (*Prunus maritima*) | —by the sea |
| montana(um)(us) | (*Clematis montana*) | —of mountains |
| palustre(is) | (*Ledum palustre*) | —of swamps or marshes |
| sylvatica(um)(us) | (*Fagus sylvatica*) | —of woods |

### Epithets describing Habit

| | | |
|---|---|---|
| arborea(um)(us) | (*Rhododendron arboreum*) | —tree-like |
| fastigiata(um)(us) | (*Cassiope fastigiata*) | —erect, the branches |
| fruticosa(um)(us) | (*Bupleurum fruticosum*) | —shrubby |
| horizontale(is) | (*Cotoneaster horizontalis*) | —horizontally spreading |
| humile(is) | (*Chamaerops humilis*) | —low-growing |
| major(us) | (*Vinca major*) | —greater |
| minor(us) | (*Vinca minor*) | —lesser |
| nana(um)(us) | (*Betula nana*) | —dwarf |
| pendula(um)(us) | (*Betula pendula*) | —pendulous, weeping |
| procera(um)(us) | (*Abies procera*) | —very tall, high |
| procumbens | (*Juniperus procumbens*) | —procumbent, creeping |
| prostrata(um)(us) | (*Ceanothus prostratus*) | —prostrate, hugging the ground |
| repens | (*Salix repens*) | —creeping and rooting |
| suffruticosa(um)(us) | (*Paeonia suffruticosa*) | —woody at base |

### Epithets describing Leaves

Many names describe shape and toothing of leaves, eg ovata, lanceolata, rotundifolia, serrata, crenata, laciniata for which see Glossary pp 24–30.

**(phylla(um)(us) and folia(um)(us) = leaf)**

| | | |
|---|---|---|
| angustifolia(um)(us) | (*Phillyrea angustifolia*) | —narrow-leaved |
| arguta(um)(us) | (*Spiraea 'Arguta'*) | —sharp |
| coriacea(um)(us) | (*Holboellia coriacea*) | —coriaceous, leathery |
| crassifolia(um)(us) | (*Hymenanthera crassifolia*) | —thick-leaved |
| decidua(um)(us) | (*Larix decidua*) | —deciduous, dropping its leaves |
| glabra(um)(us) | (*Elaeagnus glabra*) | —glabrous, without hairs |
| heterophylla(um)(us) | (*Osmanthus heterophyllus*) | —variably-leaved |
| hirsuta(um)(us) | (*Vaccinium hirsutum*) | —hairy |
| incana(um)(us) | (*Alnus incana*) | —grey-downy |
| integrifolia(um)(us) | (*Schizophragma integrifolium*) | —without teeth |
| laevigata(um)(us) | (*Rosa laevigata*) | —smooth and polished |
| latifolia(um)(us) | (*Ilex latifolia*) | —broad-leaved |
| macrophylla(um)(us) | (*Acer macrophyllum*) | —large-leaved |

## Epithets describing Leaves *continued*

| | | |
|---|---|---|
| **maculata(um)(us)** | (*Elaeagnus pungens* 'Maculata') | —spotted, blotched |
| **microphylla(um)(us)** | (*Azara microphylla*) | —small-leaved |
| **molle(is)** | (*Hamamelis mollis*) | —soft |
| **nitida(um)(us)** | (*Lonicera nitida*) | —shining |
| **parvifolia(um)(us)** | (*Ulmus parvifolia*) | —small-leaved |
| **picta(um)(us)** | (*Kalopanax pictus*) | —painted, coloured |
| **pinnata(um)(us)** | (*Psoralea pinnata*) | —pinnate |
| **platyphylla(os)(um)(us)** | (*Tilia platyphyllos*) | —broad-leaved |
| **reticulata(um)(us)** | (*Salix reticulata*) | —net-veined |
| **sempervirens** | (*Buxus sempervirens*) | —always green, evergreen |
| **splendens** | (*Cotoneaster splendens*) | —glittering, shining |
| **tomentosa(um)(us)** | (*Tilia tomentosa*) | —covered with a short dense pubescence |
| **variegata(um)(us)** | (*Cornus mas* 'Variegata') | —variegated, two-coloured |
| **velutina(um)(us)** | (*Fraxinus velutina*) | —velvety |

### Epithets describing Flowers
**(flora(um)(us)** = flower)

| | | |
|---|---|---|
| **campanulata(um)(us)** | (*Rhododendron campanulatum*) | —bell-shaped |
| **floribunda(um)(us)** | (*Dipelta floribunda*) | —free-flowering |
| **grandiflora(um)(us)** | (*Viburnum grandiflorum*) | —large-flowered |
| **macropetala(um)(us)** | (*Clematis macropetala*) | —large-petalled |
| **nudiflora(um)(us)** | (*Jasminum nudiflorum*) | —naked, without leaves |
| **nutans** | (*Rubus nutans*) | —nodding |
| **paniculata(um)(us)** | (*Koelreuteria paniculata*) | —flowering in panicles |
| **parviflora(um)(us)** | (*Aesculus parviflora*) | —small-flowered |
| **pauciflora(um)(us)** | (*Corylopsis pauciflora*) | —few-flowered |
| **polyantha(um)(us)** | (*Jasminum polyanthum*) | —many-flowered |
| **racemosa(um)(us)** | (*Berchemia racemosa*) | —flowers in racemes |
| **spicata(um)(us)** | (*Corylopsis spicata*) | —flowers in spikes |
| **stellata(um)(us)** | (*Magnolia stellata*) | —starry |
| **triflora(um)(us)** | (*Abelia triflora*) | —flowers in threes |
| **umbellata(um)(us)** | (*Berberis umbellata*) | —flowers in umbels |
| **uniflora(um)(us)** | (*Crataegus uniflora*) | —one-flowered |

### Epithets describing Colours

| | | |
|---|---|---|
| **alba(um)(us)** | (*Populus alba*) | —white |
| **argentea(um)(us)** | (*Shepherdia argentea*) | —silvery |
| **aurantiaca(um)(us)** | (*Mimulus aurantiacus*) | —orange |
| **aurea(um)(us)** | (*Salvia aurea*) | —golden |
| **bicolor** | (*Picea bicolor*) | —two-coloured |
| **carnea(um)(us)** | (*Aesculus × carnea*) | —flesh coloured |
| **caerulea(um)(us)** | (*Passiflora caerulea*) | —blue |
| **cinerea(um)(us)** | (*Erica cinerea*) | —ash-grey |
| **coccinea(um)(us)** | (*Quercus coccinea*) | —scarlet |
| **concolor** | (*Abies concolor*) | —of the same colour |
| **discolor** | (*Holodiscus discolor*) | —two-coloured |
| **ferruginea(um)(us)** | (*Rhododendron ferrugineum*) | —rusty brown |
| **flava(um)(us)** | (*Rhododendron flavum*) | —pale yellow |
| **glauca(um)(us)** | (*Picea glauca*) | —sea-green |
| **lactea(um)(us)** | (*Rhododendron lacteum*) | —milk-white |
| **lilacina(um)(us)** | (*Paulownia lilacina*) | —lilac |
| **lutea(um)(us)** | (*Cladrastis lutea*) | —yellow |
| **nigra(um)(us)** | (*Sambucus nigra*) | —black |
| **punicea(um)(us)** | (*Clianthus puniceus*) | —crimson |
| **purpurea(um)(us)** | (*Malus × purpurea*) | —purple |

## Epithets describing Colours *continued*

| | | |
|---|---|---|
| rosea(um)(us) | (*Lapageria rosea*) | —rose coloured |
| rubra(um)(us) | (*Quercus rubra*) | —red |
| sanguinea(um)(us) | (*Ribes sanguineum*) | —blood-red |
| tricolor | (*Rubus tricolor*) | —three-coloured |
| variegata(um)(us) | (*Weigela florida* 'Variegata') | —variegated, two-coloured |
| versicolor | (*Cytisus × versicolor*) | —variously coloured, or changing colour |
| violacea(um)(us) | (*Jovellana violacea*) | —violet |
| viride(is) | (*Alnus viridis*) | —green |

### Epithets describing Aromas and Scents

| | | |
|---|---|---|
| citriodora(um)(us) | (*Eucalyptus citriodora*) | —lemon-scented |
| foetida(um)(us) | (*Viburnum foetidum*) | —strong-smelling, unpleasant |
| fragrantissima(um)(us) | (*Lonicera fragrantissima*) | —most fragrant |
| graveolens | (*Ruta graveolens*) | —smelling unpleasantly |
| odorata(um)(us) | (*Rubus odoratus*) | —sweet-scented |
| odoratissima(um)(us) | (*Viburnum odoratissimum*) | —sweetest scented |
| moschata(um)(us) | (*Olearia moschata*) | —musk-scented |
| suaveolens | (*Brugmansia suaveolens*) | —sweet-scented |

### Epithets alluding to Other Plants

| | | |
|---|---|---|
| bignonioides | (*Catalpa bignonioides*) | —Bignonia-like |
| jasminea | (*Daphne jasminea*) | —Jasmine-like |
| liliiflora(um)(us) | (*Magnolia liliiflora*) | —Lily-flowered |
| pseudoplatanus | (*Acer pseudoplatanus*) | —False Plane |
| salicifolia(um)(us) | (*Cotoneaster salicifolius*) | —Willow-leaved |
| tulipifera(um)(us) | (*Liriodendron tulipifera*) | —Tulip-bearing |

### Epithets which are Commemorative

| | | |
|---|---|---|
| delavayi | (*Abies delavayi*) | —after the Abbé Delavay |
| harryana(um)(us) | (*Viburnum harryanum*) | —after Sir Harry Veitch |
| henryana(um)(us) | (*Parthenocissus henryana*) | —after Dr Augustine Henry |
| hookeri | (*Acer hookeri*) | —after Sir Joseph Hooker |
| thunbergii | (*Spiraea thunbergii*) | —after Carl Peter Thunberg |
| williamsiana(um)(us) | (*Rhododendron williamsianum*) | —after Mr J. C. Williams |
| willmottiana(um)(us) | (*Ceratostigma willmottianum*) | —after Miss Ellen Willmott |
| wilsoniae | (*Berberis wilsoniae*) | —after Mrs E. H. Wilson. |

### Miscellaneous Epithets

| | | |
|---|---|---|
| affine(is) | (*Cotoneaster affinis*) | —related (to another species) |
| alata(um)(us) | (*Euonymus alatus*) | —winged |
| amabile(is) | (*Kolkwitzia amabilis*) | —lovely |
| ambigua(um)(us) | (*Ribes ambiguum*) | —doubtful (identity) |
| amoena(um)(us) | (*Lonicera × amoena*) | —charming, pleasing |
| bella(um)(us) | (*Spiraea bella*) | —pretty |
| commune(is) | (*Juniperus communis*) | —common, occurring in plenty |
| confusa(um)(us) | (*Sarcococca confusa*) | —confused (identity) |
| dulce(is) | (*Prunus dulcis*) | —sweet |
| edule(is) | (*Passiflora edulis*) | —edible |
| florida(um)(us) | (*Cornus florida*) | —flowering |
| formosa(um)(us) | (*Leycesteria formosa*) | —handsome, beautiful |
| hybrida(um)(us) | (*Deutzia × hybrida*) | —hybrid |
| insigne(is) | (*Sorbus insignis*) | —outstanding |
| intermedia(um)(us) | (*Eucryphia × inter-media*) | —intermediate |
| media(um)(us) | (*Mahonia × media*) | —middle, midway between |
| officinale(is) | (*Rosmarinus officinalis*) | —of the shop (herbal) |
| praecox | (*Chimonanthus praecox*) | —early |

## Miscellaneous Epithets *continued*

| | | |
|---|---|---|
| **pulchella(um)(us)** | (*Agathosma pulchella*) | —beautiful |
| **speciosa(um)(us)** | (*Callistemon speciosus*) | —showy |
| **sativa(um)(us)** | (*Castanea sativa*) | —sown, planted or cultivated |
| **utile(is)** | (*Viburnum utile*) | —useful |
| **vernale(is)** | (*Hamamelis vernalis*) | —spring |
| **vulgare(is)** | (*Calluna vulgaris*) | —common |

Those wishing to pursue this subject may be interested in the following books:-

*Plant Names Simplified* by A. T. Johnson and H. A. Smith, first published in 1931, and since revised and enlarged.

*Botanical Latin* by William T. Stearn, 3rd revised edition published in 1983; a book which can be thoroughly recommended to all interested in botanical names, be he botanist or gardener.

*A Gardener's Dictionary of Plant Names* by A. W. Smith; revised and enlarged by William T. Stearn, and published in 1972.

*The Collingridge Dictionary of Plant Names* by Allen J. Coombes, 1985.

# List of Genera included by Family

(including intergeneric and graft hybrids)

**ACERACEAE**
Acer
Dipteronia

**ACTINIDIACEAE**
Actinidia
Clematoclethra

**AGAVACEAE**
Beschorneria
Cordyline
Hesperaloe
Yucca

**ALANGIACEAE**
Alangium

**ANACARDIACEAE**
Cotinus
Pistacia
Rhus
Schinus

**ANNONACEAE**
Asimina

**APOCYNACEAE**
Elytropus
Mandevilla
Nerium
Trachelospermum
Vinca

**AQUIFOLIACEAE**
Ilex

**ARALIACEAE**
Aralia
Eleutherococcus
× Fatshedera
Fatsia
Hedera
Kalopanax
Oplopanax
Pseudopanax
Schefflera

**ARAUCARIACEAE**
Agathis
Araucaria

**ARISTOLOCHIACEAE**
Aristolochia

**ASCLEPIADACEAE**
Araujia
Cionura
Dregea
Oxypetalum
Periploca

**ASTELIACEAE**
Astelia

**ATHEROSPERMATACEAE**
Atherosperma
Laurelia

**BAUERACEAE**
Bauera

**BERBERIDACEAE**
Berberis
× Mahoberberis
Mahonia
Nandina

**BETULACEAE**
Alnus
Betula

**BIGNONIACEAE**
Bignonia
Campsis
Catalpa
Eccremocarpus
Pandorea
Tecomaria

**BORAGINACEAE**
Lithodora
Moltkia

**CALYCANTHACEAE**
Calycanthus
Chimonanthus
Sinocalycanthus

**CANNABIDACEAE**
Humulus

**CAPRIFOLIACEAE**
Abelia
Diervilla
Dipelta
Heptacodium
Kolkwitzia
Leycesteria
Linnaea
Lonicera
Sambucus
Symphoricarpos
Viburnum
Weigela

**CARPINACEAE**
Carpinus
Ostrya
Ostryopsis

**CASUARINACEAE**
Casuarina

**CELASTRACEAE**
Celastrus
Euonymus
Maytenus
Paxistima
Tripterygium

**CEPHALOTAXACEAE**
Cephalotaxus

**CERCIDIPHYLLACEAE**
Cercidiphyllum

**CHENOPODIACEAE**
Atriplex
Camphorosma
Suaeda

**CHLORANTHACEAE**
Sarcandra

## CISTACEAE
Cistus
× Halimiocistus
Halimium
Helianthemum

## CLETHRACEAE
Clethra

## CNEORACEAE
Cneorum

## COMPOSITAE
Artemisia
Aster
Baccharis
Brachyglottis
Cassinia
Chiliotrichum
Eumorphia
Eupatorium
Euryops
Grindelia
Helichrysum
Mutisia
Olearia
Othonna
Oxylobus
Ozothamnus
Pachystegia
Pertya
Plecostachys
Santolina
Senecio

## CONVOLVULACEAE
Convolvulus

## CORIARIACEAE
Coriaria

## CORNACEAE
Aucuba
Cornus
Corokia
Griselinia
Helwingia

## CORYLACEAE
Corylus

## CRASSULACEAE
Sedum

## CRUCIFERAE
Vella

## CUNONIACEAE
Caldcluvia
Weinmannia

## CUPRESSACEAE
Austrocedrus
Callitris
Calocedrus
Chamaecyparis
× Cupressocyparis
Cupressus
Diselma
Fitzroya
Fokienia
Juniperus
Libocedrus
Microbiota
Pilgerodendron
Tetraclinis
Thuja
Thujopsis
Widdringtonia

## CYRILLACEAE
Cyrilla

## DAPHNIPHYLLACEAE
Daphniphyllum

## DAVIDIACEAE
Davidia

## EBENACEAE
Diospyros

## EHRETIACEAE
Ehretia

## ELAEAGNACEAE
Elaeagnus
Hippophae
Shepherdia

## ELAEOCARPACEAE
Aristotelia
Crinodendron
Elaeocarpus
Vallea

## EMPETRACEAE
Empetrum

## EPACRIDACEAE
Cyathodes
Leucopogon
Richea
Trochocarpa

## EPHEDRACEAE
Ephedra

## ERICACEAE
Agapetes
Agarista
Andromeda
Arbutus
Arctostaphylos
Arctous
Bruckenthalia
Bryanthus
Calluna
Cassiope
Chamaedaphne
Daboecia
Elliottia
Enkianthus
Epigaea
Erica
× Gaulnettya
Gaultheria
Gaylussacia
Kalmia
Kalmiopsis
Ledum
Leiophyllum
Leucothoe
Loiseleuria
Lyonia
Menzie sia
Oxydendrum
Pernettya
× Phylliopsis
Phyllodoce
Phyllothamnus
Pieris
Rhododendron
Rhodothamnus
Tsusiophyllum
Vaccinium
Zenobia

## ESCALLONIACEAE
Anopterus
Carpodetus
Escallonia

## EUCOMMIACEAE
Eucommia

667

**EUCRYPHIACEAE**
Eucryphia

**EUPHORBIACEAE**
Andrachne
Euphorbia
Glochidion
Mallotus
Sapium
Securinega

**EUPTELEACEAE**
Euptelea

**FAGACEAE**
Castanea
Castanopsis
Chrysolepis
Fagus
Lithocarpus
Nothofagus
Quercus

**FLACOURTIACEAE**
Azara
Berberidopsis
Carrierea
Idesia
Poliothyrsis
Xylosma

**GARRYACEAE**
Garrya

**GESNERIACEAE**
Asteranthera
Mitraria

**GINKGOACEAE**
Ginkgo

**GRAMINEAE**
Arundinaria
Chimonobambusa
Chusquea
Indocalamus
Phyllostachys
Pseudosasa
Sasa
Semiarundinaria
Shibataea
Sinarundinaria
Thamnocalamus

**GROSSULARIACEAE**
Itea
Ribes

**GUTTIFERAE**
Hypericum

**HAMAMELIDACEAE**
Corylopsis
Disanthus
Distylium
Fortunearia
Fothergilla
Hamamelis
Liquidambar
Loropetalum
Parrotia
Parrotiopsis
Rhodoleia
Sinowilsonia
× Sycoparrotia
Sycopsis

**HIPPOCASTANACEAE**
Aesculus

**HYDRANGEACEAE**
Decumaria
Hydrangea
Pileostegia
Schizophragma

**ICACINACEAE**
Citronella

**ILLICIACEAE**
Illicium

**JUGLANDACEAE**
Carya
Juglans
Platycarya
Pterocarya

**LABIATAE**
Ballota
Colquhounia
Elsholtzia
Lavandula
Leonotis
Perovskia
Phlomis
Prostanthera
Rosmarinus
Salvia
Sphacele

Teucrium
Westringia

**LARDIZABALACEAE**
Akebia
Decaisnea
Holboellia
Lardizabala
Sinofranchetia
Stauntonia

**LAURACEAE**
Cinnamomum
Laurus
Lindera
Neolitsea
Persea
Sassafras
Umbellularia

**LEGUMINOSAE**
Acacia
Adenocarpus
Albizia
Amicia
Amorpha
Anagyris
Anthyllis
Astragalus
Caesalpinia
Calophaca
Caragana
Carmichaelia
Ceratonia
Cercis
Chordospartium
Cladrastis
Clianthus
Colutea
Coronilla
Cytisus
Desmodium
Dorycnium
Erinacea
Erythrina
Genista
Gleditsia
Gymnocladus
Halimodendron
Hedysarum
Indigofera
+ Laburnocytisus
Laburnum
Lespedeza
Lupinus
Maackia

**Leguminosae** *contd*
Medicago
Notospartium
Ononis
Petteria
Piptanthus
Psoralea
Pueraria
Robinia
Senna
Sophora
Spartium
Sutherlandia
Ulex
Wisteria

**LEITNERIACEAE**
Leitneria

**LINACEAE**
Linum

**LOGANIACEAE**
Buddleja
Gelsemium

**LYTHRACEAE**
Heimia
Lagerstroemia

**MAGNOLIACEAE**
Liriodendron
Magnolia
Manglietia
Michelia

**MALVACEAE**
Abutilon
Hibiscus
Hoheria
Lavatera
Plagianthus
Sphaeralcea

**MELASTOMATACEAE**
Tibouchina

**MELIACEAE**
Melia
Toona

**MELIANTHACEAE**
Melianthus

**MENISPERMACEAE**
Cocculus
Menispermum
Sinomenium

**MONIMIACEAE**
Peumus

**MORACEAE**
Broussonetia
Cudrania
Ficus
× Macludrania
Maclura
Morus

**MUSACEAE**
Musa

**MYOPORACEAE**
Myoporum

**MYRICACEAE**
Comptonia
Myrica

**MYRSINACEAE**
Ardisia
Myrsine

**MYRTACEAE**
Callistemon
Eucalyptus
Feijoa
Leptospermum
Melaleuca
Metrosideros
Myrtus

**NYSSACEAE**
Nyssa

**OCHNACEAE**
Ochna

**OLEACEAE**
Abeliophyllum
Chionanthus
Fontanesia
Forestiera
Forsythia
Fraxinus
Jasminum
Ligustrum
Olea
Osmanthus

Parasyringa
Phillyrea
Picconia
Syringa

**ONAGRACEAE**
Fuchsia
Zauschneria

**PAEONIACEAE**
Paeonia

**PALMAE**
Chamaerops
Trachycarpus

**PAPAVERACEAE**
Dendromecon
Romneya

**PASSIFLORACEAE**
Passiflora

**PHILADELPHACEAE**
Carpenteria
Deutzia
Fendlera
Jamesia
Philadelphus

**PHILESIACEAE**
Lapageria
Luzuriaga
× Philageria
Philesia

**PHORMIACEAE**
Phormium

**PHYLLOCLADACEAE**
Phyllocladus

**PHYTOLACCACEAE**
Ercilla
Phytolacca

**PINACEAE**
Abies
Cedrus
Keteleeria
Larix
Picea
Pinus
Pseudolarix
Pseudotsuga
Tsuga

**PITTOSPORACEAE**
Billardiera
Bursaria
Pittosporum
Sollya

**PLANTAGINACEAE**
Plantago

**PLATANACEAE**
Platanus

**PLUMBAGINACEAE**
Ceratostigma

**PODOCARPACEAE**
Dacrydium
Microcachrys
Microstrobos
Podocarpus
Saxegothaea

**POLEMONIACEAE**
Cantua

**POLYGALACEAE**
Polygala

**POLYGONACEAE**
Atraphaxis
Fallopia
Muehlenbeckia
Persicaria
Polygonum

**POTALIACEAE**
Desfontainia

**PROTEACEAE**
Banksia
Embothrium
Gevuina
Grevillea
Hakea
Lomatia
Telopea

**PUNICACEAE**
Punica

**RANUNCULACEAE**
Clematis
Xanthorhiza

**RHAMNACEAE**
Berchemia
Ceanothus
Colletia
Discaria
Hovenia
Paliurus
Phylica
Pomaderris
Rhamnus

**ROSACEAE**
Amelanchier
× Amelasorbus
Aronia
Cercocarpus
Chaenomeles
Chamaebatiaria
Cotoneaster
+ Crataegomespilus
Crataegus
× Crataemespilus
Cydonia
Dichotomanthes
Docynia
Dryas
Eriobotrya
Exochorda
Heteromeles
Holodiscus
Kerria
Luetkea
Lyonothamnus
Maddenia
Malus
Margyricarpus
Mespilus
Neillia
Neviusia
Oemleria
Osteomeles
Peraphyllum
Photinia
Physocarpus
Polylepis
Potentilla
Prinsepia
Prunus
Pseudocydonia
Pyracantha
× Pyracomeles
+ Pyrocydonia
× Pyronia
Pyrus
Quillaja
Rhaphiolepis

Rhodotypos
Rosa
Rubus
Sibiraea
Sorbaria
× Sorbaronia
× Sorbocotoneaster
× Sorbopyrus
Sorbus
Spiraea
Stephanandra

**RUBIACEAE**
Bouvardia
Cephalanthus
Coprosma
Damnacanthus
Emmenopterys
Leptodermis
Luculia
Mitchella
Paederia

**RUSCACEAE**
Danae
Ruscus

**RUTACEAE**
Acradenia
Agathosma
Boenninghausenia
Choisya
× Citroncirus
Citrus
Coleonema
Correa
Fortunella
Melicope
Orixa
Phellodendron
Poncirus
Ptelea
Ruta
Skimmia
Tetradium
Zanthoxylum

**SABIACEAE**
Meliosma

**SALICACEAE**
Populus
Salix

**SAPINDACEAE**
Koelreuteria
Sapindus
Xanthoceras

**SCHISANDRACEAE**
Kadsura
Schisandra

**SCROPHULARIACEAE**
Bowkeria
Calceolaria
Freylinia
Hebe
Jovellana
Mimulus
Parahebe
Paulownia
Penstemon
Phygelius
Rhodochiton

**SIMAROUBACEAE**
Ailanthus
Picrasma

**SMILACACEAE**
Smilax

**SOLANACEAE**
Brugmansia
Cestrum
Fabiana
Lycium
Solanum
Vestia

**STACHYURACEAE**
Stachyurus

**STAPHYLEACEAE**
Staphylea

**STERCULIACEAE**
Firmiana
Fremontodendron
Reevesia

**STYRACACEAE**
Halesia
Pterostyrax
Rehderodendron
Sinojackia
Styrax

**SYMPLOCACEAE**
Symplocos

**TAMARICACEAE**
Myricaria
Tamarix

**TAXACEAE**
Taxus
Torreya

**TAXODIACEAE**
Athrotaxis
Cryptomeria
Cunninghamia
Glyptostrobus
Metasequoia
Sciadopitys
Sequoia
Sequoiadendron
Taiwania
Taxodium

**TETRACENTRACEAE**
Tetracentron

**THEACEAE**
Camellia
Cleyera
Eurya
Franklinia
Gordonia
Schima
Stuartia
Ternstroemia

**THYMELAEACEAE**
Daphne
Dirca
Edgeworthia
Pimelea

**TILIACEAE**
Entelea
Grewia
Sparmannia
Tilia

**TROCHODENDRACEAE**
Trochodendron

**ULMACEAE**
Aphananthe
Celtis
Hemiptelea
Planera
Ulmus
Zelkova

**UMBELLIFERAE**
Bupleurum

**URTICACEAE**
Debregeasia

**VERBENACEAE**
Aloysia
Callicarpa
Caryopteris
Citharexylum
Clerodendrum
Diostea
Rhaphithamnus
Verbena
Vitex

**VIOLACEAE**
Hymenanthera
Melicytus

**VITACEAE**
Ampelopsis
Cissus
Parthenocissus
Vitis

**WINTERACEAE**
Drimys
Pseudowintera

# Trees and Shrubs

## for Landscape and Garden Design

The approach to the choice of trees and shrubs is naturally varied. The nature of the job, public or private, town or country, the individual taste of the landscape designer or garden maker, the labour available for maintenance, all these factors and more affect the decision as to what trees and shrubs to use and all must be influenced by the nature of the soil and situation. Having produced a wide selection of woody plants we are anxious that they should be used to the best possible advantage, suited both to the chemical and physical conditions of the soil and the particular job in hand.

In addition to the symbols used in the text indicating the likes and dislikes of the plants, the following lists are intended to serve as a guide to, or perhaps merely a reminder of, species of trees and shrubs suitable for some of the many different soils and situations found in the British Isles, and even within one site. The lists of trees and shrubs with distinctive habit or bark, leaf-shape or colour etc, may be helpful to both the professional and amateur.

We wish to emphasise that the trees and shrubs mentioned in each list are merely a selection and there are numerous other examples. We would also point out that we have listed plants which are suitable for a particular situation and are not necessarily recommending them to be planted only in that situation: a great many plants grow quite happily in a variety of situations.

For further details of the plants in these lists, please refer to the individual descriptions in the text.

**cvs**=cultivars (see under Nomenclature and Classification, page 1 9 ).

### INDEX of LISTS

**TREES and SHRUBS suitable for CLAY SOILS (neutral to slightly acid)**

**TREES**
Acer (all)
Aesculus (all)
Alnus (all)
Betula (all)
Carpinus (all)
Crataegus (all)
Eucalyptus (all)
Fraxinus (all)
Ilex (all)
Laburnum (all)
Malus (all)
Platanus (all)
Populus (all)
Prunus (all)
Quercus (all)
Salix (all)
Sorbus (all)
Tilia (all)

**SHRUBS**
Abelia (all)
Aralia elata and cvs
Aronia (all)
Aucuba japonica and cvs
Berberis (all)
Chaenomeles (all)
Choisya (all)
Colutea (all)
Cornus (all)
Corylus (all)
Cotinus (all)
Cotoneaster (all)
Cytisus (all)
Deutzia (all)
Escallonia (all)
Forsythia (all)
Genista (all)
Hamamelis (all)
Hibiscus syriacus and cvs
Hypericum (all)
Lonicera (all)
Mahonia (all)
Magnolia (all)
Osmanthus (all)
Philadelphus (all)
Potentilla (all)
Pyracantha (all)
Rhododendron Hardy Hybrids
Ribes (all)
Rosa (all)
Senecio 'Sunshine'

Skimmia (all)
Spiraea (all)
Symphoricarpos (all)
Viburnum (all)
Weigela (all)

**CONIFERS**
Abies (all)
Chamaecyparis (all)
Juniperus (all)
Larix (all)
Pinus (all)
Taxodium (all)
Taxus (all)
Thuja (all)

**BAMBOOS**
Arundinaria (all)
Phyllostachys (all)
Pseudosasa japonica
Sasa (all)
Sinarundinaria (all)
Thamnocalamus

**TREES and SHRUBS suitable for DRY ACID SOILS**

**TREES**
Acer negundo and cvs
Ailanthus altissima
Betula (all)
Castanea (all)
Cercis (all)
Gleditsia (all)
Ilex aquifolium and cvs
Populus alba
        tremula
Robinia (all)

**SHRUBS**
Acer ginnala
Berberis (all)
Calluna vulgaris and cvs
Caragana arborescens
Cistus (all)
Colutea arborescens
Cotoneaster (all)
Elaeagnus angustifolia
        commutata
Erica (all)

**DRY ACID SOILS** *continued*
**Genista** (all)
**Hakea microcarpa**
**Halimodendron halodendron**
**Helianthemum** (all)
**Hibiscus** (all)
**Ilex crenata** and cvs
**Indigofera** (all)
**Kerria japonica** and cvs
**Lonicera** (all)
**Lycium barbarum**
**Pernettya mucronata** and cvs
        **prostrata**
**Physocarpus opulifolius** and cvs
**Rosa pimpinellifolia** and cvs
**Salix caprea**
      **cinerea**
      **repens argentea**
**Tamarix** (all)
**Ulex** (all)

**CONIFERS**
**Cupressus glabra** and cvs
**Juniperus** (all)
**Pinus** (all)

**TREES and SHRUBS suitable for
SHALLOW SOIL OVER CHALK**

**TREES**
**Acer campestre**
      **negundo** and cvs
      **platanoides** and cvs
      **pseudoplatanus** and cvs
**Aesculus** (all)
**Carpinus betulus** and cvs
**Cercis siliquastrum**
**Crataegus laevigata** and cvs
**Fagus sylvatica** and cvs
**Fraxinus excelsior** and cvs
**Fraxinus ornus**
**Malus** (all)
**Morus nigra**
**Populus alba**
**Prunus (Japanese Cherries)**
**Sorbus aria** and cvs
      **hybrida** cvs
      **intermedia**

**SHRUBS**
**Aucuba japonica** and cvs
**Berberis** (all)
**Buddleja davidii** and cvs
**Buxus sempervirens** and cvs

**Caragana arborescens** and cvs
**Ceanothus** (all)
**Cistus** (all)
**Colutea** (all)
**Cornus mas** and cvs
**Cotoneaster** (all)
**Cytisus nigricans**
**Deutzia** (all)
**Dipelta floribunda**
**Elaeagnus** (deciduous species)
**Euonymus** (all)
**Forsythia** (all)
**Fuchsia** (all)
**Genista cinerea**
**Hebe** (all)
**Hibiscus syriacus** and cvs
**Hypericum** (all)
**Laurus nobilis**
**Ligustrum** (all)
**Lonicera** (all)
**Mahonia aquifolium** and hybrids
**Olearia** (all)
**Paeonia delavayi**
      **lutea**
**Philadelphus** (all)
**Phillyrea** (all)
**Photinia × fraseri** cvs
**Photinia serratifolia**
**Potentilla** (most)
**Rhus** (most)
**Rosa** (most)
**Rosmarinus** (all)
**Rubus tricolor**
**Sambucus** (all)
**Sarcococca** (all)
**Senecio** (all)
**Spartium junceum**
**Spiraea japonica** and cvs
      **nipponica** and forms
**Stachyurus** (all)
**Symphoricarpos** (all)
**Syringa** (all)
**Vinca** (all)
**Weigela** (all)
**Yucca** (all)

**CONIFERS**
**Juniperus communis** and cvs
      **× media** and cvs
**Pinus mugo** and forms
      **nigra**
**Taxus baccata** and cvs
**Thuja occidentalis** and cvs
      **plicata** and cvs
**Thujopsis dolabrata** and cvs

**SHALLOW SOIL OVER CHALK** *continued*
**BAMBOOS**
Pseudosasa japonica
Sasa ramosa

**TREES and SHRUBS tolerant of both
extreme ACIDITY and ALKALINITY**

**TREES**
Betula papyrifera and forms
Betula pendula and cvs
          platyphylla and vars
          pubescens
Crataegus monogyna and cvs
Fagus sylvatica and cvs
Populus alba
          tremula
Quercus cerris
          robur and cvs
Sorbus hybrida cvs
          intermedia

**SHRUBS**
Ilex aquifolium and cvs
Ligustrum ovalifolium and cvs
Lycium barbarum
Rhamnus frangula
Salix caprea
          cinerea
Sambucus nigra and cvs
          racemosa and cvs
Viburnum opulus and cvs

**CONIFERS**
Juniperus communis and cvs
Pinus nigra
          sylvestris and cvs
Taxus baccata and cvs

**TREES and SHRUBS suitable for
DAMP SITES**

**TREES**
Alnus (all)
Amelanchier (all)
Betula nigra
          pendula and cvs
          pubescens

Crataegus laevigata and cvs
Magnolia virginiana
Mespilus germanica cvs
Populus (all)
Pterocarya (all)
Pyrus betulifolia
          communis cvs
Quercus palustris
Salix (all)
Sorbus aucuparia and cvs

**SHRUBS**
Amelanchier (all)
Aronia (all)
Calycanthus floridus
Clethra (all)
Cornus alba and cvs
          stolonifera and cvs
Gaultheria shallon
Hippophae rhamnoides
Lindera benzoin
Myrica cerifera
          gale
Neillia longiracemosa
Photinia villosa
Physocarpus opulifolius and cvs
Prunus spinosa and cvs
Salix caprea
          humilis
          purpurea and cvs
          repens and cvs
          many other bush species
Sambucus (all)
Sorbaria (all)
Spiraea × vanhouttei
          veitchii
Symphoricarpos (all)
Vaccinium (all)
Viburnum opulus and cvs

**CONIFERS**
Metasequoia glyptostroboides
Picea sitchensis
Taxodium ascendens and forms
          distichum

**BAMBOOS**
Arundinaria (all)
Phyllostachys (all)
Pseudosasa japonica
Sasa (all)
Sinarundinaria (all)
Thamnocalamus (all)

TREES and SHRUBS suitable for
INDUSTRIAL AREAS
**TREES**
**Acer** (many, but not Japanese Maples)
**Aesculus** (all)
**Allanthus altissima**
**Alnus cordata**
  **glutinosa** and cvs
  **incana** and cvs
**Amelanchier** (all)
**Betula papyrifera** and forms
  **pendula** and cvs
  **platyphylla** and vars
  **pubescens** and cvs
**Carpinus betulus** and cvs
**Catalpa bignonioides** and cvs
**Crataegus** (most)
**Davidia involucrata** and var.
**Eucalyptus** (most)
**Fagus** (all)
**Fraxinus** (all)
**Ilex** × **altaclerensis** and cvs
  **aquifolium** and cvs
+ **Laburnocytisus adamii**
**Laburnum** (all)
**Ligustrum lucidum** and cvs
**Liriodendron tulipifera** and cvs
**Magnolia acuminata**
  **denudata**
  **kobus**
  × **loebneri** and cvs
  × **soulangeana** and cvs
**Malus** (all)
**Mespilus germanica** cvs
**Morus nigra**
**Platanus** (all)
**Populus** (most)
**Prunus** × **amygdalo-persica 'Pollardii'**
  **avium**
  **cerasifera** and cvs
  **dulcis** cvs
  **Japanese Cherries**
  **padus** and cvs
**Pterocarya** (all)
**Pyrus** (most)
**Quercus** × **hispanica**
  **ilex**
  × **turneri**
**Rhus** (most)
**Robinia pseudoacacia** and cvs
**Salix** (most)
**Sorbus aria** and cvs
  **aucuparia** and cvs
**Tilia** × **euchlora**
  × **europaea** and cvs
  **platyphyllos** and cvs

676

**SHRUBS**
**Amelanchier** (all)
**Aralia elata**
**Arbutus unedo** and cvs
**Aucuba japonica** and cvs
**Berberis** (all)
**Buddleja davidii** and cvs
**Buxus sempervirens** and cvs
**Camellia japonica** and cvs
  × **williamsii** cvs
**Ceanothus** × **delilianus** cvs
**Ceratostigma willmottianum**
**Chaenomeles** (all)
**Cistus** (all)
**Clethra** (all)
**Colutea arborescens**
  × **media**
**Cornus alba** and cvs
  **stolonifera** and cvs
**Cotoneaster** (most)
**Cytisus** (most)
**Daphne mezereum**
**Deutzia** (many)
**Elaeagnus** × **ebbingei** and cvs
  **pungens** and cvs
**Escallonia** (all)
**Euonymus fortunei** and cvs
  **japonicus** and cvs
**Fatsia japonica**
**Forsythia** (all)
**Garrya** (all)
**Genista** (many)
**Hibiscus sinosyriacus** and cvs
  **syriacus** and cvs
**Hydrangea macrophylla** and cvs
**Hypericum** (all)
**Ilex aquifolium** and cvs
  **cornuta** and hybrids
**Kerria japonica** and cvs
**Leycesteria formosa**
**Ligustrum japonicum**
  **ovalifolium**
**Lonicera pileata**
**Lycium babarum**
**Magnolia grandiflora** and cvs
  × **soulangeana** and cvs
  **stellata** and cvs
**Mahonia aquifolium** and hybrids
  **japonica**
  **lomariifolia**
  × **media** and cvs
  **pinnata**
  **repens 'Rotundifolia'**
**Olearia avicenniifolia**
  × **haastii**
**Osmanthus** (all)

**INDUSTRIAL AREAS** *continued*
**Pernettya mucronata** and cvs
**Philadelphus** (all)
**Phillyrea** (all)
**Photinia davidiana**
**Physocarpus** (all)
**Prunus laurocerasus** and cvs
**Pyracantha** (all)
**Rhododendron Hardy Hybrids**
    **Knap Hill Azaleas**
    **luteum**
    **ponticum**
**Rhodotypos scandens**
**Rhus glabra**
    **typhina**
**Ribes** (all)
**Rosa** (most)
**Salix** (most)
**Sambucus canadensis 'Maxima'**
    **nigra** and forms
**Sarcococca** (many)
**Senecio monroi**
    **'Sunshine'**
**Skimmia japonica** and cvs
**Sorbaria** (all)
**Spartium junceum**
**Spiraea** (all)
**Staphylea** (all)
**Symphoricarpos** (all)
**Syringa** (all)
**Tamarix tetrandra**
**Ulex** (all)
**Viburnum** (many)
**Vinca major** and cvs
    **minor** and cvs
**Weigela florida** and cvs
    **Hybrids**


**CLIMBERS**
**Ampelopsis** (most)
**Hedera** (all)
**Parthenocissus** (all)


**CONIFERS**
**Cephalotaxus fortunei** and cvs
    **harringtonia** and forms
**Fitzroya cupressoides**
**Ginkgo biloba**
**Metasequoia glyptostroboides** and cvs
**Taxus baccata** and cvs
    × **media** and cvs
**Torreya californica**

**TREES and SHRUBS suitable for
COLD EXPOSED AREAS**


**TREES**
**Acer pseudoplatanus** and cvs
**Betula** (most)
**Crataegus monogyna** and cvs
**Fagus sylvatica** and cvs
**Fraxinus excelsior** and cvs
**Laburnum** (all)
**Populus** × **canadensis 'Robusta'**
    **'Serotina'**
**Populus tremula**
**Quercus robur** and cvs
**Sorbus aria** and cvs
    **aucuparia** and cvs
    **intermedia** and cvs
**Tilia cordata** and cvs


**SHRUBS**
**Arctostaphylos uva-ursi**
**Calluna vulgaris** and cvs
**Cornus alba** and cvs
    **stolonifera** and cvs
**Cotinus coggygria** and cvs
**Elaeagnus commutata**
**Euonymus fortunei** and cvs
× **Gaulnettya** cvs
**Gaultheria shallon**
**Hippophae rhamnoides**
**Hydrangea paniculata 'Grandiflora'**
**Kalmia angustifolia** and cvs
    **latifolia** and cvs
**Kerria japonica 'Variegata'**
**Lavatera thuringiaca** cvs
**Ledum groenlandicum**
**Leucothoe fontanesiana**
**Lonicera pileata**
**Mahonia aquifolium**
**Myrica gale**
**Pachysandra terminalis**
**Pernettya mucronata** and cvs
**Philadelphus** (many)
**Pieris floribunda** and cvs
**Prunus spinosa**
**Rhododendron Hardy Hybrids**
    **ponticum**
    **yakushimanum**
**Salix** (most)
**Spiraea** (most)
**Tamarix** (all)
**Ulex** (all)
**Viburnum opulus** and cvs

**677**

**COLD EXPOSED AREAS** *continued*
**CONIFERS**
**Chamaecyparis nootkatensis** and cvs
        **obtusa** and cvs
        **pisifera** and cvs
**Cryptomeria japonica** and cvs
**Ginkgo biloba**
**Juniperus communis** and cvs
        × **media** and cvs
**Larix decidua**
**Picea abies** and cvs
**Pinus banksiana**
        **nigra** and forms
        **ponderosa**
        **sylvestris** and cvs
**Taxus baccata** and cvs
**Thuja occidentalis** and cvs
        **standishii**
**Tsuga canadensis** and cvs

**TREES and SHRUBS suitable for
SEASIDE AREAS**

**TREES**
**Acer pseudoplatanus**
**Arbutus unedo** and cvs
**Castanea sativa**
**Crataegus** (all)
**Eucalyptus** (many)
**Fraxinus angustifolia** and cvs
        **excelsior** and cvs
**Griselinia littoralis**
**Ilex** × **altaclerensis** and cvs
        **aquifolium** and cvs
**Laurus nobilis** and cvs
**Phillyrea latifolia** and cvs
**Populus alba**
        **tremula**
**Quercus cerris**
        **ilex**
        **petraea**
        **robur**
        × **turneri**
**Salix** (most)
**Sorbus aria** and cvs
        **aucuparia** and cvs

**SHRUBS**
**Atriplex halimus**
**Bupleurum fruticosum**
**Cassinia fulvida**
**Chamaerops humilis**
**Choisya** (all)
**Colutea** (all)
**Cordyline australis** and cvs

**Corokia cotoneaster**
        × **virgata** and cvs
**Cotoneaster** (many)
**Cytisus** (many)
**Elaeagnus** × **ebbingei** and cvs
        **pungens** and cvs
**Erica arborea 'Alpina'**
        **lusitanica**
        × **veitchii**
**Escallonia** (most)
**Euonymus fortunei** and cvs
        **japonicus** and cvs
**Fabiana imbricata 'Prostrata'**
**Fuchsia magellanica** and cvs
**Garrya elliptica** and cvs
**Genista** (most)
**Halimium** (all)
**Halimodendron halodendron**
**Hebe** (all)
**Helianthemum** (most)
**Helichrysum** (many)
**Hippophae rhamnoides**
**Hydrangea macrophylla** and cvs
**Ilex aquifolium** and cvs
**Lavandula** (all)
**Lavatera thuringiaca** cvs
**Leycesteria formosa**
**Lonicera pileata**
**Lycium barbarum**
**Myrica cerifera**
**Olearia** (most)
**Ozothamnus** (many)
**Parahebe** (all)
**Phlomis** (most)
**Phormium** (all)
**Pittosporum** (most)
**Prunus spinosa**
**Pyracantha** (all)
**Rhamnus alaternus** and cvs
**Rosa** (many species)
**Rosmarinus officinalis** and cvs
**Salix** (many)
**Sambucus racemosa** and cvs
**Santolina** (all)
**Senecio** (most)
**Spartium junceum**
**Spiraea** (many)
**Tamarix** (all)
**Ulex** (all)
**Viburnum,** many, especially evergreen spp.
**Yucca** (all)

**CLIMBERS**
**Fallopia baldschuanica**
**Muehlenbeckia complexa**

**SEASIDE AREAS** *continued*
**CONIFERS**
× **Cupressocyparis leylandii**
**Cupressus** (many)
**Juniperus** (most)
**Pinus contorta**
    **mugo** and forms
    **muricata**
    **nigra**
**Pinus nigra** subsp. **laricio**
    **pinaster**
    **pinea**
    **radiata**
    **thunbergii**
**Podocarpus alpinus**
    **nivalis**

**BAMBOOS**
**Arundinaria** (many)
**Sasa** (all)

**SHRUBS suitable for HEAVY SHADE**

**Arctostaphylos uva-ursi**
**Aucuba japonica** and cvs
**Buxus sempervirens** and cvs
**Camellia japonica** and cvs
    × **williamsii** and cvs
**Cornus canadensis**
**Daphne laureola**
    **pontica**
**Elaeagnus** (evergreen)
**Euonymus fortunei** and cvs
× **Fatshedera lizei**
**Fatsia japonica**
**Gaultheria** (all)
**Hedera helix 'Arborea'**
**Hypericum androsaemum**
    **calycinum**
**Ilex** × **altaclerensis** and cvs
    **aquifolium** and cvs
**Leucothoe fontanesiana** and cvs
**Ligustrum** (many)
**Lonicera nitida** cvs
    **pileata**
**Mahonia aquifolium** and cvs
**Osmanthus decous**
    **heterophyllus** and cvs
**Pachysandra terminalis**
**Prunus laurocerasus** and cvs
    **lusitanica** and cvs
**Rhododendron Hardy Hybrids**
    **ponticum**
**Rhodotypos scandens**

**Ribes alpinum**
**Rubus odoratus**
    **tricolor**
**Ruscus** (all)
**Sarcococca** (all)
**Skimmia** (all)
**Symphoricarpos** (all)
**Vaccinium vitis-idaea**
**Viburnum davidii**
**Vinca** (all)

**CONIFERS**
**Cephalotaxus** (all)
**Juniperus** × **media 'Pfitzeriana'**
**Podocarpus alpinus**
**Podocarpus andinus**
    **nivalis**
**Taxus** (all)

**BAMBOOS**
**Arundinaria** (most)
**Phyllostachys** (most)
**Sasa** (all)

**SHRUBS and CLIMBERS suitable for NORTH- and EAST-FACING WALLS**

**SHRUBS**
**Azara microphylla**
    **petiolaris**
**Berberis** × **stenophylla**
**Camellia** (North walls only)
    **'Inspiration'**
    **japonica** and cvs
    **reticulata**
    **saluenensis**
    **sasanqua**
    × **williamsii** and cvs
**Chaenomeles** (most)
**Choisya ternata**
**Crinodendron hookerianum**
    **patagua**
**Daphne gnidium**
    × **hybrida**
    **odora**
**Desfontainia spinosa**
**Drimys winteri**
**Eriobotrya japonica**
**Eucryphia cordifolia**
    × **intermedia** cvs
    × **nymansensis** and cvs
**Euonymus fortunei** and cvs

**NORTH- & EAST-FACING WALLS** *continued*
Garrya elliptica and cvs
Garrya × thuretii
Grevillea rosmarinifolia
Ilex latifolia
Illicium anisatum
Jasminum humile and forms
    nudiflorum
Kerria japonica 'Pleniflora'
Lomatia myricoides
Mahonia japonica
    lomariifolia
    × media and cvs
Mitraria coccinea
Osmanthus yunnanensis
Photinia × fraseri and cvs
    serratifolia
Piptanthus nepalensis
Pyracantha (all)
Ribes laurifolium
Rubus lambertianus
Schima argentea
Viburnum foetens
    grandiflorum

**CLIMBERS**
Akebia quinata
Celastrus orbiculatus
Hedera colchica and cvs
    helix and cvs
Hydrangea petiolaris
Muehlenbeckia complexa
Parthenocissus (all)
Pileostegia viburnoides
Rubus henryi var. bambusarum
Schizophragma hydrangeoides
    integrifolium

**SHRUBS suitable for GROUND COVER**

Arctostaphylos nevadensis
    uva-ursi
Artemisia 'Powis Castle'
Aucuba japonica 'Nana Rotundifolia'
Berberis tsangpoensis
    wilsoniae
Buxus microphylla
    sempervirens 'Prostrata'
Calluna vulgaris and cvs
Ceanothus prostratus
    thyrsiflorus var. repens
Cornus canadensis
Cotoneaster—several including:
    'Coral Beauty'
    dammeri

'Gnom'
    horizontalis
    microphyllus and cvs
    nanshan
    'Skogholm'
    'Valkenburg'
Cytisus × beanii
    scoparius subsp. maritimus
Daboecia cantabrica and cvs
Erica (most)
Euonymus fortunei and cvs
Gaultheria (most)
× Gaulnettya cvs
× Halimiocistus 'Ingwersenii'
    sahucii
Hebe many, especially
    albicans
    pinguifolia 'Pagei'
    rakaiensis
    'Youngii'
Hedera (most)
Helianthemum (all)
Hypericum calycinum
    × moserianum
Jasminum nudiflorum
    parkeri
Leptospermum humifusum
Leucothoe fontanesiana and cvs
    keiskii
Lithodora diffusa and cvs
Lonicera pileata
Mahonia aquifolium 'Apollo'
    nervosa
    repens
Mitchella repens
Muehlenbeckia (all)
Pachysandra terminalis
Pernettya buxifolia
    mucronata cvs
    prostrata subsp. pentlandii
Pimelea prostrata
Potentilla dahurica 'Abbotswood'
    'Longacre'
Rhododendron (many, especially
    members of the Subsections
    Lapponica
    and Saluenensia)
    Evergreen Azaleas (most)
Ribes laurifolium
Rosa 'Max Graf'
    nitida
    × paulii
    'Raubritter'
    wichuraiana
Rosmarinus officinalis 'Prostratus'

**GROUND COVER** *continued*
Rubus calycinoides
    tricolor
Salix—several including:
    × cottetii
    repens and cvs
    uva-ursi
Santolina (all)
Sarcococca hookeriana var. humilis
Stephanandra incisa 'Crispa'
Symphoricarpos × chenaultii 'Hancock'
Vaccinium, many, especially
    delavayi
    glauco-album
    myrtillus
    vitis-idaea
Viburnum davidii
Vinca (all)

**CONIFERS**
Cephalotaxus fortunei 'Prostrata'
Juniperus communis, several forms,
    including—subsp.
    depressa
        'Hornibrookii'
        'Repanda'
    conferta
    horizontalis and cvs
    × media (several cvs)
    sabina var. tamariscifolia
Picea abies 'Reflexa'
Pinus strobus 'Prostrata'
Podocarpus alpinus
    nivalis
Taxus baccata 'Repandens'
        'Repens Aurea'
Tsuga canadensis 'Bennett'
        'Prostrata'

**BAMBOOS**
Indocalamus tessellatus
Sasa veitchii
Shibataea kumasaca

**TREES of PENDULOUS HABIT**

Acer saccharinum f. laciniatum
Betula pendula 'Dalecarlica'
        'Tristis'
        'Youngii'
Cercidiphyllum japonicum 'Pendulum'
Crataegus monogyna 'Pendula Rosea'
Fagus sylvatica 'Aurea Pendula'
        'Pendula'
        'Purpurea Pendula'

Fraxinus excelsior 'Pendula'
Gleditsia triacanthos 'Bujotii'
Malus 'Red Jade'
Populus tremula 'Pendula'
Prunus subhirtella 'Pendula'
        'Pendula Rubra'
    × yedoensis 'Shidare Yoshino'
Pyrus salicifolia 'Pendula'
Quercus robur 'Pendula'
Robinia pseudoacacia 'Rozynskyana'
Salix babylonica 'Pendula'
    × sepulcralis 'Chrysocoma'
        'Erythroflexuosa'
Sophora japonica 'Pendula'
Tilia tomentosa 'Petiolaris'

The ultimate height of the underlisted trees is
largely dependent on the stem height at which
they are grafted or to which they are trained.

Caragana arborescens 'Pendula'
        'Walker'
Cotoneaster 'Hybridus Pendulus'
Ilex aquifolium 'Argenteomarginata Pendula'
        'Pendula'
Laburnum alpinum 'Pendulum'
    anagyroides 'Pendulum'
Malus 'Royal Beauty"
Morus alba 'Pendula'
Prunus 'Cheal's Weeping'
    × yedoensis 'Ivensii'
Salix caprea 'Kilmarnock'
    purpurea 'Pendula'

**CONIFERS**
Cedrus atlantica 'Glauca Pendula'
        'Pendula'
Chamaecyparis lawsoniana 'Pendula'
    nootkatensis 'Pendula'
Cupressus lusitanica 'Glauca Pendula'
Dacrydium franklinii
Fitzroya cupressoides
Larix decidua 'Pendula'
    kaempferi 'Pendula'
Picea abies 'Inversa'
    breweriana
    omorika 'Pendula'
    smithiana
    spinulosa
Taxodium distichum 'Pendens'
Taxus baccata 'Dovastoniana'
Taxus baccata 'Dovastonii Aurea'
Tsuga canadensis 'Pendula'
    heterophylla 'Greenmantle'

**681**

## TREES and SHRUBS of UPRIGHT or FASTIGIATE HABIT

### TREES and SHRUBS
Acer × lobelii
 platanoides 'Columnare'
 pseudoplatanus 'Erectum'
 rubrum 'Scanlon'
 saccharinum 'Pyramidale'
Betula pendula 'Fastigiata'
Carpinus betulus 'Fastigiata'
Corylus colurna
Crataegus monogyna 'Stricta'
Fagus sylvatica 'Cockleshell'
  'Dawyck'
  'Dawyck Gold'
  'Dawyck Purple'
Ilex aquifolium 'Green Pillar'
Liriodendron tulipifera 'Fastigiata'
Malus tschonoskii
 'Van Eseltine'
Populus alba 'Pyramidalis'
 nigra 'Italica'
Prunus 'Amanogawa'
 lusitanica 'Myrtifolia'
 'Pandora'
 × schmittii
 'Snow Goose'
 'Spire'
Pyrus calleryana 'Chanticleer'
Quercus castaneifolia 'Green Spire'
 frainetto 'Hungarian Crown'
 petraea 'Columna'
 robur 'Fastigiata'
 'Fastigiata Purpurea'
Robinia pseudoacacia 'Pyramidalis'
Sorbus aucuparia 'Fastigiata'
 'Sheerwater Seedling'
 commixta
 'Joseph Rock'
 × thuringiaca 'Fastigiata'
Tilia cordata 'Greenspire'
Ulmus × hollandica 'Dampieri Aurea'

### CONIFERS
Calocedrus decurrens
Cephalotaxus harringtonia 'Fastigiata'
Chamaecyparis lawsoniana 'Allumii'
  'Columnaris'
  'Ellwoodii'
  'Erecta'
  'Grayswood Feather'
  'Kilmacurragh'
  'Pottenii'
  'Wisselii'
  'Witzeliana'

× Cupressocyparis leylandii and cvs
Cupressus glabra 'Pyramidalis'
 sempervirens and cvs
Ginkgo biloba 'Tremonia'
Juniperus chinensis 'Keteleeri'
  'Pyramidalis'
 communis 'Compressa'
  'Hibernica'
  'Sentinel'
 drupacea
 scopulorum (several cvs)
 virginiana 'Burkii'
Picea omorika
Pinus sylvestris 'Fastigiata'
Taxodium ascendens 'Nutans'
Taxus baccata 'Fastigiata'
  'Fastigiata Aureomarginata'
  'Standishii'
 × media 'Hicksii'
Thuja occidentalis 'Fastigiata'
  'Malonyana'
 plicata 'Fastigiata'
Tsuga heterophylla 'Laursen's Column'

## TREES and SHRUBS with ORNAMENTAL BARK or TWIGS

### TREES
Acer capillipes
 davidii 'George Forrest'
 griseum
 grosseri var. hersii
 negundo var. violaceum
 palmatum 'Senkaki'
 pensylvanicum and cvs
Arbutus × andrachnoides
 menziesii
Betula (most)
Carya ovata
Eucalyptus (most)
Fraxinus excelsior 'Jaspidea'
Lyonothamnus floribundus
 subsp. aspleniifolius
Myrtus luma
Parrotia persica
Platanus (all)
Prunus maackii 'Amber Beauty'
 × schmittii
 serrula
Salix acutifolia 'Blue Streak'
 alba 'Britzensis'
  var. vitellina
 babylonica 'Tortuosa'
 daphnoides and cvs
 × sepulcralis 'Chrysocoma'
  'Erythroflexuosa'

## ORNAMENTAL BARK or TWIGS *continued*
Stuartia (most)
Tilia platyphyllos 'Aurea'
        'Rubra'

## SHRUBS
Abelia triflora
Arctostaphylos (most)
Clethra barbinervis
Cornus alba and cvs
    officinalis
    stolonifera 'Flaviramea'
Corylus avellana 'Contorta'
Deutzia (several spp.)
Dipelta floribunda
Euonymus alatus
    phellomanus
Hydrangea aspera and forms
    heteromalla 'Bretschneideri'
Kerria japonica and cvs
Leucothoe grayana
Leycesteria formosa
Philadelphus (several)
Rhododendron barbatum
    thomsonii
Rosa sericea f. pteracantha
    virginiana
Rubus cockburnianus
    phoenicolasius
    thibetanus
Salix irrorata
    moupinensis
Stephanandra tanakae
Vaccinium corymbosum

## CONIFERS
Abies squamata
Cryptomeria japonica
Pinus bungeana
    sylvestris
Sequoia sempervirens
Sequoiadendron giganteum

## TREES and SHRUBS with
## BOLD FOLIAGE

## TREES
Acer japonicum 'Vitifolium'
    macrophyllum
Ailanthus altissima
Aralia (all)
Catalpa (all)
Cordyline australis
Gymnocladus dioica
Idesia polycarpa
Juglans cinerea

Kalopanax pictus
Magnolia hypoleuca
    macrophylla
    officinalis var. biloba
    tripetala
Meliosma veitchiorum
Paulownia (all)
Platanus (all)
Populus lasiocarpa
    szechuanica var. tibetica
    wilsonii
Pterocarya (all)
Quercus dentata
    frainetto
    macrocarpa
    pontica
    velutina 'Rubrifolia'
Sorbus insignis
    thibetica 'John Mitchell'
    vestita
Tilia americana 'Redmond'
    × moltkei
Toona sinensis
Trachycarpus fortunei

## SHRUBS
Aralia (all)
Chamaerops humilis
Eriobotrya japonica
× Fatshedera lizei
Fatsia japonica
Hydrangea quercifolia and cvs
    aspera subsp. sargentiana
Ilex latifolia
Magnolia delavayi
    grandiflora and cvs
Mahonia acanthifolia
    japonica
    lomariifolia
    × media and cvs
Melianthus major
Osmanthus armatus
    yunnanensis
Phormium (all)
Pseudopanax davidii
Rhododendron, several including
    grande
    macabeanum
    rex and forms
    sinogrande
Sambucus canadensis 'Maxima'
Sorbaria (all)
Viburnum rhytidophyllum
Yucca gloriosa
    recurvifolia

**BOLD FOLIAGE** *continued*
**CLIMBERS**
Actinidia chinensis
Ampelopsis megalophylla
Aristolochia macrophylla
Hedera algeriensis and cvs
Hedera colchica and cvs
Holboellia latifolia
Vitis amurensis
    coignetiae

**BAMBOOS**
Indocalamus tessellatus

**TREES and SHRUBS for AUTUMN COLOUR**

**TREES**
Acer, many, especially
    capillipes
    maximowiczianum
    platanoides and cvs
    rubrum and cvs
    triflorum
Aesculus, several, including
    glabra
    × neglecta
Amelanchier laevis
    lamarckii
Betula (most)
Carpinus (all)
Carya (all)
Cercidiphyllum japonicum
Cercis canadensis
Cladrastis (all)
Cornus controversa
Crataegus, many, especially
    crus-galli
    pinnatifida var. major
    prunifolia
Fagus (most)
Fraxinus angustifolia 'Raywood'
    excelsior 'Jaspidea'
Gymnocladus dioica
Liquidambar (all)
Malus, several, including
    coronaria 'Charlottae'
    transitoria
    trilobata
    tschonoskii
    yunnanensis var. veitchii
Nothofagus antarctica
Nyssa (all)
Parrotia persica
Phellodendron (all)

Photinia beauverdiana
    villosa
Picrasma quassioides
Populus, several, including
    alba
    × canadensis 'Serotina Aurea'
    canescens 'Macrophylla'
    tremula
    trichocarpa
Prunus, many, including
    'Hillieri'
    × juddii
    sargentii
    verecunda 'Autumn Glory'
Quercus, many, including
    coccinea 'Splendens'
    palustris
    phellos
    rubra
Rhus trichocarpa
Sassafras albidum
Sorbus, many, including
    alnifolia
    americana
    commixta
        'Embley'
    'Joseph Rock'
    scalaris
Stuartia (all)
Toona sinensis

**SHRUBS**
Acer, many, especially
    ginnala
    japonica and cvs
    palmatum and cvs
Aesculus parviflora
Amelanchier canadensis
Aronia (all)
Berberis, many, including
    aggregata
    dictyophylla
    × media 'Parkjuweel'
    morrisonensis
    thunbergii and cvs
    wilsoniae
Callicarpa (all)
Ceratostigma willmottianum
Clethra (all)
Cornus alba
    'Eddie's White Wonder'
    florida and cvs
    officinalis
Corylopsis (all)
Cotinus (all)

**AUTUMN COLOUR** *continued*
**Cotoneaster,** many, including
    **bullatus**
    **divaricatus**
    **horizontalis**
    **nanshan**
    **splendens**
**Disanthus cercidifolius**
**Enkianthus** (all)
**Eucryphia glutinosa**
**Euonymus,** many, including
    **alatus** and cvs
    **europaeus** and cvs
    **latifolius**
    **oxyphyllus**
    **planipes**
**Fothergilla** (all)
**Hamamelis** (all)
**Hydrangea quercifolia**
    **serrata 'Preziosa'**
**Lindera** (most)
**Prunus,** several, including
    **glandulosa** and cvs
    **incisa**
    **pumila** var. **depressa**
**Ptelea trifoliata**
**Rhododendron** several
    Azaleas including
    **arborescens**
    **calendulaceum**
    **'Coccinea Speciosa'**
    **'Corneille'**
    **luteum**
    **'Nancy Waterer'**
    **quinquefolium**
**Rhus,** several, especially
    **copallina**
    **glabra** and cvs
    **typhina** and cvs
**Ribes odoratum**
**Rosa nitida**
    **rugosa** and cvs
    **virginiana**
**Sorbaria aitchisonii**
**Spiraea thunbergii**
**Stephanandra** (all)
**Vaccinium** several,
    **corymbosum**
    **praestans**
**Viburnum,** many, including
    **carlesii** and cvs
    **furcatum**
    × **hillieri 'Winton'**
    **opulus** and cvs
    **plicatum** cvs

**Zanthoxylum piperitum**

**CLIMBERS**
**Ampelopsis** (all)
**Celastrus** (all)
**Parthenosiccus** (all)
**Vitis** (all)

**CONIFERS**
**Ginkgo biloba**
**Larix** (all)
**Metasequoia glyptostroboides** and cvs
**Pseudolarix amabilis**
**Taxodium** (all)

**TREES and SHRUBS with
RED or PURPLE FOLIAGE**

**TREES**
**Acer campestre 'Schwerinii'**
    **palmatum Atropurpureum**
    **'Hessei'**
    **platanoides 'Crimson King'**
    **'Deborah'**
    **'Schwedleri'**
**Betula pendula 'Purpurea'**
**Catalpa** × **erubescens 'Purpurea'**
**Cercis canadensis 'Forest Pansy'**
**Fagus sylvatica 'Dawyck Purple'**
    **Purpurea**
    **'Purpurea Pendula'**
    **'Riversii'**
    **'Rohanii'**
    **'Roseomarginata'**
**Malus 'Lemoinei'**
    **'Liset'**
    **'Profusion'**
    × **purpurea**
    **'Royal Beauty'**
    **'Royalty'**
**Pittosporum tenuifolium 'Purpureum'**
**Prunus** × **blireana**
    **cerasifera 'Nigra'**
    **'Pissardii'**
    **'Rosea'**
    × **cistena**
    **padus 'Colorata'**
    **virginiana 'Shubert'**
**Quercus petraea 'Purpurea'**
    **robur 'Atropurpurea'**

**685**

**RED or PURPLE FOLIAGE** *continued*

**SHRUBS**

Acer palmatum many including,
    'Crimson Queen'
    'Dissectum Atropurpureum'
    'Linearilobum Atropurpureum'
    'Red Pygmy'
Berberis × ottawensis 'Superba'
    thunbergii many including,
    Atropurpurea
    'Atropurpurea Nana'
    'Red Chief'
    'Rose Glow'
Corylopsis willmottiae 'Spring Purple'
Corylus maxima 'Purpurea'
Cotinus coggygria 'Royal Purple'
    'Velvet Cloak'
    'Grace'
Phormium tenax 'Purpureum' and others
Pittosporum tenuifolium 'Tom Thumb'
Salvia officinalis 'Purpurascens'
Sambucus nigra 'Guincho Purple'
Weigela florida 'Foliis Purpureis'

**CLIMBERS**

Vitis vinifera 'Purpurea'

**TREES and SHRUBS with GOLDEN
or YELLOW FOLIAGE**

**TREES**

Acer cappadocicum 'Aureum'
    negundo 'Auratum'
    pseudoplatanus 'Worleei'
Alnus incana 'Aurea'
Catalpa bignonioides 'Aurea'
Fagus sylvatica 'Aurea Pendula'
    'Zlatia'
Gleditsia triacanthos 'Sunburst'
Ilex aquifolium 'Flavescens'
Laurus nobilis 'Aurea'
Liquidambar styraciflua 'Moonbeam'
Populus alba 'Richardii'
    × canadensis 'Serotina Aurea'
Quercus robur 'Concordia'
    rubra 'Aurea'
Robinia pseudoacacia 'Frisia'
Sorbus aria 'Chrysophylla'
Tilia × europaea 'Wratislaviensis'
Ulmus × hollandica 'Dampieri Aurea'

**SHRUBS**

Acer shirasawanum 'Aureum'
Berberis thunbergii 'Aurea'

Calluna vulgaris 'Beoley Gold'
    'Gold Haze'
    'Joy Vanstone'
    'Orange Queen'
    'Robert Chapman'
    'Sir John Charrington'
Cornus alba 'Aurea'
    mas 'Aurea'
    'Aurea Elegantissima'
Corylus avellana 'Aurea'
Erica carnea 'Ann Sparkes'
    'Aurea'
    'Foxhollow'
    cinerea 'Golden Drop'
    'Golden Hue'
    × darleyensis 'Jack H. Brummage'
    vagans 'Valerie Proudley'
Euonymus japonicus 'Ovatus Aureus'
Ilex aquifolium 'Flavescens'
Ligustrum ovalifolium 'Aureum'
    'Vicaryi'
Lonicera nitida 'Baggesen's Gold'
Philadelphus coronarius 'Aureus'
Physocarpus opulifolius 'Dart's Gold'
Pittosporum tenuifolium 'Warnham Gold'
Ptelea trifoliata 'Aurea'
Ribes alpinum 'Aureum'
    sanguineum 'Brocklebankii'
Sambucus canadensis 'Aurea'
    nigra 'Aurea'
    racemosa 'Plumosa Aurea'
    'Sutherland Gold'
Spiraea japonica 'Gold Flame'
    'Golden Dome'
Viburnum opulus 'Aureum'
Weigela 'Looymansii Aurea'
    'Rubidor'

**CLIMBERS**

Hedera helix 'Buttercup'
Humulus lupulus 'Aureus'

**CONIFERS**

Abies nordmanniana 'Golden Spreader'
Calocedrus decurrens 'Berrima Gold'
Cedrus atlantica 'Aurea'
    deodara 'Aurea'
    'Aurea Pendula'
Chamaecyparis lawsoniana, many
    cvs, including
    'Aurea Densa'
    'Lane'
    'Minima Aurea'
    'Stardust'
    'Stewartii'
    'Winston Churchill'

**GOLDEN or YELLOW FOLIAGE** *continued*
  **obtusa,** several cvs, including
    **'Crippsii'**
    **'Fernspray Gold'**
    **'Nana Aurea'**
    **'Tetragona Aurea'**
  **pisifera,** several cvs, including
    **'Filifera Aurea'**
    **'Gold Spangle'**
    **'Golden Mop'**
    **'Plumosa Aurea'**
**Cryptomeria japonica 'Sekkan-sugi'**
× **Cupressocyparis leylandii 'Castlewellan Gold'**
**Cupressus macrocarpa,** several cvs, especially
    **'Donald Gold'**
    **'Goldcrest'**
**Cupressus sempervirens 'Swanes Golden'**
**Juniperus chinensis 'Aurea'**
  × **media** several including,
    **'Gold Coast'**
    **'Mordigan Gold'**
    **'Old Gold'**
    **'Pfitzeriana Aurea'**
    **'Plumosa Aurea'**
    **'Sulphur Spray'**
  **communis 'Depressa Aurea'**
**Picea orientalis 'Aurea'**
**Pinus sylvestris 'Aurea'**
**Taxus baccata,** several cvs, including
    **'Adpressa Variegata'**
    **'Dovastonii Aurea'**
    **'Elegantissima'**
    **'Standishii'**
    **'Summergold'**
**Thuja occidentalis,** several cvs, especially
    **'Europe Gold'**
    **'Rheingold'**
  **orientalis,** several cvs, especially
    **'Aurea Nana'**
  **plicata 'Aurea'**
**Thujopsis dolabrata 'Aurea'**


**TREES and SHRUBS with GREY or SILVER FOLIAGE**


**TREES**
**Eucalyptus,** many, including
  **coccifera**
  **gunnii**
  **pauciflora subsp. niphophila**

**Populus alba**
  **canescens** cvs
**Pyrus,** several, especially
  **nivalis**
  **salicifolia 'Pendula'**
**Salix alba var. sericea**
  **exigua**
**Sorbus aria 'Lutescens'**


**SHRUBS**
**Artemisia** (all)
**Atriplex halimus**
**Berberis dictyophylla**
  **temolaica**
**Buddleja,** several, including
    **alternifolia 'Argentea'**
    **fallowiana**
**Calluna vulgaris 'Silver Queen'**
    **'Sister Anne'**
**Caryopteris** × **clandonensis** cvs
**Cassinia vauvilliersii var. albida**
**Cistus 'Peggy Sammons'**
    **'Silver Pink'**
**Convolvulus cneorum**
**Cytisus battandieri**
**Elaeagnus,** several, including
    **angustifolia**
    **commutata**
    **macrophylla**
**Erica tetralix 'Alba Mollis'**
**Euryops acraeus**
    **pectinatus**
**Feijoa sellowiana**
× **Halimiocistus wintonensis**
**Halimium lasianthum**
    **ocymoides**
**Halimodendron halodendron**
**Hebe,** several, including
    **albicans**
    **colensoi 'Glauca'**
    **pimeleoides 'Quicksilver'**
    **pinguifolia 'Pagei'**
**Helianthemum** several cvs including
    **'Rhodanthe Carneum'**
    **'Wisley Pink'**
    **'Wisley White'**
**Helichrysum** (all)
**Hippophae rhamnoides**
**Lavandula angustifolia** several cvs, including
    **'Grappenhall'**
    **'Hidcote'**
    **'Vera'**
  **stoechas**
    and forms

**GREY or SILVER FOLIAGE** *continued*
**Leptospermum lanigerum**
**Olearia,** several including,
    **mollis**
    **moschata**
    × **scilloniensis**
**Perovskia atriplicifolia 'Blue Spire'**
**Potentilla arbuscula 'Beesii'**
    **'Manchu'**
    **'Vilmoriniana'**
**Romneya** (all)
**Rosa glauca**
**Ruta graveolens** and cvs
**Salix elaeagnos**
    **exigua**
    **gracilistyla**
    **lanata**
    **repens var. argentea**
**Salvia officinalis**
**Santolina chamaecyparissus**
    **pinnata subsp. neapolitana**
**Senecio,** several, especially
    **'Sunshine'**
**Teucrium fruticans** and cvs
**Zauschneria cana**


**CONIFERS**
**Abies concolor 'Candicans'**
    **'Compacta'**
    **lasiocarpa var. arizonica**
    **magnifica 'Glauca'**
    **pinsapo 'Glauca'**
**Cedrus atlantica Glauca** and forms
**Chamaecyparis lawsoniana,**
    many cvs, including
    **'Columnaris'**
    **'Ellwoodii'**
    **'Fletcheri'**
    **'Pembury Blue'**
    **'Triomf van Boskoop'**
    **'Van Pelt'**
    **pisifera 'Boulevard'**
    **'Squarrosa'**
**Cupressus cashmeriana**
    **glabra 'Pyramidalis'**
    **lusitanica 'Glauca Pendula'**
**Juniperus chinensis** (several cvs)
    **'Grey Owl'**
    **horizontalis** and cvs
    especially
    **'Bar Harbor'**
    **'Wiltonii'**
    × **media 'Blaauw'**
    **'Pfitzeriana Compacta'**

**Juniperus procumbens**
    **sabina 'Hicksii'**
    **scopulorum,** several cvs,
    including
    **'Blue Heaven'**
    **'Skyrocket'**
    **'Springbank'**
    **squamata 'Blue Carpet'**
    **'Blue Star'**
    **'Meyeri'**
    **virginiana 'Glauca'**
**Picea glauca**
    **pungens Glauca** and cvs
**Pinus koraiensis 'Glauca Compacta'**
    **parviflora 'Glauca'**
    **pumila 'Compacta'**
    **sylvestris 'Edwin Hillier'**
    **wallichiana**
**Pseudotsuga menziesii var. glauca**
**Tsuga mertensiana f. argentea**


**CLIMBERS**
**Lonicera caprifolium** and cvs
**Vitis vinifera 'Incana'**


**TREES and SHRUBS with**
**VARIEGATED FOLIAGE**

**TREES**
**Acer negundo 'Elegans'**
    **'Flamingo'**
    **'Variegatum'**
    **platanoides 'Drummondii'**
    **pseudoplatanus 'Leopoldii'**
    **'Nizetii'**
**Castanea sativa 'Albomarginata'**
**Cornus controversa 'Variegata'**
**Crataegus monogyna 'Variegata'**
**Fagus sylvatica 'Albovariegata'**
**Fraxinus pennsylvanica 'Variegata'**
**Ilex** × **altaclerensis,** several cvs,
    including
    **'Belgica Aurea'**
    **'Golden King'**
**Ligustrum lucidum 'Excelsum Superbum'**
    **'Tricolor'**
**Liquidambar styraciflua 'Silver King'**
    **'Variegata'**
**Liriodendron tulipifera 'Aureomarginatum'**
**Platanus** × **hispanica 'Suttneri'**
**Populus** × **candicans 'Aurora'**
**Quercus cerris 'Variegata'**
    **robur 'Variegata'**

**VARIEGATED FOLIAGE** *continued*
**SHRUBS**
Abutilon megapotamicum 'Variegatum'
Acer palmatum, several cvs,
    especially
        'Butterfly'
        'Kagiri Nishiki'
        'Ukigumo'
Aralia elata 'Aureovariegata'
        'Variegata'
Aucuba japonica, several cvs,
    especially
        'Crotonifolia'
        'Gold Dust'
        'Variegata'
Azara integrifolia 'Variegata'
    microphylla 'Variegata'
Berberis thunbergii 'Rose Glow'
        'Pink Queen'
Buddleja davidii 'Harlequin'
Buxus sempervirens 'Elegantissima'
Cleyera japonica 'Tricolor'
Cornus alba 'Elegantissima'
        'Spaethii'
        'Variegata'
    alternifolia 'Argentea'
    florida 'Rainbow'
        'Welchii'
    mas 'Variegata'
    stolonifera 'White Gold'
Coronilla valentina 'Variegata'
Cotoneaster horizontalis 'Variegatus'
Crataegus laevigata 'Gireoudii'
Daphne × burkwoodii 'Carol Mackie'
    and similar cvs
    cneorum 'Variegatum'
    longilobata 'Peter Moore'
    odora 'Aureo-marginata'
Elaeagnus × ebbingei 'Gilt Edge'
        'Limelight'
    pungens 'Dicksonii'
        'Frederici'
        'Maculata'
        'Variegata'
Euonymus fortunei 'Emerald Gaiety'
        'Emerald 'n' Gold'
        'Silver Pillar'
        'Silver Queen'
        'Variegatus'
    japonicus, several cvs especially
        'Aureus'
        'Latifolius Albomarginatus'
        'Microphyllus Pulchellus'
        'Microphyllus Variegatus'

× Fatshedera lizei 'Annemieke'
        'Variegata'
Fatsia japonica 'Variegata'
Feijoa sellowiana 'Variegata'
Fuchsia magellanica 'Sharpitor'
        'Variegata'
        'Versicolor'
Griselinia littoralis 'Dixon's Cream'
        'Variegata'
Hebe × andersonii 'Variegata'
    × franciscana 'Variegata'
    glaucophylla 'Variegata'
    'Purple Tips'
Hedera helix 'Little Diamond'
Hoheria populnea 'Alba Variegata'
Hydrangea macrophylla 'Tricolor'
Hypericum × moserianum 'Tricolor'
Ilex aquifolium, many cvs, especially
        'Argenteomarginata'
        'Golden Milkboy'
        'Golden Queen'
        'Handsworth New Silver'
        'Ovata Aurea'
        'Silver Milkmaid'
Kerria japonica 'Variegata'
Leucothoe fontanesiana 'Rainbow'
Ligustrum sinense 'Variegatum'
Myrtus communis 'Variegata'
Myrtus luma 'Glanleam Gold'
Osmanthus heterophyllus 'Aureomarginatus'
        'Goshiki'
        'Latifolius Variegatus'
        'Variegatus'
Pachysandra terminalis 'Variegata'
Philadelphus coronarius 'Variegatus'
Phormium (many)
Photinia davidiana 'Palette'
Pieris 'Flaming Silver'
    japonica 'Little Heath'
        'Variegata'
Pittosporum eugenioides 'Variegatum'
        'Garnettii'
    tenuifolium, several cvs, including
        'Irene Paterson'
        'Silver Queen'
        'Variegatum'
    tobira 'Variegatum'
Prunus laurocerasus 'Marbled White'
    lusitanica 'Variegata'
Rhamnus alaternus 'Argenteovariegata'
Rhododendron ponticum 'Variegatum'
Rubus microphyllus 'Variegatus'
Salvia officinalis 'Icterina'
        'Tricolor'

**689**

**VARIEGATED FOLIAGE** *continued*
Sambucus nigra 'Aureomarginata'
          'Pulverulenta'
Symphoricarpos orbiculatus 'Variegatus'
Viburnum tinus 'Variegatum'
Vinca major 'Variegata'
      minor 'Argenteovariegata'
Weigela florida 'Variegata'
      praecox 'Variegata'
Yucca filamentosa 'Bright Edge'
          'Variegata'
      flaccida 'Golden Sword'
      gloriosa 'Variegata'

**CONIFERS**
Calocedrus decurrens 'Aureovariegata'
Chamaecyparis lawsoniana 'Pygmaea
   Agentea'
        'White Spot'
      nootkatensis 'Aureovariegata'
      pisifera 'Nana Aureovariegata'
        'Snow'
Thuja plicata 'Irish Gold'
        'Zebrina'

**CLIMBERS**
Actinidia kolomikta
Ampelopsis brevipedunculata 'Elegans'
Hedera algeriensis 'Gloire de Marengo'
        'Margino-maculata'
      colchica 'Dentata Variegata'
        'Sulphur Heart'
      helix, several cvs, including
        'Adam'
        'Cavendishii'
        'Eva'
        'Glacier'
        'Goldchild'
        'Goldheart'
        'Harald'
        'Kolibri'
        'Luzii'
        'Marginata'
        'Sagittifolia Variegata'
        'Sicilia'
Jasminum officinale 'Argenteovariegatum'
        'Aureum'
Kadsura japonica 'Variegata'
Lonicera japonica 'Aureoreticulata'
Trachelospermum jasminoides 'Variegatum'

**BAMBOOS**
Arundinaria auricoma
Arundinaria fortunei
Sasa veitchii

**TREES and SHRUBS bearing
ORNAMENTAL FRUIT**

**TREES**
Ailanthus altissima
Arbutus (all)
Catalpa bignonioides
Cercis siliquastrum
Crataegus, many including,
      laciniata
      × lavallei
      mollis
      prunifolia
Diospyros kaki
Fraxinus ornus
Halesia (all)
Ilex, all females, including
       × altaclerensis 'Balearica'
         'Camelliifolia'
         'Wilsonii'
      aquifolium 'J. C. van Tol'
      latifolia
Koelreuteria paniculata
Magnolia, several, including
        campbellii subsp. mollicomata
        hypoleuca
        officinalis var. biloba
        tripetala
Malus, many, including
      'Crittenden'
      hupehensis
      'Golden Hornet'
      'John Downie'
      'Red Jade'
      'Red Sentinel'
      transitoria
Pterocarya (all)
Sorbus, most, including
      aucuparia and cvs
      commixta
      'Joseph Rock'
      'Kewensis'
      scalaris
      vilmorinii
      'Winter Cheer'
Tetradium daniellii

**SHRUBS**
Aucuba japonica (female cvs)
Berberis (most, especially deciduous)
Callicarpa (all)
Chaenomeles (most)
Citrus 'Meyer's Lemon'

**ORNAMENTAL FRUIT** *continued*
**Clerodendrum trichotomum**
**Colutea** (all)
**Coriaria** (all)
**Cornus,** many, especially
      **amomum**
      **mas**
           **'Variegata'**
      **'Norman Hadden'**
**Cotinus** (all)
**Cotoneaster** (all)
**Daphne mezereum**
      **tangutica**
**Decaisnea fargesii**
**Euonymus,** many, including
      **europaeus 'Red Cascade'**
      **hamiltonianus 'Coral Charm'**
      **latifolius**
      **oxyphyllus**
      **planipes**
× **Gaulnettya** cvs
**Gaultheria,** many, including
      **cuneata**
      **forrestii**
      **miqueliana**
      **procumbens**
**Hippophae rhamnoides**
**Ilex,** females, including
      **aquifolium 'Amber'**
           **'Bacciflava'**
           **'Pyramidalis'**
           **'Pyramidalis Fructu-luteo'**
      **cornuta 'Burfordii'**
**Leycesteria formosa**
**Mahonia aquifolium**
      **japonica**
      **lomariifolia**
**Mespilus germanica** cvs
**Myrica cerifera**
**Pernettya mucronata** and cvs
**Photinia davidiana** and forms
**Poncirus trifoliata**
**Prunus laurocerasus** and cvs
**Ptelea trifoliata**
**Pyracantha** (all)
**Rosa,** many, including
      **'Arthur Hillier'**
      **'Highdownensis'**
      **macrophylla** and cvs
      **moyesii** and forms
      **rugosa** and cvs
      **webbiana**
**Rubus phoenicolasius**
**Ruscus aculeatus**
**Sambucus** (most)

**Skimmia japonica** (female forms)
      **subsp. reevesiana**
**Staphylea** (all)
**Symphoricarpos** (most)
**Symplocos paniculata**
**Vaccinium, several,** including
      **corymbosum** and cvs
      **cylindraceum**
      **vitis-idaea**
**Viburnum,** many, including
      **betulifolium**
      **opulus** and cvs
      **setigerum**
      **wrightii 'Hessei'**


**CLIMBERS**
**Actinidia chinensis**
**Akebia quinata**
      **trifoliata**
**Ampelopsis,** several, especially
      **brevipedunculata**
**Billardiera longiflora**
**Celastrus** (all)
**Clematis,** several, especially
      **tangutica**
      **tibetana subsp. vernayi**
**Parthenocissus,** several, including
      **himalayana**
**Passiflora caerulea**
      **edulis**
**Schisandra** (all)
**Stauntonia hexaphylla**
**Vitis,** several, especially
      **'Brant'**


**CONIFERS**
**Abies,** many, including
      **forrestii**
      **koreana**
      **procera**
**Picea,** many, including
      **abies 'Acrocona'**
      **likiangensis**
      **purpurea**
      **smithiana**
**Pinus,** many, including
      **ayacahuite**
      **wallichiana**
**Taxus baccata 'Lutea'**

## TREES and SHRUBS with FRAGRANT or SCENTED FLOWERS

The scents of flowers are a wonderful part of garden enjoyment as well as being a delightful extra attraction in a flowering plant. Just as a sense of smell differs from person to person, so scents vary from flower to flower. The positioning of a plant is of importance if its scent is not to be lost to the wind. Even if the position is right weather conditions can make all the difference to the strength or carrying power of delicate scents.

### TREES
Acacia dealbata
Aesculus hippocastanum
Azara microphylla
Cladrastis lutea
 sinensis
Crataegus monogyna
Drimys winteri
Eucryphia × intermedia 'Rostrevor'
 lucida
Fraxinus mariesii
Gordonia axillaris
Laburnum alpinum
 × watereri 'Vossii'
Magnolia fraseri
 hypoleuca
 kobus
 macrophylla
 salicifolia
Malus baccata var. mandshurica
 coronaria 'Charlottae'
 floribunda
 'Hillieri'
 hupehensis
 'Profusion'
 × robusta
Michelia doltsopa
Myrtus luma
Pittosporum eugenioides
Prunus 'Amanogawa'
 'Jo-nioi'
 lusitanica and cvs
 × yedoensis and cvs
Robinia pseudoacacia and cvs
Styrax japonica
Tilia × euchlora
 oliveri
 platyphyllos
 tomentosa and cvs

### SHRUBS
Abelia chinensis
 × grandiflora
 triflora
Abeliophyllum distichum
Azara petiolaris
Berberis buxifolia
 sargentiana
Brugmansia suaveolens
Buddleja, many, including
 alternifolia
 crispa
 davidii and cvs
 fallowiana
 'Lochinch'
Buxus sempervirens and cvs
Camellia sasanqua cvs
Ceanothus 'Gloire de Versailles'
Chimonanthus praecox and cvs
Chionanthus virginicus
Choisya 'Aztec Pearl'
 ternata
Citrus 'Meyer's Lemon'
Clerodendrum bungei
 trichotomum
Clethra alnifolia and cvs
 barbinervis
 fargesii
Colletia hystrix 'Rosea'
 paradoxa
Corokia cotoneaster
Coronilla valentina subsp. glauca
Corylopsis (all)
Cytisus battandieri
 'Porlock'
 × praecox and cvs
 supranubius
Daphne, many, including
 arbuscula
 blagayana
 × burkwoodii and cvs
 cneorum and forms
 collina
 × hybrida
 × mantensiana 'Manten'
 mezereum and cvs
 × napolitana
 odora and cvs
 pontica
 tangutica
Deutzia compacta and cvs
 × elegantissima and cvs
Edgeworthia chrysantha
Elaeagnus (all)

692

**FRAGRANT or SCENTED FLOWERS** *contd*
**Erica arborea 'Alpina'**
    × **darleyensis** and cvs
    **lusitanica**
    × **veitchii**
**Escallonia 'Donard Gem'**
**Eucryphia glutinosa**
    **milliganii**
**Euonymus planipes**
**Fothergilla gardenii**
    **major**
**Gaultheria forrestii**
    **fragrantissima**
**Genista aetnensis**
**Hakea microcarpa**
**Hamamelis × intermedia** cvs
    **mollis** and cvs
**Hoheria glabrata**
    **lyallii**
**Itea ilicifolia**
    **virginica**
**Jasminum humile 'Revolutum'**
**Ligustrum,** all, including
    **quihoui**
    **sinense**
**Lomatia myricoides**
**Lonicera fragrantissima**
    × **purpusii**
        **'Winter Beauty'**
    **standishii**
    **syringantha**
**Luculia gratissima**
**Lupinus arboreus**
**Magnolia denudata**
    **grandiflora** and cvs
    × **loebneri** and cvs
    **sieboldii**
    **sinensis**
    × **soulangeana** and cvs
    **stellata** and cvs
    × **thompsoniana**
    **virginiana**
    × **wieseneri**
    **wilsonii**
**Mahonia japonica**
**Myrtus communis** and cvs
**Oemleria cerasiformis**
**Olearia × haastii**
    **ilicifolia**
    **macrodonta** and cvs
**Osmanthus** (all)
**Paeonia × lemoinei** and cvs
**Philadelphus,** many, including
    **'Belle Etoile'**
    **'Bouquet Blanc'**

    **coronarius** and cvs
    **'Erectus'**
    **microphyllus**
    **'Sybille'**
    **'Virginal'**
**Pimelea prostrata**
**Pittosporum tenuifolium**
    **tobira**
**Poncirus trifoliata**
**Prunus mume** and cvs
**Ptelea trifoliata**
**Pterostyrax hispida**
**Pyracantha** (all)
**Rhododendron,** many, including
    **Albatross** and forms
    **arborescens**
    **auriculatum**
    **calophytum**
    **'Countess of Haddington'**
    **decorum**
    **fortunei**
    **'Fragrantissimum'**
    **Lodauric**
    **Loderi** and cvs
    **luteum**
    **periclymenoides**
    **'Polar Bear'**
    **roseum**
    **viscosum**
    **Deciduous Azaleas many,**
    especially,
        **'Daviesii'**
        **'Exquisitum'**
        **'Irene Koster'**
**Ribes alpinum**
    **gayanum**
    **odoratum**
**Romneya** (all)
**Rosa,** many, including
    **'Albert Edwards'**
    **'Andersonii'**
    **'Anemonoides'**
    **banksiae** (single forms)
    **bracteata**
    **brunonii**
    **filipes 'Kiftsgate'**
    **foliolosa**
    **helenae**
    **longicuspis**
    **'Macrantha'**
    **moschata**
    × **odorata 'Pseudindica'**
    **primula**
    **rugosa** and cvs
    **wichuraiana**

**FRAGRANT or SCENTED FLOWERS** *contd*
Sarcococca (all)
Skimmia × confusa and cvs
      japonica 'Fragrans'
          'Rubella'
Spartium junceum
Syringa, many including
      × chinensis 'Saugeana'
      × josiflexa 'Bellicent'
      julianae
      × persica and cvs
      sweginzowii 'Superba'
      vulgaris cvs
Ulex europaeus
Viburnum, many, including
      × bodnantense cvs
      × burkwoodii and cvs
      × carlcephalum
      carlesii and cvs
      'Chesapeake'
      erubescens var. gracilipes
      farreri
      grandiflorum
      japonicum
      × juddii
Yucca filamentosa
      flaccida
Zenobia pulverulenta

## CLIMBERS
Actinidia chinensis
Akebia quinata
Clematis armandii and cvs
      cirrhosa var. balearica
      flammula
      montana and forms
      rehderiana
Decumaria sinensis
Dregea sinensis
Holboellia latifolia
Jasminum azoricum
      beesianum
      officinale and cvs
      polyanthum
      × stephanense
Lonicera × americana
      caprifolium and cvs
      etrusca
      × heckrottii
      japonica and cvs
      periclymenum and cvs
Mandevilla laxa
Stauntonia hexaphylla
Trachelospermum (all)
Wisteria (all)

## TREES and SHRUBS with AROMATIC FOLIAGE

Aromatic plants and those with scented leaves or wood play an important part in the make-up of a garden. Whether they give off their aroma freely or only as a result of a gentle bruising, they contribute much to the appreciation of a living plant.

### TREES
Cercidiphyllum japonicum (in autumn)
Clerodendrum (all)
Eucalyptus (all)
Juglans (all)
Laurus nobilis and cvs
Phellodendron (all)
Populus balsamifera
      trichocarpa
Salix pentandra
      triandra
Sassafras albidum
Umbellularia californica

### SHRUBS
Aloysia triphylla
Artemisia arborescens
      'Powis Castle'
Caryopteris (all)
Cistus, many, including
      × aguilari
      × cyprius
      ladanifer
      × loretii
      palhinhae
      'Pat'
      × purpureus
Clerodendrum bungei
Comptonia peregrina
Elsholtzia stauntonii
Escallonia (many)
Gaultheria procumbens
Hebe cupressoides
Helichrysum italicum subsp. serotinum
      plicatum
Illicium (all)
Lavandula angustifolia and cvs
Lindera (all)
Myrica (all)
Myrtus communis and cvs
Olearia ilicifolia
      mollis
Perovskia (all)
Prostanthera (all)
Ptelea trifoliata

**AROMATIC FOLIAGE** *continued*
**Rhododendron,** many, including
        **augustinii**
        **cinnabarinum** forms and hybrids
        **Mollis Azaleas**
        **'Pink Drift'**
        **saluenense**
**Ribes sanguineum** and cvs
**Rosmarinus officinalis** and cvs
**Ruta graveolens**
**Salvia** (all)
**Santolina** (all)
**Skimmia** all, particularly,
        **anquetilia**
        × **confusa** and cvs

**CONIFERS**
Most conifers, particularly,
**Calocedrus decurrens**
**Chamaecyparis** (all)
**Cupressus** (all)
**Juniperus** (all)
**Pseudotsuga menziesii** and forms
**Thuja** (all)

**FLOWERING TREES and SHRUBS**
**for EVERY MONTH**

A month by month selection of flowering trees
and shrubs. Many subjects flower over a long
period, but are only mentioned under the
months during which they provide a
reasonable display.

**JANUARY**

**TREES**
**Acacia dealbata**

**SHRUBS**
**Camellia sasanqua** cvs
**Chimonanthus praecox** and cvs
**Erica carnea** and cvs
        × **darleyensis** and cvs
**Garrya elliptica**
**Hamamelis** (many)
**Jasminum nudiflorum**
**Lonicera fragrantissima**
        × **purpusii**
        **standishii**
**Sarcococca** (several)
**Viburnum** × **bodnantense** and cvs
        **farreri**
        **tinus**

**FEBRUARY**

**TREES**
**Acacia dealbata**
**Magnolia campbellii** and forms
**Populus tremula**
**Prunus incisa 'Praecox'**
        **mume** and cvs
**Rhododendron arboreum** and forms
**Sorbus megalocarpa**

**SHRUBS**
**Camellia sasanqua** cvs
**Cornus mas**
        **officinalis**
**Daphne mezereum**
        **odora** and cvs
**Erica carnea** and cvs
        × **darleyensis** and cvs
**Garrya elliptica**
**Hamamelis** (many)
**Jasminum nudiflorum**
**Lonicera fragrantissima**
        × **purpusii**
        **setifera**
        **standishii**
**Mahonia japonica**
**Pachysandra terminalis**
**Rhododendron dauricum 'Midwinter'**
        **mucronulatum**
**Sarcococca** (several)
**Ulex europaeus**
**Viburnum** × **bodnantense** cvs
        **farreri**
        **tinus** and cvs

**MARCH**

**TREES**
**Acer opalus**
        **rubrum**
**Magnolia** (several)
**Maytenus boaria**
**Prunus** (several)
**Rhododendron** (several)
**Salix** (many)
**Sorbus megalocarpa**

**SHRUBS**
**Camellia japonica** (several cvs)
        **sasanqua** and cvs
**Chaenomeles** (several)

**FLOWERING TREES and SHRUBS** *continued*
Corylopsis pauciflora
Daphne mezereum
Erica carnea and cvs
    × **darleyensis** cvs
    erigena and cvs
    lusitanica
    × **veitchii** cvs
Forsythia (several)
Lonicera setifera
Magnolia stellata
Mahonia aquifolium
    japonica
Osmanthus (several)
Pachysandra terminalis
Prunus (several)
Rhododendron (several)
Salix (many)
Stachyurus praecox
Ulex europaeus
Viburnum tinus and cvs

**APRIL**

**TREES**
Acer platanoides
Amelanchier (several)
Magnolia kobus
    × **loebneri** and cvs
Magnolia salicifolia
Malus (several)
Prunus (many)

**SHRUBS**
Amelanchier (several)
Berberis darwinii
    linearifolia
    × **lologensis**
Camellia japonica and cvs
    × **williamsii** and cvs
Chaenomeles (many)
Corylopsis (several)
Cytisus (several)
Daphne (several)
Erica (several)
Forsythia (many)
Kerria japonica and cvs
Magnolia × soulangeana and cvs
    stellata
Mahonia aquifolium
    pinnata
Osmanthus × burkwoodii
    decorus
    delavayi

Pieris (most)
Prunus (many)
Rhododendron (many)
Ribes (many)
Spiraea 'Arguta'
    thunbergii
Viburnum (many)

**CLIMBERS**
Clematis alpina
    armandii
Holboellia coriacea

**MAY**

**TREES**
Aesculus (many)
Cercis (several)
Cornus nuttallii
Crataegus (many)
Davidia involucrata
Embothrium coccineum and cvs
Fraxinus ornus
Halesia (all)
Laburnum anagyroides
  × watereri 'Vossii'
Malus (many)
Paulownia tomentosa
Prunus (many)
Pyrus (all)
Sorbus (many)

**SHRUBS**
Camellia japonica cvs (several)
Ceanothus (several)
Chaenomeles (many)
Choisya (all)
Cornus florida and cvs
Cotoneaster (many)
Crinodendron hookerianum
Cytisus (many)
Daphne (many)
Dipelta floribunda
Enkianthus (all)
Erica (several)
Exochorda (all)
Genista (many)
Halesia (all)
Helianthemum (all)
Kerria japonica and cvs
Kolkwitzia amabilis
Ledum (all)
Lonicera (many)

**FLOWERING TREES and SHRUBS** *continued*
**Magnolia liliiflora**
    × **soulangeana** cvs
**Menziesia** (all)
**Paeonia** (many)
**Piptanthus nepalensis**
**Potentilla** (many)**Pyracantha** (many)
**Rhododendron** (many)
**Rosa** (many)
**Xanthoceras sorbifolium**

## CLIMBERS
**Clematis** (many)
**Lonicera** (many)
**Schisandra** (all)
**Wisteria** (all)


## JUNE


## TREES
**Aesculus** (several)
**Crataegus** (many)
**Embothrium coccineum** and forms
**Laburnum alpinum**
    × **watereri 'Vossii'**
**Magnolia**, several, including
    **acuminata var. subcordata**
    **'Charles Coates'**
    **fraseri**
    **hypoleuca**
**Malus trilobata**
**Robinia** (several)
**Styrax** (several)


## SHRUBS
**Abelia** (several)
**Buddleja globosa**
**Cistus** (many)
**Colutea** (all)
**Cornus kousa**
    **'Norman Hadden'**
**Cotoneaster** (many)
**Cytisus** (many)
**Deutzia** (most)
**Erica ciliaris** and cvs
    **cinerea** and cvs
    **tetralix** and cvs
**Escallonia** (many)
**Genista** (many)
× **Halimiocistus** (all)
**Halimium** (all)
**Hebe** (many)
**Helianthemum** (all)
**Hydrangea** (several)

**Kalmia** (all)
**Kolkwitzia amabilis** and cvs
**Lonicera** (several)
**Magnolia**, several, including
    × **thompsoniana**
    **virginiana**
**Neillia** (several)
**Olearia** (several)
**Ozothamnus** (all)
**Paeonia** (all)
**Penstemon** (several)
**Philadelphus** (many)
**Potentilla** (all)
**Rhododendron** (many)
**Rosa** (many)
**Rubus** (many)
**Spartium junceum**
**Spiraea** (many)
**Staphylea** (several)
**Syringa** (many)
**Viburnum** (many)
**Weigela** (all)
**Zenobia pulverulenta**


## CLIMBERS
**Clematis** (many)
**Jasminum** (several)
**Lonicera** (many)
**Schisandra** (several)
**Wisteria** (all)


## JULY


## TREES
**Aesculus indica**
**Castanea sativa**
**Catalpa** (all)
**Cladrastis sinensis**
**Eucryphia** (several)
**Koelreuteria paniculata**
**Liriodendron tulipifera**
**Magnolia delavayi**
    **grandiflora** and cvs
**Stuartia** (several)


## SHRUBS
**Aster albescens**
**Buddleja davidii** and cvs
**Calluna vulgaris** and cvs
**Cistus** (many)
**Colutea** (all)
**Daboecia cantabrica** and cvs
**Desfontainia spinosa**

**697**

**FLOWERING TREES and SHRUBS** *continued*
**Deutzia setchuenensis**
**Erica ciliaris** and cvs
      **cinerea** and cvs
      **tetralix** and cvs
      **vagans** and cvs
**Escallonia** (many)
**Fuchsia** (many)
**Grevillea juniperina 'Sulphurea'**
**Halimodendron halodendron**
**Hebe** (many)
**Hoheria** (several)
**Holodiscus discolor**
**Hydrangea** (many)
**Hypericum** (many)
**Indigofera** (several)
**Lavandula angustifolia** and cvs
**Magnolia virginiana**
**Olearia** (several)
**Penstemon** (several)
**Philadelphus** (several)
**Phygelius** (all)
**Potentilla** (many)
**Rhododendron** (several)
**Romneya** (all)
**Yucca** (several)
**Zenobia pulverulenta**

**CLIMBERS**
**Clematis** (many)
**Eccremocarpus scaber**
**Fallopia baldschuanica**
**Jasminum** (several)
**Lonicera** (many)
**Mutisia oligodon**
**Passiflora** (several)
**Schizophragma** (all)
**Solanum** (all)
**Trachelospermum** (all)

**AUGUST**

**TREES**
**Catalpa bignonioides**
**Eucryphia** (several)
**Koelreuteria paniculata**
**Ligustrum lucidum** and cvs
**Magnolia delavayi**
      **grandiflora** and cvs
**Oxydendrum arboreum**
**Stuartia** (several)

**SHRUBS**
**Buddleja** (many)
**Calluna vulgaris** and cvs
**Caryopteris** (several)

**Ceanothus** (several)
**Ceratostigma willmottianum**
**Clerodendrum** (all)
**Clethra** (several)
**Colutea** (all)
**Daboecia cantabrica** and cvs
**Desfontainia spinosa**
**Deutzia setchuenensis**
**Elsholtzia stauntonii**
**Erica ciliaris** and cvs
      **cinerea** and cvs
      **tetralix** and cvs
      **vagans** and cvs
**Fuchsia** (many)
**Genista tinctoria** and cvs
**Grevillea juniperina 'Sulphurea'**
**Hibiscus** (several)
**Hydrangea** (many)
**Hypericum** (many)
**Indigofera** (several)
**Itea ilicifolia**
**Lavandula angustifolia**
      (several cvs)
**Leycesteria formosa**
**Myrtus** (several)
**Olearia** (several)
**Perovskia** (all)
**Phygelius** (all)
**Potentilla** (all)
**Romneya** (all)
**Rosa** (many)
**Yucca** (several)
**Zenobia pulverulenta**

**CLIMBERS**
**Berberidopsis corallina**
**Campsis** (all)
**Clematis** (many)
**Eccremocarpus scaber**
**Jasminum** (several)
**Lonicera** (many)
**Lapageria rosea** cvs
**Mutisia oligodon**
**Passiflora** (several)
**Pileostegia viburnoides**
**Fallopia** (all)
**Solanum** (all)
**Trachelospermum asiaticum**

**SEPTEMBER**

**TREES**
**Eucryphia** × **nymansensis** and cvs
**Magnolia grandiflora** and cvs
**Oxydendrum arboreum**

**FLOWERING TREES and SHRUBS** *continued*
**SHRUBS**
**Abelia chinensis**
    × **grandiflora**
    **schumannii**
**Aralia elata**
**Buddleja** (several)
**Calluna vulgaris** and cvs
**Caryopteris** (several)
**Ceratostigma griffithii**
    **willmottianum**
**Clerodendrum bungei**
    **trichotomum**
**Colutea** (several)
**Daboecia cantabrica** and cvs
**Elsholtzia stauntonii**
**Erica ciliaris** and cvs
    **cinerea** (several cvs)
    **terminalis**
    **tetralix** and cvs
    **vagans** and cvs
**Fuchsia** (several)
**Grevillea juniperina 'Sulphurea'**
**Hebe** (several)
**Hibiscus** (several)
**Hydrangea** (several)
**Hypericum** (several)
**Genista tinctoria** and cvs
**Indigofera** (several)
**Lespedeza thunbergii**
**Leycesteria formosa**
**Magnolia cordata**
**Perovskia** (all)
**Potentilla** (most)
**Romneya** (all)
**Vitex** (all)
**Yucca gloriosa**
**Zauschneria**

**CLIMBERS**
**Campsis** (all)
**Clematis** (several)
**Eccremocarpus scaber**
**Fallopia baldschuanica**
**Jasminum** (several)
**Lapageria rosea** cvs
**Mutisia oligodon**
**Passiflora** (several)
**Pileostegia viburnoides**
**Polygonum baldschuanicum**
**Solanum crispum 'Glasnevin'**

**OCTOBER**

**TREES**
**Magnolia grandiflora** and cvs

**SHRUBS**
**Abelia** × **grandiflora**
**Calluna vulgaris** (several cvs)
**Ceratostigma griffithii**
    **willmottianum**
**Erica carnea 'Eileen Porter'**
    **vagans** (several cvs)
**Fatsia japonica**
**Fuchsia** (several)
**Hibiscus** (several)
**Hydrangea** (several)
**Hypericum** (several)
**Lespedeza thunbergii**
**Mahonia** × **media** and cvs
**Potentilla** (several)
**Vitex** (all)
**Zauschneria** (all)

**CLIMBERS**
**Clematis** (several)
**Eccremocarpus scaber**
**Lapageria rosea** cvs

**NOVEMBER**

**TREES**
**Prunus subhirtella 'Autumnalis'**

**SHRUBS**
**Erica carnea 'Eileen Porter'**
**Jasminum nudiflorum**
**Lonicera standishii**
**Mahonia acanthifolia**
**Mahonia** × **media** and cvs
**Viburnum** × **bodnantense** cvs
    **farreri**

**DECEMBER**

**TREES**
**Prunus subhirtella 'Autumnalis'**
    **'Autumnalis Rosea'**

**SHRUBS**
**Erica carnea** (several cvs)
    × **darleyensis 'Silberschmelze'**
**Hamamelis** × **intermedia** (some)
    **mollis**
**Jasminum nudiflorum**
**Lonicera fragrantissima**
    × **purpusii**
    **standishii**
**Mahonia** × **media** and cvs
**Viburnum** × **bodnantense** and cvs
    **farreri**
    **foetens**
    **tinus**

**699**

# PLANTS RAISED or SELECTED
## by HILLIER NURSERIES (WINCHESTER) LTD

(Dates in parentheses represent the approximate year of raising or selection)

Abies procera 'Glauca Prostrata' (1895)
Abutilon × suntense 'Jermyns' (1967)
Abutilon × suntense 'White Charm' (1975)
Acer × hillieri (before 1935)
Acer palmatum 'Heptalobum Lutescens' (before 1935)
Acer 'Silver Vein' (1961)
Apple 'Easter Orange' (before 1897) AM 1897
Aucuba japonica 'Hillieri' (before 1930)
Berberis 'Blenheim'
Berberis 'Goldilocks' (1978)
Berberis × stenophylla 'Etna' (before 1935)
Berberis × wintonensis (before 1955)
Buddleja 'West Hill' (before 1967)
Camellia 'Barbara Hillier' (1960)
Camellia × williamsii 'Jermyns' (1960)
Caryopteris incana 'Peach Pink' (1960)
Ceanothus 'Blue Mound' (1960)
Cephalotaxus fortunei 'Prostrate Spreader' (before 1920)
Cephalotaxus harringtonia 'Gnome' (1970)
Cephalotaxus harringtonia 'Prostrata' (before 1930)
Chamaecyparis lawsoniana 'Elegantissima' (before 1930) AGM 1969
Chamaecyparis lawsoniana 'Hillieri' (before 1930)
Choisya 'Aztec Pearl' (1982) AM 1990
Chrysanthemum 'Hillier's Apricot' (1919) AM 1921
Cistus 'Silver Pink' (1910) AM 1919 AGM 1930
Corylopsis willmottiae 'Spring Purple' (1969)
Cotinus Dummer Hybrids (1978)
Cotinus 'Grace' (1978) AM 1983 Cory Cup 1984
Cotoneaster 'Eastleigh' (1960)
Cotonester 'Salmon Spray' (before 1940)
Cupressus lusitanica 'Glauca Pendula' (before 1914) AM 1944
Cytisus battandieri 'Yellow Tail' (before 1975)
Cytisus × versicolor 'Hillieri' (1935)
Daphne bholua 'Jacqueline Postill' (1982) FCC 1991
Daphne longilobata 'Peter Moore' (1980)
Daphne 'Valerie Hillier' (1984)
Deutzia chunii 'Pink Charm' (1960)
Deutzia 'Hillieri' (1926)
Escallonia 'Wintonensis' (before 1921)
Eucryphia × hillieri 'Winton' (1953)
Euonymus hamiltonianaus subsp. sieboldianus 'Fiesta' (1967)
Fagus sylvatica 'Cockleshell' (1960)
Forsythia 'Golden Nugget' (1964)
× Gaulnettya 'Pink Pixie' (1969)
× Halimiocistus wintonensis (1910) AM 1926
Hamamelis × intermedia 'Carmine Red' (1934)
Hamamelis × intermedia 'Hiltingbury' (1934)
Hamamelis vernalis 'Red Imp' (1966)
Hamamelis vernalis 'Sandra' (1962)
Hamamelis vernalis 'Squib' (1966)
Helianthemum 'Coppernob' (1968)
Hibiscus sinosyriacus 'Autumn Surprise' (1936)
Hibiscus sinosyriacus 'Lilac Queen' (1936)
Hibiscus sinosyriacus 'Ruby Glow' (1936)
Hypericum × dummeri 'Peter Dummer' (1975)
Hypericum 'Eastleigh Gold' (1964)
Ilex × altaclerensis 'Purple Shaft' (1965)

Ilex aquifolium 'Amber' (1950)
Ilex 'Jermyns Dwarf' (before 1955)
Iris chrysographes 'Purple Wings' (1962)
Kniphofia 'St Cross' (before 1935)
Laburnum anagyroides 'Erect' (1965)
Laburnum × watereri 'Alford's Weeping' (1968)
Larix kaempferi 'Hobbit' (1960)
Leucothoe fontanesiana 'Rainbow'
Linum flavum 'Saffron' (1967)
Lonicera × purpusii 'Winter Beauty' (1966)
Lupinus 'Broadgate Yellow' (1962)
Magnolia campbellii 'Ethel Hillier' (1927)
Magnolia salicifolia 'Jermyns' (1935)
Pernettya mucronata 'Cherry Ripe' (1965)
Pernettya mucronata 'Mulberry Wine' (1965)
Pernettya mucronata 'Pink Pearl' (1965)
Pernettya mucronata 'Rosie' (1965)
Pernettya mucronata 'Sea Shell' (1965)
Pernettya mucronata 'White Pearl' (1965)
Perovskia 'Hybrida' (before 1937)
Photinia 'Redstart' (1969)
Photinia 'Winchester' (1969)
Phygelius × rectus 'Devil's Tears' (1985)
Phygelius × rectus 'Moonraker' (1985)
Phygelius × rectus 'Pink Elf' (1985)
Phygelius × rectus 'Salmon Leap' (1985)
Phygelius × rectus 'Winchester Fanfare' (1974)
Phyllocladus alpinus 'Silver Blades' (1968)
× Phylliopsis hillieri 'Pinocchio' (1960) AM 1976 FCC 1984
Pieris formosa 'Jermyns' (1950) AM 1959
Pinus cembra 'Jermyns' (1929)
Pinus koraiensis 'Winton' (1929)
Pinus parviflora 'Adcock's Dwarf' (1965)
Pinus sylvestris 'Edwin Hillier' (1920) AGM 1969
Populus 'Hiltingbury Weeping' (1962)
Potentilla 'Eastleigh Cream' (1969)
Potentilla 'Elizabeth' (1950) AMT 1965 AGM 1969
Potentilla 'Milkmaid' (1960)
Potentilla 'Ruth' (1960)
Potentilla 'Whirligig' (1969)
Primula sinensis 'Annie Hillier' (1875) FCC 1880
Prunus 'Hillieri' (before 1928) AM 1959
Prunus incisa 'Praecox' (before 1938) AM 1973
Prunus laurocerasus 'Greenmantle' (1965)
Prunus 'Spire' (before 1928)
Prunus × yedoensis 'Ivensii' (before 1929)
Quercus castaneifolia 'Green Spire' (1948)
Rhododendron campylogynum 'Crushed Strawberry' (1955)
Rhododendron kaempferi 'Highlight' (1955)
Rhododendron kiusianum 'Hillier's Pink' (1957)
Rhododendron tosaense 'Barbara' (1958)
Rhododendron 'April Chimes' (1938)
Rhododendron 'Arthur J. Ivens' (1938) AM 1944
Rhododendron 'Arthur Stevens' (1960)
Rhododendron Fittra (1938) AM 1949
Rhododendron 'July Fragrance' (1955)
Rhododendron 'Midsummer Snow' (1955)
Rhododendron (Knap Hill Azalea) 'Dracula' (1965)
Rhododendron (Knap Hill Azalea) 'Orange Truffles' (1966)
Robinia × slavinii 'Hillieri' (1933) AM 1962
Rosa 'Albert Edwards' (1937)
Rosa 'Arthur Hillier' (1938)
Rosa 'Hillieri' (1926)
Rosa 'Wintonensis' (1928)

Salix 'Mark Postill' (1967)
Santolina rosmarinifolia 'Primrose Gem' (1960)
Schizophragma hydrangeoides 'Roseum' (1933) AM 1939
Sorbus 'Apricot Lady' (1960)
Sorbus 'Autumn Glow' (1967)
Sorbus commixta 'Jermyns' (1955)
Sorbus 'Eastern Promise' (1967)
Sorbus 'Edwin Hillier' (1947)
Sorbus 'Ethel's Gold' (1960)
Sorbus folgneri 'Lemon Drop' (before 1950)
Sorbus 'Pearly King' (1959)
Sorbus 'Red Marbles' (1961)
Sorbus 'Rose Queen' (1959)
Sorbus 'Signalman' (1963)
Sorbus 'Sunshine' (1968)
Sorbus 'Tundra' (1968)
Sorbus 'Vesuvius' (1960)
Sorbus 'Winter Cheer' (1959) AM 1971
Stachyurus chinensis 'Magpie' (1948)
Syringa yunnanensis 'Alba' (1946)
Syringa yunnanensis 'Rosea' (1946)
Thuja orientalis 'Hillieri' (1920)
Thuja plicata 'Hillieri' (1880)
Torreya californica 'Spreadeagle' (1965)
Ulmus × hollandica 'Hillieri' (1918)
Verbascum 'Golden Bush' (1962)
Viburnum × hillieri 'Winton' (1949) AM 1956
Viburnum × globosum 'Jermyns Globe' (1964)
Viburnum rhytidophyllum 'Roseum' (before 1935)

# PLANTS NAMED by HILLIER NURSERIES (WINCHESTER) LTD

(Dates in parentheses represent the approximate year of naming)

Acaena 'Blue Haze' (1965)
Aucuba japonica 'Lance Leaf' (1968)
Aucuba japonica 'Speckles' (1968)
Betula utilis 'Jermyns' (1974)
Betula utilis 'Silver Shadow' (1991)
Camellia 'Winton' (1948)
Cornus mas 'Hillier's Upright' (1974)
Cotinus 'Flame' (1964) AGM 1969
Cotoneaster conspicuus 'Highlight' (1965)
Cotoneaster 'Pink Champagne' (1965)
Deutzia compacta 'Lavender Time' (1969)
Enkianthus campanulatus 'Red Bells' (1991)
Escallonia 'E. G. Cheeseman' (1948)
× Gaulnettya 'Ruby' (1967)
Foeniculum vulgare 'Smoky' (1964)
Genista tenera 'Golden Shower' (1973)
Griselinia littoralis 'Dixon's Cream' (1969)
Hamamelis × intermedia 'Moonlight' (1960)
Hydrangea heteromalla 'Snowcap' (1970)
Hypericum olympicum 'Sunburst' (1974)
Ilex aquifolium 'Green Pillar' (1970)

**Larix decidua 'Corley'** (1971)
**Ligustrum lucidum 'Excelsum Superbum'** (1908)
**Magnolia campbellii 'Sidbury'** (1970)
**Magnolia campbellii 'Werrington'** (1970)
**Magnolia × loebneri 'Snowdrift'** (1969)
**Malus 'Hillieri'** (1928)
**Olearia avicenniifolia 'White Confusion'** (1969)
**Pernettya leucocarpa 'Harold Comber'** (1965)
**Pernettya mucronata 'Edward Balls'** (1965)
**Phlomis 'Edward Bowles'** (1967)
**Pinus sylvestris 'Windsor'** (1971)
**Pittosporum tenuifolium 'Warnham Gold'** (1969)
**Prunus 'Pink Shell'** (1969) AM 1969
**Prunus 'Snow Goose'** (1970)
**Prunus verecunda 'Autumn Glory'** (1969) AM 1966
**Pyracantha 'Golden Dome'** (before 1973)
**Quercus ilex 'Bicton'** (1971)
**Reynoutria compacta 'Pink Cloud'** (1964)
**Rhododendron 'Cool Haven'** (1969)
**Rhododendron 'Lorien'** (1973)
**Rhododendron 'Mrs Edwin Hillier'** (1933)
**Santolina pinnata 'Edward Bowles'** (1968)
**Sarcococca hookeriana var. digyna 'Purple Stem'** (1968)
**Soleirolia soleirolii 'Golden Mat'** (1963)
**Sophora microphylla 'Sun King'** (1991)
**Sorbus alnifolia 'Skyline'** (1976)
**Sorbus 'Chinese Lace'** (1973)
**Sorbus commixta 'Embley'** (1971)
**Sorbus 'Wilfrid Fox'** (1964)
**Taxodium distichum 'Hursley Park'** (1970)
**Tilia 'Harold Hillier'** (1991)
**Trachelospermum jasminoides 'Wilsonii'** (before 1935)
**Tsuga heterophylla 'Laursens's Column'** (1971)
**Ulmus minor 'Jacqueline Hillier'** (1967)
**Ulmus parvifolia 'Frosty'** (1970)

# The Hillier Gardens and Arboretum

## a living resource

Although the origins and concept of the Hillier Gardens and Arboretum have been referred to briefly elsewhere in this book, the development of such an outstanding national and international environmental resource merits further description.

When the late Sir Harold Hillier came to live in Jermyns House in 1953, there was a relatively small garden, mainly lawns and shrubbery, but with some large trees and, in particular, some fine specimens of beech, planted around 1840.

His ultimate aim was to assemble and conserve the most comprehensive collection of temperate zone woody plants ever to be grown on one site, and present them in a setting in which they could be enjoyed throughout the seasons - whether by botanists, gardeners, school parties or casual visitors - an aim which, it is generally acknowledged, he attained within his lifetime.

Immediately on settling in, he embarked on a programme of development and planting. A large scree area, created for alpines and carpeting shrubs was complemented by an herbaceous border. A woodland garden was established for magnolias and camellias, along with peat and bog gardens to provide a hospitable growing environment for other plants with special needs. The basis of the arboretum was a partially-cleared 10 acre field, initially planted as a tree nursery.

As time went on, more and more land was acquired to accommodate thousands of plants. Although many of these were from Hillier's own production, others were the result of purchases from or exchanges with both UK and overseas horticultural and botanical establishments or as gifts from friends and well-wishers around the world. Yet more specimens came from the overseas plant-collecting expeditions which Sir Harold Hillier was able to undertake and enjoy in his latter years.

As the collection grew, so more features were created - a new scree, a pond, a heather garden and a collection of rhododendrons and azaleas. In 1964, to mark Hillier Nurseries' Centenary, a massive double border, 230m long, was made, running diagonally across the original 10 acres of the arboretum.

But growth and the progressive fulfillment of a dream brought inevitable problems. How could the future of such a major national and international asset, by then covering more than 100 acres, be secured and extended yet further? The answer was found in co-operation with a supportive Hampshire County Council. A charitable trust was established with Hampshire County Council acting as funding corporate trustee, advised by a committee of distinguished experts. Thus in May 1978, the Hillier Gardens and Arboretum were accepted as a gift, on behalf of the Council, by Her Majesty, Queen Elizabeth, the Queen Mother. Since then, many changes and additions have been made. The total area has been extended to some 160 acres, containing usually at least several specimens each of more than 11,000 different plants, many of them rare in the wild or in cultivation. Visitors can join guided walks throughout the year, or simply wander at will, enjoying the plants and surroundings and gathering ideas for their own gardens. Sir Harold's former home, Jermyns House, is, like the gardens themselves, continually developing as an educational resource centre, serving the needs of young and old, from school parties to adult groups, students and botanical researchers.

Extensive labelling is supported by the storage of detailed records on computer, while as visitor numbers rapidly increase so does the number of Friends of the Gardens, a keen and active group very much involved with activities there. The search for new plants continues, not only for those collected in remote parts of the world but also for new garden varieties, often originating much closer to home, and although still relatively young for a garden, the extensive collections it maintains have enabled it to be the home of 9 National Collections as part of the scheme organised by the National Council for the Conservation of Plants and Gardens. Thus the Hillier Gardens blend seasonal beauty, enjoyment, learning and leisure, offering something for everybody at all times of the year.

The Hillier Gardens and Arboretum, Jermyns Lane, Ampfield, near Romsey, Hampshire, are well signposted from the A31 Winchester to Romsey road and the A3057 Stockbridge to Romsey road.

Opening hours are 10.30am-5.00pm Monday-Friday throughout the year and 10.30am-6.00pm at weekends and Bank Holidays, March to November (inclusive). An admission charge is payable.

The gardens may be open at other times. For details of these and of current admission charges for individuals and groups, please telephone the Curator on (0794) 68787.

Many paths and routes will accommodate wheelchairs, but it is regretted that no dogs are allowed.